Contemporary
Literary Criticism
Yearbook 1996

Guide to Gale Literary Criticism Series

For criticism on	Consult these Gale series
Authors now living or who died after December 31, 1959	*CONTEMPORARY LITERARY CRITICISM (CLC)*
Authors who died between 1900 and 1959	*TWENTIETH-CENTURY LITERARY CRITICISM (TCLC)*
Authors who died between 1800 and 1899	*NINETEENTH-CENTURY LITERATURE CRITICISM (NCLC)*
Authors who died between 1400 and 1799	*LITERATURE CRITICISM FROM 1400 TO 1800 (LC)* *SHAKESPEAREAN CRITICISM (SC)*
Authors who died before 1400	*CLASSICAL AND MEDIEVAL LITERATURE CRITICISM (CMLC)*
Black writers of the past two hundred years	*BLACK LITERATURE CRITICISM (BLC)*
Authors of books for children and young adults	*CHILDREN'S LITERATURE REVIEW (CLR)*
Dramatists	*DRAMA CRITICISM (DC)*
Hispanic writers of the late nineteenth and twentieth centuries	*HISPANIC LITERATURE CRITICISM (HLC)*
Native North American writers and orators of the eighteenth, nineteenth, and twentieth centuries	*NATIVE NORTH AMERICAN LITERATURE (NNAL)*
Poets	*POETRY CRITICISM (PC)*
Short story writers	*SHORT STORY CRITICISM (SSC)*
Major authors from the Renaissance to the present	*WORLD LITERATURE CRITICISM, 1500 TO THE PRESENT (WLC)*

ISSN 0091-3421

Volume 99

Contemporary Literary Criticism

Yearbook 1996

The Year in Fiction, Poetry, Drama, and
World Literature and the Year's
New Authors, Prizewinners, Obituaries,
and Outstanding Literary Events

Deborah A. Stanley
EDITOR

Jeff Chapman
Pamela S. Dear
Jeff Hunter
Daniel Jones
John D. Jorgenson
Jerry Moore
Polly A. Vedder
Thomas Wiloch
Kathleen Wilson
ASSOCIATE EDITORS

GALE

DETROIT • NEW YORK • TORONTO • LONDON

STAFF

Deborah A. Stanley, *Editor*

...man, Pamela S. Dear, Jeff Hunter, Daniel Jones,
...D. Jorgenson, Jerry Moore, Polly A. Vedder,
Thomas Wiloch, and Kathleen Wilson, *Associate Editors*

Tracy Arnold-Chapman, John P. Daniel, Linda Quigley,
and Janet Witalec, *Contributing Editors*

Susan Trosky, *Permissions Manager*
Margaret A. Chamberlain, Maria Franklin, and Kimberly F. Smilay, *Permissions Specialists*
Sarah Chesney, Edna Hedblad, Michele Lonoconus, and Shalice Shah, *Permissions Associates*

Victoria B. Cariappa, *Research Manager*
Julia C. Daniel, Tamara C. Nott, Michele P. Pica, Tracie A. Richardson,
Norma Sawaya, and Cheryl L. Warnock, *Research Associates*
Laura C. Bissey, Alfred A. Gardner I, and Sean R. Smith, *Research Assistants*

Mary Beth Trimper, *Production Director*
Deborah L. Milliken, *Production Assistant*

Barbara J. Yarrow, *Graphic Services Manager*
Sherrell Hobbs, *Macintosh Artist*
Randy Bassett, *Image Database Supervisor*
Robert Duncan and Mikal Ansari, *Scanner Operators*
Pamela Reed, *Photography Coordinator*

Library of Congress Catalog Card Number 76-46132
ISBN 0-7876-1063-1
ISSN 0091-3421

Printed in the United States of America
10 9 8 7 6 5 4 3 2 1

Contents

Preface vii

Acknowledgments xi

IN MEMORIAM

TOPIC IN LITERATURE: 1996

Preface

A Comprehensive Information Source
on Contemporary Literature

Scope of the *Yearbook*

*C*ontemporary Literary Criticism Yearbook is a part of the ongoing *Contemporary Literary Criticism (CLC)* series. *CLC* provides a comprehensive survey of modern literature by presenting excerpted criticism on the works of novelists, poets, playwrights, short story writers, scriptwriters, and other creative writers now living or who died after December 31, 1959. A strong emphasis is placed on including criticism of works by established authors who frequently appear on syllabuses of high school and college literature courses.

To complement this broad coverage, the *Yearbook* focuses more specifically on a given year's literary activities and features a larger number of currently noteworthy authors than is possible in standard *CLC* volumes. *CLC Yearbook* provides students, teachers, librarians, researchers, and general readers with information and commentary on the outstanding literary works and events of a given year.

Format of the Book

CLC, Volume 99: *Yearbook 1996,* which includes excerpted criticism on fifteen authors and comprehensive coverage of a key issue in contemporary literature, is divided into five sections—"The Year in Review," "New Authors," "Prizewinners," "In Memoriam," and "Topic in Literature: 1996."

- **The Year in Review**—This section consists of specially commissioned essays by prominent writers who survey the year's works in their respective fields. Bruce Allen discusses "The Year in Fiction," Allen Hoey "The Year in Poetry," Julius Novick "The Year in Drama," and William Riggan "The Year in World Literature." For introductions to the essayists, please see the Notes on Contributors.

- **New Authors**—This section introduces seven writers who received significant critical recognition for their first major work of fiction in 1996 or whose work was translated into English or published in the United States for the first time. Authors were selected for inclusion if their work was reviewed in several prominent literary periodicals.

- **Prizewinners**—This section begins with a list of literary prizes and honors announced in 1996, citing the award, award criteria, the recipient, and the title of the prizewinning work. Following the listing of prizewinners is a presentation of five entries on individual award winners, representing a mixture of genres and nationalities as well as established prizes and those more recently introduced.

- **In Memoriam**—This section consists of reminiscences, tributes, retrospective articles, and obituary notices on three authors who died in 1996. In addition, an Obituary section provides information on other recently deceased literary figures.

- **Topic in Literature**—This section focuses on a literary issue of considerable public interest, the growth in popularity of true-crime literature.

Features

With the exception of the four essays in "The Year in Review" section, which were written specifically for this publication, the *Yearbook* consists of excerpted criticism drawn from literary reviews, general magazines, newspapers, books, and scholarly journals. *Yearbook* entries variously contain the following items:

- An **Author Heading** in the "New Authors" and "Prizewinners" sections cites the name under which the author publishes and the title of the work discussed in the entry; the "In Memoriam" section includes the author's name and birth and death dates. The author's full name, pseudonyms (if any) under which the author has published, nationality, and principal genres are listed on the first line of the author entry.

- The **Subject Heading** defines the theme of each entry in "The Year in Review" and "Topics in Literature" sections.

- A brief **Biographical and Critical Introduction** to the author and his or her work precedes excerpted criticism in the "New Authors," "Prizewinners," and "In Memoriam" sections; the subjects, authors, and works in the "Topic in Literature" section are introduced in a similar manner.

- A listing of **Principal Works** is included for all entries in the "Prizewinners" and "In Memoriam" sections.

- A **Portrait** of the author is included in the "New Authors," "Prizewinners," and "In Memoriam" sections, and an **Excerpt from the Author's Work,** if available or applicable, is also provided. Whenever possible, a recent, previously unpublished **Author Interview** also accompanies each entry.

- The **Excerpted Criticism,** included in all entries except those in the "Year in Review" section, represents essays selected by editors to reflect the spectrum of opinion about a specific work or about an author's writing in general. The excerpts are typically arranged chronologically, adding a useful perspective to the entry. In the "Year in Review," "New Authors," "Prizewinners," and "In Memoriam" sections, all titles by the author being discussed are printed in boldface type, enabling the reader to more easily identify the author's work.

- A complete **Bibliographical Citation,** designed to help the user find the original essay or book, precedes each excerpt.

- **Cross-references** have been included in the "New Authors," "Prizewinners," and "In Memoriam" sections to direct readers to other useful sources published by Gale Research. Previous volumes of *CLC* in which the author has been featured are also listed.

Other Features

The *Yearbook* also includes the following features:

- An **Acknowledgments** section lists the copyright holders who have granted permission to reprint material in this volume of *CLC*. It does not, however, list every book or periodical reprinted or consulted during the preparation of this volume.

- A **Cumulative Author Index** lists all the authors who have appeared in the Literary Criticism Series published by Gale Research, with cross-references to Gale's Biographical and Autobiographical Series. A full listing of series referenced in the index appears at the beginning of the index. Readers will welcome this cumulated author index as a useful tool for locating an author within the various series. The index, which lists birth and death dates when available, is particularly valuable for locating references to those authors whose careers span two periods. For example, Ernest Hemingway is found in *CLC,* yet a writer often associated with him, F. Scott Fitzgerald, is found in *Twentieth-Century Literary Criticism.*

- Beginning with *CLC,* Vol. 65, each *Yearbook* contains a **Cumulative Topic Index,** which lists all literary topics treated in *CLC* as well as the topic volumes of *Twentieth-Century Literary Criticism, Nineteenth-Century Literature Criticism,* and *Literature Criticism from 1400 to 1800.*

- A **Cumulative Nationality Index** alphabetically lists all authors featured in *CLC* by nationality, followed by numbers corresponding to the volumes in which the authors appear.

- A **Title Index** alphabetically lists all titles reviewed in the current volume of *CLC*. Listings are followed by the author's name and the corresponding page numbers where the titles are discussed. English translations of foreign titles and variations of titles are cross-referenced to the title under which a work was originally published. Titles of novels, novellas, dramas, films, record albums, and poetry, short story, and essay collections are printed in italics, while all individual poems, short stories, essays, and songs are printed in roman type within quotation marks. When published separately, the titles of long poems (e.g., T. S. Eliot's *The Waste Land*) are printed in italics.

Citing *Contemporary Literary Criticism*

When writing papers, students who quote directly from any volume in the Literary Criticism Series may use the following general forms to footnote reprinted criticism. The first example is for material drawn from periodicals, the second for material reprinted from books:

[1]Alfred Cismaru, "Making the Best of It," *The New Republic,* 207, No. 24, (December 7, 1992), 30, 32; excerpted and reprinted in *Contemporary Literary Criticism,* Vol. 85, ed. Christopher Giroux (Detroit: Gale Research, 1995), pp. 73-4.

[2]Yvor Winters, *The Post-Symbolist Methods* (Allan Swallow, 1967); excerpted and reprinted in *Contemporary Literary Criticism,* Vol. 85, ed. Christopher Giroux (Detroit: Gale Research, 1995), pp. 223-26.

Suggestions Are Welcome

The editor hopes that readers will find *CLC Yearbook* a useful reference tool and welcomes comments about the work. Send comments and suggestions to: Editor, *Contemporary Literary Criticism,* Gale Research, 835 Penobscot Building, Detroit, MI 48226-4094.

Acknowledgments

The editors wish to thank the copyright holders of the excerpted criticism included in this volume and the permissions managers of many book and magazine companies for assisting us in securing reprint rights. We are also grateful to the staffs of the Detroit Public Library, the Library of Congress, the University of Detroit Mercy Library, Wayne State University Purdy/Kresge Library Complex, and the University of Michigan Libraries for making their resources available to us. Following is a list of the copyright holders who have granted us permission to reprint material in this volume of *CLC*. Every effort has been made to trace copyright, but if omissions have been made, please let us know.

COPYRIGHTED EXCERPTS IN *CLC*, VOLUME 99, WERE REPRINTED FROM THE FOLLOWING PERIODICALS:

America, v. 167, August 8, 1992; v. 173, December 9, 1995; v. 171, November 19, 1994. © 1992, 1994, 1995, All rights reserved. Reprinted by permission of Thomas Bonner, Jr. and America Press, Inc. 106 West 56th Street, New York, NY 10019. *American Book Review*, v. 16, March-May, 1995. © 1995 by The American Book Review. Reprinted by permission of the publisher. *American Scholar*, v. 63, Spring, 1994. Copyright © 1994 by the United Chapters of the Phi Beta Kappa Society. Reprinted by permission of the publishers. *Americas*, v. 39, November/December, 1987. Reproduced by permission. *The Atlanta Journal/Constitution*, March 24, 1996. Reproduced with the permission of The Atlanta Journal and The Atlanta Constitution. *The Atlantic Monthly*, v. 278, September, 1996. Reproduced by permission of the author. *Belles Lettres: A Review of Books by Women*, v. 11, January, 1996. Reproduced by permission. *Book World—The Washington Post*, May 22, 1988; December 31, 1989; May 6, 1990; June 25, 1995; v. XXVI, January 21, 1996; v. XXVI, May 26, 1996. © 1988, 1989, 1990, 1995, 1996, The Washington Post Book World Service/Washington Post Writers Group. Reprinted with permission. *Booklist*, v. 89, December 15, 1992; July 1995; v. 92, December 15, 1995; September 15, 1996. Reproduced by permission. *BookPage*, September 18, 1996. Reproduced by permission. *Books and Bookmen*, March, 1996. Copyright © 1996 Desmond Hogan. Reproduced by permission of the author c/o Rogers, Coleridge & White Ltd., 20 Powis Mews, London W11 1JN. *Books for Your Children*, v. 26, Summer, 1991. © Books for Your Children 1991. Reprinted by permission of the publisher. *The Boston Globe*, January 5, 1993; March 27, 1996; May 1, 1996; November 19, 1996. Reproduced by permission. *Boston Review*, v. XIV, December, 1989. Copyright © 1989 by the Boston Critic, Inc. Reprinted by permission of the author. *British Book News*, February, 1986. Reproduced by permission. *Chicago Tribune*, February 3, 1994. © Copyrighted Chicago Tribune Company. All rights reserved. Used with permission; June 22, 1995. © Copyrighted Chicago Tribune Company. All rights reserved. Used with permission; October 29, 1995. © Copyrighted Chicago Tribune Company. All rights reserved. Used with permission; April 19, 1996 for "This Boy's Life Is No Fun on the Run" by Bobbie Hess. © copyrighted 1996, Chicago Tribune Company. All rights reserved. Reproduced by permission of the author; May 12, 1996. © Copyrighted Chicago Tribune Company. All rights reserved. Used with permission; July 21, 1996. © Copyrighted Chicago Tribune Company. All rights reserved. Used with permission; May 30, 1996. © Copyrighted Chicago Tribune Company. All rights reserved. Used with permission; July 28, 1996. © Copyrighted Chicago Tribune Company. All rights reserved. Used with permission; October 3, 1996. © Copyrighted Chicago Tribune Company. All rights reserved. Used with permission. *Chicago Tribune—Books*, December 13, 1992. © Copyrighted Chicago Tribune Company. All rights reserved. Used with permission. *Choice*, v. 29, 1992. Reprinted with Permission from CHOICE, copyright by the American Library Association. *The Christian Century*, v. 107, October 24, 1990; v. 112, November 22-29, 1995. Reproduced by permission. *The Christian Science Monitor*, June 2, 1988; July 27, 1990; v. 87, October 12, 1995; May 8, 1996. © 1988, 1990, 1995, 1996 The Christian Science Publishing Society, All rights reserved. Reprinted by permission from the Author. *Commonweal*, v. CXVII, November 23, 1990; v. CXXII, v. CXXII, May 19, 1995; October 6, 1995. Copyright © 1990, 1995 Commonweal Publishing Co., Inc. Reprinted by permission of Commonweal Foundation. *Entertainment Weekly*, February 16, 1996; February 23/March 1, 1996; April 26, 1996. Reproduced by permission. *Interview*, v. 26, June, 1996. Reproduced by permission. *Journal of American Culture*,

COPYRIGHTED EXCERPTS IN *CLC,* VOLUME 99, WERE REPRINTED FROM THE FOLLOWING BOOKS:

PHOTOGRAPHS APPEARING IN *CLC,* VOLUME 99, WERE RECEIVED FROM THE FOLLOWING SOURCES:

The Year in Review

The Year in Fiction
by Bruce Allen

In a year not notable for experimental or even particularly unconventional fiction, the most audacious production may well have been a straightforward retelling of one of the most familiar of all stories. Walter Wangerin Jr.'s *The Book of God,* subtitled "The Bible as a Novel," indeed reshapes the separate books of the Old and New Testaments (beginning with the story of Abraham) into a single continuous narrative that is distinguished—if such is the right word—by both reasonably crisp summary and description and numbingly anachronistic dialogue. Perhaps the best one can say of it is what Samuel Johnson said when comparing a woman preaching with a dog walking on its hind legs: "It is not done well; but you are surprised to find it done at all."

A rather more literary novel, Harry Mulisch's *The Discovery of Heaven,* grafts a plot that is quite literally made in heaven onto a richly observed exploration of intellectual and sexual kinship and rivalry. A celestial "Prologue" informs us that a disillusioned God intends to break His covenant with mankind and that angelic interference with the course of human events will produce a proto-human prodigy capable of fulfilling the divine will.

Mulisch depicts the working-out of this plan as the pattern that shapes the lives of astronomer Max Delius and linguist Onno Quist, the woman they both love, and the son she bears, in effect, to both of them. That chosen child, Quinten, is given an eerie hyperreality that's altogether convincing—as is this surpassingly dense novel's dramatic communication of the scholarly and theoretical matters that absorb its vividly drawn protagonists. In fact Harry Mulisch, an eminent Dutch writer previously best known for his superb novel *The Assault,* has here surpassed himself. *The Discovery of Heaven* was the year's most demanding work of fiction, and one of the most rewarding.

An equally learned novel, *Palinoru of Mexico,* introduced American readers to that country's forbiddingly erudite Fernando del Paso. He has here constructed a witty metafiction in which the metaphysical dimensions of medical (particularly, anatomical) study, political activism as self-creation, and the unruly relations among narrators, fictional characters, and their creators are explored at both exhausting and intriguing length. A difficult book whose extraordinary energy will likely win over even the most recalcitrant reader.

The most daunting American novel of 1996 was David Foster Wallace's gargantuan *Infinite Jest.* In braiding together the passions and fates of a family of semi-deranged overachievers and the drug-addicted inhabitants of a clankingly symbolic halfway house, Wallace—whose previous fiction included the delightfully impudent and brainy *Girl With Curious Hair*—has achieved a synthesis of vivid realism and speculative fantasy that many have compared to work of his presumable mentors Pynchon and DeLillo, though one might also imagine *Infinite Jest* as the product of an unholy union between William Burroughs and J. D. Salinger. It's heavy going, but beautifully written, and its vision of a cockeyed America hellbent on the pursuit of pleasure has great power. And Wallace has the wit to make even a supplemental hundred pages' worth of "Notes and Errata" and essential and pleasurable component of the strange adventure this big book comprises.

John Edgar Wideman's *The Cattle Killing* revisits territory previously explored in his fiction ("Fever," *Philadelphia Fire*): an outbreak of plague in late-eighteenth century Philadelphia, and the consequent near-annihilation of that city's black population. This novel is a sequence of fragmentary, impressionistic images which suggest, but do not make clear, a connection between the confused wanderings of a nameless epileptic black preacher and a haunting tale (denoted by Wideman's title) of an African tribe misled into sacrificing the herd that constituted their livelihood. The novel is written in stark, accusatory prose that masterfully creates a tone of doom-laden sorrow, but its meanings are teasingly withheld, and the result is a work of unquestionable beauty that remains frustratingly opaque.

One of the most tireless experiments among American writers, John Hawkes, offered in *The Frog* a perversely elusive fable whose narrator actually has (accidentally) swallowed a frog and subsequently experienced a life of brief furtive pleasures and fulfillments truncated by setbacks which occur whenever his disturbed corporeality (as it were) rears its head. The novel's actions take place in an exquisitely rendered early twentieth-century French provincial setting, but God alone knows what it all means—and Hawkes doesn't offer the reader much help.

In *John's Wife,* however, Robert Coover put his mandarin postmodern energies to good use in an agreeably manic chronicle of Middle American social and sexual confusion. It takes place in a close-knit small town dominated by the eponymous John, whose successful construction business and bewitching (if essentially unknown, and unknowable) wife make him the envy of a vigorously evoked host of variously moonstruck, worshipful, and lust-besotted neighbors. Coover cleverly explores the psychic driving forces that propel them all toward a catastrophic comic denouement which says all that need ever be said about the intersection of Main Street with Sodom and Gomorrah. It's one of Coover's most abrasive and accomplished performances.

Steven Millhauser's **Martin Dressler,** a more robust counterpart to his delicately crafted and richly embroidered tales of dreamlike obsession, recounts in pleasingly plain, swift sentences the story of its title character's rise from cigar-store clerk to rich hotelier, and his fall (through an act of ill-considered overreaching) back to something like his humbly expectant origins. In fashioning a tale of capitalism and its discontents that also comprises a sly parable of the creative urge and its psychic ramifications, Millhauser has managed an unique hybrid: a book that might have been co-authored by Dreiser and Borges, and that both would surely have admired.

Once past some coy authorial posturing (i.e., is it or isn't it autobiography?), there's much to be enjoyed in Paul Theroux's "imaginary memoir" **My Other Life,** an ostensibly alternative version of the career and personal life of a successful writer who grew up in Massachusetts, served with the Peace Corps in Africa, taught school in various Far Eastern and other foreign climes, and published a number of books remarkably similar to those Paul Theroux has owned up to. Intermittent theorizing about the divided identity of the book's protagonist and author grows increasingly tedious, but as a lively narrative of adventures courted and relationships painfully endured and often mishandled, it achieves a nervy and almost unqualified success.

Three other established American novelists offered new installments of multivolume works in progress. **The Flaming Corsage,** novel number six in William Kennedy's popular "Albany Cycle," weaves skillfully backward and forward in time to explore the causes and consequences of its pivotal actions: a hotel fire and the related (and notorious) "Love Nest Killings"—particularly as they affect recurring character Francis Phelan, most familiar as the protagonist of the critically acclaimed *Ironweed.* This novel features some vigorous melodrama, and lively characterizations, especially of its male figures, but will be of only passing interest to those who haven't kept up with the Albany Cycle.

Tales of Burning Love continues Louise Erdrich's portrayals of Native American life (begun with *Love Medicine*) in and near Angus, North Dakota. This time her focus is on dysfunctional charmer Jack Mauser, a Chippewa Indian, who can't seem to avoid attracting women, and the four former wives (of the five he married) who together weave a *faux*-Chaucerian tapestry of remembrance about their experiences of his seductions and misdeeds. This is a vivid novel filled with extravagant comic (and, sometimes, serious) invention, and one of Erdrich's very best.

The most remarkable novel cycle of our time is unquestionably the late Henry Roth's autobiographical **Mercy of a Rude Stream,** begun in old age decades after the appearance of Roth's single masterpiece (*Call It Sleep* in 1934) and completed shortly before his death in 1995. The story of writer Ira Stigman, whose formative experiences are indistinguishable from the known facts of Henry Roth's life, reaches a furious crisis point in **From Bondage,** which concentrates on Ira's sexual liaisons with an older woman mentor, a female cousin, and his younger sister. It's an amazing book: a raw confessional howl of pain, rendered both as it is lived and as it's guiltily remembered, long afterward. A deeply personal work that nevertheless far transcends autobiographical catharsis.

Other well-known American novelists surfaced with surprisingly accomplished new works. One was Bruce Jay Friedman, whose wonderfully droll *A Father's Kisses* portrays a middle-aged poultry distributor turned gangland hit man with the rueful comic resignation that characterized such previous triumphs as *Stern* and *A Mother's Kisses.*

Another was Albert J. Guerard, the eminent critic and novelist (*Night Journey, The Bystander*) who in **The Hotel in the Jungle** constructs an energetic symbolic drama set in Mexico over a fractious half-century of cultural and political conflict and featuring a large cast of intertwined characters that includes fictional counterparts of poet Mina Loy and heavyweight boxing champion Jack Johnson, and the notorious adventurer and malcontent William Walker. It's the sort of novel you can happily lose yourself in for several days.

John Updike's **In the Beauty of the Lilies** explores the comparative attractions and disappointments of the religious life and the fleshpots of Hollywood in an ambitious multigenerational portrayal of a New Jersey family that is, simultaneously, compulsively readable and clogged with intermittently tedious sociological detail.

Suspects is another of Thomas Berger's wry revelations of the dark underside of Middle American complacency. It's a murder mystery that blossoms into a beautifully plotted chain of coincidences, in which both the duplicitous souls of ordinary people and the bland inequities of law and order are presented with the irresistible deadpan understatement shared by such earlier delights as *Sneaky People* and *The Feud.* It's a pleasure to report that Berger's twentieth novel ranks among his most outrageously appealing.

Fred Chappell's **Farewell, I'm Bound to Leave You** revisits the rural North Carolina depicted in his best fiction for a backwoods portrait of the artist: recurring Chappell character Jess

Kirkman. In recounting tales of embattled and indomitable women (that mainly concern courtship and marriage) told him by his mother and grandmother, Jess creates both a rich patchwork portrayal of a vanished culture and an intriguing revelation of the sources of his own inquiring and receptive sensibility. This beautifully written novel was one of the year's best.

It was a typical year for Joyce Carol Oates, who published a nondescript collection of generally overwrought short stories (*Will You Always Love Me?*); a rhetorically charged and ingeniously symbolic portrait of the corruption of preadolescent innocence (*First Love*); and, in *We Were the Mulvaneys,* one of the most accomplished and haunting of her twenty-six novels. It's a large-scaled chronicle of a wealthy and seemingly blessed upstate New York family undone by an act of sexual violence and the shock waves thus sent throughout its members' later lives. Oates's tendencies toward strident melodrama and empurpled sentences are as irritating as ever, but she takes us deeply inside the variously destroyed and self-destructive Mulvaneys, and renders with remorseless clarity the subtle permutations of character that make of people either victims or survivors. This is a consistently engrossing novel, and a very rewarding one.

Joan Didion's *The Last Thing He Wanted,* her first novel in twelve years, is a savvy political thriller which makes expert use of its author's celebrated reportorial skills. It's the story—told by herself, and also seen from differently involved other perspectives —of Elena McMahon, a disaffected journalist whose initially passive involvement in her late father's business propels her into an ungodly spiral of Cuban and Caribbean—and, perhaps, global—intrigue. This compact and resonant analysis of the inevitably political character of presumably unaffiliated lives constitutes a triumphant return to fiction for one of our finest essayists.

Among other new books from veteran novelists, the most notable included Louis Begley's marvelously urbane and incisive study of a priggish and pompous (and, for all that, likable) lawyer's complex late-middle age crisis (*About Schmidt*); E. Annie Proulx's vastly ambitious, and somewhat contrived double-edged *paean* to the American immigrant experience (*Accordion Crimes*); Joanna Scott's rich Gothic exploration of taxidermy as a metaphor for enclosure and stasis (*The Manikin*); Ron Hansen's affecting character study of a widowed Colorado rancher who must also bear, and somehow understand the loss of his wayward son (*Atticus*); and Padgett Powell's delicious *Edisto Revisited,* which returns to the eccentric South Carolina backwater and addled extended family relished, and suffered by Simons Manigault, the errantly maturing protagonist of his fine first novel *Edisto*. Not much happens in this sleepy, agreeable novel, but Padgett Powell's characters are pure pleasure to spend time with, even when they're only fretfully tolerating one another.

Among several variously accomplished second novels, the most interesting was Sherman Alexie's vividly written, passionately accusatory Native American murder mystery *Indian Killer*; Alfredo Vea Jr.s' invitingly chaotic tale of culture conflict, murder, and revolution in a vividly ethnically mixed-up San Francisco (*The Silver Cloud Cafe*); and Alan Isler's *Kraven Images,* a comic roundelay of sexual pursuit and conquest in a Bronx Jewish setting that effectively explores a rather more visceral dimension of the deracinated ethnic culture portrayed in his memorable debut novel *The Prince of West End Avenue.*

Gish Jen's *Mona in the Promised Land* followed her highly praised *Typical American* with its lively account of a Chinese-American family adrift in a chameleon-like America in which everybody seems to have roots in everybody else's nationality and ancestry. It's a highly entertaining example of a novel whose humor arises with perfect naturalness from its cleverly imagined core situation.

And Dale Peck's *The Law of Enclosures* diverges successfully from the knowing portrayal of gay life that distinguished his first novel *Martin and John,* in constructing a jagged and harrowing picture of a deeply troubled marriage. The characters of "Dale" (who tells the story), his alcoholic father Henry, and embittered mother Bea are three of the most painfully, sorrowfully real characters contemporary fiction has to offer.

Of the usual plethora of American first novels, the traditional coming-of-age tale took pleasingly various forms in Max Phillip's attractive recounting of preadolescent Nicky Wertheim's fixation on a beauteous "older woman" (*Snakebite Sonnet*); Alan Brown's thin but nicely imagined story of a young Japanese artist's fetishistic maturing (*Audrey Hepburn's Neck*); and Elizabeth McCracken's widely praised portrayal of a lonely woman librarian's unconventional relationship with a deformed eight-foot-tall teenaged boy (*The Giant's House*).

Even better was Geoffrey Becker's *Bluestown,* a charmingly bittersweet narrative about bright, sardonic Spencer Markus's bumpy adolescent relationship with his vagrant father, and later tribulations as a young adult befuddled by rock 'n' roll, the mysteries of women, and the irritating persistence of unwanted family ties. It's a delightful story, told in an engagingly fresh, lively voice.

Several less categorizable first novels included Todd Wiggins's calculatedly zany *Zeitgeist,* a Kerouacian *and* Pynchonesque satire on all manner of American complacency and myopia; and Daniel Akst's *St. Burl's Obituary,* an often hilarious picaresque featuring an adipose gourmand whose rude wit intensifies his awkward relations with both women and The Mob. This is the novel that the overpraised *A Confederacy of Dunces* should have been.

And Eric Darton's *Free City,* a clever fable of technology and commercialism run rampant, set in an unspecified (though vividly evoked) seventeenth-century European seaport city, mocks the grand designs of idealistic and mercenary souls alike in a zestfully epigrammatic period style that reminded me of Voltaire.

But the majority of the year's better first novels focussed on family relations. Antonya Nelson's *Talking in Bed* observes the chance intersection of two totally different unhappy families with a knowing blend of convincing domestic realism and thoughtful introspection. Christopher Tilghman's *Mason's Retreat* fashions a moving drama of incompatibility and its consequences out of the interactions of a long-troubled family obsessively drawn back to the Maryland Eastern Shore area so vividly depicted here, as also in his earlier short-story collection *In a Father's Place.*

Judson Mitcham's *The Sweet Everlasting,* written in a beautifully spare first-person voice that precisely suggests the hesitant character of its burdened narrator and protagonist, movingly relates the struggle of a semiliterate Georgia mill worker to rebuild the sustaining family life he had all but thrown away. Mitcham's stolid, stoical Ellis Burt was one of 1996's finest characterizations.

The closely linked stories of Allegra Goodman's *The Family Markowitz* comprise an affectionate and very funny group portrait of several generations of an American Jewish clan dominated by its aging matriarch Rose, which exfoliates expertly in detailing the familial and career conflicts that absorb her children and grandchildren and often center in the varying degrees of their commitment to orthodox Judaism.

The world of Diane McKinney-Whetstone's *Tumbling* is a Philadelphia neighborhood during the 1940s and 1950s and the orbit of a black family threatened by both urban upheaval and its members' imperfect, reluctant commitment to one another. This novel's thoroughly satisfying and believable resolution is the best single feature of a story that many readers will find impossible to forget.

In *The River Beyond the World,* acclaimed short-story writer Janet Peery created a rich double portrait; of a wealthy Texas matron and the Mexican servant woman whose romantic and sexual tribulations and embattled motherhood parallel, as they become entwined with, her own.

Marly Swick, another superb story writer, produced in *Paper Wings* a lyrical account of young Suzanne Keller's confused intimacy with her dreamy, remote mother—a memorable casualty of the cataclysmic social changes that followed the 1963 assassination of President Kennedy. Swick's unerring feel for the minute emotional shifts that accompany and underscore more visible family dynamics imbues her debut novel with the same delicacy and precision that distinguish her stories.

A number of fine first collections of short stories by American writers appeared in 1996. These included wry portrayals of middle class life and domestic discord in Erin McGraw's *Lies of the Saints* and Dean Albarelli's *Cheaters*; keen analyses of cultural difference and conflict along the Texas-Mexico border in Wendell Mayo's *Centaur of the North*; Kafkaesque tales of nightmarish personal struggles in Philip Graham's *Interior Design* and of the workaday world become the soulless future in George Saunder's *Civil War Land in Bad Decline*; and an eerie presentation of the complex symbiosis that binds together humans and animals in Brad Watson's intensely imaginative *Last Days of the Dog-Men.*

An almost Faulknerian empathy with the rootless wanderers and phlegmatically self-possessed inhabitants of northern California's mountain country distinguishes the vividly metaphoric stories of Roy Parvin's *The Loneliest Road in America.* The often violent and endangered lives of Dominican American refugees hopefully resettled in New York and New Jersey are explored with terse understatement in Junot Diaz's highly praised *Drown.* The varieties of romantic obsession vis-a-vis suburban angst are the abundantly suggestive matter of Paul Griner's *Follow Me,* a frustratingly uneven collection whose high points can bring you right up out of your chair.

And in one of the year's best debut collection, *Same Place, Same Things,* Louisiana's Tim Gautreaux surveys moments of decision and crisis conditions in the baffled lives of white Southern and Cajun protagonists whose imperfect intimacies with others evolve believably out of their own solipsism and wariness.

Character is subordinated to situation and incident in Jim Shepard's very satisfying *Battling against Castro,* a hair-raisingly varied volume of stories whose characters include sexually dysfunctional college football players, a suicidal suburbanite, an incompatible couple struggling to make it in a postnuclear America, and a science-fiction freak whose hobby somehow sustained him through a painful childhood. Jim Shepard has the talent to make the unrelentingly bizarre entirely credible.

Short fiction from veteran writers included the compassionate and borderline-sentimental portrayals of separation anxiety and compromised fidelity in Andre Dubus's *Dancing After Hours*; intelligent analyses of wealthy and complacent families tested by divorce and the pangs of parenthood in Roxana Robinson's *Asking for Love*; and a beguiling further view of the scattershot emotional life of Ellen Gilchrist's recurring character Nora Jane Whittington (among other, similarly bittersweet portrayals of addled souls who might all be her second cousins) in *The Courts of Love.*

John Barth offered more of his trademark self-reflexive metafictions in **On With the Story,** an intricate and amusing collection that nevertheless seems scarcely distinguishable from the contents of his *Lost in the Funhouse* nearly thirty years ago.

Robert Olen Butler produced in **Tabloid Dreams** a smartly conceived set of tales inspired by *National Enquirer*—like kitsch and salaciousness ("Help Me Find My Spaceman Lover" is typical), but the stories' execution only intermittently lives up to their seductive premises.

Attention-getting premises also dominate the tense, menacing stories—many set in or redolent of the worlds of drug abuse and trafficking—of Edward Falco's *Acid.* And in **The Night in Question** Tobias Wolff further explores the disorienting experiences of maturing under pressure in fragmented families or the hermetic unreality of military service, and of helplessly confronting the facts of one's own solitude and mortality. The title story, "The Other Miller," and "Firelight" are on a par with the best stories Wolff has written.

The disappointed and regretful depths of everyday lives are keenly analyzed in **Distant Friends and Intimate Strangers,** a welcome second collection from Louisianan Charles East (whose only previous book of stories appeared in 1965). "A Perfect Day," "Man of the House," and "Days of Our Lives" are quietly convincing examples of the resonance this very underrated writer extracts from apparently ordinary people and situations.

Andrea Barrett's **Ship Fever** (which won a 1996 National Book Award) offers, in its seven unusually textured stories and its brilliant title novella, an enormously rich investigation into lives ruled by, and expressive of, the spirit of scientific inquiry. The experiences and examples of Linnaeus, Mendel, and Darwin among others are counter-pointed against discoveries about the material world and themselves made by disciples of such touchstone figures—particularly by women who have been discouraged from exercising their intellects. A superb and endlessly suggestive collection; easily the year's best.

Flying Home, a posthumous collection of early (1937-54) stories by the late Ralph Ellison, forms a welcome pendant, if not a worthy counterpart, to the enduring achievement of his classic novel *Invisible Man.* With the single exception of the graphic and powerful title piece, these stories are, variously, melodramatic, derivative, or inchoate. The volume's greatest value is its gathering together of rough materials that would later be magically reshaped into segments of *Invisible Man*—and it is also graced by editor and Ellison scholar John F. Callahan's informative and moving "Introduction."

Another essential American writer, Gina Berriault, was rep-

resented by **Women in Their Beds,** an omnibus collection of thirty-five precisely observed and hauntingly intimate portrayals of men, women, and children stunned into paradoxical acknowledgement of both their inescapable connections to others and their ultimate loneliness. Familiar stories like "The Stone Boy" and "The Infinite Passion of Expectation" are matched by such previously uncollected standouts as the subtly mocking "A Dream of Fair Women" and the collection's unforgettably astringent title story. Not enough people know it yet, but Gina Berriault is one of the masters.

Another of them, Canada's Mavis Gallant, offered in her **Collected Stories** a dazzlingly rich retrospective of fifty-two stories (a half-century's work) which evoke with firm clarity and generous detail the discoveries and compromises of (mainly Parisian) expatriate life and the varied and traumatizing legacy of World War II. Prominent among this big book's many delights are Gallant's brilliant autobiographical "Linnet Muir" stories, and also an informative "Preface" in which she charmingly pre-empts outside analysis of her unique and surely lasting *oeuvre.*

Several other Canadian writers produced some of the year's best fiction. Brian Moore's **The Statement** is a superbly crafted story, both thriller and moral drama, about the hunt, forty years following the war, for a former Vichy regime operative and Nazi collaborator who is sought, for various reasons, by his enemies and colleagues alike. Dialogue, action, and remembrance are seamlessly interwoven in this engrossing tale, which actually surpasses such earlier successes in this vein as *Lies of Silence* and *No Other Love.* As pure narrative, this was perhaps the year's best novel.

Indian-born Rohinton Mistry reached far beyond his previous work in the ambitious **A Fine Balance,** a sumptuously detailed portrait of four impoverished protagonists struggling to survive during Indira Gandhi's indifferent rule. This provocative and deeply felt novel falters only when Mistry's knowing vignettes of the teeming life that surrounds his principal characters usurps our interest and relegates them to the story's background.

Funny Boy, a superb first novel by Shyam Selvadurai, skillfully combines an account of its gay young narrator's coming-out and coming-of-age in its author's native Sri Lanka with a sober and deeply disturbing picture of violent rivalry between indigenous Tamil (Hindu) and Sinhalese (Buddhist) adherents. In its firm command of tone, and virtuosic blending of comic and serious materials, this is a very accomplished debut.

Veteran writer Margaret Atwood offered her finest novel yet in **Alias Grace,** a devious and fascinating reconstruction of a notorious nineteenth-century Toronto murder case. In presenting the puzzle of Grace Marks, an articulate and reserved servant girl whose complicity in the murders of her employer and his mistress remains teasingly in question throughout, Atwood has created an ingenious mystery, a meticulously detailed picture of Victorian Canada, and a witty commentary on the fates doled out to women who won't accommodate men's fantasies about them. She has never written better.

Arguably Canada's most distinguished export, Alice Munro was seen at her spectacular best in an ample *Selected Stories* drawn from such rapturously praised collections as *The Moons of Jupiter* and *Friend of My Youth.* These complex, often novella-length portrayals of usually) Ontario women obsessed by both the actual and potential lives they may have lived and men they may have loved, or at least endured, are among the best short fiction of our time. The best of this volume's contents include "The Progress of Love," "A Wilderness Station," and the unforgettably Chekhovian "Carried Away"— but not one may safely be skipped.

Munro's only rival, in this reviewer's opinion, for the title of best living short story writer is the Anglo-Irish William Trevor, whose *After Rain* contains twelve more superlative examples of his understated analyses of stunted or threatened sheltered lives. A solitary woman discovering her true nature while vacationing in Italy, a blind piano tuner at the mercy of his combative former and present wives, and a doting mother unwilling to acknowledge her beloved son's violent criminality are prominent among the damaged yet somehow resilient souls whose strategies for remaining, and feeling alive are so memorably portrayed in Trevor's consistently brilliant fiction.

The popular Irish novelist Roddy Doyle achieved in *The Woman Who Walked Into Doors* a success of a somewhat different sort from that enjoyed by his roughhouse-comic *Barrytown Trilogy.* This is the story of an abused housewife, Paula Spencer, whose feisty defiance of her brutish husband is narrated with Doyle's characteristically exhilirating vulgarity, and builds into a stunning and moving characterization of a weary survivor whose strength amazes her as much as it impresses us.

Another fine novel from Ireland, John B. Keane's *The Ram of God,* tells the vivid tale of a rural village unsettled by the complicated rivalry among a lapsed cleric eager to rebuild his wasted life, his unregenerate twin brothers, and the scheming matron who means to bend them all to her will and ensure her erring daughters' respectability. Keane skillfully combines a stinging satire on traditional Hibernian pieties with a rousingly entertaining old-fashioned melodrama.

Even more variety was displayed in fiction from Scottish-born authors. Alison Fell's *The Pillow Boy of the Lady Onogoro,* for example, concocts a hilarious fantasy of female resourcefulness and survival in her richly imagined tale

of an eleventh-century Japanese woman fulfilled and empowered by stories told her (during lovemaking) by a blind stableboy. A brilliantly mischievous variation on the *Arabian Nights,* and one of the year's most inventive fictions.

A History Maker offered another invigorating infusion of Alasdair Gray's truculent metafiction, in an enchantingly wild and crazy narrative of clan warfare set in a dystopian twenty-third century and featuring both a thick-headed Samson and his beguiling Delilah, and a generous sprinkling of Gray's medieval-surrealist illustrations. I don't quite know what to call it, but whatever it is, it's wonderful.

Shena Mackay's *The Orchard on Fire,* which was nominated for Britain's Booker Prize, is the beautifully imagined story, told from the vantage point of her subdued adulthood, of an eight-year-old girl's summer of innocence besieged by her wary relations with family, a new best friend, and a sexually predatory neighbor. It's a convincingly realistic and paradoxically reassuring picture of the peculiar resiliency of childhood, and a fine introduction to the work of a writer whom many have labelled one of today's best.

1996 saw the U.S. publication of two books by Scotland's scabrous bard of heroin addiction and calculated sociopathy, Irvine Welsh. *Ecstasy* collects three short novels that show no advance beyond such predecessors as his superb "rave" of a novel *Marabou Stork Nightmares* (though the x-rated courtship recounted in "The Undefeated" is a partial exception). But Welsh's debut novel *Trainspotting* (first published in 1993) is a one-of-a-kind winner: a fragmented, accusatory, ingeniously slangy portrait of Edinburgh's don't-give-a-damn drug culture that virtually bursts with energy and creates a burnt-out protagonist whose very hopelessness elicits our intrigued empathy.

Prominent among several fine first novels from England were *Behind the Scenes at the Museum,* Kate Atkinson's rudely comic multigenerational chronicle of a daft Yorkshire family whose members are slightly more worldly versions of the memorable rustic monsters of Stella Gibbon's *Cold Comfort Farm*; John Lanchester's urbane portrait (in *The Debt to Pleasure*) of a superbly arrogant gourmet whose meandering "culinary reflections" brilliantly tell the story of a uniquely insular life; and John Derbyshire's *Seeing Calvin Coolidge in a Dream,* a marvelously winning tale of a Chinese immigrant's infatuation with America, temptation to relive the passions of his youth, and eventual *détente* with his new country and his formidable wife. It's a charmer.

Among their countrymen, veteran writers of comparatively recent vintage produced several unusually interesting novels. *Birdsong* by Sebastian Faulks, for one, tells the involving and intricately detailed story of a lovestruck young English industrialist's grand passion and life-changing battle experiences in First World War Europe, in a splendidly romantic narrative reminiscent of, and in many ways equal to, *A Farewell to Arms.*

Tim Binding's *A Perfect Execution* is a risk-taking symbolic novel whose opaque hero struggles to reconcile his seemingly destined occupation as a merciful hangman with a less manageable personal life that values making choices and acknowledging priorities more than simple compassion. It's occasionally floridly written, but Binding's central character is a memorable figure indeed. And Paul Bryar's *In a Pig's Ear* constructs a devilishly witty portrayal of political, sexual, and artistic energies spent under the shadow of a briskly rendered generic Europe after Hitler. Bryar's narrator and antihero Milan (perhaps a homage to Kundera?) explores the mock-Arthurian dimensions of his own adventurous quests with a sophisticated deadpan obliquity that in fact resembles nothing more than one of that eminent Czech writer's understated *récits.*

Another younger British writer, Will Self, continued his *conte cruel*-like satires on contemporary deracination and ennui in the nine abrasive, borderline-surrealistic stories of *Grey Area*—at least one of which, "Inclusion," envisions the future potential of drug therapy with a comic ferocity that Mr. Self's peer and *frere semblable* Martin Amis undoubtedly envies.

Sara Maitland's *Angel Maker* collects thirty forthright and admirably varied stories which at their best (as in "Cassandra" and "The Witching Times") explore woman's fate as preserved in a rich matrix of history and legend, and at their weakest succumb to strident protofeminist argumentation.

Maitland's obvious mentor, the late Angela Carter, was a grand mistress of such associative juxtapositions, as is triumphantly evinced by *Burning Your Boats*, a marvelous omnibus volume containing forty-two of her enchantingly overripe fabulistic confections. "The Bloody Chamber," "The Fall River Axe Murders," and "Our Lady of the Massacre," among many others, reinvent our known world with a Gothic facility and outrageousness that, to be sure, turns away many readers at the outset. But if you take even a single step inside Angela Carter's seductively deranged world, you won't be able to stop reading her.

Three long-established British novelists published books that compare favorably with their best. Anita Brookner's *Incidents in the Rue Laugier* records an earnest young woman's Parisian encounters with two very different men who attract and, to differing degrees, disappoint her in an economical and rigidly controlled narrative much in the manner of her master Henry James, and reminiscent of both his *The American* and *The Portrait of a Lady.*

Beryl Bainbridge's *Every Man for Himself,* the best of the year's several books memorializing the "Titanic" disaster, retells the familiar story from the viewpoint of a fictional nephew of financier J. P. Morgan with an elliptical surehandedness that packs an enormous amount of life (and not a little social comedy and satire) into eloquent brief compass.

Graham Swift's *Last Orders,* the current Booker Prize winner, conclusively demonstrates the continuing vitality of the traditional realistic novel in its masterly interweaving of the relationships of several men thrown into friendship by their experience of the Second World War, and both tested and transformed when the death of one of them brings the survivors together, many years later, for his funeral. The characters, so alike on the surface, are expertly distinguished, and the potentially dreary and trite details of their families' interactions are made fresh by the force of Swift's elegiac respect for their simple persistence and endurance. This is a very moving story.

Three other eminent writers offered work a bit below their usual level. A. S. Byatt's *Babel Tower,* the third in her cycle of novels featuring presumable *alter ego* Frederica Potter, finds that character adrift in the 1960s London literary world and involved in *two* elaborately detailed courtroom dramas. It's willfully Dickensian, and it's a bit much. Iris Murdoch's *Jackson's Dilemma,* her twenty-sixth country-house romantic comedy, focusses on a versatile manservant whose efficiency is interpreted by the several lovers and beloveds through whose orbits he treads as evidence of his magical, perhaps divine nature. It's very swiftly done, and it feels both hurried and rather thin.

Doris Lessing's *Love, Again* analyzes the emotional and intellectual life of sixty-five-year-old Sarah Durham, a theater manager who becomes infatuated, and to some extent involved with two adoring younger men. Sarah's late-life magnetism must be taken pretty much on faith, but Lessing probes her reawakened spirit skillfully, and offers, in the subplot story of a beautiful woman musician whose life Sarah researches, a haunting image of passions unslaked that continually threatens to take center stage, as it were, and is far more compelling that the main character's story.

Finally, two superb novels from two of the world's finest writers. Guyana's Roy Heath produced in *The Shadow Bride* a brilliant chronicle of an idealistic doctor's pursuit of his own moral nature, in the face of his possessive mother's determined domination of him. Indian-born Betta Singh's dedication to improving the lives of workers exploited by a notorious sugar plantation makes for a gripping story in its own right, though it pales beside Heath's magnificent delineation of the grasping Mrs. Singh. A well-meaning woman who cannot resist the urgings of her own hunger to belong and to control, she is one of the most unusual, and greatest, characters in contemporary fiction.

And in *The Moor's Last Sigh,* Salman Rushdie created an epic polyglot comedy fully worthy of comparison to his earlier masterpieces *Midnight's Children* and *Shame.* This exuberantly inventive novel depicts the common (and, for that matter, uncommon) fortunes of a Portuguese woman folk painter, her Indian Jewish multibillionaire husband, and their doomed son (who, in the book's boldest magical-realist stroke, ages at twice the speed of a normal human), the story's sardonic and eloquent narrator, with a captivating word-drunk velocity that elevates even its melodramatic excesses to the level of gorgeous fireworks. Rushdie's third great novel is a hymn to cultural and ethnic assimilation, and an unanswerable rebuke to the separatist fanatics who demand his death. This novel ensures his immortality. And it goes, as they say, without saying that it was the richest and most rewarding fiction of the year just past.

The Year in Poetry
by Allen Hoey

Part of what keeps a round-up reviewer going year after year of reading volumes of predictably mediocre and too often inane work, both in terms of poetry and what passes for intelligent comment on poetry, is occasionally stumbling upon passages that articulate precisely and concisely exactly what one has thought. Such was my reaction while reading W. S. Di Piero's new collection of essays, *Shooting the Works*. This excerpt from the final section, "Out of Notebooks," consolidates wonderfully much that needs to be said:

> What's wrong with our poetry is that it's worried about being right. Heartthrob platitudes, huggy anec-dotalism, outraged stridencies over injustice in countries to which the poet migrates in search of worthy subjects, scrupulous self-censorship in the interest of preserving morally pristine responses to the facts of experience, lines that confuse form with metrical or sentimental purity, agonies endured (or sworn to) entirely for the "appropriate dramatic fullness" of a poem, classroom vocabularies that determine the formal emotional deliberations in the writing of poetry, valiant eloquence in defense of poetry—"our" poetry—against philistines who ask who killed poetry. . . . Poetry needs to be defended most against those who most righteously defend it and who identify the life of poetry with the life of a career. Does it matter? . . . Poetry has nothing to fear from advocates of any new formalism for whom formal mysteries exist as occasions for polemical opportunism, for ever more gleaming correctness. The new decorum declares that no argument, no line or phrase of song or great speech, disturb the pieties of the interested party. . . . Those who feel that poetry belongs to them, and that American poetry is their share of cultural real estate, may smell of success in the world and shine with the friction of praise rubbed on their surfaces by so many hands. Poetry belongs to them, and that is part of the scheme of rectitude and valor, and so may they never realize that they do not belong to poetry. Then it will be sure of going on, needless, unannounced, unprotected, unheard of.

To those whose bristle or bluster at the thought that this means them specifically, smooth your hackles or relax your pectorals and reread the paragraph. Take note: poetry is bigger than ideology (however much individual poetics may be subject to the pressures of specific ideologies), more capacious than pseudo-professionalism, more expansive than polemics and propaganda. It has weathered the exigencies of political subjugation; it will survive the annoyance of poetasters.

Our most enduring exemplar of the polar opposite of those Di Piero lambastes is Hayden Carruth, the fruits of whose forty-five years' labor as critic and literary journalist have been gathered in *Selected Essays & Reviews*, the third volume in Copper Canyon's conservancy of Carruth's work. This volume contains a generous sampling of Carruth's reviews and essays, with the exception of those concerning jazz, which have been collected in *Sitting In* and specifically autobiographical pieces which, the author's preface indicates, will be published "in a year or two." Among the exclusions, "Influences: The Formal Idea of Jazz" and "Suicide" (available in *Suicides and Jazzers*) regrettable. The latter is one of the most excruciatingly moving treatments of suicide—Carruth's own nearly successful effort—as an affirmation of existence I've read.

More pertinent to the current selection, "Influences" offers a formal definition of jazz, which provides perhaps the most succinct statement of Carruth's poetics available: ". . . the idea, in the Platonic sense, of jazz is spontaneous improvisation within a fixed and simple form, usually improvisation by more than one musician at a time, even if the ensemble comprises no more than a solo instrument and a rhythm section." This describes the working principle for most of Carruth's poems, especially the substantial oeuvre, including "Contra Mortem," "Paragraphs," and, his master work, "The Sleeping Beauty," composed in the "paragraphs" of his own devising—fifteen-line, rhymed stanzas which consist of lines of variable but determinate length. The "rhythm section" against which Carruth counterpoints his solo improvisations is, essentially, what he calls "the grand community." The paragraphs, for instance, take their unique definition against the ground of the sonnet; like Paul Goodman, to whom Carruth devotes a lengthy homage, he "reache[s] backward to go forward": "Better than anyone else [Goodman] understood the poet's need to exist *consciously* in the continuum" (emphasis mine).

Carruth's essays, taken either individually or as a whole, betray the pervasive influence of a variety of thinkers, including Nikolai Berdyaev, Max Stirner, Arthur Schopenhauer, and Albert Camus. Carruth's prose meditation on Camus, *After the Stranger*, is long out of print, but it does point to the primacy of Camus's thought to the development of Carruth's critical biases. Existence precedes essence; life comes before form, and the poet has multiple considerations, as Carruth writes in his remarkable "A Meaning of Robert Lowell," "prior to poetry." Precise definition is crucial for Carruth, and he is both ruthless and exhaustive in rendering meaning clear. And clarity is the point, not the studied murk of hyper-attenuated critical theory. Carruth demonstrates a near-encyclopedic memory for literature and philosophy (notably Western), but the essays never seem cerebral set-pieces; his knowledge operates as an instrument for ethical discrimination. In this regard, he is a disciple, as well, of William James, not in the sloppy application of relativism but in the clear regard of context and applicability. Special note should be made, in addition to the essays already mentioned, of "Ezra Pound and the Great Style," "The Writer's Situation," "The Question of Poetic Form," "The Act of Love: Poetry and Personality," "Mystery and Expressiveness," and "The Nature of Art." The last provides a representative taste of Carruth's pragmatism; of the relationship between nature and art, he notes:

> no relationship pertains between nature and art at all. . . . Relationships can exist only among things in nature, and art is one of them. Nature is everything, OK? It is all material reality, and material reality includes absolutely everything, all there is, not merely stones and oceans, butterflies and flowers, but ideas, poems, dreams, spiritual intimations. I neither know nor need a supernatural, an other-than-natural. The supernatural is by definition inconceivable, and the inconceivable is of no use to poetry—or to anything.

This insight leads to awareness of ultimate devastation— death. And such awareness leads to "lucidity" and "authenticity," terms borrowed from Camus and Sartre, respectively: "the two ideal virtues toward which conscious humanity, personally and collectively, must strain, coming even before honesty and ordinary decency, immensely important though these are." This spirit animates all the pieces gathered in this overdue compilation as completely as through his collected poems.

In tandem with his essays, Carruth has published his first collection of lyrics since his *Collected Shorter Poems* was issued in 1992. **Scrambled Eggs & Whiskey**, the National Book Award winner, extends Carruth's already considerable accomplishment and reveals a heretofore underdeveloped aspect of Carruth: the depth and breadth of his sense of humor. While many of his Vermont poems display characteristic Yankee wryness and dryness, Carruth's humorous repertoire includes the epigrammatic, such as "The Last Poem in the World":

> Would I write it if I could?
> Bet your glitzy ass I would.

The sequence "Faxes to William" contains bad puns ("They

have unmade / their beds and they must schlep in them"), farce, and a generally self-deprecating stance. Sly humor also runs through the moving sequence, "A Summer with Tu Fu," in which Carruth conducts a dialogue across centuries and an ocean with the Chinese poet, a chat between friends over chilled white wine, looking over their respective vistas:

> A swallow here
> zooms across the pond, becoming
>
> a winter jay on the farther shore.
> Snow whirls in the pass, torrential
>
> rain drenches the cabbage fields,
> the palace grounds are enshrouded
>
> with mist. Old age and final illness
> come with the swiftness of the Yangtze
>
> flooding in springtime, or like
> the quick unreeling cinematograph.

Note the compression of time and space, the seamless movement through seasons and eras, and the adept cross-cultural figures for rapid, ineluctable change. Even the doubling of the final figure reinforces the distance between our culture and that one, the displacement of a natural metaphor by a mechanical one. Also, the specific technological reference is not just mechanical but a mechanism for producing artificial imagery that itself displaces immediate experience. More than mere difference is implied, more than impoverishment.

Many of the poems speak of age and infirmity, but even in this regard Carruth is more humorous than not, as in "April Clean-up":

> He isn't quite a eunuch, but that's
> what he calls himself, this old
> two-beat codger on this spring
> afternoon picking up the winter's
> crop of twigs and bark from the lawn
> to make it "look nicer". . .

Little here suggests that this "he" ("the man I am always writing about," as Carruth notes in "Sex," from *Collected Shorter Poems*) is anyone other than the poetic stand-in for the poet himself. This character's much younger wife bears the same name as Carruth's, and she, like the book's dedicatee, is also a poet. Yet, for all the apparent seamlessness between autobiography and art, rarely does the book seem self-indulgent and never merely "confessional." These poems from late in the author's life show vigor, rigor, experimental suppleness, and rare candor. What seems to have provided the rejuvenating spark is this relationship found late in life, celebrated in the commonplaces of their rural life together, as seen in "Birthday Cake," which begins with the speaker eating "the last of [his wife's] birthday cake":

> The cake was stale.
> But I like stale cake, I even prefer it, which you
> don't
> understand, as I don't understand how you can
> open
> a new box of cereal when the old one is still
> unfinished.
> So many differences. You a woman, I a man,
> you still young at forty-two and I growing old at
> seventy.
> Yet how much we love one another.
> It seems a miracle. Not mystical, nothing occult,
> just the ordinary improbability that occurs
> over and over, the stupendousness
> of life.

Always original and thoughtful, in this book Carruth realizes himself even more fully than before, like Yeats' "wild old wicked man," coming into his element without apology and with the confidence that only the enthusiasm of the constant beginner can engender and only life-long devotion to the art and craft can support.

Rather less satisfying, W. S. Merwin's fourteenth separate collection of poems (excluding his *Selected* and the two tetralogies of early books), **The Vixen**, stands in stark relief to Carruth's volume. Where the latter employs a variety of forms, the former extends the same shape and basic size through page after unpunctuated page. While individual passages flicker with vitality, the whole becomes a monotonous blur. To his credit, Merwin almost completely eschews the vatic posturing that swamped his work beginning in the late-sixties and returns to the lyric structures which show him at his best; alas, narrative, with its demands for clarity of sequence (the sentence is the prime model for narrative structure, and Merwin's perverse insistence on erasing the traffic signs of syntax suggests the impediment to that impulse) and subordination of surface texture and color to the demands of the coherent whole. In the lyric, Merwin's eye for detail, for baroque elaboration, is not so conspicuously distracting, since the need for the reader to participate constantly as redactor, while consistent with postmodern theory and some minimalist practice, is distracting enough.

The poems are set in the South of France, where Merwin lived for much of his adult life; most seem written from the point of view of a speaker whose sensibilities resemble those of the poet; of two exceptions to this rule, "François de Maynard 1582-1646" and "Peire Vidal," the latter, with its consistent syntax-to-line correlation, is among the least challenging to read, in the most absolutely literal sense. The poem "Substance," with its almost Hopkinsesque reification of a

version of divine presence in the particular and contingent, provides a clear, brief sense of the detriments and benefits of the volume:

> I could see that there was a kind of distance lighted
> behind the face of that time in its very days
> as they appeared to me but I could not think of any
> words that spoke of it truly nor point to anything
> except what was there at the moment it was
> beginning
> to be gone and certainly it could not have been
> proven
> nor held however I might reach toward it touching
> the warm lichens the features of the stones the skin
> of the river and I could tell then that it was
> the animals themselves that were the weight and
> place
> of the hour as it happened and that the mass of the
> cow's neck
> the flash of the swallow the trout's flutter were
> where it was coming to pass they were bearing the
> sense of it
> without question through the speechless cloud of
> light

This might have been more satisfying had he dwelled more on "the mass of the cow's neck" than on the self-congratulatory perception of the ineffable and relied more on the studied accumulation of detail than on syntactic trickery to achieve intensity.

For some of the same reasons, Jane Kenyon's **Otherwise: New & Selected Poems** makes a less eloquent testimonial to her too brief life than might have been hoped. Her attention to detail, unlike Merwin's, rarely falters. Too often, however, Kenyon's generosity of spirit, which elevates the commonplace to numinosity, is not matched by mastery of craft. The poems accumulate as too much the same: the same kinds of lines, the same versifying strategies, the same mood—at once melancholy and exultant. Probably the poems gathered from her second volume, *The Boat of Quiet Hours*, and her last separate collection, *Constance*, are the best; the former because she was past her freshman awkwardness, the latter because she was operating with the mastery of a poet who had come into her own. The selection of *New Poems* is perhaps most moving read in the context during which they were composed, Kenyon's terminal leukemia. Too many of them seem incompletely realized, despite her efforts at revision; we can only imagine the ways in which her mind, without the distraction of illness, might have worked them just a little closer to fixed shape. The difficult task in reviewing a volume that is as much elegy as compilation is to separate the altogether necessary human and emotional response from the equally crucial critical remove; failure to manage that separation results in sentimentality, which serves no one.

Among the most fully realized of Kenyon's poems, "Peonies at Dusk" occurs toward the end of *Constance*:

> White peonies blooming along the porch
> send out light
> while the rest of the yard grows dim.
> Outrageous flowers as big as human
> heads! They're staggered
> by their own luxuriance: I had
> to prop them up with stakes and twine.
>
> The moist air intensifies their scent,
> and the moon moves around the barn
> to find out what it's coming from.
>
> In the darkening June evening
> I draw a blossom near, and bending close
> search it as a woman searches
> a loved one's face.

The ranks of serious poets have been that much reduced.

The poems of Terrance Keenan, a Rinzai Zen monk, also imbue the natural world with an almost mystical quality—although "imbue" suggests enhancing or adding to something not already present in full. Instead, **Practicing Eternity**, which gathers a smattering of poems from a previous full-length collection and two chapbooks with a body of newer poems, seeks to peel away the layers that separate us from the perfection already completely present in all things. No snowfall falls in an inappropriate place, one Zen case declares; even the broken watchband is perfect—if it could be otherwise, it would be. This is the world Keenan inhabits and of which he provides glimpses. And, at his best, his poems register the commonplace mystery through delicate rendering of detail, as in this passage from "Milk Jug":

> Morning slants across the table,
> flickers shadows beyond
> the clear early air.
> This old clay jug sits here
> filled with meadows
> or just empty,
> space in and around it
> the same vixen wind.
> Clay is the last touch
> of fractal dust adrift—
> no jug, no table, no wind,
> and void healing sweet
> all things together.

Other than the, to my ear, misstep of "vixen wind," the poem inheres entirely in specifics. Let the ear enjoy the music of "Clay is the last touch / of fractal dust adrift": this melody

exacted from the scientific terminology exceeds what Ammons manages, precisely because Keenan presents without preciousness a snippet of an extensive vocabulary.

Where the poems go wrong, they do so from an apparent urge to testify; they seem too self-consciously vatic, abstracted from the concrete details from which revelation or insight must emerge. Consider "Knowing a Friend on the Road":

> If I start from here
> to seek you out
> there will be nothing
> among my intentions.
>
> If you look for me
> you will find only
> self satisfying gestures.
>
> When we finally give up,
> my friend,
> like old dogs
> we will know each other by smell.

Jack Gilbert in his essay "Real Nouns" argues in favor of words that present "concrete particulars," language that can be bitten "like people used to bite coins to see if they were genuine." Where in the first seven lines can we test the poem's reliability? Only in the last stanza does Keenan steer back to the demonstrable, with a kind of wit evidenced in the first brief poem of the collection, "The Axe":

> This is the best axe
> I've ever had.
> It's lasted fifteen years.
> It's had only two new heads
> and six new helves.
> God damned good axe.

In its simplicity, we might overlook the absolute compression of language, the appropriate pitch and diction, and, once more, the music of right language—"heads" and "helves"—all of which serve a wry humor akin to but not clearly derived from Carruth's. Still, the best of these poems shine with a light of understanding and call us back and back in an act of reciprocal benediction.

Three other volumes of Zen-inspired or -related poetry have come out this year. Philip Whalen's **Canoeing Up Cabarga Creek**, subtitled *Buddhist Poems 1955-1986*, contains no previously unpublished poems but gathers a generous sampling of poems that directly derive from or reflect Whalen's devout practice. Like Keenan, Whalen is ordained and has, in fact, received transmission as a roshi, a Zen master. Not surprisingly, given the collection's focus, this aspect of Whalen's interests takes center stage; the texture of the verse, however, seems cut from the same cloth as Whalen's poetry in general, which is to say that his roots in the Beat movement remain integral to his poetic practice. If, in general, I tend to prefer the earlier poems in this volume (as in Snyder's, a review of which follows), that reflects my general preference for the early energy evidenced in Beat poetry. While a certain self-consciousness pervades most Beat writing—if nothing more than a self-consciousness of the rebellious nature of the work—something vital leaked out at some point in the sixties through the seventies. Still, Whalen's quirky perceptions and quick-cut transitions often produce effective, moving poems. This passage from "Sourdough Mountain Lookout" gives a taste of the kind of music Whalen makes at his best:

> Fire and pressure from the sun bear down
> Bear down centipede shadows of palm-frond
> A limestone lithograph—oysters and clams of stone
> Half a black rock bomb displaying brilliant crystals
> Fire and pressure Love and Strife bear down
> Brontosaurus, look away
>
> My sweat runs down the rock

Evident here are influences of both Pound and Kenneth Rexroth. While not the best poet of the Beats still active, Whalen is well worth the read, and this selection provides a good sampling of his career.

Gary Snyder's **Mountains and Rivers Without End** purports to be a book-length poem but seems more a selection of poems on related topics. Lacking is the unity of form that characterizes successful long poems; even Pound's *Cantos* (issued this year for the first time in paperback with several previously uncollected pieces) demonstrates a kind of continuity of formal concern, though, as Hayden Carruth has argued, the book may be best read as Pound's collected poems from the second half of his career. The pieces that compose this volume were written between 1956 and 1996. The initial inspiration was Chinese scroll landscapes, which provided, as he notes in an afterward, a vision of "how the energies of mist, white water, rock formations, air swirls—a chaotic universe where everything is in place—are so much a part of the East Asian painter's world." From this, Snyder has produced a scroll-work of poems that traverse the planet, including trips by freighter, hitching, and walking. Framed by a Zen sensibility, these Beat wanderings take on something of the glow of the mendicant monk, though the idiom is clearly American. The earliest of the pieces here appeal to me most, especially those, like "Night Highway 99," that capture the colloquial speech of those met on the road with an almost blues-like rhythm:

Toledo, Castle Rock, free way four lane
no stoplights and no crossings, only cars

& people walking, old hitchhikers
break the laws. How do I know. . .
the state cop
told me so

Come a dozen times into
Portland
on the bum or
hasty lover
late at night

The variety of the pieces included demonstrates greater range of expression than does Whalen's selection, a fair comparison since each book gathers poems drawn from several decades of practice. In part, Snyder seems to have a genuinely more synthetic imagination than Whalen; what he borrows, he assimilates, and his borrowings seem more eclectic, his sense of the world thus that much more enlarged.

Finally, Jim Harrison's **After Ikkyu**, his ninth collection of poems, like Snyder's volume but even more so, demonstrates the seamless continuity between the sacred and profane characteristic of Zen. Ikkyu was a fifteenth century Zen master and poet, notorious for his unconventional attitude toward authority and devotion. True to this inspiration, in his poems, Harrison (who "does not remotely consider [him]self a 'Zen Buddhist'") combines a naturalist's keen observation with an iconoclast's melding of the spiritual and profane:

> Just before dark
> watched coyote take a crap
> on rock out cropping,
> flexing hips (no time off)
> swiveled owl-like to see
> in all six directions:
> sky above
> earth below,
> points of compass
> in two half circles.
> There.
> And there is no distance.
> He knows the dreamer
> that dreams his dreams.

At times, Harrison's verse lapses into too prosaic discursiveness, a consequence of his more profitable career as novelist, and his poems betray a too easy smugness about the world, again a tendency less detrimental over the course of a several-hundred-page novel than in a smaller, tighter poem. Still, at his best, he manages the compression characteristic not only of his Japanese inspiration but of good lyric poetry in general. This is the first section of the volume's title poem:

> Our minds buzz like bees
> but not the bees' minds.

It's just the wings not heart
they say, moving to another flower.

For fans of Harrison's poetry, this collection is a welcome addition from a writer whose energies too often go elsewhere, and it's a good introduction to an underrated poet for readers otherwise new to his work.

A devotional strain has been evident through all of Denise Levertov's eighteen separate collections of poetry, but that tendency has become more pronounced in her most recent volumes and reaches a crescendo in *Sands in the Well*. Like Harrison, Levertov has an acute eye for nature though her temperament seems quieter, more attuned to the "parallel world," as she calls it, though nature alone is not the apparent reference, since these poems as much concern the parallel world of the spirit as nature; most of the poems in this collection, at least the successful ones, concern Levertov's "Sojourns in the Parallel World," times when

> we drift for a minute,
> an hour even, of pure (almost pure)
> response to that insouciant life:
> cloud, bird, fox, the flow of light, the dancing
> pilgrimage of water, vast stillness
> of spellbound ephemerae on a lit windowpane. . .

At these moments "something tethered / in us, hobbled like a donkey . . . / . . . breaks free" into a transport that allows us to re-see and re-claim a world of "Primary Wonder," as she titles another poem, an interlude in the course of days when "[p]roblems insoluble and problems offering / their own ignored solutions / jostle for [our] attention." This "mystery," however, is not unauthored; she concludes this poem, and this volume, with a note of genuine praise:

> the mystery
> that there is anything, anything at all,
> let alone cosmos, joy, memory, everything,
> rather than void: and that, O Lord,
> Creator, Hallowed One, You still,
> hour by hour sustain it.

In the face of belief this passionate, no wonder that, however melancholy the moment, Levertov cannot maintain an attitude "strictly sad."

If not all of the poems rise to the heights of the best, this is to be expected. At times the awe seems almost formulaic, and the political poems rarely transform her sense of the sanctity of life into other than relatively propagandistic terms in which, for instance, all underground nuclear tests are "Hiroshima blasts." Still, these poems, in particular, occupy only a single—the briefest—section of the book. For the most part, her eco-activism is implicit in poems that celebrate the too

often overlooked splendor of the natural world, as in the delicately handled "Threat," a poem about how one can live in proximity to nature, in this case a large pine, without appreciating fully its power. The poem concludes:

> Only when, before dawn one year
> at the vernal equinox, the wind
> rises and rises, raising images
> of cockleshell boats tossed among huge
> advancing walls of waves,
> do you become aware that always,
> under respect, under your faith
> in the pinetree's beauty, there lies
> the fear it will crash some day
> down on your house, on you in your bed,
> on the fragility of the safe
> dailiness you have almost
> grown used to.

This collection, with its "shards / of memory, scraps of once-heard lore, intimations / once familiar" ("What Goes Unsaid") is the strongest Levertov has brought out in some years.

The lineaments of Jeredith Merrin's world are much more distinctly human. In *Shift*, her first collection, we are treated to poems that track relationships, many rather different than the usual suspects in a first volume. In place of poems to parents, we have poems about a step-father from whom the speaker is "still hungry for his / never-spoken 'I love you'" ("The Best Cook"), the speaker's first lesbian encounter— "A massive shifting, / as of plates rearranging / along a continental shelf" ("Shift"), and an errant, early liberated grandmother prone to take off "for weeks / to Palm Springs and her trailer / in the desert, alone" ("Gram"). Merrin has no characteristic form—the poems range from relatively short-lined poems to roughly metered tercets with irregular rhyme—though her "style" is generally intimate, confidential, though hardly confessional, a term that suggests either shame or pride in whatever actions spur the revelations. Merrin's approach is measured, her language careful; her poems are the residual search for "The Right Words," as she titles one poem, "that finally // make up for childhood, / make the right one love you." And the elegiac mood that permeates the collection seems to emerge, at least in part, from the consequences of finding that "right one" only to have her suffer from a life-threatening illness. The frustration at being unable to effect change in matters that matter most is articulated in "Sublunar," where the speaker admits, "If something isn't right you try to fix it; / when Chance grips big things, you control the small." Finally, unable to find answers in the macrocosm, against which personal "tragedies are insignificant," she concludes:

> I don't know how to end it. My mind wanders,

then focuses on helpful minute chores,
making the coffee, laundry, next week's meals
—then drifts again. The satellites and planets,

glowing with various colors in black space,
with names from ancient myth or Shakespeare's
plays,
go about their rounds the way she goes

about her work: writing and revising,
indifferent to pain. Moons spin; lovers
love as best they can; a writer writes.

Merrin apparently accumulated the poems that comprise this volume for a long time; the care in selection and crafting shows.

David Mason's **The Country I Remember** does not suffer from the same degree of sophomore slump as the second collections of many of his New Formalist colleagues, in large measure due to the long title poem that occupies the first two-thirds of the collection. None of the poems in the second section, sadly, come close to the verbal and metrical fluency of the best of Mason's first volume, *The Buried Houses*, most notably the remarkable "Blackened Peaches." This poem, like the best of the work in both collections, is written in Frostian blank verse and spoken by a persona clearly not the poet. As a rule, New Formalists seem to fare poorly at the personal, a peculiarity a critic might profitably explore. For the purposes of this review, however, suffice it to say that Mason is at his best in the braided monologues that compose the title poem, whose speakers are modeled after the poet's relatives. In this poem, two speakers, Lt. John Mitchell and his daughter, Maggie Gresham, each recount tales of their separate escapes, he from the confines of both Libby Prison in the Confederate South and the bounded existence of a midwestern farmer, and she from the confines of sheltered life in the family home. In both cases, the tales are told at the end of a life, with the prospect of death close. To Mason's credit, he creates a believable fiction—the first measure of any story-teller. The details seem exact, the ways of speech credible. This latter is perhaps the weakest element of the poem, for the two speakers' voices are not as distinct as one might hope; the modalities of meter, including variations, caesurae, and enjambments, do not pattern speech rhythms as clearly individual as one might hope.

On the plus side, Mason handles an iambic, largely pentameter line with considerable agility. Consider this passage from the section titled "Acoustic Shadows":

We climbed Sand Mountain and could see the dust
raised by Bragg's army beating a retreat.
That night we saw the flash of cannonfire

but didn't hear a sound. "Acoustic shadow,"
the Colonel called it, hillsides all lit up
like summer lightning, but only a drizzle
hissed and the men were too dead tired to hear.

At heart, the poet's labor is to preserve and celebrate a family connection that, if worked well, will transcend the individual need and speak to a segment, at least, of our society at large. Mason allows Mrs. Gresham, in the section called "The Country I Remember," to articulate that aim:

I thought my whole ambition was to make
the past and present come together, dreamed
into a vivid shape that memory
could hold the way the land possesses rivers.
They in turn possess the land and carry it
in one clear stream of thought to drink from
or water gardens with.

These passages convey well both the strengths and limitations of Mason's craft; he usually manages a very fluid metrical line, avoiding the metronomic beat evidenced in the first line of the second sample, working within the acceptable range of substitutions to keep the numbers smooth but unobtrusive. Still, the rhythm and locutions of "Blackened Peaches" seem a step beyond the poems in this collection.

With **Trespasser**, R. T. Smith moves into new territory. Most of the poems are set in Ireland, where Smith is a decided foreigner. One of the collection's many virtues is that Smith never pretends otherwise and is able gently to mock himself for his "real-life" pretensions to the contrary. "Waterford (County Cavan)" provides an early sense of the book's tone and stance; while the speaker's Irish "hostess fetches tea," he handles a piece of her crystal,

study[ing]
the flawless polish with immigrant
glee and giv[ing] it

all my reverence for skill
and a pilgrim's mixed envy,
till I hear the kettle's

whistle and the hall
clock gongs four. Almost calm,
but finding I have nicked my

finger on one corner,
I long still, here on the northern
border, for the wintry

clarity of this Irish
vessel, fragile and dazzling

in my trespassing hands.

In another poem, drifting into sedation after breaking his arm, the speaker realizes that he "was only / a graceless tourist // who imagined somewhere / nearby . . . a terrorist's device." Toward its end, the poems in the first section migrate closer to home, including the poet's tender recollection of his mother, "Black Shawl."

Most of the poems in the volume's first section are relatively short-lined lyrics that run fluidly down the page, treating description with succinct detail and the loving care the speaker gives the piece of Waterford; the poems in the second section are somewhat more gnarled in appearance, as befits the subject of the poems, the fictional character Gristle, part Crazy Jane and part Crow. Gristle is a mystic bard out of Irish folklore, roaming the rocks and crags and woodlands, taking on the spirit of whatever he perceives. Interestingly, a poem that, in somewhat earlier form, more "personal" in its context, seemed overly self-conscious, now, slightly revised (though how telling "slight" revisions can be; see Carruth's discussion of Goodman's changes to "The Lordly Hudson"), the poem takes on different coloration as spoken by Gristle. Even the title reflects the new aspect: from "Self as Trout" in *The Cardinal Heart* to "Gristle Trout." Consider what a changed stance the new costume gives these lines:

> Soon I will be beheaded,
> a slit saint, my milt
> and viscera greasing newsprint,
> my eye eclipsed with a brittle
> lid, armor singed in
> the black skillet, yet
> the glib gill persists.

"Glib" we may still find the speaker, but the changed persona makes all the difference in how we perceive that glibness, no longer a perhaps unself-aware critique of preciousness but a distanced comment on a somewhat disreputable figure. More contemporary poets should learn the value of finding the appropriate stance and angle from which to cast a poem. If the craft that goes into the poems of this new collection shows the same workmanship apparent in Smith's earlier volumes, the new strategies of stance and tone show increasing poetic maturity.

The mythological frame for Louise Glück's **Meadowlands** is considerably different, though, more accurately, one should speak of "mythologies," for Glück uses the tale of Penelope, Telemachus, and errant Odysseus to explore the myth of contemporary marriage. While less lyrically effusive than her ground-breaking *The Wild Iris*, she successfully builds on that material. If the poems are less rhapsodic, they accurately register the tensions of a couple whose distances are measured by more than miles. As early as the second poem, Glück

sounds the essentially elegiac note of the collection. In "Cana," the woman laments the dulling of passion; looking about the home and grounds previously "lit" by forsythia and hyacinth, emblems of their love, she now realizes:

> And all of it vanished,
> reabsorbed into impassive process. Then
> what will we see by,
> now that the yellow torches have become
> green branches?

Not that the world has become blackened by the loss, merely reduced to less saturated coloration. Counterpointing the poignancy of poems like the one above are poems that see through our rehearsed poses of loss and betrayal, such as the first poem voiced by the son, "Telemachus' Detachment":

> When I was a child looking
> at my parents' lives, you know
> what I thought? I thought
> heartbreaking. Now I think
> heartbreaking, but also
> insane. Also
> very funny.

The subtle shift in register from the first "heartbreaking" to the second prepares for the wrenching "insane" and also for the startling, but finally more wrenching, "very funny." The funny but terrifying dynamic between the woman and man is revealed with unnerving acuteness in the several dialogue poems in the volume, none of which are entirely self-contained, for Glück builds one exchange on the previous, forcing us back and forth through the poems, allowing us to gain increased insight with each perusal. The only one of these conversations brief enough to quote in its entirety is "The Butterfly," in which the indented lines are the woman's:

> Look, a butterfly. Did you make a wish?
>
> > You don't wish on butterflies.
>
> You do so. Did you make one?
>
> > Yes.
>
> It doesn't count.

Such cruelties are allowed the perverse laugh of self-recognition they will doubtless bring to many readers. In her work beginning with the publication of *The Wild Iris*, Glück has demonstrated herself to be one of the very few strong voices of her generation.

If Donald Hall has never quite matched his career high of *The One Day*, his two separate collections since have displayed the consistent craft of a master, and in *The Old Life* he demonstrates an emotional openness missed in 1993's *The Museum of Clear Ideas*. Life circumstances have certainly helped push Hall in the direction of intensified emotion; the premature death of his wife, Jane Kenyon, which, although unacknowledged until the penultimate poem, saturates the mood and seems a slant reference of the volume's title. Each of the four longish poems included takes a different form, from the loosened iambic pentameters of the colloquial "The Night of the Day," in which Hall gives us a small vignette of country life through the lens of a late-night conversation regarding ownership of a group of stray cows; to the continuation of "Baseball" from his previous book in the thirteen-syllable lined, thirteen line stanzas of "Extra Innings," an offering prompted by one reviewer's comment that no one would "wish for a thirteenth" inning of the earlier poem; to the alternating three- and four-beat lines of the title poem, an autobiographical study prompted by his own disdain for McPoems—"boring prosy little anecdotes out of memory, where the poets look back on themselves, often in childhood, with *such* affection and pity, and with a continual, crepuscular melancholy"—and apparent desire to see if he could avoid the pitfalls; to the concluding elegy, "Without," written in loose pentameter but "without punctuation" or capitalization, which results in a breathless deluge of feeling.

The final poem is perhaps the most interesting, for it seems to explore distinctly different regions from his previous volumes, this form resulting from the need to find a new mode of expression for the unbearable weight of grief. The subject of the poem first enters, in the rush of the opening stanza:

> we live in a small island stone nation
> without color under gray clouds and wind
> distant the unlimited ocean acute
> lymphoblastic leukemia without seagulls
> or palm trees without vegetation
> or animal life only barnacles and lead
> colored moss that darkens when months do

The poem accumulates the way the year of the inferred subject's death does—"without punctuation"—seasons essentially meaningless when life is lived at the bedside. Even the violence of the world at large, encapsulated in "bomb shoot shell / strafe execute rape retreat and attack," is diminished by the closer "pain vomit neuropathy morphine nightmare." And, afterward, life lacks savor:

> no cathedral no hobo jungle the same women
> and men they long to drink hayfields
> without dog or semicolon or village square
> without monkey or lily without garlic

This volume constitutes as powerful and moving an elegy and romance as one could bear to read.

The poems gathered in *The World at Large: New and Selected Poems, 1971-1996*, demonstrate a range of forms and idioms almost as impressive as Hall's. Although James McMichael has published only four separate collections over the course of the twenty-five years this volume spans, the breadth and scope of his achievement more than warrant the attention a selected poems asks. If the earliest, short poems seem a piece with other brief lyrics of the time in their neo-surrealist personification of vegetables, they display a tighter craft and more lucent syntax than was common in the period; also, they accumulate with the force of careful analogy, in which the assorted greens treated in "The Vegetables," from McMichael's first collection, come to represent the growth of the fetus and child who will become the poet. By the time his second collection was issued in 1974, McMichael was already straining against the confines of period style, most eloquently in "Itinerary," the longish poem which looks forward to his two book-length poems. This poem begins with an impersonal voice surveying the contemporary West Coast and moves progressively eastward and backward to the seventeenth century through several speakers, modeled apparently on historical figures as diverse as Meriwether Lewis and Cotton Mather, whose presences in the poem are never clearly signaled; each voice subtly modulates into the next. The retrospective journey expresses not only the increasing purity of the land (or, more conventionally, the increasing pollution from then till now) in terms as grounded in the specific as the muddy runnels of contemporary California compared to the paradisal river waters of colonial Virginia. The subtext of the poem's movement concerns equally eros and loss—the explicit sexuality of nature poised against the active spirituality of nature. Not surprisingly, the final destination of the poem, or its point of nativity, is a garden in New England, in which the hand of God is discernible in every lineament. Meditating after Sunday service, the speaker confesses, "after my devotions / a walk in the garden can do much / to fill my heart with clear obedience." His relations to the earth are seen in terms of congress and procreation:

> . . . I would
> look upon such country as will show me
> nature undressed, the strata of the land,
> her lays and beds and all her privacies.
> For my wonder tells me I should be
> promiscuous, should learn by all the
> laws of bodies and by where they are
> the joyful news out of the newfound world.
> This walk is news.

The ironic culmination of this urge to go forth and be fruitful is where the poem begins, and we return to the beginning to read again with different eyes.

The shape and contents of the book are somewhat peculiar for a selected poems, which bears some comment. McMichael chooses not to organize his volume by either chronology or reverse chronology; instead, he weaves older and newer to interesting effect. We see the changes in his approach in dramatic relief but observe as well the continuity of theme, the death of the poet's mother while he was a child. The mother is the unidentified subject, along with the child present only by analogy, in the first group of poems, but her death and its import is announced directly in the first section of his most recent separate book, *Each in a Place Apart*, published in 1994. Such juxtaposition cannot be accident. This book-length poem, one of two he's issued over twenty-five years, marks another of the book's irregularities; while cullings from his first two collections seem scant, he reproduces both long poems in their entirety, a choice justified by the nature of both poems which recount narratives in a somewhat recursive and indirect form. Any excerpt would not do justice to the way the wholes accumulate. This, too, is the reviewer's burden, especially with regard to *Four Good Things*, a poem that begins with autobiography but moves through more than a simple summary could indicate, meshing personal meditation with larger social and political concerns in nearly seamless segues reminiscent of those he used in "Itinerary." Above all, McMichael works in both long poems with an unerring ear for a loosened pentameter yet manages that line to very different effect in each. *Four Good Things*, particularly, also displays McMichael's ability to include information—dense and expository information—without losing the thread of either the line or the through-line. Consider this passage from a little more than midway through the poem, a description of warehouses at nineteenth-century Liverpool docks:

> They were still in that plain geography of
> "things in their places," of bales on
> hoisting-pulleys and in ship-holds and, along the
> quays,
> the dry white scudding that they lost as waste.
> They were looking for the samenesses that make us
> feel we've
> broken through to something, through those
> unsure things that happen in a place in time to
> something like our safe impalpable and self-
> sustaining
> plans that are always future.

Taken in its entirety, this volume demonstrates an intelligence and artistic will and talent determined to make "the most of what we / know and go on learning." With both of his long poems and a tight selection of his lyrics available in a single volume, McMichael's work may begin to draw the attention it deserves.

Finally, a native Californian from further up the coast and current United States Poet Laureate, Robert Hass has brought out **Sun Under Wood**, his fourth book in twenty-three years, the same period over which McMichael published his sepa-

rate volumes. That said, a reviewer might seek other principles of comparison, and they could, indeed, be found. Like McMichael, Hass has a good eye for detail and a broad knowledge of nature and culture; like McMichael, he writes with loving attention to the California landscape; and, like McMichael, he has a keen ear for the music of language as it combines with syntax and the poetic line. Unlike McMichael, and as he acknowledges in the final poem of this new collection, Hass has little facility with metaphor or analogy. He sees things best when he sees them clearly, for what they are and what they might mean—signify, not represent. If McMichael most effectively deals with over-powering emotion through distraction into peripherally or tangentially analogous systems or incidents, Hass has tended to veer away, displacing emotion into weak, often trivial and reductive—frequently extended—metaphors. Few of these obtrude on the poems in this collection, which seems, in fact, to confront matters of personal life with greater honesty and openness than in earlier collections. For all the naming of names in earlier poems, the reader was left with little sense, other than generally, of the turbulences of the life out of which those forcibly moderated poems emerged.

Two of the personal circumstances brought into poetic light represent conflicts from childhood and from the present, first with his mother's alcoholism and, second, with his separation and divorce. Both experiences are traumatic enough that indirection and non-disclosure are understandable strategies; however, the force they exert also seems to require some release, the shapes of which are long, mixed formal sequences occurring toward the beginning and the end of the volume. The earlier conflict is first raised in the second poem, "Our Lady of the Snows," in which the speaker recalls "slip[ping]" into church "[w]hen [his] mother was in a hospital drying out" to light a candle "and bargain for [them] both." She appears again, more directly seen, in the next poem, "Dragonflies Mating," in which the poet confesses his humiliation when she would appear at basketball practice

> with her bright, confident eyes,
> and slurred, though carefully pronounced words,
> and the appalling
>
> impromptu sets of mismatched clothes she was
> given to
> when she had the dim idea of making a good
> impression in that state.

Hass explores this painful topic at even greater, more direct length in the following sequence, "My Mother's Nipples." Writing about this poem, Hass comments that when the topic was first proposed to a friend, "My first idea was to make fun of the idea, my second was the painfulness of it. These suggested a form." The "form" includes both long-lined, meditative poetry; brief, parodic lyrics; and prose passages, which circle the subject at times and at times narrow to harrowing directness. From its opening lines, the poem announces the tendency against which it will struggle:

> They're where all displacement begins.
> They bulldozed the upper meadow at Squaw Valley,
> where horses from the stable, two chestnuts, one white,
> grazed in the mist and the scent of wet grass on summer mornings
> and moonrise threw the owl's shadow on voles and wood rats
> crouched in the sage scent the earth gave back after dark
> with the day's heat to the night air.

What all this has to with the theme announced by the poem's title we might wonder until we realize that the lyricism demonstrates the very evasiveness of displacement. Not until the first of the prose sections does the poem approach the pain more directly, with two memories of the mother's institutionalization. At the climax of the poem, Hass recounts his father's death and his curiosity "to see in what ratio [his mother] would feel relieved and lost." This longest of the sections narrates the poet's trip to locate a copy of his parents' marriage license, at the end of which he discovers that they wed at the last moment before his older brother's birth and feels sorry "that their life together began in a negotiation too painful to be referred to again." In the final prose passage, Hass exemplifies his desire as a child for a normal life, against all indications to the contrary:

> I came home from school and she was gone. I don't know what instinct sent me to the park. I suppose it was the only place I could think of where someone might hide: she had passed out under an orange tree, curled up. Her face, flushed, eyelids swollen, was a ruin. Though I needed urgently to know whatever was in it, I could hardly bear to look. When I couldn't wake her, I decided to sit with her until she woke up. I must have been ten years old: I suppose I wanted for us to look like a son and mother who had been picnicking, like a mother who had fallen asleep in the warm light and scent of orange blossoms and a boy who was sitting beside her daydreaming, not thinking about anything in particular.

After this, the poet admits, "You are not her singing, though she is what's / broken in a song." Trying "to think of some place on earth she loved," the poet can "remember she only ever spoke happily / of high school." Evasion and approach—the poles between which Hass struggles with this demonic angel.

Often Hass begins with this effort at displacement against

which the poem finally defines itself. "Regalia for a Black Hat Dancer," the longest and most inclusive of the sequences, opens with the writer's effort to find words to express experience and the failure, in abstraction-laden apothegms, to realize his desire. The rest of the poem grows from his determined sitting "down to it," from which he can state lucidly and without self-pity about "the year [his] marriage ended":

> I don't think I could have told the pain of loss
> from the pain of possibility,
> though I knew they weren't the same thing.

What follows is the difficult process of distinguishing between these two kinds of pain and two kinds of emptiness: "one made of pain and desire / and one made of vacancy." Or, as he notes later:

> Emptinesses—
> one is desire, another is the object that it doesn't have.
> Everything real is nourished in the space between these things.

The poet's meditations carry him from Friday night restaurants in Berkeley filled with divorced parents and their noncustodial children to the cave of the Sokkaram Buddha in Korea, from the unpremeditated loss of his wedding band to the unexpected discovery of a new relationship with its "desperate kissings, wells of laughter." Yet the new discovery might only, at times, accentuate the old loss, felt as "pain. Physical pain, fluid; it moved / through [his] body like grassfire spreading on a hill." He comes to realize:

> I didn't know you could lie down in such swift, opposing currents.
>
> Also two emptinesses, I suppose, the one joy comes from, the one regret, disfigured intention, the longing to be safe or whole flows into when it's disappearing.

After building such structures of conflicting feelings and impulses, the poet confronts the difficulty of finding an appropriate conclusion, and Hass is often not at his best with what in the trade is called "closure." Here, he attempts, in a characteristic gesture, to ground this complex of emotions in a simple physical act; in the open market of a Korean town, the poet has a mug of beer and barbecued baby chicks. The poem ends with enumeration and fragmented phrasing:

> Two pancakes. A clay mug of the beer. Sat down under an umbrella and looked to see, among the diners
> feasting, quarreling about their riven country,

if you were supposed to eat the bones. You were. I
did.

Such elaborate structures beg a more satisfying, less patent
conclusion.

To his credit, however, Hass seems more than passingly acquainted with his short-falls, as he elaborates in the volume's
final poem, the tellingly titled "Interrupted Meditation." The
poem opens with the kind of lyrical description of nature at
which Hass excels:

> Little green involute fronds of fern at creekside.
> And the sinewy clear water rushing over
> creekstone
> of the palest amber, veined with a darker gold,
> thinnest lines of gold rivering through the amber
> like—ah, now we come to it.

Just what "we come to" will take another two pages of dialogue between the poet and an unnamed Polish survivor of
the Nazi occupation of Warsaw that treats the relation between experience and language in the context of extreme suffering. This leads to the remembered referent of the opening,
in which the unnamed interlocutor speaks:

> Of course, here, gesturing out the window, pines,
> ragged green
> of a winter lawn, the bay, *you can express what
> you like,*
> enumerate the vegetation. And you! you have to,
> I'm afraid,
> *since you don't excel at metaphor.* A shrewd, quick
> glance
> to see how I have taken this thrust. *You write well,
> clearly.*
> *You are an intelligent man. But*—finger in the air—
> silence is waiting. Milosz believes there is a Word
> at the end that explains. There is silence at the end,
> *and it doesn't explain, it doesn't even ask.*

Notice how what could be taken as self-congratulation on
Hass's part—praise of his skill at writing, his intelligence—
is rendered as left-handed compliment, the way in which it
was offered. If Hass cannot, at least cannot yet, completely
rise above his flaws, he at least can recognize the truth when
it's articulated.

This poem makes for an interesting comparison with "On
Squaw Peak," the closing poem of Hass's previous collection, *Human Wishes.* Although in general I like this poem

very much, in it he is guilty of many of the same ploys of
displacement and avoidance but without this level of self-
knowledge, which leads him, instead of facing pain directly,
to slide off into one of his lyrically inappropriate metaphors,
as in this description of the place to which aborted fetuses
go:

> I wanted to tell you
> that when the ghost-child died, the three-month
> dreamer
> she and I would never know, I kept feeling that
> the heaven it went to was like the inside of a store
> window
> on a rainy day from which you watch the blurred
> forms
> passing in the street.

How much more powerful, more honest and—more to the
point—more plausible this passage from the new poem in
which the poet remembers "the failure of [his] marriage, / the
three or four lost years just at the end and after":

> She sat on the couch sobbing, her rib cage shaking
> from its accumulated abysses of grief and thick
> sorrow.
> I don't love you, she said. The terrible thing is
> that I don't think I ever loved you.

Less lyrical, certainly, but the emotional gain is intense. If
Hass is unable to sustain this pitch through to the conclusion
of the poem, at least, now, he realizes that flaw, too:

> A vault of blue sky, traildust, the sweet medicinal
> scent of mountain grasses, and at trailside—
> I'm a little ashamed that I want to end this poem
> singing, but I want to end this poem singing—the
> wooly
> closed-down buds of the sunflower to which, in
> English,
> someone gave the name, sometime, of pearly
> everlasting.

The exponential growth in self-awareness evidenced in *Sun
Under Wood,* along with Hass's demonstrable lyrical skill
and intelligence, mark his movement from one of the best
poets of his generation to one of the best poets working in
America today; we could all afford to learn from his penetrating self-criticism, doubtless a consequence of his refusal
to publish too much and too soon, and follow as he continues
this slow but sure growth to poetic majority.

The Year in Drama
by Julius Novick

In recent years many people have worried loudly about the decline of the American musical theater. Broadway and the road have been dominated by long-running behemoths from Britain, and by loving revivals of classic American shows—the kind of shows nobody seems to be able to write anymore. Recent American Broadway musicals have tended to be uninspired recyclings of movies: *Beauty and the Beast* (the long-running Disney extravaganza, which opened on Broadway in 1994), *Victor/Victoria* (a crass vehicle for the indefatigable Julie Andrews, 1995), *State Fair* (warmed-over Rodgers and Hammerstein, albeit with beautiful songs, 1996), and *Big* (a 10.5-million-dollar flop, 1996). But 1996, a lacklustre year for spoken drama in America, was a year in which the Broadway musical, that proud but aging creation of specifically American genius, was invigorated by new energies from non-commercial off-Broadway institutional theatres. Perhaps the important thing is not to try to write 'em like they used to, but to find different ways of writing 'em, so as to have a better chance of connecting with the young audiences of the '90s. That seemed to be happening in 1996.

Unquestionably, like it or not, the great event of the year in drama was the arrival of *Rent*, with words and music by Jonathan Larson, which won the Pulitzer Prize in Drama, the New York Drama Critics Circle Award as Best Musical, Tony Awards for Best Musical, Best Book and Best Score, and just about every other award this side of the Nobel Peace Prize. Until *Rent* opened at the New York Theater Workshop in New York's East Village (after four years "in development" there), Larson was totally unknown, working as a waiter while struggling to make it in the theater. Greeted with tremendous enthusiasm by critics and audiences alike, the production was moved intact to Broadway, where it immediately became a huge hit; the first touring company opened in Boston before the end of the year, and others are planned. The movie rights were sold for a goodly sum. Bloomingdale's even opened a *Rent* boutique. But Larson was unable to enjoy his success; just hours after *Rent*'s final dress rehearsal downtown, he died suddenly of an aortic aneurysm. (Two New York hospitals are being sued for failing to realize the seriousness of his condition.) He was ten days short of his 36th birthday.

What has made *Rent* so popular (aside from the publicity bonanza generated by its creator's death) is its wonderfully adroit combination of the here-and-now up-to-date with the eternally traditional. For excellent reasons, it struck many people as the nineties' answer to *Hair*, the off-Broadway-to-Broadway surprise-hit musical of the sixties. Both are rock musicals about a group of young people, alienated from re-

spectable consumer society, living hand-to-mouth in New York's East Village (where both shows were first produced), trying to evolve a new way of living, a new sort of community that will replace the constrictions of conventional families. Both shows feature sex, drugs, rock-and-roll, and a big protest meeting. And as *Hair* did in its time, *Rent* lights up the stage with the galvanic energy and winning charm of young, previously unknown performers who, if hype is to be believed, feel themselves to be a new-style "family." (Michael Greif, the director of *Rent*, has received less credit for this than he deserves.)

But the mood in *Rent* is much darker. Instead of radiant optimism ("This is the dawning of the Age of Aquarius"), there is pessimistic malaise ("You're living in America/ At the end of the millennium"). *Hair* is a fantasy of impudent yet sensitive, high-spirited adolescence; the young people in *Rent* are adults, worrying about the rent; the innocence is gone. The East Village in *Hair* is Bohemia as Arcadia; in *Rent* it is a place of cold, poverty, homelessness, crime, sickness and death. Dope in *Hair* is the source of euphoric visions; the heroine of *Rent* is on heroin. For the kids in *Hair*, sex is like a new toy; among the things young lovers in *Rent* have in common is HIV infection. Welcome to the nineties.

The acknowledged source of *Rent*, however, is not *Hair*, but another "musical" about ardent young people living without money on the margins of society: Puccini's *La Boheme*, which Larson has artfully adapted, creating a story more complex and coherent than that of either *Hair* or *Boheme*. Rodolfo the poet has become Roger, the creatively-blocked songwriter; Marcello the painter is now Mark the film-maker, who hides from life behind his camera; Schaunard the musician is Angel Dumott Schunard, street musician and drag queen; and Colline the philosopher is Tom Collins, still a philosopher. (Angel and Collins fall tenderly in love, a possibility which did not occur to Puccini's librettists.) Mimi, Rodolfo's neighbor and then his lover, becomes Mimi, Roger's neighbor and then his lover, but instead of Puccini's shy seamstress, she is an HIV-positive junkie who dances in an s&m club. Musetta, Marcello's flirtatious mistress, is transformed into Maureen, a flighty performance artist who has left Mark for Joanne, a civil rights lawyer. Welcome, once more, to the nineties.

Borrowing only a few notes from Puccini (Roger picks out the theme from Musetta's Waltz on his guitar), Larson has managed to catch the quality that has made *La Boheme* so beloved for a hundred years: the sweet pathos of youth, full of yearning for life and love, helpless in the face of disease and death. Paradoxically, for *the* musical of the Nihilistic Nineties, **Rent** is even more extravagantly sentimental than its famously weepy source. (That is another key to its popularity.) More even than **Boheme**, **Rent** takes place in the shadow of death. In the opera, only Mimi is infected (with tuberculosis, the great youth-killer of nineteenth-century Europe), and the opera ends with her death. Almost at the beginning of **Rent**, HIV-positive Roger sings of his hope to write "One song/ Glory/ One song/ Before I go/ Glory/ One song to leave behind." (This, of course, takes on extra poignancy in the light of Larson's own early death.) Sweet-tempered Angel dies, and Collins mourns him with a heart-breaking reprise of their love duet. But at the same time, **Rent** preaches an inspirational optimism. In her performance piece, Maureen calls for a "leap of faith": "Only thing to do is jump over the moon." "How do you measure—measure a year?" asks the company in the opening number of Act II, and answers, "Measure in love/ Seasons of love." At the end, Mimi, like her predecessor, is desperately ill, but Roger is able to sing her his one song—and it revives her! She doesn't even die! And the brave bohemians, defying all the forces ranged against them, sing of seizing the moment: "No day but today."

In its own way, then, **Rent** is heir to the Rodgers-and-Hammerstein tradition of strenuous affirmation. Most people (myself included) have found it irresistible; some consider it pretentious, soft-centered kitsch. These latter tend to prefer the year's other up-from-off-Broadway innovative musical: **Bring in Da Noise, Bring in Da Funk**, created by the dancer-choreographer Savion Glover and the director George C. Wolfe. **Noise/Funk** began its career in the fall of 1995 at the Joseph Papp Public Theater/New York Shakespeare Festival, of which Mr. Wolfe is the producer, and moved to Broadway in April, '96; it is an attempt to evoke the African-American experience, from the slave ships on down, by means of tap-dancing, with some assistance from words (by Reg E. Gaines) and music (by Daryl Waters, Zane Mark, and Ann Duquesnay). "I wanted to see how tap could not just tell stories," said Mr. Wolfe, "but how it could really convey really complicated emotion." The phenomenal Mr. Glover and his tap-dancing colleagues proved that the emotional range of tap is wider than most people would have expected. The agonies and ironies and frustrations of African-American history were not trivialized. But it seemed to me that they were not deeply explored or vividly rendered, either, by all that endless, brilliantly percussive footwork. (To my mind, the best number was a wryly parodic evocation of Bill "Bojangles" Robinson and his saccharine dance with Shirley Temple, in which little Shirley was represented by a large doll held by Mr. Glover—a number specifically *about* tap-dancing.) On this subject, however, mine was distinctly a minority view.

One more American musical deserves mention in this chronicle, one very different from any previously discussed:

a tiny, three-character chamber musical entitled **Bed and Sofa**, with music by Polly Pen and words by Laurence Klavan, which opened off-Broadway, at the Vineyard Theater, and did *not* move to Broadway (where it would have been totally out of place). **Bed and Sofa** was adapted from a film—not, however, a Hollywood film, but a silent Soviet film, released in 1927, about the Moscow housing shortage—well, actually about a woman and two men sharing a very small apartment. Ludmilla is married to Kolya, but that doesn't keep her from having an affair with Volodya. **Bed and Sofa** is the fourth Polly Pen musical to be produced at the Vineyard and directed by Andre Ernotte; Ms. Pen, Mr. Ernotte, and their colleagues have distilled their own economical, graceful, sweetly whimsical aesthetic.

No outstandingly important work of spoken drama burst upon the American theater in 1996, but established playwrights and new ones were trying to confront, with varying degrees of success, the issues of our end-of-the millennium lives. As befits the state of the nation, their plays tended to be somber, full of anxiety, short of hope. Comedy had a bitter edge; high spirits and playfulness were not abundant.

Hope finally prevails in **Golden Child** by David Henry Hwang, but it does not come easily. Mr. Hwang, most celebrated as the author of **M. Butterfly**, is writing about both of his great concerns as a dramatist: the impingement of the Western world on the Chinese, and the struggle of Chinese immigrants and their descendants to make lives for themselves in America. In this play, a young Chinese-American, uneasy about becoming a father and thus taking his place in the great, fraught succession of ancestors, dreams of his Chinese great-grandfather Eng Tieng-Binh, who comes home to his village, *circa* 1917-18, after three years away "trading with monkeys and devils." Mr. Hwang vividly creates the Eng household as a nest of intrigue, hypocrisy, and cruelty, with bitter animosity crackling back and forth among Tieng-Binh's three wives, who are constantly piercing and repairing the joint facade of harmony, humility, and elaborate good manners that tradition obliges them to maintain. The contrast between facade and feeling is often sharply funny.

Tieng-Binh feels burdened by the traditions he has inherited:

> It's not that I want to forget my family, quite the opposite. But to be Chinese—means to feel a whole web of obligation—obligation?—dating back 5,000 years. I am afraid of dishonoring my ancestors, even the ones dead for centuries. All the time, I feel ghosts—sitting on my back, whispering in my ear— keeping me from living life as I see fit.

He longs to be "modern," to be an "individual"—to have only one wife, the third and youngest, whom he loves. But he is enmeshed in contradictions. When his first wife demurs at his order to unbind their daughter's feet, he finds himself shouting, "I'm still the master here." Influenced by a bumbling missionary, he becomes a Christian. And his efforts cause terrible suffering. His traditionalist first wife cries,

> I have never stood in the way of change. But tell me, Honored Husband, how much change can people endure? How much progress can you shove down their throats before they rise up, screaming "Bring back the past! Nothing is more terrible than this constant turning of the wheel!"

But by confronting this turning-point in the lives of his ancestors, Tieng-Binh's American great-grandson is reconciled to handing on their legacy to his child.
In writing about the agony—and the irony—of the transition from traditional to modern ways of life, Mr. Hwang is writing about his own ancestors—the play took its origin from family stories told by his grandmother—but he is also writing about something that is part of the heritage of almost every American. *Golden Child* was commissioned by the South Coast Repertory of Costa Mesa, California. Beautifully staged by James Lapine, it opened off-Broadway at the New York Shakespeare Festival/Joseph Papp Public Theater, transferred to Costa Mesa, and is scheduled for Broadway.

Jon Robin Baitz, author of *The Film Club*, *The Substance of Fire*, and *Three Hotels*, reworked an early play called *Dutch Landscape* into *A Fair Country*, produced off-Broadway by the Lincoln Center Theater. Mr. Baitz, an American, spent some years of his boyhood in South Africa; his play concerns an American family living in South Africa in the 1970's—the father is a diplomat—whose members are too sensitive to be comfortable in the land of apartheid. The elder son, a left-wing journalist, is furious at his mother for having called the police when their Xhosa maid went berserk; the mother is barely holding herself together. To save his family, the father makes a deal that gets them out of South Africa; like Mr. Hwang's paterfamilias, he has good intentions which lead to irreversible disaster. *A Fair Country* diverts itself into a not-quite-clear examination of the homosexual younger son's relationship with his mother, but Mr. Baitz writes with intensity, shrewdness, and wit about a fraught point where the political and the personal intersect. Apartheid is gone, but America is still unsure how to respond to foreign struggles, and family tensions, conflicting claims, devil's bargains, are all still with us.

David Ives made his name with *All in the Timing* (1994), a highly popular and widely produced sextuple bill of six witty short plays, mostly about language. His experiments with plays that last longer and go deeper have fared less well. *Don Juan in Chicago*, reviewed last year, is a lamely facetious comedy in rhymed verse. In 1996, Primary Stages (off-Broadway) presented *Ancient History* (a completely revised ver-

sion of a play first produced in 1989), in which Mr. Ives uses a device from *All in the Timing*—a bell which signals the characters to go back and play the scene again, with a difference—to probe a complicated romantic/sexual relationship. There is snappy repartee (along with some tiresome persiflage), but there are also touching moments; *Ancient History* does not quite cohere, but there is a sense about it that Mr. Ives is on to something. (A long one-act, *Ancient History* was presented on a double bill with *English Made Simple*, a characteristic David Ives language playlet that might have been part of *All in the Timing*.)

The Red Address, another new-old play by Mr. Ives, first produced by the Magic Theater, San Francisco, in 1991, was presented off-Broadway, in a revised version, by the Second Stage Theater. Its protagonist is a hard-driving, macho young businessman named E. G. Triplett, who, at times of stress, likes to "go to the red address," which means donning lacy black panties, black stockings, a flame-red dress, and matching pumps—with the enthusiastic assistance of his wife. But this is not a play full of drag gags, nor of any other kind of gags. It is written with tough authority, very different from Mr. Ives's usual style, and it is about a man who is fighting for his life. But what is the point? What does E. G. Triplett's secret transvestism have to do with the mysterious Joe Driver's threat to E. G.'s milk company? Why, after his wife is brutally murdered, does E. G. undermine himself by wearing the red dress when he goes to meet Driver? Some statement about masculinity seems to be intended—not just that even a macho businessman might want to wear a dress, but something more complicated, more interesting, richer—but what? Still, *The Red Address* suggests that there is more to Mr. Ives's talent than I would have otherwise suspected.
The New York Drama Critics Circle gave its award for Best Play of 1995-96 to *Seven Guitars*—the sixth play by August Wilson to win a Circle Award. Like all Mr. Wilson's plays, it forms part of a cycle that dramatizes the African-American experience in the twentieth century, decade by decade; this is his play of the 1940's. Like all except one early play, it was directed by Lloyd Richards, and came to Broadway after a long march through the regional theaters.

Though not a musical, *Seven Guitars* as its title implies is haunted by music—by the blues, which Mr. Wilson acknowledges as a primary influence on his work. Set in a backyard in Pittsburgh (the city where Mr. Wilson grew up, and where most of his plays take place), it examines the last days of a young bluesman (magnetically played on Broadway by Keith David) called Floyd "Schoolboy" Barton. Floyd's guitar is in a pawnshop and his "manager" is arrested for selling fake insurance. Nevertheless, Floyd is determined to get to Chicago, where a record company is waiting to put a recording studio at his disposal:

> I know what will make a hit record. I leave here on

the Greyhound and I bet you in one year's time I be back driving a Buick. . . I am going to Chicago. If I have to buy me a graveyard and kill everybody I see. I am going to Chicago. I don't want to live my life without. Everybody I know live without. I don't want to do that. I want to live with. I don't know what you all think of yourself, but I think I'm supposed to have. Whatever it is.

That sense of deprivation, and the determination to be deprived no longer, is something Mr. Wilson (and other African-American playwrights) have dramatized before, and better. *Seven Guitars* unfolds sluggishly. Characters are not deeply probed, nor—except for one muttering, poultry-slaughtering, crazy old man—are they sharply individualized. Mr. Wilson's trademark virtues—the sense of authenticity, the enveloping atmosphere, the vernacular eloquence—are amply present, but he has evidently been seduced by his own talent. There is a lot of just sitting around chewing the fat in this play. The characters trade familiar schoolyard rhymes ("One bright morning in the middle of the night/ Two dead boys got up to fight"); one even favors us with a disquisition on how to cook greens. When they do have something of interest to say, they tend to take a great many words to say it. Mr. Wilson seems to have mislaid his blue pencil.

A number of distinguished American playwrights produced relatively (or absolutely) undistinguished work in 1996. Christopher Durang, the author of *Sister Mary Ignatius Explains It All for You, Beyond Therapy,* and *The Marriage of Bette and Boo,* gave us an uncharacteristically crude satiric comedy entitled *Sex and Longing.* To satirize the moral watchdogs of the religious right, as Mr. Durang does, by showing a sanctimonious, crusading minister raping the woman he is supposed to be praying for, is easy, obvious, cheap. Lulu, Mr. Durang's heroine, is initially presented as someone who needs sex every fifteen minutes; poor, game Sigourney Weaver, who played the part on Broadway (under the non-commercial auspices of the Lincoln Center Theater), was thus forced to spend much of Act I interminably repeating the play's title, in a tone of desperate moaning, while throwing herself at strangers. At the end of Act I, Lulu is attacked by Jack the Ripper; barely prevented from murdering her, he does manage to sever her arm muscles. In Act II comes the rape, while she is in a wheelchair, unable to move her arms. The high jinks of Act III are punctuated by the screams of Lulu's homosexual friend Justin, who is tortured (onstage) by electric shocks in the midst of a Senate hearing, after which the Ripper returns to finish off Lulu. Ho, ho, ho.

Mr. Durang has written that as he worked on one of his early plays, "the extremity of suffering made me giddy, and I found the energy and distance to *relish* the awfulness of it all. This 'relish' is something that audiences do not always feel comfortable with, and I find that some people, rather than simply disliking my work, are made furious by it." In *Sex and Longing,* the balance between suffering and "relish," finely held in Mr. Durang's best work, falls seriously out of whack, and—in spite of some flashes of Mr. Durang's deadpan wit, and an exquisitely hilarious performance by Dana Ivey as a moral battleaxe— even his admirers (of whom I am one) were appalled.

Fewer people were appalled by *Fit to Be Tied,* a comedy by Nicky Silver (produced off-Broadway by Playwrights Horizons), which might also have been called *Sex and Longing.* But there were those who found it distasteful. Mr. Silver's protagonist, a youngish man named Arloc, has fallen in love with Boyd, who plays an angel in the Christmas show at the Radio City Music Hall. Arloc entices Boyd to his house, ties him up, gags him, and refuses to let him go, while insisting, "I will never hurt you. I love you." But though these are clearly the acts of a dangerous psychopath, Mr. Silver evidently wishes us to regard his hero as a charmingly neurotic, charmingly bumbling ne'er-do-well. He asks us to laugh under circumstances where laughter implies our complaisance toward, if not our complicity with, ugly deeds—ugly not because they violate sexual codes, but because they violate another person's freedom. Then he asks us to feel pity for poor Arloc, sinking the wacky goings-on (Boyd spends a lot of time in his angel outfit) under an emotional weight that they are too flimsy to bear. Raising the question of AIDS seems particularly gratuitous. Mr. Silver, who made his reputation as the author of *Pterodactyls* and *The Food Chain,* has an entertainingly antic imagination, but he too has trouble, less acutely than Mr. Durang but more consistently from play to play, with the balance of suffering and "relish."

Other disappointments of 1996:

· *No One Will Be Immune:* A bill consisting of a monologue and four playlets by David Mamet, produced off-Broadway by the Ensemble Studio Theatre. Fragmentary minor works.

· *Missing/Kissing:* Off-Broadway at Primary Stages (after a previous production by the Actors Theatre of Louisville), "Missing Marisa" and "Kissing Christine," two arch and vacuous one-act plays by John Patrick Shanley, author of the screenplays for the films *Five Corners* and *Moonstruck.*

· Janusz Glowacki, an emigre from Poland, is the author of *Hunting Cockroaches* (1986), a wry comedy, full of pointed ironies, about two Eastern European emigres, an actress married to a writer, struggling to establish themselves in New York. His new play, *Antigone in New York* (which reached New York by way of Arena Stage in Washington, D. C. and the Yale Repertory Theater in New Haven, Conn.), is also a wry comedy about emigres: two homeless men, bear-like Sasha and nervous little Flea, a Russian and a Pole. The two have an interestingly contentious relationship—Mr.

Glowacki's quirky comic talent is still evident—but though the play began (off-Broadway at the Vineyard Theater) at 8:04 P. M., the plot did not get under way until 8:47, and turned out to consist of borderline-tedious to-ing and fro-ing in search of a corpse.

Compensating for these disappointments was some promising work by newer or lesser-known writers. **Below the Belt** by Richard Dresser, for instance, which had a short commercial run off-Broadway after a previous production at the Actors Theater of Louisville: an acrid comedy, with a lot of Pinter, a little Kafka, and something original, about three men, two "checkers" and their supervisor, obsessively occupied with jockeying for position and catching each other off-guard. "Hanrahan—what have you got against me?" asks the youngest of the three. "You're alive on this planet at the same time I am," is the reply. The arena for their struggle is a walled factory, by a polluted river, that makes an unknown product. They live on the premises, separated from all other relationships, like scorpions in a bottle—vulnerable, intermittently sympathetic scorpions. The same sort of things—challenges, betrayals, quibbles over tiny points, sudden changes of attitude—happen over and over. Still, Mr. Dresser's play is a witty nightmare-fantasy of a desperately competitive future, with troubling implications for our lives in the present.

The Waiting Room, by Lisa Loomer, came to the Vineyard Theater after previous productions in Massachusetts, California, and Rhode Island. Borrowing a technique from the English playwright Caryl Churchill, Ms. Loomer brings together women from widely separated places and times. Forgiveness from Heaven, an eighteenth-century Chinese lady, is having trouble with her tiny bound feet: her toes are falling off. (Along with **Golden Child**, **The Waiting Room** makes 1996 a banner year for bound feet in American drama.) Victoria Smoot, a nineteenth-century English matron, wears a corset that hurts, she says, "Only when I breathe." Unfortunately, "The pressure from the corset's forcing my uterus out through my vagina." Wanda, breezy, outspoken, and very late-twentieth-century American, has three sets of breast implants, and breast cancer. The three meet in a doctor's waiting room. At first, all cheerfully spout the values that have induced them to reshape their bodies (and minds) for the sake of men's satisfaction, and cheerfully make light of the sufferings this has cost and is costing them. As the play goes on, each, in her own way, rebels.

At times, **The Waiting Room** seems like an anthology of feminist grievances, and some of its points get repeated all too often. On the other hand, Ms. Loomer's gift for satiric exaggeration yields sharp comedy (if sometimes a little too grisly for my taste); moreover, the evolving relationships among these three so-different women, and their stalwart nurse, are unsentimental, unsanctimonious, and pleasantly comic. With her men, Ms. Loomer is less successful. She tries to be fair

to them (the doctor is conscientious, and he has cancer too), but her heart doesn't seem to be in it. "If there's a villain in my play," she told an interviewer, "it's certainly not men, it's greed." Oddly enough, however, it's only men in **The Waiting Room** who are greedy. But if Ms. Loomer falls prey to the men-are-pigs syndrome (and bogs her play down in a tendentious drug-company-conspiracy subplot), she does manage to disprove the canard that feminists have no sense of humor.

Old Wicked Songs by Jon Marans is a two-character play built around a series of singing lessons. A tense, edgy, arrogant young American pianist named Stephen Hoffman has come to Vienna for advanced study, and is not pleased to discover that he will have to begin by studying singing with Professor Mashkan, a wry, puckish, *echt* Viennese teddy bear. As they go to work on Schumann's song cycle *Dichterliebe*, the audience seems to be in for another go-round with the old story of the brash, callow young American and the charming, worldly-wise old European who teaches him about Life. But what about charming Professor Mashkan's anti-Semitic remarks? As Stephen becomes less tense, less guarded, less hostile, more and more cracks appear in Mashkan's facade. The time is 1986; the ex-Nazi Kurt Waldheim is campaigning to become president of Austria. Gradually it becomes clear that Mr. Marans is concerned with the great paradox of Germanic culture, seedbed of classical music and Nazism.

The Holocaust is a big subject for this small play; the climax, in which Mashkan reveals his big secret, is melodramatic. Moreover, the ups and downs, the moments of anger and of friendliness between teacher and pupil, succeed each other sometimes arbitrarily. But the moments themselves, the fluctuating clashes and rapports between two men so removed from each other in age, nationality, and temperament, are entertaining in themselves, and artfully interwoven with the varying moods of the *Dichterliebe*. Hal Robinson, who remained with the play from its first production in Philadelphia, through its engagement off-Broadway at the Jewish Repertory Theater, to its open-ended commercial run off-Broadway, was the definitive Mashkan, making it easy to forgive the play its sentimentalities, its implausibilities, its unearned happy ending.

As for the new foreign plays that reached us in 1996, most of them, as always, were from England. **The Skriker** by Caryl Churchill was a major disappointment, though it was sumptuously produced by the Joseph Papp Public Theater / New York Shakespeare Festival. This newest play by the author of **Cloud Nine, Top Girls**, and **Serious Money** is an incomprehensible tale, set in present-day England, about a supernatural being who for unknown reasons persecutes two working-class young women. But in the fall, two English plays came to Broadway in which great matters were not only dramatized but discussed, argued—in which the clash of conflicting beliefs could be clearly heard.

Like *Old Wicked Songs* (discussed above), *Taking Sides* by Ronald Harwood contrasts the sublimity of Germanic music with the horror of the Holocaust—but does so more directly, with less charm but more force. Wilhelm Furtwangler (1886-1954) was a real person, a celebrated conductor who chose to stay in Germany when the Nazis came to power, which put him in trouble with the Allied authorities after World War II. In *Taking Sides*, Furtwangler is interrogated by a fictional American officer. "Why did he stay?" Major Steve Arnold wants to know. "Why did he play for them? Why was he the flag carrier for the regime? Why was he their servant?" In the course of the play various possible reasons emerge, some honorable, some not. What is the responsibility of the artist in such a situation? Mr. Harwood refuses to take sides, but the question is intensely posed, not as a matter of abstract ethics but as a question of overwhelming personal importance to the prosecutor as well as the accused. On Broadway, the play was driven by the raw, straightforward energy of Ed Harris's Major Arnold; Daniel Massey's Furtwangler, arrogant but pathetic, feeble, almost spastic, made a vivid contrast.

What is most disturbing about the play is Major Arnold's prosecutorial zeal. He contrasts himself with another officer: "He was interested in justice, evidence, facts. I'm interested in nailing the bastard—" Arnold claims to be impelled by "the smell of burning flesh" at a just-liberated concentration camp, but in that case, as his subordinate asks, "Why Dr Furtwangler? Why him?" Surely there are far guiltier Nazis than Furtwangler could ever be. And how can he dismiss as "totallly irrelevant" all the evidence that Furtwangler helped many Jews to escape? Arnold goes out of his way to insist on his contempt for culture-talk and his hatred for classical music; he delights in calling Furtwangler a "band leader." It seems as if he hates Furtwangler less for being a Nazi collaborator than for being an eminent conductor—as if he hates Hitler less than Beethoven. Are we seeing the Revenge of the Philistines disguised as a de-Nazification proceeding? That cannot have been Mr. Harwood's intention, but it is not the least of his play's fascinations.

Skylight by David Hare appears at first to be a "relationship play," abjuring the political for the personal. Kyra went to work for Tom and his wife Alice when she was just eighteen. She became part of the family, a dear friend to both spouses; she and Tom were also lovers for six years. When Alice found out, Kyra simply left, cutting off all contact with Tom. Now Alice is dead, and Tom comes knocking at Kyra's door. Between night and morning they talk, probing their rela-

tionship, challenging each other, testing to see whether they can have a future together. There are some inconsistencies here, most notably that Kyra, presented as a woman of rigorous principle who genuinely loved Alice, seems totally without remorse for six years of deceiving her. But there is a density to the relationship between Kyra and Tom, an urgency, that (most of the time) compels attention—especially when the lovers are played, as they were in London and on Broadway, by Lia Williams and Michael Gambon.

What distinguishes *Skylight* the most, however, is Mr. Hare's awareness of how people's beliefs about the public world can stem from who they deeply are, and how the resulting complex of beliefs and feelings can be crucial to the success or failure of even—especially—something as personal as a love affair. Tom is a businessman, and proud of it. "I'm an entrepreneur, he says, "I'm a doer. I actually go out, I make things happen. I give people jobs which did not previously exist." He enjoys creating, expanding, making money, and surrounding himself with what money can buy; it validates him to himself. Kyra is a teacher, working with tough, dangerous kids, making very little money, living in a shabby, chilly flat. "I can't think of anything more tragic, more stupid," says Tom, "than you sitting here and throwing your talents away." "I'm helping them because they need to be helped," she says. He accuses her of "ridiculous self-righteousness"; she thinks he is monstrously self-indulgent, and accuses him of treating people like objects. Each thinks himself/herself to be in touch with a reality that the other ignores.

Tom is the perfect New Man of the Thatcher Era in Britain; Kyra is an old-fashioned, consecrated leftist, intensely angered by social injustice, a do-gooder, a bleeding heart. What is amazing is how justly Mr. Hare, well-known for many years as a man of the left, holds the balance between them. Some have found the play schematic. To me, its fusion of public issues with personal passions makes *Skylight* both urgent and resonant. Tom and Kyra are not just mouthpieces; their lives depend on the outcome of their argument.

What, then, do we conclude from all this? Clearly, Broadway is now almost totally obsolete as a source of theatrical creativity, though it still has its usefulness in enabling dramatic works developed elsewhere to have larger audiences and longer lives. But even in this year of meager harvest, promising new works, with and without music, are continuing to emerge from subsidized, not-for-profit, resident professional theaters, off-Broadway and all over America (not to mention England). How long our society will continue to support these theaters remains to be seen. But American drama will have little future without them.

The Year in World Literature
by William Riggan

The year 1996 in world literature was not one of the most stellar in recent memory, but it did produce a good many points of light in the form of new works and important translations from a broad range of writers both established and just-emerging. Particularly impressive were the number and quality of new works of fiction by writers from Russia and the Far East.

Russian. With *Dust and Ashes* Anatoli Rybakov concluded his monumental trilogy, *Children of the Arbat*, this time taking us through the horrors of the Stalinist purges of the 1930s and early 1940s down to the fateful battle of Stalingrad and also bringing to a close the sad tale of the ill-fated young lovers Sasha and Varya. Theirs is unfortunately a somewhat mundane story compared to the riveting historical background against which it unfolds. Stalin himself occupies nearly a third of the book, and the resulting portrait of the tyrant is blood-curdling, matched perhaps only by Solzhenitsyn's a quarter-century ago in *The First Circle*.

In 1992 Mark Kharitonov won the first Russian Booker Prize for his novel *Lines of Fate*, an Eco-like metafictional detective story about the efforts of a small-town scholar to track down all the writings of an obscure provincial philosopher who scribbled his aphorisms on the backs of candy wrappers. This powerful, important, and charmingly oddball work is now available to the West in an excellent translation by Helen Goscilo. Admirers of Ludmilla Petrushevskaya's dark, pessimistic plays and fiction welcomed her new collection of stories, *Immortal Love*, a title typically ironic in its counterpoint to the often abortive loves and strangling intimacies depicted in the tales themselves. That the stories possess such strong interest and fascination is due in no small measure to the manner of telling, a relentlessly oral, colloquial, and largely uninflected style perfectly suited to the women whose experiences are recounted here.

Vladimir Makanin, who became an overnight sensation in 1993 (after nearly three decades of writing) when his novel *Baize-Covered Table with Decanter* won the second Russian Booker Prize, is continuing to receive much-belated and much-deserved attention for his subtle, haunting, often surrealistic fiction. In 1996 his two novellas "Escape Hatch" and "The Long Road Ahead" were issue together in translation, and to considerable acclaim. In the latter a young technician at a remote Soviet-style packing plant sometime in the near future exposes the factory as a glorified slaughterhouse processing and packaging real meat as meat substitute for a populace grown too squeamish for violence of any kind; that subversive narrative is later undercut, in good postmodernist style, by the revelation that it contains only the fictive outpourings of an "author" inspired by the fears and delusions of a seriously disturbed friend. In "Escape Hatch" a middle-aged intellectual living in a nightmarish, crumbling metropolis discovers a secret route to an extraordinary, well-lit, civilized underworld where writers and artists and thinkers of all kinds are free to spend whole days and nights in elegant cafés discussing such universal issues as art, politics, sex, life, and death; ultimately, however, he must choose between idyllic refuge here and the responsibilities of trying to protect his family and friends from the growing dangers of the normal world above ground.

Finally, the young Irina Ratushinskaya made an impressive debut in 1996 with a first novel titled *The Odessans*, described by the publishers as "epic" but in fact more an intimate, personal work than might be inferred from the book's size (410 pages) and sweep (from the 1905 Revolution to the start of World War II). Despite plenteous scenes of revolutionary chaos in Petersburg and the horrors of the Western Front in 1916, the author's primary focus is on the women back home, mostly in Odessa, far from the fighting and turmoil but of course closely affected by those events through the hardships and losses which war inevitably inflicts on all.

Other Slavic Languages. The exuberant and wonderfully accessible Czech novelist Josef Škvorecký treated his international audience in 1996 to his first big novel in several years, *The Bride of Texas*, a colorful saga that mixes historical fact with Schweikian invention in following the fortunes of some 300 Czech soldiers who fought with the Union Army's Wisconsin Battalion under General Sherman in the American Civil War. A parallel plot line traces the life and loves of the strong-willed Lida, a sort of Czech-born Scarlett O'Hara who time and again manages to "gamble on the wrong card" in choosing her men. Intermezzos in the period voice of the pseudonymous author Laura A. Lee, doubtless meant as a humorous evocation of much nineteenth-century American popular fiction (replete with chapter-ending cliffhangers), are ultimately more distracting than beneficial but still cannot detract seriously from the novel's thoroughgoing excellence and excitement. Also new to Škvorecký's Czech readers in 1996 was his *Nové canterburské povídky* (New Canterbury Tales), written in the 1950s but never before published until its release this year as part of a twenty-volume collected edition of his works. The author now belittles the nine tales as naïve and sentimental juvenilia, but readers and critics have embraced their lively inventiveness and irreverent humor, both strongly reminiscent of the author's now-classic first novel, *The Cowards*.

One of the few Serbian works to come to Western readers' attention in recent years, and one of the first to emerge from the 1990s turmoil in the former Yugoslavia, Vladimir Arsenijevi 's 1995 novel *U potpalublju* made its appearance in English in 1996 as *In the Hold*. Cast in the hip, engaged, but sardonic tones of a disaffected twenty-something narrator (the author himself has only just turned thirty), the work is a stunning and moving—and often mordantly humorous—portrait of a city (Belgrade) and a cluster of youthful friends "at the edge of extinction and dispersal." Drug addiction, conscription, death and maiming, shattered political idealism, enervation of the spirit, self-pity—all are dealt with, to varying degrees of success, in the course of the novel's unfolding. The resulting portrait is one not of nationalist but of generational concerns—of a youthful generation dispirited, manipulated, and impoverished by its elders and all but condemned to continue their age-old battles.

Asia & the Pacific. The young Indian expatriate Rohinton Mistry produced perhaps the finest single work of 1996 about the subcontinent with *A Fine Balance*, the tale of four ordinary people struggling to survive and make ends meet during the 1975-76 state of emergency declared by Indira Gandhi. Already being compared with Salman Rushdie's now-classic *Midnight's Children*, the work features a more traditional Balzacian mode of narration—its epigraph is from *Le Père Goriot*—that may well attract and involve even more readers more profoundly. It has already received one major prize in Canada and is sure to garner others elsewhere in the Commonwealth and the U.K. in the months to come.

Indonesian writer Pramoedya Ananta Toer's extraordinary "Buru Quartet" was brought to completion for Western readers in 1996 with the publication of *House of Glass*. The focus has now shifted from the progressive, crusading early-twentieth-century journalist Minke to Minke's antagonist, the Sorbonne-educated police commissioner Jacques Pangemanann, whose occasional pangs of conscience and constant sense of irony combine with his reactionary political stance, consummate hypocrisy, and monstrous sadism to create a narrative that is fascinatingly subversive and modern. The author's chief concern here is the corrosive influence of colonialism as embodied in Pangemanann, a cynical and self-serving opportunist yet still with at least some vestigial sense of conscience and honor that he ultimately suppresses as he succumbs to the lures of power and privilege. The result is, in one critic's apt phrasing, "an illuminating, moving account of colonial psychosis [and] a memorable analysis of the human capacity for self-destruction, anywhere and at any time."

The late Shen Congwen, considered by many as China's most

serious Nobel prospect during the 1970s and 1980s, was presented to the West in 1996 with an excellent and representative collection of his short fiction, *Imperfect Paradise*. Most of the twenty-four tales involve provincial folk and pastoral settings, but as the volume's title implies, the "paradises" presented here are far from vapid idealizations of bucolic charms and peasant wisdom. The provincial family in "Sansan," for example, possess many of the standard virtues of country folk but also show an unusually keen adaptability to changing social circumstances that is distinctly modernistic and untraditional.

Japanese author Akira Yoshimura's novel *Shipwrecks*, like Shen Congwen's stories, avoided the pitfalls of romanticized idealism in its lean, graceful account of difficult, poverty-stricken life in a medieval fishing village stricken by an epidemic of smallpox contracted from the crew and cargo of a merchant ship that ran aground on a nearby reef. Under conditions wherein mere survival is an achievement, the orphaned young hero Isaku and his fellow villagers struggle on a daily basis to retain as well some semblance of humanity.

The late Kobo Abe's final novel, *Kangaroo Notebook*, indulged in typically dark, surreal fantasy in its imaginative and vigorous account of an office-products developer sent careening on a hospital gurney through bleak realms of memory, barren alienating wastelands, and fearful underground encounters with creatures and images of the wildest kind imaginable. As in much of Abe's earlier work, metamorphosis, alienation, the problem of personal identity, the journey motif, and elements of the fantastic blend with wholly realistic features in an exasperating and unnerving amalgam.

Japan's recent Nobel laureate Kenzaburo Oe offered readers no fewer than four new books in 1996: the first English translation of his two early-1960s novellas "Seventeen" and "J," the first a tale of a disturbed young adolescent, the second on the fateful encounter between several artsy urbanites and the superstitious inhabitants of a remote fishing village where city folk are shooting scenes for a pornographic film; the first English translation of his recent novel *An Echo of Heaven*, which follows the path to sainthood of a Japanese woman who salves her personal losses and tragedies through ministering to the needs of the poor and downtrodden in Mexico; the translation of the recent novel *The Quiet Life*, presented as the diary of the daughter of a famous writer with the given name of K--- and her report on the year in which she cared for her retarded brother while her parents were away at an American university; and the publication of the novel *inaru hi ni* (On the Day of Grandeur), completing Oe's "Burning Green Tree" trilogy with the convoluted but ultimately uplifting tale of the saintly Brother Gii, whose sacrificial death reunites the warring factions within his church and sets them back on the road to salvation of both their own souls and the future of the Earth and mankind.

Romance Languages. The prolific, multilingual J. M. G. Le Clézio, recently voted "the greatest contemporary writer in the French language" in a nationwide magazine poll, produced his twentieth novel in twenty-four years with *La quarantaine* (The Quarantine), a sprawling family saga based loosely on the author's own forebears, who resettled from Brittany to the island colony of Mauritius in the late nineteenth century. The threat of a smallpox epidemic occasions the quarantining of the passengers of a ship on a small island near Mauritius, a horrifying and prolonged confinement which nevertheless spawns a beautiful love affair between the young narrator Léon and the Hindu girl Surya; even when the quarantine is finally lifted, the two choose to stay on rather than leave their "paradise of love."

The multitalented Italian polymath Umberto Eco brought out the much-awaited sequel to *The Name of the Rose* and *Foucault's Pendulum*, the intriguingly titled novel *The Island of the Day Before*. Set in the seventeenth century and filled with metafictional allusions to a host of literary, cultural, social, and philosophical artifacts relating to that baroque/picaresque era, the narrative charts the mental and physical course of the young soldier/sailor/student Roberto De La Grive, shipwrecked off the coast of a small Pacific island from which he is separated by what is now known as the International Date Line (hence the title). Forced to imagine life on the island from a distance both physical and temporal, Roberto develops a series of ever more fantastic stories and plots, one calling to life his fictitious evil twin Ferrante and others alluding slyly to such Hollywood fare as *Mutiny on the Bounty*. In sum, a brilliant demonstration of how one can simultaneously teach and entertain, and also, in its encyclopedic frame of reference and its postmodern all-inclusiveness, of the cliché that there is practically nothing new under the sun.

Eco's venerable countryman Mario Rigoni Stern presented his legion of fans and admirers with a somewhat more traditional novel, *Le stagioni di Giacomo* (Giacomo's Seasons), re-creating the life of a small mountain town as it struggled to survive and adapt during the Fascist era between the two world wars without sacrificing its integrity and its strong sense of community. Neither social upheaval nor fiscal hardship nor political repression can break down the harmony and decency of Giacomo's village, and the novel stands as a passionate homage to a civilization now unfortunately vanished.

From the eminent Mexican novelist Carlos Fuentes came *La frontera cristal* (The Glass Curtain; literally "The Crystal Border"), a "novel in nine stories" focused on the oligarchic Barroso family but ultimately concerned with the larger themes of love and perfidy, hope and disillusionment, idealism and corruption, and the problematic relations between Mexico and the United States. *Delito por bailar el chachachá* (It's a Crime to Dance the Chachachá) by Guillermo Cabrera

Infante showcased the Cuban émigré's characteristically mordant wit and incessant wordplay in three interlinked stories about a young couple dining at a Havana restaurant in the late 1950s with bolero and chachachá music blaring in the background. The real intent behind the project is to expose the faults of the Castro regime, particularly in the lengthy title story, wherein the narrator, a Cuban intellectual and authorial alter ego, holds disinterested interviews with caricaturish bureaucrats and offers firsthand reminiscences of the heady early days of the Cuban revolution. The ideological posturing sorts oddly with the fictional story line, unfortunately, and may well have been better placed in a memoir than in a work of fiction.

Germanic Languages. Far and away the most significant new work of German literature published in 1996 was Martin Walser's novel *Finks Krieg* (Fink's War). Based, like much of Walser's earlier fiction, on a true event, the work follows the agonizing six-year legal battle of a midlevel government official forcibly transferred to another office so that a patronage appointee might have his cherished current position. Resistance brings only damaging (and untrue) slanders about his past performance and further outrage to his sense of honor and duty, and each defeat and indignity only increases his obsession with obtaining justice. The grinding, glacial process of the case ultimately produces in Fink either utter exhaustion or transcendent wisdom, for by the time he finally wins on appeal, he no longer seems really to care about either rehabilitation or remuneration, having found in an idyllic Swiss abbey the inner peace that has so long eluded him.

A drastically different but equally strong impact was made by the Austrian novelist and playwright Peter Handke with the journal/pamphlet *Eine winterliche Reise zu den Flüssen Donau, Save, Morawa und Drina, oder Gerechtigkeit für Serbien* (A Winter Journey to the Danube, Sava, Morava, and Drina Rivers, or Justice for Serbia). As the subtitle indicates, Handke was aiming here to redress imbalances in press coverage of the Balkan conflict, coverage which in most cases had cast the Serbs exclusively in the role of aggressors and the Muslims and Croatians as victims. Public readings from the text in several German and Austrian cities only heightened the controversy which the work had sparked upon publication, and Handke's book became public issue number one for much of the spring in the German-speaking world.

The novelist and Swedish Academy member Kjell Espmark created one of the literary year's biggest sensations in Scandinavia—and touched a long-sensitive nerve in Sweden—with his novel *Hatet* (Hatred), the fifth installment in his "Years of Forgetfulness" series. The narrator here is a specter, a former prime minister of Sweden who was stabbed to death by a still-unidentified assailant and who now finds himself trapped within a private inferno (the Markeet Hall) desperately trying to piece together the jumbled memories of his past and his career in order to determine at least *why* he was murdered, if not by whom. The model for this narrator is of course the late Olof Palme, gunned down on a Stockholm street in 1985 and ever since the subject of endless speculation and mythologizing, since no killer was ever found and therefore no firm motive or explanation for his death ever identified with any reasonable certainty. The narrative is therefore disconcerting at least, intrusive and offensive to some, but also strangely moving and extremely adept in using a lyrical, associative prose style to convey the complexity of mind and character that marked the real-life Palme. On balance, a stunning achievement, in the judgment of most readers and critics.

Near East. The ancient practices of vendettas and blood feuds are at the heart of Egyptian writer Bahaa Taher's latest novel, *Aunt Saffiya and the Monastery*, wherein a Muslim elder and a Coptic monk join forces to oppose and end the vengeance sworn by the eponymous Saffiya against the man who killed her husband. That man just happens to be her former betrothed, Harbi, who had been brutally tortured by her late husband, an elderly bey, and the agent of her revenge is to be her son. A small local tragedy is raised by the captivating laconic style to a level of epic resonance and import. In *A Beggar at Damascus Gate* the Palestinian writer and archeologist Yasmine Zahran links the story of her people's twentieth-century struggle for a place to call home with an evocation of the ancient worlds of their ancestors. The strains in the love affair between a (female) Palestinian writer and activist and a (male) English photographer mirror on a personal level those between the strivings for Palestinian liberation and the resistance of imperial structures and authorities. Characterization and persuasiveness of argument unfortunately fall victim to cliché and hyperbole all too often, but the effort and the topic make the work eminently readable nevertheless.

Ad-She'ya'aleh Amud Ha'Shahar (*Until the Dawn's Light*),

the newest work by the Israeli novelist Aharon Appelfeld, follows the tragic fortunes of a brilliant young East European Jewish girl in the first decade of this century as she abandons her faith out of love for a gentile, suffers unbearable abuse at his hands, and eventually murders him, though more to salvage her son's future than to gain release for herself from the virtual prison that her life has become. The author's now-familiar controlled and compassionate tone only heightens the visceral shock of this sweet soul's metamorphosis into a cold-blooded killer but also makes possible and plausible the healing self-acceptance she is ultimately able to achieve.

West Indies and Africa. Nobel Prize winner Derek Walcott brought out *The Bounty*, his first new collection of verse since the book-length epic poem *Omeros* appeared in 1990. Among the reading pleasures to be found here are a moving elegy to the poet's mother and a haunting series of poems evoking his native ground, the island of St. Lucia. The biggest impact of the year 1996 in the Caribbean region, however, was made by *Jonestown*, Wilson Harris's fictionalization of the events surrounding the 1978 mass suicide in his native Guyana by some 900 followers of the Reverend Jim Jones. As usual in Harris's fiction, heavy doses of philosophy and mysticism almost overwhelm the narrative line (the narrator, Francisco Bone, is a survivor of Jonestown), and the events are subsumed within a larger context, here one of postcolonial excesses and antihumanism challenged by the unbridled spirit of the "sovereign" imagination.

And lastly, the still-new nation of South Africa gained a superb and superbly celebratory novel in 1996 with André Brink's *Imaginings of Sand*. The tension between the returned émigrée Kristien Muller and her conservative Boer brother-in-law is palpable throughout, and the convincing facility with which Brink assumes a feminine voice and viewpoint—inhabiting both Kristien and her aged, dying Aunt Ouma—is nothing short of miraculous. A magical and intensely moving performance, Brink's best in years.

Notes on Contributors

Bruce Allen is a frequent contributor of reviews to the *Chicago Tribune, The New York Times Book Review,* the *Philadelphia Enquirer,* and Monitor Radio. He is currently at work on a critical history of the American short story.

Allen Hoey is the author of *A Fire in the Cold House of Being,* chosen by Galway Kinnell as the 1985 Camden Poetry Prize winner. A Professor in the Department of Language and Literature at Bucks County Community College outside of Philadelphia, Hoey has contributed poems and essays to such journals as *American Poetry Review, Diacritics, The Hudson Review, Poetry,* and *Shenandoah. What Persists,* his most recent collection of poems, was published in 1992.

Julius Novick is Professor of Literature and Drama Studies at Purchase College of the State University of New York. The author of *Beyond Broadway: The Quest for Permanent Theatres,* Novick has written theatre criticism for *The Village Voice, The Nation, The New York Times,* and many other publications, and is a winner of the George Jean Nathan Award for Dramatic Criticism.

William Riggan is Editor of *World Literature Today* and an expert on Third World, Slavic, Anglo-American, and smaller European literatures. The author of *Picaros, Madmen, Naïfs, and Clowns: The Unreliable First-Person Narrator,* Riggan has written extensively on the history of both the Nobel and Neustadt International Prizes in Literature. He also regularly reviews new foreign poetry and fiction for several journals and newspapers.

New Authors

Alan Brown

Audrey Hepburn's Neck

Born in 1951, Brown is an American novelist.

INTRODUCTION

Set in Tokyo, *Audrey Hepburn's Neck* (1996) is told from the perspective of Toshi, a young, naive illustrator from a small fishing village in northern Japan. Raised by a reserved father and deserted as a small child by his mother, Toshi has admired America and American culture ever since he saw Audrey Hepburn in the film *Roman Holiday.* Eventually he goes to study English at the Very Romantic English Academy in Tokyo, where he meets many Americans, including Jane, an English teacher; Paul, an advertising agent; and Lucy, Jane's friend and an artist. Toshi becomes romantically involved with Jane, who, being obsessive and melodramatic, begins to stalk him. Considered a coming-of-age story, the novel also addresses such themes as cultural stereotypes and identity, deception, betrayal, and family relationships. Critics have been generally positive in their reaction to *Audrey Hepburn's Neck.* The work has been described as an intimate and authentic portrayal of Japan—Brown lived and taught in the country for seven years beginning in 1987—and has been lauded by many reviewers for its humor and complex themes. Some critics, however, have faulted Brown for clumsy prose and have contended that he attempts to address too many issues and subjects in the work. Nevertheless, most critics maintain *Audrey Hepburn's Neck* is a noteworthy first novel. As Pico Iyer stated: "With the beautiful control of a born novelist, Brown shows us that clarity, as much as charity, begins abroad." Since its publication, the screenplay rights to the novel have been sold to Wayne Wang, director of *The Joy Luck Club,* a film based on the novel by Amy Tan.

CRITICISM

Pico Iyer (review date 5 February 1996)

SOURCE: "America, from Right to Left," in *Time,* Vol. 147, No. 6, February 5, 1996, p. 72.

[*In the following positive review, Iyer praises* Audrey Hepburn's Neck *as an unstereotypical and intimate portrayal of Japan.*]

The first all but unfailing rule of foreign books about Japan is that they exult in the perspective of a bewildered outsider, not quite sure whether to be excited or exasperated by the science-fictive surfaces of that alien world. The second is that they find a focus for their mingled fascination and frustration in an unfathomable Japanese love object. The gracious and redeeming delight of *Audrey Hepburn's Neck,* a first novel by Alan Brown, an American, is that it turns all the standard tropes—and expectations—on their head by presenting Japan from the inside out, and yet with a sympathetic freshness that most longtime expatriates have long ago abandoned.

Daringly, Brown, a Fulbright scholar who lived in Tokyo for seven years, delivers his entire tale through the wide eyes of Toshi, a dreamy young illustrator from a northern village who loves America in part because he knows so little about it. He takes to drinking milk, goes to Tokyo to study at the Very Romantic English Academy (English schools in Japan really do have names like that) and falls in with various foreigners who return the compliment by idealizing him: Jane, a tattooed English teacher in red cowboy boots who mistakes intensity for intimacy; and Paul, a refined advertising agent who collects Japanese boys as if they were woodcuts.

Inhabiting Toshi's heart and soul with absolute conviction, Brown shows us how Americans might look to a confused admirer, with their "blue-tinged complexions," their "crayon-colored eyes," their habit of wishing on everything, even "when breaking dried chicken bones." In effect, he turns the usual "The Japanese are so strange!" cliché inside out. Toshi's unsteady American girlfriend suddenly says things like, "You think I'm awful, don't you? I am, I'm dreadful and I'm not pretty," and, where the Japanese tend to present images of happy families, Toshi notes, Americans "offer up their unhappy childhoods like movie plots, or like gifts." All this is set against the backdrop of the Crown Prince's dating Brooke Shields, protesting farmers dumping foreign rice, and "laid-off Toyota workers burn[ing] AMERICA=AIDS into the brush on the southern slope of Mount Fuji." While cultures fight, their products flirt.

Brown evokes the sleek surrealism of Tokyo—where dogs are rented by the hour and people eat green-tea tiramisu cake—with economical aplomb. Even better, he offsets such Tomorrow-land aspects with lyrical images of Toshi's rural home, where women eat grilled eel while watching Audrey Hepburn and go looking for candleweed and ghost mushrooms. Toshi is as much a foreigner in Tokyo as any American might be, yet his two worlds are knit together with an exacting precision, with fishermen's nets "the color of dried persimmon," and an American's blanket having "the color of squid just pulled from the sea." Like Audrey Hepburn, perhaps, Brown's art is meticulous and precise beneath its haunting surface.

[In *Audrey Hepburn's Neck,*] we pass through many of the rites of an American coming-of-age story, ... but all seen in a Japanese context, as if Brown had written an all-American tale to be read right to left.

—*Pico Iyer*

As the book continues, we pass through many of the rites of an American coming-of-age story—a confounding love affair, memories of a distant childhood, a visit from a parent, the unfolding of family secrets—but all seen in a Japanese context, as if Brown had written an all-American tale to be read from right to left. And Toshi, with his shy charm, proves much more like Audrey Hepburn than any of the foreigners he meets. Going to bed with a dream and waking up with a nightmare, he begins to plumb the ironies of loving a culture that has destroyed many of his relatives. Gently, with sensitivity and tact, the very notion of "foreignness" is peeled away to some deeper level where passports don't apply. With the beautiful control of a born novelist, Brown shows us that clarity, as much as charity, begins abroad.

Mary Jo Salter (review date 24 March 1996)

SOURCE: "Tokyo Prose," in *Los Angeles Times Book Review,* March 24, 1996, p. 6.

[*Salter is an American poet. In the following review, she lauds the imagery and figurative language in* Audrey Hepburn's Neck *but states that the book "sometimes staggers a bit under the weight of its author's desire to inject every possible theme into it."*]

"What was the pivotal event, the thing that changed the direction of my entire life, that carried me halfway around the world?," asks Paul, a gay American living in the vibrant Japan of Alan Brown's first novel. "A photograph of Yukio Mishima in a loincloth. That's what."

Paul's friend Toshi, the young Japanese protagonist of *Audrey Hepburn's Neck* has no choice but to accept the American's take on the irrationality of human attraction—and its far-reaching consequences. Toshi is himself trying without much success to get out of a passionate mess with his lunatic, arsonist English conversation teacher, Jane Borden ("like Lizzy

who chopped up her father with an ax," she explains cheerfully). She has specialized in Japanese men ever since, at the age of 15, she saw Toshiro Mifune in *Rashomon*. A gentler soul than Jane, Toshi was nevertheless sexually imprinted in much the same way: He traces his own obsession with foreign women back to his 10th year, when he and his mother, passing a thermos of green tea between them, sat spellbound before the image of Audrey Hepburn in *Roman Holiday*.

Images are at the heart of this acute and acutely funny novel. Nearly all the people in it are powerfully swayed not only by mass media images ("Jane and her friends," Toshi reflects, "offer up their unhappy childhoods like movie plots") but by their own private, romantic stereotypes of the "other." (One of Brown's implicit themes is the erotic quality of foreignness, especially of foreign languages.) Sometimes—as Toshi learns when he sets off from his father's noodle shop in rural, remote Hokkaido to make his fortune in Tokyo—the "other" can even be an alien culture within one's own people.

Toshi is also a maker of images, a talented cartoonist in the childish *manga* tradition who, as he matures, will find a way within it to address his own grave family history. But the book's most notable image-maker is its American author who, in daring to see with the eyes of a Japanese character has embraced, gingerly but lovingly, the multiple identities of Japan itself.

This is a xenophobic country, as Brown only half-amusingly shows us, where tourist guidebooks for the Japanese warn that "foreigners carry AIDS and other diseases from abroad" and the prospect of imported American rice is reason to riot. (I hope Brown is exaggerating when he presents us with a computer game in which Japanese fighter planes perpetually strafe a cartoon Pearl Harbor.) And yet it's a country where fluency in English is as desirable an attainment as, say, fine calligraphy once was and is nearly synonymous with sexual happiness. Toshi meets Jane in the Very Romantic English Academy, in the Hysterical Glamour Building. What may well be the world's most incongruous country needs a novelist with a poet's gift for linking incongruities.

Brown's similes and metaphors are unexpected, as good ones always are, and yet on reflection seem inevitable. The young woman who eventually steals Toshi's heart steals ours because she has "short hair hooked behind her ears like window curtains pulled back to let in the sunlight." At an evening picnic, under cherry blossoms, "wooden chopsticks click like cicada legs." The rightness of Brown's imagery owes much to his cultural immersion: Japanese things are often viewed in terms of other Japanese things, not Western ones. A gravel road "tapers off to nothing, like a Zen conundrum." (This is the road to Toshi's childhood home, which indeed holds a terribly sad secret within.) My favorite image is of a green kimono, "the color of the seaweed you wrap around rice."

It's not just the shade of green but the verb "wrap" that wraps kimono and seaweed together.

The book's most notable image-maker is its American author who, in daring to see with the eyes of a Japanese character has embraced, gingerly but lovingly, the multiple identities of Japan itself.

—Mary Jo Salter

On a larger scale, Brown deftly juggles subplots that are in some way images of Toshi's quest for the perfect "other" to share his life with. Though the adult Toshi, unlike the child, doesn't actually hope to win Audrey Hepburn, he's forever half-consciously linking moments in his own life to scenes in her movies. (You have to be a Hepburn fan to identify them—like that attempted suicide by carbon monoxide poisoning in *Sabrina*.) Meanwhile, as Paul looks for romance in promiscuity, the Crown Prince is accepting formal applications from prospective brides. Even he isn't immune to Hollywood images; is it really true, after so many young Japanese women have enrolled in bridal training academies, that he plans instead to marry Brooke Shields?

As often with first novels, even short and charming ones like this one, *Audrey Hepburn's Neck* sometimes staggers a bit under the weight of its author's desire to inject every possible theme into it. The book casts at least a glance at nearly every social crisis and even geological challenge that has faced modern Japan: earthquakes so powerful they nearly obliterate the past; the smoldering anger, half a century old, of Korean women forced into prostitution by the Japanese army; an overcrowding in Tokyo so extreme that people don't actually own pets, they just rent them for the day. There are wobbly moments, too, when Toshi's English seems either better or worse than we've been led to believe.

But on page after page, Brown's touch, both as observer and stylist, is sure and accurate. Ultimately, I wouldn't want to delete the earthquake from the book, for then we'd lose the collapsed lighthouse "on the rocky promontory, its inner staircase a spiraling, bleached skeleton." It's a rare writer who combines such delicacy with a zany sense of humor: "Take my wallet. Take my wristwatch. Take my leather coat, please. Please don't shoot," runs the English conversation drill at the Very Romantic English Academy. And the affecting friendship of Toshi and Paul, who is openly in love with Toshi but never attempts again to seduce him after the first "no," is just one instance of the subtlety and reticence that make this book a serious one when it must be.

Elizabeth Ward (review date 24 March 1996)

SOURCE: "A Superficial Look inside '90s Japan," in *The Atlanta Journal/Constitution,* March 24, 1996, p. K14.

[*In the mixed review below, Ward praises the plot and characters of* Audrey Hepburn's Neck *but faults Brown's prose.*]

This novel about today's Japan resembles one of those intriguing little washi-paper-covered boxes that open to reveal a smaller box nestled inside, which contains another and another and so on down to the very last box, which might be as small as a lima bean. Reading *Audrey Hepburn's Neck* is like unpacking, one after the other, every received opinion of Japan current among its foreign residents in the past few years. You are amazed that so much can be squeezed into such a slim package, yet you close the book feeling oddly unsatisfied, surfeited on surface impressions.

To his credit, Alan Brown has tried to give a new twist to his contribution to the crowded field of gaijin novels. His protagonist is not the typical wide-eyed or cynical foreigner, but a young Japanese male. Toshi is from the northern island of Hokkaido, so he is almost as much an outsider in the neon and concrete blur that is Tokyo as his American acquaintances are. The fact that he is Japanese at all lends at least the illusion of perspective to Brown's portrait of Toshi's foreign friends. But the question still nags: How authentic can the portrait of Toshi possibly be?

Brown came to Japan in 1987 as a journalist on a Fulbright fellowship and stayed seven years. Not much of what he experienced can have been left out of *Audrey Hepburn's Neck.* The title itself is a reference to the well-known Japanese adulation of the fragilely elegant actress, whose death in 1993 Japan publicly mourned. The noisy Rice Party and assorted right-wing demonstrators, all showing off Japan's oft-cited fear of foreigners' tainted rice and AIDS-contaminated blood, pop up continually. Cherry-blossom-viewing picnics, the controversial Russian-held northern islands, the crown prince's public search for a bride, Tokyo's gay subculture, the comic book craze and—most predictably, perhaps—the supersensitive issue of wartime "comfort women" succeed one another like images in a slide show.

As a result, Brown's characters are all, without exception, the kind of people journalists single out for their story leads: case studies, good for a quote, photogenic, a tad one-dimensional. Besides the representative cast of Japanese, from family to office colleagues, there is Toshi's English teacher, Jane, with her red cowboy boots and "seaweed green eyes," who turns out to have *Fatal Attraction* fantasies; Paul, the red-headed gay, lonely in his huge company-subsidized apartment; and Lucy, the sensitive artist type who saves Toshi from the legacy of his damaged childhood (details not to be revealed). Each of them is naturally a serious learning experience for the northern naif, whose rites of passage form the backbone of the plot.

The problem with the novel—plot, characters, ambience, everything—is that Brown simply does not write very well. Too often he relies on brand-name prose to do his work for him: "According to its brochure, the Very Romantic English Academy occupies the third and fourth floors of the Hysteric Glamour Building, upstairs from My Charming Home interior furnishings . . . and a Cherry Blossom Discount Camera Center." Not much better is his flat guidebook prose: ". . . the metallic skyscrapers of Shinjuku. . . . Abalone shells piled high outside a fish restaurant."

Worst of all is his earnest, post-recovery prose, which predominates toward the end, when everything starts to come together for Toshi and Lucy, not to mention Japan and the United States: "Together they are mining two languages to express new, shared ideas and beliefs. To find out that you are not the person you thought you were is exhilarating but exhausting. Who will he become? Who will Lucy become?"

Cultural ambassadors, maybe. But not, one hopes, novelists.

Deirdre Donahue (review date 29 March 1996)

SOURCE: "A Fascination for All Things Foreign," in *USA Today,* March 29, 1996.

[*In the review of* Audrey Hepburn's Neck *below, Donahue gives a brief description of the novel and provides background information on Brown.*]

Sitting in a little bar in Osaka, Japan, long before his novel was even a glimmer in his eye, Alan Brown wrote down the title *Audrey Hepburn's Neck.* It came from a conversation with the bar's owner, who explained the reason he had festooned his establishment with posters and photographs of the big-eyed star.

"'It was her neck,' he told me," recalls Brown, 45, from his New York apartment.

The eternal appeal of the other, the foreign, the alien forms the underpinning of Brown's magical first novel, *Audrey Hepburn's Neck.* Brown writes from the perspective of Toshi, a 23-year-old Japanese comic-book artist living in Tokyo and working on a strip called *Chocolate Girl.* Taking English classes at the Very Romantic English Academy, Toshi finds himself enmeshed in an affair with his drama-addicted American teacher. Stalked by the crazy Jane, he confides his troubles to his best friend, Paul, a gay American copywriter working in Japan. The novel also explores the secrets of Toshi's child-

hood on Japan's northernmost island, including the tragic reasons behind his mother's decision to live apart from him and his father when he was 8 years old.

What gave Brown the confidence to write a book from Toshi's viewpoint were in part the weekly journals he read as a teacher at Keio University, a prestigious private institution. For his writing class, Brown's students—reluctant to talk about personal issues—opened up on paper about their families, their dreams, their loves, their troubles.

"I just adored these students," says Brown fondly.

Brown spent 7 years in Japan; he first went there on a Fulbright grant for journalists. Then, he adds, "I never came home."

Ironically, the longer he lived and worked in Japan as a teacher and journalist, the less he felt like an authority on the Japanese. He dislikes the image of the Japanese as "very regimented and dour."

As befits a book with an actress in the title, its movie rights have already been sold to Wayne Wang, who directed *The Joy Luck Club.* Brown is currently writing the screenplay.

David Galef (review date 28 April 1996)

SOURCE: A review of *Audrey Hepburn's Neck,* in *The New York Times Book Review,* April 28, 1996, p. 23.

[*Below, Galef provides a negative assessment of* Audrey Hepburn's Neck.]

Toshi Okamoto, the hero of Alan Brown's first novel [*Audrey Hepburn's Neck*], is a hick from Hokkaido now living in Tokyo. His father runs a noodle shop back home; his mother left long ago to work in a rustic inn. Toshi has found his niche as a comic-strip artist by day and an English student by night, taking lessons at the Very Romantic English Academy. His small circle includes Paul Swift, a gay American advertising copywriter, and Nakamura, the comic-strip studio boss, whose idea of encouraging hominess in the office is to rent a pet dog by the hour. Toshi's own personal quirk is his fascination with Audrey Hepburn, which began when he first saw *Roman Holiday* at the age of 9. Since then, he's had a few foreign girlfriends, but nothing has prepared him for Jane Borden, his American teacher, who strikes up an acquaintance that ripens alarmingly into sadomasochistic sex. All of this is seen through the eyes of Toshi the naif, allowing Mr. Brown to slip in a lot of descriptions of modern Japan, from its comic-strip culture to the gay bar scene. Intercut with these present-day vignettes are Toshi's recollections of his lonely childhood, shadowed by the ever-present mystery of his mother's unhappiness. Yet most of the book remains curiously flat, and even its resolutions are somewhat tepid. If only *Audrey Hepburn's Neck* were as provocative as its title!

Jill Neimark (review date 18 September 1996)

SOURCE: A review of *Audrey Hepburn's Neck,* in *Bookpage* (online publication), September 18, 1996.

[*In the following positive review, Neimark states that "ultimately this charming tale of America and Japan is a tale of human tragedy and hope."*]

[An] accomplished first novel out this season is *Audrey Hepburn's Neck,* by Alan Brown, a Fulbright scholar who lived in Tokyo for seven years. It is the story of Toshi, a delicate, polite, Japanese illustrator who is fascinated by all things American, particularly the mesmerizing white beauty of Audrey Hepburn's neck, which he saw in a movie as a young boy. Seen through Toshi's eyes, America erupts, fierce and volcanic, untidy and mysterious, like the Niagara Falls in comparison to a bonsai tree. Toshi's American girlfriend, Jane, has an albino tiger tattooed on her breast, is sex-mad and manic-depressive, writes him love-obsessed letters in red envelopes, and ultimately sets fire to his flat.

Toshi's version of America, both surreal and comical, rings true: "Jane has a pocketknife. Does she have a gun too? Does it even matter? Toshi's seen it in the movies and on the news: Anything can be a murder weapon in the hands of an American. They kill each other frequently, nonchalantly, and with everyday objects—hammers and golf clubs. Plastic dry cleaning bags. He picks up his fork and examines the sharp prongs."

The novel works so well because, deep beneath the still reserve of Toshi, a reserve as perfect and flawless as Audrey Hepburn's neck, is tumult and pain, passion, and heartbreak—all that he sees as so foreign and American. His own past carries a mystery as vivid and heartbreaking as any American's. Ultimately this charming tale of America and Japan is a tale of human tragedy and hope.

FURTHER READING

Kenney, Michael. "Selling His Story to America: A First Novelist Hits the Book-Tour Road—and Feels the Miles." *Boston Globe* (11 April 1996): 73.

Journal-style account of Brown's six-week tour to promote *Audrey Hepburn's Neck.*

John Gilstrap
Nathan's Run

Born c. 1957, Gilstrap is an American novelist.

INTRODUCTION

Drawing on experience from his volunteer work with troubled children, Gilstrap's debut novel, *Nathan's Run* (1996), explores the theme of real children subjected to an often brutal penal system with little consideration of their crimes as defensive reactions to unbearable situations. The owner of an environmental consulting firm, Gilstrap outlined *Nathan's Run* during a 1994 business trip to Montana. The story begins as Nathan, orphaned at the age of 12 and placed in the custody of an abusive uncle, steals a car to escape. Captured and sentenced to a juvenile detention center, Nathan is further abused by other inmates as well as the adults in charge. When a guard attempts to stab him, Nathan kills the guard and flees, taking shelter in the home of a vacationing family. While there, he turns on the radio and learns that he is the target of a nationwide hunt. He calls the radio station to give his side of the story and finds support in a charismatic radio talk-show personality known as "The Bitch," who engenders sympathy for him among her listeners. As Nathan runs—"borrowing" cars and empty homes (though always cleaning up and leaving a note of apology), and evading the police, a self-serving prosecutor, and a mob hit man—he continues to call in to The Bitch with updates, and his flight becomes a real-life soap opera for listeners. Critical response to *Nathan's Run* has generally been favorable, with commentators praising its fast pace, likeable protagonist, and thrilling conclusion. Detractors, however, argue that the novel copies John Grisham's *The Client* (1993), and fault its characters as generic, lacking personality and psychological depth.

CRITICISM

Thomas Gaughan (review date 15 December 1995)

SOURCE: A review of *Nathan's Run*, in *Booklist*, Vol. 92, No. 8, December 15, 1995, pp. 667-68.

[*In the following review, Gaughan offers a mixed assessment of* Nathan's Run, *finding the characters shallow.*]

Nathan Bailey's life is a Dickensian tragedy updated for the 1990s. At age 11, his father dies in a car accident, leaving him orphaned and at the mercy of abusive, alcoholic, ne'er-do-well Uncle Mark. To escape further beatings, Nathan steals Mark's car and is sentenced to a juvenile-detention center,

where he is promptly gang-raped. When a drunken guard attempts to kill him, Nathan manages to kill the guard and escape. Stealing cars and hiding in the suburban homes of vacationing families, Nathan learns that he's the talk of talk radio, and as the boy hunt escalates, he begins an on-the-air dialogue with The Bitch, a nationally syndicated talk-show star. The body count rises as a sadistic hitman also stalks Nathan, and only The Bitch and a local cop believe that

> **Nathan Bailey's life is a Dickensian tragedy updated for the 1990s.**
>
> —*Thomas Gaughan*

Nathan may be a victim instead of a stone killer. This novel isn't literature, and the author isn't a new Dickens. Nathan seems too sweet and polite to be a believable 12-year-old, especially one so brutalized. Other characters, notably the callous juvey warden and the DA who thinks the death penalty for Nathan is his ticket to the U.S. Senate, are the flimsiest of cardboard constructions. That said, the book has an engaging, plucky hero and a breakneck pace, and it is likely to become both a smash best-seller and a big-budget film. Libraries should prepare for a Grisham-like run on *Nathan's Run.*

Kirkus Reviews (review date 15 December 1995)

SOURCE: A review of *Nathan's Run,* in *Kirkus Reviews,* Vol. LXIII, No. 24, December 15, 1995, p. 1718.

[*In the following review, the critic describes the ending of* Nathan's Run *as "predictable but undeniably pulse-pounding."*]

[In *Nathan's Run*] a preteen locked in a juvenile detention facility for car theft kills a supervisor, breaks out, and leads the police on a chase from Virginia to Pennsylvania.

> **Like a roller-coaster, [*Nathan's Run*] races along on well-oiled wheels to an utterly predictable but undeniably pulse-pounding conclusion.**
>
> **—Kirkus Reviews**

At least that's what it looks like—though actually Nathan Bailey is as innocent as the next 12-year-old. He stole the car only to get away from his uncle Mark, the hated guardian who's secretly after his inheritance; he killed the supervisor only in self-defense; and he's being pursued not only by the red-faced police but by a contract killer as well. Nathan doesn't know about the contract killer, but he blurts out the rest of his story at the first opportunity to Denise Carpenter, the self-styled "Bitch" of NewsTalk 990, during her phone-in radio program, and the audience, cueing the gentle reader, goes bananas (eventually, calls run 3 to 1 in his support). Gone to ground in a vacationing family's home, the slight, blond, resourceful Nathan—an obvious role model for most of the 12-year-olds you know—sweeps up the glass he broke getting in, washes the linens, and leaves an apologetic note for the surprised homeowners. (A second note to a different family remarks in passing that he's taken their handgun.) Meanwhile, county cop Warren Michaels and his good-cop friends sweat to bring Nathan in before damn-the-First-Amendment county prosecutor J. Daniel Petrelli or well-connected hit-man Lyle Pointer can pin down his location and blow him away. First-timer Gilstrap doesn't clutter this scenario with any unnecessary physical descriptions, psychological background, or moral complexity; like a roller-coaster, the story races along on well-oiled wheels to an utterly predictable but undeniably pulse-pounding conclusion.

Publisher's Weekly (review date 18 December 1995)

SOURCE: A review of *Nathan's Run,* in *Publisher's Weekly,* Vol. 242, No. 51, December 18, 1995, p. 39.

[*Below, the critic offers a favorable review of* Nathan's Run, *calling the book a "brilliantly calculated debut."*]

Gilstrap is a first-novelist, but you wouldn't know it from his brilliantly calculated debut. With the skill of a veteran pulp master, he weaves a library's worth of melodramatic clichés into a yarn that demands to be read in one sitting. Eponymous Nathan isn't any old 12-year-old; he's a kid, shades of Dickens, who was unjustly thrown into a juvenile detention center and raped his first night there. Now the boy's on the lam, having escaped the center after killing a guard who for some mysterious reason tried to stab him to death. Crying for Nathan's blood are an ambitious politician and vengeful cops, as well as a sadistic mob hit man who aims to finish what the guard botched. Luckily for the boy, the cop in charge of bringing him in is a kindly sort who recently lost a son who looked much like Nathan. Readers should find much of this familiar—even Nathan's calls to a radio host as he runs are old news (a similar ploy was used in the 1971 film *Vanishing Point*). Still, as the plucky kid fights against increasingly desperate odds, Gilstrap mixes sentiment and suspense with a wizard's touch, ensuring that Nathan's most satisfying run likely will be right up the bestseller lists.

> **Gilstrap is a first-novelist, but you wouldn't know it from his brilliantly calculated debut.**
>
> **—Publisher's Weekly**

Erna Chamberlain (review date 1 February 1996)

SOURCE: A review of *Nathan's Run,* in *Library Journal,* Vol. 121, No. 2, February 1, 1996, p. 97.

[*In the following review, Chamberlain remarks favorably on* Nathan's Run.]

Nathan Bailey, a 12-year-old boy incarcerated in a juvenile detention center on spurious charges, escapes after murdering a guard who attempted to stab him to death. A chase ensues, and along the way we are introduced to an ambitious prosecutor, some vengeful cops, a mob hit man trying to finish what the guard started, and other assorted bad guys. On the side of the young escapee is an empathetic police lieutenant who recently lost a son of the same age who bore a strong resemblance to Nathan. A charismatic shock-radio talk show hostess plays a pivotal role in influencing public opinion as well as providing a forum for Nathan's side of events. As the chase continues, the reader is forced to consider how one views the doling out of punishment, as well as judging the validity of outside influences on the rightness or wrongness of the commission of a violent crime. Gilstrap's debut work gallops along at breakneck speed to an ending that is guaranteed to evoke a strong emotional response in the reader.

Gilstrap's debut work gallops along at breakneck speed to an ending that is guaranteed to evoke a strong emotional response in the reader.

—Erna Chamberlain

Drew Limsky (review date 29 February 1996)

SOURCE: "The Copycat Crime," in *Washington Post,* February 29, 1996, p. B2.

[*Limsky is a novelist, poet, educator, and critic. In the following review, he describes* Nathan's Run *as derivative of John Grisham's* The Client.]

Few writers would envy the prose of John Grisham, marvel at the elegant ease of his language or aspire to the complexity of his characterizations, but there are no doubt hundreds of nascent pulp scribes hot to mimic the staggering commercial success of the lawyer turned bestselling author. John Gilstrap is one. *Nathan's Run* is just the kind of novel Grisham writes—in fact, he's already written it: *The Client*.

Grisham's 1993 book was about a street-smart 11-year-old who witnesses the suicide of a gangster and finds himself sought after by the mob and by a publicity-hungry prosecuting attorney; along the way, he secures as an ally a savvy female lawyer with a palpable maternal instinct. Similarly, *Nathan's Run* is about a street-smart 12-year-old who survives a botched murder attempt; after killing the would-be assassin in self-defense, Nathan Bailey becomes an unlikely fugitive pursued by, yes, the mob and a publicity-hungry prosecutor. Within hours of his flight, the boy becomes championed by a headstrong woman—this time a radio talk-show

host known by her subtle on-air moniker, "The Bitch." She reveals her maternal instinct as quickly as the author exhausts his talent for nicknames.

One begins to lose count of the number of characters that seem derived from Grisham's book: Aside from the smart-mouthed but adorable kid, the hard-luck career gal with the heart of mush, and the underhanded prosecutor with a polling booth for a brain, we are also treated to the vicious but incompetent hit man who is repeatedly foiled by the resourceful pre-teen. Unfortunately, Gilstrap adds to the story what seems like a dozen more supporting players, mainly cops with names as interchangeable as their generic personalities; the author allows each no more than one identifying trait, but somehow this doesn't make them any easier to remember from chapter to chapter.

[In *Nathan's Run,*] one begins to lose count of the number of characters that seem derived from [John] Grisham's book [*The Client*].

—Drew Limsky

Actually, Gilstrap does a fair job of shaping the personality of the young protagonist; Nathan's pop-culture mind-set and his fear of getting caught are rendered convincingly enough. The author has much more trouble with the grown-ups—Gilstrap seems incapable of writing mature, believable dialogue or evoking thought patterns for his adults, who are uniformly slow-witted and suggestible. Several of the book's ostensibly hard-boiled characters—the pair of cops who are trying to track Nathan down and the politically conservative disc jockey (it's difficult to keep referring to her as "The Bitch" with a straight face)—shed their tough skins in record time, exposing their bleeding hearts at the very thought of the precocious boy on the lam.

And who wouldn't? Nathan is so sweet-natured and polite that, whenever he breaks into a house for the night, he takes care to change the sheets and leave an apologetic note before making his exit. "I think we were all pulling for the kid," one cop admits, adding wistfully, "Boys his age are supposed to be innocent." Gilstrap's agenda—a plea for children who are mistreated by neglectful guardians and a harsh child penal system—whether cynical or sincere, is ladled out in clumsy servings. At times one senses the author dropping any pretense of fiction, such as when Gilstrap has a police sergeant lecture the warden of a juvenile detention center about the dual goals of compassion and rehabilitation.

The fun of pulp fiction is the reader's seduction by a titillating, even outlandish, story; a genre writer who entertains will be forgiven considerable lapses in language and depth. One begins to focus on the torpor of Gilstrap's prose and the shallowness of his characters only because his plot about a boy running away isn't all that diverting, particularly when one can see the outcome a mile off.

Pam Lambert (essay date 4 March 1996)

SOURCE: "Punctuation and Pretzels," in *People Weekly,* Vol. 45, No. 9, March 4, 1996, p. 41.

[*In the following essay,* Lambert *describes how* Nathan's Run *earned publication.*]

An exclamation point almost kept John Gilstrap from getting published. New York City agent Molly Friedrich was about to become the 28th to reject Gilstrap's manuscript, then called *Nathan!,* in her case without reading it because of the offending punctuation. ("It apparently screams, 'Amateur!,'" the author explains.) But Friedrich's assistant Sheri Holman noticed Gilstrap was a fellow William & Mary grad and read further. The result: a heart-pounding tale of suspense—rechristened *Nathan's Run,* about a 12-year-old murder suspect trying to elude the heat and a hit man—that has already earned more than a million dollars in book and film rights.

"I'd like to have fallen through the floor," says Gilstrap, 39, who lives in Woodbridge, Va., with wife Joy, an insurance-claim rep, their 9-year-old son Chris and black Lab Joe. "We dreamt that if we got $25,000 out of this we'd be able to finish the basement and put something away for Chris's education, and we'd call that a success."

So far the only signs of his windfall are a large stash of Gilstrap's favorite cinnamon-and-sugar pretzels and the fact that he now spends most of his time working on a new novel rather than for the environmental-consulting firm he owns. But his company played a key role in his success. During a 1994 trip to Montana, Gilstrap found himself making the 16-hour drive between two clients several times—with no radio reception. "I had nothing to do but think," he says. "I had the novel outlined within a few days."

Though Gilstrap isn't writing the *Nathan* script, he admits to some mental casting. "I think The Bitch [a radio shock jock] would be nicely played by Whoopi Goldberg. And for [cop] Warren Michaels, Harrison Ford would be great." But, Gilstrap adds, "it's hard for me to separate who I'd like to see in it and who I'd like to meet."

Bobbie Hess (review date 19 April 1996)

SOURCE: "This Boy's Life Is No Fun on the Run," in *Chicago Tribune,* April 19, 1996, p. 3.

[*Below, Hess praises Gilstrap's protagonist as "one of the most likable characters in recent fiction: an honest yet resourceful kid."*]

This emotionally charged thriller is one of the year's best.

Until he was 10, Nathan Bailey had an almost perfect life. Although his mother died when he was an infant, he was adored by his prosperous father. But when a train crashes into his father's car, Nathan's life becomes a living hell. The court awards custody of Nathan to an uncle, who beats the boy. At 11, Nathan decides to run away, steals his uncle's car, is caught and sent to a children's detention center, where he is assaulted on the first night. At 12, a guard puts Nathan into a detention room, makes him take off his shoes and socks, then tries to kill him. Nathan is small for his age, but he fights back and kills the guard, takes his keys and flees the detention center.

John Gilstrap has created one of the most likable characters in recent fiction: an honest yet resourceful kid.

—Bobbie Hess

A survivor, Nathan hunts for a safe haven. He finds a quiet neighborhood, looks for a house with lots of newspapers on the porch and breaks in. He takes off his bloody clothes, showers, finds something to eat, then goes to sleep. When he awakes, he looks for a boy's room so he can borrow some clothes. Then he settles down in the master bedroom, turns on a radio talk show and learns there is a nationwide hunt for him, with officials saying they would seek the death penalty. For 20 minutes he listens to callers say he should be tried as an adult and executed. Finally, Nathan calls the station to tell his side of the story. When talk-show host Denise Richardson asks if he killed the guard, Nathan answers yes. And he tells what really happened. Later that night, after laundering the sheets he slept in, he leaves the house's owners a letter, apologizing for breaking in, promising to repay them for the broken window, clothes and food, and saying he will let them know where he leaves the family's BMW.

Nathan takes off, knowing that the police are after him but not knowing that a hit man is also closing in.

John Gilstrap has created one of the most likable characters in recent fiction: an honest yet resourceful kid. At every turn in the story, Nathan tugs at your heart. *Primal Fear* and *The*

Client both deal with youngsters in jeopardy, but not as well as ***Nathan's Run.***

FURTHER READING

Criticism

Harris, Mark. "Write, Camera, Action." *Entertainment Weekly* 314 (16 February 1996): 54-5.
    Remarks on the film potential of *Nathan's Run.*

Caroline Knapp

Drinking: A Love Story

Born in 1959, Knapp is an American journalist and memoirist.

INTRODUCTION

In *Drinking: A Love Story* (1996) Knapp traces her experiences as an alcoholic from the time she took her first drink as a young teenager until she checked herself into a rehabilitation center at the age of thirty-four. Influenced by Peter Hamill's book *A Drinking Life,* Knapp wanted to write about the effects of alcoholism and addiction from a woman's perspective. Knapp notes in her memoir that she was not the stereotypical alcoholic; she was born into a wealthy and privileged family in Massachusetts, graduated magna cum laude from Brown University, and became a hardworking and successful columnist, writing under the pseudonym Alice K., for the Boston *Phoenix.* The often personal matters Knapp wrote about in her column may have prepared her for the revelations made in *Drinking,* in which she examines her relationships with various family members, particularly the one between her and her father, a psychiatrist, also an alcoholic, who was often distant and unemotional. He died in 1992 of a brain tumor; shortly after, Knapp's mother, an artist, died of breast cancer. Knapp notes that the deaths of her parents caused her to drink even more until she eventually sought help in 1994. In addition to her alcoholism, Knapp writes about her struggles with anorexia and the emotional impact of having an abortion and engaging in an affair. Critical reaction to *Drinking: A Love Story* has been mixed. Some reviewers have faulted the work for a lack of focus and detached, unengaging portrayals of other alcoholics. Other critics, however, have lauded Knapp's honesty, introspection, and focus on self-discovery as well as her prose style; Walter Kirn, for example, called Knapp's sentences "measured, hand-cut gems."

PRINCIPAL WORKS

Alice K.'s Guide to Life: One Woman's Quest for Survival, Sanity, and the Perfect New Shoes (journalism) 1994
Drinking: A Love Story (memoir) 1996

CRITICISM

Irene Sege (essay date 1 May 1996)

SOURCE: "Her Time in a Bottle: Caroline Knapp's Memoir

Recounts Her Painful Love Affair with Alcohol," in *The Boston Globe,* May 1, 1996, p. 61.

[*In the following essay, Knapp discusses with Sege why she wrote* Drinking: A Love Story *and details her experiences as an alcoholic.*]

Honestly, can you imagine a man describing his alcoholism like this?

"It happened this way: I fell in love and then, because the love was ruining everything I cared about, I had to fall out."

Well, that is how writer Caroline Knapp opens her memoir, titled, femininely enough, ***Drinking: A Love Story.***

The Boston *Phoenix* columnist, who is 36, had her first drink as a young teenager, 13 or 14 years old, and her last a little more than two years ago. In those intervening years she graduated magna cum laude from Brown University and has worked as a journalist. She never wrote drunk, but she has written nursing a hangover.

Knapp is—and was, through all those years of drinking—well bred and high-achieving, a closet imbiber who hardly fit the stereotypical picture of the two-fisted drinker, the two-fisted male drinker, who loses everything to too many bottles of gin. More than two-thirds of the nation's estimated 8.1 million alcoholics are men, but that still leaves 2.5 million women with drinking problems.

That is one reason Knapp wrote this book.

"I was moved and influenced by Pete Hamill's book [*A Drinking Life*], but it was such a guy story and such a guy experience with drinking," she says. "He was the boisterous hard-drinking reporter, out covering wars. There was not a lot of the stuff that women I know struggle with when they become addicted to something and try to get out of it. Fears and self-doubts and self-loathing and all that stuff.

"I felt if I had read something from a real female perspective during my own drinking it would have been really helpful to me."

The other reason that Caroline Knapp wrote this book is that what Caroline Knapp does is write about herself, and this, quite simply, is the time when finally she could tackle one of the biggest forces in her life. She is Cambridge-raised, the daughter of a psychiatrist and an artist, and her writing melds the examined life and the creative life.

Knapp has bantered in print (often through her alter ego, the thoroughly modern and perpetually insecure Alice K.) about orgasms and suntans and being a grown-up. She has written seriously about her experience with anorexia and the deaths of her parents.

But, other than a brief mention of her own alcoholism in a 1995 column on the "moderation" movement, Knapp has not written about her bout with the bottle, with the roots and comforts of her alcoholism, with the way she took to liquor like a lover, then mourned its loss.

Now that she has, all her experience with self-revelation is proving a flimsy shield against the fear with which she awaits the publication of her book this month by the Dial Press.

"I'm really scared," Knapp says. "I'm more anxious about it than I feel I have a right to be. I've written personal stuff for so long, but it's always been a fairly small audience and a more limited way of being personal. This just feels much bigger. It makes me feel terribly exposed.

"There's still a stigma around alcoholism. A big one. This is not a lot of fun to imagine people I used to drink with or work with or friends of my parents opening up the paper and saying, 'Oh, gee, look, Jean and Pete's kid is an alcoholic.'

It strips away a level of privacy I'm very used to having. It was a relief to write it, but mostly right now I'm just scared."

Knapp is sitting at the kitchen table of the house, or rather the half of a side-by-side duplex, that she bought in 1994, four months after she quit drinking. Her dog, Lucille, a German shepherd mix, her other major post-drinking acquisition, "something in my life that would have been impossible were I still drinking," is sprawled on the sofa in the living room.

Knapp lights a Virginia Slims menthol—no way she's ready to tackle another addiction yet—and sips herbal tea. Her blond hair hangs to her waist, much as it did when she was a girl, and when one sees her sitting here, her knees curled to her chest and her arm curled around her knees, one can imagine her as the child she describes in her book who found solace rocking herself, obsessively, addictively, long before she ever found solace in wine.

"I still feel newly sober," she says. "Two years isn't that long. I still feel kind of raw. In some ways rawer than in the beginning. The first year you sail through on the novelty of it and the understanding that you're doing the right thing and moving in the right direction and all that. The second year and the beginning of this year have felt a little more real and a little more raw."

In her memoir, Knapp describes a childhood of privilege and intellect, in what her father used to call the "small world" at the top. Knapp never saw her parents fight and never heard them say "I love you." Her father, a professor at Boston University School of Medicine, was intense and probing and detached. "I felt small and exposed in his presence," Knapp writes, "as though my body was transparent and fragile as air, as though I might evaporate at any moment, or blow away."

He died in 1992, almost a year after he was diagnosed with a brain tumor. One year later, in 1993, Knapp's mother died of breast cancer. By the time her father died, Knapp had been drinking daily for five years, and in the aftermath of her parents' illnesses and deaths, she turned increasingly to liquor. Finally, on Feb. 20, 1994, she checked into Beech Hill, an alcoholic rehabilitation center in New Hampshire.

Alcohol becomes infused in every aspect of your identity and your life. It's a central way of managing emotions and feelings.

—*Caroline Knapp*

Now Knapp has written the book she wishes she'd been able

to read. She writes about "the way women (at least women like me) use alcohol to deaden a wide range of conflicted feelings—longing for intimacy and terror of it; a wish to merge with others and a fear of being consumed; profound uncertainty about how and when to maintain boundaries and how and when to let them down."

She writes about meeting friends for drinks after work at the Aku Aku in Boston, then meeting another friend for drinks at David's in Brookline, usually careful not to order so many glasses in one place that anyone would look askance. She writes about hiding a bottle of Old Grand Dad behind the toilet in her parents' house.

"Alcohol becomes infused in every aspect of your identity and your life. It's a central way of managing emotions and feelings," Knapp says.

"Drinking brings out very 'unfemale' behavior in women. It makes you more aggressive. It makes you more likely to act out sexually. You're tougher, less nurturing. It resolves conflicts for women in particular ways: how sexual to be. How assertive to be. How aggressive to be. What to act like in public. What to act like in private. It just takes all that away temporarily."

"Sometimes women talk differently about their drinking. You'll get an emotional history from a woman—this is a generalization—and a chronological history from a man. What happened. The events of one's life, rather than this is how I felt and this is how I felt and then that's how I felt."

If alcoholism is primarily a male problem, then Knapp's other obsessive behavior, anorexia, is a quintessentially female ailment. She was anorexic through much of her 20s, and even now she is thin. She is 5 feet 4 inches tall and weighs 110 pounds. When she was starving herself she weighed 83 pounds.

"At heart," she writes, "all addictions are driven by the same impulses and most accomplish the same goals; you just use a different substance, or take a slightly different path, to get there. For women, that path often winds around alcohol and heads straight through food. You hear about women who became bulimic or anorexic in high school or college, then established some kind of equilibrium around food when or after they started drinking."

Knapp reached her equilibrium around food by the end of the 1980s, several years after starting to see a therapist who helped her become able to eat two bagels instead of one.

"It's more tempting to relapse into anorexia," Knapp says. "It's more subtle. You pick up a drink and you've had a relapse. You eat weirdly one day, and is that a relapse? It's much murkier. I'm scared enough about a relapse with drinking that I'll go to great lengths to avoid it, but food is something you have to make decisions about many times each day."

For all that Knapp has written a woman's story, she has also written a daughter's story. More specifically, she has written the story of her father's daughter.

Her father, like her, was a quiet alcoholic, an accomplished man with what Knapp calls "a particular fondness for martinis." For 17 years—a good decade after he told his wife he'd ended the affair—he had a mistress. Knapp was involved for years with two different men in a romantic life almost as tormented and surreptitious and complicated as her father's. Watching him die with so many regrets—and recognizing the parallels in her own life—helped propel her toward sobriety.

"I experienced alcoholism very similarly to my father, which is one of the reasons it gets murky to say women alcoholics are really different from men," Knapp says. "We got the exact same things out of it, a way out of our own heads, a way to lighten up, relax, not deal with problems and conflicts and whatever issues were knocking at the door. In many ways it served us both well. We both were hard-working, obsessive, creative people who got stuff done and then checked out at the end of the day."

Knapp is still hard-working, obsessive and creative. She still looks for ways to get out of her own head. She lives in an ordered house, clean and spare. But for a throw rug and Lucille's bed, the living room is bare-floored. But for a lacquer vase here, a vase of flowers there, she displays few knickknacks. There are no piles of papers or periodicals, only a *New Yorker* resting on a stair.

"I've always been obsessively neat and organized. The queen of lists," Knapp says. "I get obsessive about work. I can see traces of all my behaviors, sort of ritualizing my day, adhering to a rigid routine that is comforting to me. Take the dog out. Come back. Eat the muffin at the computer. Check the e-mail. Everything is done in its own order.

"A lot of trying to get better is figuring out where the line is between a behavior that's comforting and self-protective and something that spills across a line into overly self-protective and overly rigid and isolated.

"I don't think anyone will ever describe me as a spontaneous person. I would like to let go of that rigidity, lighten up a little bit. It's not as though you quit drinking and everything that got you drinking in the first place goes away."

Three or four times a week, Knapp attends Alcoholics Anonymous meetings. Initially, she went as much to fill the time she used to fill with drinking at the Aku Aku after work as to reap its therapeutic value.

"I think it's really important to stay scared, to keep it fresh, to remember what it was like because it is so easy to have a selective memory about drinking," she says. "I can still easily just evoke the good stuff and think it wasn't so bad and it really got bad because of circumstances. I could do it differently.

"I also love hearing the stories," she adds. "I never get tired of watching people struggle with their lives."

Knapp has never sipped or served liquor in the house she bought. Dinner guests bring mineral water instead of wine. The day she moved in, Knapp found a bottle of wine, a housewarming gift from the previous owner, on the kitchen counter, right in the spot where she now keeps a snapshot of her mother. She called a friend to come fetch it.

Then Knapp started unpacking boxes, and she came to one that had remained closed since she had moved the previous year to her childhood home on Raymond Street following her mother's death. Inside were her wine glasses. "I remember standing here," she says, "and thinking should I throw them away or keep them?"

She kept them. She put 11 goblets and five shot glasses on the top shelf of a kitchen cabinet.

"I still like the ritual of a wineglass," Knapp says. "I like the look of them. And I like the feel of them. And every once in a while I'll drink a club soda in one of them."

Meryl Gordon (review date 2 June 1996)

SOURCE: "Hitting Bottom," in *The New York Times Book Review,* June 2, 1996, p. 34.

[*Gordon is an American author and editor. In the excerpt below, she offers a negative assessment of* Drinking: A Love Story.]

Caroline Knapp, a journalist from a well-to-do Massachusetts family, . . . believes that her alcoholism is partly inherited, but in *Drinking: A Love Story* she nonetheless settles the score with her now-deceased parents. Ms. Knapp, a magna cum laude graduate of Brown who uses frequent literary references, describes her household as "an Updike family, a Cheever clan." Her cold and remote father, a noted Cambridge psychoanalyst, had a long-running affair; her mother was so preoccupied with her own long battle against breast cancer that she hardly noticed her daughter's starving-for-attention anorexia. Ms. Knapp's twin sister responded to the family dynamics by becoming a doctor, while the author retreated into drink.

Ms. Knapp was inspired to sober up and write by Pete Hamill's memoir, *A Drinking Life*. But while she can be a talented stylist, she hasn't recognized one basic fact: other people's hangovers are boring. Her book rambles, and too many stories of fellow drinkers begin, annoyingly: "A guy I know named William," or "A drinker I know named Mitch." The reader is grateful that Ms. Knapp is no longer careering drunk in her car through Boston, hopeful that her recovery will last and curious to see how she does tackling a topic larger than herself.

Elizabeth Houghton (review date 9 June 1996)

SOURCE: "The High Life from the Bottom of a Bottle," in *Los Angeles Times Book Review,* June 9, 1996, p. 6.

[*Houghton is an American writer. In the mixed review of* Drinking: A Love Story *below, she praises Knapp's depiction of her own addiction but faults her portrayal of other alcoholics.*]

A love story dances on water. The music moves us farther from shore, starts a twinkle in our eyes, and we are new again. Bottle that feeling and you could be King. It's the Holy Grail to an alcoholic. Caroline Knapp is the latest to throw her hat in the ring, dazzling us with her heady description of alcohol's allure and its devastating hold, a high that is near impossible to sustain. In this memoir [*Drinking: A Love Story*] by the 36-year-old recovering alcoholic, shelves of experience and feeling tend to get neatly labeled and wrapped up with a "here let me tell you what alcoholism is all about" bravado, but really, there is no need to explain; the allusive quality of this insidious, cunning disease creeps up and grabs us.

The message is a little too obvious: Even an attractive, Ivy League educated, award-winning lifestyle editor and columnist from an upper-middle-class intellectual family can be a drunk. "Sometimes, as a way of reminding myself how hidden the symptoms and effects of alcoholism can be, I'll look around an AA meeting and tick off our collective accomplishments," she writes. Revealing that an impressive résumé does not grant immunity, Caroline Knapp reports that many alcoholics have achieved enviable success. "That's not uncommon among high-functioning alcoholics: Drinkers like me tend to expend vast amounts of energy protecting our professional lives, maintaining the illusion that everything is, in fact, just fine. It's part of what keeps us going."

Perception is key to continued drinking. According to the author, most people cannot get past the image of a falling-down bum clutching a brown paper bag when they hear the word "alcoholic." Someone in a suit, or "casual chic" as Caroline Knapp's wardrobe dictated, who still has a job, a roof over his head and a car in the garage, does not compute in our lexicon of exterior values as a drunk. Nor did it in hers. The problem was not the drinking, it was the living with one man, sleeping with another, the aborted pregnancy, the back-to-back deaths of her parents, the near fatal accident with friends' children, the deadlines.

It seems to go with the territory; there must always be someone in sorrier shape, a point of comparison to finger as the alcoholic in the author wraps her hand around one more glass of wine, one more for the road, one to her depression as a 12-year-old when the au pair went back to Denmark. As an adult, Caroline Knapp could count on Elaine, a boozy next-door neighbor caught in a doomed affair with a married man, to keep her from the truth: "Some small part of me (it got larger over the years) was always secretly relieved to see Elaine that way: a messy drunk's an ugly thing, particularly when the drunk's a woman, and I could compare myself to her and feel superiority and relief. I wasn't that bad; no way I was that bad."

The habit of comparing herself to others follows her into sobriety. The dramatic stories she hears in Alcoholics Anonymous meetings leave her waiting: "I sometimes feel a little out of place by comparison, a little guilty that my narrative is so spare, and I often wish I had a story that would lay out in clearer, more vivid detail." When redacting the chaos of a fellow alcoholic's traumatic upbringing, she notes, "Mine was more along the lines of a John Updike novel or a short story by John Cheever." Pages later she continues, "It was a well-ordered household. An Updike family, a Cheever clan: calm, educated, cocktails at seven." These tag lines are not nearly as compelling as the lean prose she puts to paper about her highly charged relationship with her father.

A twin, she was her father's favorite; not a Daddy's girl, but a soul mate. "My father drank. He was a tall, distinguished man of bracing intelligence and insight and I grew scared of him, not because he was mean or violent but because he was anxious and sad himself and because he had a kind of intensity that made you feel he could see right through you." An esteemed analyst, he brought his work home. "The problem was that he got in too deep, and that left me with the feeling of being a specimen instead of a daughter, something to be investigated and shaped instead of just loved, just simply loved."

The irony is that Caroline Knapp made a career of investigating herself, shaping her experiences to fit the inches of her weekly column and reporting them as the travails of her alter ego, Alice K., a thirtysomething angst-ridden single woman who battles anorexia, deals with her dying parents and obsesses over bad men. Her take on alcoholism often

feels like this week's assignment. Get the notebook out, go to rehab, sit in AA meetings, hang out in coffee shops, research the statistics, and though it may take a year or so, you'll get the story. She sells herself short.

"A lot of AA meetings begin with what's called a 'qualification,' which means someone stands or sits in front of the room and tells their story to the rest of the group—what happened when they drank, how they changed after they stopped." When Caroline Knapp sticks to her own story, it can be as quietly moving as the mood that lifts in her family's living room after her father is into his second martini and able to talk and laugh. When she tells the stories of the other members of AA, the narrative falls remarkably flat. Without context there is no resonance, it is just information being disseminated, and much like sitting at a bar listening to a stranger's war stories, after a few too many—"a woman I know named so-and-so says this," and "a man I know named so-and-so did that," and "my friend so-and-so thinks"—interest wanes and there isn't much to hang your hat on.

In the last paragraph of the book, Caroline Knapp hints at a greater understanding, a real affection. She fondly imagines her fellow alcoholics all tucking themselves into bed that night with another sober day behind them, their collective pain put to rest. The courage that carried her here has allowed her to put her notebook down, to be alone with the truth. Love of humanity can be a powerful elixir.

Christopher Lehmann-Haupt (review date 13 June 1996)

SOURCE: "Two Lives, One Lost to Alcoholism and the Other Surviving It," in *New York Times,* June 13, 1996, p. C18.

[*In the excerpt below, Lehmann-Haupt states that Knapp's account of her alcoholism "is a remarkable exercise in self-discovery."*]

In ***Drinking: A Love Story,*** an eloquent account of her own experience with alcohol, [Knapp] writes, "The knowledge that some people can have enough while you never can is the single most compelling piece of evidence for a drinker to suggest that alcoholism is, in fact, a disease, that it has powerful physiological roots, that the alcoholic's body simply responds differently to liquor than a nonalcoholic's."

If the cause of excessive drinking really is physiological, one might wonder what the point is of reading further harrowing accounts of alcoholism's progress: After all, the disease's course has been traced repeatedly in books and movies, many nightmarishly unforgettable. One might almost conclude that if narrative could teach, no one would drink.

What complicates matters is that physiology is rarely the entire story. . . . [Ms. Knapp examines] unresolved emotional conflicts at length. What makes Ms. Knapp's book worth reading is, first of all, her fluency in writing about her addiction: "I loved the sounds of drink: the slide of a cork as it eased out of a wine bottle, the distinct glug-glug of booze pouring into a glass, the clatter of ice cubes in a tumbler. I loved the rituals, the camaraderie of drinking with others, the warming, melting feelings of ease and courage it gave me."

But more important is the portrait she offers of what she calls "the high-functioning alcoholic": "Smooth and ordered on the outside; rolling and chaotic and desperately secretive underneath, but not noticeably so, never noticeably so."

Throughout the worst years of her dependence she functioned successfully as an editor and columnist for *The Boston Phoenix* and even published a book based on her column, ***Alice K.'s Guide to Life.***

In ***Drinking,*** she writes of herself as a case study of what she considers the typical alcoholic: "We're often professionals—doctors and lawyers, teachers and politicians, artists and therapists and stockbrokers and architects—and part of what keeps us going, part of what *allows* us to ignore the fact that we're drunk every night and hung over every morning, is that we're so very different from the popular definition of a 'real' drunk."

She continues, "In fact, the low-bottom, skid-row bum is the exception, representing only 3 to 5 percent of the alcoholic population, a mere fraction." Then she concludes, "The vast majority of us are in far earlier stages of the disease: we're early- and midstage alcoholics, and we function remarkably well in most aspects of our lives for many, many years." Ms. Knapp eventually stopped functioning well, gave up drinking, joined Alcoholics Anonymous and discovered a world made up of "color instead of black and white."

Her account of this journey is a remarkable exercise in self-discovery.

Kim Hubbard (review date 1 July 1996)

SOURCE: A review of *Drinking: A Love Story,* in *People Weekly,* Vol. 46, No. 1, July 1, 1996, p. 33.

[*In the positive review below, Hubbard lauds Knapp's "heart-breaking honesty."*]

Even as a child, Caroline Knapp liked the cocktail hour. The daughter of a stern, distant psychoanalyst and his self-contained painter-wife, she looked forward each evening to her father's first martini, when his reserve would dissolve "as

though all the molecules in the room had risen up," she writes [in ***Drinking: A Love Story***], and "rearrange themselves, settling down into a more comfortable pattern."

With a transformation like that, who wouldn't hit the bottle? But in this compelling memoir, Knapp, 37, a columnist for *The Boston Phoenix,* avoids assigning blame for her own anguished 20-year duet with alcoholism. Instead, she describes with heart-breaking honesty the disease's insidious stages: the early infatuation, when liquor served as a "liquid bridge" to intimacy; the downward spiral ("You have to see all those bottles . . . and that can be a disconcerting image"); and the final debacle, when her life was a shambles and her taste for booze had become "the single most important relationship in my life."

In A.A. parlance a "high-functioning" alcoholic, Knapp never woke up in a gutter, so she denied the magnitude of her problem for years. Sober since 1994, when she went into rehab, she does not deny the pull her former passion still has on her. "The attraction doesn't die," she writes, "when you say goodbye to the drink." Like all good tales of unrequited love, ***Drinking*** is addictive.

James Marcus (review date 18 September 1996)

SOURCE: A review of *Drinking: A Love Story,* in *Salon* (online publication), September 18, 1996.

[*In the following mixed review, Marcus questions Knapp's focus and intention in* Drinking: A Love Story.]

Caroline Knapp started drinking when she was 14, and spent almost 20 years as an alcoholic. Throughout the 1980s she maintained a good front, holding down a high-pressure job at the Boston *Phoenix* and keeping her addiction under wraps. Much of the time she managed to hide it even from herself: "You know and you don't know. You know and you *won't* know, and as long as the outsides of your life remain intact—your job and your professional persona—it's very hard to accept that the insides, the pieces of you that have to do with integrity and self-esteem, are slowly rotting away." This acceptance didn't come to Knapp until the early 1990s, when she finally entered a rehab program.

Drinking, then, is a tale of recovery, with the emphasis on Before rather than After. When Knapp sticks to her own story, her writing is lucid and uncontaminated by self-pity. Her account of the way that alcohol "travels through families like water over a landscape" convinces us by its very specificity. Often, however, Knapp is unsure of whether she wants to write a literary memoir or a more general discussion of alcoholism. Over and over she interrupts herself to splice in statistics and vignettes she's collected from other drinkers, and while she delivers this stuff with requisite professionalism, it robs the book of its focus. Her story, she seems to suggest, approximates those of the other 15 million alcoholics in America. But approximations are exactly what we don't want in (as Knapp herself calls it) a love story.

Additional information on Knapp's life and career is contained in the following source published by Gale Research: *Contemporary Authors,* **Vol. 154.**

John Lanchester

The Debt to Pleasure

Lanchester is an English novelist.

INTRODUCTION

Set primarily in France, *The Debt to Pleasure* (1996) is narrated by Tarquin Winot, a middle-aged Englishman who despises his late brother Bartholomew, a famous sculptor. Tarquin argues that the true height of artistic expression is not to create things but to make them disappear. Although purportedly taking a gastronomic tour of France, it eventually becomes apparent that Tarquin is stalking a pair of newlyweds; Laura Tavistock, the bride, is Bartholomew's biographer. Divided into four sections—Winter, Spring, Summer, and Autumn—the novel incorporates recipes for each season along with Tarquin's musings on various culinary, historical, and philosophical subjects. He also offers fragments of autobiography, which gradually unveil his psychopathic nature. Critical reaction to *The Debt to Pleasure* has generally been favorable. Although some commentators have questioned the efficacy of using a menu or recipe as a structuring device for a thriller, most have praised Lanchester's technique of slowly unraveling the true nature of his protagonist. Other critics have compared the novel to the works of Vladimir Nabokov, noting similarities between the two authors in their gradual subversion of their narrator-protagonists. Michael Upchurch stated that "Lanchester has devised a near-perfect package in which to unveil [Tarquin Winot], layer by layer, lending *The Debt to Pleasure* the tension of a mystery."

CRITICISM

Jane Jakeman (review date 15 March 1996)

SOURCE: "Dishes to Die for," in *New Statesman & Society*, March 15, 1996, p. 33.

[*In the following review, Jakeman argues that* The Debt to Pleasure *lacks suspense and suffers from too little attention to detail.*]

"Who am I? Who are you? And what the fuck's going on?" The reader of John Lanchester's foodie thriller [*The Debt to Pleasure*] will inevitably sympathize with the narrator's artist brother, Bartholomew. Hamlet-like, he poses these crucial questions while embedded in a mesh of upmarket gourmandise. Lanchester was the restaurant critic of the *Observer,* so he has the foodie world at his fingertips in the

creation of his murderous anti-hero, Tarquin Winot, for whom *haute cuisine* is a ruling passion.

Tarquin is a full-blown product of the European great tradition—in food as in literature. He liberally scatters his story with rib-nudging cultural references (*hypocrite lecteur*), whereas Bartholomew represents the untamed, uncivilized, tomato-sauce-loving force of creative genius. The polarization of our society is thus crudely symbolized by the food preferences of the two brothers. So far, so clichéd; but every thriller is essentially a cliché. The question is what the writer does with the givens of the genre.

Not a lot, in this case. The book takes the form of series of seasonal recipes, and although Tarquin's preface claims an elemental role for the menu (and it is true that all structures can be seen as menus), Lanchester's real and unresolved technical problem is that the plot of the recipe is the opposite of the plot of the thriller.

In the recipe, the outcome is declared at the start. We know at the beginning that the bouillabaisse or shepherd's pie, or whatever, will result from the subsequent ingredients and operations, rather as if the name of the murderer were disclosed at the beginning of a detective story. A recipe that serves up any ghastly surprises is a failure, whereas this is precisely what the murder story should do.

And here, indeed, the identity of the murderer is not long in doubt. Barely has young Tarquin finished off the pet hamster before we know that we are dealing with a foodie-psychopath. The only subsequent narrative interest is how, and when, he disposes of his victims. These homicidal episodes occur at such long intervals, between feverish bouts of seasonal cuisine, that such faint undercurrents of tension as the story possesses are dispersed in a welter of *gigots* and *blinis,* of *lupsup* and *charcuterie.*

To give this book its due, it is a very upmarket *Year in Provence*. Many smart dinner parties will be racing to keep up with Tarquin's table, and adopting buzz-words from Lanchester's frequent multilingual outbursts of thesaurus-like alimentary vocabulary. Why serve a mere stew when you could call it *djuredi,* or *arni ladorigani,* or Bulgarian *kaparma*? As for the recipe-thriller, it is possible to visualize a new literary game of detective stories in culinary genres: the idiot snobberies of Lord Peter Wimsey rhapsodized *à la* Elizabeth David, or Delia on the solidly crafted country-house mystery.

I can't see Delia, famous for her thorough research, making the slips that pop out here. Given that Tarquin places such a premium on accuracy—this being for him one of the charms of the recipe—and considering how snobbish he is about vulgar yobs, it is odd that he is so slovenly. He, or his creator, might for example have noticed that David Embury, writer on cocktails, has his name spelled in two different ways on one page, or that a *menu du joir* is a tad peculiar. I don't think it's a subtle postmodern irony—more late 20th-century editorial exhaustion.

Great stress is laid on Tarquin's fluent French, so perhaps it's a bit daring of this uncultured slob of a reviewer to point out that a sentence such as "the etymology of 'barbecue' is *vaut le détour*" has become a nonsense because *vaut* is a verb, or that a "*soi-disant* cottage-pie" would be a terrifying creature indeed. And Tarquin, like all those who parade their knowledge, comes a terrible cropper ("arse over tip", as Bartholomew would no doubt put it) when he speaks of jostling crowds of "ignorami". The plural of "ignoramus" is "ignoramuses". Well, it must be, mustn't it, since the word already means, "we don't know?" Even a poor ignorant sod of a chip-eating reviewer knows that.

Richard Eder (review date 14 April 1996)

SOURCE: "A Fine Taste for Murder," in *Los Angeles Times Book Review,* April 14, 1996, pp. 1, 6.

[*In the following review, Eder focuses on the personality of Tarquin Winot, the protagonist and narrator of* The Debt to Pleasure.]

When Tarquin Winot was a child, his graceful and beautiful mother took him, dressed in his sailor suit, to dine at La Coupole, Paris' once-resplendent *brasserie.* Someday he would accomplish great things, she told him.

The assurance of glory, a dazzling mother who promised it and sublime food were the child's peek into a paradise never to be forgotten—and never regained. As it turned out, it was not Tarquin whom the whole treacherous world, including his mother, would recognize as a genius, but his little brother Bartholomew, who grew up to be a celebrated painter and sculptor.

Accordingly, Tarquin grew up to be the anti-Bartholomew, the anti-artist, a lucid particle of anti-matter. His exquisitely nurtured mission was to assert his own anti-universe and cause the real one, at strategic junctures, to go "poof!"

John Lanchester, a British literary editor and food critic, has done Cain and Abel as elaborate parody. In blatantly unreliable tones—urbane wit punctuated by howls—Tarquin begins his memoir as a spoof of highbrow cookbook writing. This leads, in a pastiche of Proust's celebrated madeleine, to a series of variations on food and memory. Gradually another story emerges. Tarquin's comically farfetched—and far too discursive—tale of a revengeful chase through the French landscape. It is a second pastiche: this one of Humbert Humbert's wordy pursuit of Lolita, Quilty and his own delusions through the American landscape.

The Debt to Pleasure opens as Tarquin is about to undertake what purports to be a gastronomic tour of France, in the course of which he will keep a day-by-day diary. His admirers (they will turn out to be imaginary) have persuaded him to do so, he tells us, even though food is merely an avocation—"a shaving from the master's workbench"—and not his real art.

His real art, in contrast to his sculptor brother's vulgar production of objects, consists in imagining things and *not* producing them. Not creative passion but creative dislike is the highest aesthetic force, he argues: Passion puts you at the mercy of reality, dislike keeps you free.

Tarquin's art, therefore, is not to create things but to make them disappear. Bit by bit, as he spins out theories and tendentious recollections, sets out seasonal menus, discusses the difference between stews that require sautéing and those that don't, he drops hints of how this actually works.

His first artistic act, as a child, was to smash a papier-mâché elephant his brother had made. His second was to frame his nanny over a missing bit of jewelry so that she would be fired before she could tell on him. She kills herself, and over the years various others—a cook, a tutor, Tarquin's parents and eventually his brother—die in odd assorted ways. The deaths are divulged casually, minor details in the course of Tarquin's ebullient menu writing, philosophizing and peculiarly suspect food-and-travel journal.

Lanchester provides considerable wit along the way, particularly in the gradual undermining of his narrator's urbane tone and his expansive certainty that the world will eventually recognize him as the real genius of his family. He assumes, right up to the denouement, that an attractive young writer who comes to interview him is engaged on his, not Bartholomew's, biography. He also assumes that she is secretly smitten with him.

Tarquin divides his journal with an ideal menu for each of the four seasons. He goes on to discuss the preparation and significance of the particular dishes and drifts from these to updates on the journey, which begins in Normandy, continues to Brittany and then turns southward, ending at his lavish summer home in Provence.

The food writing starts off with conviction and panache. Tarquin gives a lively step-by-step account of how to layer an Irish stew. He discusses the details of fish soups and stews around the world, noting that the English, great fish-eaters, lack a proper version of their own; even the Scots have something called *cullen skink*.

But then there is an odd droop and trailing off. For curries, he impatiently advises consulting a book. As for lemon tart, the reader is told to go buy one. It is not creation, we remember, that is Tarquin's art, but disappearance; and by the time he reaches his home in Provence, he is writing of poisonous mushrooms and omelets.

As for the trip itself, it undergoes its own undermining. At first it is all food and reminiscence; there is a nice bit about restaurants as the setting for the big emotional transactions of our lives: seductions, ruptures, life-changing proposals.

Abruptly and without comment he ducks into a shop to avoid meeting someone. He begins to refer to his trip with "we" instead of "I." Citing a manual of surveillance, he changes his rental car each day. Before long he lets us glimpse a young couple he is trailing; a little later he has broken into their hotel bedroom to bug it and attached a directional radio device to the undercarriage of their car. We are on our way to Provence and a concluding work of art.

The Debt to Pleasure is elegantly written. Lanchester describes Tarquin's aristocratic mother giving politely disdainful orders to the mouth-breathing Irish nanny, who receives them with the "faintest bat squeak of mimed reluctance." Illustrating the need to follow recipes precisely, Tarquin speaks of a pheasant emerging from the oven "terrible in its sarcophagus of feathers" when the cook failed to notice the word "pluck."

The gradual infusion of poisonous hatred into Tarquin's debonair narration is accomplished with skill and polish. It loses its suspense before long, though; the character, unlike Nabokov's Humbert, is a vessel of surprises, not mysteries. Tarquin is flat, and on a flat landscape the destination comes into sight miles in advance.

The book begins with a reference to Brillat-Savarin, the larger-than-life French chef and exponent of the theory of limitless gastronomic pleasure. He was a man so exhausting that his sisters took to their beds for three months in advance of his annual visit.

The reader may experience some of the same exhaustion in the course of Tarquin's blithely fraudulent account. At the start, the narrator enticingly proposes a game of sorts: Guess what is really going on. By the end, his "let's play" has turned—we've all been thrown in with children like that—into "watch me play."

Frank J. Prial (review date 21 April 1996)

SOURCE: "Movable Feasts," in *The New York Times Book Review,* April 21, 1996, p. 9.

[*Prial is the wine columnist for the* New York Times. *In the following review, he relates the events of* The Debt to Pleasure *and praises Lanchester's writing ability, made more impressive by the author's status as a "debutant novelist."*]

Tarquin Winot, an English esthete and gourmand, remembers the time when, as an impressionable 11-year-old, he was taken to lunch at his older brother's boarding school. It was a meal "Dante would have hesitated to invent." In particular, he recalls "the jowly, watch-chained headmaster" plunging his arm into a vat and emerging "with a ladleful of hot food, steaming like fresh horse dung on a cold morning."

"For a heady moment," he says, "I thought I was going to be sick."

It was a defining experience in young Tarquin's life. "The combination of human, esthetic and culinary banality formed a negative revelation of great power," he explains, "and hardened the already burgeoning suspicion that my artist's nature isolated and separated me from my alleged fellowmen."

Tarquin, now having achieved a self-confident and extremely loquacious adulthood, is the central figure—almost the only figure—in *The Debt to Pleasure,* a dazzling and delicious first novel by John Lanchester.

"I decided," Tarquin tells us, "to take a short holiday and travel southward through France, which is, as the reader will learn, my spiritual (and for a portion of the year, actual) homeland. I resolved that I would jot down my thoughts on the subject of food as I went, taking my cue from the places and events around me as well as from my own memories, dreams, reflections, the whole simmering together, synergistically exchanging savors and essences like some ideal *daube*."

By now, anyone familiar with the literature of food is beginning to murmur "Brillat-Savarin." And with good reason. The French lawyer and philosopher, whose 1825 treatise *The Physiology of Taste* is still the greatest of all books on food, is Tarquin Winot's muse. Brillat-Savarin called the sections of his book "meditations", Tarquin Winot speaks in terms of "culinary reflections." And what remarkable reflections they are. He informs us that "the primary vehicle" for transmitting them will be menus, "arranged seasonally."

> **To assume a superior air, to be arch for any length of time, is tough going for any writer. It's like playing faultless Mozart. For a debutant novelist, Mr. Lanchester pulls it off amazingly well.**
>
> *—Frank J. Prial*

"It seems to me," he says, "that the menu lies close to the heart of the human impulse to order, to beauty, to pattern. It draws on the original chthonic upwelling that underlies all art. A menu can embody the anthropology of a culture or the psychology of an individual; it can be a biography, a cultural history, a lexicon; it speaks to the sociology, psychology and biology of its creator and its audience, and of course to their geographical location; it can be a way of knowledge, a path, an inspiration, a Tao, an ordering, a shaping, a manifestation, a talisman, an injunction, a memory, a fantasy, a consolation, an allusion, an illusion, an evasion, an assertion, a seduction, a prayer, a summoning, an incantation murmured under the breath as the torchlights sink lower and the forest looms taller and the wolves howl louder and the fire prepares for its submission to the encroaching dark."

Prolix? Perhaps. Not many contemporary novelists work with 121-word sentences. But Mr. Lanchester is not just another contemporary novelist.

Tarquin's first menu is for blini with sour cream and caviar, Irish stew and a dessert called Queen of Puddings. In discussing blini, he invokes descriptions of Swedish, Finnish, Italian, Belgian and Polish pancakes, among others, then segues to reflections on wheat, the goddess Ceres, frying pans called placentas, Freud and David Copperfield. Moving to caviar, we learn why chess players should eat it and why a professional taster of Volga caviar will carry a dagger in his boot. Describing an outdoor meal, Tarquin wanders off into the etymology of "barbecue." It derives, he tells us, from the Haitian *barbacado,* a frame of sticks used to suspend beds and other things off the ground.

Irish stew conjures up a truly Proustian essay on Tarquin's Cork-born nanny and his actress mother. It touches on Brecht, Pinter, Ibsen and Stoppard, proceeds to his own childhood in London and Paris, considers the family's cooks ("a Dostoyevskian procession of knaves, dreamers, drunkards, visionaries, bores and frauds, every man his own light, every man his own bushel"), then gets down to the proper cuts of meat and the best potatoes ("Bishop or Pentland Javelin if using British varieties") and runs through the world's best stews, from the Belgian carbonade Flamande to the tagines of North Africa and the stufato di manzo of northern Italy. Deconstructing his Queen of Puddings, Tarquin complains— he's insufferable at times—that "it is almost impossible, in writing about or discussing it, to avoid the double genitive 'of' which used so to upset Flaubert."

As he makes his leisurely way across the Channel and on through Brittany and the Loire Valley, Tarquin drops tantalizing hints about another side of his life. He wears disguises, for one thing, and there have been violent deaths among people who are close to him. Why does he keep bringing up his brother, a successful painter? And who are the two young people he seems to be following? Suffice it to say that Tarquin is also an expert on mushrooms, those that are edible and those that are not.

To assume a superior air, to be arch for any length of time, is tough going for any writer. It's like playing faultless Mozart. For a debutant novelist, Mr. Lanchester pulls it off amazingly well. Now and then he falters, and there are clinkers. No matter; they just remind us how good the rest of his writing is.

Currently the deputy editor of *The London Review of Books,* Mr. Lanchester has been a book reviewer, a sports journalist, an obituary writer and, for three years, the restaurant critic of *The Observer*. One could say, cautiously, that he might think about giving up his day job.

Gerald Howard (review date 6 May 1996)

SOURCE: "Bulls on Bouillabaisse," in *The Nation,* May 6, 1996, pp. 66, 68.

[*In the following review, Howard remarks favorably on* The Debt to Pleasure *and compares the novel to Vladimir Nabokov's* Pale Fire.]

Ever since Humbert Humbert made his indelible assertion in *Lolita,* we've been counting on our murderers for a fancy prose style. Not only does Tarquin Winot, the tart-tongued and mesmerizingly daft narrator of John Lanchester's "gastro-historico-psycho-autobiographico-anthropico-philosophic" tour de force *The Debt to Pleasure,* not disappoint, he even provides a Lanchestrian corollary to the Nabokovian proposition—and an educated palate.

At a distance *The Debt to Pleasure* may look like the latest entry in that portmanteau genre, the novel-with-recipes, made so fashionable by *Heartburn* and *Like Water for Chocolate.* Indeed, the book is ostensibly structured as a galloping gourmet's ramble through the seasons as he discourses over-knowledgeably on all things culinary, studding his lectures with opinionated asides, erudite digressions, inflated (if mock-modest) self-assessments and discursive recipes that will send more than a few readers to the market and the kitchen. Even if most readers will twig pretty quickly to Lanchester's cleverly ironic narrative strategy, it must be said that Winot and his creator know their onions—and their shallots and their elephant garlic. In his toplofty way Winot manages to be consistently absorbing and even ecstatic on a groaning board of topics: odes to aïoli, diktats on daubes, bulls on bouillabaisse, reveries on repasts past. And not on food alone: See, for example, his riff on the personalities of French rivers, which finally proclaims with the thunk of authority the Loire to be "France's least obvious and therefore most compelling wine river." Care to argue? Part of the fun of *The Debt to Pleasure* is savoring how Lanchester, himself a restaurant reviewer and a literary editor, performs his ventriloquism, using Winot as a literal mouthpiece for his own interests and obsessions—another Nabokov specialty, of course.

We've all run into Tarquin Winot types in our lives: the compulsive lecturer who deigns to include us so flatteringly in the charmed circle of his well-buttressed snobbery, who at first strikes us as eccentrically engaging and then only gradually begins to seem more than a little . . . *off* . What initially seems to be Winot's poised self-absorption assumes by degrees the aspect of full-blown megalomania. In fact, not since the late Harold Brodkey have we encountered in art or in life such a monumental case of narcissism, so delusional a sense of the world's rapt attention and abject adoration—a lunacy quite impervious to irony or logic: "I myself have always disliked being called a 'genius.' It is fascinating to notice how quick people have been to intuit this aversion and avoid

using the term." This hits the essential cracked Brodkeyesque note.

Cocksure, obtuse, increasingly sinister, Tarquin Winot is a brilliant creation—as compelling an unreliable narrator as we've had since Nabokov set the gold standard with Charles Kinbote in *Pale Fire.* They are alike in the grandiosity of their self-effacement and the monstrosity of their intentions. Like *Pale Fire,* *The Debt to Pleasure*'s apparent subject becomes increasingly subverted by the narrator's tantalizing asides, oblique revelations and unbidden reminiscences, as Lanchester shrewdly practices his art of indirection. As Winot, writing in "real" time, crosses the English Channel and motors about France, we see, as from a corner of the eye, that he is wearing a wig, a false mustache and other items of disguise. Why? As he stumbles about Inspector Clouseau-ishly, apparently tailing a honeymooning couple, and fills us in on his family past, two inescapable themes emerge: a mammoth sibling rivalry with his deceased brother Bartholomew, a sculptor of large reputation; and the tendency of the people around him to die violent accidental deaths: subway mishaps, hunting accidents, gas explosions, wild mushroom misidentifications. . . . Pet hamsters buy the farm, loyal retainers are caught inexplicably thieving, and none of it ruffles Winot's composure.

> Ever since Humbert Humbert made his indelible assertion in *Lolita,* we've been counting on our murderers for a fancy prose style. Not only does Tarquin Winot . . . not disappoint, he even provides a Lanchestrian corollary to the Nabokovian proposition—and an educated palate.
>
> —*Gerald Howard*

It gradually dawns on us that Tarquin Winot is that familiar type beloved of ironists, the artist *manqué.* His particular specialty is the disappearing act—he just practices it on others. He loses no opportunity to denigrate his brother's accomplishments, and when questioned by a woman engaged in writing Bartholomew's biography, resolutely ignores or misconstrues her questions (to the point where he can refer to her as "my collaborator") and delivers an extraordinary apologia for what he terms "the artistic project which was to form my lifetime's work." He justifies himself as the murderer as Modernist, practicing "the aesthetics of absence, of omission," and speaks of "*genuinely* dissolv[ing] the boundaries between art and life, while *radically* challenging the boundarizing and conceptual structure of old aesthetics." (*Artforum* meets *True Detective*.) Later he develops this idea to its fullest extent: In comparison with the artist, "the murderer . . . is better adapted to the reality and to the aesthetics of the modern world, because instead of leaving a presence behind him—the achieved work, whether in the form of a painting or a book or a daubed signature—he leaves behind him something just as final and just as achieved: an absence." The murderer isn't a failed artist, the artist is a failed murderer—watch for this line of thought in the Menendez brothers' appeal.

Well, it was inevitable that somebody was going to write a high-toned serial killer novel with a literary pedigree, and considering the potential awfulness of such a book, we must be grateful to Lanchester for bringing it off so beautifully. He has conjured up an immensely stylish literary dish and served it with a wit and knowingness that will delight foodies and bookies alike. *En passant,* he has managed to compose a lovely English bouquet to French civilization; in this respect as in others, *The Debt to Pleasure* resembles another suave and intricate meta-novel of recent years, Julian Barnes's *Flaubert's Parrot.*

For almost any other novel that would be quite enough. But there remains the Nabokov problem to be disposed of—or at least raised. How to acknowledge John Lanchester's immense debt to the master without on the one hand diminishing *The Debt to Pleasure* as a kind of *Pale Fire Lite,* or on the other suggesting that the book achieves quite (or anywhere near) that level of delirious invention?

This is of course cruel. Few people would have even risked climbing into the ring with Nabokov, let alone given him a respectable few rounds, as Lanchester has. That said, a more fruitful comparison of *The Debt to Pleasure* may be to the amusingly heartless black comedies made by Ealing Studios in the late forties and early fifties, in particular *Kind Hearts and Coronets,* another droll comedy of serial murder, albeit without the fancy aesthetics. Poised deftly between pure entertainment and flat-out art, those films, like *The Debt to Pleasure,* are marvelously civilized artifacts, unflappable exercises in high British comic style. (I kept casting Alec Guinness, then Peter Sellers, as Tarquin Winot in the movie.) That is why, classify his novel as you will, a good many readers are going to be deep in John Lanchester's debt for their reading pleasure.

John Derbyshire (review date 26 May 1996)

SOURCE: "Food for Thought," in *Book World—The Washington Post,* Vol. XXVI, No. 21, May 26, 1996, p. 5.

[*In the review below, Derbyshire praises* The Debt to Pleasure, *calling it "original as well as witty and brilliant."*]

The veil and the mask; the blizzard of allusions; the dawn-

ing realization that our charming, erudite, terrifically cultured narrator is, in point of fact, barking mad—this territory looks familiar. John Lanchester, reading reviews of his book, is going to get mighty sick of the adjective "Nabokovian."

It would be an injustice to him to make too much of these echoes. *The Debt to Pleasure* is original as well as witty and brilliant, and the voice we hear—this is a first-person narrative—has a self-assurance and ruthlessness never attained by the old Slav illusionist's haunted exiles. On internal evidence, there seems to have been some drinking from common wells (Proust, Conan, Doyle); but this is a book that deserves to be taken on its own merits, which are numerous.

Leaving matters of content aside for the moment (and *The Debt to Pleasure,* more than most novels, delivers its narrative satisfaction by an exquisitely timed revelation of what is going on, so that the more fastidious reader might care to skip the last two paragraphs of this review), the book's style and structure are curious and striking. It is laid out in four sections: Winter, Spring, Summer, Autumn. Imbedded in each section are recipes appropriate to the season, extravagantly garnished with a mass of culinary, literary, historical, philosophical and geographical musings into which the narrator has adroitly slipped fragments of autobiography.

> **John Lanchester, reading reviews of his book, is going to get mighty sick of the adjective "Nabokovian." It would be an injustice to him to make too much of these echoes.**
>
> **—*John Derbyshire***

Now, you either like this kind of thing or you don't. (De gustibus . . . but no, I am going to eschew cheap gastronomic metaphors.) The late Kingsley Amis famously didn't, and it must be said that if you agree with his dismissal of Nabokov—in a nutshell, that the old boy was a show-off—you will probably not like this book.

Personally I couldn't get enough of it. In the matter of textural felicities, Lanchester is at least a match for the master. Try his description of a waitress changing the filter of a coffee machine; or the character sketch of the narrator's mother (in a paragraph whose first words are "Irish Stew"); or this abrupt, exhausted lapse into self-mockery: "Please imagine here a passage which evokes the comparative experiences of mushroom hunting all over Europe, with many new metaphors and interesting facts."

As a storyteller, Lanchester is out on his own. There is a passing resemblance to the muted menace of King Vlad's early Russian stories, but none of the mellow wistfulness of those later American novels that so irritated Amis; though I note that Lanchester's protagonist, like Pnin, nurses a melancholy affinity for failing small businesses, introduced here with a deft Tolstoyan flourish. (Is it not *Anna Karenina,* now I come to think of it, that includes a recipe for jam?)

The narrator, Tarquin Winot, is single, middle-aged, English. After a night in a Portsmouth hotel he crosses the channel to Brittany, whence he traverses France to his summer home in Provence. The novel purports to consist of rambling notes he made on his journey, organized around gustatory themes as described above.

Tarquin's elder brother, Bartholomew, recently deceased, was a painter and sculptor of some fame. A pretty young woman named Laura Tavistock has been appointed to write Bartholomew's biography and has met with Tarquin for purposes of her research. Now Laura has married Hwyl, a Welshman, and they have gone on a honeymoon tour of France—a working honeymoon for Laura, who has arranged the tour to take in some of Bartholomew's works, on view at various places in that country.

Slowly we realize that Tarquin is stalking the newlyweds, and that he is, in fact, a psychopath of terrible cunning and utter moral emptiness. He would dispute the latter point, and indeed goes to some pains to lay out a philosophy—or at any rate an aesthetic—of the murder-as-an-art-form variety.

This is not very convincing, and probably is not meant to be. The real art on display here is literary, and the quality is (aw, hell) *trois etoiles*. This reader—Francophobe and gastronomically challenged—was caught by the first sentence ("This is not a conventional cookbook") and held rapt to the last (which I would give the game away altogether by quoting). Buy the book and read it, but be warned: It owes nothing whatever to *Like Water for Chocolate*—dwells in fact in a different solar system, in orbit around a darker sun.

Pat Dailey (essay date 30 May 1996)

SOURCE: "Food Has Become a Tasty Plot Device," in *Chicago Tribune,* May 30, 1996, p. 1.

[*In the essay below, Daily discusses the prominent role that food has played in numerous literary works and cites* A Debt to Pleasure *as the most recent example of this trend.*]

"This is not a conventional cookbook," suggests the preface to John Lanchester's new novel ***The Debt to Pleasure.*** And despite carefully worded directives for making flawless lemon tarts and meltingly tender roast lamb, an entire chapter devoted to aioli, the potent French garlic sauce, and as thorough a discussion of bouillabaisse as exists anywhere, it most clearly is not a cookbook.

It's delicious to read, though, a fictional feast chronicling the life of Tarquin Winot, an Englishman with a big appetite for culinary observations ("We then sat down to a meal which Dante would have hesitated to invent") and diabolical ideas about how to use mushrooms. Lanchester serves food as the main course, with plot and characters carefully selected to simmer alongside.

Gastronomic pleasures have a long history in the world of storytelling. Marcel Proust, discreetly nibbling a tender little tea biscuit, found that the cake unleashed a lifetime of remembrances, enough for him to fill a book.

Many other writers have been similarly seduced. From Dante's discussion of apples in Eden to Henry Fielding's ribald scenes of seduction, food conveys a larderful of hungers and emotions.

In *To the Lighthouse,* Virginia Woolf wrote of boeuf en daube, with its exquisite aroma of olives and oil, a "confusion of savory brown and yellow meats." Emotions were similarly tangled and confused. Isak Dinesen wrote lavishly of food in *Babette's Feast,* in which the tragic, red-haired Babette cooked with the passion of an artist for people who barely remembered what they ate. Ironically, Dinesen is said to have starved to death. In Margaret Atwood's *The Edible Woman,* the central character starves, too, unable to eat first meat and then almost anything else. She herself was being consumed, by fears and doubts of impending marriage.

Other authors have stirred food into the fictional stewpot, among them Leo Tolstoy, James Joyce, William Makepeace Thackeray, Washington Irving, Lawrence Durrell, Charles Dickens and Nora Ephron, using repasts to explore powerful themes and relationships.

"Food is a provocative and endlessly powerful medium that everyone understands on the most basic level. In *Here Let Us Feast,* a book of food passages culled from fictional works, M.F.K. Fisher wrote that food is "honest and intrinsically necessary in any human scheme, any plan for the future." People have always feasted, she noted, as a way of admitting that "hunger is more than a problem of belly and guts."

But as readily apparent as it is, food also resonates with layers of emotions and elaborate rituals that move it beyond the obvious. Whether it's used as a meal or a metaphor, food allows a story to unfold in unexpectedly delicious ways.

These are palmy times for food to flourish as a means of

expression. Many of us, with our easy access to food wherever and whenever we desire it, have long forgotten hardscrabble times of need and want. A celebratory sense of abundance has spilled into the literary world, where it rests comfortably with our current, cult-like love affair with food.

In *Like Water for Chocolate*, Laura Esquivel begins each chapter with a traditional Mexican recipe, preparations that, like human emotions, are based on the subtle interplay of seemingly disparate ingredients. Throughout the book, which begins with Tita de la Garza being born on the kitchen table amid a profusion of onions, garlic, cilantro and bay leaves, sex and magic are wondrously woven together.

The interior scenes of the kitchen easily overwhelm the exterior ones, and in Tita's richly articulated domestic world, passion is always on the verge of boiling over. "It was as if a strange alchemical process had dissolved (Tita's) entire being into the rose petal sauce, in the tender flesh of the quails, in the wine, in every one of the meal's aromas," Esquivel wrote, a passage so powerful that it has made quail in rose petal sauce a favorite for Valentine's Day dinners a deux.

Lanchester, deputy editor of the *London Review of Books*, says that sex, food and passion often share the page for good reason.

"There's an automatic reflex between food and sex, which are two of the most fundamental appetites we have as human beings. It just so happens that food is more socially open and so we write about the food. The sexual aspects and the passions are right there on the surface, though."

He explains that for him, food, with its myriad meanings, is the absolute center of the fictional world, a means to tell a story and a vehicle for moving it along.

"In writing, there's some discussion as to whether we choose the subject or the subject chooses us," he says. "I was chosen by food because, even standing alone, it reveals so much about emotions and motivations."

Jacqueline Deval, author of *Reckless Appetites: A Culinary Romance*, a 1993 novel that includes nearly 100 historical recipes, suggests that the truest nature of a book's characters can emerge by examining their relationship to what they eat.

"Food in different social settings gives license for people to behave in certain ways—with greed, pleasure, love, generosity, even at times revenge," she explains. "It's an informal way to get into the depths of personality."

Deval gives shape to Pomme Bouquin, the book's central character, through her examinations of the lives of great writers, including Emily Dickinson, D.H. Lawrence and the

French novelist Colette. From the annals of cooking and literature, Pomme has learned "that the finest seduction engages all the senses," most certainly the sense of taste.

Deval says approaching her story from a culinary angle and interspersing it with recipes was "purely self-centered and hedonistic," a way for her to indulge her own interest in food and cooking.

"I thought at first I would write a literary cookbook, but as I researched and wrote, I found that a distinct, strong voice was emerging. It was then that I saw a fictional love story emerging," Deval says, an evolution that shouldn't be altogether surprising.

Colette, who routinely meandered into the sensual pleasures of food, wrote that there are two kinds of love, "well-fed and ill-fed." The rest, she said, "is pure fiction."

S. English Knowles (review date 18 September 1996)

SOURCE: A review of *The Debt to Pleasure*, in *BookPage* (online publication), September 18, 1996.

[*In the following review, Knowles comments favorably on* The Debt to Pleasure.]

"The role of curry in contemporary English life is often misunderstood" according to the decorously correct standards of Tarquin Winot, protagonist of John Lanchester's debut novel. In this combination memoir, food lexicon, and aesthetic philosophy, Lanchester treats us to a travelogue of the appetites, where cultural and culinary trivia arise from dusty corners worldwide to be commented upon and cataloged by his narrator's ever-tart tongue. Tarquin Winot's polished storytelling skips back and forth between past and present, anecdote and documentation, but the sensory transitions are seamless. In mid-reminiscence of a sweaty adolescent romance, he might suddenly begin to enumerate the complete range of caviar sizes, all the while reflecting on the palate-arousing character of the champagne aperitif.

Rather than recounting his life story chronologically, Tarquin chooses to structure his memoir seasonally, starting with winter and ending with autumn.

Each of the four sections is anchored at the beginning with a seasonally appropriate menu, which acts as a sort of reference point and landmark for the narrator's otherwise meandering style. A discussion of winter bouillabaisse, for example, provides opportunity for an archival listing of the various fish soups of the world. In the spring it's roast lamb, in the summer it's cold cuts and salads, in autumn it's aioli and the wild mushroom omelette.

Every pleasure, however, has its dark side, just as every peach (as we learn from Tarquin) contains a cyanide-laced pit. It is the tenuous relationship between sustenance and poison that increasingly begins to obsess our narrator, snagging the polished veneer of his sybarite's tale. Could these rich still-life descriptions be a baroque disguise for some more sinister plot? To the list of appetites evoked in this gourmet adventure one more is now added—that of horror. And of all the delectable genres that John Lanchester expertly stirs into his first novel, it is perhaps the mystery story with which his seduction is the finest.

Jane Mendelsohn

I Was Amelia Earhart

Born in 1965, Mendelsohn is an American novelist and poet.

INTRODUCTION

I Was Amelia Earhart (1996) is Mendelsohn's idea of what might have happened to famed aviatrix Amelia Earhart and her navigator, Fred Noonan, after their disappearance in July of 1937. Mendelsohn traces the pair's last day before their doomed transatlantic flight, and then picks up where the facts leave off, drawing a fantasy of what might have happened if Earhart's Lockheed Electra had managed to land on a deserted island when the pilot and her navigator lost their way. Critics see *I Was Amelia Earhart* as a story about freedom, escape, and transformation. Mendelsohn began her career as a poet, and reviewers find a lyrical quality to her writing. Most critics also discuss the blending of reality and fantasy in the novel, finding the result dreamlike. Some reviewers, however, are uncomfortable with Mendelsohn's blurring of the lines between reality and fiction, finding inconsistencies between Mendelsohn's characterization of Earhart and the real woman. Much of the credit for the book's popular success is attributed to national radio personality Don Imus, whose enthusiastic on-air praise after reading it prompted a sellout of the first 30,000 copies and a subsequent second printing of 250,000 more.

CRITICISM

Publishers Weekly (review date 18 March 1996)

SOURCE: A review of *I Was Amelia Earhart*, in *Publishers Weekly,* Vol. 243, No. 12, March 18, 1996, pp. 57-8.

[*In the following review, the critic praises Mendelsohn's first novel and calls her a writer to watch.*]

[In *I Was Amelia Earhart,*] past and present, fact and fiction, first-person and third blend into a life of the celebrated aviatrix—both before and after her famed disappearance in 1937, at age 39—that unfolds with the surreal precision of a dream and that marks first novelist Mendelsohn as a writer to watch. "The sky is flesh," begins the first of the scores of discrete vignettes and reflections that make up the narrative, an apt start to a story drenched in sensuality and the pursuit of it. The Earhart limned here is materialistic, glory-seeking, sexually hungry, outrageously self-absorbed and utterly charismatic. Telling her tale with ruthless honesty in both her own voice and that of the self she sees "from far away

. . . ghostly, aerial," she speaks of her days as America's sweetheart, as the wife of publisher G. P. Putnam. Diverting from the historical record, she also speaks of the years after she and her navigator, Frederick J. Noonan, "a drunk," crash-land on a South Sea island that they name "Heaven, as a kind of joke," but that becomes a decent approximation as the years slip by and the castaways discover happiness in nature and in each other's arms. When rescue seems eminent, Earhart and Noonan take to the air one last time, and crash one last time, perhaps into eternity but in any case into an existence defined not by control but by "abandonment"— a message in keeping with the story's theme but in fact an ironic one for a novel as calculatedly lovely and moving as this one.

Molly E. Rauch (review date 22 April 1996)

SOURCE: "Of Time and the River," in *Nation,* April 22, 1996, pp. 35-6.

[*In the following excerpt, Rauch criticizes the way Mendelsohn alternates between the first and third person narrative in* I Was Amelia Earhart.]

The mystery of Amelia Earhart's disappearance is the subject of Jane Mendelsohn's first novel. Whether Earhart lived or died is of secondary importance to Mendelsohn, who basks in the dreamy, terrifying magic of a plane roaring through the sky, then falling a mile to the sea. She basks as well in the imagination and despair of the woman—famous heroine, detached pilot—within the plane.

> **Whether Earhart lived or died is of secondary importance to Mendelsohn, who basks in the dreamy, terrifying magic of a plane roaring through the sky, then falling a mile to the sea.**
>
> —*Molly E. Rauch*

But she doesn't solve the mystery of Earhart's death. On a miraculous desert island, animals gather on the beach and communicate with Noonan, Earhart's navigator. Planes appear and disappear on the horizon; planes circle overhead; planes could rescue them; Amelia's downed Electra glints on the beach. There is solitude. There is a passionate love affair born of animosity. Then there is another flight, another crash, another desert island.

Is any of it real? Ambiguity is alluring: It highlights the impossibility of ever really knowing what happened, and makes the loss of Amelia and Noonan intensely sad. It also illustrates the expansiveness of fiction, and its limitations.

The narrative alternates between first and third person, which is disconcerting and ineffective, though explained: "Sometimes my thoughts are clearly mine, I hear them speak to me, in my own voice. Other times I see myself from far away, and my thoughts are ghostly, aerial, in the third person." But all this breaks down when, in the third person, we hear the inner workings of Noonan's consciousness, as if Mendelsohn doesn't know what she's doing with the narrator. And while there are some provocative sentences that could only come from a mind devoted to flying, like "The flight around the world contains within it everything inside me, all the life and all the death," some are repeated too often.

Mendelsohn's repetition, her confusing narrative and her melding of fantasy and reality make us feel as though we are witnessing someone else's dream: It's a little bit thrilling and a little bit boring.

Michiko Kakutani (review date 26 April 1996)

SOURCE: "Earhart as Brave, Careless, Marooned and in Love," in *The New York Times,* April 26, 1996, p. C31.

[*In the following review, Kakutani asserts that Mendelsohn manages to make her version of the fate of Amelia Earhart oddly convincing, but criticizes her "phony lyricism."*]

In the last few years, there has been a lot of speculation about what might have happened to Amelia Earhart, the famous flygirl whose plane mysteriously disappeared over the Pacific Ocean in July 1937. In *Lost Star: The Search for Amelia Earhart* (1994), the aviation industry journalist Randall Brink suggested that Earhart was on a spying mission for the United States Government, and that she was shot or forced down by the Japanese when her plane wandered into restricted airspace. He further suggested that the Roosevelt Administration helped orchestrate a cover-up of her story, and that she might have even returned to America after the war and assumed a new identity.

Other biographers have repeated the rumor that the American Government faked Earhart's disappearance in order to conduct an elaborate reconnaissance of Japanese-held territories—under the guise of a search for her body.

In her lyrical first novel, *I Was Amelia Earhart,* Jane Mendelsohn avoids taking advantage of such melodramatic possibilities: there are no glimpses in these pages of a fictional Earhart playing Mata Hari, or hiding out in New Jersey under the witness protection program. Instead, Ms. Mendelsohn has chosen to use the bare-boned outlines of the aviator's life as an armature for a poetic meditation on freedom and love and flight. Although Ms. Mendelsohn acknowledges her reliance on several source books—including Doris L. Rich's *Amelia Earhart: A Biography* and Earhart's own writings—she does not try to pass her story off as history, but rather imaginatively transfigures her material.

The resulting novel, like Gabriel Garcia Marquez's *General in His Labyrinth* or Larry McMurtry's *Anything for Billy,* invokes the spirit of a mythic personage, while standing on its own as a powerfully imagined work of fiction.

The Amelia Earhart depicted in this novel emerges as a fiercely independent woman, a woman who has dreamed since childhood of becoming a heroine like the Joan of Arc and Cleopatra she has glimpsed at the nickelodeon. She is a spirited but fatalistic woman who now finds herself trapped in a bad marriage and trapped by ambition and time. She is a woman most at home in her silver plane, gliding through the clouds in search of weather that will brighten her mood, a feminine Icarus, dreaming of "diving over the sun."

This Amelia is motivated, in equal parts, by courage and carelessness, love of danger and craving for oblivion. Her decision to fly around the world in a tiny two-seat plane is both an extravagant publicity stunt and a desperate "flirtation with death."

> **The Amelia Earhart depicted in this novel emerges as a fiercely independent woman, a woman who has dreamed since childhood of becoming a heroine like the Joan of Arc and Cleopatra she has glimpsed at the nickelodeon.**
>
> **—Michiko Kakutani**

"By 1937, at the tender age of 39," Ms. Mendelsohn writes, "she was the loneliest of heroines. She was more expressive around the eyes, and no movie star seemed as mysterious as she or wore leather and silk with such glamorous nonchalance. But she felt as though she had already lived her entire life, having crossed the Atlantic solo and set several world records, and she had no one to share her sadness with, least of all her husband."

As described by Ms. Mendelsohn, Earhart's last flight is doomed by carelessness from the start. Not only has Earhart's husband pushed her into the trip without making adequate safety preparations (he wants to get the story of her flight published in time for Christmas), but she has also recklessly jettisoned the communication devices that might have helped her get out of trouble. Her navigator, Fred Noonan, is little help: a sullen alcoholic, he spends the better part of their trip getting drunk and getting on her nerves.

Certainly Ms. Mendelsohn's Amelia and Fred are an unlikely couple: she, a self-created heroine, imperious and melancholy; he, an irresponsible womanizer, feckless and afraid. Yet when their plane loses altitude near New Guinea and crash lands on a small island, they are forced to invent a new life for themselves, as they wait to be rescued. There, on a tropical bit of sand, under a merciless sun, they become, in Ms. Mendelsohn's telling, a kind of new Adam and Eve, at home and in love in Paradise.

Although Ms. Mendelsohn's writing occasionally curdles into phony lyricism ("The sky is flesh," "Her plane gleams dully, like a barge of beaten silver"), she manages to make this highly whimsical story feel oddly convincing, by giving us snapshots of Earhart that possess the hallucinatory power of a dream: Amelia building little replicas of the Brooklyn Bridge and the Eiffel Tower with the wood she had gathered for kindling; Amelia, holed up in the remnants of her flying machine, writing down the story of her strange life; Amelia watching the birds by the lagoon, stepping "in and out of the water, delicately, like ladies."

By cutting back and forth between third-person assessments of Earhart's life and first-person reminiscences delivered from Amelia's own point of view, by cutting back and forth between the present and the past, fantasy and history, Ms. Mendelsohn invests her story with the force of fable. She has invented in these pages a heroine who may bear little resemblance to the real-life Amelia Earhart, but who remains, nonetheless, every bit the heroine she dreamed of becoming.

Deirdre Donahue (review date 2 May 1996)

SOURCE: "Earhart Is Good for Anyone Needing to Escape," in *USA Today,* May 2, 1996, p. 4.

[*In the following review, Donahue states that Mendelsohn's* I Was Amelia Earhart *is a lyrical story about escape, but points out that for those interested in what truly happened to Earhart it may seem insubstantial.*]

The romance inherent in the early days of aviation has always escaped this reader: the tiny, fragile planes, the danger of crashing, the historical figures like aviators Charles Lindbergh and Amelia Earhart in their leather jackets.

And yet Jane Mendelsohn's slim tale [*I Was Amelia Earhart*] swept me away, after something of a slow start. Nor, apparently, am I alone.

There are several reasons. Not least among them is that more and more readers enjoy books they can devour in a few hours. (Although it's hardcover, *Earhart* is barely larger than a paperback.) And radio personality Don Imus has raved about the book on air.

In fairness, though, Mendelsohn brilliantly evokes an imagined destiny for the beautiful 39-year-old aviatrix who disappeared off the coast of New Guinea in 1937 with her navigator, Fred Noonan. Moreover, she conveys a sense of what the world was like before jet travel: the distance, the strangeness, the sheer wonder of flying. "We spent our days feverish from the flaming sun or lost in the artillery of monsoon rains and almost always astonished by the unearthly architecture of the sky."

In Mendelsohn's fictional rendering, Earhart appears on the eve of her flight around the world as an unhappy, isolated woman trapped both in her marriage to the publishing scion George Palmer Putnam and in her persona as the glamorous, honey-haired pilot beloved of millions for her beauty and bravery. Her husband pushes her to write; she wants a signal placed on Howland Island to help her navigate, but he insists it will hurt her image. While Earhart craves the solitude of flying alone, Putnam insists she bring along Noonan, a handsome, dark-haired navigator with a dangerous weakness for drink. The duo heads off on its ill-fated trip; Mendelsohn captures the fury of dislike that builds between the two.

The book comes truly alive with the crash of Earhart's twin-engine Lockheed Electra. Noonan and Earhart survive, finding themselves on an island in the middle of an uncharted nowhere. This results in some of the best deserted island scenes put to paper since Robinson Crusoe. Mendelsohn lyrically evokes the heat, the storms, the sharks circling at dusk. The novella describes the changing bond between Earhart and Noonan—from contempt to hatred to a shared, almost wordless bliss. The driven Earhart and drunken Noonan enter into the sphere of the body's pleasures, isolated from time, pressure, the world.

Two caveats: Some may think the writing precious. And those fascinated by and knowledgeable about Earhart may find this literary trifle rather insubstantial. It is not an account of what probably or even possibly happened. It's more a lyrical meditation about flight, life on a desert island and the human psyche.

And to be honest, *I Was Amelia Earhart* contains an alluring element of fantasy for anyone feeling closed in by technology, pressure, people, life. The book is about escape.

Merle Rubin (review date 8 May 1996)

SOURCE: "A Refuge from Politics, as Well as a Refuge for the Imagination," in *The Christian Science Monitor,* May 8, 1996, p. 15.

[*In the following excerpt, Rubin asserts that escape is at the center of Mendelsohn's* I Was Amelia Earhart.]

Jane Mendelsohn's first novel, *I Was Amelia Earhart,* could be summed up as a paean to the ultimate escape. Taking as her starting point what is known of the mysterious disappearance of aviatrix Amelia Earhart on her uncompleted final round-the-world flight, Mendelsohn has imagined not only the fate that might have befallen Earhart and her hapless navigator, Fred Noonan, but also the thoughts, memories, emotions, and longings that propelled this woman into a life of flight.

Jane Mendelsohn has composed this novel as a sequence of short, sparely written, almost visionary passages. Third-person descriptions of Earhart and Noonan on their final voyage alternate with first-person accounts, written in Earhart's voice.

The writing throughout is terse, austerely lyrical, and the emphasis is on the subjective and psychological. Mendelsohn has chosen to view and to present Amelia Earhart's last flight as the culmination of a lifelong desire to escape. And in the adventure that Mendelsohn has invented for her, Earhart succeeds in escaping, not only from the pressures and structures of modern civilization, but from all previous failed definitions of herself.

Francis Spufford (review date 17 June 1996)

SOURCE: "Airheart," in *New Republic,* Vol. 214, No. 25, June 17, 1996, pp. 38-41.

[*In the following review, Spufford discusses how Mendelsohn fuses the individual and the legend of Amelia Earhart in* I Was Amelia Earhart.]

To a novelist, the real people of the past are coalesced masses of characteristics learnable from the work of biographers or historians; inert, yet available to be woken. But animating a celebrity, and a comparatively recent celebrity, is inevitably a double process. You enter not only the person, but also the envelope of their fame; their mind, and then their persona, a thing determined very variously in collaboration with the world, concerted between the actual body of the person and the bank of night-blooming camera flashes which greeted them at train stations. You find that you need to make some judgments—some discriminations—that aren't purely a matter of the assessment of past character. These are judgments that concern the amount of the cloud of legend that you are going to admit into the intimate movements of mind and body you attribute to that past self. How much, and in what ways, you're going to treat their fame as part of them.

Judging by Doris Rich's 1989 biography, Amelia Earhart (1897-1937) was a contained and fastidious person. Her upbringing in an imprudent Kansas family—Old Money minus the money—taught her not to rely on anyone. She would never marry, she told her friends, because no man would accept the equal importance of her ambitions. Her friends called her "boyish," meaning perhaps that she got single-mindedly excited over things as male children are encouraged to do. She kept a scrapbook of successes by women at law, medicine, pistol-shooting, business—everything. Men's looks gave her a detached pleasure; she nursed the ruined bodies of First World War gas casualties in Toronto, and became a pacifist.

> **It is impossible to tell how good a pilot Earhart was, because every contemporary judgment seems polarized by the facts of her notoriety and her gender. As an aviator, she was reflexively praised or reflexively damned.**
>
> —*Francis Spufford*

In the early 1920s she took her first flying lessons in California. But the feat that made her famous overnight was a publicity-stunt crossing of the Atlantic as a male pilot's passenger. (A London newspaper viciously remarked that she could have been replaced by a sheep, for all the difference she had made.) The real achievements that followed happened against a background of adulation. Part of this adulation was organized by George Palmer Putnam, the publisher and publicist who had recruited her for the Atlantic crossing: she married him, the only man in North America who had a direct stake in the continuation of her career. And part of the adulation simply clustered around her: glorification in a host of shadings from a Depression-era public eager to believe.

She landed her autogiro unannounced in Zanesville, Ohio, wove a ring of daisies for a small girl onlooker, helped wash the dishes in the household that put her up. Then flew on: completing an occasion with a folksy magic to it, something like a Ray Bradbury story, as if an everyday goddess had descended to bless the town. Other encounters with public appetite were ordeals, poised on the edge of hysteria. If the tone of these had had an author, though, it would not have been Ray Bradbury, it would have been Nathanael West. "Oh, I got a good look at her that time!" shrieked a woman in West Virginia who got behind the curtain after a lecture. At Newark Field in 1936, panicky police trying to whisk her away from a crowd of 3,000 rubberneckers dragged her arms and legs in opposite directions.

It is impossible to tell how good a pilot Earhart was, because every contemporary judgment seems polarized by the facts of her notoriety and her gender. As an aviator, she was reflexively praised or reflexively damned. What one can know is the determination with which, for example, she effaced the Atlantic stunt of 1928 with a genuine solo transit in 1932. She possessed an unforced reckless turn of mind ready to spend the future for the sake of the instant's bravery. She left a letter to be opened by her father if the Atlantic killed her. "Hooray for the grand adventure! I wish I had won, but it was worthwhile anyway. You know that." Earhart's life presents that satisfying trope in which a hero's mask, crass and gaudy, proves to conceal the face of a real hero.

This is the biography that has been transformed by Jane Mendelsohn into a novel. Mendelsohn has roused it to an elegant and extremely concentrated life, which allows an explicit grammatical space for the accommodation of celebrity. Told in both the first person and the third person, *I Was Amelia Earhart* loops Earhart across "I" and "she": "Sometimes my thoughts are clearly mine, I hear them speak to me, in my own voice. Other times I see myself from far away, and my thoughts are ghostly, aerial, in the third person." Even when this Earhart speaks in the first person, the "I" is sometimes a fusion of the individual and the legend. "It was 1937. I was thirty-nine. I was more beautiful than ever, but an aura of unhappiness travelled with me, like the trail of a falling comet." A star's self-summary, "I was more beautiful than ever," is not a thought that could plausibly have originated in the private woman.

By 1937 Earhart's trademark curled bob was turning to a thatch of hair; her face was baked and exhausted. She had always maintained a conscious glamour, dry Ivy-League feminine on the ground, a tough mix of silk and leather for the air, and rather enjoyed it in a skeptical sort of way—the "Amelia Earhart"-branded luggage and clothes for "active living" weren't purely schemes by her husband. A perceptive friend had praised her at 22 for "a strangely poetic beauty which did not depend on regularity of feature or perfection of bodily structure." Instead—dispiritingly, predictably, sympathetically—she thought her thighs were too fat. Beauty of a conventional 1930s variety was attributed to her because it was stipulated by her role: it was necessary that she be beautiful,

as it was necessary that Joan of Arc be beautiful. An aviatrix must be that. Mendelsohn's Earhart speaks for the role, too.

But the effect is measured. By incorporating her fame, Mendelsohn's fictional Earhart molds fame into a willed thing. The novel makes her more purely confident of herself, makes her what she is because to a stylized degree she has chosen to be it. It hushes the voices talking to Earhart and softens the buffeting of events. Incidents become decisions. The historical Earhart wore a leather coat when she was learning to fly. She deliberately wrinkled and stained it after the guys in the hangar made jokes about "dude aviators" on the coat's first outing. Their laughter vanishes in Mendelsohn's novel: "I slept in it the first night I bought it because I loved it and because I wanted to break it in."

Instead the novel reproduces the conflicts of Earhart's life, which it has taken inside the wide hoop of "I" and "she" together, as strains within that expanded selfhood. The novel translates mundane tussles into internal disturbances accessible to the tools of reflection: Mendelsohn writes prose in small mirror pieces, not worldly expanses. Her simplification is a paring of the elements of Earhart till they can be worked on by a lyric intelligence. It is also a diagnosis. Earhart had troubles in her last years. The phase of opportunity for female flyers was passing. Putnam had begun to bully: "Stop your sniveling!" someone heard him snap at her. In the novel, these problems cease to be external to her. Instead, Mendelsohn makes her experience a crisis of vocation, a loss of inner altitude: "I was risking my life without ever having lived it." Her disappearance in 1937 provides the moment at which Mendelsohn can begin to do something about that.

Of course, we want Earhart's disappearance, flying round the Equator in a Lockheed Electra with a navigator named Fred Noonan, to have been purposeful. The baldness of her radio silence over the South Pacific seems incommensurate with the importance of her death—though in other moods the immediacy of death in the air forms part of the romantic intensity of flight as we imagine it. That is why, in 1937, speculations multiplied about a secret rationale for the apparent accident: stories were told in which the Japanese captured her or she was on a mission for FDR. Mendelsohn has Earhart and Noonan float down onto a convenient desert island, and in so doing Mendelsohn may seem to be making a similar protest at the anticlimax of mortality.

But she has a more ambiguous extension to Earhart's story in mind; it's true, a further reach of life than the record allows, an extra leg for Earhart to fly during which she can sift amply among the unsolved puzzles of herself—but one conjured from dreamtime. Earhart and Noonan are in an equatorial sky shuddering with heat, lost and dehydrated. Then she's feeling the "metal skeleton" of the Electra scrape earthward through air. Then there's the island, a desert island diagram, without there being a moment of landfall between which would have forced Mendelsohn to state how real these events are. She writes with a liquid compression; and, like flailing swimmers pulling each other down into lower and lower strata of the sea, Earhart, then Noonan, then Earhart again more deeply, succumb to the delirium of isolation on the tropical shore; which is not a destructive process but a journey of the soul. On her island, Earhart passes through madness into the discovery of her own largeness. She realizes that what she "had considered to be her self all these years was only a magnified detail of an enormous painting. . . . The sky, however wide and smeared with thick painterly clouds, now seems to her only one square inch of an infinite fresco of the world." Even a renewed flight in the beached silver Electra seems possible; and perhaps another and another in endless sequence flying to remoter and yet remoter islands, in emulation of the mystics' idea of unending refinement, never-concluded passage into purer spheres of being.

Not much is known about Fred Noonan, a slender drunk fired by Pan Am, except that Earhart didn't trust him. In these pages, too, he's a sketched, hermetic presence; but he is the Other to Earhart's Self, supplying a salting contrariness if spiritual intent threatens to overwhelm persuasive experience. Lovers eventually, the two of them are engaged in a idyll that has no stable state. It tilts continually this way and that, with bickering and romantic abrasion. Mendelsohn rather savors the proximity of the Hollywood versions of castaway romance—the same palm trees might serve as props for Hepburn as Earhart, Bogart as Noonan. But Mendelsohn is unsentimental: her lovers aim at edgy autonomy. Rather than happy endings, her two castaways feel, at the end of the book, the happiness of being "able to please themselves forever because they don't protect each other from their selfishness."

At times Mendelsohn falters. Sometimes the struts of irony bracing the idyll collapse and the novel crumples into a compliant swoon. Sometimes the tone strays. Earhart performing herself in Mendelsohn's third person ("The great heroine leans against a tree") can suddenly sound like Snoopy atop his doghouse ("The Red Baron is diving out of the sun!") But then poetic prose is a repeated gamble. Since even a short novel has almost as many components as a space shuttle, it ends up being evens or better that something will go wrong.

What goes right here is worth celebrating: repeated clusters of observations whose fresh accuracy one can only salute. The book is full of the exactitude of the newly seen. A day of Californian spring when "the afternoon light felt powdery, as if it might blow away" and "skirts of breeze" brushed Earhart's face. The legs of dead bugs "shriveled like morbid curlicues." Noonan, drunk in the navigator's cabin of the wrecked plane, "passed out with his face on an open map. His head lies in the

Pacific like a dark eighth continent, and his long arms wrap around the ocean as if he were a sweetly uncoordinated god trying to scoop it up."

On the island, shadows of palm leaves move on the sand "like fish skeletons," the hot sea "rolls in folds like the back of a dog's neck"; off the doped side of the Electra, the sun reflects in "fruit-punch colors." And all these, in themselves tentative and lightly phrased specifics, are the members of a structure with its own curious rigor. Mendelsohn's narrative goes forward by revolving, counterpointing, reversing the set of selected figures by which she imagines Earhart (flying as fulfillment, as escape, as evasion, as illusion). She fugues through Earhart, subjecting the premise of the novel's beginning, that "I risked my life without living it," to the inversions and tense-shifts of the island where a heroine can outlive herself, until it resolves into an affirmation won by daring fingerwork from the expected story of death. "I believe in this life. I believe that it continues."

"The sky is flesh" is this novel's first line, and one of its chief figures. Mendelsohn makes Earhart see "the blue belly" above as several successive kinds of body. But outside the internal consistency of Mendelsohn's weave of imagining, is the sky really flesh, to heroes? You could make a case that heroes— and Earhart set out to be a female hero, not a heroine—are precisely people who choose to devote the greatest intensity of their lives to things other than those demanded by flesh, by the biological script of existence. Flying's greatest attraction might be the uncarnality of the air. It was part of Putnam's promotional shtick that Earhart looked like Lindbergh, "a Lady Lindy"; but it implied something different for a woman to want the sky than it did for Lindbergh. A woman might possess the same character as the male heroes of aviation, the same reticence concealing complete self-faith, the same set of superstitions designed to starve fate of oxygen. But she couldn't get out of the biological script just by rising up from the sticky ground into the thin air.

A woman taking to the bodyless heavens in the 1930s had an anatomy that was supposed to be her destiny. To make the same escape, she had in some sense to go against her own body, to become an exalted exception. It comes as no surprise that Amelia Earhart does not seem to have been enthusiastic about eating. She looked "like a bag of bones" in a swimsuit, someone said. But by refusing her own flesh's power to net her into childbearing and the forever-erasing actions of domesticity, she gained a body that felt more simply and uncodedly her own than many women's. Her sister Muriel remarked bitterly on the radio that Amelia looked much younger than her, because "taking care of a house and two children is more care, it would seem, than flying solo across the Atlantic." There were, too, small gains of corporeal freedom. As a consultant on careers for women at Purdue College, she liked to sit with her elbows on the table. "If Miss

Earhart can do it, why can't we?" asked a student. "You can," replied the dean of women, "as soon as you fly the Atlantic."

Rather than a perpetual mounting into new thinnesses of the empyrean, flight ends with touchdown and a return to the regime of the ground; or with a crash and the reduction of the flyer to pure mashed body, just as the end of anorexia is indignity and confinement rather than angelic escape. But before her final "crack-up" (a term that brings together the crash of a plane and the crash of a consciousness) Earhart was able to inhabit her exceptional, perhaps untenable position, arrived at by the strange compromises of fame, in a way that carried the isolation of flying into other kinds of self-possession. For reading her speeches and letters is like finding a person who somehow contrived to dispense with a large proportion of the supposedly inevitable mental furniture of her age. The actual stances she took on sexual politics startle you less with their modernity than does the underlying degree of certainty that the speaker herself is a whole human subject, not a local embodiment of a compulsory femininity. She flew: through receptions and banquets she preserved the memory of having her existence under the sole control of stick and rudder. It is this aerial identity that Jane Mendelsohn has translated into the lightness of fiction.

The historical Earhart's regret seems to have been that her devil's bargain with her husband demanded so much touring and schmoozing and flesh-pressing for so little time flying; that there were so few hours of cloud and roaring silence between one airfield where people stared at her, and the next.

Susan Heeger (review date 3 July 1996)

SOURCE: "Two 'What If' Stories of a Famous Flier," in *Los Angeles Times,* July 3, 1996, p. E5.

[*In the following excerpt, Heeger asserts that Mendelsohn's* I Was Amelia Earhart *is "a brief, brilliant study in redemption, a meditation on love and loneliness that steers far away from mawkishness."*]

Good news, Amelia Earhart fans. This summer your elusive hero flies again in two recently published novels that can be knocked off in a couple of beach days. And I do recommend the beach. Both are largely set on desert islands, the kind where palm trees sway and the only beverage comes in coconuts. Both are first novels that suggest that Amelia—who vanished in 1937 on a trans-world flight—didn't go down in a blast of fire but landed safely on some atoll with her navigator, Fred. That she and Fred, improbably, fell in love. And that's about all these two books have in common.

I Was Amelia Earhart, by Jane Mendelsohn, is a brief, brilliant study in redemption, a meditation on love and loneli-

ness that steers far away from mawkishness. In 146 quick pages, Mendelsohn keeps the focus on Amelia, the celebrated aviator, a woman trapped by the world's expectations and by a rotten marriage to a man who uses her to inflate himself. She's bored, exhausted, sick with longing. As a flier, she has no life beyond her public role—the tough beauty in a leather jacket, swinging carelessly from the cockpit with her nose powdered.

Later, as a castaway, she struggles to create herself. Who is the famous Earhart if her wings are clipped? If she's powerless against nature? If she and Fred—a gutless boozer who failed to keep them on course—are equals on an empty beach? The answer is, she's free. But it takes awhile before she knows it. First, she and Fred must try frantically to be rescued—light bonfires, fix the plane, insult each other.

> *I Was Amelia Earhart* is a brief, brilliant study in redemption, a meditation on love and loneliness that steers far away from mawkishness.
>
> —*Susan Heeger*

"I treat him more brutally than I've ever treated anyone," Amelia admits. Luckily, Fred bears up pretty well. When Amelia demands, "How did you get to be such a stinking drunk?" he calmly replies, "Two ways. Gradually and then suddenly." Which is exactly how their defenses fall away until eventually they fall together, two survivors who save each other from the "cold, ethereal strangeness of existence."

Mary Rourke (review date 18 July 1996)

SOURCE: "Taking Wing," in *Los Angeles Times,* July 18, 1996, p. E5.

[*In the following review, Rourke discusses the evolution of Mendelsohn's* I Was Amelia Earhart.]

You can tell you're in someone else's fantasy just by reading the title, *I Was Amelia Earhart.* You might even wonder if the author, Jane Mendelsohn, still answers to her real name.

Such odd concerns have only helped attract more readers to her brief, poetic novel. Within weeks of the book's . . . publication, there were paperback and movie deals, a rushed second printing and high visibility on the bestseller lists.

"I don't feel like I was ever Amelia Earhart. But once I'd gone through her journey by writing about it, I thought the title was something *she* might write," says Mendelsohn, a 30-year-old New Yorker who is married to filmmaker Nick Davis.

She uses the title to introduce an imaginary story of how circumstances changed the life of the famous aviator. When Mendelsohn describes the change, she answers not only for, but *as,* her heroine. "I used to be Amelia Earhart," she says, "now I'm someone else. I'm no longer the Amelia Earhart of the myths."

Mendelsohn is accustomed to speaking this way. She wrote most of her book in the first person. But at times she switched to the third person. And when she talks about the novel, she still switches back and forth.

"The title contains the theme of the book, which is transformation," she says. "Earhart lived a very external life as an adventurous flier. Later, she got to know herself. It's a story about fantasy and reality, history and fiction."

In the writer's fantasy, this change occurs after Earhart's plane disappears from the skies near New Guinea during a 1937 flight around the world. Earhart, 39, and her navigator, Fred Noonan, were never found. "A lot of people are willing to leave it that they went down in the ocean," says Mendelsohn. "But other things are plausible. We really don't know what happened."

The title contains the theme of the book, which is transformation. Earhart lived a very external life as an adventurous flier. Later, she got to know herself. It's a story about fantasy and reality, history and fiction.

—Jane Mendelsohn

The few facts that are available captured Mendelsohn's attention four years ago when she read a newspaper article about fragments of an airplane discovered on a deserted Pacific island. There was reason to believe they might belong to Earhart's Lockheed Electra. Over the years, dozens such reports, and even alleged sightings of the lost heroine, have proved to be false.

"I was waiting for some idea to sweep me away," Mendelsohn recalls of the days before she began her book. The newspaper article suggested to Mendelsohn the possibilities of a romance between the pilot and co-pilot—which have never been proved—and of an adventure on the island.

Writing the book took close to three years, much of it spent listening to tape recordings of Earhart's voice, looking at pictures of vintage airplanes and newspaper clippings surrounding her desk, and imagining herself climbing into the cockpit of a plane as she sat down in front of her computer. Writing began to seem like flying—a solitary adventure into empty space.

She finished one version of the book in two years, but didn't like it. "Amelia Earhart's spirit was missing," she says. In the rewrite she let Earhart tell most of the story herself.

The sky is flesh.

By this startling first line of the novel we learn that Earhart is in love with her work.

"I wanted people to know the book is about language," the author explains of the stark, erotic beginning.

Poetic lines carry the story, at times describing years of frustration in a brief confession. "I was risking my life without living it," admits the adventuring Earhart, who was married to publishing magnate and flamboyant promoter G.P. Putnam.

This is not Mendelsohn's first flight into poetry. She has been publishing since she was an English major at Yale University—she graduated summa cum laude in 1987. After college she wanted to be a full-time poet but entered Yale Law School instead. She left after a year. "I went to law school because I didn't have any real plan. I didn't really know how to be a poet."

Some of the publishers who turned down Mendelsohn's book complained about its lyrical quality. They said it was too short (146 pages), too arty. Later, some reviewers added that it was too pretentious.

Ann Close, a fiction and poetry editor at Alfred Knopf, saw it differently. But it took a strong tail wind to lift *Earhart* up the charts. That came in the form of Don Imus, a New York-based radio talk show host.

"My wife, Deirdre Coleman, gave me the book to read," he says. Intrigued by the title, she bought it the first week it was out, finished it in one day and persuaded him to try it, although he rarely reads fiction. "I was blown away by it," says Imus, who raved about the novel on his morning show and invited Mendelsohn to be a guest.

At first he wondered about recommending the somewhat obscure book to listeners. His show, "Imus in the Morning," airs nationally. . . . "Why talk about a book nobody can find in stores?" he wondered. Shortly after the show, the book went into a second printing, notching up the number from 30,000 to 250,000.

Imus remembers Mendelsohn as "charming and very bright." But he takes no credit for making her a best-selling author. "The book would be successful if I'd picked it up or not," he says. "I couldn't have taken a piece of junk and made this happen."

[Amelia Earhart] died at the peak of her importance to us. She's like Elvis, James Dean or John Kennedy.

—Jane Mendelsohn

Mendelsohn was reasonably happy about the book's reception even before Imus discovered it. "I was thrilled that the first printing was 30,000. That's considered big for a first novel. At that point I'd have been happy for it to have a little bit of a life."

She has moved on from her dramatic entry into the literary scene, to write a horror film and sketch out a second novel. But she now knows something she didn't know before, about the debutante-turned-aviator and her place as an American icon.

"She was a great feminist, a great pilot, a visionary for women who was very vocal about women's rights," says the cerebrally passionate author. "She'd be important if she hadn't disappeared. But the fact that she did gives her another tier of mystery.

"She died at the peak of her importance to us. She's like Elvis, James Dean or John Kennedy."

Katherine Whittamore (review date 18 September 1996)

SOURCE: A review of *I Was Amelia Earhart*, in *Salon* (online publication), September 18, 1996.

[*In the following review, Whittamore asserts that Mendelsohn's book "brings Amelia Earhart to life, more than any straight biography ever could.*]

"Hubris and liquor" made Amelia Earhart crash, according to Jane Mendelsohn, her literary channeler in *I Was Amelia Earhart.* "The more he (her navigator, Fred Noonan) drank, the more reckless she became, the more he drank." If you don't mind riding on thermals of speculation without a glider

of fact, you'll love this novel, which purports to tell the story of Earhart and Noonan after their plane goes down. If you do mind, *I Was Amelia Earhart* will feel indulgent and bothersome until about page 46, when the imaginative loop-de-loops arch into something higher than sheer style: "We saw the same sights and felt the same breezes," writes Mendelsohn of Earhart and Noonan, pre-flameout. "We watched the same moon dip in and out of the same clouds. We felt the same rain and heard the same silences. It was like sharing a dream with someone else."

We learn of Earhart's little-loved husband G.P. Putnam, with his "studied New York charm," and her failed inventor father. We read the telegram from the Roosevelts. We appreciate, if never warm to, the aviatrix's uncompromising personality; "I have not one self-sacrificing, maternal bone in my unwomanly, muscular body," as she says. But she loves her plane, "a barge of beaten silver," with its cruddy radio and bamboo fishing pole, along which messages were sent from tail to cockpit. We hear about the month-long trip across the world, most nights spent sleeping in hangars "on rancid cots, with sinister stains."

[*I Was Amelia Earhart*] brings Amelia Earhart to life, more than any straight biography ever could.

—Katherine Whittamore

But all this is preparation for part two of the book, where the pair ends up, yes sir, on a desert island. "TV movie," one groans, but this is where Mendelsohn's flights of fancy spiral the highest. The book now becomes a great read. Earhart and Noonan move from hope of rescue to bickering, hatred, and madness; to love and then to fear of rescue, against a backdrop of coconut palms, "slate-colored sharks," heatwaves so bad Noonan's skin bleeds, monsoons where the "clouds turned purple, bruising before our eyes," and sweaty lovemaking. He does the fishing and she builds the fires, as well as "replicas of the Hoover Dam, the Eiffel Tower, and then, when she is at her most despairing, a scale model of the Brooklyn Bridge."

It sounds like a cloying montage, but it isn't. Both realize that the booze and the flying were more escapes from life than runs at transcendence; by deplaning from the world of publicists and reporters and expected behaviors, they get their lives back. "Noonan once said any fool could have seen I was risking my life but not living it," as Earhart/Mendelsohn says. A year past the crash, after a supper of shark fin soup, the two go for a swim in the lagoon, "where they were both struck at the same moment with the realization that they had never been so happy." You may not feel quite the same way—the prose is lovely, but completely humorless—yet the book does spirit you aloft. It brings Amelia Earhart to life, more than any straight biography ever could.

FURTHER READING

Reilly, Patrick M. "Imus to the Rescue: Knopf Acknowledges the Power of Talk." *The Wall Street Journal* (9 May 1996): B10.

    Discusses the rise in popularity of *I Was Amelia Earhart* after its discovery by radio talk show host Don Imus.

Mary Morrissy

Mother of Pearl and *A Lazy Eye*

Born in 1958, Morrissy is an Irish novelist, short story writer, and journalist.

INTRODUCTION

The recipient of the 1995 Lannan Literary Award and the 1984 Hennessy Award for Short Stories, Morrissy is the author of works that are known for their evocative characterizations, Irish settings, and thematic focus on women, children, and despair. Her 1993 short story collection, *A Lazy Eye,* contains characters whose lives are defined by bleakness. In one story, a kleptomaniac steals and then destroys books; in another, an infant is abandoned in a store's Christmas display; in yet another tale, a young woman becomes infatuated with the man for whom she baby-sits and, when spurned, exacts her revenge on his newborn child. Set in Ireland in the mid-twentieth century, Morrissy's novel, *Mother of Pearl* (1995), centers on three women whose lives are likewise defined by their bleak and repressive surroundings: Irene, a former tuberculosis patient who becomes so obsessed with having a child that she ultimately kidnaps a newborn; Pearl (later renamed Mary), the baby whom Irene steals; and Rita, Pearl's biological mother. Much of the novel focuses on Pearl, who, as a child, is returned to Rita. After she is reunited with Pearl, Rita is unable to integrate "Jewel," a child she invented in her mind to replace her stolen child, with Pearl's physical presence; in Rita's mind, Pearl and Jewel are two distinct individuals, and Pearl subsequently grows up in the shadow of an older sister who never existed. As she grows, Pearl experiences confusing memories of life with another family. These events have disastrous effects on Pearl when she reaches adulthood and is expecting her own child. Morrissy has been praised for *Mother of Pearl'*s prose style and its thematic and feminist focus on obsession and neurosis; abandonment and the search for belonging; death and poverty; and the relationship between the past, present, memories, and the imagination. In a review of Morrissy's writing, Michael Harris observed: "A constricted life, a warped attempt to break out of it, a residue of essential innocence, the inevitable punishment—this is Morrissy's territory indeed."

CRITICISM

Publishers Weekly (review date 8 May 1995)

SOURCE: A review of *Mother of Pearl,* in *Publishers Weekly,* Vol. 242, No. 19, May 8, 1995, p. 283.

[*In the following positive review, the critic describes Morrissy's writing in* Mother of Pearl *as giving off "sparks of feminist insights and gimlet humor."*]

A lushly lyrical portrait of women wrestling with their inner demons, this stunning first novel [*Mother of Pearl*] begins in the Irish sanatorium where tubercular Irene Rivers stays from 1947 through the mid-1950s, even after she is cured. Terrified of the outside world and having been brutalized by her father, Irene endures furtive sexual encounters with fellow patients and employees while remaining a virgin; she sees her sexual ministrations as a mission of mercy. In time, Irene marries Stanley Godwin, a tender but impotent outpatient, leaves the sanatorium and becomes obsessed with having a baby, even lying to neighbors that she is pregnant. Then she kidnaps an infant girl from a Dublin hospital, telling Stanley that "Pearl" is her own child by another patient. The illusion is shattered four years later when police arrest Irene and return Pearl to her newly widowed biological mother. Pearl, renamed Mary, grows up believing that she and her biological sister, Stella, had a third, "lost" sister, Jewel, who mysteriously vanished. In a first-person narrative occupying the final third of the novel and extending from her preadolescence into adulthood, Mary conjures Jewel as an imaginary companion while struggling to reclaim the buried memories of the years she lived as Pearl. Morrissy's writing gives off sparks of feminist insights and gimlet humor, and her sensuous, lilting prose propels a sensitive study of obsession, betrayal, neurosis and lost innocence.

Barbara Love (review date 15 June 1995)

SOURCE: A review of *Mother of Pearl*, in *Library Journal*, Vol. 120, No. 11, June 15, 1995, p. 96.

[*In the following review, the critic relates the plot of* Mother of Pearl, *describing it as a "haunting first novel."*]

Emotionally needy Irene and Stanley meet in a tuberculosis sanitorium in 1940s Dublin [in Mary Morrissy's ***Mother of Pearl***]. Irene has remained on as an aide after recovering from the disease, and Stanley, the quintessential mama's boy, has come to sit by his mother's deathbed. Their hasty marriage soon founders when Stanley's impotence causes them both unending pain and embarrassment in dealing with the speculation of prying neighbors about a hoped-for baby. This leads Irene down a dangerous path where she first fabricates a pregnancy and is later driven to snatch an infant from a hospital nursery. Amid random acts of everyday violence, the consequences of this outrageous act resonate down through the years in this haunting first novel. [***Mother of Pearl*** is recommended] for most fiction collections.

Nancy Pearl (review date July 1995)

SOURCE: A review of *Mother of Pearl*, in *Booklist*, July, 1995, p. 1860.

[*In the following review, Pearl describes* Mother of Pearl *as "well-written, lyrical, and terribly sad."*]

Set in Ireland in the 1950s, this well-written, lyrical, and terribly sad novel [***Mother of Pearl***] is the story of Irene Rivers, who, at the age of 18, is sent away to a sanitarium to recover from tuberculosis. Long after Irene is cured, she stays on at Granitefield, which she regards as home. But when an act of kindness on Irene's part is misunderstood, she escapes by marrying the son of another patient and moving to Dublin with him. When Irene tells her impotent husband, Stanley Goodman, that she is pregnant, he inexplicably believes her. Like a rock gathering destructive force as it hurtles downhill, this one act of deception sets in motion events with lifelong repercussions for three women: Irene, the baby named Pearl, and Pearl's mother, Rita Golden. Skillfully shifting narrative perspectives between the three, Morrissy forces the reader

to acknowledge that their subsequent actions, which include a kidnapping, an abortion, and having an imaginary child, though bizarre, are, in the end, all too understandable. This novel, Morrissy's first book to appear in the U.S., will leave readers pondering the inevitability of events and wondering which of the characters deserves their pity more.

Claire Messud (review date 9 July 1995)

SOURCE: "Nobody's Child," in *The New York Times Book Review*, July 9, 1995, p. 6.

[*Messud is a novelist. In the favorable review below, in which she discusses the plot and theme of* Mother of Pearl, *Messud notes Morrissy's focus on Irish society, despair, and "the violent movement between the external and the internal."*]

The narrative of an infant stolen from its parents is necessarily a double one, demanding accounts both of one family's loss and of another's joyous gain. But ***Mother of Pearl,*** a fine first novel by the Irish writer Mary Morrissy, goes further, acknowledging the triple nature of the tale: two families live through this momentous event and its consequences, but so too does the child caught between them.

Divided into three main sections, ***Mother of Pearl*** explores the internal lives of three Irishwomen linked by the theft of a baby. Their conflicts are reflected in those of the unnamed Irish city they inhabit, "a city of tribes, like twins divided at birth. At war, at war with itself." In spite of their differences, the women have in common the bitter narrowing of their horizons. They're condemned to a world of working-class poverty where sex—brutal or voyeuristic or merely failed—provides no relief from isolation, and where the only escape is departure to the New World.

The novel's opening strand, which begins in the late 1940s, follows Irene Rivers, who is plucked from her first job, on the cruise ship *Queen Bea,* and confined to a tuberculosis sanitarium. Abandoned by her family, she remains at Granitefield long after she is cured, providing sexual favors to the inmates out of a sense of moral obligation.

The man who rescues her, Stanley Godwin, is middle-aged and impotent. To him, Irene "offered what he knew was impossible. New life." To her, he is simply a last chance at life. Yet Irene finds herself imprisoned afresh in Stanley's terraced house on Jericho Street. There she invents a child, the impossible product of a nonexistent sexual union. Once created, this girl—named Pearl—refuses to release Irene's imagination. It is only a matter of time until Irene must make her flesh, which she does by stealing an unattended infant from the city hospital.

Pearl brings happiness to Stanley and Irene both. But Irene is always aware that the intersection of her dreams with reality is precarious; and when, four years later, the police come to reclaim her precious daughter, she is waiting for them.

Ms. Morrissy's gift for the unexpected image allows shafts of light into an otherwise bleak world: when Irene undresses, she hears "the silky chattering of her slip up around her ears", a bus is "a beast driven," with wipers that "clung gamely to its snout." But it is the darker themes—of isolation, secrecy and the search for connection and control—that recur, carefully patterned, through all the sections of the novel.

In the second, Rita Spain, the child's natural mother, is struck by the confluence of her imagined and real lives. In marrying, "she felt both omnipotent and helpless—all she had done was *to wish* for this." Her child comes too soon, is not wanted; Rita's guilt over the baby's disappearance is overwhelming. She survives by manufacturing an "official version of their lives," which denies the past. When her little girl is returned to her, Rita imposes this official version on Mary (as she renames Pearl): unable to accept the fact that the child taken and the one brought back are the same, Rita separates them, inventing for Mary and her younger sister, Stella, the myth of a stillborn older sibling.

Dense, lyrical and often startlingly written, Ms. Morrissy's various narratives evoke with a relentless force the stifling enclosure of her characters' lives.

—Claire Messud

Mary, granted the novel's only first-person voice, grows up haunted by the lingering presence of this shadowy girl, whom she calls Jewel. Her father dead, her younger sister and her mother locked in a sympathy that excludes her, Mary finds in Jewel her only companion; but it is Jewel who prompts her to ruin her own life.

The novel is shot through with instances, both physical and metaphorical, of invasion, of the violent movement between the external and the internal. Its complex imagery of boats, rivers and the sea seems to promise pain and death as readily as escape. The *Queen Bea* floats into view on a number of occasions, the bearer of unattainable dreams; but it comes as no surprise to learn that she eventually "went down with all aboard."

Dense, lyrical and often startlingly written, Ms. Morrissy's various narratives evoke with a relentless force the stifling

enclosure of her characters' lives. The effect is powerful, uncompromising, but not easily likable. The obscure but ever-present menace of their torn society, the airless despair of the houses and streets they inhabit, and the loveless isolation of their circumstances give rise to the women's elaborate—and dangerous—fantasies of salvation. Ms. Morrissy allows them few moments of pleasure, and these are hard-won and short-lived. When one of the novel's minor characters, a young man named Michael Carpenter, accidentally hangs himself while masturbating, it seems, next to these women's experiences, an almost enviable fate; at least he "had the biggest orgasm of his life."

Michael Harris (review date 24 September 1995)

SOURCE: A review of *Mother of Pearl*, in *Los Angeles Times Book Review*, September 24, 1995, p. 6.

[*In the review below, Harris explores Morrissy's emphasis on character development in* Mother of Pearl.]

The Irish are inexhaustible—here comes yet another gifted writer from that buoyantly tragic isle. [With ***Mother of Pearl***] Mary Morrissy has written a novel about marginal people, thwarted hopes and cruelly deformed love that fairly bursts with the juice of language and compassion for her characters. So that the tragedy, when it comes, is all the more devastating.

Irene Rivers' parents abandon her when she gets tuberculosis. Her craving for family and stability leads her to stay in the Granitefield sanatorium even after her cure, to do sexual favors for the inmates, to marry the first decent man who comes along and, when he proves impotent, to steal somebody else's baby.

The young couple who lose the child live, no less than Irene, in worlds of pathetic and destructive fantasy. The child, Pearl, returned to her parents by the police, has no immunity from the curse; fugitive memories of having lived somewhere else, as another girl, later contaminate her love for her own unborn baby: "I would wake from the dream of [that other girl's] life and find little seams in the air as if the skin of a new world had been peeled back and then hurriedly sewn up again, leaving behind only the transparent incisions."

Nancy Middleton (review date January 1996)

SOURCE: A review of *Mother of Pearl*, in *Belles Lettres: A Review of Books by Women*, Vol. 11, No. 1, January, 1996, p. 47.

[*In the review below, Middleton examines Morrissy's focus*

on memory and the past's effect on the present in Mother of Pearl.]

This first novel [***Mother of Pearl***] is a painfully deep exploration of the power of memory—particularly childhood memory—to color and define a life. A tubercular child banished to a sanitorium, Irene Rivers decides early that "there was no God; there was only sickness and health." The patients and staff at Granitefield become her family until, miraculously, she is cured and then, almost as miraculously, "rescued" via marriage.

Irene's hopes for a "normal" life are dashed, however, when she learns that her new husband is impotent. Convinced that the child she deserves is "still out there . . . unclaimed, waiting for her mother," Irene steals a child from the hospital nursery in a nearby town, leaving the birth mother with "the terrible truth that someone had wanted her baby more than she had." The child, Pearl, grows up haunted by curiously mixed memories of two childhoods—claimed by two women and belonging to neither.

Mother of Pearl is desperate, searching, and full of questions about what constitutes both family and true memory. Children—lost, stolen, found, in the form of ghosts—serve as markers, important clues in the fragmented lives Morrissy examines. But there is no resolution, and questions lead only to other questions. The reader is left feeling uneasy, forced to draw her own lines between reality and illusion, which is just what the author intended.

Carol Birch (review date 12 January 1996)

SOURCE: "Lost and Found," in *New Statesman & Society,* Vol. 9, No. 385, January 12, 1996, pp. 38-9.

[*Birch is a novelist. In the following highly favorable review, she praises Morrissy's characterization and thematic focus in* Mother of Pearl, *describing it as an "acute, elegiac first novel."*]

In Mary Morrissy's acute, elegiac first novel [***Mother of Pearl***] she returns to territory familiar from her collection of stories, *A Lazy Eye*—illness, alienation, the emotional ambivalence of parenthood, the dangers of bargaining with God. There were one or two gems there, but even the most successful tended to suffer from a sense of having tried to do too much for the genre. With this novel, however, she spreads her wings.

Several writers have explored the theme of babysnatching in recent years but no one else has tackled it with quite so much sympathy and sophistication. This is an emotional minefield, but Morrissy is clear-sighted. The characters all have their reasons. They all want to be happy. None of them is bad. Their constellation just happens to map out tragedy.

"Baby Spain" is a few weeks old when she is abducted from the maternity unit where, premature, she has been receiving special care. Four years later, she is found living happily with her new "parents" and returned to her real mother. We approach this tangled web from every angle: that of the abductor, the real parents and the child, grown to womanhood.

There is a rich succession of characters, sensitively portrayed: Stanley Godwin, husband of the babysnatcher and the ageing innocent; Mel Spain, the irresponsible young father who "missed the boat" literally and figuratively; and Rita, the mother, torn between buried relief, guilt and horror at her baby's disappearance. When her child reappears, Rita has mentally buried her and given birth to another. She becomes "the mother of three": the second, established child, the grieved baby, and a four-year-old stranger "who had been suckled by wolves".

Mary Morrissy builds an intricate picture, layer on layer, with an energy and absolute conviction that grips after the first, bleak 25 pages or so. Unsentimental, powerfully emotional, even-handed and generous, [*Mother of Pearl*] has a rare compulsive quality.

—*Carol Birch*

It is in this child, Mary—grown up and unaware of her strange beginnings—that Morrissy explores the intricate interplay between memory and dream, fantasy and reality, conscious and unconscious. All of this is skillfully and yearningly evoked.

For Mary, it's as if a past life echoes inside her, a dim primeval longing for a lost Eden and her "first parents, Adam and Eve". But the book's feet are firmly on the ground. Adam and Eve are Stanley and Irene, an impotent shipyard worker and his wife, a lonely, withdrawn woman with a history of illness, abandonment and institutionalization. In the brief inklings that memory allows to trickle down, we see a world of lost warmth, of buttons done up wrong by clumsy hands, of muddy boots on oilcloth and the carving of a loaf by workworn hands: "the steady thrum of identical days". We see the ghost-child, focus of love, "on her wooden throne". Half remembered, half believed in, she can never be pinned down, only glimpsed: "a dark child grasping at the air for a mother's hand".

Mary Morrissy builds an intricate picture, layer on layer, with an energy and absolute conviction that grips after the first, bleak 25 pages or so. Unsentimental, powerfully emotional, even-handed and generous, the novel has a rare compulsive quality. It's extremely unusual for a book to bring tears to my eyes these days, but *Mother of Pearl* managed it on the very last page, quite taking me by surprise. It is a very fine novel indeed and deserves wide recognition.

Charlotte O'Sullivan (essay date 28 January 1996)

SOURCE: "Quite Contrary," in *The Observer*, No. 10658, January 28, 1996, p. 16.

[In the following essay, drawn from an interview with the author, O'Sullivan relates details of Morrissy's upbringing and her views on family, writing, and children.]

Irish writer Mary Morrissy does for the nuclear family what *Jaws* did for midnight dips. Her first novel *Mother of Pearl* picks up where her collection of short stories, *Lazy Eye,* left off: in a landscape of unerring dysfunction.

Morrissy distrusts ideas of normality. When I meet her in a Soho cafe—a corpulent figure in a shapeless gingham coat, with a crop of dulled red hair—she greets me with 'It's very chilly, isn't it?' Her brow wrinkles. 'It's been ever so mild in Dublin—*very odd'*. It's as if, in her mind, mildness itself is a breeding ground for trouble.

Her novel, set in an unidentified Irish town in the Fifties, is, among other things, a brilliant book about mothering. Morrissy takes a story—the tale of a barren housewife kidnapping another woman's child—that might occupy a few lines in a tabloid, and explodes it. Woven throughout is the Biblical view on the subject: Solomon's money-back-guaranteed way to spot a 'real' mother. In Morrissy's novel no such rules apply: biological ties are no more binding than the fanatical, fantastical desire to parent and be parented.

Not that she romanticizes the obsessive imagination. In *Mother of Pearl* lies and secrets multiply like tumors and ultimately cause a botched birth that left this reader weak. Morrissy has been accused of wilful pessimism. Is she surprised? 'My characters, Irene and Rita, are not happy bunnies. They're women without many options and little independence. People who are trapped tend to turn to desperate measures.'

She has, she says, no idea what a typical Mary Morrissy reader would be like, but she assumes they'd probably be female. She explains, very slowly and cautiously, that her father died when she was 13 (*Lazy Eye* is dedicated to him). 'My sister and I were the last in the family. I suppose I had a much more female upbringing than my brothers, who were older. My mother is a very, very important influence in my life.' (*Mother of Pearl* is dedicated to her.)

The other, less positive, influence has been the Catholic church. She lost her faith at 21—'I realised there was a way out of all those terrible moral dilemmas that centered around boys, you know'—and she's glad to be rid of her spooks. She has fought to make her writing 'not Irishy, Irishy, but mythic, universal'.

Some would say this goal has already been reached. Last year Morrissy won a Lannan Literary Award in the States, a prize worth $50,000. It's one of the few awards that you don't have to apply for, which is wonderfully fitting—you can't imagine Morrissy putting herself forward for it. As she says, 'I go through troughs where I don't feel it's justifiable to describe myself a writer—I guess that's the absolutist Catholic in me. So this is an endorsement.' Then again, Morrissy is still working as a journalist for the *Irish Times:* 'You get addicted to the pay packets. I've not made any decisions about what I want to do next. The boss keeps coming round'—she mimics herself timidly typing—'saying "are you still here?"'

She imagines a future involving many more books, 'I'm a monster when I'm not writing, I feel so guilty.' Her worst nightmare is that she will repeat herself. 'There are writers who just keep writing the same book. I admire people like Philip Larkin who say, "Right, I've said now what I wanted to say, there it is." I've got a feeling even if I got to that point I'd still be sitting down at the desk writing dementedly thinking "I'm sure there's something else".'

Now that she has writing in her life, there's very little room for anything else, and that includes children of her own. Morrissy believes that even in 1996 there's still a lot of pressure on women to reproduce—often from other women. 'I was married at one stage and friends would often say, "any news?" It's a very intimate question and I used to think, what right have you to ask me that?'

She is also convinced that it would have been harder to write *Mother of Pearl* as a mother. 'For some reason it's all right to say we feel ambiguous towards friends or lovers but it's not acceptable to say "I feel very ambiguous about this child and sometimes I feel like killing it, sometimes I hate it." ' She struggles to put it another way. 'We all like to think we're the product of great love and cherishing, but the fact is that most of us don't know how we were conceived, whether we were wanted.' She thinks for a moment. 'Perhaps if I had children I might not be able to write in such a detached way about them.'

Would she consider having children in the future? 'It doesn't escape my notice that here I have all this equipment and that it's unlikely that it's going to be used. But I'm 38 now, nearly

39, and time is ticking on and I wouldn't want to have a child on my own, you know. I wouldn't want there to be an absent father.'

And yet the fathers in her novels are half-sentient beings, swallowing lies like greedy children. 'Yes, they lack imagination. But there are good fathers: the doctor who cures Irene, and Rita's father.'

I point out that both men act as single parents; good parenting is thus always equated with isolation and claustrophobia. Morrissy smiles. 'I've got my babies,' she says, and points to my copy of *Mother of Pearl*. It does seem the perfect arrangement—after all, a book demands a single parent.

Michael Harris (review date 15 July 1996)

SOURCE: "Tragic Irish Stories Blended with a Dash of Sly Humor," in *Los Angeles Times,* July 15, 1996, p. E3.

[*In the review below, written upon the occasion of the U.S. publication of* A Lazy Eye, *Harris offers a thematic discussion of the work, finding the collection weaker than the novel* Mother of Pearl.]

Those who read Mary Morrissy's first novel, *Mother of Pearl,* and saw that Ireland had produced yet another powerful voice—tragic and lyrical and slyly humorous in the Irish tradition, yet completely original—will be disappointed a little by these 15 stories [in *A Lazy Eye*].

For some reason, the weakest tales seem to come first. They begin with a novelistic amplitude and abruptly peter out, or they conclude shockingly but flatly. In **"Bookworm,"** the narrator steals and shreds books; in **"Possibilities,"** a woman catches a venereal disease from her lover; in **"Rosa,"** the narrator's sister leaves an unwanted baby to die in a Christmas creche.

We miss how, in *Mother of Pearl,* one fully realized world gave onto another. The very title suggested this depth and luminescence, as well as being a literal description of the heroine—a girl who grows up in a sanitarium when tuberculosis ravaged Ireland, longs for a normal family life and, when released, seizes her chance to steal a baby, whom she renames Pearl. *That* girl, returned by the authorities to her real parents, grows up in turn with a mysterious sense of having once been somebody else.

A Lazy Eye wins us over, however—in part because the worlds of the different stories serve as the sections of the novel did: as variously colored decanters for Morrissy's sensibility.

Then, too, the stories get better. The turning point is the title story, about Bella Carmichael, one of 11 siblings in a poor Dublin household, whose only distinction has been a childhood case of "lazy eye," soon corrected. Traveling alone in Europe in vain hopes of adventure, she is thrown off a train for "bleeding in public"—she has run out of tampons.

"She was determined to be dignified. She had, after all, been waiting for this moment all of her life." But as the train pulls away, Bella's exhilaration fades:

> She thought about home—the ramshackle house . . . the crowded bedrooms, the lack of privacy and space, the pans of white bread and the cheap cuts of meat . . . *these* were what had marked her out. There would be no large, singular event to validate her existence. There would only be more of this—official retribution. . . . She felt as she did when the doctor had first taken the glasses with the eye patch off: her vision unobscured.

A constricted life, a warped attempt to break out of it, a residue of essential innocence, the inevitable punishment—this is Morrissy's territory indeed.

It's no accident that babies figure so prominently in these stories. Stolen babies, sick babies, drowned babies, yet-unborn babies arousing jealousy in their parents and siblings. The critic Edwin Muir once said of Dostoevsky that he wrote "as if the unconscious were conscious." Morrissy writes as if the primitive passions that lie coiled even in civilization's innermost redoubt, the nursery—snakes among the teddy bears—are hardly disguised at all.

In **"Invisible Mending"** a man who was abused as a child uses his knowledge of fear to extract false confessions from immigrants detained by the police. In **"A Marriage of Convenience,"** an English-speaking tourist marries a waiter, to help him flee the war-torn Central American country of El Quistador. Later, the waiter narrating his version of things, tells us that he truly loves her. Just as we begin to sympathize with his plight, Morrissy wickedly turns the tables with the story's last two lines:

> I sometimes fear that Judith will never recognize my love and that in the end I shall have to force it on her. I am, after all, her husband.

The best story here is probably the last, **"A Curse."** Clara, a girl from a poor Dublin family, babysits for an affluent one and falls in love with its whole lifestyle. While the wife is having a new baby, the teenager's love focuses on the husband, who has stayed at home. When the wife returns, he makes light of the girl's declaration of love for him; she interprets his jocularity as ridicule. Before leaving her job for good, she sticks a pin in the newborn child. "Clara had drawn blood." And, since this is a Mary Morrissy story, that, too, has its consequences.

James Marcus (review date 18 September 1996)

SOURCE: A review of *A Lazy Eye,* in *Salon* (online publication), September 18, 1996.

[*In the mixed assessment below, Marcus discusses thematic and stylistic aspects of* A Lazy Eye.]

The Irish have always had a gift for depicting blighted lives, and Mary Morrissy, whose novel **Mother of Pearl** won a Lannan Foundation award in 1995, is right in the tradition. Even a quick scan through the stories in *A Lazy Eye* is enough to make you grateful for your own, comparatively unblighted existence.

In **"Bookworm,"** a tightly-wound kleptomaniac makes a career of stealing books and shredding them to pieces in the privacy of her apartment. **"Rosa"** revolves around an unwanted pregnancy, and concludes with the baby being abandoned in a department store Christmas display: "When they dismantled the crib in the new year they would find the creature as dead and as frozen as the one originally placed there."

After a while this bleakness grows unrelenting, as if the author were out to prove that misery (to paraphrase Joyce) is general all over Ireland. But much of the time Morrissy compensates the reader with her prose, which is full of sensuous accuracy.

In the title story, for example, the lazy-eyed protagonist is forced to wear some low-tech corrective glasses "with the right lens patched over with sticking plaster." Morrissy does a marvelous job recording her apprehensions: "[The glasses] gave her a lopsided, partial view of the world—a huge, pinkish blur before her and a sensation of an obstruction looming ahead which was never encountered but yet never went away." What's more, the glasses do the job they're designed for, which in this context qualifies as a deliriously happy ending.

Sapphire

Push

Born Ramona Lofton in 1950, Sapphire is an American poet and novelist.

INTRODUCTION

A controversial novel even before its publication, *Push* (1996) is set in the harsh world of Lenox Avenue in Harlem during the 1980s. It relates the miserable existence of Claireece "Precious" Jones, an overweight, African-American sixteen-year-old girl who dreams of learning to read so she can graduate from high school and find independence. Precious's story begins with her discovery that she is again pregnant by her own father, who also is the father of her first child, Mongo, a girl born with Down's syndrome. Not only has Precious's mother, who is not married to her father, been aware of his routine sexual abuse, but she beats Precious for stealing her man. After the birth of her second child, Precious learns that her father has died of AIDS and that she is HIV positive. Despite all the degradation she has endured from her abusive family and cruel classmates, she is not psychologically destroyed. A ninth-grade dropout due to her first pregnancy, Precious by chance gains entrance to an alternative school, where she is befriended by Blue Rain, a reading teacher who restores a sense of self-respect and hope in her students by encouraging them to keep a journal, "to live in language." Precious eventually joins an incest survivors support group. A lengthy postscript contains the life stories of other students in Precious's reading class. Critical reaction to *Push* generally has been favorable, but debate about the book's literary merits and its intense focus on incest, abuse, and prejudice has continued. Although many publishers thought that the unrelenting despair of Precious's existence was greatly exaggerated, reviewers have often compared *Push* to Alice Walker's *The Color Purple*. Critics have frequently commented on the angry yet intimate voice of Precious and her blunt, graphic language, to which many readers have attributed the emotional power of *Push*. "Without benefit of intricate plot or beautiful language, masterly structure or terribly complex characters," remarked Rosemary Mahoney, "Sapphire has created in *Push* an affecting and impassioned work that sails on the strength of pure, stirring feeling." Sapphire also wrote a collection of prose and poetry, *American Dreams* (1994), which explores similar themes of racism, misogyny, and the despair and injustice suffered by the poor. One poem in particular, "Wilding," scandalized critics with its frank description of a Central Park gang rape. Margaret Randall found the book "startlingly raw in places, imbued with a haunting power."

PRINCIPAL WORKS

Meditations on the Rainbow: Poetry (poetry) 1987
American Dreams (poetry and prose) 1994
Push (novel) 1996

CRITICISM

Margaret Randall (review date March-May 1995)

SOURCE: "Dreams Deferred," in *American Book Review*, Vol. 16, No. 6, March-May, 1995, p. 26.

[*In the excerpt below, Randall discerns "considerable craft" in the poems of* American Dreams.]

Sapphire's *American Dreams* is a first book and as such suffers from some of the problems such endeavors often display. It is also startlingly raw in places, imbued with a haunting power. . . . Sapphire is African-American; . . . concerned with the ugliness of race hatred, the mindless misogyny of woman-hatred, the despair of poverty-induced disease and injustice. The landscapes of these American Dreams range from the tenement bed to South Central LA, from the shabby stage of "lesbian love teams" to the girl child who tries to substitute her own story of sexual abuse for the fairy tale her mother insists upon forcing down her throat.

Sapphire is at her best in her rich prose. There are stories in *American Dreams* that stay with you, like **"A New Day for Willa Mae," "There's a Window"** and **"Eat."** Prose poems like **"Reflections from Glass Breaking"** and **"Human Torso Gives Birth"** are as close to perfect as anything in the book. This writer is less successful when she combines prose and the poetic line; some narrative pieces dwindle into several pages of lines rambling to no purpose I could discern. I have a feeling hearing Sapphire read might help to resolve some of my questions about why she has chosen this particular style. On the page it doesn't work.

Still, as I say, there are poems in *American Dreams* that are splendid in their language and strength. The "Gorilla in the Midst" series is very fine, particularly **"1989 cont./Gorilla in the Midst #6"** and **"1965 cont./Gorilla in the Midst #3."** Sapphire's work is unrelenting. Fucking and being fucked (by both women and men), disembodied penises, wilding, battery, rape, drugs, betrayal, S & M, sickness and death far outweigh connection, creativity, the retrieval of memory or the power of righteousness in this book. Most of the action is played out against a sordid backdrop or is itself sordid.

Often (though not often enough) a person in *American Dreams* comes through so multidimensional and real as to be worth the entire reading. Such is the case of Willa Mae, the non-narrating prisoner in **"There's a Window,"** and Leroy in **"Wild Thing."** I look forward to a second book by Sapphire. Something tells me she will have cut and pared by then, further honed her considerable craft and weeded out much of what now seems superfluous.

Terese Svoboda (review date Spring 1995)

SOURCE: "Try Bondage," in *Kenyon Review,* Vol. XVII, No. 2, Spring, 1995, pp. 157-59.

[*In the following excerpt, Svoboda observes of* American Dreams, *"These are not nice poems. But they are rarely not good poems."*]

Every word costs in *American Dreams,* a High Risk book by Sapphire, published [in the United States] and in London. The title is the screen on which she projects both the shattering of those dreams and the dream of re-making them. The title poem yields yet another reading:

> The woman looked at me & hissed,
> "Stand up for the general!"
> I said, "My father's in the army, not me."
> & I remained seated.
> & throughout 38 years
> of bucking & winging
> grinning & crawling
> brown nosing & begging
> there has been a quiet
> 10 year old in me
> who has remained seated.
> She perhaps is the real American Dream.
>   **("American Dreams")**

"Nobody said that what was cannot be changed," Sapphire writes in the opening poem, **"Are You Ready to Rock?"** This is a brave premise for a woman with a childhood of extreme sexual abuse who lives in a society which values her little as a black lesbian.

American Dreams unfolds with the spectacle of a black, middle-class family gone sordid, the father attacking all his children, male and female, with a complicit mother who never wanted them standing by. These are not nice poems. But they are rarely not good poems. Sometimes the imagery weaves too far from its frighteningly concrete base, as in **"Rabbit Man,"** and sometimes the prose is not urgent enough, as in **"A New Day for Willa Mae,"** but the breadth of the poet's sympathy overwhelms any flaws:

> now you know why
> with a job on Wall Street,
> nice white boy husband
> & a house in the country
> she tore her
> wrists apart
> & bled into
> the nite
> dying
> alone
> on the
> bathroom floor
> you had scrubbed
> earlier that day.
> now you know
> now you know
> & now that you know
> you can begin
> to heal.

"Autopsy Report 86-13504:" is a strong eulogy crafted from Sapphire's brother's autopsy, his notes, and what the poet remembers of him. **"There's a Window"** is a near prose piece about prison lovemaking that bursts into vulnerability as the woman with the gray crewcut reveals she is afraid of being naked in prison, and the young woman cries because it has been six months since she has seen the moon. "I was a cave girl riding a dinosaur across the steamy paleolithic terrain snatching trees with my teeth, shaking down the moon with my tongue."

The speaker insists "i am that type of girl" in **"poem for jennifer, marla, tawana and me."** For a woman to admit she likes sex is dangerous—in the world of poetry where only the most asexual or secretly sexual are revered (think Marianne Moore, Emily Dickinson, Elizabeth Bishop)—but especially in the everyday world that implicitly condones the rape of "that type of girl."

Sapphire attacks colonialism obliquely but at its contemporary root in **"Questions for the Heart of Darkness."** It's Saturday morning TV where "a bunch of black African cartoon characters with bones through their noses and huge white lips like donuts spring out of the tangled underbrush." The poem ends with "The black child feels the wind blowing backwards, turns the tv off; tries to tell her mother something."

"Strange Juice (or the murder of Latasha Harlins)" describes the shooting of a child who shoplifts in a Korean grocery. "Listen to the gasoline on the wind / Listen to my blood rhyme—drip drop on the sidewalk." Sapphire gives voice to a girl so silenced that at the trial the murderer receives only community service and probation.

American Dreams presents the spectacle of a mind creating itself out of the sacrilege of sex, the very ground of identity. As if we won't believe her or have already forgotten, Sapphire provides notes at the end on the public atrocities: the bombings in Philadelphia, the Tuskegee syphilis experiment, the deaths of Tawana Brawley, Lisa Steinberg, and Latasha Harlins. But the most potent validation of her own experience comes at the end of **"One Day."** Having avoided children all her life for fear of abusing them, and now menopausal, the speaker hears the baby upstairs cry, a child who's been taken in for money:

> If it was mine, I say slowly
> and see the tiny child body safe in my warm brown
> arms
> If it was mine, I whisper again
> Maybe the baby hears me cause the crying
> downstairs, in my soul, stops as I hold
> my work, the work of a lifetime close to me.

Michiko Kakutani (review date 14 June 1996)

SOURCE: "A Cruel World, Endless Until a Teacher Steps In," in *The New York Times,* June 14, 1996, p. B8.

[*In the following review, Kakutani suggests that an ideological subtext diminishes the emotional impact of the narrative in* Push, *which makes it "disturbing, affecting and manipulative all at the same time."*]

What do you get if you borrow the notion of an idiosyncratic teen-age narrator from J. D. Salinger's *Catcher in the Rye* and mix it up with the feminist sentimentality and anger of Alice Walker's *Color Purple*? The answer is *Push,* a much-talked-about first novel by a poet named Sapphire, a novel that manages to be disturbing, affecting and manipulative all at the same time.

Like Celie in *The Color Purple,* the heroine of *Push* is the survivor of a brutal childhood and youth; at the age of 16, Claireece or "Precious" as she calls herself, has already had two children by the man she knows as her father. Her mother has not only allowed these rapes to occur, but also beats Precious for stealing her man. She, too, sexually abuses Precious, and treats her as a maidservant around the house.

It's hard to imagine how things could get much worse, but in the course of *Push,* Sapphire throws a lot more misfortune Precious's way. Little Mongo, Precious's first child, to whom she gave birth at the age of 12, turns out to have Down's

syndrome and is quickly taken away from her. A week after her second child, Abdul, is born, Precious finds herself out on the streets of Harlem, without a place to live. Not much later, she learns that her father has infected her with H.I.V.

Given these circumstances, it's no surprise that Precious often feels as if her mind has become a television set, playing and replaying videos that offer her a brief respite from the bleak realities of her daily life. In these daydreams, she is thin, not fat; white, not black; loved, not mocked.

Push, however, is not the story of a helpless or self-loathing victim. It's meant to be a story of female empowerment and triumph. Through the help of a gifted teacher named Rain, Precious learns to read and write. She learns how to write down her own experiences and turn them into poetry. She also gets hooked up with an incest survivors' support group, and a H.I.V.-positive support group. She gains friends, self-respect and the hope of one day going to college. "Push," the paramedic says to her when she's giving birth. "Push," says her teacher, when she despairs of making anything of her life.

What prevents all this from sounding as cloying as the characters' names is Precious's street-smart, angry voice, a voice that may shock readers with its liberal use of four-letter words and graphic descriptions of sex, but a voice that also conjures up Precious's gritty, unforgiving world. Sapphire somehow finds lyricism in Precious's life, and in endowing Precious with her own generous gifts for language, she allows us entree into her heroine's state of mind.

Precious talks of the neighborhood addicts with "kraters like what u see wen you look at spots on the moon" on their arms, and girls in her incest support group who sit in a circle with "faces like clocks, no bombs." She speaks of time seeming "like clothes in the washing machine at laundry mat—round 'n round, up 'n down," and the television in her own head, "always static on, flipping picture."

"I'm walking across the lobby room real real slow," Precious recalls. "Full of chicken, bread; usually that make me not want to cry remember, but I feel like crying now. My head is like the swimming pool at the Y on one-three-five. Summer full of bodies splashing, most in shallow end; one, two in deep end. Thas how all the time years is swimming in my head. First grade boy say, Pick up your lips Claireece 'fore you trip over them."

Although the reader comes to feel enormous sympathy for Precious, one is constantly aware of the author standing behind the scenes, orchestrating her heroine's terrifying plummet into the abyss and her equally dramatic rescue. The first time we see Precious with a book at school, she is having difficulty sounding out the words in a picture book and learning the alphabet. Only pages later, her teacher is trying to get her to read *The Color Purple* in class.

For that matter, Alice Walker's ghost hovers more and more insistently over **Push** as the novel progresses, lending Precious's story a blunt ideological subtext. We learn that white social workers are foolish, patronizing liberals, and that men are pigs who only think about sex. Though it's easy to understand how Precious might hold all of these views, it soon becomes clear that Precious's creator, Sapphire, is also stacking the deck.

Sapphire somehow finds lyricism in Precious's life, and in endowing Precious with her own generous gifts for language, she allows us entree into her heroine's state of mind.

—Michiko Kakutani

In a lengthy postscript in which Precious's classmates tell the story of their lives, we are treated to a recitation of crimes committed against women by men. Rita's father kills her mother in front of her eyes, and Rita begins working as a hooker at the age of 12. Rhonda is raped by her brother, then thrown out of the house by her mother; when she gets a job taking care of an old white man, he asks her for sexual favors. Jermaine is molested by a boy at the age of 7, then raped by a friend's father a few years later; at 19, she is assaulted by six men.

No doubt this rapid-fire sequence of horrifying stories is supposed to mean that Precious has finally found a community of friends with shared experiences. Instead, they leave the reader with the feeling that one has abruptly exited the world of the novel and entered the world of a support group. In trying to open out her heroine's story and turn it into a more general comment on society, Sapphire has made the tale of Precious decidedly less moving than it might have been.

Dinitia Smith (review date 2 July 1996)

SOURCE: "Playing the Hand She's Dealt," in *The New York Times*, July 2, 1996, pp. B1, B4.

[*In the review below, Smith discusses the controversy over some of the themes and perspectives in Sapphire's novel and poetry.*]

This is the realm of "the voiceless," Lenox Avenue between 133d and 134th Streets in Harlem, where Precious, the teenage heroine of **Push**, a new novel by the poet Sapphire, lives.

"She lives *there*," Sapphire, also known as Ramona Lofton, said recently, pointing at a dowdy building over a check cashing store. Sapphire spoke as if Precious really existed. In the book, Precious, whose given name is Claireece, has a baby, "Little Mongo," who was conceived with her own father. The baby has "Down sinder" (Down's syndrome). Now Precious is pregnant again, by "my fahver," as she puts it, and attending an "insect survivor group."

Alfred A. Knopf paid Sapphire $500,000 for **Push** as part of a two-book deal and gave it a first printing of 75,000, big for a first novel. It is as unconstrained as anything that the house, better known as John Updike's publisher, has issued.

Even before publication, Sapphire, 45, was censured for her portrayal of a big, dark-skinned Harlem girl to whom almost every conceivable form of degradation occurs. When Precious goes into labor, her mother kicks her. Her mother also sexually abuses her. And it gets worse.

When Sapphire was working on the novel as a graduate writing student at Brooklyn College, her classmates would "be dissing me," she said. "These guys thought it was overkill. They'd says: 'Do you hate men? Do you hate white people?'" When the manuscript was auctioned last year, some publishers found the story exaggerated. Michiko Kakutani, reviewing the novel in *The New York Times*, found it "affecting and manipulative all at the same time."

Only a few feet from the plain stretch of Lenox Avenue where Sapphire says that Precious lives are side streets with nice houses, hydrangea, children bicycling. The suggestion that her character represents all of Harlem makes Sapphire angry. There are children like Precious everywhere, she says. "The common kid in Harlem actually makes it," Sapphire said. "The typical underclass kid is not in trouble. But the American family as a whole is in trouble, and black people are part of America."

Push, unlike some novels by black writers who have dealt with incest, carries a message of hope: Precious, unlike the abused child in Toni Morrison's *Bluest Eye*, is not psychologically destroyed. Nor does she find her salvation by falling in love, as the character Celie did in *The Color Purple*, by Alice Walker.

"This book could not have existed if I had not read Alice Walker and Toni Morrison," Sapphire said. "But Precious learns to deal the hand she's dealt." This heroine is spunky and irreverent, and she sees through grown-ups' cant. She finds help within her own community, through the vestiges of Great Society programs, from public health to literacy, that remain intact. And there is her teacher, "Miss Rain," who loves Precious and teaches her to read.

"I don't have to answer to the black middle class," Sapphire said.

It is not the first time her work has stirred indignation. Gripped by the 1989 rape and near-fatal beating of a jogger in Central Park, Sapphire wrote a poem, **"Wild Thing,"** from the imagined point of view of a would-be rapper who commits such an attack. "I had a young black woman ask, 'How is what you are writing different from what white people are writing about black men?' I was devastated."

Then the Rev. Donald Wildmon, head of the American Family Association, spotted the poem, which included a homoerotic passage involving Christ, in *The Portable Lower East Side Queer City,* a journal that received financing from the National Endowment for the Arts. He circulated the journal in Congress as part of a campaign that led to the dismissal of John E. Frohnmayer as chairman of the endowment in 1992.

At one time Sapphire might have seemed destined to write another kind of novel, about an educated child of the black working class who comes of age in the 1960's, perhaps.

She was born in Fort Ord, Calif., part of a church-oriented, tightly disciplined family. "My father was very much into being a father on the surface," said Sapphire, the second of four children. "My mother was a housewife, wanted us to have nice clothes, do well in school. They had a deep need to appear normal."

When she was 13, her mother "abandoned us" and became an alcoholic, Sapphire said.

Raised in the era of black power and student demonstrations, Sapphire began reading the work of such black poets as Sonia Sanchez and Jayne Cortez. She attended San Francisco City College, thinking she might be a doctor, but grew more interested in dance. Eventually she dropped out and, inspired by the hippie scene in San Francisco, started calling herself "Sapphire."

In 1977 she moved to New York with only $20 in her pocket, and worked as a topless dancer, becoming a prostitute, she says. She also took part in the lesbian scene. "This was going to be a way out of living your parents' life," she said.

Sapphire started writing poetry in notebooks. She published her work in feminist journals and read her poetry aloud in Village cafes.

She studied modern dance at City College, graduating with honors in 1993, and then took a job with the Children's Aid

Society as "a parent-child mediator." The experience allowed her to enter the private lives of white people and black.

In 1986, Sapphire's mother died, and her brother, who was homeless, was killed. Sapphire said she began to "remember things," specifically "an incident of violent sexual abuse" by her father when she was 3 or 4 years old. She confronted him, she added, but "he said it never happened." Her father died in 1990.

Was her mother aware of such an incident? "She didn't stop it," Sapphire said, "but I don't know if she knew." Later a sister confided that she, too, had been abused by their father, she added.

Around this time, Sapphire began teaching reading to children in Harlem and the Bronx, among them many "Preciouses." "Seven years of telling me their stories! But I don't hear this story back!" she said. She enrolled in graduate school at Brooklyn College in 1993 and in 1994 *American Dreams,* a collection of prose and poetry, was published.

When she started work on *Push,* her teacher, the novelist Susan Fromberg Schaeffer, read a draft and told her she had a novel. "I didn't know what a novel is; Susan says, 'It's 150 pages!'" Translation rights to the novel have already been sold in six countries.

But "I didn't write this book for the rent," Sapphire said. "I wrote it to feel this girl's voice. As an artist you have the responsibility."

Rosemary Mahoney (review date 7 July 1996)

SOURCE: "Don't Nobody Want Me. Don't Nobody Need Me," in *The New York Times Book Review,* July 7, 1996, p. 9.

[*Below, Mahoney calls* Push *"an affecting and impassioned work that sails on the strength of pure, stirring feeling."*]

Intrepid will and raw intelligence ring forth in Claireece Precious Jones, the narrator of *Push,* the poet and performance artist Sapphire's first novel. Precious, as she prefers to be called, is a teenager in Harlem during the 1980's, and the numerous violations she has withstood in her young life have left her bereft of resources, utterly lacking in self-command and virtually unable to communicate. Black, poor, angry, profoundly illiterate, notably fat, rejected, enslaved by the cruel and violent mother she lives with, raped repeatedly by her father since she was a first grader and now, at the age of 16, pregnant by him for the second time. Precious Jones may have only one thing to be thankful for; that she has not also been struck blind. The world, however, is blind to Precious, and the resultant invisibility she suffers is, by her own assessment, her greatest obstacle.

Push is written in her halting dialect, a hobbled, minimal English that defies the conventions of spelling and usage and dispenses with all verbal decorum. At the outset, this occasionally uneven stylistic device threatens to obstruct the narrative, but the intensity of Precious' persona swiftly overrides whatever irritation the reader may feel at having to puzzle through her not always convincingly misshapen words. Precious speaks in a darting stream of consciousness that ranges over the events of her life, summarizing and classifying what affronts and interests her. By her own admission she knows nothing—"How we gonna figure anything out," she says of herself and her classmates. "Weze ignerent"—yet it becomes clear to the reader that Precious is smart, perceptive, curious and capable of expressing the bitter rhythm of her days in an exceptionally evocative fashion. Her sardonic voice is blunt and unadorned, sorrowful as a foghorn and so wholly engulfing that despite its broken words it generates single-handedly the moving power of this novel. Too debased and self-loathing to reveal them to anyone else, Precious lays her undressed emotions before the reader with fervent intimacy; we fairly feel her breath in our ears.

As a young child, Precious withdraws, taunted and ridiculed by her classmates for her size, her appearance, her jumbled speech. "First grade boy say, Pick up your lips Claireece 'fore you trip over them. Call me shoe shine shinola. Second grade I is fat. . . . No boyfriend no girlfriends. I stare at the blackboard pretending." Paralyzed with shame, Precious sits mutely at the back of the classroom in a dirty dress; rather than rise and attract attention when she has need of a bathroom she stays in her seat and urinates on herself. She hears television voices in her head. Abandoned as a hopeless case, she falters at school. At 12 she gives birth to her first child—engendered by her father—on the kitchen floor, while her mother, jealous of the sexual attention her husband has turned toward Precious, savagely kicks and beats her. The infant girl, called Mongo ("short for Mongoloid"), is passed off to the care of Precious' grandmother. Precious' mother, a horribly obese ("she ain' circus size yet but she getting there"), noxiously unwashed, lazy, controlling recluse, does little but watch television and inhale the huge greasy meals she commands Precious to cook for her. She beats Precious without provocation, abuses her sexually and verbally, accuses her of stealing her husband and greedily collects the welfare checks intended for the care of Precious and her retarded child. Precious attends to her mother, awaits the next sexual assault from her father.

At 16 and expecting her second child, Precious reflects on her life. "I big, I talk, I eats, I cooks, I laugh, watch TV, do what my muver say. But I can see . . . I don't exist. Don't nobody want me. Don't nobody need me. I know who I am. . . . Ugly black grease to be wipe away." "My fahver don't see me really. If he did he would know I was like a white girl, a *real* person, inside." "Sometimes I wish I was not alive. But I don't know how to die. Ain' no plug to pull out. 'N no matter how bad I feel my heart don't stop beating and my eyes open in the morning."

Precious countervails. While her father rapes her, she escapes into daydreams as amusing as they are heart-breaking. She imagines herself a graceful dancer in a video, slim, virginal, pretty ("like a advertisement girl on commercial") and light-skinned ("Light even more important than being skinny; you see them light-skinned girls that's big an' fat, they got boyfriends"). She imagines herself married to her white math teacher, living in "Weschesser, wherever that is," or out on a date with John Kennedy Jr. or Tom Cruise; she imagines having Aretha Franklin or Tina Turner for a mother. But her greatest dream is simply to graduate from high school and find independence, to learn to read, to become visible. Her plans for the future, remarkable by their very existence, are marked by tender hope and dauntless determination.

> **Too debased and self-loathing to reveal them to anyone else, Precious lays her undressed emotions before the reader with fervent intimacy; we fairly feel her breath in our ears.**
>
> —*Rosemary Mahoney*

Suspended from the ninth grade because of her pregnancy and wary of the teachers and social workers who decide her life for her, Precious lands by chance at an alternative school, where at last one teacher reaches her, a caring black woman from California who goes by the name of Blue Rain. It is her job to teach her class of disadvantaged young women to read, but she does more: she entreats them to live in language, to write and record their dreams and stories in a journal. She introduces them to black history and culture. Precious responds, aware somehow that in knowledge and literacy lies her redemption. "You can do anything when you talking or writing," she says in wonder, "it's not like living when you can only do what you doing." Precious' first written sentence, the start of her emergence into the world, is "li Mg o mi m": Little Mongo on my mind. Suddenly Precious enjoys school. The accounts of what goes on in Ms. Rain's motley classroom prove the most vivid and entertaining sections of the novel. Together the students read Alice Walker's novel *The Color Purple,* which demands great effort on Precious' part. "Most of it I can't read myself," she says. "But how Ms Rain hook it up I am getting something out the story. I cry cry *cry* you hear me, it sound in a way so much like myself."

Push is a novel about acceptance, perseverance, self-discovery and the ways in which the three are intertwined; Sapphire has managed to work into her short book a number of divisive social issues: homosexuality, class prejudice, racism, welfare, misogyny, imperialism, drug abuse—issues difficult to treat without preaching or cynicism. In Precious' unsophisticated hands they are surveyed with irony and subtlety, yet when Blue Rain enters, the social commentary turns somewhat proselytizing. Indeed, as the catalyst for Precious' awakening Ms. Rain is an inexplicably underdeveloped character with some surprisingly wooden dialogue. But this is one of the novel's few flaws. (Another is a brief section early on when the narrative moves for no apparent reason out of the first person and into a decidedly more eloquent third person, which nonetheless slips erratically and puzzlingly back into Precious' rudimentary speech patterns. Perhaps we're meant to understand this as a future, more literate Precious portraying herself and exercising her own notions about the freedom and flexibility of writing. Whatever the case, the interlude is distracting and its purpose unclear.) In her journal Precious writes poetry and heartfelt letters to Ms. Rain, and Ms. Rain responds with enthusiasm both over-earnest and oddly undistinguished; nevertheless, as their relationship grows, so grows Precious. Upon the birth of her second child, a healthy boy, Precious leaves her mother's apartment and takes her beloved son to a halfway house. Things improve until Precious discovers that her father is dead of AIDS and that she is H.I.V. positive. Her brave response to this news is the measure of all she has learned.

Without benefit of intricate plot or beautiful language, masterly structure or terribly complex characters, Sapphire has created in *Push* an affecting and impassioned work that sails on the strength of pure, stirring feeling from a girl who should long ago have had all the feeling knocked out of her.

Paula L. Woods (review date 7 July 1996)

SOURCE: "Pushed to Survival," in *Los Angeles Times Book Review,* July 7, 1996, pp. 1, 9.

[*In the following review, Woods calls* Push *"an impressive yet deeply flawed debut," pointing to inconsistencies in narrative voice and use of language.*]

"I was left back when I was twelve because I had a baby for my fahver."

The opening line of Sapphire's first novel hits the reader like a Mack truck, and it clearly signals that the literary ride ahead won't be in your father's Oldsmobile. The journey of Harlem teenager Claireece Precious Jones is sickening and confusing, painful and hopeful. By turns thought-provoking and horrifying, *Push* is sure to provoke passionate debate about

the book's literary merits and the author's talents—as well as issues ranging from incest to teen pregnancy, literacy programs and welfare reform. Despite its shortcomings, *Push* is a stunningly frank effort that marks the emergence of an immensely promising writer.

At its most fundamental, *Push* is an up-by-the-bra-strap success story, predictable as a TV movie refashioned for the downbeat '90s. It features the understandably enraged, savagely funny, totally unique voice of its protagonist. When we meet her, 16-year-old Precious is anything but what her name implies—she's obese, illiterate and pregnant by her father for the second time. She's physically and sexually abused by her equally depraved mother, who keeps the young girl virtually trapped in her own home, feeding the mother's culinary and sexual appetites: "She ain' circus size yet but she getting there," Precious notes.

> **Despite its shortcomings, *Push* is a stunningly frank effort that marks the emergence of an immensely promising writer.**
>
> **—*Paula L. Woods***

Although right-wingers might dismiss the real-life Preciouses of this world as the Willie Hortons of welfare, Sapphire gives the fictional Precious something that surveys and case studies do not—a mind, a heart and a ferocious rage to survive that ignite the book and make it strangely compelling for all of the horror Precious relives in the telling.

Precious finds salvation when she is expelled from Harlem's P.S. 146 and enrolls in an alternative school, Each One/Teach One. Sensing the opportunity to escape from her abusive mother, Precious must push aside the memories of cruel molestation swimming in her head—the images she carries of herself as invisible, black and ugly, her fear of becoming a target of ridicule—and make her way into the classroom that first day:

> "I takes in air through my nose, a big big breath, then I start to walk slow to the back. But something like birds or light fly through my heart. An' my feet stop. At the first row. An' for the first time in my life I sits down in the front row." Precious' guide out of her living hell is Blue Rain, the instructor in her pre-G.E.D. reading class, who encourages the teenager to keep a journal. Her initial entries are so indecipherable that Rain transcribes the words the badly abused girl can barely form: "li Mg o mi m" (Little

Mongo on my mind), a pained reference to her retarded firstborn, always on the young mother's mind.

Astute readers will draw parallels between Precious' emerging identity and language skills and those of Celie in Alice
Walker's *The Color Purple.* Sapphire almost invites the comparison when she places Walker's novel in Precious' book-
case, and later liberally quotes Walker's characters, along
with the poetry of Harlem Renaissance writer Langston
Hughes. But while it is interesting to see how Walker, Hughes
and novelist Audre Lorde influence the fictional Precious,
Sapphire could learn much from these masters—especially
when it comes to creating an internally consistent black dialect for Precious to speak and write.

As it stands, *Push* is wildly inconsistent in its narrative voice
and use of language. The criticism, however, is leveled reluctantly and with much sympathy for the author's dilemma:
How do you write a book about a protagonist who can barely
read or write? The author's solution is to mostly write in Precious' voice, although there is a lengthy section of the first
chapter that inexplicably—and annoyingly—shifts to a distant third-person narrator.

Sapphire's attempt to replicate her character's speech on the
page is even more unsettling. In *Push,* Precious sometimes
drops the final G (as in "gettin'"), sometimes not. In some
passages she says "that's" and later "thas." Occasionally, the
conceit works to great effect—it makes perfect sense that
Precious wouldn't want to know how to spell the reviled words
"mother" and "father" over the names of heroes Louis
Farrakhan, Harriet Tubman and Alice Walker. But trying to
figure out why she can spell "Mongoloid," "intercourse" or
"dungeon" and not "electric" interferes too frequently with
the intense narrative that Sapphire works hard to achieve.

This is a dilemma other writers have handled with success.
The well-crafted and well-edited novels of Walker, J. California Cooper, A.J. Verdelle's "The Good Negress" and the
poetry of Hughes solved the problem by developing a grammar consistent in usage and context albeit unfamiliar to some
readers.

Another shortcoming in *Push* is the lack of narrative balance. The scenes of Precious' torment at the hands of her
parents are retold in horrific detail and searing imagery. But
her hard climb upward to even the middle of life's crystal
stair—to borrow, as does the author, from Hughes' famous
poem "Mother to Son"—seems almost remotely experienced
by comparison.

Still, the novel is intense and unflinching in its portrayal of
abuse suffered by women and children. To her credit, Sapphire provides much-needed balance and a sense of triumph
in *Push* through a highly charged scene at an incest survi-

vors' group late in the book. There is also an appendix, "Life
Stories," which includes excellent poetry by Precious and
the writing of other students that opens up the narrative,
revealing the diverse lives of the young women who have
slipped through society's illusory safety net. For this reader,
being privy earlier to the transformation of these characters—
by experiencing their interaction and writing—would have
made me care even more about their fates, making their
achievement ultimately more moving and satisfying.

Regardless of the controversy that may surround the book's
themes, perspective or language, *Push* is an impressive yet
deeply flawed debut. One hopes Sapphire will continue to
nurture her original voice, while incorporating difficult themes
like incest and abuse—which she also explored in her earlier poetry collection, *American Dreams*—into a broader
vision of the black and human experience.

Achy Obejas (review date 21 July 1996)

SOURCE: "Living Hell," in *Chicago Tribune—Books,* July
21, 1996, p. 3.

[*In the review below, Obejas briefly outlines the themes in*
Push, *praising Sapphire's portrayal of inner-city life.*]

Push is a story about hell.

It's about Precious Jones, a 16-year-old girl whose life is
damned before she's even born. It's about economic and spiritual poverty, about violence and incest, about ignorance and
prejudice, pregnancy and AIDS and death. It's the kind of
story that gets more intense and infernal with every page.

Yet the miracle of *Push* is that, even at its most devastating,
it is also a story about faith and possibility, about the way
even the most scarred and scabbed human beings can respond
to the lightest touch of love.

Written by Sapphire, a black poet best known for *American
Dreams,* a book-length prose poem, *Push* is a quick 179 pages
that often read like a slammer's angry verse in a smoky urban bar. It has rhythm and snap, rage and sensibility.
Sapphire's choice is less black English than poor English—
the speech of American-born city dwellers who live in indigence, with little or no education and virtually no exposure
to or knowledge of any other kind of life. In *Push,* Sapphire
gives us the voice of America's internal exiles.

To add to the relentlessness of *Push,* Precious' tale is told in
often uncomfortably intimate first person. We are inside Precious' head and body, inside her anger and pain, inside her
awe and occasional disassociation from reality. When we see
Precious, we see her through her own eyes, through her take

on how others see her. It is to Sapphire's credit that Precious is able to give us vital glances of herself without being overly self aware.

Like *American Dreams,* which scandalized with its raw, first-person description of the Central Park gang rape that introduced the word "wilding" to America, *Push* will also shock with its frank descriptions of incest and the ambivalence of Precious' desire.

But it should shock as well for its exposé of a world in which children are born without the slightest hope of a caress, never mind nurturing, an education or a job. In the world Sapphire describes, there is often little to distinguish the parents from the children, and virtually nothing divides wrong from right.

Sapphire begins Precious' story as she discovers she is pregnant again. She had her first child at age 12, a girl with Down's syndrome whom she calls Little Mongo. Like Little Mongo, the new baby's father is Precious' own father. The babies are the result of his constantly raping her.

Precious' mother, who is not married to her father, is aware of the situation but, although she has wild bouts of jealousy (yes, jealousy) about it, tolerates it, using Precious as bait so he will come to their miserable, stinky apartment. (She also uses Precious, and Little Mongo, who doesn't live with them, to get more money out of welfare.) No sooner does he leave, though, than she beats the daylights out of Precious, blaming her for stealing her man. On at least one occasion, Precious lands in the hospital as a result of her mother's blows.

As Precious attempts to negotiate her world, we discover she is barely literate. She has managed to get through elementary school and most of junior high with good grades but can't distinguish one page from another in a textbook. How does something like that happen? With just a handful of scenes, Sapphire deftly demonstrates how even the best intentions can contribute to this cycle of despair.

In the midst of all this madness there are good people who make a difference in Precious' life. The most vital is Blue Rain, a teacher at an alternative school who takes Precious into her pre-GED class. Ms. Rain, as her students mostly call her, is a committed teacher, part social worker, part angel, who helps Precious and a handful of other wounded and deprived young women realize that, even in hell, there are choices.

Ms. Rain is no Sidney Poitier, though, and *Push* is not a contemporary *To Sir With Love.* Although there are many lessons learned, there are no family reconciliations, no tidy resolutions and no happy ending in *Push.* If Precious' world still seems like a Stygian creek, at least now she has a paddle.

FURTHER READING

Criticism

Roiphe, Katie. "Making the Incest Scene." *Harper's Magazine* 291, No. 1746 (November 1995): 65, 68-71.
> Discusses the theme of incest in works of contemporary fiction including *Push.*

Prizewinners

Literary Prizes and Honors
Announced in 1996

Academy Awards in Literature

Bestowed by the American Academy and Institute of Arts and Letters.

August Kleinzahler
For poetry
Paul Muldoon
For poetry

American Academy and Institute of Arts and Letters New Members

Louise Gluck, Kenneth Koch, John Russell, Oliver Sacks, Edmund White, Elie Wiesel

James Tait Black Memorial Book Prize

Scotland's oldest book award, bestowed by the University of Edinburgh; two prizes of £3000 each awarded annually.

Alan Hollinghurst
In fiction, for *The Folding Star*
Doris Lessing
In biography, for *Under My Skin*

Booker Prize for Fiction

Britain's major literary prize for fiction, established in 1968; £20,000 awarded annually.

Graham Smith
For *Last Orders*

Georg Buchner Prize

Established in 1923; 60,000 German marks awarded annually.

Sarah Kirsch

Witter Bynner Foundation Prize for Poetry

Established in 1979 and bestowed by the American Academy and Institute of Arts and Letters; $2500 awarded annually.

Lucie Brock-Broido
For *The Master Letters*

Commonwealth Writers Prize

Administered by the Association for Commonwealth Literature and Language Studies; £10,000 awarded annually.

Rohinton Mistry
For novel *A Fine Balance*

Faulker Award for Fiction

Bestowed by the PEN American Center; includes $15,000 award to winner and $5000 each to four runners-up.

Richard Ford
For novel *Independence Day*

E. M. Forster Award in Literature

Established in 1972 by Christopher Isherwood and bestowed annually by the American Academy and Institute of Arts and Letters to enable a young British writer to travel to the U.S.

Jim Crace

Goncourt Prize

Established in 1914 by Edmond de Goncourt and awarded annually to recognize young French writers; considered among the most prestigious of French literature awards.

Pascale Rose
For "Le Chasseur Zero"

Governor General's Literary Awards

Established in 1936 by the Canadian Authors Association; $10,000 awarded annually.

Marie-Claire Blais and Guy Vanderhaeghe
In fiction
E. D. Blodgett and Serge Patrice Thibodeau
In poetry
Normand Chaurette and Colleen Wagner
In drama
Michel Freitag and John Ralston Saul
In nonfiction

Guggenheim Fellowships

Awarded in recognition of exceptional ability and talent to recipients in the U.S., Canada, and Latin American/ Caribbean nations; awards based on need and the scope of the recipient's project.

Lucy Brock-Broido, Mark Rudman, Agha Shalid Ali, David Ferry, Susan Howe, Robert Wrigley, Jennifer Egan, Jonathan Franzen, David Guterson, Kathryn Kramer, Ralph Lombreglia, Chris Offutt

Ernest Hemingway Foundation Award

Established in memory of Hemingway and bestowed by the PEN American Center to recognize the first publications of young or developing writers; $7500 awarded annually.

Chang-rae Lee
For *Native Speaker*

Hugo Awards

Established in 1953 to recognize notable science fiction works in several categories.

James Patrick Kelly
For novelette *Think Like a Dinosaur*
Maureen F. McHugh
For short story "The Lincoln Train"
Neal Stephenson
For novel *The Diamond Age*
Allan Steele
For novella *The Death of Captain Future*

Sue Kaufman Prize for First Fiction

Established in 1979 in memory of Kaufman and bestowed by the American Academy and Institute of Arts and Letters; $2500 awarded annually.

Peter Landesman
For novel *The Raven*

Ruth Lilly Poetry Prize
Established by Lilly in 1986 to honor young college or university poets; $75,000 awarded annually.

Gerald Stern

National Book Awards (a.k.a. American Book Awards)
Administered by the National Book Foundation; $10,000 awarded in each of three categories.

Andrea Barrett
In fiction, for *Ship Fever and Other Stories*
James Caroll
In nonfiction, for *An American Requiem: God, My Father, and the War that Came Between Us*
Hayden Carruth
In poetry, for *Scrambled Eggs and Whiskey: Poems 1991-1995*

National Book Critics Circle Awards
Awarded annually to recognize outstanding books in five categories.

Robert Darnton
In criticism, for *The Forbidden Best-Sellers of Pre-Revolutionary France*
Stanley Elkin
In fiction, for *Mrs. Ted Bliss*
Jonathan Harr
In general nonfiction, for *A Civil Action*
Robert Polito
In biography/autobiography, for *Savage Art: A Biography of Jim Thompson.*
William Matthews
In poetry, for *Time and Money: New Poems*

National Book Foundation Medal
Awarded for distinguished contribution to American letters

Toni Morrison

Nebula Awards
Established in 1965 to honor significant works of science fiction published in the U.S.

A. E. Van Vogt
Grand Master
Esther Friesner
For short story "Death and the Librarian"
Elizabeth Hand
For novella *Last Summer at Mars Hill*
Ursula K. Le Guin
For novelette *Solitude*
Robert J. Sawyer
For novel *The Terminal Experiment*

Neustadt International Prize for Literature
Bestowed by the University of Oklahoma for outstanding achievement in several categories; $40,000 awarded biennially.

Assia Djebar
Algerian poet and fiction writer

New York Drama Critics Circle Awards *Presented annually in several categories.*	**Jonathan Larson** For musical *Rent* **August Wilson** For play *Seven Guitars*
Nobel Prize in Literature *Awarded annually to recognize the most distinguished work of literature of an idealistic nature; includes prize of 6.7 million Swedish kronor.*	**Wislawa Szymborska** For body of work
Antoinette Perry ("Tony") Awards *Established in 1947 and bestowed by the American Theatre Wing in recognition of outstanding Broadway plays.*	**Jonathan Larson** For best musical, *Rent* **Terrence McNally** For best play, *Master Class*
Edgar Allan Poe Awards *Awards in numerous categories bestowed in recognition of achievement in mystery, crime, and suspense writing.*	**Dick Francis** For best novel, *Come to Grief* **David Heffernan** For best original paperback, *Tarnished Blue* **David Housewright** For best first novel, *Penance*
Pulitzer Prizes in Literature and Drama *In the literature and drama categories, $3000 awarded annually for fiction by an American author on American life and for a drama by an American author preferably dealing with American life.*	**Richard Ford** In fiction, for *Independence Day* **Jorie Grahm** In poetry, for *The Dream of the Unified Field* **Jonathan Larson** In drama, for *Rent* **Jack Miles** In biography, for *God: A Biography* **Tina Rosenberg** In nonfiction, for *The Haunted Land: Facing Europe's Ghosts after Communism* **Alan Taylor** In history, for *William Cooper's Town*
Rea Award *Established in 1986 by Michael Rea to recognize a writer who has made a significant contribution to the short story as an art form; $30,000 awarded annually.*	**Andre Dubus** For body of work

Rome Fellowship in Literature
Bestowed by the American Academy and Institute of Arts and Letters to allow artists a year of study at the Academy in Rome.

Randall Kenan
Fiction writer

Richard and Hilda Rosenthal Foundation Award in Literature
Bestowed by the American Academy and Institute of Arts and Letters for a work of fiction considered a literary achievement but not a commercial success; $5000 awarded annually.

David Long
For short story collection *Blue Spruce*

Tanning Prize
Established in 1994; the largest prize for poetry in the U.S.

James Tate

United States Poet Laureate
Established by the Library of Congress in the 1930s to recognize an outstanding American poet.

Robert Hass

Whitbread Literary Awards
Established to encourage and promote English literature among authors in Great Britain and Ireland; £2000 prizes in several categories and £20,000 awarded to the overall winner.

Kate Atkinson
For best first novel and Book of the Year, *Behind the Scenes at the Museum*
Roy Jenkins
In biography, for *Gladstone*
Bernard O'Donoghue
In poetry, for *Gunpowder*
Salman Rushdie
For best novel, *The Moor's Last Sigh*

Morton Dauwen Zabel Award
Established in 1966 to recognize progressive, original, and experimental tendencies in writing; $5000 awarded.

J. D. Landis

Kate Atkinson

Behind the Scenes at the Museum

Award: Whitbread Awards for Fiction for Book of the Year and First Novel

Atkinson is a British short story writer and novelist.

INTRODUCTION

Atkinson, described at times uncharitably as a middled-aged chambermaid, was awarded the Whitbread Prize over fellow nominee Salman Rushdie with some critical disapproval. When the clamor abated, however, positive reviews of *Behind the Scenes at the Museum* dominated. Described as an ambitious, well-crafted first novel, *Behind the Scenes at the Museum* follows the life of the irrepressible Ruby Lennox from conception (an event of which she is aware, and opinionated) well into adulthood. Ruby is gifted with an omnipotence beyond her years, as well as the ability to see the ghosts of her ancestors who inhabit the tiny home she shares with her parents and siblings above her father's pet shop. Critics remarked on the richness of Atkinson's characterization as well as her skill in conveying the multigenerational connections established as everyday objects and events spark memories or preview future additions to the family. Ben Macintyre remarked that the setting and everyday events of Ruby's story are typical of Yorkshire, a place of "grimness, grit, and grandeur." "Like Yorkshire itself," Macintyre remarks, "*Behind the Scenes at the Museum* is all sharp edges; it is a caustic and affectionate portrayal of a world in which bleak but nourishing wit is the only safety net." In addition to the Whitbread Award, Atkinson is also the recipient of a 1993 Ian St. James Award for short stories.

PRINCIPAL WORKS

Behind the Scenes at the Museum (novel) 1995

CRITICISM

Publishers Weekly (review date 30 October 1995)

SOURCE: A review of *Behind the Scenes at the Museum,* in *Publishers Weekly,* Vol. 242, No. 44, October 30, 1995, p. 46.

[*In the following review, the critic offers a positive assessment of* Behind the Scenes at the Museum.]

The narrator's insistent voice and breezy delivery animates this enchanting first novel [*Behind the Scenes at the Museum*] by a British writer who won one of the 1993 Ian St. James Awards for short stories. Ruby Lennox is a quirky, complex character who relates the events of her life and those of her dysfunctional family with equal parts humor, fervor and candor—starting with her moment of conception in York, England, in 1959: "I exist!" Ruby then describes the family she is to join. Her parents own a pet shop; her mother, Bunty, bitterly rues having married her philandering husband, George, and daydreams about what her life might have been. Ruby has two older sisters, willful Gillian and melancholy Patricia. Through its ambitious structure, the novel also charts five generations and more than a century of Ruby's family history, as reported in "footnotes" that follow relevant chapters. (For example, a passage about a pink glass button reveals the story of its original owner, Ruby's great-grandmother Alice, who will abandon her young family and run off with a French magician.) Ruby's richly imagined account includes both the details of daily life and the several tragic events that punctuate the family's mundane existence. Though the "footnote" entries are not quite as gripping as those rendered in Ruby's richly vernacular, energetic recitation, Atkinson's ebullient narrative style captures the troubled Lennox family with wit and poignant accuracy.

Georgia Jones-Davis (review date 27 December 1995)

SOURCE: "From the Mouth of a Babe, Details of Ordinary Lives," in *Los Angeles Times,* December 27, 1995, p. 5.

[*In the positive review below, Jones-Davis describes* Behind the Scenes at the Museum *as "a powerhouse of storytelling."*]

Ruby Lennox, the heroine of Kate Atkinson's stunning first novel, out-Copperfields *David Copperfield.* While Dickens' David began narrating at his birth, Atkinson's narrator begins working at the moment of her conception.

And hers is indeed a quest to see if she will be the hero of her own story. For the first 40 pages of *Behind the Scenes at the Museum,* we are being guided by an embryo with an all-seeing, wise-guy take on the world. She's living in York, England, a place so rife with history "there's no room for the living."

She knows the future, she knows the past. Her mostly tragic narrative about a completely ordinary, working-class family will hop, skip, and swirl backward and forward through time. Every member of the various generations introduced will fall into his or her place in a huge, albeit confusing family tree. (Is Clifford Bunty's uncle or brother? Whose son is Adrian? Whatever happened to Auntie Eliza? Auntie Eliza—"about as common as you can get. We know this has something to do with the fact that her blond hair has coal-black roots and she is wearing immense rhinestone earrings.")

Ruby, our narrator, is the third child of George and Bunty, who met in 1944. When the novel opens in the early '50s, lean, gray years in postwar Britain, they live in a dark, dank, cramped, ancient building above the family pet shop. Ruby alone sees the ghosts of all of the occupants from over the centuries. They don't bother anybody, and tend to congregate on the many winding narrow staircases.

To the little girl, the spirits inhabit the place; somehow they seem more comforting than her family. Her oldest sister, Patricia, is a dour 5-year-old; imperious Gillian is already a terror at 3; father George sells budgies, puppies and kittens with no more feeling for his merchandise than the medical supplies he will sell later, after the disastrous pet-shop fire. He plays around with the ladies too, on nights out with his old mate Walter, the meat man. So he's not around the night that Bunty gives birth to his third daughter, Ruby.

Remember, we're hearing all this from an embryo, now a newborn: "The midwife goes away, the neat, tip-tapping of her black lace-up shoes on the linoleum of the corridor gradually fades and we are left alone. We lie in our cots, wrapped tightly in white cotton-cellular blankets, like promises."

Promise is the key word here. Atkinson's first novel is a powerhouse of storytelling, a treasure chest bursting with the painful, pitiful, sad, always fascinating details of the most ordinary of lives—farmers, shopkeepers, stepdaughters, salesmen, simple soldiers. She's telling tales that sweep from the 1890s through the 1980s. Stories that range from the moors of Yorkshire to the trenches of World War I to the remote west of Canada in the '50s and '60s. At the same time we never escape the center of Ruby's world, in the crowded heart of York, with its winding, crooked streets and buildings that lean into each other like gossiping women.

We never escape Bunty, the mother from hell. "My real mother is roaming in a parallel universe somewhere, ladling out mother's milk the colour of Devon cream," Ruby writes. "I don't like porridge," 5-year-old Patricia says to her mum at breakfast one day. "As fast as a snake, Bunty hisses back, 'Well, I don't like children, so that's too bad for you, isn't it?'" (She doesn't like animals much either. Even though they own a pet shop, the Lennox children are never allowed a pet.)

Ruby's sisters vanish one by one—by death, by intention. Ruby is already a typically pained adolescent in the early '60s, burdened with a tragic family history, when she loses her father. Left alone with Bunty, her teenage angst is aggravated by panic attacks, low self-esteem, her mother's emotionally abusive boyfriend and a hunger for a mother's love.

> **For the first 40 pages of *Behind the Scenes at the Museum,* we are being guided by an embryo with an all-seeing, wise-guy take on the world. She's living in York, England, a place so rife with history "there's no room for the living."**
>
> **—*Georgia Jones-Davis***

Atkinson's revelation of what lies at the heart of the bitter relationship between Bunty and her youngest daughter proves only one of several riveting surprises that conclude this novel.

My only quibble with Atkinson's otherwise marvelous story is what we don't learn about Ruby's own emotional and sexual maturity. We never hear her thoughts on boys (or girls, for that matter). We know more than we'd like to about the sex lives of her relatives and family. Ruby's hasty marriage takes place off-stage and leaves one hungry for more detail about her mysterious adult life.

This past summer when I visited York with my husband and daughter, I went to the Castle museum, where previous eras are brought to life through tableaux. I remember a re-creation of a working-class family's sitting room prettied up with a new telly and festive tea things for the coronation of Queen Elizabeth. What a sad, cramped little room, I thought. After reading *Behind the Scenes at the Museum,* it will always be the Lennox family I see in that claustrophobic room, gathered around that ancient television set, little Ruby parading in one of the homemade, crepe-paper flower coronets all-too-common Auntie Eliza made for the little girls.

Merle Rubin (review date 10 January 1996)

SOURCE: "New Voices Spin Tales of Fiction, Mostly Fiction," in *The Christian Science Monitor,* January 10, 1996, p. 14.

[*In the following excerpt, Rubin offers a mixed review of* Behind the Scenes at the Museum.]

From England, more specifically the cathedral city of York, comes an ambitious, exuberant first novel that takes the form of a young woman narrating her autobiography, starting with the moment of her conception and dipping into past generations of her family while moving forward through her own girlhood.

The narrator of Kate Atkinson's *Behind the Scenes at the Museum* is Ruby Lennox, youngest daughter of a family that lives "above the shop," in this case, a pet shop. Dad is a hard-drinking skirt chaser, Mom a mean-spirited bundle of resentments, big sister Patricia a model of moral and scholastic rectitude, and middle sister Gillian a bratty egotist. As for Ruby—she is, in her own words, "alive . . . a precious jewel . . . a drop of blood," with an uncanny ability to perceive and describe, everything going on around her, even before she is born!

It doesn't take the fetal Ruby very long to notice—with some dismay—that she is not an eagerly anticipated arrival. "Still, never mind—the sun is high in the sky and it's going to be a beautiful day again," remarks the optimistic embryo. "The future is like a cupboard full of light and all you have to do is find the key that opens the door." Birth, however, proves difficult: "My tender skin, as yet untouched by any earthly atmosphere, is being chafed by this sausage-making process. (Surely this can't be natural?)"

Ruby's young life, growing up in England in the 1950s and '60s, is interspersed with vignettes from the lives of her mother, aunt, grandmother, and great-grandmother. Going backward and forward in time, Ruby's vivacious, tartly funny narrative manages to include some of the main events of the past century: two world wars, bombing raids, lost brothers and sweethearts, the coronation of Elizabeth II, the lure of Elvis and the Beatles.

Despite Ruby's evident cheerfulness, it is not a pretty story: Bickering, neglectful parents, sudden deaths, reversals of fortune, and broken hearts abound, but all are conveyed in a brisk, breezy style that at times conceals bitterness beneath a mask of blitheness.

Well received in England, where it won the Whitbread award, *Behind the Scenes at the Museum* may be a little too relentlessly flippant for some tastes, and not quite as brilliantly written as all that (I squirmed at a few grammatical faux pas). But it marks the debut of a distinctive new voice that should appeal to readers who enjoy the panache of a Fay Weldon or the witty inventiveness of a Carol Shields. And it strikes a nice balance between fantasy and reality.

Ben Macintyre (review date 31 March 1996)

SOURCE: "Yorkshire Terrors," in *The New York Times Book Review,* March 31, 1996, pp. 13-14.

[*In the following review, Macintyre praises Atkinson's portrayal of Yorkshire life in* Behind the Scenes at the Museum.]

Yorkshire has an established and self-nurtured reputation as a place of heroic complaint. Nothing is ever quite so bad as it is in Yorkshire. The weather is worse, life is harder, the coal mines are deeper and darker and the scenery harsher, you will be told, than in other, softer lands.

Until, of course, someone unlucky enough to be born outside Yorkshire should dare to chime in to this litany of grievance, at which point the Yorkshire native will point out that the beer and cricket are better, the emotions richer, the history deeper, the women kinder and the men braver than anywhere else on earth. The sheer bloody awfulness of life is a badge of honor, to be worn with grim humor in the knowledge that while existence may be easier elsewhere, it could not be better.

It is this sardonic understanding that informs Kate Atkinson's remarkable first novel, a work full of the grimness, grit and grandeur of Yorkshire life. *Behind the Scenes at the Museum* is a multigenerational tale of a spectacularly dysfunctional Yorkshire family and one of the funniest works of fiction to come out of Britain in years. The book has already, and deservedly, won the prestigious Whitbread Prize.

The tale of Ruby Lennox's family begins with her own conception, an unglamorus event in the year 1951, involving George (philanderer, in thrall to his own libido) and Bunty (dreamer, in thrall to housework), which takes place Above the Shop, as they call their flat in the shadow of the York Minster cathedral. It happens after George gets back from the pub, having successfully worked his way through "five pints of John Smith's Best Bitter."

The chronicle then dives back to the previous century, when Bunty's grandmother, the racked, beautiful Alice Barker, is fighting to bring up her vast brood in hopeless rural poverty but decides to go off with an itinerant French photographer instead, as, frankly, anyone would. Even by traditional standards of Yorkshire gloom, what happens to the intervening generations of Ruby's family is pretty dire. Most end up married to people they cordially detest or with children they did not expect or much want; many die violent, early deaths and almost all are miserable, some quite happily so.

Ms. Atkinson has a superb ear for the deprecating Yorkshire aside (usually offered in at least one set of parenthesis). Her eccentric and sometimes bewilderingly large cast of characters is rendered affectionately, but red in tooth and claw as well as complexion: Ruby's sister Patricia, a quiet and well-behaved duckling who grows into a splendidly Bolshie swan; her other sister, Gillian, grumpy and doomed; a Wodehousian array of eccentric uncles and aunts.

The author is at her best and sharpest when juxtaposing the dreary frustrations of daily life with the searing horror of men and women caught up in the careless wreckage of this century's history. Her description of Ruby's male forebears staggering blindly through the mud of the Somme without a notion of why they are there, but convinced, in some cases rightly, that they will die, is one of the most gripping and sincere depictions of war I have read. The same ruggedness of tone is brought to the quotidian strains of Lennox family life: Bunty, slaving away in the kitchen in an adamant refusal to buy "shop-bought cakes," although she detests cooking because "it's too much like being nice to people."

Few of these characters are strictly likable, all are believably honest and fragile. But under the black hilarity of this world is richer and far sadder fare. This is a novel about loss; the holes that are left by missing lives, love, innocence, but also the enduring meaning of objects and events that anchor each of our personal histories to the past. The artifacts in Ms. Atkinson's "Museum" range from a series of photographs of her great-grandmother to the buttons from Alice's shirt to the golden curls that crop up repeatedly on new shoots of the family tree, often in the most unexpected places. The swift narrative is cleverly played out against the backdrop of defining moments in ordinary lives: the coronation of Queen Elizabeth II in 1953, England playing Germany in the World Cup in 1966, births and funerals.

Sometimes, as in the case of Ruby's relationship with a favorite teddy bear, the evocation can come perilously close to whimsy, just as the humor can border on burlesque, most notably when George expires while *in flagrante delicto* with a waitress during a family wedding reception. But anyone who has struggled to find a missing voice in an object, an image or a work will appreciate Ms. Atkinson's clever cataloguing.

Almost every character in this book is damaged and cauterized, desperately papering over the holes. Ruby's voice, sassy, falsely omniscient and brittle, also hides a loss of which even she is unaware until the book's hallucinatory but powerful ending.

[Atkinson] is at her best and sharpest when juxtaposing the dreary frustrations of daily life with the searing horror of men and women caught up in the careless wreckage of this century's history.

—Ben Macintyre

Like Yorkshire itself, *Behind the Scenes at the Museum* is all sharp edges; it is a caustic and affectionate portrayal of a world in which bleak but nourishing wit is the only safety net. The small-town, big-dream novel is one more often associated with North American women novelists, but Kate Atkinson succeeds here in a different context and with only a trace of sentimentality. Bunty will never be Vivien Leigh, George will never understand what he did wrong, Ruby will never quite find her lost other half and England will probably never reach the World Cup final again. But behind all the half-filled holes and broken or lost things lies a rich, funny seam of hope, like the coal beneath the moors.

Hilary Mantel (review date 4 April 1996)

SOURCE: "Shop!," in *London Review of Books,* Vol. 18, No. 7, April 4, 1996, pp. 23-4.

[*In the following positive review, Mantel lambastes the London critics who mistreated Atkinson upon her winning of the Whitbread Award for* Behind the Scenes at the Museum, *then presents an extensive analysis of the book.*]

On the day after Kate Atkinson's first novel [*Behind the Scenes at the Museum*] won the Whitbread Prize, the *Guardian*'s headline read: 'Rushdie makes it a losing double.' Thus Rushdie is reminded of his disappointments, Atkinson gets no credit, and the uninformed reader assumes that this year's Whitbread is a damp squib. But read on. 'A 44-year-old chambermaid won one of Britain's leading literary awards last night.'

Was this the *Guardian?* Was this 1996? One felt spun back in time to, say, 1956: up jumps a saucy little piece with a feather duster, whisking a notebook from under her frilly apron and pencilling a few lines of a craggy-jaw-and-warm-baritone book, her pretty brow puckered in concentration and her tongue-tip just visible. But wait. This is a 44-year-old chambermaid, so would she have a vast bosom, varicose veins, a vengeful sniffle? Yes indeed: she sounds the sort who would pen what is (according to the *Times*) 'a chronicle of working-class life in York over several decades'.

Then began what the *Scotsman* referred to as 'Scenes from a Maul'. The London media descended on Atkinson. A man from the *Daily Express* asked her to explain what Post-Modernism was; Richard Hoggart, chairman of the Whitbread judges, said that Atkinson had written a Post-Modern novel, but might not know it. (She did the whole thing absent-mindedly, perhaps, while polishing brass doorknobs.) The *Daily Mail* sent a woman who found the author 'pale, rather pimply, her hair unwashed'. Atkinson's private life was probed. She was found to be divorced, with two children, and happy with that arrangement. She was dubbed 'antifamily', and abused accordingly. Julian Critchley, one of the Whitbread judges, wrote an article in which he blamed the 'Corps of Lady Novelists' for her victory. The book, he said, 'resembles the Life of Jackie Charlton as written by Beryl Bainbridge'. He clearly meant this as a huge insult—but to whom?

Interviewers who had not had time to look at the book went to see Atkinson with a set of expectations which she quickly shattered. Atkinson has a degree in English literature, and has done postgraduate work in the field of American contemporary fiction. The job as a chambermaid was a holiday job, and the other menial occupations cited were those which any would-be writer takes up to pay the bills—and which, in the case of young men, are thought to broaden experience and convey prole credentials. 'She doesn't even have a Yorkshire accent,' wailed the woman from the *Independent,* who had clearly expected some kind of idiot savant. As the interview wore on, Atkinson became 'chippy and cussed'. This is not surprising. 'Never,' she has written, 'have my hair, my nails, my clothes, my marital status been of as much interest to anyone as they were to the women of the London press.' The *Sunday Times* quoted Anita Brookner recently: 'I think literature is without gender.' Think again. Hundreds of thousands of words have been written about Salman Rushdie—and we know nothing of his manicure.

Now Atkinson is back in Edinburgh, where she lives. She speaks of the London press as 'evil and morally corrupt'.

From Whitbread winner to John Knox in four easy weeks. Even the friendlier Scottish papers were apt to harp on rags-to-riches, overnight success. Commentators should take this truth to heart: no novelist ever has an overnight success. Atkinson has been writing for fifteen years, and it is clear that, in one sense, her book has taken a lifetime. It is not autobiographical, but an uncanny reproduction of autobiography. It is not a chronicle. It is not about the working classes. It is not—as the interviewers assumed—slice-of-life realism. This assumption is made because the book is set in the North of England. If it were set, say, in Sri Lanka—Ondaatje's *Running in the Family* comes to mind—it would not have been described as if it were the literary equivalent of suet pudding. If it were from South America, it would be evaluated quite differently. There is a double standard operating here; the exoticism of everyday life is overlooked. And the Atkinson v. Rushdie fight is not a mismatch. In its fantastic and magical conceits, its energy and tireless invention, its echoes of dream-worlds and genetic mysteries, the Whitbread winner is more like a book by Salman Rushdie than the writers of the lowering headlines could imagine. Like Rushdie's work, it makes most English fiction look chlorotic, green-sick, an exhausted swooner fanning herself in the twilight of a tradition.

When the book was first published it received a number of favourable reviews. No one took to the rooftops, bellowing 'Atkinson is a genius,' but there is a good reason for this. Reviewers are paid to read books, and they often feel guilty about it—lolling before the gas-fire, as they do, sultans of syntax, while their less fortunate contemporaries are out braving the sleet and the IRA. The guilt abates when they feel that they are earning their money, and they feel this only when they are stunned by boredom, or itching with irritation. Atkinson's book does not provoke these reactions—and so critical panic sets in. What—reached page 39, and no yellow sticky note stuck? No felt-tip scrawl saying 'Debt to Murdoch is crippling,' or 'X is to Self as Self is to Amis' or 'vivid, charming, but lacking in force'? What, page 100 reached, and nothing done? Nothing to say, except 'I am really enjoying myself'?

Anyone who reads, let's say, Joanna Trollope will be able to read and enjoy Kate Atkinson. Her novel delivers to the populace its jokes and its tragedies as efficiently as Dickens once delivered his, though Atkinson has a game-plan more sophisticated than Dickens's, and her handling of a child's death scene forestalls any Wildean scorn. ***Behind the Scenes at the Museum*** is very unusual: a book that would have pleased the 18th century, the 19th century, and pleases our own.

The story begins with a cry of triumph from the narrator, Ruby Lennox. 'I exist! I am conceived to the chimes of midnight.' Tristram Shandy, of course, the reader thinks. Both Sterne and Proust are read in the course of the novel, by

Ruby's clever older sister, Patricia. Many reviewers must have longed to write: 'The scene is York, and a crumpet/pikelet/ muffin must stand in for Proust's madeleine.' But Atkinson, who quite certainly knows what Post-Modernism is, has a way of diverting her reader from the easy, pre-set response. Just when you think you have begun to understand how her book works, she will undeceive you. She is not so much standing on the shoulders of giants, as darting between their legs and waving her own agenda—and talking all the time, with a voice that is absolutely her own: waspish and wry, street-smart and down-beat, sometimes brutal and sometimes (perhaps just once) tender.

Ruby's parents are George and Berenice, who own a pet shop. They are not working-class people; they belong to the shop-keeping classes, which are different. By the date of the Queen's coronation—Ruby is one of the first babies of the new Elizabethan Age—they own a refrigerator and a TV set. Berenice is always known as 'Bunty', which doesn't seem to suit her sour character at all; in fact it is an inspiration, because we are constantly reminded of the little girl inside the grown woman, and that child is still present in our minds when her aged carapace has departed to 'planet Alzheimer.'

Bunty does not like children. Her first reaction to the infant Ruby is 'Looks like a piece of meat. Take it away.' Her marriage is unhappy, fraught with so many arguments that Ruby wishes 'that I could accelerate my evolution and develop earlids'. Bunty is 'a slave to housework', and hates cooking—it is 'too much like being nice to people'. She steeps her husband's underwear in a bucket of Dettol before allowing it to join the family wash. George is an uncouth philanderer, 'scraping and grovelling' when he is in the shop and ripping off the mask of geniality when he comes backstage. The parents' lives are entirely a performance, of a play scripted by themselves, which might be called 'Everything is nice and normal'. But it is not. Their shop, in a medieval building under the shadow of York Minster, has tilted walls and sloping ceilings, like a malign enclosure in a fun-fair. The shades of Roman legionnaires tread the streets, and the household ghosts cluster on the staircase, waiting to catch Ruby as she climbs up to bed: the ghosts sleep 'curled up in the corners and stretched out along the curtain rails'. And throughout her childhood Ruby sleepwalks—always looking for something, someone, conscious of a loss she cannot articulate, of a shadowy presence, of whispers in her blood and intimations of other times, other lives.

The stories within the book embrace the lives of four generations, running from before the Great War to almost the present day; they are linked together by a system of 'footnotes' which direct the reader backwards and forwards in time. Often it is the mention of a household object or a small personal item like a button or a locket which sends the narrative on one of its great loops. This technique is much more ingenious and

hard to manage than straightforward flashback—which Atkinson also employs—and her dexterity is considerable. When one reads the book for the first time, some identities blur, there is sometimes an aunt or an uncle too many, but only a Gradgrind will stop to make a family tree and calculate the dates. On a second, anatomist's reading, the book's articulation shows clearly, its bones and joints almost perfectly aligned; Atkinson cares for structure, and here is a delicate but robust skeleton on which hangs the muscle of narrative force and the tissue of loss and sadness and indecent merriment.

Atkinson is a contemporary of her heroine Ruby, but she writes about everyday life in earlier times with a precision which is eerie. Objects here have their own stories, their secret lives. Three buttons burst from the bodice of the dress of Ruby's great-grandmother and go rolling down the generations in three separate directions. A soldier on leave sees the delicate flower pattern of the china tea-set over which Ruby's grandmother presides; he is about to tell her of life in the trenches, but suddenly sees that there is no point. Two generations on, the family cat eats from the remaining saucer, another inarticulate witness to the tribulations the years have brought.

The nature of memory is a central issue in the book. Atkinson understands that the habit of 'mystification' that Laing observed in the families of his schizophrenic patients is in fact common in 'normal' families. There are gaps in children's memories, because adults—sometimes from the best of motives—conspire to create them. Instinct makes things fit, gives endings to stories; any fabulous nonsense is wheeled in to fill the gaps. Years pass, and the fabrications take on the colours of sober truths. These truths then become an instrument of power, governing how life should be lived—in our family, people say, we have *always* done so and so. Again, the power of the half-word, or the unspoken word, governs a child's construction of the universe it inhabits. Ivy Compton-Burnett, who needed no subject other than the power-play of family life, had a quirk or habit of writing that a character 'barely uttered' some significant and usually hurtful remark. Atkinson's characters are always 'barely uttering', though she never uses the formulation. And when parents speak out loud and clear, who can make sense of what they say? In the space of one day, Ruby is told a) that girls should not cross their legs and b) that the Labour Party is more dangerous than the Catholic Church. No one must pass within two feet of a paraffin heater, even when it is not alight—*that makes no difference.* Why do Ruby's parents shout 'Shop!', she wonders, when one of them walks in at the front door. Surely that is what the customers should shout? One day Ruby will realise that there is no reason, no reason at all—and that day will be the beginning of her growing up.

But growing up to be what? Her foremothers have hardly

relished the traditional womanly role. Ruby develops a particular dread of a doll's house owned by her twin cousins, weird little girls who she fears are extra-terrestrials. When she shares a bedroom with them, she is afraid that they will miniaturise her and trap her inside it, and that she will be condemned for ever to be one of the pretty ringletted girls taking a piano lesson or—even worse—the scullery maid eternally blacking the range. Atkinson contrives to explore the changing nature of women's lives without being either obvious or schematic, and she can do this because she respects all her characters. Even those who seem to have no redeeming features are treated with wry humour; the book is never depressing. It is, in fact, outrageously funny on almost every page, and this is a wonder, when you consider what is actually happening. Of Bunty's four daughters, two die violently and prematurely, one becomes pregnant, has her baby adopted and then leaves home for good, and the fourth makes a serious suicide attempt at the age of 16. The horrible, casual randomness of sudden death rips through the text, and Atkinson fells her people artlessly, casts them off with a phrase: 'In 1945 George's father died by falling under a tram on a day trip to Leeds.' That is typical of an Atkinson character—to survive a world war, but not notice that a tram is coming. The West's biggest disasters leave them unimpressed; a Great War soldier writes home: 'The battle of Ypres is over now, and we are all very glad.'

Some practitioners of tragi-comedy manipulate their readers, pushing and pulling them firmly towards the viewpoint that the writer wants them to see. Atkinson's method is more like that of Escher, where, as the artist said, 'black and white only manifest themselves together and by means of each other.' An Escher design contains two realities, opposed to each other but both true; the viewpoint is constant: the trick is in the mind's eye. In his *Sky and Water,* birds become fishes and fishes become birds, but one cannot see both bird and fish simultaneously. In the Atkinson set-piece that one might call 'Christmas Eve at the Pantomime' she produces her most glittering and savage comic writing, and yet the reader knows—because we have been tipped off, in Sparkian fashion, in the book's earliest pages—that this is the last night of sister Gillian's life. The reader is transfixed, spitted, by laughter and horror in turn. The pork chops are charred, the pudding is tinned peaches; if only they'd known what was going to happen, Ruby remarks, they could have had Christmas dinner early, just for Gillian.

Just occasionally, there is a misfire. In one episode, Ruby's Uncle Ted finds to his disgust that he has agreed to be married on the very Saturday afternoon, in the summer of 1966, that England are to meet Germany in the World Cup final. The ceremony is performed, the buffet is laid out, and slowly all the men at the reception drain away, as if a giant plug has been pulled and they have been swirled into the sewers. They have found a television set, of course, and when the women locate them their wrath is terrible. It is a wonderful idea, and works brilliantly until Uncle Ted falls into the cake—this physical extravagance goes just beyond what one can bring off on the page. It is a small miscalculation. A greater one is Atkinson's decision to prolong the narrative into Ruby's adulthood. Even this capacious book cannot contain it, and once the peak of intensity has passed, in Ruby's 16th year, neither we nor the author have the emotional energy to see her into the calm waters of middle age. The result is that, close to the end, there is some slightly underpowered, perfunctory narration.

It hardly seems gracious to complain. The best indication of Atkinson's talent lies in the novel's spirited generosity. The average cautious beginner would have chipped three novels out of the material. Combining vast creative energy with a cast-iron technique, this is a book which will survive any amount of ignorant carping and boorishness, and will dazzle readers for years to come. It is almost as good, in fact, as that as yet unborn masterpiece, for which the millions will queue: the Life of Jackie Charlton, as written by Beryl Bainbridge.

Richard Ford

Independence Day

Awards: Pulitzer Prize in Fiction and PEN/Faulkner Award for Fiction

Born in 1944, Ford is an American novelist, short story writer, essayist, and critic.

INTRODUCTION

In *Independence Day* Ford continues the story of Frank Bascombe, introduced in his earlier work *The Sportswriter.* Bascombe is a middle-aged, middle-class American, a short-story writer who published just one book before quitting to become a sportswriter. Having lost a son, his marriage, and finally his job, Bascombe attempts to carry on with a career in real estate sales. The story takes place over a Fourth of July weekend, which Bascombe intends to spend visiting the baseball and basketball halls of fame with his remaining, deeply troubled teenage son. In the process, he considers the nature of independence in people's lives and takes stock of his own life.

Critics have praised Ford's ability to evoke sympathy among readers for a protagonist as common, unremarkable, and un-heroic as Bascombe. While some reviewers have dismissed the plot of *Independence Day* as sketchy and uninteresting, others have found in its plainness a metaphor for the quiet desperation of everyday life. Critics have also praised Ford as masterful in his use of descriptive detail in *Independence Day,* particularly in his depiction of the book's setting and his understanding of the real estate business. "With *Independence Day,*" Michiko Kakutani observed, "Mr. Ford has written a worthy sequel to *The Sportswriter* and galvanized his reputation as one of his generation's most eloquent voices."

PRINCIPAL WORKS

A Piece of My Heart (novel) 1976
The Ultimate Good Luck (novel) 1981
The Sportswriter (novel) 1986
Rock Springs: Stories (short stories) 1987
Wildlife (novel) 1990
Independence Day (novel) 1995

CRITICISM

Richard Ford with Molly McQuade (interview date 18 May 1990)

SOURCE: "Richard Ford," in *Publishers Weekly,* Vol. 237, No. 20, May 18, 1990, pp. 66-7.

[*In the following interview, Ford talks about the act of writing, his career, and his life.*]

In Richard Ford's fiction, characters wince at a painful moment, extract its grudging truth, and scramble to survive. Ford, whose fourth novel, **Wildlife,** is due out next month from Atlantic Monthly Press, writes about "the smaller lives," their redeeming aches, and the luck or grit his people need to know themselves.

"I'm an optimist," Ford insists, but is rueful about what he calls, with amused chagrin, his "solemnity." It is something that permeates his stories and novels and also makes its presence felt in the author's soft-spoken yet hard-bitten Southern drawl. "I would rather be the guy who says 'I'm happy,'"

Ford avows, "but I'm not much of a hoper. Rather than hope, I try to *do* something."

Since 1968, doing something has meant writing, and it came about fairly innocently. "When I decided to write, it wasn't larky, yet it was quixotic," Ford says. "I didn't have any notions of making a life out of it. I had the idea of writing stories, one at a time." Briefly a law student at Washington University in St. Louis, he had grown dissatisfied with the "answers" the law prescribed. Having been away for a spell from his home in the South—he was raised a salesman's son in Jackson, Miss., and Little Rock, Ark.—and separated from his Michigan State University sweetheart, Kristina Hensley, whom he later married, Ford felt "itchy and curious." So he left the place where he was living and changed his life.

"Turning my life toward writing books was a pretty strenuous turn. I was wrenched around," Ford concedes. But by temperamental decree, the man seems to need to move. He has been called "peripatetic" with a swaggering romanticism that Ford fights shy of, claiming that such talk is "very tedious to me. I don't think I'm restless. I live in the U.S., and wherever I am, I am." (These places have included New York City, Chicago, Ann Arbor, Princeton, Missoula and now New Orleans.) Protesting that "your preconceptions about a place are not exactly what happens," he explains his roving by stating, "I need to be certain that I have new stimulus. New places give me something I can use." But the self-described fatalist grew up with "an awe of the unknown" that may have predisposed him to rapid transits. His awe, Ford says, "was useful. There were a lot of things I didn't understand, and I got accustomed to living with that. I discovered that the virtue of writing can extinguish the vice of ignorance."

Ford swears that "I wasn't an extraordinary young man at all, and I didn't strive to be. I liked to write because I could do it by myself." But he acknowledges the help he got—and the salutary boot out the door he received—from such mentors as E. L. Doctorow, with whom he studied at the University of California at Irvine, earning an M.F.A. in 1970.

Doctorow proved a useful teacher because, Ford says, he taught his students that once class ended, they had to make their own way in the world. "It seems like you're getting left out in the cold, yet you're supposed to be left out in the cold—and get your work done." A popular writing instructor himself at Princeton, Williams College and the University of Michigan during the '70s, Ford quit in 1981 because his yen for "the cold"—and his wish to concentrate his energies on writing—got the better of him.

"I was always a hard worker when I was young, and my ethic was to work hard at writing. But to make literature your life's habit is a fairly fragile habit," Ford observes. "You get to the point where you're doing it the best you can, and then you can't do much else. It's like walking down a road that gets narrower and narrower. As you get further out on that limb, it becomes precarious, but writing is a precarious life—and all life is precarious." Or, as a character in Ford's acclaimed short story collection *Rock Springs* put it, "The most important things of your life can change so suddenly, so unrecoverably, that you can forget even the most important of them and their connections, you are so taken up by the chanciness of all that's happened and by all that could and will happen next."

Ford broods, "Writing is the only thing I've done with persistence, except for being married to Kristina—and yet it's such an inessential thing. Nobody cares if you do it, and nobody cares if you don't. And the way you 'make yourself up' to be the author of your books, especially when you're young, depends on the stars coming into alignment. Life tugs at you. It's not as if there's a profession for writers out there; there isn't even a fraternity. You may have friends who are writers, but they can't write your books. I don't think writers *have* careers—my work doesn't exist separately from my life."

Ford's first book was *A Piece of My Heart,* brought out by Harper & Row in 1976, and nominated for the Ernest Hemingway Award for Best First Novel. *The Ultimate Good Luck* followed five years later; *The Sportswriter* was published in 1986. *Rock Springs* came out in 1987. All have been issued in trade paperback by Vintage.

As he has roamed, so have Ford's books. *A Piece of My Heart* was hailed by the *Boston Globe* as a Faulknerian "collision course with destiny set in the swamp-ridden Mississippi Delta." *The Ultimate Good Luck,* called by one critic "a bruiser of a novel replete with gun-metal dialogue and drug deals gone sour," takes place in Oaxaca, Mexico, and was completed while the Fords were living in Cuernavaca and Yahualica. *The Sportswriter* has New Jersey as its locale; Ford came to know Princeton well while teaching there. The backdrop of *Rock Springs* and *Wildlife* is Montana, where Ford moved in 1983 when his wife accepted a job as planning director of Missoula.

While Ford has changed addresses often, much of *The Sportswriter* and some of *Rock Springs* were written in a house in the Mississippi Delta, one of Ford's longtime favorite spots despite his reluctance to be classed as a Southern writer. Jackson, Miss., his boyhood home, continues to hold his affection—as does Jackson resident Eudora Welty—and many of his relatives are in northwestern Arkansas. Though Ford's attachment to Mississippi may be circumstantial (his parents settled there because it was located at the center of his father's sales territory), his ties to the South are such that his 1987 Mississippi Academy of Arts and Letters' Literature Award came as a special pleasure. Still, regardless of where he is,

Ford aims "to write a literature that is good enough for America."

But no literature can be good enough for everyone. Ford recalls, with impenitent cheer, the reaction of "a famous New York editor" to the first hundred pages of *The Sportswriter,* later to sell upwards of 50,000 copies: "He told me I was wasting my life." Ford concludes, "I got bit there. But you'll always get bit." When his publisher, Simon & Schuster—for whom Morgan Entrekin had acquired *The Sportswriter* before leaving S & S—requested changes in the novel, Ford resisted. Gary Fisketjon, then at Random House, now Ford's editor at Atlantic—and soon to join Knopf—finally acquired the book as a Vintage Contemporaries Original. Agent Amanda Urban's entreaty—"You need a book that's going to do well"—was thus satisfied.

Not all critical response to *The Sportswriter* was ardent, but sportswriters made their enthusiasm known, writing fan letters to Ford (who, after college, had hoped to be a sportswriter for the *Arkansas Gazette*). Their testimonials? "'I lay in bed with my wife and we read your book back and forth for a month," reports the author bashfully, "It hasn't made me rich, but it's made me read." Somewhat less gratifying was critic James Wolcott's fierce sally at Ford's accomplishments to date in the August 1989 issue of *Vanity Fair.* Deemed "a totally nasty piece of work" by Ford's publisher, "Guns and Poses: A Revisionist View of Richard Ford, the Lauded Novelist" was read by Kristina Ford, who told her husband not to try it. After letting fly with a few choice bits of invective, Ford philosophizes, "There are certain things that people are going to say about you that you can't redeem—you have to get used to it."

It was easier to get used to the praise of *Rock Springs* offered by such critics as the *New York Times*'s Michiko Kakutani, who cited his "wholly distinctive narrative voice . . . that can move effortlessly between neat, staccato descriptions and rich, lyrical passages," and novelist John Wideman, who lauded the way Ford fashioned a "concentrated, supple, ironic" prose style from "everyday speech."

In fact, some of the credit for that style should go, Ford says, to the poets he has read and admired over the years. Once merely "mysterious" to Ford, poetry became clarified when "I saw people *doing* it"—James Wright, Galway Kinnell, Gregory Orr, Charles Wright, Donald Hall. "I saw how useful it could be to exercise such care over phrases and utterances and lines." In his own sentences Ford seeks a comparable "level of intensity, an economy of language and maximum effect."

Ford's "maximum effect" will soon extend to film; he has just finished wrapping up post-production work on *Bright Angel,* an adaptation of two stories (and a new one) from

Rock Springs. Starring Sam Shepard and Valerie Perrine, the movie was directed by Michael Fields and shot on location in Montana.

Also an essayist, Ford recently served as guest editor of Houghton Mifflin's forthcoming *Best American Essays 1990.* With typically gentle self-mockery, he recalls trying to say no to his first essay assignment, from Rust Hills of *Esquire.* The year was 1983, the magazine's 50th anniversary issue was in the planning stages, and Hills approached Ford with the idea of writing a piece on Faulkner, Hemingway and Fitzgerald. "Oh, you're making a big mistake," Ford dodged. "That's just an opportunity to hang myself." "Well," Hills countered, "you've been likened to Faulkner, you've been likened to Hemingway, you've been likened to Fitzgerald." Besides, he added, "Philip Roth turned it down."

Other recent projects include Ford's introduction to *Juke Joints,* a collection of photographer friend Birney Imes's work to be published in July by the University Press of Mississippi. And in January Ford was recognized for his lifetime achievements with an American Academy and Institute of Arts and Letters Award for Literature.

So he sits and works in his New Orleans townhouse, where the crime of the French Quarter is "scary." With his reputation as a "tough guy"—hotly disputed by Ford himself—and as a skillful evoker of male voices and violence, perhaps it's not surprising to hear Ford talk of a recent near fistfight. "This man was threatening to beat up his girlfriend in front of our house. I just kind of stepped out the door and asked him to quit. So there we were, nose to nose. And the police came and wanted to arrest *me.* We settled it, though." Ford pauses. "Maybe I am a primitive and don't know it." He hunts and fishes "to forget about what's bugging me, because my father and grandfather did it, because Kristina likes to do it," and for the fun of raising bird dogs.

"Writers' lives are such pedestrian affairs," Ford complains. "You want to mine out everything you can, but then broaden your ways. In an effort to be demanding on myself, I create an aura of difficulty, in which things won't turn out right. But I would like language to be, in some secular way, redemptive. Writing is an act of optimism: you make a thing, make it well, give it to someone, and it has a use. They need it—though they didn't know they did."

James Bowman (review date 16 June 1995)

SOURCE: "One Man's Cavalcade of Really Deep Thoughts," in *Wall Street Journal,* June 16, 1995, p. A12.

[*In the following review, Bowman criticizes Ford's* Independence Day *as an example of the "Ruminative School of fic-*

tion" in which plot and character development are sacrificed for deep thinking.]

A good rule of thumb for readers of contemporary fiction is to avoid anything written in the first person whose main character is a failed writer. Actually, I would avoid anything whose main character is any kind of writer, but failed or blocked writers purporting to write about themselves are the worst. Richard Ford enjoyed his biggest success as a novelist with *The Sportswriter,* in which Frank Bascombe, author of one book of short stories, retreats from art to sportswriting. In *Independence Day,* he has brought Frank back as a real-estate salesman. Now that's what I call blocked!

Both these novels belong to what might be called the Ruminative School of fiction. In novels by ruminants nothing much happens, but lots of Deep Thoughts get thought and often lots of fine writing gets written. Introducing a genuinely dramatic element would seem phony and inauthentic to writers of the Ruminative School. Such traditional forms of literary excitement as plot and character development are presumably beneath the dignity of those who have Deep Thoughts to think and fine writing to write. They write about what they know, and what they know is themselves.

Mind you, lots has happened *before* the novel begins. Without his memories of death and divorce, of pain and loss, of sex and writing gone bad, the Ruminative hero would be a cow without a cud. But nothing much is happening as we read, at least not to the hero, and the banal, everyday events of his life are little more than the medium or stock in which his meaty thoughts are suspended. To taste them, we must consume lots more filler than we really want to about, say, the real-estate market in New Jersey in the late 1980s.

Frank Bascombe's new occupation is meant to be the guarantee of his authenticity. Writers get paid for thinking Deep Thoughts, while real-estate salesmen, we may assume, must think them solely for love. Also, Frank's profession has been chosen as being particularly appropriate to what he calls "the Existence Period" of his life. Theorizing about the Existence Period comprises the deepest of his thoughts, though there is no thought of how pretentious it is to divide one's own life up into periods.

Frank is sincere even in his pretensions. He sees the Existence Period as that phase of his middle age during which his practice "has been to ignore much of what I don't like or that seems worrisome and embroiling," or as "the high-wire act of normalcy, the part that comes after the big struggle which led to the big blow-up" and is characterized by "the small dramas and minor adjustments of spending quality time simply with ourselves."

Frank may in fact hold some kind of record for spending qual-

ity time with himself. But he also has a son, Paul, to whom he feels he owes some of this precious commodity, and the drama of the novel, such as it is, consists of his taking this troubled teenage boy to visit as many sports halls of fame as they can in two days (i.e. two). That's about it. It is one of those ideas that exhausts itself in being stated. What is there to say about the actual visiting of these places that is more interesting than the idea of visiting them?

So the father-son expedition, which doesn't even begin until more than halfway through the novel, is cut short with its one quasidramatic event, which puts Paul in the hospital. There are, however, no lasting consequences to this moment of action—beyond making Frank think even deeper thoughts about himself and life and everything. These remind us that, as he tells a client who thinks he may have a gift for selling real estate himself, the realty business is "like being a writer. A man with nothing to do finds something to do."

It is this sense of surrounding vacancy, of busywork, of the commonplace unnecessarily rendered into self-conscious prose, that is the characteristic feature of the Ruminative style. Its tortured, introspective meanderings finally become exasperating and at times degenerate into a paragraph full of speculative questionings about what if this or that had happened, followed by some such colloquial formula as: "God only knows, right? Really knows?"

My favorite passage of Frank's speculative self-questioning, which almost rises to the height of self-parody, is where he spends a paragraph wondering what it would have been like if he and his ex-wife had bought a Volvo that they looked at years before and then didn't buy. Nothing from his more youthful past is beneath the notice of his Existence Period, it seems, though he fantasizes about reaching a Permanent Period in which he will have become more like an "ordinary person." My guess is that it is a delusion characteristic of the Existence Period to suppose that there is a Permanent Period. The bad news for readers is that it is Frank's interminable self-examination that has become permanent.

Charles Johnson (review date 18 June 1995)

SOURCE: "Stuck in the Here and Now," in *The New York Times Book Review,* June 18, 1995, pp. 1, 28.

[*In the following review, Johnson discusses Ford's characterization in* Independence Day, *and asserts that "Frank Bascombe has earned himself a place beside Willy Loman and Harry Angstrom in our literary landscape."*]

When we last saw Frank Bascombe, the angst-ridden antihero of Richard Ford's highly praised 1986 novel, *The Sportswriter,* he was 38 and about to cast himself adrift. A journalist and onetime short-story-writer, Frank was a perfectly ordinary man with an extraordinary gift for social observation. Served up in highly original language, his perceptions lifted him above what he called "the normal applauseless life" to illuminate the "psychic detachment" caused by his divorce and by his own relentless self-doubt. At the time, *The Sportswriter* was an entertaining CAT scan of the shellshocked American psyche. It remains so today.

And now there's a sequel. Frank has returned, 44 years old but still unconvinced that "life's leading someplace," to narrate Mr. Ford's spirited fifth novel, *Independence Day.* The time is 1988, and Frank is looking forward to the Fourth of July weekend, when he's arranged to meet with his girlfriend, Sally Caldwell, and then take his 15-year-old son, Paul, to the basketball and baseball halls of fame. Paul has never recovered from the death of his brother, Ralph; occasionally barks like a dog; and has been labeled by a team of therapists as "intellectually beyond his years" yet "emotionally underdeveloped." He has recently been arrested for shoplifting "three boxes of 4X condoms ('Magnums')" and is being taken to court by the female security guard who captured him, who's accusing him of assault and battery.

Frank's little excursion with his son is, as he puts it, "a voyage meant to instruct." Somewhat unrealistically, he has sent Paul, among other things, a copy of Emerson's *Self-Reliance,* to help him see that the Fourth of July is "an observance of human possibility, which applies a canny pressure on each of us to contemplate what we're dependent on . . . and after that to consider in what ways we're independent or might be; and finally how we might decide—for the general good—not to worry about it much at all."

As in *The Sportswriter,* Frank appears both as a survivor of the 1960's and as a descendant of T. S. Eliot's *Hollow Men*; in his own words, he is a man who has "yet to learn to want properly." These things we know about Frank: he is a New Deal Democrat who believes that life's choices are limited, that getting old is humiliating and that the nearness of death is downright terrifying—though, like any decent man, he's determined not to complain too much. He has abandoned sportswriting and returned to conservative Haddam, N.J., to live in the home of his ex-wife, Ann, and work as a realtor, a profession (and point of reference) that provides as many opportunities for sardonic commentary on the human condition as his previous job did. "You don't sell a house to someone," he observes, "you sell a life." But he has also learned that "a market economy . . . is not even remotely premised on anybody getting what he wants."

One thing Frank wants is for Paul, a boy "you'd be sorry to encounter on a city street," to come live with him so he can straighten things out. Another thing he wants is a second chance with Ann, which seems highly unlikely since she feels

that he "may be the most cynical man in the world." There's also the small matter of her remarriage, to a 61-year-old architect named Charley O'Dell. "I divorced you," Ann tells Frank, "because I didn't like you. And I didn't like you because I didn't trust you. . . . I wanted somebody with a true heart, that's all. That wasn't you." For Frank, a third hankering is "to form a new grip, for a longer, more serious attachment" with his girlfriend, Sally, but here too there are problems. "Life seems congested to me," she confesses. "Something's crying out to be noticed, I just don't know what it is. But it must have to do with you and I. Don't you agree?"

To be sure, Frank's relationships with women—indeed, with most people—are as puzzling to him as ever. He speaks with his best friend in Haddam, Carter Knott, for no more than 90 seconds every six months; Frank prefers to keep things this way because he has happily entered what he calls the "Existence Period," "the part that comes after the big struggle which led to the big blowup," a sort of holding pattern characterized by "the condition of honest independence."

With a mastery second to none, Richard Ford has created, and continues to develop in *Independence Day,* a character we know as well as we know our next-door neighbors.

—Charles Johnson

His other problems involve trying to collect rent from Larry McLeod, a black former Green Beret, and his white wife, Betty, who live in one of two houses Frank owns in Haddam's solitary black neighborhood. Although Frank fondly remembers an affair he once had with a black realtor, whose murder remains a mystery throughout the novel, he is clearly less sympathetic to the mixed-raced McLeods, because they give off a scent of self-righteousness. To him, Betty always seems to wear "a perpetually disappointed look that says she regrets all her major life choices yet feels absolutely certain she made the right moral decision in every instance, and is better than you because of it. It's the typical three-way liberal paradox: anxiety mingled with pride and self-loathing. The McLeods are also, I'm afraid, the kind of family who could someday go paranoid and barricade themselves in their (my) house, issue confused manifestoes, fire shots at the police and eventually torch everything, killing all within. (This, of course, is no reason to evict them.)"

Frank is no less critical of Joe and Phyllis Markham, two "donkeyish clients" he has guided through 45 houses and is urging to close on a place located next to a minimum security prison. The Markhams watch their dreams and their marriage unravel; they come to know firsthand "the realty dreads," and after so many house showings realize they are "just like the other schmo, wishing his wishes, lusting his stunted lusts, quaking over his idiot frights and fantasies, all of us popped out from the same unchinkable mold."

We have come to expect brilliant character sketches from Mr. Ford, and he doesn't disappoint us. In addition to the principal players orbiting like moons around Frank Bascombe's planet-sized ego, there are memorable cameo figures like his former boss, old man Schwindell, who alternates between sucking on Pall Malls and the nozzle of an oxygen tank, and Char, a saucy chef Frank meets in the Deerslayer, an inn in Cooperstown where he stumbles upon a copy of his "now-old book of short stories" and makes a discovery that leads to one of the novel's most richly ironic scenes.

But there is only the thinnest of story lines in the 451 pages of *Independence Day.* The novel often bogs down in repetitive descriptions of place and setting. Some events—Frank's effort to collect his rent from the McLeods, his arrival at a motel in Connecticut just after a killing has occurred and the mystery of the realtor's murder—lead nowhere. On the other hand, plot (or the notion of life's events leading much of anywhere) would violate Frank's basic belief that "you can rave, break furniture, get drunk, crack up your Nova and beat your knuckles bloody on the glass bricks of the exterior wall of whatever dismal room you're temporarily housed in, but in the end you won't have changed the basic situation and you'll still have to make the decision you didn't want to make before, and probably you'll make it in the very way you'd resented and that brought on all the raving and psychic fireworks."

Predictably, then, Frank's meeting with Sally is inconclusive. (Sally hopes someday he'll "get around to doing something memorable.") The Markhams lose the house they were looking at to a Korean family. And Frank's effort to help his troubled son veers toward tragedy and irreparable loss.

In the end, however, the small problems in the world of Frank Bascombe resolve themselves for the best—or at least in the best ways that can be expected for a man who knows that "it's not exactly as if I didn't exist, but that I don't exist as *much*" as other people. Despite this alienation, which Mr. Ford uses effectively for memorable comic moments, Frank has, by the novel's final scenes, managed to take his first tentative steps from the Existence Period toward a sense of community and the possibilities of the "Permanent Period," which he defines as "that long, stretching-out time when my dreams would have mystery like any ordinary person's; when whatever I do or say, who I marry, how my kids turn out, becomes what the world—if it makes note at all—knows of me."

With a mastery second to none, Richard Ford has created, and continues to develop in *Independence Day,* a character we know as well as we know our next-door neighbors. Frank Bascombe has earned himself a place beside Willy Loman and Harry Angstrom in our literary landscape, but he has done so with a wry wit and a *fin de siècle* wisdom that is very much his own.

John Blades (essay date 22 June 1995)

SOURCE: "House Calls," in *Chicago Tribune,* June 22, 1995, p. 9C.

[*In the following essay, Blades discusses Ford's novel* Independence Day *and asserts that Ford's "migratory habits have only enriched his life and fiction."*]

By loose definition, Richard Ford is a displaced writer, but his migratory habits have only enriched his life and fiction. For one thing, they relieved him of the need to do extensive research for his latest novel, *Independence Day.*

The book's central character, Frank Bascombe, is a real estate agent, an occupation with which the 51-year-old Ford has acquired a more than passing familiarity over the decades, as he moved from Mississippi to New Jersey to Montana to Louisiana, with various intermediate stops.

By lighting out every couple of years for a new territory, Ford has been able to diversify, to "learn and write about the whole country." In the process, said the novelist, who was briefly in Chicago this week to promote his new book, he has also avoided the regional stereotyping that handicaps so many fiction writers.

Of his nomadic life, Ford said: "I haven't bought very many houses, but I've looked at a jillion. And when I started *Independence Day,* I discovered how much I knew about real estate. I guess it's a habit of being a writer. You just begin to soak stuff up."

Selling houses represents a dramatic career change for Frank Bascombe, who was "The Sportswriter" in Ford's 1986 novel of that title. For the sequel, *Independence Day,* Ford decided to retire Frank from sportswriting and immerse him in real estate.

Next to sportswriting, selling houses sounds like a resoundingly dull business, hardly the stuff of lively or sympathetic fiction. But Ford disagrees, calling real estate "an index to our national character. . . . As Frank says, a large portion of every American's life is spent in the company of realtors."

Ford's faith in his ability to invigorate not only the subject but also his fictional characters was largely affirmed by the reviews for *Independence Day.* Perhaps the most positive was the one in *Publishers Weekly,* which called the novel "often poetic, sometimes searing, sometimes hilarious."

Though well-grounded in the fundamentals of real estate, *Independence Day* is more concerned with Frank Bascombe's psyche than his occupation. The novel catches him six years after the close of *The Sportswriter,* still living in Haddam, N.J., still troubled by his divorce and the death of a son from Reye's syndrome.

As the title indicates, Ford's long, introspective novel takes place over a Fourth of July weekend. During the holiday, Frank compulsively meditates on his "psychic detachment" and the nature of personal independence, while embarking on an inglorious pilgrimage with his surviving teenage son to the basketball and baseball halls of fame.

Although he has never sold real estate, Ford did spend a year as a sportswriter with *Inside Sports* magazine, beginning in 1980. At the time, his first novel, *A Piece of My Heart,* though generously received, was out of print, leaving him in need of a regular income, said the author (whose 1995 income got a welcome boost with the $25,000 Rea Award for short fiction).

When the magazine was sold, Ford was out of a job, but his brief inning as a sportswriter provided him with the raw material for a novel. As a number of reviewers pointed out, *The Sportswriter,* with its consuming focus on moral and spiritual issues rather than physical action, tried to do for sports what Walker Percy's *The Moviegoer* did for movies.

At various places in *Independence Day,* Frank Bascombe expresses his preference for real estate transactions over sportswriting, which offers at best, he says, "a harmless way to burn up a few unpromising brain cells." Ford may tacitly endorse that sentiment, but not so eagerly that he'd ever apply for a real estate agent's license. "Given a choice," he said, "I'd still probably want to be a sportswriter."

A native of Jackson, Miss., who grew up in Eudora Welty's neighborhood, Ford naturally used the South as background for his first novel. Since then, he has deliberately avoided the region in his fiction, setting subsequent books in places like Mexico (*The Ultimate Good Luck*) and Montana (*Wildlife, Rock Springs*) as well as New Jersey.

Before he settled in New Orleans five years ago, Ford was called "America's most peripatetic fiction writer." By one interviewer's tally, he and his wife, Kristina, had lived in a dozen places in 22 years, with Chicago; St. Louis; Princeton, N.J.; Missoula, Mont.; and Oxford and Cahoma, Miss., among their many transient postmarks.

According to Ford, the chief reason he has traveled around so much is not to satisfy his own literary wanderlust so much as accommodate the career moves of his wife, an urban planner currently employed by the City of New Orleans. "We're not really migratory," Ford said. "She just goes places for a better job, and I take my work along with me."

For all its dark threads, *Independence Day* is a hopeful novel. Taking inventory of all his misfortunes, Frank Bascombe concludes that he's "still as close to day-to-day happy as I could be. . . . I made one promise to myself, and that was that I'd never complain about my life, and just go on and try to do my best, mistakes and all."

Although Ford distances himself from Frank in other matters, he does admit to sharing his resilient optimism. "Writing a book is an optimistic gesture," he said, "because it presumes that people will have the time to read it and that it will have a good effect on them."

Michiko Kakutani (review date 22 June 1995)

SOURCE: "Afloat in the Turbulence of the American Dream," in *The New York Times,* June 22, 1995, p. 1.

[*In the following review, Kakutani praises Ford's accomplishments in* Independence Day, *asserting that Ford moves beyond Frank's state of mind to create a portrait of middle-class America in the 1980s.*]

Perhaps the highest compliment a sportswriter can bestow on a basketball player is "he's unconscious!"—meaning, he's on one of those rhapsodic shooting streaks where instinct and reflex have combined to produce a blissful state devoid of doubt and hesitation, a state of pure immediacy where touch is everything and every shot falls with perfect, unthinking grace.

It was the fate of Frank Bascombe, the title character of Richard Ford's highly acclaimed 1986 novel, *The Sportswriter,* never to experience that state of grace, which is why he became a writer instead of the athlete his youthful prowess promised. Indeed, Frank emerged in that lucid novel as one of the most self-conscious, self-annotating characters to make his debut in contemporary American fiction since Binx Bolling appeared in *The Moviegoer,* by Walker Percy, in 1961.

Bascombe is back in Mr. Ford's powerful new novel, *Independence Day,* and though some seven years have passed since the death of his oldest son and the subsequent breakup of his marriage, Frank seems worse off than ever, sunk deep into a morass of spiritual lethargy. Although Frank's existential gloom and talent for self-pity can sometimes makes him an irritating (not to mention long-winded) narrator, Mr. Ford expertly opens out his story to create a portrait of middle age and middle-class life that's every bit as resonant and evocative of America in the 1980's as John Updike's last Harry Angstrom novel, *Rabbit at Rest.*

Since he and his wife, Ann, spilt up, we learn, Frank has suffered a kind of breakdown, quit his sportswriting job, bummed around Europe with a young woman, returned home to Haddam, N.J., and stumbled into the real-estate business. Ann, meanwhile, has remarried and moved their two remaining children, 12-year-old Clary and 15-year-old Paul, to Connecticut. All these changes have served only to magnify Frank's sense of detachment, his determination to remain cautious, careful, in control. He has entered what he calls his "Existence Period," a fancy term for going through the motions without really caring or connecting, and letting "matters go as they go."

"I try, in other words," he says, "to keep something finite and acceptably doable on my mind and not disappear. Though it's true that sometimes in the glide, when worries and contingencies are floating off, I sense I myself am afloat and cannot always touch the sides of where I am, nor know what to expect. So that to the musical question 'What's it all about, Alfie?' I'm not sure I'd know the answer."

Frank warns his girlfriend, Sally, that he may well be "beyond affection's grasp." As for his children, he says he wants to be a good father, wants to impart to them some sort of wisdom, but feels exiled from their daily lives. He is especially worried about Paul, who has been arrested for shoplifting, and who has fixated on his dog that was run over by a car almost a decade before. Paul has grown fat and slovenly, and has shaved off most of his hair; he has also taken to barking like a dog.

Frank decides that over an Independence Day weekend, he will take Paul on a father-and-son trip to the Basketball Hall of Fame in Springfield, Mass., and the Baseball Hall of Fame in Cooperstown, N.Y. Along the way, he hopes, he will "work the miracle only a father can work."

"Which is to say," he explains, "if your son begins suddenly to fall at a headlong rate, you must through the agency of love and greater age throw him a line and haul him back."

Like *The Sportswriter, Independence Day* takes place over a couple of days, though Frank's ruminations move freely backward and forward in time, navigating his entire life and the lives of his neighbors and friends. His actual actions may seem banal in the extreme: he shows some houses to a disagreeable couple named the Markhams; he tries to collect rent from another troublesome couple, the McLeods; he checks in with Kari Bemish, his partner in a root-beer-stand operation; he spends an unsettling evening with Sally, and

he sets off on the long drive to his ex-wife's house to pick up Paul.

On the way there, Frank comes close to witnessing a brutal murder in a motel. As in many of Mr. Ford's short stories, such acts of random violence percolate throughout this novel, grisly reminders not only of our own encroaching mortality but also of the innate precariousness of life, the fragility of the bonds of love and order and logic. Frank's co-worker Clair, a young black woman with whom he had an affair, was raped and murdered at a housing site several months before, and Frank worries, too, about the more prosaic dangers of radon, E. coli, hydrocarbons and black ice. Given such all-too-palpable perils, he reasons, why subject oneself to the further dangers of emotional hurt; better, he thinks, to avoid regret and disappointment by expecting and volunteering nothing.

If one were to describe **Independence Day** in outline, it might sound schematic and strained. The title and holiday backdrop baldly underscore the hero's quest for self-reliance, as does his reading of Emerson; and over the Fourth of July weekend, a traumatic event brings this man's relationship with his family into sharp and sudden focus, even as his midlife anxieties are echoed and reinforced by the problems of his friends and clients. Yet happily for the reader, the spindly armature on which **Independence Day** has been so methodically constructed quickly melts into the background, so persuasively does Mr. Ford conjure up the day-to-day texture of Frank Bascombe's life.

Not only does Mr. Ford do a finely nuanced job of delineating Frank's state of mind (his doubts and disillusionments, and his awareness of those doubts and disillusionments), but he also moves beyond Frank, to provide a portrait of a time and a place, of a middle-class community caught on the margins of change and reeling, like Frank, from the wages of loss and disappointment and fear. Mr. Ford uses his consummate ear for dialogue to give us a wonderfully recognizable cast of supporting characters (from the obnoxious yet oddly touching Markhams to the justifiably paranoid Bemish, from Frank's put-upon girlfriend to his troubled, troubling son), and he orchestrates Frank's emotional transactions with them to create a narrative that's as gripping as it is affecting.

With **Independence Day,** Mr. Ford has written a worthy sequel to **The Sportswriter** and galvanized his reputation as one of his generation's most eloquent voices.

R. J. Smith (review date 2 July 1995)

SOURCE: "You Can't Drive Home Again," in *Los Angeles Times Book Review,* July 2, 1995, pp. 1, 7.

[*In the following review, Smith praises Ford's* Independence Day *for features he says Ford's readers have come to expect—the mimetic dialogue and telling detail—but points out that "the book can be a hefty sulk."*]

A central dread of Frank Bascombe's life in Richard Ford's new novel, *Independence Day,* is that his ex-wife has married an architect. Bascombe is a realtor, someone who by his own description sells dreams. But his ex has left him for somebody who builds them, and somehow manages to bring those dreams to life. The question of what makes a house a home, and a group of people a family, animates Ford's novel.

Bascombe goes on an air-conditioned drive across New England, in a sense looking for the architect who might animate his own life. It's a parody of the journey to knowledge— Bascombe is a pilgrim more lost than he knows on his way to the shrine. Bascombe is on an idiot mission over the Independence Day weekend of 1988, driving with his son and trying to hit as many halls of fame as they can in 48 hours. Along the way, he thinks he'll: save his son from the life of crime he fears is ahead by reading Emerson to him; rendezvous with his girlfriend; and maybe get back together with his wife. His Ford Crown Victoria becomes his secret Mayflower on his voyage into the soul of independence. But instead, Bascombe gets a royal comeuppance, ends up crying three times in less than 24 hours and has to take his son to the emergency room.

Independence Day picks up five years after Ford's celebrated 1986 novel, *The Sportswriter.* Bascombe is still living in Haddam, the New Jersey commuter town where he feels at home in his cheerful invisibility. By having Bascombe end up a sportswriter after a promising start as a fiction writer in the earlier book, Ford hit an ominous bass-chord of failure. (You could have made a drinking game out of how frequently Ford homed in on that chord in the earlier novel—every time somebody asks Frank why he doesn't write short stories any more, the reader downs a shot. Bascombe himself would have liked that.) And yet Ford here has extended the feat, finding a chord resonating even lower than the last one. Bascombe has quit his unnamed sports magazine and become a real estate agent. And if the intended fall, from man of letters to man of ledgers, is meant to be calamitous, it is also oddly rich with possibility—rarely has real estate seemed so tethered to the very mysteries of life.

Bascombe is knee-deep in what he calls the Existence Period, an epoch lodged between the Pleistocene and the Great Beyond. He is existing but hardly more, shutting out those who get too close, effortlessly mangling the lessons of his life, rotting from the inside out. "When you're young your opponent is the future," he offers, "but when you're not young, your opponent's the past and all you've done in it, and the problem of getting away from it." Forward to the deep freeze.

Where the Bascombe of *The Sportswriter* would at times shriek and squeal over what was slipping away—his wife, youth, self-esteem; he imagined himself translucent, walking the streets of Haddam—now the middle-aged realtor tries to focus on the good he imagines he's doing setting people up in new homes. Failing that, he concentrates on the fixed mortgage rates. He's no happier, but he's resigned to disappearing, and that steadies his voice.

Fumbling his own life choices while fancying he's helping strangers with theirs, Bascombe himself has only gotten more pathetic in the years since he gave up sportswriting. When his ex-wife moved out of Haddam, Bascombe sold his home, bought hers and moved in. He has an intricate definition of "home" he's trying to sell himself; by owning hers, he thinks, he is creating a fresh life with her. He'd like nothing more than to start all over again with his wife.

As Bascombe and his son drive the turnpikes and side streets, an awful lot of architectural detail is described along the way. Ford looks attentively at the dormers and mullions, the redwood decks and picket fences, only then to look beyond appearances. Ford explores the idea of what "home" means to people, and how finding a home isn't nearly the same as finding a place for yourself in the world. The way Bascombe sees it, maybe it all comes down to a business motto he quotes, that selling real estate is the "True American profession coping hands-on with the fundamental spatial experience of life: more people, less space, fewer choices." That's a lesson from the late-80s market, but it finds its home in this painful novel about reconciling yourself to life's final offer.

At the end, the tour is a mess. In a batting cage outside the Baseball Hall of Fame . . . Bascombe's son intentionally steps into a fastball and winds up with a detached retina. Yet it's his father who seems struck by something possibly more violent, a shard of responsibility that he suddenly can't shut out any longer. Maybe it will stick and maybe not; but he seems to have navigated an amicable break with his wife, and perhaps built a new bridge to his son. He's cut a fresher start from himself than he managed at the end of *The Sportswriter.* You can bet on another book yet, as Bascombe grows older and snaps up the estate left by Updike's Harry Angstrom. He's ready to move in.

Independence Day is an easy novel to inhabit, a harder one to love. Bascombe lives deeply within shallow confines; Ford's observations are broader than they are deep. Bascombe's talk on the fly, racing past like the scenery on the Yankee Expressway, is invariably sharper and closer to heart than the long ruminations that dapple the book. Ford ribbons a bittersweet tone with Bascombe's biting sarcasm— the longer Ford writes, the funnier his fiction gets. Still the book can be a hefty sulk. The place Bascombe shared with his wife is never just his home, it's "my old once-happily married house." Parked before that address, Bascombe asks himself, "And yet and yet, do I sense, as I sit here, a melancholy?" After some 450 pages of the Crayola spectrum of melancholia, you can just bet the mortgage he does.

The accomplishments here are many and familiar to Ford's readers. There is the exquisitely mimetic dialogue, his ease with a telling detail, and the life found at the world's extremities. Ford makes the Vince Lombardi Rest Area on the New Jersey Turnpike seem like a world unto itself (or is it hell on earth?). But maybe there's no greater proof of skill than how he makes Bascombe's base elements seem like universal essences. By the end of the book, the realtor's self-pity, his fear that any break in the day's routine could lead to unspeakable dread he'll never recover from, even his urge to fish with his son, may well seem like the American experience, rather than the circumscribed experience of the white suburban male. Maybe nobody more than a provided-for white guy could be so certain that his crises were those of the world.

Merle Rubin (review date 3 July 1995)

SOURCE: "Frank Bascombe Awakes to Lessons of Independence," in *The Christian Science Monitor,* July 3, 1995, p. 13.

[*In the following review, Rubin praises Ford's* Independence Day *as "a fully realized portrait of modern American life as filtered through the mind and heart of a unique, yet typical American man."*]

It's the early summer of 1988, year of the Dukakis-Bush presidential election and five years since we've last heard from Frank Bascombe, the protagonist of Richard Ford's memorable novel *The Sportswriter.*

Frank, who started out as an aspiring novelist with a book of short stories to his credit, then opted for journalism and became a sportswriter, has recently changed careers again [in *Independence Day*]. He is now a realtor. Forty-four years old, divorced, still living in Haddam, New Jersey, he feels he is entering a new, rather cheerless, phase of his life, which he calls his "existence period:" a time when unrealistic dreams have been given up and clear-eyed coping begins.

Frank is looking forward to the coming Fourth of July holiday. He plans to take his son, an increasingly troublesome teenager, on a trip to the basketball and baseball Halls of Fame in the hope that the excursion will be a chance to communicate with the boy. Armed with a copy of Emerson's "Self-Reliance," he imagines he will find a way to teach his son the lesson of independence.

Frank's own "independence" has been brought home to him not by his divorce from his wife, Ann, but by Ann's subsequent remarriage and move to Connecticut. Prior to this unwelcome wake-up call, Frank had somehow managed to kid himself that they were still the same two people "only set in different equipoise: same planets, different orbits, same solar system. . . . My life was (and to some extent still is) played out on a stage in which she's continually in the audience (whether she's paying attention or not)." By removing herself and their two children to her new husband's home in Connecticut, Ann has dismembered "the entire illusion . . . leaving me with only faint, worn-out costumes to play myself with."

The narrator, if not quite the hero, of his own story, Frank wryly yet seriously portrays his current life in sharply-observed detail, from the workings of the real estate business to the fluctuations of his skittish relationship with a woman he's not sure he loves. And, it is Richard Ford's great gift as a novelist that makes the details matter: first, in the way that they are used to create a profoundly convincing picture of particular people at a particular time and place; second, in the way that even seemingly trivial occurrences, words, gestures are shown to have significance.

Frank's career in real estate, for example, bears some relation to his moral and political beliefs. He likes to think of himself as someone who helps people find homes they can afford. He owns rental property in the town's black section and conscientiously keeps it in top-notch repair. He's also helped a redneck entrepreneur finance his birch-beer stand in the countryside. One of the few remaining Democrats in a town growing ever more Republican, Frank entertains some hope that Dukakis (whom he finds uninspiring) will defeat Bush (whom he finds even more so).

In the weeks leading up to Independence Day, however, Frank's patience is being sorely tried by an extremely indecisive, hard-to-please couple from Vermont, who find fault with every house he shows them. The Markhams are in the sad, but all-too-common position of being unable to afford the kind of house they would like. Frank perceives his job as getting them to face up to reality and take the plunge—much as he has embraced the diminishing dreams of his "existence period."

Frank's undeclared war of attrition with the Markhams, however, is pushed aside by a family crisis involving his ever-more-difficult son. Despite his revulsion for the boy's buzz-saw haircut, filthy clothes, disturbing pranks, and fresh tattoo, Frank has a sneaking affection for someone who, like Frank himself, hates "Mommy's new husband." But his son is in deeper trouble than Frank first is willing to understand.

An assiduous and accomplished practitioner of contemporary realism, Richard Ford is at the top of his form, brilliantly and believably evoking all the social, psychological, and moral nuances of Frank Bascombe's world. (Speaking as someone not usually interested in sports or real estate, I can attest to the fact that both fields seemed quite fascinating as depicted here.)

Ending on a note of cautious, hard-earned optimism, *Independence Day* is a fully realized portrait of modern American life as filtered through the mind and heart of a unique, yet typical American man.

Guy Lawson (review date 10 July 1995)

SOURCE: "Teenage Wasteland," in *Maclean's,* July 10, 1995, pp. 42-3.

[*In the following excerpt, Lawson compares and contrasts the adolescent angst suffered by Paul in Ford's* Independence Day *to that of Chappie in Russell Banks's* Rule of the Bone *and discusses the literary merits of each work.*]

There isn't a name for them yet—those early teen years of 14 and 15 when a boy's voice drops, he grows two shoe sizes every six months and he begins to see and judge the world through his own eyes. "An ass-o-lescent" is how Frank Bascombe, the narrator of Richard Ford's latest novel, *Independence Day,* describes his 15-year-old son, Paul. Chappie, the plain-speaking and compelling 14 year old narrator of Russell Banks's *Rule of the Bone,* doesn't have a word for his stage of life, and he doesn't have a witty father to mint one for him. Chappie doesn't have a father at all.

That is just one of the contrasts between these very fine, very different new works of American fiction. The stories of two white man-boys, the kind one might see hanging out at a mall on a school-day afternoon, sharply illustrate the vast and growing divide between rich and poor, haves and have-nots. *Independence Day,* the sequel to Ford's much-praised *The Sportswriter,* finds Frank Bascombe, a divorced, 44-year-old former short story writer and sports journalist, selling real estate in a posh New Jersey town. It's the Fourth of July weekend in 1988, and Bascombe is emerging from what he says is his "Existence Period," a kind of mid-life crisis, a time of uncertain desire and lost love and regret, when treading water is the most that can be hoped for.

It is his son, Paul, a troubled, pudgy rich kid living with his mother and stepfather in a mansion in Connecticut, who seems to be drowning. Busted for shoplifting three boxes of extra-large condoms, Paul has his hair cut "in some new, dopey, skint-sided, buzzed-up way" and sports a tattoo that says "insect" on the inside of his right wrist. "In the next century," Paul tells his father, "we're all going to be enslaved by the insects that survived this century's pesticides. With this I ac-

knowledge being in a band of maladapted creatures whose time is coming to a close."

Driving up to spend the Independence Day weekend touring the baseball and basketball halls of fame with his son, Bascombe tells himself that at least Paul does not suffer from what he calls "the big three:" he does not play with fire, wet his bed or torture animals. But Bascombe finds a dead bird at the gate of Paul's stepfather's mansion and knows instantly that it is his son's handiwork. Paul does torture animals.

Paul also reads *The New Yorker,* barks like a dog from time to time, and asks his father questions such as "Do you think I'm shallow?" When Paul steals one of his stepfather's Mercedes and crashes it, no charges are brought. The incident is hushed up, consequences avoided. Paul has suffered the pain of a brother's death and his parents' subsequent divorce. But despite his strong self-destructive streak, Paul has second chances in life and is loved by his mother and father.

In Russell Banks's *Rule of the Bone,* 14-year-old Chappie, like Paul, has an attention-grabbing hairdo—a Mohawk cut. He also has a pierced nostril and ears. Chappie shoplifts useless goods, too—in his case, "a silky green nightgown" from a lingerie store. In the course of the novel, Chappie gets a tattoo on the inside of his left forearm. But getting his tattoo—a pirate's crossed bones without the skull—is not an ersatz nihilistic gesture like Paul's. It is a way of remembering the innocence of his childhood, the time when his grandmother read *Peter Pan* to him, and of constructing his new identity as "the Bone," as he comes to call himself.

Chappie, or Bone, doesn't get second or third chances in life, or much in the way of love. Abandoned as a baby by his father, he lives in a trailer with his mother and stepfather, Ken, "basically a Nazi with a drinking problem plus a few others." He lives there, that is, until he is kicked out of the trailer for stealing his mother's rare coin collection.

Homeless and suffering, he says, from "wicked low self-esteem," Chappie sets out into the world with nothing but his wits. . . .

In one of Banks's earlier works, *The Sweet Hereafter,* a character says, "In my lifetime something terrible happened that took our children away from us. I don't know if it was the Vietnam War, or the sexual colonization of kids by industry, or drugs, or TV or divorce, or what the hell it was: I don't know which are causes and which are effects; but the children are gone, that I know." In a post-industrial, postmodern, pre-nothing culture, that is the sentiment that underlies Banks's *Rule of the Bone* and Ford's *Independence Day.*

Still, despite the superficial similarities, there is an enormous gap between Paul's and Chappie's lives. Middle-class Paul hurts himself to get his divorced parents' attention; rejected by his family, Chappie seriously contemplates, then nearly commits, suicide. When Paul steals a car he is protected; Chappie, who steals a pickup truck, would be sent to one of the boot camps popular with politicians these days to have the spirit beaten out of him if he were caught.

Taken separately, *Independence Day*—cracking with insights into everything from what to look for when buying a house to the special ring of hell reserved for divorced spouses who still love each other—is one of the year's best novels. *Rule of the Bone* is a work of great humanity and empathy, and Chappie is a character who will stay vividly lodged in the memory. . . .

Taken together, *Independence Day* and *Rule of the Bone* prove that growing up in America is not getting any easier.

Elizabeth Hardwick (essay date 10 August 1995)

SOURCE: "Reckless People," in *The New York Review of Books,* Vol. XLII, No. 13, August 10, 1995, pp. 11-14.

[*In the following essay, Hardwick praises Ford for his talent as a storyteller, tracing his use of lavish detail, strong characterization, and sense of time and place throughout his work.*]

From the stories in Richard Ford's collection *Rock Springs:* "This was not going to be a good day in Bobby's life, that was clear, because he was headed to jail. He had written several bad checks, and before he could be sentenced for that he had robbed a convenience store with a pistol—completely gone off his mind." Bobby's ex-wife is giving him his last breakfast and the man she is now living with is telling the story, with some disgruntlement (**"Sweethearts"**).

In the title story, the narrator, Earl, with his daughter, Cheryl, her dog, Little Duke, and Earl's girlfriend, Edna, are driving through Wyoming in a stolen car.

> I'd gotten us a good car, a cranberry Mercedes I'd stolen out of an opthamologist's lot in Whitefish, Montana. I stole it because I thought it would be comfortable over a long haul, because I thought it got good mileage, which it didn't, and because I'd never had a good car in my life.

The car develops trouble in the oil line and they have to abandon it in the woods. Somehow the little group gets to a Ramada Inn, and after a bit of food and lovemaking Edna accepts Earl's offer of a bus ticket and takes off.

There he is, Earl, with Cheryl, the dog, and no car. They might as well be dead, as immobile as the stone urns for geraniums

outside the inn. In the dark of night in the parking lot: "I walked over to a car, a Pontiac with Ohio tags, one of the ones with bundles and suitcases strapped to the top and a lot more in the trunk, by the way it was riding." Standing beside the car, Earl's inner soliloquy runs:

> What would you think a man was doing if you saw him in the middle of the night looking in the windows of cars in the parking lot of the Ramada Inn? Would you think he was trying to get his head cleared? Would you think he was trying to get ready for a day when trouble would come down on him? Would you think his girlfriend was leaving him? Would you think he had a daughter? Would you think he was anybody like you?

Another story, **"Optimists,"** begins: "All of this I am about to tell happened when I was only fifteen years old, in 1959, the year my parents were divorced, the year when my father killed a man and went to prison for it, the year I left home and school, told a lie about my age to fool the Army, and then did not come back." The father was working in the railroad yards when a hobo tried to jump off a train and was cut into three pieces. The father comes home ashen and trembling from the horrible accident he has seen. At home some recent acquaintances of his wife are playing cards. The visitor, more or less a stranger to the father, turns out to work for the Red Cross. He interrupts with a pedantic interrogation about tourniquets, resuscitation, all the while insisting that technically, as it were, the hobo didn't have to die if the father had acted properly.

In a rage of grief and the presumption of the lecture, the father hits the man, and the blow kills him. He goes to prison, comes out in a state of deterioration, begins drinking and brawling, and disappears, off somewhere. The years pass and one day the son sees his mother with a strange man shopping for groceries at a mall. The son and mother talk briefly, but with a good deal of inchoate affection. And that is more or less it. "And she bent down and kissed my cheek through the open window and touched my face with both her hands, held me for a moment that seemed like a long time before she turned away, finally, and left me there alone."

The smooth and confident use of the first person narration in these brilliant stories is especially remarkable when they are told by petty thieves, the stranded and delinquent. Here the "I" is not remembering or recasting, but living in the pure present, in the misbegotten events of the day. The focus is of such directness, the glare of reality so bright, that the shadow of the manipulating author does not fall inadvertently on the deputed "I"—who is in no way a creature of literary sensibility. The tone and rhythm of the composition, the feat of being inside the minds, or the heads, as they make their deplorable decisions and connections, infuse the pages with a kind of tolerance for false hope and felony and rotten luck.

The Montana landscape in *Rock Springs* is empty and beautiful and lonely. The men do whatever kind of work turns up and are always being laid off. There is nothing but hunting and fishing, sex, and drinking and fighting. Wives go off to Seattle or Spokane, just for a change. Young girls and not-so-young men turn up in the taverns and get into a lot of trouble for themselves and others. So your wife has taken off with a groom from the dog track and a couple of huge, rough women turn up at your door with a deer gruesomely slain lying in their pickup; and you will be glad for their knock, for the company, which will be a mistake. Recklessness is the mode of life, but what the stories seem to be saying is that people are not always as bad as what they do, something like that. No judgment is solicited, and yet the desperation and folly arouse pity, the pity that everywhere sends girlfriends, mothers and children, grandparents and old pals trundling out to the prisons for visiting hours.

In the novel *Wildlife,* a son is the observer of the sudden defections and panics of his parents. "In the fall of 1960, when I was sixteen and my father was for a time not working, my mother met a man named Warren Miller and fell in love with him." The tactful, muted eloquence of the tone is a sort of balance for the unstable inner and natural landscape. It is Great Falls, Montana, and the forest fires of summer are still smoking and glowing in the autumn sky. The parents have lived and been to college in Washington state and have come to Montana from Idaho, thinking money could be made from the oil boom. But prosperity does not extend itself to them and so the father works at the airbase for two days a week and otherwise as a golf pro at the local country club. He is rudely laid off at the club because of a false accusation. In Ford's fiction the West, with its fabled openness under the big sky and all that, is a place of emotional collapse from forced or glumly accepted idleness, an invitation to dangerous brooding over the whiskey bottle. After such an acute brooding and character upheaval the father somehow gets a chance to save his soul, or self-image, by being allowed to take a place with the knowledgeable firefighters in the forest, although he has no experience beyond the flaming egos on the golf course.

The mother is alone for three days. She and the son visit the voracious Warren Miller, a man with a limp and soon to die of a "lengthy illness," a man with lots of money, grain elevators, and other assets, and a wife who has gone off somewhere, a man with a house. In the house the mother and the son spend the night after the older folks have been drinking and dancing. The unresisting mother is seduced and on the spot decides to leave her husband and set herself up in a rented flat, there to accommodate what she foolishly believes will be a better life with Warren Miller. Shifts in direction, improvisations, sleepwalking into calamitous consequence seem to be in this fiction part of the effect the Western states

have upon the mind. The characters are still pulling the wagon across the frontier, looking for a place to settle.

The father comes down from the burning hills to meet his domestic surprise. In a fury ignited by betrayal and alcohol, he picks up a can of gasoline at the local pump and, thinking his wife is inside, sets fire to Miller's house; the fire is not serious and no charges are filed. Miller indeed fled the scene with another woman in tow, not the wife. After some years of wandering, the mother returns to Great Falls, and the son reflects that something has died between them but something remained. "We survived it." A benign accent in the style of narration covers *Wildlife* in a forgiving mist. The quiet pacing through the threat of the landscape and the predatory challenge of experience is a compromise, the rain falling on the blackened trees.

Before he went West, so to speak, in his stories and in the novel *Wildlife,* Richard Ford had published three books of fiction: *A Piece of My Heart, The Ultimate Good Luck,* and *The Sportswriter. A Piece of My Heart,* the first, is an elaborate, stylistically ambitious, and complex novel, somewhat in the Southern Gothic vein. The setting is Mississippi and there are two old people in their decayed mansion, the man a relentlessly loquacious, cursing, shrewd old fellow. The estate is connected by boat to an island where people from town pay to hunt duck and for the turkey shoot in season. Two young men, each of whom has an alternating section of the book, come to the spread. One is a Columbia graduate enrolled in the University of Chicago Law School; he's in a slump and his girlfriend thinks that, since he is a native Mississippian, he might pull himself together by a spell at the estate, owned by a relation of hers. This character, perhaps an echo of Faulkner's Quentin Compson, is not entirely successful, owing to the mingled yarn in the knit of his rather far-flung situation.

The other young man, named Robard, might be a character in one of the stories in *Rock Springs.* His fate is powerfully and alarmingly conceived in the intense thicket of the action. Robard wakes up in the dark of early morning, looks at his wife peacefully sleeping, and, although he has gentle feelings for her, takes off without leaving a word. His journey, his hardscrabble trek to the swamp of sex, has come about from a curious, oblique feeling of obligation to experience. Some years before, Robard had picked up a young woman on the road when her car broke down. They ended up in a motor court for a raw, lascivious night or two, and for Robard that was the end of it, but not for her, Beuna by name. Beuna is a seriously dreadful encounter, a sex fiend, a sort of barnyard creature of befoulment—illustrating, if such is the need, the joke of the assertion that the pornographic imagination and desires arise from books and movies rather than from the somehow inevitable contents of the human mind.

Time has passed and Beuna is married to W. W., a broken-down bush league ballplayer and a deputy sheriff. Beuna does not find much satisfaction in W. W., and since she knows where Robard lives she begins to send messages to him and to make disturbing phone calls, delivered with a panting absolute demand for a reunion. Robard finally takes off to meet her. His emotions are murky and guarded and he means to return. Beuna's insistence over the weeks and months gives Robard the sense that something has entered his life he can't altogether deny. He is broke and to complete his destiny he takes a job at the estate, acting as a guard on the island to keep poachers away.

His true "business," as he calls it, is to go into town in the evening to find Beuna. They meet and bed down in a scabby rent-a-cabin place, where she says the proprietor wouldn't care if you took a "goddamn sheep in here." For the tryst, Beuna has brought a plastic bag of excrement. There is a merciful blackout of the subsequent congress, but at last it is the cue for Robard to climb out of the pit of Eros, find his truck, and get back to the island. W. W. is nosing after him in his Plymouth, shotgun at the ready. Almost free of the pursuing Furies Robard meets his death, his release, when he is shot as a poacher by a boy who is taking his place as guard on the island.

The backcountry landscape, the waters of the river at night, the woods, the sullen towns are rendered with a tireless fluency. As a principal in a sordid tangle of compulsion, Robard, nevertheless, is conceived in tragic terms and is the most touching of Richard Ford's doom-stricken young men, rushing to certain destruction, to Beuna, who, by the unfortunate meeting on the road, has become "a piece of my heart."

Ford's second novel, *The Ultimate Good Luck,* is another trip altogether, this time to Mexico, around Oaxaca. It is a steamy ride through the south of the border labyrinth, with characters who are defined by situation, plot, intrigue, and denouement. They have a certain brittleness as they act out their roles; and there is a cinema noir aspect to the landscape of drug smuggling, prisons, bribery, disappearances, threats of murder, and actual murder. Quinn, a Vietnam vet, and his mistress or whatever, Rae, are engaged in an effort to get Rae's brother, Sonny, out of the hell of a Mexican prison.

Sonny has been picked up for drug smuggling and his escape or release is to be accomplished by bribery, mysterious connections, and enigmatic maneuvers under the direction of a shadowy lawyer named Bernhardt, who, along the way, is murdered for his efforts in the matter or perhaps for some other malfeasance. Also there is a character, a "spade," to use the locution of the drug world, named Deals. Deals is out to get Sonny since, as a partner, he believes Sonny has skimmed the profits of one of their big drug exchanges. He also thinks Sonny wants to be in jail to escape the serious

retribution he, Deals, has in mind. The language is rich, there is, or so it seems, a deep saturation in the countryside, the bars, the alleys, the prison, the midnight world. No one is sympathetic; there's not much to be said for Quinn, and Rae, embarked on her act of charitable rescue, is stoned most of the time. Sonny is not an object of moral concern since he is stupid, greedy, and a natural loser. *The Ultimate Good Luck* has a curious sheen of high glamour as a genuinely imaginative example of a genre, if that is the proper word for this visit to the underworld.

The Sportswriter followed the first two novels and preceded the Western stories and the novel *Wildlife.* Frank Bascombe is the sportswriter, living by choice in Haddam, New Jersey, a pleasant suburban town of moderate physical and social dimensions, suitable to Bascombe's moderate expectations from life. He has published a book of stories which did moderately well, started and abandoned a novel, and is moderately content to be something of an oddity in the arts, where an early kiss from the Muse is likely to leave a lifelong discoloration on the cheek. He is not a failed writer but one who fails to write another fiction or poem. What is to prevent your writing, dear? the forlorn wife in George Gissing's *New Grub Street* asks of her miserable husband trapped in the period of the three decker novel. Bascombe's answer would have been a cheerful: I prefer not to.

But even Bascombe's cheerfulness is moderated by the dark wings of melancholy, after the death of his son Ralph, and the divorce from his wife, here called X. The most remarkable aspect of this engaging character is his remove from paranoia, the national and literary mode of the time. Bascombe is offered a job on a well-known sports magazine, published in New York, to which he chooses to commute. Needless to say he does not take sports or sportswriting with undue seriousness.

> I make my other calls snappy—one is to an athletic shoe designer in Denver for a "Sports Chek" round-up box I'm pulling together on foot injuries. . . . Another call is to a Carmelite nun in Fayetteville, West Virginia, who is trying to run in the Boston Marathon. Once a polio victim, she is facing an uphill credentials fight in her quest to compete, and I'm glad to put a plug in for her in our "Achievers" column.

The scene shifts, as it often does in this work crowded with incidents and people met along the way, shifts to a trip to Detroit to interview Herb Wallagher, an ex-lineman who lost his legs in a ski-boat accident and is now in a wheelchair. The interview is not profitable, even though the sportswriter tries to rouse Herb about the game of football: "But I'd still think it had some lessons to teach to the people who played it. Perseverance. Team work. Comradeship. That kind of thing." To which, Herb replies: "Forget all that crap, Frank."

The trip to Detroit is made with Vicki, cute and with far greater common sense than Bascombe, she being a nurse in the local hospital. She talks about a "C-liver terminal, already way into uremia when he admitted, which is not *that* bad cause it usually starts 'em dreamin about their pasts and off their current problem." Scenes and characters float into this suburban novel on the wide stream of Bascombe's obstinate receptiveness. The Divorced Men's Club, which Bascombe attends, brings him into an encounter with poor Walter Luckett, whose wife has taken off to Bimini with a man named Eddie Pitcock. Walter has a secret he wants to share. After a few drinks with a Wall Street colleague, he finds himself going to bed with him, not once but again and again in the fellow's New York apartment. Walter is troubled and as naive as a country-boy sailor on his first shore leave in Naples or some such place. In what could be called a sentimental confusion, for that is his nature, he commits suicide one night.

One of the most brilliant scenes is Bascombe's Easter Sunday visit with Vicki's family. Her father, a turnpike toll-taker, has somehow gotten an old Chrysler into his small, wet basement and is restoring it fin by fin, with full attention to broken and rusted chrome. Her brother, Cade, a boat mechanic, is on the wait list at the Police Academy. Cade has already "developed a flateyed officer's uninterest for the peculiarities of his fellow man." Lynette, the father's second wife, is working on the crisis line at the Catholic church. She has "transformed her dining room into a hot little jewel box, crystal candle chandelier, best silver and linens laid" for "the pallid lamb congealed and hard as a wood chip and the . . . peas and broccoli flower alongside it cold as Christmas." In the midst of all this, Bascombe's thought is: "what strange good luck to be reckoned among these people like a relative welcome from Peoria."

The Sportswriter is a sophisticated book that celebrates life as it comes and speaks in its voice, often with devastating humor, and a hypnotic sinking into every spot of the turf. Easter Sunday: "the optimist's holiday, the holiday with the suburbs in mind" and the sermon about the Resurrection: "Well now, let's us just hunker down to a real miracle, while we're putting two and two together . . . let's just let plasma physics and bubble chambers and quarks try to explain *this* one." The vitality of the novel lies in the freedom and expressiveness of this first-person excursion through New Jersey, Detroit, the Berkshires, and the bearable shambles of Bascombe's life.

Independence Day, Richard Ford's new novel, returns to Frank Bascombe. *Rabbit Redux*?—not quite. Bascombe is an upscale ruminant, now in his forties, with opinions about everything, and Emerson's "Self-Reliance" in the glove com-

partment. There is no outstanding typicality in him; instead he has the mysteriousness of the agreeable, nice person, harder to describe than the rake, the miser, or the snob. As a professional, or a working man, his resume is unsteady—short-story writer, sportswriter, and now a "realtor." The wobbly nature of Bascombe's status makes him a creditable collector; nothing need be rejected, not the trash of the road signs, clichés produced with a ring of discovery, the program on TV, the decor of the Sleepy Hollow Motel on Route 1, or the "fanlights, columned entries and Romany fluting" of the houses on the better streets.

Selling real estate is a good way to get about town, but a poor way to reach "closure." The business is a serial plot of indignities—tune in tomorrow. Joe and Phyllis Markham have decided to get out of their hand-built house in Vermont, "with cantilevered cathedral ceilings and a hand-laid hearth and chimney, using stones off the place," to try a suburban New Jersey life style and better schools for their daughter. They "have looked at forty-five houses—dragging more and more grimly down from . . . Vermont." The fearsome negotiations, or lack of them, provide a miserably comic underpinning to Bascombe's days and nights.

The other block of the story is a hazardous trip, a Fourth of July journey with his son, Paul, to the Basketball Hall of Fame in Springfield, Massachusetts, and the Baseball Hall of Fame in Cooperstown, New York, where they stay in The Deerslayer Lodge. Paul is a thoroughly complicated and unpredictable young man of fifteen. He has stolen boxes of condoms, for which he had no use, from a pharmacy; he barks like a dog in memory of his dead dog and probably in memory of his dead brother, Ralph. Underneath his basket of misdemeanors and off-tone noises, he is a gentle teen-ager and will probably come to resemble his father's more acceptable waywardness. At the Baseball Hall of Fame, Paul seriously damages an eye in the batter's cage, a tourist attraction that allows one to seem to swat a ball like Babe Ruth. His mother, now remarried to a rich architect, comes up in a helicopter and takes him to New Haven for surgery.

There are many other diversions: Sally, Bascombe's girlfriend, the renters of a house he owns, old friends, and new passersby. And as always with Richard Ford, the sense of place, towns, houses, highways is luminous in lavish, observed detail.

> I drive windingly out Montmorency Road into
> Haddam horse country—our little Lexington—where
> fences are long, white and orthogonal, pastures wide
> and sloping, and roads . . . slip across shaded, rocky
> rills via wooden bridges and through the quaking
> aspens back to rich men's domiciles snugged deep in
> summer foliage. . . . and here, wedges of old-growth
> hardwoods still loom, trees that saw Revolutionary

armies rumble past, heard the bugles, shouts and defiance cries of earlier Americans in their freedom
swivet, and beneath which now tawny-haired heir-
esses in jodhpurs stroll to the paddock with a mind
for a noon ride alone.

In passing it might be remarked that Ford is the first, if memory
serves, to give full recognition to the totemic power in American life of the telephone and the message service. At one
point he pauses at the Vince Lombardi Rest Area, across from
the Giants Stadium, to check his messages. There are ten of
them, listed with content, among them obscenities from Joe
Markham, client. Often Bascombe will interrupt the plot to
make a dreamy call to a former lover, who may not immediately place him or may be cooking dinner. In *The Sportswriter* the call is to Selma, a friend from his spell as a teacher
at Berkshire College. In the present novel, he gets on the line
to Cathy, a medical student he spent time with in France a
few years back. He's hoping for "a few moments' out of context, ad hominem, pro-bono phone 'treatment.'" Ring, ring,
ring, click, click, click, and the machine answers: "Hi. This is
Cathy and Steve's answering mechanism. We're not home
now. Really. I promise." In Frank Bascombe's world a good
deal of the information necessary to move forward is given
over the phone.

(Recently, in the O. J. Simpson trial, the prosecution, following week after wearying week, month after month building
its beaver dam of circumstantial particulars, spent quite a lot
of time with the record of O. J.'s car phone around the time
projected for the murders. The record keeper for the phone
company dutifully went down the list, the purpose seeming
to be that the number of busy signals and no answers might
slip into the mind of the jurors as yet another twig forming
the rage that led to double homicide. No answer motivation.)

Independence Day, if you're taking measurements like the
nurse in a doctor's office, might be judged longer than it need
be. But longer for whom? Every rumination, each flash of
magical dialogue or unexpected mile on the road with a stop
at the pay phone, is a wild surprise tossed off as if it were just
a bit of cigarette ash by Richard Ford's profligate imagination. *The Sportswriter* and *Independence Day* are comedies—not farces, but realistic, good natured adventures,
sunny, yes, except when the rain it raineth everyday. The
new work, *Independence Day,* is the confirmation of a talent as strong and varied as American fiction has to offer.

Richard Ford with Dinitia Smith (interview date 22 August 1995)

SOURCE: "A Nomad's Ode to Soffit and Siding," in *The
New York Times,* August 22, 1995, pp. C13, C17.

*[In the following interview, Smith talks to Ford about his
life, his career, and his novel* Independence Day.*]*

After a lifetime of itinerancy, living in 9 states and some 14
homes, the novelist Richard Ford knows the language of real
estate by heart. "I try to be someone upon whom nothing is
lost," he said the other day in his present hometown, New
Orleans, borrowing a phrase from Henry James.

"Richard watches everything," said his wife, Kristina.

In *Independence Day,* his sixth work of fiction, Mr. Ford has
tapped into the imagination of his contemporaries in their
late 40's and early 50's who are obsessed with real estate and
the buying and selling of houses. It is a generation for whom
real estate has become a metaphor for human fulfillment.

He takes Frank Bascombe, the main character from his third
novel, *The Sportswriter,* and transposes him to another time,
about five years later, where, having failed in his career as a
writer, he is now selling real estate in Haddam, N.J., a fictional town that bears many similarities to Princeton.

Frank, Charles Johnson wrote in *The New York Times Book
Review,* is "a character we know as well as we know our next-
door neighbors. Frank Bascombe has earned himself a place
beside Willy Loman and Harry Angstrom in our literary landscape."

He is a survivor of the 1960's and all its enthusiasms. "Holding the line on the life we promised ourselves in the 60's is
getting hard as hell," Frank muses. In the space of four days
over a Fourth of July weekend, he carries on a love affair,
longs for his ex-wife and drives his son—a 13-year-old who
has been arrested for shoplifting condoms and has taken to
barking like a dog in memory of a dead pet—on a trip to the
Baseball Hall of Fame in Cooperstown, N.Y. He also tries to
sell a house to an unhappy couple, the Markhams. He has
shown them 45, none of them "right." Frank is a forgiving
man with a saintly patience.

Mr. Ford makes virtual poetry out of real-estate nomencla-
ture in *Independence Day*: "1,900 sq. ft. including garage,"
he writes, in a kind of song, "three-bedroom, two-bath, ex-
pandable, no fplc." The words "unsolvable structural enigmas, cast-iron piping with suspicions of lead" take on a gently
ominous tone; "grounded wall sockets" and "Ten-four on a
30-year fixed, plus a point, plus an application fee," have a
kind of melody. He meditates lovingly on "belvedere," "oriel,"
"aluminum flashing" and "soffit vent." For Mr. Ford, these
are words you can roll your tongue around and relish.

Mr. Ford is 51, tall, with longish, straight, thin gray hair,
pale blue eyes and a high domed forehead. At the moment,
he owns a town house here with an interior courtyard and a

gallery overlooking Bourbon Street; sometimes he works in a room that was part of the residence's old slave quarters. He also owns a bungalow in Montana, where his 1988 collection of short stories, ***Rock Springs,*** was set. A native Mississippian, he leases a big white plantation house in the Mississippi Delta as well so he can stay close to his roots.

"Whenever we go to a town," said Mrs. Ford, a 40-year-old urban planner and former model, "Richard really likes to go to the real estate office. We've lived in so many places that our best friends are Realtors."

Mrs. Ford is executive director of the New Orleans City Planning Commission. "Her interests made it seem to me that the business of how land is used is a fit subject for one's concerns," Mr. Ford said.

"Some people think of real estate salesmen as sleazeballs and shysters," he went on. "A profession in which a human being finds shelter for others is in fact important. Real estate agents are in the business of helping us all find ways to realize our dreams."

"I'm also sensitive to the fact that these are desperate human situations," he added. "If you have a balloon mortgage, it's a nightmare!"

At one point in Mr. Ford's book, Frank Bascombe observes, "You don't sell a house to somebody, you sell a life."

It was in 1991, when he had just finished two novellas, that Mr. Ford realized from his notebooks that Frank was speaking to him again. "I was on the sniff of a book," he said. "A feeling about the Northeast overtook me. It seemed fragrant in a way. I took a month and went up to Princeton and rented a room in a bed-and-breakfast."

He had lived in Princeton from 1976 to 1982, while Mrs. Ford was teaching at New York University and Rutgers. He had worked as a sportswriter then and taught writing at Princeton University.

To research ***Independence Day,*** he drove around New England and New York State registering his impressions in a tape recorder. He made numerous trips to Cooperstown because "I wanted to see it in different seasons."

"My job as a writer was to find language for that which did not seem to invite it," Mr. Ford said. "To describe Connecticut Route 9 was the challenge of a lifetime. To describe U.S. Route 7 between North Ridgefield and Danbury as seen at night, in the work of a writer, is equal to Edward Hopper painting," he said with a laugh.

Itinerancy is in his blood. His father was a traveling salesman

for a starch company, and Mr. Ford was born in the middle of his route, in Jackson, Miss. He grew up across the street from a house where Eudora Welty had lived. When he was little, his mother pointed Ms. Welty out to him: "I could tell from the tone of my mother's voice that being a writer was something estimable."

"Mississippi is very kind to its writers," he said. Today he and Ms. Welty are close friends.

Mr. Ford was an only child. He was also dyslexic. "My mother stood over me and made me learn to read," he recalls. Being dyslexic may even have helped him as a writer: "It makes me pore over words, sound words out in my mind."

The South of his childhood was a culture of "mouthing and punning, a lot of play on words, disrespectful jiving about our elders," he said. "I began to realize how much pleasure there was to language."

When he was 16, his father died, and he spent some time in Little Rock, Ark., with his grandparents. At Michigan State University, he met Kristina Hensley, a daughter of an Air Force pilot who had herself moved every three years. He tried law school but dropped out after less than a year. He went on to study writing with E. L. Doctorow at the University of California, Irvine.

His first two novels were ***A Piece of My Heart,*** about the rural South on the cusp of modern life, and ***The Ultimate Good Luck,*** about drug dealers in Mexico. All of his novels have a common thread: the men are wry, wistful, vaguely melancholy, the women viewed mostly through the prism of the men's needs.

The two books were not commercially successful. "The first two novels didn't go into paperback at a time when you could put snow tires into paperback," he said. "I felt they were as good a books as I could write; this is the world talking to you!" So in 1981, he decided to "hang it up."

"I wasn't downcast," he said. "I don't take being a writer for granted." He wrote for *Inside Sports* but lost the work when the magazine was sold. He was still living in Princeton, and "I thought, 'What am I going to do?' Maybe write a book about a guy who's a sportswriter." ***The Sportswriter,*** set in New Jersey, was written in Montana after the Fords left Princeton.

"Richard always writes backward," said Mrs. Ford, who plays an integral part in his work. After finishing a novel, he sometimes reads the entire work aloud to her, though ***Independence Day,*** a 700-page manuscript, was too long for that.

They even go bird hunting together. "We spoil each other,"

he said of their relationship. Still, he often spends weeks apart from his wife so he can concentrate. "When Kristina walks into the room, everything changes. I have to get up and see what she's doing. I have to erect a barricade around myself."

They have no children. "I'm not crazy about kids," he said. "It's easier to imagine them than to raise them yourself." But in Frank Bascombe's son, Paul, Mr. Ford has imagined an awkward, rude, unwashed teen-ager with vividness. "The condition of 15-year-olds in American culture is not a secret," he said. "It's in the American air."

For the moment, *Independence Day* has emptied Mr. Ford's novelistic reservoir, so he is writing a screenplay. Next winter he plans to write a novella and an essay about his father. "If I could find something else to do, I could not do it," he says of his writing. "Nothing is promised to me."

Geoff Dyer (review date 24 August 1995)

SOURCE: "Realty Meltdown," in *London Review of Books,* August 24, 1995, p. 23.

[*In the following review, Dyer praises Ford's ability to capture the psychological dynamics of a situation by describing a few simple movements.*]

Richard Ford's narrator, Frank Bascombe, quit serious writing to become a sportswriter. This was the making of Ford. It wasn't until he became Bascombe, the sportswriter, that Ford turned himself into a major novelist.

At odd moments in *The Sportswriter,* Frank looks back on his abandoned literary career. He had published a 'promising' collection of stories, *Blue Autumn,* and had then started on a novel which he never finished. It was going to be about an ex-Marine in Tangiers, a place Frank had never visited but which he 'assumed was like Mexico'. In his late thirties, with the abandoned manuscript in a drawer, Frank looks back with bemusement at these efforts to sound 'hard nosed and old-eyed about things'.

This is an accurate enough diagnosis of what was wrong with Ford's first two books, *A Piece of My Heart* and *The Ultimate Good Luck,* both of which were published in Britain only in the wake of the success of his third, *The Sportswriter. A Piece of My Heart* was swamped by low-lit contrivances, by loading the banal with a freight of what Frank comes to call 'hard emptinesses':

'I ain't hot,' he said, keeping his head sealed against his wrist and spitting in the dust.

She got quiet, and he decided to let things be quiet awhile.

'I'm waitin,' she said.

'What're you waitin on?' he said . . .

She sat staring straight out at the long curve in the road, breathing deeply.

Set in Oaxaca—a place like Tangiers?—*The Ultimate Good Luck* is harder ('Quinn wanted the money put away fast') and emptier: 'Money gave him nerves. It was too important to fuck with.' Quinn is a Vietnam vet (naturally) who, in the opening pages, takes a girl he's just met to a boxing match. 'He wanted this fight to be over and better fighters to come in, and so did the Mexicans.' The boxer has an eye put out but Quinn doesn't even blink. After the fight the girl sucks him off in his room, and after that there's a lot of bad-ass chat and some shooting. In both these early novels, incidentally, cigarettes are not 'put out' or 'stubbed out' but 'mashed'.

According to Frank Bascombe, the problem with his earlier stories was that he could always 'see around the sides' of what he was writing, just as we can see around the sides of what Ford was doing in his first books: when male American writers take us to a boxing match, it's generally so we can watch them squaring up to Hemingway. Writing about sport, though, Frank hit on a style that was entirely his own, 'a no-frills voice that hopes to uncover simple truths by a straight-on application of the facts'. That was Hemingway's intention too, of course, but by now Papa's has become a frill-a-minute legacy; sparseness has itself become ornamental. No, this is an ambition that all writers have to fulfil—unfrill—for themselves. For Ford this was the discovery of writing frankly, or Frankly. If anything of Hemingway survives into this phase of Ford's writing it is what John Cheever (himself an influence) claimed you could sniff in all of Hemingway's work: the smell of loneliness.

Ford had always been a writer with a message, in the sense that there was always a mood, a resolution, his fiction was drawn towards; he wanted to put over a generalised sense of the way things tended. But he had done this through people (like the hero of Bascombe's unfinished novel) on the edge of things. With Frank Bascombe he was able to realise this ambition through a man who was in the middle of everything: born in the middle of the century, middle-class (Ford's earlier protagonists were drifters), suburban, stalled in the middle of life's journey. Born into 'an ordinary modern existence in 1945', he is 'an ordinary citizen' living the 'normal applauseless life of us all'. Years ago, in the Marine cadets, he was 'somewhat more than average'—and still is in the sense that his is an achieved ordinariness, an ordinariness Ford renders with extraordinary precision.

Emptiness, here in the suburbs, is not hard but delicate, manageable even. *The Sportswriter* opens on Good Friday, when Frank and his ex-wife meet at the grave of their dead child. The whole book circles around the loss (of child, of wife, of literary ambition) and the 'terrible searing regret' that underwrites—but is all the time threatening to undermine—Frank's accommodation with the everyday. Not least among the novel's remarkable achievements is the way that, for Frank, acknowledgment and evasion are indistinguishable from each other. Ford sustains a tone in which numbness, comfort, desolation and contentment are present in equal measure. This complex of antinomies generates tremendous, unrelieved suspense—we never know where the consequences of the smallest actions will end—which leaves the reader of this awful almost-comedy in an appropriately compounded state of relaxed and exhausted admiration.

The sequel, *Independence Day,* finds Frank in his so called 'Existence Period'. Having abandoned serious writing for sports journalism, he has now given up sportswriting to sell real estate. He's in his forties, still living in Haddam, New Jersey (in his ex-wife's house), going about his unremarkable business: collecting rent—or trying to—on a house he owns, showing properties to a couple of increasingly wretched clients, and preparing, as in *The Sportswriter,* for a holiday weekend away. Not, this time, with a 'lady friend' but with Paul, his troubled teenage son.

Since Ford locates the novel so precisely, on a Fourth of July weekend in 1988 with elections looming, you think initially that Frank, like John Updike's Rabbit, will serve as some kind of litmus test for America's larger fortunes. This turns out not to be Ford's intention, or at most it is only tangential. He battens everything down, anchors the details of every action to a particular historical moment, because he needs to hold his novel tightly in place while simultaneously allowing Frank's monologue to drift where it will. A digressive novel by most standards, *The Sportswriter* was, by comparison, wire-taut. It hummed. Ford's version of suspense in *Independence Day* is to leave things hanging. He seems to pay out the narrative willy-nilly, carelessly, haphazardly. When calamity strikes and the novel snaps, the wrench is even harder because of all the apparent surplus that has been piling up in harmless coils and loops. Only then do you realise that the narrative rope has been measured out inch by inch.

It's a risky business, though. At times *Independence Day* nudges too close to the ordinariness it depicts. When Frank advises us of every twist and turn of his itinerary—'up to 80, where untold cars are all flooding eastward, then west to Hackensack, up 17 past Paramus, onto the Garden State north (again!), though eerily enough there's little traffic; through River Edge and Oradell and Westwood, and two tolls to the New York line, then east to Nyack and the Tappan Zee, down over Tarrytown'—we switch off, let it wash over us without

registering where he's going. Whisking us off on a 'bystander's cruise' through town, he succumbs to what is either an exhaustive short (or a highly abbreviated long) hand:

> past the closed PO, the closed Frenchy's Gulf, the nearly empty August Inn, the Coffee Spot, around the Square, past the Press Box Bar, the closed Lauren-Schwindell Office, Garden State S & L, the somnolent Institute itself and the always officially open but actually profoundly closed First Presbyterian, where the WELCOME sign out front says, *Happy Birthday America!* * 5K *Race* * HE Can Help You At The Finish Line!*

As narrator, in other words, Frank is carrying some extra weight these days, suffering a little middle-page spread. Not that it bothers him. In his semi-resigned way he's actually pretty chipper, 'larruping' down the ole highway, heart going 'ker-whonk' as he notices a girl sway '*waaaay* back' on her heels. When prose is as easy on the ear as this you have to attend carefully lest, lulled by the lope of Frank's voice, you miss important turns (of phrase, of action). In the itinerary passage quoted earlier, it turns out, there were none; but it is by tailgating the quotidian like this that Ford captures these interludes, too vague and drifting even to be termed states of mind, the aggregate of which gives the Existence Period its characterless character.

Frank's voice also proves surprisingly flexible. With no perceptible change of gear it can cry out like Rilke before gliding back into the humdrum:

> My heart has begun whompeting again at the antiseptic hospital colours, frigid surfaces and the strict, odourless, traffic flow yin-yang of everything within sight and hearing . . . And *everything's* lugubriously, despairingly *for* something; nothing's just for itself or, better, for nothing. A basket of red geraniums would be yanked, a copy of *American Cage Birds* magazine tossed like an apple core. A realty guide, a stack of *Annie Get Your Gun* tickets—neither would last five minutes before somebody had it in the trash.

Lucky American writers, for whom the dominant narrative voice of literature is so close to the lives of the people within the narrative! 'Every time I talk to you I feel everything's being written by you,' complains Frank's ex-wife at one point. 'That's awful. Isn't it?' Skew things round a little, though—everything Frank writes sounds as if it could have been said by someone in the book—and it becomes anything but awful. Think of the hoops James Kelman has had to wedge himself through to close the gap between narrative and dialogue; then think of Ford and that all-accommodating, middle-of-the-road voice that is equally at home either side of inverted commas.

As in *The Sportswriter,* much of the action of *Independence Day* involves Frank chatting with people he bumps into. Characters—even those with walk-on parts like Mr Tanks, the removal man, his wristwatch 'sunk into his great arm', or Char, the cook with whom Frank almost gets something going—step into the book and are instantly, vividly present. They don't even have to be present to *be* present: when Frank phones through to check messages on his answering machine, a deserted motel lobby is suddenly jostling with six or seven people, all breathing down his neck. (Ford, as far as I know, is the first novelist to have tapped the potential of this relatively recent technological innovation; I'm surprised Nicholson Baker hasn't made a whole book out of it.)

I mention these messages because of the way they reveal Ford's skill at conveying entire lives in very few words. (Nothing in *The Sportswriter* is more suggestive of the gulf/bond between Frank and the world than the exchanges with his near-suicidal acquaintance Walter Luckett, each of them finishing everything they say with the other's Christian name.) He also has an uncanny ability to make what characters say somehow contain the light or weather that surrounds them. A gesture is implied by a voice, a state of mind by a gesture. In *Wildlife,* the fine short novel Ford published in 1990, between the two Bascombe books, the teenage narrator sees his mother on the phone to her lover, 'winding the phone cord around her finger and looking at me through the door as she talked to him'. The new book is dense with moments like this, where the psychological dynamics of a scene are inherent in a few simple movements—as when Frank is ferrying around a couple of housebuyers who are close to 'realty meltdown':

> 'Maybe we *should* think about renting,' Phyllis says vacantly. I have her in my mirror, keeping to herself like a bereaved widow. She has been staring at the hubcap bazaar next door, where no one's visible in the rain-soaked yard, though the hubcaps sparkle and clank in the breeze. She may be seeing something as a metaphor for something else.

> Unexpectedly, though, she sits forward and lays a consolidating mitt on Joe's bare, hairy shoulder, which causes him to jump like he'd been stabbed. Though he quickly detects this as a gesture of solidarity and tenderness, and lumpily reaches round and grabs her hand with his . . . It is the bedrock gesture of marriage, something I have somehow missed out on, and rue.

The journey made by Frank and his son both locates *Independence Day* quite consciously within the tradition of the American novel and implicitly tugs that tradition towards Ford's own preferred territory. From Haddam they head to Cooperstown, to the dawn, as it were, of the American novel, where James Fenimore Cooper's name is preserved in dozens of variants of the Leatherstocking Giftshop or the Deerslayer Inn, where Frank and Paul spend the night. Frank is struck by the geography involved in their journey from Haddam, by the way that 'in three hours you can stand on the lapping shores of Long Island Sound, staring like Jay Gatz at a beacon light that lures you to, or away from, your fate; yet in three hours you can be heading for cocktails damn near where old Natty drew first blood—the two locales as unalike as Seattle is to Waco.'

And in the middle of these two literary poles, of course, is Haddam, New Jersey, where Ford stakes his own claim to literary greatness. It's tantamount to his saying—to making exactly what the book's title commemorates: a declaration—that he is right up there. I would not dispute the claim: it's not just that Ford deploys the he-did-this, she-did-that traditional tools and qualities of the writer's art so abundantly; also, and perhaps more important, he reminds us that these qualities are themselves difficult to surpass. You can go beyond them but you cannot better them.

Raymond A. Schroth (review date 6 October 1995)

SOURCE: "The Poetry of Real Estate," in *Commonweal,* Vol. CXXII, No. 17, October 6, 1995, pp. 27-8.

[*In the following review, Schroth notes that although the characters of Ford's* Independence Day *are searching for their independence, they are actually very interconnected.*]

One of my regrets about not having money is that I'll never be able to buy a house. Still, I cannot jog the oak-lined streets of Uptown New Orleans or bike up Storm King Mountain at Cornwall-on-Hudson without casing every house I pass and asking if that house is "me."

Which is why, perhaps, Richard Ford, in his new novel, *Independence Day,* his continuation of *The Sportswriter,* has moved Frank Bascombe, his narrator and protagonist, from sports magazine journalism into the real-estate business. For the realtor, if he has moved his science to the level of art, is part social historian, part character analyst. He daily redraws the line of the shifting American Frontier—charts the highways, Shop Rite malls, suburban enclaves, shrines, motels, trailer parks, and honky tonks which speckle the skin over the American soul—and matches this particular acre with its two-bedroom clapboard bungalow with this particular migrant family's dream.

When we left Frank Bascombe in Easter week six years ago,

he was thirty-eight, a Haddam (Princeton), New Jersey, recently divorced father of a boy and girl and a dead son whom he and his ex-wife (called "X") still mourned. He was a good, though rootless, man, a seeker who struck others as having a "sense of ethics," though he consistently denies having the admirable traits which others perceive. Then he was ready for a fling in Florida with Cathy Flaherty, a Dartmouth student who admired his writing. We liked Frank, perhaps because he didn't judge, and we thought he might like us; and we wondered—hoping—whether he would return to his wife and to the serious fiction from which sportswriting had distracted him.

Though they celebrate "independence," Ford's characters are obviously dependent on one another, as if each one were a bird with one wounded wing who by hooking up with the other birds could flutter to safety.

—Raymond A. Schroth

When we pick him up this 1988 fourth-of-July weekend, Frank is forty-four, and he and the nation which he both embodies and meticulously observes have, like an untended piece of property, gone down. Bush and Dukakis are squabbling for the presidency; Frank's wife Ann has married a rich, sixty-one-year-old architect, who "knows Bush," and taken the children to Connecticut. Frank has moved into Ann's former house in Haddam, has had his fling with Cathy in France, had another affair with a black real-estate partner who was later raped and murdered, keeps a girlfriend Sally in Mantoloking, and strives to apply his Good Samaritan instincts to real estate, taking good care of his two properties in a black neighborhood and dealing fairly and patiently with a thuggish client couple from Vermont. His plan: "to do for others while looking after Number One." Friends describe him as "sweet" and "priestly"; but we like him a little less. Perhaps as a sign of how American culture has coarsened, so has Frank's narrative vocabulary, and he occasionally addresses us in a vulgar lingo—of which *The Sportswriter* was relatively free.

Though *Independence Day* opens with Frank's seriocomic analysis of the Haddam real-estate business as the town gears up for the holiday weekend, the novel's focus soon becomes Frank's troubled fifteen-year-old son Paul. Frank fears the boy, once a lover of pigeons, may have killed a grackle just for kicks. Paul has grown fat, sloppy, and injury-prone, been arrested for shoplifting condoms, slugged his stepfather, and wrecked the family car. He goes around barking for his long-dead dog, and, in banter with his father, likes to talk dirty.

By his own lights as good a parent as he can be, Frank plans

to "rescue" the boy by taking him on a holiday tour of the Basketball Hall of Fame in Springfield, Massachusetts, and the Baseball Hall of Fame in Cooperstown, New York. He will impart his fatherly wisdom, and, at the same time, by having Paul read the Declaration of Independence and Emerson's "Self Reliance," and by chatting in the car about Thomas Jefferson and John Adams, he will enlist American history in his struggle for the boy's salvation. Ironically, Frank is also reverting to sports nostalgia, which Ford eviscerated in *The Sportswriter,* as if Cooperstown were an American Mecca, or Rome, or Lourdes, where exposure to the Great Pastime in its purest form could heal the scars of death and divorce.

Displaying again his astonishing mastery of New Jersey, Connecticut, Massachusetts, and New York roadmaps—their physical as well as moral landscapes—Ford sweeps us in a four-day whirl through an election-year America which de Tocqueville foretold—filled with ambitious men but empty of lofty ambitions: Where Roy Rogers is not a cowboy hero but a fast-food joint on the Jersey Turnpike, where virtually everyone is divorced, where murder is almost as commonplace as the car alarm whining and whooping in the night, where the suspicious-looking Mexican youths cruising by your hot dog stand really are getting set to rob you, where the neighborhood cop or the "polite" security guard with the gold stud in his ear symbolizes not security but the intimations of the coming police state.

And where, especially if we have read Ford's other books, we sense a catastrophe lurking around the bend. Yet Ford's men and women, though they suffer from the American virus of excessive individualism, yearn to be connected. In one startling, yet plausible, surprise, Frank's long-lost Jewish half-brother appears like a biblical angel at a moment of crisis to remind him of the hidden continuity that has linked his life. Though they celebrate "independence," Ford's characters are obviously dependent on one another, as if each one were a bird with one wounded wing who by hooking up with the other birds could flutter to safety. The implements of their connectedness—cellular phones, gas station pay phones, voice mail, helicopters, sex manuals, the *Trenton Times,* a discarded volume of Frank's short stories, routes 1, 91, and 84, and a people-mover in the Basketball Hall of Fame arena from which the tourists shoot baskets—are hardly spiritual. But occasionally they make possible what Ford terms that "Sistine Chapel touch," when two fingertips meet, and Richard Ford continues to create, in this stunning book, what William Dean Howells stated as his own goal, a "literature worthy of America."

Richard Ford with Susan Larson (interview date 5 November 1995)

SOURCE: "Novelist's View: Real Estate and the National Psyche," in *The New York Times,* November 5, 1995, sec. 9, p. 7.

[In the following interview, Ford talks about the realty industry and how he used his experience with real estate agents to create the character of Frank Bascombe in Independence Day.*]*

When the novelist Richard Ford sees Michael Wilkinson showing French Quarter property to potential clients, he stops his car and sticks his head out the window to say hello. "I always ask him, 'Read my book yet?'" Mr. Ford said, "And he always says, 'No.'"

So much for the great relationship between literature and life. Real estate agents who read Mr. Ford's new novel *Independence Day,* published by Alfred A. Knopf, may think that the author is one of them. He's not. And his closest friend in real estate, Mr. Wilkinson, hasn't even read his book. But the New Orleans-based Mr. Ford says that if his protagonist, Frank Bascombe, strikes a responsive chord, the author has done his job. That he did it so well springs out of a lifelong interest.

"My father, who in many ways had come up in the world from small-town life in Arkansas, thought that looking for houses meant progress," Mr. Ford said. "When I was a little boy in Jackson, Miss., we moved into the middle of town. Later, my father began to want to move to the suburbs. So every Sunday we'd pile into the car. We looked at all kinds of houses—houses under construction, model homes, even floor plans. My father equated that with a better life, and it became quite clear to me that looking at houses represented people's good aspirations for themselves."

So when Mr. Ford was looking for a new occupation for Frank Bascombe, also the protagonist of his critically acclaimed 1986 novel, *The Sportswriter,* real estate came to mind. "The first thing I always have to know is what a character does for a living." Mr. Ford said. "I guess that proves what a middle-class guy I am.

"Real estate worked for me because Frank could do it with very little formal training, it was something one could learn by doing, and it could be accomplished well with good instincts and good will, both of which are Frank's strengths."

Mr. Ford has said that real estate marks the intersection of business and the American dream. "I wanted to write a large novel that was really about the entire country." he said. "Realty is not a metaphor; it's a literal thing in the book. It became clear to me that exploring these issues—shelter, money, as well as our sense of well-being and placement on the planet—I could write a book that had in it an inquiry about the American spirit. Frank's professional philosophy is encapsulated by the business motto that realty is the true American profession engaging hands-on with the fundamental spatial experience of life: more people, less space, fewer choices."

The holiday weekend described in *Independence Day* covers a broad cross-section of American society and human relationships along with lengthy ruminations about real estate and the American dream in the late 80's. Frank shows a Vermont couple a house in his home town of Haddam, N.J., which bears a strong resemblance to Princeton; tries to collect rent from the racially mixed couple occupying his rental house; visits his business partner at their hot dog stand; spends an evening with his lady friend at the Jersey shore; goes to his ex-wife's house in Connecticut to pick up his troubled son for a trip to the Baseball Hall of Fame in Cooperstown, N.Y., before heading home for the holiday celebration.

Critics have praised Mr. Ford's attention to the details of Frank's professional life—from his familiarity with the psychology of buying and selling to the trunk of his Crown Victoria filled with yard signs. But Mr. Ford says that while he has known many real estate agents over the years, "I'm writing about a guy who's a realtor, not trying to make a portrait of reality."

"If it's persuasive I'm glad," he added. "But I'm making somebody up. I'm not trying to peg a typical realtor."

Mr. Ford said that when he married his wife, Kristina, the executive director of the City Planning Commission of New Orleans, they lived in many places and in many houses. "So I know what houses cost in virtually any city and whether I could afford to live there," he said. "I enjoyed doing this. It became a sort of divertissement."

So did the language of real estate and architecture, which lends such color to *Independence Day.* "I've always been interested in architecture and the lingo of architecture," Mr. Ford said, "When we bought our first house in Princeton, I had the 'Dictionary of Architecture,' and I went around the house looking at all the parts. The language of architecture—words like corbel, bracket, threshold, lintel, and soffit—is so wonderful and imaginative. And sometimes the terminology of realty is hilarious, those expressions like 'eating into your down.'"

The Fords have owned five houses. "I don't think that's so very many," Mr. Ford said. "But I've lived in many more and I must have looked at a jillion others. I've toured large parts of the earth with realtors, and I've always seen these as potentially good relationships, possible friendships. After all, days spent with a realtor are part of a person's life."

These days aren't always pleasant, as Mr. Ford's wickedly funny portrait of the Markhams, Frank Bascombe's clients, demonstrates. After looking at 45 houses, they're at the point of what Frank calls "realty death." But, as he asks himself and the reader, "What more can you do for wayward strangers than to shelter them?"

Mr. Ford knows what emotional baggage attends the issue of shelter. "Realty becomes sort of gathering and rallying point for all basic human desires and anxieties and pains and frustrations and joys," he said. His own history reflects those complex emotions. "What the house I'm living in right now means to me is freedom," he said, referring to his house in Chinook, Mont. "It's a small bungalow in a rather remote, tiny town on the northern high line of Montana. It's a place I can go and just be in a wonderful community in a purely anonymous way and be free.

"My first house in Princeton was probably our first act of superficial adulthood. And that house we owned in Missoula, Mont., I considered our real estate disaster."

That 5,000-square-foot house, with an indoor swimming pool, was on 100 acres. It required a year's renovation, and the Fords lived in it for only a year before selling it.

"It's basically the nicest house in Missoula, but it was too remote," Mr. Ford said. "I like to be down amongst people, though I think the French Quarter may be too much amongst them. But from that experience in Missoula I learned—oh, my God!—the terrible anxiety of owning a house I didn't want to own and wanted to get rid of."

"Our house in the French Quarter is really Kristina's dream house and I hope I survive it," Mr. Ford said. The elegant New Orleans home was the last of some 45 houses the Fords looked at before settling there in December 1989. "Yes, you could say I was at the point of realty death when we settled on Bourbon Street," he said.

Thomas Bonner, Jr. (review date 9 December 1995)

SOURCE: A review of *Independence Day,* in *America,* Vol. 173, No. 19, December 9, 1995, pp. 26-7.

[*In the following review, Bonner praises Ford as a storyteller and calls Ford's* Independence Day *"a work at the edge of philosophy but far enough away that its art still lives."*]

"I was trying to address the country in as large a way as I can imagine—intellectually as well as spiritually. It was the way I defined myself a challenge," observed Richard Ford about his novel ***Independence Day*** during a *New Orleans Times-Picayune* interview. The mission suggested in his comments

gives his fiction a life beyond the story and makes his narrative part of a tradition of consciously merging stories with ideas.

American literature through the late 19th century, as represented by Hawthorne and Melville, for example, repeatedly gives us writers engaged with balancing these elements. The works of Emerson, too, remind us that the American reading public once had a taste for the direct exploration of ideas in essays. Emerson's words and ideas emerge often in ***Independence Day*** as do those of Jefferson's Declaration of Independence and de Tocqueville's *Democracy in America.*

Independence Day begins with Bascombe closing up the details on a private rental, trying to close a company sale on a home, seeing his current romantic interest, preparing to pick up his troubled son from his former and now remarried wife and celebrating the nation's birthday with his son by visiting nearby basketball and baseball halls of fame. The holiday weekend has almost as much thinking as driving. Ford persistently reminds us that we are going somewhere and seeing something on this holiday journey.

Consciously political, the narrative reflects the disappointment, strained hope and confusion of life in the late 1980's. Ford sets the novel during the summer before the Democratic National Convention that nominated Governor Dukakis of Massachusetts. The author explains, "I came to sense how badly misled Americans had been by Ronald Reagan and that the choices in the election of 1988 were not a good set of choices." Contributing to this atmosphere is Haddam, N.J., a place remarkably like Princeton with its university the site of an early congress, its seminary a powerful presence and its affluent residences a contrast with its poor and minority neighborhoods.

Bascombe may work as a character who represents Ford's ideas and experiences, but he is not an Everyman. The cosmic and conscious first person ("I myself, Frank Bascombe") brings us into this story, this vision of American life that seeks an ideal amid the flora and fauna of self-interest and materialism. The poet Whitman is successful in creating an epic voice in "Song of Myself" because he emphasizes the vision itself in its varied and organic parts. Bascombe is too much an individual whose particulars and accidentals obscure the universals. In creating Bascombe, Ford reaches into the epic tendency in American culture to make a statement about this vast and challenging land. The details of Bascombe's life come in vivid and unrelenting force, allowing readers to see only parts of themselves in the character, but not enough to cause them to identify with Bascombe.

The story in its meandering is simple. In space, we go a short distance; in time, a long weekend. For a lengthy novel we encounter a limited number of characters. The situation is conventional for contemporary American life: a divorced parent exercising visitation rights with a child. The complications emerge from the protagonist's past as it affects the present, especially in the father-son relationship. Ford tells a good story (he is an especially accomplished writer of short fiction), but the landscape of the narrative provides the garden for his and Bascombe's generally liberal and often "politically correct" thinking. Events nearly always lead us into an exploration of larger and less concrete realities.

Readers of Walker Percy's novels will find here a familiar tension between narrative and idea. *Independence Day,* its title pregnant with meaning, suggests a summer novel, but it is fictional inquiry into things that matter, a work at the edge of philosophy but far enough away that its art still lives.

FURTHER READING

Biography

Weeks, Linton. "A Novel Hit the Jackpot." *The Washington Post* (17 April 1996): pp. C1, C24.

Additional coverage of Ford's life and career is contained in the following sources published by Gale Research: *Contemporary Authors,* Vols. 69-72; and *Contemporary Authors New Revision Series,* Vols. 11 and 47.

Robert Hass

United States Poet Laureate

Born in 1941, Hass is an American poet, essayist, editor, and translator.

For further information on his life and career, see *CLC,* Volumes 18 and 39.

INTRODUCTION

A respected American poet, Hass has served two terms as U.S. Poet Laureate. Following the example of former Laureate Rita Dove, Hass took the opportunity afforded by the position to play an active role in American literary affairs. Hass pursued his goal of raising awareness of the importance of literacy with a countrywide speaking tour and a number of events at the Library of Congress.

Much critical attention has been focused on Hass from the beginning of his career. Upon the publication of his first poetry collection, *Field Guide* (1973), which won the Yale Series of Younger Poets Award, Hass was identified as an important new poet. In explaining his approach to writing poetry, Hass has remarked, "Poetry is a way of living . . . a human activity like baking bread or playing basketball." Critics quickly recognized the influence of all aspects of life, both mundane and extraordinary, in Hass's work, and lauded the conciseness, imagery, and clarity of expression in his poems. Hass's reputation broadened with the release of *Twentieth Century Pleasures* (1984), a collection of previously published essays and reviews which earned him the National Book Critics Circle award in criticism. Many reviewers remarked that the insight into poetry-writing Hass demonstrated in this work was both informed by and further illuminated his own poetry. Hass expanded in yet another direction with *The Essential Haiku,* translations of representative works by the most famous masters of haiku, a form of short poetry that has been influential in his own poetry writing. "Hass has noted his own affinity for Japanese haiku," Forrest Gander has remarked, "and his work similarly attends to the details of quotidian life with remarkable clarity."

Hass was nominated to the post of United States Poet Laureate in 1995 and 1996, and served both terms. "My first reaction was reluctance," Hass told David Streitfield. "It's a great honor and it seemed like a massive distraction. But it was also an opportunity to be a spokesperson for the literary community." Following his predecessor Rita Dove's example as an active, high-profile Laureate, Hass chose to use his position to raise awareness of literacy issues among community and civic groups across the country, going "where poets don't

go." "I thought the thing to talk about is not poetic 'uplift,'" he told interviewer Francis X. Clines, "but the fact that basic literacy in this country is in a serious crisis." On the road most of the time, Hass found that, ironically, his duties as Poet Laureate interfered with his poetry writing, an uncomfortable situation made more so by the experimental nature of his project. As he neared the end of his second term, he remarked to Clines, "Did it do any good? Was I wasting my life? Should I have been home writing poems? It's like teaching. You have no idea."

PRINCIPAL WORKS

Field Guide (poetry) 1973

Praise (poetry) 1979

Twentieth Century Pleasures: Prose on Poetry (essays) 1984

Human Wishes (poetry) 1989

The Essential Haiku: Versions of Basho, Buson, and Issa [editor and translator] (verse) 1994

Sun under Wood (poetry) 1996

CRITICISM

Edward Hirsch (review date March 1985)

SOURCE: "Praise," in *Poetry,* Vol. CXLV, No. 6, March, 1985, pp. 345-48.

[*In the following review, Hirsch discusses the essays and reviews collected in Hass's* Twentieth Century Pleasures, *considering what they reveal about Hass and his work.*]

Recently, I wrote a memorial speech for a close friend who had died of cancer. Reading the piece aloud, I discovered that I could deliver it with a modicum of calmness when I was speaking in generalities, but that I wavered whenever specific images of him were summoned up: my friend giving me a high five at a basketball game, or carrying a steaming cup of coffee across campus in the early evening. These images were so clear and palpable that I could feel him in front of me again. "Images haunt," Robert Hass tells us in *Twentieth Century Pleasures.* They are also, by their very nature, phenomenal, standing for nothing else but themselves, reaching down into the well of being and affirming, *this is.* It is a permanently startling fact that language can give us back parts of our own world, full-bodied. "Images are powers," Hass also writes, emphasizing that they are metonymic glimpses, fundamental acts of imagination, moments of pure being. The image is the primary pigment of the lyric poet and in its purest form it is the enemy of time, of discourse, of all narratives that seek to surround and distill it. No wonder that an image could cut the fabric of a memorial speech. Yeats claimed that the intensity of images actively bordered on the visionary, an intersection between two worlds. In a different tradition, one of Tu Fu's colleagues told him, "It is like being alive twice."

The nature of the image—its surprising fullness of being and phenomenological significance—is one of the leitmotifs of *Twentieth Century Pleasures,* Robert Hass's collection of prose pieces about poetry. The book brings together ten essays and four reviews, all of which were commissioned by various editors over the past five years, and consequently it has the character of an omnibus, weaving together a number of essays about individual poets—Lowell, Wright, Tranströmer, Kunitz, Milosz, Rilke, and others—with a memoir about the San Francisco Bay Area as a cultural region and three larger meditations about poetic form, prosody and rhythm, and images. Most of these essays are what used to be called "appreciations"—if we mean by the term something along the order of Randall Jarrell's essays on Frost, Auden, and Whitman. Like Jarrell, Hass is often at his best when he is both reconsidering a poet's work and rescuing it from a myriad of surrounding assumptions. His extended meditation on "The Quaker Graveyard in Nantucket," for example, should forever lay to rest the received opinion that Lowell's

early poems "clearly reflect the dictates of the new criticism" while the later ones are "less consciously wrought" and "more intimate." In a somewhat different vein, his indispensable essay on James Wright helps to define the inward alertness, luminous intelligence, and clarity of feeling in Wright's work; but it also unmasks some of the unspoken assumptions and limitations in his aesthetic, in particular the unconscious insistence on a "radical and permanent division between the inner and outer" worlds. For Hass, this Calvinist division—which is anyway denied by Wright's best work—is one of the recurrent problems in American poetry. Indeed, *Twentieth Century Pleasures* is held together not only by Hass's uniquely personal and unified sensibility, but also by his ongoing conviction that the division between inner and outer can be healed in post-romantic poetry and that human inwardness needs to find a viable shape in the external world. One of his persistent concerns is the relationship between looking and being, his sense of how the image comes together and how the mind—through the medium of the lyric poem—recovers and creates form.

Hass is the most intimate and narrative of critics—each of his essays begins with a personal example or story—and he writes with an unusually vivid sense that "Poems take place in your life, or some of them do, like the day your younger sister arrives and replaces you as the bon enfant in the bosom of the family. . . ." So, too, he writes always as a man situated in a particular place at a particular time, a Wordsworthian poet, only partially off-duty, who is taking a specific occasion—a symposium, the publication of a book—to think about his art. As a native Californian with a formalist training (Kenneth Rexroth and Yvor Winter are two California presences who shaped his sensibility), Hass often seems to be standing at the edge of the continent, facing west. Throughout *Twentieth Century Pleasures* the Japanese haiku poets serve as his primary touchstones and models. Thus Chekhov's notebook entries are praised for being "close to the temperament" of Japanese poets, and Whitman's "Cavalry Crossing a Ford" is demonstrated to be "in the spirit" of Buson; Gary Snyder's "August on Sourdough, A Visit from Dick Brewer" is located in a tradition of Oriental leave-taking poems, and James Wright's "Outside Fargo, North Dakota" is compared to a haiku by Basho which gets at the same feeling. Hass's essay on **"Images"**—which is the concluding and arguably the most important piece in the book—weaves together a series of radiant personal memories with a mini-discussion of Japanese poetics. Poems by Buson, Issa, and Basho are the essential examples in his argument that images are not so much "about" anything as they are things-in-themselves, "equal in status with being and the mysteriousness of being." At times Hass sounds like an intuitive Bachelard, a phenomenologist transplanted to California and turned into a mid-century American poet.

One recurrent problem for modern poets is the relationship

between image and discourse, epiphanic moment and narrative time, song and story. Hass is particularly alert to the issue, noting in one piece that "The *Cantos* are a long struggle between image and discourse" and in another that "Winters never solved for himself the problem of getting from image to discourse in the language of his time." The problem is crucial for poets who seek to transcend Imagism (and deep Imagism) and want to carve forms in time, to build from the individual to the community and to incorporate into their work aspects of natural, social, political, and historical life. The "perilousness of our individual lives," Hass declares, "is what makes the insight of the isolated lyric untenable." One of the secondary dramas in *Twentieth Century Pleasures* is watching the essays circle the problem of image and discourse, finding different solutions in different poets. Thus, Hass argues that Tranströmer's *Baltics* solves the problem through a series of wandering fragments or islands, Wordsworth's *Prelude* by knitting together being and looking, giving the poet's own inwardness "a local habitation and a name." He finds that Rilke finally lets the world come flooding through him in the *Duino Elegies* and that Milosz circumnavigates the problem in "Separate Notebooks," continually returning to the issue of "whether one should try to rescue being from the river of time by contemplating or embracing it." The Japanese haiku poets serve as another type of model by organizing their anthologies seasonally; as a result each poem reaches out "toward an absolute grasp of being" but also takes its place in a larger seasonal cycle. In this way the stillness of the moment is given special poignance by the velocity of time. What is crucial to Hass in all of these works is the basic idea of poetic form, the mind making connections, creating rhythmic texture and shape out of diverse fragments.

Twentieth Century Pleasures begins by discussing the difficulty of talking about favorite poems, and it ends by affirming "the fullness and emptiness of being." Its very title sets itself against our twentieth-century experience of fragmentation, and one of the book's key subjects is the mind's capacity for "wonder and repetition," the way the best poems can focus an attentive and self-forgetful consciousness. Hass's own most successful poetic mode has been the meditative lyric which, as he notes in an essay on Stanley Kunitz's work, "can step a little to the side and let the world speak through it, and the world has no need to cry 'Let be! Let be!' because it is." Hass has an acute sense of the perils of twentieth-century history, but this is always tempered by his abiding faith in "the absolute value of being." He has a long memory for happiness and returns often to experiences of well-being, radiance, fullness, health. As his most well-known poem, **"Meditation at Lagunitas,"** puts it: "There are moments when the body is as numinous / as words, days that are the good flesh continuing. . . ." *Twentieth Century Pleasures* is informed by a deep faith that the greatest poems can capture the numinousness of the world and ultimately it is this faith

which makes Robert Hass a critic—as well as a poet—of praise.

Anthony Libby (review date 3 March 1985)

SOURCE: "Criticism in the First Person," in *The New York Times Book Review,* March 3, 1985, p. 37.

[*In the following review, Libby remarks favorably on* Twentieth Century Pleasures.]

Twentieth-century pleasure is not precisely what we expect from a book of criticism, which often has a distinctly 19th-century quality and offers secondary pleasures at best. But as the California poet Robert Hass recounts and analyzes his complex joy in poets from Basho to Rilke to James Wright [in *Twentieth Century Pleasures*], he creates a very special pleasure of his own. This results partly from the almost fictional tendencies of his criticism. As Mr. Hass tends to locate poets in their times and places, so he locates his reading for us, giving up the illusion of objectivity to place the reading in his life. In a piece about Robert Lowell, Mr. Hass complains about the difficulty of judging the value of poetry "when it's gotten into the blood. It becomes autobiography then." So his criticism contains many snatches of autobiography, for instance as he introduces a study of the poetry and politics of Czeslaw Milosz with a memory of participating in a 1966 antinapalm demonstration or when he begins a piece on prosody with a quick, funny glance at dirty saloon repartee. Conversely, he writes only one overtly autobiographical piece for this collection, and it is mostly about poetry.

Mr. Hass's complexity shows not so much in his autobiographical gestures as in his thinking about the poems. We are conscious of a whole mind before us, presented in a style that is both elegant and plain, enlivened by a freely metaphorical imagination and magisterial one-liners. (About rhythm: "The first fact of the world is that it repeats itself.") Deep intelligence and wide knowledge serve Mr. Hass's particular vision of poetry, a vaguely Tory one that has been unfashionable for much of the past two decades, though it is coming dramatically into its own now.

Unlike the early modern Imagists and such recent neo-Surrealists as Robert Bly, Mr. Hass cares more for the line than the image. Not that he opposes Surrealism, but he argues that what is genuinely basic, what gets to the unconscious, what defines "revolutionary ground," is rhythm more than visual representation. Mr. Hass admits that "images haunt," but he remains clearly less drawn to pictures than to ideas. This inclination has one unfortunate effect: the piece called **"Images,"** despite some thoughtful meditations on haiku, is less compelling than the others. Even the tone of its personal reminiscences—which are too obviously rhetorically calculated, habitual—seems askew.

Another, more interesting effect of Mr. Hass's interest in thought is his ambivalence about modernism, partly an inheritance from the poet and critic Yvor Winters, with whom he briefly studied. But Mr. Hass moderates Winters's rather ill-tempered scorn for everything Romantic or post-Romantic. (He also does a little restorative work on Winters's image as a poet, trying in one review to remember "the fierce old curmudgeon of Palo Alto" as a young Romantic.) Whatever his position in the poetry wars, Mr. Hass remains devoted to the massive poems of modernism, like Lowell's "Quaker Graveyard in Nantucket" or Rilke's "Duino Elegies." But because of his interest in the moral implications of ideas and because he locates poetry so squarely among the central experiences of existence, he worries about modernism's infatuation either with intense self-examination or with the inhuman—the darkness of instinct, not the light of reason, and finally death.

Mr. Hass argues with a rationalist's insistence on the value of reason as opposed to more mysterious ways of knowing. But unlike excessively rationalist critics, he understands precisely the appeal of mystery and admits the aesthetically generative power of dark forces in the self. Even while amusing himself by accusing Mr. Bly of describing "imagination as a kind of ruminative wombat," he tends to grant the general validity of Mr. Bly's Romantic insistence on the deep roots of poetry—though Mr. Hass insists that "the imagination is luminously intelligent." But there remains a problem. As he says in a moment of impatience in his wonderful essay on Rilke, at times he feels "a sudden restless revulsion from the whole tradition of nineteenth- and early-twentieth-century poetry" because of its narcissistic obsession with inwardness and death.

The great skill of this critic is his willingness to entertain such judgments, as well as many small, fair, precise judgments of individual poems. His final intention is not merely to judge but to give a picture of the writer's mind. He begins with a balanced assessment of flaws in a particular vision and articulates a complex understanding of the way those flaws are inseparable from—genius. Among the transcendent contradictions of poetry, human or even esthetic weakness can be one of the springs of esthetic power.

Because he is so concerned with the absence of human relationships in so much poetry, Mr. Hass sometimes tends to welcome suggestions of sexual desire with an uncharacteristically uncritical enthusiasm. He is a stern judge of Surrealist sentimentalism about darkness and otherness, but when he finds traces of the erotic, Mr. Hass sometimes lets sentimentalism pass (in James Wright, for instance), and he does not always see the dangers of narcissism in the contemplation,

especially male and abstract, of the sexual other. But it seems unduly crabby to insist on this small failing; let me suggest, as Mr. Hass does when he points to poetic flaws, that it is in ways inseparable from the strengths of Mr. Hass's own luminous sensibility.

Because of the range of that sensibility, many of these essays, especially the introduction to Rilke but even the rather too long discussion of prosody, are both interesting enough for a general audience and rigorous enough for professionals. Correspondingly, Mr. Hass's style balances conversational directness and eloquent complexity. However readers might argue with the details of his responses, his writing appeals. That comes naturally—if his highly self-conscious rhetoric can be described as natural—from his pleasure in poetry and in talking about poetry, always frankly mixed with enjoyment in talking about the self. The two are indivisible. Mr. Hass believes that poetry is what defines the self, and it is his ability to describe that process that is the heart of this book's pleasure.

Dick Davis (review date 15 March 1985)

SOURCE: "Arguing in Unknown Quantities," in *The Times Literary Supplement,* No. 4276, March 15, 1985, pp. 293-94.

[*In the following excerpt, Davis commends Hass for a collection that demonstrates his desire "to serve poetry—not appropriate it or crow over it or show off at its expense."*]

We enter a different world, and one I think most readers of poetry would much rather live in, when we open Robert Hass's **Twentieth Century Pleasures**; his first sentence, "It's probably a hopeless matter, writing about favourite poems", establishes the tone—colloquial, welcoming, inviting complicity; and if you don't have favourite poems read no further. Hass is a poet himself and it shows; his love for poetry, his intimate awareness of how it is made and the kinds of effects it is capable of, are obvious on almost every page. This [book] . . . constantly sent me back with fresh understanding to poems I thought I knew, and in search of poems I had not known before.

The writing is relaxed, almost belletrist, certainly free of jargon: there are some brilliantly illuminating passages—the comparison of a James Wright poem with Truffaut's *L'Enfant Sauvage,* for example, and the scansion of a poem by Snyder. It may be that the writing will prove too personal for some readers (we learn a great deal about Hass's children in the course of the book), but the personal moments are often the most telling, as in the essay describing his own discovery of poetry during adolescence. An adolescent hunger for poetry is something he values and he quotes Octavio Paz with evident approval: "Young boys read verse to help themselves express or know their feelings, as if the dim intuited features of love, heroism or sensuality could only be clearly contemplated in a poem"; out of his own hunger a fine critical intelligence has grown. The book is helped by the fact that Hass writes almost entirely about poems and poets he likes: often his assurance is a little breathtaking (he confidently discusses poems he can read only in translation) and some of his aphorisms can seem more glib than true (particularly his dismissal of Herrick) but these are minor cavils. One reads here the prose of an intelligent man who wishes to serve poetry—not appropriate it or crow over it or show off at its expense—and this is a rare enough experience to arouse gratitude and admiration.

John Matthias (review date Spring 1986)

SOURCE: "Reading Old Friends," in *Southern Review,* Vol. 22, No. 2, Spring, 1986, pp. 391-406.

[*In the following excerpt, Matthias, who is a personal acquaintance of Hass's, presents a thorough analysis of* Twentieth Century Pleasures.]

Robert Hass begins one of the pieces in *20th Century Pleasures* by saying that he has been "worrying the bone of this essay for days" because he wants to say some things against the poems he has agreed to discuss in a special issue of a journal celebrating the work of James Wright. I have been worrying the bone of this essay for days as well, but not because I want to say anything against the work I intend to discuss. I have decided to write in an autobiographical way [in this issue of the *Southern Review* and in the next] about three books . . . which are themselves autobiographical in different respects and which are, as it happens, all by old friends. I thought at first that it would be a very simple business to give a strictly personal and subjective account of these books. There would be no need to feign anything like a critical disinterest; it was specifically agreed that I should write about the work of friends from the perspective of a friend. But this is not an easy task. The chief reason why it isn't is that years ago all these books began for me as conversations or as an exchange of stories growing out of conversations—long talks with Hass first at Stanford and then later in the pubs and coffee shops of Cambridge about the art of poetry, stories traded back and forth with [Michael] Anania driving in Chicago traffic jams, accounts exchanged with [Jiri] Wyatt in the London of the later sixties as we struggled for a language to articulate a politics and to describe our primal childhood memories—and not as something printed on a page. Reading these conversations back into the texts, which is something that I find I cannot keep myself from doing, I am acutely aware that other readers are *not* doing this, though some are doubtless reading different, even contradictory, conversations back into the texts. Should my account include the conversations or re-

strict itself to the texts? If I am to be the autobiographer of my reading, as Robert Hass often is of his in *20th Century Pleasures,* I must risk talking about a book that no one else can read. For example, there is a point in Hass's essay on Robert Lowell's "Quaker Graveyard in Nantucket" where he deprecates "the slough of poetry" engendered by *Life Studies* beginning typically "Father, you. . . ." I remember his making that point in a coffee shop across from Trinity College, and I remember saying: "Yes, but your father is still alive." Then he said—but it doesn't really matter *what* he said; he went on to qualify or modify the remark by saying something else. What began in conversation and was open to the natural processes of conversation becomes a telling point, decisively made, in an essay where I still hear the resonance and backwash of an exchange which occurred ten years ago. This conditions my reading and my response and, while both can be communicated, the second probably cannot be fully shared. It also suggests that it may be more difficult to talk about work by someone you know than by someone you don't.

Then there is the question of voice, or, as the theorists like to say, the question of presence. The related questions of voice, conversation, and presence are taken up by Denis Donoghue in his recent book on current theory and ideology called *Ferocious Alphabets.* This has suddenly become a very useful book to me precisely because the form of language which Donoghue wishes to privilege, which in fact he thinks *is* privileged, is conversation. Arguing that conversation is so radically different from the notion of communication proposed by such early twentieth-century theorists as Jacobsen and Richards that we should regard it as communion rather than communication, Donoghue writes that conversation is made memorable "by the desire of each person to share experience with the other, giving and receiving."

> All that can be shared, strictly speaking, is the desire: it is impossible to reach the experience. But desire is enough to cause the reverberations to take place which we value in conversation. . . . The resonating force in a genuine conversation is not admiration, but desire. In conversation . . . the words enact desire . . . the "I" and "you" are constantly changing places; not only to maintain the desire of communion but to keep it mobile. The two voices are making a music of desire, varying its cadences, tones, intensities.

When you separate these two communing and fully embodied voices in such a way that one becomes a writer and the other a reader, certain kinds of compensation must occur. The writer's compensation for the lack of conversation's true communion is style. The reader in his turn "makes up for the tokens of absence which he finds in written words. . . . He is not willing to leave words as [he] finds them on a page [but] wants to restore words to a source, a human situation involving speech, character, personality. . . . We read to meet the other. The encounter is personal, the experience is satisfying in the degree of presence rather than knowledge."

If this kind of reading, which Donoghue has an ugly word for—he calls it *epireading*—commits one not only to the *epos* of speech but to the logocentrism attacked by the kind of reader engaged in an activity he has an even uglier word for, *graphireading,* the objections of the graphireaders might be summarized in the most severely reductionist terms by a bit of graffiti appearing in a recent *Times Literary Supplement* that looks to have been written by a deranged graduate student:

> D'ya wanna know the creed 'a
> Jacques Derrida?
> Dere ain't no reada
> Dere ain't no wrider
> Eider.

I don't know if I can be an "epireader" in general, but I think I am unavoidably and inescapably an "epireader" of my friends. I hear their voices and I feel the pleasure of their presence in their words. At the end of *Ferocious Alphabets,* Donoghue says that he detests the "current ideology which refers, gloatingly, to the death of the author, the obsolescence of the self, the end of man, and so forth. . . . To be sure that I exist, all I have to do is catch a cold or stumble on the pavement. Pleasure achieves the same effect more agreeably. . . . Knowledge is debatable, pleasure is not." Robert Hass calls his book **20th Century Pleasures** and, I think, shares most of Donoghue's basic assumptions about the nature of literature and language. Still, he writes in his essay on Robert Creeley that underneath some of the typical pleasures of our time are uncomfortable things "which the mind must, slowly, in love and fear, perform to locate itself again, previous to any other discourse." And in his best known poem he writes:

> Longing, we say, because desire is full
> of endless distances.

In reading the work of friends, something of desire's communion in the pleasure of familiar voices is very present and very real; but so, of course, is the longing, and so are the distances. We fall asleep in the middle of a conversation and awake with a page of prose in our hands.

I am surprised that Helen Vendler in a recent review of **20th Century Pleasures** and some other books about contemporary poetry feels that Hass fails to engage some of the questions and assumptions touched on or alluded to above. Taking the part of the theorists in the November 7, 1985 issue of the *New York Review of Books,* she argues that all practical criticism "assumes positions silently taken" about basic premises

and says that she would like to see Hass and the others consider first principles or at any rate make the reader confident that "the theoretical questions had been silently put, and satisfactorily answered, before the writing was undertaken." Vendler is also worried about the autobiographical element in Hass's writing—its familiar tone, its "determined effort toward the colloquial," its attempt through what she calls "interpolated narratives" to communicate the idea that the texts under discussion have some connection with his own sensual life and the life of the times, that the books have literally been lived with for a while and not just read and rapidly reviewed to meet a deadline. Actually, Hass engages the fundamental premises of the theorists and implies his own in any number of his essays. The piece on Creeley, for example, deals in Lacanian and Derridian terms with a poetics "which addresses the tension between speaking and being spoken through language," but also makes clear through some "interpolated narratives" why such an "austere and demanding" poet as Creeley could communicate with a large and often uninstructed audience during the 1960s. The "interpolated narratives" imply a "premise" as fundamental as anything in Lacan and Derrida—namely, that art unfolds both in individual lives and our collective history, and that factors which only narrative can reveal condition our response to it. But of course there is no systematic statement of principles, no prolegomenon to any further study of contemporary poetry, in a book like this. It achieves its unity and authority from the manner in which art is shown to intersect with life. It *is* an autobiography of sorts.

Epireader of this text that I must be, the first thing I am conscious of in **20th Century Pleasures** is a voice. It is a familiar voice, and it sounds like this:

> I've been trying to think about form in poetry and my mind keeps returning to a time in the country in New York when I was puzzled that my son Leif was getting up a little earlier every morning. I had to get up with him, so it exasperated me. I wondered about it until I slept in his bed one night. His window faced east. At six-thirty I woke to brilliant sunlight. The sun had risen.

> Wonder and repetition. Another morning I was walking Kristin to her bus stop—a light blanket of snow after thaw, the air thick with the rusty croaking of blackbirds so that I remembered, in the interminable winter, the windy feel of June on that hill. Kristin, standing on a snowbank in the cold air, her eyes alert, her face rosy with cold and with some purity of expectation, was looking down the road. It was eight-fifteen. Her bus always arrived at eight-fifteen. She looked down the road and it was coming.

Helen Vendler objects to what she feels marks a difficulty in controlling tone in a passage similar to this one taken from the final and most fully autobiographical essay in this book, which I am going to quote a little later on. It is an intentionally vulnerable passage and functions, along with others like it, to make clear exactly what elements, insofar as Hass is conscious of them, combine to condition his reading and his response, to make it *his* reading and *his* response rather than mine or Helen Vendler's or someone else's. It tells us some of what we need to know in order to understand his perceptions, his reactions, and his judgments. And it is especially in passages like it, and like the one quoted above, that I hear the familiar, amused, vigorous, disarming voice often touched with a Chekhovian irony and sadness that I know. I sense the presence of a friend and not a difficulty in controlling tone. One function of the passage about Hass's children is, of course, to get an essay about form begun in a relaxed and graceful way. No academic categories introduced, no pedagogical solemnities. But we are also persuaded by this kind of writing that his coincident experiences of "trying to think about form" and remembering the power of repetition in the lives of his young children yield the surprised perception out of which the essay grows, that "though *predictable* is an ugly little word in daily life, in our first experience of it we are clued to the hope of a shapeliness in things. . . . Probably, that is the psychological basis for the power and the necessity of artistic form." But let me take an example from the first essay in the book to demonstrate more fully the usefulness of narrative and autobiography:

On these terms, Lowell's prayer moved me.

What are "these terms," and what conditions them? The prayer which Hass is moved by occurs in Part V of "The Quaker Graveyard in Nantucket"—"Hide / our steel, Jonas Messias, in Thy side"—and the terms of his being moved are conditioned by the way in which his own inherited Catholicism has been modified or transmuted by a range of experiences and some important reading by the time it meets the intense but unorthodox Catholicism of a convert's poem. At the beginning of his essay, Hass says that it's difficult to conduct an argument about the value of music in favorite poems once it's gotten into the blood: "It becomes autobiography there." But so does the meaning of favorite poems become a kind of autobiography—so conditioned is it by the times and places and the circumstances of initial or repeated readings—and only narrative can really show us how this happens. After explaining the "enormously liberating perception" found in Robert Duncan's prose that "the mistake of Christianity was to think that the soul's salvation was the only human adventure" and, Christ seen therefore on an equal footing with the other gods, Pound's idea that they all were "forms of consciousness which men through learning, art and contemplation could inhabit," Hass writes this paragraph:

I got my Catholicism from my mother's side, Foleys

from Cork by way of Vermont who drank and taught school and practiced law on the frontiers of respectability until they landed in San Francisco at the turn of the century. My father's side was Protestant and every once in a while, weary probably with the catechisms of his children, he would try to teach us one of his childhood prayers. But he could never get past the first line: "In my father's house there are many mansions. . . ." He would frown, squint, shake his head, but that was as far as he ever got and we children who were willing to believe Protestants capable of any stupidity including the idea that you could fit a lot of mansions into a house, would return to memorizing the four marks of the true church. (It was one, holy, catholic, and apostolic.) But that phrase came back to me as a way through the door of polytheism and into myth. If Pound could resurrect the goddesses, there was a place for a temple of Christ, god of sorrows, desire of savior, restingplace of violence. I could have the memory of incense and the flickering candles and the battered figure on the cross with the infinitely sad and gentle face and have Aphrodite as well, "the fauns chiding Proteus / in the smell of hay under olive trees" and the intoning of Latin with which we began the mass: "*Introibo ad altare Dei.*" On these terms, Lowell's prayer moved me: "Hide our steel, Jonas Messias, in thy side."

The essay on Lowell is important for a lot of reasons. It is the generative essay of the volume, written in England in the cold winter of 1977 when Hass and his family were living in the Cambridgeshire village of Little Shelford in a huge house owned by the master of St. John's College, which I had lived in two years before. The essay may be as personal, as autobiographical, as it is in part out of compensation for not being able to write, there in Little Shelford, the poems he had hoped to write in the course of the year away from his familiar turf in Berkeley and San Francisco. Actually, I feel vaguely guilty about this. I persuaded Hass to go to Cambridge for the year rather than to York where his Bicentennial Fellowship was really supposed to take him, thinking that it would be good to spend the year near one another—I was once again to be in the area—and that the big house in the little village would be as productive a place for him to live and work in as it had been for me two years before. Once the weather turned, all the poems were frozen out of his system—the house "has central heating," but the system is in a permanent state of disrepair—and he wrote very little poetry until the San Francisco sun had warmed his blood and spirit again eight or nine months later. He did, however, write a lot of prose, and he wrote this first essay of the present book which, I think, led to his wanting to write the others and established their characteristic tone and point of view. It begins and ends with recent and more distant memories of voices—that of a mild-looking schoolteacher in the Shelford pub who, when the subject of favorite poems came up one night, treated the locals to a recitation of Kipling's "Gunga Din," and the surprise of Robert Lowell's when Hass finally got to hear it at a reading, which sounded "bizarrely like an imitation of Lionel Barrymore" or "like a disenchanted English actor reading an Elizabethan sonnet on American television." So much, perhaps, for the possibility of being an epireader of poets whom we haven't heard give readings or of those we don't or cannot know. Hass's own poems returned to him again once he was back in the world where he and his brother, as he remembered in the pub, had also, like the Shelford teacher, loved as children reading Kipling aloud "on summer nights . . . in our upstairs room that looked out on a dusty fig orchard and grapevines spilling over the wooden fence." I suppose it would have been even colder in York than it was in Cambridgeshire. Anyway, the one piece in **20th Century Pleasures** actually called a memoir returns Hass to "the San Francisco Bay Area as a culture region." It is a rich and evocative autobiographical essay, and it connects with the important reading of Milosz that comes just before and the remarkable **"Images"** which comes after.

In his Bay Area memoir, Hass is dealing in the most delicate and often amusing and ironic way with the fundamental mysteries of our common world as they were given a local habitation and a name in the area where he grew up. The memoir glosses his desire, in the Lowell essay, to have "the battered figure on the cross . . . and Aphrodite as well," and provides a context both for the way in which he deals with the gnostic side of Milosz and his celebration of the image in the final essay of the book. It begins, in fact, recalling Hass's attempt to write another essay—for one Sister Reginald to enter on his behalf in a competition sponsored by the National League for Decency in Motion Pictures about how fine a film could be made from a book called *Stranded on an Atoll.* In his comical account of the revisions and reversals of attitude while working on this junior high school project, Hass's memory connects Sister Reginald's austere Dominican habit first with the order itself, "founded in the 12th century as a kind of Papal CIA to root out the gnostic heresy of the Cathars," and then, to his surprise, with the modest dress of the Cathar women who had been burned alive at Montségur and elegized, as he had found years later, by both Pound and Robert Duncan. Hass's essay, revised at school but recopied at home before his favorite radio show came on—*I Love a Mystery,* heard ritually each night against the family rules but with his father's visible acquiescence—won a ten-dollar money order from a local bookshop where he bought, dizzy and confused by all the possibilities, *A Comprehensive Anthology of American Poetry.* Unable to understand any of the poems, he stumbles onto Stevens' "Domination of Black" with its cry of the peacocks. Though the young Hass does not at first remember the cry of the peacocks from the front yard of his Portuguese babysitter, the reader does at once, having read about them

in the first paragraph of the memoir "trailing their tails in the dust" under a palm tree. Stevens' peacocks seem to announce the existence of another world. Hass read the poem again and again. "I read it exactly the way I lined up for a roller-coaster ride with a dime tight in my fist at Playland across the bay." It made him, he says, "swoon"—and it made him "understand what the word 'swoon' meant" a year before he found himself actually riding the Playland roller coaster beside a girl in his ninth-grade class he thought "the most beautiful being I had ever come close to in my life, which may also account for some of the previous year's swooning." Mysteries, then: The young boy's fascination with the Sister's habit and her "long beautiful hands which she waved in the air like doves when she conducted us at Mass in the singing of the *Tantum Ergo* and *Pange Lingua,"* the Cathars at Montségur, the theosophical and gnostic writings standing behind the poetry of Robert Duncan later given association with these early memories, the hypnotized amazement at the sound of peacocks crying in what seemed to be an incomprehensible poem read over and over again like a mantra nevertheless, the similarly hypnotized amazement at the existence—at the otherness—of a beautiful girl, a radio program called *I Love a Mystery* mysteriously allowed to be heard even though it violated family rules, and the sound of peacocks crying in a babysitter's yard unconnected with the ones that cried in the poem, even unnoticed. In the same year he won the essay prize, Hass and his friends were playing baseball on teams sponsored by businessmen's clubs and insurance companies with hilarious names, especially when seen stitched on players' uniforms in competition, like *Optimists* and *California Casualty.* Playing center field, he heard the "irritated, prenocturnal cries of the peacocks" in the yard of the Portuguese babysitter. And the grown man writes:

> I never once associated them with the Wallace Stevens poem. Art hardly ever does seem to come to us at first as something connected to our own world; it always seems, in fact, to announce the existence of another, different one, which is what it shares with gnostic insight. That is why, I suppose, the next thing artists have to learn is that this world is the other world.

Beside the baseball field ran a creek called Papermill. By the time Hass reads a poem by Kenneth Rexroth, who published "the first readable book of poems by a resident" of San Francisco in 1941, he is a little older. But reading that "Under the second moon the / Salmon come, up Tomales / Bay, up Papermill Creek, up / The narrow gorges to their spawning beds in Devil's Gulch" moves him deeply, and in a way very different from that in which he had been moved by "The Domination of Black" before. It is the presence of Papermill Creek in the poem that provides the final jolt and makes it "seem possible that the peacocks in Wallace Stevens and the scraggly birds under the palm tree could inhabit the same world."

These are some of the factors that condition the mind—the being-in-the-world—of the man who will read Milosz for us (and Rilke and Wright and Transtromer and Brodsky) and tell us about the nature of images, the music of poetry, and a poetic form which is "one body." We learn to trust his voice because he does not seek to mute its characteristic tones and intonations in the idiom of critic-talk or theoreze, and because, as they used to say in the sixties, we know—we are specifically told—where he's coming from. One of the places he is coming from *is* the 1960s, and Helen Vendler is right to point this out in her review. But she is wrong to stress the notion that Hass's aim is to rehabilitate the familiar essay. The familiar essay may be rehabilitated along the way in some of these pieces—and very winningly so at that—but the *aim* of the autobiography and "interpolated narratives" is to dramatize as vividly as possible the inevitable historical conditioning of both the texts to be read and the perceptions of the reader who intends to talk about them. Hass does not attempt to clear his mind of everything that's in it before turning to the poem on the page; instead, he gives us an account of what is in his mind when he begins to read and how it comes to be there. He does not stop living while he struggles with intractable profundities in Milosz or in Rilke; he shows us daily life as an illumination of the struggle. Even poems that do announce the existence of another world have got to be perceived in this one, and the history—both personal and social or political—which shapes the circumstances of their being read by this particular reader in this particular time in this particular place becomes, in Hass's writing, essential to the work at hand. The premises which Helen Vendler is looking for are found, essentially, in the narrative and autobiographical passages of the book. And not only premises, but a whole implied poetics. There is a moment—and Vendler doesn't like it; it is the passage she objects to in terms of what she regards to be a descent into bathos and a failure of tone—when Hass the particular reader becomes for a brief moment the perfectly average American of his time and place, which is one aspect of his existence as person and poet and reader of poems which he knows he must acknowledge.

> I am a man approaching middle age in the American century, which means I've had it easy, and I have three children, somewhere near the average, and I've just come home from summer vacation in an unreliable car. This is the *selva oscura.*

That is the passage which Vendler quotes. But it goes on: "Not that it isn't true, but that it is not the particular truth. It is the average, which is different from the common; arbitrary, the enemy of form." And Hass is the friend of form.

In the Milosz essay, the Berkeley native, conditioned by a life that makes him in some ways a hostage to what he calls "the seemingly eternal Saturday afternoons of *l'homme moyen sensuel*" and in others a gifted and utterly displaced member of the diaspora of poets and readers of poems still half listening for the peacock's cry that announces the existence of another world, must deal with the fiercely isolated and visionary Berkeley immigrant from Lithuania who refuses "in the privacy of his vocation as a poet to become an accomplice of time and matter." This last, says Hass, is a difficult step for the American imagination to take.

Hass's imagination as a poet does not take that step, but his imagination as a critic follows with deep sympathy and understanding the voyage of Milosz as *he* takes it. The essay on images which ends the book probably comes closer than anything else to being Hass's *Ars Poetica.* The essay on Milosz, to use a word borrowed I think from Robert Duncan in these essays, gives "permission" for its affirmation of the world—of time and matter—by testing the most typical manifestations of the American poetic imagination against Milosz's "leap into dualism or gnosticism" seen against the full history of the poet's life and thought and, again, the factors conditioning the critic's reading. "It might be useful," he says, "to begin by invoking a time when one might turn to the work of Czeslaw Milosz."

The time turns out to be the later 1960s, and the first scene recalled is a protest march to the napalm plant in Redwood City which I remember very well participating in. Bearing our pathetically inadequate signs and listening to the hopelessly inane or merely rhetorical speeches, we did indeed "feel sheepish between gusts of affection for this ragtag army of an aroused middle class." In three pages of narrative and description as good as anything in *Armies of the Night,* Hass evokes the atmosphere of guilt, commitment, generosity, illusion, disillusion, cynicism, and craziness culminating in what he calls "a disease that was on me." He remembers the Second World War veteran who shaved his head, smeared himself with red dye, and began attending Quaker meetings carrying an American flag; the careerist professor who returned from a European antiwar demonstration "to wear jeans, T-shirt and a Mao cap to teach his course in Victorian bibliography"; a friend arrested with dynamite in his trunk driving off to blow up a local air base. On his way home from the Redwood City demonstration, he even catches a glimpse of his loathed double twenty years before its time, a version of "the man approaching middle age in the American century" from the essay on images in the form of a vacationing paterfamilias driving his wife and somewhere-near-the-average-number-of-children off to enjoy dinner "on a deck from which you can admire green pines, grey granite, blue sky . . . thousands of miles away [from] fear, violence, brothels, villages going up in an agony of flames." He thinks about myth and decides that "myth is about eating each other . . . man's first tool for sanctifying the food chain. . . . The world was a pig-out; or the matter-universe was a pig-out. As if there were some other universe to distinguish this one from."

The disease that was on him had various names—philosophy, theology, eschatology—and the one thing he felt he knew about them "was that they were the enemies of poetry." But they were the enemies of a poetry inherited from Williams and Pound, an American modernism which sought to render things rather than ideas, to build a poetry out of natural objects or pictographs "as if no one had ever thought before and nothing needed to be thought that was not shot through with the energy of immediate observation." The problem was that the things and objects and pictographs of an imagist or imagist-derived poetics threw "the weight of meaning back on the innocence and discovery of the observer, and something in the dramatic ambivalence of that gesture rhymed with the permanent unconscious of the man with the boat," the vacationing paterfamilias noticed while returning from Redwood City. Hass felt "vaguely ashamed" when he saw this in the poems he was reading. "I wanted to read a poetry by people who did not assume that the great drama in their work was that everything in the world was happening to them for the first time." He finds such a poetry in the work of Milosz, but also a poetry willing to postulate a universe different from this one, different from the pig-out matter-universe of Hass's eschatological disease which the medicine of American poetry didn't seem to cure.

Hass discusses or alludes to twenty-nine books by Milosz in his long and loving consideration of the full career, and I haven't space enough to outline the entire argument. For my own purposes, I want to focus on the end of the piece, the pages where Hass's poetic imagination sidles up most closely to Milosz's own, but where—because Milosz really does locate the disease Hass was suffering from in the matter-universe itself, and not in a particular subjective aberration caused by a particular objective moment in a nation's history—the two imaginations also must part company.

Hass argues that Simone Weil's lesson to Milosz that "contradiction is the lever of transcendence" gave the poet, who had also taken eros as one of his teachers, permission to dwell in contradiction: "and once that happened, eros—in the form of dream, memory, landscape—comes flooding back into his work" after the years in Paris during the 1950s. But since erotic poetry "is usually intense because it is narrow and specific, mute and focused," when the focus of Milosz's work "widens through a terrible and uncompromising love of his own vanished experience, the poetry, refusing to sacrifice the least sharpness of individual detail to that wider vision, makes a visceral leap into dualism or gnosticism." Hass writes three closely argued pages explaining exactly how this happens, concluding thus:

If you do not want one grain of sand lost, one mo-

ment lost, if you do not admit to the inexorable logic of the death or suffering of a single living creature, then you might, by a leap of intuition, say that it is *all* evil, because then nothing could be judged. Because it all dwelt in limitation or contradiction or, as Blake said, in Ulro. But the universe could be saved if you posited a totally independent but parallel universe of good in which each thing also had an existence. Thus, when the matter-universe fell away, the good universe survived.

Again, if you like, the cry of peacocks. But for Hass himself the other world announced has got to be this very world he's living in, the other universe the only universe we know.

In the final essay in the book—and I am passing over a brilliant reading of Rilke which falls between the Milosz essay and the essay celebrating images, not to mention half a dozen others of enormous interest—Hass becomes "an accomplice of time and matter." To praise things is not necessarily, as it comes to be in Milosz, "to praise the history of suffering; or to collude with torture and mutilation and decay." The American will out (with a little help from the Japanese), his illness purged perhaps by contemplating all the implications of the *gnosis* vouchsafed to the Lithuanian. But the most extraordinary thing about this essay is that it requires from life a vision as remarkable as any given to a Catholic mystic or a gnostic prophet, and that life cooperates with all the urgency that literature could possibly require of it.

It's difficult to know even what to call the essay on images. Like other essays in the book—but maybe here more fully achieved—it may invent a new nongeneric form of writing in its combination of vivid anecdote, personal reminiscence, literary history and analysis, meditation on life and death and imagery found in poetry, fiction, painting, sculpture, mythology, and ordinary quotidian experience. Hass begins by gathering some images from his recent domestic life and running them through his mind along with others found in Chekhov, Buson, and Issa to demonstrate their power and the extent to which we may be haunted by them. He examines the nature of "the moment, different for different memories, when the image, the set of relationships that seems actually to reveal something about life, forms." Then he picks out such a moment: a woman camping with him and his family in a canyon about to tell a story of early sorrow: a frying pan in one hand, a scouring pad in the other, a Stellar's jay perched in the tree above her, Hass's son playing card tricks, a long granite moraine behind them, a meadow in the distance. Then Issa, then Buson, then Tu Fu who said of the power of images: "It's like being alive twice." Neither idea, nor myth, nor always metaphor, images do not explain or symbolize: "they do not say this is that, they say this is."

Hass walks through the rooms of his house feeling his life to be in part "a long slow hurdle through the forms of things." It is a sensation he resists because it implies a kind of passivity, but he would doubt the absence of the sensation because he knows his life is lived among the forms and facts and objects of the natural world. "The terror of facts is the purity of their arbitrariness. I live in this place, rather than that. Have this life, rather than that. It is August not September." Then comes the sentence about being a man approaching middle age in the American century having come home from a summer vacation. The true haiku of his recent domestic life would have to go, he says, something like this: "Bill and Leif want to climb Mount Allac and Karen and I are taking the Volkswagen to go fishing, so can you and Mom walk to the beach now and pick up Luke at Peter's later in Grandma's car?" Collecting images, beginning his essay, these distracting twentieth-century pleasures had begun to eat him up. He felt "a means to a means to a means" and longed for a little solitude in which to think about poems as arresting as Basho's haiku written just before his death: "Sick on a journey, / my dream hovers / over the withered fields."

At this point, Hass breaks off writing. The second part of his essay begins by unexpectedly incorporating an experience which has just occurred: "Because it is summer," he says, "I have been in the mountains again and am now back at the typewriter." The experience in the mountains has been shattering. Walking a path in Desolation Wilderness, Hass began to feel the prickly sensation and notice the rash of an allergic reaction which he sometimes gets. He ignored it and kept walking until the inside of his mouth began to swell, the sign of a generalized reaction which can end in one's throat closing up. He took two antihistamines, but the reaction intensified nevertheless, and he began to feel dizzy and frightened. He thought of the worst that might happen: that his son would have to punch a hole in his trachea with a knife; no, that he would die. The images and attendant memories that he had been collecting passed through his mind, including Basho's dream that "hovers over the withered fields." Then his legs gave way and he was on his back looking at the hillside and the sky: "everything green in the landscape turned white, and the scene flared and shuddered as if it were on fire." Later, after the antihistamines had taken hold and he had recovered, he felt as if he had been granted a vision of death: "White trees, white grass, white leaves; the snow patches and flowering currant suddenly dark beside them; and everything there, rock, tree, cloud, sky, shuddering and blazing. It was a sense, past speaking, past these words, that everything, all of the earth and time itself, was alive and burning."

This is an amazing passage to encounter in the middle of a literary discussion, and it ought finally to make clear that phrases such as "interpolated narratives" or categories like "familiar essay" don't begin to say enough about how Hass's writing works on us. After the death vision—and it *is* a vi-

sion of death, not resurrection, not the vision of Czeslaw Milosz where "the demiurge's workshop will be stilled . . . / And the form of every single grain will be restored in glory"— Hass returns gratefully to time and things and human beings to celebrate the world of the peacocks in the babysitter's yard, the other world which is this world, and the sensation great art and image-making give us of marrying that world, of living in the grain at the permission of eros and "in the light of primary acts of imagination." He doesn't give up the idea from the Milosz essay that many things bear thinking about that are not "shot through with the energy of immediate observation," but he does, here, affirm that energy as one of the supreme values in poetry. In spite of this, or maybe even because of it, the essay is death-haunted to the end, and this is one of the things that makes it so exceptionally memorable. "The earth turns, and we live in the grain of nature, turning with it. . . . When the spirit becomes anguished or sickened by this cycle, by the irreversibility of time and the mutilation of choice, another impulse appears: the monotheist rage for unity. . . ." One sometimes finds this rage in Hass's work both as poet and critic, but not very often; not, at any rate, unless it appears as the "fuel" which he says can power "the natural polytheism of the life of art." Remember the essay on Lowell's monotheistic rage in "The Quaker Graveyard" and the terms according to which Hass was able to be moved by the prayer at the end of its fifth part. For the rest, the essay delicately builds a collage of images from the haiku masters, from Pound and Williams and H.D., from Whitman and Chekhov and Cézanne, and comments on them, bringing life's experiences—his own and those of the artists whose work he loves—to bear upon that commentary. If we are lucky, he says, the images in terms of which we live our lives "are invisibly transformed into the next needful thing." (The danger is in clinging just to one, to the exclusion of yet others which should naturally compose themselves.) Though there is something of Basho's spirituality and a lot of Issa's humanity in the prose of *20th Century Pleasures,* I associate the author of these essays most of all with the spirit of Buson whose "apparent interest in everything that passed before his eyes and the feeling in his work of an artist's delight in making" provide a sense of "something steadying and nourishing" for Hass. I am similarly steadied and nourished by his own work here, and by the sound of a voice that I think I know. Concluding his book by quoting a final Buson haiku about whale-watching, Hass remembers his own participation in a West Coast version of that ritual and says: "We go to glimpse being." And of the poet himself, whose whale-watchers in the haiku find no whales: "Buson is not surprised by the fullness and the emptiness of things."

Carolyn Kizer (review date 12 November 1989)

SOURCE: "Necessities of Life and Death," in *The New York Times Book Review,* November 12, 1989, p. 63.

[*In the following excerpt, Kizer praises Hass's* Human Wishes.]

Robert Hass is so intelligent that to read his poetry or prose, or to hear him speak, gives one an almost visceral pleasure. He is the master of what I call the reticule poem. A reticule is a capacious bag carried by some of our grandmothers, which might contain knitting, cough drops, gloves, a tin of cookies, a volume of Wordsworth or Jane Austen or a missal, coin purse, shopping list, makeup and a folder of family snapshots. In short, necessities of life. One can say that all these articles go together because they are together, in one bag. But it is Mr. Hass's associative processes, his associated sounds and his strategies that enhance, combine and weave together these elements to give his poems their rich and singular flavor.

> when Luke was four or five
> he would go out . . . still in his dandelion
> yellow pajamas on May mornings
> and lie down on the first warm stone
>
> Later, on street corners,
> you can hardly see the children, chirping
> and shivering, each shrill voice climbing over
> the next in an ascending chorus "Wait, you guys,"
> one little girl says, trying to be heard
> "Wait, wait, wait, wait, wait" . . .
>
> Richard, who had recently divorced,
> idly rolling a ball with someone else's child,
> healing slowly, as the neighbor's silky mare
> who had had a hard birth in the early spring,
> stood quiet in the field as May grew sweet,
> her torn vagina healing

[The poems in **Human Wishes**] need to be heard, spoken resonances, pauses, intonations, the vocal music. Mr. Hass is a poet of domestic passion—for children, friends, the household, the neighborhood, for women as lovers, women as friends. His publisher speaks of his work as poems of loss, of mutilation. Rather, he is a poet of abundance, a romantic of the breakfast table, of a companionable walk in his California hills. Perhaps his publisher was bemused—as well she might be—by his elegy to a vanished life, a miscarried child, called **"Thin Air."** This noble poem, which defies paraphrase and should not be amputated by quotation, is the keystone of a remarkable book.

David Barber (review date December 1989)

SOURCE: A review of *Human Wishes*, in *Boston Review*, Vol. XIV, No. 6, December, 1989, pp. 28-9.

[*In the following review, Barber compares* Human Wishes *to Hass's earlier work.*]

While not quite as rare as a lunar eclipse, a new book of poems by Robert Hass isn't likely to escape notice. In his first two collections, *Field Guide* (1973) and *Praise* (1979), Hass helped ignite a running dialogue between the possibilities of the lyric and the demands of the intellect. And the intellect, in his case, seemed to have won out. Over the past decade Hass's prominence has owed less to his distinctively crafted poems than to his determined undertakings as a critic (*Twentieth Century Pleasures,* a volume of gracefully erudite essays, won the National Book Critics Circle Award for criticism in 1984) and translator (most notably, by way of his working partnership with Berkeley neighbor Czeslaw Milosz).

At an age by which many of his contemporaries are starting to cobble together their selected poems, Hass's restrained literary enterprise has had about it an air of almost monkish detachment. Naturally, then, one is tempted to regard the conspicuous hiatus between collections as the product of either painstaking ambitions or painful reservations. *Human Wishes,* as it turns out, provides ample evidence on both sides.

"I think I must have thought / the usual things," Hass muses early in **"On Squaw Peak,"** a supple elegy for a miscarried child that closes the book. It's a moment that could serve as a refrain. *Human Wishes* teems with Hass's "usual things": studious observations of his native California landscape, reflections on the failed paradigms of language and desire, dilemmas over art's relation to social circumstance, appeals to a muscular sense of history and memory. But what gives the line its signature ring and the book its familiar cast is Hass's characteristic attempt to eavesdrop on his own intelligence, his impulse toward incessant revision and quiet skepticism. Nor has this most self-conscious of poets broken the mold of his colloquial yet elliptical meditative manner: more than ever, Hass seems to want to be overheard more than he wishes to address us, so absorbed is he in the workings of his mind, the sifting of his experience, and the act of articulation itself.

What's always righted Hass's tilt toward solipsism is his infectious zest—verging at times on fetish—for the world's sensual particulars. Happily, *Human Wishes* draws nourishment from a bulging horn of plenty—"sweet hermaphrodite peaches and the glister of plums," "the frank nipples of brioche," "chunks of cooked chicken in a creamy basil mayonnaise a shade lighter than the Coast Range in August." Riffs like these tell us unmistakably that we've happened onto a Hass poem. Where else can the mandarin break bread with the mystic, the Epicurean sit down with the Stoic? Yet *Human Wishes* confirms that there's more to Hass than courtly efforts to keep body and mind on speaking terms. The give and take of passionate dialectics lends this book its very grain, abstraction answering to detail, pleasure to pain, clarity to mystery, epiphany to commonplace. Then there's Hass's noted penchant for fleshing out contraries by way of the flesh itself, his candid tracking shot into bedrooms where lovers entwine in a blur of ardor and desperation. This time around, in two of the volume's finer poems, Hass opens the door on a couple who are "trying to become one creature / and something will not have it" (**"Misery and Splendor"**) and who "close their eyes again and hold each other, each / feeling the mortal singularity of the body / they have enchanted out of death for an hour or so" (**"Privilege of Being"**).

Obsessive though Hass is, mulish he's not. Despite unquestionable similarities in theme and manner, *Human Wishes* is at once a more ingratiating and disquieting book than its predecessors. Paradoxically, it appears as if Hass's poems now rest easier in their skins even as they feel sharper chills in their bones. He's more assured than ever, for example, in quarrying poems out of the personal and the local, in naming names and limning intimacies, all but pulling up a chair for us at the family table in his conviction that poetry begins at home. Hass's wife, children, and friends not only are routinely invoked but generously quoted, even, as in **"Santa Barbara Road,"** when words are barely within reach: "Household verses: 'Who are you?' / the rubber duck in my hand asked Kristen / once, while she was bathing, three years old. / 'Kristen,' she said, laughing, her delicious / name, delicious self." It's difficult to think of any poet since Williams who so persuasively brings the pulse of daily common life to the page.

A good portion of that daily life, however, teeters on doubt and resignation. In Hass's previous books melancholy lapped at the poems' edges; here it wells up at almost every step. One trace of this residual sorrow can be detected in the nearly complete absence of Hass's once customary delight in marrying refined poetic measure to unpruned organic forms, the best efforts of which (*Praise*'s **"Weed"** comes to mind) suggested a sturdy hybrid of hothouse prosody and wayside vernacular. In *Human Wishes,* he's given himself over almost entirely to the long line and block stanza, steadfastly adhering to unadorned, prose-like rhythms throughout the sinuous paragraphs and strict prose poems of the first half of the book and the sequences and monologues of the second. Nothing if not resourceful, he's cultivated a more open, intimately epistolary verse that makes room for everything from strenuous metaphysics, beguiling storytelling, and wry recollections to haiku-like snapshots, flinty epigrams, and tremulous lyricism. Yet, on another level, the self-effacing withdrawal from poetic shapeliness, the occasionally stolid essayistic manner, betrays a sensibility increasingly consumed with diminishment and flux. "There is no need for this dream-compelled narration," writes Hass abruptly at the close of **"Late Spring,"**

biting off the poem's lulling seasonal evocation: "the rhythm will keep me awake, changing."

Change Hass has, though time and age alone cannot account for the somber hues of *Human Wishes.* Even the youthful Hass was wise to how myths and hopes exhaust themselves, how language turns in on itself, how mindfulness is a mixed blessing. Here his concessions run deeper: provisionality and mutability make hash of human will and insight, not to mention human wishes. And where does that leave the poet? In part, prematurely autumnal (there's no small irony in the fact that so many poems here are spring and summer set pieces); in part, tempering his reckonings with a poetry unashamed of bordering here and there on prayer. Frost, you'll recollect, aspired to verse that might provide "momentary stays against confusion." Hass's new poems, whether zeroing in on the "interval created by *if,* to which mind and breath attend," or reaching to embrace "the blessedness of gathering and the blessing of dispersal," strive for equilibrium amid disorder— and reward us more often than not with something we might call equipoise.

Don Bogen (review date 11 December 1989)

SOURCE: "A Student of Desire," in *Nation,* Vol. 249, No. 20, December 11, 1989, pp. 722-23.

[*Bogen is an author and educator. In the following review, he remarks favorably on* Human Wishes.]

What's immediately striking in Robert Hass's work is the sheer abundance of pleasures. Who else among our poets would bring together the delights of landscape, climate and food in a salad "with chunks of cooked chicken in a creamy basil mayonnaise a shade lighter than the Coast Range in August" (**"Vintage"**) or include a recipe for onion soup— complete with shredded Samsoe and advice on how to eat it with friends—as a **"Song to Survive the Summer"**? In his incisive collection of essays, *Twentieth Century Pleasures,* Hass set our engagement with poetry squarely in the context of other forms of satisfaction—in domestic life, in nature, in the senses. The title of his new book of poetry, *Human Wishes,* reveals his basic concerns: He is a student of desire, of what we want and how likely we are to get it.

If one pleasure of poetry is the evocation of beautiful things, Hass's work definitely satisfies. From his first book, *Field Guide,* which won the Yale Series of Younger Poets Award in 1973, through *Praise* in 1979 and now *Human Wishes,* he has shown a mastery of sensory description, combining the light touch of a calligrapher with the specificity of a botanist. Place—particularly northern California, where he grew up and now lives—has always been central in Hass's poetry, and few writers capture the special qualities of this environment as well. **"January"** gives a fine sense of that gorgeous oddity, a Bay Area winter:

> Back at my desk: no birds, no rain,
> but light-the white of Shasta daisies,
> and two red geraniums against the fence,
> and the dark brown of wet wood,
> glistening a little as it dries.

Hass's continuing engagement with Japanese poetry is evident here. Casual in tone, the lines seem almost transparent, as if they were just a moment's observation. Yet their arrangement is exquisite. The contrast between the blank monosyllables of the first line and a half—"no birds, no rain"—and the sudden appearance of those specific, polysyllabic Shasta daisies; the step-by-step expansion of the color scheme—"white," "red," then "dark brown"; the subtle echoes of sound in "red" and "wet," "daisies" and "dries"; and the hint of blank verse for closure in the last line show a rigorous and self-effacing craftsmanship. The lines have been written so well they hardly seem "written" at all.

With his California subjects and his skill at evocation, Hass could easily have settled for the reproduction of a predictable and popular verse "product." Indeed, a few years after *Field Guide* came out, a small fad for poems with references to food, accounts of hikes and other surface elements of his work flourished in the literary magazines. But Hass is after something more than sensuous word painting. The mind behind the description is analytical, probing, unsatisfied with the conventional stances language often provides. The poems in *Human Wishes* are energetic and full of surprises. They turn on themselves suddenly, breaking into self-consciousness or rejecting their initial visions, as when the idyllic reverie of **"Late Spring"** is revealed to be a fabrication that keeps the poet awake at night, or the list of pretty images at the start of **"Spring Drawing"** and again in **"Spring Drawing 2"** implies but then fails to generate a sentence.

Hass's awareness of the limits of language helps fuel his restless exploration of different poetic strategies. Each of his books makes use of a range of approaches and forms, from rhymed iambic pentameter to haiku, from brief lyrics to sequences of fragments to long discursive meditations. In *Human Wishes* he consolidates the strengths of his earlier work while pushing on into fresh territory. The first section of the book, for example, develops a new kind of line: lengthy, proselike in its rhythms and set off in a stanza by itself. These lines function as independent postulates in an argument, some plush and physical like the one about chicken salad, others gnarled with abstraction like these from the first poem in the book, **"Spring Drawing"**:

> as if spirit attended to plainness only,
> the more complicated forms ex-

hausting it, tossed-off grapestems
becoming crystal chandeliers,

> as if radiance were the meaning of
> meaning, and justice responsible to
> daydream not only for the strict
> beauty of denial,

> but as a felt need to reinvent the inner
> form of wishing.

Hass has never shied away from the language of theoretical discourse. In fact, he finds a rarefied music in the polysyllabic abstractions, long clauses and parallel constructions of his argument. This is not a music everyone will enjoy. It can be daunting to encounter a passage like the one above on the first page of a book of poetry. But if the demands on a reader are high, they signal Hass's commitment to his enterprise: an art that can both evoke and analyze the complexity of human desires.

The second section of *Human Wishes* consists of prose poems, a form prefigured in some of the work in *Praise* but not developed consistently until now. Rimbaud is the father of this type of poem, and much American work in the genre still reads like a bad translation from the French. Hass has avoided the portentousness and easy surrealism that can afflict paragraphs trying too hard to be poetic. Instead, he looks to narrative models—the short story, the anecdote—as well as to allegory and the personal essay as guideposts. A few of the shorter prose poems—**"Duck Blind," "In the Bahamas"**—can seem a little thin, but the longer pieces give him room to juxtapose scenes and events, building up a constellation of meaning. **"The Harbor at Seattle,"** for example, looks at friendship and personal tragedy within different contexts of history, art and work. Each paragraph in this beautifully structured poem works like a controlled reaction as the poet puts two elements together, notes the effects, then moves on to the next step. In the title poem of *Human Wishes,* Hass achieves a more dense interactive texture. This page-long paragraph uses rapid shifts of focus, from the Upanishads to a Cambridge pub, to expose a web of varied individual desires—for beauty, for understanding, for wealth, for a good time with friends—in all its intricacy and imperfection.

The unspoken element in all "human wishes" is, of course, vanity. Hass may not be as explicit as Juvenal on this point—he finds beauty in some of these wishes, flawed as they are—but he's well aware of the devastating power of time and human failings. In the extended meditations that make up the last two sections of *Human Wishes,* he traces pleasures and their loss—in love, in family life, in the living world—with intelligence and a deft control of tone. Despite the wealth of personal detail in these poems, there is little overt self-dramatization. The poet is not set up as the tragic hero of his own life. His presence in the work is rather that of a man *thinking*: remembering, describing, defining, comparing, imagining.

As in the prose poems, the strength of these meditations lies in Hass's ability to handle several themes at the same time and his exploration of the range of possibilities the form presents. In one of the most intriguing, **"Berkeley Eclogue,"** he takes on the hoary literary convention of the pastoral dialogue. The decorous speech of stylized shepherds becomes an internal argument, with a harsh second voice—a kind of nagging muse—prodding the poet toward more clarity and depth with italicized comments such as *"You can skip this part"* and *"Do you believe in that?"* Other meditations are symphonic in structure. **"Santa Barbara Road"** introduces, repeats and varies several different motifs—the poet building a bench, children and their parents, classical Chinese thought, June weather, various walks—in an extended reflection on the abundance and impermanence of family life.

Hass's sense of the interrelatedness of all human endeavor gives his book a breadth of perspective and a distinct focus. Even the man brewing one cup of tea and immersing himself in his own memories at the end of **"Thin Air"** is connected to the frustrated warehouse worker who packed the tea leaves. This is not liberal sympathy but a recognition of how things work, of the context of suffering and loss in which we live. It is a mark of Hass's integrity as a poet that he rejects the usual consolations here. Art, nature, love—these are certainly pleasures but not solutions. They are parts of what he calls in **"On Squaw Peak"**

> . . . the abundance
> the world gives, the more-than-you-
> bargained-for
> surprise of it, waves breaking,
> the sudden fragrance of the mimulus at
> creekside
> sharpened by the summer dust.
> Things bloom up there. They are
> for their season alive in those bright
> vanishings
> of air we ran through.

If the first half of the passage is as rich and surprising as its subject, the last sentence stumbles on the perfect awkward placement of "for their season." In **Human Wishes** Robert Hass captures both the brightness of the world and its vanishing.

John Ash (review date 31 December 1989)

SOURCE: "Going Metric," in *Book World—The Washington Post,* December 31, 1989, p. 6.

[*In the following excerpt, Ash offers a negative appraisal of the poems in* Human Wishes, *with the exception of "Natural Theology."*]

[**Human Wishes**] raises disturbing questions about what can be said to constitute a poem today. I am not referring to the fact that the first two of its four sections are written in prose. In fact the opening sequence of prose poems is by far the best part of the book. The prose here is elaborate and compacted in such a way that we are left in no doubt that we are reading poetry, but, despite some good moments, the pieces in the second section obstinately refuse to catch fire. Inconsequential anecdotes (a visit to the doctor, an upper-middle-class dinner party, remarks the neighbors made) are recorded in prose that is unremarkable when not actually clichéd. Hass seems to have fallen victim to confused intentions and weakly sentimental failings.

Sentimentality is often taken as evidence that the writer's heart is in the right place, that he is just too close to his material. But Wallace Stevens's stern definition of sentimentality as "a failure of feeling" is the correct one. This failure also infects the verse that follows in parts three and four. When Hass remarks of "the famous night / we first made love" that "I think I remember / stars, that the moon was watery and pale," it isn't the facile romanticism that irritates so much as the inauthenticity betrayed by that "I *think* I remember." One either remembers or one does not. Hass is being coy.

His habit of continually mentioning family and friends by name also makes the poems a little too cozy for comfort. Hass has made the common mistake of assuming that the details of middle-class, intellectual domesticity are innately interesting. This is writing that is confined by class, writing that routinely signals "sadness," "love" and "loss" in fluent, characterless language. Attempts at a more heightened style only result in unconvincing mannerism. The opening lines of **"Privilege Of Being"** suggest that Rilke has a lot to answer for:

> Many are making love. Up above, the angels
> in the unshaken ether and crystal of human longing
> are braiding one another's hair, which is strawberry
> blond
> and the texture of cold rivers . . .

After reading this it is impossible to believe any thing that Hass says in the rest of the poem. What follows is in any case a concatenation of some of the hoariest clichés in the poetic lexicon (subcategory: making love), for example, "awkward ecstasy," "mortal singularity of the body" and "unspeakable sadness." I will not go on. But it is worth dwelling on this failure since Hass is a poet of real talent. He proved this in his last collection, **Praise,** and he proves it again, here, with **"Natural Theology,"** a genuinely affecting poem that addresses itself with impressive eloquence to "the imagination of need from which the sun keeps rising into morning light." Let us hope that this poem will set the tone for his next collection.

Darcy Aldan (review date Spring 1990)

SOURCE: A review of *Human Wishes,* in *World Literature Today,* Vol. 64, No. 2, Spring, 1990, p. 313.

[*In the following review, Aldan praises Hass's imagery in* Human Wishes.]

The delicacy and sensibility of Robert Hass, as exemplified in his new volume of poetry, **Human Wishes,** is a distinct joy to experience in this time when so many published works deal with violence, aberration, and alienation. His elegant gleanings of essence, often impressionist in tone, make us aware once again that beauty and meaningful silence still exist; that the day's events, as they progress into weeks, months, seasons in the cycle of life, are timeless and universal. What is required is that one remain attentive. Hass has done so, and has used his skill to record, and to remind us.

The collection is divided into four parts, through which various themes weave in flowing rhythm and resonance of imagery, among them the theme of progression, of metamorphosis. In mingling the sublime with the "everyday," as Mallarmé called it, the inner life is revealed, and we are grateful to acknowledge that this does not occur computerlike. Careful selection of details and image placement here lead not to naturalism but to art, to the true poem. Thus Hass succeeds in achieving what Mallarmé attempted: to depict "non la chose, mais l'effet qu'elle produit." Hass's poems, however, are not the convoluted, complex, multimeaning structures of the French poet, but rather an easy-flowing form consonant with the English language and the evolution of poetic structure.

Parts 1 and 4 contain the most successful poems, the latter section being a veritable apotheosis toward which the rest of the collection ascends. At the very start, in **"Spring Dawning,"** Hass states: "A man thinks *lilacs against white houses* . . . and can't find his way to a sentence, a brushstroke carrying the energy of *brush* and *stroke*. . . . as if radiance were the meaning of meaning, and justice responsible to daydream not only for the strict beauty of denial but as a felt need to reinvent the inner form of wishing." Later, in **"Spring Dawning 2,"** he will say, "A man says *lilacs against white houses,* two sparrows, one streaked, in a thinning birch, and can't find his way to a sentence."

In part 2 an attempt is made to create the prose poem. Hass's is not the prose poem of Mallarmé, Poe, or even W. S. Merwin, but rather similar to those of the Swiss poet Albert Steffen, who calls his creations "little myths." Among those, the one called "January," with its combination of structured verse and narration, is an evocative experience. This section contains observations, nostalgia, memories, dreams, in sudden beautiful images, as in the poem **"Calm"**: "The meadow, you remember the meadow? And the air in June which held the scent of it as the woman in religious iconography holds the broken son? [That is amazing!] . . . You can go into that meadow, the light routed by a brilliant tenderness of green." Another enjoyable image occurs in **"Novella"**: "It lay in her memory like one piece of broken tile, salmon-colored or the deep green of wet leaves, beautiful in itself but unusable in the design she was making."

In part 3 the poet returns to the familiar verse structure, but in a free projected line and rhythm. **"The Apple Trees at Olema"** alone would make the volume worth owning. A magical atmosphere and tone are created by such lines as "She is shaken by the raw, white, backlit flaring / of the apple blossoms" or "a thin moon of my dismay / fades like a scar in the sky to the east of them." Moments of sadness, love, and communion are captured and re-created with economy, suggestion, and skill. Hass weaves events as a spider might weave a delicate silken net and depicts "so many visions / intersecting at what we call the crystal / of a common world."

In part 4 the profusion of exquisite images is so great I can only recommend that any poetry lover purchase the collection, for choosing an image or two to quote seems inadequate. Perhaps the following lines from **"Natural Theology,"** however, will whet the appetite for beauty:

> . . . and the fluting of one bird where the road curves and disappears,
> becoming that gap or lack which is the oldest imagination of need, defined more sharply by the silvergrey region just before the sun goes down and the clouds fade through rose to bruise to the city-pigeon color of the sky going dark and the wind comes up in brushstroke silhouettes of trees and to your surprise the window mirrors back to you a face open, curious, and tender. . . .

In **"Tall Windows"** the secret of Hass's creative esthetic is revealed: "What kept you awake was a feeling that everything in the world has its own size, that if you found its size among the swellings and diminishings it would be calm and shine." Hass finds the size of disparate experiences and renders them calm—and they shine.

Bruce Bond (essay date Fall 1990)

SOURCE: "An Abundance of Lack: The Fullness of Desire in the Poetry of Robert Hass," in *Kenyon Review,* Vol. XII, No. 4, Fall, 1990, pp. 46-53.

[*In the following essay, Bond centers on Hass's manipulation of language as he discusses themes of desire, loss, and redemption in Hass's poetry and prose.*]

The word "clarity" is often unclear. If by "clear" we mean "under the clarifying light of reason," placed with quieting control in a world promoted as stable, without contradiction, then Robert Hass's poetry is repeatedly unclear. But if by "clear" we mean "lit by an immanent light," creating a persuasive model of consciousness in all its disjunctions, wonder and loss, paradox and uncertainty, then Hass's poetry has a clarity which puts its language under immense pressure. Through Hass's clarifying lens, we see words as gestures of longing rather than vestiges of truth, as motivated by a sense of their own failure, a sense of lack that no discourse can finally fill. As though always on the threshold of saying what it cannot, Hass's language is both haunted and invigorated by an "immense subterranean" absence, an absence which we imagine nevertheless as a kind of presence, a "counter-pressure" akin to a displaced unconscious. If his view toward language as both the product and producer of desire, as driven by a sense of lack at the core of its being, appears strikingly Lacanian, it may come as small surprise that Hass recalls, in his essay on Robert Creeley [in *Twentieth Century Pleasures*], the arrival of Jacques Lacan's *Ecrits* on the Anglo-American shore as revolutionary, full of both astonishing and troubling notions that struck the contemporary nerve.

The distinguishing generosity of Hass's work lies in how he turns the everpresence of lack, both as reflected and created by language, into not only a testament of loss, but also an occasion for praise—that which endears the ephemera of our lives. By way of language, absence eroticizes the world. Despite how we may feel troubled in Hass's poetry by what language cannot accommodate, his is not the austere, archetypal, syntactically pared-down universe we often find in so-called poetry of silence—much of W. S. Merwin's verse, for instance. Hass's world is abundant, expansive, richly textured with unexpected detail, philosophical and intimate, unmistakably anchored in daily life yet appealing to our lust for wonder, astonishing us with, what Hass calls in his description of Yosa Buson's poetry [in *Twentieth Century Pleasures*], "the fullness and emptiness of things."

Thus language in its failure to tell the whole truth appears in Hass's poetry as nevertheless redemptive, since such failure animates the imagination and inspires its continual revisions. In Hass's later work, we feel the imaginative urge to renew let loose with particular abandon and an especially disjunctive logic. But although desire may cause disjunctions in consciousness, bringing to mind always the next needful thing, there are complicating moments in Hass's verse where desire appears briefly, paradoxically, as a connecting medium, a bridge made of the distance to be bridged. It joins what cannot logically be joined: self and other, past and present, word and the signified world.

Hass's view of words as gestures of longing, as both empty and full, animated by loss, is perhaps most familiar to his readers by way of his second collection of poems, *Praise*—in particular, the much anthologized poem **"Meditation at Lagunitas"** with its potently aphoristic claims that yield to an affectionately particularizing language, language which, as Hass makes explicit, can never be particular enough to bridge the gap between word and world:

> All the new thinking is about loss.
> In this it resembles all the old thinking.
> The idea, for example, that each particular erases
> the luminous clarity of a general idea. That the
> clown-faced woodpecker probing the dead sculpted
> trunk
> of that black birch is, by his presence,
> some tragic falling off from a first world
> of undivided light. Or the other notion that,
> because there is in this world no one thing
> to which the bramble of *blackberry* corresponds,
> a word is elegy to what it signifies.

The word's longing to cross that impermeable Saussurian bar, to embrace the signified world on the other side, resembles a desire to retrieve a lost past, as though that past harbored an original unity of self and other—a paradise lost, "a first world of undivided light."

The paradox of desire characterizes the paradox of language in that each presupposes a distance between opposites—self and other, past and present, signifier and signified—while creating the very basis for their intimacy. In the life of words, a greeting is always a farewell, an elegy. As Lacan claims, "the being of language is the non-being of objects" ("The direction of the treatment . . . ," *Ecrits*). And this non-being strangely discloses itself as a presence, a yearning, the very conveyance of the abundance of the world:

> Longing, we say, because desire is full
> of endless distances. I must have been the same to
> her.
> But I remember so much, the way her hands
> dismantled
>   bread,
> the thing her father said that hurt her, what
> she dreamed. There are moments when the body is
> as
>   numinous
> as words, days that are the good flesh continuing.
> Such tenderness, those afternoons and evenings,
> saying *blackberry, blackberry, blackberry.*
> (*Praise*)

Desire is full, freighted with the stuff of memory, that which seems both immanent and distant. In reciting a text of remembered things, we are thus made up of a world we lack.

The phrase "numinous as words" recalls the Latin word *numen* ("the spiritual"). Since the numinous world is by definition contradistinguished from the physical, to call the body "numinous as words" is to blur the very concept of numinosity, to confuse so-called inner and outer domains. Such "crossbreeding" is in keeping with a typically Romantic conception of the imagination, that which invests the world with consciousness and consciousness with the world. By way of the image as the point of fusion, the word is made flesh. In his essay **"Images"** [in *Twentieth Century Pleasures*], Hass writes, "that confusion of art and life, inner and outer, is the very territory of the image; it is what an image is. *And the word was made flesh and dwelt among us.*" Bound up inextricably in its lost presence, the word *blackberry* is itself sweet and palpable.

The notion of the body as numinous derives the power to astonish from its illogic—the fact that Hass in one stroke asserts and denies a distinction. Even the most intimate relation between inner and outer, present and past, self and nature, signifier and signified presupposes a distance—a difference. And it is this difference which drives the imagination forward. In his essay **"One Body: Some Notes on Form"** [in *Twentieth Century Pleasures*], Hass claims that he doesn't share Wordsworth's belief that a childlike alliance with nature represents "the first / Poetic spirit of our human life." According to Hass, the urge to create grows rather out of a broken alliance. Hass states, "I have none of [Wordsworth's] assurance, either about the sources of the order of nature or about the absolute continuity between that first nurturing and the form-making activity of the mind. It seems to me, rather, that we make our forms because there is no absolute continuity, because those first assurances are broken. The mind, in the act of recovery, creates."

"Meditation at Lagunitas" pays tribute to memory as such an act, a creative and affectionate response to a fall from the first world of undivided light. Hass's poem **"Natural Theology"** from his third collection of poems, *Human Wishes,* offers a similar tribute, though exploring in more detail the evolutionary pattern of a consciousness:

> White daisies against the burnt orange of the
>   windowframe,
> lusterless redwood in the nickel gray of winter,
> in the distance turbulence of water—the green
> regions
> of the morning reflect whatever can be gained,
> normally,
> by light, then give way to the blue regions of the
>   afternoon

> which do not reflect so much as they remember,
> as if the light, one will all morning, yielded to a
>   doubleness
> in things—

In this first world, "the green regions / of the morning," the images, with their precision of coloristic detail, appear designed to dazzle us, not with their symbolic weight, but with their mere presence, their visual sweets. They have a primary potency to them. In his essay **"Images,"** Hass explains:

> It seems to me that we all live our lives in the light of primary acts of imagination, images or sets of images that get us up in the morning and move us about our days. I do not think anybody can live without one, for very long, without suffering intensely from deadness or futility.

In **"Natural Theology,"** Hass's way of describing the mode of this world's first appearance works to circumvent the perceiver/perceived distinction associated with "the second world," the world of language and the broken alliances that language presupposes. Not a perceiver, but the green regions themselves "reflect," and the degree to which this reflection implies transformation in the process of emergence is ambiguous. The regions, according to Hass, simply "reflect whatever can be gained, normally, by light." What *is* clear is that, as time passes, this light and its green regions yield to an increasingly associative consciousness. Once again, Hass's essay enlarges our reading of the poem:

> I think that, for most of us, those images are not only essential but dangerous because no one of them feels like the whole truth and they do not last. Either they die of themselves, dry up, are shed; or, if we are lucky they are invisibly transformed into the next needful thing.

Secondary acts of the imagination, being more transformative, are more obviously metaphorical, and thus we find ourselves more obviously in the realm of language.

Although Hass does not explicitly associate the "green regions" with infantile experience, such a world resembles the imaginary order which Lacan claims precedes a child's "mirror stage." The mirror stage marks not only the advent of language, but also the emergence of selfhood, made precarious since images of the self are always "out there," mirrored back from the world. In Lacan's words, the "I" "is objectified in the dialectic of identification with the other" ("The Mirror Stage," *Ecrits*). Hass's poem dramatizes a similar mirror stage, a point at which the dynamics of memory make possible the perception of similitude and difference and thus the tension between the two as language. With an associative consciousness, identification becomes possible, and the nar-

cissistic imagination perceives a mirroring sheen on the surface of the other:

> images not quite left behind rising as an undertow
> of endless transformation against the blurring
> world
> outside the window where, after the morning
> clarities,
> the faint reflection of a face appears; among the
> images
> a road, repetitively, with meadow rue and yarrow
> whitening its edges, and pines shadowing the
> cranberry
>   brush,
> and the fluting of one bird where the road curves
> and
>   disappears,
> becoming that gap or lack which is the oldest
>   imagination
> of need, defined more sharply by the silver-gray
> region
> just before the sun goes down . . .
>
> (***Human Wishes***)

Though one's literally reflected physical bearing provides a
metaphor for the self as discrete, that independence is threatened by the otherness of the reflective surface. In Hass's poem,
we feel the dissonance implicit in the emergence of selfhood
as the reflected face floats tentatively over a restless flux of
images.

Like the self, the other too is characterized by lack—in Hass's
poem, that place out there where the road curves and disappears. As Lacan states in his typically elliptical style, "the
subject has to find the constituting structure of his desire in
the same gap opened up by the effect of the signifiers in those
who come to represent the Other for him, insofar as his demand is subject to them" ("The direction of the treatment . .
."). For Lacan, demand includes more than mere physical
need. That margin of demand which stretches beyond need is
what he calls desire, and desire is infinite. Those who are
subject to one's desire are always perceived as lacking.

The bird at the threshold of lack—what Hass calls, "the oldest imagination of need"—invites a cultural memory of birds
that serve as correlatives to the poetic imagination. Keats
and Whitman most obviously come to mind, but also Stevens,
in part by parallel contrast. In Hass's essay **"What Furies,"**
he describes Wallace Stevens's bird in the poem "On Mere
Being" as "both an alien being and the one true resident; it
sings its song without human meaning at the edge of space,
its feathers shining." What is remarkably similar between
Hass's and Stevens's birds is how they are both situated spa-
tially at the limits of consciousness, positioned to imagine
what no imagination successfully can. Paradoxically, extreme

artifice, in the guise of a gilded bird, provides a vocabulary
for the real, that which, as a nonhuman realm, spells the
death of artifice:

> The palm at the end of the mind
> Beyond the last thought, rises
> In the bronze distance,
>
> A gold-feathered bird
> Sings in the palm, without human meaning,
> Without human feeling, a foreign song.
>
> You know then that it is not the reason
> That makes us happy or unhappy.
> The bird sings. The feathers shine.
>
> (*Opus Posthumous*)

On its spare, remote threshold, Stevens's bird sits posed like
an undying piece of formal glamor. The lines are short; the
poem, full of silence. By contrast, Hass's bird appears but
briefly, swept into the afternoon's "undertow of endless transformation." In contrast to the quiet posture of Stevens's lines,
Hass's poem leads breathlessly down forty-one largely
heptameter, cataloging lines before pausing at a period. Hass's
expansiveness offers us a hymn to possibility, but possibility
as grounded in the thingness of everyday life:

> . . . dance is defined
> by the body's possibilities arranged, this dance
> belongs to the composures and the running down
> of things
> in the used sugars of five-thirty: a woman straight-
> ening
> a desk turns her calendar to another day, signaling
> that it is another day where the desk is concerned
> and that there is in her days what doesn't belong to
> the desk;
> a kid turns on TV, flops on the couch to the tinny
> sound
> of little cartoon parents quarreling; a man in a bar
> orders a drink, watches ice bob in the blond fluid,
> he sighs and looks around; sad at the corners,
> nagged by
> wind,
> others with packages; others dreaming, picking
> their
> noses
> dreamily while they listen to the radio . . .
>
> (***Human Wishes***)

Whereas Stevens's poem tends toward paring away the mean-
ingfully charged details of the everyday world, Hass's tends
toward including them all. Since neither absolute elimination
nor inclusion of such detail is possible in language, both
poems create a sense of irresolution.

As in **"Meditation at Lagunitas,"** **"Natural Theology"** imagines the failure of images to tell the whole truth as potentially redemptive, since such failure sparks the urge to renew. But in **"Natural Theology,"** as in much of Hass's newer work, we feel that urge working forcefully on the syntax itself. Hass's new poems have a particularly disjunctive logic, broad canvas, and rich texture of detail. In **"Natural Theology,"** the poem's syntactic momentum and associative skips create the sense of an unseen pressure causing the verbal ground to shift:

> The religion
> or region of the dark makes soup and lights a fire,
> plays backgammon with children on the teeth or
> the
>   stilettos
> of the board, reads books, does dishes, listens
> to the wind, listens to the stars imagined to be
> singing
> invisibly, goes out to be regarded by the moon,
> walks
> dogs, feeds cats, makes love in postures so various,
> with such varying attention and intensity and hope,
> it enacts the dispersion of tongues among the
> people
> of the earth—compris? versteh'—and sleeps with
> sticky genitals
>
>   (*Human Wishes*)

Images rapidly displace one another, unpredictable though not entirely unguided, as though we had been dipped into the lively workings of a symbolic unconscious.

In such a world, Hass tells us, it is "the dark" which "enacts the dispersion of tongues." Thus language enjoys a degree of autonomy from conscious control. It is as though language were speaking itself into existence. The autonomous nature of language, its emergence as an alien self, is yet another Lacanian theme which, as Hass points out [in *Twentieth Century Pleasures*], finds its poetic dramatization in the verse of Robert Creeley:

> The system of analogies derived from Levi-Strauss
> and Lacan and Derrida seems to assert that conscious-
> ness carries with it its own displaced and completely
> symbolic unconscious, that is, the structures of lan-
> guage by which consciousness is constituted. . . . This
> is what Creeley's mode and the attractiveness of his
> mode have to do with, at least much of the time; it is
> a poetics which addresses the tension between speak-
> ing and being spoken through language.

In Lacanian terms, this tension is the tension between the "je" and the "moi," the self that speaks and the self that is spoken, "the object of the other." Most obviously in our

dreams, we feel ourselves "being spoken" by an uncontrollable other, the forms of consciousness enjoying a level of abandon but nevertheless informed by some kind of organizing syntax and symbolic logic.

An element of abandon in the forms of consciousness makes possible their seductive play. In Hass's poem, the French question *compris?* stands posed with a semantic yearning answered by its parallel contrast in German, *versteh'*. The semantic resolution, albeit temporary, of parallel opposites corresponds to a sexual consummation, a metaphor made explicit as the poem then turns to an image of love's aftermath. It is comically appropriate that the question, like a seductive envoy, is in French whereas the response, offering reassuring closure, is in German:

> -compris? versteh'-and sleeps with sticky genitals
> the erasures and the peace of sleep: exactly the
> half-
> moon
> holds, and the city twinkles in particular windows,
> throbs
> in its accumulated glow which is also and more
> blindingly
> the imagination of need from which the sun keeps
> rising
> into morning light,
> because desires do not split themselves up, there is
> one
> desire
> touching many things, and it is continuous.
>
>   (*Human Wishes*)

Just as erotic desire rises again, so does the craving for understanding since no understanding is complete. The whole truth is always deferred, inhabiting an imaginary realm "out there."

Appropriately, Hass's closure in **"Natural Theology"** offers us an image dramatizing the permanent revisionism of consciousness: as the ephemeral sense of sexual and semantic resolution, the erasures and the peace of sleep, give way once again to the climbing light of morning, we are reminded that the cycle of desire is infinite. The sun's movement, slow, inevitable, mirrors an inevitable yearning, rising, as Hass states, from "the imagination of need." Much of the power of Hass's final image lies in the tension it creates between closure and irresolution. The rising sun marks the end of a cycle, a completion which signifies the impossibility of completion. We end with a beginning.

Hass's idea that there is one desire that is "continuous" makes explicit the notion that desire is everpresent—continual. But also there is a way in which desire, being singular and touching many things, provides an associative continuity among the contents of a consciousness. In Hass's final lines, desire is credited with creating a sense not only of variety and disjunctiveness but also of coherence and belonging. In its everpresence, desire appears as a connecting medium, a subtle, undying force of contact between signs and what they bring to mind. Desire joins, albeit loosely, the many into a long and singular chain of signs and their displacing transformations, each yielding to and yet to some degree setting into motion "the next needful thing."

As we have seen, Hass's essay **"Images"** claims that primary acts of the imagination are transformed into "the next needful thing" only "if we are lucky." Throughout Hass's work, feelings of "connectedness," of intimacy between the past and present, signifier and signified, self and other, word and flesh, recur as ephemeral blessings, matters of luck—as when momentarily the body seems "numinous as words" or when words appear as "days which are the good flesh continuing." Naturally, the good flesh dies, as do words, as does the sensation that our words are made flesh. The explicit failure of Hass's claims to tell the whole truth humbles them to being. They gesture affectionately toward the inscrutable nature of things charged by language and thus by our desire to see them always more clearly, to retrieve them, to understand. His opulent catalogs are likewise devotional in tone, expressing an immense affection for the world, a longing to name it all. With a kind of devotional alchemy, Hass's poetry excels at creating out of humility, out of uncertainty and loss, a recovering sense of reverence and reverie.

David Streitfield (essay date 8 May 1995)

SOURCE: "The Poet of the People," in *Washington Post,* May 8, 1995, p. D1.

[*In the following article, announcing Hass's appointment to the position of U.S. Poet Laureate, Streitfield describes the duties of the post and anticipates how Hass will follow the work of his predecessor, Rita Dove.*]

The nation's next official cheerleader for all things verse will be Robert Hass, a 53-year-old Berkeley professor, translator, critic and poet. The eighth person to hold the post of poet laureate, Hass responded with the by-now-traditional trepidation when approached by Library of Congress officials.

"My first reaction was reluctance," Hass admitted by phone from the University of Iowa, where he is teaching in the Writers' Workshop this semester.

"It's a great honor and it seemed like a massive distraction," he said. "But it was also an opportunity to be a spokesperson for the literary community."

As for his duties? "I cannot even say I know what my task is." He'll spend from now until October, when he officially starts at the library, figuring it out.

Rita Dove, the outgoing laureate, has some basic advice for Hass: Don't get overwhelmed. Early in her two-year stint, she was twice hospitalized from exhaustion. "I got kind of used to writing in the front of ambulances," the 42-year-old Dove said lightly during an interview last week at her office in the library.

Both incidents happened in the summer of 1993, after she was selected and had endured the initial onslaught of media attention but before she learned to pace herself.

The first time was at a writers' conference in Squaw Valley, Calif., where the altitude was blamed. The second was at home in Charlottesville, when Dove was trying to answer hundreds of letters from an eager public before traveling to the West Coast.

"I fainted, passed out, and [her husband] Fred couldn't rouse me," she remembered. "I woke up in the morning and then immediately went out again." The first thing she did after coming home from the hospital that afternoon was another interview, propping herself up on the couch.

"What that told me is, don't overextend yourself, because then you aren't any good for anybody," Dove said. "I learned it's better to let the letters sit for three months, to answer them bit by bit."

One thing the outgoing and incoming laureates share is a belief in the power and the popularity of poetry. Said Hass: "I often feel when I'm in the East that people talk about the situation of writing as if it were in trouble. But from my perspective it seems pretty healthy. First of all, there's a lot of urgent and interesting writing being done in a variety of modes. And there are audiences for it among people who don't live in the mass media."

His own poetry fits on a compact shelf: three books. The first, *Field Guide,* won the Yale Series of Younger Poets Award. The second, *Praise,* appeared in 1974. The most recent, *Human Wishes,* was a finalist for the National Book Critics Circle award in poetry in 1990. "I never wanted to have, like John Updike said about T. S. Eliot, 'a reluctant oeuvre,' but I do seem to be slow," the poet said. "I tend to write a lot and throw away a lot."

What remains has been praised. "He writes in many shapes, moods, even styles. Yet everywhere one recognizes this reverence for the power of language, words in their full-flight of syntax, what we—or our ancestors—used to call eloquence," wrote Hayden Carruth in *Harper's* magazine.

Hass, who was born in San Francisco and has lived near there most of his life, is the first laureate from the West Coast. "In some ways I take this as a representative honor—that I'm to stand for a whole bunch of writers and a tradition of writing," he said.

Like everything else in the West, poetry doesn't have much of a past. Robinson Jeffers, issuing his jeremiads against the modern world in the first decades of the century, is the first real California poet. It wasn't until the '50s that a critical mass of poets developed, and almost immediately San Francisco rivaled New York as the poetry capital of the country.

"It was an incredibly lively place to grow up wanting to be a writer," said the new laureate. "And there were people around, audiences, so it didn't feel like a strange vocation."

It also didn't feel like an insular activity. Hass has reached out both to Japan, translating a book of haiku, and to Europe, where he has collaborated with Czeslaw Milosz to render seven of the Nobel laureate's collections into English. "I'm really not very good at any language," he confessed. "Sometimes I say I don't really translate but I 'de-Polandize' other people's poems."

In 1984, Hass won the National Book Critics Circle award for criticism for *Twentieth Century Pleasures: Prose on Poetry.* Unlike most poets, he is also a frequent reviewer. "Writing prose is a way of engaging questions about the practice of poetry in the life of readers. It's all part of the same enterprise—trying to live imaginatively in poetry and in my time."

Now, as laureate, he'll be seeking ways to help others live in poetry as well. While Dove has expanded the position, it's still stuck with the sort of vagueness that nearly every previous laureate and, before 1986, what was then termed the "consultant in poetry" has complained about. James Dickey, consultant from 1966 to '68, once said he had finally figured his role: "You walk around so people can point to you and say, 'That's him.'"

Yet why should the poet laureate's task be clearly defined when the very place of verse in our national life has been endlessly debated? It's booming, it's in decline, the audience has never been bigger, the audience has never been smaller, everyone's writing it, no one's reading it, no one cares, everyone should care.

Dove elevated the post of laureate by bringing a new level of energy to the chronically underfunded and largely ceremonial position. In return for a $35,000 annual stipend—a sum that hasn't changed in a decade—the laureate is required only to give one reading, deliver one lecture and organize a reading series.

But Dove went far beyond this in being intensely visible, at least for a poet. She appeared on "Sesame Street" and with Garrison Keillor, read at the White House and worked with schoolchildren on closed-circuit TV, and wrote and delivered a poem for a ceremony commemorating the restoration of the Freedom Statue on the Capitol.

This happened partly because Dove, as a black woman, was a symbol in ways that Hass, a white man, cannot be, but it was also due to her enormous energy. She figures she did more than 200 interviews and personally answered more than 2,000 letters about poetry.

She did this without much institutional support. While the Library of Congress gives great lip service to the program, in recent years the laureate's staff has been cut in half—from two people to one. (Dove also had help from her secretary at the University of Virginia, as well as considerable assistance of all sorts from her husband Fred, a novelist.)

Unlike some of her predecessors, however, Dove declined to blame the library's management for a failure to offer more assistance. Instead, she wondered if the media had fully done their job. While a tremendous amount of coverage was focused on her, there was relatively little on her programs. A poetry and jazz festival that drew 200 people, a ceremony involving eight young Crow Indian poets from Montana reciting their verse in full regalia—these received minimal or no attention.

"It seems to me that interest in a lot of things is created by focusing attention on them," Dove said. "I felt that if you give people half a chance to like poetry, they will."

William Grimes (essay date 8 May 1995)

SOURCE: "Robert Hass Is Named Poet Laureate," in *The New York Times,* May 8, 1995, pp. C11, C15.

[In the following article, Grimes announces Hass's appointment as Poet Laureate and comments on Hass's career.]

Robert Hass has been named the poet laureate of the United States by James H. Billington, the Librarian of Congress. Mr. Hass, the author of the poetry collections *Field Guide, Praise* and *Human Wishes,* succeeds Rita Dove, whose second one-year term as poet laureate ends this month.

"It's a daunting honor," said Mr. Hass (whose name rhymes with grass), in a telephone interview from the University of Iowa in Iowa City, where he is teaching at the Iowa Writers Workshop for the spring semester. "On the one hand, I'm quite pleased, and on the other I'm fearful of the distraction. I think Joseph Brodsky said that the job is ill-paid, ill-defined and irresistible." Mr. Brodsky was the poet laureate in 1991.

The post of poet laureate was created in 1937 to provide the Librarian of Congress with advice on the library's poetry collection, but in recent years it has come to be regarded as a platform for raising national awareness of the importance of poetry and the written word. Laureates receive a salary of $35,000. By design, their duties are loosely defined except for the requirement that they give a reading of their work at the Library of Congress upon assuming the job, deliver an address upon stepping down and organize literary programs at the library. Mr. Hass will open the library's annual literary series on Oct. 12.

Mr. Hass's poetry reflects what he once described in an essay as "the pure activity of being alive." He is deeply concerned with the nuances of perception and the potential for language to adequately describe the sensory and emotional landscape. His subjects tend to be humble and close to home: the landscape of northern California, the routines of family life, the love between men and women.

Carolyn Kizer, writing about Mr. Hass in *The New York Times Book Review,* called him the master of the "reticule poem," alluding to his gift for weaving together seemingly unrelated objects, events and images. He once wrote in an essay on poetic images that in the best poetry, "what perishes and what lasts forever have been brought into conjunction, and accompanying that sensation is a feeling of release from the self."

Mr. Hass, who is 54, was born in San Francisco and earned a bachelor's degree from St. Mary's College in Moraga, Calif., and a master's and a doctorate from Stanford University. He taught at the State University at Buffalo from 1967 to 1971, and at St. Mary's College from 1971 to 1989, when he joined the faculty of the University of California at Berkeley.

Mr. Hass attracted notice with his first book, *Field Guide,* a collection of lyric encounters with the California landscape. The book was published the year after he won the Yale Series of Younger Poets Award. His two other poetry collections, *Praise* (1979) and *Human Wishes,* which also includes a section of short prose meditations (1989), where published to wide acclaim. His essay collection, *Twentieth Century Pleasures: Prose on Poetry* (1985), won the National Book Critics Award for criticism.

For the last decade he has devoted much of his time to translating the poetry of Czeslaw Milosz, working closely with the author. He has also published *The Essential Haiku: Versions of Basho, Buson and Issa* (1994).

"I don't know how much you can do in a year," Mr. Hass

said. "I hope I can intensify people's sense of the vitality and importance of American writing of all kinds."

Kurt Shillinger (essay date 12 October 1995)

SOURCE: "New Laureate Wields Bully Pen for Poetry," in *The Christian Science Monitor,* Vol. 87, No. 222, October 12, 1995, pp. 1, 16.

[*In the following essay, Shillinger presents a profile of Hass on the occasion of his appointment as Poet Laureate.*]

Perhaps everyone is at the football game nearby. At any rate, the cafe is unhurried. Robert Hass bites a sandwich, crunching its wedges of green-skinned apple. He pauses, then recalls the heroes of his youth, none of whom wore cleats.

"One thing about growing up in the Bay Area in the 1950s was the Beat thing in San Francisco," he says. "There were poets around. It seemed like something you could be."

Today's youths may feel differently. In a culture where heroes are increasingly defined by their shoe contracts, poetry may seem out of place, a quaint art from the days before MTV.

Mr. Hass, who today becomes the nation's eighth poet laureate, hopes to change that perception. He wants to make his art more accessible—via everything from poets in schools to more verse in newspapers.

An English professor at the University of California at Berkeley, Hass is considered a skillful translator of classical haiku and, more recently, the poetry of Czeslaw Milosz. As a poet, his influences range from Beat to bebop to Bob Dylan.

He has long found art in the distractions of the ordinary. From neglected apple trees along the Pacific Coast, to couples eating drowsily in museum cafes, to the simple act of picking up his children after school, it is day-to-day detail that drives Hass's poems.

"Hass is able to talk in a conversational way about everything from the mushrooms he's picking one minute to heavy philosophical subjects the next," says Dan Halpern, an editor at Ecco Press, which publishes the poet's works.

As poet laureate, he may be able to bring to a wider audience the joy he finds in language. From his earliest days of discovery, when he and his brother would stay up late on summer nights reading Robert Lowell and Rudyard Kipling to each other, Hass was captivated by the musical aspect of verse.

Poetry "has a feeling of true things being said in powerful ways that are very measured," he says in an emery-board voice. If it hits home, he says, "something happens to you and you say, 'Oh, it would be great to make other people feel it.'"

Hass's central theme is his perception of the coincidence of pleasure and pain in the human experience, a mixture he calls "bewildering."

Admirers, such as Lee Briccetti of Poet's House in New York, call Hass's works "nourishment for the soul and mind." They count him among the leading influences for young poets.

Critics say he is too sentimental, prosaic, and self-conscious. "Hass thinks about Jacques Lacan while picking blackberries," notes Boston poet William Corbett. "He's reaching there. I don't think all poets mull over things like that."

But few who are familiar with either his work or the man himself doubt that Hass, in his capacity as laureate, will make an eloquent spokesman for his art. The American poetry community is vibrant, spreading through the Internet and urban cafes in as many different directions as there are political and social interest groups.

Following African-American poet Rita Dove, Hass's selection as the first laureate from the West Coast continues a celebration of that diversity. Yet the poetry community remains, in large part, a community of participants, overshadowed by Brad Pitt and Hootie & the Blowfish.

"There's lots of activity in American poetry," Mr. Corbett says. "But it's an art in search of an audience outside itself. The energy and vitality that used to go into poetry is now going into movies and rock-and-roll."

With a demeanor as easy as well-worn jeans, Hass has a gentle, witty way of making poetry accessible. "He is a great thinker on American culture," Ms. Briccetti says, "one of the best essayists on the art. He reaches out to a broad audience."

As laureate, Hass has four ideas about how to make poetry more accessible. One involves giving inner-city students in Washington the same kind of models he found in the Beat poets.

"It would be great to get interesting young black poets and some of this sensational emerging generation of jazz musicians together in Washington over a stretch of time to do concerts for the schools," he says.

One performance, for example, might team artists such as poet Rita Dove and saxophonist Joshua Redman. Students would be encouraged to mingle with the performers during rehearsals. The shows would be taped for a video archive.

"It's often the situation with the American kid who wants to be a poet that he comes from a place where his father would think he was a flower-sniffer if he wanted to do that," Hass says. "There are no models."

Hass also hopes to recapture a role poets played in the 19th century and again in the 1950s: major influences on public-political thought. He wants to organize a week of readings and seminars in Washington next spring with the best environmental writers in the United States.

"Everybody's getting to hear what the lobbyists have to say about Alaska," Hass says, "but nobody's talking about how mountains and rivers and bays fit into community values—about what we preserve when we talk about preserving."

To encourage the structures of American poetry, Hass wants to establish a series of annual awards for publishers, critics, and community figures who promote the art.

Finally, he would like to see poetry reemerge in newspapers and is trying to find a format for syndicating poems "reflecting the whole range of writing that is going on—Asian American, Chicano, African American, Latino."

The constraints, of course, are time and money. The poet laureate receives some private funding, but traditionally has had to raise additional funds to implement the kind of programs Hass has in mind. With Republicans swinging their budget ax at arts and humanities programs, Hass says, fund-raising has taken on a political dimension.

"I don't have any illusions about how much good any of this is going to do," he says. "But the question is, do you do something or nothing? If you ever did have this dream of a literate electorate that could entertain complicated ideas because it knew how to read complicated books . . . we haven't done so well."

A melody played on strings floats down from the cafe stereo, and the discussion shifts course. "Not only is the San Francisco tradition full of Western images and our more intense personal relationship with the natural life," Hass says, commenting on the shaping of himself as an artist, "but it has always been more friendly to international, experimental impulses."

He is talking, in a manner, about the Beats again.

Growing up in Marin County in the years right after World War II, Hass felt displacement at the swift pace of development. The principle of the shortest distance paved over the logic of roads that followed the contours of valleys. Dusty Italian-style gardens with fig trees and fennel started disappearing, and it didn't make sense to the young Hass.

But poetry did. At the same time development was remaking the Bay area, Beat poets like Gary Snyder and Kenneth Rexroth, in addition to writing their own pieces, were translating Asian and Eastern European poetry. As early as high school, Hass was struck by the clarity of such verse.

"There's a tremendous tendency, especially in our hurried-up society, to abstract, to not see, not notice," Hass says. "I was attracted to Japanese poetry because it was the poetry of ordinary attention. And it was hugely arresting . . . for me, the way to anchor and clarify is with a poem—my so-called Zen-clear way of noting detail."

If there is a mythology in Hass's poetry, its central point may be that numbness is the worst kind of pain. In his pieces, details arouse feelings—some pleasant, some discomforting. Sometimes a single image provokes both.

There is a verse by the 18th century Japanese poet Kobayashi Issa that Hass translates as "In this world we walk on the roof of hell, gazing at flowers."

It is close to Hass's central themes. Gazing at flowers implies a slowing down, as if the simple pleasures of deliberate living are an antidote to painful experiences.

Hass's poem **"Museum"** hints at the same problem.

A young couple sits in a museum cafe having breakfast. She cradles a sleeping infant; he reads the Sunday paper and eats fresh fruit. Then he holds the child and she finds a section of the paper and butters a roll. They are drowsy, almost automated.

All around them, Hass writes, is an exhibit of carved wooden faces "of people with no talent or capacity for suffering who are suffering the numbest kind of pain: hunger, helpless terror.

"But this young couple is reading the Sunday paper in the sun, the baby is sleeping, the green has begun to emerge from the rind of the cantaloupe, and everything seems possible."

They are oblivious to the contorted images around them. They also seem unaware of the pleasures of the moment: atmosphere, sunlight on their table, release from the workday schedule. They seem incapable of feeling.

Now that he is in the midstream of his career, Hass hopes a shape is emerging to the body of his work.

His poetry chronicles the phases of a man trying to make sense out of the world: a youth sifting through the rigidity of a Roman Catholic education and the bustle of Western society; a father seeing the world through the eyes of his children; a man in midlife dealing with "the accumulation of rues and woes and mistakes and damaged icons."

"Either you wrestle and cope with friction and pain, or you just go straight ahead," he says, drinking the last swallows from a steaming mug. "And it's a question of what do you praise."

Kurt Shillinger (essay date 12 October 1995)

SOURCE: "The Legacy of Poet Laureates," in *The Christian Science Monitor,* Vol. 87, No. 222, October 12, 1995, p. 17.

[*In the following essay, Shillinger describes the Poet Laureate position.*]

To call Robert Hass the eighth poet laureate of the United States is somewhat misleading. The office has existed in one form or another since 1937. Prior to 1986, when Robert Penn Warren returned to the office after 40 years and first accepted its current title, his predecessors were known more blandly as "consultants in poetry."

The poet laureate is a spokesperson for his or her craft, a custodian of poetry in American culture. The job is fairly and deliberately unstructured. The office, which is privately funded, requires the holder to act as a consultant to the Library of Congress, advising the institution in regard to the forces and trends in American literature.

Each year, the laureate helps select new poets to read in the Library's series and to be added to the archives of artists reading their own work.

Beyond that, the officeholder is free to pursue special projects—limited, of course, by the funds he or she can raise.

Rita Dove, the outgoing laureate, conducted a special symposium entitled "The Black Diaspora" and a reading by Crow Indian poets. Allen Tate, consultant from 1943 to 1944, edited an anthology of American poetry of the early 20th century. Joseph Brodsky, laureate from 1991 to 1992, tried to spread poetry in supermarkets, hotels, and airports. His funds—and tenure—expired before he caught up with the Gideons.

Among those appointed to the office have been Robert Lowell (1947 to 1948); William Carlos Williams (who was named in 1952, but did not serve); Robert Frost (1958 to 1959); Howard Nemerov (1963 to 1964); Stanley Kunitz (1974 to 1976); and Maxine Kumin (1981 to 1982).

Term of office lasts one year. That few have served a second term may have something to do with the intense demands of the position. From the day he was chosen last May, Professor Hass has received floods of mail, manuscripts, requests for interviews, and invitations to speak. Lately, his answering machine has been logging more than 30 calls a day.

"All my predecessors warned me that you'll be immediately deluged with millions of letters and requests to do all sorts of things," he says. "And that's been the case."

Linton Weeks (review date 14 October 1995)

SOURCE: "Something Ode, Something New," in *Washington Post,* October 14, 1995, p. D1.

[*In the following essay, Weeks recounts Hass's first public reading as U.S. Poet Laureate.*]

When the tall man in the black suit stood to introduce Robert Hass, the new poet laureate of the United States, the tall man said, "Welcome to another year of poetry at the Library of Congress."

In the back of the room someone whispered, "This reading's going to last longer than I thought."

But in truth, Hass's first public appearance in Washington revealed a witty, provocative, to-the-point guy whose conversation is poetic and whose poetry is conversational.

More than 250 people—lots of bearded, ponytailed men, and women in black sweaters—gathered in the mundane Montpelier Room on the sixth floor of the library's James Madison Memorial Building Thursday night to hear Hass read for 1 1/2 hours.

Some of the poems were written by Hass, others by two poets Hass has translated—the Japanese haiku master Basho and Polish poet Czeslaw Milosz, who has written of poetry as an expedition "as necessary as love."

Dressed in a dark shirt, dark coat and dark tie, Hass stood behind a blond-wood lectern flanked by towering Yamaha speakers, and in a thin, lilting voice led the audience through an expedition of longing and lust, of nature and shame.

Two Basho haikus:

What voice,
what song, spider,
in the autumn wind?
and
Teeth sensitive to the sand
in salad greens—
I'm getting old.

The reading fulfilled one of the poet laureate's official obligations. During his tenure, Hass, who will also be poetry consultant to the Library of Congress, must mount a reading series. This fall he will bring nine poets to town, beginning with Karen Alkalay-Gut of Israel and Iowa poet Jorie Graham on Thursday. In the spring he will usher in another batch, to include poet, critic, playwright and novelist Ishmael Reed. Then, before he leaves, Hass must deliver a closing lecture. For services rendered, he'll receive a $35,000 stipend. The appointment is for one year. Some poets stay two.

As poet laureate, Hass may occasionally be given the opportunity to commemorate a historic event with a bit of verse. But the official duties are minimal, and that's fortunate. He will continue to teach two courses this fall at the University of California at Berkeley, where he has been on the faculty since 1989.

Hass has a hard act to follow. His predecessor, Rita Dove, who served as poet laureate for two years, not only fulfilled her requisite duties, but she also led a crusade to make poetry more visible and more vital. She showed up on "Sesame Street" and on Garrison Keillor's radio program. She organized a poetry reading by District schoolchildren. She did everything but recite the national anthem at the World Series. She stretched herself so thin, she was hospitalized twice for exhaustion.

On Thursday night, Hass looked pretty relaxed. He said he was excited about being in Washington. He looked out the window toward the Capitol dome twinkling in the night sky. "I get to lobby for the mind and the heart. I don't think they're in danger, but I think the country is in danger in relation to them."

The great truth about translation is that foot doesn't rhyme with grass.

—*Robert Hass*

He read a poem about the free-market system. "Markets don't make communities," Hass said. "Imagination makes communities. Markets make networks of self-interested individuals."

There were times when Hass's observations and his poems ran together and the audience couldn't really tell the difference. He spoke of eavesdropping on a fragmented conversation that wound up in his poem **"The Beginning of September."** The line he used was, "He didn't think she ought to and she thought she should."

Glasses low on his nose, a wisp of blond hair pasted on his

forehead, Hass read poem after poem from his several books, including *Field Guide, Praise* and *Human Wishes.* He paused now and then for an aside or to pat his heart Cal Ripken-style. During his longer poems, he sometimes looked up from his text and continued reciting the verse by memory, rapt in his own words.

Many of his poems are autobiographical. He was born in San Francisco in 1941 and has spent most of his life there. He went to St. Mary's College in Moraga, Calif., and Stanford University. Besides writing poetry, he has penned essays, reviews and literary criticism. He has won a bunch of awards including the Yale Younger Poets Award and the National Book Critics Circle Award for criticism. He's received a Guggenheim Fellowship and a MacArthur Fellowship.

One of the poems that especially appealed to the Thursday audience was the unpublished **"Forty Something."** Hass prefaced his reading by saying, "This poem is not about me and these words were not spoken by my wife."

She says to him, musing, "If you ever leave me, and marry a younger woman and have another baby, I'll put a knife in your heart." They are in bed, so she climbs onto his chest, and looks directly down into his eyes. "You understand? Your heart."

Hass's wife, poet Brenda Hillman, was with him on his first official visit to Washington. At a luncheon yesterday she stood across the room and watched folks swarm around her husband. She explained that Hass will fly to town every other week, "and he'll do his own laundry." She has written four collections. The latest is "Bright Existence." She teaches creative writing at Hass's alma mater, St. Mary's.

The luncheon was a sunny affair. Former librarian of Congress Daniel Boorstin and his wife, Ruth, were there. The current librarian, James Billington, and his wife, Marjorie, were there. So was Jack Shoemaker, associate publisher and editor in chief of the newly created Counterpoint publishing house, and Reed Whittemore, who was a poetry consultant to the library in 1984.

Over baked chicken and steamed vegetables, Hass and Whittemore moved from a discussion of mythology to personal childhood stories of dressing in capes and dashing about. Hass said he often appropriated a baby diaper and so his brother called him "Diaper Boy."

After lunch, Billington rose and said he hated to interrupt the sparkling conversation that was going on over the pumpkin tarts—"the desserts, not the people"—but he wanted Hass to say a few words about the art of translation.

Hass told of sitting down with another translator and trying

to capture the excitement of a Polish poem in English. "The great truth about translation," he said, "is that foot doesn't rhyme with grass."

Hass spoke for a few more minutes, answered a few more questions, and then in conclusion said he hoped as poet laureate to do some more translation, to translate the excitement of American literature into something everyone can understand.

Donna Seaman (review date 15 September 1996)

SOURCE: A review of *Sun under Wood,* in *Booklist,* September 15, 1996, p. 205.

[*In the following review, Seaman describes Hass's focus on "the most ordinary aspects of life."*]

Poet laureate Hass is continuing the effort of his predecessors, Rita Dove and Joseph Brodsky, to bring poetry back into the realm of everyday life by writing a weekly column for the *Washington Post* and sponsoring many programs and projects. A true democrat, Hass values education, the power of language, and the most ordinary aspects of life: the warmth of the sun, the call of a bird, love and even its loss, and all the oddities of consciousness. Hass' firm grounding in life is expressed in his unusually anecdotal, conversational, and stylistically prosy poetry. He weaves in dialogue, comments on his activities during the writing of a poem, and even offers variations on two poems in the form of "Notes," but make no mistake, each and every word counts as it must in poetry, and Hass' perceptions into the nature of emotions are at once as fine as gossamer and as resilient as vines. He is a giving, honest, sensual, moody, and plainspoken poet, a tireless bard who sings of our sorrows and joys, our perversities and strengths.

Publishers Weekly (review date 30 September 1996)

SOURCE: A review of *Sun under Wood,* in *Publishers Weekly,* Vol. 243, No. 40, September 30, 1996, p. 82.

[*In the following review, the critic praises Hass's "quirky, imaginative incarnaitons of grace."*]

Hass is Poet Laureate of the United States, a position through which he has worked to enlarge the cultural presence of poetry. Much the same ends are served in his new collection, which contains a remarkable range of themes and styles, all of them generous-hearted and friendly of access. Although Hass's work can be positioned somewhere between the rural lyricism of William Stafford and the precise, Zen-like economies of Gary Snyder, he seems, most of all, a California poet.

There is a distinctive ease and optimism in his poetic attentions, and his voice is as comfortable musing about ethnicity as it is detailing marital peccadilloes or extolling the allure of "my mother's nipples." In this, his first volume since 1989's *Human Wishes,* Hass shows that he can write a perfect sonnet (**"Sonnet"**), but seems to revel more in an idiosyncratic free-form of blank verse broken by sharp apercus. Hass is careful not to allow his poems to be reducible or predictable. Most remarkable in this collection is **"Faint Music,"** in which the poet attempts "a poem about grace," and then wanders through a meditation on self-love, an anecdote about a failed suicide, an infidelity and porch sounds at night. In the end, the poet concludes, "the sequence helps, as much as order helps— / First an ego, and then pain, and then the singing." Such quirky, imaginative incarnations of grace are all we need ask of a poet or a laureate.

Fred Muratori (review date 1 October 1996)

SOURCE: A review of *Sun under Wood,* in *Library Journal,* Vol. 121, No. 16, October 1, 1996, p. 82.

[*In the following review, Muratori describes* Sun under Wood *as "a disarming, disturbing, memorable book of poems."*]

Like Robert Frost, Gary Snyder, and the haiku masters before them, current U.S. Poet Laureate Hass (***The Essential Haiku,*** Ecco, 1995) discerns in nature's random blossomings and processes a "beauty unconscious of itself," all the more attractive for its autonomy. Combining an almost Zen tranquility of expression with a naturalist's eye ("Creekstones practicing the mild yoga of becoming smooth."), Hass seems engaged in "an activity of incessant discovery" whether he's meditating on a surprised raccoon, the circumstances surrounding a divorce, or a parent's debilitating alcoholism. "It is good sometimes," he writes coyly, "that poetry should disenchant us," an ironic observation given his special—and subversive—talent for disenchanting the reader at the moment of deepest enchantment, knowing that "We live half our lives / in fantasy, and words." Though he often strives for a lyricist's concision, Hass will let his poems wash widely into prose (**"My Mother's Nipples"**) if necessary, as if the urgency of his thought refuses containment. For the fourth time, he has given us a disarming, disturbing, memorable book of poems. Recommended for all collections.

Michael Coffey (essay date 28 October 1996)

SOURCE: "Robert Hass: Bard on the National Stage," in *Publishers Weekly,* Vol. 243, No. 44, October 28, 1996, pp. 51-2.

[*In the following essay, drawn from an interview with Hass during his second year as Poet Laureate, Coffey relates the author's views on the current state of poetry in the United States.*]

As Poet Laureate of the United States, Robert Hass's mandate is to raise national awareness of the importance of poetry and the written word. Such a task, at a time when most households have 70 TV channels and many others are plugged into the global village prophesied 30 years ago by McLuhan, surely is daunting. But being the frontman for a quaint art that barely has a profession tied to it—unless it's called teaching—does not faze Hass. Rather, it is a task to which he has taken naturally. In fact, there may not be a better poet today working with such catholic tastes, boundless energy and open aesthetics as Hass.

Perhaps this sense of openness is grounded in Hass's California roots. Born in San Francisco of German and Irish stock, he grew up mingling with kids of myriad backgrounds and then found himself in his impressionable teens living in the suburb of San Rafael, reading Kerouac and watching the rise of the Beat movement nearby. Having attended graduate school at Stanford in the heady 1960s, Hass emerged with a sensibility that is pan-poetic and insatiably curious, at once as alive to the poetry of Japan as to that of Eastern Europe, as much a devotee of the California poetries of Rexroth and Jeffers as to the austere wintering of Robert Frost.

Acclaim came early for Hass. His first book, ***Field Guide,*** won the Yale Younger Poets competition in 1973 and was lauded by one reviewer "as a means of naming things, of establishing an identity through one's surroundings, of translating the natural world into one's poetry." Since then, he has built upon that early promise, prompting Carolyn Kizer to observe in the *New York Times Book Review* that "to read his poetry or prose, or hear him speak, gives one an almost visceral pleasure."

Hass, despite the peripatetic nature of his poetic interests, has stayed close to his roots. The father of three children from a first marriage, he still lives in the Bay-Area, with his second wife, the poet Brenda Hillman, and her daughter.

Somehow, Hass manages to write and to think deeply about his craft despite his Laureate obligations in the nation's capital, his full-time teaching position at Berkeley and his participation in poetry and literacy events all over the country. When *PW* catches up to Hass, whose latest book, *Sun Under Wood,* just out from Ecco Press, is an NBA finalist in poetry, he is lecturing to hundreds of poetry teachers and would-be poets under a large tent in New Jersey. The venue is the Geraldine R. Dodge Poetry Festival, and Hass's gentle, impassioned presentation lays out the depths of his engagement with the questions of poetry and what he sees as its place not only in the culture but in the development of self.

"History," he says, "can be reclaimed in the rhythms of a poem." As a person who has thought deeply about such issues, Hass offers a wonderfully winding exposition of the idea: "In the history of writing in the European tradition, as I understand it, what happened is that, up until the 1780s, the idea was that truth and knowledge came from reason or revelation and poetry was an attractive way to say those truths. But with romanticism the idea that poetic knowledge precedes reason came to the fore. Now, if the source of all knowledge is poetic insight, where does it come from? Inside or outside? The mind or the world? And why does the question matter?"

The audience stirs, perhaps a bit unaccustomed to pondering such elemental questions, perhaps more accustomed to seeing poetry as simply heightened self-expression.

"The issue," Hass continues, "is literally a matter of life and death to poets like Czeslaw Milosz," one of Hass's mentors at Stanford and with whom, in true mentor-student fashion, Hass still jousts. For Milosz, "the only purpose of poetry is a perfect description of reality. The adequacy and presence of the physical world is something I wanted to believe in," Hass confesses. He takes a long sip of coffee standing at the podium. "But is this just mere record-keeping?" he asks, more of himself than of the audience.

Hass will continue for another hour, discussing his beloved haiku poets—Basho, Buson, Issa—who, like Milosz, describe only the real (or as Hass puts it, "the frog, the hyacinth, the pond"), eschewing metaphor and interpretation, the reach for a meaning beyond the images. But Hass will give equal time to poets in the romantic tradition who seek out metaphors in order to transform reality, like Wordsworth, or create something to stand in its place, like the modernist romantic Wallace Stevens. Hass would have it that the movement away from the "realism" of William Carlos Williams ("no ideas but in things") is dangerous if it leads merely to a solipsism. He wows the audience with an anecdote about a Stevens poem: "The palm at the end of the mind / beyond the last thought / rises in the bronze distances," pointing out that when Stevens crossed out "bronze distances" and replaced it with "bronze decor," he entered a troublingly hermetic impressionism. Hass concludes by wondering at the extremes of a poetry bent upon transforming rather than describing, asking, somewhat on Milosz's behalf (whose work was censored in his native Poland): "Why did so many surrealists become communists?" Metaphor, in this instance, has taken up arms as revolution.

The talk is a brilliant performance, but delivered in such a humble, self-effacing manner by the lean, tanned man in a pony tail that some teachers in the crowd may not remember the disquisition on Roman Jakobsen, or that Hass, in the course of extolling the relevance of figures like Whitman and Frost, also praised Language poet Lyn Hejinian and young

Chinese-American poet Li-Young Lee. Hass, whose essay collection, *Twentieth Century Pleasures,* won the NBCC award for criticism in 1984, represents the best in literary intelligence, blending an ecstatic tolerance with discriminating judgment. Sitting at a picnic table over black coffee and a cigarette, Hass would clearly be happy to talk about the intricacies of his chosen craft all day; but when asked about literacy and poetry, he musters his characteristic enthusiasm and does not speak in vague generalities or without passion.

"When I got the [Laureate] job," he says, "I did a lot of reading about literacy and I went to a lot of places poets don't normally go, speaking to corporations, for example. And one of the things that struck me was just how powerful a presence poetry has had in the culture.

"You have to remember that, at the beginning of the 19th century, less than 60% of American males could write their name, and that was far higher than in most of Europe. If you were black, you could get killed for reading. Once the ideals of puritanism transferred to the ideology of democracy, the engines of literacy geared up. Capitalist investment in printing presses led to the widespread agitation for the establishment of public schools and public libraries, just as now we have similar forces pushing for computer literacy and access to cyberspace. And the goal of advocating literacy was to expand audiences, to expand markets."

And poetry, says Hass, was very much a part of this push. "It was everywhere: in newspapers, magazines; businesses did poetry pamphlets. You can see Burma Shave signs as a relic of a public poetry, leading people down the road with the promise of soap. To have access to the culture, to get the jokes, you had to be able to read."

Although one can sniff beneath this analysis a certain anti-corporatism, Hass believes that, in the end, "as a democratic experiment in building literacy, there is no equivalent to the U.S."

He notes, however, that the landscape appears to be changing. "At the beginning of this century, the new media began to break the hold of the publishing business as the monopoly purveyor of information and entertainment and celebrity creation. Today, there are so many faces in other media that there is little room for a culture of writerly celebrity."

Even if poets aren't among America's celebrities, issues of fame and main-streaming have always riven the poetic community. Jealousies, turf mentality and a sense of privilege in marginality enliven discussions wherever poetry lovers meet. At the moment, there is, if not a poetry war, at least a lively skirmish, with one side being the American Academy of Poets and their new formalism, and the other being those poets who see themselves as inheritors of a tradition that overthrew the constrictions of form years ago. Hass has alliances in both camps, and for good reason, he says: the conflict rages within. When *PW* asks him where the poetry wars are being fought, Hass responds: "In the guts of the living," quoting Eliot, but declines to say more.

"I don't have too much interest in choosing up sides" Hass says, careful to steer clear of poetry politics. "But something I am very concerned about is what's happening with bookselling. Everyone is getting clobbered right now," he says of publishers large and small, "with all the expansion on the retail level. Clearly, the bet is that the superstores aren't just poaching on the small stores—some independents have been hurt badly—but expanding the readership. However, it seems they have expanded before the market did. And the danger is that, after this ordeal, we'll just return to the mall-store model. I just hope everyone can be patient, and, of course, I hope they are right: I hope the creation of attractive, book-lovers' bookstores does expand readership and that bookselling remains healthy."

Hass, who is 55, describes his childhood in Northern California as a battle against the "ferocious anti-intellectualism" of the time as well as the Catholic grade school he attended. If not for the encouragement of his older brother, Hass says, he would not have been able to pursue his fantasy of being a writer. "I started out imagining myself as a novelist or essayist, but then Gary Snyder and Allen Ginsberg came along; and poetry, imbued with the whole lifestyle of the Beats, was so much more exciting." Hass could go down to the Surf theater and see Ginsberg standing in line for a Kurosawa film; the poetry community in San Francisco was national news, and as an aspiring writer, Hass wanted to be part of it.

After earning an undergraduate degree at St. Mary's College, he got his doctorate in English at Stanford in 1971, where he audited courses given by haughty and exacting Yvor Winters. Hass then went on to a teaching job in the English Department at SUNY Buffalo, where Robert Creeley was laying out a counter-cultural poetics with an enchanting metrical music and an austere precision. There, someone told Hass about the Yale Younger Poets competition; he sent in his manuscript for *Field Guide.* Stanley Kunitz selected it as winner.

Since then, Hass has published exclusively with Daniel Halpern's Ecco Press. *Praise* came out in 1979, *Human Wishes* in 1989. *Sun Under Wood* is his first collection in seven years. Halpern has also published four Hass-edited volumes on Milosz, the classic *Essential Haiku: Versions of Basho, Buson and Issa,* as well as the award-winning *Twentieth Century Pleasures.* "I've been lucky," says Hass. "New Directions was my model of what a publisher should be and Dan has stepped right in."

As to how poetry, or good literature, will fare as we enter the 21st century, Hass is hopeful, or perhaps trusting is the word. "For all the talk of the time of the 'gentleman publisher' of yore, what I have learned is that publishing has always been predominantly an urban phenomenon clustered around cities and capitalists and entrepreneurial places; the spread of literature as well as literacy has been market-driven. As these things go, that makes sense. I'd love to see a comparison of how 'literary' the publishing was in economies that weren't market-driven. Did they publish only the best literary work, being free of the market? Or is it the market that in some ways tells us what is important to people?"

It's a good question. As a poet skeptical of how truths are formulated, Hass leaves the answering to the reader.

Francis X. Clines (essay date 9 December 1996)

SOURCE: "A Poet's Road Trip along Main Street, U.S.A.," in *The New York Times,* December 9, 1996, pp. A1, B8.

[*In the following article, Clines relates Hass's observations on his two years in the post of U.S. Poet Laureate and its impact on his poetry writing.*]

Sometimes he hits upon a lyrical scrap of haiku amid the hum of the crosstown subway. But essentially the Poet Laureate of the United States has put aside consulting his muse in favor of proselytizing Rotarians.

"I thought an interesting thing to do would be to go where poets don't go," explained Robert Hass, heading into his final four months in one of the odder capital jobs, one that he has shaped to become more like a missionary drummer in the provinces of commerce than as a performing bard in celebrity coffeehouses.

"I thought the thing to talk about is not poetic 'uplift,'" he said, "but the fact that basic literacy in this country is in a serious crisis."

With that, Mr. Hass, a celebrated 55-year-old poet and critic, offered a vivid scholarly synopsis of the decline of American literacy as he paid a rare visit to his office at the Library of Congress. He celebrated the "heroic" literacy levels of a century ago, when there was a national hunger to read and general literacy was at 95 percent. He deplored the bleak evidence of current life that finds half the eighth graders in Texas reading at the fourth-grade level.

"This is the Office of Poetry and Literature; this has to stop," Mr. Hass said, in a desperate emphasis of his concern as he sat in solitude in his attic office overlooking the Capitol dome and described his attempt to be an activist laureate.

Ostensibly, he is one of the more powerless loners among the legions of appointees in Washington. But Mr. Hass chose to resort to the basic stuff of his art, mere words, and to spend much of the last two years in the laureate's post traveling to business and civic meetings across the nation with a straight-prose alarum that literacy standards have been plummeting.

"One thing I found out about this country was that there are thousands of business and service organizations that have to come up with a speaker every week," said Mr. Hass, who opted to exploit the mundane curiosity out there about this figure dubbed Poet Laureate to shop his warning.

In this, he has been politely citing as a most obvious factor the tax-cutting mania so popular with American candidates and voters alike. He is asking community leaders what they intend to do, beyond freezing property taxes, to see that their children can read paragraphs or poems. How well, he asks, will they be able to use their imagination, which, in this poet's outlook and his years of work, is the very taproot of community?

"I had never been to a Rotary Club in my life, but now I've been to dozens," the poet said, recounting those and assorted other civic gatherings. "And, you know, I had the prejudice they're all Babbitts. But I discovered they're downtown business people who raise money for schools, most of them, and I made some friends."

The personal price for that has been that Mr. Hass has mostly stopped creating poems and can barely wait to resume "writing and dreaming" in May, after his tour ends. His new book of poetry, **Sun Under Wood** by the Ecco Press, is a result of 5-year-old labors. "The life I've led is the opposite of a writer's life," he said. "I've been on the road more or less constantly."

On the other hand, Mr. Hass now counts doubly poetic his new friendship with mid-America moguls like Gordon West, chief of the Bon Ami company, which historically sold its turn-of-the-century laundry goods by offering patriotic "readers," or pamphlets, to an avidly literate America.

"He's a friend of Newt," the poet said, smiling in amazement at how far afield a laureate can roam.

"The guy put up money to bring kids to Washington to read their poems, and he was excited," Mr. Hass said gratefully, referring to a well-attended conference in the spring called Watershed, when the Poet Laureate gathered writers, environmentalists and students to focus on the nation's deep literary tradition of nature writing.

Admitting to "terror" at not writing much, Mr. Hass has made himself jot down something, anything, however light, whenever he rides public transportation here. On long airport rides,

he writes 14-line taxicab sonnets. On the Metro subway, the poet—a recognized haiku scholar and translator—concocts "Metro haikus." He declines to sing the results thus far.

He prefers another genre he calls "found haiku," random snatches of overheard dialogue from life that serendipitously ring with the 17-syllable haiku formula.

"Two guys in $500 overcoats get on at the Farragut North Station," he recounted, merry-eyed at one gem. "And one says to the other, 'Well, if he *had* been focused, he wouldn't even have *considered* it.' Seventeen syllables!"

The poet sounds more like a lepidopterist in offering narrative glimpses of what he sees and hears in Washington life.

"Flying here, I see whole planefuls of guys with laptops coming in, furiously writing these arguments about, you know, why they should keep letting the whole in the ozone get bigger for five more years," he said. "I see what the business is here. It's the hustle, the business of lobbying."

The poet has had scant contact with the city's politicians, but when they inevitably pump his hand and croak, "Nice to see you!" Mr. Hass thinks that he has fathomed their art. "They *shine* on each person they meet."

He was touched when one senator suddenly admitted envy, taking the poet aside, Mr. Hass recalled, to confess: "I don't have time to think, to read. I'm just responding all the time. I would love to have your life."

As a roving missionary for literacy, Mr. Hass can still flash the striking phrase. As a professor at the University of California at Berkeley, he cites reams of statistics on the fall of his state's public school standards after the freezing of property taxes a generation ago.

"They put a lot of disposable income in peoples' pockets," he said.

"They generated a restaurant boom. California cuisine was created, smoked salmon and arugula," he continued in mock exultation, then starkly drove his point home: "It's perfectly clear what happened. People were eating their children."

Summarizing this blunt laureate's song, Mr. Hass said, "My mantra was, capitalism makes networks. It doesn't make communities. *Imagination* makes communities."

The poet will spread this word into the spring and then quit his Rotarian rounds. "Did it do any good?" he has to ask. "Was I wasting my life? Should I have been home writing poems? It's like teaching. You have no idea."

FURTHER READING

Criticism

Ford, Mark. "Reality Bites." *The New Republic* (31 October 1994): 48-51.

> Reviews Hass's *Essential Haiku: Versions of Basho, Buson, and Issa.*

Perry, Tony. "Poetry Man." *Los Angeles Times* (20 October 1996): E1.

> Personal profile of Hass.

Additional coverage of Hass's life and career is contained in the following sources published by Gale Research: *Contemporary Authors,* Vol. 111; *Contemporary Authors New Revision Series,* Vols. 30, 50; *Dictionary of Literary Biography,* Vol. 105; and *Poetry Criticism,* Vol. 16.

Jonathan Larson

Rent

Awards: Pulitzer Prize for Drama; New York Drama Critics Circle and Outer Critics Circle Awards for Best Musical; Drama Desk Awards for Best Musical, Best Book of a Musical, Best Music, and Best Lyrics; Antoinette Perry ("Tony") Awards for Best Musical, Best Book of a Musical, and Best Score of a Musical; Obie Award for Outstanding Book, Music, and Lyrics.

An American dramatist, Larson was born February 4, 1960, and died January 25, 1996.

INTRODUCTION

Winner of the 1996 Pulitzer Prize for Drama, *Rent* was hailed by the critics as the breakthrough musical of the 1990s when it premiered at the off-Broadway New York Theater Workshop; within three months it opened on Broadway. *Rent* also has become something of a theatrical legend: Larson, who worked on the words and lyrics of his play for over seven years, died of an aortic aneurysm at the age of 35 on the night of the last dress rehearsal. Consequently, he never saw the phenomenal success of his play. Larson's sudden death "has undoubtedly deepened the emotional power of the musical's central motif, the struggle of doomed young people to find love with time running out," according to Peter Marks. Based loosely on Giacomo Puccini's opera *La Boheme, Rent* tells the stories of a group of struggling artists in New York's East Village who celebrate life despite suffering the effects of drugs, poverty, and AIDS. Among the characters are Roger, an HIV-infected punk rocker desperate to write one great song before he dies; Mimi, a drug-addicted dancer at an S & M club, also HIV-positive; Angel, a drag queen dying of AIDS who loves Tom Collins, a computer science teacher; Maureen, a performance artist in a violent relationship with her lesbian lover, Joanne; Mark, Maureen's ex and would-be filmmaker who narrates the play; and Ben, an eccentric landlord who threatens to evict the artists from their loft. Billed as "the rock opera of our time," and often called "the *Hair* for the '90s," *Rent* is admired for its unique blending of show tune traditions and rock music. "[Larson's] gift for direct, compelling, lyrical statement seems to prove that the show tune can once again become both pertinent and popular," remarked John Lahr. While many critics have pinned their hopes on *Rent* for the survival of music theater, John Gardner responded that "despite its studied hipness and its aspirations to be the voice of the Nineties, *Rent* . . . is pretty much the same old showbiz fare." Nonetheless, *Rent,* as Richard Zoglin put it, "is the most exuberant and original American musical to come along this decade."

PRINCIPAL WORKS

Superbia (drama) 1988
Tick, Tick . . . Boom! (drama) 1990
J. P. Morgan Saves the Nation (drama) 1995
Rent (drama) 1996

CRITICISM

John Lahr (review date 19 February 1996)

SOURCE: "Hello and Goodbye," in *New Yorker,* Vol. LXXII, No. 1, February 19, 1996, pp. 94-6.

[*Below, Lahr examines the theatrical implications of* Rent's *popularity, hinting at Larson's possible influence on musical theater.*]

By some terrible irony, the restaurant next to the Minetta Lane Theater, where a memorial service for the composer-lyricist Jonathan Larson was held last week, is called La Bohème. Puccini's opera was the inspiration for *Rent,* Larson's rock opera (at the New York Theater Workshop), and the show features, among forty well-sung numbers, three songs that are as passionate, unpretentious, and powerful as anything I've heard in the musical theater for more than a decade. Larson died of an aortic aneurysm on January 25th, a few hours after the dress rehearsal of *Rent.* He was thirty-five. Larson's name is new to me, but his talent and his big heart are impossible to miss. His songs spill over with feeling and ideas; his work is both juicy and haunting. That's why, after seeing *Rent,* I ended up at his memorial service. I found out that Larson was a rangy, goofy-looking guy with jug ears and a funny grin; that he grew up in White Plains; that he had the capacity to love and to be loved; that he'd done six downtown musicals with suitably quirky titles like *Tick, Tick . . . Boom!, J. P. Morgan Saves the Nation,* and *Superbia*; that he waited tables at a SoHo diner to support his musical habit; that he dreamed of earning enough money from his writing to splurge on cable TV; and that he believed, like Gatsby, in the green light and the orgiastic future. "Count the green flags, not the red flags," he told his friends. He also talked about his crazy ambition to bring the musical up to date: *Rent* is billed as "The Rock Opera of the '90s." Larson is certainly not the first composer to take aim at that elusive target, but he may be the first to have hit it. His gift for direct, compelling, colloquial lyrical statement seems to prove that the show tune can once again become both pertinent and popular. Over his desk Larson had posted the motto "Make the familiar unfamiliar, and make the unfamiliar familiar." Whatever the problems of the production, the score of *Rent* achieves the astonishing feat of marrying the musical's old sense of blessing to the society's new sense of blight.

The landscape of *Rent* is a gray and dishevelled loft space and environs in the Lower East Side's Alphabet City. "The curtainless set seems more like a pile of junk than a set," Larson's stage direction says; and waste is the right metaphor for this soiled, threadbare world of artists, addicts, and the homeless—the compost out of which the lost souls in *Rent* try to grow their dreams. Here poverty, and not abundance, is the musical's issue. "No Visa No Mastercard / No Amex / No travellers' checks / No dollars / No cents / No," a chorus of Village vendors sings. It's Christmas, and the holiday provides an ironic frame for the uncharitable events of *Rent,* which include the eviction of a group of artists from their loft. In fact, every assumption of the traditional musical has been stood on its head. The old romance of triumph has been replaced by the new romance of despair. Now lovers don't meet cute, they meet infected. Roger (Adam Pascal), a young songwriter struggling to write one good song before his light is snuffed out, falls for Mimi (Daphne Rubin-Vega), a strung-out dancer; both are H.I.V.-positive. The drag queen Angel (Wilson Jermaine Heredia) camps up catastrophe in his seduction of Collins (the smoky-voiced Jesse L. Martin), a young teacher who ends up giving him safe harbor. "Yes," Angel sings. "This body provides a comfortable home / For the Acquired Immune Deficiency Syndrome." Mark (Anthony Rapp), a would-be filmmaker who bears witness to the group's eviction battle and earnestly tries to take the moral temperature of his times, asks, "How can you connect in an age / Where strangers, landlords, lovers, your own blood cells betray?" Death is the climate in which this musical lives. The air is full of loss—loss of home, loss of dreams, loss of life. If it sounds like Sondheim territory—well, in a way, it is. Larson won a Stephen Sondheim Award for *Superbia* and a Richard Rodgers Development Award for *Rent.* Although he wasn't a Sondheim clone, he was definitely a disciple; he even works his decidedly uptown mentor—a Broadway baby if there ever was one—into a rhymed catalogue of downtown bohemian icons: "To Sontag / To Sondheim / To anything taboo . . . " (At the memorial service, a college friend recalled long late-night talks with Larson about "why Stephen Sondheim was God and Jerry Herman the enemy.") If Larson doesn't have the word hoard or the technical skills of a Sondheim, neither does he have the glibness. Larson was more emotional than his showy hero. His songs have urgency—a sense of mourning and mystery which insists on seizing the moment. "No day but today" is the show's last sung line—at once a plea and a philosophy.

The aroma of *Rent* may not be sweet, but it is also not sour. Larson's gift was for the elegiac, which celebrates both grief and gladness. He uncovers the poignance in his characters' panic—a manic quality that suits rock's electrified sound. This combination of gravity and grace is best expressed in the opening of Act II, where fifteen actors come to the foot of the stage and perform Larson's gospel song **"Seasons of Love."** ("I broke up with a girlfriend because she said I couldn't write a gospel song," Larson is reported to have told a friend. On the evidence of the inspired and subtle simplicity of **"Seasons of Love,"** he was right to leave.) The song is an anthem and also a kind of epitaph:

> Five hundred twenty-five thousand
> Six hundred minutes
> Five hundred twenty-five thousand
> Moments so dear
> Five hundred twenty-five thousand
> Six hundred minutes
> How do you measure—measure a year?
>
> In daylights—in sunsets
> In midnights—in cups of coffee
> In inches—in miles
> In laughter—in strife
>
> In five hundred twenty-five thousand
> Six hundred minutes
> How do you measure
> A year in the life?

Larson's answer is "How about love? / Measure in love," and Gwen Stewart, in the chorus, embellishes the lines with elegant gospel riffs. In Steve Skinner's shrewd arrangement, the song is reprised in the middle of the act in counterpoint with a reprise of a beautiful, heartbreaking blues, **"I'll Cover You."** Larson really seems to have known about love. By merging the refrains of the two songs, he combines the sense of time passing with the sense of affection. The moment of connection is powerfully immediate and reverent. Collins sang the words to Angel in Act I. Now, at Angel's funeral, he sings to the coat that was Angel's gift before laying it on the drum that substitutes for his dead lover's casket:

> Open your door—I'll be your tenant
> Don't got much baggage
> To lay at your feet
> But sweet kisses I've got to spare
> I'll be there—I'll cover you.

In a few cunningly harmonized phrases, Larson evokes both love's gift of solace and the longing for it. "With a thousand sweet kisses I'll cover you," a soloist sings along with Collins' testament to his unequivocal love: "If you're cold and you're lonely / You've got one nickel only." Collins and the company continue, "Oh lover / I'll cover you / Oh lover," as the refrain merges with the eloquent "Five hundred twenty-five thousand six hundred moments so dear." The tenderness of the singer and of the song hits an audience like a punch to the heart.

At the memorial service, a *Rent* cast member said that he once gushed to Larson, "I think you're going to change the American musical theater," and Larson replied, "I know." Perhaps Larson might have—but not, I think, with the din of rock opera. The problem is not with Larson's songs but with the nature of song itself. The pleasure of rhyme runs counter to analysis. The audience can't really reflect while it's being ravished. As a result, character detail dissolves into a few brushstrokes of attitude; plot points are briefly addressed, only to be lost as one song piles on top of another. *Rent* tells eight separate stories, but as a structure the through-sung musical can't support that kind of narrative overload. Inevitably, the theatrical shorthand of *Rent* makes it wobble. What you get is a song cycle tricked out into a notional story whose events are not so much dramatized as indicated. The musical becomes a kind of soap opera of song. The artists are evicted, then not; Mark sells out to network television, then doesn't; the quarrelling lesbian lovers Maureen (Idina Menzel) and Joanne (Fredi Walker) break up, then don't; Mimi resolves to shake her drug habit, then doesn't. In all this to-ing and fro-ing you can feel Larson and his director, Michael Greif, struggling to take the musical to a new dramatic place—and if it's not a total victory it's also not a defeat. Greif and the lighting designer, Blake Burba, seem to have fallen under a brutalist downtown spell, and display a kind of willful disregard for entertainment values. Many of the stage pictures are smudged, but, despite its shambolic action and slovenly set, there's a weird power to the piece. This impact could have been magnified by a more rigorous cutting and rearranging of Act I: its rhythm is off kilter, and it should end with **"La Vie Bohème,"** Larson's uptown Broadway number extolling downtown life. Here Greif's staging is crisp and funny. "To riding your bike, midday past the three-piece suits," Mark sings. "To fruits, to no absolutes / To Absolut, to choice, to the *Village Voice,* to any passing fad / To being an us, for once / Instead of a them / La Vie Bohème." The song builds to one last raspberry at the straight world: "To sodomy," the cast sings (just in case we didn't know we were teetering on the brink of fashion). "It's between God and me / To S & M / La Vie Bohème."

Rent could use more streamlining, more color, more revision. But all that hardly matters. By the end of the evening, Larson's talent has taken the audience to places where the musical, with its boulevard frivolity and its boulevard nihilism, never ventures these days. *Rent* dares to embrace the ugly and the beautiful, the sin and the miracle. And, if it naïvely rants at American capitalism at thirty dollars a seat ("And when you're living in America / At the end of the mil-

lennium / You're what you own"), at least it's asking about justice, and not, like *Starlight Express,* about whether a steam engine can find happiness with an electric train. Larson clearly had his eye on the prize. He wanted to be great, and he had great ambitions for the musical theater. He puts this single-minded pursuit of his craft, this drive to redeem his time on earth, into Roger's **"One Song Glory,"** an apotheosis that now feels eerily prophetic:

> One song
> Glory
> One song
> Before I go
> Glory
> One song to leave behind . . .
> Find
> Glory
> In a song that rings true
> Truth like a blazing fire
> An eternal flame.

Larson would have been thirty-six last week. He was just beginning. Go see his musical and remember his name.

New York Times (review date 25 February 1996)

SOURCE: "*Rent* Is Brilliant and Messy All at Once," in *The New York Times,* February 25, 1996, sec. 2, pp. 5, 22.

[*In the following review, the critic describes* Rent *as "a lot of things: brash, brilliant, sweet, canny and messy."*]

It's odd to have joined the generations that talk about what "the young" are doing, saying and going through these days, and how that is reflected in art and entertainment. When *Hair,* the counterculture antiwar musical, opened to the late 60's, I was pleased but a little patronizing as well you always are when you're part of a subculture that suddenly goes mass culture. So I wonder what today's counterculture young think when they see themselves or a facsimile of themselves on stage in *Rent,* the rock opera of the 90's now playing at New York Theater Workshop.

What do they think of this portrait of avant-garde experiment and rock-bottom desperation on the Lower East Side of New York? Call it the East Village. Call it Alphabet City: it is a montage of performance artists, abandoned buildings, upwardly mobile landlords, firm makers and rock-and-roll bands, homeless people, policemen, drug dealers and drug addicts, free-thinking, free-form multiculturalism, homo-, hetero- and bisexuality, life-support groups and safe sex, privilege side by side with poverty and open-hearted exhilaration in the face of death and H.I.V.

I think *Rent* is a lot of things: brash, brilliant, sweet, canny and messy for starters. Messy enough to make you crazy at times (too long on plot, too short on musical resources), and rich enough (it has passion, principles and daring) to send you home believing you've experienced something like a catharsis.

Jonathan Larson, the 35-year-old composer and librettist of *Rent,* was absolutely right to choose Puccini's 1896 *Boheme* as the foundation for his 1996 homage to artists, rebels and outsiders. This lavishly romantic, melodic work is as close to pop culture as opera gets. Like Puccini's heroine, Mimi, Mr. Larson died as the opera ended; he watched the last dress rehearsal on Jan. 24 and was dead of an aortic aneurysm hours later.

He has turned Puccini's band of expansive, Italian-speaking French rebels into high-strung East Village Americans who talk every kind of slang (nerd slang, soul slang, Nuyorican slang, gay slang, college-girl and street-girl slang). Now the rebel artists are Roger Davis, Mark Cohen and Tom Collins. They are a songwriter, a film maker (Mark constantly turns his camera on the other characters and tells us what we need to know about them) and a computer guru. They are played by Adam Pascal, Anthony Rapp and Jesse L. Martin with (in that order) sullen charm, forthright savvy and wry bravado.

Roger and Tom are H.I.V. positive; so are their respective lovers, Mimi (the ravishing Daphne Rubin-Vega) and Angel, a street drummer and drag queen whom Wilson Jermaine Heredia plays with the insouciance that the Artist Formerly Known as Prince had when he first became known as Prince.

Musetta, the vamp-coquette to whom Puccini gave a heart of gold plus one of the loveliest waltzes yet written (its opening notes find their way into Roger's guitar riffs), has become Maureen (Idina Menzel). Maureen does protest-performance art, wears black vinyl with chic, struts like Sandra Bernhard and hits raspy high notes like Janis Joplin. Maureen has thrown Mark over for Joanne (Fredi Walker), a lapsed Ivy Leaguer and Talented Tenther who practices civil liberties law when she's not filming Maureen's performances and having vehement lovers' quarrels with her.

Most of the lovers are quarreling here, with each other and with their acquisitive landlord, Benny (Taye Diggs), who was once their penniless cohort. They are also quarreling with the fact that death is never far away.

They are surrounded by a polyglot band of street people, vendors, inquiring parents and prospective employers, played by an ensemble of seven additional performers. What a strong, sure polyglot cast: they can all move, they can all sing, and nothing they do feels hyped or gussied up in a relentless "let's sell it, kids, this is show business!" way.

They move through Paul Clay's industrial gray landscape of a set: it serves as a street with clusters of Christmas lights and a rack of used clothes; it serves as the inside of an abandoned apartment building or the cafe where they celebrate "la vie boheme." The choreographer, Marlies Yearby, sees that they move from dance to everyday attitudes and gestures (the showy kind and the quiet kind) with conscious but not self-conscious ease.

And how well they wear their grunge-meets-salsa-meets-B-Boy-meets-Riot-Grrrl-clothes: plaid pants, plastic pants, print pantyhose, jeans, layered tops, slip dresses, ankle-high, knee-high and thigh-high boots, and caps of various kinds. My thanks to the costume designer, Angela Wendt, and to the cast for wearing her clothes as if they belonged on the street, not the fashion runway.

One of the nicest things about seeing *Rent* on East Fourth Street is that when you leave (Cafe La Mama is right across the street), you feel a genuine link between theater and life. (Another nice thing is that New York Theater Workshop, under its artistic director, James C. Nicola, regularly gives inventive productions to innovative works.) The director, Michael Greif, preserves this link and this tradition by keeping the spectacle—the look, the sound, the pace of the whole—attuned to the strengths of each performer.

Rent does need more shaping: the subplots get fuzzy and so do some of the quick but intense encounters between characters. And it doesn't need all of its 35 songs: the words keep us going because even when they're corny they tell the story forthrightly. But the musical resources grow scant as the second act goes on.

Never mind for now. There's time to fix all of this. And I'll take imperfections amid talent, courage and charm over pristine miniaturism any day. Once upon a time, American musicals were fresh and daring, eager to take the culture's temperature and catch its tempo. I'm beginning to see this happen again. The millennium approaches, and *Rent* augurs well for 1996.

Jack Kroll (review date 26 February 1996)

SOURCE: "A Downtown 'La Bohème'," in *Newsweek,* Vol. CXXVII, No. 9, February 26, 1996, p. 67.

[In the review below, Kroll focuses on the characterization in Rent.*]*

During rehearsals of his musical *Rent,* composer-writer-lyricist Jonathan Larson was told by his excited producers, "Jonathan, you're the new voice." Larson smiled: "Yeah? That's good." Hours after the dress rehearsal on Jan. 24,

Larson, 35, was found dead of an aortic aneurysm in his Greenwich Village apartment. After the show's opening last week at the off-Broadway New York Theater Workshop, the new voice, now stilled, was greeted with the most feverishly enthusiastic reviews for any new American musical in many years. With tragic irony, Larson's death echoed the spirit of *La Bohème,* the Puccini opera about penniless young artists which was the basis of **Rent.** Where Puccini's heroine Mimi died, Larson has his Mimi live. Instead he perished.

There is death in **Rent**—death from AIDS, the modern plague that has supplanted the tuberculosis that killed Puccini's Mimi. But by "resurrecting" Mimi, Larson emphasizes the irrepressible surge of life. The first impact of **Rent** is the astonishing humane violence of its vital spirit, embodied by the youthful multicultural cast who perform with an ecstasy of commitment that is irresistible. In a way they are playing themselves: Puccini's 19th-century Left Bank bohemians have become late-20th-century struggling artists in New York's Alphabet City in the East Village.

Rent focuses on three couples. Roger (Adam Pascal), a musician desperate to write one great song before he succumbs to the plague, falls for Mimi (Daphne Rubin-Vega), a dancer at an S&M club who is doomed by drugs and HIV. Another HIV victim, the drag queen Angel (Wilson Jermaine Heredia), loves Tom Collins (Jesse L. Martin), a computer teacher dubious about the cyberworld of virtual reality. Performance artist Maureen (Idina Menzel) has a stormy relationship with her lesbian lover Joanne (Fredi Walker). Maureen's ex-lover Mark (Anthony Rapp) is a would-be filmmaker who serves as spokesman to the audience. Ben (Taye Diggs) is the landlord who threatens to evict the artists from their loft. Any whiff of artists' superiority is dispelled by the homeless, who scorn the young people as "bleeding hearts."

Did you just mutter that you don't give a damn about these people? You do, as Larson presents them in their juicy, confused, sexy, sex-scared, hopeless, hopeful humanity. His songs (there are 33 numbers) seem to leap straight from his characters' hearts. The title number is a fierce anthem of rebellion in a world where "Strangers, landlords, lovers / Your own blood cells betray." Larson writes several kinds of love songs: Roger's and Mimi's yearning **"Without You,"** Angel's and Collins's compassionate **"I'll Cover You,"** a blazing, witty duet for Maureen and Joanne, **"Take Me or Leave Me."** Director Michael Greif has a fine feel for the dynamic theatricality of Larson's music: a song will start as a solo, become a duet and ignite into a choral outpouring driven by a great onstage band led by Tim Weil, reinforced by the funky, un-Broadway choreography of Marlies Yearby.

Larson's score is the post-Sondheim musical's most successful attempt yet to fuse the eclectic energies of contemporary pop music with the needs of the theater. His versions of gos-

pel, rock, reggae, even a tango, add up to a brilliant portrait of the crazy cubistic face of today's pop. **Rent** completes a marvelously fortuitous trilogy that started with *Hair* and went on to *A Chorus Line.* All these breakthrough musicals deal with "marginal" Americans: the flower children of the '60s, the gypsy dancers who sweat and smile on Broadway, and now the young people who follow the often quixotic dream of art in a chilling time for soul and body. These shows make their characters emblems of a striving that's at the center of the American mystique. Larson, who never stopped striving (he was working as a waiter two months ago), was one of these people. His simultaneous death and triumph is a metaphor for the heartbreak and hope, the paradox of the American Dream.

Peter Marks (review date 26 February 1996)

SOURCE: "Looking on Broadway for a Bohemian Home," in *The New York Times,* February 26, 1996, pp. C9, C11.

[*In the following review, Marks describes the frenzy surrounding* Rent's *premiere.*]

On the opening night of **Rent** two weeks ago, the phones in the offices of the New York Theater Workshop began ringing off the hook. They haven't stopped since.

Theater producers, record promoters, film directors, actors, musicians and ordinary theatergoers have been jamming the phone lines in search of tickets to the critically acclaimed rock musical, in a clamor unlike anything the people who run the nonprofit theater on East Fourth Street have ever experienced. Sylvester Stallone showed up early in the run. Whitney Houston's assistants came to check out the score.

The demand was so intense that the 150-seat Off Broadway theater immediately raised the ticket price from $30 to $45 and brought in a small army of volunteers to handle the volume. "The phones were ringing from 8 o'clock in the morning until 10 o'clock at night," said Nancy Kassak Diekmann, the theater's managing director.

Rent, a raucous 1990's version of *La Bohème* set on the Lower East Side and populated by drug users and performance artists and drag queens, has burst on the theater scene with a breakout force that few shows muster. Until a few weeks ago, hardly anyone had heard of the musical. Then its 35-year-old composer and librettist, Jonathan Larson, died suddenly of an aortic aneurysm on the night of the final dress rehearsal. And now, buoyed by waves of glowing reviews and strong word of mouth, **Rent** is the hottest show in town.

Commercial producers are already making final arrangements to move it to Broadway, where it is to open in late April, a transfer so eagerly anticipated that Broadway's two biggest landlords, the Shuberts and Nederlanders, are in a head-to-head contest to win the musical.

The rapid rise of *Rent* is the story of the theater season, a surprise triumph in an industry short on sensations and starved for a fresh, home-grown musical hit. Like *Hair* and *A Chorus Line* and *Dreamgirls* before it, *Rent,* with its lush untamed score and vibrant, young 15-member cast seems to have re-kindled faith in the American musical when many in the theater business, particularly younger people, believed it had reached an artistic dead end.

"It's a phenomenon already," said Daryl Roth, one of the producers of another recent Off Broadway hit, *Three Tall Women.* "It's something to get excited about when a new young voice is able to bring something to the public's attention, when the subject is so rooted in today. It's the same kind of chill that you had with *Hair* and *Jesus Christ Superstar.*"

With the graying of their audience, Broadway's elders are desperate for something that hooks the young, so the youthful appeal of *Rent* is one of several factors that is propelling the show uptown. Another is the music itself. While the drawing power of George C. Wolfe's *Bring in da Noise, Bring in da Funk,* the other breakthrough musical that opens on Broadway in April, is its use of tap to tell the story of an entire culture, the strength of *Rent* is its score. Already its rich rock melodies have attracted widespread interest from the recording industry; the movie and record producer David Geffen appears to have the inside track on the right to make the cast album.

And while the sudden death last month of the show's composer, Mr. Larson, devastated the cast, the calamity has undoubtedly deepened the emotional power of the musical's central motif, the struggle of doomed young people to find love with time running out.

"I think this show is a lot of different things to a lot of different people," said James C. Nicola, the artistic director of the New York Theater Workshop. Mr. Nicola, whose theater specializes in supporting new works and emerging artists, had been helping Mr. Larson develop *Rent* for several years. "I think what it does is it takes the kind of fear and despair that's rampant in America and transcends it."

Although Mr. Nicola had hoped to hold onto *Rent* a while longer before the show's commercial producers moved it uptown, he and others involved in the production say they are confident it will thrive beyond East Fourth Street. Nonetheless, he and others acknowledge that Mr. Larson had not finished work on the piece, and that there is some "incompleteness" to it. Several critics who praised the show overall also made note of this rawness; a few took the director, Michael Greif, to task for what they saw as an unfocused staging. (Some involved in the show say that, in fact, Mr. Greif played an important role in helping Mr. Larson shape the musical).

Mr. Nicola says many of those involved in the project felt strongly that *Rent* had to be staged in a theater space that had a connection to the bohemian, downtown world the musical conjures. After its run at the workshop, he said, the initial plan was "to create a space" for it to run somewhere in the city that reflected that world. One of the reasons the creative team was drawn to Kevin McCollum, Jeffrey Seller and Allan S. Gordon, he said, the producers Mr. Larson selected to move the show, was that they shared that vision of the musical.

Finding an appropriate space to convert proved financially unrealistic. Now, the producers say, they are trying to find a vacant Broadway theater that might have some of those ramshackle characteristics. The Nederlanders and Shuberts are courting the producers with a variety of playhouses that are normally considered to be among the less desirable. The producers say they will make their choice this week.

Whatever theater they choose, the people behind *Rent* think they will attract a new audience to Broadway and thereby stake a claim to it for a new generation.

"Some of the naysayers have warned us that our audience doesn't go to Broadway," Mr. Seller said. "Our response has been, they haven't gone to Broadway because there hasn't been anything to see. We think they'll come to Broadway for this."

Frank Rich (review date 2 March 1996)

SOURCE: "East Village Story," in *The New York Times,* March 2, 1996, p. A19.

[In the following review, Rich describes the theatrical and political significance of Rent.*]*

In an age when almost every showbiz event is predigested and presold by the media long before the public can decide for itself, the truly spontaneous pop-culture phenomenon is almost extinct. Almost but not quite. Two weeks ago, at a 150-seat theater in the East Village, a rock opera called *Rent,* written and performed by unknowns, came out of nowhere to earn the most ecstatic raves of any American musical in the two decades since *A Chorus Line.* And now the world is rushing to catch up: *Rent* will quickly move to Broadway to accommodate the insatiable demand for tickets, even as Hollywood titans fight to bring it to the screen.

Rent is all the critics say it is. There's a moment that often comes early in thrilling musicals—call it the "Something's Coming" moment, in honor of *West Side Story*—when a performer steps forward, grabs the spotlight and demands what he wants from life, no matter the obstacles. In *Rent*, which loosely transposes the story of *La Bohème* to Manhattan's present-day downtown bohemia, that moment arrives when a young, H.I.V.-positive punk rocker sings of how he lives only for "one song / glory / one song / before I go." Such is the naked yearning of this anthem that it would induce chills even if you didn't know that its lyrics proved eerily prescient: Jonathan Larson, the 35-year-old author of *Rent*, is dead.

The story of Mr. Larson's death on the eve of the triumph for which he had hungered all his life is unspeakably sad. He died suddenly and inexplicably of an aortic aneurysm a month ago, hours before his show's first performance. As Michael Greif, who directed *Rent*, recalled in an interview punctuated by tears this week, Mr. Larson had sacrificed his life to his work, waiting on tables for years, sustaining himself with the "sunny belief" that his talent would one day lead to his breakthrough. "He wanted it bad," said Mr. Greif. "It's cruel that he's not here to enjoy it."

Yet the significance of *Rent*, the phenomenon, derives not from its author's tragic death, or from what the show may say about the American theater, or from its superficial resemblances to *Hair*. For all the talk about how *Rent* speaks for the cyber-AIDS-Doc-Martens Generation X of Alphabet City as *Hair* allegedly did for 60's flower children, Mr. Larson's songs are bigger than their milieu. Stephen Sondheim, who became the young songwriter's mentor, this week recalled how he "welled up" when he first heard Mr. Larson's work on a tape—in part because it was "generous music," lovingly merging the musical theater traditions of past generations, including Mr. Sondheim's own, with rock.

The night I saw *Rent* at the New York Theater Workshop, few theatergoers in the house demographically matched the castoffs on stage. But neither did the audience seem like the desperately hip on a slumming expedition. People were riveted, as I was, by the raw exuberance of characters who keep fighting and creating and reaching out no matter how strong their fears—whether of death in a plague or of marginalization in the ruthless new post-industrial economy that frightens many Americans on the lower rungs, not just those living on the edges of St. Mark's Place.

If anything, some of the turn-of-the-millennium fears given powerful voice by the dispossessed bohemians of *Rent* resemble those of what we now call Pat Buchanan voters. Brilliant artists and politicians do, after all, share the ability to divine and then articulate the unspoken hopes and fears of the society around them, moving audiences powerfully as they do so.

But Mr. Larson's artistry doesn't leave the audience angry, as Mr. Buchanan's demagoguery does. The songwriter takes the very people whom politicians now turn into scapegoats for our woes—the multicultural, the multisexual, the homeless, the sick—and, without sentimentalizing them or turning them into ideological symbols or victims, lets them revel in their joy, their capacity for love and, most important, their tenacity, all in a ceaseless outpouring of melody.

At so divisive a time in our country's culture, *Rent* shows signs of revealing a large, untapped appetite for something better. It's too early to tell. What is certain is that Jonathan Larson's brief life belies the size of his spirit. In the staying power of his songs, he lingers, refusing to let anyone who hears his voice abandon hope.

John Simon (review date 4 March 1996)

SOURCE: "All in the Family," in *New York*, March 4, 1996, p. 65.

[*Below, Simon gives a mixed review of* Rent.]

In September 1914, Puccini got wind of an abridged version of *La Bohème* to be mounted in Lucca, and promptly wrote his publisher, "I beg you not to give them the opera. You will do me a real favor." How would he have felt about a version called *Rent*, which updates the Giacosa-Illica libretto, transplants the action to the East Village, and keeps only a few bars of his music, strummed on a guitar—just enough to put the rest of the score to shame? Well, with the copyright lapsed, it would not matter what he felt.

Jonathan Larson, who wrote both words and music, died at 35 of an aortic aneurysm upon returning from the final dress rehearsal a month ago. This is doubly sad when you consider that the gifted young man was groping his way to a unified personal style that this uneven, scattershot show does not yet achieve. For although *Rent* profits from the *Bohème* infrastructure, it is also hampered by it, as the author is obliged to think up clever parallels or disheveled variations that invite unfavorable comparison with the original. Still, even this partial success holds a genuine promise cut off from fulfillment.

The poet Rodolfo becomes Roger, the punk rocker; the painter Marcello, Mark Cohen, a filmmaker brandishing his camcorder. The philosopher Colline is now Tom Collins, a black mechanic of some sort; the musician Schaunard is Angel Schunard, a Hispanic transvestite and street drummer who succors the mugged Collins and becomes his lover. Mimi is still Mimi but is now a performer in an S&M nightclub, and a junkie afflicted with AIDS. Roger, Collins, and Schunard are all HIV-positive. Benny (i.e., Benoit), the landlord, is a homeboy gone yuppie, full of bohemian-unfriendly schemes, and a rival for Mimi's favors. Maureen (Musetta), a performance artist, has left Mark for a black lesbian lawyer, Joanne.

There are all sorts of approximations of the opera but also a few radical departures. Thus it is Angel who dies of AIDS, whereas Mimi merely seems to die. Her fever breaks, and she revives to join the rest of the cast in the finale, "There is no future, there is no past. / I live each moment as my last." This copout makes a mockery not only of logic but also of death and Jonathan Larson's own tragedy. It is, however, not the only thing that doesn't make sense in *Rent.* Let us, however, judge the show on its own terms. The music is both eclectic and erratic as it tries to embrace every form of pop. It is most successful in some ensemble numbers and in tributes to (or takeoffs on?) show tunes, such as **"Tango: Maureen"** and **"Santa Fe,"** a fantasy about starting a restaurant in that city. Also in Maureen's performance-art number, **"Over the Moon,"** which Idina Menzel performs with infectious comic brio. Other fine performers include Wilson Jermaine Heredia (Angel), Taye Diggs (Benny), and Jesse L. Martin (Collins), with the rest of the cast of fifteen mostly pleasant or better. Only Anthony Rapp, as a smarmy Mark, and Daphne Rubin-Vega, as an inconsequential Mimi, disappoint.

Michael Greif's staging, despite inventive moments, does not quite keep the action that sprawls over a large and inflexible stage in proper control, and Marlies Yearby's rudimentary choreography is no help at all. There are savvy and sassy costumes (by Angela Wendt) and scenery (by Paul Clay) to which Blake Burba's lighting does not do full justice. The five-piece band led by Tim Weil is in fine fettle. *Rent,* which opened just as *La Bohème* celebrated its centenary, will probably prove less perdurable but is not without its quirkily perky charm.

Richard Zoglin (review date 4 March 1996)

SOURCE: "Lower East Side Story," in *Time,* Vol. 147, No. 10, March 4, 1996, p. 71.

[*In the following favorable review, Zoglin praises the life-affirming message of* Rent.]

Jonathan Larson was looking tired and pale all week, but it might have been just the stress of preparing for the opening of his new musical, *Rent.* Twice he went to the hospital, complaining of chest pains and a fever; his trouble was diagnosed as food poisoning, and he was given a battery of tests. He managed to drag himself to the last dress rehearsal, but colleagues were concerned: Larson, who rode his bicycle even on the coldest winter days, came in a taxi. "You could see he was trying to conserve his strength," says director Michael

Greif. The next morning, when Greif arrived at a production meeting, he got the shocking news. Larson, 35, had been found dead in his apartment—the victim, it was later determined, of an aortic aneurysm.

The death of a promising theatrical talent is always tragic, but Larson's legacy makes his all the more painful. *Rent,* a rock opera based on Puccini's *La Bohème,* opened in New York City just three weeks after Larson's death and got an ecstatic reception. Critics hailed it as the breakthrough musical of the '90s. Theatergoers began streaming downtown, to the way-off-Broadway New York Theater Workshop; within a week, the show had sold out its entire run, through the end of March. Hollywood studios and record executives began calling, as did Broadway. By late last week, the producers were finishing up negotiations to transfer the show to a Broadway house in mid-April, just in time for the Tony nominations. "*Rent* belongs in front of as many people for as long as possible," said coproducer Kevin McCollum. For once, a producer may get his wish.

Rent may not be quite the groundbreaker, or have the melodic richness, of *Hair* or *Jesus Christ Superstar.* But it is the most exuberant and original American musical to come along this decade. Larson has updated *La Bohème* and set it among the artists, addicts, prostitutes and street people of New York City's East Village. In place of Puccini's Mimi, dying of tuberculosis, is Larson's Mimi (Daphne Rubin-Vega), a drug-addicted dancer in an S&M club who is suffering from AIDS. The Rudolfo she falls for is Roger (Adam Pascal), an HIV-positive rock singer who longs for one great song to leave behind.

AIDS is the shadow hovering over all the people in *Rent,* but the musical doesn't dwell on illness or turn preachy; it is too busy celebrating life and chronicling its characters' efforts to squeeze out every last drop of it. Tom Collins (Jesse L. Martin), a gay teacher, hooks up with Angel (Wilson Jermaine Heredia), a high-spirited transvestite. Joanne (Fredi Walker), a lesbian attorney, gets together with Maureen (Idina Menzel), a performance artist who has just broken up with Mark (Anthony Rapp), a video filmmaker who acts as the musical's narrator and guide.

Rent is a bit overloaded with characters and subplots; the central love story, between Mimi and Roger, gets all but lost in the bustle. But the energy and passion of Larson's music make up for it. A five-piece band on the open, cluttered stage drives an insistent rock beat. The lyrics (there is no spoken dialogue) are resonant but not sanctimonious, with snatches of easy wit. When Roger tells Mimi he has too much baggage for a relationship, she replies, "I'm looking for baggage that goes with mine." In songs like **"La Vie Bohème,"** a rousing celebration of the bohemian life, Larson shows a knack for clever, rolling rhymes that never sound forced:

"Compassion, to fashion, to passion when it's new / To Sontag, to Sondheim, to anything taboo."

Stephen Sondheim was a mentor to Larson, who grew up in White Plains, New York, and had six musicals (among them *Superbia* and *Tick, Tick . . . Boom!*) produced in downtown workshops and cabarets before *Rent.* In the summer of 1992 Larson showed an early draft to James C. Nicola, artistic director of the NYTW, which was renovating its performance space. Says Nicola: "He saw the construction, stuck his head in the theater and knew immediately that this was the perfect spot for *Rent.*" They worked together on the show for two years, then called in Greif, who last year staged Randy Newman's *Faust* at San Diego's La Jolla Playhouse.

Rent is a surprising pick-me-up for another poverty-stricken season of Broadway musicals, dominated by revivals and reworkings of old movies (*Victor/Victoria*). It's Broadway's dream come true: an audacious, really *new* musical with crossover appeal and half a dozen starmaking roles (Rubin-Vega's sexy, strong-voiced Mimi stands out in the excellent cast). All that's missing is its creator to take a bow—and promise us more. "I sit every night in that theater and think about what was to come that's now denied to us," says Nicola. "Thirty years of great theater have been lost." But *Rent,* at least, has been found.

Donald Lyons (review date 6 March 1996)

SOURCE: "*Rent,* New Musical Is Deserved Hit," in *Wall Street Journal,* Vol. CCXXVII, No. 46, March 6, 1996, p. A18.

[*Below, Lyons distinguishes between "*Rent *the phenomenon and* Rent *the show," claiming that the production's "artlessness is a sophisticated achievement."*]

There's *Rent* the phenomenon and *Rent* the show. The phenomenon: Limousines and taxis snake through East Fourth Street, a strip of tenements and bodegas, toward the New Theater Workshop, where the new musical is the town's toast. It's an updating of Puccini's *La Boheme,* which, exactly a century ago, celebrated the defiant struggles of Paris bohemians. Composer-lyricist Jonathan Larson (his earlier, misfired satire on Wall Street, *J.P. Morgan Saves the Nation,* was actually staged on Wall Street) transposed it all to the grungy East Village—a few blocks or so east of the theater. Now, in a plot development right out of its own story, it's to move uptown in late April, but only to a theater on the lower outskirts of that co-opting entity called Broadway. It will forsake its 150-seat home for a 1206-seat space: it will be eligible for uptown awards: commercial temptations will assail it. There's irony, of course, in the quick embrace of rebelliousness by celebrity, but *Rent,* in truth, begs to be embraced:

it's a good boy at heart. The saddest irony of all is that, on the very eve of glory, on the evening of the last dress rehearsal, Larson, 35, died suddenly and shockingly of an aneurysm.

Rent the show: If your heart sinks at the phrase "rock musical," buck up, for *Rent* does not belong to that dreary, hybrid litter. Almost 30 years ago *Hair* was supposed to have revolutionized the musical by wedding it to rock, but it was a shotgun and short-lived union. *Hair* now seems stupidly complacent and sounds not unlike the Partridge Family. *Rent* is a musical, one influenced by many styles including rock and reggae and salsa and tango and opera, but Larson was a protege of Stephen Sondheim, the bringer of psychological complexity and literate doubt to the form, and that's the tradition it works in—and surpasses. It's the best new musical since the 1950s, the time of Leonard Bernstein's *Candide* and John Latouche's *The Golden Apple.* Director Michael Greif (he did a vivid, complex *Pericles* at the Public a while back) has had a lot to do with the clarity, the force, the crisp definition with which *Rent* presents itself. It flaunts the bareness and spareness: bare stage, granite blocks, stylized Christmas tree, bandstand stage right at which the five musicians in black casually assemble. It's as if we're about to see a rehearsal, and what we do experience has the raw, ragged, slightly unfinished, excited, urgent feel of a late but coalescing runthrough: This seeming artlessness is a sophisticated achievement.

There's no book; some 35 songs, sung by 15 young singers, propel the story, which is indeed stronger in emotion than narrative, as it follows the vicissitudes of a band of artists in and around an East Village squat. It's Christmas, and our roommate heroes, filmmaker Mark (Puccini's poet Rodolfo) and songwriter Roger (Puccini's painter Marcello), can't pay the rent to their new yuppie landlord, who wants to turn the building into a cyberspace for artists. Mark has lost his performance-artist girlfriend Maureen (Puccini's Musetta) to soundwoman Joanne. During a power outage Mimi comes to Roger looking for a match: he's an ex-junkie; she's a junkie; it's love at first squint, but a shadowed love, for both are HIV-pos as they find out later, only when their AZT beepers go off simultaneously.

Maureen's performance-piece protest song about Elsie the Cow in Cyberland sparks a riot, which Mark films so brilliantly that he's offered a network job. Uptown, Faustian temptations beckon our downtown rebels. The Roger-Mimi romance stalls as she goes back on the needle and he splits for healthy Santa Fe.

It's in the intimate but charged personal songs that *Rent* excels, as when Mark and Joanne share the pains of loving an egoist in **"Tango Maureen"** or when Roger paints his musical vision in **"Glory"** or Roger and Mimi exchange

"Light My Candle" and **"I Should Tell You."** What Mr. Larson knew so well and Mr. Greif stages so electrically is that each song must contain and enact a conflict. Every minute of *Rent* is energized by polarized pain; someone's constantly in someone else's face. Under Mr. Greif's no-frills direction and Marlies Yearby's bare-knuckles choreography, bare tables are sites of conflict, and microphones are vessels of rage. This is no smug, *Hair*-like celebration of a culture, but an angry anatomizing of a culture's internal and external stresses. "This is not Bohemia, but Calcutta," in the words of **"La Vie Boheme,"** the exultant, choric first-act finale that proclaims allegiance to icons like [filmmaker Michelangelo] Antonioni, [Bernardo] Bertolucci and the Sex Pistols even as those mortal beepers beep. The second half brings tragedy, recrimination and a final, paradoxically life-affirming resurrection of Mimi.

There are flaws, and large ones: There's a transvestite named Angel whose love for an NYU prof and death from AIDS is supposed to be a key moral anchor for everyone, but the character is barely there and is a cliche at that: even Mimi, with her relapses, is largely unexplained: the Christmas ironies are trite: much plot is literally inaudible. But who cares? So much fresh air blows through *Rent*! If *Sunset Boulevard* was the twilight of the old musical and *Victor/Victoria* its midnight, if Sondheim's sterile cleverness has proved a dead end, this is both smart and alive.

Daphne Rubin-Vega's Mimi has spunk and poignancy. Fredi Walker and Idina Menzel are terrific as Joanne and Maureen; they've got a wonderful number together, **"Take Me or Leave Me."** (One of *Rent*'s cheerful virtues is its eagerness to cast players of color in a lifelike, but still surprising variety of roles: Ms. Walker's Joanne is a good guy, but Taye Diggs's yuppie landlord is perhaps not.) Ms. Menzel's show-stopping sing-along ode to Elsie is hilarious. *Rent* likes to laugh at itself. Central are the vocal-dramatic performances of Adam Pascal as Roger—he's an actual musician and gets exactly their solipsistic intensity—and of Anthony Rapp as the hot, angry idealist Mark. Alert and savage, with presence to burn, Mr. Rapp runs through the show like a jolt of illicitly hooked-up electricity.

Bernard Holland (review date 17 March 1996)

SOURCE: "Flaws Aside, *Rent* Lives and Breathes," in *The New York Times,* March 17, 1996, sec. 2, p. 31.

[*In the following review, Holland discusses* Rent *in terms of its relation to high art.*]

Who has musical culture and who doesn't? A letter to the editors of this newspaper recently complained that young people don't. Its author used opera on the radio as a measur-

ing stick. "I . . . remember walking from one end of the Yale campus to the other on a warm Saturday afternoon without missing a beat of the Metropolitan Opera broadcast through open dormitory windows," the offended correspondent writes. "Thirty years later, the same trip yields loud rock." A strong indictment, but of what?

Possibly the very culture the writer is trying to defend. Not that paying attention to long-deceased Italian composers is a waste of time. Study and appreciation of them and their music have meant a valuable life's work for listeners, musicians and scholars alike. But to hold up the dead and the distant as exclusive standards by which educated end-of-the-20th-century young people are to be judged gives culture and art a slightly provincial tone.

I wonder if those first visitors to *La Boheme* at the Teatro Regio in Turin a century ago reacted much differently from the audiences currently being wowed by Jonathan Larson's *Rent,* the rock-and-roll knockoff of Puccini at the New York Theater Workshop in the East Village. Sure, a number of them must have said: "What is this vulgar nonsense? Let's go back to 'Don Giovanni'." But I suspect that many were kindred in spirit to the crowd I mingled with at *Rent* not long ago; 40 or under, inventively dressed, well-spoken and clearly educated. It was a crew genuinely curious about what the world around it right now had to offer.

Rent, as you may know by now, transplants Puccini's beloved Bohemians to East 11th Street, gives them AIDS, rats and roaches, and sends them out into the world to a rock-and-roll beat. Critics have smiled; audiences have showed up. *Rent* is soon moving to Broadway.

> **Whether or not *Rent* succeeds as an opera, a musical or anything else is beside the point for present purposes. The effort behind it and the sense of adventure it represents say something serious about a sophisticated culture trying painfully to create a more inclusive art.**
>
> **—*Bernard Holland***

From a musical viewpoint, I wanted *Rent* to be better than it is. A lot of the music is warmed over: somewhat tame and secondhand for its rough, drugged-up and disease-ridden Alphabet City surroundings. I live around the corner from the real thing, and what I see and hear on the streets has an edge that the earnest practitioners of *Rent* can't quite summon. My companion at the performance—and she is a bona-fide rock-and-roller—said it better than I, likening the music of *Rent* to one of those bar bands that play at roadside Holiday Inns on Saturday night.

There is also a college-dorm patness to the show's social politics: the victim-victimizer, good-evil, us-against-them dichotomies that seem a little too symmetric. Yet just as *Rent* starts trying the patience, it gathers energy. The cast is young, attractive and filled with talent. It works endearingly hard. The ensemble interchange, a hip version of recitative style, is alternately clever and clumsy. The ghost of *Tommy* hangs over this show. *Rent* has no Pete Townshend to send it soaring, but it brims with good will.

Whether or not *Rent* succeeds as an opera, a musical or anything else is beside the point for present purposes. The effort behind it and the sense of adventure it represents say something serious about a sophisticated culture trying painfully to create a more inclusive art. If its young men and women do not listen to the Met on balmy Saturdays—if they do not know [Italian composer Giuseppi] Verdi and [German composer Richard] Wagner—that is distinctly a shame. But the way to get Verdi and Wagner into their heads is not through letters like the one here.

Classical music, having carefully developed a two-centuries-old cult of the past, now finds itself in an ambivalent position. It rightly defends a repertory of great music by dead composers, but it has become distinctly inept at handling the present. The righteous indignation of our letter writer abets the suicidal tendencies of so-called high culture. High culture places its artifacts at the peak of a mountain and proceeds to push away the ascending creative minds that are not of its direct bloodline. Art like this retains its identity as do all closed societies: by rejection.

And here is another question. Can young people's ignorance of the classical tradition be any more ignominious and alarming than the classical-music establishment's ignorance of the popular music that surrounds its everyday life and, indeed, dominates the world's attention? Almost all the thinking pop-music fans I know have a working knowledge of [German composer Ludwig van] Beethoven and are curious to know more. Most classical-music people of my acquaintance either bridle or stare blankly at anything outside their ken.

What, I wonder, does our writer understand of the subtle differentiations in Brazilian popular style? He says in his letter that present students "haven't a clue as to what the arts mean and their importance to a civilization." Maybe we should amend that thought to say that students do not necessarily enter the walled-in cultural space in which the writer has decided the right kind of art should reside.

This letter, as you may have noticed, makes me mad, and for reasons that are a little oblique. As someone who has spent

his life with classical music, I am alarmed for the future of its important artifacts. I don't know how we are going to save them. Isolating them with a sneer and a shrug from what responsive young people find important for themselves is a poor solution. Inferred from our writer's cry of cultural pain is an old refrain: "They don't make them like they used to." Maybe they are not supposed to.

Patrick Pacheco (review date 14 April 1996)

SOURCE: "Life, Death and *Rent*," in *Los Angeles Times*, April 14, 1996, p. 4.

[*In the following review, Pacheco recounts the history of* Rent *as the production prepared for its Broadway premiere.*]

It was closing night for the new musical *Rent* at the New York Theater Workshop, a 150-seat East Village theater where the pop opera, loosely based on Puccini's *La Boheme*, opened in February. Onstage, friends and creative personnel, including director Michael Greif, mingled with the youthful cast and band in the kind of pizza-and-beer ritual that has been repeated countless times in experimental theater spaces.

But this celebration was distinctly different. For one, television cameras and reporters were present at what had all the giddy earmarks of a bon voyage party. And indeed, this was not just a closing: *Rent* was on its way into previews for its Broadway opening April 29, and, though no one could have known it at the party, it was also on its way to winning the Pulitzer Prize for drama last week, two more stops in what has been one of the most extraordinary journeys in recent theater history.

But amid the celebration, a palpable ghost was in the room.

"This has been an insane experience—it's like having been struck by a bolt of lightning," said 25-year-old Daphne Rubin-Vega, who plays Mimi Marquez, an S/M dancer at the Cat Scratch Club. "I just wish Jonathan were here. He's the one person responsible for all of this, and it sucks that he's not here to enjoy it with us."

The Jonathan on the minds of almost everyone in the room was Jonathan Larson, the 35-year-old author and composer of *Rent.* It is his life and the lives of his friends that are reflected in the musical, a raw and exuberant celebration of bohemian East Village artists—drag queens, drug addicts, performance artists and vagrants—living on the edge. The prevalence of violence and HIV in the stories of these characters suffuses the musical with the fragility of life, the theme of Puccini's opera. Indeed early in *Rent,* a character sings of writing one song " . . . before I go, one song to leave behind. . . . " All the more affecting, therefore, that on Jan.

25, the day *Rent* was to begin previews at NYTW, Larson died suddenly of an aortic aneurysm.

While Larson had previously shown promise with two comparatively modest shows (***Superbia, JP Morgan Saves the Nation***) and had won prestigious theater grants, he was largely unknown among New York's theater-going public at the time of his death. But that changed dramatically after *Rent* opened on Feb. 13. Glowing reviews hailed Larson's swan song as the "*Hair* of the '90s" and soon limousines were wending their way past the East Village bodegas and coffeehouses to the tiny theater on East 4th Street. Uptown theater owners began fiercely bidding, courting the show's neophyte producers, and David Geffen or Ahmet Ertegun became the odds-on favorites to produce the show's original cast album.

While there was talk of opening the show in a West Village theater, the heat and momentum made Broadway all but inevitable. Yet questions remain about how well the show will do on Broadway, with its very different demographics. After all, Broadway ticket buyers hardly seem to be hungering for a musical in which four of the seven leads are HIV-positive, the central romantic couple meets over a bag of heroin and vagrants snarl out Christmas carols.

Capitalized at a paltry $3.5 million at the Nederlander Theater, situated in Broadway's shabbiest area, *Rent* is in minimalist contrast to the glitzy revivals and over-produced musicals of recent years. Even *The Who's Tommy,* its closest antecedent, seems grandfatherly compared to this brash Generation X upstart, with its cast of unknowns, some of whom had never done theater before.

"You know, if someone had told me two months ago that this show was moving to Broadway, I'd have said they were nuts," said Adam Pascal, a rock musician making his theater debut in the role of Roger, the tortured songwriter in love with Mimi. "But now it makes a weird kind of sense to me. I think we're going to draw a really bizarre mix of people, some who've never set foot in a theater."

Shortly after *Rent* opened at the NYTW, director Greif sat down at NYTW's offices to chat. As the phones rang persistently from callers asking about tickets, the director looked emotionally wrung out but gratified by the show's success and intrigued by its commercial possibilities.

"I think it's a really important conversation to have, where the new audience for theater is going to come from," Greif said. "How do we get them to find something of value in their lives in the theater?

"That's why I got so excited about *Rent,*" he added, noting that two years ago, NYTW's artistic director James C. Nicola and Larson had sent him a tape and script of the show. "Here

was an opportunity to express things you generally don't find expressed in musical theater, yet it was a wonderful hybrid of some very operatic impulses, some very conventional musical theater impulses, and some not very conventional musical theater impulses, such as collage and nonrealistic storytelling. As I read on and listened, the doors of possibility opened."

Larson's pop opera began to evolve in the late 1980s, when he seized the concept that some of the themes and plot points of Puccini's *La Boheme* reflected his own life. Larson had had a relatively privileged upbringing in Westchester, but after graduating from New York's Adelphi University he waited tables and lived in a shabby TriBeCa apartment with, as Greif put it, "one extension cord going out of the window and a cavalcade of roommates, some of whom were addicts and some of whom were not and some of whom had HIV and some of whom did not."

In a note, written for the NYTW program, Larson stated his aims: "With this work, I celebrate my friends and the many others who continue to fulfill their dreams and live their lives in the shadow of AIDS. In these dangerous times, where it seems the world is ripping apart at the seams, we can all learn how to survive from those who stare death squarely in the face every day, and we should reach out to each other and bond as a community, rather than hide from the terrors of life."

When Larson won a Richard Rodgers theater grant in early 1994, a musical workshop of *Rent* became possible. He had already found a champion in NYTW's Nicola, who suggested Greif as the workshop's director. Greif, who had just been appointed artistic director of the La Jolla Playhouse in San Diego, had very little experience in musical theater aside from having assisted his La Jolla predecessor Des McAnuff on *Big River* in the early '80s. (He has since directed Randy Newman's *Faust* at La Jolla.) But his inexperience played in his favor, said Nicola and Larson.

"His understanding of how a Broadway musical worked was a good thing," Nicola explained. "But it didn't form his style. Michael has a downtown sensibility, a way of telling stories in a way that is very stripped down and simple yet theatrically bold. Jonathan and I both thought this was absolutely the right style for the narrative."

The workshop in the fall of 1994 was successful enough to become a prelude to a full-scale production at NYTW the following season. By this point, too, two young producers, Jeffrey Seller and Kevin McCollum of the Booking Office, and their older partner Allan Gordon, won the rights for a commercial production. Even with their added capital, the budget for the NYTW production was minimal—$200,000—and sets and costumes were, aptly enough, as threadbare as the show's have-nots.

Paul Clay's set, which will be scaled up for Broadway, is largely an impressionistic steel framework and walk-through scaffolding decorated with found objects, one corner of which is taken up by the band. It is left to the actors and some clever lighting to suggest the settings, which include a loft, a performance club and vacant lots.

"We didn't want it to become over-literal," Greif said. "As Jonathan was fond of saying, 'Make something out of nothing,' and I wanted to celebrate that kind of theater. We didn't want to get away from that concert-like presentation even if we had a gazillion dollars to spend."

More problematic to all concerned was how best to focus the narrative, which meandered through the emotional ups and downs of three couples, against a chorus of nudging parents, HIV support groups and local junkies and homeless people. The question was how to balance the primary relationships in *Rent*: Roger, the aspiring songwriter, and his relationship with the sultry and self-destructive Mimi; Angel, the life-embracing joyous drag queen (Wilson Jermaine Heredia) who finds a soulmate in Tom Collins (Jesse L. Martin); and law student Joanne (Fredi Walker) who steals Maureen, the performance artist (Idina Menzel), away from Mark Cohen (Anthony Rapp), the filmmaker who is obsessed with recording his friends' lives before they are prematurely snuffed out.

"How do you tell all those stories so they're not just a blob?" asked Greif, adding that two years of debating such questions ended with Larson's death just before the critical phase of previews began. "Ultimately, the consensus led to the conclusion that it was about the community itself, about people and artists struggling to live with disease in dignity and wholeness and to honor that without being sanctimonious.

"It would've been easier if that had not been the focus," he added. "But that came directly out of Jonathan's material, and while I wish he'd been around so that I could've fought with him about certain things, I'm also sure I would've lost those battles. These questions of how you tell the story of a community continue to challenge me. The show has flaws, certainly."

Whether Greif will have enough time before the show opens on Broadway to smooth out some of those flaws is another question. Producer Jeffrey Seller has dubbed the swift move "Operation Desert Storm" and the onslaught has begun. The ads for the show are simple: the title, stenciled in crooked block letters, and a number to call for tickets. It is a low-key antidote to the avalanche of hype that has set up *Rent* as the musical to beat for the Tony, though it stands to get a run for its money from another unconventional transfer, off-Broadway's *Bring on Da Noise/Bring on Da Funk,* the tap-rap musical directed by George C. Wolfe at the Ambassador Theater.

The media attention and the Pulitzer have not only boosted ticket sales—the show has a respectable $4-million advance—but also increased the heat surrounding the movie sale. Agent Bill Craver of Writers and Artists, who is handling the negotiations, had no comment, but producer McCollum confirmed reports in the trades that Warner Bros. is actively bidding on behalf of Joel Schumacher and that Fox's Searchlight Division and Danny DeVito's Jersey Films also have been negotiating. McCollum added that there are more companies expressing an interest.

Greif says he isn't worried about a possible backlash from either East Villagers who may not recognize themselves on the stage or from a public primed on hype. It's Jonathan's friends who are up there, not a ZIP Code, he says.

"On the other hand, Jonathan had a very far-reaching soul," Grief said. "I don't think he was writing for White Plains or Scarsdale, but he came from there and that's part of him. So *Rent* doesn't affront parents. It tries to be inclusive."

"I just hope they get the same experience as audiences had here," said Nicola, hoping that the media spotlight and career ambitions will not swamp the ensemble work of the young cast. "Losing Jonathan at the moment we did is a tremendous strength in the onslaught. I think it keeps everybody with their feet on the ground—that sadness that the person who really deserves most of these accolades is not here. In the face of either scorn or acclaim, for better or worse, we've had a real reality check built into this."

Indeed, on the day Jonathan Larson died, the shocked cast and creative team gathered at the theater in the evening for an impromptu memorial tribute to the composer. He was remembered warmly and wittily by his stricken friends, details of whose lives he had put into *Rent.* Then the cast sang through the score of the musical, with its anthems of longing and regret, love of life and celebration of community.

"I think we all felt Jonathan's spirit that night, absolutely," Nicola said. "And he was here with us on opening night and has been every night. I really believe that."

Paula Span (review date 18 April 1996)

SOURCE: "The Show Goes On," in *Washington Post,* April 18, 1996, p. C1.

[*In the following review, Span relates the genesis of* Rent *and its phenomenal growth.*]

Opening night looms, and at the Nederlander Theater all is chaos.

An artist with one name (Billy) and two earrings is painting graffiti-ish murals on the mezzanine ceiling to invoke that gritty downtown ambiance. Workers are installing cheetah-spotted carpeting in the lobby. Onstage, 24-year-old Wilson Jermaine Heredia rehearses a dance number that calls for him to hop onto and off a table, no small feat in a Santa jacket, zebra-striped tights, a wig and huge platform heels. The theater reeks of sawdust.

Understandable disorder. The new musical *Rent*—a rock-and-roll reimagining of the Puccini opera *La Boheme,* set among the video artists, junkies, musicians and homeless people of the East Village—has careened onto Broadway. It began previews this week, after a series of events so singular and stunning that its cast, crew and producers are still shaking their heads.

On the day they began rehearsals here on 41st Street, after weeks at the off-Broadway theater downtown where the show was born, nurtured and unveiled, director Michael Greif asked cast members to sing **"Seasons of Love."** Their rendition of an anthem that asks "How do you measure a year in the life?" was both a benediction and a remembrance of its writer, composer and lyricist.

Jonathan Larson died of an aortic aneurysm on the night of *Rent*'s first dress rehearsal in January, a few days shy of his 36th birthday. He never read the celebratory reviews or knew that the show he'd been working on since 1989 was Broadway-bound. "It was so extraordinary and so cruel that he wasn't with us that day that I wanted to include him in some way," Greif says.

Then last week, rehearsal was interrupted when a producer walked onto the stage to announce that Larson had been awarded the Pulitzer Prize for drama. The actors applauded and embraced. The media threatened to inundate the Nederlander. Ticket sales, already brisk, doubled the next day.

"It's disorienting," actress Fredi Walker, watching from the rear of the theater, says of the whole barely fathomable progression. "It's incredibly intense, amazingly intense. This is beyond normal Broadway success—it has the emotional impact of Jonathan's death, the intensity of the extreme acclaim. It's bizarre."

She has never performed on Broadway before; others in the young cast have never acted before, period. Like the characters in the play, she's behind in her rent after months of working for off-Broadway wages ($305 a week, "$5 more than unemployment"). She didn't expect to move uptown, to the realm of *Cats* and Julie Andrews, while playing a lawyer-turned-manager of the bisexual performance artist she's fallen in love with.

But bringing a raucous rock musical, populated by mavericks and misfits, to a gilded Broadway theater is exactly the sort of synthesis Jonathan Larson had in mind all along.

In photos, he was a slender man with a broad grin and a mop of dark curls. Stage-struck ever since he starred in school plays, a composer from the time he scored college cabarets at Adelphi University, Larson had grown up revering the aristocracy of the musical theater: Jerome Robbins, Leonard Bernstein, Stephen Sondheim. His favorite shows, he told friends, were *West Side Story, Fiddler on the Roof* and *Gypsy.*

At the same time, he routinely ridiculed contemporary Broadway, home of endless revivals and mammoth British imports, for being terminally out of touch with his generation. Broadway audiences have been aging for years: A survey by the League of American Theaters and Producers in 1991 found that only a third of ticket-buyers were under 35. "Those are not our people uptown; those are not our stories uptown; that's not our music," he told his pal Jeffrey Seller, now one of *Rent*'s producers. "Why would we go?"

Larson and his circle were not apt to spend 70 bucks to see *Sunset Boulevard.* In fact, really trying to succeed in show business had kept him in a state of semi-poverty. He knew firsthand the culture of artistic aspiration, voluntary indigence and frequent tragedy—Puccini's Parisian romantics were threatened by tuberculosis, Larson's downtown friends by AIDS—that both *La Boheme* and *Rent* portray. "I hate to tell you what his total income was last year," says his father, Al Larson, left with the unhappy task of settling his son's accounts.

For nearly a decade, Jonathan supported himself as a waiter at the Moondance Diner in Greenwich Village and lived in a grungy walk-up loft. "He had a bathtub in the kitchen," says his father, a retired businessman living in Albuquerque. "Not the kind of place I would have chosen, but he loved it." To pay the $1,400-a-month rent, Jonathan always had two roommates, recruited through ads in the *Village Voice.* "Over 10 years he probably had 30 different people," his father says. "All kinds, including one guy who evidently was a junkie and stole stuff from him." His favorite mode of transportation was a banged-up old bicycle.

But he harbored a serious, soaring ambition: "a desire to somehow reunite popular music and theater, which divorced somewhere back in the '40s," says James Nicola, artistic director of the New York Theater Workshop, where *Rent* was developed and staged. "My belief was, this might be the guy who could do it."

Larson had made several earlier attempts to achieve that fusion, with limited success. But he boldly predicted that *Rent* would be "the *Hair* of the '90s." And he had just finished the first draft in 1992 when he biked past the old garage that the New York Theater Workshop was renovating for its new home. Intrigued by the space—raw brick walls, shabbily elegant velvet seats—he sent Nicola the script and a tape of the score.

"He was an amazingly fully formed songwriter," Nicola decided. "And his skills as a dramatist were not nearly so advanced." Nicola, who'd spent eight years as a producing associate at Washington's Arena Stage, offered his help with the substantial revision he thought *Rent* needed. It was a process that would consume another three years.

"The amount of work Jonathan did was astounding," Nicola says. "And you could see the quality getting better and better." Among those offering encouragement was one of Larson's heroes, Sondheim, who had critiqued one of his earlier shows at a workshop and had served as an informal adviser and booster since. He also helped steer a Richard Rodgers Production Award in Larson's direction.

That was a turning point: Unlike other grants and honors that had come Larson's way, this one provided enough money, $50,000, to actually put the show—albeit briefly and in barebones fashion—on the stage. In late 1994, the New York Theater Workshop presented seven performances of *Rent,* directed by Greif of California's La Jolla Playhouse. Seller brought his producing partner, Kevin McCollum, down to the East Village to see it, hoping he'd share Seller's enthusiasm for Larson's work. "At intermission," Seller recalls, "Kevin said, Get out the checkbook.'"

A deal was struck: The NYTW would give *Rent* a six-week off-Broadway run that could be extended if the box office boomed. The modest $250,000 budget included a small salary for the playwright-composer, who last fall was finally able to give notice at the Moondance Diner. His co-workers threw him a fond farewell bash.

"It was a very magical time for him, that last few months," his father says. "Seeing [the show] take shape with such a brilliant cast, all the pieces falling into place—it was everything he had envisioned."

It was also grueling work, sometimes leading to arguments over the inevitable revisions. Thus when Larson complained of severe chest pains in the days before the first preview, Nicola thought that sheer tension might be playing a part. During a technical rehearsal Sunday, Jan. 21, Larson collapsed, saying he thought he was having a heart attack. "He seemed frightened and pale," Nicola recalls. As they waited for an ambulance, Nicola speculated that Larson "was exhausted and getting the flu that was going around, and certainly there was no more stressful moment in his life."

At the hospital emergency room, doctors said Larson might be suffering from food poisoning. They pumped his stomach and sent him home. He skipped rehearsals Monday, went back to an emergency room Tuesday. This time the diagnosis was, indeed, a bad flu.

Larson managed to attend the dress rehearsal on Wednesday. "The first act was a total mess," Greif says. The invited audience cheered, which was reassuring, but "it was very, very not-finished." Afterward, the creative team met to discuss the work that remained. "I could see Jonathan getting paler and paler and more and more tired," Nicola says. They agreed to continue the discussion the next morning at a 9:30 breakfast.

Instead, Nicola got a phone call at 8 a.m.: Larson's roommate had found him dead on the floor of their scruffy apartment. His parents were already flying in from New Mexico. It was Nicola's task to call the cast and crew, one by one, and tell them what had happened.

They convened at the theater, "devastated, weeping, stunned," Nicola says. "Like the people in the play, we've all had to deal with people dying young—because of AIDS. The big difference is, that's a slow progression toward death. . . . This just came out of nowhere." They could not perform that night's first preview, the cast agreed. But they wanted Larson's music to be heard, and invited friends and his parents to an impromptu sing-through.

"It was a fantastically moving experience," Al Larson says. "They started out just sitting at tables and singing, but by the second act they were up bouncing around. They couldn't sit still." Everyone, says Nicola, felt and still feels "a commitment to make the extra effort, go beyond what you think your limits are, out of care and love for someone that's not here."

A more formal memorial service, held a few days later, was lavishly and lovingly catered by the Moondance Diner.

The rest is rapidly becoming theatrical legend. When the show opened the following week, the critics were elated. Though they noted the lingering messiness, most agreed that Larson had indeed written the *Hair* of the '90s. "The most exuberant and original American musical to come along this decade," said *Time.*

The six-week run sold out in four days, a four-week extension shortly thereafter. Theatrical and film producers, music industry VIPs and celebrities began a steady pilgrimage downtown, sometimes watching from folding chairs at the rear of the theater. *Rent* was the season's hot ticket.

How much did the drama of Jonathan Larson's death, such an echo of the show's seize-the-day spirit, contribute to the sensation? "I've given up trying to speculate," Nicola says.

"There's no answer to it; it's become a myth." What was clear, as "Entire Run Sold Out" signs went up on East Fourth Street, was that *Rent* would have a future.

Originally, hoping to preserve its funky atmosphere, its producers scouted old concert halls downtown and checked out abandoned Times Square theaters. But such spaces were either too small or required daunting amounts of renovation. "It frankly became bigger than all of us," says Seller. "The play had to go to Broadway to meet the demand."

Now *Rent,* which easily packed a 150-seat theater downtown, faces the challenge of filling the 1,180-seat Nederlander and recouping a $3 million investment. It also faces questions: How many tourists and middle-aged theatergoers want to see a rock musical that features drug users, rent strikers, gays and homeless people? How many of the people who would be drawn to an unorthodox show with a rock score will pay up to $67.50 to see it—and will they find it insufficiently avant-garde if they do? Nicola also worries about "the kind of hype that surrounds it now. . . . Can it match those expectations?"

Especially since the problems the critics pointed to—overcomplicated subplots, loose ends, several expendable songs—couldn't really be tackled head-on without Larson. The creative team has made "adjustments, rather than changes," Greif says. "Tinkering is a good word."

But so far, say the producers, so good. Advance sales will pass $3 million this week. Winning the Pulitzer "broadens our appeal," Seller says. The April 29 opening makes *Rent* eligible (by two days) for a Tony nomination, which would mean a spot on the Tony broadcast, which might also help lure ticket buyers. Taking the award for best musical would help even more.

Meanwhile, Seller and his co-producers are experimenting with unconventional marketing techniques—from ad campaigns on alternative-rock radio stations to stencil-style, graphics in its print ads—to reach the young. At every performance, the first two rows of orchestra seats will be sold for a cut-rate $20 to people standing in line at the theater. A soundtrack album, to be produced by David Geffen, will be rushed into record stores in hopes, Seller says, "that '**Seasons of Love**' becomes a song everyone in America knows"— the way everybody under 30 could hum "The Age of Aquarius" in 1968. And Bloomingdale's will sell East Village-style clothing and *Rent* T-shirts and caps in a boutique at its flagship Manhattan store.

Integrating rock and theater has been a frustrating and decades-long effort. It's had only scattered triumphs, even if you count *Jesus Christ Superstar,* which was a '70s hit but didn't rock much harder than the Cowsills. *Tommy* ran for more than two years and won praise for its imaginative staging, but Peter Townshend of the Who is evidently not composing future projects for the stage. Even if *Rent* settles in for a long run, it might prove to be one of a kind, a singular sensation.

But that's not what Jonathan Larson had in mind. "He wanted to be the pied piper, leading his generation and the one behind him back to Broadway, back to musical theater," says his father, who with the rest of the family will be in the audience opening night. "He ought to be here for this."

Robert Brustein (review date 22 April 1996)

SOURCE: "The New Bohemians," in *New Republic*, Vol. 214, No. 17, April 22, 1996, pp. 29-31.

[*Below, Brustein questions the popularity of* Rent, *disparaging Larson's lyrics and the production's use of rock music.*]

The American theater chases after a new musical sensation with all the messianic fervor of a religious sect pursuing redemption. And when the composer/librettist dies the day before his show begins previews, we have all the conditions required for cultural myth-making—a martyred redeemer, a new gospel, hordes of passionate young believers and canonization by *The New York Times,* which devoted virtually all the theater columns of a recent Arts and Leisure section to *Rent,* the "rock opera for our time."

Jonathan Larson's premature death at the age of 35 from an aortic aneurysm was a misfortune from many points of view. He was a young man on the brink of a strong career who did not live to enjoy the early fruits of his talents, a promising artist who would undoubtedly have gone on to write much more finished works. I hope it will not be construed as coldhearted when I say that his death was also a sad day for contemporary criticism, being another instance of how it can be hobbled by extra-artistic considerations.

Rent (now playing at the New York Theater Workshop before it moves to Broadway) is an updated version of *La Bohème,* substituting the multicultural denizens of New York's East Village for Puccini's Latin Quarter Bohemians. It is good-natured, fully energized, theatrically knowing and occasionally witty. It is also badly manufactured, vaguely manipulative, drenched in self-pity and sentimental in a way that makes Puccini and his librettists ([Luigi] Illica and [Giuseppe] Giacosa) look like cynics.

Rent is being advertised as "*Hair* for the '90s," and there are indeed certain similarities between the two musicals. Both idealize their socially marginal characters, both are poorly constructed, and both fail to penetrate very deeply beneath a colorful and exotic surface. Larson was a sophisticated librettist, if a somewhat sloppy architect (there is twice as much incident in his brief second act as in the much longer section that precedes it). But his score for *Rent* struck me as the musical equivalent of wallpaper, the rock version of elevator music ("tame and second hand," as Bernard Holland wrote in the only *Times* dissent). Compared to Galt McDermott's exhilarating compositions for *Hair,* Larson's songs—except for the moving **"Another Day"**—show little lyric genius. Their impact derives less from intrinsic inspiration than from extrinsic amplification. Whenever the show begins to flag, the appealing cast lines up downstage to holler into microphones.

The cast, in fact, is highly amplified throughout the entire evening, often leaving us in bewilderment over whose lips are issuing the sounds. The principals wear head mikes, which not only makes them look like telephone operators but makes any physical contact between them (such as a hug or a kiss) sound more like a scrape. *Rent* has a lot to say about the need for human communication, but nothing very human is allowed to emerge from all this acoustical racket. "You're living in America where it's like the Twilight Zone," notes one character, while another (cribbing from Philip Roth) asks, "How do you document real life when real life is getting more like fiction every day?" What isn't probed is how these people also contribute to a sense of the American unreality, especially when they are so superficially examined.

Although warm-hearted, Larson's book is basically superficial and unconvincing. In this piggyback *Bohème,* the painter Marcello becomes Mark, a documentary filmmaker; Rudolfo the poet turns into Roger, a rock composer; Colline the philosopher emerges as Tom Collins, a black anarchist expelled from MIT for his work on "actual reality"; and Schaunard, the musician, metamorphoses into Angel, a black sculptor by profession and transvestite by disposition. As for the women, Musetta evolves into a bisexual rock singer named Maureen who has left Mark for Joanne (Puccini's Alcindoro transformed into a black lawyer from Harvard), while Mimi, the mignonette, has turned into Mimi Marquez, a Latino strip dancer and heroin user (when she enters Roger's apartment with frozen hands, carrying a candle, she's looking for her stash).

The background for all this interracial, intersexual character grunge is a rent strike. Blacks, Latinos and whites alike, whether gay, bisexual or straight, all stand in common opposition to the uptight Benjamin Coffin III, who, though also black, is, like his Puccini prototype Benoit, a grasping landlord and rent gouger. What they protest is his hard-heartedness toward the homeless ("Do you really want a neighborhood where people piss on your stoop every night?") and his desire to gentrify the surroundings ("This is Calcutta. Bohemia's dead").

Aside from this easy mark, and similar simplistic oppositions, what virtually all these people have in common is AIDS (an analogy for Mimi's tuberculosis in *La Bohème*). Some have contracted the disease from sexual activity, some from drug use, but in *Rent* it seems to be an East Village epidemic. During an AZT break, the entire cast pops pills. Most of them are dying. Angel, minus his wig and connected to an IV, is provided with a protracted death scene, after which Mimi memorializes him as "so much more original than any of us." (Following [Tony] Kushner's *Angels in America,* Phyllis Nagy's *Weldon Rising,* the PBS documentary *The Time of Our Dying* and other such theatrical artifacts, it is doubtful how "original" black drag queens really are any more.)

The death of Angel (the angel of death?) sets the stage for Mimi's demise. She and Roger have finally consummated their love after discovering they are both HIV positive and therefore can't contaminate each other. Still, Roger decides to leave for Santa Fe to write one great song before he dies. Upon his return, he learns that Mimi has been living on the street, in deteriorating health. Maureen carries the dying girl into Roger's apartment, and all the comrades gather round for the obligatory death scene. Roger declares his love in song ("Who do you think you are, leaving me alone with my guitar"), Mimi falls back on the couch, and the concluding strains of *La Bohème*—the most powerful music of the evening— swell up over the sobs and groans.

Fear not. Unlike bel canto opera, American musicals allow resurrections and require happy endings. Mimi awakes. Her "fever has broken." Love has triumphed over immune deficiency. And the show concludes with the lovers in each other's arms, as movie memories are projected onto an upstage screen.

We don't ask our musicals to be like real life unless they pretend to be: *Rent* is offered to us as an authentic East Village *tranche de vie.* This pretense makes the final Puccini musical quotation seem cheap and the ending sentimental. George Meredith once defined the sentimentalist as "He who would enjoy without incurring the immense debtorship for the thing done." He accurately describes the emotions forced upon the audience in *Rent*: a ghastly disease is exploited for mawkish purposes.

Michael Greif's highly charged production employs a host of gifted young performers: Daphne Rubin-Vega as a dejected Mimi in skin-tight Spandex pants; Adam Pascal as the rock-and-rolling Roger; Anthony Rapp as the camera-toting Mark; Wilson Jermaine Heredia as the transvestite sculptor Angel; Idina Menzel (a Sandra Bernhard look-alike) as the sexually ambivalent Maureen; and Taye Diggs, Fredi Walker and Jesse L. Martin in other roles. The energy of the entire cast is prodigious. I hope that energy can be sustained over what promises to be a long Broadway run.

Larson has been hailed for creating the downtown equivalent of Bohemian life. I fear he has only created another fashion. Bohemia used to be celebrated not just for flamboyant life-styles but also for artistic innovation. Many Bohemian artists ([Henrik] Ibsen, [Edouard] Manet) dressed like burghers and lived exemplary lives. It was [Gustave] Flaubert who famously said that he was peaceful and conservative in his life in order to be violent and radical in his work. Alas, Larson's New Age Bohemians display nothing but their life-styles. As for their art, it's just a little daunting to note that most of them have no greater ambition than to dominate the rock charts.

Laurie Winer (review date 30 April 1996)

SOURCE: "*Rent* Goes Up—to Broadway," in *Los Angeles Times,* April 30, 1996, p. F1.

[*Below, Winer ponders whether* Rent *would be as popular if Larson had lived, suggesting that "what would have been merely moving in* Rent *is made almost unbearably bittersweet by the knowledge."*]

When **Rent,** a rock musical version of Puccini's *La Boheme* opened off-Broadway last February, Jonathan Larson garnered the kind of rave reviews that young, struggling composer-lyricists pray and dream for.

Larson wasn't there to read the reviews—he died of an aortic aneurysm on the night of the final dress rehearsal at the age of 35. His opus depicts the life he knew—the disease- and drug-plagued but joyous Bohemia of New York's East Village, circa 1995. More than one reviewer dubbed the show a watershed event in the history of the American musical and declared Larson the posthumous savior of the form. The press celebrated a fabulous story, more dramatic even than when choreographer Gower Champion died hours before the opening of *42nd Street* 16 years before.

A Pulitzer Prize soon followed, and a phenomenon was born, producing extreme curiosity and understandable skepticism among theater-goers who could not get a ticket to the tiny East Village theater where **Rent** played a sold-out run. Monday night **Rent** opened on Broadway, at the Nederlander Theater, the most anticipated opening in several years. Anyone who hasn't seen it cannot help but ask: Would this musical be the red-hot ticket it is if Jonathan Larson had lived?

What an incalculably strange and sad question that turns out to be. Muscular, chilling and energizing, **Rent** is as full of death, and the prescience of dying, as any musical has ever been. The show focuses on a group of young people clinging fiercely together while living a difficult, exhilarating existence on the brink of poverty. And, as it turns out, Jonathan

Larson is the main character in this wonderful but imperfect show. What would have been merely moving in **Rent** is made almost unbearably bittersweet by the knowledge, apparent in almost every song, that Larson had grappled profoundly with the meaning of life and art in his final years. His death should be irrelevant to his achievement, and yet it is not.

"I'm writing one great song before I go . . . one blaze of glory," sings Roger (Adam Pascal), an HIV-positive songwriter, in an act-one ballad. Soon he meets the similarly infected Mimi (the appealing and vulnerable Daphne Rubin-Vega), and the lovers come together to sing, "There is no future / There is no past / I live each moment as my last." "How do you measure a year?," asks a chorus line of poverty-ridden young people, in a simply beautiful number called **"Seasons of Love."** After suggesting the number of minutes and hours in which a year can be calculated, they suggest that you "measure your life in love."

Larson, director Michael Greif, and a fresh and talented cast give us a desolate, kinky and creative world, light-years away from the sanitized and monied fantasy worlds of *Big* and *Victor/Victoria,* two of the season's other new musicals. In Larson's version of the Puccini opera, consumption has been replaced by the AIDS virus. Mimi, a diminutive and wild-haired S&M dancer, cements her attraction to rocker Roger not by dropping her key in his apartment but by dropping a little bag of heroin.

Meanwhile, Puccini's Marcello becomes Mark Cohen (Anthony Rapp), a pale young filmmaker from Scarsdale who looks a lot like the young Elvis Costello, and is as cool and emotionally post-modern. Mark's ex-love is Maureen, in Idina Menzel's energized performance, a big-voiced and sexually open performance artist who has taken up with Joanne (Fredi Walker), a law student. Colline becomes Tom Collins (Jesse L. Martin), a computer whiz in love with Angel (Wilson Jermaine Heredia), an exceptionally attractive and sweet transvestite who has AIDS.

With one jokey exception, **Rent** does not quote directly from *La Boheme,* but its score nevertheless embraces the passion and tenderness of Puccini and straddles the world of rock as well, with its five excellent musicians pumping out the percolating, sometimes soaring melodies onstage. But while the show borrows the musical vocabulary and vocal stylings of rock, it is unlikely anyone would mistake it for actual rock music. It is a hybrid, and it tells its story in terms clearly defined by the musical form.

Its most direct antecedent is in fact the rock musical *Hair,* which opened on Broadway on the same night, April 29, in 1968. Like the hippies immortalized in *Hair,* the Bohemians of **Rent** wear their youth, poverty and creativity like a cloak around them, shielding them from judgment by the enemy—

anyone who has "sold out" and has money. Very much modeled on the song "Sodomy" from *Hair,* the terrific act-one closer, **"La Vie Boheme,"** is a list of things celebrated by this Generation X, including Uta and Buddha, Sontag and Sondheim, sodomy ("It's between God and me") and Lenny Bruce. This generation's Vietnam is the AIDS virus and the rampant materialism they see all around them.

In fact, one of the show's most unconvincing and simplistic plot points involves Mark's decision whether or not to "sell out" by selling footage to an air-head TV show or to make his own film. But such issues—and even the superficiality of the characters, who are more spirited attitude than well-drawn people—are not the point. *Rent* is a rousing anthem to living each day as it comes.

Under designer Paul Clay, the stage is used as an expansive overlapping living area for the artists, the onstage band and a chorus of family, friends, cops, the homeless and dispossessed, who merge with the action both onstage and above on two scaffolds. Greif proves an effective orchestrator of mass humanity, but at times he overextends or indulges the show's sentimentality, such as when he has an AIDS support group look down from a scaffold and comment on the meeting of Mimi and Roger below.

Rent, the thing that most of its characters don't have the money to pay, is a blissfully overloaded hodgepodge of emotion and life and talent. "How do you figure a last year on Earth?," asks a plaintive chorus in the show's most beautiful number. "Figure in love. Measure in love."

Rent is a memorial service as a work of art, clearly and authentically created in love.

Gregory Beals (essay date 13 May 1996)

SOURCE: "The World of *Rent,*" in *Newsweek,* Vol. CXXVII, No. 20, May 13, 1996, pp. 58-9.

[*In the essay below, Beals, a former roommate of Larson's, reminisces about the playwright with cast members and friends.*]

In December of 1995, Jonathan Larson wrote his good friend Victoria Leacock a touching Christmas card. This was typical of Larson; even when he was entirely consumed with his work, he still made the effort for his friends. He'd been working on *Rent,* obsessing over it, since 1989. Now it was finally going to open. But for both Leacock and Larson, the season was a difficult one. They'd lost two close friends to AIDS since September. Their lives and deaths had been on his mind; he spoke at their memorial services, and wrote both into the fabric of *Rent.* So when it came time to compose a Christmas

greeting for Leacock, he wrote, "Vic, darling Vicks, '96 will be our year. And no more funerals." She received the card the day after his memorial service.

Larson spent the last weeks of his life over-stressed by the demands of his work, and poor as the characters in his show. Ten days before his death he had to sell some books to buy a ticket to *Dead Man Walking.* His health was deteriorating. A friend brought him care packages—chicken soup, noodles, Mylanta—to combat the dizziness and stomach problems he was suffering. Final preparations for the show were typically chaotic. In late January, Larson and director Michael Greif were singing one of the songs from the production when Larson felt an acute pain in his chest. "You better call 911," he said. "I think I'm having a heart attack." He was rushed to the hospital, but an ECG revealed no heart irregularities. His friend Eddie Rosenstein, a documentary filmmaker who visited him in the hospital, thought the problem was psychosomatic. This, too, would be typical of Larson. "He blacked out once before a tryout and thought he was having a heart attack." The lyrics Larson and Greif had been singing ran: "We're dying in America to come into our own . . . " Three days later, on Jan. 25, the day of the final dress rehearsal, Larson died in his apartment of an aortic aneurysm. He was 35.

I lived with Jonathan in that apartment on Greenwich Street in downtown Manhattan from February through July 1994. It was a loft space, converted into a three-bedroom apartment. Roommates tended to come and go. The doorbell didn't work, so visitors had to call from the phone on the corner, and we'd toss the keys down. The claw-foot bathtub was in the middle of the kitchen; the roof leaked. Jonathan was from a middle-class background—he grew up in suburban White Plains, N.Y., and had a childhood of drama clubs and trumpet lessons—but he seemed to thrive on the improvisational clutter. Sometimes he tried to impose some order on the decay. He ran fat orange extension cords around the place to make up for lack of electrical outlets; when the seat covers on the kitchen chairs wore out, Jonathan replaced them with leopard-skin vinyl. But disorder ruled. I remember once watching the news with Jonathan when suddenly he blurted out, "Did you know that this ZIP code has the second highest AIDS rate in the country?" He began telling me about a woman he knew who had contracted the virus sexually at the age of 16. Then, just as abruptly, he started talking about Madonna's outrageous recent appearance on Letterman.

The bohemia of *Rent,* though liberally exaggerated, came out of characters whom Jonathan knew and loved. He was sometimes an odd man out in this world: he was as passionate about Broadway and his mentor, Stephen Sondheim, as he was about downtown. We went to a very hip East Village party one time, full of young filmmakers, actors, dancers, artists. When anyone asked what he did, he'd say, "I'm making a rock opera for the '90s." People just turned away. Finally he learned just to say he was a rock songwriter. Yet he was fiercely engaged with the multiracial, multisexual world downtown, determined to bring it to the stage with sensitivity and affection. Lisa Bonacci, an old girlfriend of his, remembers his telling her that one of the actresses auditioning for the role of Mimi, the HIV-positive dancer at an S/M club, was squeamish about the part. She'd never known anyone who was into S/M. "Oh, really," he joked. "I think all my friends are."

Anthony Rapp, who plays Mark, lives in this world. Rapp, 24, is one of two openly gay members of the cast. (The major gay characters are played by straight actors.) He lives in an East Village apartment, where for three years he was a squatter. Last week, like many of the players, Rapp seemed tired from the recent publicity blitz; he was also depressed that he'd been snubbed for a Drama Desk award nomination. "If you walk down St. Mark's Place," he says, "you're going to see a lot of people who look like people in the play: our haircuts, our clothes. We recognize this play is a theatricalization of something, but we feel like we're being represented. My friends and I, we want something alive, something relevant, something meaningful, and thrilling and sexy, and sad." He says he related to the no-big-deal sexual fluidity in the show. "My generation is sort of making our own rules about all that stuff," he contends, "and hopefully doing it with safety and respect."

In fact, the cast members—several of whom were not actors—supplied a lot of the energy and breadth of their characters. Wilson Jermaine Heredia, 24, who plays the transvestite Angel, the show's guiding spirit, says that "you see more of the person than the [skills of the] actor with most of us." Heredia, who was born and still lives in the Williamsburg section of Brooklyn, says that for him the East Village is "the only place I felt normal." He settled into the role of Angel without much difficulty. A number of his friends are gay or transvestites, so he was close to the material; the challenge was more to grasp the character's soul. To that end, Angel became Heredia. "People are baring their heart and soul onstage," he says. "We've given at least 70 percent of our own personal character. We're almost all ourselves in different circumstances."

When production began on *Rent,* Jonathan called his friend Timothy Britten Parker to offer him a role in the ensemble. He told Parker, "Toby, I'm so happy. I finally have a life in the theater." Larson would have loved to see the way his cast and his characters grew together, changing each other in the process. He was fascinated with other people's tales. The actress Molly Ringwald, a friend of his for the last four years, remembers his helping her move into her apartment. "I knew him as the person who'd hang up my Dust-buster," she says. The day of the move, he sat around her living room with a big smile on his face, looking at all her stuff. "He wanted to know where everything came from," she says. "It wasn't like he was interested in the deco, but in the stories." This was Larson: always devoted, always curious. His stories, and those of his friends, are now the freshest, most loving show on Broadway. He'd have loved to see that, too.

Jon Wiederhorn (essay date 16 May 1996)

SOURCE: "A New Rock Opera Celebrates Life after the Death of Its Creator," in *Rolling Stone,* May 16, 1996, pp. 54-8.

[*In the following essay, Wiederhorn examines* Rent *in terms of Larson's life and death.*]

The day before his rock opera, **Rent,** was scheduled to begin previews at a small off-Broadway theater in New York's East Village, the composer and playwright Jonathan Larson felt like he was coming down with the flu. Tired, pale and feverish, he had also experienced chest pains and had visited two emergency rooms earlier in the week. His symptoms had been diagnosed as food poisoning, but some of his colleagues thought he might be suffering pre-show jitters. After all, Larson had poured seven years of soul-searching work into **Rent,** an emotionally stirring story about young East Village artists struggling to celebrate life in the shadow of drugs, poverty and AIDS. Within days, the show and its 31 songs incorporating dance pop, salsa, R&B and hard rock would be dissected by a roomful of snobby critics.

Larson needn't have worried. A mere 24 hours after opening night, the box office had sold $38,000 worth of tickets—the entire five-week run. By the end of the week, a month-long extension was sold out as well. The show received gushing reviews and has since been attended by such luminaries as Steven Spielberg, Al Pacino, Sylvester Stallone, Ivan Boesky, Danny DeVito and Rhea Perlman, and a slew of record-company executives vying for the rights to the soundtrack. What's more, there are reports that Jody Watley wants to cover songs from the show, and sources say Whitney Houston is interested in securing the film rights. The production, which recently won the Pulitzer Prize, has just moved uptown to Broadway's Nederlander Theater.

Unfortunately, Larson will never reap the rewards of his hard work. While preparing a kettle of tea, he suffered an aortic aneurysm and died on Jan. 25, 1996. Only 35 years old, he was considered to be in good physical health. It's both tragic and ironic that Larson, who was only able to quit his day job as a SoHo waiter two months before he died, never saw ticket holders enjoy his show. Even more uncanny are the parallels between Larson's life and his characters', many of whom cling to life knowing that it could end at any moment. "One song before I go / One song to leave behind," sings Roger, an HIV-positive punk rocker, in **"One Song Glory,"** near the beginning of *Rent.* And at the show's conclusion, the song **"Finale/Your Eyes"** reiterates the idea with the lines, "There is no future, there is no past / I live this moment as my last."

"It's almost like Jonathan wrote his own funeral," says Nancy Kassak Diekmann, the managing director of the New York Theater Workshop. "The play is about his life in every way." Larson was born in White Plains, N.Y., and after graduating from Adelphi University, he decided to devote his life to the theater. Over the years, Larson composed two musicals, *J.P. Morgan Saves the Nation* and *Superbia,* and a rock monologue, *Tick, Tick . . . Boom!,* which he performed at the New York Theater Workshop, where *Rent* would open several years later. While living in New York's East Village, he befriended many AIDS sufferers, whose strength and courage inspired him to create the characters in *Rent.*

To a certain degree, Larson's demise served as a catalyst for the success of the rock opera. The press turned the event into an epic tale of life imitating art, with *Time, Newsweek* and the *Wall Street Journal* devoting an unusual amount of coverage to the off-Broadway play. In addition, the cast members were drawn closer together by the desire to do justice to Larson's striking script.

"It became a lot more real, and it really stripped away a lot of the bullshit," says Daphne Rubin-Vega, who plays Mimi, one of the show's romantic leads. "All the words in the play made sense, so it wasn't just a story anymore. The day after he died was supposed to be opening night. We all went to the theater early and huddled together like animals in a fucking storm. It was weird and galvanized in the sense that it was bigger than us. All of a sudden it was, 'Oh, shit, we're in something that's bigger than us.'"

Instead of staging a performance that evening, the producers of *Rent* scheduled a sing-through memorial for the benefit of Larson's friends and family. "They were all crying, and we were crying, and we were trying to sing these songs, which are really beautiful," says Adam Pascal, who plays Mimi's love interest, Roger. "It felt so wonderful because it was so cathartic. I'm not one to lose it, but you can't help it in a situation like that. It was probably one of the most moving experiences in my whole life."

Rent is loosely based on the Puccini opera *La Bohème.* Rodolfo the lovelorn poet becomes Roger the punk rocker; Marcello the painter is Mark Cohen the videographer; Mimi the tuberculosis victim is transformed into Mimi the HIV-positive, heroin-shooting S&M dancer; and Musetta the callous flirt resembles Maureen the sexually ambivalent performance artist who leaves Mark for Joanne, a yuppie

lawyer and sound engineer. Then there's Puccini's philosophical Colline, who becomes Tom Collins, a college professor who falls in love with Angel, a transvestite street drummer.

Rent also contains several plot references to the original opera. Where Puccini's Mimi drops a key to attract Rodolfo, Larson's Mimi intentionally loses a heroin bag, and in both productions the main characters are threatened with eviction and burn their written work to stay warm. But enjoyment of the production requires no knowledge of opera. In fact, the music and message are directed primarily at frustrated twentysomethings, an age group not generally thought of as avid theater-goers. Throughout, Larson refers to such youth-culture fixtures as IMAX, e-mail, the *Village Voice* and latex sex. And the music for *Rent* is played by a five-piece band that alternately soothes, swings and rocks.

"I live in the East Village, and a lot of my friends do, and we feel for once we have the opportunity to go to the theater and see ourselves up on that stage," says Anthony Rapp, who plays Mark. "It's a life that we can recognize. It's not like *Friends,* which is about youths that have a lot of money and live in a loft and never have any serious problems. It's about something a lot more real."

"Hopefully the show will have a positive effect on Broadway theater," adds Pascal. "Broadway doesn't know from rock & roll—except maybe for *Tommy,* and that's really sugarcoated. I hope we can put a little of the spirit and energy of rock & roll into theater for other plays to come along and do the same thing."

Rent confronts a number of sobering issues—AIDS, drug addiction, romantic disillusionment, artistic struggle, death—but it's not overly moralistic. It's also not a downer. Sure, there are several tear-inducing scenes, but Larson places more emphasis on love, friendship and survival. "People need to realize that if you're dealing with these problems, it doesn't mean your life has to be dark and black and gloomy," says Pascal. "If you're suffering with AIDS, the time you have left doesn't need to be wasted."

The second act of *Rent* opens with **"Seasons of Love,"** a gospel number in which the company sings, "525,600 minutes / How do you figure a last year on earth? / Figure in love." One of the production's most heart-rending songs, it sums up the spirit and pathos of the show. Larson may not have lived long enough to alter the face of Broadway, but his empathy and compassion profoundly affected everyone he was involved with. "Jonathan gave us something that changed our lives," says Rubin-Vega. "And it wasn't just a really fierce career move. It was the real fucking thing, and it's left us with a great pleasure: a very strong prayer every night."

John Guare (review date May 1996)

SOURCE: "Smash!," in *Vogue*, May, 1996, pp. 305, 347.

[*In the following review, Guare considers the tragedy of* Rent *and of Larson's death.*]

I'm sitting in the Truck and Warehouse Theater on East Fourth Street in New York City's East Village, a.k.a. Lower East Side, a.k.a. Loisaida. The matinee performance has just ended for the new smash hit *Rent,* which reviews have ballyhooed as the most important musical since *A Chorus Line.* I can't help going back 25 years to when I sat in this same theater (now the home of the New York Theater Workshop) in the same cold month, waiting for my play *The House of Blue Leaves* to open. In 1971, I was in my early thirties and felt that everything depended on my play's reception. Stephen Sondheim's telegram—"Have a wonderful opening tonight. Your entire future depends on it"—made me roar with laughter but also cringe with horror because it was true. I had worked for five years on my play. It had to work.

On January 24, Jonathan Larson, the 35-year-old composer and lyricist of *Rent,* saw the final dress rehearsal of the show he had worked on for five years. The rehearsal was good. Afterward, Larson congratulated the cast, went home, and, out of the blue, was stricken by an aortic aneurysm that killed him instantly. The musical went on to a rapturous reception—and to Broadway's Nederlander Theater in late April. In fact, everything about *Rent* has become the stuff of theater legend.

What knocked me out is that *Rent* more than lives up to its reviews. Except for the occasional lightning bolt from Sondheim, the American musical in the Reagan-Bush years took a somnolent detour to London, with high-tech musicals dangling their production values—falling chandeliers and spaceships—like gaudy costume jewelry. But *Rent,* inspired by Puccini's *La Bohème,* comes along on East Fourth Street on a cold winter's evening, and everything is alive again.

Rent is a rock musical, but it's theatrically savvy, taking a tradition and pushing it into new areas. The joy is hearing, in the words of Daphne Rubin-Vega, who plays *Rent*'s sensational Mimi, "a divine dovetailing of great rock music with theater music and theater lyrics." Every generation has to invent its version of Paris in the twenties, and Larson does for his what Fitzgerald and Hemingway did for theirs. It is a shock to realize that this cast, all born in the early 1970s, are the first generation to come into maturity never having known a world without the specter of AIDS. There's a recklessness, a doomed fatedness in their joy. Coming from Long Island and Westchester, from the projects as well as from Harvard, these kids have elected to find their lives and freedom in

Alphabet City. Mimi and Rodolfo (called Roger here) have one dreaded point of communion: They are both HIV positive. Raised in the eighties, they are truly "Reagan refuse." Nancy's "Just say no"? Forget it. These kids say yes to everything no matter the consequences.

Daphne Rubin-Vega says she auditioned for *Rent* on a dare because her music-loving dad said he did not like his opera messed around with. She liked that this Mimi was no tender waif but a junkie stripper dying of AIDS. She hadn't auditioned for musicals because, she told me, they had become corny and "not cool." When Mimi sings "I'm gonna take you out tonight," Rubin-Vega makes the phrase sound like the cry of a paid assassin. The rest of the cast, under the astute direction of Michael Greif, is uniformly wonderful, too, beginning with Anthony Rapp, as the young filmmaker who is recording it all. And Adam Pascal, a newcomer, sings Roger/Rodolfo terrifically.

I met Jonathan Larson only once, in the most unlikely place, the magnificent Beaux Arts home of the American Academy of Arts and Letters. Founded 98 years ago with such original members as Mark Twain and Henry James, it is about as far as you can get from the world of *Rent.* But Richard Rodgers left the Academy $1 million, with the interest on that money to be awarded annually for the development of a new American musical. In May 1994, Jonathan Larson came to the Academy to collect his award for *Rent.* On that day, this young guy who had the world ahead of him told me that he had written his musical in response to the deaths of so many of his young friends. I remember his great goofy smile of joy as he collected $45,000, which would pay for a studio production at the prestigious New York Theater Workshop.

Roger, the doomed hero, wants to write one great song—"one blaze of glory," he calls it—before he dies. The joy of *Rent* is that Jonathan Larson did it. The tragedy is that there won't be any more.

James Gardner (review date 3 June 1996)

SOURCE: "Lowering the Rent," in *National Review,* Vol. XLVIII, No. 10, June 3, 1996, pp. 56-7.

[*In the review below, Gardner dismisses* Rent *as mostly hype and little substance.*]

I have this theory: in any given musical after 1970, there will come a moment in which the protagonist is on stage alone and sings the words, "Who am I?" This may be called the hokey-identity-crisis moment, when the character is torn between his principles and his self-interest, and tempted to take the easy way out, which threatens to damn his soul and shave twenty minutes off the second act.

In *Rent,* the new great hope of the American musical theater, this does not happen—or at least not quite. The protagonist, Mark, an aspiring video artist who cannot pay his rent and has no electricity or food in his house, is offered a lucrative assignment from some cheesy network news magazine. Will he take the job and end his financial plight, or will he preserve his principles—though we never quite learn what those are—and turn the job down? At this point, Mark, on the verge of accepting, turns to the audience and says, "What am I doing?" Then his roommate, Roger, an equally insolvent rock poet, comes on stage and asks, "Who are you?" Now since he has known Mark for years and is not suffering from any psychotic disorder, despite a healthy drug habit, we assume that this question is meant metaphorically.

My point: there seems to have been a tacit agreement among twenty or thirty powerful people on Broadway that *Rent* is to be the Next Big Thing and everyone else is docilely toeing the line. And yet, despite its studied hipness and its aspirations to be the voice of the Nineties, *Rent,* which is an updating of *La Bohème,* is pretty much the same old showbiz fare, though with almost formulaic inversions. Instead of boy meets girl, you now have girl meets girl and boy meets drag queen. The audience is almost explicitly invited to say, "Look at that! Lesbians. Say!" And whereas earlier generations acknowledged the archetype of the annoying mother-in-law, as in *Barefoot in the Park,* here one is beset with the Annoying Jewish Mother archetype who endeavors to stifle with self-centered affection the young hero's artistic ambitions. Then there's the overbearing landlord with the heart of gold, who, in a cutesy reversal of type, is a black yuppie. Combine that with myriad references to AZT, Prozac, and Pee Wee Herman and you can positively hear the Generation Xers in the audience as they "relate." The low point in this process comes in the form of Mark's nutty ex-girlfriend, Maureen. Protesting the landlord's desire to transform their tenement into a studio space, she does a performance piece which we know we are supposed to find silly, though in fact it is not much sillier than the rest of the musical. Well, at one point Maureen imitates a cow (I forget why) and delivers what is perhaps the one genuinely funny line in the play, "C'mon. Moo with me!" This would be fine except that then, sure enough, the majority of the terminally hip audience started lowing like a stable of prize Guernseys.

As for the music, it is standard rock fare of the sort that pleases some people more than me. For what it's worth, I found myself enjoying *Hair* and *Jesus Christ Superstar,* also rock operas, far more than I did this, which means that I am not totally averse to the art form. The staging, furthermore, seems surprisingly drab and lifeless, an impression that the dull, vaguely industrial set does little to mitigate.

Like most people who saw *Rent,* I was expecting a great deal, since the musical had won the Pulitzer Prize and had been praised by all and sundry. Furthermore, knowing the genuinely tragic circumstances of the life and death of the author, Jonathan Larson, his having waited on tables in obscurity for years while struggling in vain to get his musical produced, and then dying at age 35 of an aortic aneurysm the day it was supposed to open—I wanted to like the play. And I was and remain sincerely happy for the author that all these people, who probably wouldn't even have tipped him properly if he had waited on their tables, were now clamoring to get the few remaining tickets, not to mention the few remaining *Rent* T-shirts and *Rent* buttons that were being hawked at the entrance.

But I found that I could never get past what seemed to be the essential bad faith of the musical, its trying to be the *Hair* of the Nineties. You just know that the chorus that ends the first act, **"La Vie Bohème,"** wants desperately to be taken as the anthem of some nonexistent youth movement. But the bohemian life glorified in *Rent* looks no more vital than it did before, and Broadway itself, whose fortunes this musical was said to revive, appears about as moribund as ever.

Stefan Kanfer (review date 3-17 June 1996)

SOURCE: "Tragedy and Art," in *The New Leader,* Vol. LXXIX, No. 3, June 3-17, 1996, pp. 22-3.

[*In the following review, Kanfer faults* Rent *on the basis of its form, characters, and the theater building, suggesting that the play is "only a mainstream entertainment disguised as avant garde art."*]

Plot *A:* An earnest polymath—playwright, composer and lyricist—struggles for recognition. He writes a musical and takes it to producer after producer, hoping for a showcase somewhere, anywhere. After many disappointments he finally attracts the attention of a director and a vigorous little theater group. They get him a production at a 150-seat Off-Broadway house. Actors are chosen, rehearsals begin, new lines and songs are added under pressure. During rehearsals the writer complains of chest pain. Emergency room physicians assure him that it's just a case of food poisoning and send him home. Less than 24 hours before the first preview he is struck by a fatal aortic aneurysm. The show becomes a posthumous triumph: Critics and the public are so enthusiastic that new investors clamber aboard and move it to Broadway, where it carries on with even greater audience response.

Plot *B:* Afflicted with AIDS, a young musician tries to compose one great song before he goes. Around him are other sufferers—of poverty, disease, neglect, prejudice. In a '90s restatement of *La Boheme,* the stories of the doomed youth and his drug-hooked girlfriend, a drag queen and his cyberwhiz lover, a performance artist and *her* lesbian lover, and an eccentric landlord as well as other white, black and Hispanic East Village personae, unfold under the lens of an aspiring video cameraman.

As unlikely as it sounds, *A* is the true story of Jonathan Larson (1960-1995), who died just before the curtain rose on *B,* his creation, **Rent.** Not since 1984, when director Gower Champion died on the opening night of *42nd Street,* has there been such a theatrical tragedy in every sense of the words. I wish it were possible to give *A* and *B* equal value; alas, it is not. There is no question that Larson possessed talent. Had he survived, perhaps he might some day have created musicals of enduring value. As it is, the story he lived is far more moving than the one he wrote. **Rent,** for all its flashes of promise, is the most overpraised production of the '90s: modish, attitudinizing, full of unripe social criticism—*Hair* redux.

One of the show's central problems is its form. Larson originally conceived **Rent** as a romantic confederation of East Village types—saintly addicts, saintly homosexuals, saintly misfits, radicals, homeless. These people eke out lives of noisy desperation, unsure of next month's payment on apartments in "Alphabet City," the neighborhood of Avenues A, B, C, and D. Advisers persuaded Larson to superimpose the plot of *La Boheme* on the songs and characters. The result is a procrustean affair, with Mimi transformed into a dancer under the shadow of heroin, Rudolfo into Roger, an HIV-positive guitarist, and . . . but you get the idea.

The trouble is, what worked for Puccini's neglected bohemians seems ludicrous in an age of grants, AIDS lobbyists and advocates for the homeless. Indeed, **Rent** has become a "crossover show" (one for which folks pay $50 to watch actors play outcasts) because society has become tolerant of—and often sympathetic to—Alphabet Citizens on the margins of society. Moreover, **Rent** does not even have the guts of its predecessor. Mimi refuses to perish after all: She is miraculously restored to the living, like Jimmy Stewart in *It's a Wonderful Life,* a movie that celebrates the middle class and therefore stands for everything **Rent** ostentatiously puts down.

Another difficulty is the characters. As Angel, Wilson Jermaine Heredia is a terrific looking drag queen. But after he does the "letting out the more female side of me that every male has if they're willing to let go," he becomes something of a bore. Even so, he is far less irritating than Maureen (Idina Menzel), a "performance artist" who stops the show in the wrong way, giving a moribund imitation of those yammering standup comediennes who have no idea what a joke is, let alone how to tell it. In the role of Roger, Adam Pascal does somewhat better; he has a small but true voice, having sharpened it with his own heavy metal band before going legit. As Mark, the video artist, Anthony Rapp projects an appealing and pleasant personality and singing style: and as Mimi, Daphne Rubin-Vega has a couple of numbers that bring down the house, most notably the howling, vixenish **"Out Tonight."** Still, she and the male leads are part of an ensemble, and their big moments are followed by undistinguished chorus work, or by performers less gifted and songs less diverting.

The third difficulty is the house itself. The Nederlander Theater is a place where *Showboat* might dock, or *The King and I* might waltz. Bringing a cabaret musical to the massive dimensions of a Broadway stage is like taking an a capella quartet to Grand Central Station. The only way to be heard is to shout, or to be so profoundly amplified that words become a cascade of indistinguishable sounds. Michael Greif's cumbrous restaging and Marlies Yearby's ungainly choreography are of little help in this uptown cavern. The cast members not only move uncertainly but chant into their body mikes with unbalanced ardor, as if the smallest love song and the harshest ensemble piece were of similar value.

Those numbers, shrewdly arranged by Tim Weil, vary in quality and substance. Occasionally lyrics remain in the mind— "You are what you own" seems a fair summary of '90s avarice. And one or two melodies will rise from the original cast album to have a life of their own. For the most part, however, the show Larson called "a rock opera" is neither rock nor opera, only a mainstream entertainment disguised as avant garde art, made palatable by the energy of its young stars and, more significantly, by the irony and poignance of its author's biography.

Molly Ringwald (essay date June 1996)

SOURCE: "Jonathan Larson," in *Interview,* Vol. 26, June, 1996, p. 104.

[*In the essay below, Ringwald offers reminiscences of Larson and her perspective on* Rent.]

Recently, my best friend, Victoria Leacock, woke me from a nap. When I answered the phone, I was still disoriented, halfway between sleep and waking. She asked, "Did you hear about Jonathan?" Her voice was trembling and sounded oddly grave. My first thought was, *Oh God no, he died.* And then, *No, it couldn't be.* "He won the Pulitzer," Victoria told me. I felt a huge rush of happiness. But then, of course, our friend Jonathan *had* died.

I met Jonathan Larson through Victoria, his college sweetheart, longtime champion, and dear friend. Later, he became an extraordinarily dependable friend to me, helping me move into my new apartment, introducing me to the neighborhood hardware store, and appointing himself my handyman. I remember one hilarious afternoon we spent attempting to put together a closet, without instructions, that I had carted back from France. Not an easy task. Somehow, at last, we succeeded, and headed down to the corner bistro to celebrate. I treated him to a beer while he enthusiastically explained the entire opera *La Bohème,* which I had never seen, and how his upcoming musical, **Rent,** differed from it. He died just two weeks later.

I can't imagine what he would have made of what has happened. During our last dinner, I remember him breathing a sigh of relief that Frank Rich had moved to another section of *The New York Times,* and was unlikely to be reviewing this work. A couple of weeks later, Victoria and I cried while reading out loud to each other the glowing piece Mr. Rich wrote in the *Times* op-ed page.

It's a strange thing when a friend becomes a celebrity/phenomenon; stranger still when they aren't here when it happens. I would give anything to have him here, watch him bask in the glory, and maybe even become swell-headed for awhile. There are some who have called **Rent** a masterpiece and who have said it marks the end of a brilliant, heretofore unknown career. But Jonathan Larson was far from finished; he was just beginning. He would have already been working on something else, thrilled that he would actually get paid for it, thrilled that he wouldn't have to go back to work as a waiter at the Moondance Diner.

I love **Rent.** I wish I could have told Jonathan so. I saw it a half-dozen times in the last few months, when it was at the New York Theater Workshop, and I imagine that I will continue to see it now that it's on Broadway. It speaks to me in the way only a few contemporary rock artists have. I get the same feeling I had as a teenager when I was sure Elvis Costello or R.E.M. wrote that song just for me. A Broadway show has never stirred me in the same way. Who could ever put on the soundtrack to *Evita* and rock out? *Hair* never moved me personally, but I wasn't born when it premiered on Broadway, and watching revivals as a young girl was confusing. "Mommy, what are hippies? . . . What's Vietnam?" I can't help but imagine, years from now, taking my children to see revivals of **Rent** and hearing them ask, "What's AZT? . . . What's AIDS?" I hope they will have to ask these questions; I hope that they will not have a reason to know.

It was Jonathan's dream to make Broadway popular again. In the same way that *Damn Yankees* was popular in his grandparents' day and the same way *Hair* was in the following generation. He was right in believing that there was no impetus for young people to go to Broadway and listen to something they couldn't relate to. Why not just stay home and watch MTV? But television can isolate and, thankfully, we still need to be together and share in an experience. Our generation may have given up on Broadway, but not, I believe, by choice. *Tommy* was the most recent offering of something resembling contemporary music on Broadway—and that was written more than twenty years ago.

Jonathan listened to what he heard around him—the need for a community, the paralyzing fear of AIDS—and he created **Rent** out of that. He wasn't born without money, but he chose his work over money, which meant that he lived without it right up until the day he died. He wasn't HIV-positive himself, but one of his close childhood friends is, as were other mutual friends whose lives found their way into **Rent.** The play deals specifically with their *lives,* rather than their deaths—it's a tribute to their courage and their capacity to love one another in the face of a frightening, uncertain future. I have encountered the occasional doubter who asks how anything happy can come out of AIDS or who doesn't want to share in the enthusiasm surrounding **Rent.** I think the doubt arises precisely because **Rent** *is* optimistic, idealistic even. To me, it's a bit like the difference between a Catholic wake and a New Orleans funeral. One is a mourning of death, the other is a celebration of life. **Rent** decidedly celebrates. But it never forgets the pain and loss.

There are unforgettable, heartbreaking moments. I defy anyone to listen, truly listen, to the character Collins (Jesse L. Martin) sing **"I'll Cover You"** to his dead lover at his funeral and not cry, or not want to cry, for someone they have loved and lost. And the theater literally vibrates when Mimi (Daphne Rubin-Vega) screams out the song **"Out Tonight"** so beautifully. Delivering this overwhelming, energetic testament to life and living, I half expect her to fly off the stage. I want to fly with her.

On the night that Jonathan's Pulitzer was announced, my friend Victoria and I ended up going out for dinner to celebrate his win with the producers of **Rent** and some of Jonathan's closest friends. We tried to connect this extraordinary achievement to the memory of our friend, but it wasn't so easy. There were heated debates concerning whether or not **Rent** should be called a musical or a rock opera, and whether a chorus member should begin the despairing song **"Will I?"** on Broadway, as it had been done at the New York Theater Workshop, or if it should be sung by the main character, Roger. Afterward, we stopped by the theater where the cast was finishing rehearsal. Victoria had been there earlier that night with the director, Michael Greif, and the cast. It's funny, but half of these kids didn't even know what the Pulitzer Prize is. What they do know, perhaps better than any of us, is Jonathan's music and just how sweet it is.

Francis Davis (review date September 1996)

SOURCE: "Victim Kitsch," in *The Atlantic Monthly,* Vol. 278, No. 3, September, 1996, pp. 98-100, 102-104, 106.

[*Below, Davis argues that* Rent *is not the solution to Broadway's problems.*]

As everyone has surely heard by now, Jonathan Larson's **Rent**—the seventh musical ever to win a Pulitzer Prize for drama and the first to do so in advance of its premiere on Broadway—is a rock musical in the tradition of *Hair* but with even grander pretensions to opera, "sung through" by an energetic young cast that plays East Village versions of the artists and paupers in Puccini's *La Bohème*. The painter Marcello and the poet Rodolfo have been transformed into Mark, a documentary filmmaker, and his roommate Roger, a rock singer and songwriter and a former junkie. Their friend Tom Collins, a computer whiz fired from MIT and now homeless, is based on Puccini's philosopher, Colline. Musetta, Marcello's former lover, is Maureen, a performance artist who has decided she's a lesbian. The seamstress Mimi, Rodolfo's tubercular inamorata, is still Mimi, but now she's an exotic dancer trying her best to stay off the needle. She's also HIV-positive, as are Collins, Roger, and a Latino street drummer and drag queen named Angel, who corresponds to Puccini's Schaunard.

This Mimi doesn't die—or not exactly. She's brought back from a near-death experience by her self-absorbed Roger, who tells her, "Hey, babe, don't die—you ain't heard my song yet." The one who does die is the drag queen, who, like so many fatally ill people on stage and screen nowadays, is a life force whose role in the grand scheme of things is to instill in others the courage to live.

A rock opera isn't exactly a new idea. Whether we're talking concept albums or actual Broadway productions (*Tommy,* you'll recall, was both), there have been too many of them to count, none of them very good. Andrew Lloyd Webber's scores borrow the volume and aerobicized pulse of disco, and twenty-six years ago Stephen Sondheim built his score for *Company* around brass figures and bass lines that would not have sounded out of place on a Dionne Warwick record (almost nobody noticed, because he did it without saying so in *Playbill*). Staging *La Bohème* in modern dress isn't exactly unprecedented either, though one has to wonder if those who have tried it realize that Puccini's opera was a period piece to begin with (first presented in 1896, it was set sixty years earlier, in keeping with the Henri Murger serial novel on which it was based). Legend has it that operagoers were initially scandalized by Puccini's glorification of people they regarded as lowlifes. The truth seems to be that *La Bohème* had a lukewarm reception because its Turin premiere closely followed the Italian premiere of Wagner's *Götterdämmerung;* despite Puccini's artful synthesis of traditional Italian and modern French elements *La Bohème* must have sounded positively quaint by comparison. So might **Rent** to anyone passingly familiar with current trends in performance art or rock-and-roll. Except for a few bars of "Musetta's Waltz"

played twice on guitar to comic effect (if you're like me, you first heard it as "Don't You Know," a Della Reese hit in 1959), **Rent** borrows none of Puccini's music, just his characters and stray narrative details. Using the story of a great opera for a new musical might be as pointless as watching a Fred Astaire and Ginger Rogers movie for the plot. But this is something that could be charitably overlooked, if it were **Rent**'s only problem.

I've seen the show twice now, the first time last winter, at a close friend's urging, when—already a hot ticket—it was still being presented off-Broadway, at a downtown performance space blocks from Larson's grimy Alphabet City setting. There and on Broadway, where remarkably little about the show has changed, the first act ended with a bouncy song called **"La Vie Bohème,"** Larson and the director Michael Greif's one stab at a big production number. This finds the entire fifteen-member cast at a banquet table following an offstage demonstration against a landlord (Mark and Roger's former roommate, turned yuppie) who's trying to evict them from their apartments and to remove an encampment of the homeless from the vacant lot next door. The scene corresponds to one in which Puccini's bohemians feast in a Latin Quarter café and then flee into the crowd when presented with the bill. **"La Vie Bohème"** is nothing if not catchy, but having it buzz around in my head all through intermission allowed me to place exactly where I had heard that sporty, nonstop bass riff before—in "Cool Jerk," a 1966 dance hit by the Capitols, which I suspect is also where Larson first heard it. Todd Rundgren's remake from seven years later is another possibility, given that almost every number in **Rent** sounds vaguely like a tune Larson would have heard on the radio as a teenager in the 1970s. (A tail-end Baby Boomer, he died in January, just short of his thirty-sixth birthday, after attending the final dress rehearsal for his show. So much has been made of his death in conjunction with his creation of characters facing imminent death from AIDS that some people probably think he was a casualty of the disease. But the aortic aneurysm that killed Larson isn't part of his show's zeitgeist.)

A story endlessly retold in the reams of copy devoted to Larson following **Rent**'s debut has it that he broke up with a girlfriend when she doubted his ability to write an authentic gospel tune—the implication always being that **"Seasons of Love,"** Larson's second-act opener, proves that he was right to ditch a woman of so little faith. But **"Seasons of Love"** is just Curtis Mayfield's "People Get Ready" stripped to the bone and reharmonized into something bland and blue-eyed enough to serve as a jingle for Hallmark or the friendly skies.

I don't think Larson was guilty of plagiarism; he was just being derivative in much the same way I was when, in my younger and more vulnerable years, I unwittingly wrote *The Great Gatsby*. Like the books we love, our favorite songs won't let go. Larson's previous shows, ***Superbia, Tick, tick***

... boom! and *J. P. Morgan Saves the Nation,* opened and closed quickly, in out-of-the-way venues. I haven't heard their scores, so I don't know if *Rent* marked a departure for Larson. Given his worship of Stephen Sondheim (another recurring theme in the articles about him), my guess is that he was a songwriter working more or less within the conventions of Broadway who, having decided to write a rock musical, wound up imitating the rock songs he remembered from his adolescence, which was probably the last time he had paid much attention to rock. Because I read over and over that Larson waited tables for ten years at the Moondance Diner, near the foot of Sixth Avenue, while waiting for his big break, another of my hunches was that the golden oldies on the diner's jukebox permeated his consciousness. A hike to the Moondance hours before I saw *Rent* on Broadway disproved this theory, because the place doesn't have a jukebox. Even so, in the theater that night I felt as if I were listening to a seventies jukebox.

With its echoes of Meat Loaf, Bruce Springsteen, David Bowie, Billy Joel, Gamble and Huff, *Flashdance,* and *The Rocky Horror Picture Show, Rent* is a musical in which the hits keep coming, but not ones we haven't heard before. The first time I saw *Rent,* I overheard a fellow intermission smoker exclaim to a companion, "To think that out of the death of theater, *this* can grow." It goes to show that everyone is a critic these days, though perhaps only when the licensed critics are unanimous.

About *Rent* they were almost unanimously ecstatic, paying it the ultimate compliment of pinning on it their hopes for the survival of music theater. Their logic went something like this: by virtue of being up-to-the-minute musically and in its depiction of characters for whom race, sexual orientation, and T-cell count present no barriers to friendship, *Rent* would sell tickets to young adults unlikely to pay to see Julie Andrews in *Victor/Victoria,* Carol Channing in *Hello, Dolly,* or anyone in *The King and I* (true of most young adults, I would think).

Another show making the transition from downtown to Broadway which was supposed to help get the fabulous invalid up and boogieing was *Bring in 'da Noise, Bring in 'da Funk,* the latest offering from George C. Wolfe, who in his capacity as producer for the Joseph Papp Public Theater/New York Shakespeare Festival is emerging as the David Merrick of identity politics. Fast on its feet if somewhat soft in the head, *Noise/Funk* is a dance musical in praise of rhythm—rhythm as a survival tactic, as a moral principle, as the secret ingredient in black life—with very few songs as such. Still running on Broadway as I write, the show was assumed by critics to be of special interest to younger black audiences for having captured not just the sound of hip-hop but a good deal of hip-hop's combative street posture. Reviewers were enthusiastic about *Noise/Funk,* and especially about the hoofing and

choreography of its star, Savion Glover, who makes palatable a series of brilliantly staged but preachy vignettes on four centuries of pain and degradation inflicted upon African-Americans, beginning with slavery.

Rent was praised to a degree that would have seemed unrealistic even for *The Threepenny Opera.* In the opinion of *Time, Rent* was only "the most exuberant and original American musical to come along this decade." In the eyes of *The Wall Street Journal,* it was "the best new musical since the 1950s." Michael Sommers, of the Newark *Star-Ledger,* enjoyed himself so much that he forgot to take notes, and Michael Feingold, of *The Village Voice,* was reduced to tears, presumably by Angel's death scene and its bitter reminder of Larson's own death hours away from triumph. The *Voice* was one of several papers to devote team coverage to *Rent,* with both the classical critic Leighton Kerner and the rock critic Evelyn McDonnell giving it their blessing. (McDonnell did complain that because "two of the main characters [Roger, the romantic hero, and Mark, who serves as the narrator] are straight white guys . . . for the umpteenth time, the stories of 'others' are made palatable by a dominant-voice narration." That Larson was a straight white guy himself is no excuse.)

The worth of *Rent* is one of very few issues on which the *Voice* and *The Wall Street Journal* have ever seen eye to eye. Not that the opinion of either paper counts for very much when it comes to theater. Only *The New York Times* can make or break a show, and the smitten paper of record began blowing kisses *Rent*'s way even before the show's official downtown opening, on February 13. A lengthy advance feature on Larson and Ben Brantley's initial rave review were only the beginning. A Sunday Arts and Leisure section preceding the Broadway opening looked like a *Rent* supplement; in addition to yet another feature recounting the show's past from the moment of conception on, the section included head shots and thumbnail biographies of all the cast members and a large front-page color photo of them in costume, performing **"La Vie Bohème."** The whole thing was reminiscent of those team photos that lesser newspapers tuck into the Sunday funnies to celebrate a victory in the World Series or the Super Bowl.

Rent emerged as a legitimate source of news when it became the prize in a bidding war between Broadway's two largest theatrical organizations, and then when it won four Tony Awards, including one as the season's best new musical and two others for Larson's book and score. (It was such a shoo-in that the producers of *Charlie Rose* and *The Late Show With David Letterman* didn't wait for the awards ceremony to book the show's principal cast members for post-Tony appearances.) But hardly a day seemed to go by early last spring without some mention of *Rent* in the *Times,* whether it was only Margo Jefferson telling us how much like genuine Lower East Siders the cast looked in their "grunge-meets-salsa-meets-B-Boy-meets-Riot-Grrrl-clothes" or Frank Rich arguing on the op-ed page that even though

> some of the turn-of-the-millennium fears given powerful voice by the dispossessed bohemians of *Rent* resemble those of what we now call Pat Buchanan voters . . . [Mr. Larson] takes the very people whom politicians now turn into scapegoats for our woes—the multicultural, the multisexual, the homeless, the sick—and, without sentimentalizing them or turning them into ideological symbols or victims, lets them revel in their joy, their capacity for love and, most important, their tenacity, all in a ceaseless outpouring of melody.

Rent was soon everywhere, including the cover of *Newsweek*. Just over a week after the show's April 29 Broadway premiere the cast—even at that point the most overexposed group of fictional young people since the cast of *Friends*—turned up in the *Times* once again, this time striking poses in a nearly full-page Bloomingdale's ad announcing the opening of a *Rent* boutique. It was less a case of life imitating art or of couture imitating thrift-shop dishabille than of advertising imitating editorial.

I've been telling friends that *Rent* is not as good as the *Times* says it is but probably not as bad as I make it sound. A number that almost everyone but me finds especially moving, **"One Song Glory,"** has Roger, the HIV-positive songwriter, who we're told used to sing with a punk-rock band, expressing his desire to write one great song in the little time he may have left. **"One Song Glory,"** like the song Roger ultimately writes, is a preening, melodramatic rock ballad of the sort that punk was supposed to stomp to smithereens. Still, this is one of those instances in which good theater doesn't necessarily require a good song. Tim Weil, the show's music director, has provided a starkly effective orchestration, with guitar reverb suggesting the steady drip of an IV. Blake Burba's lighting increases the chill by dwarfing Roger in his own shadow—the shadow of death. Frank Rich wasn't the only theatergoer to equate Roger's desire for one final blaze of glory with what might have been Larson's, had the composer known that this would be his last triumph as well as his first.

The problem is that Roger could be *Rent* the show, and his bigger-than-life shadow *Rent* the phenomenon. So much has been written about *Rent* that audiences may find themselves a little sick and tired of it on their way into the theater. The show could fall victim to the media's tendency to follow each binge with a purge. Already some of *Rent*'s most ardent early champions, including Brantley and Jefferson, have begun to question whether the show lost some of its purity or charm or social relevance in its transfer to Broadway. (The answer is no: it's a Broadway musical that happened to have its debut off-Broadway.)

I find it significant that the only *Times* writers to express strong reservations to begin with were the classical columnist Bernard Holland and the pop critic Jon Pareles. It may be that rock is impervious to emulation, something they both recognized. *Rent* may look like rock-and-roll, with its spandex- and flannel-clad cast wearing head mikes and shouting lyrics into one another's faces above a live band, but, like *Hair* almost thirty years ago, it sounds more like Broadway.

Judged as Broadway, Larson's score does not lack simple virtues. Stephen Sondheim praised his late disciple's music as "generous," a word that strikes me as particularly apt, though Sondheim probably meant something different by it than I would. Larson's melodies give themselves up very easily. Even someone who isn't especially taken with the songs might hum them on the way out, and this is all that many theatergoers ask of a musical. Larson's songs stick in your head, and not all of them are unwelcome there. (That they're also extremely easy to sing probably means that *Rent* will eventually be a favorite of college music and theater departments.) But this generosity is achieved at a cost. Larson's melodies are too close to the surface. Nothing harmonically complicated of the sort that goes on in Sondheim's songs goes on in Larson's. Although his lyrics are occasionally clever (when he's not making lists or settling for easy rhymes), his meanings are very close to the surface too. Unlike Sondheim's songs, Larson's are never shaded by the context in which they're sung. His lyrics are never revealed to be delusional; they mean exactly what they say. These may be faults common to all young composers, however talented, but still Larson seems not to have learned very much from his mentor. This doesn't seem to bother reviewers and audiences, who distrust what they perceive to be Sondheim's frosty intellectualism.

In *Rent*'s book Larson's generosity takes the form of big-heartedness toward his characters. Only two are beyond redemption, both of them peripheral and, in this context, stock villains: a drug dealer who tempts Mimi back onto junk and a pastor who refuses to bury Angel and condemns Collins as a "faggot." Even Benny, the nouveau-yuppie landlord, does a good deed or two by the end, and the casting complicates our reaction to him by giving the part to an extremely affable black actor named Taye Diggs. If nothing else, *Rent* is laudably unstereotypical in its characterization. Collins, the homeless MIT hacker, is black, and one of the other black characters (Joanne, the performance artist's lesbian lover) is an attorney. The show's music is another story: as soon as we hear the opening bars of **"Seasons of Love,"** we just know that one of the black actresses is going to step forth to supply a few gratuitous melismatic flourishes. This has become such a cliché that it even turned up in the 1995 Broadway revival of *How to Succeed in Business Without Really Trying,* on the song "Brotherhood of Man."

Larson's bigheartedness, which I imagine was a joy to his friends, worked to his disadvantage as a playwright. In ***Rent*** he indulged in a sentimentality of the sort that has always gone over big on Broadway, regardless of what social ills are being addressed (it's the same sort of sentimentality that keeps some of us from enjoying *La Bohème*). The show's title comes from an early song in which Larson's would-be artists defiantly refuse to pay their back rent. That they identify with their neighborhood's teeming homeless population is a given, yet the issue of social class is virtually ignored. Typical of ***Rent***'s lack of political sophistication, Larson's bohemians—the voluntarily, and probably only temporarily, poor—oppose gentrification without realizing that aspiring artists like themselves are inevitably gentrification's advance guard.

This is a show in which the observation that "the filmmaker cannot see, the songwriter cannot hear" passes for a profound insight. It's as though Larson believed that his characters faced no problems they couldn't solve by getting in touch with their feelings. Angel, the drag queen envied by artists for being his own canvas, is a character we've met countless times, and so is Mark, the filmmaker who wishes to document life but is afraid to participate in it. Mark, the show's narrator, is a stand-in of sorts for Larson and a surrogate for the audience. He's also the one principal character who isn't gay, HIV-positive, a woman, or a member of a racial minority. It's a difficult role, in that it asks the actor to be as self-effacing as a person in such company might be, for fear of being denounced as "privileged." Anthony Rapp, an energetic blur of an actor who's the best thing about ***Rent***, may have succeeded too well in conveying his character's desire for inconspicuousness. The Tony nominating board overlooked him in favor of four others in ***Rent***'s ensemble who sang louder and did a showier job of emoting: Adam Pascal, as Roger; Daphne Rubin-Vega, as Mimi; Idina Menzel, as Maureen; and Wilson Jermaine Heredia, the only one of the four nominees who won (in the featured-actor category), as Angel.

Unlike Pascal, who according to his program bio used to sing and play guitar with a rock band called Mute, and Rubin-Vega, who once reached No. 1 on *Billboard*'s dance chart, Rapp is a child of the theater and not pop music. Yet he's the only performer in ***Rent*** who looks comfortable singing rock on stage—maybe because he's the only one with sufficient stage experience to realize that behaving naturally while singing material of any kind in a theatrical context requires a great deal of acting technique. He obviously glanced at rock videos; with his hunched shoulders and slightly pigeon-toed gait, he has exactly the right look. Rapp is called on to deliver Larson's attempts at recitative, and he displays a real knack for this style of singing. He makes even **"La Vie Bohème"** satisfying, which is no easy trick, given its endless and dated roll call of artists who were evidently favorites of Larson's but who have little resonance for today's young adults (Bertolucci? Kurosawa? Stephen Sondheim? Susan Sontag?).

Music and contemporary youth culture aren't the only areas in which ***Rent*** seems hopelessly out of touch. The character of Maureen, the performance artist, epitomizes everything that rings false about the show, even though it's fun watching Idina Menzel perform Maureen's act at the demonstration against Benny, the landlord. Maureen represents Larson's chance to poke fun at the excesses of performance artists like Annie Sprinkle, who puts her feet into stirrups and invites her audiences to conduct a gynecological examination, and Karen Finley, infamous for supposedly committing unnatural acts with yams. But Maureen's act is annoyingly tame: she doesn't scream obscenities, smear anything on herself, or bleed on anyone. And since performance artists are exhibitionists practically by definition, wouldn't one who has only recently come out make her lesbianism the focus of her act?

Larson could have demonstrated with the character of Maureen how well he knew his way around the Lower East Side, but he seems to have been too genuinely nice a person to take much glee in wicked satire. Besides, it's tough to be a satirist when you're always going for the goo. In a song called **"Will I"** an unnamed AIDS victim who is eventually joined by the entire company wonders if he'll lose his dignity along with control of his body. The song is meant to be moving, but finally it's only embarrassing. The friends I've lost to the epidemic, no matter how needy they were at the end, had too much dignity to make such a naked appeal for pity (or perhaps I just prefer to think so). Larson wanted to blast audiences out of their apathy, with the help of rock-and-roll. But his show comes dangerously close to romancing the virus—to downgrading it to one more symptom of post-adolescent disengagement. In the sixties, *Hair*, while inviting theater groups to cluck in wonder at that era's young people, with their free love, their psychedelics, and their loud music, reduced all the world's evils, including the carnage in Vietnam, to the musical question "How can people be so heartless?" ***Rent***, for all that's supposed to be new about it, similarly invites theater groups to cluck in wonder at today's young people, with their bisexuality, their faulty immune systems, and their performance art.

Say what you will about *Hair* (and I'll say worse), that prototypical rock opera was transgressive in ways that ***Rent*** only imagines itself to be. In its own day *Hair* was as notorious for its nudity and its quasi-tribalism-elements borrowed from experimental theater, notably Julian Beck's Living Theater—as it was for its facsimile of the big beat. In some ways *Hair* was nothing more (but also nothing less) than an amplified, optimistic, mainstream version of the Living Theater's *Paradise Now*.

Rent serves a similar function in regard to today's experimental forms of performance art, but does so far less obviously and in a manner that promises to be far less liberating for mainstream theater. Two years ago Arlene Croce, the dance critic for *The New Yorker,* created a tempest by condemning as an example of an unfortunate trend a work by the HIV-positive dancer and choreographer Bill T. Jones that she admitted to not having seen. This was *Still/Here,* a performance in which Jones's choreography was interspersed with videotapes of people with fatal illnesses talking about their impending deaths. I think Croce misrepresented *Still/Here,* which I found to be moving largely for the videotaped interviews to which she categorically objected (the dancing itself struck me as mannered and earthbound). But I think she was right to complain of being "*forced* to feel sorry for . . . performers, in short, who make out of victimhood victim art" and in defining this art as "a politicized version" of the "blackmail" practiced by even as great an artist as Charlie Chaplin when he asked audiences to share in his self-pity. Like *Noise/Funk,* with its pep talks on black pride and its calculated appeal to a peculiar sort of pleasure that disguises itself as outrage at injustice, *Rent* neutralizes and mainstreams avant-garde victim art by sentimentalizing it into what I'm tempted to call victim kitsch.

Will *Rent* revitalize Broadway by persuading young adults who have grown up with rock-and-roll that music theater has something to offer them? I doubt it, because rock is itself a form of theater for such young adults, just as the street is a form of theater for the B-Boys and gang members whose moves are emulated in *Noise/Funk.* Thirty-nine years ago did teen hoods flock to Broadway to see their likenesses sing and dance in *West Side Story?*

Shows like *Rent* and *Noise/Funk* represent Broadway's attempt to colonize off-Broadway—to reap its perceived riches. A relic of art before the age of mechanical reproduction, the theater has been dying for as long as anyone can remember, though despite Broadway's constant state of peril it contributes greatly to New York's tourism industry and the city's sense of itself as an artistic mecca. Music theater now seems in greater peril than ever, in large part because of the staggering cost of staging a new show and the consequent high cost of tickets (for $67.50, the price of a good ticket to *Rent,* you can see ten movies or buy five CDs). Originating shows downtown and then moving the most successful of them to Broadway must appeal to producers as a sensible means of minimizing start-up costs.

But this doesn't explain why *Rent* has sparked such enthusiasm among reviewers and others with no direct stake in its box office. The only explanation I can think of is that they love music theater so much they wish it to have what Larson's Roger wishes for himself—one great song on which to go out. Either that or both they and Broadway are so out of

touch that they mistake the mere hint of social relevance for genius, and the slightest twitch for resurrection.

Ed Siegel (review date 19 November 1996)

SOURCE: "*Rent* Has a Lease on Energy," in *The Boston Globe,* November 19, 1996, p. D1.

[In the following review, Siegel analyzes Rent's *blend of show tunes and rock music.]*

There is one characteristic of rock music that it alone possesses. It's the jolt at the beginning of a song, from Chuck Berry's "Reelin' and Rockin'" to Cracker's "Teen Angst" that shoots the audience onto the dance floor, or at least into the middle of the living room playing air guitar. It's as if the electric instruments have created a musical energy field.

Show music has its own form of up-tempo energy, consisting of hummable tunes that get your toes tapping while you're in the theater and that you can't get out of your head for days afterward. The great accomplishment of Jonathan Larson's *Rent* is that it is successful in melding those two musical idioms. Rock fans find something they can relate to in musical theater and show-music fans find a relevance that had seemingly disappeared.

In the successful road-company version which has now debuted in Boston (but which wasn't ready to open to the press until last night), those virtues were apparent when the audience gave the cast members a standing ovation before it began. The ovation did appear to be somewhat accidental. Some members of the audience stood up for the New York cast who came in just as the show was beginning. The New Yorkers, in a very classy way, redirected the applause to the cast members who had just come out onstage.

It turned out to be appropriate because the Boston version is quite comparable to New York's and in one important regard infinitely better: The acoustics of the restored Shubert Theater are to New York's Nederlander Theatre what Symphony Hall's acoustics were to the late Boston Garden. (The one black eye for the Shubert's reopening were pickets protesting the theater management's lack of recognition for the union representing theatrical press agents and managers.)

What both versions capture so well is the spirit of rock music, even though *Rent* is not great rock music and, arguably, isn't even rock music at all. Is there anyone who doesn't know the story of its origins, how Larson set out to make a rock musical based on Puccini's *La Boheme,* capturing the lives of fellow struggling artists in New York's East Village, many of whom were HIV positive? And how he died at 35 of an aortic aneurysm hours after the production's final dress re-hearsal?

By this point, though, **Rent** has to stand on its own two feet and though it's able to do so, it can be awfully wobbly. The fusion of rock and show music is also one of its biggest flaws—it's a musical hybrid that isn't as solid as a real rock score that borrows a show-tune format (*Tommy*) or show music that draws on other elements (*West Side Story*). While **Rent** is always tuneful, it is rarely exciting, the anthemic **"La Vie Boheme"** being the primary example. At times it's downright tedious. How many different ways can you sing **"Seasons of Love"**?

The cast does bring an excitement to the proceedings. Simone, daughter of Nina Simone, is a very hot Mimi, a drug abuser apparently dying of AIDS who has fallen in love with Roger, a rock musician, who's HIV-positive and whose previous lover has killed herself. C. C. Brown and Stephan Alexander as the gay lovers are exceptional, particularly Brown, whose Richie Havens voice is one of the few with any special char-acter. (There are adult themes here so you might want to think about bringing the kiddies. They probably won't be embar-rassed but you might be embarrassed that they're not.)

Documenting all this is Mark, a filmmaker whose girlfriend Maureen has left him for a woman. Carrie Hamilton, Carol Burnett's daughter, is the one weak link in the cast as Maureen, particularly when measured against Idina Menzel, who domi-nated the stage every minute she was on, particularly in her satire of Laurie Anderson. Hamilton just blends in with the scenery. Or lack thereof. (The stage is a grungy loft, which is easily convertible when the young bohemians go out on the town.)

But the biggest flaw with **Rent,** if not with the ethos it is pro-moting, is the emptiness of its bohemianism. It wants us to recognize gay people as normal, which is all to the good, but so does prime-time television. It wants us to have compas-sion for people with AIDS, which we should, but so did the Republican Convention.

When nothing is shocking anymore what is there to be bohemian about? The freedom to wear tight pants? In terms of content, **Rent** is little more than a fashion state-ment. One leaves the theater humming the clothes along with the tunes.

In terms of form, though, **Rent** is a success. Musical theater has needed this kind of goose for the better part of 25 years. And all of us can use the kind of rejuvenating jolt that rock music delivers. Even when the voltage isn't as high as it could be.

FURTHER READING

Biographies

Rosenthal, Elisabeth. "2 Hospitals Fined in Wake of Death of 'Rent' Creator." *New York Times* (13 December 1996): A1, B6.
> Outlines preliminary legal and punitive action taken in the year after Larson's death against the two hospitals that misdiagnosed his fatal heart condition.

Tommasini, Anthony. "The Seven-Year Odyssey that Led to 'Rent'." *New York Times* (17 March 1996): sec. 2, pp. 7, 37.
> Details the creation of *Rent.*

Interview

Galvin, Peter. "How the Show Goes On: An Interview with 'Roger,' 'Mimi,' and 'Mark.'" *Interview* 20 (June 1996): 105.
> Interview with original cast members Adam Pascal, Daphne Rubin-Vega, and Anthony Rapp.

Wislawa Szymborska
Nobel Prize for Literature

Born in 1923, Szymborska is a Polish poet.

INTRODUCTION

Winner of the 1996 Nobel Prize for Literature, Szymborska, a private—some would say reclusive—widow, has been described as "the Mozart of poetry . . . [with] something of the fury of Beethoven." Although she is perhaps Poland's most popular female writer and valued as a national treasure there, she is little known by English-speaking readers, and only three books of her poetry have been translated: *Sounds, Feelings, Thoughts* (1981); *People on a Bridge* (1986); and *View with a Grain of Sand* (1995). "Polish poetry in the 20th century has reached a strong international position on the European continent," observed renowned Polish poet Czeslaw Milosz. "Szymborska represents it well." Szymborska emphasizes and examines the chance happenings of daily life and of personal relations in her poetry, which spans five decades. "She is a master at recognizing the importance of the insignificant. . . ," explained James Beschta, "it is the innovative, playful use of language that dominates her style." While Szymborska treats a wide variety of subjects in as many different styles, her method remains constant: her lyrics usually build from some small detail, then expand into revelations about the larger universe. Szymborska published her first poem in 1945, but she later renounced her first two volumes of poetry as attempts to conform to tenets of social realism. The Swedish Academy acknowledged that it awarded the Nobel Prize to her on the basis of her poems written since 1957, when she published her third collection, *Calling out to the Yeti,* which the Academy cited as a reaction against Stalin. "Of course, life crosses politics, but my poems are strictly not political," Szymborska said in a rare interview. "They are more about people and life." Beata Chmiel concluded that the Nobel was given "to an unknown poet of Poland, but this poet can be very close to people all over the world: men, women, black and white."

PRINCIPAL WORKS

Dlatego zyjemy (poetry) 1952
Pytania zadawane sobie (poetry) 1954
Wolanie do Yeti (poetry) 1957
Sól (poetry) 1962
Wiersze wybrane (poetry) 1964
Sto pociech (poetry) 1967
Poezje wybrane (poetry) 1967
Poezje (poetry) 1970

Wybór poezji (poetry) 1970
Wszelki wypadek (poetry) 1972
Wybór wierszy (poetry) 1973
Lektury nadobowiazkowe (lectures) 1974
Tarsjusz i inne wiersze (poetry) 1976
Wielka liczba (poetry) 1976
Sounds, Feelings, Thoughts: 70 Poems (poetry) 1981
Poezje wybrane (II) (poetry) 1983
Ludzie na moscie [People on a Bridge] (poetry) 1986
*Poezje = Poems (poetry) 1989
The End and the Beginning (poetry) 1993
View with a Grain of Sand: Selected Poems (poetry) 1995

*This work is a bilingual edition.

CRITICISM

Alice-Catherine Carls (review date Summer 1991)

SOURCE: A review of *Poezje=Poems,* in *World Literature Today,* Vol. 65, No. 3, Summer, 1991, p. 519.

[*In the following review, Carls detects "a grim reminder of taboos that are still bridling Polish society" in* Poezji = Poems.]

Polish publishers have a tradition of publishing original works written in foreign languages. The present volume, a reprint of a 1981 bilingual selection of Wislawa Szymborska's verse (*Sounds, Feelings, Thoughts: Seventy Poems*), belongs to that category. Given the present shortage of paper in Poland and the resultant price tag of 2,500 zlotys—a student's entire monthly stipend in the 1970s—such an undertaking can only be justified by Szymborska's status as one of the finest postwar Polish poets and by the desire to acknowledge her popularity abroad.

Surprisingly missing from the Polish edition, however, are the comments and the bibliographic note contained in the American edition; the Polish volume remains silent as well about the translators, on whom a note would have been appropriate, especially in light of the recent death of Magnus J. Krynski, a prominent Polish émigré. The American edition's introduction by the translators has now become the afterword. Its opening lines about Polish critics' unabating praise for Szymborska have been deleted. Later, one paragraph referring to the poems written under Stalinist rule and two paragraphs mentioning political themes, the poet's recent protest against Stalinist politics, and her involvement in the Flying University have been deleted. As a result, the footnotes have been considerably abridged. Szymborska's poetry stands bare here, a grim reminder of taboos that are still bridling Polish society.

Bogdana Carpenter (review date Winter 1992)

SOURCE: A review of *People on a Bridge,* in *World Literature Today,* Vol. 66, No. 1, Winter, 1992, pp. 163-64.

[*In the following review, Carpenter finds* People on a Bridge *"subtle, witty, and ironic."*]

Long recognized in Poland as a leading voice in contemporary Polish poetry, Wislawa Szymborska has not achieved the same popularity in the English-speaking world as other poets of her generation such as Zbigniew Herbert and Tadeusz Rózewicz. Still, *People on a Bridge* is not the first introduction of Szymborska's verse to English readers. Czeslaw Milosz included poems by her in his seminal anthology *Postwar Polish Poetry* (1965), and in 1981 Princeton University Press published a selection of her poems translated by Magnus Krynski and Robert Maguire. Let us hope that the present volume, a welcome addition to those earlier translations, will help bring Szymborska the recognition that she deserves.

The poems selected by Adam Czerniawski come from four different collections and span a period of twenty years. Rather than adhere to chronology, Czerniawski has grouped the poems according to recurring themes, most prominently the problem of art's relationship to time, death, and reality. Thematic unity is further emphasized by a ring composition. The poems opening and closing the book (the only two given both in English translation and in the Polish original) deal with the precariousness of human life, symbolized both times by the image of a bridge, and the inability of art—despite its futile attempt to resist the flow of time—to penetrate the mystery of death and existence.

> **In the opposition between reality and art, life and intellect, Szymborska declares herself on the side of reality and life.**
>
> —*Bogdana Carpenter*

At the center of Szymborska's attention is the disparity between the limitations of the poetic imagination and the unlimited vastness of reality: "Four billion people on this earth, / but my imagination is as it was" (**"Big Numbers"**). The mathematical value of [pi] comes closer to expressing the infinite richness of the universe than does the poetic imagination: "It cannot be grasped *six five three five* at a glance, / *eight nine* in a calculus / *seven nine* in imagination, / or even *three two three eight* in a conceit, that is, a comparison." Art catches only individual facts and existences, a fraction of reality. Poetry, marked by insufficiency and imperfection, is a selection, a renunciation, a passing over in silence, and a "sigh" rather than a "full breath." The poet, like anyone else, is unable to transgress his or her own "I," his own particular existence. Being himself, he cannot be what he is not.

In the opposition between reality and art, life and intellect, Szymborska declares herself on the side of reality and life. Ideas are most often pretexts to kill, a deadly weapon, whether under the guise of an artistic experiment (**"Experiment"**), a political Utopia (**"Utopia"**), or ideological fanaticism (**"The Terrorist, He Watches"**). Szymborska sides with reality against art and ideology, and this choice situates her in the mainstream of postwar Polish poetry alongside Milosz, Herbert, and Bialoszewski.

Like Bialoszewski, although in a different idiom, Szymborska extols the everyday and the ordinary. Her "miracle mart" is made of barking dogs, trees reflected in a pond, gentle breezes and gusty storms, the world "ever-present." Even in dreams she appreciates most of all their ability to create the illusion of reality. In the theater she is moved by a glimpse of actors caught beneath the curtain more than by tragic tirades. Her poetry reverses the accepted view of what is important and what is unimportant; it puts forward common and humble reality at the expense of history and politics: "Pebbles by-passed on the beach can be as rounded / as the anniversaries of insurrections" (**"May Be Left Untitled"**).

Pervaded by the spirit of contestation, Wislawa Szymborska's poetry thrives on paradox. A mixture of "loftiness and common speech" (**"Unwritten Poem Review"**), it is subtle, witty, and ironic.

M. G. Levine (review date January 1992)

SOURCE: A review of *People on a Bridge,* in *Choice,* Vol. 29, No. 5, January, 1992, p. 752.

[*In the review below, Levine briefly compares* People on a Bridge *to the earlier* Sounds, Feelings, Thoughts.]

Szymborska is a distinguished Polish poet, admired for her witty, often wry, coolly intellectual poems—poems that at the same time radiate warmth and, through their attention to the particular, often subvert the intellectual categories through which we view the world. Adam Czerniawski has translated 36 of Szymborska's poems published over the last two decades. The present volume is not the first collection of Szymborska's poems in English translation. *Sounds, Feelings, Thoughts,* a selection of 70 poems (the earliest of them from the mid-1950s) in translations by Magnus J. Krynski and Robert A. Maguire, was published ten years ago (1981). That volume offered a much richer introduction to Szymborska's poetry, having a more varied and therefore more representative selection and an essay by the translators that is both longer and more informative than Czerniawski's crisp five-page evocation of Szymborska's "particular imagination." *Sounds, Feelings, Thoughts* had the additional virtue of being a facing-page, bilingual edition. Of the 36 poems in *People on a Bridge,* 20 also appear in *Sounds, Feelings, Thoughts*. But Czerniawski's translations are more felicitous, and his selection includes 16 new poems written in the 1980s; thus, *People on a Bridge* will enhance college and public library collections of poetry in translation.

James Beschta (review date September 1995)

SOURCE: A review of *View with a Grain of Sand: Selected Poems,* in *Kliatt,* Vol. 29, No. 5, September, 1995, p. 29.

[*In the review below, Beschta praises* View with a Grain of Sand, *calling the volume "a joy."*]

Although her work has been translated into English before, Szymborska has not been widely recognized here in the States.

Here, her selected poems, wonderfully translated by Stanislaw Baranczak and Clare Cavanagh, might well change that situation, bringing America into step with Europe, which acknowledges her as arguably Poland's leading female poet. This collection presents 100 poems taken from seven separate volumes. As such, it offers a broad perspective on her career, one which maintains an optimism and sense of wonder about the world while recognizing the trials of reality. In 1957 she says, "We've inherited hope— / the gift of forgetting . . ." and in 1993 she points out that

This terrifying world is not devoid of charms,
of the mornings
that make waking up worthwhile.
The grass is green
on Maciejowice's fields,
and it is studded with dew, . . .

Through the writings of nearly 50 years, her sense of humor is as evident as her sense of wonder, and her urge to speculate, to find alternative possible causes for what the rest of us would tend to ignore or accept as evident, makes her as unique as she is delightful. She is a master at recognizing the importance of the insignificant, and though her subtle insights alone are justification for her success, it is the innovative, playful use of language that dominates her style and resonates through these translations. This volume is a joy. Szymborska deserves to be heard and recognized, and this book is a great introduction.

Virginia Quarterly Review (review date Winter 1996)

SOURCE: A review of *View with a Grain of Sand,* in *The Virginia Quarterly Review,* Vol. 72, No. 1, Winter, 1996, p. 29.

[*In the review below, the critic briefly considers Szymborska's poetic style.*]

"So much world all at once—how it rustles and bustles!" Szymborska is constantly amazed and challenged by life's plenty, and in capturing it in language, her poems employ all the "inventiveness / bounty, sweep, exactitude, / sense of order—gifts that border / on witchcraft and wizardry" that she praises in life itself. Though claiming only to have "borrowed from the truth," Szymborska writes lyrics that build from small details, such as a grain of sand, into visions of the wider universe. Her styles, like her subjects, are many, ranging from satire to elegy, meditation to play. She is especially deft at composing brief, spare allegories that have all the emotional force of extended narratives. In rendering this multi-faceted Polish voice into English, the translators (Stanislaw Baranczak and Clare Cavanagh) deserve high praise. There is nothing strained or awkward here, and lines like, "Oh how grassy is this hopper, / how this berry ripely rasps," work so well in English it's hard to believe they were conceived in any other language. Culling work from between 1957 and 1993, [*View with a Grain of Sand*] is the third selection of Szymborska's poems to appear in English. One hopes it won't be the last.

Helen Vendler (review date 1 January 1996)

SOURCE: "Unfathomable Life," in *New Republic,* Vol. 214, No. 1, January 1, 1996, pp. 36-9.

[*Below, Vendler comments on Szymborska's evolution as a poet and establishes a context for her art.*]

"Again, and as ever, . . . the most pressing questions / are naïve ones." The remarkable poet Wislawa Szymborska closes, with this remark, a late poem, **"The Century's Decline,"** on the collapse of Marxist utopian hopes, after uttering one of her deliberately "naïve" questions: "How should we live?" Szymborska, one of a generation of notable Polish poets (she was born in 1923), was brought to American attention by Czeslaw Milosz in his history of Polish poetry, by two slim collections of translations, and by Stanislaw Baranczak in *Spoiling Cannibals' Fun,* his recent anthology of Polish poetry of the last two decades of Communist rule. Now Baranczak and Clare Cavanagh, his collaborator in that anthology, have brought out the largest selection of Szymborska—100 poems—in English [*View with a Grain of Sand: Selected Poems*].

They draw from seven of Szymborska's volumes, ranging from *Calling Out to Yeti,* her third collection, which appeared in 1957, through *The End and the Beginning,* which appeared in 1993. Their admirable versions, most of them readable as English poems owing to the exceptional gifts of the translators, make it possible to follow Szymborska's career, as she evolves from the high-spirited young poet-inspired equally by Marxist aspirations and by an antic sense of words-through the mature poet asking, in her "naïve" way, embarrassing political questions, to the older poet grieving for companions lost and hopes betrayed.

In spite of the translators' inventive substitutions, Szymborska's language-play as rendered in English is probably only a shadow of the felicitous original. Szymborska "translates well" because her poems, with all their local linguistic liveliness, adhere to a determined simplicity of narration. They are also resolutely "anonymous": their speaker is identified only rarely by gender, and never by age or nationality or ethnicity or local habitation. No lyric writer has ever been more confident of the universality of human response. Szymborska writes not for Poles alone, nor for women alone, nor for the twentieth century alone: she believes fiercely

in a common epistemology and a common ethic, at least within the Western culture she writes from and to.

This new collection, regrettably, lacks an introduction that would set Szymborska in context for English-speaking readers. In a brief essay on the poet published in 1994 in *Salmagundi,* Baranczak recalls her beginnings:

> Under the circumstances of Poland's own version of Stalinist culture, any literary work that dared be either innovative or candid was doomed. Even though she was a sincere believer in Communism at this point, Szymborska was also too good a poet not to have sinned on both these accounts at once. The first collection that she prepared for publication was initially accepted but later scrapped, as aesthetically and ideologically not orthodox enough. Her debut, a heavily re-worked collection titled, with characteristically Socialist-Realist self-assertion, *That's What We Live For,* came out at last in 1952, much later than the first books of most of her coevals. Symbolically enough, Szymborska's second collection, published in 1954, was titled *Questions Put to Myself.* . . . [In a recent interview], she sums up the "mistake" underlying her early writing by saying that she tried then "to love humankind instead of loving human beings."

The difficulty in writing anonymously and generally—allegorically, almost—is that one will distance oneself from the personal, the local, the intimate. Szymborska feared, early on, her own tendency toward the overview, and the lofty aloofness it fostered. As she (in an early poem) ascends to the chilly Himalayas, she addresses the Yeti who is thinking of visiting the earth:

> Yeti, we've got Shakespeare there.
> Yeti, we play solitaire
> and violin. At nightfall,
> we turn lights on, Yeti.
>
> Up here it's neither moon nor earth.
> Tears freeze.
> Oh Yeti, semi-moonman,
> turn back, think again!

The still void of the Himalayas appeals to her, yet she half-ironically defends the earth's virtue and its "sentences," even as she flees its crime and its unjust "justice":

> Yeti, crime is not all
> we're up to down there.
> Yeti, not every sentence there
> means death.

Later, speaking through the voice of Cassandra, Szymborska admits the prophetess's distance in relation to her countrymen, a distance she fears in herself:

I loved them.
But I loved them haughtily.
From heights beyond life.

Despite her aesthetic fastidiousness, and the intellectual haughtiness that is natural to her, Szymborska reluctantly admits, in her most famous early poem, that her "final exam" will be a historical and ethical one: as long as there is cruelty, her voice must be at the service of suffering. Here is the poem entire, which includes (as a simpler protest poem would not) the recurrent temptation to a skeptical impatience with ethical imperatives. The poem incorporates, besides its moral import, that necessary component to art, imagination's dream (here stimulated by the Brueghel painting described in the first stanza):

"Breughel's Two Monkeys"

This is what I see in my dreams about final exams:
two monkeys, chained to the floor, sit on the windowsill,
the sky behind them flutters,
the sea is taking its bath.

The exam is History of Mankind.
I stammer and hedge.

One monkey stares and listens with mocking disdain,
the other seems to be dreaming away—
but when it's clear I don't know what to say
he prompts me with a gentle
clinking of his chain.

Szymborska's narrative manner will not change notably over her writing life, but her rendition of suffering will enlarge as she sees the full brutality of life in Poland from the '40s through the '80s. A poem of 1985 called **"Tortures"** begins each of its five stanzas with the sentence, "Nothing has changed." The first stanza remarks on the unchangingness of the body over the centuries: "it has a good supply of teeth and fingernails; / its bones can be broken; its joints can be stretched." The second concerns the body's responsiveness: "The body still trembles as it trembled / before Rome was founded and after, / in the twentieth century before and after Christ." The third notes the contemporary multiplication of offenses "requiring" torture—"new offenses have sprung up beside the old ones—/real, make believe, short-lived, and nonexistent"—yet the body's cry "was, is, and will be a cry of innocence." The poem rises to a climax in its fourth stanza:

Nothing has changed.
Except perhaps the manners, ceremonies, dances.
The gesture of the hands shielding the head
has nonetheless remained the same.
The body writhes, jerks, and tugs,
falls to the ground when shoved, pulls up its knees,
bruises, swells, drools, and bleeds.

The universality of suffering is Szymborska's chief life-theme, and reiterative narration (interspersed with epigram) is her usual rhetorical mode. Of course, neither theme nor mode, nor both together, would suffice to make a poem. Every lyric poem is the trace left by an emotion; and the entire trace (not merely the thematic or narrative content of the poem) defines the emotion, as a footprint defines a foot. Szymborska is a most ingenious constructor of traces. And her ingenuity is not factitious; it is, rather, philosophical. Each line in a poem-and each white space in a poem-must be weighed for the new imaginative information they bring.

Szymborska writes not for Poles alone, nor for women alone, nor for the twentieth century alone: she believes fiercely in a common epistemology and a common ethic, at least within the Western culture she writes from and to.

—Helen Vendler

Consider **"Utopia,"** surely one of the classic treatments of the Soviet utopia as it was consolidated in Poland. The poem begins with the promise and desirability of utopia, both moral and intellectual, but sees that each promise has left suffering in its wake. Szymborska does justice both to the initial suffering under the ancien régime that provoked a hope for a new system, and to the later suffering caused by that system's betrayal of its utopian promises. Each successive line bears meditation, as—in the fiction of the poem—a populace, wrung by their destructive experience in the (politically irrational) ocean, at last comes ashore on a (Marxist) island:

Island where all becomes clear.

Solid ground beneath your feet.

The only roads are those that offer access.

Bushes bend beneath the weight of proofs . . .

If any doubts arise, the wind dispels them instantly. . . .

Unshakable Confidence towers over the valley.

Its peak offers an excellent view of the Essence of
Things.

And then, after twelve such dawning statements about utopia, the poem makes its bleak sardonic turn:

> For all its charms, the island is uninhabited,
> and the faint footprints scattered on its beaches
> turn without exception to the sea.

> As if all you can do here is leave
> and plunge, never to return, into the depths.

> Into unfathomable life.

Utopia is uninhabitable. It will always lose to unfathomable, dangerous, and chaotic life. Szymborska's poem
enacts both the conviction of the early Marxists and their
gradual disillusion, step by step, space by space, thought
by thought.

Since Szymborska's sibylline and oracular sentences—formed
in that same apodictic mode so congenial to universal system—risk being themselves examples of Unshakable Confidence, her admission that life is always unfathomable means
that her sentences must also consider themselves provisional.
An unexpected energy, often reactive (as in the case of her
plunge into the ocean, away from the totalization of utopia)
upsets and revivifies her lines. We deduce the extent of the
anterior suffering by the energy needed to counteract it. Plunging into the sea—"never to return"—is usually a figure for
suicide: Szymborska, writing **"Utopia"** in the '70s, is in a
Poland where self-liberation and suicide are hardly distinguishable.

For intellectuals—and Szymborska is one—epistemological
perplexity is also a form of suffering. The clean and perpen-
dicular lines of her poetry reflect her wish to be absolutely
exact, even transparent. "Don't bear me ill will, speech, that
I borrow weighty words, / then labor heavily so that they
may seem light." And yet language is heavy with anthropo-
centric perspectives. Thus the simplest sentence—"The window has a wonderful view of a lake"—immediately sets up
Szymborska's rigorous denials:

> but the view doesn't view itself.
> It exists in this world
> colorless, shapeless,
> soundless, odorless, and painless.

> The lake's floor exists floorlessly,
> and its shore exists shorelessly.
> Its water feels itself neither wet nor dry

and its waves to themselves are neither singular nor
plural.

How, then, can one speak of the view, the floor of the lake,
the shore, the waves? Is it possible to de-anthropomorphize
language, and not say "the sun sets," or "time passes"?

> Time has passed like a courier with urgent news.
> But that's just our simile.
> The character is invented, his haste is make-
> believe,
> his news inhuman.

Every poem by Szymborska is a struggle against taking common ways of expression for granted, or thinking that a single
phrase can cover all the possibilities. In a revolt against her
own genre—the generalizing poem—she multiplies instances
in order to cover all bases, certain that any one example will
be humanly insufficient. Her poem **"Clothes,"** about medical suspicion and relief, wittily offers a multiple-choice check-
list which will certainly, she intimates, cover your
apprehensive visit to the doctor as well as hers:

> You take off, we take off, they take off
> coats, jackets, blouses, double-breasted suits,
> made of wool, cotton, cotton-polyester . . .
> for now, the doctor says, it's not too bad,
> you may get dressed, get rested up, get out of town,
> take one in case, at bedtime, after lunch . . .
> you see, and you thought, and we were afraid that,
> and he imagined, and you all believed;
> it's time to tie, to fasten with shaking hands
> shoelaces, buckles, velcro, zippers, snaps,
> belts, buttons, cuff links, collars, neckties, clasps
> and to pull out of handbags, pockets, sleeves
> a crumpled, dotted, flowered, checkered scarf
> whose usefulness has suddenly been prolonged.

It is the awful normalcy and generality of the dreaded ver-
dict-visit that comes through in Szymborska's rendition: all
over the world people are stripping in doctor's offices and
expecting the worst. For Szymborska, the awful is, all too
often, the normal, and her even tone embraces, in one of her
most accomplished poems, the act of terrorism itself—which
is, of course, entirely normal to its perpetrator:

> #### "The Terrorist, He's Watching"

> The bomb in the bar will explode at thirteen twenty.
> Now it's just thirteen sixteen.
> There's still time for some to go in,
> and some to come out.

> The terrorist has already crossed the street.
> The distance keeps him out of danger,

and what a view—just like the movies:

A woman in a yellow jacket, she's going in.
A man in dark glasses, he's coming out.
Teenagers in jeans, they're talking.
Thirteen seventeen and four seconds.
The short one, he's lucky, he's getting on a scooter,
but the tall one, he's going in.

Thirteen seventeen and forty seconds.
That girl, she's walking along with a green ribbon
in her hair.
But then a bus suddenly pulls in front of her.
Thirteen eighteen.
The girl's gone.
Was she that dumb, did she go in or not,
We'll see when they carry them out.

Thirteen nineteen.
Somehow no one's going in.
Another guy, fat, bald, is leaving, though.
Wait a second, looks like he's looking for something in his pockets and
at thirteen twenty minus ten seconds
he goes back in for his crummy gloves.

Thirteen twenty exactly.
This waiting, it's taking forever.
Any second now.
No, not yet.
Yes, now.
The bomb, it explodes.

A poem such as this one was inconceivable, stylistically, before the twentieth century; it defines an epoch, a type, an
ethic. It stands for Lockerbie and Belfast, Jerusalem and
Oklahoma. It was, one could say, hanging in the air waiting
to be written, one of those poems that inscribes itself without
effort on the mind receiving it.

Though Szymborska excels in such grim impersonal narratives, she is equally able to evoke—always obliquely, always
originally—intense tenderness. The death of someone beloved, for example, is narrated from the point of view of his
"Cat in an Empty Apartment":

Nothing seems different here,
but nothing is the same.
Nothing has been moved,
but there's more space.
And at nighttime no lamps are lit. . . .
Someone was always, always here,
then suddenly disappeared
and stubbornly stays disappeared. . . .

Just wait till he turns up,
Just let him show his face.
Will he ever get a lesson
on what not to do to a cat.
Sidle toward him
as if unwilling
and ever so slow
on visibly offended paws,
and no leaps or squeals at least to start.

The equally wrenching elegy for Krzysztof Baczynski, a poet
who died at 23 in the Warsaw Uprising in 1944, exhibits
another of Szymborska's characteristically unexpected angles
of approach. She heartbreakingly creates the poet as he would
be had he continued to live till now, imagining him "Goateed,
balding, / gray-haired," eating his lunch:

Sometimes someone would
yell from the doorway: "Mr. Baczynski, phone call
for you"—
and there'd be nothing strange about that
being him, about him standing up, straightening his
sweater,
and slowly moving toward the door.

Szymborska is not sentimental. She sees that the 65-year-
old man would have coarsened "as if clay had covered up the
angelic marble" of his exalted youth: "The price, after all,
for not having died already / goes up not in leaps but step by
step, and he would / pay that price, too." She speaks from
the knowledge of the price that she has herself paid for aging. But the ethical observation would be inert were it not
for the poet's initial leap of imagination extending
Baczynski's short life—a human wish so powerful it creates
a full-scale scenario, down to the yearning phone call.

It would be wrong to consider Szymborska without asking
whether, the anonymity of her stance notwithstanding, she
does not sometimes write "as a woman." The answer is yes
and no. Yes, she writes as Cassandra and as Lot's wife, she
writes on Isadora Duncan, on a prehistoric figure of the Great
Mother, and on Rubens's women; and all of these could le-
gitimately be taken as reflections on femaleness. Yet the poem
on Cassandra is chiefly a meditation on how prophets, any
prophets, are hated; and Lot's wife accounts for her halt by
citing her "age . . . Distance. . . . / The futility of wandering. Torpor. / . . . in desolation. / In shame"—all of them
gender-neutral factors. It seems to me that Szymborska writes
most "as a woman" when she chooses a "humble" subject
such as an onion (as a symbol of a non-dualist conception of
nature); or when her imagination darts to a fantasy on Hitler's
actual baby-photograph:

And who's this little fellow in his itty-bitty robe?
That's tiny baby Adolf, the Hitlers' little boy! . . .

Whose teensy hand is this, whose little ear and eye
and nose? . . .

A little pacifier, diaper, rattle, bib,
our bouncing boy, thank God and knock on wood,
is well,
looks just like his folks, like a kitten in a basket,
like the tots in every other family album.
Sh-h-h, let's not start crying, sugar.
The camera will click from under that black hood.

The Klinger Atelier, Grabenstrasse, Braunen.
And Braunen is a small but worthy town—
honest businesses, obliging neighbors,
smell of yeast dough, of gray soap.
No one hears howling dogs, or fate's footsteps.
A history teacher loosens his collar
and yawns over homework.

"Hitler's First Photograph" is not Szymborska's best poem,
but its opening is startling and daring, its black humor confronting—as only a woman might think to do—the mystery
of how babies turn out. Szymborska often approaches ethical
issues from just such an odd (and perhaps implicitly female)
vantage; her poem **"Voices,"** about what we now call ethnic
cleansing, simply lets us in on conversations between Roman governors:

> You can't move an inch, my dear Marcus Emilius,
> without Aborigines sprouting up as if from the
> earth itself. . . .

> These irksome little nations, thick as flies.
> It's enough to make you sick, dear Quintus
> Decius. . . .

> They drive us mild-mannered sorts to sterner
> measures
> with every new mountain we cross, dear Gaius
> Cloelius.

> If only they weren't always in the way, the
> Auruncians, the Marsians,
> but they always do get in the way, dear Spurius
> Manlius. . . .

> Little nations do have little minds.
> The circle of thick skulls expands around us.
> Reprehensible customs, Backward laws.
> Ineffectual gods, my dear Titus Vilius. . . .

This seditious little poem of communications among the
Spurious and the Vile was probably protected from the cen-
sors in 1972 only by its historical setting. It may be that
Szymborska's resolute impersonality, anonymity and alle-

gorical stance were forced into being by Polish censorship;
but it is equally possible that her view of lyric as that which
describes the irreducible human invariables evoked her geo-
metrical abstraction of voice and her aloof narrations "from
above."

In a time when it is being metaphysically denied that any
human universals exist, it is salutary to read Szymborska on
the ancientness of human evil. Mercifully, Szymborska also
notes the perpetual resurgence of hope and the deep rewards
of human attachment. "My identifying features," she says in
the poem **"Sky,"** "are rapture and despair." Both are found
here, but perhaps more despair than rapture, in Szymborska's
stern and unforgiving scan of the savage world that she has
learned to understand.

Edward Hirsch (essay date 18 April 1996)

SOURCE: "Subversive Activities," in *The New York Review
of Books,* Vol. XLIII, No. 7, April 18, 1996, pp. 35-6.

[*In the following essay, Hirsch provides an overview of
Szymborska's career, analyzing subversive elements in her
poetry.*]

Wislawa Szymborska, with Zbigniew Herbert and Tadeusz
Rózewicz, is one of the major living Polish poets of the generation after Milosz. Of the four Szymborska is the least well-
known in America, perhaps because she has remained in
Poland, and because she shuns the public eye. Little is known
about her private life; she has rarely been interviewed. Yet,
as in the case of Elizabeth Bishop, her reticence is accompanied by considerable literary ambition. Like Herbert, she has
mounted in her work a witty and tireless defense of individual subjectivity against collectivist thinking, and her poems, like his, are slyly subversive in a way that compels us to
reconsider received opinion. In both, the rejection of dogma
becomes the basis of a canny personal ethics.

Szymborska was born in 1923 in the small town of Bnin in
the Poznan area of western Poland. She moved with her family
to Cracow when she was eight years old and has lived there
ever since. She attended school illegally during the German
occupation, when the Nazis banned Polish secondary schools
and universities, and after the war studied Polish literature
and sociology at Jagiellonian University. From 1952 to 1981
she worked on the editorial staff of the cultural weekly *Zycie
Literackie* (*Literary Life*). She has published nine collections
of poems and several editions of her selected verse, as well
as a volume of newspaper reviews and columns. She is also
known to Polish readers as a distinguished translator of French
poetry, mostly of the sixteenth and seventeenth centuries.

View with a Grain of Sand, translated by Stanislaw

Baranczak and Clare Cavanagh, brings together a hundred poems spanning nearly forty years of Szymborska's work. It is by far the most extensive and readable edition of her poems yet to appear in English. The translators haven't included anything from Szymborska's early books, *That's What We Live For* (1952) and *Questions Put to Myself* (1954), and only three poems from her transitional third collection, *Calling Out to Yeti* (1957). The later volumes, published after she managed to break free of political pressures to conform, are well-represented here: *Salt* (1962), *No End of Fun* (1967), *Could Have* (1972), *A Large Number* (1976), *The People on the Bridge* (1986), and *The End and the Beginning* (1993).

Szymborska comes through well in translation, but Baranczak and Cavanagh are the first to convey the full force of her fierce and unexpected wit. Their versions reproduce the rhythm and rhyme schemes of some of her early poems. They have come up with deft equivalents for her pervasive wordplay, and have recreated the jaunty, precise, deceptively casual free verse of her late work. My only complaint about this splendid book is that it comes without any supplementary information. It has no introduction, no commentary or notes, no afterword—the reader who wants help with Szymborska's Polish references, or a sense of the biographical, linguistic, and political overtones of her work, has to look elsewhere.

Szymborska came of age during World War II, and spent much of her life under Stalinism. Thus she saw her country twice destroyed. She made her literary debut in 1945 with a poem in a Cracow newspaper and in 1949 her first volume was scheduled for publication, but it never appeared. That year Socialist Realism was imposed on Polish artists and, as Czeslaw Milosz has written, "the world of Orwell ceased to be a literary fiction in Poland." Szymborska's manuscript was attacked for being morbidly obsessed with the war and inaccessible to the masses, and was therefore unpublishable.

The poets of Szymborska's generation responded to authoritarian pressures in different ways. Some, like Zbigniew Herbert and Miron Bialoszewski, chose internal exile, or "writing for the drawer"; others, like Rózewicz, who was already famous, and Szymborska, who was virtually unknown, tried to conform. The poems that subsequently went into *That's What We Live For* and *Questions Put to Myself* range from dogmatic denunciations of the old order to strident condemnations of Western imperialism, and they take the Party line on any number of subjects—from the Allied release of German war criminals, to the Korean War, to the sufferings of working people under the capitalist system. *Questions Put to Myself* contains a few reflective lyrics, largely love poems, but most of the poems are on contemporary issues and make discouraging reading. One critic has

described Szymborska's style in these early books as "agitation-propaganda in a chamber-music manner."

But with her third collection, published after the "thaw" of 1956—the year that censorship famously loosened its grip on Poland—Szymborska began to sound her own note. The three poems that Baranczak and Cavanagh have included from *Calling Out to Yeti* reveal a disillusion with Stalinist politics, and are marked by mordant humor and a deep skepticism. The figure of Yeti, the Abominable Snowman, is the book's central metaphor for Stalinism. Believing in communism is like believing in the Abominable Snowman: neither offers any human warmth or artistic comfort. **"Notes from a Nonexistent Himalayan Expedition"** ends:

> Yeti, we've got Shakespeare there.
> Yeti, we play solitaire
> and violin. At nightfall,
> we turn lights on, Yeti.
>
> Up here it's neither moon nor earth.
> Tears freeze.
> Oh Yeti, semi-moonman,
> turn back, think again!
>
> I called this to the Yeti
> inside four walls of avalanche,
> stomping my feet for warmth
> on the everlasting
> snow.

The opening poem of *Calling Out to Yeti,* **"Brueghel's Two Monkeys,"** takes off from the painting *Two Monkeys in Chains,* in which a pair of monkeys are chained by the waist in the embrasure of a fortress wall. One is turned toward the misty panorama of Antwerp in the background, the other away from it, emblems perhaps of the poet's divided consciousness.

> This is what I see in my dreams about final exams:
> two monkeys, chained to the floor, sit on the
> windowsill,
> the sky behind them flutters,
> the sea is taking its bath.
>
> The exam is History of Mankind.
> I stammer and hedge.

Brueghel's painting has been understood as a protest against the Spanish occupation of the Netherlands in the mid-sixteenth century; so, too, in 1957 Szymborska's poem was widely interpreted as a protest against Stalinist repression.

> One monkey stares and listens with mocking
> disdain,

the other seems to be dreaming away—
but when it's clear I don't know what to say
he prompts me with a gentle
clinking of his chain.

In the Sixties Szymborska truly hit her stride. From that time her voice has increasingly taken on the sharp sting of experience, while she has not so much developed as perfected her strategies. In many of her poems she first considers a subject, next embraces it, then she reverses herself, undercutting what went before with sharp, disillusioned comment. "See how efficient it still is, / how it keeps itself in shape— / our century's hatred," she writes, and "Our twentieth century was going to improve on the others":

A couple of problems weren't going
to come up anymore:
hunger, for example,
and war, and so forth.

There was going to be respect
for helpless people's helplessness,
trust, that kind of stuff.

Anyone who planned to enjoy the world
is now faced
with a hopeless task.

Stupidity isn't funny.
Wisdom isn't gay.
Hope
isn't that young girl anymore,
et cetera, alas.

God was finally going to believe
in a man both good and strong,
but good and strong
are still two different men.

                              (**"The Century's Decline"**)

Szymborska is a highly conceptual poet, and an idiosyncratic one. Reading the great twentieth-century poets—Eliot, for example, or Vallejo—one feels the language moving mysteriously ahead of the thought, the combination of words unlocking perceptions deeper than the conscious mind; hence the high premium these poets place on the irrational and the unconscious in the creative process. In Szymborska's case the governing rationale of a poem comes first and then develops in unexpected directions, while the poem quietly shifts to close range. **"Could Have"** appears to be set in wartime Poland during the German occupation:

It could have happened.
It had to happen.
It happened earlier. Later.

Nearer. Father off.
It happened, but not to you.

You were saved because you were the first.
You were saved because you were the last.
Alone. With others.
On the right. The left.
Because it was raining. Because of the shade.
Because the day was sunny.

You were in luck—there was a forest.
You were in luck—there were no trees.
You were in luck—a rake, a hook, a beam, a brake,
a jamb, a turn, a quarter inch, an instant. . . .

So you're here? Still dizzy from another dodge,
close shave, reprieve?
One hole in the net and you slipped through?
I couldn't be more shocked or speechless.
Listen,
how your heart pounds inside me.

While the poem recalls the brutal uncertainty of the Nazi period, it also addresses the radical contingency of experience itself—the "sheer dumb luck"—that leads to one's survival. So, too, there is a sense of the vast distance between simple things ("a rake, a hook, a beam, a brake . . . ") and how much life depends on them. Even the most innocuous objects can become sinister or hazardous, while ridiculous coincidences can account for one's survival. It's as if we're all actors in an unrehearsed slapstick comedy. But the poem ends in bitter irony, for the speaker has had her share of unwitting reprieves, and ruefully pays for them with an incurably guilty conscience.

Szymborska's mastery of the conditional lends her poetry its wit and its experimental feeling. She will run through all the ramifications of an idea to see what it will yield; indeed, she pursues large, unanswerable questions nonchalantly, with an offhand charm. She typically begins a poem with a simple paradoxical assertion—"The Great Mother has no face" (**"A Paleolithic Fertility Fetish"**) or "Four billion people on this earth, / but my imagination is still the same" (**"A Large Number"**)—which the poem breezily sets out to explore. Just as often a philosophical question is raised: Can time be stopped by a work of art? (**"The People on the Bridge"**); Is there an afterlife? (**"Elegiac Calculation"**) Because of her method there's not much descriptive writing in her work ("Save me, sacred folly of description!" she cries in **"Clochard"**), though she is capable of quick, precise brushstrokes.

Often she meditates on huge general subjects such as "Hatred" and "True Love" and ranges from the mathematical concept of "Pi" to the socialist ideal of Utopia to the joys of composing poetry. Characteristically a poem is made up of questions (**"Plotting with the Dead"**). Or of apologies, as in **"Under One Small Star"**:

> My apologies to chance for calling it necessity.
> My apologies to necessity if I'm mistaken, after all.
> Please, don't be angry, happiness, that I take you as
> my due.
> May my dead be patient with the way my memories
> fade.
> My apologies to time for all the world I overlook
> each second.
> My apologies to past loves for thinking that the
> latest is the first.
> Forgive me, distant wars, for bringing flowers
> home.
> Forgive me, open wounds, for pricking my finger.
> I apologize for my record of minuets to those who
> cry from the depths.

As this poem progresses the speaker keeps shifting from one category to another. She begs forgiveness from inanimate objects, and even concepts, then from places and from groups of people—everything is anthropomorphized. She herself feels unequal to the world's sufferings, and fears that by narrowing her focus on the world to make it manageable, she has trivialized it. But all viewpoints are incomplete, all efforts inadequate: "My apologies to everything that I can't be everywhere at once. / My apologies to everyone that I can't be each woman and each man." The poem's conclusion amounts to a small *ars poetica*:

> Don't bear me ill will, speech, that I borrow
> weighty words,
> then labor heavily so that they may seem light.

Szymborska plays with scale and changes in voice throughout her work. She will take a nonhuman perspective in order to expose what people are really like, speaking through some small animal like a tarsier, or from the point of view of a god observing human beings from a vast height and in a bemused outrage, as in **"No End of Fun"**:

> So he's got to have happiness,
> he's got to have truth, too,
> he's got to have eternity—
> did you ever!

The miniaturization of human beings gives a Swiftian quality to Szymborska's work, as she shifts the scale to examine humanity under a magnifying glass. And she is an especially keen ironist of sentimentality and political cant.

> And who's this little fellow in his itty-bitty robe?
> That's tiny baby Adolf, the Hitler's' little boy!

(**"Hitler's First Photograph"**)

The key to Szymborska's style may well be her subversive variations on familiar rhetoric, as she enters a debate already in progress or responds to a well-known story with a surprising perspective. In **"An Opinion on the Question of Pornography"** she turns the argument for legalizing pornography on its head to include the scandalous pleasures of thought itself: "There's nothing more debauched than thinking," the speaker declares; "This sort of wantonness runs wild like a wind-borne-weed / on a plot laid out for daisies." The context is the growing underground intellectual dissent of the late Seventies, and the period of martial law in the early Eighties when people gathered in private apartments to talk about forbidden books. Sometimes the secret police parked outside to intimidate participants in this orgy of thinking. The poem is filled with double entendres ("It's shocking, the positions, / the unchecked simplicity with which / one mind contrives to fertilize another!"), but there is a sinister undertow:

> Only now and then does somebody get up,
> go to the window,
> and through a crack in the curtains
> take a peep out at the street.

One of Szymborska's most daring poems, **"Lot's Wife,"** retells the biblical story from the vantage point of the main character.

> They say I looked back out of curiosity,
> but I could have had other reasons.
> I looked back mourning my silver bowl.
> Carelessly, while tying my sandal strap.
> So I wouldn't have to keep staring at the righteous
> nape
> of my husband Lot's neck.
> From the sudden conviction that if I dropped dead
> he wouldn't so much as hesitate.
> From the disobedience of the meek.
> Checking for pursuers.
> Struck by the silence, hoping
> God had changed his mind.

Each new reason displaces the ones before, and we can't reliably tell whether Lot's wife turned back from torpor or desolation, from shame or loss. It may be too complicated even for her to comprehend ("I looked back for all the reasons given above"); or it may have been inadvertent ("I looked back involuntarily"). The intimacy with which Szymborska treats the legend here transforms it, and for all its playfulness it echoes with the tragedy of a woman's bitter fate:

> No, no. I ran on,
> I crept, I flew upward

until darkness fell from the heavens
and with it scorching gravel and dead birds.
I couldn't breathe and spun around and around.
Anyone who saw me must have thought I was
dancing.
It's not inconceivable that my eyes were open.
It's possible I fell facing the city.

Szymborska's poetry takes place much of the time, as here, on the edge of an abyss. It is the poetry of the close shave. And it's not only accidents we contend with, but history itself, with its hatreds and more deaths than we can count ("the impeccable executioner / towering over its soiled victim"), catastrophes that defy the imagination. Yet the world keeps mysteriously renewing itself. This is the theme of **"Reality Demands"**:

Reality demands
that we also mention this:
Life goes on.
It continues at Cannae and Borodino,
at Kosovo Polje and Guernica.

There's a gas station
on a little square in Jericho,
and wet paint
on park benches in Bila Hora.
Letters fly back and forth
between Pearl Harbor and Hastings,
a moving van passes
beneath the eye of the lion at Cheronea,
and the blooming orchards near Verdun
cannot escape
the approaching atmospheric front.

There is so much Everything
that Nothing is hidden quite nicely.

Eventually even the worst of destructions can recede: "On tragic mountain passes / the wind rips hats from unwitting heads / and we can't help / laughing at that."

Yet for all Szymborska's bitter awareness of human fallibility, time and again commonplace miracles happen: fluttering white doves, a small cloud upstaging the moon, mild winds turning gusty in a hard storm. Szymborska slyly entitles a poem about evolution **"Thomas Mann."** "Dear mermaids, it was bound to happen. / Beloved fauns and honorable angels, / evolution has emphatically cast you out." But Nature never anticipated such a creature as the German novelist: "She somehow missed the moment when a mammal turned up / with its hand miraculously feathered by a fountain pen." So, too, coming upon Szymborska's work, with its strange mixture of world-weariness and exhilaration, can seem something of a miracle.

Amy Gamerman (essay date 4 October 1996)

SOURCE: "Pole Wins Nobel Literature Prize," in Wall Street Journal, Vol. CCXXVII, No. 68, October 4, 1996, p. A5.

[*In the following essay, Gamerman reviews the themes of Szymborska's poetry.*]

In **"Evaluation of an Unwritten Poem,"** Wislawa Szymborska, the Polish poet who won the Nobel Prize for Literature yesterday, writes of a poet who contemplates the cosmos—and comes up short:

"In her depiction of the sky, one detects a certain
helplessness,
the authoress is lost in a terrifying expanse,
she is startled by the planets' lifelessness,
and within her mind (which can only be called
imprecise)
a question soon arises:
whether we are, in the end, alone
under the sun, all suns that ever shone."

The authoress's intentions, the narrator confesses, "might shine brighter beneath a less naive pen. / Not under this one, alas."

It seems fitting that in naming its new laureate, the Swedish Academy hailed the 73-year-old Ms. Szymborska as a poet for whom "no questions are of such significance as those that are native." The author of 16 collections of poetry, Ms. Szymborska asks big questions about life, death and the meaning that poetry can claim in the face of them, in language that is direct, lucid and surpassingly modest. Citing the rich inspiration and fluid grace of Ms. Szymborska's verse, the academy hailed her as the Mozart of poetry—with "something of the fury of Beethoven."

Although hardly a household name here, Ms. Szymborska has popped up at Nobel time as a potential candidate for years. She's certainly well-known in Poland, where her work is said to have inspired everyone from rock musicians to the late film director Krzysztof Kieslowski, whose movie *Red* was launched by her poem **"Love at First Sight."** The 1996 laureate was born in 1923 in the small western town of Bnin (now a part of Kornik), but has lived in Cracow since she was eight years old. She published her first poem in a newspaper supplement while she was studying Polish literature and sociology at the Jagiellonian University in 1945. Her first effort was titled, appropriately enough, **"I seek the word."**

Ms. Szymborska has made seeking words her life's work, both as a poet and as the author of a magazine column called "Non-compulsory Reading," in which she reviewed everything from cookbooks to T.S. Eliot's cat poems from 1953 to 1986. Some words, however, the poet has chosen to discard. She disavowed her 1952 debut collection, *That's Why We Are Alive,* and the 1954 collection that followed it as attempts to conform to communist-sponsored doctrines of social realism. That gesture was not lost on members of the Swedish Academy, who specified that they were awarding the Nobel to Ms. Szymborska on the strength of the poems written since 1957—"when censorship had lost its stranglehold."

Although the academy cited the poet's 1957 collection, *Calling out to Yeti,* as a reaction against Stalin ("Yeti, crime is not all / we're up to down there," the narrator of one poem insists to the abominable snowman), Ms. Szymborska's poetry is not overtly political. Three English editions of her poetry have been published here, most recently, *View With a Grain of Sand,* translated by Stanislaw Baranczak and Clare Cavanagh. Spanning some 36 years, the poems in this collection leapfrog from one unlikely subject to another: Rubens's nudes, a poetry reading, an onion. The poems in her 1962 collection, *Salt,* capture an opera singer mid-aria— "Though doom be nigh, / she'll keep her chin and pitch up high!"—and a sweaty bodybuilding contestant, who "grunts while showing his poses and paces. / His back alone has twenty different faces."

The poems are vivid, witty and even funny, but mortality often laps at their edges. In **"View With a Grain of Sand,"** from the 1986 collection, *The People on the Bridge,* Ms. Szymborska seems to find even poetry itself a vain exercise in the face of death, musing:

> Time has passed like a courier with urgent news.
> But that's just our simile.
> The character is invented, his haste is make-
> believe,
> his news inhuman.

The poems in her 1993 collection, *The End and the Beginning,* tackle the subjects of war, ethnic hatred and the foretaste of death the poet experiences in her own loss of memory. But time and again, her verse returns—as if drawn by an invisible magnet—to the elusive miracle of the life all around her: like the "Ants stitching in the grass" and the "white butterfly . . . fluttering through the air / on wings that are its alone" in **"No Title Required."**

Most striking, in **"Maybe All This"** the poet returns to the question posed by the hapless authoress in her **"Evaluation of an Unwritten Poem"** and turns it upside down: What if we're not alone? What if the cosmos is contemplating us? Wondering if our evanescent lives could possibly be of interest to heavenly spectators, the poet—an optimist in spite of herself—answers yes.

> They've got a taste for trivia up there?
> Look! on the big screen a little girl
> is sewing a button on her sleeve.
> The radar shrieks,
> the staff comes at a run.
> What a darling little being
> with its tiny heart beating inside it!
> How sweet, its solemn
> threading of the needle!
> Someone cries enraptured:
> Get the Boss,
> tell him he's got to see this for himself!

Dean E. Murphy (essay 4 October 1996)

SOURCE: "Reclusive Polish Poet Awarded Nobel Prize," in *Los Angeles Times,* October 4, 1996, p. A1.

[In the following essay, Murphy relates the reponses of other Polish writers to the announcement of Szymborska's award.]

Polish poet Wislawa Szymborska, a reclusive widow whose seductively simple verse has captured the wit and wisdom of everyday life for the past half century, has been awarded the 1996 Nobel Prize in Literature, the Swedish Academy announced Thursday in Stockholm.

Unassuming, shy and obsessively protective of her privacy, Szymborska had been considered a longshot for the prestigious prize, which was presented to another poet, Irishman Seamus Heaney, last year. Although she is perhaps Poland's most famous woman writer, Szymborska is often overshadowed in Polish literary circles by poets Zbigniew Herbert and Tadeusz Rozewicz, both of whom have been mentioned as Nobel contenders.

"She has gone through a long evolution and has reached maturity," said renowned Polish poet Czeslaw Milosz, a professor at UC Berkeley, who won the Nobel Prize in 1980. "Polish poetry in the 20th century has reached a strong international position on the European continent. Szymborska represents it well."

Szymborska reacted to news of her award with characteristic humility and humor. She granted several brief telephone interviews from a faraway mountain retreat she frequents in southern Poland, then took an afternoon nap—with strict orders not to be disturbed.

"I have accepted it with surprise, of course with great joy, but also with bewilderment and embarrassment," she told a gathering of reporters later in the day, after relenting to demands for a public appearance. "My poetry is quite private. I am a private person. . . . I will have to be a bit of an offi-cial person, and I don't like this, because I'm not a movie star."

At 73, Szymborska is the matriarch of Polish poets, with her first collection of poems published in 1952 and her latest still being penned when the telephone call came from Stockholm. Although the volume of her work is relatively modest, the Swedish Academy referred to it as powerful art that combines "esprit, inventiveness and empathy."

Critics describe her poetry as emotional, striking—sometimes even arresting—but rarely personal. Milosz characterizes Szymborska's style as "reverse-confessional," directing her art from a carefully detached perch. When her poems do erupt from the depths of her soul, the result is so distilled that only her closest associates recognize the inspiration.

One recent poem about the death of a longtime companion, for example, told the story of their cat suddenly finding itself alone in an empty apartment. To the unknowing reader, the poem offers no clue to its intensely personal subject matter.

"This poem really moved me very much, because I knew the story behind it," said Jan Jozef Szczepanski, a prominent Polish author and friend of Szymborska. "They both cared very much for this animal, and it was her way of dealing with the death."

As with many Polish writers of her generation, Szymborska briefly dabbled in social realism—two early works glorified communism—but she quickly went on to write critically about totalitarianism, including one poem that likened Josef Stalin to the Abominable Snowman. In a later verse, **"Children of Our Age,"** Szymborska cast politics as the obsession of our time.

> Whether you like it or not,
>
> your genes have a political past,
> your skin, a political cast,
> your eyes, a political slant.
> Whatever you say reverberates,
> whatever you don't say speaks for itself.
> So either way you're talking politics.

In the 1980s, Szymborska collaborated under a pseudonym in a Polish samizdat, or underground publication, as well as an exile magazine published in Paris. Earlier, she worked for nearly four decades as a book critic for a now-defunct Polish literary magazine, reviewing everything from T. S. Eliot cat poems to gardening manuals.

Her keen wit, clever mastery of the Polish lexicon and no-nonsense commentary on basic issues of human existence

have made her Poland's most popular woman poet, with her most recent collection of works in its second printing.

"She writes very wise poetry, and part of its magic is that it doesn't give you any resistance when you read it," said Ryszard Krynicki, a Polish poet who publishes Szymborska's Polish-language works. "This doesn't mean that it is sim-plistic poetry—just that the more of her poetry you read, the more you discover new meanings."

Her poems have been translated into numerous languages, including English, but she remains relatively obscure out-side her homeland. The subtleties of her poetry, the Swedish Academy said, do not always translate well, something that may contribute to her lack of an international reputation. The academy acknowledged, however, that a 1989 Swedish translation of selected poems strongly influenced members' impressions of her writing, and Szymborska credited her Swedish translator with securing the Nobel.

"If this had been a mediocre translator, we would not be talk-ing today," she said.

Three books of her poetry have been published in English, including **View With a Grain of Sand,** released last year by Harcourt Brace & Co. Last January, the Village Voice de-scribed Szymborska as "a tremendous find" when preview-ing a public reading of her translated work in New York. "Her humor is mournful, her sadness antic, her sense of in-teriority completely available to the senses," the newspaper said.

In announcing the award, the Swedish Academy praised Szymborska for poetry that "with ironic precision allows the historical and biological context to come to light in frag-ments of human reality."

The academy drew special attention to a 1980 poem, **"Noth-ing Twice,"** as illustrative of "a streak of lightning" in her art. The final stanza reads:

> With smiles and kisses, we prefer
>
> to seek accord beneath our star,
> although we're different (we concur)
> just as two drops of water are.

Los Angeles Times (essay date 4 October 1996)

SOURCE: "Near a People's Heart," in *Los Angeles Times*, October 4, 1996, p. B8.

[*In the following essay, the critic considers the significance of Szymborska's award to Polish letters.*]

"Poets are the unacknowledged legislators of the world," Percy Shelley once said. He was speaking from early 19th-century Europe, a world away from 1990s America, where unacknowledged power is more likely to lie with spin doctors and political action committees. What Shelley said, however, largely remains true in Poland today: The country has been carved up so many times by invaders since the late 18th century that its heart has remained whole only in its literature.

This is what makes Wislawa Szymborska, who Thursday was awarded the Nobel Prize for Literature, both a political and artistic leader. The intellectual Polish writer Czeslaw Milosz may be better known abroad, but Szymborska is the real "people's poet" of her nation.

You wouldn't guess this from the Swedish Academy's amusingly incomprehensible statement that it was honoring Szymborska "for poetry that . . . allows the historical and biological context to come to light in fragments of human reality." Maybe it was the translation.

The intellectual Polish writer Czeslaw Milosz may be better known abroad, but Szymborska is the real "people's poet" of her nation.

—Los Angeles Times

But her work speaks for itself. **"In Praise of Feeling Bad About Yourself,"** for instance, begins with this observation of some carefree animals: "The buzzard never says it is to blame . . . / When the piranha strikes, it feels no shame." The poem goes on to defend the animals' failure to reflect: "Why should they when they know / they're right?" Finally, the poem concludes that "On this third planet of the sun . . . / a clear conscience is Number One." Is the poem a spirited defense of gut instinct, of living in the moment? Or is it a subtle indictment of humans for living instinctively rather than conscientiously?

Unlike those Eastern European writers who moralize in heavy-handed prose, the genuinely humble Szymborska lets us answer the question for ourselves.

David Streitfield (essay date 4 October 1996)

SOURCE: "Szymborska? It Means 'Famous'," in *Washington Post,* October 4, 1996, pp. F1, F3.

[*Below, Streitfield introduces the Nobel Prize winner to English-speaking readers.*]

Vihs-WAH-vah sheem-BOHR-skah.

Pronouncing the name of the 1996 Nobel laureate in literature is the hardest part. Once that's done, Wislawa Szymborska's poetry slips down like melted snow. From **"Writing a Résumé"**:

> Concise, well-chosen facts are de rigueur.
> Landscapes are replaced by addresses,
> shaky memories give way to unshakable dates.
>
> Of all your loves, mention only the marriage;
> of all your children, only those who were born.

To praise the Polish poet, the Swedish Academy resorted to musical comparisons. It called her a "Mozart of poetry" and said she combined elegance of language with "the fury of Beethoven."

The 73-year-old Szymborska tackles the most difficult subjects—hatred, love, the persistence of memory, the charms of life as well as its ravages—in the simplest language. Her poems affirm what she calls "The joy of writing, / The power of preserving. / Revenge of a mortal hand."

Still, for the English-speaking world, Szymborska qualifies as the most obscure Nobel selection since the Czech Jaroslav Sifters in 1984. If you want to be generous and include things like a special issue of the *Quarterly Review of Literature,* she's had four books published in this country.

Someone from NBC Radio called a local literary editor on Wednesday to arrange for some commentary on the winner but withdrew the request after learning it was Szymborska. Too little known in America, he explained. It's poetry, it's Polish, no one cares.

> Twelve people in the room, eight seats to spare—
> it's time to start this cultural affair.
> Half came inside because it started raining,
> the rest are relatives. O Muse.
> —from **"Poetry Reading"**

In Poland, of course, it was a different story. Szymborska's honor, which translates into $1.12 million and a better-than-average shot at literary immortality, topped all the news programs and soothed even the most contentious of political debates. A critical day-long argument in the country's senate over relaxing abortion restrictions was silenced, at least for a few moments, by the surprise news from Speaker Adam Struzik. Applause erupted on the senate floor.

The goodwill spread even to the most no-nonsense of Polish officials, Finance Minister Grzegorz Kolodko. He said he was sending Szymborska 21 red roses and promised to exempt her from taxes on the prize.

The announcement by the Swedish Academy at 1 p.m. in Stockholm set loose a band of reporters in search of the poet, who happened to be at a resort for writers in the Polish mountain town of Zakopane. A news conference was organized.

"My plans?" Szymborska responded to a reporter. "It's so nice to be asked about my plans. I have no idea about my plans." She later described the prize as "an extremely big honor. This means happiness and responsibility." But she fretted: "From now on, I will have to become an official person, which I don't like to be. It's against my nature."

This attitude has led to a certain obscurity. The poet doesn't do readings or appear at poetry conferences. In the first three decades of her career, she gave exactly one extensive interview. In a rare comment, she described her method: "I borrow words weighed with pathos, and then try hard to make them seem light."

> The body is a reservoir of pain;
> it has to eat and breathe the air, and sleep;
> it has thin skin and the blood is just beneath it;
> it has a good supply of teeth and fingernails;
> its bones can be broken; its joints can be stretched.
> In tortures, all of this is considered.
>
> —from **"Tortures"**

Most of the time, she's not keen on explanations. "The fact that with one writer, the words fall together into units, that are alive and enduring, and with another, they do not, is decided in a realm that's not easily comprehensible to anyone," she wrote in a 1973 book review.

Szymborska is only the ninth woman to win a Nobel in literature since the prize was first awarded in 1901, although she's the third in the past six years. She's the fourth Polish laureate, after Henryk Sienkiewicz in 1905, Wladyslaw Reymont in 1924 and Czeslaw Milosz in 1980.

"Again, Poland was noticed," former president Lech Walesa bragged to Radio Zet. He said Szymborska was "so modest as a person and so great in spirit."

But the greatness wasn't always so apparent. In the 1983 edition of Milosz's *History of Polish Literature,* the senior poet basically dismissed Szymborska, saying, "It would be unjust to present her as a poetess of narrow range.... Yet she often leans toward preciosity."

There's evidence Milosz has since revised that harsh judgment; in a new anthology, *A Book of Luminous Things,* he uses five of her poems. Perhaps he is no longer angry at how

she had briefly hewed to the communist line early in her career.

Szymborska published her first poem in 1945; by the end of the decade, she had a book ready. The communists, however, were asserting control over the country's cultural life. The young poet was found guilty of dwelling morbidly on World War II and being less than gung-ho about the great socialist world to come.

Publication was canceled. In 1952, a more politically acceptable collection was published under the title *That's What We Live For.* The book was dismissed by one critic as "agitation-propaganda in a chamber-music manner," and later cut loose by the poet as well: Nothing from it appears in her collected works.

By 1956, she was comparing Stalin to the Abominable Snowman, and writing much better poems in the bargain. Her collected work, the critic Edward Hirsch wrote in the *New York Review of Books* last year, takes place much of the time "on the edge of an abyss. It is the poetry of the close shave. And it's not only accidents we contend with, but history itself, with its hatreds and more deaths than we can count . . . Yet the world keeps mysteriously renewing itself."

At a luncheon yesterday at the Library of Congress for U.S. Poet Laureate Robert Hass, a number of poetry buffs confessed they either hadn't heard of her or hadn't read her. But Hass himself was full of praise.

"This is an unusual case of justice being done," he said. "I thought this was a year they would take care of politics. Instead, they took care of poetry." He added that last spring he had invited Szymborska to the library, but she had declined.

The only book of the poet's that has been readily available in English is *View With a Grain of Sand,* published by Harcourt Brace a year ago. It was well received—this newspaper called it "brilliant"—and won a PEN/Book-of-the-Month Club Translation Prize. The publisher sold about 4,000 paperback copies, quite good for a translated poet.

Local bookstores had a single copy, at most, on hand yesterday; they were immediately gone. By noon, Harcourt had orders for 12,000 more. "For a Polish poet, that's not bad," said Harcourt publicist Dori Weintraub.

Jane Berlez (essay date 4 October 1996)

SOURCE: "Polish Poet, Observer of Daily Life, Wins Nobel," in *The New York Times,* October 4, 1996, p. C5.

[*Below, Berlez offers reminiscences of Szymborska from friends and writers in Poland.*]

Wislawa Szymborska, a self-effacing 73-year-old Polish poet who collects trashy postcards because she says trash has no pretensions, won the Nobel Prize for Literature today.

This year's prize is the biggest ever, $1.12 million The announcement by the Swedish Academy surprised some in the literary world who had expected the 1996 award to go to a novelist because last year's winner was the Irish poet Seamus Heaney.

Ms. Szymborska, whose name is pronounced vees-WAH-wah sheem-BOR-ska, is little known outside Poland, where she is revered as a distinguished poet from the intellectual center of Cracow. She stresses the quirks and unexpected nature of daily life and of personal relations in poetry that spans five decades. Her early work, which she has since renounced, embraced the Socialist Realism of the Stalinist era.

In its award citation the Swedish Academy noted that Ms. Szymborska has been described as "the Mozart of poetry, not without justice in view of her wealth of inspiration and the veritable ease with which her words seem to fall into place."

Word of the prize reached Ms. Szymborska in the southern mountain town of Zakopane, where she was staying at a writers' retreat. Staff members there said she was having lunch and could not be disturbed.

But after a flurry of congratulatory phone calls, including one from Czeslaw Milosz, the Polish-born poet who won the Nobel Prize for literature in 1980, Ms. Szymborska, a diminutive woman with slightly graying hair, a cigarette always between her fingers, got up the gumption for a news conference.

"I don't think much of myself, but I'm afraid that saying that will be taken as trying to charm the audience," she said. But she added, "The poet as a person is in a way self-conceited: she has to believe in herself and hope she has something to say."

The citation quoted one of her poems, **"Nothing Twice,"** from 1980, the year before martial law was declared in a crackdown on the democracy movement in Communist Poland.

The final stanza reads in the English translation:

> With smiles and kisses we prefer
> to seek accord beneath our star,
> although we're different (we concur)
> just as two drops of water are

In a telephone interview from Zakopane, Ms. Szymborska said her work was personal rather than political.

"Of course, life crosses politics," she said, "but my poems are strictly not political. They are more about people and life."

An ebullient Mr. Milosz said in an interview from his home in Berkeley, Calif., that Ms. Szymborska's award represented a "triumph for Polish poetry in the 20th century" and added, "Two Nobel poet laureates from a given country is quite good"

Ms. Szymborska's first poem was published in a Cracow newspaper in 1945 Her early work dealt with Western imperialism and depicted the suffering of the proletariat under capitalism.

But in 1954 in a collection, ***Questions Put to Myself,*** there were glimmers of the sparse style that characterizes her later work. By 1957 she was disillusioned enough to draw a parallel between Stalin, who died in 1953, and an Abominable Snowman in a collection titled ***Calling Out to Yeti.***

The literary critic Edward Hirsch noted in *The New York Review of Books* earlier this year that Ms. Szymborska had concluded that believing in Communism was like believing in the Abominable Snowman: neither offered human warmth or artistic comfort.

Mr. Milosz said that Ms. Szymborska passed through a long evolution as a poet. "I didn't like her early work," he said. "She went through a Stalinist phase. But every volume is better." Her later work was unusual for the 20th century, he said. "As a person and in her poetry, she is very attenuated. It is just a whisper."

One of Ms. Szymborska's handful of close friends, Jan Pieszczachowicz, the president of the Cracow branch of the Polish Writers' Union described her as "delicate" and "sensitive," with "a wonderful sense of humor."

"In her poems there is a certain sadness, and nostalgia, a general fear of civilization and the crisis of values," Mr. Pieszczachowicz said. "But contrary to other poets, Szymborska says that one can still live nobly in her poems, she talks about ordinary everyday things, which, according to the poet, live their own separate lives. In her poetry there is no cheap sentimentalism."

Ms. Szymborska, who also won the Polish PEN club's poetry award this week, lives in a modest two-room apartment in the center of Cracow, where a cherished tall poplar grazes the balcony

She avoids literary gatherings and conferences and traipses

around in old coats and sweaters, Mr. Pieszczachowicz said. As much as she disdains crowds, she likes to surround herself with a few friends "She likes herring, beans Breton style and a glass of vodka," he said.

In a poem, **"Kiczowaty"** (**"Kitschy"**), dedicated to his daughter, Mr. Pieszczachowicz said, Ms. Szymborska referred to the intrinsic value of the postcards she collects, explaining that "trash does not pretend to be anything better than it is."

Born in 1923 in Kurnik, a small town near the western city of Poznan, Ms. Szymborska moved with her parents to Cracow at the age of 8. She attended Jagiellonian University there.

Mr. Pleszczachowicz said Ms. Szymborska was married twice. Her first husband was a poet, Adam Wlodek, whom she divorced. Her second husband, Kornel Filipowicz, was a writer with whom she shared a love of fishing. Mr. Filipowicz's death in the early 1990's inspired a collection of poems that appeared in 1993, *The End and the Beginning.*

Beata Chmiel, the editor of *Ex Libris,* a leading Polish literary magazine, said that collection included **"Cat in the Empty Apartment,"** which she described as "the best poem I have read about death." Ms. Chmiel translated the first lines thus:

> To die
> This we cannot do to a cat
> What can a cat do in the empty apartment.

"Her poetry is something very personal," Ms. Chmiel said, "and this is the victory of the Nobel Prize committee. They have given the prize to an unknown poet of Poland, but this poet can be very close to people all over the world: men, women, black and white."

In an interview with Ms. Chmiel in *Ex Libris* in 1994, Ms. Szymborska scoffed at the idea that there should be anything like "womanly" poetry.

"I think that dividing literature or poetry into women's and men's poetry is starting to sound absurd," she said. "Perhaps there was a time when a woman's world did exist, separated from certain issues and problems, but at present there are no things that would not concern women and men at the same time. We do not live in the boudoir anymore."

Ms. Szymborska is the fifth Polish-born writer to win the Nobel literature prize. The novelist Henryk Sienkiewicz won in 1905 for his book *Quo Vadis,* and Wladyslaw Reymont won in 1924 for his rendition of rural life, *The Peasants.* Isaac Bashevis Singer, who wrote about Polish-Jewish life

from his perch in New York City, was awarded the prize in 1978, and Mr. Milosz, who is based at the University of California, Berkeley but keeps an apartment in Cracow, won in 1980.

The elusive Ms. Szymborska confessed that the prize would bring some unwelcome changes. "I have no defense mechanism," she told Mr. Milosz when he called from California. "I'm a private person. The most difficult thing will be to write a speech. I will be writing it for a month. I don't know what I will be talking about, but I will talk about you"

By the end of the day, Ms. Szymborska said she had had enough, and was retreating to a place in Poland even more remote than Zakopane, where nobody, and certainly not reporters, could find her.

Dinitia Smith (essay date 21 October 1996)

SOURCE: "Competing Versions of Poem by Nobelist," in *The New York Times,* October 21, 1996, pp. C13-14.

[*In the following essay, Smith focuses on the difference between two translated versions of a poem by Szymborska that appeared in both* The New Yorker *and* The New Republic.]

There was a wee contretemps in the literary world last week when *The New Yorker* and *The New Republic* inadvertently published the same poem by Wislawa Szymborska of Poland, winner of this year's Nobel Prize for Literature. Not only that but the two translations had subtly different tones, and the endings, depending on how seriously one takes these things, had slightly different meanings in the end, though, the whole matter proved to be something of a post-structuralist's dream.

The poem, called **"Some People Like Poetry"** in *The New Republic* and **"Some Like Poetry"** in *The New Yorker,* is a gentle riff on the fact that while people cannot agree on a definition of poetry itself, there are those who love it nonetheless.

The *New Yorker* version was translated by Joanna Trzeciak. The one in *The New Republic,* which was translated by Stanislaw Baranczak and Clare Cavanagh, had been submitted to *The New Yorker,* but not published, before Ms. Szymborska's recent fame.

Traditionally a magazine prides itself on being the first and only one to print a poem.

"What?" said Alice Quinn, *The New Yorker*'s poetry editor, when first told of the similarity. "If I'd known about it I wouldn't have published the same poem."

Technically, *The New Yorker* was first out of the gate. Its poem came out in a special double issue on politics dated Oct 21. *The New Republic's* issue was dated Oct 28. Still the two translations are on the newsstands at the same time.

At *The New Republic,* the literary editor, Leon Weiseltier, seemed less concerned than Ms. Quinn. "I knew about it," he said, "but I don't look to my right and left. *The New Yorker* can do what they want to do."

How, then, did this come to pass? After Ms. Szymborska won the Nobel Prize on Oct. 3, editors all over the world scrambled to find poems of hers to publish.

"Some People Like Poetry"

Some people—
that means not everyone.
Not even most of them, only a few.
Not counting school, where you have to,
and poets themselves,
you might end up with something like two per thousand.

Like—
but then, you can like chicken noodle soup,
or compliments, or the color blue,
your old scarf,
your own way,
petting the dog.

Poetry—
but what is poetry anyway?
More than one rickety answer
has tumbled since that question first was raised.
But I just keep on not knowing, and I cling to that
like a redemptive handrail.
   —translated, from the Polish, by Stanislaw
      Baranczak and Clare Cavanagh

New Republic, October 28, 1996, p. 40.

Ms. Quinn said that when she received **"Some Like Poetry,"** from Ms. Trzeclak, "I was very happy," and quickly accepted it. Nevertheless, Ms. Quinn phoned Mr. Baranczak, whose translations of Ms. Szymborska's work had appeared before in *The New Yorker,* to let him know she was using a Szymborska poem translated by another person.

But, Mr. Baranczak said, he and Ms. Cavanagh did not submit their translation to *The New Republic* until the following day, after they knew that Ms. Quinn was planning to use Ms. Trzeclak's translation.

"He didn't tell me," Ms. Quinn said, sounding a bit taken aback.

But for Mr. Baranczak, at least, the duplication seemed like sweet literary revenge. "My translation was sent to her a couple of years ago," he said on the phone from Cambridge, Mass., where he is a professor of Polish language and literature at Harvard, "but Ms. Quinn didn't want it."

As for what exactly Ms. Szymborska's poem does mean, to people in the poetry world at least, the differences in the two translations seem significant.

"SOME LIKE POETRY"

Some—
that means not all.
Not even the majority of all but the minority.
Not counting school, where one must,
and poets themselves,
there will be perhaps two in a thousand.

Like—
but one also likes chicken-noodle soup,
one likes compliments and the color blue,
one likes an old scarf,
one likes to prove one's point,
one likes to pet a dog.

Poetry—
but what sort of thing is poetry?
More than one shaky answer
has been given to this question.
But I do not know and do not know and clutch on to it,
as to a saving bannister.

  (Translated, from the Polish, by Joanna Trzeciak.)

New Yorker, Vol. LXXII, No. 32, October 21 & 28, 1996, p. 156.

For one thing, *The New Republic's* poem has a slightly more conversational tone "What is poetry anyway?" the poet asks. In *The New Yorker,* the same lines are translated a bit more formally: "What sort of thing is poetry?"

But it is in the ending that the chief difference apparently lies. In *The New Yorker's* version, the poet seems to say that even though some people do not know what constitutes a poem, they cling to poetry anyway "as to a saving banister."

In *The New Republic,* the poet appears to say that even though the definition of poetry is ultimately unknowable, it is to the question itself to which the reader clings.

Mr. Baranczak, referring to Ms Irzeclak said, "My translation clings to the uncertainty, she clings to poetry itself." This is the stuff upon which translation seminars at universities are built. As the post-structuralists might say, there is no right reading of any text, the truth is in the language anyway.

Stanislaw Baranczak (essay date 27 October 1996)

SOURCE: "The Reluctant Poet," in *The New York Times Book Review,* October 27, 1996, p. 51.

[*Below, Baranczak discusses Szymborska's poetics, citing the poet's wisdom for realizing "that what attracts people to poetry today is . . . its art of asking questions."*]

"The Greta Garbo of World Poetry," trumpeted a headline in the Italian daily *La Repubblica;* it has so far been easily the most amusing among the attempts of the news media worldwide to attach some identity tag to this year's Nobel laureate in literature. What makes the comparison genuinely funny is that it's true and untrue at the same time. Those who know Wislawa Szymborska personally will be the first to admit that she indeed has something of the famous Swede's charm and subtlety. Yet her reticence and dislike of being in the spotlight have never turned her into a recluse. Wit, wisdom and warmth are equally important ingredients in the mixture of qualities that makes her so unusual and every poem of hers so unforgettable. We love her poetry because we instinctively feel that its author genuinely (though by no means uncritically) loves us.

I have mentioned reticence, and the 1996 decision of the Stockholm committee represents, among other things, a triumph of quality over quantity. Ms. Szymborska is among the least prolific major poets of our time; there has perhaps been no Nobel Prize-winning poet who has written less verse. Over the past three decades she has published very sparingly in the Polish literary press, and her slim collections, published at seven- to ten-year intervals, recall in their infrequency those of Philip Larkin or Elizabeth Bishop. This has nothing to do with writer's block: rather, she writes deliberately little because she holds the highest standards for herself. Wislawa Szymborska, quite simply, does not write irrelevant poems. She is a poet for whom each and every poem matters.

Born in 1923, she made her debut with a Socialist Realist collection titled *That's What We Live For* in 1952. (The manuscript was initially considered not ideologically correct enough, and its publication dragged on for years.) Her second collection, *Questions Put to Myself,* came out in 1954. It is in the semantic hiatus between these two titles that we can catch the first glimpse of the genuine Szymborska, who reached her maturity with her third collection, in 1957, *Calling Out to Yeti.* The youthful self-confidence of the first book's title gives way to self-doubt; perhaps most significant, the plural "we" is replaced with the singular "myself."

In one of the very few interviews Ms. Szymborska has given in the course of her career, she said that in her early writing she tried to love humankind instead of human beings. One might add that the esthetics of Socialist Realism demanded love for nothing less than humankind while at the same time, ironically, narrowing the multidimensionality of human life down to just one, social, dimension; it is Ms. Szymborska's focus on the individual that allows her to view human reality in all its troublesome complication.

The most extraordinary thing about her achievement is that, in some mysterious and enviable way, the uncompromising profundity of her poems never prevents them from being accessible. Over the past decade her popularity in Poland has reached staggering proportions; some of her recent poems, like the amazing and moving **"Cat in an Empty Apartment"** (in which the absence of someone who is dead is presented from the perspective of the house pet he left behind), have already acquired the status of cult objects among Polish readers. As a rule, a poet's popular appeal is a commodity purchased in exchange for some concessions, for the poet's renunciation of at least a part of what constitutes the natural complexity of his or her self. In contrast, Ms. Szymborska seems to be endowed with an almost superhuman ability to be complex yet comprehensible, ambitious yet approachable, individualistic yet involved.

If this secret can be explained, it will have to do with Ms. Szymborska's being wise enough to realize that what attracts people to poetry today is not its potential for making statements but rather its art of asking questions. The model of inquiry or self-inquiry makes its presence felt with striking frequency and insistence throughout her entire work. In the concluding part of her poem **"The Century's Decline"** she uses an apt but surprising adjective to denote the specific quality that marks all the questions she asks:

> "How should we live?" someone asked me in a letter.
> I had meant to ask him
> the same question.
>
> . . . The most pressing questions
> are naive ones.

The accessibility of Ms. Szymborska's poetry stems from the fact that the pressing questions she keeps asking are, at least at first sight, as naive as those of the man in the street. The brilliance of her poetry lies in pushing the inquiry much farther than the man in the street ever would. Many of her poems start provocatively, with a question, observation or statement that seems downright true, only to surprise us with its unexpected yet logical continuation. What can be more banal than noting that nothing happens twice? And yet the next three lines, by pursuing this thought to its end, offer a startling view of human existence:

> Nothing can ever happen twice.
> In consequence, the sorry fact is
> that we arrive here improvised
> and leave without the chance to practice.

Similarly, the title poem in Ms. Szymborska's latest collection, *The End and the Beginning* (1993), opens with a statement that sounds so disarmingly trivial that it seems not to contain any revelation at all:

> After every war
> someone has to tidy up.
> Things won't pick
> themselves up, after all.

Yet the naive question implied in this poem concerns no less pressing an issue than the meaning of human history or perhaps the senselessness of it. What makes this poem typically Szymborskian is that its initial naiveté almost imperceptibly moves to another plane. The action of cleaning up the mess turns, by metaphoric equation, into the process of forgetting. Just as you must remove the rubble after the war, you must remove the remembrance of human evil; otherwise, the burden of living would be unbearable. But this means that we never learn from history. Our ability to forget makes us, at the same time, repeatedly commit the same tragic blunders.

The typical lyrical situation on which a Szymborska poem is founded is the confrontation between the directly stated or implied opinion on an issue and the question that raises doubt about its validity. The opinion not only reflects some widely shared belief or is representative of some widespread mindset but also, as a rule, has a certain doctrinaire ring to it: the philosophy behind it is usually speculative, anti-empirical, prone to hasty generalizations, collectivist, dogmatic and intolerant.

Ms. Szymborska's finest point is that it is the very dogmatism of the opinion that prompts the naiveté of the question. Being dogmatic, the opinion is naturally self-confident and categorical as well, and may end up patching its logical, moral holes with blatant oversimplifications, unjustified generalizations and blindly optimistic (or blindly pessimistic) predictions. Such patches, particularly easy to discern, almost invite the irony of the skeptic. Thus, Ms. Szymborska's notion of the function of the poet: the poet should be a spoilsport. The poet should be someone who calls any bluff and lays bare any dirty trick in the game played by the earthly and unearthly powers, where the chief gambling strategy is dogmatic generalization and the stakes are the souls of each and every one of us.

FURTHER READING

Criticism

Dobyns, Stephen. "Poetry." *Book World—The Washington Post* (30 July 1995): 8.
> Appreciative review of *View with a Grain of Sand.*

McKee, Louis. Review of *View with a Grain of Sand. Library Journal* 120, No. 12 (July 1995): 85.
> Concludes that "it is about time more readers found the poetry of Szymborska."

"Writing a Résumé for a Nobel Winner." *U.S. News & World Report* 121, No. 15 (14 October 1996): 32.
> Brief account of Szymborska's career.

In Memoriam

José Donoso

1924-1996

Chilean novelist, short story writer, essayist, poet, and critic.

For further information on Donoso's life and career, see *CLC,* Volumes 4, 8, 11, and 32.

INTRODUCTION

One of the most influential figures of the Latin American literary boom of the 1960s and 1970s, José Donoso constructed tales of human foibles and social disintegration that often employed elements of fantasy. Compared to authors such as Gabriel Garcia Marquez, Carlos Fuentes, and Mario Vargas Llosa, Donoso is known for his denouncement of regionalism, a style prominent among Latin American writers. One of the most noted features of his writing is his move towards experimental fiction that contains surrealistic fantasies, myths, and legends. The writer of over twenty novels, Donoso created plots that feature saints, magicians, monsters, and other bizarre characters who struggle against class boundaries and rigid societal structures.

Donoso was born in Santiago in 1924 to parents who were members of the professional middle class, and for the first ten years of his schooling he attended the Grange, a private school in Santiago. The literary interests of his father and his mother's ties to the Chilean aristocracy helped Donoso become acquainted with both the importance of education and the distinct class boundaries that existed in society. Donoso attended Princeton University on a scholarship, and then returned to Chile where he worked as a journalist for five years. Donoso published his first work, *Summertime and Other Stories,* in 1955, with the financial support of family and friends. In 1957, he published his first novel, *Coronation,* again with the financial support of his family and associates. In 1971, he experienced his first great success with *The Obscene Bird of Night*, a story contrasting the aristocratic residents of a decaying Chilean estate with the old crones who inhabit a crumbling convent. Enlarging upon themes developed in *Coronation,* in which he contrasted an outmoded oligarchy and an emerging middle class, *The Obscene Bird of Night* employs decrepit hags, monsters, and witches coupled with the narration of an ailing and delusional writer to examine social, political, and economic power. In 1972, Donoso produced a nonfiction examination of emerging Latin American writers entitled *The Boom in Spanish American Literature: A Personal History.* The book was highly praised for its detached point of view and for its cov-

erage of the writers of the period. In his fiction, Donoso drew on personal experiences, his extensive travels, and his family's history to help craft his narratives. His move away from realism to magical, surrealistic narratives has defined the modern Chilean novel. Certain works such as *Curfew* and *The Garden Next Door* have been viewed as more straightforward and realistic than others, yet still retain many of the macabre, mystical elements that typified his earlier novels. Critics have commented on the straightforward narrative of *The Garden*—and on its surprise ending. Tony Talbot wrote: "In almost documentary fashion, Mr. Donoso depicts exiles who are torn by eroding political commitment, unable to transmit to their children an identity with their homeland, nostalgic for their native country and yet fearful of going back." In his review of *Curfew,* Christopher Leland also noted Donoso's turn toward more realistic narratives: "[T]he book depends little on the magical, on that dreamlike mix of the quotidian and the supernatural we have come to expect in much Latin American literature. Magic is here, however, woven sparingly throughout the text, and, is, finally, the sign of the very faint hope with which Donoso concludes."

PRINCIPAL WORKS

Summertime and Other Stories [*Veraneo y otros cuentos*] (short stories) 1955

Coronation [*Coronacíon*] (novel) 1957

This Sunday [*Este domingo*] (novel) 1965

The Obscene Bird of Night [*El obsceno pájaro de la noche*] (novel) 1970

Hell Has No Limits [*El lugar sin límites*] (novel) 1972

Sacred Families: Three Novellas [*Tres novelitas burguesas*] (novella) 1973

The Boom in Spanish American Literature: A Personal History (memoir) 1977

A House in the Country [*Casa de campo*] (novel) 1978

The Garden Next Door [*El jardín de al lado*] (novel) 1981

Four for Delfina [*Cuatro para Delfina*] (novellas) 1982

Curfew [*La desesperanza*; also translated as *Despair*] (novel) 1986

Poems of a Novelist [*Poemas de un novelista*] (poetry) 1992

Taratuta and Still Life with Pipe (novellas) 1992

Where Elephants Go to Die (novel) 1995

INTERVIEWS

Ricardo Gutiérrez Mouat with José Donoso (interview date Summer 1992)

SOURCE: "Beginnings and Returns: An Interview with José Donoso," in *Review of Contemporary Fiction,* Vol. XII, No. 2, Summer, 1992, pp. 11-17.

[*In the following interview, Mouat questions Donoso about his novels (particularly* Curfew *and* The Obscene Bird of Night*), his feelings about his native Chile, and other topics related to being a writer of the Latin American "boom" period.*]

The following conversation with José Donoso was held at the writer's house in Santiago in November of 1990, when the Chilean spring was blossoming in the gardens of the *barrio alto* and in the political arena of the whole country. It was conducted in English and it has been slightly edited for inclusion in this issue. My explanatory notes are indicated by brackets. I wish to record my gratitude to Pepe and to his wife María Pilar for their generosity and help.

[*Ricardo Gutiérrez Mouat:*] *You left Chile in the early sixties a Chilean writer and returned in 1980 a Latin American author. How has your relationship with the public changed?*

[José Donoso:] In the first place, my relation with the public

was nil, there was nothing to it, it was just a question of a few people from Chile and a few people from Latin America to whom I sent my books because they knew somebody I knew and so on and so forth. So I sent the first batch of books out to Benedetti [Mario Benedetti, the Uruguayan essayist and short story writer], I remember, some people in Argentina, all over Latin America, about fifty books I think. That was with *Coronation,* which is where I really think my career started. What happened then? My name began to be talked about, they read this book and they were of the same mind that people in Chile were, that it was a good novel. And then, what did I do? I went away from Chile, I left Chile, got entangled with María Pilar, and then I wrote the second volume of stories, and I found that my name was very much talked about and my presence acknowledged. Forever I was the author of *Coronation* and I have continued to be that for a lot of people, here in Chile especially. I suppose that is because *Coronation* in a way is a naturalistic novel, and the public here, the middle class here, is very fond of seeing themselves portrayed in a book: this is just like my Uncle Juan, this is just like my cousin Teresa, you see? That's what they like about books, that's one thing they do like. Everybody had a grandmother more or less like *misiá* Elisita Grey. Then I went away, I started on *This Sunday* and finished it, and had it published in Mexico, which was a great step forward. I broke the ice of Latin America. Then I wrote *Hell Has No Limits* and I found by then I was already a well-known writer in the circles of Latin America. Then I left Mexico for Barcelona and changed over to Seix Barral, and they published *Coronation* at once, and talked about my new novel and they were very enthusiastic and interested in what I was doing, so I started writing for that hungry public. But it was after publication of *The Obscene Bird of Night* that I found my reputation had grown immensely.

How has your relationship with your fellow writers of the Boom changed over the years?

No, it's more or less the same, we haven't seen much of each other for a long time. I continue to see Mario Vargas Llosa whenever I go, whenever I leave Chile; I see García Márquez with no problem; Carlos Fuentes, whenever he is in Argentina, calls up. It's very theoretical but it's still there, and María Pilar keeps track of everybody.

And how has your view of Chile changed?

Well, necessarily because Chile itself has changed so much. This is not the Chile I left back in, what, '64 or '65.

What's the biggest difference?

Consumerism. A lack of respect for whatever is literary. People are *not* interested in literature in Chile at all.

Is that because of the growth of the communication or TV or culture industry?

No, funny enough I think it's because the importance of politics is so big.

Your exile was not political, yet Chile underwent a political crisis in the seventies and you responded to it. How can you describe your response?

As the response of what seems to me a responsible intellectual. I wasn't active in politics but I threw my lot in with the people who were against Pinochet. So if I was not active my name was, and that gave me a lot of security.

How did your novels respond to the political crisis in Chile?

Well, you can see in my novels a response either to the crisis itself or to the conditions that led up to the crisis.

Are you speaking of **A House in the Country***?*

There is more to *A House in the Country* than that. I mean, there are actually certain speeches by Allende and Pinochet which have been lifted out of the newspaper.

Did you feel that your literature could ever become pamphleteering?

No, I've never been a staunch upholder of anything at all. I've been against the Pinochet thing but I have no ideology to which I can turn. So I am a democrat without ideology.

Or perhaps a liberal, a classic liberal?

A classic liberal . . . I hate the idea, but yes, I would accept that.

Several interesting things have happened to you upon your return to Chile: you got involved in theatre, in film (and just two nights ago the film you wrote the script for won the "Chilean Oscar"), and you've been shaping a new generation of writers in your workshops. What can you tell me about these activities?

Certainly the most impassioned involvement comes with the workshops. I feel it is through them that I speak, that I reach a wider public. They help me in many ways. I've been growing older and I get more and more separated from youth, from what's in the air, you see. I don't know what people read nowadays, or what they talk about, or what their idiosyncracies are. But through these workshops, this involvement with younger people, I get the feeling of what's really to be young, to be in the center of things.

Have any of these budding writers who have studied with you become important voices in Chile?

Yes. Marco Antonio de la Parra, Agata Gligo, Arturo Fontaine, Alberto Fouquet . . .

You've been an intensely private writer . . .

Yes.

. . . yet in the eighties it seems that you have blended that approach to writing with a more collective approach to creativity. I mean theater and film and workshops. Have you sensed this?

I don't feel it, really. I feel that having a workshop is another kind of privacy.

What about theater?

Well, theater, I just work with another guy.

But you must have been involved in the production itself.

I was involved in the first production, which was *Sueños de mala muerte*.

Let us review your work from the perspective of **Curfew***, your most recent novel and one of your most successful ones. What was the genesis of this novel?*

We were planning to go down to Chiloé for the holidays, my wife and I; we took flowers to Matilde Neruda, who was then quite sick in bed. She didn't let us see her but she sent messages of thank you, so on and so forth. Then she wrote us a letter saying that the flowers we had taken her perfumed all her house. Then we moved on to Chiloé, and then I began writing starting from this woman who is an ex-society girl who works with people, with women. She triggered that book. And then I got a feel for other characters, Lopito, for instance, and my desire to work with somebody who belonged to the more popular classes and yet had the sensibility of an intellectual.

And that was Lopito.

That was Lopito. But he was also Mañungo.

Are they in any way doubles in the novel?

No, they don't work as doubles, I think . . . As foils, perhaps.

What about the references to chilota [*i.e., from the island of Chiloé in southern Chile*] *folklore and legends?*

I got involved with them down in Chiloé that summer and enjoyed that tremendously. I befriended a family who put me in touch with all these people who had the keys, so to speak, to *chilota* folklore. And I did want to use some kind of myth in this novel, as I have used the *imbunche* in another novel [the legendary entity with all its orifices sewn up that figures in *The Obscene Bird of Night*], and here I use the *caleuche* [a local variation on the ship-of-fools motif blended with Charon's ferry and Rimbaud's drunken boat].

What is your understanding of the caleuche?

Well, in the first place it is very much of a story, something that moves: if you do this, this will happen to you; if this happens to you, you'll go to this place, you see? It gave me a stepping stone, a structure.

How do you think the myth functions in the novel itself?

It works as a reference constantly because Mañungo is a *chilote* and consequently immersed in these childhood stories. Things of childhood you take into adulthood. Probably he doesn't get lost because he has this anchorlike thing in his past. And people interpret life according a little bit to myth. You see, when you get together with somebody or live with somebody, that other person brings in a whole lot of myths that are different from yours. These people will have heard some myths or some legends or some stories, some riddles, which belong to the old country. And this is what gives the person a kind of floe to stand on.

It's funny because when I asked you how the novel came to be, most people would've expected you to talk about the politics of it.

I'm not interested in politics, it's something nobody can accept. Politics has not formed a deep vision in me. I feel things like these are more in depth. If you notice, the political questions all have political answers; if you can also notice, legendary aspects have no answer whatever . . .

Mañungo and Judit are divided characters, and there is a theme that runs through your work from **Coronation** *on: role-playing, simulation, alienation, the disjunction/conjunction of Self and Other. . . . Do you see this continuity and what do you make of it?*

Sure, I see it in Judit trying to be a woman of the people being herself very middle-class; Mañungo trying to be middle-class *malgré lui*, no?, and not being able to be that nor a folksinger, a folklore hero.

In a novel like **Hell Has No Limits**, *role-playing is intimately tied up with sexual politics, with the power game*

between the sexes. What is your interpretation of the transvestite?

Difficult, I really don't know myself why at that point in my life I did that. Funny, the things that are real and the things that aren't; things that are verbatim in that novel are the whorehouse, the little village, the little railroad, the countryside, the vineyards. But in that village that I know la Manuela didn't exist; I brought her over from another set of experiences.

How do you see the relationship between the roles that she plays—which are of both genders—and the violence in the novel?

Well, I feel that transformation is always punished with violence. God didn't put us here to be transformed, He put us here to be what we were told to be.

What you're saying is that authority cannot accept metamorphosis, it's a transgression, no? And speaking of authors and authority, I'd be very interested in hearing your interpretation of the power game in **The Garden Next Door** *between the male author (who cannot write the novel we're reading) and the female one who does write it.*

Well, I think that all men carry inside them a lot of other men, a lot of possibilities. I think that in *The Garden Next Door* transformation takes on not what happens in *Hell Has No Limits* but something very near it.

In what sense?

I've been asked this question several times: why is it that you, who are a successful writer, can draw a picture of a writer *manqué*? My reply is that I hope I'm still a writer *manqué*. I carry inside me the shape of a *fracasado*. If I lose that, my irony and my humor and my sarcasm, maybe, or my cruelty, everything that is more or less impassioned in me would fail. I am a failed writer; I'm also a successful one.

That doesn't explain the fact that a woman ends up writing the novel.

I may have wanted to be a woman at one point . . .

You said before that you give your stories to read to two people in particular, both of whom are women: Delfina Guzmán and your wife. Does that mean anything?

Yes, I have a better relationship with women than with men, far and away. I'm much more interested in women than I am in men.

Do women make it easier for you to be creative?

They are more intelligent, somehow; they have a greater panoply of . . . I don't know, desire, or possibilities.

How do you think women were portrayed by the novelists of the Boom?

There isn't a true woman in the pages of the writers of the Boom. The women in Vargas Llosa are not women, they are sketches!

And the women in One Hundred Years of Solitude?

Not plausible, not felt. They have no freedom, they transgress nothing. And La Maga [from Cortázar's *Hopscotch*], look at the name . . .

Do you think that any woman writers were excluded by the Boom?

No, no. I don't see any women writing at the same time. Clarice Lispector, perhaps . . .

Can you name some interesting women writers today in Latin America?

Yes, Rosario Ferré, for instance.

What interests you in her?

People speak of two poles in Latin America: civilization and barbarism. I think she's both.

In **The Obscene Bird of Night** *you were trying to write a* miserabilista *novel. Why did you feel you wanted to do that at that point?*

Because I've always been very attracted by poverty and by what I call the underside of power. I'm interested in *clochards,* hobos, the servant class, in people with no means, who have nothing because they are afraid to be stripped of everything.

Like the imbunche *fantasy in* **The Bird,** *right?* **A House in the Country** *is the luminous face of* **The Obscene Bird**. *Here role-playing is not just an existential/psychological theme as in* **Coronation** *and* **Curfew** *but the aesthetic of the novel as a whole, in the sense that language itself is mask, disguise, carnival. Can you tell me something about the genesis of* **A House in the Country**?

It's a story I've told many times. The truth is that we had gone to Italy with my wife. And Poland. And in the Warsaw station we had a telegram saying that the *"once"* [the military coup on 11 September 1973] had happened, that things had turned topsy-turvy in my country. In Italy I met Antonioni who had read **The Obscene Bird** and had found it a very

powerful novel. He wasn't interested in any of the themes I wrote about; he liked the way I wrote, the power of the novel. I was very thrilled. I went back to Calaceite and shut myself in with the purpose of writing a scenario for Antonioni. And I spent a lot of time in my reclining chair out in the garden, listening to the rumors from the village. Then Vargas Llosa's children came to stay in the house. Mario and Patricia were going to Mexico and they asked us to babysit for them. We tried to rest in the afternoon but they had such a rumpus, the kids, that we couldn't sleep at all. There were some very strange things going on. . . . Alvarito and Pilarcita both had a leg in the same pair of underwear; they were completely naked. Then they went out to the street and I fantasized with the rumors in this large house, in the many rooms of this house. And also there was pampas grass. . . .

So **A House in the Country** *is the conjunction of the world of childhood—with its little perversions—and Chile's political nightmare?*

That and the feeling of being completely away from everything that mattered. I was trying to complete a thought. There is also a twist, there is also a transgression, an underside. In *A House in the Country* I use a discourse which is in itself quite refined and is sometimes superelegant, exquisite. And I decided that this whole novel was going to be exquisite, to write exactly the other side of what I had written in *The Obscene Bird of Night*. I wrote it with this rococo thing in mind, it's more a rococo novel than anything else: vain, artificial, pretentious—Fragonard.

Is that something postmodern in your estimation?

No, I don't think we need to worry about that at this juncture. As I began writing *A House in the Country* I started to feel that I needed a language which is completely opposite to that of the *Bird,* to give this effect I wanted. Because the superfluity of the rococo seemed to parallel the *miserabilismo,* so there are two things pitched against each other. And, again, the language was the language used by the florid writers of the nineteenth century, the Spanish, for example. And then you get the language of the marchioness. Somebody said, and I don't know who it was, that you can't write novels that begin: "La Marquise est sortie à cinq heures . . ."

Valéry . . .

Valéry, right, he said that. And then I set out to prove that novels can be written in that way.

In **The Boom in Spanish-American Literature: A Personal History** *you wrote: "The new generation finds the novel of the 60's excessively literary, and they devote themselves, like those in all avant-garde movements, to writing an 'anti-literature,' an 'anti-novel'." This kind of epitaph of the Boom* *was written in 1971. Are you alluding here to what later was called postmodernism?*

I think so.

What is your understanding of postmodernism? Do you think you have written postmodern novels?

Probably *A House in the Country.* It has all the ingredients: it's eclectic, it's humorous, it apes the forms of classic novels, it is artificial and self-conscious, it is a novel about writing, and there is a spoof in it.

In fact, John Barth makes you a postmodernist on the basis of that novel. When I quoted the passage from **The Boom** *I was alluding to the fact that right after you wrote* **The Bird,** *you wrote* **Sacred Families** *which can be said to mark a departure in some other direction.*

I was trying to write about a milieu that was falsely refined, falsely intellectual, so I took up this other kind of artificiality.

The beginning of one of these novellas parodies the beginning of Pride and Prejudice, *so here we have a contemporary milieu and a literary representation with nineteenth-century roots. Is this postmodernism?*

Could be. The whole caricature thing, perhaps.

Do you find the term, the label "postmodern" valid?

I think so, I mean we have to try all sorts of terms to try to get at these things.

The final question: yesterday the National Prize for Literature was delivered to your door. What's the meaning of this prize for you?

It's as if somebody had driven a nail into the wall to hang my posthumous portrait.

Marta Mestrovic with José Donoso (interview date 30 November 1992)

SOURCE: "José Donoso," in *Publishers Weekly,* Vol. 239, No. 52, November 30, 1992, pp. 30-1.

[*In the following interview, Mestrovic questions Donoso about* The Garden Next Door. *Speaking about the novel's autobiographical content, its use of realistic characters and details, and his education and life in general, Donoso provides the interviewer with details about his career.*]

In *The Garden Next Door,* a middle-aged Chilean writer

who has never quite achieved the popularity of other Latin American authors of the same generation fails at writing the "great Chilean social novel," the masterpiece that is supposed to secure his place in modern literature. Simultaneously, through a blur of alcohol and Valium, he and his wife watch their marriage dissolve, then resurrect itself.

The Chilean writer José Donoso is the author of *The Garden Next Door.* Since he is known for his experimental works, readers may well suspect that despite the realism with which events are depicted, nothing here is quite what it seems. Indeed, in a satisfying surprise ending, the reader discovers that this is a novel within a novel; rather than being related by an embittered male narrator, the story has actually been written by the protagonist's wife. And the novel does turn out to be a successful work, one snapped up by the Spanish literary community.

The switch of narrators, which lifts the novel from a minor to a major key, is one of the clever literary devices of the book, just out from Grove Press. Meeting Donoso in his publisher's offices in Manhattan, *Publisher's Weekly* is prompted to ask him why he decided to end his book in this way.

His answer is hesitant, musing. "I guess I always wanted my wife to be a writer. She has always been a very literary person, and I always had a feeling that if she had become a writer, she'd be on better terms with herself. After I wrote this book she did write a book of her own—an entertaining, wonderful book of memoirs."

The Garden Next Door, first published in Spain in 1981 by Seix Barral, marks a departure in Donoso's use of narrative. "This is my first venture into just telling a plain story, while also dealing with characters who are mimetic. Before, I worked with emblematic characters, but there's no emblematic quality about these characters. They are just very plain people undergoing crises." In addition, Donoso acknowledges, *The Garden Next Door* is his most autobiographical novel. In a soft, modulated voice, he observes that many of the incidents in the novel, which is set in Spain, where the Donosos spent several years, were drawn from his own life. "We lived in a little town called Sitges, and the experience was not unlike the experience that I describe in the book." While daily life there did not have the supercharged atmosphere of a dramatic narrative, there was a garden next door where interesting people often appeared.

"People ask me why I say this is an autobiographical novel, since the writer who appears there is a failed writer—and I haven't exactly failed. The answer is that in order to write one has to cultivate inside oneself the idea of oneself as a failed person. I have the seeds of failure in myself.

"Success," on the other hand, "is something I decide. There

is another side of success, which is the outward side, celebrity. Celebrity to me is dangerous." This is an interesting and telling statement, coming from a man who belongs to a generation of writers who suddenly found themselves objects of international esteem, as the Latin American novel assumed almost a cult status in the '60s and '70s.

Donoso writes about this ambivalence in his assessment of this period, *The Boom in Spanish American Literature: A Personal History.* "On the whole, the boom was a blessing," he observes. "We all took a lot of things from each other. There was a lot of pinching going on, which is part of the vitality of Latin American novels of my generation. The fact that we read each other voraciously, imitated each other, wrote about each other, and went to parties together, did a lot to cement what happened.

"We were all out of our own countries. We were all in exile—some for political reasons, others not—so we could have an overall view. We could work with the bricks of reality. The outcome was something completely to do with poetry and the imagination."

He attributes the initiation of "the Boom" to the efforts of the Spanish publisher Carlos Barral, "a man of great literary taste and know-how," whose firm, Seix Barral, first published many of these Latin American writers. Agent Carmen Balcells, who represents many of them—Donoso included—is credited as well. "We've been together a long time," he says. "My books are in 23 languages, which is mostly due to her effort."

Now 68, Donoso wears his graying, unruly hair combed back. In a tweed jacket, pinstriped shirt and tie, he looks very much a successful scholar. Currently a fellow at the Woodrow Wilson Center's Latin American Program in Washington, D.C., he has indeed held teaching posts at universities in the U.S. and in Chile.

Donoso's career as a writer can be traced to his childhood in Santiago. The oldest of three brothers, he grew up in a household dominated by women—"dotty great-aunts" and a grandmother who slowly descended into madness. He remembers his parents as charming society people who did not directly involve themselves with their children.

"The tone of the house was set by these old women and the servants. I picked up stories when I was a young boy from the old servants, who sat around the fire and talked about the farms [Donoso's family were landowners from the south], and about their own native backgrounds. Strange things: why this aunt had been put into a convent to ask forgiveness of God for another aunt who had misbehaved—how one person can pay for the sins of another. I realized what it was to

be poor, what it was to be a servant. I learned that the real truth is what is told, not what happens."

After romantically trying his hand as a shepherd in Patagonia and as a dockhand in Buenos Aires, Donoso entered the University of Chile. In 1949 he received a scholarship to attend Princeton, where he studied under R. P. Blackmur and Allen Tate. Henry James was just coming back into vogue and "Princeton was rife with talk" of his work. Donoso fell under the influence of the American writer.

"I had already read Proust, who was a big influence for many years, so much so that when I got married—I married rather late; I was 35, my wife [Maria del Pilar] was a year younger—I said, 'If you want to marry me there are two things you have to do. One is to learn how to drive, because I will never learn how to drive a car. And another thing is to read Proust, because if you don't read Proust we won't have anything to talk about.'"

After completing his studies, Donoso returned to Chile and tried to find a niche for himself in a literary community dominated by a tradition of regional realism. "I remember going to the home of a very well-known writer of the *criollista* school—the naturalistic school—and she said, 'I understand that you are the great inheritor of Chilean realism.' I shuddered; I must have been about 22; this was the last thing I wanted to be."

He persevered, however, and eventually published a first novel, *Coronation,* which drew upon his family experiences and launched his career as a writer. Issued in Chile in 1957, *Coronation* was published here by Knopf in 1965, and won the William Faulkner Foundation Prize. Ironically, this novel and several collections of short stories were the only works to be published in his homeland. He recalls that he had to help pay for, sell and promote those efforts in Chile, a country that even today has only 80 bookshops—"a shocking thing." Had he not been published and encouraged by Barral, Donoso's career would have been quite different.

In 1962, he made the acquaintance of the Mexican writer Carlos Fuentes at a writers' conference. Two years later, he attended another writers' congress, in Mexico. He was unaware when he left Chile that he was beginning a self-imposed exile that would last until the early 1980s.

The catalyst was an invitation from Fuentes to stay with him. While living in a house on Fuentes's property, Donoso wrote his next novel, *Hell Has No Limits.* It concerns a brutal incident in the life of an aging male transvestite. Many critics view this novel as a thematic dividing point between the author's early and later works.

Donoso's relationship with the Mexican writer is complicated. Although he credits Fuentes's novel *Where the Air is Clear* with providing the impetus for his own style, there is also a touch, perhaps, of competition. Donoso remembers once accusing Fuentes of stealing his ideas. Fuentes laughed and said, "Don't you realize we are all writing different parts of the same big Latin American novel?"

It was Fuentes who sent Donoso's first novel, **Coronation,** to Knopf. "Alfred snapped it up at once. It was owing to Carlos Fuentes that I broke the barrier," Donoso acknowledges. But unlike Fuentes, who was heavily influenced by the classics of Spanish literature, Donoso found his inspiration in Anglo-Saxon literature. "That is my book culture," he says.

Donoso had already begun what would turn out to be his masterpiece, **The Obscene Bird of Night**, a loosely structured, phantasmagoric novel about the nature of power. In it Donoso identifies many of the images he absorbed as a young child. "I try to build a world of those old crones, to show the way women control the underside of power because it is the only one available to them. It was a difficult book for me to visualize, because it was a novel about writing a novel."

The events of September 11, 1973, changed the course of his writing. "I had been in exile for 10 years," Donoso says, speaking of the coup that plunged Chile into military dictatorship. "Since the Pinochet coup I have been writing political novels. It has invaded my emotion and my subconscious." He was compelled to set aside another book he was working on at the time to write *A House in the Country,* an allegorical novel about the Chilean sociopolitical situation. "I accept all the political interpretations given that book. There are things I'd change today, but I think it holds water."

Although Donoso spent 14 years in Spain, he never felt totally accepted there. "Spaniards admired a lot of what the Latin Americans were doing, but they had a very ambivalent relationship towards us. We were doing something with the Spanish language that they had not yet begun to do. They felt ambivalent—so much so that there is now a general rejection in Spain of the Latin American novel."

What was it then that brought him home? "I suppose it was the effect of both my parents dying. The old house was done away with [as in a prominent incident in **The Garden Next Door**], so I was nobody's son anymore. My daughter, who was then 13, had never been to Chile. She had begun to date boys in Spain, and it was either we leave and become Chileans again, or we just throw this little girl into this life which we don't really control. I was very much a foreigner in Spain. I feel great kinship with Spain, it's the same language finally, but the mother country is too far away."

When Donoso returned to Chile, he found himself "com-

pletely welcomed back. One tends to become a mythological figure in Chile." Donoso explored this ambivalent feeling towards exile in **Curfew**. The book was poorly received in Chile, however, probably because its criticism of Chilean society was too close to home.

Undaunted, Donoso continues to add to his sizable oeuvre. Two novellas, **Taratuta** and **Still Life with Pipe,** will be published next year by Norton. (Donoso says: "Grove didn't want these. Norton is a very good house; they made me an offer and I accepted.") This pragmatic point of view previously propelled Donoso from Knopf, the publisher of five of his books: "I had the feeling that Knopf wasn't loyal to me. They didn't make an effort to make my books better known. I was very angry at one point. I'm not anymore."

With an eye toward posterity, Donoso, who has always kept a writer's diary, has donated his personal papers to Princeton University, where they are available to scholars. Does he think Henry James would have been pleased with his work? "Henry James is my mentor. He's my teacher, and one can write for or against one's teacher. The rules are all set by Henry James—you can either break them or take them."

OBITUARY

Robert D. McFadden (obituary date 9 December 1996)

SOURCE: "José Donoso, 72, Fantastical Chilean Novelist," in *The New York Times,* December 9, 1996, p. B13.

[*The following obituary presents an overview of Donoso's life and career.*]

José Donoso, one of Chile's best-known authors, whose novels and short stories used dark surrealism and social satire to explore the haunted lives of exiles and writers and a world of aristocratic excesses, died on Saturday in Santiago. He was 72 years old.

Mr. Donoso died of cancer at his home, his niece Claudia Donoso told The Associated Press.

One of the major figures of the Latin American literary boom of the 1960's and 1970's. Mr. Donoso crafted multilayered visions of social disintegration and human fallibility that were sometimes compared with those of Colombia's Gabriel Garcia Márquez, Mexico's Carlos Fuentes and Peru's Mario Vargas Llosa.

After a youthful wanderlust that took him across South America, the United States and Europe, Mr. Donoso began writing short stories and novellas in the 1950's. But his first great success—regarded by critics as his masterpiece—was *The Obscene Bird of Night,* a 1971 novel about characters on a run-down Chilean estate and a residence for elderly women it contrasts sterile embittered old age with the decadence of aristocrats, all of whom are afflicted with some physical deformity.

While his earlier work had been praised as imaginative and unified by themes of death and decay in Chile's rigidly structured society. *The Obscene Bird of Night* was more ambitious, critics said when it was published in English by Knopf in 1973. It transcended Chilean boundaries, they said, and carried its author into the emerging stream of Latin American writers experimenting with legends, myths bizarre plots, multiple identities and grotesque fantasies.

In *The New York Times Book Review* Robert Coover called it "a dense and energetic book, full of terrible risk-taking populated with legendary saints and witches, mad old crones and a whole estate-ful of freaks and monsters, and narrated by a disturbed deaf-mute."

Mr. Donoso's more than 20 novels and collections of short stories, many of them translated into English, include *Coronation, Charleston and Other Stories, Hell Has No Limits, A House in the Country, The Garden Next Door* and *Curfew.*

In dense, elaborately constructed plots sometimes compared with works by Henry James and Marcel Proust, Mr. Donoso's books were peopled with upper-class families clinging to privileges, children exposed to the hypocrisy of adults, expatriates searching for identity, and a nightmarish gallery of criminals, widows, prostitutes, political bosses, magicians and dreamers.

Mr. Donoso had a long association with the United States, attending Princeton University and later teaching there and at the University of Iowa. One of [his] last works was *Where Elephants Go to Die,* about a Chilean professor who goes to teach in the United States.

The scion of a wealthy, eccentric Santiago family, José Donoso was born in a Santiago suburb on Oct. 5, 1924, and grew up in a privileged world of servants, limousines and English tutors. As a young man, he flitted from the life of a social dandy in Santiago to shepherding in Patagonia and hobnobbing with sailors and stevedores on the docks of Buenos Aires.

In 1949, he won a scholarship to study at Princeton, where he was not a good student but wrote short stories in English for a literary journal that became his first published works. Returning to Chile, he was a journalist for five years in Santiago, covering, as he put it, "everything from earthquakes to new books, from fashion shows to revolutions."

But he also continued to write fiction. In 1962, four years after its publication, his novel *Coronation*—a strange tale of the mock crowning and death of an aged widow and her grandson's descent into madness, at the hands of their servants—won the William Faulkner Foundation Prize, giving the author his first wide international recognition.

Convinced that his work was being stifled by his surroundings, Mr. Donoso moved to Mexico City, where he became a close friend of Carlos Fuentes. He later moved to Europe, and for many years in the 1960's and 1970's lived in Spain, mostly in Barcelona, where he wrote many of his most famous works.

Mr. Donoso returned to Chile in the early 1980's. Though he had never seen himself as a political exile, he was a passionate critic of the authoritarian regime of Gen. Augusto Pinochet, who overthrew President Salvador Allende Gossens in 1972. Mr. Donoso was not a spokesman for Chilean leftists, but he occasionally wrote anti-Government articles and he was arrested briefly in a 1985 protest against the dismissal of dissident writers from teaching jobs.

He also criticized what he regarded as the crass commercialism of Chile's relatively prosperous society in the 1990's, and accused some publishers of chasing profits at the expense of good writing. "Chile is a country that has forgotten its soul," he said in an interview last year.

In 1990, Mr. Donoso was awarded the Chilean National Literature Prize, his nation's highest literacy award. But he conceded in October of last year that writing had become a psychological torment for him. Bearded, bespectacled, weakened by illness, he said: "The agony of having to write is terrible, of feeling empty, that you amount to nothing."

Mr. Donoso is survived by his wife the former Maria Pilar Serrand, whom he married in 1961, and by a daughter, Pilar.

OVERVIEWS

Priscilla Melendez (essay date Fall 1987)

SOURCE: "Writing and Reading the Palimpsest: Donoso's *El jardin de al lado,*" in *Symposium,* Vol. XLI, No. 3, Fall, 1987, pp. 200-13.

[*In the following essay, Melendez provides a detailed discussion of* The Garden Next Door *as a palimpsest. Focusing on the different narrative points of view in the novel, the dialectic between reading and writing, and the meaning of the garden, Melendez examines the concept of the palimpsest at length.*]

To introduce the concept of palimpsest in a technological and computerized era might be perceived as an unnecessary irony or as the sign of reliance on an already exhausted metaphor. But the proliferation of intertexts, both perceptible and veiled, in José Donoso's *El jardín de al lado* (1981) reveals an archaic system, the palimpsest, linked to a process of writing or "publishing." This system functions as a literary metaphor in which the substitution of the object and its referent for one or more other objects and referents does not imply the disappearance of the first set. Although in the medieval practice of "scraping again" the text substituted is not necessarily linked to what it covers, the dialectical implications suggested by the palimpsestic metaphor in Donoso's novel connect and unmask the multiple covert/overt texts that demand to be read. The recognition of texts over a text is, in essence, an incomplete enterprise, since the established fictive boundaries between them disappear with the identification of each fragment as a single entity. This contradictory phenomenon—boundaries vanish just as they are discovered—leads us to juxtapose the multiple texts and their readings and simultaneously reveals the subordinate nature of both the explicit and implicit discourses. Therefore, within this framework, literary intertextuality becomes a useful notion only if conceived not exclusively as an echo of other texts or as mere sharing of a stock of literary codes and conventions, but as a nonhierarchical interplay of discourses. The illusory discovery of footprints, of ruins, submerges the observer (reader) in a world that has apparently disappeared and upon which new worlds—or texts—have been built or written.

The recognition of a consequent multiplication of texts and subtexts imposed by the palimpsestic metaphor obliges us to heed warnings in Paul de Man's *Allegories of Reading* against the debate that opposes intrinsic to extrinsic criticism, which in formalistic terms states that "form is now a solipsistic category of self-reflection, and the referential meaning is said to be extrinsic." From the standpoint of the inherent plurality implied in the title of the present essay, my concern is the "obligation" of reading and decoding both the superimposed text and the one(s) being removed. That is, I shall be dealing, not with the inside/outside metaphor that de Man seriously questions—although he often has recourse to it—but with the notion of covert and overt writing, which has more to do with a rhetorical development than with a structural one. The relationship between the act of interpretation and the use of the metaphor of the palimpsest suggests a process of elucidation, of revealing something else.

But my goal is not to "translate" into intelligible or familiar language what has been explicitly presented or indirectly concealed, even less to put the overt discourse in the place of the one that remained obscured. It is to expose a proliferation of texts that thematically and formally clash with one another and, in this encounter, to examine their genesis/de-

struction as linguistic and fictive entities. Nevertheless, the possibility of reading these multiple "manuscripts" that are constantly emerging and simultaneously being substituted presents the reader with a rhetorical dilemma. The metaphorical and/or literal nature of the text's language creates another level of intra- and extra-textual structures that are part of the overt/covert writings. The garden, for example, not only characterizes the proliferation and elusiveness of its meanings but also questions the distinction between what is understood as literal and what is figural. In other words, which one is the "real" garden, who represents the authoritative voice of the text, which novel are we, in any case, reading?

In *El jardín de al lado* the protagonist and narrator, Julio Méndez, is a slightly recognized Chilean writer whose most recent novel has been rejected for publication by the well-known editor from Barcelona, Núria Monclús, although she encourages Julio to revise and rewrite his text. Five of the first six chapters of Donoso's novel consist of Julio's narration of the ordeal of revising his manuscript during a summer in Madrid. Parallel to his need for writing, the other strong force in Julio's life is his wife, Gloria. Fusion and confusion of past and present events transforms Julio's narration of his professional and personal life into an autobiography. But when, in the sixth chapter, we discover that it is Gloria who has written and implicitly narrated the entire preceding text, *El jardín de al lado*'s clear commentary on its self-begetting and fictional nature becomes problematic. What was first taken for Julio's autobiography—Julio's text and narrative voice—turns out to be Gloria's recreation of their survival as writers. This moment of recognition, which coincides with the end of Donoso's novel—and also with that of Gloria's work—invites the reader to look for an alternate and more reliable writing that has been concealed. The act of rereading, either literal or metaphoric, implies substitution of the former interpretative text (where the garden was observed by Julio) for a text where the narrative discourse has been drastically altered and where the point of view (that of the observer of the garden) has been replaced. "Erasing" the first reading to set forth a new interpretation is reminiscent of Julio's painful exercise of rereading and rewriting his rejected text.

Overt thematization of the acts of writing, reading, publishing, and interpreting in *El jardín de al lado* leads us to pose a question similar to the one de Man proposed while trying to "explain" the passage in Proust's *A la Recherche du temps perdu* where Marcel engages in the act of reading a novel: "The question is precisely whether a literary text is *about* that which it describes, represents or states." In his attempt to answer his query, de Man examines the possible coincidence between the meaning read and the meaning stated in the *Recherche*. If, as de Man says, "reading is the metaphor of writing," then *El jardín de al lado* is a clear example of an act of reading both explained and redefined by its counterpart, the act of writing. The process of interpretation becomes, therefore, a paradigm of both reading and writing. De Man's Proust is comparable to Donoso: *El jardín* is a work in which the story-telling and the story-told are intermingled, the meaning read and the meaning stated blend together. Gloria's fictionalization of Julio's political and existential dilemmas documented in his rejected novel reveals the difficulty of writing about a writing saturated with historical and political overtones. It is Julio-narrator who reproduces part of Núria Monclús' verdict of his novel: "Falta una dimensión más amplia, y, sobre todo, la habilidad para proyectar, más que para describir o analizar, tanto situaciones como personajes de manera que se trasformen en metáfora, metáfora válida en sí y no por lo que señala afuera de la literatura, no como crónica de sucesos que todo el mundo conoce y condena, y que por otra parte la gente está comenzando a olvidar. . . ." De Man's concerns for autobiography as a genre—"what is at stake is not only the distance that shelters the author of autobiography from his experience but the possible convergence of aesthetics and of history"—highlight not only the autobiographical connections between Donoso's own life and *El jardín* but, more substantially, Julio's inadequacy to recreate his political experience within his literary creation. On the other hand, to what extent does Gloria's own text succeed or fail to make of her literary discourse a metaphor—something that, as she immediately discovers, Julio is incapable of doing? Can we, as readers of Donoso's novel, recognize our own forgetfulness of historical events that are foreign to our experience, or that, even if experienced, are eventually buried in our memory? Can we describe the ethical/aesthetical dialectic that obsessed Julio and Gloria as an aporia which, in spite of its contradictions, they both try to reconcile in their writings—Julio through overt incorporation and description and Gloria through a false act of rejection?

Julio's "intention" in writing his novel-document (as he alludes to it) is precisely to transform the six days spent in a Chilean jail into what he calls a source of telling, in other words, a discourse. But this enterprise is threatened not only by the course of time (which turns the narration pale and causes it to fade away), but more evidently by the superimposition of other texts, by the invasion of other "experiencias menos trascendentes y más confusas, mezquinas experiencias personales que no me aportaban otra cosa que humilliación . . ." The weakening of Julio's "heroic experience," the weakening of his initial hate produced by the imprisonment, begins to transform itself into a marginal text where the remains and footprints are being replaced by other writings: "todo este cúmulo de vejaciones se había sobreimpreso a aquella experiencia cuya jerarquía yo tan desesperadamente trataba de mantener mediante las páginas de notas que escribía como quien riega una planta moribunda, pero que, ay, al fin se iba secando pese a tanto esfuerzo" It is not until Julio completes

the version of his novel that he is able to criticize his manuscript, recognizing in it the lack of two central aspects of the creative process: "Al avanzar por mi copioso escrito se me fue haciendo indudable que la pasión que pretendía animarlo no era ni convincente como literatura ni válida como experiencia."

As de Man suggests, Marcel's act of reading reconciles imagination and action. Marcel realizes that the sedentary act of reading is powerful enough to recreate the outside world and even to draw a more holistic perception of it. Although in *El jardín de al lado* Julio's ethical conflict between imagination and action is restructured in a different manner, it also dramatizes the confrontation of the inner and the outer worlds (jail-garden) as experienced by the protagonist. Julio's anxiousness to transform his political experience—which is not transcendental—into a transcendental writing is precisely what establishes the parameters and the inevitable failure of his text. But one of the ironic forces of *El jardín* is that Julio not only fails to recreate aesthetically his Chilean imprisonment, but also fails to participate, while in self-imposed exile, in an active political life. Gloria constantly accuses him of his ideological "impotency," of his weak liberalism, and describes his "moderate humanism" as pedantic cowardice. Therefore, the emptiness of both his literary work and his own life is filled neither by imagination nor by action. Contrary to Marcel's relationship with the act of reading, neither of these activities is capable of satisfactorily replacing the other. When Julio mentally blames Gloria for living her life in his shadow—that is, through him—he is ironically describing his own pseudoliterary discourse which lies under the shadow of historical facts and, indeed, is eclipsed by Gloria's successful story. In a similar way, the garden translates into metaphor and simultaneously deconstructs its own allegorical meaning, particularly in its dual incarnation of the literal and the metaphorical and of the action and the imagination.

After a long period of procrastination, provoked by his weaknesses, his abuses of drugs and alcohol, his mother's death, his contemplation of the garden, Julio completes the revision of his novel. But his second version is the result of an imprisonment different from the one that inspired the original text. The endless series of dramatic events in Gloria's life—from Julio's refusal to sell the family house after the death of his mother to Bijou's theft of one of Salvatierra's paintings—pushes her to a state of depression, having as one of the consequences her absolute silence, particularly towards Julio. In their own special ways, both Julio and Gloria become convalescents from different "diseases," prisoners of different jails where, as Julio says: "Incomunicada [Gloria], sólo tolera su situación de encarcelamiento dentro de su enfermedad. Pienso en mis seis días de calabozo en Santiago, en lo distinto y en lo igual a esta enfermedad que fueron, y lo igual que son, también, a esto en que se está transformando mi novela." Not by mere coincidence, *El jardín* is divided into six chapters. This fact suggests the possible infinite exchange between the literal and figurative vision of the garden and the six days spent by Julio in jail—a substitution that can even take place in the title. Julio asks himself: "¿Hubiera podido terminarla sin el silencio de su enfermedad, sin la paz que me ha proporcionado su dolor y su encarcelamiento?" Once his novel is revised and Julio recognizes his wife's symptoms of recovery, he gives his new text to Gloria, whose muteness is now directed only toward him. Gloria's reading is staged, as de Man would have it, in his *Allegories of Reading* in "an inner, sheltered place . . . that has to protect itself against the invasion of an outside world, but that nevertheless has to borrow from this world some of its properties." The jail, in Gloria's text, has become a garden. But the garden turned out to be as oppressive for Gloria as she had intended to make it for Julio. In other words, the metaphorical connotation of the garden has expanded to include both the creation and the creator.

Gloria's reading of the new manuscript—that took place after Julio's revision of his own text—questions the first act of rereading that he experiences, since it suggests that the end result will not only be an act of criticism on her part but also of re-writing. We are forced to ask then: to what extent is Gloria's novel—that is, her writing—the consequence of her reading of Julio's novel? Is her own creation a "revision" of her husband's defective text? Núria's negative response to Julio's novel comes precisely from Julio's inability to "see" his own creation. Since he is incapable of "looking over" his text, his rewriting is as faulty as the first version: "No sé lo que he escrito, ni lo que a mí me ha ocurrido al escribir. No logro verme, ni 'verla'."

But the reader does "see" and recognize the confused causality of the acts of (re)reading and (re)writing in the identities, also confused, of Julio and Gloria. Their marital struggles, where harmony and discord coexist as a single entity and where dissatisfaction with the physical and sexual decadence of the partner's body can only be destroyed by the other's presence, dramatize their battle to reconcile their antagonistic discourses in a single body—or text—as a means of becoming one. Julio repeatedly questions himself about his tendency and Gloria's to invade the other's very being, to deny it by their intrusions: "¿Por qué sólo nos satisface la devoración mutua, el escarbar incansable de uno dentro del otro hasta que no queda ni un rincón turbio ni oscuro ni privado, ni una sola fantasía conservada como algo personal, sin exponerla?" The duality—reading and writing and their repetition—exercised both by Julio and Gloria, represent part of that struggle of identity where there is a confusing relationship between creator and reader. Within this profusion of readings, writings, and interpretations, Gloria raises these acts to the level of themes in her novel and experiences them in her chaotic life:

Escribí mis quejas en mi diario, tan desgarrador que ahora no me atrevo a releerlo; pero al releerlo entonces para escarbar mi rencor, y al volver y volver a escribir esas páginas, y darles vueltas y más vueltas, fui como depurándolo todo, en ese tiempo tan largo que las estaciones me han obsequiado junto al Mediterráneo, depurando la imagen de mí misma, la de Julio, la de nuestro matrimonio, hasta darme cuenta de que para que este examen tuviera fuerza de realidad era necesario que yo construyera algo fuera de mí misma, pero que me contuviera, para "verme": un espejo en el cual también se pudieran "ver" otros, un objeto que yo y otros pudiéramos contemplar afuera de nosotros mismos, aunque todo lo mío sea, ahora, en tono menor.

This is precisely why the famous editor of Latin American fiction, Núria Monclús, is willing to publish Gloria's novel. In opposition to the accomplishments of her text, Gloria realizes that the only footprint left by Julio's manuscript was a vague chronicle of injustice. But is Gloria's success, in any case, the result of her refusal to give Núria access to her diary and in a way risk a rewriting of her text by an "outsider," as they both did to Julio? Or is this not what actually happens when, during a meeting between editor and writer, Núria expresses dissatisfaction with the end of Gloria's novel, and after listening to her narration of Julio's vicissitudes in Tangiers, suggests that this become the end of the novel:

—¡Please do not disturb! ¡Qué irónico final feliz para una novela tan amarga!—dijo [Núria].

—¿Cómo . . . ?

—Bueno, ¿ño es éste el capítulo que falta, el que no has escrito . . . ? preguntó Núria Monclús.

Needless to say, this also happens to be the end of *El jardín de al lado*. Ironically, Núria-(re)reader has provided her own writing; she has imposed her own ending to Gloria's novel. But, is this a metaphor for what the reader of fiction experiences while engaged in the act of (re)reading—that is, the imperative to interpret and rewrite what (s)he is reading? When Núria suggests that Gloria's real challenge is to write a second novel, is she implying that the public's reading of her first text will immediately produce an infinite number of rewriters demanding their active participation in the process of creation?

This "struggle for authority," or even the recognition of it—to use Lucille Kerr's terms—is not limited to the two narrator-writers, Gloria and Julio, who represent the overt powers. But the causal line of development between the act of (re)reading and the need to (re)write unveils the fragility of those powerful overt structures of creation which, ironically, become subject to the strength of other readings and writings, such as Núria's or even our own. The "new" texts discovered do not represent the substitution of the original one, but an interplay of discourses that weakens the entire system of authority, including the authorial figure.

According to Kerr, when we finish reading *El jardín de al lado* and discover Gloria's voice as creator and manipulator of the narration, "we virtually see one image of authority usurp the position of the other: an apparently secondary subject of authority replaces another whose primary position seems to have been authorized and then denied by that very subject who literally follows, but also virtually precedes, him as the 'original' author(ity)." The truth of this statement is subject to an endless process of substitution that is not limited to Julio and to Gloria's manipulations or even to the direct or subtle allusions to Donoso's reality as a Chilean writer, but to the very nature and power of reading and writing. In this case, Donoso is equally subject to the process of substitution, and his text is also threatened by our reading and inevitable rewriting. The ironic overtones of the readers' discovery of Gloria's new position provoke the dismantling of the first reading, where the autobiographical first-person narration becomes a biographical account presented by one of the characters of the "former" text. Gloria's takeover demands an act of rereading—which for de Man is "a play between a prospective and a retrospective movement"—an act of revising not the truth or falseness of the overt and covert texts, but their rhetorical structures. As already implied, Gloria's literary account is also subject to a process of dismantling and reconstruction.

To decode the layers of rhetorical structures that a plurality of narrations—through the proliferation of readings and writings—imposes on the text, has been one of my tasks. Let us turn now to the recurrent trope of the garden. The first allusion to the duke's garden, which is next to Salvatierra's apartment, is immediately diverted to a different garden populated by other flora and by other figures:

> Mientras Gloria termina de abrir la cortina me levanto de la cama y miro: sí, un jardín. . . . Florecillas inidentificables brotan a la sombra de las ramas. . . . Ramas de un jardín de otro hemisferio, jardín muy distinto a este pequeño parque aristocrático, porque aquélla era sombra de paltos y araucarias y naranjos y magnolios, y sin embargo esta sombra es igual a aquélla, que rodea de silencio esta casa en que en este mismo momento mi madre agoniza.

Julio's memories of his Chilean house and its inhabitants (his dying mother, his dead father, his German-speaking niece, himself as a youth) come forth through the presence of an immediate and physical space already mentioned in the title. In addition, the fusion, confusion, and multiplica-tion of gardens and feelings remind the reader of a parallel proliferation of texts and narrative voices in *El jardín.* But this frantic reproduction of spaces and referents ironically creates a sense of oppression, isolation, claustrophobia, which is reflected in Julio's perception of the outside world through various windows or, as he later says, "desde mi ventana chileno-madrileña de exilado." As a space of enclosure, the garden is where Julio's historical past, his political experience, and his imaginative world clash to recreate the linguistic and narrative paradox of the text.

When Monika Pinell de Bray, that is, "la condesita," leaves with her family for the traditional summer vacation out of Madrid (their departure also coincides with the death of Julio's mother), Julio experiences a profound emptiness as he faces the deserted garden. His new enigma is how and with what he should fill the empty space. Surprisingly, what comes to Julio's mind is Marcelo Chiriboga's poetics of writing: "Al fin y al cabo uno no escribe con el propósito de decir algo, sino para saber qué quiere decir y para qué y para quiénes." The uninhabited garden, in Julio's words, is available now for a luminous inquisition; he is now "free" to write his own text—his own garden.

The garden represents the linguistic and narrative paradox of the text. Throughout the novel, this particular space is destroyed as a single unit while its various expressions become the paradigm of the emerging texts already conceived in the palimpsestic metaphor. In other words, the literal and metaphorical presence of the garden also works as a mirror image of the figural and literal meanings of the multiple overt and covert texts. Within this rhetorical distinction, what has to be taken into account is that *El jardín,* with all its linguistic and literary images—above all, the garden—is inherently metaphorical and its literal dimension impresses us also as a metaphor. The notions of reading and writing—an overt theme in Donoso's novel—compel Gloria and Julio (characters, writers, narrators) and us as readers, to engage in a process in which both of these activities are challenged by their own repetition. Rereading and rewriting endlessly multiply those subtexts that we have been in search of through the medieval practice of "scraping again." The text's deconstruction of its own writing is achieved in the infinite replacement and flow of previous writings that show no hierarchical bounds but which have been rhetorically concealed.

De Man's allusion to the traditional meaning of the metaphor sheds light on *El jardín*'s ultimate expression of the palimpsestic structure: "Conceptualization, conceived as an exchange or substitution of properties on the basis of resemblance, corresponds exactly to the classical definition of metaphor as it appears in the theories of rhetoric from Aristotle to Roman Jakobson." The exchange or substitution that takes place in the act of conceptualizing, of metaphorizing, leads the reader to ascertain Julio's strong desire to become someone else (Bijou, Pato, Gloria, Chiriboga, or the "guapo-feo"), to possess other people's bodies, discourses, identity, as he simultaneously erases his own decadent codes and footprints, which had traced his failure as a writer, a father, a husband, and as a political activist. Julio suddenly discovers the meaning of his attraction for Bijou: "De repente comprendí . . . que no era tan sexual mi atracción por Bijou sino otra cosa, un deseo de apropiarme de su cuerpo, de *ser* él, de adjudicarme sus códigos y apetitos, mi hambre por meterme dentro de la piel de Bijou era mi deseo de que mi dolor fuera otro, otros que yo no conocía o había olvidado; en todo caso, no mi código tiránico ni los dolores que me tenían deshecho . . ."

Julio's desire for transmutation is not only dramatized by his obsessive desire to become a Cortázar and write a *Rayuela* for Gloria, or to possess García Márquez or Vargas Llosa's literary discourse. It is in Julio's last chapter as narrator that the reader is confronted with his almost insane willingness to get lost in a jungle of unintelligible codes, which, in the eyes of a Westerner, are represented by the enigmas of the Arab world. Julio's desire for anonymity is not provoked by his fame as a writer but, ironically, by his endless failures. As he constantly suggests, his disappearance alone will guarantee freedom from his unsuccessful life. But is the need for transformation a way of searching for another mask, for another disguising source, or is it an act of unmasking that is indirectly linked to the activity and nature of literature?

His eagerness to unfold himself and experience a mental and physical metamorphosis reaches its highest point when, on a Tangiers street, he glimpses a scene in which a beggar is lying beside a rubbish dump and is accompanied by a naked one-year-old child who is feeding (his father?) with garbage: "Envidia: quiero ser ese hombre, meterme dentro de su piel enfermiza y de su hambre para así no tener esperanza de nada ni temer nada, eliminar sobre todo este temor al mandato de la historia de mi ser y mi cultura, que es el de confesar esta noche misma—o dentro de un plazo de quince días—la complejidad de mi derrota . . ." Julio goes a step further and even contemplates the possibility of killing the beggar. He recreates the scene: while he exchanges his breath and soul with the dead man, they also exchange their identities, allowing Julio to walk away from himself. The garden—in all its forms—and Tangiers are the two spaces in which signs are deprived of their traditional meaning and values: the former by the juxtaposition of past experiences with an unreadable present (the duke's garden with all its characters), and the latter by cultural differences. Who is Núria Monclús or Marcelo Chiriboga, Julio asks himself, in a space ruled by a completely different set of codes? Parallel to the unexpected narrative transition from the fifth to the sixth chapter in *El jardín de al lado,* which demands a rereading and reinterpretation of signs and "messages," the mysterious gardens

and the indecipherable happenings at Tangiers challenge the reader to retune his/her reading codes or habits.

Similarly, the narrative, psychological, and existential unmasking that characterizes Julio's discourse can be compared with his claim for physical transformation. Julio's writing tries arduously to detach itself from bourgeois codes and Western standards as a way, among other things, of challenging the "boom" writers. But as readers watch Julio disappear from the scene, witness Gloria's takeover, and later discover her husband's return to the hotel at Tangiers, they realize that Julio's search for otherness has also been a failure. What he seems incapable of appreciating is that one of the effective ways to become someone else (a metaphor of himself) is achieved through writing. Even Gloria's success does not come without pain and a certain fear of experiencing that same transformation that she will later embrace with determination: "Tuve la certeza, en esos minutos que siguieron a su desaparición del hotel, que no volvería a ver a Julio nunca más. . . . ¿En qué se transformaría Julio? ¿En ese mendigo que ni siquiera sé si vio, tirado a la puerta de una mezquita, mientras yo me transformaba en una señora latinoamericana, sola y madura, dedicada a traducir o a los telares en Sitges?"

The profound irony of *El jardín de al lado* is that Gloria, the writer of Julio's desire for transformation, is ultimately the one who experiences metamorphosis. As the creator of Julio's narrative voice, she (to some extent out of envy) impersonates his discourse, codes and sufferings, but only to free herself from anonymity. She happens to be the observer, the *reader* of the next-door garden which, as she suggests at the end, inspired the *writing* of her novel. As I have been stressing, the proliferation of intra- and extra-textual readers, narrators, and writers in *El jardín* and their constant exchange of roles not only creates a flow of texts within texts demanding to be read but also gives language a sense of otherness, where a frequent transformation toward aesthetic discourse takes place: the garden is framed through the image of the window; Gloria becomes the perfect "Odalisca de Ingres"; Bijou the *angelo musicante;* and Monica Pinell "la Brancusi."

Because *El jardín de al lado*'s main concern is the dialectic between reading and writing and the endless repetition of these two acts, the characters' explicit discussion of the ethical/aesthetical question in relation to both art and their own lives cannot be ignored. For example, it is Julio, himself, who poses the ethical/aesthetic conflict at the beginning of the novel: "¿Por qué—me preguntaba cada vez que hablaba con él [Pancho Salvatierra], cada vez que veía su casa o su pintura—, por qué Pancho tenía la terrible virtud de replantearme el problema, que yo ya daba por resuelto, de la relación entre arte y ética?" In Pancho's world—by contrast with Julio's philosophical views of art and life—things lack history, purpose, and even future. And it is in this absence that the antagonism between Pancho's art and Adriazola's becomes even more evident. The tension between Adriazola's weekly murals, permeated with propaganda against political and social injustice, and Pancho's lack of compromise represents one of Julio's moral conflicts. Julio's attachment to his political experience in Chile hinders his writing. But, ironically, when Gloria confronts him with his lack of political commitment, he indirectly associates himself with Pancho's perception of art and life: "No nací para héroe, ni siquiera para tener razón, lo que puede sañalarme como un ser limitado y comodón, pero qué le voy a hacer: es lo que soy. Después de todo lo que ha pasado, es muy duro darse cuenta que me interesa más la música de piano del romanticismo y las novelas de Laurence Sterne que tener razón en cualquier campo que sea." Julio's allusion to Sterne should not go unnoticed, since that eighteenth-century author's art represents one of the most important efforts to break with traditional literary codes. *Tristram Shandy* is an overt exaltation of literariness and of self-conscious fiction that has often been interpreted as a departure from a contextual commitment.

Not by mere coincidence, one of Salvatierra's most discussed paintings in the novel is precisely the one that reproduces a deceptive reality: between the two symmetrical and barred windows of his apartment there is a painting—of the same dimensions as the windows—that reproduces the white curtains of the entire house. Pancho Salvatierra, through his paintings, and, surprisingly, Gloria, through the text that "we" are reading, are perceived by Julio and Núria, respectively, as successful reconcilers of the "dual" scheme of art and ethics. Gloria acknowledges: "Te quiero explicar que yo, como persona, no es que no siga exaltada, políticamente, y sobre todo en relación a Chile. Haría cualquier cosa para que la situación cambiara en mi país. Pero sé que eso es ajeno a la literatura, quiero decir, ajeno por lo menos a mi literatura." Far beyond this confession, what she actually does is closer to what Julio and Núria perceive than it is to her own statement. Gloria's achievement is the incorporation of a political discourse through apparent rejection. That is, her own text about Julio's failure as writer incorporates—through storytelling—those same elements that contributed to his novel's unsuccessful outcome. Although Gloria theoretically pretends to stay away from nonliterary discourse, the reader is constantly exposed to the ideological developments of the protagonist creating, not a contradictory level of expression, but a dynamic relationship between ethics and art.

Within a thematic context the ethical issue is frequently translated into a deep sense of guilt, particularly expressed by Julio. Although he forcefully condemns Bijou's immoral behavior, Julio commits similar crimes. Directed by Bijou, Julio uses a "fixed" phone to call his mother in Chile; he steals Salvatierra's painting the way Bijou stole one sometime be-

fore, but with the additional burden that Julio falsifies the object painted, selling it as Gloria's portrait. Directly or indirectly, the idea of fraud is always present: fraud in the political development of Latin America, in Julio and Gloria's marital relations, in the subtle allusions to plagiarism, and even fraud on the part of the narrator-creator, inevitably posing the question of the intrinsic falseness of literature.

But our interest goes beyond strict concern for a moralistic view of ethics, to the multiple texts and subtexts unveiled and substituted, and their demand to be read and deconstructed. The "reconciliation" of ethics and aesthetics that the reader experiences both in Donoso's novel and in Gloria's is not the result of a mere fusion but the claim of each text to be (re)written and (re)read. The act of writing and reading represents the literal and figurative space where the creative process is conceived. But it is simultaneously the space that also generates its own destruction. The reader's perception of Julio's guilty conscience is not so much the recognition of the protagonist's incapacity to write a text that accurately fuses the ethical/aesthetical dialectic, but the realization that Gloria's multiple levels of narration, of writing, and of reading incarnate the ethical demands of a fictional enterprise; that is, to reread and rewrite Donoso's and Gloria's *El jardín de al lado*.

Paul de Man's discussion of the image of the fountain in Proust's *A la Recherche du temps perdu* suggests that the fountain—similar to the garden in *El jardín de al lado*—is not subject to the synthesis of the literal and the figural senses:

> The shimmering of the fountain then becomes a much more disturbing movement, a vibration between truth and error that keeps the two readings from converging. The disjunction between the aesthetically responsive and the rhetorically aware reading, both equally compelling, undoes the pseudo-synthesis of inside and outside, time and space, container and content, part and whole, motion and stasis, self and understanding, writer and reader, metaphor and metonymy, that the text has constructed. It functions like an oxymoron, but since it signals a logical rather than a representational incompatibility, it is in fact an aporia. It designates the irrevocable occurrence of at least two mutually exclusive readings and asserts the impossibility of a true understanding, on the level of the figuration as well as of the themes.

Beyond de Man's notion of unreadability, both the garden and the novel(s) studied characterize the proliferation of texts and intratexts in which to write, to read and to narrate about writing, reading, and narrating become the story-telling and the story-told. To write and to read the palimpsest is to rewrite and to reread *El jardín de al lado*.

Marcela Kogan (essay date November/December 1987)

SOURCE: "Stormy Adventures of the Spirit," in *Americas,* Vol. 39, No. 6, November/December, 1987, pp. 8-13.

[*In the following essay, Kogan relates comments made by Donoso in a Washington, D.C. lecture. Kogan also provides an overview of Donoso's career and details about his wife and family.*]

Back in the 1960's, when many Latin American writers were living in Europe, José Donoso accused Carlos Fuentes of stealing his ideas from a review he read on Donoso's book. Those were the days when Latin American writers, later dubbed the "Boom generation," stunned the world with dozens of novels all published at once—novels whose magical realism, intertwining metaphors and dazzling reflections cast a spell over the international literary community.

"Carlos told me I was being ridiculous," said the 63-year-old Chilean writer to a room full of avid fiction readers in Washington, D.C., where he spent four months earlier this year as a visiting scholar. "He said 'Nobody is stealing anything. All of us Latin Americans are writing one and the same novel.' In that period we were writing very different parts of something which was one thing."

At that time many Latin American writers were living abroad, away from the political turmoil in their own countries. They stuck together, meeting in cafés to talk about politics, literature, change. The group of exiles shared one feeling: nostalgia, and a need to express this profound sadness in writing.

Things have changed. Since then, everybody has had a different story to tell, and they have been telling it in dozens of books. Along with the works of the other Boom writers—García Márquez, Julio Cortázar, Carlos Fuentes and Mario Vargas Llosa, to mention a few—Donoso's books have been translated into dozens of languages, including Chinese.

Donoso broke with the traditional narrative in literature and exposed a new realm of possibilities: literature did not need to be limited to writing poetry about the land or testimonials (the vogue at the time). Dreams, fantasies, myths, nightmares were all sources of day-to-day reality, and a rich form for expression.

Donoso's critics call his work "original." Since the conversation he had with Fuentes, however, Donoso has given the issue of originality some thought. "I no longer care about originality," he says in British accented English while crossing his legs and stroking his gray beard. "I realized that we are all constantly stealing from others. I squeeze out of all forms—absurd, ironic, realism, grotesque. How can anybody

claim to be original? It's ridiculous. Originality is rated over quality. In our times, if somebody dabs green on a piece of canvas, a minute after it's televised [and] the world knows about it. Originality is not that much fun."

Neither is talking about the Boom. After decades of discussing the contribution Boom-generation writers have made to Latin American literature, Donoso has grown cynical. "Perhaps the moment has passed and we no longer have to continue talking of the Boom," he says in his book *The Boom in Spanish American Literature: A Personal History.* "The Boom has been a game; perhaps more precisely, a cultural broth, that nourished the tired form of the novel in Latin America for a decade."

Looking the part of the worldly intellectual that he is, Donoso wears a tweed jacket, shirt and tie. When he talks about literature, his words flow like a ream of paper through a typewriter, and he gets the dreamy look of a man in love with his work. His voice is soft and musical, and he punctuates conversation with hand gestures.

"We Latin Americans write about the snow storm while North Americans write about the snowflake," he continues. "There is something really exciting about the way we write, as we try to find out who we are, as we try to see what answers exist in the way of metaphor. We Latin Americans have a feeling of adventure in our novels."

His books are full of psychologically stormy adventure in which the reader can expect to encounter huge opulent mansions full of ghosts, myths, witches, nuns. Born into a wealthy family of doctors and lawyers, Donoso writes about the decadence of aristocracy, the repulsion of aging, the mysterious universe of maids, the grimness of a fated world.

His characters do ordinary things: visit friends, go on vacation, take naps. But behind these activities lurk destructive impulses. A man is overpowered by his passion for sleep, a materially successful couple begins losing their possessions without reason. The natural and the supernatural merge to create figures that are too grotesque to appear real but who, in fact, represent the ugly side of human beings.

Donoso transforms this pessimism into insight. People may not be able to control events in their lives, but they can at least understand them. And this is what he has spent most of his life doing—trying to understand himself and his surroundings.

Despite his greatest efforts, Donoso hasn't escaped from all the ghosts of his past. His childhood recollections are full of sick family members, bed-ridden aunts who got out once a year to visit Europe, poor relatives who came around to claim inheritances.

"I still think about death," he winces, his voice losing the melody. "My own death. My sickness, aging, degeneration. Things like that. I hate them. They scare me. I try to deal with it in my writing. It gets it out of my system for a while. But I pay heavily for it in stress. It becomes part of all that is negative."

"I'm not really that unhappy," he tries to cheer himself up, transforming another grim thought into a philosophy. "But I would like to know why I feel I've been given the instrument to find out but not the right. People have a chance to find out who they are, to know when they may die, but they haven't been given the right to find out. The open-endedness keeps people asking."

His characters share his dilemma as they pursue their "right to know." With unyielding introspection, they start probing into themselves, penetrating layers of knowledge and feeling. But when they reach the level underneath all that is definable, they panic and, as if blinded by the light, freeze. Few can transcend that state. There comes a point at which the politics of the country ties their hands behind their backs. They are too strapped to change.

But in real life, as well as in fiction, this soul searching becomes tiring. In a private interview, Donoso, who calls himself a "reluctant politician," refuses to talk about the difference between politics and literature, claiming that in 30 years he hasn't been able to answer that question, and that he finds such conversation "bloody boring."

Politics are implied throughout his works with metaphor. In *House in the Country,* for instance, children left alone in a mansion while their parents go off on an excursion break the rules and fight with the servants to seize control of the house. The "takeover" resembles a military coup overthrowing an incumbent government.

Donoso may be bored with certain subjects, but never with words. Fascinated with different ways of phrasing thought, Donoso experiments with his audiences, giving them a sense of the author at work. "A writer is a very confused person," he says, shifting into poetic gear while answering a question about his working style. "A novel happens to him. We are not very rational people. A novelist is a man who is involved with words and words that lead to words, which leads him to some memory, which he thought was forgotten. The words and sentences and the rhythm of what he is saying stem from a dark world, rains of many seasons, many streams. You want to make something out of clay, but you are not really sure what it is."

He wasn't sure what he was after when he started writing *Obscene Bird of Night,* his most accomplished work. The narrative is told from the point of view of Humberto, once secretary of a wealthy Chilean family, who helps the family's monster child feel normal by building him a monster world.

"The book almost killed him," says his wife, a tall, striking woman with high cheekbones and gray hair pulled back into a bun. "He was exorcising all his childhood ghosts. One day he came home and said he was so fed up with that book that he was going to burn it. Thank God I stopped him. I looked at him and said, 'If you burn that book you won't get rid of it.'"

The happy couple, who met in church with a baby in their arms when a mutual friend chose them as godparents, moved 22 times over the past 20 years of marriage, hopping around from Europe to the United States as Donoso tried to overcome the writing block he suffered while writing *Obscene Bird of Night.*

They spent time in Madrid, Majorca, Paris. They covered university networks in the United States, from the University of Iowa, to Princeton, to Dartmouth. They attended book parties in New York and Mexico celebrating the launching of novels he managed to write despite his block. But always, their goal was to finish *Obscene Bird of Night.*

Walking around their efficiency apartment with a pink bathrobe on, the television news blaring in the background, his wife remembers how timid Donoso used to be about his writing, especially after he met Carlos Fuentes at a writers' conference.

"Carlos was very impressed with Pepe's book and told him to send a copy to his publisher in the United States. But Pepe didn't do it. He never thought anything like that could happen to him. So I sent it there. Several months later Carlos calls to congratulate us for having our book accepted by the largest gringa press in the U.S."

The Donosos made themselves at home in Washington, D.C., right away, hanging on the wall frameless prints purchased at the National Gallery of Art, along with photos of their daughter and pets. Plastered on one wall with thick black headlines that read "Donoso & Donoso" was a centerpiece of a magazine showing Donoso escorting his adopted daughter to the altar, where she was to wed her cousin.

"She is ashamed that I'm a writer," Donoso once said about his daughter. "She told me that my books all sound the same. That's all right. She is only 20. She has time to learn."

"Pilarcita adores Pepe," says his wife, waving away his wisecrack. "When she is sad, Pepe gets paralyzed. He can't write."

Growing up in Chile, Donoso had no idea he would someday be talking to García Márquez about writing blocks, showering at Pablo Neruda's house, accompanying Jorge Borges to the house of the great-granddaughter of José Hernández, author of the classic *Martín Fierro*.

In fact, he had never heard of them. Like many of his contemporaries, Donoso felt frustrated with his university education, which required readings of well-known writers like Faulkner, Hemingway and Camus and ignored Latin American authors. Back in the 1950's most companies published Spanish translations of European and U.S. classics and invested in local, popular commercial writers.

In the Boom book he analyzes the problem. "The regionalists wanted to raise the barriers that separated one country from another, literally isolating them, praising xenophobia and chauvinism and confusing these concepts with nationalists."

What resulted was a "defensive and arrogant Olympus of writers," he says. "We were orphans. But this orphanhood, this position of rejecting what we forced on us as 'ours,' a position in which we were placed by the novelists who preceded us, produced an emptiness in us, a feeling of not having anything exciting in our writing. And I don't believe I'm wrong in maintaining that my generation of novelists looked not only outside Latin America but also outside our own language toward the Anglo-Saxon countries, toward France and Italy in search of sustenance. . . ."

He left Chile in his early 20's to explore the world. And explore he did, diving into his new life the way he delves into his characters. He worked as a truck driver, shepherd, delivery boy, subconsciously beginning to collect details he would later use in developing characters. In a half-demolished room in the back of the writers association in Buenos Aires, Donoso picked up Borges for the first time. Literary vistas stretched open before him, the possibility that Chile was not an island, that it existed within the context of Latin America, and that Latin America existed within the context of the world.

When he was ready to publish, the companies weren't interested. His work was considered "difficult," and he wasn't well known. But Donoso convinced his publisher that he could sell enough copies to cover costs.

In his late 20's, when most friends were settled down with full-time work and a family, Donoso stood on street corners in Santiago trying to sell his first collection of short stories. His buddies helped by standing on other busy intersections.

He sold enough copies. The next year he won a prize for the short stories. When he was ready to publish *Coronation,* he contacted the publishers, but nobody returned his calls. Again, he hit the streets, this time expanding his marketing plans to

include his father, who agreed to take a stack to his club, where gentlemen with canes came to play cards.

Coronation became a big hit. The impact it had on Latin American literature was immediate. The story, about a Chilean woman who retains the vision of her glorious aristocratic past even while she is dying, starts out with traditional narrative. But the author pushes this form into the grotesque at the end of the novel when, in a mocking celebration, the maids crown her.

In his later novels, Donoso begins to play with notions of ambiguity, showing how different interpretations of one incident can coexist, despite the contradictions—a technique he admired in Faulkner's works.

In *Obscene Bird of Night,* he stretches ambiguity to the limit, and his characters can no longer be viewed in traditional terms. Grotesque elements interact with the imaginary world, and the reader no longer knows what is real and what is fiction.

In retrospect, Donoso, who was enraptured after reading Carlos Fuentes's *Where the Air is Clear,* now understands that his writing block partially stemmed from the feeling that he lagged behind other writers.

"The book [*Where The Air is Clear*] brusquely tore me away from the aesthetic to which I was still attached," he writes in the Boom book. "So much so that on a purely intellectual level I think it was this trauma, uprooting me from my homespun aesthetic in order to land me within a broader ethic, that left me incapable of finishing the *Obscene Bird of Night,* incapable simply because I was afraid of not being able to live up to the literary demands then suggested to me as superior to the ones I had come to think of as my own."

Donoso is now ready to return to Chile, despite the love-hate relationship he has with his country. His last book, *Desesperanza* (*Desperation*) features a Chilean singer who returns to his homeland after years of exile in Europe. This is one of the first times Santiago, Chile, will appear in literature as a main setting. Donoso has finally given his home a place in the classics.

But his fame hasn't made him happy. "I can't say I'm unhappy," he says, making yet another attempt to understand his feelings. "I never would have thought that I'd make a living off my writing, that I would have such a wonderful marriage and meet so many wonderful people. Yet there is a part of me that feels unsuccessful as a writer. It's good. I think. I hate what comes with too much loving yourself. I feel that I carry within me the seeds of an unfulfilled man, which accounts for so much of my pessimism."

The character he most relates to is Julio Mendes from *Jardin de al lado* (*The Garden Next Door*), who suffers from a writer's block that directs his attention from his typewriter to his neighbor's garden, where he begins to hear the voices of family long since dead. Obsessed with the ghosts of his past, Mendes and his wife nurse themselves numb with liquor and drugs.

Will he ever write any stories with happy endings?

"I don't think so," he says. "Not really. To have a happy ending, I would have to be a bad writer. If there had to be a happy ending, I'd have to stop writing."

"One doesn't write because one is happy," he says, amusing himself with the play on words. "One wants to know why he isn't happy, which means one doesn't know, you see. So one can't be happy without knowing."

Rosemary Geisdorfer Feal (essay date March 1988)

SOURCE: "Veiled Portraits: Donoso's Interartistic Dialogue in *El jardin de al lado*," in *MLN,* Vol. 103, No. 2, March, 1988, pp. 398-418.

[*In the following essay, Feal discusses the "meta-confessional" nature of the narration in* The Garden Next Door, *and the masking, or mediated figure of the male author.*]

José Donoso has characterized *El jardín de al lado* as his "most realistic novel to date; it is a psychological study and there are few masks although I imagine scholars will find them." He also claims that it is "the portrait of a middle-aged literary couple whose love is starting to give way and the political defeat somehow breaks them but they stick together." Donoso's classification of this work as a portrait is far from arbitrary, and he is right in imagining that students of the novel will find masks where he consciously placed few. On close examination, the novel engages in a lively dialogue between two arts—literature and painting—that attempts to answer the question: how can the eye/*I* see itself? The confessional mode, which entails intimate revelations, here becomes a device that instead produces a textual disguise of remarkable complexities. Julio Méndez, the primary narrator of *El jardín,* documents his failed efforts to produce a publishable version of his novel, whose subject is the military coup in his native Chile. But the whole of *El jardín* revolves around the hidden female narrator-author, Gloria Echeverría de Méndez, Julio's wife, who steps forward in the final chapter. In telling the story of exile, Donoso thus takes flight from his own *I*—always a potential empty shifter in literature, and always an other, as Rimbaud tells us—to take refuge in his writer-protagonist who himself is filtered through the eyes of an overriding narrator.

In this confessional work, then, the figure of the male author is twice masked or mediated in the text: through the narrative disguises of a male character with a fictional name and through a female author-character who purportedly writes the novel finally accepted for publication by literary agent Núria Monclús. Thus *El jardín* centers on a meta-confessional act: Gloria writing about Julio writing about his struggles to write an autobiographically-inspired novel. This great unwritten novel of the Chilean experience, which is only spoken about in *El jardín,* constitutes the elusive core of the work in that it escapes both Gloria, Julio and perhaps even Donoso to remain trapped in layers of narrative and psychological cover. When the novel first opens, Julio is seen avoiding his typewriter, the taskmaster that demands either a new version of his "novela-documento . . . ya rechazada una vez por la formidable Núria Monclús" or the "tediosa traducción de *Middlemarch* de George Eliot, hecho en *tandem* con Gloria, labor que parecía eterna . . ." In tandem: one behind the other, or a team: but for the team to operate, one partner must assume a dominant position. And the apparent forerunner, Julio, wears blinders, since he remains unaware that throughout the entire work he is a textual object for his wife, the successful author. Interestingly, Julio's and Gloria's translation is of a work by a female author who goes by a male pseudonym, which previews in ironic fashion the gender crossing that is unveiled in the final chapter of Donoso's novel.

In her insightful analysis of the structure of authority at play in *El jardín,* Lucille Kerr concludes that "the contingent and mobile quality of the authority apparently held or wielded by the principal subjects undermines any notion of its absolute or permanent nature, even when the final inversion, the surprising reversal, would seem to put an end to its movements." Yet, we may add, it is precisely the unconscious fantasy of an integral and infallible narrative anchor that undergirds the novel: this figure is clearly related to the pre-oedipal or phallic mother, whom Jane Gallop describes in Lacanian terms: she is "apparently omnipotent and omniscient until the 'discovery of her castration,' the discovery that she is not a 'whole' . . ." Omnipotent and omniscient: what better words to characterize the hidden Gloria, who has managed to pass off a convincing first-person narration in her husband's voice? She then becomes the all-seeing eye, the spy whose gaze penetrates into the most remote corners of Julio's being. It would be she who has Julio engage in ruthless self-examination, she who authors the devastatingly ironic remarks about herself: "la odio porque está fea o mal vestida o porque saló demasiado el tomate . . ." In keeping with modern functions of the first person, the *I* of Julio's text fails to be self-referential and really stands for another: thus, the masculine *I* harbors a latent *she,* who eventually dislocates the unstable *I* to subordinate it as a third person, *he.* The narrative filter is thus a veil that cloaks the shocking, naked reality of the female author at the work's core. Here we have two veiled portraits, as the cover of *El jardín* graphically symbolizes with its version of René Magritte's *The Lovers*. In this extratextual sign system, Magritte's painting is superimposed on portions of a draft of *El jardín;* these typewritten lines, containing crossed out words and hand written corrections, extend from the front cover of the book to the back. The couple's shrouded faces partially block the traces of the text-in-progress, thus mirroring the process that occurs within the novel. In *El jardín,* words, both in their semiotic and semantic powers, remain buried, literally under cover. The association of text to art constitutes a most important medium through which Donoso explores the couple's relationship to each other and to writing, and it is through an interartistic analysis that we may gain access to the deep structure of desire in *El jardín de al lado.*

The apartment in Madrid, home to Julio and Gloria for the summer, belongs to Chilean Pancho Salvatierra, a painter. Julio describes one wall of his friend's apartment: "En el salón, dos ventanas simétricas, desnudas, que descubren sólo cuadrados de *verdure* como si fueran tapices, y entre ellas, de exactamente las mismas dimensiones, un cuadro que reproduce los cortinajes blancos de toda la casa, cuadro en que reconozco la maestría para reproducir la engañosa realidad que es don de Pancho Salvatierra." Bijou, son of Chilean exiles living in Paris, bursts into laughter when he first spots Pancho's *trompe l'oeil* painting. Bijou's reaction gives Julio cause to reflect on Pancho's apparent success: "Poseer un punto de vista tan original que se acerque a lo cómico . . . , pienso en Dalí, en Chirico, en Magritte, que también son envolventes e instantáneos y divertidos. . . . Eso envidio." Pancho's *trompe l'oeil* consists of false curtains that cover nothing (except empty wall space), while the bare windows in the room create a painting-like impression as they open on the lush garden next door. Donoso's novel, itself a study in trickery with regard to characters and readers alike, also plays with the notion of naked revelations and veiled portraits. But to equate Pancho's work with Magritte's, as Julio does, is to err significantly, for while there are similarities in theme, an important difference stands out. Magritte creates not the *trompe l'oeil,* which hinges on deceiving one's perception of physical reality, but instead cultivates what Picasso has called the *trompe l'esprit,* a type of metaphysical questioning. Pancho's work of art may best be compared to one of Magritte's paintings, such as *The Gioconda* that show what would be a physically impossible reflection. In this painting two free-standing black curtains are placed against a dark background; the superimposed panel in the shape of a curtain appears to be an isolated patch of sky with clouds. Of course, the black curtains in *The Gioconda* do not fulfill their traditional function of shading out light, whereas the curtain-shaped sky panel defies even more dramatically the function of real draperies. Magritte's *The False Mirror* depicts a giant human eye, but filling it is a reflection of blue sky and clouds. The "painting philosopher" challenges the seeing function of the eye and instead turns it into the object viewed. Similarly, in *El jardín,* the fascinating woman in the garden next door, the Countess Monika Pinell de Bray, has Magritte-like eyes, which serve as false mirror to Julio: "como en una cabeza clásica de mármol, sus ojos son vacíos. Pero con una diferencia: en vez de ser un vacío de piedra en blanco, son dos ventanas abiertas al cielo por el cual transitan nubes o donde juegan niños o . . . , cuando mi amor es más doloroso, los agujeros almendrados me dejan ver olas rompiendo sobre riscos, y más allá, el horizonte del mundo entero." Like Magritte, Donoso takes up the problematics of "seeing" in *El jardín,* where the subject sees himself reflected in the eyes of the (female) other, who in turn views herself through the male's desire.

To pursue the painting analogy, central to the confessions in Donoso's work, we must now turn to the Odalisque paintings of Jean-Auguste-Dominique Ingres; it is here that we find the interplay of desire and vision carried out in full depth. Julio first associates Gloria with Ingres' Odalisque on their wedding night, an image he continues to evoke throughout the decades of their marriage. He describes Gloria as she showers: "el torneado de la otrora perfecta Odalisca de Ingres—deleitosa cadera plena, largo arco de la espalda para acariciary pierna larga, largo cuello, y ojo alargado bajo el turbante envuelto en la cabeza volteada—se dibujaba más allá de esa puerta, pero, sóbre todo, más allá del tiempo, por el reconocido roce de la ropa al caer por los contornos de aquel cuerpo. Hasta que, contemporánea, doméstica, imperfecta otra vez, la oí dar la ducha y meterse debajo." This description corresponds most exactly to the *Grande Odalisque* (Fig. 1), but may also be related to like paintings such as the *Valpinçon Bather* or *Odalisque with the Slave.* For Julio, Gloria lives on as the imperfect, deformed Odalisque whom he attempts to resuscitate through physical contact and mental fantasy.

This comparison between Gloria and the Odalisque rests on a solid basis, as revealed by Julio's knowledge of the artist's technique: "Ingres, pienso al mirarla ahora, sabía dibujar como nadie: le bastaba la más sutil modulación de una línea, variar su espesor, su densidad, hacerla más profunda o casi eliminarla, para hacer real la sugerencia de masa y de peso y el satinado y la sensualidad y el calor de la espléndida carne de su modelo . . ." While the equation Gloria-Odalisque serves to keep Julio's wife attractive to him but at the same time to show painfully how she has aged and changed, the association also keeps Gloria in her marriage, as she discloses in the last chapter to Núria Monclús during their meeting to discuss Gloria's accepted manuscript: "¿Y por qué no abandonaste tú a Julio?", inquires the literary agent of Gloria, who responds: "La Odalisca, que tan orgullosa me hace, no existe fuera del recuerdo y la fantasía de Julio. . . . ¿Qué otro ser puede restituirme mi cuerpo de entonces, hacer presente la realidad de esa Odalisca del pasado, sino Julio?

Un beso, la toalla envuelta en la cabeza, basta." The subtle implications of this linkage become apparent when we examine Ingres' paintings, which reveal a remarkable similarity in artistic vision to Donoso's portrait of Gloria in *El jardín*. For example, Robert Rosenblum makes these comments on the *Grande Odalisque:* "the prodigious ductility of the line . . . suggests a flesh of voluptuous malleability, yet this pliant stuff is polished to a marmoreal firmness, so that it seems alternately warm-blooded and cold, slack and taut, a fusion of opposites." Is not Gloria forged precisely as a flesh-and-blood woman whom her husband believes to know completely, yet simultaneously as the unknowable, unreachable, *unreadable* controller of the text and consequently of its primary narrator? And while the *Grande Odalisque* has been compared to a titillating pin-up girl, most critics instead agree that these paintings "generate erotic power precisely because they elude the imagination's hot embrace," as John Connolly puts it. More radical is Norman Bryson's opinion that sexuality in Ingres "is not a positive or *plenary* force, but a force of *vacuum*"; he claims that the *Grande Odalisque* "is not offering herself at all," but rather is presented in terms of highest unreality, and "constitutes a radical disruption of the standard and homogeneous image of woman." This self-dissolving and self-unravelling movement that Bryson sees in the implausible physical form of the Grande Odalisque causes her to be Ingres' most impossible creation.

Paradoxically, it is this impossible creation that incarnates the structure of desire both in Ingres and Donoso. And returning to our original thesis, what would represent the structure of desire better than the fantasy of the phallic/castrated woman who threatens the male protagonist or viewer with a terrifying *manque-à-être*? Any text, Sarah Kofman argues, "is always a tissue that, for fear of castration, disguises a terrible and most tempting nudity . . ." Like the spider, a phallic mother symbol, Gloria spins narrative threads to cover her nakedness and perhaps to entrap her victim. But she is also the Odalisque, who, let us remember, is a female slave or concubine in a harem, to which men are forbidden access. This is Gloria speaking in Tangiers, near the end of Julio's part of the text: "¿Qué pena que el idiota de Carlos Martel ganara en Poitiers! . . . Si no, andaríamos todos vestidos así, yo viviría cómodamente en un harem precioso. . . . En fin . . . por lo menos andaríamos con la cara velada." Julio wonders to himself, "velada para disimular la vergüenza . . .": that is, the facial veil has been displaced upward from the true locus of corporeal shame. So it becomes clear that Donoso's evocation of the Odalisque is far from casual: it symbolizes Gloria's conflictive double role as tempting slave and terrifying slave-driver. Looking back at Ingres' paintings, we notice that the Odalisque indeed remains partially veiled, but not her face: it is her genital nudity that remains out of sight, either because she has her back to us (*Grande Odalisque*) or because she is shrouded by the diaphanous cloth that extends provocatively from her thighs to other regions (*Odalisque with the Slave*). Ingres did indeed paint total nudes, but the Odalisque guards her mysteries, like Gloria. Lacan tells us that "the phallus can only play its role as veiled, that is, as in itself the sign of the latency with which everything signifiable is struck as soon as it is raised to the function of signifier." Ingres and Donoso touch upon a common fantasy when they cast their Odalisques in the mold of a veiled woman who defies man's attempts to possess her, and who remains alluringly attractive because of what she hides, or more accurately, because she hides it.

This hidden schema of temptation and terror, of strength and impotence, of hostility and affection, goes beyond the immediate duo of Gloria and Julio. Let us consider the role of Núria Monclús, the literary agent who twice rejects Julio's novel. She is intimately associated with Gloria, first by Julio, who proclaims of his wife: "ella y Núria son, igualmente, mis verdugos." A mythical devouring female, Núria represents all that is terrible: she preys on weaklings like Julio with her "carnívoro sadismo." While Julio finds some comfort in the *vox populi* that makes Núria out to be a frigid, avaricious and opportunistic woman, he cannot escape her tyranny: "¿Si recupero mi facultad de sentir placer en vez de aceptar pasivo mi ciudadanía en esa provincia tan extrañamente reglamentada que es la del fracaso personal . . . podré adquirir la libertad para escribir otra o la misma novela . . . ? No: aunque saque ahora mismo los papeles de la maleta, la figura de Núria Monclús con la telaraña velándole los ojos y la espada de fuego en su mano ensangrentada se interpondrá entre yo y el placer." Julio feels himself imprisoned in his novel, with Núria as his jailor. Unlike his wife, this spiderwoman shows no positive reverse side to Julio: Núria is *par excellence* the castrating, phallic mother who impedes the son's absolute pleasure. Núria admonishes Julio to "see" his novel: "verla," she says from beneath her own veiled eyes. And yet sight belongs specifically to the phallic order, since the discovery of castration revolves around a vision, a prizing of that which is seen above all. What Julio ultimately sees is himself as failed writer: "Soy inerte, castrado, malescritor . . ."; "el falso triunfador el macho falsificado, el ladrón, el delincuente, el mentiroso . . ." And while Julio struggles to assume his own failure, as he puts it, he nevertheless incriminates Núria, agent of his literary nonexistence.

Julio's failure extends to Gloria, not only spouse but also collaborator and reader of his fiction: "El fracaso es de ambos, yo no la arrastré a él, yo tengo esperanza aún, y hasta ella suele tenerla, sólo que a veces todo se torna negro, como si todo ocurriera detrás del antifaz sin ojos . . ." Gloria's black night mask is one way of seeing, or rather, of blocking out a vision. For if Gloria "sees" Julio's novel when he reads it to her during her recovery from severe depression, she also is blinded because, as she states, "no puedo juzgarla porque es tan mía como tuya y te quiero . . ." Or rather, the successful novel is hers alone: Julio is blinded to the fact that Gloria will write a triumphant version of their intimate story. Julio dons his wife's black mask to obliterate all visual sensations, a symbolic gesture that represents the overall irony of his textual predicament. In his naiveté, he fears that Núria's rejection of his novel would be an equally terrible blow to his wife: "Núria tiene la culpa, puesto que ella me impide triunfar: ella tiene atrapada a Gloria en una telaraña, que es su cárcel." But, instead, the two web-spinning women form an alliance in the book's final chapter. Gloria's opening line undoes the frightful picture Julio had painted of Núria: "Ninguna de las terribles leyendas que circulan sobre ella son verdad: es fina, encantadora, generosa, sensible." Thus, the portrait of Gloria that Julio sketched throughout "his" part of the narration is shown to be distorted as well: no longer ensnared in anyone's net, she has instead become the trapper. Julio's derogatory comments about Gloria's creative abilities turn ironically against him when their source is revealed. Or do they? Must we disavow the authority who really engenders these transfigurations? Does not the figure of the male author—not the fictional Julio, but José Donoso—stand clearly behind the many masks assumed by the writer-characters in the text of *El jardín?* After all, Gloria *is* his creation. Could we not apply to *El jardín* and Gloria what Donoso himself has said of Manuela, the protagonist in his *El lugar sin límites:* "a man who poses as a woman who poses as a man who poses as a woman." *El jardín* harbors a futile search that crosses gender boundaries: much like Ingres' Odalisques, who exude desire and yet thwart it, the narrators and their masks seek through the Other a knowledge impossible to attain. Every object of desire, according to Lacan, will show itself to be "necessarily ephemeral and destined to be supplanted because it is incapable of stopping up the lack inscribed in the subject from the start . . ." Donoso's characters cannot fathom the nature of lack in the Other, precisely because they fail to recognize it in themselves, and their incessant search for (phallic) plenitude edges them closer to the void.

If Gloria's apparition at the end of the work symbolizes the male narrator's blocked access to knowledge, vision, or truth, then so does the garden nextdoor to the apartment building in Madrid where the couple is staying. Much like the self-representative figure of Hieronymous Bosch above the abyss in *The Garden of Earthly Delights,* Julio observes the spectacle of the neighbors as they dance, laugh, and splash about in the pool, a veritable "Pond of Lust," and he wishes to join them: "El anhelo es de pasar al otro lado del espejo, que ellos habitan . . ." This hallucinatory garden next door serves as a cruel mirror that forces Julio to "see" himself as incomplete or disassembled, the same image that Núria reflects back to him. Julio's fascination with this garden centers on the young Countess, who changes before his ever-watchful eyes from ordinary *hausfrau* into passionate adultress. In a reversal of the classic primal scene, Julio, the middle-aged adult, glimpses the youthful participants in their orgy: "me

abro en una oquedad de melancolía al darme cuenta de la irreparable exclusión de mi cuerpo y mi mundo del desenfadado vigor de esos cuerpos que continúan nadando . . . abrazados en racimos."

Julio describes the Countess and her lover as follows: "el hombre desnudo toma en sus brazos a la mujer de la túnica que se entrega a su cuerpo en un abrazo tan sexual como el de la pareja de Klimt, en que sólo se ven las cabezas envueltas por la algarabía de colores de oro, pero que los ojos cerrados de la mujer describen como el placer de la entrega total." Klimt's *The Kiss* indeed transmits the total self-laden of the embracing pair as they merge into one gold-laden sphere. But this bliss in Klimt is short-lived: the erotic, the "doomed-to-transiency embrace," as Alessandra Comini calls it, leads to the spectre of aging, destruction, and death. This stifling, colorful ornamentation in works like *The Kiss* engulfs the couple in an over-lush garden, one that gives way to the stark, deathlike embrace of, for example, the clinging pair in Klimt's Beethoven frieze, done mostly in *grisaille.* According to one critic, Klimt's female is sexually destructive, "her eroticism cloaked, layered and ultimately kept untouchable by a glittering surface of elaborate gold painting," a vision close to Ingres' and Donoso's. It comes as little surprise at the end of *El jardín* when Gloria reveals that the Countess had committed suicide. Gloria thinks: "tal vez no haya pasado de ser una fantasía cuya clave se encuentra en *El abrazo,* de Klimt. . . ." This fantasy, as we will see, interconnects with the other artistic themes so richly woven throughout Donoso's novel.

When at the end of Chapter 2 Julio, from his darkened room, hears the sounds of splashing water in the pool, he mentally recites part of the third stanza of T. S. Eliot's "East Coker": *The laughter in the garden, echoed ecstasy / Not lost, but requiring, pointing to the agony / Of death and birth."* Donoso's interartistic dialogue once again strikes deep chords; T. S. Eliot's *Four Quartets,* which belong to the confessional mode, treat precisely the writer's struggle to "see" his work and himself. Further ahead in "East Coker" we read: "So here I am, in the middle way . . . Trying to learn to use words, and every attempt / Is a wholly new start, and a different kind of failure / Because one has only learnt to get the better of words." Julio's lost garden, like Eliot's, is a paradise of words that could somehow magically take shape on the page to transmit feelings or to communicate experiences. But words, for both writers, remain insubstantial signs that call attention to themselves, that constantly threaten to unveil their status as "shabby equipment always deteriorating," as Eliot says. Julio, like all humans, must mediate himself through words—doubly so, since he is writer. When he becomes caught up in the other's look in his attempt to see himself, he only becomes further alienated from the truth he so desperately seeks. This may explain Julio's desire to exchange himself, to become another, be it the adolescent Bijou the Bachic revellers next door, or the ailing beggar in Tangiers: "quiero ser ese hombre, meterme dentro de su piel enfermiza y de su hambre para así no tener esperanza de nada ni temer nada, eliminar sobre todo este temor al mandato de la historia de mi ser y mi cultura, que es el de confesar esta misma noche . . . la complejidad de mi derrota . . ."

Yet the deepest level of surrender to another, or of disappearance into another, occurs metafictionally when Gloria steps out as the "real" author of Julio's story. May we then say that she, too, wishes to be another, to trade in her identity for, perhaps, that of her husband, whose narrative voice she usurps? This undoubtedly is one reading the novel allows. Let us not forget that Gloria presents herself as a potential author: "¿Si supieras cuántas novelas no escritas tengo encerradas dentro de mí, como gatos locos en un saco, que pelean y se destrozan . . . !" This remark meets with Julio's scorn: "¡No digas leseras! ¿Me quieres convencer ahora de que eres una escritora frustrada?" Gloria mockingly retorts: "En fin, ¿quién sabe? Puede ser sólo la clásica envidia del pene . . ." That writing is a phallic activity has of course been questioned by feminists, and even silence has been called woman's true voice. Silence serves as a way for Gloria to avenge herself: it is a weapon she uses effectively against Julio. But, as Kerr demonstrates, Gloria breaks silence and turns to a more powerful weapon to achieve her final revenge: writing her own and Julio's story. Through writing, Gloria shuns her exclusive role as Odalisque, object (and creation) of man's desire. By writing herself, Domna Stanton points out, woman may reappropriate the female body, "which man has confiscated as his property." These issues of gender and writing are firmly planted and debated on the multiple narrative planes of *El jardín,* not as detached, theoretical constructs but as an intimate portrait of two people's trials and triumphs.

But this gender-writing conflict leads not to the destruction of the couple's relationship, but to reconciliation and a "Glorious" triumph. Julio realizes that his wife has shared his vision of Tangiers and most likely would be able to write a superior chronicle of the experience; thus he encourages her to take up where he trails off. So the gender-crossing in *El jardín* must also be considered as a positive force, since it touches on an androgynous spirit, which, Heilbrun says, may be identified in literary works "where the role of the male and female protagonists can be reversed without appearing ludicrous . . ." In his reversal of narrative voices Donoso perfects this structure of androgyny: Gloria is not only plausible, but also *invisible,* in as much as she actually passes unnoticed under Julio's cover.

Despite Gloria's decision to stay with Julio, she nevertheless expresses dissatisfaction with her marital role, and formulates this wish: "Ser yo, por fin, no parte incompleta de lo que Lawrence Durrell, falsamente, llama '*that wonderful two-headed animal that is a good marriage*', ideal que durante tanto tiempo me sirvió para apoyar mi matrimonio." Yet, ironically, the two-headed animal must be seen as the purported creator of this fragmented novel, for neither of the two main voices in *El jardín* would be possible without the other. When joined they form what may be called, in Melanie Klein's terminology, a fantasy of combined parents, in which the mother retains her phallic powers through her link to the father. But if on the one hand the image of combined parents in *El jardín* stands for phallic power, on the other it disguises a lack-in-being. Much like the hydra, which reproduces a slain head with two new ones, the fused narrative authorities of *El jardín* only manage a thin cover for their individual wounded selves. For in order to generate new phallic heads, the hydra must first suffer decapitation: and that is precisely what Gloria undergoes by means of the portrait that Julio calls *Retrato de la señora Gloria Echeverría de Méndez.*

After Julio learns from Núria that his novel has been rejected for a second time, he enters Pancho's study, where he spots a painting with an electric, phosphorescent blue background: "un bello cuerpo de mujer desnuda, sentado, pero invadido por cientos de insectos meticulosamente pintados que cubren como joyas la carne fresca y bella de esa mujer, cochinillas, libélulas, moscardones, escarabajos, grillos, saltamontes, arañas. La figura sentada tiene un batracio sobre una rodilla, de modo que le cubre el sexo: los ojos del bicho son penetrantes, y la boca húmeda y lívida, abierta. El marco es un listón de plata que decapita la figura, cuya cabeza queda fuera del cuadro." On the back appears Pancho's title, *Retrato de la condesa Leonor de Teck,* which Julio promptly blackens out and replaces with Gloria's name: he then wraps up the painting and proceeds to bootleg it. This is not the first time a painting of Pancho's disappears from the apartment: Bijou apparently stole the one depicting a package wrapped in Manila paper, which Julio and Gloria desperately tried to recover (exactly like the couple in "Atomo verde número cinco.") Nor is the Countess's portrait the first object to be wrapped up and shipped off: Julio's novel manuscript received the same treatment. After hearing it read, Gloria exclaimed: "Mandémosla ahora mismo. En la despensa hay un rollo de papel de Manila y una madeja de cordel . . ." The manuscript, in its package form, is a material sign that reproduces the one contained in the painting Bijou stole: both packages disappear, their insubstantiality confirmed in loss.

Julio's description of the portrait of Leonor/Gloria does not, as far as I know, refer to a real painting but to the work of a character in a novel, and as such is just a verbal construction. It nevertheless may be related to paintings by artists such as Bosch, Magritte and Dalí. Bosch of course captured on canvas the images of the nightmare of humanity in his *Garden of Earthly Delights,* including bestial torments not so different from the insect-covered body of Pancho's painting. Following Bosch's lead, the surrealists, particularly Salvador Dalí, cultivated horrifyingly beautiful dream imagery. In Dalí's *Hallucinogenic Toreador,* with its shocking blue background (also present in a good number of his other works), we may appreciate affinities to the fictional *Retrato de la condesa Leonor de Teck.* Like Magritte, Dalí often studies the duplication of a figure; in *Hallucinogenic Toreador,* multiple versions of the Venus de Milo are depicted in floating positions throughout the center band of a coliseum-bullring, her lower torso draped in bright garb. Twice she is shown frontally; four figures of the status in descending proportions appear with their backs to the viewer. Also visible are several heads and faces (one of whom represents Gala, the painter's wife), and tiny replicas of the Venus de Milo posed like classical statues around the upper ring of the coliseum and below the large female figures. What disturbs this serene beauty is the juxtaposition of life-sized flies at the base of the large statues; the motif is repeated in the sections of dots covering much of the painting that sprout wings as they menacingly approach the Venuses. Most interesting is the misproportioned figure seen from a lateral angle posed between two of the large Venuses: this human form is the only one to possess arms, which are raised, with hands fused to an oval-shaped object. Covering the upper torso of this figure are hundreds of the winged dots, creating the impression that the body is victim of an insect attack. Typical of Dalí's work, in which erotic elements are often bound up with counterparts from the realm of the sadistic or the destructive, the *Hallucinogenic Toreador* comes very close to the fantasies expressed in Pancho's portrait.

We have made numerous references to the fantasy of the phallic woman and to the discovery of her castration, themes that manifest themselves in both paintings. In Dalí's the multiplicity of the Venus de Milo, with her truncated (castrated) arms, creates poliphallic cover for feared loss; Pancho's painting severs the woman's head, leaving it outside the frame. Dalí's abundance of winged insects serves as grotesque cover for the profiled figure, much as Pancho's bugs and creatures provide a hideous cloak for his Countess. The frog that obstructs view of the Countess's sex organs itself creates a bulge where there is none; its eyes are described as "penetrating." This horrid phallic creature sees, but the woman who is the subject of Pancho's portrait is deprived of sight, much like the woman's face in Magritte's *The Rape,* which is composed of breasts for eyes, and sex organs for mouth. Turning back to Magritte, we may discover a possible source for Pancho's painting style: *The Dangerous Relations* (*Les Liaisons dangereuses*), which depicts a nude woman holding a mirror that almost completely hides her. The frame of the mirror cuts off part of her head, which is downcast, with her eyes half-shut. The woman shown in the mirror appears in profile, an impossible angle of reflection, given that the woman is holding the looking glass in a frontal position. The reflected image is completely headless,

and like the holder of the mirror, she attempts to shield her nude body from view. This deformation, according to Mary Ann Caws, may be read as central to the self, "for the woman divided is also watching herself—without seeing us see her from behind." Caws proposes that Magritte's painting may be aptly named *Woman Reading Woman*; in Donoso's novel, which could be called *Woman Writing Man,* it is Julio (and the reader) who cannot perceive the female observer-author until she chooses to reveal herself.

Michel Foucault remarks of *The Dangerous Relations*: "Through all these scenes glide similitudes that no reference point can situate: translations with neither point of departure nor support." Pancho's painting also reveals a lack of departure point or support. Does not the woman whose head is cut off by the painting's frame represent the whole-hole of *El jardín,* where the female author rears her head only outside the main frame of the work, in the final chapter? And isn't woman's body covered over with layers of narration that shield her from view and turn her into a type of fetish? Julio never sees Gloria in her role as triumphant writer, nor does he witness the unveiling of her nakedness at the work's end. He manifests affection and hostility (normally accompanying fetishism) toward that obscure, shifting, supportless construction that arouses insatiable desire in him but that he can never "see" or totally possess. The fetish is of course the metaphor for the maternal phallus, a notion we have linked to several female figures in Donoso's work. We have also stressed Julio's ambivalence toward woman, and so if we interpret Gloria's writing as fetish, it comes as no surprise that "like all other compromises, the fetish can never be totally satisfying for either of the two positions, castration or its denial." Julio's text mutates before him into the female body, the other against whom man defines himself. The loss of mother, one key to Julio's crisis in *El jardín,* also signifies the loss of the garden of youth, the "beautiful land" of Melanie Klein's theory of artistic creation. The work of art, then, would stand for the mother's body, repeatedly destroyed in fantasy but restored or repaired through the act of creation.

If the text takes on the form of a palimpsest or, to use the artistic metaphor, a pentimento, then perhaps we have succeeded in uncovering a layer or two. Donoso charts the course for readers, following Julio's and Gloria's lead, to "see" *El jardín* from a variety of angles, including some impossible ones similar to those of Magritte's paintings. Ingres said: "art never succeeds better than when it is concealed." Magritte supplies a possible corollary: "What is invisible cannot be hidden from our eyes." Donoso tells us that we must go through the way of ignorance and dispossession to arrive at a vantage point from which we may contemplate the hallucinatory garden next door or within, a place that perhaps is devoid of ecstasy but never lacking in humanity.

Juan Carlos Lértora (essay date Spring/Summer 1989)

SOURCE: "José Donoso's Narrative: The Other Side of Language," in *Salmagundi,* No. 82-83, Spring/Summer, 1989, pp. 258-68.

[*In the following essay, Lertora discusses several of Donoso's works, focusing on the unusual approaches in narrative and structure that the author employed. Lertora notes Donoso's departure from realism, his use of magic and surrealism, and comments on the multiple narrators or points of view presented in Donoso's novels.*]

A characteristic trait of the narrative produced by Spanish American writers like Gabriel Garcia Márquez, Julio Cortázar, G. Cabrera Infante, M. Vargas Llosa, and José Donoso, is its attempt to explore human experience by way of the secret codes associated with the instincts, the unconscious and magic. The discourse that founds these narratives is situated in the labyrinthic space of the characters' consciousness. Characters are no longer conceived as representatives of social class or as psychological types, but as subjects of inner conflicts for which they cannot always find lucid or logical understanding or expression. Consciousness is assumed as chaos; it has its corollary in the language that expresses it, whose categories contradict the rational, "objective" thinking of a positivistic discourse in order to explore a new "logic" that, as paradoxical as it may seem, has its constantly changing center in human ambiguity. There is where this new coherence dwells, in the inner space created by new, sometimes dizzying associations that generate new meanings.

The narrative discourse is not monologic and assertive about the world it deploys, but polyphonic (in Bakhtin's sense of a "plurality of voices and consciences independent and distinct, expressing different worldviews"). The space of the discourse is shared by multiple narrators (or different and contradictory manifestations of one consciousness) that sustain different view points without a prevalent enunciating instance (or authoritarian narrative voice) that would sanction one particular discourse as carrier of the truth about the represented world. This multiplicity of discourses is yet another expression of the fundamental ambiguity that Donosian narrative develops and that has as a corollary the manifold or labyrinthine confusion of personal identity.

To this consideration of human being, unreachable in its complexity, corresponds a treatment of a narrative time that, heavily influenced by Henri Bergson's theory, flows and stands still at the same time. A broken chronology, inconstant flow, that disperses itself repeatedly, is consonant with the nature of the human situations it narrates: time and space are conceived as inseparable entities, constituting, as Bakhtin

defines it, the *chronotope.* It is in this coordinate that José Donoso's narrative should be placed.

From the outset Donoso's narrative fiction has challenged the institutions and conventions that regulate language and determine our response to it. Even in such early works as *The Blue Woman* and *The Poisoned Pastries* (both written in English), as also in his collection of short stories—**Summertime**—, and his first novel, **Coronation,** a number of characteristic concerns begin to appear.

These early works deploy a constellation of recurrent meanings, which are also present in the later works, according to which the world is perceived as ominous, deteriorating, mad, grotesque. These categories signal the fundamental precariousness of the world and of human existence. They form the basis of a nihilism that finds expression in the merciless destruction of myths and beliefs which are customarily introduced in order to hide from us the tragic ambiguity of the human condition.

In Donoso's narrative, human relations and social institutions are considered by means of a discourse which finds, in the rupture of conventions, its best definition. In Donosian fiction characters who defend (and believe in) an apparent order of the world are relentlessly destroyed. Tragedy is brought on by the search for rational meaning in a world dominated by instinct and irrationality. The world is inevitably destined to end in the decadent, the absurd and the abominable, the zones whence characters derive their definition and destiny. The tragedy of human being is basically provoked by an obstinate search for a rational explanation in a world in which the instinctual and irrational prevail.

Already in **Coronation,** with its grotesque and carnivalesque ending (the crowning of a dying crazy old woman by her servants who dress her as a Queen), Donoso's narrative sets itself apart from the characteristic traditional realism of the previous generation of Latin American novelists. It explores yet other existential dimensions which place the fiction in a marked frame of irrealism, penetrating reality from a new, obverse perspective. Another work entitled *This Sunday* subverts the interior consciousness of its characters while revealing their degraded existence and their anguish before the terror which alienates them from the world they inhabit. Later works would refine tendencies that are unmistakably a part of Donoso's distinctive voice and vision.

Given the nature of the world he depicts, the exasperating quality of his narrative situations, and the ambiguous condition of his characters, the Donosian narrative is connected in a decisive way to the carnivalesque tradition, with all it contains of spectacle, transgression, fragmentation, transvestism, defiance of all rules and hierarchies, inversion of whatever is established; in sum, *le monde á l'envers.* That is why, in Donoso's fiction, antithesis and parody are central figures. Certain categories of the carnivalesque, again as formulated by Bakhtin, are central to the understanding of this aspect of Donoso's narrative: "eccentricity, like intimate relations, is a special category for perceiving the carnivalesque nature of the world; it allows itself to open up (and to express itself in concrete form) to all that is normally repressed [. . .] It is necessary to add another category, that of profanity, sacrilege, and the whole system of debasement, carnival mockery, and the inconveniences having to do with generational forces of the land and of the body, the parodies of texts and sacred words."

El lugar sin limites represents a considerable breakthrough for Donoso into the realm of the carnivalesque as described by Bakhtin. Its pessimistic portrayal of the condition of personal existence through the presence of the absurd and the total disintegration of the self goes further than his earlier works in its depiction of a world corroded in all its components. This novel is itself an anguished metaphor of an inverted utopia, an impossible paradise without God, love or solidarity; it is a version of a lost Paradise, or the antibiblical prediction.

Desecration in the novel works at all levels: that of the body, of identity, and of the official discourse that attempts to impose a false sense of order and generosity. The novel depicts the inversion (which along with transvestism and antithesis are, at the figurative level, its basis) of all social roles, and bitterly shows the absurdity of absolutes.

By showing the impossibility of categorically limiting dichotomies such as man/woman, good/evil (which in Donoso's earlier works functioned as structuring principles based on a clear appearance/reality opposition), *El lugar sin limites* presses towards a radical perception of the ambiguity which, for Donoso, is essential to the human condition. There is no one identity; there is no authenticity; we are all fragments, pieces, a human kaleidoscope.

This conception generates narrative structures without center, works in continuous self-transformation and mutation, and a discourse in constant displacement that shows the emptiness of everything, the nothingness which finds its greatest expression in *The Obscene Bird of Night*. In this work, the reader cannot differentiate between what is dream or hallucination, "reality" or fantasy; between what supposedly has taken place, and what can only be conjectured. This is a novel in which Donoso's grotesque realism achieves the standard defined by Bakhtin: "The images of the Romantic grotesque," Bakhtin writes, "usually express fear of the world and seek to inspire their reader with this fear"; "madness acquires a somber, tragic aspect of individual isolation" and "discloses the potentiality of an entirely different world, of another order, another way of life. It leads men out of the

confines of the apparent (false) unity of the indisputable and stable." Donoso's obsession with the diffuseness of individual identity gives shape to an alienating view in which the monstrous and the obscene ritual and magic, regularly interact with objective reality.

The novel depicts a world of hallucinatory indeterminacy, of constant interruption of narrative sequences, the elimination of absolute dichotomies, so that the "same" and the "other" complement each other, "are" each other. The rupture of chronology, and the total elimination of the narrator-protagonist-witness are but components of a relentless procedure in terms of which reality and fantasy freely intermingle. This is, of course, also the case for much contemporary Latin American fiction, a tendency described by the labels of "Magical Realism" or the "Fantastic."

In this novel reality is perceived from its underside, as it were, at a level prior to, even resistant to, that of coherent formulation. It depicts profanation of the body, or identity, but also profanation of any official language that attempts to impose the appearance of order, of harmony, of human generosity. Chaos rules, relentlessly producing substitutions, transformations, and distortions of personality. "El Mudito" is the unreliable narrator, character and witness of different stories that have, as a common element, ambivalence and sequential instability. Inversion, transvestism and transgression are structuring categories of the novel; accordingly, the configurating narrative discourse is also ambiguous, the "other side" of what traditionally constitutes narrative discourse. In *The Obscene Bird of Night* the reader has no way to formulate valid reading hypotheses, or to come up with definitive answers to the questions raised. Everywhere the reader is confronted by narrative procedures that interrogate themselves and continue to open up disturbing questions.

The Obscene Bird of Night expresses a deeply pessimistic conception of the world and of human being as essentially anchored in the absurd. The ceaseless, maze-like changes in spatial structure are just one more manifestation of the novel's lack of center; the subject of discourse is plural; in the discourse there is always a displacement of center. If there is any order in the novel, it is of a precarious sort whose fragile membrane is constantly threatened. At best, we are given an illusory, transitory order which in the end cannot sustain itself. Most of the story corresponds to the delirious inner discourse of the narrator-protagonist-witness, a discourse delivered without sequential organization and originated from different levels of a fragmented inner consciousness, the reflection of a disintegrated identity. Donoso creates a series of substitutions at both the level of *énonciation* and the level of *énoncé* (—Humberto Peñaloza/writer/secretary/the seventh hag/giant head of papier maché/son of Iris Mateluna/dog of Iris Mateluna/"imbunche"/light ashes dispersed by the wind—) so that the subject of the narrative enunciation is never fixed, and the narrative discourse does not have a stable generating center. Julia Kristeva explains this narrative feature when she says that "The mechanism of this mutation is insured by a *shifter* or specific connector: the MASK, which is the mark of alterity, the rejection of identity". Bakhtin claims that the mask is related to "the merry negation of uniformity and similarity; it rejects conformity to oneself. The mask is related to transition, metamorphoses, the violation of natural boundaries."

In *The Obscene Bird of Night,* the mask does not have a single specific symbolic value; it does not constitute a concrete entity. It gives way to other masks but there is no concrete personality at the end of this permutation process, no unique or authentic identity. As Donoso puts it: "It is my obsession with the no unity of human personality. Why am I so interested in disguises? Because they are ways of dissolving the unity of human being, of undoing the psychological unity, that horrible myth we have invented".

This view of human life as fragmented is sharply shown in *Sacred Families:* In **"Chatanooga Choo Choo"** the characters are like manikins whose faces can be erased and later be painted in different ways *ad infinitum,* and whose limbs can be assembled and disassembled whichever way one wants. In **"Gaspard de la nuit,"** the main character exchanges his identity with a *clochard* of identical appearance, thus losing his own identity while "the other" is now "himself". With this, Donoso expresses his rejection of the myth that assures the unity of the self and emphasizes, instead, dispersion and ambiguity as main features of our condition.

By refusing to acquiesce in a stable image of apprehensible reality, Donoso's narrative questions the mimetic nature of fiction in general, and poses new ways to explore its possibilities. One interesting aspect of the larger theoretical problem is nicely signalled in *The Obscene Bird,* where the character "El Mudito" ("The Mute") is the narrator; but as his words can't be spoken, there can be no communication. And if that is so, can there be narration? At this level the *Obscene Bird* stands as a metaphor of the impossibility of conveying deep inner experience, the experience of an identity in crisis, for example. What seems real is narrated from the other side of language, not from the side that "tells" but from the side that cannot "tell," that can give at most only an incomplete view of what we might call "Reality."

By denying the traditional mimetic condition of narrative, Donoso seeks to convey what is essentially a project of liberation or, in bakhtinian terms, the "carnivalesque spirit": "The carnival-grotesque form exercises the same function: to consecrate inventive freedom, to permit the combination of a variety of different elements and their rapprochement, to liberate from the prevailing point of view of the world, from conventions and established truths, from clichés, from

all that is humdrum and universally accepted. This carnival spirit offers the chance to have a new outlook on the world, to realize the relative nature of all that exists, and to enter a completely new order of things." It is this freeing of the individual from the stifling weight of conventions, from the rigidity and falseness of institutionalized rituals, a salient aspect of Donoso's fiction, which finds its best expression through a discourse that seeks to break away from that other discourse, generated from power, that presumes to hold the truth.

The image of power and its carnivalesque transgression is the organizing principle of *A House In The Country.* The novel is organized by means of a narrative-authorial discourse that attempts to control all components of the represented world, but which the fiction itself contradicts. Complementary to this discourse there is another, multilevel discourse, which gives the novel a polyphonic structure, generated by different groups of characters. Characters are organized in a series of circles, or rings, which in turn correspond to the structures of power in the society; accordingly, their discourses represent the variety of social discourses, the social heteroglossia. The novel becomes, then, the space in which different discursive practices meet. The old members of the Ventura family, representative of the old aristocracy, owners of the gold that they exchange for money to foreign investors, are at the outer circle. Inside this hierarchical ring we find the younger thirty-three Ventura cousins, who already are, in essence, a micro version of what they will be when they grow up: just like the old Venturas. At the time the story takes place, they plan an endless game whose title corresponds to Valéry's well known line: "La marquise est sortie á cinq heures." Among them, there are transvestites and homosexuals, some sadistic, some greedy, in anticipation of what their life will be.

The next circle consists of the servants who, by not owning anything (not even their lives), have no identity; they are anonymous to the Venturas, and they are "recognized" only by the function they have in their domestic tasks. However they do have some power: to watch the children after a certain hour at night and punish those who are caught breaking the house rules.

House In The Country is the space whose limits separate two worlds, two intertwined social orders, generating a chaotic rebellion which is quickly quelled, and whose end is also the dissolution of an aristocratic dynasty which gives birth to another that, in turn, destroys the former. This example of social cannibalism belies the standard understanding of cannibalism used by the aristocracy as a way of reinforcing its power. Ironically enough, the so-called "cannibals" of the novel, who constitute the last of the three "circles" of characters, are revealed to us late in the novel as "vegetarians."

House In The Country is a novel open to different readings; it transcends a simplistic interpretation which would bind it, in a mechanical way, to a historical pre-text that might function as its referent; that is to say, to Chilean history after the military coup. Even so there are plenty of "winks to the reader's complicity," as Cortázar would put it, and a number of "coincidences": The initials of *A*driano *G*ómara, the doctor being held in a tower for the "insane" and "dangerous," correspond to the initials of the assassinated President, *A*llende *G*ossens; the servants would be the military; the Venturas, the richest of Chilean society; the darkening of the home, an allegory of Chile's isolation, an image of death, etc. More important, the novel symbolizes the structuring of human relations based mainly on the exercise of power at all interpersonal levels. But the different discourses that organize the novel are structured in such a way that ultimately *it is the nature of fiction* that emerges as the text's final objective. The narrative discourse explores its own structuring possibilities as textual productivity regulated by the needs of writing.

It is this same principle that supports the represented world of *La misteriosa desaparición de la marquesita de Loria,* and certain *novellas* included in *Sacred Families* and *Cuatro para Delfina*. These are not political texts in any traditional sense. However, they do express both an "historical and ethical responsibility," quite as Roland Barthes saw it as the task of writing to do. The more overt manifestation of this responsibility is to be found in *Curfew,* Donoso's latest novel. The action takes place in twenty four hours, and is centered on the wake and burial of Matilde Urrutia, Pablo Neruda's widow. As an allegorical novel, *Curfew* depicts life in Chile after more than a decade of dictatorship, showing social contradictions, misery, and most importantly, hopelessness. The main character, Mañungo Vera, is a returned exile who embodies many characteristics of the well know composer and singer Victor Jara, brutally assassinated by the Military Junta in the first days of their murderous coup. Here, as elsewhere in Donoso, political concerns are enmeshed in a matrix which contains a range of other issues, equally compelling and disturbing.

Donoso constantly questions the ontological status of fiction and challenges its traditional mimetic function. This questioning informs his conception of reality as incapable of allowing for true insight and of power as the main obstacle to genuine human interaction. The obsession with power, inauthenticity, masquerade, irrationality, and the fragmentary makes for a persistent and painful exploration of the dark side of human existence. The language, which is equal to the large purpose assigned to it, is the final mark of Donoso's mastery and of his commitment to the excesses and obliquities of the carnivalesque.

Ricardo Gutierrez Mouat (essay date January 1991)

SOURCE: "Aesthetics, Ethics, and Politics in Donoso's *El jardin de al lado*," in *PMLA,* Vol. 106, No. 1, January, 1991, pp. 60-70.

[*In the following essay, Mouat discusses the "artistic crisis" presented in* The Garden Next Door, *which focuses on "a contradiction between modernist and postmodernist aesthetics." Mouat concludes that the novel successfully explores "the ground that separates politics from the autonomous work of art."*]

José Donoso's *El jardín de al lado* [*The Garden Next Door*] dramatizes an artistic crisis that has ethical and political implications. The novel focuses on the contradiction between modernist and postmodernist aesthetics in the context of political upheaval and on the attendant challenge to literary intellectuals to choose between representing their individual self-contained subjectivities and representing a collective subject repressed by dictatorship. This ethical choice, furthermore, must be made in a milieu alien to the modernist ethos, that of the literary marketplace promoted by the culture industry. Here exchange value subverts the narrator's more traditional values and undermines narrative authority. Simultaneously, the culture industry reinterprets the notion of artistic autonomy by divesting it of its traditional "aura," to which Donoso's narrator remains attached. Thus this narrator, who is also represented—deceptively, we discover—as the author of the novel, disappears from it when his narrative project reaches a dead end. Yet at a different level the novel finds a way out of its contradictions and sublates them by replacing the authority of the canonical author with that of the subaltern. Reading *El jardín de al lado,* then, implies a dialectical movement from erasure to inscription and reveals the collapse of the hierarchies that supported the modern bourgeois novel.

The method of this essay is both heuristic and dialogic to the extent that our elucidation of the complex interaction among aesthetics, ethics, and politics relies on a counterpoint between *El jardín de al lado* and one of its implicit subtexts, Thomas Mann's "Death in Venice." This approach allows us to insert Donoso's text in the mainstream of European modernism and to view *El jardín de al lado* as a troublesome supplement to that tradition. The essay is divided into two main parts, each of which focuses on a dialectic shared by both texts but worked out differently by Donoso and Mann: bohemian pleasure versus bourgeois discipline and textual production versus textual reception. Each of these areas of inquiry subsumes all or part of the contradictions dramatized by *El jardín de al lado* and permits us to move freely between the two texts. But first the intertextual pertinence of "Death in Venice" must be established.

El jardín de al lado is both the story of a failed novel and a trompe l'oeil text that reflects and refracts itself and several other texts situated within Donoso's cultural horizon. The narrator's allusive strategy appropriates the literary images that surface on his reflecting mirror and roots an insecure creative project in the solid ground of canonical literature. T. S. Eliot, Mallarmé, Joyce, Proust, and Henry James, together with the great figures of the Latin American "boom," parade through the novel's pages as cultural signposts leading back to a text whose identity remains undefined. The most significant borrowing, however, is from "Death in Venice," a text whose name is repressed in *El jardín de al lado* but whose blurred image hovers over the novel and can be appropriated as an interpretive tool.

Both works deal with the crisis of an author driven to spend a summer holiday in foreign surroundings in the hope of replenishing his creative energies. In Mann's Venice and Donoso's Madrid a middle-aged protagonist meets a perturbing youth who challenges his social authority and ultimately leads him to destruction. Aschenbach dies in Venice, but Julio Méndez (Donoso's tortured protagonist and the narrator of all but the last chapter of *El jardín de al lado*) disappears in the clandestine mazes of Tangiers after fleeing his literary failure in Madrid. Julio's imagined guide in his descent to hell is Bijou, the youth he had met earlier in Madrid and who had destroyed his certainties. The scene replicates Aschenbach's pursuit of Tadzio through the labyrinthine streets of Venice in Mann's novella, especially as Mann endows his Venice with oriental traits similar to those that characterize Donoso's Tangiers.

Other incidental details contribute to the affinity between the two works, though there are obvious differences as well. Tadzio's Polish family in "Death in Venice" includes his mother (a lady of aristocratic bearing and finery) and a governess, characters who recall Donoso's duchess of Andía and her Austrian daughter-in-law (a baroness who serves as governess of the duchess's grand-children), two of the figures Julio scrutinizes from his observatory window. The lyrical association between Tadzio and the sea contemplated by Aschenbach from his own observatory post, on the Venetian beach, is replayed ironically in the opening chapter of *El jardín de al lado,* where Bijou is found not as we might expect, bathing on the Mediterranean coast of Spain, but, rather, sleeping prosaically in a parked car. And there are other, more subtle elements shared by both works, such as the dynamic motif of passage. The narrator of "Death in Venice" speaks of Aschenbach's passage to Venice, a journey invested with symbols of death and enveloped in an uncanny, fearful atmosphere. Donoso's passages, by contrast, are phantasmic and framed by the window through which the novel's narrator constantly stares at the garden scene below. This window marks the division between the inside and the outside worlds, Chile and Spain, the past and the present, even while inviting reflection on these categories. The Spanish garden is also the lost garden where the narra-

tor spent his childhood and where now his mother lies dying, just as the window is also the trompe l'oeil paintings that decorate the Madrid apartment and the blank page where a deceptive writing is inscribed and the mirror that both tricks the reader and returns Julio's tortured image. The ultimate passage for Julio, of course, is through the mirror, into which he disappears, leaving his wife, Gloria, as the narrator of the final chapter and as the "author" of *El jardín de al lado*. Mann also uses specular tactics to trace the progress of his protagonist's deterioration, particularly in the scene where Aschenbach is repelled by the sight of the old wigged and bejeweled reveler making merry with a group of young clerks on the steamer to Venice. Aschenbach becomes this sorry figure at the end of the tale, when he accepts the ministrations of the Italian barber who dyes his hair and applies cream to his wrinkles and carmine to his cheeks. (Another link between the works is Julio's proposed trip to Venice to recuperate from his failed attempt at having the revised version of his novel accepted for publication.)

"Death in Venice" dramatizes a transvaluation of values affecting the protagonist. This crisis is described in grotesque terms by a narrator who wavers between parody and direct statement and who becomes progressively more distant from the character. Much of the novella's complexity, in fact, stems from the way that the authority of the narrative voice shifts, reproducing the ideological contradictions inherent in Mann's conception of the artist's role. These contradictions are aesthetic, ethical, and political, though politics becomes an issue for Mann only after "Death in Venice." The same contradictions resurface in Donoso's novel, but from a different source. If Mann's Aschenbach is a writer who is canonized by the traditional literary institutions, who represses in his life and works the very pleasure necessary for artistic creation, and who takes his public, magisterial role too seriously, Donoso's Julio is the practitioner of a traditional bourgeois literature that is radically challenged by historical crisis and by the rising authority of the culture industry, whose market mechanisms eclipse the literary institutions.

Bohemian Pleasure versus Bourgeois Discipline

"Who shall unravel the mystery of an artist's nature and character! Who shall explain the profound instinctual fusion of discipline and dissoluteness in which it rests?" asks the narrator of "Death in Venice," who describes the protagonist's crisis as the gradual imposition of a formal discipline at the expense of the primordial joy of composition and expression that has the "power to delight the receptive world":

> As time passed, Gustave Aschenbach's presentations took on something of an official air, of an educator's stance; his style in later years came to eschew direct audacities, new and subtle nuances, it developed toward the exemplary and definitive, the fastidiously

conventional, the conservative and formal and even formulaic.

Not that discipline has no legitimate role to play in the production of aesthetic pleasure. Without its agency, form could not be achieved or, alternatively, form would be excluded from the domain of bourgeois morality. Ethics would be separated from aesthetics, a split already latent in the notion of form itself:

> And is form not two-faced? Is it not at one and the same time moral and immoral—moral as the product and expression of discipline, but immoral and even antimoral inasmuch as it houses within itself an innate moral indifference, and indeed essentially strives for nothing less than to bend morality under its proud and absolute scepter?

Aschenbach succeeds in repressing desire to become a model of bourgeois morality and accede to the highest honors that bourgeois society can bestow on the artist. He even condemns the pursuit of knowledge, because knowledge subverts the will and promotes the forgiveness of transgression. And yet Aschenbach is wholly dedicated to the pursuit of artistic form, an endeavor that ultimately cannot be separated from the risk of the abyss. But he is no Baudelaire or Rimbaud. Aschenbach explicitly renounces "all sympathy with the abyss" for the sake of conventional morality, an effort that the narrator finds problematic because of the ambiguous morality of form itself and because such exclusion of psychological material would actually constitute a forbidden realm and hence a temptation bound to corrode the ethically acceptable self. When Tadzio appears to Aschenbach in the guise of an aesthetic vision of sublime perfection, the truth of art (the truth according to the universalizing logic of the ideological discourse) is revealed. As the passage from the *Phaedrus* quoted near the close of the narrative states, "[F]orm and naiveté . . . lead to intoxication and lust; they may lead a noble mind into terrible criminal emotions . . ." It is true that neither the narrator nor the implicit author accepts responsibility for the quoted passage; nevertheless, the implication is clear: Aschenbach in his canonical works sacrifices the integrity of art because to acknowledge it would mean subverting the moral economy of bourgeois society and the artist's privileged social position. The novella's dialogic narrative and ambiguous texture defer the resolution of the ethical-aesthetic dilemma, but the antinomy between a repressive conventional morality and an aesthetic libertinism points up the possibility of a greater and more authentic participation by the artist in society, a possibility that would require the artist's abdication of the throne on which the bourgeoisie seats its cultural heroes. At least this potential is implicit in Mann's own evolution as public figure and writer. As Charles Neider affirms, Mann's "work and life constitute the devel-

opment of the isolated artist-type into the artist as one of and provider for the people."

The same critic writes that Mann's entire artistic and didactic output is based on the burgher-bohemian contradiction afflicting the bourgeois author:

> Because of his burgher forbears and his own naturally conservative temperament Mann tends to regard the artistic impulse in himself as something suspect, verging on the criminal. . . . [This] has led him to a personal variation of the artist myth, a consideration of himself (and the artist in general) as the middleman between burgher and bohemian, nature and spirit, tradition and revolt. It has also led him to attempt to bring the artist back into the fold of good society after his nineteenth-century escapades. . . .

The reference to Mann's progenitors recalls a passage from "Death in Venice" in which Aschenbach brings the genealogical law to bear on his "illicit" attraction to Tadzio. Recollecting his ancestors' "decent manliness of character," Aschenbach asks himself:

> What would they say? But for that matter, what would they have said about his entire life, a life that had deviated from theirs to the point of degeneracy, this life of his in the compulsive service of art, this life about which he himself, adopting the civic values of his forefathers, had once let fall such mocking observations—and which nevertheless had essentially been so much like theirs!

The artist's deviation or degeneration is not outside the genealogical law but is inscribed in it according to the naturalist discourse "quoted" by the novella's narrator. Thus, if Aschenbach's ancestors on the paternal side "had all been military officers, judges, government administrators," those on the maternal side included a Bohemian musical conductor whose daughter is the author's mother. The synthesis is contradictory: "It was from this marriage between hard-working, sober conscientiousness and darker, more fiery impulses that an artist, and indeed this particular kind of artist, had come into being."

This contradiction, developed further in "Tonio Kröger," unfolds itself in *El jardín de al lado*. Julio Méndez represents an entrenched bourgeois subjectivity confronted by the same type of nineteenth-century nonconformist verging on the criminal that both repels and fascinates Mann's bourgeois artist. The role of bohemian in Donoso's novel is played by Bijou, whose literary model is Rimbaud. The descriptions of Bijou emphasize both the beautiful ("sus rizos dorados de *angelo musicante*" 'his golden ringlets of a music-playing angel') and the corrupt ("la malvada suciedad rubia, los inmundos dientes defectuosos" 'the wicked blond dirt, the rotten filthy teeth'), the aristocratic and the déclassé ("pese a susuciedad, a su aire malévolo . . . tiene la *allure* de un señorito" 'despite his filth, despite his malevolent air . . . he has the allure of a young lord')—traits that are physical and moral, underscoring the ambiguity that unnerves Julio's monologic subjectivity and that extends into sexuality. Julio's response to this hybrid creature (hybrid also in his Franco-Chilean nationality) traces a path from irritation and rejection to desire. The narrator's fantasy of "breaking through the mirror," formally realized by the novel through its authorial inversion, gradually becomes the exasperated need to exchange identities with the "low Other," to find liberation from the rigid structure of bourgeois (inter)subjectivity but also from the oppositions conjugated in Bijou's body and morality. Not the least important aspect of the fantasized exchange of identities (which takes the form of a descent into hell, into the abyss, thus recalling Aschenbach's plunge into the abysmal depths of his illicit passion) is liberation from history, since Bijou rejects the political defeatism of Julio's generation and dismisses his elders' commitment to a historical past that holds no meaning for him. Thus in both "Death in Venice" and *El jardín de al lado* the protagonist must traumatically shed the bourgeois ethic and aesthetic of composure in order to achieve what he desires—artistic truth or productivity.

In Mann's novella the contradiction inherent in the bourgeois artist leads to the repression of desire and ultimately of aesthetic joy. A contradiction between ethics and aesthetics also seizes Donoso's authorial subject, who is consequently unable to experience pleasure: "Puritano receloso del placer en que me ha transformado nuestra historia reciente" 'Our recent history has turned me into a Puritan suspicious of pleasure.' Historical crisis (namely, Chile's military coup of 1973) imposes on the erstwhile authors of domestic novels and stories (both the early Donoso and Julio Méndez) an ethical imperative, which Julio fails to express in an adequate aesthetic form. His first attempt to write the crisis is only an obsessive repetition of it, a mere chronicle of well-known and roundly condemned events that lacks aesthetic value Núria Monclús, the Catalan editor who rejects Julio's manuscript, passes the following judgment on the novel: "falta . . . la habilidad para proyectar . . . tanto situaciones como personajes de manera que se transformen en metáfora, metáfora válida en sí y no por lo que señala afuera de la literatura . . ." '[the novel] lacks . . . the ability to project either situations or characters so that they become a metaphor valid in itself and not for what it refers to outside literature . . .' Instead of an autonomous work of art Julio produces a record of his brief incarceration, which occurred immediately after the military takeover. There is no liberating transformation of the prison experience by means of artistic creation, but instead Julio's novel becomes its author's prison.

The revised version of the manuscript does not so much represent the Chilean political crisis as it does the "petite histoire" of the Chilean bourgeoisie before the September coup, intimately shared by Julio and his wife but lacking in public validity. Although Gloria finds in this novel an "authentic political exaltation", the contradiction between ethics and aesthetics is suspended, especially in the light of Núria Monclús's devastating evaluation of the novel's aesthetic merits. Politics has become sexual politics in Donoso's novel, and the denunciation of authoritarianism has turned into a struggle for authority whose object is the text. As Lucille Kerr remarks in her analysis of narrative authority in *El jardín de al lado,*

> The combatant in whose defeat and virtual capture Julio's powers to write seem to be generated is thus not one of the literary rivals about whom he obsessively ruminates throughout his narration . . . It is instead Gloria, his spouse, the apparently powerless woman. . . . The significant point here is that when Julio tells how he finally begins to write his novel the description coincides with the description of his wife's nervous breakdown and slow recovery. It seems that it is only when Gloria appears to be defeated or virtually imprisoned . . . that Julio no longer is blocked nor defers writing.

Gloria's emergence as author in the final chapter of *El jardín de al lado* yields what can be considered a third version of Julio's novel, one whose condition of possibility is the resolution of the contradiction between ethics and aesthetics that had undermined the production of the previous versions:

> Te quiero explicar que yo, como persona, no es que no siga exaltada, políticamente. . . . Pero sé que eso es ajeno a la literatura, quiero decir, ajeno por lo menos a mi literatura. Asumí esta ambivalencia analizando mi enfermedad de Madrid desde mis cuadernos de Sitges, y dándome cuenta que fue mi cárcel. Y asumir el "tono menor" fue, tal vez, mi salvación.

> I want to explain to you that it's not that I as a person have ceased to be politically exalted. . . . But I know that that is alien to literature, I mean, alien at least to my literature. I became aware of this ambivalence while analyzing my Madrid illness in my Sitges diary and realizing that [the ambivalence] was my prison. And to assume a low-key style was, perhaps, my salvation.

Gloria's statement is an implicit criticism of her husband's second version of the novel. Earlier she had approved that version on the strength of its "political exaltation," the very notion that she now calls "alien to literature." Gloria's liberation from the "prison" of her subjectivity results, then, from a displacement of the ethical question, specifically from the detachment of ethics from politics. At this point *El jardín de al lado* is about the (re)emergence of narrative authority, a process grounded on an ethical insight: namely, that politics is beyond the ken of the novel's "author"—Gloria—and perhaps of Donoso as well. The honest thing to do is to acknowledge this limitation, an act that permits the construction of a valid artistic object freed from the constraints of subjectivity—that is, freed from any suspicion of authoritarianism. The form of the framing novel duplicates and legitimates Gloria's position to the extent that *El jardín de al lado* is an autonomous work of art that formally sublates the political novel. That is, the mimesis and the testimonial mode of authority that characterize Julio's narrative project are transformed in the novel's Magritte-like structure into the (self-)representation of a distorted mirror—a mode in which perspective is refracted and the referent oscillates. (For more on the analogies between the novel and its references to painting, see Feal.)

This emphasis on form, however, does not mean that *El jardín de al lado* is an aestheticist novel or that its authorial subject is exposed to the formal temptation that dooms Mann's Aschenbach. Insofar as a working theory of the novel can be disengaged from *El jardín de al lado,* it is a psychological theory that envisions literary creation as the exorcism of private obsessions:

> Tortura, injusticia, derechos humanos, sí, desgarrador, es necesario tomar parte en esa lucha. Pero a mi modo, por favor, a mi modo y no ahora; . . . déjenme tranquilo, por lo menos hasta que la demencia de Gloria haya logrado exhumar del acertijo de este jardín sus propios, y tal vez nuestros, fantasmas.

> Torture, injustice, human rights, yes, it's necessary to join that struggle. But in my own way, please, in my own way and not now; . . . leave me alone, at least until Gloria's madness manages to exhume from the puzzle of this garden her own, and perhaps our own, ghosts.

A stronger, somatic formulation of exorcism can be found in the many references to disease in the novel: "Yo también, como quien convalece, voy llegando al fin de mi novela. . . . Sólo sé que me quedan las llagas de una prolongada enfermedad. . . . Eso sí, siento que me he extirpado algo maligno que era necesario extirpar" 'I'm arriving as someone who convalesces at the end of my novel. . . . I only know that I'm left with the ulcers of a prolonged disease. . . . But I feel that I have extirpated something malignant that had to be extirpated.' The psychological burden of the novel is not limited to Julio as author-narrator but is also transferred to Gloria, who assumes the authorial position only after she has managed to evict the narrative material out of her interi-

ority, to a space where the novel becomes a mirror of the crises that she and others undergo. Therefore the authorial subject's legitimation of the novel as politically inoperative cannot be dissociated from the text's therapeutic function, which bears exclusively on the individual (bourgeois) subject. Julio's remark that the Chilean historical crisis has for the first time allowed him to identify himself with a collective destiny is symptomatic of the contradiction between the bourgeois and the collective subjects, which is resolved by collapsing collective experience onto the individual's inner space and later expelling the intrusive material in a mediated form.

All this is important because it allows us to generalize the ethical-aesthetic contradiction beyond the confines of Donoso's novel. Suffice it to recall the early 1970s debate between Mario Vargas Llosa and Angel Rama on the contradiction between a subjective, bourgeois aesthetic and a sociopolitical legitimation of literature. Rama objects to the "theological" view of the author put forth in Vargas Llosa's massive study *García Márquez: Historia de un deicidio,* the concept of the author as a suprahuman individual who recreates reality and writes to exorcize personal ghosts or demons. For Rama, who regards literary production as a mediation of social reality, his opponent's poetics is idealist and archaic. Vargas Llosa retorts that the writer's "demons" have a sociohistorical origin and can be rationally "hunted down," so that an author can be both a "deicida" 'god killer' and a social laborer.

Both antagonists miss the historical logic of their debate. If literature can be considered autonomous, it is because literature was institutionalized in the historical development of the bourgeoisie, a fact that comes fully into view with the rise of aestheticism in the middle of the nineteenth century (Bürger). Autonomous art is a legitimate by-product of societies characterized by the economic and political ascendancy of the middle classes. In Latin America this rise was sufficiently advanced at the turn of the century to generate a distinctly modern poetry. The novel had to wait another fifty years to undergo the same modernization and still longer to come to terms with the contradictions of autonomous art in underdeveloped societies. Rama's call for a sociopolitical ethic of literary production is a symptom of these contradictions, but his argument fails to take into account the institutional status of modern literature.

Textual Production versus Textual Reception

Mann is quite aware in "Death in Venice" of the central role played by the institutions that regulate artistic production. To a large extent, in fact, Aschenbach's output is the product of its public, his texts determined by the possibilities of their reception: "His talent, equally-remote from the commonplace and from the eccentric, had a native capacity both to inspire confidence in the general public and to win admiration and encouragement from the discriminating connoisseur." As a young man Aschenbach writes for his contemporaries and fascinates "twenty-year-olds with his breathtaking cynicisms about the questionable nature of art and of the artist himself." His more mature work wins the approval of serious critics and later becomes conservative and exemplary enough to be canonized as textbook material, even as its author is conferred the letters patent of nobility. At this point the relation between the artist and his public is mediated by the academy (itself linked to the state), and Aschenbach becomes a national figure to whom foreign countries pay homage.

But the exalted position of the artist is not ethically safe. On the contrary, "Death in Venice" is an exploration of the moral risk inherent in such a status, a risk that bears equally on the work and on the artist. The theme is explicitly stated in the *Phaedrus* passage:

> The magisterial poise of our style is a lie and a farce, our fame and social position are an absurdity, the public's faith in us is altogether ridiculous, the use of art to educate the nation and its youth is a reprehensible undertaking which should be forbidden by law. For how can one be fit to be an educator when one has been born with an incorrigible and natural tendency toward the abyss?

The danger of corruption underscored here assumes the identity of the work and its producer, while "Death in Venice" thematically separates the artist and the work. Socrates wants to eject the poets from the republic because they either would corrupt their charges with the kind of knowledge that poets have access to or would have to betray the integrity of their aesthetic mission in the service of the state. Poetic "nature" is anarchic and licentious because poets "cannot tread the path of beauty without Eros" and therefore can be neither "wise nor dignified." Poetic integrity, in addition, requires that the text reflect the true image of its maker—that is, that poets must be in a position to guarantee their words. This contract is feasible for Socratic instruction but becomes more problematic when a written text mediates the relation between master and disciple. In "Death in Venice" it is precisely in the space of this mediation that a moral gap opens up between the artist and the work, showing that the magisterial elevation of the poet endangers not only youth and the populace but also the poet (who is potentially deformed by a responsibility that is not necessarily consubstantial with art), as well as the work, which must conform to its canonical status by repressing its formative impulses.

That art and morality are not consubstantial is asserted, however reluctantly, by Mann himself in a lecture given in 1952, four decades after he wrote "Death in Venice." the lecture returns to the aesthetic and ethical issues raised by the novella and by his other works from the first quarter of the century, issues that by the 1950s had become political as well. The lecture's title is "The Artist and Society," but already in the opening paragraph Mann slides uncomfortably from society to politics and from politics to morals, attesting the indissoluble totality of social existence, of which art forms a part. Mann was traditional enough to perceive this totality (and of sufficient stature to operate authoritatively in its several dimensions) but modern enough to realize that art is, nevertheless, an autonomous sphere, for he states that the "essence" of the artist is aesthetic and not moral, just as the "essence" of art is free play and not virtue. But only the aesthete (the "bohemian") would force a rupture between a dependent art and an autonomous one. Mann (quoting Goethe) preserves a link between them by stating that if artistic production does not have to legitimate itself by a recourse to ethics or politics, art may nonetheless have moral consequences.

Mann pursues this theme by pointing out a moral contradiction between the production of art and its reception, its institutionalization. Recounting his experience with *The Magic Mountain,* the novel that earned him the Nobel Prize in 1929, he implies that the artist who writes a novel is not the same one who is rewarded for it later. During its production a novel is the scrawl of a private subject, a network of private allusions, to be read in the intimacy of the author's circle of family and friends. At this stage the artist is assimilated to bohemian psychology, characterized by "social disorder, a bad conscience dissolved in frivolity, humor, and self-irony with respect to bourgeois society and its demands" ("Künstler" 328). But this bohemian is transformed into a bourgeois by the successful reception of the work and by its subsequent canonization. This is the gap that Aschenbach cannot cross. He gives in too readily to external demands and accepts the risks of social recognition, prematurely relinquishing the risks that are just as inherent in the pursuit of art. In his 1952 piece Mann counsels modesty as the appropriate ethical response of the artist to this dilemma. Mann's own life constitutes a similar response:

> It does Mann no moral dishonour to say that his campaign for truth and human decency was always inwardly qualified by his participation in Nietzsche's belief that human life wins dignity only in proportion as it is lifted up "into the significance of works of art," into the sphere signifying for Mann a "matter-of-factness undisturbed by any moralism."

In *El jardín de al lado* the traditional cultural institutions are not represented as mediating the exchange between artist and reader, and in fact the very notion of artist loses its validity or becomes presumptuous. In the postindustrial and cosmopolitan ethos surrounding the production of fiction in Donoso's novel, the forms of authority developed by traditional bourgeois society are corroded by the power of the culture (or consciousness) industry that tends to collapse the aesthetic and ethical value of cultural productions into exchange value. The emergence of a culture industry in Latin America coincided with the modernization of the Latin American novel, a revival that culminated in the boom of the 1960s, to which Donoso was a latecomer and which he equivocally portrays in *El jardín de al lado* from Julio's perspective, that of the writer excluded from the boom's movable feast.

Julio sees the boom as an outmoded literary fashion engineered by mercenary publishers such as Núria Monclús and characterized by formal experimentalism devoid of substantial value. This perspective, not fully authorized by the narrative discourse and in fact contradicted by it, generates an aesthetic paradigm that not every critic would consider fair to the novels of Fuentes, García Márquez, Vargas Llosa, and "Marcelo Chiriboga" (the fictitious embodiment of literary superstardom propagated by news media fascinated with the boom). But it does allow Donoso's authorial subject to vindicate his own narrative project as ethically (if not aesthetically) superior:

> No podía adaptar el dolor que mi país había experimentado a las exigencias de las modas literarias preconizadas por Núria Monclús. . . . ¿Cómo impedir que se esfumaran y palidecieran mis seis días de calabozo, que eran como el trazo que definía el contorno de mi identidad?

> I could not adapt the pain that my country had experienced to the literary fashions proclaimed by Núria Monclús. . . . How could I keep my six days in jail from going up in smoke and paling away, when they were the outline that defined my identity?

The opposition between political content and aesthetic form dooms the first draft of Julio's novel, as his inability to connect with the public dooms the second. Julio recognizes that he lacks the talent he attributes to the likes of Chiriboga, to Salvatierra (a painter friend), and to certain key figures of modern painting:

> Poseer un punto de vista tan original que se acerque a lo cómico . . . pienso en Dalí, en Chirico, en Magritte, que también son envolventes e instántaneos y divertidos. . . . ¿Es por eso que Núria Monclús no me incluye, porque elimino ese estrato de inconciencia y humor que se relaciona como un chispazo que conecta con el público? . . .

> To have a point of view so original that it might approach the comic . . . I think of Dalí, of De Chirico, of Magritte, who are also involving and spontaneous

and funny. . . . Is that why Núria Monclús doesn't include me, because I eliminate that unconscious stratum of humor that like a spark connects with the public? . . .

Dalí, De Chirico, and Magritte, of course, represent the aesthetic paradigm that Julio cannot realize but that Gloria achieves by fruitfully exploiting her husband's multiple failures. In this sense *El jardín de al lado* is about the production of success from failure and of aesthetic form from political crisis. Gloria's novel, moreover, exchanges the currency of modernism (as embodied by Julio's literary references) for that of the commercially successful avant-garde, thereby articulating an implicit critique of the author figure in postmodern mass culture.

Jean Franco identifies three "technological" paradigms present in the boom novel, three competing versions of narrative authority that also function as allegories of social formation. One is the archaic storyteller, whose skill is derived from an oral culture and who serves as a repository for collective memory; another is the founder or creator of an original universe text, a figure conditioned by the emergence of print culture and closely linked to history; and the final type is the superstar, produced when the age of mass culture overtakes the Latin American novel in the 1960s. There is no doubt that according to this typology Donoso's failed author is located in the problematic transition between cultural hero and media star. The author as cultural hero is concerned with the life of the individual in society (and particularly of the artist in the historical moment known as modernism), while for the author as media star (at least for the consumer of mass culture) individualism and even the sense of history have become inoperative. This contradictory transition can readily be grasped through the notion of aura that Walter Benjamin associates with the traditional authority of art and that comes to an end with the advent of modern technology. The development of film, photography, and mass communications makes late-nineteenth-century aestheticism obsolete by creating a new popular audience for artistic production, an audience excluded by the "negative theology" of autonomous art. According to Benjamin's argument, aestheticism is forced to deny the social function of art while attempting to preserve the aura linking art and cult or ritual. Thus what comes to an end in the modern age is the concept of art as something mysterious and distant that subjects the viewer or reader to its transcendental authority. Modern art dispels the transcendental illusion and offers itself as materially produced, changing the role of the addressee from contemplative subject to critical or participatory agent.

Now, Donoso's narrator is dazzled by the novelist's aura: "[P]ara mí el escritor . . . está dotado de un aura incomparable" 'The writer for me . . . is endowed with an incomparable aura.' Julio is caught between the mirror images of

Rimbaud and of Marcelo Chiriboga, who is the novel's aura-bearing figure. He also confesses and reiterates that his "idol" is Chiriboga,

> este escritor . . . que habla de igual a igual con el Papa y con Brigitte Bardot, con Fidel Castro, Carolina de Mónaco o García Márquez, y cuyos pronunciamientos sobre política o sobre cine, o sobre moda causan tempestades. . . .
>
> this writer . . . who speaks face to face with the Pope and Brigitte Bardot, with Fidel Castro, Caroline of Monaco or García Márquez, and whose pronouncements on politics or movies or fashion unleash storms. . . .

Appropriately, this tropical media star appears surrounded by rare silver antiques representing mythological and probably Christian motifs. Julio describes Chiriboga as "one of those figures created by Renaissance artisans," a statement attesting that Julio has a talent for appreciating beauty even if he is unable to create anything resembling the objet d'art that is Marcelo Chiriboga, a curious blend of ritualistic and pop art. But the novel as a whole does not fully legitimate the literary figure's aura and particularly questions its own aura-endowed status as a work of art. *El jardín de al lado* is characterized by an unstable and deceptive point of view, modeled on the trompe l'oeil paintings that decorate the narrative space, and this strategy is intimately linked to narrative demystification, achieved by denying the reader a central perspective from which to consume the "beautiful illusion" of the novel. The demystification, however, is not total, for the "author" safeguards at least one secret, that of the surprise reversal of perspectives in the final chapter. This withholding of information ensures a certain mastery, a control over readers, at the same time that it preserves the work's aesthetic integrity (autonomy). Thus, on the one hand, the scene of writing is opened to direct scrutiny by readers, who get the impression that they too can be authors. If the novel stuck systematically to this path, it would be an avant-garde work, in the historical sense of the term: it would be "close to the state of freedom, of something that can be consciously produced and made." But, on the other hand, the "author" refuses to yield entirely to this democratic and materialist temptation, and the novel retains something of the fetish character imputed by Adorno (following Benjamin) to autonomous or aura-endowed art. Self-mirroring is the narrative device that lodges the novel's aura. *El jardín de al lado* is symmetrically composed around a clearly identifiable central scene: the fortuitous meeting in the marketplace (which is also a hall of mirrors) between Julio and Marcelo Chiriboga, attended by Gloria, Bijou, Núria, and other minor characters. The description of Julio's "vision" of Chiriboga mimics the language of photography (or film) and painting and thus joins the artistic technologies that compete with the written

word in the marketplace. Onomastic signifiers also reflect one another, as in the Rimbaldian play of vowels between Julio and Bijou, or they reflect larger narrative units. "Gloria" refers to the literary glory denied to Julio but achieved by Chiriboga, a name whose last two syllables form the word meaning "vogue."

Thus, *El jardín de al lado* takes the modernist author who is the protagonist of "Death in Venice" farther down the road of history, where modernity crosses over into postmodern mass culture. There, at that liminal boundary, Donoso's modern author battles the twin forces of political engagement and the ethics of the marketplace but succumbs to the aporia of a modernism that cannot transform itself into a viable form of reading and writing. At a different level, of course, *El jardín de al lado* is a successful exploration of the contradictory ground that separates politics from the autonomous work of art, an exploration carried out by the transference of the notion of crisis from the political realm to the aesthetic.

Antonio Benitez Rojo (review date Summer 1992)

SOURCE: "*The Obscene Bird of Night* as a Spiritual Exercise," in *Review of Contemporary Fiction,* Vol. XII, No. 2, Summer, 1992, pp. 50-5.

[*In the following essay, Rojo defends his idea that* The Obscene Bird of Night *can be read as a spiritual exercise in which the reader imagines an experience of self-annihilation. Rojo asserts that this experience represents a grappling with death, and is similar to religious observances such as Lent, Sabbath, or Ramadan.*]

From time to time, in accordance with the prescription of the majority of the world's religions, all believers must perform a ritual of self-annihilation. This has to do, of course, with the enactment of death. Accordingly, practices such as fasting, sexual abstinence, physical penitence, silence, worldly withdrawal, and meditation often play a role. In general, these practices not only limit to a greater or lesser degree the natural appetites of the body, but also affect the social activities of the individual in everything from work to recreation. For a period of time the believer is supposed to remain in a state of limbo in which he negotiates with death, and one can call this Lent, Sabbath, or Ramadan.

After this metaphysical plunge the pious individual emerges convinced of the futility of worldly values and fortified in his faith. Though results are not usually enduring, the various religions provide innumerable opportunities to strengthen the soul in the daily renouncement of small pleasures and worldly honors. Any hour of any day can be used for prayer, penance, sacrifice, mystic trances, or meditation. In the

Catholic faith one may recall the spiritual exercises instituted by Saint Ignatius of Loyola.

Of course not all of humankind believes in an afterlife; there are those who are atheists or agnostics, and those who subscribe in only a nominal fashion to some religion or belief. By this I mean to say that millions and millions of human beings do not feel obligated by any religious code to simulate death, in even the most trivial way. And yet all simulations of death, including deep reflections on the subject (which implies dying a little), are productive experiences. In effect, one must agree with the ancients that to submerge oneself under the crust of the earth, if possible while fasting, skeptically leaving behind the bulky garments of vanity, pride, and self-importance—even if only for a short time—will be more enlightening than any moral harangue arising from the fear of divine punishment. To approach death without the hope of eternal life, and brush against the ashen folds of its cloak as a ritual initiation to a higher plane of earthly existence, is the best moral exercise that anyone could undertake if one is sincere.

If one accepts this proposition, what incentive do the incredulous have to experiment with this useful and economic initiation? Here literary creation doubtless performs an important role, because it provides a half-dozen models that can successfully substitute for the most demanding spiritual exercises. Notice, from the Bronze Age to the present, the enormous number of heroes and heroines who descend to gloomy depths and later resurface in the warm light of victory. Or the affectionate feelings that characters like Don Quixote, Hamlet, and Colonel Aureliano Buendía arouse by the mere fact of having lived exemplarily in their madness, which is to say, in death. Or, beginning with the minotaur and ending with the lugubrious entities of Stephen King, the fascination that otherworldly creatures have for us, as if those who traffic in them are part of an unmentionable pact. Or the disturbing compassion we bestow on human freaks, no matter how low their condition. Isn't having been born Quasimodo a case of starting life half dead from the beginning? Or the suspicious tenacity with which we read expiatory books like *Crime and Punishment* and *Under the Volcano,* whose realism is perhaps more awful than any fantastic monstrosity ever imagined. Anyway, to continue, it's obvious that without being aware of it, the most skeptical reader has died and revived to his heart's content through the medium of literary catharsis. And of course for those who only read the newspaper, there are always the radio, movie, and TV versions.

In any case, world literature produces every now and then truly exceptional works within this popular and varied genre. In my experience as a reader, for example, I treasure the readings of the first editions of *Nausea,* Curzio Malaparte's *Skin, The Tin Drum, The Subterraneans, The Plague,* and

The Obscene Bird of Night. If including this last work leaves me open to a charge of regionalistic or linguistic chauvinism, I can only respond sincerely that I have never read any book by a contemporary author more devastating than that novel by José Donoso.

On what do I base my judgment? Well, I think it's a matter of density, of saturation. This in the sense that Donoso's book superimposes several of the aforementioned models to induce in the reader the imaginary experience of self-annihilation. To begin with, there is the epigraph chosen by Donoso to inform the reader from where he took the title of his novel and, in passing, to prepare him for one of the most anguished journeys to nowhere ever seen in the history of literature. The quote isn't brief (it comes from a letter by Henry James, Sr., to his sons Henry and William) but it is necessary to recall it in its entirety to allow us to approach the novel productively:

> Every man who has reached even his intellectual teens begins to suspect that life is no farce; that it is not genteel comedy even; that it flowers and fructifies on the contrary out of the profoundest tragic depths of the essential dearth in which its subject's roots are plunged. The natural inheritance of everyone who is capable of spiritual life is an unsubdued forest where the wolf howls and the obscene bird of night chatters.

The remaining 500-plus pages of text should be read as a pragmatic reflection on James Senior. If a reader, through excessive haste or carelessness, misses that passage, he could end up thinking that Donoso's novel is unnecessarily long, that it is repetitive, that its settings hardly differ among themselves, that the subject matter lacks suspense and excitement, that its characters are intolerably paradoxical, that its narrative structure is chaotic, and that its discourse is abstruse. However, it would never enter the reader's mind that he had just finished reading a minor work: frivolous, badly written, unoriginal, in short, forgettable. It is indeed possible that the reader will arrive at an unjust conclusion: too bad about that book; it could have been a masterpiece but the editor wasn't very good. Of course, if the reader considers the James quote as the first paragraph of Donoso's text, he will know very well what to expect. He will know that he has just entered Diogenes' tub, where he will have to accommodate himself for several days in order to meditate upon the irreparable indecency of the world and of that which we call reality— that abject convention we use to deny ourselves the most elementary answers: where did we come from? why are we here? where are we going? This takes for granted that the reader "has reached his intellectual teens" and "is capable of spiritual life."

In any case, Donoso connects the epigraph with a shadowy

antechamber to facilitate the reader's entrance to the rigorous labyrinth that is the novel. In effect, upon turning the page, one suddenly encounters the death of the aged Brígida, and one has no option but to attend her wake in the chapel or the House of Spiritual Exercises. Forty decrepit old women, three nuns, and five orphan girls live there. But, most importantly, the principal character, Humberto Peñaloza, lives there as well. His tortured body will serve as a sarcophagus for the readers both male and female through the grace of catharsis. It is obvious in the previous sentence that I have emphasized the idea that the reader's gender is not important. Either sex will be able to identify with the protagonist. The same thing happens with particulars such as age and profession because Humberto Peñaloza, like the narrator in Borges's "Lottery in Babylon," has performed the most diverse moral roles (victim, executioner, sinner, penitent) and has worn the masks of man, baby, crone, giant, deaf-mute, and writer. In short, Humberto Peñaloza is everything and nothing, and his physical disappearance in the last night of the novel—a necessarily eschatological night—symbolizes the ethical initiation of which I have spoken, beyond which the individual has to go on living with the gnawing certainty that nobody knows anything and that life is nothing more than this: the existential frustration of knowing that nobody knows anything, beginning with oneself. Once the anguish has reached this extreme point, one should reach a kind of hopeless serenity that has favorable repercussions on the individual and, by extension, on society.

In reality, Donoso's novel is an inverted epic where the laurels do not belong to the victor but to the vanquished, to him who knowing from the start that all is lost tries, as Ernest Hemingway would say, to give it his best shot. And not to win accolades but for the sake of self-fulfillment. History, of course, counts for naught here since every event, once extracted from its manipulating discourse, lacks all organic meaning. For Donoso, in accordance with his fortunate metaphor, history is no longer anything more than a miserable sack stuffed with old newspapers whose photos and headlines tell us nothing.

To comment at length upon what happens in the novel goes beyond the intent of this quick rereading. Nevertheless, I would have to point out that the paradoxical behavior of the characters is due to the fact that in the text several worlds— or, if one prefers, spaces of seclusion—coexist: for example, the space of the Rinconada and that of the House of Spiritual Exercises, each with its own language and narrative model. The first is a kind of bestiary full of deformed and lewd people (dwarfs, giants, the grotesquely obese, hunchbacks), nightmarish creatures who drag their monstrosity through the luxurious pavillions and gardens of the place. But the lives of these defective beings are not far removed from our own. In reality, these beings are the moral monsters we carry within, that dark Other that wavers between elemental passions and the grossest sentiments, this perverse and crippled Mr. Hyde whom we do not always succeed in keeping at bay; this obscene bird of night of which James spoke to his sons.

Superimposed on the Rinconada is the House of Spiritual Exercises, a labyrinth of humid cells, tumbledown rooms, and patios full of rubble. At one time it was a structure of piety dedicated to perfecting souls. Now it barely functions as a shelter for a group of invalid and sterile women. In my reading—and possibly in Donoso's as well—these useless cellars that are about to be abandoned symbolize religion. I'm not referring only to Christianity but to any religion or belief, to any hope for a hereafter, or to any faith in a transcendental locus of eternal redemption. One could say that God once lived in these ancient cellars or, rather, someone passing himself off as God, taking advantage of kind souls. But that God, false or inefficient, has died and all that is left are his remains: tattered angels, one-armed virgins, patched sheets, rags, bits of string, burlap bags, old newspapers, broken objects, and leftovers.

Humberto Peñaloza resides simultaneously in both spaces. He suspects he is a sinner but doesn't know what his sin is. His life, minuscule and mediocre, never quite comes together in the eyes of reason; it is a coming and going full of sound and fury signifying nothing. From this precarious observatory Humberto Peñaloza mythicizes reality, that is to say, whatever he doesn't understand inside or outside himself. So his desire to become someone worthy (like Don Jerónimo de Azcoitía) and to be desired by someone estimable (like Doña Inés) not only compels him to live in La Rinconada and in the House of Spiritual Exercises, but also in a third space which, like the others, has its own language and narrative codes: the space of myth. In effect, lost in the night and the turns of an indecipherable labyrinth, Humberto Peñaloza lives the life of the minotaur. As in myth, the notions of time and space are blurred. Furthermore, the characters with whom he interacts allude more to transpersonal symbols than to real people. There inside, in the shadowy passages of the labyrinth, one never quite knows who is who and who is the Other. Consequently, all life is multiple, a sequence of masks that one must put on so that one can try to know oneself better. In the end, with the years and the vicissitudes of life, things seem to become simpler. The masks begin to disappear by dint of resembling themselves. It is precisely at this critical juncture that Donoso's narrative discourse apprehends Humberto Peñaloza. For a moment, the reader who accompanies him in his anguished adventure has the illusion that he is going to emerge from the text with an answer. A futile hope. Suddenly an old woman comes, grabs Humberto Peñaloza by the scruff of the neck, and stuffs him in a burlap sack. She immediately sews the mouth of the sack closed and puts the package in another bag, and so on. Then the old woman throws the bundle on her shoulder and begins to wander about aimlessly. Outside the bundle (which suffocates us and denies us access to any revelation) it is dark and cold. The old woman huddles over a bonfire, falls asleep, and soon everything turns into ashes which the wind disperses. In the end Humberto Peñaloza and the reader are reduced to a black smear on the stones, and the spiritual exercises that Donoso proposes for unbelieving humanity end right here.

Is *The Obscene Bird of Night* a pessimistic novel? I think not, but one must conclude that it lacks the sugary flavor of metaphysical explanation. Perhaps it could be taken for a pessimistic work if nothing remained of the human being. But something does remain: a black smear that the trip to nowhere does not succeed in blotting out. Well—the reader with certain expectations will say—a black mark and nothing are the same. And I nevertheless would say no, they aren't the same, and I would refer the reader to a curious belief of the Navajo Indians.

This belief or tradition is related to the beautiful blankets that the Navajo weave and that can be purchased in any store specializing in handmade textiles. These Indians believe that the weaver's dedication in carrying out her task is so intense that, thread by thread, her spirit passes into the cloth. So that she won't lose her spirit in the symmetrical labyrinths of the design (which to the Navajo implies losing one's reason) the weaver leaves a loose thread that interrupts the pattern of the cloth in some place. The Navajo believe that this loose thread provides the spirit with an escape route, and thanks to it the spirit can return to the artisan's body. Perhaps the most interesting aspect of this belief is that the "lifeline" is, at the same time, the weaver's signature. Naturally one will say that such a practice is useless, given that ultimately the loose thread becomes part of the geometric pattern of the design. But it is also true that the thread, even though it can be read as a necessarily unsuccessful path of escape, also speaks of the individual's desire to leave an identifying mark, a signature, as an irrevocable record of his plan of escape. It is in this sense that I read in the black spot the name of Humberto Peñaloza and also that of the reader.

Charles Bowden (review date 29 November 1992)

SOURCE: "An Autopsy of a Generation," in *Los Angeles Times Book Review,* November 29, 1992, p. 7.

[*In the following review, Bowden gives a brief plot summary of* The Garden Next Door, *and asserts that the book relies on images that conjure up "the emptiness of modern life."*]

They sag with failure, are in their fifties, and live as exiles trapped in Spain with no money and no future. They possess but one asset-their pasts. Julio and Gloria fled Chile after Allende's fall. Julio had been a university professor of En-

glish literature, the author of two promising books, the son of a congressman, and she had been raised to be the proper wife of a professional man.

In Chilean José Donoso's bittersweet novel *The Garden Next Door* this does not prove to be sufficient material for starting a new life. Or even remembering their past lives. Julio struggles to rewrite a massive novel which pivots on his six days of incarceration in one of Pinochet's prisons. An earlier version of his tale had been rejected by Spain's leading agent as lifeless. Now he suspects he will be a flop, a drop-out from the Boom generation of Latin American writers. Their teen-age son despises them for their fixation on the failed left government of Allende and has disappeared into Marrakech. They wonder if he is now a male whore. Julio's mother is dying in Chile and he lacks both the money and the will to visit her deathbed. Then, a rich friend offers them his luxurious apartment in Madrid for the summer and they grasp desperately at this opportunity.

The flat in Madrid looks down on the lush garden of a neighboring Duke and this green sanctuary becomes a metaphor for a lost Chile, for a dead marriage, for lives either in decline, or possibly never truly lived. "Why not accept failure once and for all?" Julio thinks. "I have nothing to say. Nothing to teach. I can't create beauty, but I know how to appreciate it." So Julio proceeds to drink the summer away, swallow valiums and putter at his novel. Gloria slides into a mental breakdown. This mutual descent is punctuated by experiences with characters seemingly more alive: the aristocratic woman next door in the garden who takes lovers easily and moves gracefully in her nakedness by the pool; a vagabond friend of their son named Bijou who is a male prostitute, thief, peddler of drugs and resolutely apolitical; a famous Ecuadoran writer who ostentatiously enjoys the rewards of his fame.

Donoso's book moves by images more than actions and the images all conjure up the emptiness of modern life—"From the terrace above we could see the reddish sky . . . with its festive summer lights: international jazz or horror film festival?" Solutions are systematically rejected: youth culture proves an empty mannerism; literature is both unreachable and unreal; politics are bankrupt; the flesh a fraud betrayed by age; personal integrity a fantasy that cannot be sustained without status and money. Julio and Gloria cling to memories of favorites snatches of classical music which they hum almost as prayers as they confront a world in which they no longer have a place. Donoso, born in 1924 and a leading member of the South American crop of writers called the boom generation, operates as a pathologist performing his generation's own autopsy. He writes very deftly and yet coldly. The novel has a clinical, morning after feel to it.

Julio ends his summer a total failure, just as the garden next door goes to temporary ruin during the August holiday of the aristocratic family. His revised novel is scorned by every major house in Spain and so he steals to taste the rewards of a success he has not achieved. Gloria utterly breaks down. The memories of Allende's fall prove inadequate for either fiction or a life. "I'll be the one," Julio decides, "for whom revolutions will catch fire, yet not the one who commits himself to fight or defend the rights of others with his blood. No: I'll remain outside the struggle and outside history."

In almost a wicked sendup of both magical realism and pulp fiction, all is made right in the end and Julio and Gloria are either restored to their proper standing, or-depending on the reader's point of view-condemned to their limited lives. Money and station descend, classical music once again seems to correctly express the actual world. The plot hardly matters in a book that insists history does not matter, a novel which ends with the injunction, "Please do not disturb!" This is not the book for Fidel Castro or Ronald Reagan but it seems appropriate for this weary moment at the end of a bloody century.

Lawrence Thornton (essay date 22 December 1992)

SOURCE: "The Muses Answered the Missus," in *Washington Post,* December 22, 1992, p. C2.

[*In the following review, Thornton provides a plot synopsis of* The Garden Next Door, *and defends his view that there is "no better meditation on the agonies of writing" than the one presented in this novel.*]

The entrance to Writers' Hell isn't marked by Dante's "Abandon Hope, All Ye Who Enter Here!" but by the resounding "No!" thundered by an agent. Out of that little damnation the Chilean novelist José Donoso has fashioned a bittersweet story laying bare the psyche of an artist on the verge of failure, a man well past 50 who is deeply aware that his life's blood is going into every sentence of a book that may not be good enough to publish.

Donoso has already produced seven books to considerable praise, and this latest novel to be translated into English will further burnish his reputation. There is no better meditation on the agonies of writing than in *The Garden Next Door,* which explores the fortunes of one writer on his way to rejection and another on her way to fame.

Julio and his wife, Gloria, are Chilean exiles living in a small Spanish town where they worry about money, the sexual proclivities of their son and their contentious marriage. Drinking too much, able to sleep only with the aid of liberal doses of Valium, they are both rapidly going downhill when an old friend offers them his Madrid apartment for the summer.

This elegant retreat boasts a view into the garden of an estate next door where beautiful people spend their afternoons in erotic play.

As the book opens, Julio is nursing a wounded ego after the first draft of his novel has been turned down by Nuria Monclus, a powerful agent whose disdain has made it almost impossible for him to work. Speaking of his visit to her office he says, "She had let me know, without saying it, that I didn't interest her as an author for her stables, something it hadn't been difficult for me to predict when I saw her surrounded by portraits, framed manuscripts, personal mementos, gifts, inscriptions, fetishes from all the 'greats' and their families; this made my hopes come crashing down right there, even before she had passed sentence." Fortunately, the apartment and garden give him new hope, enough to begin revising the novel, which deals with his imprisonment during Pinochet's rule.

As much as he wants the book to be his masterpiece, Julio is acutely aware of its weaknesses and he vacillates between despair and the conviction that he can still make a name for himself. One of Donoso's achievements is his ability to render the anguished envy of a writer who has never quite been successful and alternately hates and admires those who are. At one point or another, Julio castigates Garcia Marquez, Fuentes, Cortazar and others associated with the Latin American Boom. He sees conspiracies among agents, argues that publishers invented these writers to make fortunes, while in the next breath admitting that they can all do things that are beyond him.

His problem, as Gloria points out, is that he "only knows how to live within structures imposed on him from outside and can't create for himself the imaginary world that answers only to its own laws, the artist's world." When she proves to be right and Nuria Monclus turns down his manuscript a second and final time, Julio is so despondent that he cannot tell Gloria. Instead, he sells one of his host's paintings, claims the money is an advance and hustles his wife off to Tangier.

By shifting the point of view at this point from Julio to Gloria, Donoso allows us to revisit the period when Julio was writing and Gloria had started drinking so heavily that she finally had a breakdown. From time to time she had mentioned her own creative ambitions, which Julio discounted, arguing that she ought to be content plying her trade as a translator. But in the depths of Gloria's depression she had begun keeping notes on herself, on Julio, on everything of importance in her life, and out of that work emerges a novel that Nuria Monclus finds exceptional.

One of the things that makes this book so fine is Donoso's refusal to look away from the hope and fear that accompany the artist's enterprise. But while *The Garden Next Door* is a cautionary tale for both published and aspiring writers, there is a feeling that even though we may not hear again from Julio, he has made peace with his muse while Gloria has just begun courting hers. Her spiritual rebirth and Julio's acceptance of his limitations as an artist are poignantly and profoundly rendered.

Tony Talbot (essay date 10 January 1993)

SOURCE: "Caught in a Sweet Trap," in *The New York Times Book Review,* January 10, 1993, p. 11.

[*In the following review, Talbot contends that* The Garden Next Door *is about exiles who have fled dictatorships to live out their lives in more pleasant places. Commenting on the autobiographical aspects of the story, Talbot claims the novel to be about "our universal terror of disintegration when everything seems to be losing its meaning."*]

Latin American fiction, since the boom of the 1960's, has been identified with the novel that is bigger than life: Jungles teeming with extravagance, grotesqueness, fantasy and absurdity. How else to make sense of the Latin American reality? José Donoso, Chile's most prominent fiction writer, is the author of one of these multilayered books, the highly acclaimed 1973 novel *The Obscene Bird of Night.* But in his 1981 work *The Garden Next Door*, the novel bigger-than-life retreats into the backyard of his protagonist's imagination.

Mr. Donoso's narrator, Julio Mendez, is an exiled Chilean writer. He and Gloria, his wife of more than 20 years, have been living amid a circle of other exiles in Sitges, a coastal town near Barcelona, for seven years. Julio is trying to revise a novel about the six days he spent in a Santiago jail after the fall of Allende, a novel that has been rejected by the formidable Catalan literary agent Nuria Monclus, who finds that it needs "a wider dimension." Gnawed by self-doubt and money concerns, constantly bickering with his wife, obsessed by their estranged teen age son (who has vanished into the maze of Marrakesh), guilty because he can't return to his dying mother in Chile, adrift with other uprooted Latin Americans. Julio finds scant relief in his menu of stimulants, tranquilizers and sleeping potions. Just as Gloria does in alcohol. Escape, at least for the summer, comes when they are offered the use of a luxurious apartment in Madrid by Julio's childhood friend Pancho, now a famous artist.

Through the bedroom window, Julio discovers the garden next door: a luminous, erotic realm inhabited by a young blond aristocrat and her charmed coterie. Julio's fantasies about the days of his childhood and adolescence—about his mother's lovingly tended house and garden—grow around

this magical Eden, where all is fertile and transcendent. But the messiness of his real life inexorably intrudes. Gloria plunges into depression and requires treatment from a Uruguayan psychoanalyst friend who flies in regularly from Barcelona. 'Julio's rewritten manuscript is turned down for good by the literary agent. His mother dies and his brother in Chile presses him to sell the family homestead. Julio commits a theft out of desperation and flies to Tangier with Gloria. There, after five introspective chapters, *The Garden Next Door* might plausibly have concluded. But the twist ending of the sixth chapter gives the book a juicy narrative spin.

This deftly translated *roman a clef* is primarily about exile—about those former guerrillas, writers, painters and intellectuals who have fled dictatorships to lead their lives in places like Sitges, "a sweet trap as sticky as flypaper." In almost documentary fashion, Mr. Donoso depicts exiles who are torn by eroding political commitment, unable to transmit to their children an identity with their homeland, nostalgic for their native country and yet fearful of going back. But he also relentlessly exposes a writer in his 50's who has lost his bearings and vigor, detailing his bitterness, envy, hypochondria, depression and paralysis—and, finally, his reconciliation to defeat and failure. *The Garden Next Door* is about our universal terror of disintegration when everything seems to be losing its meaning.

Twenty years ago, recalling his childhood home. José Donoso wrote that the "house and especially the garden, which became beautiful under my mother's care, is identified in my emotions with her fancy and delight in things. Only when that garden no longer exists shall I feel finally, really on my own." This brutally honest novel may be that final purging.

David Streitfield (essay date 8 April 1993)

SOURCE: "Writing from the Gut," in *Washington Post,* April 8, 1993, p. D1.

[*In the following article, Streitfield provides a brief commentary on Donoso's life, specifically focusing on the lies he told as a youngster about stomach problems, and his real ulcer later in life.*]

When José Donoso was a boy, back in his native Chile almost six decades ago, he hated school. So the clever lad invented an ache in his gut.

For a time, the malady did its job; Donoso didn't have to eat with the rest of his classmates or participate in sports. But there came a day when faking wasn't necessary. It was real, all right, this sharp spasm in his belly.

Maybe early on it was psychosomatic. Yet as the decades

passed, the ulcer became genuine. Finally, during a lecture in Colorado in 1969, Donoso had a hemorrhage and nearly died. He left the hospital with only part of his stomach.

Donoso sees this as a truly painful lesson about the nature of fiction. "I was creating something out of nothing, out of my own innards, which then had to be taken out. Isn't that just like writing a novel?"

It was also, he adds, a little like a macabre fairy tale, one that warned how easily the roles of master and servant can be reversed. "You tell the story, and at some point the story becomes true. You write the book out of your life, and then the book gains control of your life and begins to throttle you."

He's sitting in his office at the Woodrow Wilson Center, that unlikely publicly funded think tank ensconced in the Smithsonian's castle on the Mall. It's a plain place, almost a cubicle, with the only idiosyncratic note two postcards, each of which depicts an enormous woman—inspiration for a projected novel about "a nice American big fat girl."

Across the hall, behind a half-closed door, a seminar is taking place. Droning voices contemplate the post-Cold War economy or the Russian crisis or maybe the post-Cold War Russian economy. The Wilson Center is egghead academic, which makes Donoso a bit of an oddball. Of the 30 or so current fellows, he's the only novelist.

That's partly because not many apply, but the selection criteria are also fairly narrow. "Every novelist we've had—and there's never been a year we've had two of them—has been historically or politically oriented," says Wilson Center Director Charles Blitzer. "The idea is, you can learn as much if not more from a first-rate fictional treatment of historical events as from a social historian."

Donoso, now 68, is possibly the finest novelist living in the metropolitan area. Over a 40-year career, he has published about 20 distinguished works of fiction, half of which have been translated into English. But only three are in print, including the newly issued novellas *Taratuta/Still Life With Pipe,* and publishers aren't exactly assaulting him for new work. . . .

At a distance of 20 years, the Boom has taken on the dimensions of myth. Cortazar is now dead, Vargas Llosa and Fuentes influential statesmen, Garcia Marquez probably the most acclaimed author in the world. And Donoso?

"I lead a much more inner life, a more subjective life, than novelists generally do," he maintains, comparing himself in this regard to Flaubert, another writer with "a strange devouring thing inside him."

He was gravely ill last year, which only made the situation worse. "I still haven't got myself together. I used to be a much more outgoing person, much more willing to relate to people. I don't do that much anymore. I ache, to put it bluntly."

In the way that couples over the years begin to resemble each other, perhaps novelists start to take on the qualities of their characters. In *The Obscene Bird of Night,* there's something called the "imbunche," a nightmare creature born with all its orifices sealed. It's a metaphor for being unable to create, for having work inside that you're unable to release.

This is Donoso's greatest fear. "For several periods, I felt I wouldn't be able to write—that I'd be hampered by something physical. And that would be the death of me. I have nothing else to fall back on."

Donoso would like to be remembered as a street in Chile. Many of them bear the names of people, so why not his?

"I see myself as about two blocks long," he says. "Maybe with a few trees."

"Or a little plaza?" asks Maria Pilar.

"A very small plaza," the writer agrees. "Maybe something secluded. Hidden places have a sort of unity, I think . . .

"I'll be happy as a street. Even though people may not read me, they will walk me. They'll still speak my name."

REVIEWS OF DONOSO'S RECENT WORK

Christopher Leland (review date May 15 1988)

SOURCE: "Stay and Fight, or Leave and Love?," in *Los Angeles Times Book Review,* May 15, 1988, pp. 3, 13.

[*In the following review, Leland gives a plot synopsis of* Curfew *and comments on the political structures described in the novel as they relate to Donoso's own experiences.*]

Fifteen years have passed since the overthrow of Chile's last elected government, the Popular Unity regime of Salvador Allende. Other Latin American nations—Argentina, Uruguay, Bolivia—have passed in this period from democracy through dictatorship to democracy again. Chile, however, which for more than half a century maintained one of the continent's proudest liberal traditions, has remained under the heel of the military. An entire generation has now matured beneath the gloomy authoritarianism of Gen. Augusto Pinochet.

It is into this world that José Donoso, Chile's most famous living author, thrusts us [with] his new novel, *Curfew*. Mañungo Vera, a famous protest singer, returns to his native land after a 15-year Parisian exile. His relationship with the mother of his son at an end, his career in abeyance due both to a recurring tinnitus and a personal crisis before the prospect of middle age, he arrives in Santiago the day of the wake of Matilde Neruda, the widow of the nation's greatest poet, Pablo Neruda, dead himself in the earliest days of military rule.

In the 24 hours that follow, we witness Vera's re-entry into a world no longer his. At the wake of his old friend from the days of the Nerudas' residence in Paris, Vera is drawn to Judit Torre, a former revolutionary herself returned from exile, apparently reintegrated in the society and yet secretly involved in a complex and intensely personal conspiracy. At the Neruda house, amid the crowd of mourners, the two individually confront old comrades-in-arms, young radicals with romantic revolutionary visions, the privileged opposition distrusted by their more intensely politicized friends. Later, after a chance meeting on the street, Vera and Torre together come in contact with other elements of Pinochet's Chile: the ever-growing army of the country's dispossessed, ragtag ragpickers whose only hope must be apocalyptic revolution, as well as those who to a greater or lesser extent have made their peace with the gray and implacable monstrousness of institutionalized repression, informing, torture.

Donoso, who himself spent long years as an expatriate, documents the perverse effects of a decade and a half of dictatorship. A government which, as most of its ilk, sees itself as above politics, has created a society in which politics permeates and predetermines everything. He shows us the uneasy alliances and furious infighting among various factions of the Left, which reduces all the groups to equal impotence as the country stagnates in economic and spiritual torpor. Among the regime's supporters, meanwhile, there is an equivalent kind of jockeying, the peevish concern for minor privilege which can determine life or death for someone run afoul of the authorities. Trapped in a world in which, overtly, the personal is political and vice versa, in which one's fate can be determined by bad timing or caprice, Donoso's characters can make no plans, live with no assurance. Judit Torre, for example, embodies the contradictions of life in a military police state. Of privileged family, she nonetheless became a revolutionary and the companion of one of the movement's leaders. Captured, she was arbitrarily saved from rape, released from her secret prison by bureaucratic oversight, issued a passport by a sympathetic functionary himself later disappeared. Anxious for revenge for a violation that never in fact occurred, yet ravaged by a sense of unworthiness beside those who have suffered more gruesomely, she still imagines almost against her will a possible happiness with Mañungo Vera in Paris: safe, distant, private. Vera is him-

self torn, tempted constantly to flee back to the Rue Sevastopol at the same time he is drawn further and further into the drama of his martyred homeland.

Unlike much of Donoso's other work, including his most famous, *The Obscene Bird of Night,* this book depends little on the magical, on that dreamlike mix of the quotidian and the supernatural we have come to expect in much Latin American literature. Magic is here, however, woven sparingly throughout the text, and, is, finally, the sign of the very faint hope with which Donoso concludes. Magic. Children. Art. These are perhaps the means by which Chile and its people may achieve some future redemption. Yet, this is a land, for the last 15 years, populated by people who "defined themselves through hatred, (and so) their lives gave them intolerable pain because of this sad mutilation history had imposed upon them." The novel ends not with love consummated, but merely with the notion that, in a day not too far distant, the word might be uttered aloud. It is a bleak but fitting conclusion to this dark and moving novel.

Donoso is fluently served by his translator, Alfred MacAdam, though, interestingly, *Curfew* is not what the book is called in Spanish. Perhaps the translation of the original title seemed to publishers here too grim or dramatic for the American audience, so many thousands of miles from the realities of Santiago. There, in Chile itself, the book is called *La Desesperanza.* It means despair.

Joanne Omang (review date 22 May 1988)

SOURCE: "Home to Santiago: The Return of the Exile," in *Book World—The Washington Post,* May 22, 1988, p. 7.

[*In the following review, Omang discusses the plot of* Curfew, *noting that this work is more accessible than any of Donoso's other novels. Containing less "magic realism" than his other books, Omang maintains that* Curfew *is a work of "riveting clarity."*]

For two or three years after the 1973 coup that brought Augusto Pinochet to power in Chile, the Chilean left was more or less in hiding, frightened, but somehow smug. In the slum apartments that hid them in Santiago, in their mountain hideouts and their Parisian exile cafes, the activists knew the dictator would fall any day now: there would be a popular rising, there would be revolution. There was no need to change tactics.

There was no need, in other words, to do more than paper over the doctrinal chasms and personal feuds that split the dissidents' families and kept everyone arguing late into the curfew hours, always too late to do anything today.

Twelve years after the coup, in 1985, the sobered leftists of José Donoso's new novel, **Curfew**, are no longer smug, but paralyzed, taking their cranky children to the amusement park, drinking too much, despairing of change, dreaming bitter dreams.

Mañungo Vera, an exiled singer of revolutionary songs, comes back to Santiago with his young son, born and raised in France, for the funeral of the widow of leftist Chilean poet Pablo Neruda. Mañungo has lost his convictions over the years, and his career as revolutionary symbol is slipping. He wants to find "the mutilated pieces of his history" among the graying radicals who gather to fight over the relics of the departed Neruda saints.

After several obscure, mannered novels smothered in just too much magic realism, Chilean writer José Donoso has produced in **Curfew** a work of riveting clarity. It is a keen and compassionate look at a single day in the lives of those educated, cultured Chileans whose anguish after a dozen years under Pinochet is that they have survived.

"We keep telling ourselves that the people united will never be defeated, when for more than ten years they've had us more defeated than I can imagine," says Lopito, Mañungo's lost and repellent old buddy. With his greenish teeth and drunken opportunism, Lopito is doomed by his guilty, passionate rage: he embodies the defeat of all his friends. In Chile, Donoso says, "all personal pain had to have at least a political subtext."

Mañungo also, encounters the aristocratic guerrilla legend Judit Torre, an old lover whose cold fire hides the torturing secret that she too escaped torture. "I'd like to talk about music," she says, "but in my heart I'm afraid it would be frivolous." She drags Mañungo through the ominous no-man's-land of Santiago's deserted streets after the midnight curfew, when bodies are dumped on sidewalks and helicopters chug over the gardens with searchlights. Together they stalk the army officer who years ago made Judit pretend to scream in pain, crippling her beyond the rapes inflicted on her friends. But like everything else in today's Chile, he turns out not to be what they expected.

Watching Judit, watching all of them with a greedy eye for everyone's price, is Judit's cousin Freddy Fox, the overweight, overbearing and all-knowing government official. His comfortable arrogance and easy access to all of them demonstrate far more effectively than any torture scene the dictatorship's unassailable strength.

Chile is a place, Donoso says, of convents "where nuns embroider sheets for brides who no longer stain them" and where "everyone can be the incarnation, if he or she dares, of history." He shows the way history can turn in Chile on an issue as obscure as whether William Randolph Hearst secretly funded Leon Trotsky in Mexico.

People's index fingers are growing shorter in Chile, Lopito says, worn down like those of the Spanish Republicans who pounded their fingers against the table for 40 years, saying "this year Franco will fall, this year he will fall." Donoso's novel ignores those who are happy in the new Chile; this is a story of those whose political goals "wasted away and became impoverished in a kind of prolonged verbal masturbation."

Donoso brings all the forces together at the great chaotic funeral of Matilde Neruda, held before the cameras of muscular men in gray-glassed cars without license plates. The aging firebrands are distracted by their difficult children: Mañungo's truculent son, Lopito's ugly little girl and Judit's anxious preteen daughter, who for all their appalling flaws are the country's future. In this story Donoso celebrates the crippled half-people, dwarves and freaks weaving pathetic, futile plots, and the toothless lions roaring out complaint to an uncaring world: a people not quite repressed enough to die.

Donoso, now 64, lived in Europe for 15 years before returning to Chile with his wife and daughter. Several passages are, annoyingly, left in French in the otherwise excellent translation by Alfred MacAdam, and Donoso's prose can sometimes recall an unpruned wisteria: a little too exuberant in spots, a puzzling twist here and there. But the occasional excess stands out for its rarity, and the novel is the most accessible of any yet to come out from under Pinochet's enduring dictatorship.

Suzanne Ruta (review date 29 May 1988)

SOURCE: "What's Become of Chile," in *The New York Times Book Review*, May 29, 1988, p. 9.

[*In the following review, Ruta asserts that* Curfew *is a study of "the many ways politics mutilate and distort the private lives of [those] confronted by Pinochet." In her review, Ruta lauds the novel as "an urbane comedy of manners, a love story, a fairy tale," and praises the book's romantic themes, as well as its commentary on dictatorships.*]

The exile's return to his native land is the subject of some of the best writing from Latin America in recent years. Julio Cortazar in *Hopscotch* and Alejo Carpentier in *The Lost Steps* have played brilliant variations on the theme "you can go home again." José Donoso returned to Chile in 1980 after 15 years in Europe. He now lives in Santiago. In **Curfew** he has created a small masterpiece in the familiar genre. The book's protagonist is a famous singer of protest songs named

Mañungo Vera, just returned to Chile after 13 years in Paris. He hasn't been off the plane an hour when someone asks him the inevitable question: "How does it feel to be living under a dictatorship?" We already know by then that *Curfew* is both the story of a man's search for his roots and a portrait of Chile in the second decade of a military dictatorship no one knows how to get rid of.

Behind Mr. Donoso's engaging fictional hero stands, unmentioned but unmistakable, the shadow of Victor Jara, the young Chilean songwriter, voice of the Allende years, murdered within days of the 1973 anti-Allende coup. With such a ghost at his side, the invented hero Mañungo Vera links those the Pinochet regime destroyed and those it has allowed to go on living, maimed in body and spirit. *Curfew* examines the many ways politics mutilate and distort the private lives of the generation that was confronted by Pinochet head-on. But the historical figure who haunts the book is the late, great poet Pablo Neruda. Neruda and Pinochet, art and repression, are the immovable landmarks around which the fictive characters must find their way.

Known for the lavishly Gothic imagination of his earlier works (like *The Obscene Bird of Night*), Mr. Donoso doesn't have to invent in his new novel. It's enough simply to record the facts of life in a country under a state of siege, where not the sleep of reason but the apparatus of state terror breeds monsters. The pivotal events in the plot are the funeral of an old woman—Neruda's widow—and a young man's death by torture. And yet this is not a grim book. To turn somber politics into lively art is some kind of triumph over the politicians. *Curfew* is a political novel that is also an urbane comedy of manners, a love story, a fairy tale, a thriller, a lyric evocation of landscapes. The large cast of characters spans three generations, both sides of the political spectrum and whole social scale. Chilean place names, legends, food, class accents, literary fads—Mr. Donoso describes it all with the appalled and loving Rip Van Winkle eye of someone just back from a long time away.

The action is concentrated into the 24 hours following the death of Neruda's widow, Matilde, in January 1985. The book divides, like a sonata, into three sections—"Evening," "Night" and "Morning"—each with its own tempo and tone and complement of gripping scenes. "Evening" takes place in the civilized atmosphere of Neruda's house in Santiago, during the wake for Matilde. Mr. Donoso goes into chatty detail about Neruda's tastes in furniture, foods, women, landscapes, friends. He contrasts the poet's humanity and breadth with the shrunken, joyless lives of the next generation.

Was Neruda mixed up in a plot to kill Trotsky in some way? One of the characters raises the question and answers in the negative. To underscore the point and to rescue Neruda from sectarian claims, José Donoso spins an intrigue about the poet's wife's death that is a sly allusion to the plot to kill Trotsky. A Communist Party official plants his mistress in the Neruda household to make sure the party will draw full benefit from Matilde's impending death. The funeral of Neruda's wife will provide a rare opportunity for a show of opposition to the regime. Rather than lose control of the event, the party hack overrides the dying woman's last wishes, blackmails his mistress and sabotages a chance for unity among groups opposed to the Pinochet regime. The party hack has an unwitting ally in a member of Pinochet's inner circle, a greedy culture vulture who collects—a lovely comic touch—Trotsky memorabilia, but who, when push comes to shove, resorts to violence. Repression on the right and stagnation on the left combine to shore up the intolerable status quo in Chile.

There is a sense, Mr. Donoso suggests, in which all politicians, in or out of power, are buffoons. This satirical strand of the plot is urbane and slightly dated comedy, 1920's Evelyn Waugh or 1950's Anthony Powell. But then, one effect of dictatorship in Chile is to have made the country a graveyard of old fashions, political, literary and sartorial.

Another strand of the plot romantically involved the singer Vera with Judit Torre, a former revolutionary who is a daughter of one of Chile's most powerful oligarchical families. If Vera is a singer whose repertory and public image have grown stale and stifling, Judit is an activist who, after arrest, torture, exile and return to clandestinity, finds herself a burntout case. Hatred takes the place in her life that love might have occupied in kinder times. She prowls the city at night looking for the man who tortured her cellmate in jail, in order to seduce and perhaps kill him.

A dark Dantesque concatenation of images, ideas and allusions sets the tone for the second part, "Night," which takes place during the witching hour after curfew, when Judit pursues her obsessions while armored cars patrol the streets and helicopters circle overhead. Bands of guerrilla youth scavenge for salable garbage in wealthy neighborhoods, where they want to plant bombs. Mr. Donoso seems to take these desperate youngsters, doomed to a life where fear and hatred are the ruling emotions, altogether more seriously than he does the old left, with its rote ideological optimism. By the end of a terrifying night on the streets with Judit, Mañungo Vera is ready to take the plane back to Paris. He wants her to come along. Are they in love? In Paris, it won't matter.

In "Morning," the time of clear sight and harsh revelation, the fairy-tale romance shatters against the banal cruelties of daily life in a police state. The two lovers are united in feeling, separated in fact, by the death, under casual torture, of a mutual friend. Lopito is a character out of Dostoyevsky, an insidious mixture of fake and real humility, a petty thief, a coward, a father who can't help abusing the child he adores.

He embodies perhaps a well-known Chilean type, the *roto*, the guy at the bottom of the heap whom people respect because, since he has nothing to lose, he tells the truth with flair.

Lopito also incarnates everything Chile has to teach Vera, the pop idol whose fame has kept him from danger and discomfort but also from self-knowledge. It's a lesson in powerlessness, frustration, bitterness, despair. Within less than 24 hours of his arrival from Paris, Vera has his moment of truth, his homecoming, in the Santiago police station his friend will not leave alive. *Despair (La Desesperanza)* is the Spanish title of this beautifully realized and deeply moving work. Alfred MacAdam's translation accurately conveys the many subtle shifts in tone and pace.

Marjorie Agosin (review date 2 June 1988)

SOURCE: "Latin America Seen through the Eyes of Contemporary Writers," in *The Christian Science Monitor,* June 2, 1988, p. 20.

[*In the following review, Agosin discusses Donoso's description of Chile in* Curfew, *and provides a brief plot summary. Asserting that the novel "manages to combine chaos, absurdity, and the reality of life under a dictatorial government in a masterly way," Agosin lauds Donoso's descriptive passages and attention to detail.*]

José Donoso is one of Chile's foremost novelists, and one who is beginning to receive the attention he richly deserves. His story *Curfew* is very different from Dorfman's "Last Waltz in Santiago." Yet once again the theme, one might say their literary obsession, is their native land. Donoso writes with splendid subtlety. *Curfew* gravitates around two poles: the wake of Matilde Neruda, widow of the Nobel laureate Pablo Neruda, and the love relationship between Mañungo Vera, an exiled pop singer, and Judit Torre, an aristocrat involved in revolutionary activities against the junta. In an opening scene that is written with almost documentary realism as well as with irony and humor, Mañungo Vera returns to Santiago from exile in Europe on the day of Matilde Neruda's wake.

Few recognize him and his revolutionary songs. Mañungo confronts his own conscience. The feelings aroused by his return to a chaotic country unfold as the reader looks through Mañungo's eyes as he walks through Neruda's house and sees the poet's collection of marvelous objects and rare first editions.

Donoso presents many contradictions. Neruda is a communist and one of the richest poets of the 20th century, and Vera as a singer is now unknown, because the revolution no longer needs him. Politics and the sometimes harsh realities of political culture are revealed, as well as the mythical life of the Neruda family. Opposed to the childlike and magical universe of the Nerudas, a Chile of beggars and destitute shantytowns emerges through the confessional voice of Judit Torre, who desperately tries to heal the pain of torture and agony through memory and love.

But Vera is the center of the story. He—and so the reader—feels and understands the agony of a nation in despair. The concluding episode, a tour de force, begins with Matilde's funeral, which is turned into a political rally. The title of the Spanish original; *Despair,* is much more appropriate than *Curfew*, the title chosen for the English translation.

This novel manages to combine chaos, absurdity, and the reality of life under a dictatorial government in a masterly way. At the end, the reader feels he is being told about an almost unreal place: "It was a beautiful toy country, the trees and lakes, the snow-capped mountains made of papier-mâché, the delicacy of the historical buildings. . . ."

Perhaps Chile has become an almost demented fantasy besieged by memories of past glories exemplified by Pablo Neruda, a country tormented by a present sunk in hopelessness. In any event, *Curfew* is an intriguing book. Above all, it invites thinking and reflection on the many ways in which politics criss-crosses between imagination and a maddening reality.

John Updike (review date June 13, 1988)

SOURCE: John Updike, "In Dispraise of the Powers that Be," in *New Yorker,* Vol. LXIV, No. 17, June 13, 1988, pp. 112-14.

[*In the following review, Updike faults* Curfew *for "too much sticky, tangled prose," and for failing to fulfill its "Dostoyevskian ambition."*]

It is sometimes urged upon American authors that they should write more politically, out of a clearer commitment or engagement or sense of protest. Two foreign novels, one by a Chilean and the other by a Nigerian, demonstrate that having a political subject does not automatically give a novel grandeur, urgency, or coherence. *Curfew*, by the Chilean José Donoso, takes place in 1985, in a crowded time span of less than twenty-four hours bridging the wake and the funeral of Pablo Neruda's widow, Matilde. The occasion collects a number of varied friends and admirers—Mañungo Vera, a folksinger returned from twelve years in Europe; Judit Torre, a blond, aristocratic revolutionary who looks like the young Virginia Woolf; Fausta Manquileo, a matronly literary figure of distinction; Don Celedonio Villanueva, her husband

and a literary figure of perceptibly less distinction; Juan López, called Lopito, a former poet and present drunkard and abrasively obnoxious hanger-on; Lisboa, a Communist Party zealot; Ada Luz, his girlfriend and a docile handmaiden of the late Matilde Neruda; and Federico Fox, a corpulent cousin of Judit Torre's and the only significant character who actively works with the ruling Pinochet regime instead of hating and resisting it.

Pinochet (who is never mentioned in the novel's text) came to power in 1973, in a bloody coup that ousted and killed President Salvador Allende, so by 1985 the dissidents have had time to go into exile and return, to be imprisoned and released, to grow middleaged in their youthful fury and frustration, to lose faith and make ironical accommodations and die of natural causes. Lopito says, "All of us have retired from the political scene, even though we keep telling ourselves that the people united will never be defeated when for more than ten years they've had us more defeated than I can imagine, Mañungo. This is total defeat. . . . A bomb here, another there, but they don't do anything, like swearing by nonviolent protest or violent protest, or the opposition, or the people united, et cetera. They broke our backs, Mañungo."

Pablo Neruda, the triumphant embodiment of Chilean culture and leftwing conscience, "returned to Chile to die of sadness." Now his widow, Matilde, whom he had nicknamed "La Chascona, the wild woman . . . because of her tangled mop of hair"—Matilde, who had been "a young, desirable woman of the people, as juicy as a ripe apricot," who "took long, wine-soaked siestas with the poet"—has died in a Houston hospital, after receiving last rites and confiding to Ada Luz that she wants a Mass said at her funeral. The suppression of this request—by Lisboa, because the presence of a revolutionary priest at the graveside would detract from Communist domination of the ceremony—is the main political thread wound around the funeral. The main cultural thread is Federico Fox's acquisition of control over Neruda's valuable papers and letters, in exchange for his removal of bureaucratic roadblocks in the way of establishing a Pablo Neruda Foundation. The main romantic thread is the coming together again of Judit Torre and Mañungo Vera, who had first romanced in their student days. The principal moral event, I suppose, is Mañungo's decision to stay in Chile, with his seven-year-old French-speaking son, after his round-the-clock experience of life under the regime. In his youth, Mañungo was a rock star, a "guerrilla singer . . . possessed by the potency of his guitar-phallus-machine gun;" his career, pursued since the coup in America and Europe, has been lately bothered by a "softening of his politics" and a chronic tinnitus in his left ear, a subjective sensation of noise that he identifies as "the voice of the old woman"—a certain wheezing sound made by the sea on the coast of Chiloé, his native island—calling him home.

Among these many—too many—threads, the most interesting psychological one traces Judit Torre's peculiar form of political and erotic deadness, induced by a traumatic episode when she was being held for questioning with some other members of her shadowy little group of anti-regime women. Tied and hooded and naked, she hears in her cell the other women being tortured and raped; but *her* torturer merely tells her in his nasal voice, while he puts his warm moist hand on her knee, to shout as if she were being raped. She remembers:

> I waited for his hand to touch me again, my skin waited to be caressed by that viscous, tepid hand that never went further although the nasal voice whispered, Shout more, as if you were enjoying yourself, as if you wanted more, as if I were hurting you but you wanted more, and I shout my lungs out howling like a bitch because I'm reaching a shameful pleasure I'd never felt before, not even with Ramón [her lover, a slain resistance leader]. Shout, shout, he repeated, and I call for help because his whisper threatens me if I don't shout, and I shout with terror at myself, because in this totally unerotic situation I shout my shame at my pleasure while in the other cells my friends are howling like me, but because of tortures different from the torture of being exempted from torture. . . . I didn't shout because of the tragedy of the other women, I didn't take part in the feast of that majestic collective form, from which the soft hand excluded me in order to satisfy God knows what fantasies, this impotent monster who demanded I shout with greater and greater conviction without knowing that my shouts of terror and pleasure were real.

This moment of feigned torture evidently constitutes Judit's supreme orgasm and forms the novel's most intimate and meaningful vision of the relation between the regime and its enemies. It also warrants revenge. Judit is given a pistol by her women's group and goes forth in the night to find and slay the impotent torturer whose "complex humanity" robbed her of solidarity and unqualified revolutionary purpose: "Sensitive, the bastard with the nasal voice. His sensitivity tore away my right to hatred and revenge." This loss is cause, in the murky atmosphere of contemporary Chile, for murder.

Curfew packs a baggage of Dostoyevskian ambition which its action and conversations do not quite carry. Judit seems not so much tormented as whimsical, in the way of wellborn beauties. The novel in Spanish was titled *La Desesperanza* (*Despair*), but the English title refers to a section of the narrative which shows Judit and Mañungo wandering the "green ghetto" of an upper-class Santiago neighborhood during the five hours of curfew, from midnight to five. The curfew, to judge from the number of people they encounter and noisy incidents that take place, isn't very effectively enforced. With her feminist pistol Judit shoots not her impotent torturer/ savior but a skylight and a little white bitch in heat who has attracted a disgusting crowd of nocturnal dogs. This eerie section, called "Night," in which the hiding, sometimes sleeping couple haunt the empty streets and merge with the vegetation, is the one effortlessly magical passage of the novel. The hard-breathing prose evokes a dreamlike atmosphere: "On the sidewalk, in their pale clothes, their arms around each other, hidden by plants that were so strong they looked carnivorous, Judit and Mañungo resembled inhabitants of a strange universe which barely needed the flow of love and sleep." Latin-American writers have a way of seeing their major cities as desolate and powerful, as wastelands of a natural grandeur—one thinks especially of Borges' Buenos Aires but also of Vargas Llosa's Lima, Cabrera Infante's pre-Castro Havana, and the Buenos Aires meticulously traversed in Humberto Costantini's "The Long Night of Francisco Sanctis." Donoso here does something like that for Santiago.

Elsewhere, however, his will to significance generates too much sticky, tangled prose. "The only sure way to eliminate his demons was to eliminate himself, to drown in the slow green waters of the Cipresales River that mirrored the vertigo of the air tangled with the vines of madness; waters in which the tops of the oaks and elms sank, and out of whose lazy current emerged trunks of tortured pewter, bearded with moss and covered with a cancer of lichens and fungus." Just across the gutter of the book, a shorter sentence also numbs the mind: "Five years ago, Bellavista seemed immersed in the anachronistic anorexia of oblivion." The translator, perhaps, should share the blame for such heavy-handed conjurations as "Sartre, with whose words he had fertilized the Chiloó dirt from which he'd sprung" and "She gave him only the scrap of her body, which she did not succeed in relating to herself, leaving Mañungo outside the tangle of her feminine failure." Donoso's touch has lost lightness and impudent ease since *The Obscene Bird of Night,* written during the democratic rule of Eduardo Frei and published in 1970, the year Allende took power. In *Curfew*, the dominant metaphor—a mythical "'ship of art,' the *Caleuche,* which was manned by a crew of wizards"—fails to float. The symbols in the background of the book—Carlitos, the toothless lion in the Santiago zoo; Schumann and his attempted suicide in the Rhine; the floods and fogs and witchcraft of Chiloó—have more life than the foreground. The links between history and the novel's character disorders seem forced: "Nadja [Mañungo's former lover]'s coldness was gratuitous, an aesthetic, an experiment with her own limits and the limits of others, while in Judit it was a vertiginous destiny that someone else, or perhaps history, had established." Woolf-like Judit and Mañungo with his "rabbitlike smile" are rather pale and wispy posters to be blazoned with such portentous words as "the incarnation of the despair the current state of affairs was pushing them to" and "lives with no meaning more complex than the simplifications wrought by obses-

sion." Most unfortunately, the novel's climax of political violence befalls a character, Lopito, so repulsive, verbose, adhesive, and tiresomely self-destructive that the reader is sneakily grateful when the police do him in. The surge of indignation and sympathy that the text indicates should greet his demise does not come. Lopito makes a poor martyr.

Jacobo Timerman wrote in these pages seven months ago, in whole-hearted praise of *Curfew*, that in it Donoso "reveals that even those who fight against the dictatorship may be cowards and antiheroes. Most important of all, he shows that not everything in Chile is clear—there is also confusion and despair. . . . No individual act of political protest is more telling than the sad lives that Chileans are forced to lead." Perhaps in Spanish the novel is more persuasive, less wordy and diffuse and slack, than in English; but in any translation the unhappy revolutionaries must quarrel and drink and seethe and drone in a political vacuum. Donoso, who returned to Chile in 1981 after an absence of eighteen years, generously credits the personnel of the regime with "human complexity," and perceives that the anti-regime forces can sink into "a hatred of all for all." In his exposition, however, the regime has little face and less philosophy, and those who oppose it have no dream or memory of good government. How things came to this claustrophobic pass is not explained, nor is a way out indicated. What human virtue we see resides in the oldest characters, the two venerable writers, Fausta and Don Celedonio, survivors from a more gracious time; in the last chapter, they are taking care of the novel's children, since nobody else will.

Selden Rodman (essay date 23 January 1989)

SOURCE: "Tale of a Politicized Bard," in *The New Leader,* Vol. LXXII, No. 2, January 23, 1989, pp. 21-2.

[*In the following review, Rodman discusses the plot of* Curfew. *Faulting it for not adequately fleshing out the two main characters, Rodman feels the novel does succeed in the end because of the change produced in the protagonists.*]

Pablo Neruda, the great poet, divided his time while in his native Chile between two houses he owned. In the one at Isla Negra, south of Valparaiso on the Pacific Ocean, he kept his collection of monumental mermaids, angels and ships' figureheads, wrote most of his poems, and entertained those of his friends who could appreciate his art. In the one in Santiago, high on the outcropping called San Cristóbal, near the zoo, he and his lovely wife Matilde held more formal functions and (presumably) conferred with officials of the Communist Party, to which Neruda belonged for 40 years.

I met the poet and his wife in the San Cristóbal house in 1967, and I spent several delightful weeks with them during the two following years at Isla Negra. Our friendship foundered following a violent argument about the Soviet invasion of Czechoslovakia and the party-line politics of his friend Salvador Allende, who had begun to campaign for the presidency. Coincidentally, Neruda died of cancer in San Cristóbal on the very day in 1973 that Allende was overthrown by the Chilean military—who are still in power under General Augusto Pinochet's dictatorship.

José Donoso's novel opens in January 1985 with a conclave in the San Cristóbal house where Matilde, who has just died, lies in state; and it concludes the next day with every faction from Right to Left at the funeral trying to capitalize politically on the event. The time and place are well chosen. Chilean democratic liberalism has always been a house divided. Allende, whatever his good intentions, was overthrown because the 400-600 per cent inflation that threatened to wipe out the most prosperous middle class in Latin America was followed by a last desperate attempt to give free rein to the extreme Movement of the Revolutionary Left (MRI), engaged in seizing unconstitutionally the rich individual farms of the south. Up to that point the military had stood by.

Neruda's double identity symbolized, and still symbolizes, liberalism's split. Was he the great bard of national unity and all-encompassing love? Assuredly he was. But he was also the party loyalist who, as Chilean Consul in Mexico in 1938, gave the Communist painter David Alfaro Siqueiros, the leader of the armed attack on Leon Trotsky, a passport and a commission to paint murals in Chile until he could safely return to Mexico. And what about those fulsome odes to Stalin? And what about the millionaire poet's role in his friend Allende's rise to power and ultimate attempt to subvert democracy in Chile?

All of these contradictions are alluded to, although not too explicitly, in the politicking that surrounds Matilde's obsequies. Donoso, who had lived abroad and achieved fame both as a novelist and as an anti-Pinochet activist, finally came home and was permitted to publish *Curfew* in Santiago. It was a courageous act. He does not pull his punches. About one character, eligible for a national prize, he writes: "The regime, of course, had refused to hear of it, since she was a Communist—something she never was—or because she was a dissident, which for the government was the same thing as being a Communist."

The principal characters are Judit, who has rebelled against her aristocratic family almost from birth, and has witnessed the torture of her fellow militants in jail; and Mañungo Vera, born on the primitive island of Chiloé but an internationally famous pop singer just returned to Chile to expiate his guilt for making a fortune out of his "revolutionary" songs. Mañungo seems an obvious stand-in for the author, though

he may also be modeled after Victor Jara, a pro-Allende songwriter killed within days of Pinochet's coup.

Mañungo's son, Juan Pablo (named after Sartre, not Neruda), has never recovered from the Paris experience. His mother "made him choose so many times that the poor kid viewed any situation that presented more than one option with horror-stricken eyes." Here in Chile, how could Mañungo "demand that the boy be decisive, when even he isn't sure where his acoustic nightmares could take him?" Where did Mañungo belong? In Paris' rue Monsieur le Prince? Among the fishermen and weavers of Chiloé? Or here with the would-be revolutionaries?

Judit's neurotic behavior perfectly complements Ma ungo's. He first embraces her after watching her fearlessly fondle and even provoke a sex-maddened Doberman watchdog: "Mañungo felt that Judit took danger as the raw material for play." They toy with the idea of escaping to Chiloé or to Paris, rather than yielding to the romanticism of the famous song Ma ungo had been goaded into singing in Neruda's house:

> I shall walk the streets again
> Of a Santiago bathed in blood
> And in a beautiful plaza now free
> I shall stop to weep for the dead.

What finally eases the two into an opposite decision, to face the (ambiguous) music, is a ludicrous yet tragic encounter at a local police station. The hopeless alcoholic, Lopito, is being beaten with sticks in the courtyard because he refuses to stop insulting the police, who had arrested him to begin with for provoking them in the streets. Even when Judit first encountered Lopito years before, as an informer for the MRI who gave her access to the revolutionary Left, he was a repulsive creature. He begged her to let him see her naked so that he could masturbate dreaming of her. Judit yielded to him then, out of pity, and four months later the MRI had expelled Lopito for stealing money from a student union. Still, now Judit pities the drunken Lopito again when she sees him being carried inside to die after suffering a heart attack in the courtyard.

Judit and Mañungo accuse the police of one more brutal murder. They are allowed to go only because the police feel threatened by the enormous publicity that would result from holding the famous pop singer under arrest. ("Did everything have to be used, then? Wasn't even a drop of pain allowed to go to waste?") In a closing scene Mañungo lifts Lopito's daughter to his shoulders, his face transformed by his decision to stay in Chile. Mañungo and Judit will go underground to pursue the revolution together.

All of this would be a little more credible if the author had taken the time to tell us more about the early lives of Judit and Mañungo. Why was Judit's family so repulsive? What caused her to rebel and become a loner? Did Mañungo fail to take Judit to Chiloé in the beginning because he had to do more than seek redemption in the primitive existence there that apparently meant so much to him? Did both of them have the need to expiate their guilt violently? Was Matilde Neruda's deathbed request for a priest ignored because politics in Chile rules everything?

José Donoso's novel, despite these loose ends that are never pursued, succeeds because his two principal characters do change. To see them gain a sense of purpose in the final chapters is a moving experience. Neither of them is likable, but they do become believable. Chile's future, if it has a future as a pluralistic society, is in their hands. And the author's.

George Roth (review date 10 September 1989)

SOURCE: "The Burden of Chile's Night," in *Los Angeles Times Book Review,* September 10, 1989, p. 15.

[*In the following review of* Curfew, *Roth reminisces about his years as a student and friend to Donoso. The critic also focuses much of the review on the political climate in Chile, General Pinochet, and the poet Pablo Neruda.*]

I had not seen José Donoso for 30 years. Then, late last year, I visited him at U.C. Davis as he finished leading a three-month graduate seminar on himself and his work and prepared to return to Santiago. I remembered my high school teacher, a man in his early 30s, wearing alien Ivy League suits from Princeton, rocking from foot to foot as he yelped at the class to shut up and pay attention. I found one of *El Boom's* grand old men (aren't they all GOM's by now?), complete with white beard and hair curling over his collar.

The 30 years have yielded Donoso a harvest including Spain's gloriously bejeweled Order of Alfonso X the Wise, four New Yorker magazine pages of John Updike's faint praise, more than 500 theses, and a catalogue listing 800 separate writings about him and his opus, and status as a "banner" to Pinochet's opposition.

Because the Pinochet government doesn't allow me to visit Chile, my awareness of Donoso's fame there was incomplete. He was frozen in my mind as the dear teacher who persisted in opening a window out of Santiago's provincial smother; who kept alive hope that there really was a world "out there" where people discoursed coolly, meaningfully-and with precision, about literature, philosophy, justice and taste.

To my classmates and myself, Donoso was unquestionably a writer. We granted him that status long before concrete evidence emerged as a slim paperbound volume of *cuentos* (stories) which, like his first novel, **Coronación,** a few years later, the faithful peddled to friends, relatives, and anyone who came up with the equivalent of a couple weeks allowance. I seem to remember selling 18 copies. Maybe 50.

Donoso said he had rehearsed the writer's role since he was 12: lectures, literary prize acceptances, awards, lionizing . . . the whole thing. As a teacher, he would warn his students not to confuse life and literature. For at least one of them this truth remained hidden until the rebirth that middle age is for the lucky. I wonder still how "Pepe" Donoso, then a mere boy of 30-odd, acquired that wisdom.

El peso de la noche, "the burden of night" was another of Pepe's gifts. He attributed the phrase to Diego Portales, a dictator assassinated after he cudgeled Chile out of anarchy in the 1830s. Portales, a merchant, wrote in his letters, Donoso told us, that he created order solely to pursue his passions for women and money more smoothly. Exasperation must have driven him to coin *el peso de la noche:* exasperation at his naturally gifted countrymen, suffocating in their miasmas.

There are countries and regions that are overlush or too harsh. (*La banana es el peor enemigo de la civilización:* "Bananas are civilization's worst enemy," my junior high school teacher, Maria Marchant, a militant Communist, used to say, explaining why Central America is more at U.S. mercy than the rest of Spanish America). Much of Chile is just challenging enough. The young Donoso once complained that the land is inhospitable, at least compared to the friendly green pastures of New Jersey. Nowhere in Chile can one live off the (uncultivated) land, except perhaps spiritually. Much of it is heartbreakingly beautiful, a land that won't harm you but won't feed you. The web of Chilean society, on the other hand, pervades everything and lies over everything, and never stops demanding.

Donoso's latest novel, **La Desesperanza,** (**Curfew**) is really about *el peso de la noche,* the burden of night under the Pinochet regime. Characters act out fear, greed, the search for love, with the dictatorship casting a straining, nightmare glow, as in an Edward Hopper painting. The scenes are uniquely and thoroughly Chilean, developing naturally from a curiously immobile social order that only lets you go in one direction: away. And even that takes some effort.

Donoso (an oligarch born and bred) left and stayed away—mostly in Spain—for 20 years. He went home because Chile is a highly rewarding habitat for literary lions, particularly of the home-grown variety. One of the more literate peoples in the world, Chileans uncritically revere internationally known (home-grown alone don't qualify) writers and poets, no matter where they are from. Arnold Toynbee, the historian, remarked to Donoso at Princeton that Chile had to be a fascinating country: It was the only one where Thomas Mann's "Magic Mountain" was a best seller.

Where successful intellectuals are concerned, Chileans trade their whiplash wit for craven awe. Donoso said he went home from Spain because he wanted recognition, to "be what one is." In Santiago, he is recognized on the street as the reigning king of the literary jungle who is a member of the oligarchy. He is also, as his wife proudly declared, a "banner," a rallying point, for Pinochet's opponents. And he is also the survivor of the trio (with Nobel Prize-winning poets Pablo Neruda, 1971, and Gabriela Mistral, 1945) of Chile's unofficial equivalents of Japan's National Treasures.

Although Chileans love jokes—the more irreverent and dirtier the better—and tell them constantly, not once in 20 years did I hear a joke about Mistral or Neruda (or Donoso, for that matter). Neruda's absence from the pillory is specially surprising because he was, from all accounts, a pompous, self-indulgent ass who allowed himself, while flaunting his lifelong Communist Party membership, to be kept in a luxurious Paris mansion as ambassador to France.

Poverty is the norm in Chile and always has been, no matter what the government; working people live on hunger's edge. Still, the wolfish humor of the poor and the constantly dispossessed middle class tenderly avoids literary idols. The savage wit is the bastard twin of an almost religious reverence of education which, in turn, is bonded to Chile's national self-esteem. This secular religion of education produced what used to be and maybe still is one of the best elementary-through-university education systems in the world.

Like other peoples, Chileans use literacy (statistically at the level of the more developed European countries and much higher than the United States) and an avid interest in the outside world to help cope with a reality often too painful or dreary to take straight. That reality stems primarily from being semi-willing prisoners of a minority that has ruled for 200 years by, first, owning the land and monopolizing politics, then by extruding itself into a class system that taints every relation and weights lives with the leaden pervasiveness of nightmare: This is the burden of night . . . *el peso de la noche.*

Pinochet has named an office building for Portales: Both forcibly brought an arguable order from inarguable chaos. But Portales merely wanted the country to go about business; Pinochet attempts to restore intact the feudal social order. And, somewhere deep in the Chilean psyche there's a thin but unfailing source of nourishment for such an enterprise.

Perhaps that same source animates whatever it is that prevents a mass uprising against military rule. In one Machia-

vellian scenario, the dictatorship's strategists plumb their imaginations for ways to let imagination make cowards of their countrymen: They let *la copucha* (Chilean bush radio) spread the stories of live rats pushed bodily up vaginas, besides better-known and more subtle tortures. Under the burden of night, terror doubles its effectiveness and keeps resistance to the level of gesture, and in the cities. The strength of **Curfew** is in illustrating how terror and the temptation of survival undermine the will to resist. Judit, **Curfew**'s antiheroine, is unable to shoot the man who had her friends raped by dogs in the dungeons of the secret police. She feels she is an accomplice: The man made her scream as if raped while he sat sweating at her side.

Another **Curfew** character is Lopito, a former hanger-on at the university. Ugly and poor but tolerated—even to the point of having once slept with Judit, who recollects only his stench and her pity—Lopito is almost literally taunted to death by police who make him pull a turf-roller until his heart bursts. He doesn't even get the dignity and drama of a death by legitimate torture. Lopito (like everyone else in the novel except some background figures) fights Pinochet only with thoughts and words. And as a *roto,* a low-class person, Lopito gets no comfort from the secular religion that the class system is. Only in death does he set down the burden of night.

Malcolm Coad (review date 19 October 1990)

SOURCE: "Chile's Hour of Despair," in *New Statesman & Society,* Vol. 3, No. 123, October 19, 1990, p. 34.

[*In the following review, Coad asserts the political setting of* Curfew *is a departure from the imaginary worlds typically used in Donoso's novels. Coad praises certain elements of the novel, such as the descriptions of landscapes, and faults other parts such as the psychological portraits of the main characters.*]

In one sense, this is an unexpected novel from José Donoso. Normally, Donoso—justly billed on the dust-jacket as "Chile's greatest living writer"—steers well clear of allusion to actual events, preferring entirely imaginary settings for his enigmatic fables of the psychosocial pathology of the Chilean bourgeoisie. While a firm opponent of General Pinochet's recently ended dictatorship, he has always stoutly declared himself a "non-political" writer.

This time, however, not only does Donoso opt for something like realism, but he sets the novel directly amid one of the most immediate and poignant events lived by Chile's artistic community in the latter years of Pinochet's rule: the death and funeral in January 1985 of Matilde Urrutia, widow of the great Nobel prize-winning poet, Pablo Neruda.

Urrutia's death came at a particularly low moment for the Chilean opposition, just as the first serious anti-government protest movement since the 1973 coup was fading without direction. Neruda himself, the over-arching symbol of the country's democratic culture, had died shortly after the coup, seen off by a funeral which was the first open demonstration against the military. The death of his widow was therefore both a new symbol of a truncated past and the opportunity for a similar demonstration.

The novel spans 24 hours before and after the funeral. It spares few feelings. Leaders of Neruda's own political party, the communists, plot to wrest control of the funeral from Matilde's friends and ensure that her last wish to have a priest, albeit left-wing, say a mass is suppressed. Neruda's friends and literary colleagues bribe a pro-government collector with part of the poet's private papers (some supposed letters from Trotsky) to unblock permission to set up a Pablo Neruda Foundation.

But such glimpses of petty intrigue are not Donoso's main concern. This centres on the more existential conflicts of three central characters, all of whom represent the ambiguous nature of responsibility in dramatic events like those lived in Chile before and after the collapse of Salvador Allende's socialist experiment.

Mañungo Vera is an internationally famous singer returning to Chile to rediscover his roots after a sham career pandering to Europe's taste for Latin American revolutionary culture. At Neruda and Matilde's house, he meets a former girlfriend, Judit Torre—an upper-class revolutionary considered a heroine by many, but who never suffered the torture she is believed to have gone through while under arrest.

The third character is Lopito, a decaying poet whose revolutionary commitment has given way to a state between despair and nihilism.

Much of this threesome's journey from self-disgust—"the despair" which is the literal translation of the novel's Spanish title, **La Desesperanza**—to the beginning of a kind of authenticity, at least in the cases of Mañungo and Judit, is telling and true. Many Chileans in the darkest days did feel that their country "seemed on the point of foundering, sinking and disappearing with all of them aboard". The failure of intensely lived utopias, the sterility of exile and its encouragement of false but comforting images of home—such experiences have fractured the lives of countless Chilean leftists since 1973. Donoso has a clear eye for the myths that Chileans use to sustain the triumphalism about themselves which all too readily would re-emerge under Pinochet whenever he showed signs of weakness.

At the same time, Donoso's own fascination with the landscape and legends of his country is finely used in the novel, especially as the memory of the foggy mystery of the myth-bound southern archipelago of Chiloé, Mañungo's home, reflects his psychological state.

In the end, however, the novel falls too far towards an opposite, but equally Chilean, characteristic: a kind of paralysing psychologistic self-doubt. The constant analyses of characters almost before they have time to think are external and wearing. All action tends to be reduced to pathology—to the distinctly tacky extent of making Judit's motive for revenge against her torturer that she enjoyed his sexual abuse of her and wanted more to make her equal with her fellow prisoners.

Increasingly, the well-heeled Santiago suburbs where the novel is set begin to feel like one of Donoso's imaginary locations. There are, for example, groups in Chile who use bombs; but they cannot be reduced to these shadowy networks of lumpen and physically disabled nihilists from the surrounding slums. At this point, the bourgeois fear and loathing which Donoso understands so well appears to have seeped debilitatingly into his own perceptions.

Patrick Parrinder (review date 6 December 1990)

SOURCE: "Superhistory," in *London Review of Books,* Vol. 12, No. 23, December 6, 1990, pp. 24-6.

[*In the following review, Parrinder lauds Donoso's* Curfew, *saying the art is "richly crafted" and that the novel "remains an enchanted space," despite faulting the book for its reliance on history, and for problems in the translation.*]

All novels are historical novels, as my late teacher Graham Hough used to say; but some are more historical than others. Novelists can improve on history, and if they are Science Fiction writers they can anticipate it. History can be invented, but most novelists only do so within strict limits. According to Hough, they would tend to invent a Prime Minister but not a major political party, a provincial town but not a capital city. A writer like Joyce can put together an immensely painstaking reconstruction of the past without linking it in any way to a historical narrative, while other novelists treat strictly contemporary events as history-in-the-making, much as journalists do. Rather like Joyce in *Ulysses,* José Donoso in *Curfew* tracks his protagonist's adventures during a 24-hour period in the life of a modern city, but there the resemblances stop.

Recognised as the leading Chilean novelist, Donoso seems to have drawn heavily on his own experience of returning from political exile in the writing of *Curfew*. The novel describes events in Santiago in 1985, the year in which it was composed (it was first published in Spanish in 1986). Mañungo Vera, a famous revolutionary singer, has been absent from Chile for 13 years, having left the country in 1972 to appear at a peace concert in San Francisco with Joan Baez. Mañungo must be seen as a more fortunate version of Victor Jara, the singer murdered in the aftermath of the military coup which overthrew the Allende regime. Donoso's protagonist is a former teenage idol who has given up his repertoire of guerrilla and protest songs, and has lost his youthful certainties. He has settled in Paris, he has a wife and a son, and his politics have gone soft.

Mañungo's return to Santiago coincides with the death and funeral of Matilde Neruda, widow of the great poet who was Chile's only other modern cultural superstar. For an outsider it is impossible to say how far *Curfew*'s vivid portrayal of Pablo Neruda's surviving friends and the members of his entourage constitutes a *roman à clef*. Many of Donoso's characters expect to draw either personal gain or political advantage as a result of their association with the dead poet. Don Celedonio and the poetess Fausta dream of setting up a Neruda Foundation to serve as a beacon for subsequent generations, while the various political factions are more concerned with orchestrating the massive funeral procession, which may or may not help to undermine the military dictatorship. Most of these characters have a strong sense of the potential historical significance of their actions, but Donoso gently deflates their pretensions. Whatever their real-life originals, most of these squabbling, down-at-heel literati would be comfortably at home in the pages of Olivia Manning.

To the extent that it offers a kind of instant history, *Curfew* must already be a period piece. The nightly curfew, with its silence broken by the wailing of sirens and the droning of police helicopters, was lifted before the end of the Pinochet years. Donoso's tense and intricate plot turns on routine incidents of torture and police brutality which one must hope are now a thing of the past. If Chile is indeed entering a new period of stable democracy, Donoso's registration of the cowed and vengeful atmosphere of Santiago in the mid-Eighties may itself become a historical resource, once individual memories have faded.

Vengeance is represented here by Judit Torre, a mysterious beauty known as the 'Chilean Virginia Woolf', who is the leader of a group of female terrorists bent on killing a member of the security police. Mañungo falls under Judit's spell and finds himself, within hours of his return, joining the scavengers and thugs lurking in the streets of a wealthy residential district of the city after midnight, at the risk of being shot on sight if he is spotted by the police. Judit, who has been tipped off to watch out for a blue Mercedes, decides that Mañungo will make a useful decoy. The Mercedes turns out to contain a pleasure-seeking couple of off-duty officers,

one of whom may have sexually humiliated Judit and tortured her fellow detainees several years before. Mañungo is recognised, and is invited indoors for a drink in exchange for a private command performance; and Judit, still unsure that she has correctly identified her victim, tremblingly reaches for her gun.

Though Judit's mixture of violence, sexual readiness and high-cultural frigidity owes rather a lot to male fantasy, the night of the curfew combines elements of the political thriller with a degree of witchcraft and a farcical unmasking of daytime identities. It is a rite of passage through which Mañungo has to pass if his return from exile is to lead to a possibility of personal and artistic renewal. Sometime after dawn he finds a temporary resting-place in Judit's apartment, but on the morning of the great funeral they are both caught up in the machinations and petty intrigues of Neruda's circle. During his lifetime the poet trod a dangerous path between art and Communism, between connoisseurship and ideology, and one of his legacies is a rich collection of books, paintings and manuscripts which both Right and Left would like to get their hands on. Are the letters that Trotsky sent him in the late Thirties as valuable as is rumoured, and could these and other documents play their part in a final discrediting of the Communist cause, and of Neruda with it? Was he, indeed, implicated in Trotsky's murder? Mañungo tries to preserve his independence from party-political commitment while these and other questions are being debated, but finally, thanks to Judit and to the raffish poet Lopito with whom he renews his acquaintance, he finds himself inescapably, passionately involved. A 'wicked wizard' has transformed him into someone who can no longer stand aloof from the Chilean experience.

Mañungo grew up on the fogbound island of Chiloe, a last outpost on the way to the glaciers in the remote south of the country. The islanders are fervent believers in witchcraft, and Mañungo, by becoming a famous musician, has pursued their legend of the *Caleuche* or 'ship of art', with its crew of wizards bound for a distant paradise beyond the ice-bound horizon. Only one chapter of *Curfew* is set among the witches of Chiloe, and Donoso manages to employ the notion of metamorphosis or magical transformation while sedulously avoiding the style of unrestrained 'magic realism' that we have come to expect of Latin American novels. 'It was so easy to imitate Garcia Marquez, and everyone was doing it,' the narrator remarks of the mourners gathered at the Nerudas' house: but the scene from which this comment is taken is less reminiscent of Marquez than of Balzac and Galsworthy. Just as Chile is still perhaps the least American of Latin American countries, so Donoso's art is richly crafted and somewhat old-fashioned, like a racy European *grande dame* from a previous era.

The notions of the 'ship of art' and of the curfew as a theatre or zone of transformations may not impede Donoso's fictional realism, but they do mark the difference between the novel and journalism or documentary writing. Equally important, in a fiction which often stresses the Lilliputian scale of Chilean culture, is Donoso's use of the figure of the historical microcosm. In a moving final scene, he takes us with Judit's, Lopito's and Mañungo's children to visit the 'toy country' of Chile in Miniature, a tourist attraction in a Santiago park which transforms Pinochet's country into a natural paradise of mountains, beaches, forests and deserts. The architects of Chile in Miniature, Donoso explains, had to leave out the poor and monotonous and uninteresting areas of the country, since there was not enough room: 'not everything can fit into a miniature, and unpleasant things should be left out.' Donoso, who is adequately though far from faultlessly served by his translator, has put back fear and corruption and many unpleasant things, but his novel remains an enchanted space.

Michael Wood (essay date 4 January 1991)

SOURCE: "Purity at a Price," in *The Times Literary Supplement,* No. 4579, January 4, 1991, p. 16.

[*In the following review, Wood faults* Curfew *for being "a discursive and rather windy novel," but credits it for providing an in-depth look at the political history of Chile.*]

There is a moment which occurs again and again in José Donoso's novels, an instant of malign or obscure carnival, a scene of ruin or disguise. We can think of magical realism in this context, but only if we darken the notion, let go of its implications of whimsy and liberation. The real turns to phantasmagoria without ceasing to be real. We step suddenly into waking, historical nightmare, unfamiliar to us only because it is so close and so insistently denied.

In *Curfew,* for example, we are in a street in Santiago de Chile, high fences protecting large houses and gardens. A boy opens a gate as we follow him through:

> There was no house: an empty lot with the remains of a pool from which the tiles had been ripped, the ruins of a grape arbor, a terrace and a balustrade, the outline of a foundation and holes from the old basements, invaded now by the shoots of sycamore trees, young agaves, and scrub oak. . . .

The trees in the garden seem to move, but there is no magic here, only small-time criminals and conspirators hiding during curfew. The house has been demolished but not replaced, witness to an interrupted speculation. The empty pool is a relic of luxury but also hints at a social order which has been not so much overturned as abandoned. The trees themselves have changed their allegiance, joined the outlaws.

Curfew is a discursive and rather windy novel, not nearly as powerful or haunting as Donoso's wonderful *Obscene Bird of Night* and *House in the Country.* It does, however, embody his major themes—class, authority, rebellion, monstrosity—and it does take us into intimate reaches of recent Chilean history, the alluring shallows rather than the depths of terror and repression. The chief narrative occasion of the book is the wake and funeral of Matilde Neruda, the great poet's widow, in 1985. Warring factions want to take over this event as propaganda, and we follow their murky conversations and evasions, elaborated by Donoso with lugubrious affection. The minor poet, friend of the great; the literary *grande dame;* the Communist operator; the noisy literary layabout; the timid lady companion; the repulsive banker; boastful policemen; various children—all are observed making their way through the evening and the night before, and the day of the ceremonies. The central figures are Judit Torre, a woman repeatedly said to look like Virginia Woolf, but a Woolf turned into an angular 1960s saint in jeans and black shirt, and Mañungo Vera, a famous protest singer who on this very day has returned to Chile from thirteen years of exile. Judit is seeking to bury her upper-class guilt in revolutionary politics, Mañungo is trying to rediscover his music and himself. The two spend the night cheating the curfew, talking, remembering. They fall in love by agreeing not to fall in love; attend Matilde's funeral; wait helplessly while the police harry a drunken friend to death from a heart attack; and decide not to leave together for Paris.

The Spanish title of the novel, *La Desesperanza* (*Despair*), reflects the unbearable moral and political alternatives of the time of its first publication, 1986. Exiles from Pinochet's Chile were out of touch with their country and preserved their purity at that price; those who stayed at home were softened or embittered by the years of impotence. "Despair has no music", Mañungo thinks; and later he comes to feel that private life has died in Chile. Everything is politics, Judit argues, "we repress all other themes, blocking out the horizon with our political obsessions". Another character claims that his countrymen need to learn to live without hope, that a deep *desesperanza* is the only way to start again, to avoid the futility and violence of actions based on a tiny optimism. This is a darker thought than the present, improved situation calls for, but a good indication of the way thought went in the dark times.

"My road had to be rougher, and I had to wander on it forever"; "he knew this rebellious, taciturn traitor hated him, but he also knew she possessed a power over him, a power incarnated in her excessive beauty": even in elegant Spanish, these sentences sound soupy and verbose—a sign, I think, that Donoso has not imagined his characters quite thoroughly enough. They talk like sketches for a novel, refractions of an essay. But the sketches and the essay are those of a major writer.

Fernando Alegria (essay date Summer 1992)

SOURCE: "Goodbye to Metaphor: *Curfew*," in *Review of Contemporary Fiction,* Vol. XII, No. 2, Summer, 1992, pp. 77-9.

[*In the following essay, Alegria asserts that* Curfew *serves as Donoso's clear statement about Pinochet's military dictatorship in Chile. Discussing the controversial images and stark description in the novel, Alegria praises the novel's ambitiousness and its explanation of Chilean history.*]

For years José Donoso has beaten the path of metaphor to express his way of feeling and understanding Chile, a path both difficult and dangerous. In a bold effort he produced a beautiful and well-structured synthesis of nostalgia, emotions, and sorrows. It was called *A House in the Country.* It deeply impressed readers in Spain and Latin America, but Chileans did not seem moved. They were dazzled and amused by the novel; yet they couldn't get over a feeling of playfulness, of clues to be deciphered, and failed to grasp the profound tension that surely seized the author when he opened and closed the doors to his risky maze.

Today Donoso lays cards on the table that the reader will have to stack up again but that in the process will open wounds and leave scars, for *Curfew* is a detailed account of a love affair with Chile that Donoso held in reserve up to now. But the matter is no longer the loose threads that lead to the ruin of aristocratic families confronted by the onrush of lower-class daring. The uneasiness is of a different kind. The sadness that reverberates like an echo in Donoso's stories here begins to be recognized not in the issue of origins and traditions but in wrongs committed, lack of will, and recent failures in today's Chile.

For those who wonder if Donoso finally makes a pronouncement in this novel on the bleak record of Pinochet's military dictatorship, the answer is loud and clear: not only does he take a stand but states it in the harshest terms. Such a change, which might surprise some of his readers, was to be expected. The general's image—coarse, stubborn, cranky—is crumbling today, at century's end, eaten away from within. The country of *Curfew* is the survivor of a bloody and brutal nightmare in which everything is possible—torture, disappearance, treason, murder—under the drab cloak of a clever and monstrous lie. Perhaps the important thing is not so much to remember the facts (the media repeats them constantly) but to examine objectively what those crimes have done to the character of the Chilean people as they deal with the crisis.

It is in this connection that Donoso abandons his typical metaphoric strategy and confronts the collapse of Chilean society in images and portraits bound to cause a stir—and resentment?—among his compatriots. Let me make clear that I'm not referring to literary clues of the kind proffered by the book's jacket to serve as bait for the reader's curiosity. Donoso is too experienced and skillful to fall into that trap. His portraits are like Picasso's: multiple planes and angles, a nose where one expects an eye, a grill in place of a head of hair, a profile that is not a profile but the smudge of a face, and a resemblance dissolved along collective lines.

Who are the characters, the singer Mañungo Vera, the collector Freddy Fox, the minor poet Don Celedonio, the tragic Judit, the legendary Fausta? Those familiar with Santiago's social and literary menagerie will have a field day identifying them—a somewhat useless pastime. To my mind, it is not the *who* that matters but the *what* they represent. Mañungo, for instance, is the artist who lost the motivation and inspiration for rebellion in his years of exile. So much time passed! So many guitars wielded like machine-guns! People got tired, but the charismatic performer grew even wearier, and now he suddenly returns to Chile without knowing the why or the wherefore. He will find the reason—will he ever! He will inadvertently become part of the drama, he will plunge into it, thinking to save himself thanks to his art and his boldness—he, the superstar of guerrilla rock—without realizing that he has fallen headlong into a fight to the death against the dictatorship. And Mañungo dives into it with Judit and Fausta, the ugly duckling Lopita and Don César, and the cherub Jean Pablo. In Chile no one seems to be able to help coming face to face with abuse, derision, the thrust of the knife, or escape hearing the death knell of curfew.

The narrator seems not to take sides. But in his own way he does. He skillfully keeps his distance in "Evening"—one of the three parts of the novel—and a little less in "Night." In "Morning," after a scene of torture, imprisonment, and death, the narrator goes along with Judit and joins the resistance. He covers a lot of ground. And he rubricates his commitment with a master stroke: the metaphoric tableau entitled "Chile in Miniature."

History is smoothly framed by the description of Matilde Neruda's funeral [January 1985—Ed.]. Neruda and Matilde always received José Donoso with a cordial embrace and offered him an unwavering friendship. Donoso witnessed the outrages committed against Matilde and watched her struggle till the end. Matilde and Pablo unwittingly gave the Chilean people the occasion to protest with all their strength and soul and without risking a major confrontation: their funeral in Santiago's General Cemetery. As is well known, Neruda and Matilde are buried in a wall just a short distance from Victor Jara [the popular folksinger tortured and killed by military henchmen in the National Stadium in the hours following the coup—Ed.], in the grounds that elsewhere I've called "the slum of death." It is the field of the poor, of wooden crosses, red geraniums, and little paper flags.

Donoso gathers his characters in La Chascona, the Nerudas' house at the foot of the San Cristóbal [a hill just blocks from downtown Santiago—Ed.]. There he lays out their lines of communication and alienation; that is the stage for their loving and forgetting, for their disdain and their rebelliousness; there one can measure what's left of the old social classes, and more than one life falls apart as others come together. From there the characters go out wandering through the leafy streets of the Barrio Alto [Santiago's wealthy district—Ed.] surrounded by the fragrance of flowers and watered lawns. They stop off at garbage dumps that once were palaces, share in the tasks of beggars and trash can inspectors, conspire, make love, flee, and disappear. La Chascona is an island: breached, devastated, besieged, defending with invisible weapons the integrity of an already defunct Chile. Its owners don't rest and neither do their living kin. The city is the site of a free-for-all between the living and the dead.

To orchestrate this vast and agitated *danse macabre* Donoso displays arresting allegories: a hellish interlude in which an aroused pack of street dogs rape an aristocratic but seedy little bitch. Judit saves her by shooting her dead, Judit, who lives in order to avenge her own interrupted violation. A ghost ship, the *Caleuche,* signals its witchery from the waterways of Chiloé, and a small scale model of Chile, inspired by Walt Disney, shows off next to a Burger King.

The final dialogue between Mañungo and the journalists defines the novel:

> "Why did you come back to Chile at this particular time?" the reporters asked.
> "To stay here."
> "For how long?"
> "Forever."
> "Didn't you say last night in Neruda's house that your visit would be short because you didn't understand the situation your country was in?"
> "Now I understand it." He thought for an instant and then went on. "I've changed my plans. In any case, after twenty hours in my country, I can assure you that I have never been clearer on any subject than I am on this matter of staying."
> "In order to define your political action?"
> "Could be."
> "Armed struggle?"
> "No, except in self-defense or to defend someone else."
> "Songs?"
> "I'd like that. But who knows if bombs won't turn

out to be the only alternative? It's their fault. Because what can we do when they force us into violence by taking away all our hope? I am not justifying bombs, but I do understand them."
> (trans. Alfred MacAdam)

This dialogue defines *one* novel among others, because there are several novels in **Curfew**. The main one is explanatory, mournful, and one might say, tough, if it didn't leave such a lump in one's throat.

Marjorie Agosin (essay date Summer 1992)

SOURCE: "The Poems of José Donoso," in *Review of Contemporary Fiction,* Vol. XII, No. 2, Summer, 1992, pp. 70-6.

[*In the following essay, Agosin discusses Donoso's* Poems of a Novelist, *praising the author's willingness to write in a genre that is not his usual form.*]

Donoso is a narrator of images, of hallucinatory scenographies that take on life beyond the text, beyond writing and the reader. From his early stories to the majestic **Obscene Bird of Night** Donoso appears as a great seeker of portraits, of bewitching and overwhelming images; but the images of old houses predominate, houses through which memory perambulates like the typically phantasmagoric and unreal characters. This is why readers and critics alike were surprised when Donoso published a book of poems.

A kind of collective tenderness took hold of the Chilean literary milieu regarding this novelist who seemed to have returned to an innocent adolescence in order to write poems, whose title reflects his implacable metier: **Poemas de un novelista**. Why should we be surprised that this master of Chilean letters should get it in his head to write poems when his whole narrative enterprise is an immense metaphor of foundation, of creation; that is, a great poem rooted in the myth of a decadent culture recreating itself mythically?

The question takes on added importance because Donoso's poems have little to do with that obsessive and fertile narrative that characterizes his work, but instead retrieve experiences and moods. They seem to be visions from which the typical stage of his previous fiction disappears to allow the birth of an already mature poet who radiates freshness and a voice that allows him to escape the "monstrous demands of prose." [All prose quotations are from Donoso's preface to his book of poems—Ed.]

It is wonderful to sit down and read this collection of poems by a novelist who is also a poet because they contain the most purified language, centered on simplicity, on clean and beautiful imagery, delicately constructed in terms of commonplace images. These poems of a novelist have nothing to do with the prose writer but they belong to a common pattern; they are born of the same essence that inaugurates and celebrates them.

José Donoso writes his own preface and does so modestly as if, taken by surprise, he were trying to explain to his readers why he is writing poetry. Thus he produces a novelist's poetics of poetry. He affirms that

> the experience of writing poetry is so distinctively different from that of writing a novel. Why, for instance, did the experience of seeing a pig killed become so markedly split into two? Here, in these verses, that experience has the imprint of a realistic chronicle, an absence of imagination—the characters appear with their real names and are bound to be recognized—a being *myself* without recourse to metaphor. On the other hand, in my novel *A House in the Country* the killing of the pig also appears, which is the same killing of the pig in the poem, that scene lived in a wintry night in the stone streets of the town of Calaceite, in the province of Teruel, Spain. But in the novel—in prose—the fact is transubstantiated, made into metaphor, full of disguises and masks, stuffed with meanings, a part of the world of fantasy, the episode and backbone of a sequence.

Donoso's preface brings us closer to the exploration of a language devoid of the baroque and scenic vision.

Repeated readings of *Poemas de un novelista* betray an unequalled beauty of place because, though Donoso tries to avoid scenography and lavish ornament, *Poemas* is made up of brief territorial stories in which the somber old houses open their doors and start to talk among themselves as if part of the same landscape. Then the autobiographical fuses with a sense of place and the poet's voice travels through a space that might be populated by the dimensions of a novel:

> These poems are then the fruit of at least two things: of my impossibility to write autobiography, to project my intimacy as mine, and let my solitude and tenderness course through my novels, which are never immediate and always metaphorical. On the other hand, these verses are the fruit of my respect for poetry as a perhaps more serious and less bastardized genre than the novel, and my fear, also, of being over my head. I have looked for a tone: I think I found it but since I'm not a professional I don't have at my disposal the required diapason to prove it. The diction and the lexicon also do not appear to have missed their mark. But what about the rest, the important thing, that which constitutes the poet's vision and that is embodied in his rhythm and cadence, or in his rejection

of them in order to create another rhythm and another cadence, the vision that stands for personality, style, and for the creation of a poetic universe—these essential things, are they present? I'm afraid not. The plotting of sound at different levels that constitutes the essence of poetry is here frequently replaced by chronicles and anecdotes, itineraries and memories—elements that belong to the novel.

The book presents itself as a travel diary with a perfectly discernible itinerary and geography, but the territories envisioned by the poems are rather portraits of the soul and of the flesh that lure the reader with gestures of love and good faith. "Diario de invierno en Calaceite (1971-1972)" [Diary of Winter in Calaceite, the first of the four parts in which the book is divided—Ed.] is the first stop, a geographical and metaphysical description of the desert region of Aragón where Donoso bought an old house in which he "lived four very poor and isolated years":

> The eyes uninhabited.
> The skin a void:
> the ivy climbs the stone wall
> which can't feel it climb.
>
> It is the season of feeble,
> silent hurricanes.
> The cloud passes by,
> it seals the landscape in its cold shell.
>
> The light sharpens eaves and corners:
> through sudden trapeziums of shadow
> people pass hastily stooping,
> turned inward like a glove:
> every surface worn out and unpolished.
>
> What's left?
> Whom to touch?
> What glance that might crack
> suddenly open like the laughter of a watermelon?. . .

I touch on this poem, initiation of the rites of solitude at the beginning of the journey. It possesses the lucidity of the lonely and the virtues of a poetry concrete, meditated, and simple, devoid of grandiose adjectives. The images are sparing and delicate; the sound resembles more and more the cadences of silence.

In the second poem Donoso speaks of tenderness, of the need to write these poems as if yanking them away from his interior to let himself be. Then the voice of the woman is heard, whose body becomes the outpost of the territory, the house itself. And in the hollow, the body, warmth, writing:

Surprise to find you here,
though I have brought you.

We entered through our stone arch:
we closed it because you and I so wished it.
I probe into the house as if it were
the hollow under your arm . . .

Are we all here?
Yes, let me count:
daughter, pictures, dogs, and the music
that determines our limits.
This that shelters us is the blanket.
The paternal refuge of so many books.
Our sleep devours
the reversible wakefulness that we are, you and I,
ten fingers in a hand,
single glass for the red wine. . . .

The poet's house, space, and fantasy only follow the dictates
of love because

Within this archaic organization
of stones, rooms, and corridors,
the world of warmth is reduced
to a certain sector of your neck,
to my clenched fist,
to an amusing phrase.
It is necessary to eliminate space. . . .

Donoso's concrete and detailed realism conjures up the over-
flowing image of the killing of a pig. Although Donoso means
to establish differences between poetry and prose, the realism of poem 9 is so brutal that it unfolds into two:

Julia came up to tell us
that tonight
Emilio kills the pig:
as soon as it is dark
the ceremonial crime
is going to consecrate hunger.
We are invited
because we are friends . . .

The second scene begins with the phantasmagoric tableau of
A House in the Country, where the names for the world are
violence and orphanhood. The ceremony is inaugurated by
the atavistic signs of death, with a ripping pain always in
relation to the solitary hostility of winter during which the
poem takes place. An interplay of voices mitigates the scene
but endows it with the attributes of horror and delirium:

The bloody ritual is displayed
in the narrow and steeply scenic street:
gorged with the fragrance of burning rosemary

the children play rough.
Voices boom and give orders:
quick, corner him,
don't let him go downhill;
tell Espina to bring the fire and the bucket closer.
The struggle of the men
—tougher than last year,
twice as hard as the neighbor's—
raises the beast on the altarstone:
tame on the old table of dark blood and dark smoke
and generations of boiling water
that kills the beast while ennobling the pinewood.
It kicks—as if it knew—in the middle of the street
so narrow, so crowded,
so cruel, so intimate. . . .

Curiously, in this poem the ritual forms part of the landscape of Calaceite, where village and culture are deeply fused;
the children function as a backdrop, as a vital force in the
future, as if evolving towards the presages of death:

The children I know over there
would fear a squeal like the one here.
The hugging night
is not an adequate stage for its rites.
They ignore the relation between pain and hunger,
death and cold.
But the brutal children of this winter
know those secrets without fear:
stones, bursts of rosemary, war,
hunger and fullness,
grapevine, cypress, olive tree.
It is the timeless night of ancient villages
where hunger is fought with a knife
and they talk of wolves howling at doors
though proudly they add
that they no longer exist. . . .

Poemas de un novelista offers a brief interlude of poems
written in 1952 [dedicated to Mario Vargas Llosa—Ed.], but
soon the motif of the journey reappears: the third section is
called "Madrid, 1979." In this section there is an ever sharper
movement towards characterization, barely suggested in the
preceding sections. The texts speak of love or of the plaints
of love, taking the form of tactile and olfactory sensations, of
habitual places that become imprecise in the light of day,
dislocated in the poet's rapid memory. The poet notes the
austerity of the landscape in order to go into another territorial space, this time more rooted in the idea of the body itself
than in objects and belongings. Thus **"My Hand"** is explored
as if for the first time:

And to sum it up
it is this:
Not beauty,

of course.
And yet a certain modesty
eloquent in its restraint.
It is here daily.
Weaver? Engineer?
Did I build it
or did it build me?
Yes, daily I have no
other choice
but to accept its guidance.
I touch people with it.
It touches me, it brings me news
of all that surrounds
this distant border of mine
that when all is said and done
is me.

Hot when it grips.
And when extended,
the palm draws healthy, fervent lines.
The knuckles hurt when it's about to rain
(age, they say . . .)
And it throbs with the
ever renewed exaltation
when someone makes the tentacles of my fantasy
climb like ivy.

The landscape as such only appears in the section "Diario de invierno en Calaceite" but it rounds out the book as a concordance to the preface focusing on the poetics of realism. [The book's fourth section is entitled "Retratos," Portraits] That's why Donoso chooses family albums and photographs since only by means of the camera can a visible relation to worldly reality be maintained. Under the influence of Diana Arbus's demented vision and Susan Sontag's aesthetic, the portraits become part of the book and of the real like **"Roman Busts in the City Museum"** [the title of one of the poems—Ed.]. To reflect on a photograph or daguerreotype is a way of approaching the immemorial, as in the case of **"Photograph of My Great-Great-Grandmother Carmen Fantobal de Donoso, Dead at the Age of One Hundred Years in Talca, on 22 November 1867, at 11:30 A.M."** The poem's initial question is related to the beginning of the preface where Donoso wonders how it is that all these poems turned up, and thus the coffer is a magic box, a gentle Pandora's box that when opened reveals a profusion of birds, stories, and photographs:

How did it turn up in my coffer?
Dead, toothless, furrowed visage.
Great-great-grandmother of a thousand colonial years,
fading ochre,
so old that not even of your surname
are there memories or survivors left.

I know nothing about you.
You are your nun's habit.
the centuries
that leap on to the cardboard.
No bond joins us
except for the expendable coincidence
of blood;

no anecdotes, no lands, no affection,
no ennobling tradition.

And yet somebody loved you:
a careful handwriting
recorded your name,
and the day and the hour of your death
in the back of your effigy
by now almost faded.

This person is
alive, she talks to me.

Who was she?

Susan Sontag writes in *On Photography:* "People robbed of their past seem to make the most fervent picture takers, at home and abroad. . . . Photography has become one of the principal devices for experiencing something, for giving an appearance of participation." Donoso rounds out the *Poemas* with the recovery of a past both real and mythical through photographic realism.

I always remember my conversations with José Donoso in Santiago, surrounded by young poets, and it was beautiful to see him there with his quiet demeanor. Donoso listened to the young poets as they recited their somewhat old-fashioned and perversely romantic verses, but he always felt fascinated by the rhythms of poetry and love. Some of that tenderness is in *Poemas de un novelista,* and the preface is to some extent the apology of a novelist hounded by his own language. *Poemas de un novelista* inscribes the stories/poems of a great writer in love with the language of poets and in love with a solitude like a dream, and like a Calaceite winter.

We celebrate these poems and this unheard of phase of José Donoso, and we open *Poemas de un novelista* as if we plunged into a great coffer and upon opening it dreams appeared, poems, enticing beds in grand old houses, and Donoso's hand writing a luminous verse.

Brad Hooper (review date 15 December 1992)

SOURCE: A review of *Taratuta* and *Still Life with Pipe*: Two Novellas," in *Booklist,* Vol. 89, No. 8, December 15, 1992, p. 714.

[*In the following excerpt, Hooper briefly outlines the plots of* Taratuta *and* Still Life with Pipe.]

Donoso is probably the most highly esteemed contemporary Chilean novelist. His latest book to be translated for U.S. publication is actually two novellas. *Taratuta* is concerned with a Russian revolutionary of that name whom the novelist-narrator has come across in his desire to learn more about Lenin. The character of *Taratuta* has beguiling aspects that make the narrator want to ponder and write about him, but the man's historiography is incomplete. The narrator tracks down a fellow who just might be a descendant—but that person proves nearly as illusory as details about Taratuta. The fact that the project must remain incomplete teaches the narrator and the reader an important lesson in life—a lesson Latin American fiction teaches time and again—that separation of fact from fantasy is often impossible and usually less desirable than allowing them to remain in magical blend! The second novella, *Still Life with Pipe,* is no less cerebral. In the midst of a difficult relationship with his fiancée, bank employee Marco Ruiz Gallardo attempts to revitalize the rather moribund Association for the Defense of the National Artistic Heritage, of which he is a member, but in the process ruins his reputation while at the same time becoming custodian of a museum dedicated to the work of a forgotten Chilean painter. The twists and turns of irony make this tight little tale a brilliant mirror of life's incongruities.

Fernando Gonzalez (review date 5 January 1993)

SOURCE: "A Realistic Fantasy of Vivid Ideas, Shrouded in Gray Words," in *The Boston Globe,* January 5, 1993, p. 65.

[*In the following brief review, Gonzalez discusses* Taratuta *and* Still Life with Pipe.]

This new book by Chilean writer José Donoso comprises two short works: *Taratuta,* which spins from the name of an obscure figure in the Russian Revolution, and *Still Life With Pipe,* the story of a bank clerk's fascination with the work of a minor painter. From these modest starting points, Donoso attempts nothing less than a meditation on the power of the word and the role of fantasy in everyday reality, the renewing energy of art.

The results are mixed. Donoso is a master craftsman, but his tone here is so muted, his arguments built on such small details, that when he succeeds he can only succeed modestly.

When his revelations emerge they feel undefined, almost like the faint aftertaste of a mediocre wine. More troubling, while the issues at hand are vital, especially for a writer, Donoso seems merely curious about them, rather than passionate.

In *Taratuta,* the narrator, Donoso himself, becomes intrigued with the improbable name of a man who appears briefly, and then only tangentially, in the life of Vladimir Lenin. When they mention him at all, historians seem unable to agree on his name, his character or his role in Bolshevik politics. Rather than as a dead end, Donoso sees this as an opportunity. He publishes an article speculating on *Taratuta* and, surprisingly, adding to the intrigue, a reader named Taratuta writes Donoso a letter.

From then on, Donoso creates a delicate, three-dimensional tableau: In one plane he is the narrator; in another one he is the writer, free to create and elaborate; and in yet another there is the historical reality. They intersect at odd angles and as Donoso moves between them the paradoxes become apparent.

The historical characters, perhaps fictional, are vivid and memorable. The real characters are ciphers or read like literary conceits. Taratuta had red hair, smoked a pipe, drank absinthe, had ambiguous morals. There's an aura of authority around Lenin, even as Donoso mocks his near-sainthood status.

The living Taratuta, perhaps a long-lost descendant of the revolutionary, is unremarkable. We forget the details of his face and his past as soon as we learn them. La Zonga, a fortuneteller of the wealthy, is a breathtaking sexpot who, on a closer look and minus the makeup and the wig, becomes "a country schoolteacher a few years before her retirement."

Yet with so much life swirling around him—real and imagined, present and past—Donoso speaks with the tone of a starchy professor and the urgency of a career bureaucrat.

His approach feels on the mark in *Still Life With Pipe,* in which the storyteller, Marcos Ruiz Gallardo, is a low-ranking bank employee mired in mediocrity but with upper-class aspirations. On an escapade with his girlfriend to a working-class beach resort, Ruiz finds a house museum dedicated to the work of Larco, supposedly a near-great painter who never fulfilled his promise and became a footnote in the art history of Chile.

Ruiz is unimpressed with the artwork and put off by the museum's caretaker, Larco's longtime valet-assistant-confidant, though he fantasizes about the potential financial gain in his discovery. But little by little, almost imperceptibly, Ruiz is moved by the ugly beauty of the paintings. Then the caretaker dies. Soon Ruiz's life is changed.

Like the paintings it describes, Donoso's language is in soft colors, mostly the grays seen by a gray man. In the story, the pain, the joy, the passion in the paintings transcend form and color. Donoso's ideas are rich and potentially powerful, but they never quite overcome his words.

Los Angeles Times Book Review (review date 14 February 1993)

SOURCE: A review of *Taratuta* and *Still Life with Pipe,* in *Los Angeles Times Book Review,* February 14, 1993, p. 6.

[*The following article provides a brief review of* Taratuta *and* Still Life with Pipe.]

Does art imitate life or vice versa? Or is the relationship between the two subtler and more playful than either of these maxims suggests? This is what José Donoso, one of Chile's leading novelists (*The Obscene Bird of Night*), would conclude, offering us these two novellas as evidence.

In *Taratuta,* a writer tries to uncover the truth about a minor character in the Russian Revòlution, a red-bearded crony of Lenin's whose specialty was "expropriating" (stealing) money for the Bolshevik treasury. The man's true name, character and activities slide into the chinks of biased or slipshod histories and disappear. The narrator's reconstruction of the revolutionaries' exile in Paris is almost entirely fiction, but the fact that Taratuta did, in some sense, exist is enough to give a possible descendant—a wan and disconnected young man the narrator meets in Madrid—a whole new "plot" to live by. And, indeed, the youth's story displaces Taratuta's as the novella's central focus.

In *Still Life With Pipe,* art comes to the rescue of a stilted bank clerk and his old-maidish fiancée, via a rascally old artist who poses as the caretaker of a museum of his own paintings. Art itself is nothing, the old man maintains; *life* is art. What does this mean? Well, the strange, ugly Surrealist or Cubist paintings work on the couple until eventually they start a new life within the frame of the old man's vision: a bohemian, Parisian life of wine bottles, checkerboards, guitars and kimonos. Not that their old life wasn't also a work of art. It was just as "framed," as artificial, as the new one. Their new life, Donoso implies, is simply *better* art; brighter, less kitschy, unsettled enough to give amorous blood room to stir.

James Polk (review date 8 April 1993)

SOURCE: "Labyrinth of the Narrative," in *Washington Post,* No. 124, April 8, 1993, p. D2.

[*In the following review, Polk lauds the two novellas* Taratuta *and* Still Life with Pipe. *He asserts that Donoso continues*

to focus on the relationship between an artist and his art, and social realism, in the two works.]

First, a confession: Although I've reviewed all manner of contemporary fiction over the years, I'm still uneasy about using the word "postmodern" in a sentence.

But surely something different is going on in the work of the Chilean novelist José Donoso, perhaps even something that warrants the term. The richly imagined tapestry of *The Obscene Bird of Night,* his best known novel, is a tight fabric of ambiguity, stitched through with surreal highlights of switched identities and a meandering plot that falls apart and reassembles itself in unexpected places.

A recurring theme in much of Donoso's fiction is the nature of inspiration and the ambivalent relationship between the artist and his art. *The Garden Next Door,* for instance, describes a novelist first searching for and then mishandling a theme. The supposed creator and his supposed creation keep intersecting at odd junctures until the former is overwhelmed by the latter and the tale is left to be told by an unforeseen third party.

The novelistic process is also central to *Taratuta,* the first of these impressive short works. While looking through material about pre-revolutionary Russia, the writer-narrator stumbles across Taratuta, a historically obscure comrade of Lenin's.

Perhaps using a pseudonym, the man was mixed up in a plot to transfer a sizable inheritance to revolutionary coffers. Glimpsed through the fog of distant history, the story is a fun house of mirrors and darkened passages that awakens in the narrator "the impenitent spinner of intrigue that's present in all novelists. . . ."

While the incipient fiction percolates, he writes a magazine article about Taratuta's shadowy adventures along with the obscurities and contradictions he has uncovered. Hardly is the piece published when the novel comes to the novelist.

A letter arrives from one Horacio Carlos Taratuta pleading for a history, "a foundation stone on which to build the table of his origins." This modern Taratuta exists in a void, orphaned in Buenos Aires by a father who revealed nothing of his roots before disappearing in the turmoil of Argentina's Dirty War. Now the son is left with only a peculiar name and a few weakly grounded suspicions about where it came from. Suddenly, in the magazine, he sees that name; maybe there's a reality to it after all.

For the narrator, reading the young man's plea places him in the middle of his own fiction. A "writer's arrogance can make him challenge dragons and work miracles," he says, "and the disorientation of that boy condemned to live a story without any beginning moved me."

Soon, however, the disorientation consumes the writer's own plot, and by the end the young man's story becomes the only story, as the historical saga the narrator had once imagined fades into oblivion. He makes one last stab at reasserting control, but fails and the novella meanders toward what appears an end of its own determining.

Taratuta, in fact, often seems independent of any author's voice. This is not true, of course; it is a creation of José Donoso. Yet the issues it raises take us to the extremes of fiction and to questions about the nature of that beast which sound very postmodern after all.

Still Life With Pipe is more conventionally structured, with clear antecedents, particularly in fiction by such Argentine writers as Humberto Costantini and Vlady Kociancich. But one of Donoso's most singular techniques is to apply his own brand of surrealism to themes more common to social realism—class struggle or the deadening life of the bourgeoisie—with unique results.

We are introduced to the pompous bank clerk Marcos Ruiz Gallardo, who very much wants to become part of the cultural elite. Unfortunately, he has no real idea who the elite is or what it does, although he suspects art may be involved.

Imagine his good fortune then, while on a vacation in the faded resort of Cartagena, to stumble across the paintings of Larco, a forgotten Chilean artist. He has never heard of the man, nor, as it happens, have many others. Although Marcos sees little to recommend the work, it is 'art' and thus may lead him to his goal. The obscure clerk quickly becomes an expert on the obscure painter.

He does not make it to the elite, but the attempt allows Donoso some insightful observations about art, society and human nature. By the end, our perceptions of all these things are not quite what they were at the beginning.

These short works, smoothly translated by Gregory Rabassa, show the author at his near best, challenging, provoking, forcing reexamination. Both are complex but intensely readable, told with generous amounts of irony and wit. All of this may or may not be postmodern, but it certainly is striking.

John Updike (review date 16 August 1993)

SOURCE: "Shadows and Gardens," in *New Yorker,* Vol. LXIX, No. 26, August 16, 1993, pp. 86-9.

[*In the following review,* Updike contends that The Garden Next Door *is "ruthless, deep and tender." The novel draws on several experiences of Donoso's life according to Updike, and centers the processes surrounding artistic creativity.*]

In these last three or so decades, the novel has looked for urgency and energy to two bedevilled backwaters, Eastern Europe and Latin America. The rollback of Communism has left Eastern Europe's artistic compasses spinning, and the rollback of the dictators in South America has left the social terrain there somewhat flat, dreary, and ambiguous—of a piece with the bourgeois prairies to the north and in the over-farmed Old World. So it seems, at least, in two short novels by authors from the cone of our shapely sister continent: *Shadows,* by the Argentinian Osvaldo Soriano and *The Garden Next Door,* by the Chilean José Donoso. Soriano's earlier venture into black comedy, *A Funny Dirty Little War* was a chilling astonishment—a village bloodbath rendered with the hectic, fluid speed of a Keystone Cops comedy. *Shadows,* too, suggests a silent movie—a parade of clowns on the desolate Argentine pampas, tracing in their dilapidated vehicles vast dusty circles that implausibly keep intersecting. It is *On the Road* without Kerouac's youthful buoyance and North America's roadside abundance; the first sentence runs "Never in my life had I been on the road without a penny to my name," and one of the two epigraphs displays the late Italo Calvino's opinion that "now the only kind of stories which exist in the world are those that are unresolved and get lost on the road."

Shadows is nothing if not modernist, in the classic, Beckettian manner. Our narrator-hero has no name, save the one that another lost traveller, a former circus proprietor and performer called Coluccini, gives him: Zárate. We learn that this Zárate is a software expert, has been living in Italy, and has a daughter in Spain about whom he feels guilty because he never communicates with her. A train he was riding through the pampas to a town called Neuquén has stopped "in the middle of nowhere." After the second night of non-movement, he begins to walk, lights a fire, is told by a farmhand that this is against the law, finds a semi-abandoned Shell station, washes himself and his underpants at a pump out back, and encounters Coluccini, who drives a Renault Gordini piled high with suitcases and announces, *"L'avventura è finita!"* Zárate accepts a ride, and is off on a closepacked series of adventures in a virtually endless, homogeneous landscape: "I tried to identify a point of reference along the road, but it was all the same: wire fences, cows, the occasional tree, a dumb cloud drifting along." He encounters, among others, a truck driver who, his truck having broken down, hopes to sell his load of watermelons to a passing empty truck; a man with "a smooth, insipid face, the kind you forget instantly," who drives a Jaguar, is unlucky in love, and is named Lem; a dog that bites him (Zárate); a priest who feeds him; a travelling fortune-teller called Nadia, who drives an old Citroën Deux Chevaux; two kids called

Rita and Boris, who are on their way to Cleveland in a Mercury; some thieves stripping telephone poles of their copper wire; and, the most bizarre of all, a big man called Barrante, who wears a Perón pin, a suit "missing almost all its buttons," a "wide, shiny mourning band," and a length of hose "wrapped around him up to his neck, [so] he looked like a roll of dried beef."

For two-thirds of the way, *Shadows* is a beguiling farce, an uncanny exaggeration of the shadowy, sleepy, muffled, flimsy, gray quality of modern life, especially life on the road, as the landscape dulls down and lives meaninglessly pass and repass: "It all seemed to be taking place at a distance, as if it were happening to someone else or as if I were seeing it in a movie." But the point is not one, perhaps, that can be made at length; at less than two hundred pages, *Shadows* is a third too long. A muddled sting operation that Coluccini and Zárate pull off in a town called Colonia Vela and then a no doubt satirical Independence Day involvement with some stray members of the Argentine armed forces exhaust the reader's appetite for the inconsequential; the line keeps playing out, but we are no longer hooked. Soriano is fascinated by messiness, by messes. The civil mayhem of *A Funny Dirty Little War* was a bloody mess; the messes of *Shadows,* though there is a fatal shooting, primarily concern automotive malfunction, squalid poverty, drink, food, and flood. Nadia's Citroën is swept off the road by a downpour:

> The car floated awhile, then slammed against a hummock, and I landed on top of Nadia because there was nothing for me to hold on to.... Muddy water began to seep in through the floor, carrying away our sandwiches and covering our feet.... I had to dry the ham with a rag. The mayonnaise jar was lost under the seat, but the bread was safe because it had been caught between two cans of oil.

In this dishevelled setting occurs the novel's one scene of lovemaking. Its tenderest scene of healing, stranger still, comes when Barrante removes a speck of dirt from Zárate's eye:

> He turned on the lamp and brought it closer while he raised my eyelids with two pudgy and filthy fingers. His breath was bitter, and his teeth were covered with yellow plaque. Everything he had on was falling apart, and the Perón button was just about to fall off his lapel.

The word "filthy" is recurrent: "Two farmhands riding horses followed by a filthy dog were driving some cattle"; "Coluccini grabbed the gin and staggered out of the store, his shirt hanging out of his trousers, a sheet of filthy yellow newspaper stuck to his shoe"; up above hangs "the gray sky, where a rather filthy slice of moon was shining through." Such filth confirms the characters' sensation that they are, as Coluccini says, "in the asshole of the world." On the next page, it is said of Argentina, "A country where finding a fortune is a waste of time isn't a serious country." Zárate has known exile, as has Osvaldo Soriano, and, like him, has returned. There is no place like home. He avows that on the vacant, derelict pampas he has "met more people in the past few days than I had in all the years I lived in Europe." And there are certain magical moments in the provincial wasteland: Nadia's wonderfully insouciant and accurate card-reading, Coluccini's acrobatic bicycling on the wires above the ghost town of Junta Grande, and, in that same desolation, the appearance in a lonely mailbox of a letter from Zárate's little daughter, addressed to him simply "*Poste Restante, República Argentina.*" In such moments, the novel reclaims its hapless, drab territory for magic realism. As in the surreal desert of "Krazy Kat," life absurdly persists.

José Donoso's *The Garden Next Door,* as the title suggests, offers a more palpable texture. It begins far from the wastelands of the New World, in the snug Catalan resort of Sitges, which is overrun by European tourists and Latin-American political refugees. In addition to our central characters, the Chilean writer Julio Méndez and his wife, Gloria, and their set of expatriate Chileans, there are:

> Argentinians of all stripes and colors, with conflicting ideologies, but intelligent and very well prepared for exile: the tragic Uruguayans who fled in large numbers, emptying their country; the Brazilians and the Central Americans, all of them running away like us, some of them persecuted, most going into voluntary exile because back home it was impossible to live and go on being yourself, with the ideas and feelings that made you who you were.

To fill their days, the exiles scrape out a living at what jobs they can find, sell handicrafts to tourists, sit in cafés admiring the parade of "Belgians, Germans, and Frenchmen, stuporous from a whole day lying in the sand . . . looking as if they'd been squeezed into their reddened skins, shiny with foul-smelling sun cream," attend Argentine barbecues, sleep with "the blond dryads who came down from the urban forests of the north in search of rest or fun, or of their 'sexual identities,'" lament the way their children are becoming Europeans and losing their Latin-American roots, and endlessly rechurn the political issues and antagonisms that have landed them in Spanish exile. In the backward glance of an unusually successful expatriate, the painter Pancho Salvatierra, Chile is—like Soriano's Argentine pampas—"the asshole of the planet." Salvatierra offers the Méndezes the use of his elegant Madrid apartment for the summer, and the impoverished middle-aged couple, worn down by too much booze and Valium and Sitges partying, gratefully accept.

It is the summer of 1980; seven years have gone by since Allende's fall and his loyalists' flight from the Pinochet government. The luxurious apartment, in the center of Madrid, is reminiscent of the Santiago of Julio's past. The floors, he observes, are parquet and have "the eloquence of the wooden floors of another time, lost so many years ago in the silence of Mediterranean tile floors." Back in Chile, "all the floors creak; as well as a characteristic voice, everyone has a characteristic sound, his or her own tread on wood, a personal signature that follows one around, as inseparable as a shadow." The garden next door, an unexpectedly ample and bucolic park belonging to the Duke of Andía, reminds Julio of the garden of his old home on Rome Street, where his mother lies dying, begging in vain for Julio and his family to come for one last visit: "Why don't they come to close my eyes?" For a time, the garden is inhabited—by the duke's youngest son and blond daughter-in-law and their two children, who live in a smaller house apart from the mansion. Julio, instead of working to revise the novel that has become the repository of all his hopes, gazes into this green paradise and falls in love with the young blonde, who is conducting, Julio comes to see, an affair with a dark young man, a "handsome brute." The novel has a number of surprises, which should be reserved for its readers. As a portrait of a struggling writer, of an embittered yet still viable marriage, and of an exile's paralyzing nostalgia, *The Garden Next Door* is ruthless, deep, and tender. Donoso, like many another writer of the so-called Boom in the Latin-American novel, was infected by Faulkner's circling indirections and cavalier time jumps; this potentially tiresome manner works well enough here, as the meditative Julio obliquely drifts, in his borrowed milieu, toward defeat and renewal.

In an even shorter and more frankly autobiographical recent work, a novella titled *Taratuta,* Donoso's narrator speaks of "the cultural references without which reality is only a sketch." Like him, Julio is a compulsive alluder, who fondly sees his blond dryad in the duke's little forest and her smooth young friends as "Brancusiesque," and who, when she is folded in the embrace of her lover, instantly thinks of a painting by Klimt "in which all you see is the heads wrapped in a riot of colors and of gold." His own wife, the tall and patrician Gloria, is appreciated in terms of Ingres's famous "Odalisque" so consistently that she plays to it, winding her head in a towel and presenting her nude back to him. An amoral young drifter called Bijou appears to Julio first as a curly-haired *angelo musicante* from some medieval fresco and then as a Rimbaud-like decadent: "I'd thought I'd recognized the evil blond filth, the perverted defiance in those clear eyes, the dirty uneven teeth of the character in *Coin de table!*" Magritte, Scott Fitzgerald, and Mallarmé's "L'Après-Midi d'un Faune" are repeatedly mentioned—stroked like lucky stones. A sensibility for which life is already so saturated in art has natural difficulty in creating fresh art. The Boom weighs cruelly upon Julio, who may have some of

Donoso's sensibility but does not have his secure high reputation. Julio is especially tormented by the fictional maestro Marcelo Chiriboga, "the most insultingly famous member of the dubious Boom," and by the Barcelona superagent Núria Monclús, a literary discriminator of fearsome chic and decisiveness. Artistic ambition is felt as a joyless burden, and release from it as a longed-for blessing:

> Not to go on being a slave to my desire to evoke a poetic universe governed by its own resplendent laws, like the one—in spite of all the unbearable commercial lies—García Márquez, Carlos Fuentes, Marcelo Chiriboga, and Julio Cortázar are sometimes able to create. To surrender: the sweetness of accepted failure.

The garden next door to reality is art, and the mysteries of artistic creativity—its inhibition, its successful activation—lie at this novel's center. As in "Shadows," blankness has its paradoxical fertility. When the Brancusiesque young woman dominating Julio's fantasy life departs from Madrid, he reflects, "Since the important thing about beautiful things is the pain of the deep wounds they leave, her presence in the garden may have been an obstacle for me; with her now gone, the empty park may be fruitful." For the writers of the Boom, the New World was a garden where fantasy had flourished from the start. At first, America was taken for Asia and the East Indies, then as a source of endless gold and slave-produced wealth and, later still, as a political proving ground populated by noble savages and unprecedentedly free men. Its history is one long disillusionment, broken by spells of renewed enchantment; ideas and dreams have always been part of its unsteady, colorful reality. The final twist of perspective, in *The Garden Next Door,* is a drastic one, and the reader may boggle at its plausibility, but there is no denying Donoso's essential point: it takes imagination to live as well as to write.

FURTHER READING

Criticism

Friedman, M.L. "Curfew: A Novel." In *Choice,* Vol. 26, No. 2, (October 1988): 321.
    Brief description of Donoso's *Curfew.*

Friedman, M.L. Review of *The Garden Next Door.* In *Choice,* Vol. 30, No. 7, (March 1993): 1155.
    Brief description of Donoso's novel *The Garden Next Door.*

Larisch, Sharon. "Old Women, Orphan Girls, and Allegories of the Cave." In *Comparative Literature,* Vol. 40, No. 2, (Spring 1988): 150-171.

An essay comparing Plato's *Republic* (specifically "The Allegory of the Cave") and Donoso's *The Obscene Bird of Night.*

Levitas, Mitchel. "Writers and Dictators." In *The New York Times Book Review,* (14 August 1988): 1, 22-23.

Levitas describes the political climate in Chile since 1973, and provides some details about the publishing industry in the country.

Additional coverage of Donoso's life and career is contained in the following sources published by Gale Research: *Contemporary Authors,* Vols. 81-84; *Contemporary Authors New Revision Series,* Vol. 32; *Dictionary of Literary Biography,* Vol. 113; *DISCovering Authors Modules: Multicultural Authors; Hispanic Literature Criticism; Hispanic Writers;* and *Major Twentieth-Century Writers.*

Shusaku Endo

1923-1996

Japanese novelist, playwright, short story writer, essayist, and biographer.

For further information on Endo's life and works, see *CLC,* Volumes 7, 14, 19, and 54.

INTRODUCTION

Endo is regarded as one of Japan's premier contemporary novelists and as one of the world's great Catholic writers. Born in Tokyo, Endo spent his early childhood in Manchuria. After his parents divorced, he and his mother returned to Japan to live with a Catholic aunt. His mother soon converted to Catholicism, and at the age of 11, Endo was baptized, an event he later described as the most critical of his life. At the time, however, Endo felt pressured to become a Catholic and compared the feeling to putting on an ill-fitting suit. Endo was uncomfortable with his Catholicism for many years, but instead of abandoning his faith, he clung to it, exploring his doubts and his faith in his writing. Endo battled lung disease his entire life, and because of his ill health was exempted from service in World War II. He studied French literature at Keio University and later became one of the first postwar Japanese students to attend a foreign school, enrolling in the University of Lyon in 1950 to pursue his interest in twentieth-century Catholic fiction. Endo's first novel, *Shiroihito* (1955; *White Man*), won the Akutagawa Prize, an award for promising young Japanese writers. Endo was a prolific writer, although not all of his works have been translated into English. He won nearly every major Japanese literary award and was nominated for the Nobel Prize in literature several times before his death at the age of 73.

Much of Endo's work is autobiographical in nature, drawing on his experience as a member of the Catholic minority in a largely Buddhist country. Often compared to such writers as Graham Greene and Francois Mauriac, Endo wrote passionately moral fiction in a realistic style that he frequently embellished with lyricism and humor; much of his writing explored the tension between Western Christianity and Japanese temperament, Eastern and Western morality, and belief and skepticism. Endo often portrayed Japan as lacking spirituality and morality. In his novels *Kazan* (1959; *Volcano*) and *Chinmoku* (1966; *Silence*), Christian Westerners are unable to survive in Japan, forced to martyr themselves or apostatize. In the same way, in *Foreign Studies* (1989), the Japanese cannot survive in the Christian West. The Japanese Christians who appear in these stories are alienated from

Japan, the Christian West, and even themselves. The struggle between defiance and cowardice, martyrdom and apostasy, consume these earlier works, and the reader is left with very little hope that faith can survive. However, as Endo's faith took root, the characters in his fiction began to embrace their faith. More Christlike characters appear who love even in the face of rejection and betrayal, as seen in *Obaka-san* (1959; *Wonderful Fool*). Endo began to express a Christ with compassion for the sinful and weak, a maternal Christianity with the focus on forgiveness. His portrayal of this more maternal aspect of Christianity made it more understandable to an Eastern audience and more compatible with Japanese culture. Endo said that he used short stories to work out an idea or theme which he later intended to develop into a novel, and the seeds of many of his novels can be found in his short fiction.

Endo is perhaps the most popular Japanese writer in the West, and many critics theorize that it is his Christianity that makes his work more accessible to the Western reader. Many reviewers assert that the issues of cultural conflict prevalent in his fiction are universal themes which make his work powerful and substantive. Endo has been praised as courageous in addressing questions of faith and sin in his work, in which his delicate, understated style and his infusion of humor prevent his moralizing from becoming off-putting to the reader.

PRINCIPAL WORKS

Shiroihito [*White Man*] (novel) 1955
Umi to Dokuyaku [*The Sea and Poison*] (novel) 1958
Kazan [*Volcano*] (novel) 1959
Obaka-san [*Wonderful Fool*] (novel) 1959
Chinmoku [*Silence*] (novel) 1966
Seisho no Naka no Joseitachi (essays) 1968
Bara no Yakat (play) 1969
Ougon no Ku [*The Golden Country*] (play) 1969
Iesu no shogai [*A Life of Jesus*] 1973
France no daigakusei (essays) 1974
Kuchibue o fuku toki [*When I Whistle*] (novel) 1974
Yumoa shosetsu shu (short stories) 1974
Seisho no naka no joseitachi (essays) 1975
Kitsunegata tanukigata (short stories) 1976
Watakusi no Iesu 1976
Watashi ga suteta onna 1976
Yukiaru kotoba (essays) 1976
Nihonjin wa Kirisuto kyo o shinjirareru ka 1977
Kare no ikikata 1978
Kirisuto no tanjo 1978
Ningen no naka no X (essays) 1978
Rakuten taisho 1978
Usaba kagero nikki 1978
Ju to jujika (biography) 1979
Juichi no iro-garasu [*Stained Glass Elegies*] (short stories) 1979
Marie Antoinette (fiction) 1979
Shinran 1979
Chichioya 1980
Endo Shusaku ni yoru Endo Shusaku 1980
Kekkonron 1980
Sakka no nikki (diary excerpts) 1980
Samurai [*The Samurai*] (novel) 1980
Tenshi 1980
Ai to jinsei o meguru danso 1981
Meiga Iesu junrei 1981
Okuku e no michi 1981
Onna no issho [*The Life of a Woman*] (fiction) 1982
Endo Shusaku to Knagaeru 1982
Fuyu no yasashisa 1982
Scandal (novel) 1988
Foreign Studies (short stories) 1989
The Final Martyrs (short stories) 1993
Deep River (novel) 1994

INTERVIEW

William Johnston with Shusako Endo (interview date 19 November 1994)

SOURCE: "Endo and Johnston Talk of Buddhism and Christianity," in *America,* Vol. 171, No. 16, November 19, 1994, pp. 18-20.

[*In the following interview Endo and Johnston discuss the relationship between Buddhism and Christianity.*]

[Shusaku Endo:] Are you still interested in Buddhism, Father?

[*William Johnston, S.J.:*] *Yes, of course. I don't think I'll ever lose my interest in Buddhism.*

What aspect of Buddhism interests you most?

The meeting of Buddhism and Christianity. The dialogue. Aren't you interested in that?

I certainly am. In Europe and America scholarly studies of Japanese Buddhism keep appearing. . . .

Dialogue is the great discovery of the 20th century. Dialogue between nations, dialogue between capital and labor, dialogue between husband and wife—and dialogue between Buddhism and Christianity.

Little by little the dialogue is getting under way. A while ago in Sophia University I heard Buddhist monks chanting the sutras during Mass instead of Gregorian chant. If that had happened 20 or 30 years ago, there would have been an awful rumpus. But tell me, when did you first get interested in Buddhism? Was it before the Second Vatican Council?

Yes. The pioneer was Father Lassalle [Enomiya Lassalle, S.J.]. He influenced me a lot.

He built the Zen center outside Tokyo. But apart from Lassalle there wasn't much interest before the council. What makes people interested in Buddhism today?

Meditation is highly developed in Buddhism and modern people are looking for meditation. Often they don't find it in their own religion.

But when Lassalle began, it must have seemed heretical for Christians to practice Buddhist forms of meditation.

Not heretical, but progressive.

But what did the other missionaries think? I suppose they were indifferent. Or did they not think it was dangerous?

Some considered it dangerous. But aren't modern people attracted by danger? Don't they like risk?

[Laughing] There was a stage in the Japanese church when we thought we had to avoid all risks. But you seem to have done away with that idea. Was it because of the Second Vatican Council?

Of course. But you yourself are known for your interest in inculturation. There can be no inculturation of Christianity in Japan without dialogue with Buddhism.

Yes, but my efforts at inculturation got me into trouble with my fellow Catholics. [Laughing] You seem to have escaped. I wonder why. . . . Anyhow, I'm joking. . . . Thanks to people like you, we can talk freely about dialogue with Buddhism. In fact Japanese Catholics are now very happy with the idea. I have no doubt that dialogue is a very fine thing. But it has its limits. After all, when we Christians talk to Buddhists and learn from them, we must know where to draw the line. I would like to hear something about that.

Yes. . . .

There are vast differences between Buddhism and Christianity. Buddhism talks about abandoning the self. It talks about getting rid of all attachments and it even claims that love is a form of attachment. We can never say that. Moreover, the Buddhist approach to evil is quite different from ours. Then there is the question of reincarnation versus resurrection. Again, Buddhists claim that the Buddha is working dynamically at the core of our being, and we say that the Holy Spirit is working at the core of our being. Are we saying the same thing or are we saying different things? There are endless questions.

Yet I believe that you yourself have the basic answer. When I was in the United States a few years ago I heard a Catholic priest say that the interesting thing about Endo is that he is fascinated with the person of Christ. He is always talking about Christ, struggling with Christ, trying to understand Christ, experiencing the presence of Christ. Now it seems to me that the main thing for a Christian in dialogue with Buddhism is a deep commitment to Christ and the Gospel. If this is present, other problems will solve themselves. Besides, when we come to dialogue, we must distinguish between Christianity as a living faith and Christianity as theology. The living faith is expressed in the prayer and worship of the people who say, "Our Father, who art in heaven" or recite the Jesus prayer. This does not change. Theology, on the other hand, is reflection on religion at a given time and in a given culture. It changes from culture to culture and from

age to age, as we have seen so dramatically in the 20th century. Our task at present is to create an Asian theology.

I agree with that completely. Theology has been based on Western thought patterns for too long. We Japanese were taught that it was dangerous to depart from them. That was good medicine, but like all good medicine it had unpleasant side effects. But, as you say, if our commitment to Christ is firm other problems will be solved. But in the West, particularly in California, people are fascinated by oriental thought. They are interested in Zen, in esoteric Buddhism and in the Buddhist description of the Great Source of Life. When I read their books I see little commitment to Christ. They are creating sects that have little in common with Buddhism or Christianity or Islam . . . something that transcends the traditional religions. But I suppose the main influence is from Buddhism. Aren't people in Europe and America drawn to these sects because they are tired of traditional Christian thinking? Haven't they had enough of Aristotelian ethics and Aristotelian logic? And so they are attracted to Buddhism.

But let me return to the theological difficulties. I spoke about the vast differences between Buddhism and Christianity, and I would like to hear more about that.

At this point in history I don't think I can answer all those questions. I don't think anyone can. It will take time. Dialogue is a process and we are at the beginning. Looking back in history we now see that Christianity has been in dialogue since its inception. Jesus was a Jew. He spoke like a Jew, thought like a Jew and acted like a Jew. Christianity was at first seen as a Jewish sect. The person who brought it into the Greek world and initiated the first great dialogue was St. Paul. Then in the 13th century, when Aristotle was introduced into Europe, Aquinas initiated a dialogue that resulted in a Thomism that dominated Catholic theology until the Second Vatican Council. Now, even as we speak, Christianity is in the process of extracting itself from one culture and becoming incarnate in another. The new culture is deeply influenced by Asian religions and the work of dialogue is only the beginning.

It seems to me that Buddhism and Christianity have in common the belief that what Buddhists call the Great Source of Life and what we call the Holy Spirit dwells within us and surrounds us. Yet there are differences in the two religions and these differences must be made clear: otherwise something fundamental might be lost.

We must rely on the Holy Spirit. Any Christian who would enter deeply into dialogue must have true Christian experience—contemplative or mystical experience. Otherwise he or she will have nothing to offer. Besides, Buddhism is a very fascinating religion. Roughly, there are two kinds of dialogue. One is the interior dialogue of a person who lives in a new culture, who reads the newspapers, talks to the people, breathes the air. The other dialogue is exterior, where people meet, share ideas, say what they believe and what they practice. They don't force anything on one another but adopt a "take it or leave it" attitude. For example, Christians are now learning the role of the body in meditation. They are learning to sit in the lotus, to regulate the breathing, to enter into unitive silence, to get a glimpse of oriental wisdom. To what extent we can imbibe Buddhist philosophy is not yet clear.

Buddhists claim that the Buddha is working dynamically at the core of our being, and we [Christians] say that the Holy Spirit is working at the core of our being. Are we saying the same thing or are we saying different things?

—Shusaku Endo

I think you have practiced some Zen. You know that when one sits in silence for some time the unconscious begins to surface and one can come into considerable turmoil. Eventually one is liberated ("Body and soul have fallen away" they say) and one reaches enlightenment. Now tell me, is there anything like that in Christianity?

Of course. You get this kind of experience in the Christian contemplatives.

But is the experience of the Christian mystics like St. Teresa and St. John of the Cross the same as the Zen experience or is it different?

This is a much debated point. I can only give you my opinion. I believe that mystical experience is conditioned by one's faith. If one believes that God is love and that the Word was made flesh, this will enter into the experience. It certainly enters into the experience of St. John of the Cross, who speaks of the Incarnation at the summit of the mystical life and whose mystical experience is finally Trinitarian. In short, even though profound mystical experience is silent, imageless and ineffable, it has content. The experiences of St. John of the Cross and Zen master Dogen are not the same. To anyone who reads their writings this is obvious. Precisely because they are different, dialogue is meaningful.

I believe that in dialogue with Buddhism we can learn a lot about psychology. From the fifth century Buddhism has been preoccupied with the self, whereas Christianity has spoken principally about the relationship between God and human beings and has put all the emphasis on a God who is out-

side. *In the knowledge of the self, Buddhism has made much more progress. Take, for instance, psychoanalysis. Buddhism has been practicing it since the fifth century. Whether one can precisely call it psychoanalysis I am not sure. Anyhow, Buddhism has seen layers of consciousness in the human psyche, and in the area of psychology it is far in advance of Christianity. When it comes to Zen, however, I have no experience. I am just a theoretician talking out of my head.*

Neither do I practice Zen. Perhaps it could be said that I practice a Christian contemplation with some influence from Zen. Throughout Japan now there are people—mainly priests and sisters—who sit silently in Zen style before the Blessed Sacrament, regulating their breathing and stilling their mind. They are not practicing Zen, but perhaps it could be said that they are practicing a Zen influenced Christian contemplation. Of course there are others, though not many, who have practiced pure Zen under the direction of a Buddhist master.

But you have written books about Zen.

I would prefer to say that I have written books about Christian contemplation, with the Zen Christian dialogue in the background.

Tell me, what kind of letters do you get from your readers?

I sometimes get letters asking questions about Zen and Christianity. People in the West often ask where they can find a Christian Zen master or they ask me to recommend a place in which they can practice Christian Zen. It is difficult to give answers. I sometimes say that we are pioneers in this whole area. We are still groping and trying to find our way.

Always I come back to the same question. The Great Source of Life—what are we to call it? Do we call it the Christ or the Buddha? That is the central question.

If I am a Christian, it is because of Jesus Christ. I already spoke about the centrality of the commitment to Christ. Let me tell you something that illustrates the point. When I translated your novel **Silence**—you remember it was a controversial book because you seemed to sympathize with the Portuguese priest who apostatized by stepping on the crucifix. Well, after I translated that book I got a letter from a contemplative nun in the United States. She said that for her **Silence** was a novel about prayer. Prayer, she said, is a struggle with Christ. Magdalene struggled with Christ and then surrendered. Likewise, Peter denied Christ and then surrendered. Then there was Thomas and, of course, St. Paul. They all had their struggles before they made their commitment. Similarly the hero of **Silence** struggled with Christ. He never lost his faith but made a deep commitment.

Yes, you told me about that sister's letter many years ago, and I never forgot it. In fact, what she wrote about prayer being struggle influenced a novel I wrote subsequently, called The Life of a Woman *(Onna no Issho). In this novel a girl is in love with a Nagasaki Christian boy who has a great love for the Virgin Mary. The girl becomes very jealous of Mary and says to her: "I hate you! I hate you! You have stolen my lover." In the end she dies peacefully before a statue of Mary. But her prayer was one of struggle. She could never have said, "I hate you" if she had no faith. Hatred can always change to love. When one can say to God, "I hate you," it is like saying, "My God, my God, why have you forsaken me?" With these words authentic prayer begins. So I was impressed by that sister's comments. If ever you meet her, tell her that Endo is terribly pleased with what she wrote and sends his gratitude.*

OBITUARIES

Sonni Efron (essay date 30 September 1996)

SOURCE: "Shusaku Endo; Japanese Novelist, Humorist," in *Los Angeles Times,* September 30, 1996, p. A22.

[*In the following essay, Efron gives a brief overview of Endo's life and career.*]

Shusaku Endo, the Roman Catholic novelist who has been called the Japanese Graham Greene, died Sunday after a long illness. He was 73.

Endo was one of Japan's most acclaimed novelists and had a wide international following. He won nearly every major Japanese literary award, had at least nine books translated into English and other languages, and was nominated several times for the Nobel Prize for literature.

Endo was both a novelist and a humorist. The book for which he is best known in the West—*Chinmoku,* published under the English title *Silence* in 1969—deals with Japanese Christians in 17th century Nagasaki, and the problems of faith and apostasy.

The book, which seemed to argue that Christianity would have to change radically if it were to put down deep roots in Japan, was a sensation here. It prompted wide debate and some outrage among Japanese Christians, and won Endo the Tanizaki Prize for literature.

Endo was born in Tokyo in 1923, but his family moved to Manchuria when he was a child. Although his mother was a devout Catholic, his parents divorced and he returned to Japan in 1933 to attend elementary and high school in Kobe. He was baptized a Catholic at age 12.

Poor health kept Endo from serving in the military during World War II. He was admitted to Keio University on his fourth try after failing the famous college's entrance exam three times. He majored in French literature and in 1950 won a Catholic scholarship to University of Lyon in France. Endo returned to Japan to become a novelist. In 1955 he won Japan's prestigious Akutagawa Prize for *Shiroi Hito* (*White Man*).

In 1957, he published *Umi no Dokuyaku,* (*The Sea and Poison*), in which he wrote about Japanese doctors vivisecting a captured American pilot. The book was a searing condemnation of the Japanese lack of moral conscience, a theme that Endo continued to explore.

Critic Jun Eto wrote that Endo's work was notable for the lack of a father figure, commenting that "his Jesus is a mother-like figure." Endo frequently said he wanted to create the image of a compassionate, forgiving Christ whom Japanese could more easily embrace.

Endo often said he was writing literature, not theology, but his works explored the problems the writer had in coming to terms with his foreign religion.

Father William Johnson, who translated *Silence,* wrote of the author's conflict between "his Japanese sensibility and the Hellenistic Christianity that had been given to him."

Endo wrote: "This problem of the reconciliation of my Catholicism with my Japanese blood . . . has taught me one thing: that is, that the Japanese must absorb Christianity without the support of a Christian tradition or history or legacy or sensibility.

"Even this attempt is the occasion of much resistance and anguish and pain. No doubt this is the peculiar cross that God has given to the Japanese."

Endo had an older brother who excelled at everything and left the writer with an enduring sense of inferiority but also a sense of humor and compassion, the Nikkei Shimbun newspaper commented in today's editions.

"His works reflect the viewpoint of the weak and the inferior," the paper wrote. "In that sense, they can be seen as a literature of love."

Endo's best selling *Deep River,* published in 1993, was made into a movie that was released this year. Among the other works that have been translated into English are *Scandal, Wonderful Fool, Final Martyrs* and *Samurai.*

Endo died Sunday of respiratory failure after having been in and out of the hospital since last spring. He is survived by his wife, Junko, and son, Ryunosuke.

Eric Page (essay date 30 September 1996)

SOURCE: "Shusaku Endo Is Dead at 73; Japanese Catholic Novelist," in *The New York Times,* September 30, 1996, p. B8.

[*In the following essay, Page gives a brief overview of Endo's career and the themes that consumed his work.*]

Shusaku Endo, a leading Japanese novelist who wrote about faith and faithlessness, East and West, heritage and modernity, died yesterday at Keio University Hospital in Tokyo. He was 73 and lived in Tokyo.

The cause was complications of hepatitis, The Associated Press reported.

Mr. Endo was born in Tokyo and grew up partly in China. When he was 11, a Roman Catholic aunt persuaded him to be baptized. After World War II, during which ill health kept him out of the fighting, he attended Keio University and went to Lyons, France, to study French Catholic authors' writing. In time he was called modern Japan's most distinguished Catholic novelist.

The British novelist Graham Greene, also a Catholic, hailed him as "one of the finest living novelists." Mr. Endo was considered a contender for the 1994 Nobel Prize in Literature, but it went to another Japanese writer, Kenzaburo Oe.

Mr. Endo also wrote plays on religious themes, was a humorist and won numerous important literary prizes in Japan.

His novel *Deep River* accompanies soulless modern Japanese voyagers to the Ganges River in India, where they come to know the humanity and the sufferings of some who have faith. His writing in that work was praised by the psychiatrist Robert Coles, in a review in *The New York Times Book Review,* as "a soulful gift to a world he keeps rendering as unrelievedly parched."

Appraisals of the role of Christianity in Mr. Endo's writing have differed. Dr. Coles noted that in an epigraph to *Deep River,* Mr. Endo "by implication dismisses those critics who have made much of his relatively unusual situation as a Christian intellectual living in a nation far from the West."

But the British critic John Gross wrote in 1988 that with Mr. Endo, as with the Japanese author who is the hero of the Endo novel *Scandal,* "his Catholicism colors everything he writes."

In that book, the hero goes on a quest in the red light district of Tokyo, seeking to learn how a lewd portrait of him (or of a Doppelganger) was put on exhibition. He comes to conclude that "deep in the hearts of men lay a blackness they themselves knew nothing about." Mr. Gross wrote that he found the book "extremely gripping."

Over the years, critics repeatedly said Mr. Endo was the Japanese author whose works were the most comprehensible to readers in the West, possibly because his Catholicism brought Western traditions to bear on his thinking.

His novel *Silence* was about a young Portuguese missionary in the time of the persecution of Japanese Christians early in the 17th century. The novelist John Updike has called that book "somber, delicate and startlingly empathetic."

Mr. Endo is survived by his wife, Junko, and a son, Ryunosuke.

OVERVIEWS

Francis Mathy (essay date 8 August 1992)

SOURCE: "Shusaku Endo: Japanese Catholic Novelist," in *America,* Vol. 167, No. 3, August 8, 1992, pp. 66-71.

[*In the following essay, Mathy traces the relationship between Christianity and Endo's work throughout his career.*]

Shusako Endo, the 1989 winner of the Champion Award, conferred each year on a distinguished Christian person of letters by the editors of the Catholic Book Club, a subsidiary of America Press, is duly recognized both in Japan and abroad as a "Catholic novelist." The award citation carefully avoided this phrase and stated merely that "his Roman Catholic heritage has charged his artistic sensibilities with a vision and power rarely seen in contemporary writers of whatever nationality." Born in Tokyo in 1923, Endo subsequently lived with his Catholic aunt in Kobe after his parents divorced when he was 10. Under his aunt's influence, young Shusaku was enrolled in a children's catechism class. With little preparation, he was eventually baptized. In later years, he compared this event to being outfitted in an ill fitting suit of Western clothes, and characterized his literary career as a lifelong attempt to convert these clothes into Japanese dress in which he could feel at ease.

Endo was not a particularly good student and had difficulty getting into college, but on his third try he was admitted into Keio University, where he decided to study French literature. While at Keio he became interested in the modern French novel, especially the novels of Francois Mauriac and

George Bernanos. In his junior year of college, he wrote and managed to get published in reputable journals two critical essays, which, he says, "introduced the themes that would later occupy me in my novels." In the following two years, another 10 articles were accepted for publication. In 1950, at the age of 27, he was given the opportunity to study in Lyons, France. For a little more than two years he made an intensive study of French Catholic writers, especially Mauriac, but his study was interrupted when he came down with tuberculosis and had to return to Japan.

Back on native soil, he soon recovered sufficiently to write his first novel, *White Man,* for which he received the Akutagawa Prize, awarded to promising new writers. *Yellow Man* followed, and then *The Sea and Poison,* which won him both the Shincho Literary Award and the Mainichi Cultural Award. Endo's career as a writer was now established, and succeeding works brought him not only critical acclaim but also an enthusiastic readership. From the beginning, Endo followed the longstanding custom of Japanese writers—of dashing off, in the intervals between more serious works, light "entertainments," which are usually serialized in newspapers or magazines. In the case of Endo, the plots and themes of these "newspaper novels" counterpoint those of his more serious works, and despite the speed and casualness with which they were written, many readers, and even some critics, consider these—and *Wonderful Fool* is a good example—his best work.

Endo has always been a prolific writer. In the 38 years of his literary career, he has written on the average one full length novel a year. He has also published several plays, about a dozen volumes of short stories, a number of critical biographies and innumerable essays on a wide variety of subjects. In addition to the novels mentioned above, his principal novels are *Volcano* (1959), *The Woman I Abandoned* (1964), *And You, Too* (Part Three in the English translation *Foreign Studies,* 1965), *Silence* (1966), *On the Shore of the Dead Sea* (1973), *When I Whistle* (1974), *Samurai* (1980), *Life of a Woman* (1982), *Scandal* (1986) and *First Lady* (1988). His three major plays are *The Golden Country* (1966), *The House of Roses* (1969) and *The Japanese of the Menam River* (1973). His principal nonfiction works include *A Life of Jesus* (1973) and *The Birth of the Christ* (1978); the collections of critical essays entitled *Religion and Literature* (1963) and *Stones Speak* (1970), and three biographies—of the Christian daimio Yukinaga Konishi (1977), the Japanese Jesuit martyr Peter Kibe (1979), and the commander of the Japanese colony in 17th-century Siam, Nagamasa Yamada (1981).

In addition, Endo has a weekly newspaper column, writes articles for many magazines and journals and makes frequent appearances on television. For a year he was host interviewing prominent religious thinkers and leaders on NHK's weekly "Religion Hour." Many of his stories have been made into movies and television dramas. Endo, a member of myriad literary committees and a past president of the Japanese P.E.N. Club, has himself received many awards, including the Order of St. Sylvester, conferred upon him in 1971 by Pope Paul VI. In the United States, he has been awarded honorary doctorates by Santa Clara University, Georgetown and John Carroll. The two essays Endo wrote as a university student did, as he says, introduce the themes that would occupy him in his novels. In his essay **"God and Gods,"** Endo states that there is so great a gulf between the Western monotheistic world and the Eastern pantheistic world that neither the Eastern nor the Western writer can borrow successfully from the other. He cites as examples Rilke and Tatsuo Hori, his admirer and imitator in Japan.

Though both affirmed the same pantheistic universe, there is an unbridgeable gulf between them. Rilke for all his avowed pantheism is heir to a worldview according to which mankind is forever fixed in its grade of being. A person can become neither angel nor bird; he or she must fight with the angels and subdue nature. Men and women must always engage in positive actions. Hori, however, inherits a world view in which individual human beings are part of a whole in which there are no distinctions as to grades of being and therefore no need to fight. For Hori, the passage into the eternal occurs naturally without any struggle. A Christian, on the other hand, whose return to God is not passive, rejects pantheism. Thus, a Christian has always to fight, against himself, against sin, against the devil—even, like Jacob, against God. When Japanese read literature rooted in such a worldview, something in their pantheistic blood rebels and they feel great antagonism.

In a second essay, **"The Problems of a Catholic Writer,"** Endo states that the Catholic writer must go beyond the physical and psychological depiction of his characters to reveal the hidden traces of God in their souls. Such a writer must journey to that hidden center of each person in which the saving love of God is at work, even in those who have fallen into terrible sin. But such a writer must also witness to the light that is beyond the sin and evil, which purifies and sanctifies the sinner. In Mauriac's novels, for example, the dark shadow of sin that falls over his characters is encircled by a faint light that can also be seen in Rembrandt's paintings. The Catholic writer can only hope that this light will enter his work; he or she cannot make it do so. Characters in a novel are free and cannot be coerced. Mauriac was finally unable to portray Therese Desqueyroux as saved. In such a case, all the Catholic novelist can do is depict the terrifying misery of a person without God.

Early in his career, Endo realized the great responsibility the Catholic writer must assume, while at the same time he experienced within himself the passive attitude toward salvation that characterizes Eastern pantheism. He saw that almost all the Christian writers of Japan who preceded him had, in the end, succumbed to pantheism and abandoned their Christian faith. One of the reasons for this, he thought, was that they had not been sufficiently aware of the immensity of the chasm that separated the two sensibilities, and so the first chore he set himself as a novelist was to "take our Eastern world without a Supreme Being and contrast it as vigorously as possible with the Western world, which affirms such a Being." By "vigorously," he meant that he must put aside any philosophy or theology that fosters the delusion that the Eastern and Western worlds are the same. Endo held that the Japanese must not think of the Christian West as being in their cultural stream, nor at the same time are they to hold it off at a respectful distance.

In his novels, Endo sets out to dramatize this dilemma: to present as vigorously as possible the Japanese world without distinctions and boundaries, a world that is, as he states in another essay, insensitive to God, sin and even to death. The next step is to contrast this world with the world of the Christian West. When one reads Endo's works in their chronological order, it is clear that there is a twofold progression in them.

First, there is a progression in the dialectic between East and West, as depicted in the early novels, where Japan is portrayed as a swampland in which everything foreign, including Christianity, is swallowed up or transformed. The Japanese who try to survive out of their native soil seem doomed to perish. Yet, in succeeding novels, Christianity gradually comes not only to survive but even to triumph. Second, Endo's fictions, despite the rich invention and occasional exoticism that characterize them, belong to the stream of the confessional literature—the *watakushi shosetsu* (the "I" novel)—that has long dominated Japanese literature. The hero, or at least one of the principal characters, is never far removed from Endo himself. The very situations and experiences that Endo records in his nonfiction appear with a minimum of disguise in his stories. And the faith of this character can be seen growing from work to work.

Initially, the Japanese swampland prevents any growth or faith in Endo's fictional characters. In *Yellow Man,* for example, the French missionary Durand abandons his priesthood to marry a Japanese, while his fellow priest, Father Brou, fails in his ministry. Chiba, a student who resembles Endo himself, tells Brou that a yellow man has absolutely no consciousness of sin. "All we experience is fatigue, a deep fatigue—weariness as murky as the color of my skin, dank, heavily submerged." Durand, in turn, asks Brou if he really believes his God "can sink roots into this wet soil, into this yellow race." In Volcano, a companion piece to Yellow Man, the foreign priest not only defects, but turns tempter and tries to get others to give up their faith. In the end, he com-

mits suicide. The only optimistic note in these two novels comes from Father Brou's statement that the Japanese gods will be conquered: "Christianity will swallow up this pagan pantheism in another miracle of Cana."

Just as the Christian Westerner does not fare well in the Japanese swampland, the Japanese finds it equally difficult to survive in the Christian West. The hero of *And You, Too* arrives in France wanting nothing more from life than peace and security—and promotion when he returns to his college. His term of study in France, which should have been the quickest route toward advancement, turns out to be just the opposite. Contact with Western culture makes him completely dissatisfied with his ideal of "ordinary happiness," and almost makes him despair of achieving anything greater. He is shattered by his experience and returns to Japan broken in body and spirit, convinced that it is as impossible to assimilate Western culture as it is to receive blood from someone who has a different blood type.

Silence, at first glance, might seem to be as pessimistic about the ability of the Japanese to assimilate either Western culture or Christianity as in the previous novels. Father Ferreira, the former Jesuit provincial superior, now turned apostate, tries to convince the younger missionary Roderigo to do as he did—that is, to step on the fumi-e [a small plaque picturing the face of Christ] and reject his faith. His arguments are clear cut: The Japanese are unable to become Christians, and they have transformed the Christian God into a god of their own making. "The Japanese have no notion of God and never will have. . . . The seedlings which we brought to this country eventually began to rot in this mudswamp called Japan." But, for the first time, there appears an element of hope. When the young missionary is about to step on the fumi-e, God's silence is finally broken. Roderigo hears him say, "Go ahead and step on it." and he realizes that even in his sin God will not abandon him.

Gradually, Christlike characters begin to appear in Endo's fiction. They continue to love even when their love is rejected or abused. These are wonderful fools, like Gaston in the novel of that title; Mitchan, in *The Woman I Abandoned;* the Baron, escaped from an insane asylum but more sane than the swamp dwellers, in *One, Two, Three,* and Brother Houssin in the play *The House of Roses.* Through the power of love, these characters are able, in varying degrees, to lift others out of the swamp and help them realize their better selves. In *Wonderful Fool,* Gaston not only rescues the professional killer Endo from drowning in an actual swamp, but even pulls him out of his inner swamp by turning his heart away from revenge. Self sacrificing, trusting, gentle love offered without measure saves the denizens of the swamp and makes them also capable of love—and of action.

A corresponding growth in faith can be found in the 1973

novel *On the Shore of the Dead Sea.* A middle aged Japanese novelist, similar to Endo in almost all respects, journeys to Israel in search of the answer to the question, "What do you think of Christ?" What he learns there concerning the final moments of Rat, a completely self centered, cowardly, physically and spiritually unattractive Pole who is executed by the Nazis, convinces him that he himself is loved by Jesus and will never be abandoned by Him.

The Jesus Endo depicts in alternate chapters of this novel and in his *A Life of Jesus,* which was published in the same year, is a person to whom a yellow man can relate. This Jesus lacks the power that the Japanese find so intimidating and difficult to accept. (Endo rejects all of Jesus' miracles.) Rather, Endo's Jesus is a man with tired sunken eyes that emit a sad radiance. "He was the man who could accomplish nothing, the man who possessed no power in this visible world.... He was never known to desert other people if they had trouble.... And with regard to those who deserted him, those who betrayed him, not a word of resentment came to his lips. No matter what happened, he was the man of sorrows, and he prayed for nothing but their salvation."

Endo next attempted to come to terms with the power of the Resurrected Christ in *The Birth of the Christ,* and was able finally to depict Japanese characters who were triumphant in their faith. The most interesting of these is the 17th-century Japanese Jesuit Peter Kibe, who, unable to enter a seminary either in Japan or Macao, traveled by an overland route to Rome—the first Japanese ever to do so—where he entered a seminary, was ordained a priest, became a Jesuit and, though he knew he would eventually be captured and killed after a long odyssey involving him in many adventures, returned to Japan to minister to the persecuted Christians. Eventually he was apprehended and subjected to the same horrible torture that Ferreira underwent, but, unlike the latter, he persevered to a martyr's death. Endo was so fascinated by Kibe that he wrote a biography of him, *The Rifle and the Cross* (a very strange kind of biography that tells us as much about Endo as it does about Kibe), made him one of the two central characters in his play The Japanese of the Menam River and featured him, once again, in his biography of Nagamasa Yamada, entitled *The Road to a Kingdom.*

The next novel, *Samurai,* is in a sense, a step backward. The samurai of the title is sent as an emissary to Mexico to try to establish trade relations with the Mexicans. Though he lacks faith, he receives baptism as a political expedient to help achieve his end. But when he returns to Japan, he finds that the climate has changed. The authorities apprehend him and condemn him to death for being a Christian. Though still without faith, he is haunted by the face of the sad man he saw hanging on the cross in all the lands through which he traveled. His servant Yozo, who has become a Christian, speaks words to his master that once again depict Endo's Jesus: "I suppose that somewhere in the hearts of men, there's a yearning for someone who will be with you throughout your life, someone who will never betray you, never leave you—even if that someone is just a sick, mangy dog. That man became just such a miserable dog for the sake of mankind." The samurai goes to his death with the words of Yozo ringing in his ears: "From now on he will be beside you. From now on he will attend you." He becomes a martyr in spite of himself. In this novel, a Western Franciscan missionary, a counterpart of Ferreira, is allowed to die a heroic martyr. This proud and powerful friar repents of his sins and goes bravely to his death at the stake. The yellow man and the white man each finds God in his own way.

A fitting climax to the various depictions of martyrdom that has preoccupied the later Endo takes place in *The Life of a Woman.* The weak who give up their faith under torture continue to experience God's love even after their defection. As expected, the strong who avail themselves of God's grace remain faithful to the end, in spite of the great suffering they are made to endure. Endo even goes so far as to show that those who persevere in loving Christ have the power to convert their enemies.

Endo has been influenced by Graham Greene, as seen most clearly in *Silence.* Unlike Greene, however, Endo does not see Christ as an outsider, intervening with "special actions." Endo's Christ is always present to Endo's characters, accompanying them wherever they go, even to and from the places of sin.

Through his writings, Endo has been a great apostolic force in Japan. Not only has he helped a large number of his fellow writers and intellectuals to find their way into the church, but his books and his public persona have undoubtedly changed the image of Catholicism in Japan and made it easier for the average Japanese to approach it. Quite different from Greene, Mauriac, Bernanos and Walker Percy, he reflects the climate of Catholicism in Japan, so different from what Westerners expect. But that is matter for another article.

Joseph R. Garber (review date October/November 1994)

SOURCE: "In a State of Sin," in *San Francisco Review,* Vol. 19, Nos. 4 & 5, October/November, 1994, p. 40.

[In the following review, Garber discusses how Endo works out his themes of sinners struggling with morality in the form of a short story before developing them into a novel. Garber uses the short stories from Endo's collection The Final Martyrs *to illustrate his point.]*

Western morality is proscriptive, more concerned with what thou shalt not do than with what thou shouldst. In Japan things are different; morals are shaped by a sense of duty; honor and obligation take pride of precedence; and virtuous behavior has little to do with the dictates of those who claim to speak for God.

Therein lies the dilemma that haunts Shusako Endo, the most respected of living Japanese authors. Endo is a Roman Catholic, a devout member of a minority sect whose members were, until the 1870s, hunted, tortured, and butchered with unimaginable ferocity—because in worshipping a pale Western deity they denied the supreme godhead of their emperor, thus violating their duty and falling, by Japanese lights, into a state of sin.

The Final Martyrs, the latest of Endo's books to be published in this country, collects eleven short stories spanning most of the writer's lengthy career. They remind us how central Endo's anguish at the gap between Christian and Shinto senses of good and evil is to all his work. The title story of the collection tells the tale of nineteenth century Catholic villagers brutalized for their beliefs. One villager, the weakest, crumbles under torture. He apostatizes, only to find himself cursed by the double sin of first having failed in his duty to the state, and then having failed his duty to God. The apostate, torn by guilt, resents both God and society for presenting him with a moral puzzle that he cannot hope to solve. "What can a coward like me do?" he thinks. "Why was I born to such a fate?" In the end, damned regardless of his decision, he presents himself before the stockade in which his few surviving fellow friends are held captive. If neither God nor government can forgive him, perhaps they will.

Endo wrote this particular tale in 1959. He has returned to its theme many times since, most notably in his searing novel, *Silence.* So too has he returned to the themes of the other stories collected in *The Final Martyrs.* It is, as he admits in his introduction, his habit to work out plot and characterization in short story form long before committing them to a novel. Thus, for the reader familiar with Endo's works, *The Final Martyrs* is a fascinating study of how the writer's mind works.

For example, two stories lay the groundwork for Endo's most recent novel, *Deep River,* yet unpublished in the United States. The first, **"A Fifty Year Old Man,"** tells of a character whose younger brother is unexpectedly stricken with what promises to be a lethal disease. Then, nearly miraculously, the brother recovers. As he does so, the protagonist finds that his dog, dearly beloved and loyal, has died. Was the death owed? Did the dog accept it, and take upon itself the sin and guilt of its master? One does not know. Endo is not yet certain, and will not say.

"A Fifty Year Old Man" was written in 1976. Eight years later Endo revisited it in **"Last Supper."** Now a character lies in a hospital ward dying of much the same disease as afflicted the brother in **"A Fifty Year Old Man."** The character's sole hope of survival is to stop drinking, but he will not stop; the ghosts of the past will not let him. During World War II, in the jungles of Burma, he committed a terrible sin. Only liquor lets him forget. And rather than confront his memories, the man would much prefer to die.

Finally, in the novel *Deep River,* the two plots, themes, and characters are fused. The dog becomes a Myna bird, and, yes, the pet accepts the fate intended for its master. Over the course of two pieces of short fiction, one novel, and fifteen years, Shusako Endo has worked and reworked his material, finally bringing to perfection an already exquisite narrative.

The best two stories collected in *The Final Martyrs* are, perhaps, autobiographical. In one, the first person narrator, a sixty year old Catholic author writing a life of Christ, accidentally meets a teenaged temptress in a park. As the two talk, the nymphet hints that she might accommodate a distinguished elderly gentleman, but only one of a generous nature, a well to do writer, for example. A second meeting is arranged for the following week, and the narrator is obliged to confront unpleasant questions of age and youth, duty and sin.

In the second tale, another (or more likely the same) first person narrator finds in an antique store a box containing a worn out Bible, some fifty year old postcards, and an aged photo album. He reads the postcards, is drawn to visit the landscape they portray, and ultimately uncovers ambiguous evidence of uncommon heroism during the second World War. It is a haunting yarn, eerie, and a fine specimen of the short story at its very best.

And yet, it is not finished. I am sure of that. It contains no fall from grace, no irreconcilable conflict between duty and morality. What it is—what it must be—is Shusako Endo taking his first tentative steps on his way to a new novel. But first he must find the sinner, and first he must find the sin. Then, and only then, will he know what the novel is.

REVIEWS OF ENDO'S RECENT WORK

Kirkus Reviews (review date 1 March 1990)

SOURCE: A review of *Foreign Studies,* in *Kirkus Reviews,* Vol. LVIII, March 1, 1990, p. 288.

[*In the following review, the critic asserts that Endo's sto-*

ries of isolation in Foreign Studies *are universal to the problems of communication between different cultures.*]

An accomplished piece of writing—as well as an instructive insight into Japanese reactions to Western religion, culture, and the tolls these reactions can exact.

European in setting, except for a brief interlude in Japan, the novel is divided into three complementary sections, which illustrate the theme rather than share any common narrative. In the first part, Kudo, a young Japanese student—a Christian—has come to France, just after the end of WW II, to study on a scholarship provided by the Far Eastern Mission of the Roman Catholic Church. Staying with a French Christian family, Kudo is aware not only of the great gulf between the two cultures but is depressed by these good and well meaning people's implicit wish that he become a priest who will return to Japan to proselytize. In the second section, set in the 17th century, Japanese apostate Araki Thomas, of whom the Church expects great things, is appalled by the brutal persecution of Christians in Japan. Araki feels that the Church in distant Rome, which does not appreciate the tremendous sacrifice Japanese Christians are making, is asking too much of Japanese converts. Tanaka, of the third and longest section, visits France on a research grant. He increasingly feels not only isolated from the French, but from his fellow Japanese in Paris, and doubts whether his projected study of the Marquis de Sade is even possible, given the great gulf he perceives between the two cultures. The futility of the whole experience is further underlined when he has to return prematurely to Japan because he has tuberculosis.

Endo's delineation of isolation, of feeling terribly and irrevocably foreign, is moving and effective, with implications that go beyond the specificity of his Japanese characters to the wider problems of communications between all cultures. A thoughtful and timely book.

Publishers Weekly (review date 30 March 1990)

SOURCE: A review of *Foreign Studies*, in *Publishers Weekly*, Vol. 237, No. 13, March 30, 1990, p. 50.

[*In the following review, the critic discusses the universal truth in Endo's* Foreign Studies.]

Elegantly divided into three sections, this 1965 novel by the celebrated Japanese author of *Scandal* calibrates the dislocation of Easterners transplanted to the West. **"A Summer in Rouen,"** set shortly after WW II, follows the recipient of a church sponsored scholarship that has brought him from Japan to France to study Christian literature; his interest in the West is returned by his well intentioned hosts' paralyz-

ing inability to view him as more than a blank canvas for their own designs. **"Araki Thomas"** tells of the first Japanese student in Rome, a Christian sent there at the dawn of the 17th century who, realizing that the importation of the foreign religion brings with it certain death, renounces his faith after he returns home, choosing survival for himself and for his people. The themes of these two sections are deepened in **"And You, Too,"** in which an ambitious academic named Tanaka goes to Paris in the 1960s to become an authority on the Marquis de Sade. Despite the presence of a community of Japanese scholars and artists, Tanaka feels as alienated as the hero of **"Rouen,"** "constantly experiencing the sense of distance between himself and [a great] foreign spirit, and keenly aware of his own inferiority." The effort destroys his health; as in **"Araki Thomas,"** the price for integrating the force of a foreign culture is life. Paradoxically, Endo transcends all cultural barriers; far from foreign, his work has the intimacy and the vastness of the universally true.

Rachel Billington (review date 6 May 1990)

SOURCE: "A Long Way from Tokyo," in *The New York Times,* May 6, 1990, p. 34.

[*In the following review, Billington states that Endo's "Foreign Studies does not show Mr. Endo at his most intricate and brilliant, but it adds a further dimension to his later great works."*]

Shusaku Endo is a writer who replays a small repertoire of a strong themes. As a Japanese Roman Catholic with a close experience of Europe, he has always found an audience in the West. He writes about the possibility of true understanding between East and West. In a particularization of this theme, he questions the effect and strength of Christianity in an Oriental society. And, in a personalization of the same ideas, he examines the psyche of a Christian and the nature of the unconscious mind in which sin, as defined by a believer, or evil, as defined by someone without faith in redemption, manifests itself. These themes are familiar from his more recent novels, but Mr. Endo was already developing them in the three stories in ***Foreign Studies,*** published in Japan in 1965 and now translated by Mark Williams.

In the first story, **"A Summer in Rouen,"** a young Japanese Catholic called Kudo spends the hot summer months in a French provincial town with a strongly Catholic family. It is soon after the war, and the presence of a Japanese is extraordinary. Kudo's hostess views him as the reincarnation of her dead son, Paul, and calls him by that name. Forced to conform or break Japanese and Catholic codes of good behavior, he retreats farther and farther into secret misery. It seems to him there can be no understanding between East and West. The story is descriptive and highly emotional, but somewhat crude in its unvarying tone.

The second story, **"Araki Thomas,"** is set in the same world as that of Mr. Endo's famous later novel *Silence.* Araki is a Japanese who studies to be a priest in Rome in the 17th century. He returns to Japan during a period when being a Catholic means immediate torture and death. Burdened by the expectations aroused by his stay at the heart of the true faith, he apostatizes soon after his arrest and torture. His fame as a Japanese studying theology in Rome changes into notoriety as the fallen padre. Contact with the West has weakened rather than strengthened the man. **"Araki Thomas"** is told as if it were historical fact, with no dramatic flourishes. It is impossible that its 12 pages should build up to the power of *Silence,* but it adds a strand to the overall theme of *Foreign Studies.*

The final story, **"And You, Too,"** is far more substantial. It will be most interesting to readers of Mr. Endo's latest novel, *Scandal,* a masterpiece combining the attributes of thriller, moral treatise and philosophical investigation. **"And You, Too"** does not rise to these heights. Tanaka, a professor of European literature in Japan, goes to France to study the Marquis de Sade in 1965. During winter months of unmitigated gloom, rain and fog in Paris, he meets another Japanese academic who, exhausted by trying to reconcile Eastern and Western values, has succumbed to tuberculosis and is forced to return to Japan. In contrast, Tanaka's life briefly overlaps with that of a group of Japanese who feel no difficulty in assimilating Western values and look forward to using their European experience to advance their careers at home. But the solitary, obstinate Tanaka, like Kudo and Araki, cannot reconcile East and West until, in a brilliantly symbolic scene, he climbs up to Sade's castle near Avignon in the snow. As Tanaka wanders among the ruined rooms, a red stain catches his eye. In his imagination, it was left by Sade, a positive link between himself and that mysterious world. As he stumbles wearily down the hill, he coughs and a blob of red blood falls on the snow. He too must return defeated to Japan.

In many ways Tanaka is a younger version of the 65 year old protagonist of *Scandal.* Each man feels himself out of touch with the unconscious, "unredeemed" part of his mind. Tanaka hardly lifts the corner of the veil that covers the Marquis de Sade and what he represents, whereas in *Scandal* the older man, a novelist, feeling the grip of death approaching, tries to understand this side of himself and reconcile it with the outward form he presents to the world.

Ostensibly, *Foreign Studies* tackles the vast separation between East and West, but there are constant undertones of this more personal theme. The hardest problem for Christian creative artists is to avoid imposing their moral code on their characters. In an introduction to *Foreign Studies,* Mr. Endo describes the change in his point of view over the last 20 years: "As a result of continuous consideration of the concept of 'the unconscious' in my literature, I am now convinced that meaningful communication between East and West is possible. I have gradually come to realize that, despite the mutual distance and the cultural and linguistic differences that clearly exist in the conscious sphere, the two hold much in common at the unconscious level."

Everything Shusaku Endo writes is worth reading—as good literature (although I find it difficult to judge his style, which seems to vary according to translator) but, more importantly, for his exploration of human nature. As the novelist in *Scandal* says (before suffering from horrifying self-doubt): "The most important thing is to write about humanity.... To probe into the uttermost reaches of humanity—that, I think, is [the writer's] ultimate duty." *Foreign Studies* does not show Mr. Endo at his most intricate and brilliant, but it adds a further dimension to his later great works.

John B. Breslin (review date 6 May 1990)

SOURCE: "Pilgrim between Two Worlds," in *Book World— The Washington Post,* May 6, 1990.

[*In the following review, Breslin discusses the relationship between East and West as seen in Endo's* Silence *and* Foreign Studies.]

I had just finished teaching Shusaku Endo's novel *Silence* in an undergraduate course on Catholic fiction when *Foreign Studies* arrived for review. As always, *Silence* provoked a variety of responses among the students who found its hero, the 16th century Portuguese Jesuit Sebastian Rodrigues, alternately an arrogant Westerner intent on winning glory as a missionary or martyr, and a sympathetic victim of a cruel religious persecution and a culture he little understood. In the end, Rodrigues accepted the judgment that Christianity could not flourish in the "mud swamp" of Japan—a judgment enunciated by his canny inquisitor, Inoue, but clearly shared by the novel's author.

Foreign Studies was originally published in Japan in 1965, a couple of years before *Silence.* In his preface to this translation, the first in English, Endo describes **"And You, Too,"** the third and by far longest of the stories that make up this book, as "a prelude to *Silence.*" What he means is that his own experience as a foreign student in France after the war, the germ of that story, convinced him that East and West could never really understand one another on the deep level of "culture," only on the relatively superficial level of "civilization." Rodrigues, then, became a European mirror image of the unhappy Tanaka, the alienated Japanese student in Paris who attempts to insinuate himself into the French world of thought and feeling by studying the life and works of the Marquis de Sade. Cruelty in theory for the Japanese student, cruelty in practice for the Portuguese missionary. A nice symmetry.

Curiously, however, there are even stronger parallels with *Silence,* unmentioned by Endo, in the two brief curtain raisers that introduce **"And You, Too."** In both instances young Japanese Christians, one a seminarian, find themselves uncomfortably welcome in Europe as exotic specimens of the success of the church's missionary efforts. As such they feel constantly under pressure to live up to their status and beyond their personal convictions. Indeed the 17th century seminarian, Araki Thomas, is confidently expected by his hosts to return to Japan to become a martyr; he becomes an apostate instead. His counterpart, Kudo, comes to Europe three centuries later, like Endo, right after the war, but encounters the same overestimation. It is summer in Rouen, and the oppressive heat Kudo suffers from reflects the naive passion of his hosts for the conversion of his country. Unable to master enough French to explain the subtleties of Japanese culture to these self confident French Catholics, Kudo silences his objections and accepts his uneasy situation.

In **"And You, Too"** Tanaka has no such theological problems to deal with in Paris in the mid 1960s. His are entirely cultural and psychological. But the underlying dilemma of cultural incomprehension remains, heightened for him by doubts about the value of his profession as a student of foreign literature and about his status in his own university in Japan. Early in the story, Tanaka engages in a heated exchange with his fellow Japanese expatriates. Mocked by a mediocre novelist for being a detached critic rather than an engaged artist, Tanaka responds: "The world is full of writers, but the only time they justify their existence is when they create a masterpiece." If that weren't provocative enough, he confirms his countrymen's deepest suspicions when he awards the palm to French writers and critics as unquestionably superior to the Japanese. And all this on his first night in Paris.

Shunned and shunning, Tanaka becomes ever more isolated in his attempt to penetrate French culture through the writings of Sade. His one Japanese friend, the failed architecture student Sakisaka, takes him to his favorite museum filled with skillful reproductions of cathedral statuary arranged in chronological order. Sakisaka is ill and knows he will have to return to Japan an apparent failure, but he wants Tanaka to be drawn into what he has experienced in this "insignificant little museum"—"the great flow of European history spanning all those centuries." In ominous words, he spells out for Tanaka the cost of such discipleship: "In order to

enter that great flow, we foreign students have to pay some sort of price. I've paid for it with my health."

After Sakisaka leaves Paris, Tanaka occasionally returns to the museum, but his special shrine becomes Sade's ruined castle at LaCoste and other sites connected with the master. At each of these, Tanaka feels moved to a kind of giddy sexual ecstasy which he promptly subdues but recognizes as "the most real" part of himself. Near the end of the story, as he becomes aware that he, too, is ill, Tanaka climbs through the snow to the ruins of LaCoste: "Like a blind man groping in the dark, Tanaka passed his frozen hands over the remains of the walls and windows. He just wanted to touch and squeeze his lips against something that still retained a hint of the fragrance of Sade." He then notices a spot of red on the wall and recognizes it as blood, but of a vividness that calls up the "lips of someone sated with pleasure"—Sade or one of his victims.

But the blood does not long remain merely a sexual symbol. As Tanaka descends the hill he begins to spit up blood on the white snow. Art and life meet here in a disconcerting symbiosis, and the initial sexual identification with Sade turns pathological. Tanaka has paid the same price as Sakisaka and must now face the similar disgrace of returning to Japan with his work incomplete.

Writing a quarter century later Endo admits in his introduction that he now views his former self as "a pitiful younger brother," who did not fully appreciate that "at the unconscious level" East and West have much in common. This seems to imply that, even deeper than "culture," there exists a human dynamic that unites individuals; but, Endo suggests, it is as often demonic as celestial. Tanaka's shadow figure here is Sade, just as, in Endo's most recently translated novel, *Scandal,* it is a perverse doppelganger who haunts a popular contemporary Japanese novelist. Endo has moved inwards in his quest for the line that divides good and evil, but the awareness of the struggle remains the same. History helps us to localize the conflict, but it deceptively suggests that the forces of evil may be precisely identified. Not so, Endo insists, and offers again and again his own fictionalized story as proof.

Richard Eder (review date 13 May 1990)

SOURCE: "Japan Bitten by Europe," in *Los Angeles Times Book Review,* May 13, 1990, pp. 3, 11.

[*In the following review, Eder discusses how the stories of Endo's* Foreign Studies *dramatize the painful relationship between the East and West.*]

Who is this Japanese traveler, wearing a beret and thick

glasses, standing outside the airline terminal in Paris, drenched by the freezing rain and too wretchedly shy to hail a taxi?

He is Tanaka, that's who. Tanaka: lecturer in literature at the university back home, protege of the powerful Professor Ueda, and owing to this and to his foresight in selecting a specialty not already spoken for (the works of the Marquis de Sade), conqueror of one of those intermediate positions of vantage on the academic chess board: a year or two of research in France.

Tanaka has it made, in other words, or temporarily made. He has bested his fellow players; particularly Suganuma, who is only an assistant, and who has not yet been chosen to come to France but cannot be entirely dismissed, since his mentor, though junior to Tanaka's, may in chess terms be more strategically placed.

Homesick, splashed, bewildered, Tanaka thinks of his colleagues who had gone to Europe to study. "On their return, they made no mention of feelings of shame and self pity when they had spoken of their experiences abroad. . . . It was as though, from the moment they had arrived in Paris, they had as a matter of course been respected as members of the intelligentsia."

Whereas "The man who now stood at his wit's end in the pouring rain on a Paris street corner with heavy luggage in both hands, totally incapable of hailing a taxi, was not the university lecturer who had left Japan. . . . What was left of him was like a statue from which the plaster had been ripped off, leaving only an ugly skeleton. But at least, with a statue, the skeleton remains even after the plaster has been torn off."

Tanaka is no misfit sailor run aground on his own timid incompetence. He is the true circumnavigator, sailing nakedly around the world and finding it is flat and you fall off. It is his colleagues who are trimmers, and who survive by never leaving their own shore, even while having aperitifs at the Dome and boasting that Sartre had nodded to them.

Tanaka's story, entitled **"And You, Too,"** is the comic and disquieting is the centerpiece of Foreign Studies. Like its two companion stories, but more profoundly, it is a statement by Japanese writer Shusaku Endo about the pain between East and West. Each, experiencing the other, misappropriates the other.

"And You, Too," novella length, begins by watching Tanaka from the point of view of half a dozen Japanese businessmen at an in flight airport bar at Hamburg. They are Philistines; camera wearers, clinging together and boasting of their prospective exploits with French and German prostitutes.

Tanaka, sitting alone, won't join them. Pretentious snob, they figure. Un Japanese.

But there is another kind of Philistinism. Tanaka and his academic colleagues may speak of France as their spiritual home, visit all the right places, read the right books. But these are acquisitions; goods bought at an intellectual duty free shop to be exchanged, once back home, for promotions and prestige.

Tanaka, who finally gets his taxi and registers at a modest hotel, is a would be duty free shopper as well. But something strikes him down. Perhaps it is the fact that his hotel was the house where Proust shut himself up to write and die. Perhaps it comes from following the tracks of Sade—that other artistic extremist—from the prison at Vincennes to the madhouse at Charenton, to the ruined family castle near Avignon. Perhaps it is Sakisaka, the odd, ill compatriot who stays at the same hotel.

Sakisaka, an architect, is in Paris to better his prospects by studying at the Sorbonne. He is a loner, though, pale and distracted. He is a man with snakebite. The snake is European culture. Sakisaka has not merely filled his notebooks with useful sketches of Gothic cathedrals and Baroque palaces. He has filled himself as well. He has experienced what he calls the profound "flow" of the European soul. It has devastated him; he has, not incidentally, caught tuberculosis and will be shipped home.

"But here is the real pain that is all part of the experience of studying abroad," he tells Tanaka. "In order to enter that great flow, we foreign students have to pay some sort of a price. . . . I've paid for it with my health."

"And You, Too" is a battle for its protagonist's soul. Like most real battles, the results are both devastating and ambiguous. Tanaka tries to hold onto his purposes. He follows avidly his wife's mailed reports of his rival, Suganuma, and is horrified by the news that he too will come to France. He visits the cafe where the Japanese writers and academics hang out—as clannish as the businessmen and, in their own fashion, as crass.

But his heart is not in it. He has caught Sakisaka's illness; figuratively at first, then literally. His entanglement with Sade becomes more and more profound, and finally, on a second visit to his ruined castle, he finds himself spitting blood. He too will have to be shipped home, a failure; his rival, meanwhile, is doing all the right French things—just lightly enough.

There are oddly awkward bits in the story; among them, an unremarkable 10 page essay on Sade that dams up its fictional current. Sometimes, Tanaka's anguished reflections seem stagnant, sometimes repetitive.

Yet the cumulative effect is astonishing. **"And You, Too"** wields a variety of effects, from a comedy of academic intrigue, to a Jamesian portrait of cross cultural misunderstanding, to the hauntingly surreal quality of Tanaka's pilgrimage around France in pursuit of Sade's presence, to a real and profound sadness.

Of the two lesser companion pieces, **"A Summer in Rouen"** is a beautifully suggestive account of a Japanese boy brought to a French town just after World War II. He—like the author—is Catholic; his sponsors hope he will study and return to Japan to propagate a French provincial brand of Catholicism. He finds himself and his culture totally misperceived by his well meaning bourgeois provincial hosts; polite and sweating, he retreats into himself. When the daughter tries to teach him "correct" table manners—eat slowly, make conversation—his head feels "like a waste basket."

"Araki Thomas," much sketchier, sets a similar theme back in the 17th Century. A Japanese youth, converted by Catholic missionaries, is sent to Rome to study. When Japan's rulers begin to persecute its small Catholic community, he returns unwillingly to face what his Roman sponsors glowingly prescribe as glorious martyrdom. Upon arrival, he promptly abjures the faith.

In an introduction, Endo notes that these stories, written 25 years ago, present a starker picture of the divide between Japanese and Western culture than the one he has come to hold. Now he sees hopes of transcending it, he writes, perhaps by studying the subconscious.

Yet to the Western reader, the flash of revelation is as remarkable as ever. There are moments in these stories where the author is able to make us feel Japanese ourselves. Perhaps that is an exaggeration. But he does make us feel, at times, as much of a suffering stranger inside our own culture.

Scott Baldauf (review date 27 July 1990)

SOURCE: "Between Two Cultures," in *The Christian Science Monitor,* July 27, 1990, p. 13.

[*In the following review, Baldauf discusses how Endo's* Foreign Studies *makes valid points about the tension between two cultures in its three stories of Japanese Christians.*]

When Portuguese missionaries landed in Japan in 1549, they proclaimed the Japanese to be the most spiritual race in Asia. Peasants and noblemen converted by the hundreds of thousands.

Fearing a loss of sovereignty, Japanese warlords booted the Portuguese out in 1614, and Japanese converts were forced to recant or face torture and death. Until the arrival of Admiral Matthew Calbraith Perry's warships some 240 years later, Japan's doors were shut to the white man. Some would argue that the doors remain shut today.

The persecution of Japanese Christians has been fertile subject matter for novelists, but perhaps no one addresses it better than Shusaku Endo.

Converting to Roman Catholicism after his parents' divorce, Endo soon realized that by worshipping an "alien" god, he had ripped himself out of the fabric of Japanese society. And as the initial euphoria of conversion wore off, Endo discovered that Europeans themselves fail to practice many of the teachings he valued most in Christianity. Little wonder that many of Endo's fictional characters struggle with a dual identity, Asian and Western.

> **The best of Endo's novels, including the chilling *Silence,* and *The Samurai,* are plot-driven, semi-historical fiction, and Japanese readers have consumed them like rice cakes.**
>
> *—Scott Baldauf*

The best of Endo's novels, including the chilling *Silence,* and *The Samurai,* are plot-driven, semi-historical fiction, and Japanese readers have consumed them like rice cakes. The stories retain their verve and directness, even in translation. Writing mainly for a non Christian Japanese audience, Endo steers away from preaching. He describes such religious symbols as crucifixes or church top gargoyles through Japanese eyes. The effect can be startling.

An early book, *Foreign Studies* has only recently found an English translator. It is composed of three separate narratives in France and Italy from the early 1600s to today.

In the first story, **"Kudo,"** a Japanese seminarian in France during the 1950s struggles against the cultural arrogance of his well meaning host family as he enters the Roman Catholic priesthood. Endo then shows us Araki Thomas, a Japanese priest fully 300 years before, dispirited because Rome is more interested in him as a future missionary than as a recent convert. The third and most developed story follows Tanaka, a timorous lecturer in French literature who travels to Paris in the 1960s to do research on the Marquis de Sade.

Each character suffers from an isolation that goes beyond homesickness. And because the Japanese value not showing emotion or weakness, their Western acquaintances assume that all is well.

Endo presents the West in general, and the Catholic Church in particular, as exploiting Japanese respect for authority. Obligations to the church merely replace the obligation they once felt to family and country. Defeated while their faith is still uncertain, Endo's Japanese grudgingly admit that Christianity is unsuited to their culture.

But he makes his readers wonder if Western culture has learned much from the religion it preaches. After all, the Europe that embraced Christ also toyed with the ideas of the Marquis de Sade.

And that leads us to Tanaka, a bumblingly shy man who lacks popularity even with his fellow Japanese in Paris. Many post war French intellectuals like Simone DeBeauvoir and Jean Paul Sartre saw parallels between fascism and the unabashed evil of the Marquis, and Tanaka thought he could enhance his position at his university in Japan by becoming a Sade specialist. Although lacking Sade's assertiveness to act, he shares Sade's emotional depravity.

Endo has disavowed the pessimism of *Foreign Studies,* but by releasing it to the West some 25 years after its Japanese debut, he clearly felt the novel could help us understand those who are torn between their own and a Western identity. And he's right. The points it makes are valid and harrowing, and beautifully developed.

Jeffrey Bernard Allen (review date 24 October 1990)

SOURCE: A review of *Foreign Studies,* in *The Christian Century,* Vol. 107, No. 30, October 24, 1990, pp. 973-74.

[*In the following review, Allen asserts that Endo's true subject in* Foreign Studies *is the mystery of identity.*]

The clash of cultures is an old theme of universal relevance. Shusaku Endo is a Japanese Roman Catholic who writes about the social and cultural distances between the East and the West. This book is a collection of three stories first published in Japan in 1965 and now translated by Mark Williams. All three stories concern Japanese intellectuals who experience alienation in the West—a very personal theme for Endo, who studied for several years in Lyon, France.

In the first story, **"A Summer in Rouen,"** a young Japanese student named Kudo is invited to stay with a devout Roman Catholic family in the provincial town. It is soon after the war and Kudo is forced to endure the family's ethnic misconceptions as well as their attempts to mold him into a good

Catholic. The story concludes with his almost unbearable feelings of alienation.

The second story ends on a similarly pessimistic note. Narrated in a journalistic style, the story is a speculative biography of a real figure from Japanese history, Araki Thomas, who studies for the priesthood in 17th century Rome. Angered at the West's attempt to introduce Christianity to Japan by any means, the emperor starts persecuting Christians. Thomas's contact with the West makes him a marked man, though it gains him an almost saintly status with Japanese Christians. Thomas finds himself burdened by a devotion to his faith. He returns home and is eventually executed.

The final story, **"And You, Too,"** is the longest and most substantial look at the burden of Western culture. Tanaka, a timid Japanese scholar of French literature, comes to Paris in the mid '60s to research the life and work of the Marquis de Sade. Where Kudo and Thomas had problems understanding Western notions of virtue, Tanaka has equal problems understanding Western ideas of sin. His inability to decipher Sade is symbolic of an overall failure to penetrate the heart of European beliefs, customs and practices.

Whereas another of Endo's books, *Silence,* suggests the possibility of genuine understanding between East and West, this book offers no such vision. But the failure is part of a larger failure, expressing the workings of Endo's true subject: the mystery of identity. If Endo's characters are alienated from the West, they are equally alienated from themselves. Given the dark recesses of the soul, we are all foreigners.

Elizabeth Beverly (review date 23 November 1990)

SOURCE: "The Tyranny of Our Incarnation," in *Commonweal,* Vol. CXVII, No. 20, November 23, 1990, pp. 700-02.

[*In the following review, Beverly asserts that Endo's* Foreign Studies *is about what she calls "the tyranny of our incarnation" in which we are born into one existence and yearn to reach to each other as well as ourselves.*]

Consider this book. The author calls it a novel even though it consists of one twenty five page long, perfectly realized short story, one swift historical account in twelve pages, and a long (one hundred seventy nine page) narrative that is primarily novelistic in impulse. The book was written in the mid sixties, in Japanese; finally, in 1989, the English translation appeared. In the preface, the author likens his former authorial self, the one who penned this novel, to "a pitiful younger brother." And the author is Shusaku Endo, the ardent and prolific Japanese Catholic whose most recently written novel *Scandal* concerns the subject of sexual perversion in contemporary Japan, whose masterwork *Silence* explores the apostasy of a seventeenth century Portuguese missionary, and whose Life of Jesus derives its warmth from a consideration of the mother like qualities of Christ.

Consider the plight of the reviewer who in a short space is asked to bring the book to life for you. Should I tell you what it feels like to read *Foreign Studies*? Tell you that the experience is rather like setting off on a somewhat brisk but steady trek with an acquaintance whose personal habits are both rigorous and ascetic, someone who expects you to trust him every step of the way? The terrain is somewhat rocky, unfamiliar, so you do, and just as you think that your footing is sure, Endo stops and says, "Look!" Naturally you look up, expecting to see some grand vista or unsuspecting animal. But Endo directs your eyes downward, to a spot not far from your own feet where flourishes a startling patch of language and thought, at once familiar but bizarre, and therefore oddly beautiful:

> In the winter evening light (Tanaka) could make out a couple of grooves like railway lines, which had apparently been created by the wheels of passing traffic. He had never seen such a road in Tokyo. He was convinced that no such road existed in Japan. He had never before experienced such a road, tinged as it was with the smell of human habitation and the sweaty odor of human feet. If it had been possible, he would have liked to dig up this road . . . and take it home with him. And had he not felt so inhibited, he would even have liked to run his tongue over it.

Within this patch of language from **"And You, Too,"** the third section of *Foreign Studies,* and within Endo's insistence that we linger with him over such a spot, lies his challenge to us as readers: we must read with the same awareness of the need for the conscious, moral life which preoccupies Endo as he writes. Our primary task is not to be distracted by twists in plot or the development of the protagonist, typical novelistic endeavors. Our job is to bear witness to the predicament of a particular person in a particular situation. In this instance, the person is Tanaka, an assistant professor of literary studies who has come to France to continue his research on the Marquis de Sade. And at this instant, a surge of bodily longing has caught Tanaka totally and uncharacteristically off guard.

Tanaka is a worrier; he frets over his advancement, he plans his strategies for research. He's fussy and judgmental, disheartened by the dreariness of Paris, unwilling to be embarrassed by Japanese who haven't "made it" in the expatriate life. In the midsixties enough Japanese have thrived in Europe in the two decades since the Second World War to create a known community. But Tanaka cares nothing for them.

He sees Paris as a necessary way station on the path to academic success in his homeland. He's convinced that he studies Sade only to offer an eighteenth century European commodity.

But as Tanaka worries his way through this long narrative, we see that the remarkable combination of self absorption and alienation from deeper feelings of sympathy for self and others renders Tanaka oddly reminiscent of Sade, not in his monstrousness, but in the mindlessness that allows monstrousness to take root and grow. Estranged from himself and from those impulses that serve to sweeten life (Tanaka focuses periodically on the snapshot of his baby son), he literally errs, strays from the community that might help him.

But for the Endo who wrote *Foreign Studies,* the plight of the "stranger" is to be estranged. The collision of culture with culture, of the lone Easterner with the historically dense West, promises a suffering that enters the body itself. The three protagonists: Kudo, a fifties' student who finds his housing with a devout Catholic family in **"A Summer in Rouen"** to be an invitation for shame; **"Araki Thomas,"** the first Japanese student to study in Europe in the seventeenth century and return to a homeland in which the banning of Catholicism now requires of him either martyrdom or apostasy; as well as Tanaka in **"And You, Too,"** all find that one's true spirit may be alienated from one's body as long as there are others to please or to satisfy, as long as appearances must be kept up, as long as one must hide oneself.

But for some, the body in its sorrow and aloneness can no longer lie, and asks the spirit to join it. This is the mystery of physical suffering, and the gift for a character such as Tanaka is his inability to transcend his suffering body; he must claim it, know it, feel it, and in this way must begin to intuit his common tie with the imprisoned Sade, his own dark brother. Time and cultural difference may separate, but lone suffering brings together. When Tanaka feels his body thrill to the scent of a well traveled road, we suspect that only the surprise of the embodied life can save him, but we don't necessarily suspect that his salvation will reside in an almost predictable sickness. Still, Endo closes his narrative before he allows any salvation to mar the studied cynicism of the text.

Although Endo's conscious intention in this novel is to elaborate the agony and risk of cultural conflict in which the "other" is devalued by the ascendant culture, his profound achievement is in his portrayal of what could be called the tyranny of our incarnation. That we must be born into one body, in one place, at one time, seems to determine our lot. We yearn to reach each other across these baffling distances, and cannot reach even ourselves. Foreign Studies provides a wise and compelling exploration of the problem, but Endo does not bother with hope.

Ironically, Endo, in his striking ability to bring his Japanese characters so fully to our lives, undercuts his own pessimism. If you choose to follow him, you will discover that the pleasure of reading lies not in finding out "what happens to whom," but rests in the simple act of accompanying another person, letting your pace imitate his pace, slowly matching your breathing to his, feeling his sense of the trek enter you, so that your mind can fill with the questions, with the disturbances, with the affections, with the life that floods his sight as he guides you. Endo is a rare novelist, a determined thinker who quite simply ranges over territory no one else even knows is there.

For this reason it would be wise to give yourself the chance to consider this book.

Paul Binding (review date 30 April 1993)

SOURCE: "Sad in Japan," in *New Statesman & Society,* Vol. 6, No. 250, April 30, 1993, p. 44.

[*In the following review, Binding discusses the stories in Endo's* The Final Martyrs *and asserts that Endo gives a view of the power of suffering and insight into late 20th-century urban life.*]

"Dogs and little birds still appear frequently in my fiction," says the novelist narrator of the story **"Shadows"**, "but they are no mere decorations . . . Even today, the moist grieving eyes of dogs somehow remind me of the eyes of Christ. This Christ I speak of is, of course, not the Christ filled with assurance of his own way of life. It is the weary Christ, trampled upon by men and looking up at them from beneath their feet."

These lines are of Endo's very essence; the attraction, in a Japanese middle-class milieu, to the Catholic Christianity bequeathed by his mother is precisely in its moral and spiritual elevation of the confused, the downtrodden, the insulted and the injured. And in its forgiving inclusion of the errant.

The Church was founded by one who betrayed his master; Japanese Catholicism was kept alive in secret by those who, converted by Portuguese or French missionaries, had capitulated out of cowardice to the cruelties of the authorities and apostates. In the title story, the large elephant like protagonist who so easily becomes terrified in the face of trouble is almost given dispensation for his weakness. Christ, it's suggested, will be made happy merely by the times (before he runs away again) when he keeps company with his fellow believers. It is not difficult for a non Japanese to appreciate how, against the cultures first of Tojo and the war lords and then of Japan's postwar "miracle", such aspects of Christianity would have their appeal.

In an interesting preface, Endo explains that he writes short stories to familiarise himself with the material he will turn into novels. Certainly each of the stories in this wonderful volume has something of a novel's richness and discursiveness. Readers will see openings to one novel or another throughout the book. Endo is a writer who works very much from his experimental grammar of metaphors. The Catholic priest in a non-Catholic society; "colonial" childhood in Manchuria; the unease of the graduate in the immediate postwar years; the appalling paraphernalia of illness; the contemporary writer trying to establish the moisture of spiritual life in an arid materialist society—all these predicaments are to be found here.

Endo is unflinchingly autobiographical. The moving **"A Sixty Year Old Man"**, for instance, was written when the author had turned 60 himself, extending his so ample charity even to his own ageing self as he records his pathetic hankerings after young girls witnessed in bars or parks.

Three stories in particular seem strong and generously worked in precisely the same way as his novels. **"Lies"**, from Endo's Manchurian boyhood, deals with the long term significance of interactions with those seemingly on the margins of our lives. **"The Last Supper"** and **"The Box"** present the unmanageable anguish consequent on certain compulsory immersions in the violent events of contemporary history.

The main characters here have had their whole beings defiled by the moral anarchy unleashed by war (in Burma and in mainland Japan in the second world war's last stages). It is Endo's triumph that his sense of the totalitarian power of suffering does not diminish his insights into quotidian, late 20th century urban life—and vice versa.

Kirkus Reviews (review date 1 July 1994)

SOURCE: A review of *The Final Martyrs,* in *Kirkus Reviews,* Vol. LXII, No. 13, July 1, 1994, p. 865.

[*In the following review, the critic points out the autobiographical nature of the stories in Endo's* The Final Martyrs.]

Somber, haunting stories that resonate with compassion, eloquence, and metaphor.

Once again, Endo (*Foreign Studies,* 1990, etc.) explores the themes for which he is famous: Roman Catholics in Japan, the illness and fear of aging, the pain of divorce, the loneliness of childhood. In this collection of 11 stories written over the last 30 years, autobiography continues to take a front seat: Endo finds inspiration in his own experience with lung disease to address physical suffering; in his parents' loveless relationship to address loss of innocence and compromise; in his own experience with Christianity to address, as the apostate in the almost epic title story, the question of whether or not it is all right to be afraid and run away from a commitment to Christianity in the face of persecution; and in his increasing age to tackle nostalgia, regret, and resignation. To make these heavy topics even murkier, they often overlap in ways that would be overwhelming to someone without Endo's fresh and gentle touch. Spiritual decline feels natural as **"A Fifty Year Old Man,"** a disillusioned husband, offers an almost comic look at watching his dog die a slow death. In **"Shadows,"** it's a relief when a writer finally understands that he doesn't understand the priest who was his childhood mentor, nemesis, and betrayer. And we recognize the writer in **"The Box"** who follows the trail of postcards he finds in an antiques shop to discover love, betrayal, and espionage while wondering if "perhaps I think up such nonsensical, irrational things because I am getting old." What might otherwise feel like giving up becomes giving in to the unrecognized power of the human condition. This is the precious uncertainty of all of Endo's delicate dreams.

A strange celebration of life and death that is wise but never weary.

Peregrine Hodson (review date 9 July 1994)

SOURCE: "Heavy Themes with a Light Touch," in *Spectator,* Vol. 273, No. 8661, July 9, 1994, pp. 33-4.

[In the following review, Hodson points out that Endo writes about heavy themes in his novel Deep River, *but that he "explores them with a lightness of touch that avoids sensationalism."]*

Shusaku Endo is a strong candidate to win Japan's next Nobel prize for literature. He's also a Christian. So far, so good. But sitting in the shade beside a pool in Umbria, or huddled on the beach at Southwold, *Spectator* readers might think twice before choosing his book—about a group of Japanese pilgrims going to Benares—for holiday reading. Japan, Christianity, India . . . it all seems a bit too much like hard work. Why not settle for the real stuff that's safe, familiar and predictable—another helping of exclamation marks from Julie Burchill, or something nice and undemanding by Amanda Craig?

The author of ***Deep River*** is unafraid to write about the things which most of us prefer to ignore, like death, guilt, and the inability to love—hardly topics to enliven a villa party. Endo is a serious writer. Cannibalism, religion, sex and reincarnation are heavy themes, but he explores them with a lightness of touch that avoids sensationalism.

The story is simple and elegantly structured. Each character has a secret wound which, one way or another, they hope to heal; the husband grieving for his dead wife, the writer recovering from a terrible illness, the woman who believes in nothing, and the old soldier represented by ghosts of the past. Their paths converge on Benares, by the banks of the Ganges, where a young Japanese man, Otsu, lives in poverty, carrying the sick and the dying to the river.

In the course of their respective journeys, Endo explores the limitations of Eastern and Western attitudes to suffering and, it has to be said, the meaning of life. This willingness to test the deeper currents of existence may seem foolish to people used to the shallows of contemporary writing. Big ideas are faintly embarrassing—much better if they remain where they belong, below the surface. Besides, big ideas don't make big money—unless they fit the fashionable formula. Apart from the Bible, Christianity is rarely the ingredient for a bestseller. But in Japan, *Deep River* has sold 300,000 copies in hardback.

The hyper-materialism of Japan is strange ground for Endo's mysticism. But perhaps the Japanese recognize, in his vision of the world, something absent from their own. It may not be what they want, but it might be what they need. In the same way, *Deep River* might just be the book to have beside the pool, or the sea. The translation is natural and unobtrusive. Lose some inhibitions. Forget inertia. Find out more about the Onion.

Publishers Weekly (review date 15 August 1994)

SOURCE: A review of *The Final Martyrs,* in *Publishers Weekly,* Vol. 241, No. 32, August 15, 1994, p. 88.

[In the following review, the critic discusses the different topics covered in Endo's short story collection The Final Martyrs.]

In a calm, delicate, unobtrusive manner, several of these 11 deceptively simple stories by Japanese novelist Endo (***The Golden Country***) show people wrestling with spiritual crises, extreme situations or life's central issues. In **"The Last Supper,"** an alcoholic corporate executive confesses to a psychiatrist the source of his torment: as a starving soldier in WW II, he ate a dead comrade's flesh. In **"Heading Home,"** a man exhumes his mother's body, buried 30 years earlier, in order to cremate her remains and place them with the ashes of his recently deceased brother. In the title story, set in the 1860s, when the Meiji government outlawed Christianity, a village coward recants his Christian faith to avoid the torture meted out to his fellow converts, but he ultimately redeems himself through an act of quiet courage. This deftly translated collection, comprised of stories written as early as

1959 and as late as 1985, also includes semi autobiographical tales in which Endo deals with the traumatic impact that his parent's divorce had on his boyhood. He also writes with grace, compassion and gentle humor about old age, love betrayed, Japanese tourists and the marks we leave on the lives of others.

Karl Schoenberger (review date 18 September 1994)

SOURCE: "A Voice of Moral Reasoning," in *Los Angeles Times Book Review,* September 18, 1994.

[*In the following review, Schoenberger discusses how Endo guides his characters in a search for the moral truth without sounding pompous or preachy in his collection of short stories* The Final Martyrs.]

In a country where the conservative Establishment remains unapologetic about the stain of naked aggression during World War II, and where a ranking cabinet minister recently denied the veracity of the Nanking Massacre, Shusaku Endo stands out as a lonely voice in a wasteland of moral reasoning. This Roman Catholic writer, often described as Japan's Graham Greene, has been struggling with the slippery themes of right and wrong, defiance and cowardice, martyrdom and apostasy since his country emerged, psychically burned and morally bewildered, from the debacle of war.

His fiction may not translate with the brilliance of a twisted artist such as Yukio Mishima. But Endo is one of the rare living Japanese intellectuals who truly grasps the absolute moral values that the Western World has enshrined—and betrayed—for two millennia, and which the colicky collective consciousness of Japanese society has only partially digested over the last 150 years.

Endo's journey through Japan's postwar spiritual malaise is reflected darkly in *The Final Martyrs,* a collection of short stories originally published between 1959 and 1985, now available in translation for American readers in an edition brought out by New Directions. The reader should be warned, however: these are not short pieces of fiction in the conventional sense. Endo is less concerned with entertainment value than with his message.

Indeed, these are not short stories at all, but rather character sketches and rambling essays in the confessional *zuihitsu* style, a stilled genre that is unfortunately far too prevalent in contemporary Japanese literature. Copiously detailed footnotes grace one of these stories, apparently part of the original text. It should be noted that Endo made his mark as a man of letters in the genre of historical fiction. It pays to be patient with his dull, gray sincerity.

Endo's emblematic work is the 1966 novel *Silence* (*Chinmoku*), which is perhaps his answer to Greene's The Power and the Glory, exploring the psychological horror of the persecution of Christian martyrs in 17th Century Japan. In this novel, Endo introduces his most powerful metaphor: the "swamp" of Japan, which consumes and obliterates the alien ideal that an individual has a right to stand against the crowd with a politically unpopular conviction.

The novel's theme was foreshadowed in the title story of this collection, **"The Final Martyrs,"** first published in 1959. It describes the ruthless persecution of the supposedly liberated "hidden Christians" in Southern Japan, who practiced their faith in secret during the 250 years that Christianity was outlawed by feudal authorities. The story is set in the small village of Nakano, near Nagasaki, in the early Meiji era, when the new oligarchic regime felt the same urge to suppress dangerous thoughts.

Significantly, Endo suggests a continuity of social management from feudal barbarism to modern thought control, which persisted through the ugly war years and, I would argue, is alive and well beneath contemporary Japan's veneer of liberal democracy.

Endo uses the final martyrs to show how difficult it is to embrace an absolute moral truth in the swamp of Japan. The villagers mix and muddle the absolute values of faith and devotion to Christ with the traditional, diffuse loyalties to the social group. The village ethos is clearly grafted onto the remnants of the Christian ethic, transmitted clandestinely over the generations.

A mentally disabled lad, Kisuke, is the prop demonstrating this cultural confusion. The village idiot is at first ridiculed and ostracized by his peers in the youth organization because he is mentally weak and cowardly, in a classic example of group bullying. "He has a weakness for pain, after all, and so I imagine he'd whimper in agony. Why, maybe he might even abandon the Lord Jesus and topple," says one of Kisuke's detractors.

But in the end Kisuke finds a reserve of courage, and he is shown true mercy by one of the final martyrs, as both face torture and death.

The last story in the collection, **"The Box"** (1985), is a musing essay that weaves in and out of a another parable of Christian charity. We hear a doddering Endo wonder whether talking to the plants in his study will help them grow, as he recounts the tale of an old box of pictures and postcards he once bought in the resort town of Karuizawa. The contents of the box take him on a trail of intrigue, espionage and betrayal, all involving a half Japanese foreign woman who was harassed by the thought police in wartime Japan.

"A dark, gloomy, at times even dismal atmosphere hung over Karuizawa during the war," Endo writes. "Foreigners of various nations, on the pretext they were being evacuated from military targets, were assembled here, and while on the surface they led normal lives, in reality they were under surveillance by the Japanese secret police and military police."

Endo's didactic technique, a blend of first person narrative with anecdotal fiction, is tolerable because his own voice is restrained and understated. The writer is not pompous, preaching from a pulpit high above his frail characters but a humble guide to the moral conundrum of his people.

"Over the years," Endo writes in the preface to the English edition, "I have forged intimate familial ties with [my] characters, who are a reflection and a portion of myself."

Frank Tuohy (review date 28 October 1994)

SOURCE: "Good Girls," in *The Times Literary Supplement,* October 28, 1994.

[*In the following review, Tuohy recommends reading Endo's* The Girl I Left Behind, *but asserts that* Deep River *will disappoint Endo's devotees.*]

With a dozen or so of his books translated into English, Shusako Endo must now be the best known Japanese novelist in the West. In his own country, however, his reputation is hedged around with qualifications, some of which may be reactions to the very things which attract and interest the foreign reader. These doubts on the home front would have prejudiced Endo's chances of becoming what his countrymen like to call a "Nobelist". Instead, this year's prize has gone to Kenzaburo Oe, a more avant garde writer, less successful but possibly for that reason more quintessentially Japanese.

V. S. Naipaul once wrote that "the Japanese are possessed of a way of looking—that curious literalness which adds up to a detachment formidable enough to seem pointless". Even so, he concluded, this involves a hunger for the seen and a concern with humanity. It is this concern which is in strongest evidence in Endo's work. He may be Japan's first writer to move outside the limiting social structures of his own culture and to write confidently about the outside world, depicting Polish prostitutes and French landladies as readily as his own countrymen. He is harshest in his judgment of the latter, evoking persecution and torture—as in his great novel *Silence*—and minimizing the aesthetic aspects which other writers have stressed. In *The Sea and Poison,* about wartime atrocities, there is a memorable moment when a young GI prisoner of war is introduced to a bunch of Japanese doctors. Brought up to respect the medical profession, he is polite and friendly, while their intention is to test his capacity for survival until he dies.

Endo's writing is tirelessly, repetitively, autobiographical. Born in the puppet state of Manchuria, he returned to Japan with his mother after his parents' divorce. At fourteen, he was converted to—one might say dragooned into—the Roman Catholic faith. During the war he lived in a Christian dormitory, followed by university and a period in France. Prominent Catholic novelists of the post war scene, such as François Mauriac and Julien Green, have clearly had a strong influence. He shares with Graham Greene a view of his faith as something equivalent to a viral infection. His religion is hardly joyous—nothing much in Endo is—but it is inescapable. There is a recurrent image of the sadness in Christ's face, which is compared to the expression of the dog the boy Shusaku left behind in Manchuria.

Endo has written extensively about the tragic and anomalous situation of Christianity in Japan. Silence deals with the apostasy, under torture, of a Christian missionary. The martyrdoms continued when the country was in isolation, until some years after the arrival of Commander Perry and his black ships. The very survival of garbled versions of the faith in isolated villages on the island of Kyushu is proof of its enduring power. History is full of forgotten suffering, and Endo finds a modern equivalent in the cancer ward, an example of unmentionable pain in ordinary society.

Christian novelists veer towards the dangerous edges, to paradox, doubt, apostasy. Endo's *Scandal* shows him doing this. The idea is to be found in a story by Vladimir Nabokov and an experience recorded by Graham Greene: a famous writer discovers that a stranger is using his name, passing himself off as the genuine article. *Scandal,* a Manichaean fable of insistent power, ends by casting doubt on the division of the two selves, true and false.

It is more powerful, it has to be admitted, than either of the two novels at present under review. In a new afterword to the English translation of *The Girl I Left Behind,* itself written some thirty years ago, Endo states that Mitsu, the young woman who is its central character, "has continued to live with me ever since and can be seen reincarnated in my most recent novel *Deep River* in the person of the protagonist Otsu". Both Mitsu and Otsu, a male theological student, are efforts at depicting pure goodness. A difficult task, for even Dostoevsky failed to make Alyosha Karamazov as interesting as his brothers.

The Girl I Left Behind misleads us with its dust jacket and end papers showing an elegant beauty of the Showa period. Mitsu is very different, one of those plain, pigeon toed young women you see asleep on their feet in the Tokyo Metro or, if seated, obsessively examining their long hair for split ends. As students, they wear ankle socks, carry pencil boxes ornamented with Paddington Bear and hang their heads if spoken to. Full of romantic dreams, love for them is a mixture of hope, despair and impossibility. They pursue ecstatically the "male" stars of the Takarazuka girls' theatre, and a few years ago, they packed out the cinema which was showing the Merchant Ivory film of *Maurice.*

Through an advertisement in a movie magazine, Motsu meets Yoshioka, an impoverished, sex starved young man who shares a room with a fellow student in the chaotic squalor which descends on Japanese males when they have no women to look after them. The whole relationship is bungled: sexual love is low on Endo's scale of values. Mitsu falls in love, but Yoshioka only goes back to her when he can't find anyone else. Gradually we learn that Mitsu has performed a number of completely selfless actions until, one day finding a strange mark on her skin, she is dispatched to a leprosarium run by Catholic nuns. She learns to live among the other patients, then is told that she has been wrongly diagnosed. Thrust back into the world, she gets as far as the local railway station. Then she returns; without converting to Christianity, she spends the rest of her life among the lepers. Endo tells us that the original of Mitsu was a well to do young woman from Kyoto. He has heightened the picture by making his heroine one of the despised and rejected. In spite of some technical clumsiness, one is ready to believe in her all the way.

Deep River presents the Japanese as the rest of the world has come to see them—as tourists. This tour group is visiting Buddhist sites in India, which turn out to be rare—Buddhism, like Christianity having abandoned the birthplace of its founder. It is no surprise to find that these tourists are all seeking or fleeing from the meaning of their lives. Isobe's dying wife whispers: "I know I'll be reborn somewhere else in the world. . . . Look for me." Armed with the information that an Indian child has been heard speaking Japanese, he joins the tour. Mitsuko, a shallow, self confident divorcee, seduced a young man called Otsu when they were both students, under the influence of a novel, *Moira,* by Julien Green. She fails to deflect him from his vocation, though some pre Vatican II instructors in France nearly succeed. Otsu has found his true calling in helping the dying on the banks of the Ganges. Numada, a writer, is another self portrait, recycling once more the childhood in Manchuria. There is the usual tourist whose wife wants to go shopping, and whose insistence on taking photographs leads to Otsu's death in a riot.

I read ***Deep River,*** believing in the characters more than their motivation, which seems factitious. There are some over informative descriptions of India. But most of the time there are echoes of bygone bestsellers—Louis Bromfield, James

Hilton or *The Razor's Edge,* Somerset Maugham's popular success which used Indian imprecision to keep its metaphysics warm. ***Deep River*** has sold 300,000 copies in Japan, but I think it will disappoint Endo's devotees. They should certainly read ***The Girl I Left Behind,*** with its moving portrayal of the saintly Mitsu. Beginners are better advised to go for ***Silence*** or ***Scandal,*** or some of the excellent short stories.

Kirkus Reviews (review date 1 February 1995)

SOURCE: A review of *Deep River,* in *Kirkus Reviews,* Vol. LXIII, No. 3, February 1, 1995, pp. 89-90.

[*In the following review, the critic praises the strong and original characters in Endo's* Deep River.]

Japanese writer Endo (***The Final Martyrs,*** 1994, etc.) continues his exploration of faith and anomie—in a deceptively simple and well told story of spiritual inquiry that movingly explores all the big questions.

The opening pages briefly introduce four people who will shortly, for varying reasons, join a Japanese tour-group travelling to India: Isobe, a businessman whose deceased wife, believing she would "be reborn somewhere in this world," made him promise he would look for her; Mitsuko, a volunteer at the dead woman's hospital, who is troubled by her own past and her obsession with a former classmate; retired industrialist Kiguchi, still haunted by wartime memories of Burma's notorious Highway of Death; and Numanda, a gentle writer of children's books who wants to repay his debt to the bird that saved his life when he was desperately ill. The book investigates the role religion plays in contemporary Japan, where relatives attending a funeral politely question the Buddhist priest conducting the service, while "not one of them really believed anything the priest was saying." As the trip gets under way, more disquiets are explored: Isobe can't forget how he ignored his wife when she was alive; Mitsuko hungers for love but can't abandon her cynicism; Kiguchi recalls a fellow veteran who saved his life by eating human flesh but then drank himself to death trying to forget what he had done; and Numanda muses on the central role nature has played in his life. The four finally experience their epiphanies on the banks of the Ganges at Varanasi, where the old and afflicted come to die and the faithful immerse themselves in the river. In this richly detailed setting, Endo offers a faith that, using the river as metaphor, comfortingly blends all the great religions together.

Conflicts a bit too neatly resolved, but saved from mawkishness by strong and original characters.

Patricia O'Connell (review date 19 May 1995)

SOURCE: "Deep Endo," in *Commonweal,* Vol. CXXII, No. 10, May 19, 1995, pp. 34-5.

[In the following review, O'Connell asserts that in Endo's Deep River *and his* The Final Martyrs *the author is reiterating, although sometimes expanding on his major theme: the struggle to fuse Christianity and Eastern culture.]*

In two newly translated volumes, a novel and a story collection, Japanese Catholic Shusaku Endo reiterates and sometimes expands upon his major theme—the frustration of trying to fuse Western Christianity and Eastern culture.

The novel *Deep River* may take its title from the Negro spiritual that provides its epigraph, but the setting here is not the American South—it is India, the destination of a Japanese tourist group, and the river is the Ganges, "so deep," in the words of the sometimes cynical character Mitsuko, "I feel as though it's not just for the Hindus but for everyone." This shift of locale from Japan, which provides the backdrop for most of Endo's fiction, offers the author an opportunity to move beyond his typical exposition of the East West dichotomy, to explore how yet another culture and religion can rattle expectations and provide new self revelations for his characters.

Among the tourists are Isobe, a non-demonstrative office worker who's recently lost his long-neglected wife, Keiko, to cancer; and, on the trip by chance, Mitsuko, a divorced volunteer at the hospital where Keiko died. Mitsuko's leisure time do goodism with patients seems at odds with her coldness and lack of faith, but the complexity of her character and the terrible loneliness with which she lives are convincingly revealed as the novel progresses. Also making the trip are Numada, a writer of animal stories who's often mistakenly ghettoized in the book world as a children's author, and Kiguchi, a former soldier obsessed with his experiences on the Highway of Death in Burma during World War II. What would otherwise be a central-casting stereotype—the photosnapping tourist from hell—is here transformed into a pivotal role in the person of Sanjo, an ambitious, obnoxious newlywed; even his wife is just another stepping stone in his well orchestrated and utterly compassionless life plan. Another interesting spin in the character mix is Enami, the guide from Cosmos Tour Company, who secretly despises the travelers he leads through this foreign land.

Most intriguing of all, however, is Otsu—not a member of the tour group but Mitsuko's former schoolmate who is now a Catholic priest living in an ashram. An outsider while a college student because of his religious fervor, Otsu ironically becomes another kind of outsider while studying for the priesthood because, for example, he cannot shed his East-

ern belief in the commingling of good and evil; this notion is dangerously "Jansenistic or Manichaeistic," he is told by more traditional Catholic teachers. He fulfills his priestly vocation in carrying the bodies of dead Hindu pilgrims, outcasts, to funeral pyres near the river Ganges for cremation. When asked how he reconciles the Hindu belief in reincarnation with Christianity, he explains, "Every one of [the disciples] had stayed alive by abandoning [Jesus] and running away. He continued to love them even though they had betrayed him. As a result, he was etched into each of their guilty hearts. He died, but he was restored to life in their hearts."

The letters between characters in this novel reinforce Endo's reputation as a marvelous epistolary writer; he would have given Paul et al. some stiff competition had he lived in New Testament times. And he once again proves himself the master of the quirky, unforgettable detail: when Isobe learns his wife has terminal cancer, he simultaneously hears outside the hospital window "the voice of a street vendor peddling roasted sweet potatoes—*Yaki imo o o.*" Any reader acquainted with Endo's work knows of its highly autobiographical nature. This attention to sounds in his latest writing reminds us that Endo spent a good deal of time in his life listening to painful silences (or arguments) before his parents' divorce, to the unfamiliar Mass that his mother chose as his form of worship when he was a schoolboy in a Buddhist country, to the medical professionals who have operated on and muttered ominously over his lungs for too much of his life, to the French spoken during his adult years as a student in Lyon, where he willfully exposed himself to a culture imbued not only with that prickly Christianity but also a fierce national pride, and where he must have felt even more an outsider than as a Catholic in Japan.

Familiar themes also resonate throughout his second story collection. In the title story of *The Final Martyrs,* Endo again reveals his fascination with apostasy. In **"Shadows,"** an epistolary piece, we see a grown man writing to a priest, now separated from the church, who loomed large in the man's childhood after his parents had split up and his mother had arranged for herself and her son to convert to Catholicism (which his father refers to as "one of those 'Amen' churches"). Two stories here, **"A Fifty Year Old Man"** and **"A Sixty Year Old Man,"** are march-of-time semisequels to **"A Forty Year Old Man,"** which appeared in Endo's first story collection, *Stained Glass Elegies* (1987); the oldest protagonist in these stories is in fact the author of *The Life of Jesus* (1979), nonfiction that Endo himself wrote. **"Japanese in Warsaw,"** which includes a tourist loathing guide (this time Shimzu of the Orbis Travel Bureau), has certain parallels with *Deep River* and also with **"Fudano Tsuji"** in *Stained Glass Elegies.* Both involve the Polish saint, Maximilian Kolbe, who at one point served in Nagasaki as a missionary and later sacrificed his life at Auschwitz. In **"The Last Supper"** we see Kiguchi, somewhat transformed from his role in Endo's latest novel, but still entangled in a tale of the Burmese Highway of Death. Indeed, the similarities between these stories and Endo's other works are too numerous to mention. Whether one considers the repetition among the stories, novels, drama, sketches, and memoir pieces intriguing or exasperating is up to the individual reader.

The historical novel **Silence** (1980), concerning the apostate Jesuit missionary Christovao Ferreira and his former seminary student Sebastian Rodrigues in seventeenth-century Japan (and reportedly being filmed by director Martin Scorsese), remains Endo's masterpiece, but these two new works, beautifully translated by Van C. Gessel, are welcome additions to the author's *oeuvre* in English. Let's hope that New Directions continues to publish the award winning Endo in this country and that such publications spur more lengthy analysis of this writer's life and work.

Michael Harris (review date 22 May 1995)

SOURCE: "The Various Paths that Lead to God," in *Los Angeles Times,* May 22, 1995, p. E4.

[*In the following review, Harris complains that two of the main characters of Endo's* Deep River *"are the sort of people we bump into only in religious novels," but he asserts that the powerful images at the end of the novel redeem it.*]

For Western readers, Shusaku Endo has long been one of the most accessible Japanese novelists, and not just because of his straightforward style and deft, economical plotting. Endo is a Christian. He deals with issues of faith and morality that we feel at home with, and even his occasional preachiness has a familiar ring.

Indeed, Endo has often seemed alienated from his own culture. Beginning with his most famous novel, **Silence,** about Japan's 17th Century Catholic martyrs, he has complained that the Asian mind is a "mud swamp" in which Western ideas of good and evil, sin and redemption lose their clear cut outlines and sink without a trace.

Deep River, though, signals a healing of Endo's inner split, a reconciliation between East and West, Christianity and other faiths. His chief spokesman in the novel, the outcast Catholic seminarian Otsu, searches for "a form of Christianity that suits the Japanese mind" and concludes that Jews, Muslims, Hindus and Buddhists also have valid paths to God.

The story is about a modern-day pilgrimage. In 1984, at the time of Indira Gandhi's assassination, a group of Japanese tourists visit Buddhist and Hindu holy places in India, notably Varanasi, a city on the Ganges where crowds

of the faithful come to bathe in the river or be cremated on its shore.

Less outwardly colorful than Chaucer's pilgrims, Endo's tour bus passengers all carry grave inner burdens.

Kiguchi, an ex soldier, survived Japan's disastrous 1944 invasion of eastern India. He is haunted by memories of the retreat through the Burmese jungle, where starving, malaria ridden troops killed themselves with grenades and others ate the dead. He wants to hold a memorial service for them.

Isobe is mourning his wife, whom he took for granted until she died of cancer. With her last breath, she asked him to find her as soon as she was reincarnated. Impelled by the love he failed to show her when she was alive, Isobe embarks on what he knows to be a foolish quest—pursuing reports of an Indian child who claims to have been Japanese in a previous life.

Numada, a writer of children's stories, has relied on relationships with animals during a life filled with painful separations. Dogs and birds provide him with the companionship that others find in God. Newly recovered from tuberculosis, he feels indebted to a myna bird who, he fancifully believes, has died in his place.

Mitsuko, beautiful and cynical, seduced Otsu in college in an attempt to destroy his faith. He strikes her as clumsy and ludicrous, if sincere, and she doesn't understand why she has kept in touch with him—even now, when he lives in poverty with Hindus in Varanasi and spends his days nursing the dying who have dragged themselves to the sacred river.

Though not all the pilgrims find what they seek, all are moved by the primal experience of India.

Deep River is a story of a kind usually dared only by veteran writers—a direct, seemingly guileless inquiry into the meaning of life. Tolstoy's *The Death of Ivan Ilyich* is the best known Western example, but it's a Japanese tradition, too: Witness Natsume Soseki's *Light and Darkness* and Akira Kurosawa's film *Ikiru* (*Living*).

Endo's achievement here is mixed. Kiguchi, Isobe and Numada are realistic characters, and their stories are quietly effective. Otsu and Mitsuko, though, are the sort of people we bump into only in religious novels.

Like Gaston Bonaparte in Endo's **Wonderful Fool,** Otsu is a clownish figure who believes he's a failure when we know he's actually a saint. (It doesn't help that Gaston himself, or a clone of him, appears in **Deep River** in a secondary role.) Mitsuko's skepticism, her self conscious and self lacerating lovelessness, is only too obviously a sign of her spiritual hunger.

Since the relationship between these two is at the center of *Deep River,* it suffers a little. Nor is Endo always able to resist the temptation to slight people's everyday concerns ("cars and golf") or to dismiss the young as superficial simply because they are young. But the ending redeems the novel with powerful images—a "river of humanity" being carried away by the all accepting Ganges; the Hindu goddess Chamunda, wasted by disease but just as much a mother as the queenly Virgin Mary, suckling children with her withered breasts.

Robert Coles (review date 28 May 1995)

SOURCE: "The Great Tide of Humanity," in *The New York Times Book Review,* May 28, 1995, pp. 1, 21.

[In the following review, Coles discusses the psychological aspects of Endo's Deep River.*]*

With the epigraph to his latest novel the Japanese writer Shusaku Endo not only signals his story's intention, but by implication dismisses those critics who have made much of his relatively unusual situation as a Christian intellectual (he was baptized a Roman Catholic at the age of 11 and educated by priests) living in a nation far from the West, and for a long time successfully resisting its ever probing cultural (not to mention economic and political) assertiveness. Mr. Endo calls on a "Negro spiritual" for that epigraph and, indeed, for his book's title: "Deep river, Lord I want to cross over into campground." He is suggesting that his story will tell of a universal vulnerability, and the yearning that goes with it—the desire for a redemptive journey, a passage into more promising, secure terrain. The river in this instance is the Ganges: for Hindus a sacred setting, a way station toward new kinds of life to be assumed rather than a spot that marks the end of things, but for modern Japanese as well as Americans, reared on antisepsis and biotechnology, a place of absurdity if not danger—funeral pyres everywhere, and bodies of human beings and household pets floating downstream

Before he brings his characters to that scene. Mr. Endo explores their contemporary bourgeois, cosmopolitan lives in an almost clinical way (they are called "cases"). These are troubled, restless people, no matter their privileged situation. Each of them has known disappointment, loss and psychological and moral jeopardy. Even as bodies float on the Ganges, these four men and one woman are perplexed, uneasy, pursued by demons of a past life—adrift in their own ways.

Isobe is a middle aged businessman whose wife died of cancer. He had always been cool, detached, all too self absorbed—making money, climbing higher on the social and economic ladders. He and his wife had learned to stay together, but to keep a substantial distance. With her death, more than the expected sadness overcame Isobe. A rigid emotional control, a determined practicality that had little use for playfulness or imaginative speculation, was challenged by a moment of overwhelming fatefulness, which, in this instance, seemed to make a mockery of all the carefully tended rituals and habits, if not compulsions, that had constituted a life and that were meant to preclude any hard, searching look into its meaning or purpose.

Taking aim at an agnosticism rooted in science and its pervasive rationalism, which these days is proving to be transnational and transcultural, Mr. Endo puts his finger on Isobe's spiritual pulse this way: "Because he lacked any religious conviction, like most Japanese, death to him meant the extinction of everything."

Before she died, Isobe's wife, Keiko, was haunted by disturbing dreams, and became persuaded (hope against hope) that death would not be final after all: "I'll be reborn somewhere in this world." She asked her husband to try to find her after death—thereby, of course, remaining loyal to her, remembering her in a decisive rather than cursory or occasional manner. When she was to be cremated, a Buddhist priest, in ceremonial attendance, explained his religion's assumptions: "When an individuals dies, their spirit goes into a state of limbo. Limbo means that they have not yet been reincarnated, and they wander uneasily about this world of men. Then, after seven days, they slip into the conjoined bodies of a man and a woman and are reborn as a new existence." Such a deduction is, of course, no more easily accepted by Isobe and millions like him in Japan than it would be by most Westerners.

This atmosphere of skeptical materialism informs the thinking of the others who figure in Mr. Endo's evocation of late 20th-century Japanese life. Mitsuko is an attractive divorcee, highly intelligent, relentlessly cynical, forbiddingly calculating—and yet, unbeknownst to herself, desperately vulnerable. She left a marriage that was ideal in secular terms; her husband is another of Mr. Endo's prosperous burghers. Now she does volunteer work in a hospital (she took care of Isobe's dying wife), and is haunted by memories of a relationship she had as a college student with Otsu, another "case"—a young man who would ultimately enlist as a seminarian in a Catholic religious order. Mitsuko had become Otsu's temptress, a derisively callous one at times. But she was also increasingly intrigued by, then taken with, this exquisitely innocent and generous person, so much her opposite. Together they discussed religion; and their chosen code name for God, Onion, becomes a symbolic theme that threads its way through the narrative: the many layers of faith, the humility faith asks of the believer, the connection between belief and tragedy—all of that conveyed through the ordinary, lowly onion, which one can peel and peel, though with tears. Onion addressed by those two youths eventually becomes Onion pursued with great passion, by Otsu within the Christian tradition, by Mitsuko within the confines of a willful and manipulative self centeredness that psychiatrists would find unsurprising—and very hard to challenge clinically.

All these people but Otsu are headed by plane for one of those sadly banal excursions meant to distract people already more distracted (ironically) than they might realize. To them, filling out his cast, Mr. Endo adds Numanda, a writer and naturalist who can put his heart into the construction of storybooks for children and converse passionately with birds while holding himself aloof from his wife and, it seems, all other fellow humans; and Kiguchi, a survivor of the Highway of Death in Burma, where cannibalism was rampant at the end of World War II—a terrible finale to Japan's ill fated effort to conquer the Asian mainland.

Taken together, these people make up their creator's take on modern man—as in Jung's "modern man in search of a soul." (Mr. Endo has studied psychoanalysis with interest, especially its Jungian variant.) All of these "cases" (again save Otsu) have tried to live conventional, reasonably successful secular lives and have failed—not in a dramatic way (an ostentatious turn to an "alternative life style," a collapse into madness), but with muffled cries of vague apprehension betraying a despair they don't even know, never mind acknowledge. Under such circumstances they are curiously restrained combatants, a seemingly unpromising crew for a traditionally constructed novel with a specific plot: a trip to a strange land; a tour guide who is a religious teacher of sorts; some minor but instructive, even emblematic characters (a young honeymooning couple, the husband a greedily prying photographer, the wife callow and spoiled, who give their creator a chance to comment on the self indulgent fatuousness of a certain type of Japanese—and not only Japanese—youth. Yet Mr. Endo is a master of the interior monologue, and he builds, "case" by "case," chapter by chapter, a devastating critique of a world that has "everything" but lacks moral substance and seems headed nowhere.

As his characters in India confront the great mysteries of Hinduism and Buddhism, including their notion of the migratory life of the soul, Mr. Endo gives life once more to some of his earlier characters, and to his longstanding metaphysical passions. Mitsuko has appeared in previous Endo fictions, and here, as before, the author explicitly connects her to one of his mentors, Francois Mauriac. She is a version of Mauriac's Therese Desqueyroux, whose sinful preoccupations and behavior, and whose capacity for evil, have been of no small interest to him. Mr. Endo himself was educated in

France, and here, as in other fiction, for a spell he takes a Japanese character to a Europe (Lyons) that is for him quite familiar, even congenial, territory. In fact, Otsu, the failed seminarian who was such an easy prey to Mitsuko in his youth, and later an obsession of hers, is very much a character out of another French novelist's literary and religious imagination: the cure in Georges Bernanos's *Diary of a Country Priest*. That cure, too, seems to be a bumbling innocent, no match for the guile of various high and mighty folk, especially certain church bureaucrats who can't for the life of them comprehend him, his nature and his manner of being. This is the Judeo-Christian story, endlessly retold—by the prophet Isaiah, by the writers of the four Gospels, by a succession of novelists (Dostoyevsky and Tolstoy and Dickens)—and given by Bernanos the expository life of a rural French parish in the early years of this century: Christ foretold, Christ remembered, Christ evoked.

The unnerving, voluntary marginality of the man Jesus, His topsy turvy embrace of the weak, the "despised and the scorned" as against the big shots of church and state alike, has sent shudders down the backs of all sorts of people long after His death—among them, presumably, plenty of bishops and the functionaries who do their bidding. This is the situation Catholic novelists (as opposed to apologists) of whatever national or racial background have had to confront: on one hand, the spiritual truth that emerged from an informal community of humble Jews who were peasants and fishermen, inspired by a radical teacher and healer who was rather quickly hounded down; and on the other hand the later historical truth of a tight knit, powerful organization that has been, supposedly for His sake, in the thick of things for all these centuries and that has often enough wandered from the straight and narrow. What the Catholic theologian Romano Guardini said ("the church is the cross on which Christ was crucified") Shusaku Endo has given us in novel after novel—in his brilliantly original Silence (which takes on that subtlest, maybe most pernicious version of pride, Christian smugness) and now, more than 25 years later, in this tale that has Otsu, like his Saviour, dying young and badly misunderstood.

All through *Deep River* Otsu's pilgrimage haunts Mitsuko, his secular antagonist, and through her, the other characters in this beautifully wrought, lyrically suggestive story, so charged by the moral energy of its maker—who (like Thomas Merton at the time of his accidental death in Asia) wants to bring a Catholic sensibility to the shores of Hinduism and Buddhism. Not that this is a novel of easy grace. Doubt, Shusaku Endo has always known, is very much an aspect of faith. In the last pages, his sardonic, shrewd, embittered heroine glimpses "the sorrows of this deep river of humanity," realizes herself to be a part of it and takes a momentary step away from the tenacious pride that has prompted her to be so standoffish. Soon enough, we know, she will be aiming again for her solitary, privileged perch above it all, revealing the defiance of the egoistic observer. If Christianity holds up to us the lonely individual challenged by a God who entered history, Buddhism gives us people who are ready to surrender, finally, a measure of their human and spiritual particularity and who, with acceptance, join their follow creatures as part of the great tide of humanity. Mr. Endo manages to merge both of these streams of faith, bringing them together in a flow that is, indeed, deep. His work is a soulful gift to a world he keeps rendering as unrelievedly parched.

Andrew Greeley (review date 25 June 1995)

SOURCE: "Passage to India," in *The Washington Post Book World,* June 25, 1995.

[*In the following review, Greeley asserts that "Endo is one of the world's greatest novelists, a wizard with plot and character and description, who writes a simple story about simple people and packs it densely with drama, challenge and finally faith."*]

A group of Japanese tourists comes to the town of Varanasi (once called Benares) on the Ganges River in India. Among them are a man mourning a wife to whom he had never admitted his love, a former soldier who ate human flesh on the "Highway of Death" in Burma, a writer of nature stories for children who feels his life was saved by a myna bird, and a woman (Mitsuko) who has had much pleasure in life and much wealth but no happiness. They are hardly what one would call pilgrims. Yet they all are seeking something to give them hope.

One more Japanese character encounters these quasi-pilgrims: a misfit priest—probably Jesuit, but Endo only hints at this by placing him at one time in a well known Jesuit house in Lyons. In his arguments with his superiors before his long delayed ordination, Otsu may be in part a voice for Endo himself. Otsu is a familiar character, appearing with other names in other of the great novelist's stories: a fool, a clown, a bumbling and inept loser who also happens to be a saint. Disowned by his order, he lives in a house of prostitution and spends his time carrying the bodies of dead or dying Hindus to the funeral pyres on the banks of the Ganges so that they may find their own salvation. At one time, when he and Mitsuko were together in college, she seduced him and then cast him aside contemptuously. Yet she cannot get him or the "skinny man" on the cross out of her mind. Uncomfortable with "God," she uses the word "Onion" instead.

Endo is one of the world's great novelists, a wizard with plot and character and description who writes a simple story about simple people and packs it densely with drama, challenge and finally faith. Not only is he Japanese, but, surprisingly

for a venerated Japanese novelist, a Catholic. Beginning with his first great novel, **The Silence,** Endo has been a fierce critic of Japanese culture and an equally fierce critic of the rigidities of institutional Catholicism. Yet he seems to be well-loved in Japan and in Catholic literary circles, is respected as one of the best Catholic novelists of the century, and has even been described as "a Japanese Graham Greene" (a comparison which in this reviewer's judgment is unfair to both men).

In **Deep River** Endo discovers grace in this convergence of three world religions—Hindu, Buddhist, and Catholic Christian—on the banks of the Ganges. He does not seek to combine the three religions into one. Endo is a Catholic, and Otsu is a Catholic saint. But Endo absorbs the wisdom of all three faiths into his vision and makes salvation available to all his pilgrims. Immersing herself in the deep river, Mitsuko finds humankind and the transcendent and finally some as yet unexpressed purpose for her life. She grasps that the river—like the skinny man on the cross and her sometime lover—reveals each in its way what life means:

> *What I can believe in now is the sight of all these people, each carrying his or her own individual burdens, praying at this deep river.* At some point, the words Mitsuko muttered to herself were transmuted into the words of a prayer. *I believe that the river embraces these people and carries them away. A river of humanity. The sorrows of this deep river of humanity. And I am part of it.*
>
> She did not know to whom she directed this manufactured prayer. Perhaps it was towards the Onion that Otsu pursued. Or perhaps it was towards something great and eternal that could not be limited to the Onion.

Then, as she watches from a distance, Otsu is beaten, perhaps to death, by Hindus enraged by a pompous young Japanese photographer who has taken forbidden pictures of their funeral rites. She is angry at him because he has thrown away his life for "some Onion." She adds, "now in the end you break your neck and get carried away on a dead man's litter. When it comes down to it, you've been completely powerless." However, she finally encounters some of Mother Theresa's nuns tending a sick woman and realizes that though the "Onion" had died long years ago he had been reborn in the lives of other people for 2,000 years and not only in these nuns and in Otsu.

Endo has written so many wonderful novels that it would be patronizing to suggest that one is better than others. But surely **Deep River,** this moving story about a pilgrimage of grace, must be rated as one of the best of all of them.

Kirkus Reviews (review date 1 October 1995)

SOURCE: A review of *The Girl I Left Behind,* in *Kirkus Reviews,* Vol. LXII, No. 19, October 1, 1995, p. 1380.

[*In the following review, the critic asserts that while Endo's* The Girl I Left Behind *is a "simplistic apprentice work," there are some redeeming qualities to the novel.*]

In a frank afterword, the eminent Japanese author (of *Deep River,* etc.) concedes that this early novel—written "some thirty-five years ago"—appears by contemporary standards both politically incorrect and technically immature. It's a bit better than that. In tracing the almost lifelong relationship between Yoshioka Tsutomu, a thoughtless salesman, and Mitsu, the credulous village girl whom he seduces and abandons—and whose path continues to cross his long years afterward—Endo makes clear that rejecting the selfless and generous Mitsu was tantamount to denying Christ, and that such is not done lightly. This unfortunately simplistic apprentice work is thus redeemed both by some incisive character analysis and by its fervent exploration of conflicted religiosity and of the protean forms spirituality takes. It also shows us in the making the accomplished later novelist for whom the exploration of embattled religious faith has become both his obsessive subject and his greatest strength.

David L. Swain (review date 22-29 November 1995)

SOURCE: "The Anguish of an Alien: Confessions of a Japanese Christian," in *The Christian Century,* Vol. 112, No. 34, November 22-29, 1995, pp. 1120-25.

[*In the following review, Swain discusses Endo's* Deep River *and* The Final Martyrs, *paying particular attention to Endo's confessional style of exploring his doubts and his faith in his fiction.*]

When World War II ended in 1945 there was not a single active Christian writer in Japan. By 1972, when the Christian Literature Society (Kyo Bun Kwan) began publishing its 18-volume anthology of contemporary Christian literature, there were over 20. Of the 12 novelists included in the series, seven are Catholic and five Protestant; of five playwrights, three are Catholic and two Protestant. The anthology was edited by novelists Rinzo Shiina, a Protestant, and Shusaku Endo, a Catholic who is undoubtedly the most popular and widely read Christian writer in Japan.

In a recent issue of *Japan Christian Quarterly,* Kaname Takado, publisher of the anthology, describes "a Japanese Christian writer's life and work, in a 'heathen' land where Christians are less than 1 percent of the population, as a threefold struggle: to be a Christian, to be a Japanese and to

persevere as a writer." That more than 20 Christian writers had emerged from this struggle was in itself "a miracle," Takado said.

The pre-World War II generation of Christian writers faced the same complex struggle. With the exception of influential Christian apologist Kanzo Uchimura, who had little use for literature anyway, all others lost the battle. Their faith eventually gave way to a kind of humanism, or to a special mode of thought and style known in Japan as "naturalism." None of the Christian writers in the 1945-95 period, however, has renounced the faith. Takado attributes their survival to a clearer grasp of and commitment to the faith.

Endo's readiness to confess gnawing doubts about his own faith or faithfulness suggest an affinity with his prewar predecessors. While genuine, this affinity is partly one of style, a confessional style that issued from the Christian encounter with Japan of the Meiji years (1868-1912). A brief look at that encounter may be useful to appreciating Endo's tenacity.

Literary critic Katsuichiro Kamei has identified five developments in the Meiji era that helped shape modern Japanese literature. The first was the translation of the Bible into Japanese; another was Masahisa Uemura's Japanese translation of Christian hymns. Other factors were the translation of Russian literature by Shimei Futabatei, translations of German poetry by Ogai Mori and essays by Tohoku Kitamura, one of the first Japanese writers attracted to Christianity. These factors all helped to shape what Kamei called the "spiritual revolution" that followed the political and social revolution carried out by Meiji leaders.

A spiritual revolution involves the emotions, and it was in the concomitant "emotional revolution" of the late Meiji years that translated hymns played a crucial role, providing a new poetic language that allowed adequate expression of the faith confession that lies at the heart of Christian experience. From this language, says Kamei, a Buddhist, the Japanese learned about the act and meaning of confession, something which had no precedent in Japanese tradition. Buddhism has a sense of penitence, but nothing like the awakening of self in the modern European sense. From the hymns and the Bible, and from the church attendance common among young intellectuals at the time, aspiring Meiji writers came to realize that, as Kamei says, there is such a thing as "the freedom to confess."

Kamei also realized that it is impossible to transpose meaning fully from one language to another. Words in each language have nuances that are linked to native concepts and customs. The appeal of translations is "the spell they cast on us by the mirage-like charm of taking the language, thought and feelings of another place and people and grafting them into the life and pulse of our own." Kamei claims that "excellent translations of the Bible and hymns possessed the power to penetrate the hearts of Japanese people and actually evoked responses of faith."

Along with the reformation of language born of the emotional and spiritual revolutions, there was another crucial formative factor: the freedom of romantic love. In the strict Confucian world of premodern Japan the straightforward literary treatment of sexual matters was taboo, and open treatment of sexuality did not appear in literature until after World War II. But the reality of romantic love, so widely acknowledged in prewar literature, provoked a heightened sense of sin. This gave rise to a serious tension between religion and literature, then to the exaggerated tendency among a large coterie of writers to dwell on the ugly and harsh dimensions of human nature, the trend known as naturalism.

Some of the writers immersed in this naturalist mode seemed grossly egocentric and self-indulgent. Yet at its best this mode became a secularized tell-it-like-it-is confessional style that contemporary Japanese writers have adopted as a way of attesting to their own sincerity. Endo has made himself a master of this style: much of his writing is autobiographical in its source if not in its specifics. What sets Endo apart from prewar writers is that he uses the confessional expression of his doubts and failings as a way of indicating how doggedly determined he is to hang on to his faith. This point is particularly evident in the 11 stories compiled in *The Final Martyrs* and in the novel *Deep River,* ably translated by Brigham Young University scholar Van C. Gessel. (*Deep River* has recently been made into a film by Kei Kumai.)

In a 1973 essay, Endo described his sense of distance from both Christianity and its European cultural setting. At his mother's insistence and his sister's bidding, he was baptized at age 11. He enjoyed an untroubled boyhood until he entered prep school, where he discovered that his faith was a "ready-made suit that did not fit." At the university he majored in French literature and read many European "conversion accounts." They seemed to him like a return to one's hometown. By contrast, his own journey of faith was not a homeward-bound journey; instead, it filled him with "the anguish of an alien." The first Japanese student to study overseas after the war, he was in France for two and a half years and his loneliness was acute. But his main problem was his intense sense of distance not only from European culture and sensibilities, but even more from Westernized Christianity. Hence his first aim as an aspiring writer was to make "far-away Christianity" into something close and familiar for the Japanese.

In this endeavor he needed to develop a suitable style, and in his first medium-length novel, *White Man* (1955), he apparently found the key, for it won him the coveted Akutagawa Prize for promising new writers. The crowning success of this initial phase of his writing was *Silence* (1966), the story

of a foreign missionary in Nagasaki during the early 17th century persecution of the Christians. The missionary's inherited image of Christ is of a Jesus of majesty and power, an orderly Jesus who is himself governed by order. The hero, like many of his Japanese associates, is forced by his persecutors to tread on a *fumie* plaque with an image of Christ or the Holy Mother Mary. Refusing to step on the plaque meant torture and death; the alternative was betrayal and renunciation of faith. The threatened hero sees in the *fumie* an image worn smooth by the footsteps of broken spirited apostates: the face of a Christ who suffers as we suffer.

Endo credits critic Jun Eto with having clearly seen that "the face of Jesus on the fumie is the mother's face in Japan." He notes Erich Fromm's distinction between mother-religion and father-religion. In the latter, God is to be feared; he gets angry, judges and punishes. Mother religion is different: God treats us as a mother treats a bad child. She forgives and suffers with us. For this distinction Endo need not have relied on Fromm alone. Most East Asian countries have a strong shamanistic tradition wherein the gods, often female, are nurturing and forgiving. In contrast to this is the enduring and dominant Confucian tradition, which is more interested in order than in deity; like a traditional father, it is ethically rigid and demanding, and fully capable of anger and punishment.

In any case, Endo found that European Christianity overemphasized the paternal, judgmental aspect of religion, and neglected the maternal, nurturing, forgiving side of faith. *Silence* marked the end of the period in which he focused on rectifying this imbalance.

Most of Endo's themes recur throughout his works, as evidenced in *The Final Martyrs.* The title story concerns the "far away Christianity" resisted by Japanese culture, and the pain of apostasy. **"Adieu"** reflects the alienation he felt while studying in France. In **"Shadows"** and **"The Last Supper"** we find the compassion of Jesus for sinful weaklings. Endo's confessional style is particularly vivid in several stories that draw on his childhood in China, and his parents' divorce in 1933. The theme of paternal-maternal tension underlies **"Heading Home,"** a story of his mother's funeral. A Japanese priest serving in the Philippines returns home, a stolen dog finds his way home and now his mother has headed home (heaven). Maybe, Endo implies, he too will someday make it home. The more forthrightly autobiographical **"A Sixty Year Old Man"** suggests Endo's struggle to be a faithful Christian/Japanese/writer by exposing his vague temptations to flirt with teenage girls at the very time he was trying to rewrite his Life of Jesus. Only **"The Box"** touches on the problem of indigenous worldview: it depicts a sincere European woman, trapped in wartime Japan and desperate for food, who is cruelly betrayed by the secret police—an ugly picture of a supreme state that renders all else relative and thus dispensable.

The stories of *The Final Martyrs,* with publication dates ranging from 1959 to 1985, are a good sampling of his style and themes. But there is no distinct thread that indicates Endo's own consciousness of the evolution of his work. The inclusion of an essay like **"The Anguish of an Alien"** would have served this purpose well.

Endo has labored to depict Jesus as one who is not the all-powerful, majestic Jesus, but one who stands with us an ever-faithful companion. He undertook seven visits to Israel with a twofold goal: to create a portrait of Jesus that would ring true to Japanese readers, and to construct a background that drew on more than his own subjective feelings. The result was a novel, *Around the Dead Sea,* and a critical biography, *The Life of Jesus,* both issued in 1973.

What impressed Endo most during his sojourns in Israel was the absence of rivers like those he knew in Japan. The one river that looks like a river, he said, is the Jordan; but it is too small to be called a river, and it is framed by bleak wilderness, not fields and villages. It falls short of the river as the image of the flow of humanity. But then he visited India, where he saw people burn their dead and throw the ashes into the Ganges. "I also saw them lay the corpse of a child in a small boat and set it adrift in that mother river. The land that gave birth to the religion in which Jesus was brought up is a land without a mother river. I think perhaps Jesus himself suffered from this lack."

If it sounds audacious to suggest that Jesus suffered a cultural handicap, consider this: Endo suggests that Jesus found a substitute for a mother river in the Sea of Galilee. It was from this lake region that Jesus drew together his community of followers—those who would betray and forsake him, but then become men of conviction and boldly spread their faith in him.

Deep River grew from Endo's discovery of the Ganges and from his effort to rediscover a face of Jesus that would appeal to the "pagan" sensibilities of the Japanese. His confessional instincts produce in the novel a generous range of Japanese characters. They are brought together when they happen to join the same sightseeing tour of India. Isobe has recently lost his wife to cancer, and is on a vague and somewhat guilty search for her in some reincarnated form. Mitsuko is a bitchy divorcée who has faked everything in life, including love; she has no admitted goal except a curious longing to find a man named Otsu, whom she once seduced. Kiguchi seeks expiation; during a desperate retreat in Burma during Japan's Asian war, he had eaten the flesh of a fallen comrade. The tour guide Enami came to India to study religion, but he works as a guide to make a living; he is both the prism that provides the reader with insights into India's realities and the mirror that reflects the crassness of culturally illiterate tourists.

While each member of the party finds some solution to his or her problem, the story focuses on the strange reunion of Mitsuko with Otsu, whose former awkwardness as a student is now magnified by his status as a Catholic priest—or his nonstatus, for he is constantly reprimanded by his superiors for some discrepancy or perversion of traditional doctrine or practice. An outcast from his own religious community, Otsu locates the corpses of the poor who have no one to carry their bodies to the cremation site, and casts their ashes into the Ganges. He does this because he believes that if "that man" were here, he would do the same.

Deep River grew from Endo's discovery of the Ganges and from his effort to rediscover a face of Jesus that would appeal to the "pagan" sensibilities of the Japanese.

—*David L. Swain*

The Japanese tourists are appalled that he puts the ashes of the dead into a river teeming with worshipers who not only bathe in but also drink from its waters. Mitsuko is equally repelled by Otsu's weird calling, for she sees Otsu's God as impotent and pathetic. Yet in the end she wades into the murky waters.

> Mitsuko turned her body it the direction of the river's flow.
>
> "This is not a real prayer. I'm just pretending to pray," she rationalized, embarrassed at herself. "Like my fabrications of love, this is just a fabricated prayer."
>
> At the end of her range of vision, the river gently bent, and there the light sparkled, as though it were eternity itself.
>
> I have learned, though, that there is a river of humanity. Though I still don't know what lies at the end of that flowing river. But I feel as though I've started to understand what I was yearning for through all the many mistakes of my past.
>
> She clutched her fist tightly and searched for the figure of Otsu beside the funeral pyres.
>
> *What I can believe in now is the sight of all these people, each carrying his or her own individual burdens, praying at this deep river.* At some point, the words Mitsuko muttered to herself were transmuted into the words of a prayer. *I believe that the river*

embraces these people and carries them away. A river of humanity. The sorrows of this deep river of humanity. And I am part of it.

She did not know to whom she directed this manufactured prayer. Perhaps it was towards the Onion [Otsu's playful word for God] that Otsu pursued. Or perhaps it was towards something great and eternal that could not be limited to the Onion.

When *Silence* was first published, its harshest critics were Catholics. *Deep River* may also spark criticism, for Endo suggests that the many faces of God are seen not only in Christianity and Judaism but also in Hinduism, Buddhism and Islam. Worse, he has embraced universalism: the whole of humanity is ultimately embraced by the eternal arms of the mother river. Acceptance of Endo's version of Indian spirituality is also uncertain in the pragmatic, materialist ethos of Japan. Still, an emphasis on the awesome mystery of godhead and the wondrous ambiguity of humanity may be welcomed in a jaded postmodern world.

That, however, is not Endo's primary concern. He has always been suspicious of the term "Christian literature," for that generally turns out to be mere apologetics. There is only literature, and sometimes the writer is a baptized Christian. "If the Christianity that I believe in, that I am trying to believe in, that I want to believe in all my life, is really the truth, then it is not a violin solo that plays the tune of only one aspect of [our] inner self. Rather it should be an orchestra that responds to all the chords of [our] being, just because it is [ours], good or bad."

If literature is to deal with the fullness of humanity, then it must be able to go beyond psychological novels, or those which tackle the unconscious. It must forge its way into a third dimension: "the territory of demons." Endo does not boast that his work always gets into the demonic, but he feels that his efforts to do so set his work apart. If it does, it is because, as he says, "I have to read the Bible. It is the supreme work of literature. It excels Greek tragedy and other drama in describing man's struggle with the transcendent."

Leslie Schenk (review date Winter 1996)

SOURCE: A review of *Deep River*, in *World Literature Today*, Vol. 70, No. 1, Winter, 1996, p. 240.

[*In the following review, Schenk admits that there are some fascinating aspects to Endo's* Deep River, *but complains that "a faint air of absurdity hovers over the entire enterprise."*]

Endo Shusaku is considered by many Japanese to be the last of his generation's great novelists, and indeed some expected him to be his nation's next Nobel Prize winner. Whether any Japanese critics or common readers entertain doubts about Endo's pseudophilosophic religiosity we shall never know, for Japanese critics are not there to criticize but to praise; anything less would be shitsurei or impolite. The fact remains that Endo is a Roman Catholic writer in a nominally Buddhist country. Up till now, his distinguished career has been entirely consecrated to the study of "the extraordinary difficulty that Christianity has had in taking root in Japan" (*Cambridge Encyclopedia of Japan*).

In *Deep River* Endo tackles various faiths—Christianity, Buddhism, Shinto, Hinduism, and whatever it is that Shirley MacLaine believes in—omitting Islam. The question surely must arise in some minds whether the novel is the appropriate forum for such exposition and development, but the novel is Endo's medium and he sticks to it. Endo really is a great novelist—he knows how to set up a scene, differentiate his characters, make the reader care what happens next, handle dialogue, et cetera—but alas, in *Deep River* at least, his characters become little more than bearers of their creator's ideas. We are given thumbnail sketches of these characters from the river of life, who all become pilgrims to the river of death, the Ganges. Consider:

1) While Numada underwent a possibly fatal operation, his caged myna bird died *in his place,* he thinks, and Numada goes to India to buy another caged myna to release it into nature, to repay his debt. Now this is a lovely tale in the context of Shinto, a celebration of life and nature, but in a contemporary, supposedly realistic novel . . . ?

2) Isobe's wife's last words to him before dying were, "I know for sure I'll be reborn somewhere in this world. Look for me, find me, promise!" Isobe hears of a "scientific" study of "previous lives" at the University of Virginia, according to which an Indian child claims her previous life was lived as a Japanese. Isobe sets off for India to find her. Reincarnation along the wheel of *samsara* while awaiting Nirvana is of course a beautiful link with other aspects of Buddhism, but in a contemporary novel . . . ?

3) Otsu was a Catholic novice who could never achieve ordination due to his stubbornness in maintaining that all religions contain some truths leading to the same goal. He calls Jesus his Onion (*sic*). He ends up helping Hindus bear corpses to the burning ghats of the Ganges. The one justification for his pantheistic view is a quotation from Gandhi, fortunately in its original English, so that it rings out as the one unassailable statement in the entire novel—not exactly a tribute to Endo's philosophic ingenuity.

4) It occurs to Mitsuko that her life parallels the life of the eponymous Therese Desqueyroux in François Mauriac's novel, from which many passages are quoted in support of

her theory. Borrowing another novelist's characterization is rather a cheap way of characterizing one member of a new novel's cast of characters, is it not?

5) Finally, coincidences abound and are supposed to have deep significance beyond words. Well, a word does exist for this particular stretch of the imagination, and it is *blarney.*

Do these pilgrims to the Ganges find what they are looking for? Does Endo? *Deep River* has its fascinating aspects, I would not deny, but for me a faint air of absurdity hovers over the entire enterprise.

To boot, Endo is only partly well served by his translator, notwithstanding that Gessel is probably one of the best around. Typical of so many American translators from the Japanese, including the dean of them all, his hold on his source language is stronger than his hold on his target language, his native tongue. He does not translate into the level of International Standard English commensurate with his highly literary Japanese text, but rather into a kind of middling American vernacular (although punctuation and spellings in this edition are British). Stuff rather than things, stretch her wings rather than spread, and ambiguous contractions like he'd proliferate not only in dialogue but even in narrative passages, which is unforgivable. Frequently the plural their avoids the "sexist" his or her, as "When an individual dies, their spirit goes into a state of limbo." (Yet there are such easy ways to avoid this: "The spirit of an individual who dies goes into a state of limbo.")

Nevertheless, *Deep River,* highly praised elsewhere, is to be read, if with a grain of salt. Here is a passage, perfectly translated, that will tell you whether to plunge in:

> While [Isobe] was killing time in the gift shop . . . he discovered both Shirley MacLaine's *Out on a Limb* and Professor Stevenson's *Children Who Remember Previous Lives* propped in a corner of the display window, labelled as best-sellers. This seemed less like a coincidence than the workings of some invisible power [and] he couldn't stifle the feeling that his dead wife had been pushing him from behind, directing him towards the display window. Without even thinking, he bought the books.

If you can take that, this book is for you.

FURTHER READING

Criticism

Mathy, S.J., Francis. A review of *The Final Martyrs. America* (19 November 1994): p. 28.
   Discusses the themes found in Endo's *The Final Martyrs* which can be traced to Endo's other work.

Additional coverage of Endo's life and career is contained in the following sources published by Gale Research: *Contemporary Authors,* **Vols. 29-32R, 153;** *Contemporary Authors New Revision Series,* **Vols. 21, 54;** *DISCovering Authors Modules: Novelists;* **and** *Major Twentieth-Century Writers.*

Mary Lavin

1912-1996

American-born Irish short-story writer and novelist.

For further information on Lavin's life and works, see *CLC,* Volumes 4 and 18.

INTRODUCTION

Lavin was one of Ireland's most respected contemporary writers. Although her short stories explore everyday events in the Irish countryside, the thoughts and actions of her characters often spark a deep personal resonance with her readers. She describes convincingly the eccentricities and illogic of average people and it is this character development, rather than her plots, which gained her critical acclaim. Born in Massachusetts, Lavin immigrated to Ireland as a child and grew up in the environs of Dublin. In 1934 she received a degree in English, with honors, from University College in Dublin. She continued her studies there, earning an M.A., with honors, in 1936. While writing her dissertation, she wrote and published her first story, "Miss Holland" (1938), which received favorable attention. Lavin subsequently abandoned her graduate studies to write fiction, and, in 1942, married William Walsh, with whom she had three daughters. Widowed twelve years later, Lavin continued to write, publishing thirteen short story collections and two novels. Best known for her short stories and novellas, the form she preferred, Lavin received three Guggenheim Fellowships, the Katherine Mansfield Prize, and the Aos Dana Award. Critics praised her ability to create contained, even isolated settings for her characters with great brevity and efficiency. She often wrote about poignant moments in the lives of families; not necessarily instances of dramatic action, but moments of profound insight. The sparse style of her work and its melancholy mood lead critics to compare it to that of some Russian writers, particularly Anton Chehkov. As Jean Stubbs wrote, Lavin "invites us to contemplate with her the infinite sadness and beauty of the world, the divine inconsequences of life."

PRINCIPAL WORKS

Tales from Bective Bridge (short stories) 1943; revised edition, 1978

The Long Ago and Other Stories (short stories) 1944

The House in Clewe Street (novel) 1945

The Becker Wives and Other Stories (short stories) 1946

At Sallygap and Other Stories (short stories) 1947

Mary O'Grady (novel) 1950

A Single Lady and Other Stories (short stories) 1951

The Patriot Son and Other Stories (short stories) 1956

A Likely Story (juvenilia) 1957

Selected Stories (short stories) 1959

The Great Wave and Other Stories (short stories) 1961

The Stories of Mary Lavin 3 vols. (short stories) 1964-85

In the Middle of the Fields and Other Stories (short stories) 1967

Happiness and Other Stories (short stories) 1969

The Becker Wives (short stories) 1971

Collected Stories (short stories) 1971

The Second-Best Children in the World (juvenilia) 1972

A Memory and Other Stories (short stories) 1972

The Shrine and Other Stories (short stories) 1977

Mary Lavin: Selected Stories (short stories) 1981

A Family Likeness and Other Stories (short stories) 1985

In a Cafâe (short stories) 1995

OBITUARIES

James F. Clarity (obituary date 27 March 1996)

SOURCE: "Mary Lavin, 83, Wove Tales of Irish Experience," in *The New York Times,* March 27, 1996, p. D21.

[*In the following obituary, Clarity provides an overview of her life and career and comments on the style and major themes of her fiction.*]

Mary Lavin, whose short stories and novels about the conflicts in the hearts of her fellow Irish men and women transcended mere tales of life in Ireland, died on Monday at a nursing home here [Dublin, Ireland]. She was 83.

Ms. Lavin was the author of 19 collections of short stories and three novels. She won three Guggenhelm Fellowships and a number of literary awards, including the Katherine Mansfield Prize, in 1961. Her stories appeared regularly in *The New Yorker.*

Her death was front-page news in *The Irish Times,* whose chief book critic, Eileen Battersby, called her "one of modern Irish fiction's most subversive voices" and said, "Her art explored often brutal tensions, disappointments and frustrations dictating the relationships within socalled 'normal' families."

Ms. Lavin's favorite form was the short story, which she once likened to "a flash of lightning lighting up the whole landscape all at once." In a 1976 interview she was quoted as saying "Publishers are definitely unfair to short-story writers. Since the essence of the short story is its conciseness, an addiction to change is an occupational disease and not the self-indulgence publishers think." She also said: "I don't think a story has to have a beginning, middle and end. I think of it more as an arrow in flight."

Critics often compared Ms. Lavin's work to that of other acclaimed Irish writers, including Liam O'Flaherty and Sean O'Faolain, and also perceived echoes of Balzac, Chekhov and Saki. Her writing influenced the work of others, as well, including the novelist William Trevor.

Ms. Lavin said her childhood reading of Jane Austen influenced her writing. She said that, as a realist, her writing was "only looking closer than normal into the human heart, whose vagaries and contrarieties have their own integral design." In an appreciation in *The Irish Times,* Maurice Harmon, professor emeritus of Anglo-Irish Literature at University College in Dublin, wrote, "She drew upon her own experience. Her stories explore and reflect the patterns of her life: the return of the little girl from America to the strange, puritanical society of her mother's people" in Western Ireland.

"At the high point of her career," he continued, "She wrote about widows who refuse to be passive in the face of death, who keep their memories of love and go forth to encounter experience with openness and with the wisdom of years."

Mary Lavin was born on June 11, 1912, of immigrant parents in East Walpole, Mass. When she was 10 the family moved back to Athenry, in Western Ireland. She wrote her first short story in 1938. Her first collection, *Tales from Bective Bridge,* won the James Tate Black Memorial Prize in 1942 and helped establish her career.

Her short-story collections include *The Long Ago* (1944), *The Becker Wives* (1946), *A Single Lady* (1957), *In the Middle of the Fields* (1966) and *The Shrine and Other Stories* (1976). She published her first novel, *The House in Clewe Street,* in 1945, her second, *Mary O'Grady,* appeared in 1950.

She served as president of the Irish Academy of Letters in 1971.

Ms. Lavin's first marriage was to William Walsh, a lawyer, who died in 1954. They had three daughters, who survive. In 1969 she married Michael McDonald Scott, a former Roman Catholic priest, who died in 1990. In recent years her health failed and she lived in a nursing home.

Her stories were characterized by arresting opening and closing lines. One story, **"Happiness,"** begins with "Mother had

a lot to say" and ends: "Mother made the last effort of her life and grasped at Bea's meaning. She let out a sigh, and, closing her eyes, she sank back, and this time her head sank so deep into the pillow that it would have been dented had it been a pillow of stone." Another, **"A Memory,"** begins, "James did all right for a man on his own," and ends, "Under a weight of bitterness too great to be borne, his face was pressed into the wet leaves and when he gulped for breath, the rooted leaves were sucked into his mouth."

Los Angeles Times (obituary date 27 March 1996)

SOURCE: "Mary Lavin, 83; Prize-Winning Irish Author of Novels, Stories," in *Los Angeles Times,* March 27, 1996, p. A15.

[In the obituary below, the critic comments on Lavin's literary career.]

Mary Lavin, who depicted the narrow subtleties of Irish small town life in short stories and novels, has died. She was 83.

The prize-winning writer died Monday in a Dublin nursing home.

In a *Los Angeles Times* review of a book about Irish women writers in 1990, Thomas Cahill characterized Lavin's work as representing "surely the boldest tradition of women writers in all literature.

Born in East Walpole, Mass., Lavin moved to Ireland as a child and was educated at Loreto College and University College in Dublin.

In 1942, she published her first collection of short stories, *Tales from Bective Bridge.* It won the James Tait Black Memorial Prize and established her literary reputation.

Spurred by its success, she wrote prolifically. Her 19 collections of short stories included *The Long Ago* in 1944, *The Becker Wives* in 1946, *A Single Lady* in 1957, *In the Middle of the Fields* in 1966 and *The Shrine and Other Stories* in 1976.

Her first novel, *The House in Clewe Street,* was published in 1945. The second, *Mary O'Grady,* appeared in 1950.

A recognizably Irish Catholic writer, she created such characters as forlorn spinsters, sprightly nuns, mothers mourning long-dead sons, and bitterly antagonistic sisters. Subtle, lucid and shrewdly observed, her writing featured themes that combined a sense of sorrow with hints of mystery.

Among her many awards were Guggenheim Fellowships in

1959, 1962 and 1972 and the Katherine Mansfield Prize in 1961.

In 1971, she was president of the Irish Academy of Letters.

OVERVIEWS

Mark D. Hawthorne (essay date Fall 1994)

SOURCE: "Words that Do Not Speak Themselves: Mary Lavin's 'Happiness'," in *Studies in Short Fiction,* Vol. 31, No. 4, Fall, 1994, pp. 683-88.

[*In the essay below, Hawthorne focuses on language and meaning in Lavin's story "Happiness," arguing that the story suggests an incongruence between language and meaning.*]

In the short story **"Happiness"** (1969) Mary Lavin constructed a text in which the characters', and especially the narrator's, bewilderment over and confusion of the signification of key words points both to the arbitrariness of the words themselves and to the narrator's inability to understand the story that she tells. The narrator's attempt to account for her mother's enigmatic use of the word "happiness" illustrates the futility of trying to comprehend verbal constructs; the speaker's original construct and the narrator's reconstruction of what she thinks that construct signifies negate each other in such a way that the reader must accept that, in the final analysis, words cannot communicate. If "the main purpose of the narrative . . . is to capture and evaluate Vera's philosophy of life," Lavin has made the inability to communicate a major part of that purpose.

Lavin unabashedly based the story on her own experience: like Vera, she was left after the death of her husband in 1953 with the responsibility of raising her three daughters; during the first years of her widowhood, Lavin, like Vera, took the girls to Florence. Nevertheless, Lavin's narrative seriously alters her experiences: the story is narrated by an unnamed daughter, and Vera, who dies at the end of the story, does not marry Father Hugh despite the neighbors' thinking that their relation is too intimate. In 1969, Lavin married Michael Scott, who had applied for and was granted laicization. These deviations from Lavin's autobiographical experience should warn us that the story is more complex than it appears at first, even while it provides a striking picture of her own despair and renewed commitment after William's death.

Vera, the widowed mother who teaches the enigmatic lesson that happiness is the essence and goal of life, seems at first to be a truth-sayer. Her name derives from the Latin *verax,* "truthful," and she seems earnest, however unclear her lesson. As a librarian, she works with words, an occupation

also suggested by her study and the sheaf of paper that preoccupies her as if she were, like Lavin herself, a writer. But if she is truthful, her inability to communicate clearly suggests that truth cannot easily be shared: neither Father Hugh nor her three daughters understand what she means by "happiness." Her name also suggests the Latin *ver,* "youth" or "springtime," a reading that Lavin supports in repeated references to spring, spring flowers, and the rejuvenation of spring following winter's desolation. As youthful or springlike, her name carries an obvious double or paradoxical meaning: she is old (and getting older as the story progresses), yet she is youthful in her attitude and springlike in her ability to bounce back from despair. As her name suggests, she is a fulcrum that contains opposites without fully embracing the contradictions that those opposites define.

As in the case of the main character, the narrator frequently uses words that can be read with contradictory significance, thus generating what Augustine Martin called "vibrations in the mind and the imagination which continue in the reader's mind long after the story has been put down." Twice, for example, she uses the word "rhetoric" in such a way that the reader cannot distinguish whether it signifies Vera's skill in using language effectively or an insincerity concealed behind a grandiloquent barrage of words. The first use of "rhetoric" occurs just after Vera declares that "Happiness drives out pain, as fire burns out fire," a cryptic statement obviously beyond the understanding of her daughters who, nevertheless, "thirstily drank in her *rhetoric*" (emphasis added). Here the word seems to denote the narrator's distrust of her mother's glib reply, but in the second use of the word, there is no hint of glibness: here Vera, on her deathbed, speaks of the nun and the daffodils in such a way that the daughters are mystified, Vera's language seeming to conceal a secret that she cannot or will not communicate. In the first passage Bea is skeptical, trying in vain to understand but failing because she takes Vera's statement too literally, but in the second Bea recognizes Vera's signification, a comprehension of Vera's "rhetoric" that makes her joyous and strong in facing her mother's death, the very reactions that Vera had wanted in the passage in which the narrator first uses "rhetoric."

Likewise, "father" means both the priest—as in *Father* Hugh—and the father of the family, but this particular distinction becomes blurred when Father Hugh takes on the role of the father of the family, growing to play an intimate role in the three girls' childhood even while he remains chaste and faithful to his priestly vows. If we have no trouble seeing the priest as a spiritual father, Father Hugh's role takes on broader domestic implications that have generated gossip even though he has remained fully faithful to his priestly vows. In other words, though he is not the girls' natural father, he becomes their father in every other way.

Equally significant is the narrator's use of "mother"—on the one hand, because she is a daughter telling about her own mother. But she is also married, and possibly a mother herself, thereby playing a double role of daughter to her mother and mother to her own children, a double role that she does not develop. On the other hand, she develops a verbal ambiguity between her mother and grandmother. While Vera clearly takes the role of mother, her own mother calls her "mother," thus creating a situation in which the daughter is verbally the mother of her own mother. Yet Vera confesses to her daughters, "I would never have put so much effort into rearing you, because I wasn't a bit maternal." That is, the character whom the narrator develops as mother rejects the verbalization of her role even while she clearly fulfills it. Though such reversal may be commonplace as a sign of humility, Lavin uses the change in the noun from describing a familial relation to signifying a behavioral relation to emphasize her treatment of other words that have changing or shifting significations. That the same woman can be both mother and daughter merely indicates the shifting of generational perspective, but that the woman can be called mother by her own mother reflects either a confusion in attribution or a shift from familial relation through which the mother lets her daughter the dominant role of decision-maker.

Still another blurring of family names—similar to the blurring of "father" and "mother" but more grotesque—is with the word "kid." Though the children see themselves as kids, the word, of course, also refers to young goats. When Linda mistakes goats for children, her mistake is humorous, but it is also rather frightening because it involves the slaughter of the young. The change in "father" points toward a double role played by Father Hugh; the change in "mother" points toward shifting dependencies; but the change in "kid" points toward the inexplicable terror of a child who must leave childhood to become an adult. Thus the mistaken signification suggests one of Lavin's major themes in the short story—the inability of the children to understand their mother's use of language, their inability to understand the lesson that she strives to teach.

If words that normally carry unambiguous denotations are wrenched from their usual signification, we should not be surprised by other words that carry double, contradictory meanings. Vera finds "rest" in her garden where she works and where she finally finds the "rest" of death. Like "kid," "pillow" in the final symbol of the story suggests a gap between signifier and signified. Ordinarily, a pillow is a soft object whereon to rest one's weary head; here, however, the pillow is a stone marking both Vera's death, her movement from softness, and her grave, her final resting place. This choice of words, like Lavin's use of familial words, derives from a domestic, homey vocabulary in which we usually do not expect such double meanings.

In addition to the words that have double meanings, Lavin's narrator also uses words that are misleading because they are not clearly defined; that is, either a character or the narrator uses some words that are left for the reader to interpret because the text does not given enough clues to determine a definitive signification. These words, unlike those with double meanings, often carry the appearance of a signification that they do not actually have in the context in which they appear. For example, when Vera refers to the Alps, she calls them "hills," a word that hardly describes their size and magnificence, but when the narrator corrects her, she does acknowledge her "mistake." On the one hand, she may simply confuse the two nouns, an unlikely confusion for a woman whose working life centers around words; on the other hand, she may be making a judgment in which her use of "hills" is intended to be pejorative, an attack on the spectacle that the daughters fail to comprehend. In this latter sense, Vera's word choice is a reversal of the hyperbole that enables us to talk about the "Dublin mountains" when that geological feature is merely a range of hills compared to the Alps.

When the girls try for the umpteenth time to ascertain exactly what their mother means by "happiness," Bea concludes, "It's a sham!" While a sham is something false that pretends to be genuine, it is also a curtain or decorative cloth that *conceals*. Because the context does not develop Bea's statement further, we cannot resolve whether she is making a moral judgment on her mother's advocacy of happiness or describing her mother's use of happiness as a quality that acts like a pillow sham to conceal something from view. That is, Bea may have an insight that her sisters lack, the same sort of insight that enables her to understand her mother in the final scene. Along the same lines, when Vera says she is "foolish" after the nun's revelation that her husband is dying, we have no context for determining the exact signification of her adjective. On the one hand, she may be saying that she is ridiculous, but, on the other, she may be suggesting her own insignificance. In the first, she may recognize her absurdity, a self-mocking that results from a context of denial, but, in the second, she may recognize that humility forces her to deny the importance of what she recognizes. Or, contrary to either of these readings, she may suggest that she is, indeed, the fool that we associate with a certain freedom from ordinary or material matter-of-factness or with an other-worldliness that seems simple or naïve.

Mary Lavin wrenches words from their expected denotations to shape some of the most striking images of the story. The ordinary experience of turning on a light in a dark room turns a window into a mirror: Bea turns on the light to distract Father Hugh from Vera, who has stayed in the garden after the sunset. Instead of looking *through* the window at Vera, the narrator, Bea, and Father Hugh see themselves reflected *in* the window. Structurally, this shift from transparency to opacity marks the moment when Vera's philosophy faces its most demanding test. Just as Bea turns the light on so that they can no longer see Vera in the garden, Bea, not the narrator, will be the daughter who tells her mother that she can die in peace. Bea holds Vera's "face between her palms as tenderly as if it were the face of a child" (another mother/daughter inversion) while she tells her that "You don't *have* to face it!" The combination of the imagery of seeing and this play on "face" pass Vera's legacy to the middle daughter, the only one who comprehends what Vera had been striving to teach.

The narrator uses this tendency to blur denotation to confuse the difference between tangible objects and intangible ideas. As a pillow can be a stone or a soft object on a bed, a rosary can be the beads that Grandmother says or the growing list of "if only" wishes. The object and the idea thus become inseparable: the word invokes the object even while the object exists only through its name. Thus Vera can carry her daughters "by magic" to the "small girl with black hair and buttoned boots" just as Robert, "while he lived, had cast a magic over everything." This magic, objectification through words, transforms the ordinary into the unusual, the commonplace into the extraordinary. If Vera can use words as magic, then her words about happiness turn the words themselves into the objects that they represent just as the narrator's use of words to tell about her mother's lessons makes those lessons palatable. Daffodils are both harbingers for new and refreshed life and the brutal awareness of death; Vera's swimming carries both an escape as she hovers birdlike over a rushing stream and the temptation to die when she wades into the moonlight sea after the death of her husband; a snowdrop is both "a bleak bud that had come up stunted before its time" and a summation of "the whole point of happiness."

Bea, whose name recalls the Latin *beata,* "happy" or "happiness," is the character who finally grasps the meaning of her mother's lessons, but the narrator remains nameless. Because even the grandmother takes on a nickname—Miss Imperious, Lavin implies that this lack of a name is important. Throughout, the narrator has been "loving yet occasionally skeptical," an ambivalence showing in her tone that forces the reader to question whether she has ever learned what her sister discovers at Vera's death. Vera proclaims happiness although her life does not seem happy: after the death of her husband, the girls even fear that she will commit suicide when she is swimming at night. Likewise, Bea does not understand her message until she mentions the daffodils, a word that invokes her memory of Vera's story about her husband's death. Because the word connects the past and present, Bea understands, not the word but the emotions that the word indirectly signifies: knowing that the cruel nun had made her aware of her husband's dying, Vera associated daffodils with death so that Bea can tell her that she herself can let go of life "confident that her tidings were joyous, her voice was strong." Looking on without speaking, the narrator merely reports because, unlike her sister, she has not mastered the

rich confidence of language. In short, the narrator fails to understand her mother and consequently provides us with the sort of ironic contrast that Thomas Murray described as a "point of view [that] works well to maintain an almost extremely cruel distance from the characters to the extent that at times it is impossible to say where [Lavin's] true sympathies are as judged from the distanced and neutral point of view."

Lavin's choice of a narrator is especially interesting if Vera is, as we have no reason to doubt, her "autobiographical heroine," an assumption that seems well validated by her appearance in other stories. However, if Lavin used the medium of language to describe her own philosophy that enabled her to go on after her husband's death, she seems to distrust the very medium, not the content that Vera passes on to Bea. Likewise, if the story is, indeed, "the work most revelatory of Lavin's attitude toward her own life and art," then we must read through the ironic juxtaposition of narrator and misunderstood subject. The daughter who tells the story, another wordmonger, fails to grasp her mother's throwing of manuscripts from a train window or her meaning, a meaning that falls silent, unable despite many efforts to communicate itself through language. The narrator's words, like Vera's, defy their medium: as Bea discovers, they suggest but do not contain the message.

Jeanette Roberts Shumaker (essay date Spring 1995)

SOURCE: "Sacrificial Women in Short Stories by Mary Lavin and Edna O'Brien," in *Studies in Short Fiction,* Vol. 32, No. 2, Spring, 1995, pp. 185-97.

[*In the following excerpt, Shumaker focuses on the protagonists from Lavin's stories "A Nun's Mother" and "Sarah" and argues that the "martyrdoms" of both heroines can best be understood in the context of Catholic notions of the suffering Madonna.*]

Edna O'Brien's "A Scandalous Woman" (1972) ends with the statement that Ireland is "a land of strange, sacrificial women." Like O'Brien, Mary Lavin features sacrificial women in her short stories. The disturbing martyrdoms of the heroines created by both writers stem, in part, from Catholic notions of the Madonna. The two writers criticize their heroines' emulations of the suffering Virgin. Julia Kristeva's "Stabat Mater" (1977) and Marina Warner's *Alone of All Her Sex: The Myth and Cult of the Virgin Mary* (1976) scrutinize the impact of the Madonna myth on western European women. Their feminist scholarship illuminates short stories such as Lavin's **"A Nun's Mother"** (1944) and **"Sarah"** (1943), as well as O'Brien's "Sister Imelda" (1981) and "A Scandalous Woman." In each story, female martyrdom (en)gendered by the Madonna myth takes different forms, from becoming a nun to becoming a wife, mother, or "fallen woman."

Kristeva comments upon the fluidity of the Madonna, who encompasses diverse female roles, as do the Irish female characters who emulate her. Discussing the dimensions of the Madonna—Virgin, mother, wife—Warner describes the primary effect of the Madonna myth: "By setting up an impossible ideal the cult of the Virgin does drive the adherent into a position of acknowledged and hopeless yearning and inferiority." The heroines of Lavin's and O'Brien's stories fit the pattern of self-hatred that Warner describes. Their varieties of sacrifice stem from self-disgust fostered by failing to reach the standards of the Madonna myth. . . .

"Sister Imelda" suggests that girls want to become nuns to experience the high drama of religious renunciation rather than the low comedy of becoming a sexual commodity. Lavin's **"The Nun's Mother"** presents a related explanation for why girls want to become nuns—to avoid male predation. More painfully than O'Brien, Lavin exposes the inescapability of patriarchal power, whether in the home or the convent. The story concerns a nun's mother's meditations after leaving her daughter, Angela, at a convent. Angela's mother, Mrs. Latimer, never dared to ask Angela why she chose such a career, when all of Angela's life she appeared to dislike going to mass. The girl's father, Luke, is horrified that his daughter is renouncing the physical joys of marriage without realizing what they mean. Like Mrs. Latimer he does not dare to question Angela. Mrs. Latimer reflects on her happiness in marriage, noting its rarity. She is both glad that her daughter will not have to risk a marriage failure, and sorry that she won't know intimate love. Although the parents do not realize it, a reason for Angela's choice is given at the end of the story, when the father notices a flasher who has been operating near their home for months.

Angela apparently wishes to escape a world of invasive male sexuality for a sexless world in which wearing a swimsuit into the bathtub will safeguard her. The daughter's acceptance of such prudish defenses can be explained by "the terrible reticence about the body between mothers and daughters, a reticence based on revulsion, and not, as with mothers and sons, upon respect and mystery." Shame over their bodies keeps Angela and Mrs. Latimer emotionally distant. Hence, Mrs. Latimer cannot ask Angela why she is becoming a nun: "She [Mrs. Latimer] was conscious of this revulsion [about the body] every time she was alone with her daughter during the last month." As a result, Mrs. Latimer says nothing to Angela about her decision. Mrs. Latimer pretends to her husband that she has spoken to Angela, for Mrs. Latimer feels humiliated by her inability to be as intimate with her daughter as Luke expects. Mrs. Latimer knows that if Luke had a son, Luke would talk to him easily, since men lack women's

shame about sexuality. At the story's end, Mrs. Latimer can't even imagine Angela being disturbed by the flasher near their home, because she never thinks of Angela as a sexual being capable of noticing a nude man. Mrs. Latimer's and Angela's revulsion against their bodies comes from the self-hatred engendered by a religion that regards female sexuality as evil. It is the same self-disgust that causes the narrator of "Sister Imelda" to hide from her once-beloved nun, and that perhaps caused Imelda to join her order. Only by denying her body as a nun can a woman preserve it from becoming that of a temptress.

Angela's fear of violation by the flasher or other men can be linked, through Warner, to the Church's "historical fear of contamination by outside influences, and its repugnance to change" that is symbolized by the Virgin's (and nun's) chastity. It is a fear of contamination that Angela's mother shares. Mrs. Latimer believes that the appeal of becoming a nun is gaining sexual independence from men. "And so, for most women, when they heard that a young girl was entering a convent, there was a strange triumph in their hearts . . . they felt a temporary hostility to their husbands." However, Mrs. Latimer denies that she herself ever felt the allure of sexual emancipation. She would not give up her memories of passion with Luke for anything. Luke is gentle; both Angela and her mother seem to see him as an exception to typical male aggressiveness. Despite the presence of Luke, the story countenances Angela's fear of men in that the flasher epitomizes all the varieties of perverts who do in fact hurt women; that flashers themselves usually don't rape women physically, however, suggests Angela's naïveté about men. Angela's other naïve belief is that nuns are immune from sexual attacks.

The story ends with Mrs. Latimer's fantasy of Angela as a water lily about to be picked by the flasher. That Mrs. Latimer associates Angela with water lilies shows that Mrs. Latimer sees the female experience as a conflict between beautiful nature and a degraded civilization that endangers it. Mrs. Latimer's essentialism appears in her aligning of woman with nature. The danger for the female flower is not just one of being picked, but of withering in a selfprotective, ossifying ideology of asceticism that the Irish Catholic Church endorses for women. Angela avoids the physical threat of rape but not the mental one of ossification, choosing her own form of sacrifice. Angela will be a water lily in a bowl on the convent's altar, her life a slow withering. With Angela's sexual independence from men comes intellectual dependence on the male-dominated Church. Angela's payoff will be the high status which Warner and Kristeva agree that emulating the Virgin earns.

Angela's mother will get that high status too. Mrs. Latimer realizes this upon arriving home, when her housekeeper treats her with a new deference. Yet this status is seen satirically by Mrs. Latimer, who abhors the pretentious acts of piety she may be expected to perform now that she is the mother of a nun. Mrs. Latimer fantasizes, "'Meet Mrs. Latimer, who has a daughter in the convent.' She would be quite an exhibit at church bazaars and charity whist drives. She might even have to assume an attitude." The pathetic requests for prayers that Angela receives from her dressmaker, plus the stereotypical gifts of rosary beads, quartz angels, and holy pictures, fill Mrs. Latimer with dismay. By association, Angela's mother is supposed to be aligned with the Madonna as a holy mother of a sacrificial child. But because the circumstances of Angela entering a convent in twentieth-century Ireland are portrayed with mundane humor, they contradict any glorified image of nuns and their mothers. Such images of transcendence are sold to girls by bestsellers like *The White Sister,* according to Mrs. Latimer. Transcendence of what? Of being a Mrs. Latimer—the reader knows her only by her married name, as though marriage had consumed her identity. Yet the story portrays Mrs. Latimer's marriage as a happy one in which the husband is the subordinate party if anyone is, whereas Angela's nunnery is seen not as a refuge from male dominance but as a museum.

For any mother, the ultimate price of bearing a nun might be knowing that her line ends with her daughter, as Christ ended Mary's. Mrs. Latimer will not have the pleasure of having grandchildren to love. In her odd relief at this apparent misfortune, her likeness to her daughter appears: both fear contamination above all else. At the birth of Angela, Mrs. Latimer had imagined her descendants falling into lurid varieties of wickedness that she can only observe, but not interrupt. "For the lives they led had suddenly seemed evil in every case. Some were prising open drawers and looking over their shoulders. Some were stealthily crossing the 'ts' of letters that were forged." Mrs. Latimer's relief comes from knowing that her daughter's pure choice will eliminate any responsibility for future generations. Her relief at Angela's chastity vows outweighs her regret that she will no longer need to stay young for Angela.

The story's initial image of Mrs. Latimer is telling: her eyes are closed as she leaves Angela at the nunnery, as though Mrs. Latimer is afraid to face reality. This image reveals Mrs. Latimer's compulsion to control what she knows and experiences, as well as the actions of her descendants. Perhaps Mrs. Latimer chooses not to see the pathetic reason for Angela's vocation, as that vocation allays Mrs. Latimer's anxieties about her posterity. Mrs. Latimer would have been a good mother but for her fear of the future that she unconsciously passed onto her daughter. Mrs. Latimer's obsessive desire to control the future contradicts the healthy side of the Madonna myth that Kristeva describes as its connectedness to past and future through "a flow of unending germinations, an eternal cosmos." Fertility is lost to the paranoid nun and her mother, as the virginal side of the Madonna excludes the

maternal side. Whereas Angela imagines herself a victim of male predators, Mrs. Latimer dreams of being their ancestor. This is a dark turn to the story that makes Angela's desire to become a nun seem a result of her mother's pathology, not of an actual vocation. . . .

Whereas a spiritually dead woman is the heroine of O'Brien's "A Scandalous Woman," an actual murder victim is the heroine of Lavin's **"Sarah."** As a widow who struggled to raise her children and eventually remarried a man who left the priesthood for her, Lavin can confront the paralyzing Irish middle-class conformity that Joyce critiqued. But Lavin presents a female point of view. As Zack Bowen writes, "Given Mary Lavin's lifelong concern with practicalities, money problems, responsibilities, and the effects of death, her vision of reality is harsh and closely circumscribed by an acute awareness of social class, and society's sanctions and rules." **"Sarah"** is one of Lavin's most hard-hitting pieces of social criticism. In her village, unmarried Sarah is respected for her piety and for her diligence as a cleaning lady. Yet Sarah dies from exposure while bearing her baby in a ditch during a rainstorm. The baby also dies. Sarah's angry brothers had kicked her out of their home, after depending on her cleverly efficient housekeeping for years. Although Sarah was already raising three sons whom she bore out of wedlock, this is apparently the first time Sarah had informed the father of his paternity. Sarah is no longer willing to claim sole responsibility for her children, or to pretend that she was honored by virgin births. As a result, Sarah's brothers can no longer hide behind their previous myth that the men who slept with Sarah were "blackguards" who took advantage of her. Her "fall" thus becomes a public shame that her brothers must acknowledge.

Sarah's brothers' violence is only a step beyond that of Eily's family. Since Sarah's paramour is a married man, her brothers cannot force a marriage as Eily's did. Sarah inflames her eldest brother by reminding him that her lovers are none of his business. What bothers him more than Sarah's affair is her defiance of his authority. But he hides his irritation at not being able to control his sister behind worry over their family's honor that is more socially acceptable. He regards Sarah's adultery as much more dishonorable than her previous affairs with single men, as he tells his younger brother: "No one is going to say I put up with that kind of thing." Concern for their reputation motivates the cruelty of Sarah's brothers and Eily's family. O'Brien and Lavin suggest that Irish families punish scandalous women without compunction. Eily's and Sarah's scandalousness comes from their insubordination to their families as much as from the premarital sex that is the proof of their defiance.

The wife of the man Sarah slept with, Mrs. Kedrigan, writes to Sarah's brothers to protest Sarah's letter to Mr. Kedrigan informing him of her pregnancy. Mrs. Kedrigan is angry in part because her neighbors had warned her not to hire Sarah, but Mrs. Kedrigan had wanted to show them that her husband was entirely trustworthy. Sharing a belief in the double standard with Sarah's brothers, Mrs. Kedrigan does not blame her husband for his affair; nor does she believe his denial of it, or she would have ignored Sarah's letter. The illusion that Sarah is the sole culprit lets Mrs. Kedrigan avoid fighting with her husband about his affair. As Mrs. Kedrigan relies on him for physical and psychological support, it is in her interest to keep the peace. Without a job to support their baby who will soon be born, Mrs. Kedrigan can't leave her husband. But she gets back at him indirectly by telling him the news of Sarah's death with vengeful relish, saying that the ditch is the place where Sarah belongs. Mrs. Kedrigan can be seen as a victim of patriarchal restrictions that are whitewashed by the Madonna myth, to the point that she becomes a caricature of the wronged wife. Warner notes that the Virgin myth's influence is greatest in countries where women are primarily wives and mothers; Ireland would certainly qualify. Janet Egleson Dunleavy says that Lavin's stories from the 1940s focus on "the universal truth of restricted vision"; petty, vindictive vision is clearly Mrs. Kedrigan's flaw, as much as it is Sarah's brothers'. Mrs. Kedrigan condemns Sarah because, as Warner writes of the Madonna myth, "There is no place in the conceptual architecture of Christian society for a single woman who is neither a virgin nor a whore."

Lavin questions the ideology that allows Mrs. Kedrigan and Sarah's brothers to label Sarah a whore, much as O'Brien does in "A Scandalous Woman." As Richard F. Peterson writes, Sarah's tragic death represents "the triumph of the unnatural over the natural." Oliver Kedrigan kindles Sarah's animal attraction to him by complimenting her red cheeks; he laughingly asks her whether she rubs them with sheep-raddle. At the end of the story, when Mrs. Kedrigan tells Oliver of Sarah's death, he yells at her to give him the sheep-raddle, cursing it. Oliver is cursing the instinctive lust which led him to cause Sarah's and his baby's death. He also curses the unnaturalness of those deaths, which were fostered by an unforgiving man-made morality that is supported by Mrs. Kedrigan's jealousy and Sarah's brothers' shame. And Oliver is cursing his cowardice for denying his natural family outside of wedlock. Lavin suggests that Sarah is destined by nature for motherhood by contrasting her healthy pregnancy with that of the sickly Mrs. Kedrigan. The village women had predicted that Mrs. Kedrigan could never become a mother, and had wondered why the earthy farmer had married her. Her hysterical illnesses during pregnancy cause her to rely on her husband's ministrations even though she calls him "a cruel brute" for making her pregnant, whereas Sarah cheerfully works as hard as usual during pregnancy, without the help of any man. Perhaps Sarah's natural fitness for motherhood explains why upright matrons had delivered all of her previous births, and why they continued to hire her to clean their houses. Yet when the protection of her brothers and lover is withdrawn, self-reliant Sarah and her baby die; unnatural patriarchy triumphs over the natural mother.

Trying to show their disgust with Sarah, her brothers exceed her sin of lust with one of violence. Mrs. Kedrigan also tries to prove that her value is beyond Sarah's, but fails for the same reasons that Sarah's brothers do. Lavin exposes how respectable women such as Mrs. Kedrigan reconcile themselves to the low status of their gender by seeing themselves as worthy like the Virgin, whereas "fallen women" are despicable. Kristeva might call this regarding oneself as unique among women like the Virgin herself. For Mrs. Kedrigan, it is a self-delusion of superiority with horrible consequences for Sarah, Sarah's baby, and herself.

Sarah's martyrdom draws attention to the malice and artifice latent within the virginity ideal. However unconsciously, the village priest acts in accord with the cruelty of that ideal by nagging Sarah and her brothers about her affairs. The priest tells Sarah's brothers that their sister should be put into a Home. This idea encourages them to view Sarah as less than human—as criminal trash that should be thrown away. The brothers exile Sarah from their home to prevent their priest from continuing to blame them for Sarah's behavior. The priest also helps to cause Sarah's death through having repeatedly chastised her for not revealing the names of the fathers of her older children. Like Sarah's brothers, the priest hates Sarah's lack of submissiveness as much as her so-called fallenness. For although Sarah is pious, she will not accept the repentant Magdalen role that the priest dictates. Instead, Sarah gets pregnant out of wedlock again and again. To the priest, Sarah is an embarrassment—a rebel against the notions of proper womanhood that the Madonna myth promotes. Writing Kedrigan about his upcoming fatherhood may be Sarah's half-compliant, half-defiant response to the priest's exhortations. The priest's role as an underlying cause of Sarah's death suggests that the Church teaches Irish families to murder their own "fallen women."

For Lavin and O'Brien, the demand for virginity enforces the punishment of the rebellious "fallen woman," whereas it restricts the life experience of the well-disciplined nun. Although critics have noted that the alternatives to marriage for women in Ireland rarely go beyond the brothel or the convent, nuns and "fallen women" in O'Brien's and Lavin's stories don't recognize the economic factors that shape their choices; instead, they act masochistically to pay for the evil they perceive as inherent to their female bodies. The high status of the nun is achieved through the low status of the "fallen woman," through contrasting the hard-bought virtue of one with the so-called sinfulness of the other. The nun's convent may seem imprisoning, but so may the home of the respectable wife or the ditch of the "fallen woman."

Whereas O'Brien's heroines are captivated by two forms of romance—the religious and the sexual—Lavin's heroines seem impervious to both. The Madonna myth may be regarded as a source for both the religious and the sexual romances critiqued by O'Brien's stories. As the central model for the Irish woman, the Virgin fosters the ideal of chastity to which the nun aspires and from which the "fallen woman" falls short. O'Brien's Eily is led to a lobotomy through sexual passion. Lacking Eily's heterosexual fantasies of romance, Imelda and her admirer mingle religious and sexual romance in ways that question the standard formulations of both. In contrast with O'Brien's yearning heroines, Lavin's Angela becomes a nun out of fear of the romantic side of men, Sarah has affairs without expecting courtship, and Mrs. Kedrigan places revenge above both love and religion. Whereas O'Brien deconstructs religious and sexual romance by merging the two, Lavin shows the paucity of experience that lacks any form of romance. Lavin focuses upon the least glamorous effects of the Madonna myth—killing rivalries between women and ossifying chastity. Lavin and O'Brien share an awareness of the unrealistic desires—whether for superiority or sacrifice—that the Madonna myth fosters in Irish women, along with the women's guilt at never reaching their ideal of purity and selflessness.

Desmond Hogan (essay date March 1996)

SOURCE: "Sources of Happiness," in *Books and Bookmen,* No. 365, March, 1996, pp. 24-5.

[*In the essay below, Hogan reflects on Lavin's works and concludes that the overall mood of her stories and novels is agnostic.*]

A fitting introduction to the work of Mary Lavin might be an emblem from a mesmeric and lonely short story by a contemporary of Mary Lavin, 'The Bride of the Innisfallen' by Eudora Welty, a story of journeying and estrangement and newness, the newness of place, and the newness of self away from familiar surroundings and ingrained relationships. 'You must never betray pure joy the kind you were born and began with either by hiding it or by parading it in front of people's eyes; they didn't want to be shown it. And still you must tell it.' With the republication by Virago in April of Mary Lavin's second and last novel *Mary O'Grady* and the recent publication by Constable of the third volume of Mary Lavin's stories it would seem an appropriate moment to take a bold look at the work of Mary Lavin and its unifying obsession with happiness and inner life, the fierce admonition her work seems to give that inner life should be protected at all costs. One of her most complete later stories, contained in volume three of her collected stories, is in fact called '**Happiness**', and in this the heroine who has forged a path through all of her volumes of stories is prostrate and dying, seeing psychic daf-

fodils on the bedroom floor. 'Her theme was happiness: what it was, what it was not; where we might find it, where not; and how, if found, it must be guarded.' The opening of '**Happiness**' could be an appraisal of Mary Lavin's lifetime struggle. Frank O'Connor's description of Mary Lavin is not altogether different. 'Like Whitman's wild oak in Louisiana, she has stood a little apart from the rest of us "uttering joyous leaves of dark green".'

Mary O'Grady, first published in 1950 when Mary Lavin had already published three volumes of stories and one novel, written in a month while her father was dying, is unusually frenetic among her work a series of mosaics, a description of family, an attempted analysis of family relationships, and particularly a portrait of an Irish mother who consumes joys and tragedies, rewards and afflictions into the treadmill of Irish motherhood.

'There are only two valid relationships, blood and passion' one of Mary Lavin's stories insists; and it seems in *Mary O'Grady* that anyone, like the son Patrick, who does not bow to these twin authorities is destroyed by their profligacy. The biographical fact that *Mary O'Grady* was written while Mary Lavin's father was dying is more than interesting for it is a father character, in various shades, who provides most surprises in her work. In *The Shrine* (1977), there is a story called '**Tom**' in which a father writes a letter in aberrant English to his daughter, on pink paper, on the eve of the Grand National:

> You Seem to wait till the Ball Came to you
> that is Rong you should Keep Moving and
> and Not to Stay in the One Place. God Luck,
>   Dadey.

In Mary Lavin's work there are people who move and people who are still like Mary O'Grady people trapped by stillness and people obliterated by movement like the son Patrick in *Mary O'Grady.* But it is not so much the darers who have Mary Lavin's admiration as those whose state of either movement or stillness comes from complex, integral decisions. Miss Lomas in '**The Mock Auction**' and Vera in '**One Summer**' are among those who are still and yet, despite the contradictions, achieve felicity in their stillness.

One of those who went the furthest is Lally in an early story, '**The Will**'. She went from Athenry to Dublin, the 'heart of that mystery', is spurned by her mother for making a bad marriage, and for sinking so low as to have lodgers, is cut out of the will. But Lally realises that despite the revulsion of her family towards her that 'You were you always, no matter where you went or what you did . . . you don't change' and so makes a manifesto for the Irish artist in declining a compromised family offer of money to her. She anticipates Edna O'Brien's personal and grieved manifesto in *Mother Ireland.*

'Those who feel and go along with the journey of their feelings are richer than the seducers who hit and run.' Instead of taking money she sinks her own pittances into lighting 'some holy lamps at the Covent of Perpetual Reparation', for her mother died in bitterness and nonforgiveness towards her. Someone who is forgiven but too late is the happy-go-lucky young man in the magnificent **'The Little Prince,'** driven across the 'vast Atlantic' because he is a spendthrift. 'Many a young man like him went out in danger to come home a different man altogether; a man to be respected: a well-to-do man with a fur lining in his top coat, his teeth stopped with gold, and the means to hire motor cars and drive his relatives about the countryside.' Years later his sister makes the same journey to try to find him only to come up in her searchings with a corpse which might or might not be him. 'But if it was her brother something had sundered them, something had severed the bonds of blood, and she knew him not. And if it was I who was lying there, she thought, he wouldn't know me. It signified nothing that they might once have sprung from the same womb. Now they were strangers.' The myth of blood bonds is unassailably contested. A strange room is opened in Irish fiction. The rage is Faulknerian. There is no rest for the conscience in Athenry.

The middle stories are concerned with efforts to protect the self and inner life against the loneliness of the body, against incursions from strangers, against an obtusely unsympathetic society. A 'dowdy, lumpish and unromantic figure' wanders through these stories, often stumbling on unexpected moments of triumph, unexpected epiphanies composed from everyday details. The story 'Happiness' seems to obliterate this heroine as if the struggle has gone on long enough and acknowledgement of ultimate triumph is made with a death-bed scene in which a mother finally communicates to a hitherto uncomprehending daughter her Tolstoian vision of happiness 'Nor think sorrow its exact opposite' thus preserving the continuity of things, injecting a personal vision into the family tree, sublimating the self into the general. Mary O'Grady doesn't let go of life until she knows her youngest daughter Rosie is pregnant, thus family continuity is preserved. The nightmare of self is dissolved in the omnipotent family tree. But this I would suggest is longing more than a reality in Mary Lavin's work. One of her saddest stories is another recent one, **'Eterna'**, in which a doctor befriends a woman who has become a nun because the nuns were the only people who ever took an interest in her, showing her she could paint. Years after their friendship the doctor sights a strange, wrecked creature in the National Gallery in Dublin whom he presumes to be that nun. 'People had to clip their wings if they wanted to survive in this world', he smugly remarks, recalling the nun's onetime embarrassing idealism.

The fundamental and integral mood in Mary Lavin's work, though, is not of effulgent happiness or of moral contraction. For all the priests and nuns and brothers who inhabit it

it is agnostic. It seems to say, at its most intense and unhindered, 'I don't know'.

REVIEWS OF LAVIN'S RECENT WORK

Craig Brown (review date 29 November 1985)

SOURCE: "Breathing Hope and Despair," in *The Times Literary Supplement,* No. 4313, November 29, 1985, p. 1353.

[*In the following review of* A Family Likeness, *Brown comments on Lavin's themes and style.*]

There is something rather un-Irish about Mary Lavin's prose: it doesn't sing or soar or weep, it has no lilt, no twang even, and the sentences straggle and falter and thud. There is hardly a sentence in her new book of short stories, her first for eight years, which could be described as "beautifully turned", and she salvages no aphorisms or last-line truths from the sadness of her tales. The only poetic line in the book—"Nature ever was a deceiver"—is uttered by a newly-wed young woman. "Surely this was a strange thing for a young girl to say on her honeymoon?" her husband thinks, years later. V.S. Pritchett recently said that his own short stories are concerned with those moments in which there is a change in his characters' lives; in general, Mary Lavin's could be said to concern those moments when it becomes clear—though not always to the characters—that things will never change. Lavin's sadnesses are too personal to be fêted by rhythm, too isolated to be relieved by a moral, too sparse for beauty.

She writes mainly of marriages and families. Her characters are not alone in a social sense: the possibility of a deep love is forever there, but with contact turns to something smaller and meaner, like indifference or irritation. In the best story in the new collection, **"A Marriage"**, a wife of many years confronts her increasingly irritable husband, a university professor, with the news that she has paid a secret visit to the doctor. All the petty, disloyal thoughts from a long and weary marriage fly away:

> The doctor? James was stunned. He fell back against the pillows. Such a rush of blood came to his head, his sight blurred and he thought for a moment blood had gushed into his eyes. . . . Distraught, he looked at her and their eyes met. James was momentarily distracted. How young her eyes had remained. They were the eyes of a girl. How was it that they never looked into each other's eyes nowadays? Maybe that was where love took refuge when the rest of the body was drained of the power to evoke it. "Oh Emmy, Emmy, what is the matter? Tell me. Tell me." His

eyes still clinging to hers, he went to clutch her to him.

Gently Emmy pushed him away. "I must explain something, James. It was not to consult him about myself I went. I went to make an appointment with him for you."

"Me?" James was first dumbfounded, then outraged. "How dare you interfere in my life, attempt to interfere I mean."

In Lavin's world, profound emotions make speedy, bit-part entrances and exits while less fulsome feelings—tetchiness, disappointment and undefined longings for something other—dominate. Lavin has such a keen sense of the irrational, disordered workings of the mind, and the way in which it is activated more often by misinterpretation and defiance than by truth, that occasionally when reading her, one has the uncanny sense of being confronted by something previously secret to oneself and from oneself. Her characters are more often than not hopelessly misrepresented by their efforts at speech.

Lavin's sadnesses are too personal to be fêted by rhythm, too isolated to be relieved by a moral, too sparse for beauty.

—Craig Brown

In those few Lavin stories where the reality behind this quirkiness has to submit itself to straightforwardness, or to too great a scheme, the writing jars. This happens only once in *A Family Likeness,* in **"The Face of Hate"**, set in Belfast in 1957, against a background of increasing civil unrest. Employing a young girl as the voice of wisdom and honesty ("The land was here before any of us, Catholics and Protestants"), Lavin is forced to deprive her of the subtleties and contradictions that make other characters so true and convincing. As robust and simple and articulate a voice of right as this seems less likely than ever after the stories it follows, the girl's final statement of impending doom too overtly a message from the author, and that message wrapped a little too neatly in the bleakness afforded by hindsight. Elsewhere, the characters breathe hope and despair, hope and despair as surely as they breathe in and out.

Reva Brown (review date February 1986)

SOURCE: A review of *A Family Likeness, and Other Sto-*ries, and *The Stories of Mary Lavin Vol. 3,* in *British Book News,* February, 1986, pp. 110-11.

[*In the review below, Brown comments favorably on Lavin's talents as a short-story writer.*]

Mary Lavin is a superb storyteller. She has the capacity to take an apparently ordinary, even banal, situation and to compress within the few pages of her short story an entirely credible small world. Such is the honesty and reality of her creation that we believe in the lives led by her characters both before and after the incidents that make up the core of the story she tells us about them. Not only has she a sensitive insight into the human condition but she also shows an appreciation of the beauty of the countryside in which many of her stories are set. She writes about contemporary people, involved in present-day situations, and there is something honourable and honest in her approach to her characters and their problems, emotions, involvements, triumphs and failures. Nothing extraordinary happens to them, but their lives and feelings are portrayed with a clear vision and empathy that transforms these 'ordinary' people into something special.

The 'plots' of the stories are simple: an elderly woman visits the nearby woods with her daughter and grandaughter to see if the cowslips are out (**'A Family Likeness'**); a courting couple, out on an evening stroll, see a house to let (**'A House to Let'**); a young woman describes her mother's sisters, and their lives (**'A Bevy of Aunts'**); a middle-aged woman visits her daughter and son-in-law for the first time soon after their marriage (**'A Walk on the Cliff'**); a young man meets a middle-aged widow and they both let slip the possibility of 'something more' between them (**'The Cuckoo-Spit'**); two students at Dublin University warily approach romance (**'The Lucky Pair'**); a middle-aged woman agrees to marry the man who jilted her twenty years before (**'Heart of Gold'**).

[Lavin] writes about contemporary people, involved in present-day situations, and there is something honourable and honest in her approach to her characters and their problems, emotions, involvements, triumphs and failures.

—Reva Brown

Within these ordinary, often commonplace, situations, Mary Lavin explores the motive, thoughts and feelings of her characters, rendering even the most complex of them comprehensible and clear. Her people are fully rounded and believable, depicted with a subtle wit and humour that sets up echoes of irony, pathos or recognition in the reader. Mary Lavin was born in Massachusetts, came to Ireland when she was ten, and has lived there ever since. Her stories, many published in the *New Yorker,* are set in small towns or the countryside of Massachusetts or Ireland. On a practical level, *A Family Likeness,* which contains six stories, has a larger print-size and is consequently easier to read than *The Stories of Mary Lavin,* which has thirteen stories and is only around seventy pages longer.

Richard F. Peterson (review date Spring 1987)

SOURCE: A review of *A Family Likeness and Other Stories* and *The Stories of Mary Lavin,* in *Studies in Short Fiction,* Vol. 24, No. 2, Spring, 1987, pp. 170-71.

[*In the following review, Peterson remarks on the themes of Lavin's stories and praises them as "remarkably insightful and intimate."*]

With the publication of *A Family Likeness and Other Stories* and the third volume of *The Stories of Mary Lavin,* Constable has something new and something old for Mary Lavin readers.

While a new collection of short stories by a writer of major reputation in the genre is bound to excite her readers, a volume of previously collected stories can be equally interesting and even more satisfying if the stories are among the writer's best. The third volume of *Stories* does have the virtue of containing several of Mary Lavin's finest short stories, though it suffers from the same quirks of selection and arrangement that bother the earlier Constable volumes. With the exception of "Lilacs," a leftover from Lavin's first collection of stories published in 1943, and the autobiographical "Lemonade," from a 1961 collection, the third volume collects, though not in their original order, all of the short stories and novellas from *In the Middle of the Fields* and *Happiness.* These eleven stories, published in the late 1960s, represent a major phase in Mary Lavin's career in which she added new power and control to her fiction by occasionally dramatizing her painful adjustment to widowhood.

If read in the order in which they were first collected, Mary Lavin's widow stories begin with "In the Middle of the Fields," include "The Cuckoospit," one of her most successful studies of widowhood, and conclude with "Happiness," one of her most personal narratives. In these three stories, Mary Lavin reveals the intense loneliness of the widow immediately after the death of her husband, then the emotional complexities, four years later, in the opportunity for a new intimate relationship, and finally the spiritual and physical resignation of the widow after a lifetime of joy and grief. The common thread drawing the three stories together is the powerful influence of memory on the emotions of Mary Lavin's widows, especially in preserving the pleasure of married life and the pain of loss.

The remaining entries in Constable's third volume represent Mary Lavin's diverse approaches to fiction writing, including formula stories, like "The New Gardener," impressionistic portraits of human isolation, especially "One Evening" and "A Pure Accident," and novellas, including "One Summer," "The Mock Auction," and "The Lost Child." Of these stories, the novella "The Lost Child" stands out as one of Lavin's most experimental and successful long narratives. This story of a woman's emotional and spiritual crisis during her miscarriage is told with such artistic balance that both the external events and the inner state of the central character are rendered vividly, while the narrative itself raises several difficult questions about the human spirit. "The Lost Child" and Mary Lavin's widow stories highlight the third volume of *Stories* and make it an important, even if uneven, addition to the Constable series.

> The short stories in *A Family Likeness* explore the problems of growing old, especially the persistent and growing doubts of the aging of their value and place in a world that now apparently belongs to the young.
>
> —*Richard F. Peterson*

Mary Lavin's latest collection of stories, *A Family Likeness,* offers a microcosm of the delights, perplexities, and occasional problems in her fiction. The volume holds six new stories, including a novella, "A Bevy of Aunts." While the novella is interesting because it adds one more measure to the fictionalized chronology of Mary Lavin's youth, in this case, her life with her mother's relatives in Athenry, the most intriguing stories are those reflective of her present age and concerns. With the exception of "The Face of Hate," with its contrived plot based on the troubles in Northern Ireland, and "A House to Let," with its overstated epiphany of the adolescent's acceptance of adult responsibilities, the short stories in *A Family Likeness* explore the problems of growing old, especially the persistent and growing doubts of the aging of their value and place in a world that now apparently belongs to the young. Indeed, the two best stories in the collection, "A Family Likeness" and "A Walk on the Cliff," concentrate specifically on the dilemma of the mother who struggles with either her feeling of being a nuisance in the raising of her daughter's child or her dread of interfering with her daughter's marriage.

With their sensitive narratives of the aging mother's fear of displacement from family and home, **"A Family Likeness"** and **"A Walk on the Cliff"** exemplify, more than the other stories in the collection, the sustaining power of Mary Lavin's vision and craft after the accomplishment of her widow stories. They also reveal, once again, a courageous artist at work, drawing from her own experiences, no matter how difficult and painful, to create remarkably insightful and intimate stories.

FURTHER READING

Criticism

C. L. Innes. "Living in Separate Worlds." *Irish Literary Supplement* 7, No. 2 (Fall 1988): 20.
> Favorably reviews *The House in Clewe Street,* which, Innes argues, "begins to fill a substantial gap in the subject matter of Irish fiction—the world of middle class Catholics in the towns and cities."

Patricia K. Meszaros. "Woman as Artist: The Fiction of Mary Lavin." *Critique* XXIV, No. 1 (Fall 1982): 39-54.
> An overview of Lavin's work focusing on feminist themes in her fiction.

Additional coverage of Lavin's life and career is contained in the following sources published by Gale Research: *Contemporary Authors,* Vols. 9-12R, 151; *Contemporary Authors New Revision Series,* Vol. 33; *Dictionary of Literary Biography,* Vol. 15; *Major Twentieth-Century Writers;* and *Short Story Criticism,* Vol. 4.

Obituaries

In addition to the authors represented in the In Memoriam section of the *Yearbook,* the following notable writers died in 1996:

Quentin Bell
August 19, 1910—December 16, 1996
British author, artist, critic, and biographer

Bell is best known as the biographer of his aunt, Virginia Woolf. The son of Woolf's older sister, Vanessa Bell, and Clive Bell, his childhood was influenced by the writers and artists who made up the Bloomsbury Group, including Woolf, E. M. Forster, Lytton Strachey, Roger Fry, Duncan Grant, and Vita Sackville-West. Upon its publication in 1972, Bell's *Virginia Woolf: A Biography* became a definitive source among Woolf scholars and established Bell as a careful, fair-minded writer. As was the case with the other Bloomsbury personalities, Bell was accomplished in a number of fields. In addition to nonfiction writing, which included studies of fashion, art, and design, Bell wrote a novel, *The Brandon Papers* (1985), and a memoir, *Bloomsbury Recalled* (1996). Bell was a lecturer in art education at King's College and professor of fine art at Oxford and the University of Leeds, and also served as chair of history and theory of art at the University of Sussex.

Erma Bombeck
February 21, 1927—April 22, 1996
American journalist and humorist

By finding humor in life's most annoying situations, Bombeck became one of America's most popular writers. Her syndicated column, "At Wit's End," which debuted in 1965, was a light-hearted look at the challenges of family life and led to more than a dozen best-selling books of her collected essays, including *At Wit's End* (1967), *The Grass Is Always Greener Over the Septic Tank* (1976), *If Life Is a Bowl of Cherries, What Am I Doing in the Pits?* (1978), *Family: The Ties That Bind . . . And Gag!* (1987), and *When You Look Like Your Passport Photo, It's Time to Go Home* (1991). Bombeck donated her $1.5 million advance fee and all proceeds from *I Want to Grow Hair, I Want to Grow Up, I Want to Go to Boise* (1989), in which children with cancer and their families recount their stories, to cancer research; she received the American Cancer Society Medal of Honor in 1990. Bombeck had lived with polycystic kidney disease since age 20; she died of complications after a kidney transplant.

Joseph Brodsky
May 24, 1940—January 28, 1996
Russian-born American poet, author, and educator

Brodsky's poetry earned him the wrath of the government in his native Russia and the love of critics, peers, and readers in his adopted America. After enduring ten years of persecution, a trial, and sentencing to an Arctic labor camp for his poetry, deemed inflammatory by the Russian government, Brodsky was exiled and emigrated to the United States in 1972. Settling in Michigan with the help of W. H. Auden, Brodsky began his academic career as poet-in-residence at the University of Michigan. He became a U.S. citizen in 1977. Brodsky's writings brought him considerable acclaim, including the 1981 MacArthur Award, the 1986 National Book Critics Circle Award (for the 1984 memoir *Less Than One*), and the 1987 Nobel Prize in Literature. He became the first foreign-born person to serve as U.S. Poet Laureate in 1991. Among his best-known works are the poetry collections *A Part of Speech* (1977) and *To Urania* (1988), and *Less Than One*. His most recent publications included a play, *Marbles* (1989), and a book of prose, *Watermark* (1992). For the last fifteen years of his life, Brodsky was Andrew Mellon Professor of Literature at Mount Holyoke College. Though he traveled widely, Brodsky never returned to Russia. [For further information on Brodsky's life and career, see *CLC,* Volumes 4, 6, 13, 36, and 50.]

Georges Duby
October 7, 1919—December 2, 1996
French historian, author, and editor

Duby was a medievalist noted for his ability to bring history to life. "A fine and prolific writer, in France he did more than almost anyone else to stimulate popular interest in history," a *London Times* obituarist noted. Among his writings were *Rural Economy and Country Life in the Medieval West* (1962), *The Age of the Cathedrals: Art and Society 980-1420* (1976), and what many consider his finest work, *Le dimanche de Bouvines* (1973), translated as *The Legend of Bouvines* (1990).

Hannah Green
1927—October 16, 1996
American novelist and educator

Green published just one novel in her lifetime, but it was, according to Robert McG. Thomas Jr., "one slender novel of such delicately distilled perfection that she could hardly bring herself to compose another." *The Dead of the House* met with widespread critical acclaim upon its initial publication in 1972 and again when it was reissued in 1996. Critics lauded Green's painstaking attention to the craft of fiction writing, noting that the "new author" was a forty-six-year-old creative writing teacher who had studied with Vladimir Nabokov and Wallace Stegner and had worked on *The Dead of the House* for close to twenty years. Green began a second book in 1971 and spent twenty-five years perfecting it. *Golden Spark, Little Saint: My Book of the Hours of Saint Foy,* a fact-and-fiction account of the life of a twelve-year-old French girl betrayed by her father and martyred when she refused to renounce her faith, is scheduled to be published by Random House next year. [For further information on Green's life and career, see *CLC,* Volume 3.]

Eugene "Guy" Izzi
1953(?)—December 7, 1996
American mystery writer

The death of "Guy" Izzi, a crime writer whose own tough upbringing in a steel-mill neighborhood on Chicago's South Side provided much of the gritty background for his novels, was officially ruled a suicide but remains a mystery to many. Izzi was found hanging outside the window of his locked fourteenth-floor office in Chicago, an apparent suicide, but he was wearing a bulletproof vest and carrying chemical defense spray and brass knuckles in his pocket, and his face and body were bruised, prompting some to suspect murder. Izzi's friends and family said he had no reason to kill himself—he had a wife and children and a new book set for publication—and also said that Izzi had recently received threats from a militia group angered by his undercover investigation of their operations. A third theory, that the author's death was accidental, was prompted by investigators' discovery at the scene of several computer diskettes containing an unfinished novel which ends with the protagonist, a Chicago mystery writer, suffering an attack by militia members who tie a noose around his neck, attach the rope to a metal desk, and throw him from his office window. The story ends, however, with the writer pulling himself back up the rope and killing his attackers. The similarities of the story and Izzi's death prompted some to speculate that the author may have been attempting to simulate the action in the story in an effort to add realism to his writing. Izzi's novels include *Bad Guys* and *Eighth Victim* (1988), *The Booster* and *King of the Hustlers* (1989), *Invasions* and *Prime Roll* (1990), *Tribal Secrets* (1992), and *Tony's Justice* (1993). *A Matter of Honor: A Novel of Chicago,* Izzi's last work, was published May 1, 1997.

Walter Kerr
July 8, 1913—October 9, 1996
American journalist, author, playwright, and drama critic

Respected for his vivid, involving accounts of theatrical productions, Kerr earned a Pulitzer Prize in 1978 for the body of his critical work. Kerr received bachelor's and master's degrees in speech from Northwestern University, then joined the faculty of Washington, D.C.'s Catholic University, where he directed, wrote, and adapted plays for student productions, some of which reached professional theaters and even Broadway. Having developed Catholic University's drama program into what was described in *Time* magazine as "the finest nonprofessional theater in the country," Kerr began his career as a critic in 1949 with *Commonweal,* but built his reputation writing for the *New York Herald Tribune* from 1951 to 1966. When the *Herald* ceased publication, Kerr moved to the *New York Times,* where he worked until his retirement in 1983. In addition to his collected criticism, Kerr wrote books including *How Not to Write a Play, Criticism and Censorship,* and *The Silent Clowns,* now considered the definitive source on the comedians of the silent film era. The Ritz Theater in Manhattan was restored and renamed the Walter Kerr Theater in 1990. Upon the announcement of his death, Broadway theaters' marquee lights were dimmed in his honor.

Paul Henry Oehser
1904—December 4, 1996
American writer, editor, and conservationist

Oehser was affiliated with the Smithsonian Institution, serving in the editorial division from the early 1930s until his retirement as editor in chief in 1962. Before joining the Smithsonian staff, he had worked as a scientific editor for the Bureau of Biological Survey in the U.S. Agriculture Department. After his retirement, Oehser edited scientific reports for the National Geographic Society until 1975. Oehser was a member of a number of conservationist groups, and served on the Governing Council of the Wilderness Society. Among his writings were the history books *Sons of Science* and *The Smithsonian Institution* and two poetry collections, *Fifty Poems* and *The Witch of Scrapfaggot Green.*

Margret Rey
May, 1906—December 21, 1996
German-born American children's author and illustrator

Rey and her husband, H. A. Rey, were the creators of "Curious George," the much-loved, mischievous monkey of children's stories. Both Reys were artists, but for the Curious George books she wrote the stories and he created the illustrations. The couple wrote the first Curious George adventure in the 1930s while living in Paris; they rode bicycles out of town to escape the German occupation in 1940, carrying the unsold manuscript with them. After making their way to New York, the Reys sold *Curious George* to Houghton Mifflin, which published it in 1941. The pair went on to pen six more original Curious George stories, and Rey created 28 more tales with Alan J. Shalleck. The series has sold more than 20 million copies in 12 languages. Rey also published five other books, including *Spotty* and *Pretzel,* and oversaw the large merchandising program of Curious George products. Shortly before her death, Rey contributed $1 million each to the Boston Public Library to improve the children's rooms in its branches and to Beth Israel Hospital's Center for Alternative Medicine for Research.

Carl Sagan
November 9, 1934—December 20, 1996
American physicist, astronomer, and author

An astronomer who brought the universe's "billions and billions" of stars into the nation's living rooms with the television series *Cosmos* in 1980, Sagan became a best-selling and Pulitzer Prize-winning author and a popular television personality. Bruce Alberts, president of the National Academy of Sciences, remarked, "Carl Sagan, more than any contemporary scientist I can think of, knew what it takes to stir passion within the public when it comes to the wonder and importance of science." Among Sagan's research topics were the search for life elsewhere in the universe, the origin of life on Earth, and the potential for a devastating cooling of the atmosphere, or "nuclear winter," after a nuclear war. In addition to his numerous nonfiction works, including *Cosmos, Pale Blue Dot,* and *Comet,* Sagan wrote a novel, *Contact,* which became a best-seller and will be released as a film next year. Along with his Pulitzer, Sagan received numerous awards from the scientific community, including the National Academy of Science's highest honor, the Public Welfare Medal, and the NASA Medal for Distinguished Public Service twice. [For further information on Sagan's life and career, see *CLC,* Volume 30.]

George Starbuck
June 15, 1931—August 15, 1996
American poet and educator

Once described as the "thinking man's Ogden Nash," Starbuck was known for poems that "explored profound themes with such a dazzling display of pun, parody and pyrotechnic wit that critics seemed too busy laughing out loud to take him seriously," Robert McG. Thomas Jr. noted. Starbuck began college at age 16 intending to become a mathematician, but soon turned to poetry writing. He spent years at Cal Tech, the University of California at Berkeley, the University of Chicago, and Harvard, where he studied with Archibald MacLeish and Robert Lowell and associated with fellow students Sylvia Plath and Anne Sexton, but never received a degree. He did, however, receive the Yale Younger Poets Award in 1960 for his first collection, *Bone Thoughts.* Later collections included *White Paper* (1968), *Elegy in a Country Church Yard* (1974), and *The Argot Merchant Disaster: New and Selective Poems* (1982). Starbuck taught at several schools early in his career and served almost twenty years as director of the graduate writing program at Boston University. [For further information on Starbuck's life and career, see *CLC,* Volume 53.]

Diana Trilling
July 21, 1905—October 23, 1996
American essayist, editor, and literary critic

A respected author, editor, and critic in her own right, Trilling fought to build a reputation for herself apart from that of her husband, Lionel Trilling, one of the century's leading literary critics and authors. She often joked that the headline of her obituary would read, "Diana Trilling Dies at 150. Widow of Distinguished Professor and Literary Critic Lionel Trilling." Trilling was hired as the *Nation*'s book reviewer on the recommendation of her husband; there she began the work that would lead to five books and three collections of essays and reviews, while gaining respect among readers and other critics as an uncompromising, intelligent and insightful writer. After her husband's death in 1975, Trilling edited a twelve-volume edition of his work. The book that brought her the greatest amount of public attention was *Mrs. Harris: The Death of the Scarsdale Diet Doctor* (1981), a journalistic account of the trial of Jean Harris for the murder of her husband, Herman Tarnower. In 1993, as macular degeneration robbed her of her sight, Trilling dictated her memoir, *The Beginning of the Journey: The Marriage of Diana and Lionel Trilling.* Early in 1996, she finished her last book, *A Visit to Camelot,* about an evening at the White House during John F. Kennedy's presidency.

Laurens van der Post
December 13, 1906—December 15, 1996
South African poet, linguist, philosopher, anthropologist, and explorer

In a life filled with a variety of experiences and accomplishments, Van der Post grew up in South Africa, survived for over three years in a Japanese concentration camp during World War II, later attained the rank of lieutenant-colonel and served on the staff of Lord Mountbatten, and became a trusted advisor to Britain's Prince Charles and former Prime Minister Margaret Thatcher, who knighted him in 1981. At age 21, he began writing what would be the first anti-apartheid novel ever published, *In a Province* (1934); in later writings he sought to prevent the destruction of the Kalahari Desert and its indigenous Bushmen (*The Lost World of the Kalahari,* 1958, and *The Heart of the Hunter,* 1961), and encouraged forgiveness for his Japanese torturers in the memoir *The Seed and the Sower* (1971), later filmed as *Merry Christmas, Mr. Lawrence.* Van der Post was a proponent of Carl Jung's theory of the collective subconscious, and influenced Prince Charles's thinking on that and a number of other topics, from multiculturalism to the need for modern Britain to tolerate non-Christian religions. [For further information on van der Post's life and career, see *CLC,* Volume 5.]

Topic in Literature: 1996

True-Crime Literature

INTRODUCTION

"True crime" is a recently coined term used to refer to non-fictional accounts of actual crimes, usually murders. There has been little systematic study of the genre or its readers; critics and publishers offer contradictory theories about true-crime literature. Although the term and the popularity of the genre are relatively new, factual accounts of crimes are not. True-crime accounts date back as far as the 18th century, and such writers as Edmund Pearson, William Roughead, and Jonathan Goodman described the exploits of criminals earlier in the twentieth century. Critics agree that Truman Capote's *In Cold Blood* (1966) gave birth to the genre. Called a non-fiction novel, the book was a not-strictly-factual account of the murder of a Kansas family in which Capote focused on the killers—not the victims, as was the norm previously—in attempting to explain why the killers acted as they did. Capote's work and Norman Mailer's book *The Executioner's Song* (1980) are considered classics of the genre.

In the 1980s, the true-crime book market enjoyed an unprecedented popularity. Many critics suggest that the advent of tabloid television, the desensitizing of violence, and the rise in media coverage of crimes led to an increase in demand for factual accounts, particularly of serial killings. Although some critics contend that the popularity of the true-crime genre is a uniquely American phenomenon, other commentators point out that true-crime books are very popular in England, a country with a low homicide rate. Some scholars have suggested that readers are reassured by writers' descriptions of killers as monstrous and inhuman, placing them outside the realm of normal society. However, writers like Capote and Mailer have focused almost sympathetically on how incidents in the criminals' youths transformed them into killers. Most commentators agree that the most popular true-crime books feature victims who are ordinary Americans, not unlike the readers themselves; focus on a crime which is violent and gruesome; end in a conviction of a criminal; and offer commentary on some aspect of contemporary society. Some of the most popular true-crime writers today are Ann Rule, Jack Olsen, and Joe McGinniss.

REPRESENTATIVE WORKS DISCUSSED BELOW

Baker, Mark: *Bad Guys: America's Most Wanted in Their Own Words* (nonfiction) 1996

Berkow, Ira: *The Man Who Robbed the Pierre: The True Story of Bobby Comfort* (nonfiction) 1987

Bolitho, William: *Murder for Profit* (nonfiction) 1926

Capote, Truman: *In Cold Blood* (nonfiction) 1966

Davis, Don: *The Milwaukee Murders* (nonfiction) 1991

Defoe, Daniel: *True and Genuine Account of the Life and Actions of the late Jonathan Wild; not made up of Fiction and Fable, but taken from his own Mouth, and Collected from Papers of his own Writing* (nonfiction) 1725

Egginton, Joyce: *From Cradle to Grave: The Short Lives and Strange Deaths of Marybeth Tinning's Nine Children* (nonfiction) 1989

Elkind, Peter: *Death Shift: The True Story of Nurse Genene Jones and the Texas Baby Murders* (nonfiction) 1989

Englade, Ken: *Beyond Reason: A True Story of a Shocking Double Murder, a Brilliant and Beautiful Virginia Socialite and a Deadly Psychotic* (nonfiction) 1990

Goldfarb, Ronald: *Perfect Villains, Imperfect Heroes: Robert F. Kennedy's War against Organized Crime* (nonfiction) 1996

Graysmith, Robert: *The Sleeping Lady: The Trailside Murders Above the Golden Gate* (nonfiction) 1990

Hammer, Richard: *The CBS Murders: A True Story of Greed and Violence in New York's Diamond District* (nonfiction) 1987

Jesse, F. Tennyson: *Murder and Its Motives* (nonfiction) 1924

Kaminer, Wendy: *It's All the Rage: Crime and Culture* (nonfiction) 1995

Lewis, Craig A.: *Blood Evidence: A Story of True Crime in the South* (nonfiction) 1990

Linedecker, Clifford L.: *Night Stalker* (nonfiction) 1991

Mailer, Norman: *The Executioner's Song* (nonfiction) 1980

McGinniss, Joe: *Fatal Vision* (nonfiction) 1983; *Blind Faith* (nonfiction) 1989; *Cruel Doubt* (nonfiction) 1991

Michaud, Stephen G., and Hugh Aynesworth: *The Only Living Witness* (nonfiction) 1989

Mones, Paul: *Stalking Justice* (nonfiction) 1995

Olsen, Jack: *Son: A Psychopath and His Victims* (nonfiction) 1985; *Doc: The Rape of the Town of Lovell* (nonfiction) 1989

Pearson, Edmund: *Studies in Murder* (nonfiction) 1924

Potter, Jerry Allen, and Fred Bost: *Fatal Justice: Reinvestigating the MacDonald Murders* (nonfiction) 1995

Roughead, William: *Malice Domestic* (nonfiction) 1928

Rule, Ann: *Small Sacrifices: A True Story of Passion and Murder* (nonfiction) 1987

Shimomura, Tsutomu, and John Markoff: *Takedown: The Pursuit and Capture of Kevin Mitnick, America's Most*

Wanted Computer Outlaw—by the Man Who Did It (nonfiction) 1996

Thompson, Tommy: *Blood and Money* (nonfiction) 1976

Wolfe, Linda: *Wasted: The Preppie Murder* (nonfiction) 1989

HISTORY AND ANALYSIS

William Goldhurst (essay date Fall 1989)

SOURCE: "The New Revenge Tragedy: Comparative Treatments of the Beauchamp Case," in *The Southern Literary Journal,* Vol. 22, Fall, 1989, pp. 117-27.

[*In the following essay, Goldhurst remarks on several literary treatments of the Beauchamp-Sharp murder case, which transpired in Kentucky in 1825.*]

Poe's strategy of setting an American literary situation in a remote and exotic environment has a special and complex application in the verse drama *Politian,* written in 1835. Set in Rome during the Renaissance, the play is a retelling of the Beauchamp-Sharp murder case, which took place in Frankfort, Kentucky, in 1825 and is known to historians as the Kentucky Tragedy. The story has attracted the notice of numerous authors from Poe's day to our own, including Thomas Holley Chivers, William Gilmore Simms, Charles Fenno Hoffman and Robert Penn Warren.

The lurid aspects of the sordid affair needed little blowing up to please sensation seekers of the period. Sex and violence are the foundation, while seduction, pregnancy, desertion, slander and revenge all play vivid roles in the elaboration. There is no single climax: but a bloody murder and then a trial ending in a guilty verdict, a suicide pact, and a public hanging are high points of intensity near the conclusion.

Two components of this story line are perhaps more compelling than the others: the idea that the seducer must die, and the character of Ann Cooke, who offered herself to Beauchamp on the condition that he kill for her. Of course young Beauchamp made her quarrel his own, and swore that he was acting on moral principle, as if Sharp had wronged not only a provincial maiden, but all decent men and women. Most likely Beauchamp eventually came to believe his own internal propaganda; but it was Ann Cooke who breathed life into his anger and kindled his blood lust.

According to Beauchamp's *Confession,* Cooke told him her heart would cease to ache only when Colonel Sharp was killed and not by a stranger to her tragedy, but by *her* agent acting under her direction. She was willing to kiss the hand of the person who avenged her, Ann was; and furthermore would remain forever in his debt. Later Beauchamp taught her how to shoot his pistol and she contemplated killing Sharp herself. But this plan was soon scrapped and the agent idea reinstated. When Beauchamp inquired if he should kill Sharp's brother, too, Cooke said no—not because she cared to spare the innocent, but knowing how the brother worshipped the colonel, she thought he would suffer more if left alive.

Eventually the plan was put into effect, Sharp was tricked into opening his front door and stabbed in his own vestibule, and a triumphant Beauchamp returned to an ecstatic Ann Cooke, who fell to her knees, kissed Beauchamp's hand, and begged to hear all the details of "the glorious deed."

At the end, Cooke visited Beauchamp in prison, bringing laudanum. The dose did not "take," and upon recovering they agreed to use a knife, which Cooke had smuggled into the cell. "I can refuse her nothing she prays of me to do," writes Beauchamp as his execution hour approaches. He raises the dagger and plunges it into his side, but Cooke deflects the blow, grabs the blade and directs the thrust into her own abdomen. Cooke dies of her wound; Beauchamp goes bleeding to the gallows.

The Letters of Ann Cooke provides an interesting glimpse (if they can be believed) into Cooke's feelings as she went from innocent maid to mistress to avenger. On the fatal night of her seduction, Sharp invited her to a ball, where she was "carried away" with the lights, the music, the dancing, and the wine her escort forced upon her. Acting under the influence of all these powerful and unaccustomed stimuli, Cooke says her "reason was subdued by the power of a resistless passion," etc. Before the year was out, she heard that Sharp intended to marry someone else. When she learned from Sharp himself that this was true, she sank to the floor in a faint and spent the next several weeks in her bed with a raging fever. Some months later, her baby died and Ann Cooke began to lapse into "a settled melancholy."

Eventually she emerged from her depression sufficiently to entertain Beauchamp's proposals. Yet she told him she felt she could never again experience happiness in this life, so deep was the trauma Sharp had inflicted. She believed Beauchamp thought her "degraded and unworthy" because she had been another man's fool.

Still, she was beginning to enjoy life again until she learned of Sharp's latest treachery: he was circulating a story that her baby was fathered by a negro and had even had a forged birth certificate drawn up as proof of her indiscretion. According to the *Letters,* it was at this point that Cooke invoked the Erinyes. "We took a solemn oath," she says, "that nothing but the heart's blood of the slanderer and betrayer should atone for the deep and horrible injury he had inflicted." As Beauchamp evolved from visitor to suitor to fiancé he and Cooke shared her gradually mounting anger over the injustices done her by Sharp. In calmer moments, she reminded Beauchamp that the world regarded her as "guilty and polluted." He responded by insisting that she was the innocent victim of a scoundrel's treachery.

They marry. The plan to avenge her wrongs is set in motion. Sharp is killed. Beauchamp is tried and convicted. Cooke commits suicide in his presence and he is soon afterward hanged as a felon.

Ann Cooke represents the dark side of the naive American *Frauendienst*—the habit of dehumanizing women of the time by investing them with an unrealistic purity, spirituality and vulnerability. Individual women who swallowed the mythology whole and then exaggerated its effects could easily assume a becoming narcissism with attendant feelings of self-pity over life's injustices and a brutal attitude toward the men who had wronged them.

The real Ann Cooke is difficult to identify. Certainly she did not resemble the portrait circulated by Sharp's defenders, where she is pictured as a "waning flirt of 35" who had lost her front teeth and had no chin, etc. Most likely she was average in appearance, if not beautiful, and Sharp did seduce her and then left her to marry another woman. Perhaps a healthy attitude at that point might have been a sense of shared irresponsibility. But the very definition of seduction, with its implication that the man took advantage, pressured the woman to succumb, etc. involves the idea of misconduct on the part of the male acting out a power charade against the passive female. From this assumption to: the seducer must pay! is only a short logical step.

To be sure, the early American seduction novels placed some of the blame upon the female victim, implying or stating explicitly that she was guilty of romantic fantasizing or frivolity. Still, the notion of exploitation of the female persisted, with many of Poe's contemporaries sharing the view that seducers deserved to die for offending against morality and violating the integrity of the social structure.

George Lippard certainly endorsed this view. His *The Monks of Monk Hall* concludes with the murder (or as Lippard would have us believe, the execution) of the seducer Gus Lorrimer by Byrnewood Arlington, brother of Lorrimer's victim, Mary Arlington. Byrnewood gloats over the corpse of the seducer with typical Lippard verbosity: "Ha, ha! Here is blood warm, warm, aye, warm and gushing—that gushing of the Wronger's blood!" And so on.

Earlier, Mary's seduction is accomplished with all the imagined sentiments of the stereotyped sexual villain. "Force—violence" muses the handsome Lorrimer, who says he has deeper means than force. "My victim is the instrument of her own ruin—without one rude grasp from my hand, without one threatening word, she swims willingly to my arms!"

Not only did Lippard celebrate the murder of Lorrimer in his novel, but his inflamed rhetoric resulted in a wave of public opinion (according to Leslie Fiedler's Introduction to *Monks*) that led to passage of an anti-seduction law in New York state in 1849. Death to the seducer became an ingrained formula in the urban consciousness at least, often invoked to explain the sudden or mysterious death of popular controversial figures. An irate husband or brother beat him to death: so people whispered about Poe following his collapse in Baltimore. Years later the same rumor would be circulated about Louis Gottschalk, who in fact suffered peritonitis from months of overwork.

"The seduction of a poor and innocent girl is a deed altogether as criminal as deliberate murder. It is worse than the murder of the body, for it is the assassination of the soul. If the murderer deserves death by the gallows, then the assassin of chastity and maidenhood is worthy of death by the hands of any man, and in any place," says the *Monks* author.

Lippard's revenge melodrama has much in common with the Kentucky Tragedy: the author might have had Sharp and Beauchamp and Cooke in mind when fashioning Lorrimer, Byrnewood and Mary. One conspicuous difference, however, is in his portrayal of the ruined maid. Mary Arlington, while suffering from severe depression after her "fall," assumes that her pollution and worthlessness are irredeemable; but unlike Cooke she tries to prevent any moves toward retaliation. "The wrong has been done," says Mary to her brother, "but do not, I beseech you, visit his (that is, Lorrimer's) head with a curse—." In Lippard's scheme of things, most women are pure, long-suffering, uncomplicated, and forgiving. The concept of a vindictive woman he found not unthinkable, but offensive.

Other authors of Poe's time discovered similar difficulties in attempting to portray Ann Cooke in drama or fiction. After all, weren't women, according to the popular stereotype, flawless, as well as spiritual, sentimental, loving, caring, uplifting, weak, helpless, ill, refined and self-sacrificing? How, then, with this idealized image in the popular mind, depict a vengeful, vindictive, obsessed, insane, bloodthirsty female without surrendering reader sympathy in the portrayal? It would seem that Poe and his contemporaries in this extremely revealing instance had three alternatives: 1) paint her black, make her the villain; 2) change her character, as Lippard did, omitting whatever ugly motives and emotions readers might find objectionable; or 3) complicate her character; make her vindictive, but with mitigating traits—confusion, distraction or insanity. Most authors, as we shall see, chose this third alternative.

In his verse drama *Conrad and Eudora; or The Death of Alonzo,* (1834), Thomas Holley Chivers believes along with Lippard that the crime of seduction is grievous and deserves to be punished by death. Early in the play Conrad (Beauchamp) is talking to a friend who says Alonzo (Sharp) is guilty of murder, treason, rape because he seduced Eudora and thereby "ruined the sweetest thing on earth." Conrad has a moral scale upon which he measures the degree of a seducer's guilt: "If she loved him well, and he deceived her / The crime falls heavier on his heart / Than on them both, did both love equally." Later another friend tells Conrad that "a woman's virtue robbed, like loss of sight. / Can never be restored." When Conrad says he will try to cheer Eudora up, the friend says "You can not mend a broken egg." Still later, the Innkeeper hears that Conrad might be the man who murdered Alonzo and suggests that the fault might be Eudora's; he flatly asserts that no man should be killed over a woman. But when he is told that Alonzo promised to marry Eudora and then ruined her, he says: "Then damn him—let him die." All Chivers's characters are in accord on the severity of Alonzo's crime.

The character of Ann Cooke as portrayed by Chivers is predominantly vengeful and vindictive, as she appears in Beauchamp's *Confession*. In fact she seems more bloodthirsty in *Conrad and Eudora* than she was in real life. After Conrad confronts Alonzo for the first time, issuing a death threat but relenting and letting Alonzo go, Eudora says:

> Had I been with thee, he had died so sweet
> Where he within this proud arm's reach—this stroke
> Should be effected and bring his lowness low.
> I'd tramp me in his blood, and smile with joy.

Of course, earlier Eudora tells her mother, "I would not harm the simplest thing on earth!" But she follows this statement with a lengthy speech about how deeply she has been wounded by Sharp, for whom she feels "endless hate"; and she closes with a promise to pursue him to the ends of the earth to make him pay with his life. Her mother replies: "Oh! my child! my child! thou art run mad!" Eudora denies that she is mad, but reminds her mother that "Revenge in woman hath no limitations!"

But a moment later Eudora breaks down and asks her mother to teach her how not to hate. Eudora's mother says: "Thou art distracted—oh! that I were dead!" By such means as these the playwright can have it both ways. The heroine is possibly estranged from her true nature (passive and loving) by reason of insanity. At the same time she is sane but driven by extreme emotions to act our her homicidal plan, which makes for good melodrama.

The key to this solution was provided by Cooke herself (or by the anonymous author of *The Letters*) when Ann says that Beauchamp spoke to her about the cruel treatment she had received from Sharp. "That was a chord that was never struck without producing agony and madness." The single sentence inspired more than one author of the time who was struggling with the problem of making Cooke palatable.

Greyslaer: A Romance of the Mohawk, by Charles Fenno Hoffman, originally published in 1840, is so long and diffuse that one can truthfully say the Kentucky Tragedy is buried in the narrative. Hoffman's novel is devoted more to the theme of America's emerging independence from Great Britain, with an emphasis upon Indian ways and outlaw life along the New York frontier, than it is to the affair of a wronged woman. Nonetheless some of the familiar ingredients are immediately apparent. The seduction of the heroine, Alida de Roos, leaves her scarred, psychologically speaking, for years. After her "fall," her eyes have a "bright and glassy stare," as if to indicate that she lives in a state of shock. She confesses to the hero, Greyslaer, that she is practicing with a pistol in order to avenge herself on someone; at which point Greyslaer says he loves her and would willingly become the agent of her revenge. In this version of the story, as in *Monks of Monk Hall,* the seduction of Cooke-Alida is accomplished by means of a faked marriage ceremony; and the villain undergoes character-splitting, emerging as the German immigrant Voltmeyer and the rejected suitor Bradshawe. When Alida and Greyslaer fall in love, the sentiment has a softening influence: she yields up all thoughts of retribution, and his hunger for revenge grows fainter as he enlarges his circle of acquaintances and meets more sophisticated men and women.

However, when Bradshawe hears that Alida and Greyslaer are contemplating marriage, he circulates the story that Alida has borne a child to an Indian. The slander "unhinges" Greyslaer and he begins to think of nothing but revenge. Eventually he confronts Bradshawe, but they are interrupted by Voltmeyer, whom Greyslaer kills. Arrested for this crime, Greyslaer receives a visit in prison from Alida. She expresses regret that she ever planted the idea of revenge in his mind. He says it was all an "hallucination" of her earlier years. She begs him to give up all thought of harming Bradshawe. (Later Bradshawe is shot and killed in battle.)

Hoffman's intention in *Greyslaer* was clearly to humanize the main characters of the Kentucky Tragedy. Alida's passion for blood is lukewarm most of the time; she is basically the sweet and loving woman of the sentimental tradition. Greyslaer's obsession with vengeance is short-lived and the result of temporary insanity. The author has an obvious affection for both characters; and at the end he has them fall in love, get married and live happily ever after. Like Chivers, Hoffman wants his heroine both ways—sweet and vicious. But instead of accommodating this concept by making Alida insane when she concentrates on murder, he transfers the madness to the hero and has his heroine achieve true feminity through the love of a good man. Still, for all the thought that went into Hoffman's portrayal, Alida remains a flat character, undeveloped and relatively uninteresting. In this work, at least, the author is better at portraying action than character.

The most interesting, fleshed-out depiction of Ann Cooke appears in William Gilmore Simms's novel, *Beauchamp or The Kentucky Tragedy,* published the same year as *Greyslaer.* Beauchamp is introduced as a young attorney who under extreme circumstances is capable of wild behavior. Cooke is sensitive, melancholy and capable of subtle feeling: at first she resists falling in love with Beauchamp because she fears she will use him to fulfill her "dark purpose." As other authors of the period attempted by various means to present a two-sided or ambiguous Ann Cooke—by having her basically loving, with her revenge obsession emerging out of temporary insanity, so Simms makes his heroine a combination of paradoxical traits—strength and weakness. After telling Beauchamp her story and making murder a condition of intimacy, she faints. She was "wonderfully strong," says Simms, but she was "yet a woman"—a diagnosis that explains her "sinking to the sward unconscious."

Later, her vengeful impulse becomes softened, as with Hoffman's heroine, under the influence of love; but Simms gives his heroine additional motives that help to round her out. She wants Beauchamp to *avoid* Sharp because she fears the consequences of their actions. In all the treatments of these characters from that period, including the real life models, none express this sort of very likely apprehension about the community's reaction to the murder of a high state official. The usual presentation shows Cooke and Beauchamp relishing the idea of homicide with only faint thoughts, or none at all, about consequences. The way Simm's Cooke is drawn, she qualifies as the most intelligent and the most human of all the portrayals. She is also long suffering and tolerant, far beyond what one would expect from a knowledge of the original. Simms's Cooke releases Beauchamp from his blood oath and begs him to remain with her in the country, obscure and happy, rather than highly visible in town, where he is bound to confront Sharp.

Toward the conclusion, by a complex twist of the plot, Sharp winds up a houseguest in the Beauchamp home, his crime against Ann concealed from her husband. Sharp renews his attempts at seduction of Ann; he promises to make her husband's fortune, then threatens to tell Beauchamp the truth if Cooke does not yield. Carried away by physical desire, ironically Sharp does not stop to consider what will happen to *him* if he reveals his part in Ann's ruin. Simms is the only author of the period to display the feelings involved in the Kentucky Tragedy in an ironic light.

Simms also portrays Sharp more realistically than the others. In Beauchamp's *Confession,* in the *Letters,* and in fictional or dramatic portrayals, Sharp is an abject coward. In Simm's novel, he is gutsy, sneaky and opportunistic.

The actual homicide is committed by a "maddened" Beauchamp; Cooke has begged him to leave her and avoid risking his life for her. After Beauchamp departs on his mission of murder, Cooke delivers a soliloquy showing her confusion. What good will come of this crime? she asks. But then, thinking of the way Sharp intruded into her home, even at this late stage of their history, she wonders if she will ever be free of his evil presence. Cooke concludes the speech with the idea that it might be best to kill Sharp, after all; and Simms concludes the passage by saying: "the world will not willingly account this madness. It matters not greatly by what name you call a passion which has broken bounds and disdains the right angles of convention." Unmistakably one senses that the highly civilized Simms wishes he could alter the story a la Charles Fenno Hoffman, and spare his heroine the guilt of complicity and the gruesome fate of the real Ann Cooke. Not that Simms creates profound characters in *Beauchamp,* but his Sharp and Cooke are deeper and more lifelike than other depictions of the period.

Poe's Ann Cooke, called Lelage in the verse drama *Politian,* bears little resemblance to her real-life counterpart in the Kentucky Tragedy. Instead of the depressed, melancholy, vindictive and obsessed heroine of the *Letters* and the *Confession,* Lalage is much simpler, less visible, and more pathetic than Cooke or any of her fictional incarnations.

We first hear of her from one of the servants in the home of the Duke di Broglio, Lalage's custodian:

> I saw her yester eve thro' the lattice-work
> Of her chamber-window sobbing upon her knees
> And ever and anon amid her sobs
> She murmured forth Castiglioni's name
> Rupert, she loves him still!

Later, as if to emphasize her sense of what today we call low self-esteem, her servant-girl abuses her, leaving Lalage to bemoan her altered physical appearance and imminent death as a "ruined maid." Today's readers might identify all of these character traits as obvious neuroses, but the nineteenth century audience found the pathetic heroine appealing. Or was Poe playing psychologist here, consciously endowing Lalage with sick attitudes because he believed Ann Cooke to be unappetizing? We know Poe was not satisfied with *Politian,* that he left if unfinished, and years later in a review of Simm's *Beauchamp* he observed: "Historical truth has somewhat hampered the artist." Poe might have experienced the same difficulty himself, attempting to create a sympathetic heroine from a model he could not admire.

As for Lalage's vengeful feelings and craving for the blood of her seducer—elements that form the foundation of the living story—Poe has a scene where a friendly monk enters Lalage's apartment and asks her to think of her soul and pray. Lalage says she can only think of her present misery. When the holy man offers her a crucifix, she draws a dagger and holds it high by the blade. "Behold the cross wherewith a vow like mine / Is written in Heaven!" she cries, adding that the deed, the vow, and the symbol of the deed should tally. Thus Poe preserves the essential character element of vengeful feeling, but reduces it to an oblique reference and a metaphorical gesture. Still later, in Scene VII, after Politian has declared his love for Lalage and she has revealed to him the cause of her anguish, he begs her to come away with him to America. Lalage replies: "A deed is to be done—Castigioni lives!" To which Politian says "And he shall die!" Then he exits in a rage.

The speech that follows is extremely revealing of Poe's attitude toward his heroine. Although Lalage displays none of the fury of Ann Cooke, she has stipulated that Politian avenge the wrong she has suffered by killing Castiglioni. The fact that the promise is exacted offstage is itself significant, for it spares the audience a view of the vicious original while adhering to the basic story line. Furthermore, as soon as Politian exits on his homicidal mission, Lalage immediately regrets their compact. She calls out,

> Thou art gone—thou art not gone, Politian!
> I feel thou art not gone—yet dare not look,
> Lest I behold thee not; thou couldst not go
> With those words upon thy lips. . . .

Next, after showing Lalage as a tender and regretful, nonviolent version of Cooke, Poe has her conclude the speech with something of Cooke's resolution:

> Gone—gone [referring to Politian]
> Where am I? 'tis well—'tis very well!
> So that the blade be keen—the blow be sure—
> 'Tis well, 'tis very well—alas! alas!

The final exclamations reverse the image of the heroine yet again, so that the audience might conclude that Lalage is a) in a distracted, deeply confused state of mind or b) at the mercy of forces she can not control, even though she is an active participant in and inspirer of the events that now overwhelm her.

At the conclusion, when it is clear that Politian is planning to murder Castiglioni while his marriage ceremony is in progress, Lalage cries, "Farewell, Castiglioni, and farewell my hope in heaven."

All these details of presentation—from Lelage's introduction into the drama singing sweet and mournful tunes, to her suffering abuse from her servant, to her eliciting the fateful pledge from Politian offstage, to her swearing an oath the content of which is left unspecified, to her terrible confusion when Politian goes off to avenge her, to her obvious repentance at the conclusion—accumulate to create a much softened, pathetic, vulnerable and humanized Ann Cooke. Poe's attitude toward women as ethereal, as evidenced in such early poems as "Al Aaraaf" and "To Helen," might explain his reluctance to deal with the ugly aspects of the Kentucky Tragedy, while his concern over audience reaction to his work might also have played a part in the Lalage characterization.

Of all the treatments of Cooke considered here, Lippard's is the most innocent and at the same time the most insipid. Chivers's is the most bloodthirsty, but this is mitigated (in *Conrad and Eudora*) by the possibility that she is mad. Hoffman's portrayal is the most sentimental and nonthreatening; Simm's is the most intelligent, rounded, and interesting, while Poe's is unquestionably the most pathetic.

Elizabeth Mehren (essay date 8 April 1990)

SOURCE: "Making a Killing Off True Crime," in *Los Angeles Times Book Review*, Vol. 237, April 8, 1990, p. 9.

[*In the essay below, Mehren suggests why the true-crime genre is so profitable, noting that there is no shortage of supply or demand.*]

Hours after Chuck Stuart splashed into Boston Harbor from the Tobin Bridge last January, the phone at our house began ringing with fierce determination.

Stuart was the hero-turned-villain of Boston's spiciest murder in years: the man who first insisted that he and his seven-months-pregnant wife had been shot by a black assailant who leaped into the back seat of the Stuarts' Toyota Cressida, but who later, it seems, turned out to have done the shooting himself.

That's part of the fascination, that this could be the neighbor next door. You rarely think, "This could happen to me." But you do think, "This could be my neighbor."

—*Neil Nyren*

Our telephone was ringing so insistently because my husband and I both are journalists. Apparently that fact alone—or that plus our Massachusetts residency—qualifies us to be described as true-crime writers. This is at least what one would infer from the telephone calls that came to us from an extraordinary parade of half-frantic agents, publishers, editors and movie producers:

"Hello, is your husband there?"

"No, I'm sorry, he's not."

"He's not. Well, hmmm, would *you* like to write a book?"

"No, I'm sorry, I think not. Would you like to speak to the dog?"

The calls would have been at least a boost for the ego were it not for the fact that just about anyone with even tangential involvement with any Boston-area newspaper or magazine, or anyone who is based in this area and does any reporting at all, seems to have faced the same flood of solicitations. One reporter at the Boston *Globe* told me that he received 11 inquiries about possible books or movies—and that was just in the first week after Stuart's apparent suicide. A reporter at another paper put me on hold while she took another call from still another Hollywood producer.

"It's not a question of 'tasteless' or 'tacky,'" one editor remonstrated when I used those words before referring him to our 73-pound Samoyed. "It's a question of people wanting to read this story. And it's a helluva story."

But of course it is not just this story. More and more, readers and publishers seem to be swimming in the same collective pool of blood and gore. It is hard to say which came first, the supply or the demand. But it is clear that the thirst for real crime—true crime, gory, gross and disgusting crime—appears to be insatiable.

"My theory is that it is somehow connected to the rise of tabloid television," Neil Nyren, editor-in-chief and publisher of G. P. Putnam's Sons, said. Putnam's is the publisher of one of the titans of true-crime writing, Joe McGinnis, of *Blind Faith* and *Fatal Vision* notably.

The reason those two books by McGinnis did so well is the same reason so many people were interested in the Stuart story, Nyren suggested. Chuck and Carol Stuart had worked themselves up from blue-collar beginnings to all the comforts of true yuppiedom. They had a house with a swimming pool and a wreath made out of teddy-bears on the front door. Chuck Stuart, a former dishwasher, wore suits from the fanciest men's store in Boston and had his prematurely graying temples touched up at a salon overlooking the Boston Public Garden.

"That's part of the fascination, that this could be the neigh-

bor next door," Nyren said. "You rarely think, 'This could happen to me.' But you do think, 'This could be my neighbor.'"

Harry MacLean, the author of the best-selling *In Broad Daylight* (Harper & Row, cloth; Dell, paper) about the 1981 murder of the town bully in a small town in northwest Missouri, agrees. MacLean was "just another hack lawyer" practicing in Denver when he decided to switch to true-crime writing, in part because of what he saw as the universal appeal of the genre.

In a recent lecture about true-crime writing at the Tattered Sleeve bookstore in his hometown of Denver, MacLean said he turned the question on his audience of nearly 200 people and asked them why they like to read this stuff. Their answer confirmed his suspicions.

"For one thing, they said a lot of these stories involve ordinary people, the people next door," MacLean said. He noted that he was calling from Foster City, Calif., where he was investigating a case involving "a fireman and a housewife."

Echoing that motif, Pocket Books Hardcover has been promoting one title as an example of "ordinary people, extraordinary crimes." The book, *Without Mercy: Obsession and Murder Under the Influence,* by Gary Provost, deals with a waitress at a pancake restaurant who joins her homosexual supervisor in plotting two brutal murders. Carlton Stowers' *Innocence Lost,* also from Pocket Books Hardcover, recounts the murder of an undercover policeman posing as a high school student in a small Texas town.

The reading public's appetite for this kind of book truly does seem insatiable. Day after day, press releases come in announcing new books about "shocking deaths," murders in a pediatric intensive-care unit, matricide, fratricide, patricide, psychopathic killers and crimes of vengeance, jealousy, avarice or old-fashioned passion.

But the flip side of the phenomenon is that not only does the public expect this kind of delicious fodder, so do the subjects. It's as if anyone with the slightest involvement in a potentially marketable crime of any kind figures that he or she can, pardon the expression, make a killing off it.

MacLean said that one reason he chose to back away from the Charles Stuart case, for example, was that "I heard that the assistant DAs were faxing their stories out to Hollywood." It was "too bizarre," he said. It seemed that "the process was going to taint the story."

Lawyers and crime victims—even friends and relatives of crime victims—now flock to literary agents and true-crime writers on their own. It may be that they actually enjoy the attention, that this is their personal and proverbial 15 minutes of fame. But as MacLean observed, "It feels kind of sick, in a way."

Conversely, many print journalists, not notoriously among the most overpaid of professionals, have come to see the perfect true-crime story as the vehicle that will vault them out of penury and into the ranks of true-crime giants—writers, they say in wistful tones, such as Truman Capote or Norman Mailer. Words like *miniseries* or *feature film* invariably accompany discussions of books about true crimes. The implication is that even the most starving of starving journalists will be able to junk that old Toyota and cruise around in the Mercedes he or she secretly covets.

Covering a story they think might be lucrative, journalists come to feel possessive about the cast of characters. It becomes "my murder" or "my book." Certainly this has been true in a number of recent well-publicized crimes, such as the Steinberg murder-and-child-and-wife-abuse case in New York City; the preppie murder in New York City; Boston's Stuart case; the Yom Kippur murders in Los Angeles.

Not every true-crime book is a guaranteed ticket to financial heaven, however. Books that come out as little more than a string of newspaper articles seldom make big waves. As greedy as readers may be for these stories, they do demand writing skills from the authors.

What most captures the public fancy is a book that transcends the facts of a single case and deals with bigger themes. Ideally, the story also should serve as a mirror of some segment of American life as well.

The "sudden burst" in true-crime stories "caught us by surprise," Neil Nyren said, so much so that "there's no way to tell where it's going."

But as long as there is tabloid television, and as long as there are savory stories to tell, the pace seems unlikely to slow.

In the meantime, my dog would like it known that he is a very good writer and that he is thinking of hiring an agent.

Rosemary Herbert (essay date 1 June 1990)

SOURCE: "Publishers Agree: True Crime Does Pay," in *Publishers Weekly,* Vol. 237, June 1, 1990, pp. 33-6.

[*In the following essay, Herbert discusses the characteristics of the true-crime genre, focusing her analysis on who reads it and why.*]

What's black and white and read all over? The answer is true crime. According to many top executives, editors and publicists, the success of this category is so phenomenal, it's almost criminal! As *PW* made the rounds of publishing houses and crime writers, the same word was used repeatedly to diagnose the current health of the genre: "hot." And feverish activity in the field seems to be contagious, with at least 30 trade imprints seeking to satisfy the true crime cravings of readers from all segments of the American population.

Both frontlist and backlist are booming, and mass market titles seem to do equally well in bookstores and ID markets. Hardcover and paperback publishers agree, however, that the real explosion within the genre is happening at the paperback end of the business. Putnam v-p and publisher Neil Nyren says, "In hardcover it's pretty much the same as it's always been. There are certain titles that become very strong, but the majority sell at moderate levels. It's in paperback that true crime has really blossomed during the past two years." Barry Lippman, president and publisher, Macmillan adult trade, adds that "the unusual thing about the genre is that there are both good hardcover *and* paperback audiences."

Even recently established houses are getting in on the act. The newly founded Knightsbridge, for example, has taken a hefty gamble this spring in releasing a first printing of 200,000 hardcover copies of Daniel J. Blackburn's *Human Harvest: The Sacramento Murder Story. Human Harvest* is typical true crime fare, in which an elderly lady is alleged to have murdered other residents of her retirement home and buried them in her garden.

But the veterans aren't exactly resting on their laurels. Dell just released Jack Olsen's latest paperback, *Doc: The Rape of the Town of Lovell*—about a local gynecologist's systematic rape of a large portion of the women in a Mormon community—in a print run of 950,000, a decision made *before* it won an Edgar in late April as the best nonfiction book of 1989. And St. Martin's, another stalwart, printed an initial 275,000 copies and has gone back to press for another 25,000 of its May release, *Murder in Boston* by Ken Englade, which bills itself as an "interim report" on the as-yet-unresolved Stuart case.

Dell's president and publisher, Carole Baron, says, "We've been doing true crime paperback originals and reprints all along, for at least eight or nine years. Typically, when we published Jack Olsen's *Son: A Psychopath and His Victims* back in 1985, we did it neither as a 'lead lead' nor as a 'mid-midlist' title. Then we found that it was *really* backlisting, unlike many mass market books. So it's been around since 1985 in many, many printings."

If the bestseller lists are any indication, it appears that a wide range of true crime publishers have their fingers on the pulse of many Americans' taste in nonfiction. And Berkley Books' v-p and editor-in-chief Leslie Gelbman says, "There's no question that the surge of true crime bestsellers over the past few years has given publishers and booksellers an opportunity to expand the category. There are now special sections in bookstores, and publishing programs devoted to true crime; and the books don't have to be top of the list to sell or to be profitable."

In Cold Blood

Among our interlocutors, there was strong general agreement about which books are classics of the true crime genre and which authors have been particularly exciting in recent years. Again and again Truman Capote's 1966 novel *In Cold Blood* is cited as the genre's real progenitor, although it was a "fictionalized" account of a brutal murder. According to Neil Nyren, "There may already have been some true crime books, but Capote's marked a watershed. It was the first one to make the genre really respectable. *In Cold Blood, Blood and Money* by Tommy Thompson [Doubleday 1976 and Dell, third printing 1989] and *Fatal Vision* by Joe McGinnis [Putnam 1983 and Signet 1984, with 2.3 million copies in the Signet edition] are the three giants of true crime and there will be others to come. I think the first hint of the trend might have been when Ann Rule's books started selling very well in paperback, including books that had been published years and years before. It was as if all of a sudden a whole library was there to sell." Rule was first published in NAL's True Crime Annals in 1983, under the pseudonym Andy Stack; presently several of her titles, including *Possession* and *The Stranger Beside Me,* are with the Signet imprint. Many agree that Rule's success set the stage for those who followed.

Who Reads True Crime—And Why

Just what lures so many readers into literature concerning aberrant and extreme behavior, matricide, patricide and even infanticide? Why the healthy appetite for blood and gore? Priscilla Ridgway, executive secretary of the Mystery Writers of America (MWA), reckons that "media coverage about some pretty dreadful crimes has inured the public to their horror *and* tweaked interest." Neil Nyren agrees that "the rise of tabloid television—basing program content on true crime—has had a symbiotic relationship with the rise of the books in paperback."

Irwyn Applebaum, president and publisher of Pocket Books, is pleased to see that readers' appetites are not yet "sated by some of the other media," including daily news reporting and television programs such as *911, Cops* and "some of the other cinema vérité or pseudo-cinéma vérité." In fact, an interesting example of the television/publishing connection was the Harper Paperback April release *America's Most Wanted*

by Jack Breslin, which describes the making of the popular television program of the same name.

Avon president and publisher Carolyn Reidy speaks for many when saying, "I don't know if more crimes are actually being perpetrated or whether more are being detected and reported, but something is making them greatly impinge on our consciousness, which in turn is fueling the desire to know how and why all of this is happening. Therefore, it's almost self-protective to wish to understand how it happens."

Nyren, for his part, believes successful titles must have an immediacy "that gives readers the feeling this is something that could be happening in *their* neighborhood." Charles Spicer, senior editor at St. Martin's, adds, "Frankly, there's an element of voyeurism, the appeal of gossip and a 'there but for the grace of God go I' frisson." All agree that the hallmark of successful true crime is nonfiction that packs all the traditional appeal of the novel.

> **In looking over the books that have worked particularly well over time, I don't think there's any question that murders explored within the context of family life offer the most drama, the most titillation, and I think, probably reach to people's deepest fears.**
>
> **—Roger Cooper**

Just who are the readers of true crime? Maryann Palumbo, v-p for advertising, promotion and publicity at NAL, says the genre appeals "very much to a middle America kind of audience." Bantam v-p and mass market publisher Lou Aronica believes the books are reaching "a broad section of the market. There are very literate, studied pieces like Joe McGinnis's work and then there are the far more lurid, *National Enquirer* kind of projects. They sell equally well—but I *cannot* believe that the same readers [turn to both]." All agree that the crossover of readers of mystery fiction into the true crime area is insignificant, since, as Applebaum put it, "Readers who like their details filtered through fiction are often after a more genteel depiction of crime."

The Serial Phenomenon

How often does the discussion at a publishing conference center not on the bottom line but rather on metaphysical questions of good and evil? At the recent MWA/John Jay College Symposium on true crime, that was certainly the case. According to Richard Hammer, author of *The CBS Murders: A True Story of Greed and Violence in New York's Diamond District* (Morrow 1987 and NAL 1988), and Ira

Berkow, author of *The Man Who Robbed the Pierre: The True Story of Bobby Comfort* (Atheneum, 1987), the personalities of the murderers, rapists and other criminals depicted within the books vary wildly. Some have surprising senses of humor, others are extremely intelligent and still others are just plain nasty, seeming to lack any sort of human conscience. In a society where many taboos have broken down, true crime stories seem to satisfy a hunger for clearly defined bad guys and good guys or, as it were, forces of good and evil in our lives.

Patricia Daniels Cornwell, whose novel *Postmortem* (Scribners, January 1990) draws on her experiences as a crime reporter and computer analyst in the Virginia medical examiner's office, subscribes to the latter theory, noting that an informal subgenre seems to have sprung up around the ultimate in really bad guys, the serial killer.

Some of the more notable books focusing on serial murders are the recently released *From Cradle to Grave: The Short Lives and Strange Deaths of Marybeth Tinning's Nine Children* by Joyce Egginton (Morrow, 1989; Jove, May 1990), and Ann Rule's *Small Sacrifices: A True Story of Passion and Murder* (NAL, 1987 and Signet, 1988), both dealing with infanticide perpetrated by disturbed mothers upon their own offspring. And *Death Shift: The True Story of Nurse Genene Jones and the Texas Baby Murders* by Peter Elkind (Viking, 1989 and Onyx, May 1990) examines infanticides carried out by a pediatric nurse in San Antonio, Tex.

Other studies of serial murders look at killers who seem to choose victims more randomly, although evidence often reveals that even in these cases there is method in the madness of their selection processes, as in the murderous work of David J. Carpenter, whose deeds are chronicled by Robert Graysmith in *The Sleeping Lady: The Trailside Murders Above the Golden Gate* (Dutton, April 1990). Carpenter went on a three-year rape and killing spree along hiking trails in the Bay Area and was captured after one of the greatest manhunts of this century.

All in the Family

"In looking over the books that have worked particularly well over time, I don't think there's any question that murders explored within the context of family life offer the most drama, the most titillation, and I think, probably reach to people's deepest fears," advises Roger Cooper, senior v-p and publisher of the Berkley Publishing Group. *Wasted: The Preppie Murder* by Linda Wolfe (Simon & Schuster 1989, and Pocket Books, August 1990); and *Beyond Reason: A True Story of a Shocking Double Murder, a Brilliant and Beautiful Virginia Socialite and a Deadly Psychotic* by Ken Englade (St. Martin's, May 1990), deal with young people who have everything that money can buy but who lack discipline and

direction and are not convinced that their parents love them. They end up forming dangerous liaisons with other disturbed young adults that eventually lead to murder.

Both of these authors document the mentalities of their subjects and present a picture of the legal and social ramifications of the crimes. Avon's Carolyn Reidy notes that for many people, part of the appeal of these books "lies in the realization that the rich can be victims, too."

Many titles take a peek at family murder with a regional dimension. Craig A. Lewis's *Blood Evidence: A Story of True Crime in the South* (August House, June 1990) is an example of a regional murder story in which the atmosphere of a particular place—in this case, Shreveport, La.—adds a special character to the book as a whole.

The Woodchipper Murder by Arthur Herzog (Holt, 1989; to be published in paperback by Zebra) investigates a Connecticut scene of the crime and a case in which a husband who lies about the disappearance of his wife is quickly caught up in a net of incrimination. And *Murder in the Carolinas* by Nancy Rhyne (John F. Blair, 1988) proves that local cases can have universal appeal, presenting, rather unusually, 13 cases of family treachery in an anthology format.

And Warner senior editor Rick Horgan highlights another aspect that seems to contribute to the popularity of many titles: "The more innocent and vulnerable the victim, the more likely the success of the book." *Abandoned Prayers: The True Story of Obsession, Murder and Little Boy Blue* by Gregg Olson (Popular Library, December 1990) is a case in point. It's the story of a young boy murdered by his father, an Amish man who, the publisher tells us, "disappeared from his community and crisscrossed the country abusing his child. The locals who discovered the boy's corpse buried him under a headstone marked 'Little Boy Blue.'" This is a clear example of a book with an extremely sympathetic victim.

Another title that looks at innocent victims—but this time outside the family—is the story of a disturbed woman who gunned down school children at play in Illinois in 1988. *Murder of Innocence: The Tragic Life and Final Rampage of Laurie Dann* by Joel Kaplan, George Papajohn and Eric Zorn, is scheduled for hardcover publication from Warner this fall.

Drugs, the Mafia and Spies

Harper & Row publicity director Karen Mender points out that most publishers do not distinguish subcategories as such within true crime. But readers are often drawn to a particular type of book within the true crime spectrum, for instance, drug-related titles. A notable example is *Kings of Cocaine: An Astonishing True Story of Murder, Money, and Corrup-*

tion by *Miami Herald* reporters Guy Gugliotta and Jeff Leen (Simon & Schuster, 1989 and Harper Paperbacks, May 1990). Unusually long for the genre at 680 pages, this book documents the workings of the $8-billion-a-year Colombian drug cartel.

Espionage-related crime is chronicled in such books as Clifford Stoll's *The Cuckoo's Egg: Tracking a Spy Through the Maze of Computer Espionage* (Doubleday, 1989 and forthcoming from Pocket Books, November 1990). While many true crimes are cast in the form of police procedurals, this book recounts the stalking of a computer "hacker" who was methodically prowling national networks to gain access to American databases. The computer-whiz author becomes the hero of his own story.

Mafia crime also has its share of reading fans. *The Plumber: The True Story of How One Good Man Helped Destroy the Entire Philadelphia Mafia* by Joseph Salerno and Stephen J. Rivele (Knightsbridge, 1990) and *"Please Don't Kill Me": The True Story of the Milo Murder* by William C. Dear and Carlton Stowers (Houghton Mifflin, 1989 and Ballantine, 1990) are examples of this category.

Aiding & Abetting: Promoting Crime

Donna Gould, publicity director at Berkley, is convinced that true crime is "a publicist's dream." And while many have already credited television with igniting the public's interest in the genre, publicists also see television as an ideal medium for further promoting their wares. Susan Richman, v-p and director of publicity at Macmillan, finds that national talk shows are very receptive to true crime authors, "especially if the writers are accompanied by one or more of the principals in the crime." Adam Rothberg, senior publicist at Pocket Books, says, "I think that by its very nature, the subject of true crime makes it attractive to certain media outlets that otherwise are often *not* interested in working with books: the television tabloid shows as well as tabloid magazines."

But Michaela Hamilton, executive editor of NAL/Dutton, warns of the perils of overexposure. "I think it's very tricky to bring a book out on a case that's gotten front-page headlines, because in so many cases consumers feel they already know the story inside out before the book appears."

The True Colors of True Crime

Virtually every category of publishing today seeks to have a look that announces to the reader, subliminally or otherwise, the sort of book to expect. In true crime you absolutely *can* tell the book by its cover, both in cloth and paperback. The jacket of a true crime hardcover tends to reflect the more probing, psychological nature of its content through a softer, more sensitive portrait of an individual or of the scene of the

crime, while a paperback jacket tends towards the more lurid, with bloody photographs of the victims or perpetrators, and screaming headlines. But both share one predominant attribute: they are black, white and red all over.

But between the covers, are these books solely concerned with blood and gore? The emphasis on the grisly varies, of course, but a significant majority have another agenda as well: they explore the darkest corners of our lives and try to give them some meaning or context. Ann Rule, the author most often cited by publishers as a major influence today, has a good insight into the genre's fans: "I've taken an informal poll of readers who come to my autographing sessions, and find that very many of them are women. Often they confide, 'I don't know *why* I'm fascinated with these books about terrible crime!' And I ask them, 'If you found a spider in your bathroom what would you do with it?' And do you know, most say they would gently remove it, and let the spider go free outdoors!"

In the end, perhaps the broad middle American audience keeps reading true crime to understand the extremes of human behavior, to be advised of danger and, yes, to experience a visceral horror that makes us grateful for our more ordinary lives.

Jane Caputi (essay date Fall 1990)

SOURCE: "The New Founding Fathers: The Lore and Lure of the Serial Killer in Contemporary Culture," in *Journal of American Culture*, Vol. 13, No. 3, Fall, 1990, pp. 1-12.

[*In the essay below, Caputi discusses the place of serial killers in contemporary culture.*]

> Jack the Ripper
> He was the first.
> —cover blurb from a 1988 collection
> of stories on the Ripper

> Ted Bundy—A Man With Vision
> —A Man With Direction
> —A Prophet of our Times
> —flyer advertising a student program
> on Bundy, University of New Mexico,
> Albuquerque, April, 1989

Freddy's [from the "Nightmare on Elm Street" Series] fame—make that notoriety—was confirmed by the National Coalition on Television Violence, which in a recent survey found that children ages 10 to 13 are more familiar with Freddy and his Paramount counterpart Jason of "Friday the 13th" than with such famous historical figures as George Washington, Abraham Lincoln or Martin Luther King, Jr. Jason was recognized by 72 of the 100 children surveyed and Freddy by 66, while poor Honest Abe was identified by 36.

—*Albuquerque Tribune*

Recently, as I watched an MTV show, "The Week In Rock" (Sept. 16, 1989), I was taken aback as the announcer commented, "Now for some news from Boston—home of baked beans, B.U., and at least one renowned serial strangler." How blithe, normalizing, and easy a reference to atrocity. Yet, why should I have been surprised? Just one year earlier, in autumn, 1988, Great Britain and the United States "celebrated" the centennial of the crimes of "Jack the Ripper." Mourning, which might seem appropriate to the occasion, was notably absent (except in feminist demonstrations and writings). Rather, light-hearted Ripper paraphernalia, such as a computer-game, T-shirts, buttons, mugs, and a blood-red cocktail, appeared throughout England. Most strikingly, in both the United States and England, the legend of the Ripper was ubiquitously retold and millions were refamiliarized with its elements—in a massively promoted made-for-TV movie, innumerable newspaper accounts, an exploitation thriller, *Jack's Back,* and scores of new books on the master killer.

This recent mythicization of the Ripper continues a process that has been in motion since 1888. Elsewhere, I have argued that "Jack the Ripper" is father to an "age of sex crime" and that his status as an ambiguous (both heroic and monstrous) cultural icon legitimates male violence against women. The crimes of the Ripper have provided a cultural category for a new type of crime (the territorial, ritualistic, nicknamed, serial sex slayer) and acted as a role model for subsequent killers, including "The Boston Strangler," the "Son of Sam," the "Yorkshire Ripper," the "Green River Killer," the "Hillside Strangler," and so on—killers who then go on to generate legends and attract cult-like behavior of their own. Serial sex killers such as these are celebrated (sometimes covertly, sometimes overtly) along a cultural gamut including made-for TV movies, rock 'n' roll songs horror fanzines, jokes, pornographic magazines such as *Hustler,* and extreme sadist publications. Simultaneously, a parallel cult can be discerned in the adulation given (primarily by teenage boys) to the fictional screen counterparts of the modern sex killer, such as "Freddy Krueger," the child molester/murderer from the *Nightmare on Elm Street* movie and television series, and "Jason," the hockeymasked multiple murderer from the *Friday the 13th* film series.

While such mythmaking proceeds unabated, serial murder itself has become an increasingly prevalent reality in modern, Western life. Justice Department official, Robert O. Heck, sums up the general situation:

We all talk about Jack the Ripper; he killed five people [sic]. We all talk about the "Boston Strangler" who killed 13, and maybe "Son of Sam," who killed six. But we've got people [sic] out there now killing 20 and 30 people and more, and some of them just don't kill. They torture their victims in terrible ways and mutilate them before they kill them. Something's going on out there. It's an epidemic.

Although Heck's statement is superficially correct, his language works to obscure what actually is going on out there, for the "people" who torture, kill, and mutilate in this way are men, while their victims are predominantly females, women and girls, and to a lesser extent, younger men. As these hierarchical lines indicate, these are crimes of sexually political import, crimes rooted in a system of male supremacy in the same way that lynching is based in white supremacy. That recognition, however, is impeded by longstanding tradition for, as Kate Millett noted in her classic work, *Sexual Politics:*

We are not accustomed to associate patriarchy with force. So perfect is its system of socialization, so complete the general assent to its values, so long and so universally has it prevailed in human society, that it scarcely seems to require violent implementation. Customarily, we view its brutalities in the past as exotic or "primitive" custom. Those of the present are regarded as the product of individual deviance, confined to pathological or exceptional behavior, and without general import. And yet . . . control in patriarchal societies would be imperfect, even inoperable, unless it had the rule of force to rely upon, both in emergencies and as an ever-present instrument of intimidation.

The most commonly analyzed form of such patriarchal force is rape. Early feminist analysts of rape asserted that rape is not, as the common mythology insists, a crime of frustrated attraction, victim provocation, or uncontrollable biological urges. Nor is it one perpetrated only by an aberrant fringe. Rather, rape is a direct expression of sexual politics, a ritual enactment of male domination, and a form of terror which functions to maintain the status quo. Similarly, the murders of women and children by serial killers are not the result of inexplicably deviant men. On the contrary, sexual murder is a product of the dominant culture. It is the ultimate expression of a sexuality that defines sex as a form of domination/power; it, like rape, is a form of terror that constructs and maintains male supremacy.

Heck's statement invokes shared knowledge of a tradition of serial murder beginning with Jack the Ripper, that, as he puts it, "we all talk about." Indeed, we all do. In this essay, using several representative killers, I will trace some of the ways that modern culture talks about the sex killer. I will survey the folklore and popular culture representations of these killers (both actual and fictional), and interpret these for what they tell us about male supremacy, cultural constructions of monstrosity and horror, as well as fears of the future.

Father to An Age

Two women cops working twice as hard for half the glory . . . TONIGHT: Decoys for a Jack the Ripper.
> —*TV Guide* ad for the premiere episode
> of *Cagney and Lacey,* 1982

Imagine . . . a study of feminism from the point of view of Jack the Ripper . . . a novel that bristles with irony and wit.
> —*New York Times,* review of
> *Confessions of a Lady-Killer* (1979)

A third class of strangers are so utterly beyond the pale that they seem alien not only to the group, but to the human species. I refer to *monsters,* indicated by names like: pervert, degenerate . . . psychopath . . . fiend, demon, devil . . . Jack the Ripper.
> —Orrin Klapp, 1962

[Jack the Ripper] that great hero of my youth, that skilled human butcher who did all his work on alcoholic whores.
> —Charles McCabe, *San Francisco Chronicle,* 1971

Jack the Ribber
> —a restaurant in New York City

I need some help here. Some hands. Just send me anybody. Jack the Ripper. I'll take anyone who's good with a knife.
> —Hawkeye on M*A*S*H, c. 1973

And Jezebel the nun, she violently knits,
A bald wig for Jack the Ripper, who sits,
At the head of the Chamber of Commerce.
> —Bob Dylan, "Tombstone Blues," 1965

The ghost of Jack the Ripper hovered over Washington today.
> —ABC Nightly News, 29, Nov. 1984
> (in reference to Federal budget cuts)

Knock. Knock.
Husband: Who's there?
Voice: Jack the Ripper.
Husband: It's for you dear.
> —*The Benny Hill Show,* c. 1980

Mrs. Hanson . . . had always worn an extra enforcement of petticoats against an ever-potential Jack the Ripper.
> —Fannie Hurst, *Imitation of Life,* 1933

Traces of the Ripper's presence constantly intrude into urban women's consciousness. Walking down my street in Manhattan recently, I came upon graffiti emblazoning the Ripper's name on a side of a building. That same week the Lesbian Herstory Archives forwarded to me a threatening letter from "Jack the Ripper" "THE ORIGINAL JACK not a cheap imitation. I've conquered death itself and am still on this earth waiting to strike again."
> —Judith Walkowitz, 1982

As just this brief sampling of references indicates, the figure of Jack the Ripper preoccupies this culture in the form of a pervasive and particularly all-embracing metaphor (though, obviously, with different meanings for women and men). The mythic Ripper inspires awe and laughter, he is viewed as both hero and monster, and he is hailed by many as a key innovator, not only in the annuals of true crime, but also in the imagination of modern horror. In a recent discussion of that genre, two of its practitioners, writers Harlan Ellison and Gahan Wilson, traced the origins of modern horror to Jack the Ripper:

> ELLISON: Everything that scares us today dates back to Jack the Ripper. He is still the operative icon of terror. He may be small potatoes by current standards . . . but the Ripper started it. He created the form.

> WILSON: Just as no one paints landscapes the same way since Turner, a creative monster like the Ripper changed the landscape of what scares us. He inspired generations.

Wilson and Ellison seem quite vicariously thrilled by the Ripper, if not actually heroizing him as a "creative monster" who blazed their path into the realms of horror. But, of course, this is an expedient and gender specific thrill; as men, they personally have little to fear from the Ripper and do not have to suffer any consequences of that aggrandizing mythicization.

The crimes of the Ripper occurred in the Whitechapel district of London, an area well-known as a center of poverty and prostitution. The still unknown killer has been credited with as many as twenty murders, although probably only five were the work of the one man; others were imitative or unconnected crimes. The killer made no attempt to cover up his actions. Rather, he left the bodies on display, out on the open street in four instances. Furthermore, he (or, far more likely, someone pretending to be the killer) advertised his crimes by writing letters to police, press, and citizen groups, nicknaming himself in one letter, taunting the police, predicting future crimes, and even mailing in half of a human kidney to the chief of a Whitechapel vigilance group (the letter writer claimed to have eaten the other half). The victims, all prostitutes, were not raped; their throats were slit from behind and then the sexual and other organs were severely mutilated. While similar atrocities indubitably had occurred before, indicated, perhaps, in legends of werewolves and vampires, or tracked as isolated incidents of "lust murder" in the nineteenth century, it was not until 1888 in London that the idea of a sexually motivated criminal, specializing in mutilation, dismemberment, and murder, first took shape as a cultural icon.

Many have asked why Jack the Ripper, more than other sex criminals, has left such a mark? Nigel Morland avers: "The melodramatic name of Jack the Ripper . . . is largely the reason for his immortality, that and the imaginative folk lore which has always surrounded him." In truth, the identity of the Ripper never has been established; this evocative anonymity has been a source for much of the Ripper lore as self-proclaimed "Ripperologists" and "Ripperophiles" continually sift over the known information, proposing improbable and often highly romanticized possible identities (e.g., a member of the royal family).

Another factor, along with this anonymity, further enabled the mythicization process: the crimes of the Ripper stand as one of the first media events. As historian Judith Walkowitz noted: "One cannot emphasize too much the role of the popular press, itself a creation of the 1880s, in establishing Jack the Ripper as a media hero, in amplifying the terror of male violence, and in elaborating and interpreting the meaning of the Ripper murders to a 'mass' audience." A key feature of that elaboration was the wedding of the crimes to traditional horror images and formulae. "Unable to find historical precedents for the Whitechapel 'horrors,' commentators resorted to horrifying fictional analogues." Here are the beginnings of the Ripper mythos—the sex killer as human monster, master criminal, immortal being—as well as the origins of his role as a stock character in twentieth century literature. Jack the Ripper has been a recurring figure in popular and serious fictions (beginning with Frank Wedekind's *Die Busche der Pandora,* 1904, and Marie Belloc Lowndes' story "The Lodger," 1913), in films (e.g., Nicholas Meyer's *Time After Time,* 1979), television dramas, (most notably as an immortal alien entity on *Star Trek*), and songs (e.g., Link Wray's "Jack the Ripper," 1959, Screamin' Lord Sutch and the Savages, "Hands of Jack the Ripper," c. 1969).

Still, the reasons why the Ripper has become so solidly entrenched as a cultural icon go beyond his colorful nickname or the fortuitous collaboration of the 19th century popular press. His enduring popularity, instead, primarily is rooted in the patriarchal foundations of the modern world and his essential meaning is as an emblem of misogynist terrorism. Horror writers might expediently celebrate the mythic ripper as a "creative monster" who "inspired generations"—I assume they mean of horror writers. Yet, the Ripper legend also has inspired generations of misogynist men, both armchair criminals who enjoy identifying with the Ripper in the various fiction portrayals as well as actual killers who directly indicate that they were emulating the Ripper.

As time goes by, the Ripper's mythic representations have only increased and a bibliographic essay listing all of the forms in which the Ripper makes an appearance would run well into hundreds of items. Three interconnected themes recur in this accumulated Ripper Lore: (1) the immortality of the Ripper; (2) the confusion of the historical and fictional criminal; and (3) the establishment of a sex-murder tradition, built upon the Ripper's original crimes.

In 1905, British children jumped rope to this chant: "Jack the Ripper's dead/ And lying on his bed. He cut his throat with Sunlight Soap/ Jack the Ripper's dead." Still, that is one of the very few times the Ripper has died in the popular mind. Rather, his primary persona is that of an immortal and continually lethal presence. This notion was introduced to a mass audience by Robert Bloch in his 1942 short story, "Your's Truly, Jack the Ripper" and subsequently has been imitated countless times. In the 1979 film, *Time After Time,* Jack the Ripper actually travels into the present through his unsuspecting friend H. G. Wells' time machine. The horrified Wells is finally able to dispatch him via that very machine, sending him, as perfectly befits a mythic creature, "into *infinity,* where he really belongs."

> **Just as Bundy's young, white, generally middle-class victims were stereotypically (and with marked racist and classic bias) universalized as "anyone's daughters," Bundy himself was depicted as the fatherland's (almost) ideal son—handsome, intelligent, a former law student, a rising star in Seattle's Republican party.**
>
> **—*Jane Caputi***

A startling juxtaposition of stories in the Oct. 30, 1979 issue of *US Magazine* illustrates both the second and third themes. The first, a news story on a series of sex slayings in Yorkshire claims: "A New Jack the Ripper is Terrorizing England." On the very next page, a headline for a story on the film *Time After Time* reads: "The Stars Really Fall in Love in a New Jack the Ripper Flick." This placement collapses the "New Jack the Ripper" almost imperceptibly into the "New Jack the Ripper Flick," as if there really were no substantial difference between the two. Such juxtapositions may lead us to consider the ways that the incessant mythicization/heroization of the misogynist killer encourages the emergence of "New Jack the Rippers," men eager to fill out the archetype of the criminal genius/monster, whose exploits are reviled but simultaneously celebrated in the popular culture.

A number of writers from a variety of perspectives have surveyed the lore surrounding the Ripper and it is not my intention to recapitulate that material in any greater depth here. Rather, having established the prominence and prevalence of Ripper lore, I want to concentrate on the much less analyzed personae and lores of several men who come from the "generations" inspired by Jack the Ripper, killers such as Ted Bundy and David Berkowitz.

"America's Jack the Ripper"

So let's salute the mighty Bundy,
Here on Friday, gone on Monday.
All his roads lead out of town.
It's hard to keep a good man down.
—An Aspen folk singer, celebrating
Bundy's first prison escape, 1978

In 1981, when the *Reader's Digest* published an original article on Ted Bundy, its cover blurb announced: "Caught: America's Jack the Ripper." In some ways, this seemed mere hyperbole. The two killers were not that alike: Bundy selected college coeds, not prostitutes, as his victims and he hid the bodies, rather than display them. Nevertheless, just as Jack the Ripper seemed to personify the underside of Victorian England, so too Ted Bundy epitomized his society, presenting a persona of the superficially ideal, all-American boy. Ironically, it was just months after the 1988 centennial celebration for the mythic father of sexual murder, that the focus effortlessly shifted to that paradigmatic son, Bundy—to the drama leading up to his execution, January 24, 1989, and the revelry that accompanied it. In the days preceding his death, Bundy's story dominated the mass media, memorializing and further mythicizing a killer who had already been the subject of scores of book chapters, articles, five books, and a made-for-TV movie (where he was played by Mark Harmon, an actor whom *People Weekly* once gushed over as the "world's sexiest man"). On the morning Bundy went to the electric chair, hundreds (from photographs of the event, the crowd seemed to be composed largely of men) gathered across the street from the prison. Many wore specially designed costumes, waved banners proclaiming a "Bundy BBQ." or "I like my Ted well done," and chanted songs such as "He bludgeoned the poor girls, all over the head. Now we're all ecstatic, Ted Bundy is dead." The most common

journalistic metaphors for the overall scene were that of a carnival, circus, or tailgate party before a big game.

This sort of spontaneous outpouring of folk sentiment regarding Ted Bundy was not without precedent. In the late 1970s, when he was awaiting trial for the murder of Caryn Campbell in Aspen, Colorado, Bundy managed to escape twice. The first time he was caught and returned to custody; the second time he was successful and traveled to Florida. But upon the news of his escapes (particularly the first) a phenomenal reaction occurred. All observers concur: "In Aspen, Bundy had become a folk hero." "Ted achieved the status of Billy the Kid at least"; "Aspen reacted as if Bundy were some sort of Robin Hood instead of a suspected mass murderer. A folklore sprang up out of the thin Rocky Mountain air." T-shirts appeared reading: "Ted Bundy is a One Night Stand." Radio KSNO programmed a Ted Bundy request hour, playing songs like: "Ain't No Way to Treat a Lady." A local restaurant offered a "Bundyburger" consisting of nothing more than a plain roll: "Open it and see the meat has fled," explained a sign. Yet after his second escape, the FBI took Bundy seriously enough to name him to their 10 Most Wanted List, seeking him "in connection with 36 similar-type sexual slayings throughout several Western states."

Just as Bundy's young, white, generally middle-class victims were stereotypically (and with marked racist and classic bias) universalized as "anyone's daughters," Bundy himself was depicted as the fatherland's (almost) ideal son—handsome, intelligent, a former law student, a rising star in Seattle's Republican party. And although that idealization falls apart upon examination—he had to drop out of law school due to bad grades; he was chronically unhappy and habitually abused alcohol; he was a nailbiter and a nosepicker—it provided an attractive mythic persona for purposes of identification. As several feminist analysts have noted, a recurrent and vivid pattern accompanying episodes of sensationalized sex murder is ordinary male identification with the sex killer, as revealed in "jokes, innuendoes, veiled threats (*I might be the Strangler, you know*)." Such joking followed Bundy's murder of two sorority women at the Chi Omega House at the University of Florida, Tallahassee. As one woman who lived there at the time remembered:

> Probably the most disturbing thing was the series of jokes and innuendoes that men traded about the murders. My boyfriend at the time was a public defender, and it was his office that represented Bundy at trial. He heard a lot of comments by virtue of being male and working close to the investigation that I probably would never have heard otherwise. We talked recently and he said there were basically two kinds of humor about the killings: (1) sorority-related jokes (2) jokes which connected the violence of torn-off

nipples and bite marks on the victims to Bundy's sexual "appetite" as in "eating" the victims sexually or sometimes, literally. One such joke was: "What do you get when you have a Tri Delt, a Chi O, and a Phi Mu? A three-course dinner for Ted Bundy." What could possibly be behind this kind of humor? I really don't buy the theory that these jokes help to reduce the stress of a horrible event. I think they just reduce the horror of the event in order to make it acceptable.

After his first escape, the male identification was with Bundy as a rebel, an outlaw hero. When he was on trial for murder in Florida, as the joking there indicated, he provided fodder for some sadistic sexual fantasies. But subsequently, Bundy did the supremely unmanly thing of confessing to his crimes and manifesting fear of death. No longer qualifying as hero, Bundy was now cast into the complementary role of scapegoat. The "bloodthirsty revelers" who partied outside as Bundy was executed, through their objectification and disrespect for the victims and lust for death, still mirrored Bundy, but now delightedly demanded that the all-American boy die as a token sacrifice for his and their sins.

Elements, frequently obscure, of Bundy lore now can be found in various places. Students in a popular culture class tell me that they are sure that the name of the family (Bundy) on the Fox network's parodic sitcom "Married With Children" deliberately recalls the notorious Ted Bundy and is a subtle reference to the down side of "happy" American family life. The punk band, "Jane's Addiction," on a 1988 album, includes a song, "Ted, Just Admit It." (This was before Bundy had confessed.) Here, they sing of television news being "just another show with sex and violence" and chant over and over that "sex is violent." But I encountered the most startling mythicization of Bundy last spring at the University of New Mexico in Albuquerque, where I teach. There I found a flyer advertising a program on pornography, held in the dorms and sponsored by a student group, showing the tape of Bundy's last interview. The flyer displayed a likeness of the killer under the logo: "*A Man with Vision. A Man with Direction. A Prophet of Our Times . . . Bundy: The Man, The Myth. The Legend (sic).*" Unfortunately, I was unable to attend this program, having gotten the flyer only after the fact. I was given the names of two male students who organized the program, but my attempts to find and contact them were unsuccessful; they were seniors and the semester had ended. Therefore, I cannot say with certainty what the tone of the program was. The flyer itself combines elements of a seemingly serious agenda, e.g., "film, informed speakers, discussion" with patently "sick" humor, e.g., the references to Bundy as a visionary prophet. The sponsor for the event was the Entertainment Program Committee, a dormitory student group, so I imagine that it was put on primarily as a way for, primarily male, students to get together to joke about Bundy,

particularly his claim that pornography led him to sexual violence.

As previously noted, the mystery behind the actual identity of Jack the Ripper has generated a considerable amount of his lore. Although his identity is clear, other factors about Bundy provide legendary fodder. Bundy confessed to thirty murders, yet he also has been implicated in at least twenty other murders by the authorities; moreover, without much corroborating evidence, some relatives of missing women are sure that their loved ones were killed by Bundy. For example, Sophia Mary Healey disappeared at Royal Gorge in Colorado in 1979. The *Denver Post* reports that her mother "clings to the notion her daughter was murdered or abducted by a man seen entering the park in a tan VW immediately after Healey. That man, she believes, was notorious serial killer Ted Bundy, who had recently escaped from a Colorado jail." Like his predecessor, Jack the Ripper, Bundy has become something of a "collective for murder." Finally, Bundy was "illegitimate" and his mother has never revealed the identity of his birth father. Such obscure paternal origins are an open invitation to mythicization as happened recently when an article in *Vanity Fair* (May 1989) broadly suggested (without any actual evidence) that Louise Bundy was impregnated by her abusive father and Bundy was thus a child of incest.

Finally, the greatest myth surrounding Bundy is one that we encounter nearly everywhere in the mainstream press—the concept that Bundy, and others like him, are complete "enigmas." This was constantly reiterated in refutation of Bundy's claim—which he had made consistently since his capture in 1978—that pornography had influenced his evolution into a sex killer. For example, *Playboy* approvingly quotes one of his lawyers, James Coleman: "He [Bundy] didn't know what made him kill people [sic]. No one did." Similarly, a *New York* editorialist, after pooh poohing the "deadly dangers of nude centerfolds, X-rated movies, and bottom-rack periodicals," averred: "I don't believe that Ted Bundy or anyone else understood what made him commit and repeat the crimes he confessed to, which were rape murders of an unimaginable violence and cruelty." First of all, such cruel violences are verifiably *imaginable* (and even erotic and/or entertaining) in this culture—consider the pornographic snuff film or soft-core snuff, such as the slasher film; Bundy's fame is more than matched, particularly among children, by that of the extremely cruel and violent fictional serial killers, Freddy Krueger or Jason. Secondly, a feminist analysis would not find Bundy and his ilk to be inexplicable deviants, but rather, logical, if extreme, products of a systemically misogynist culture: one that promotes an ideology of male supremacy; objectifies women; repeatedly associates violence and virility; eroticizes weaponry and various forms of violence and murder; and immortalizes and heroizes such men as Jack the Ripper.

Bundy ceaselessly demanded that people see him as just like them, as "sharing a common humanity." As he told evangelical minister Jim Dobson in his final interview: "Those of us who are ... so much influenced by violence in the media, in particular pornographic violence, are not some kind of inherent monsters. We are your sons, and we are your husbands, and we grew up in regular families." While part of Bundy's appeal is his overwhelming facade of normalcy, another sex killer from the 1970s deliberately cultivated a diametrically opposed persona—that of the inherent and committed monster.

"I am the 'Monster'"

I am deeply hurt by your calling me a wemon [sic] hater. I am not. But I am a monster. I am the "Son of Sam" . . . I am the "Monster"—"Beelzebub"— the chubby behemoth.
    —David Berkowitz, letter to police (1 April 1977),
            printed in the *Daily News,* 5 June 1977

During his spree as the "Son of Sam," the killer who randomly shot young women as they walked alone on the street, or sat in parked cars with other women or men, David Berkowitz wrote highly dramatic and disturbing letters to both police and press, letters which were subsequently printed in the daily papers. One such letter was sent to columnist Jimmy Breslin of the *Daily News:*

Hello, from the cracks in the sidewalks of New York City and from the ants that dwell in these cracks and feed on the dried blood of the dead that has settled into these cracks.

Hello from the gutters of New York City, which are filled with dog manure, vomit, stale wine, urine and blood.

Don't think that because you haven't heard from me for a while that I went to sleep. No, rather, I am still here, like a spirit roaming the night. Thirsty, hungry, seldom stopping to rest; anxious to please Sam.

The first day that just a part of that letter was printed, the *Daily News* sold a record-breaking 1,116,000 copies, a record that stood until the day Berkowitz was apprehended in mid-August. Actually, an extraordinary number of newspapers was sold throughout that entire summer as the *Post* and the *News* vied in a circulations war, turning their most sensationalist attention to this story. So intense was their coverage that the *New Yorker* charged the city's tabloids with what we might think of as "self-fulfilling publicity," of possibly encouraging the killer, or another of like mind, to strike again "by transforming a killer into a celebrity . . . into a seemingly omnipotent monster stalking the city." While such criti-

cism may seem to be merely enacting the social class differential between the prestigious magazine and the tabloids, a few years later, Berkowitz indicated that the *New Yorker* might have been right. He avowed that after his fourth shooting:

I didn't much care anymore, for I finally had convinced myself that it was good to do it, necessary to do it, and that the public wanted me to do it. The latter part I believe until this day. I believe that many were rooting for me. This was the point at which the papers began to pick up vibes and information that something big was happening out in the streets. Real big!"

The attention of the people of New York throughout the summer of 1977 was riveted on the "Son of Sam." Men wearing T-shirts bearing the police sketch of the suspect's face walked the streets. Talk of the killer had become "the staple of conversation." Then mayor Abraham Beame summed up the melodramatic fascination of that time: "Son of Sam. I even liked the name and that in itself was terrifying. I knew it would stick—would become his trademark—you could see it all building, the fears of the people, including my own, and the headlong rush of the press to create a personality, someone they could build a story around." Significantly, that movement to create a narrative was facilitated not only by Berkowitz's self-articulated monstrosity, but also by his style and choice of victims, for the killer who preyed on parked teenage couples seemed the very embodiment of that most common bogeyman of teenage horror—the stalking maniac of the popular urban legend, "The Hook." In journalistic accounts of the shooting of several Berkowitz's victims the basic elements of "The Hook" clearly structure the narrative. The boy and girl pull into a lover's lane to neck and begin to talk about the killer. The boy plays it cool but the girl gets scared and begs the boy to leave. The boy doesn't take her fear seriously, but finally agrees. Just then the killer approaches and shoots them.

After Berkowitz was captured in August, 1977, reminders of the terror continued to haunt New York women, some deliberately planted by big business. Berkowitz had claimed that he "liked to shoot pretty girls," a remark that was widely quoted in the press. Incredibly, just a few months after his arrest, Max Factor introduced a new face moisturizer called "Self-Defense." As the billboards throughout the city threatened: "Warning! A Pretty Face Isn't Safe In This City. Fight Back With Self-Defense." In this campaign, the cosmetics firm unabashedly tried to cash in on the fear generated by the sex killer, and, at the same time, implanted some all by itself.

Again, in Albuquerque, I have observed several references to Berkowitz in the local youth subculture. Currently, one of the most popular local punk bands is called "Cracks in the Sidewalk"; it is common knowledge among their fans that the name derives from Berkowitz's "hello from the cracks in the sidewalk" letter to Jimmy Breslin. When Berkowitz was caught, he claimed that he was possessed by demons and under orders to kill from a man named "Sam" who communicated with him through a barking dog. (Later, he confessed that he had made all of this up.) Ten years later, on public access cable television in Albuquerque, a group of local amateur filmmakers showcase their works (frequently short horror films featuring a serial/slasher killer) on a program they call "Son of Sam Theater." A man, who bears some resemblance to Berkowitz, hosts the show. He holds a dog hand puppet whom he calls Sam and talks with during brief addresses to the audience. Occasionally, another man will enter and chat with him, proclaiming himself to be another serial killer, e.g., Ed Gein (the murderer on whom the killer in *Psycho* was based). The general tone is one of high camp and hilarity, as when "Berkowitz" slashes "Gein" to death with a knife in a mode reminiscent of *Psycho's* famous shower scene.

Son of Sam. I even liked the name and that in itself was terrifying. I knew it would stick—would become his trademark—you could see it all building, the fears of the people, including my own, and the headlong rush of the press to create a personality, someone they could build a story around.

—*Abraham Beame*

This cross referencing between actual serial killers and horror film is itself significant. For the most common monster of contemporary horror film is a serial killer, beginning with Norman Bates in *Psycho* (Alfred Hitchcock, 1960). We now see the immortal or at least regenerated serial killer in *Silent Rage* (Michael Miller, 1982), in the phenomenally popular Freddy and Jason of the *Nightmare on Elm Street* and *Friday the 13th* series, as well as *Child's Play* (Tom Holland, 1988) and *Shocker* (Wes Craven, 1989).

"Pop Culture Heroes"

Freddy is pollution. Freddy is evil. Freddy is what's wrong with the world. . . . Racism, pollution, child molestation, child abuse, alcohol, drugs.
                                        —Robert Englund

Nowadays, the good guys seem to be fighting a losing battle, and teenagers appear to like it that way. Jason, the goalie-masked, knife-wielding fiend of the

"Friday the 13th" series of movies, and Freddy Krueger, the hideous-looking killer in the "Nightmare on Elm Street" movies are pop-culture heroes.
                                        —*New York Times,* Oct. 1989

Our heroes and their narratives are an index to our character and conception of our role in the universe.
                                        —Richard Slotkin

As noted earlier, a key factor in the mystique of Jack the Ripper has been his incorporation into the horror genre as a stock character. Indeed, by the latter part of the twentieth century, one of the most common monsters, as Robin Wood has observed, is a "human psychotic." Moreover, even the traditional monsters—the vampires, werewolves, and phantoms—now are being overtly portrayed as sex killers. If patriarchal legend has immortalized the Ripper (and is in process on Bundy, et. al), his screen brethren too are deathless, surviving seeming demise in feature after feature, resurrecting to dispatch those intrepid teenage girls who vanquished them in earlier installments, and gloating, as does Freddy in *Nightmare on Elm Street IV,* "I am eternal."

Like Bundy and Berkowitz (and their fictional forbear, Norman Bates), Freddy and Jason have identifiable mothers—but not fathers. Jason, the young son of a female cook at a summer camp, drowned while the camp counselors neglected him in favor of sexual satisfaction. His mother begins a vengeance campaign in the first *Friday the 13th* (Sean Cunningham, 1980), only to be beheaded by the sole surviving girl. Jason, however, isn't dead. In *Part II,* we meet him as a deformed teenager who keeps a candle-lit shrine to his mother's head. His first action is to gore to death the surviving girl from the original film and then to begin the silent reign of terror that has lasted through seven sequels (he doesn't even get his famous hockey mask until *Part III*). The loquacious Freddy Krueger of *Nightmare on Elm Street* originated as a child molester and murderer in an affluent suburban community. Tried for his crimes, he was freed on a technicality, so some local parents got together and burned him death. Now Freddy preys upon the children of these parents through their dreams. In *Nightmare, Part III,* we meet Freddy's mother, a ghostly nun who explains that as a young girl working in a madhouse, she accidentally was locked in with the inmates and repeatedly raped. Freddy was thus, "the bastard son of a hundred maniacs."

It is mythically necessary to leave the paternity of these killers nebulous and even multiple, for their true father is indeed a collective entity—the patriarchal culture that has produced the serial killer as a fact of modern life. Moreover, these deranged sons must themselves stand in for that absent father, assuming the punitive paternal role. As Wes Craven (director and writer of the first *Nightmare on Elm Street*) has indicated: "Freddy is the most ruthless primal father. The adult who wants to slash down the next generation."

In Craven's original conception, Freddy was "the most evil human being you can imagine, someone who goes after children." He had no plans to make Freddy invincible and eternal; rather, as he planned it, the extremely resourceful heroine of the first film, Nancy (Heather Langencamp), defeats Freddy by denying him, by turning her back on him and forbidding him reality. However, producer Nick Shaye wanted sequels and insisted upon a ludicrous ending where Freddy resurrects and the teenagers are doomed. (The heroic Nancy is killed off in *Part III*). Craven points out that under Shaye's direction, the movement was to "soften Freddy and make him a little bit more of a buffoon. . . . Now in a sense, he's embraced by younger kids. And they can make fun of him. In a way he's dangerous and in a way he's a joke. It's probably safer to deal with him that way." Craven's rationale is the same one that is used to explain the disturbing joking about serial killers such as Ted Bundy. Yet, it is women who would most need to find ways to manage fear about sex killers and in my experience women rarely if ever make these jokes. Such joking is a means of normalizing the sex killer and identifying with him. Softening Freddy only softens and makes palatable the sexual abuse and murder of children. Incidentally, Freddy is not the first serial killer to be perceived as ironic and witty; that role was originally written for the mythic Jack the Ripper. Nor is he the first figure to double as buffoon and evil terror. John Wayne Gacy, rapist, torturer, and killer of thirty-three boys and young men, frequently performed for children as a clown.

Most commentators speak quite loosely about the "kids" who embrace these filmic killers, yet we should be wary of the facile generic and the gender differences it conceals. Although there is no comprehensive study of the demographics of the slasher film audience, all observers agree that it is mostly between the ages of twelve and twenty and largely male. Without undertaking extensive interviews, it is difficult to discern in any conclusive way what Freddy and Jason mean to the, disproportionately male, children and teenagers who are so fascinated by these films in which a couple making love signals an imminent assault, where there are virtually no permanent survivors, and where both sexes are targets, though it is on the women's bodies and (usually more prolonged) deaths that the camera lingers. Film critic Robin Wood discusses the types of identification operating for the slasher film audience, but first distinguishes these current products from traditional horror:

> There the monster was in general a creature from the id, not merely a product of repression but a protest against it, whereas in the current cycles the monster, while still produced by repression, has essentially become a superego figure, avenging itself on liber-

ated female sexuality or the sexual freedom of the young. . . . Where the traditional horror film invited, however ambiguously, an identification with the return of the repressed, the contemporary horror film invites an identification (either sadistic or masochistic or both simultaneously) with punishment.

One element operating in viewers' masochistic identification is to pledge allegiance to the punitive father, hoping quite hopelessly that this will save you. We see this in the stories of those women who "fall in love" with killers such as Ted Bundy (his wife actually married him after he had been convicted of the Chi Omega murders). The other, and probably more common, strategy (the sadistic one) is to identify with the violator and his role, to be titillated by his excesses and turned on by his depredations.

In October, 1988, nineteen-year old Sharon Gregory was murdered in Greenfield, Massachusetts, when an eighteen-year-old white man, Mark Branch stabbed her over fifty times. Branch, at the time, was undergoing psychological counseling due to his obsession with slasher films; he particularly identified with "Jason" the murderer of the *Friday the 13th* series. When his home was searched, police found over 75 slasher videos, and 64 similar books, three knives, a machete, and three hockey goalie masks, like that worn by Jason. Branch eluded the police for about a month and then hanged himself in a local woods. Perhaps significantly, the murder took place around Halloween. This factor created additional havoc in Greenfield and caused town officials to ask parents to cancel traditional trick or treat activities. The officials requested this not because they were afraid Branch would strike again: "Instead, they are afraid pranksters may dress up as Jason . . . and scare young children or cause edgy residents to overreact and hurt someone in the dark." Branch's sadistic identification with Jason (as well as the expected pranksters' identification with Branch) is, assuredly, extreme, yet not completely unexpected. A hero, after all, is a role model, one who acts out the fantasies of his fans, one who inspires emulation.

For obvious reasons, Freddy and Jason are often discussed together: each is a powerful and compelling contemporary symbol of evil. Yet, the two series and the two monsters are quite distinct. The *Friday the 13th* movies are pure gorenography; the thin stories and cardboard characters exist only to give flesh to the slaughter scenes. It is difficult to imagine anything but sadism to be behind an identification with Jason. But, the original *Nightmare on Elm Street* movie (and to some extent the sequels), although not free of the slasher film's fixation on the coupling of teen sex with elaborate female death, is far more visually and philosophically interesting. Freddy is no mere death machine. As Robert Englund (the actor who plays Freddy) puts it: "He is the nightmare in suburbia. He is the nightmare in white America and he's reminding you that you can't escape IT!" As such, Freddy may invite some identification as a completely unrepressed individual, a revolutionary figure who disregards and destroys traditional mores and values, one who exposes as fraud the image of the happy nuclear family and ideal suburban community.

A rather astonishing poem, "A Nightmare on Sesame Street," seems to stem from such a perspective and displays a sense of apocalyptic humor akin to Freddy Krueger's own. It was written by a ten year old African-American boy in 1988 and turned in as a classroom assignment (along with his accompanying illustration).

> It was a pleasant day, everybody was happy. "Play Ball," shouted Big Bird one bright sunny day. But his friends disagreed. Which game should they play? Grover spoke first. He said, "Please let's play catch." But Henry suggested a quick soccer match. "Hey buddies," said Ernie, holding his bat, "how about baseball?" I'd really like that. "I agree," Betty Lou said, flexing her mitt. But Oscar retorted, "Not enough grit." Cookie completely ignored the debate. While he munched on a frisbee that looked like a plate. "I get a kick out of football," said Bert. But Oscar continued, "Not enough dirt." "My racket is tennis," said Oscar persisting. Big Bird interrupted, "Let's try co-existing!" We'll take turns," Big Bird said averting a brawl. And that's what they did. And they each had a ball . . . until . . . There he was Freddy Cruger (sic). He said, "A is for Aim, B is for Blades. C is for Cut and D is for Dead. He popped Grover's ball then he sliced him. He stabbed Ernie and threw him somewhere. He stabbed Bert when he said he wanted to play football. He sliced Cookie Monster's cookies. "What's going on here," said Big Bird. "Run," said Henry. "He will kill you." "Nonsense, I'll ask him to be my friend." "Will you be my friend," Big Bird said. Not a chance, ffft ouch I'm, dying. Cruger kills the rest of the people at sesame street. And his next stop is Mr. Rogers Neighborhood.

This piece certainly bespeaks a rage against the TV-version of banally happy children's culture and experience. Yet if this poem is a rebellion, it is one that is programmed for self-defeat. For Freddy Krueger—the child molester and murderer—is no genuine stranger to that world, but a direct product of it. He is the alter ego, not the true opposite, of that other cultural icon, the all-knowing and authoritative suburban "good dad"; Krueger is Ward Cleaver unrepressed, running amok, wielding a cleaver. He is the incestuous/alcoholic/abusive/murderous father, hidden behind the placid facade of Elm Street, U.S.A. Moreover, he is the consummate "nuclear father," threatening imminent apocalypse.

By killing women and children, Freddy and Jason, as well as the actual killers whom they reflect, are symbolically destroying life and the future itself. Robert Englund tells the (again predominantly young male) readers of the skateboard magazine, *Thrasher*:

> Child Killer? What are children? Children are the future. Freddy's killing the future. Freddy hates beauty. He hate youth. He hates the future . . . It's kinda political y'know. Freddy hates the future. He's killing the future. Parents are weary. They don't want to defend the future anymore. The kids see it, and Freddy's killing the kids.

Killing the future. Psychologist Robert J. Lifton points out that the fear of "futurelessness" (the belief that oneself and the world has no future) is a condition particularly afflicting children and teenagers in the nuclear age. It is commonly accepted that monsters from 1950s horror and science fiction—Godzilla or giant ants—were metaphors for "the Bomb." Yet, current film monsters continue to carry those nuclear meanings. As murderer of the future, Freddy is a symbolic evocation, not only of the reality of rampant child abuse and murder, but also of the everyday potential of nuclear annihilation, of radical futurelessness.

The delirious embrace of the sex killer (factual or fictional) is a phenomenon closely related to what Lifton has described as the "nuclear high": the desperate attempt to deny or escape destruction through identification with the agent of that destruction. Thus, the consummately lethal nuclear weapons are mythicized as beautiful, awesome, even divine, as the "only form of transcendence worthy of the age." Lifton illustrates this "nuclear high" by pointing to one of the final images of *Dr. Strangelove* (Stanley Kubrick, 1963), "in which man rides bomb to its target while uttering a wild Texas yodel." Interestingly, an episode of "Freddy's Nightmares," (a television series spin-off from the films), tells the story of a young girl who dreams presciently of nuclear holocaust. Throughout that episode, our commentator, Freddy Krueger, appears, first with a mushroom cloud coming out of his head, and then out in space, riding a nuclear missile down to the planet Earth to blow it up. He takes off his hat and waves it, calling "Yee ha," clearly in homage to that well-known *Dr. Strangelove* scene. Then, he reconsiders, turns the missile around, and says, "Nah, I'd rather get you little buckaroos one at a time." Freddy, we then realize, is something like a personalized nuclear bomb.

One other fact must be mentioned: in *Dr. Strangelove,* the madman general who engineers world nuclear destruction is the aptly named General Jack D. Ripper. How fitting that these icons of sex murder so frequently merge with those of nuclear annihilation, for both of these atrocities are apocalyptic—both kill the future. Moreover, both are based in male supremacist sexuality and are marked by the equation of "un-imaginable" cruelty and violence with power, eroticism, and ecstasy. Freddy Krueger and Jason join Jack the Ripper and Ted Bundy as the founding fathers and sons of an unremit-tingly apocalyptic culture, pointing to a future consisting of no safe sex ever, beaches spiked with toxic waste, extinct species, global warming, and nuclear war.

Atomic scientist Leo Szillard once commented regarding the heroization of his fellows after World War II: "It is remark-able that all these scientists . . . should be listened to. But mass murderers have always commanded the attention of the public, and atomic scientists are no exception to this rule." Yet, why must mass murderers rule our attention. Like the originally efficacious heroine in the first *Nightmare on Elm Street,* we might instead ourselves take command and deny them that aggrandizing focus. Such denial would not be the passive and self-defeating kind that merely pretends that they don't exist, but an *active* denial, one that negates their lure, deconstructs their lore, and does not perpetuate, but dimin-ishes their reality.

Gayle Feldman (essay date 17 May 1991)

SOURCE: "11 Houses Bid, Doubleday Wins *Shot in the Heart,*" in *Publishers Weekly,* Vol. 238, May 17, 1991, pp. 33-4.

[*In the essay below, Feldman discusses the interest surround-ing Mikal Gilmore's upcoming book* Shot in the Heart.]

Perhaps it's not so surprising that on April 23-24, 11 houses engaged in feverish bidding, and one house—Doubleday—finally agreed to pay a reported $700,000, for the right to publish a nonfiction book based on a 100-page proposal by a *Rolling Stone* senior writer named Mikal Gilmore. True, $700,000 for a first book is rather a lot of money, and 11 houses in an auction are rather more than the norm. It *was* a little unusual that three seemingly very different Random House Divisions—Knopf, Crown and Turtle Bay—were re-portedly each willing to offer more than $600,000 for the prize. And this is the first occasion that this writer has ever heard of when a literary magazine—*Granta*—snapped up the rights to extract and reprint part of a *proposal*—which Bill Buford did just over a week after the auction occurred.

But in these days when novels about serial killers reverber-ate through the editorial pages and reach the bestseller lists; when movies about serial killers become box-office smash hits; and when America's love affair with the gun—Brady bill or no Brady bill—is as fatally potent as ever, a book by the brother of Gary Gilmore is certainly not lacking in hard-boiled commercial potential. The story, however, doesn't end there.

For at a time when so much that is written or portrayed about violence and killing in this country is purely exploitative, Mikal Gilmore's *Shot in the Heart* hopes to be something else again. Yes, his brother murdered many innocent people and then, in 1977, became the first judicially executed pris-oner in America in over a decade—at his own urging. Yes, his brother's life and death were chronicled after a fashion by no less than an American literary lion—Norman Mailer in *The Executioner's Song*—and subsequently in a televi-sion film. But what enthused so many publishers about the 100-page proposal is neatly summed in the subtitle, "The Story of an American Family, in Murder," for Gilmore very much places the emphasis on "family."

In a quiet but intense telephone interview a week after the auction, Gilmore told *PW,* "I never kid myself that a book can change the world—I don't have any high aims that way. I know there are a lot of people who will look at a story like this and regard my family as extremely abnormal—an Ameri-can family gone wrong. But I also believe that we were an extreme example of an American norm that isn't clearly rec-ognized.

> I want people to understand that murder is a complex event—it very rarely occurs just as a single solitary response born of the moment. The seeds were sown long before, in the murderer's family and emotional history and environment, and also in the way the culture around that family embraces or punishes violence.
>
> —*Mikal Gilmore*

"I want people to understand that murder is a complex event—it very rarely occurs just as a single solitary response born of the moment. The seeds were sown long before, in the murderer's family and emotional history and environment, and also in the way the culture around that family embraces or punishes violence. We do live in a time and place where violence is seen as an effective means to deal with our prob-lems, while at the same time it is greatly feared and thought to be out of control.

"The usual response is that if we could just put people away who commit these crimes we would be okay. I understand that impulse, but it doesn't seem to stop the crimes or the violence. I think you have to understand the sources of mur-der, and that in some ways we are all part of it."

Agent Richard Pine, who "essentially spent about a year selling this proposal," looks back on the week of the auction as one unique in his experience. "It was as though the publishing business had fallen in love. Even the people who didn't get the book [Houghton Mifflin and Hyperion were also offering serious money] wished us well. There was a lot of metaphorical back slapping.

"And yet, this is the one book I thought Mikal was never going to write. I always thought his books would be about the world of music, the world he's written about for *Rolling Stone* since 1976. But in the end, I guess he had to start his book career with this one."

Gilmore himself muses, "It came as a surprise to me that I would do this book. For many years, I put myself at a distance from my family; I felt they were a bad-luck outfit and that the only way to escape was to reject them. In some ways, that really did save me. But as we all know, our families catch up with us. Certainly, in 1977, with what happened to Gary, it caught up with me in a pretty forceful way.

"Later, I tried rejecting the family all over again. It was painful and shameful—I told myself I didn't have to be shaped by it, didn't have to be known as Gary Gilmore's brother. But I kept going through cycles of depression and disappointment, often tied to hopes of marriage and family that didn't work out. My past kept caving in on me and I realized that I was more of a brother to Gary than I had ever anticipated, that some of the dark forces in his life were also in mine. We had both been shaped by a longing for family, a longing that broke each of us in different ways. I realized that if I didn't figure out where I learned these patterns, I wouldn't be able to go on with my life in an effective way."

Gilmore went into "serious therapy," and recognized that "this was a story I wanted to write as a first book. I had tried over the years to write books about music and each time I would grind to a halt in confusion and despair. But I wrote this proposal in eight or nine days, and odd though it may sound, doing it was a real pleasure. I surprised myself with what came out: it was liberating."

Although the attention he will no doubt receive—the labeling as "Gary Gilmore's brother"—will not be something he anticipates with pleasure, Mikal says he's "very much looking forward to" the actual writing of the book.

Looking forward is also something the folks at Doubleday are doing a lot of regarding this book. From publisher Steve Rubin to editor-in-chief David Gernert to acquiring editor Paul Bresnick, the pleasure at snaring this project is palpable. Gilmore makes it clear that Doubleday's was the winning bid not solely by dint of being the highest, but also because Bresnick is editing Greil Marcus, whom Gilmore calls his "favorite living American critic. I figured if an edi-

tor was working with Greil, understood him and could handle him, that was a good sign. I can be strong-willed myself, and I want this to be handled seriously."

The manuscript is due in early 1993, with fall publication anticipated. Doubleday bought North American rights, and already Pine has sold British and Commonwealth rights "for a six-figure sum in pounds" to Viking Penguin. Although a lot can happen between the writing of a proposal—even one a hundred pages long—and the delivery of a finished manuscript, the odds seem fairly good on this project making it through to the home stretch. David Gernert reckons that Doubleday's Herman Gollob said it best: "Not only is *Shot in the Heart* a potential bestseller—more importantly, it has the potential for becoming a classic as well."

Jack Miles (essay date December 1991)

SOURCE: "Imagining Mayhem: Fictional Violence vs. 'True Crime'," in *North American Review,* December, 1991, pp. 57-64.

[*In the following essay, Miles discusses the popularity of true-crime literature, what its popularity suggests about American culture, and the moral issues raised by the genre.*]

During the 1980s, America got tough on crime. As a result, our prison population has doubled, and the U.S. now ranks first in the world—ahead of South Africa and the Soviet Union—in the proportion of its populace behind bars. Does this mean that ours is the most criminally violent society in the world? Or are we simply the most punitive society in the world?

Criminal violence in America, flourishing despite massive efforts against it, defies easy comprehension. As anyone knows who has watched a jury being empaneled for a murder case, it is difficult, these days, to find twelve Americans whose lives have not been touched by violent crime. both menacing and deeply baffling, crime as public topic and as private experience quite literally forces itself upon us. And yet, even knowing this, someone who observes—as the book editor of a major newspaper is uniquely able to observe—the torrent of violence-preoccupied popular literature in our country can only wonder at what it may mean, or portend.

The recent controversy over Bret Easton Ellis's "spatter novel" *American Psycho* (1991) brought the relationship between crime on the page and crime in the streets briefly to the front of the national mind, but there was much to wonder at long before that controversy broke. Ellis has shocked readers, especially female readers, with his scenes of torture and mutilation; but Stephen King—by every measure the most popular writer of his generation and perhaps of this century—makes only somewhat milder scenes a staple of his writing. *The Stephen King Encyclopedia* (Spignesi, 1991) contains a special section on "death, torture, and mutilation" in his work. As I write, Mary Higgins Clark—a novelist who receives almost no critical discussion but whose contracts run to the high eight digits—is no. 2 on the fiction best seller list with *Loves Music, Loves to Dance* (1991), a novel that, like Ellis's, is about a serial killer. All this may mean nothing, but then again, it may mean something after all.

Have all publics been quite so bloody-minded as the American public is just now? Or do our bloody popular literature, our quick recourse to war, our restoration of the death penalty . . . , and our vast and steadily growing prison population spring from some common, uniquely American cultural root?

—Jack Miles

At the 1991 American Booksellers Association convention, I learned that three contracts have been signed for books by different authors on the slaying of San Francisco pornographer Artie Mitchell. A fourth contract, brokered by the biggest-bucks agent in town, may soon follow.

You don't get four books on any single subject under contract at the same time unless publishers are confident the public has an insatiable appetite for that subject. True, the public at all places and times has never been less than bloody-minded: Look at the corpse-strewn closing scenes of Shakespeare's tragedies. But have all publics been quite so bloody-minded as the American public is just now? Or do our bloody popular literature, our quick recourse to war, our restoration of the death penalty against the pattern of all the other industrialized democracies, and our vast and steadily growing prison population spring from some common, uniquely American cultural root? It is the thought that the answer to this question may be affirmative that makes a book editor hesitate over how much attention to devote to horror and gore. Negative reviews or reviewer neglect may be no more than flies on the carapace of a juggernaut like Stephen King. Civic responsibility dictates nonetheless that the reviewing media be on guard both against worsening the impact of crime on its actual victims and against enhancing the likelihood of further crime. Both outcomes are at the very least conceivable.

"Language is a pistol," Ben Cheever is quoted as saying to his sister, Susan, in her recent memoir *Treetops* (1991). "A pistol is a fine thing if you use it to defend yourself, or for

robbing from the rich if you are poor. It's not so fine if you shoot your little son and daughter with it." In John Cheever's story "An Educated American Woman," a little boy apparently modeled on Ben dies as a result of criminal neglect by his mother. In Cheever's story "The Hartleys," a little girl apparently modeled on Susan is brutally dragged to her death in a ski lift. All three of the Cheever children resented the use that John Cheever made of them and their mother in his fiction at the time he was writing it, and they continue to resent it now, many years later.

All three, I hasten to add, are not unacquainted with the typical defenses of such use. Susan writes of her father: "Suggestions that his or other writers' characters were modeled on real people infuriated him. 'You are reducing literature to gossip,' he would say." And Susan astutely joins her father's words to a long and apposite quote from Philip Roth's subtle *Deception,* including the line "because you're you doesn't mean I didn't make *you* up." Plainly, the children of John Cheever are not unsophisticated about the nature of fiction. Nonetheless Fred Cheever does not shrink from saying that what John did to his wife and Fred's mother, Mary, through his work "is a major wrong. It's right up there with slavery." Literary sophistication seems not to preclude deep resentment when one ends up feeling, as Ben Cheever does, "as if I was a minor character in someone else's book."

What have the Cheever children to do with the popular literature of violence? I submit that they give unusually articulate expression to the *sort* of feeling that the victims, including the collateral victims, of crime have when they find themselves built into quasi-novelistic "true crime" melodramas, and it is with these works rather than with blockbuster novels that I would begin this discussion.

John Cheever did not put his wife or children into his fiction under their real names, nor for that matter did he ever write a "true crime"—or, as it would have to have been, a "true misery"—version of his own and their lives. Whatever his children may have suffered, it has not involved actual violence. All the more reason to assume, however, that those whose sufferings have indeed included actual violence must harbor an even more intense resentment against those who have retailed their sufferings to the world.

The victims of the crimes that "true crime" writers put on display rarely have their opinion about these works solicited. But their situation is worth a moment's thought; for if these works have any social utility, they ought to have it first and foremost for those most directly affected by the crimes in question. And "true crime" continues to be a boom area in American publishing.

On April 9, 1991, a *Los Angeles Times* reporter married to a *New York Times* reporter and living in Boston published a piece in the *Los Angeles Times Book Review* entitled "Making a Killing Off True Crime." She polled an assortment of industry leaders on the growing popularity of this genre, taking as the occasion for her piece the media feeding frenzy that followed the slaying of Carol Stuart by her husband, Charles, and Charles Stuart's suicide after his failed attempt to pin the blame on a fictitious black assailant. Both Elizabeth Mehren and her husband, Fox Butterfield, received book offers by telephone, offers of which Mehren wrote as follows:

> "The calls would have been at least a boost for the ego were it not for the fact that just about anyone with even tangential involvement with any Boston-area newspaper or magazine, or anyone who is based in this area and does any reporting at all, seems to have faced the same flood of solicitations. One reporter at the *Boston Globe* told me that he received 11 inquiries about possible books or movies—and that was just in the first week after Stuart's apparent suicide."

The so-called Son of Sam law has permitted crime victims in New York state to lay claim to their victimizer's royalties, but surely it is of some note that sales of crime stories have risen so high that such a law had to be passed in the first place. When sales were smaller, no one noticed or cared; but sales have been growing.

A public consensus has formed around the thesis that criminals should not profit even in this way from their crimes. There is, however, little in the way of a consensus around the notion that the victims of crime should not have their suffering compounded by popular entertainments built around their trauma. And, by and large, popular entertainment is just what "true crime" is as a genre.

"True crime" writers, no surprise, have a rather more exalted view of what they do. Janet Malcolm, in a sensational series in *The New Yorker*, accused Joe McGinniss of bad faith in his dealings with convicted murderer Jeffery McDonald, the subject of McGinniss's book *Fatal Vision*. When the paperback edition of *Fatal Vision* appeared in 1989, it contained an epilogue in which McGinniss replied to Malcolm, comparing his deceptions to the disguises that a spy behind enemy lines might adopt. Quoting from a letter he had received from a former criminal investigator, McGinniss wrote:

> "In a very real sense, whether one is appointed by government, law enforcement bureaus or Life, itself, certain persons are called forward as undercover agents to investigate crucially important crimes. They are required to enter a variety of alien or enemy territories for the purpose of gaining vital information as to the ways and means used by adverse, hostile or criminal forces for injurious or illegal purposes. A disguise, in such matters, of one sort or another, becomes mandatory. In every case such undercover work is literally impossible without inducing trust in those to be investigated: a trust which, by its very nature, must be abused or betrayed in service to a larger purpose of reporting the truth. . . ."

McGinniss may count himself lucky to have such an uncritical supporter. The fact remains that this defense of "true crime" and its deceptions is grotesquely overblown. McGinniss did not write his book to bring a criminal to justice. At no small cost to others, Jeffrey McDonald had already been brought to justice when McGinniss began to write about him and was in fact behind bars when McGinniss conned him. *Fatal Vision* is not a public service, it is—like most "true crime" offerings—a public entertainment. Like McGinniss, however, most "true crime" authors do not identify themselves as entertainers but as unofficial intelligence agents. Ours is a nasty job, they imply, but someone has to do it. Someone has to stare the horror in the eye so that we may all know what it looks like. Society would be content to live in a fool's paradise were it not for the messages we bring from hell.

Inconveniently, of course, the very fact that these works command an immediate and large audience and that likely "properties" such as the Stuarts and the Mitchells arouse such hot competition suggests that the public already knows what true crime artists would teach them. True crime books, in fact, frequently address cases around which huge and essentially in-the-know audiences have already gathered: It is just this which makes these properties so commercial. More important, many of these works are written with little real regard for the victims. The focus, as in Truman Capote's *In Cold Blood,* which all but created the genre, is usually on the criminal. Even when attention shifts to the victims, direct or indirect, it is rarely attention that arrives at a time when they want or need it.

Joe McGinniss's later book, *Blind Faith,* describes the struggle of three young brothers to face up, during the course of a long trial, to the fact that their father has murdered their mother. How do they feel about having their trauma in all its most intimate aspects made as public as McGinniss made it in his book? After Janet Malcolm attacked McGinniss in her *New Yorker* article, one of these brothers wrote the *Times* that McGinniss had conducted himself as a consummate professional and a trusted friend in his dealings with the family. I tried several times to reach this young man by telephone and invite him to give a fuller exposition of his views in print, but he never returned my calls, and I think I know why. The youngest of the three brothers, only twelve when McGinniss was trying and failing to secure his cooperation, has never admitted that his father was guilty. Perhaps the older brother decided, on a moment's reflection, to defer to the younger brother's painfully different feelings about what McGinniss had done.

Detailed and protracted portrayal of a murder and its aftermath almost inevitably renews the pain and the humiliating exposure of those close to the murderer's victims, whatever may be the gain in such portrayals for society as a whole. Endorsements of true crime books and movies are sometimes forthcoming from such collateral victims of the actual crimes, but to quote Susan Cheever again, "If someone doesn't mind if you murder them, that doesn't make it all right to murder them."

"True crime" books, like all books, must be evaluated one at a time, but I confess that my skepticism about them has steadily grown. I find that more often than not they feed rather than check the personal and social pathologies they depict. Obviously, this broad subject matter deserves the best attention we can provide it, but these works excuse themselves from both the difficult challenge of sociological or criminological analysis and the even greater challenge of true art. Other things equal, a vividly detailed, quasi-novelistic, non-analytic, non-judgmental depiction of real people in their real agony may be the more deplorable the more entertaining it becomes. The facts do not speak for themselves. What they do for themselves is divert, and diversion is not what the case requires.

McGinniss is a writer of real talent, who has grown more skillful with each successive book. His *Blind Faith* makes poignant and compelling reading. And yet I wish he had not written it. We learn nothing of social utility through it, precisely because of the abstentions he enforces in the interests of a smooth narrative surface. I feel of my own warmly emotional initial response to the book rather as I might feel of my response to an illustrated pornographic essay portraying, against their will, people whom I actually knew. That is to say, the subject matter, if handled with sufficient pictographic virtuosity, may induce an almost autonomic response; but at even a single remove, one cannot help thinking about the feelings of real people thus involuntarily exposed.

It has been a progressive disenchantment with true crime and pornography (or what we might call true sex) that has left me, a bit to my own surprise, progressively more tolerant of explicit sex and violence in fiction. The portrayal of violence and sexual abuse in fiction may have several justifications, but one surely is that it obviates the need to talk about violence and sexual abuse in the persons of the actually violated and abused.

Susan Cheever, without denying her own bitter memories and after hearing out her two brothers about their father's work, comes to a similar conclusion after a discussion with her husband.

> "'There's nothing wrong with what your father did in those stories,' he says. . . .
>
> "'You don't think a writer should be bound by any rules at all?' I ask. . . .
>
> "'Just what he can get away with,' my husband says. . . .
>
> "My husband has never been negatively written about in fiction—never seen his intimate physical and emotional flaws skewered on the page to create a character. I don't think he'd like it. But as we talk, I realize that I have always agreed with the extreme position he's taking. . . . I realize as I argue with my husband that I take what my father did with his family as a license for what I do."

I believe that Susan Cheever has taken the correct position, and she is the more persuasive as she takes it because she has so fully earned it. More is involved, however, in "getting away with it" than just getting away with it legally. There is, in other words, a reply lying in wait for the writer in Philip Roth's *Deception* who says,

> "Because you're you doesn't mean I didn't make *you* up."

The reply is:

> "Yes, it does mean you didn't make *me* up—because you aren't as good a writer as you think."

A strong writer may re-invent characters who already exist, but who can deny that a weak writer, unable to invent, may resort to low-grade, cub-reporter copying, not to speak of exploitation or vendetta? And whether any writer in any given book deserves to make what we may call Roth's Boast is not for the writer to judge. This judgment is, quintessentially, the critic's to make.

For a sense of outrage comparable in tone and intensity to what the Cheever children felt about their role in their father's work, we need look no further—in fact, we should look nowhere else—than to the outrage that writers feel toward their reviewers. "I've ended up feeling as if I was a minor character in someone else's book," Ben Cheever says: *me, my whole life, years of time, an entire personality*. What the word "minor" conjures up is not so much the experience of misrepresentation as that of diminution. This is just how writers feel when entire novels are reduced to raw material for someone else's occasional essay, which is, of course, just what a book review is. That "skewering" to which Susan Cheever alludes may or may not take place; the shrinkage, however, cannot fail to take place and with it the transformation of one writer's full and finished product into another writer's raw material.

This is, of course, precisely as it should and must be in criticism. What art does to life—shattering it and reconstructing it—just that does criticism do to art. The fact that your novel exists does not mean that I have not invented it. But the analogous and severe conditions also apply. That is, a strong critic may re-invent the novel he criticizes, but a weak critic may certainly fall from that tightwire into a tarpit of distortion, reductionism, condescension and slander. Nothing is forbidden. You just better be good.

All this bears on the current glut of "true crime" pseudo-fiction and actual fiction on criminal themes in at least two ways.

> *American Psycho* was published . . . to reviews expressing truly unprecedented contempt and disgust. . . . The Los Angeles chapter of the National Organization of Women created headlines by recording excerpts from the book on a call-in number and calling for a boycott of all Random House books. The boycott went nowhere, but the critical rejection of the work was nearly total.
>
> —*Jack Miles*

First of all, it needs to be noted that the moral ante, so to call it, is much higher for "true crime" writers than it is for novelists. "True crime" writers may begin with a set of givens that novelists must invent. Still, if a novelist must reach a high pitch of invention before the work into which a reinvented real person has been inserted can pass muster as art, a "true crime" writer must reach some other kind of high pitch—call it what you will—before the re-use of real people under their own names can pass muster as something other than exploitation. There may be a social utility in such writing; but recall that when psychiatrists write up their cases for the professional literature, they change the names. If the authors of "true crime" wanted to spare the victims or collateral victims of violent crime further unwelcome notoriety, rather than building on just that notoriety to build the audience for their books, it would certainly be possible for them to change names as well. There were good reasons behind the convention, now so little observed, of changing the names to protect the innocent. Fiction, which typically changes much

more than just the names, gives no hostages here. "True crime" gives many.

Second, it should be noted that similarities between individuals in real life and in fiction are not the only similarities that count. There are also group resemblances. Any woman may feel, as she reads a torture-murder scene in Bret Easton Ellis's "spatter novel" *American Psycho,* a shudder like the one the young Susan Cheever felt when she read John Cheever's story "The Hartleys." What Ellis merely dreamed, some armed and sadistic reader may dream and do. Fiction, whether "didactic" or not. cannot fail to teach if a given reader chooses to learn. William Butler Yeats wondered: "Did that play of mine send out / Certain men the British shot?" Ellis's early readers have wondered whether he might not send men out to do much worse than fight the British.

American Psycho was published in Spring, 1991, to reviews expressing truly unprecedented contempt and disgust. Simon & Schuster had belatedly canceled its contract to publish the book. Vintage Books, a Random House imprint, picked it up; but in the interim copies of the proofs found their way into circulation, and the Los Angeles chapter of the National Organization of Women created headlines by recording excerpts from the book on a call-in number and calling for a boycott of all Random House books. The boycott went nowhere, but the critical rejection of the work was nearly total.

The much-noted violence against women in *American Psycho* is indeed against women as such, but Patrick Bateman, Ellis's protagonist, also kills an Asian just because he is an Asian, a child because he is a child, and so forth. He despises blacks, the homeless, Jews, homosexuals, and ultimately even himself. What makes the novel an artistic failure is, however, not the misogyny and racism of its protagonist but its lack of a plot, of even a single character other than Patrick Bateman himself, of a workable prose style or an ear for the spoken word, and of any insight into criminal madness. The violence of the novel is not required by the rest of what happens in it: instead, the violence makes up for what the rest lacks. Imagine someone playing "Chopsticks" on the piano for hours at a time: FOODfoodfood FOODfoodfood CLOTHESclothesclothes CLOTHESclothesclothes GABgabgab GABgabgab KILLkillkill KILLkillkill FOODfoodfood FOODfoodfood, etc. Now imagine that at every tenth occurrence of KILLkillkill, a gun is fired three times. You may be as bored as ever, but that gun will keep you from going to sleep.

American Psycho has a texture rather than a plot, but to say that about it is to name something that might join it to certain avant-garde trends in contemporary musical composition and painting. The publisher who canceled Bret Easton Ellis's contract is the same one that has published Mary Higgins Clark's *Loves Music, Loves to Dance.* It may be that Ellis's offense was not the offending scenes alone but their conjunction with presumptively serious literary ambitions, ambitions beyond anything to which the smoothly commercial Mary Higgins Clark seems to aspire. The editor who came to Ellis's rescue was Sonny Mehta, editor-in-chief at Alfred A. Knopf, Inc., perhaps the most hallowed imprint in American publishing. I may be wrong, but I doubt that Mehta would have rescued Clark.

And despite its crippling flaws, *American Psycho* has a few dazzling moments. There is a rare, if bizarre, talent at work, first of all, in the book's notorious mutilation scenes themselves. They leave one physically nauseated: their effect is like what the effect of first surgery is said to be on beginning medical students: it takes talent to duplicate that effect. But there is a similarly rare talent on display in at least one or two other scenes. One of these is an almost Proustian tour de force presenting the astounding array of products that late-twentieth-century America can mobilize for the narcissism of a wealthy and pretty young man at his three-hour morning *toilette*. If Tom Wolfe was born to shop, Bret Easton Ellis was cosmically predestined to shop. An abuser of various substances, Bateman owes his deepest narcosis to material abundance itself. The worst of his atrocities does not awaken him from it, nor does it awaken his friends. When he tries to confess, or at least mention, his pathology to them, they literally cannot hear him through the din of plenty.

These few moments are not enough to save the novel; but to have recourse to the artistic failure of *American Psycho* is to duck the moral question. Granted that this novel is such a misbegotten object that no allowance should be made for its purported offenses against taste and morality, can we imagine any novel artistically, intellectually strong enough to justify a scene like the following:

> I start by skinning Torri a little, making incisions with a steak knife and ripping bits of flesh from her legs and stomach while she screams in vain, begging for mercy in a high thin voice, and I'm hoping that she realizes her punishment will end up being relatively light compared to what I've planned for the other one. I keep spraying Torri with Mace and then I try to cut off her fingers with nail scissors and finally I pour acid onto her belly and genitals, but none of this comes close to killing her, so I resort to stabbing her in the throat and eventually the blade of the knife breaks off in what's left of her neck, stuck on bone and I stop. While Tiffany watches, finally I saw the entire head off—torrents of blood splash against the walls, even the ceiling—and holding the head up, like a prize, I take my cock, purple with stiffness, and lowering Torri's head to my lap I push it into her bloodied mouth and start fucking it, until I come, exploding into it. Afterwards I'm so hard I can even walk around the

blood-soaked room, carrying the head, which feels warm and weightless, on my dick. This is amusing for a while but I need to rest so I remove the head, placing it in Paul's oak and teak armoire, and then I'm sitting in a chair, naked, covered with blood, watching HBO on Owen's TV, drinking a Corona, complaining out loud, wondering why Owen doesn't have Cinemax.

Is it possible that someone, somewhere, reading a passage like that one, may be led to do what Ellis merely imagines? It is indeed possible; and, notably enough, Ellis presents Patrick Bateman as obsessively interested in the stories of actual serial killers, especially Ted Bundy. It is as if Ellis were building into his own book a reminder of what might be the extrinsic, public-safety argument against its publication (though it may also be significant that what Bateman follows is "true crime" and not fiction). Given that possibility, is it nonetheless possible to imagine a novel that, morally and artistically, could earn the right to include such a scene?

I believe that the answer to that question is Yes. In *High Risk: An Anthology of Forbidden Writings* (New York: Plume, 1991: edited by Amy Scholder & Ira Silverberg), one of the contributors recalls the first pornography he ever produced. It was a little short story he wrote on a ruled pad while sitting on his family's front porch. He left it, unfinished, while he went to get a drink in the kitchen. When he returned, his grandmother rebuked him: "How dare you even think these things!"

If torture as imagined by a novelist and represented on the page is nothing more than the vicarious experience of being a torturer or, worse, a prelude to actual torture, then it is the product of a diseased or abused imagination. But "thinking these things" may have worthier purposes than those, and thinking can never dispense with imagining. Given the right context, I, for one, think that even such a scene—even given the mentioned risks—could indeed be justified.

One of the artistic shortcomings of *American Psycho,* of course, is that it refuses to make do with just one such scene. Bret Easton Ellis may perhaps regret that the atrocity descriptions in his book, which scarcely constitute a sixth of it, have so monopolized critical discussion of the book. But the fault is in the book far more than in the criticism. Extraordinary violence has just that effect: Its noise and horror tend to block out everything else. I once heard Isaac Bashevis Singer comment on the effect of explicit sexual description. He had nothing against such writing, he said, but he rarely attempted it because the risk was so great that readers would be distracted from everything else he might be trying to tell them.

A single such scene, even a single such incident conveyed by other means than blow-by-blow description (no one's description deserves the adjective *blow-by-blow* more than Ellis's), can carry a great charge of meaning. Such is the case in Paul Theroux's recent novel, *Chicago Loop.* Theroux's protagonist, like Ellis's, is a psychotic killer of a particularly grisly sort: He kills a woman by literally biting through the tendons in her neck. This killer is also, potentially, a serial killer. He has other murders obsessively on his mind. But just one actual murder—and that one conveyed in a far more artful way than by step-by-step, quasisurgical description—is as much as Theroux requires for the deeply disturbing psychological profile he proceeds to draw. Like Patrick Bateman, Theroux's Parker Jagoda is a wealthy, obsessive businessman, flirting with homosexuality, incapable of responding sexually to the principal woman in his life and toying, oddly, with the husks of political liberalism. But Parker Jagoda, driven mad by remorse and revulsion, descends to transvestism, adopting the name and seeking to repeat the experience of the woman he murdered. This quest, this struggle at the heart of the novel, gives it structure and provides it suspense. *American Psycho,* largely without structure and entirely without suspense, is burdened with perhaps twenty slayings. No wonder readers have reacted as they have.

Again, however, I do not mean to duck the moral question by moving to the artistic one. If fiction is to exist at all, novelists must have the freedom to fail, and publishers must have the right to make mistakes. Speaking less as a critic than as a citizen concerned about the violence of American society, I want novelists to enjoy the greatest latitude in imagining violence because, as it seems to me, the risks are smaller in that medium than in any other and, without running some risks, we cannot hope to achieve any understanding.

It may be, as noted, that someone could be incited to violence by his or her reading of *American Psycho.* But consider how much greater the potential harm would be if *American Psycho* were a "true crime" pseudonovel and its ghastly descriptions had been put together from police reports and photographs. (Such photographs are, by the way, a familiar tool of the "true crime" trade.) The insult to the memory of the victims and the renewal of the mental trauma in the survivors would represent certain, actual harm far greater than the potential harm of criminal imitation.

Fiction remains, I believe, a uniquely powerful and—particularly as measured against its power—a uniquely safe medium for the representation of criminally violent behavior. We tend to think of drama and, especially, of the cinema of gory special effects as more powerful than mere words on a page, but I will go so far as to say that the more horrendous the subject matter, the further fiction surpasses cinema or drama as a vehicle for it.

A scene like the one quoted earlier could only be presented on a stage by a departure from drama-as-usual. Most likely, in today's dramaturgy, it would be achieved by some kind of mime and would require a more than usually active exercise of imagination on the part of the audience. It could not possibly be as detailed and literal as it is on the printed page.

On the screen, it could be done by special effects; but the closer the enactment came to reality—with real power drills, real chain saws, real mace, real acid, etc.—the greater would be the risk to the actors. Stuntmen and stuntwomen do sometimes suffer injury and even death. In any event, no matter how perfect the illusion, there would be an inevitable break in every viewer's perception of the action. When the actor playing Patrick was talking to the actor playing Torri, he would produce real words with his real lungs, throat, and mouth; and she would hear them with her real ears. But when he walked around the room with her severed head impaled on his erect penis, whatever our eyes saw, our minds would know that it was not really her head or his penis. A perceptual discontinuity of this sort is simply unavoidable.

The involvement of real people in the dramatic or cinematic presentation of imagined people thus imposes a surprisingly low ceiling on what a dramatist or film-maker may enact of the violence he has imagined. We are accustomed to tolerate pornography as the staging or filming of real rather than simulated sex acts, but real rather than simulated torture and murder?

Here we draw the line. The techniques of stage and screen must change at this point, while, very notably, the techniques of fiction need not. Not only are the techniques that Bret Easton Ellis uses to convey Patrick Bateman's non-criminal activities the same as the ones he uses to convey his criminal activities, those techniques are the same ones he would use if these were the crimes of an actual person and Ellis were reporting them. I mean simply to say—though I insist that the point is a crucial one—that in every case the sole technique is words on a page.

There is thus something uniquely undiminished about fictional violence: It seems, on the page, far more like real violence than theatrical violence seems like real violence on the stage or—given the perceptual break and despite the pictorial vividness—even filmed violence seems like real violence on the screen. If one endorses in principle the thesis that the imagination and representation of violence may be a part of the solution rather than a part of the problem of actual, widespread social violence in this country, then it is precisely in fiction that such representation should be welcomed, for it is there that the representation can go furthest with least risk—albeit not without some risk—to any actual person.

Within the ominously large American popular literature of violence, accordingly, works like (but better than) *American*

Psycho deserve greater attention, in principle, than works like *Blind Faith*. The protection of the innocent aside, the best reporter cannot report what anyone is thinking in the silence and privacy of his or her own mind. Novelists can indeed do that; and when the mind being imagined and entered is a criminal mind, a novelist may attain what no crime reporter, certainly none who sticks to the truth, can attain.

Something in me, I confess, recoils at the parade of talented novelists reaching the conclusion, one after another, that to write at all these days a novelist must write about the most violent and hideous kinds of crime: Paul Theroux, Peter Mathiessen, Don De Lillo, Joyce Carol Oates, Denis Johnson . . . the list is long. Bill Gray, the writer character in De Lillo's *Mao II* says of terrorists: "The danger they represent equals our own failure to be dangerous." There is a mawkish machismo in the notion that to be successful a writer must be dangerous, and Bill Gray is not without his real-life analogues.

But if crime novelists need not be feared as dangerous dudes, they may nonetheless be honored for taking up a genuinely difficult assignment. There is indeed a nasty job here that by no means everyone is ready to do. The writers I have just named can, when they want to, go toe-to-toe with Stephen King or Bret Easton Ellis both in explicit, dripping gore and in the more elusive mood of paranoia and horror. What sets them apart both from the commercial giants of fictional violence and from the merchants of "true crime" is psychological depth. Putting on—living in—the mind of a bloodthirsty killer cannot be either easy or especially enjoyable for a normally humane man or woman.

"True crime" writers are barred from the further reaches of this exercise by the nature of their genre. No contractual release, no set of interviews, however searching, no inference from past actions and words can make the reconstructed interior monologue of a criminal anything other than a doomed exercise of hubris. When the writer begins writing the subject's thoughts, either the writer becomes a novelist and forgoes the thrill factor and market boost of true crime's truth, or he fails. You-as-you and you-as-I-have-invented-you cannot co-exist under the same name in the same book. They are not the same person.

It is, finally, because the interiority of another person cannot be directly known that it must be invented. Invention is our only form of access, and it is the novelist's privilege. Few novelists, unfortunately, are really up to that task when the interiority to be invented is of a criminal character. Most novelists aren't criminals and don't really know what criminals are like. "Write what you know" is the first rule of fiction, and most novelists don't know crime. What they tend to know, obviously enough, is literature. A policeman-turned-novelist like Joseph Wambaugh knows more than most, but

even he knows policemen better than he knows criminals. The challenge is massive and built in. Novelists who overcome it deserve very serious attention indeed.

Writers who simply linger over the lurid exterior of crime, by contrast, whether "true crime" writers or novelists, do not deserve serious attention at all; and some of them should almost certainly be seen as symptoms of some kind of national obsession. Los Angeles, in an average year, loses proportionately more of its population to murder than Belfast lost in the very worst year, 1972, of its political violence. More than a little American fiction simply gapes at this carnage, and the same goes for most "true crime." One need not draw a specifically cause-and-effect connection to postulate some connection between these words and these deeds. Surely, in other words it cannot be entirely a coincidence that a country as violent and dangerous as ours favors the popular entertainments that we favor. Safer countries do indeed seem to have gentler literatures. If "true crime" ever had a message to deliver, we have all long since received it.

Lingering critically over the lingerers over crime-as-spectacle serves little purpose. Much crime fiction and perhaps most "true crime" nonfiction is so entirely without an agenda that there is little to discuss: There is only a questionable entertainment to promote. On the other hand, those few novels that take up the personal and social pathologies behind American crime in depth are probably the most serious fiction now being written; and fiction, as argued earlier, is the medium of choice in this area. The best novelists may rarely find it necessary to "go as far" as Bret Easton Ellis goes in *American Psycho* simply because they will not find his literalist direction the right one. But if and when they do, the risk will be worth the potential gain. Novelists represent the national imagination at its most powerful, and this country is dying from a lack of imagination about its own bloody behavior.

Jane Caputi (essay date Winter 1993)

SOURCE: "American Psychos: The Serial Killer in Contemporary Fiction," in *Journal of American Culture,* Vol. 16, Winter, 1993, pp. 101-12.

[*In the following essay, which won the Kathleen Gregory Klein Award in 1992 for best unpublished work of feminist criticism, Caputi remarks on the depiction of serial killers in contemporary literature, focusing on such themes as feminism, ecocide, and the place of serial killers in apocalyptic narratives.*]

> [*The Silence of the Lambs* is] no more than escapist entertainment, brilliantly made.
> —Caryn James, *New York Times* (10 March 1991)

> [Jeffrey Dahmer] was a quiet man who worked in a chocolate factory. But at home in apartment 213 a real-life *Silence of the Lambs* was unfolding.
> —cover blurb, *People Weekly* (12 August 1991)

Despite the reigning cliché, fiction about serial killers constitutes anything but "escapist entertainment." First of all, these texts frequently mirror actual crimes, suggesting that the border between representation and reality is more porous than conventional thought allows. Thomas Harris's 1981 *Red Dragon* anticipated the 1985 crimes of the "Night Stalker," just as his *The Silence of the Lambs* uncannily mirrored Jeffrey Dahmer's atrocities. Second, what are we allegedly escaping when we fall into these narratives? Are women eluding our fears of random, or not so random, sexual violence? Are any of us evading thoughts of chemical contamination, economic depression, the devastation of the rainforests, the imminent decline of the American empire, nuclear waste, nuclear war or fears of the end of the world? Hardly. Quiet as it's kept, serial killer fiction is, as the *New York Times* noted in April 1991, "all the rage" because it allows us not to escape, but to face and sometimes even to befriend these interconnected modern terrors.

Elsewhere I have argued that the contemporary era is an "age of sex crime," marked by an increasing rate of serial sex murder and the ascendancy of the serial killer to mythic/heroic status (*The Age of Sex Crime* [1987]; ["The New Founding Fathers: The Lore and Lure of the Serial Killer," *Journal of American Culture* (1990)]). The founding father of the age is the unknown British killer, "Jack the Ripper," who murdered and mutilated five prostitutes in London 1888. The Ripper's crimes were not immediately recognized as a series of "sex crimes" because he did not rape his victims. Nevertheless, within a few years (with the theoretical aid of both Freud and Krafft-Ebing), the assaulting weapon was understood as a phallus and the murder and mutilation of a female body were comprehended to be the "equivalents of the sexual act." Subsequently, patriarchal culture has enshrined "Jack the Ripper" as a mythic hero; he commonly appears as an immortal figure in literature, film, television, jokes and other cultural products. Such mythicization terrorizes women, empowers and inspires men, even to the point where some choose to emulate him, and participates in a cultural propagation of frequently lethal misogyny. The unprecedented pattern laid down during the Ripper's original siege now is enacted with some regularity in the United States: the single, territorial and sensationally nicknamed killer; socially powerless and scapegoated victims; a signature style of murder or mutilation; intense media involvement; and an accompanying incidence of imitation or "copycat" killings. Ripper-type killers include: the "Boston Strangler," the "Son of Sam," the "Hillside Strangler" and the "Green River Killer," to name only a few. Moreover, new branches of serial murder practice continue to be refined, such as the housebound killer (John Wayne Gacy or Jeffrey Dahmer) or the traveling "killer on the road" (Henry Lee Lucas or Ted Bundy).

In 1984, Justice Department official Robert O. Heck warned Americans that we were in the grip of an "epidemic":

> We all talk about Jack the Ripper; he killed five people (sic). We all talk about the "Boston Strangler" who killed 13, and maybe "Son of Sam," who killed six. But we've got people (sic) out there now killing 20 and 30 people and more, and some of them just don't kill. They torture their victims in terrible ways and mutilate them before they kill them. Something's going on out there. It's an epidemic.

Although Heck's statement is superficially correct, his language works to obscure what actually is going on out there, for the "people" who torture, kill and mutilate in this way are virtually all men, while their victims are predominantly females, and to a lesser extent younger men. As these hierarchical lines indicate, these are crimes of sexually political import, murders rooted in a system of male supremacy in the same way that lynching is based in white supremacy. Moreover, whether the victims are female or male, when murder itself becomes a sexual act, this is the paradigmatic expression of a belief system that has divided humanity into two erotically charged and unequal gender classes, thereby constructing sex itself as a form of masculine domination and defeat of the feminine, even when the feminine is embodied by males.

A surge in serial murder is recognized by criminologists to have begun in the 1950s and has become a characteristic phenomenon of the late twentieth century in the United States. Correspondingly, the mythic serial killer—the preternatural, enigmatic, eternal genius—has become an ever more common figure in film and fiction. My previous study of 1970s male-authored serial killer literature analyzed the ways that these narratives reiterated and refined the mythos of the serial killer and legitimated misogyny and femicide. Here, I will address three related themes as they occur in several key works from the 1980s: 1) the role of feminism—in the text itself or as ideological context for reception of the work, 2) serial murder's relationship to *ecocide,* that is normal, civilized depredations against the Earth, and 3) the serial killer as a central figure in a confluence of apocalyptic narratives, a glaring sign of the (end) times of the world as we know it. Finally, I will explore the themes and implications of several recent works featuring women who, avenging sexual abuse, commit murder against men.

Feminism

On December 6, 1989, at the University of Montreal, 25-

year-old Marc Lépine, dressed for combat and heavily armed, rushed the college of engineering. In one classroom, he separated the women from the men, ordered the men out, and shouting "You're all fucking feminists" opened fire on the women. During a half-hour rampage, he killed 14 young women, wounded nine other women and four men, then turned his gun on himself. Lépine resented women's advancement in a traditionally male profession and blamed women for "ruining his life"; his suicide note included a hit list of prominent Canadian feminists. As I read of this atrocity, I wondered if Columbia University English professor George Stade was satisfied with the news. His 1979 novel, *Confessions of a Lady-Killer*, a work that Mark Schechner in the *New York Times* described as "a study of feminism from the point of view of Jack the Ripper," blatantly celebrates one man's deliberate targeting of feminists as the victims of a proudly anti-feminist serial killer. Its protagonist introduces himself at the outset: "My name is Victor Grant. I am the hero or villain of the narrative to follow, depending on whether you are a feminist or a human being." Denying humanity to one's scapegoats is the classic legitimation for mass murder and that is precisely what Grant has in mind. His wife, Samantha, has left him, run off to work on a feminist magazine and establish her own identity. Victor vows revenge, quits his job in the university bookstore and begins a regimen of a nearly all-meat diet, exercise and mental conditioning in order to be born again as an heroic slayer of prominent New York feminists.

Grant does eventually murder three women before regaining his wife; he then impregnates her and ensconces her in patriarchal pastoralism on his father's self-sufficient enclave in upstate New York. Not only is there no retribution for his crimes, but the novel presents Grant as perfectly justified, indeed as heroic. At first it seems as if this might be only an absurdist parody, yet, as John Leonard commented [in the *Village Voice* (24 December 1979)], "What begins in farce, ends in cruelty, with no accounting." Essentially, this novel promotes the Lépine rationale: Terrorism, taking the form of serial sex murder, provides aggrieved men with a legitimate and final solution to feminism.

In the summer of 1991 publications ranging from the *New York Times* to *Entertainment Weekly* noted the glut of serial killer books on bestseller lists. In order for this to occur, publishers stressed, both women and men needed to comprise the audience. *The Silence of the Lambs* was one such crossover bestseller. Many critics attributed this to the story's inherent feminism and appeal to women through several strong female characters, including a United States Senator, her daughter, a kidnap victim who fights back, and the central investigator and hero, FBI student Clarice Starling. This assessment certainly has merit and undoubtedly it is gratifying to many female readers to identify with a heroine who forcefully opposes and ultimately dispatches a serial killer of

women. Still, any estimation of the novel's feminism must be balanced by a feminist critique of its central figure, the hero/monster Dr. Hannibal Lecter.

The Silence of the Lambs is dedicated by Harris to "the memory of my father" and, despite the strong female presence, it is the patriarch who rules this text. He appears variously in Starling's fondly remembered father (a slain night watchman), Jack Crawford, her boss at the FBI, and Dr. Hannibal Lecter, the infamous multiple murderer and cannibal whom she must petition to aid her in her current search for Jame Gumb, a killer who kidnaps, kills and skins large young women so that he may sew up a "girl suit" for himself to wear. Lecter, as befitting his name, then becomes her teacher, as well as her therapist, psychic lover and father figure.

Since, Jack the Ripper, the serial killer (in both fact and fiction), has been endlessly romanticized—as genius, artist, core soul of mankind, preternatural demon, outlaw hero, an undefeatable and eternal entity. The very effective characterization of Lecter in *The Silence of the Lambs* benefits from 100 years of this mythmaking process. Lecter, as the story goes, is a "genius," possessing powers both mental and sensory that transcend human limitation; he is godlike, the ultimate mystery; and by novel's end he is at large. One distinct factor has been added to make him palatable to women readers. Although he murders both women and men, the only murders described are those of men. Thus, *The Silence of the Lambs* positions its readers as torture victims by confounding us with that classic deceptive duo, here not so much good cop/bad cop, but good serial killer (Lecter)/bad serial killer (Gumb).

Where, we might ask, is the feminist value in thus immortalizing a sadistic cannibal? Moreover, where is the feminist value in featuring a central female figure when she must depend upon, bond with and achieve self-awareness through her interactions with the centennial version of Jack the Ripper? Although Starling is the putative heroine, without Lecter's reading of the evidence, she would have been incapable of solving the mystery and identifying Jame Gumb as the killer. Lecter demands payment for that assistance; his price is Starling's "worst memory of childhood." Essentially, Starling is asked to sell her soul—that is her core constitutive memory—to the devil (Lecter) in order to succeed. At the same time, the narrative asks the reader to feel fascination, empathy, awe and even love for that "devil." By novel's end, not surprisingly, it is Lecter, not the reader, who has "escaped." The "wolf" has been unbound; the serial killer once again is cast into myth as simultaneously omniscient, omnipresent and omnipotent, rather like God the Father. Female readers once again have been given to understand that their only hope of salvation lies in being dutiful daughters, bonding with and paying homage to abusive father figures.

As is well known, *American Psycho* (1991) by Bret Easton Ellis was met with a boycott by the National Organization of Women who cautioned that the graphic depictions of lethal misogyny might prove inspirational to some readers. Reading it, I was at first surprised to find that Ellis in some ways refuses the standard mythicization of the serial killer and actually deconstructs many aspects of that lore. Typically, the fictional serial killer is presented as the ultimately mysterious psychopath, adamantly undetermined by his culture, his monstrosity, if anything, the result of early abuse by a Bitch mother. Frequently, this fictional serial killer suffers from gender confusion (also due to that *bad* mother), projects a feminine affect and exhibits a tendency to cross dress (exemplified by Norman Bates in Alfred Hitchcock's *Psycho,* 1960, as well as by the "bad" killer, Jame Gumb, in *The Silence of the Lambs*). This constitutes an extraordinary reversal, for, as Gordene MacKenzie points out, in a world constructed along bipolar essentialist gender categories, statistically the cross-dressed man is far more likely to be slain by a "psycho killer" than to be one (*Transgender Nation* [1993]). Although popular misogynist narratives scapegoat the "feminine" by aligning femininity with serial killers, that killer in truth represents an extreme of patriarchal *masculinity* and masculinity's valued traits of independence (loner mentality), sexual aggression, emotional detachment, affinity for violence and objectification and hatred of the feminine.

A surge in serial murder is recognized by criminologists to have begun in the 1950s and has become a characteristic phenomenon of the late twentieth century in the United States. Correspondingly, the mythic serial killer—the preternatural, enigmatic, eternal genius—has become an ever more common figure in film and fiction.

—*Jane Caputi*

Serial murder is primarily a Western phenomenon; the United States boasts 74 percent of the world's serial killers. The hero of the well-titled *American Psycho* is Patrick Bateman, a man who epitomizes the "best" of American society. He is masculine, homophobic, white, rich, profoundly materialistic, "pornacious" (that is, salaciously and insatiably interested in pornography), Harvard educated, a Wall Street broker and an unemotional man who wonders: "If I were an actual automaton what difference would there really be?" The novel thus offers an accurate, if partial, critique of the serial killer as the product of U.S. American consumer ideologies and class hierarchies. Yet, at the same time, the novel ignores

any gender analysis of the origins or behaviors of the serial killer and becomes itself a work of femicidal pornography. When Bateman murders men, the scenes are relatively short, take place outside and are asexual. When women are murdered, the sequences are extensive, take place in private and frequently follow upon several pages of basic sadomasochistic sexual description clearly aimed at arousing the reader. With the reader sexually primed, Ellis then offers scenes of unmatched violence wherein the women are tortured and killed in ornate and highly sexualized ways. In one, the killer nails a former girlfriend to the floor, cuts out her tongue and then orally rapes her. In another, he forces a starving rat up a woman's vagina. Ironically, then, Ellis becomes what he purportedly critiques. Between boring riffs satirizing designer clothes, expensive consumer products and yuppie lifestyles, he suddenly crackles to life, churning out top-drawer, designer gore-porn—and capitalizing nicely on it too. Generally, awareness that this society is a patriarchal one, that is, one committed to committing atrocities against women, is repressed. When such material as *American Psycho* hits the best seller lists, such an event cannot help but reveal the normalcy of femicidal violence. Still, this notorious passage of femicidal pornography into the mainstream represented a significant symbolic assault on American women. The Clarence Thomas and Willie Smith spectacles would not be far behind.

Ecocide

> I start by skinning Torri a little, making incisions with a steak knife and ripping bits of flesh from her legs and stomach while she screams in vain. . . . I force my hand down, deep into her throat, until it disappears up to my wrist—all the while her head shakes uncontrollably, but she can't bite down since the power drill ripped her teeth out of her gums—and grab at the veins lodged there like tubes and I loosen them with my fingers and when I've gotten a good grip on them violently yank them out through her open mouth, pulling until the neck caves in, disappears, the skin tightens and splits though there's little blood. Most of the neck's innards, including the jugular, hang out of her mouth and her whole body starts twitching, like a roach on its back, shaking spasmodically, her melted eyes running down her face mixing with the tears and Mace, and then quickly, not wanting to waste time, I turn off the lights and in the dark before she dies I rip open her stomach with my bare hands.
> —Bret Easton Ellis, *American Psycho*

Deforestation in the 1990s will claim roughly 110,000 acres per day in the tropics alone. . . . Forest disintegration of this magnitude ripples throughout the global ecosystem. The visual metaphor that comes to mind is an earth skinned alive, its lungs ripped out . . .

—Stephen J. Pyne, reviewing *Trees of Life* [*New York Times* (21 April 1991)]

On Sept. 4, 1988, an editorial appeared in the *Los Angeles Times* urging global strictures against environmental depredations. The headline read: "To Save the Earth from Human Ruin Enact New World Laws of Geo-Ecology." To illustrate this concept, the *Times* artist, David Tillinghast, rendered the globe impaled upon a huge knife. One hardly need consult Freud to grasp the message: The (Mother) Earth is in the death grip of an ecocidal Ripper.

The mythic serial killer embodies not only femicidal but also ecocidal intent. The endless numbers of women, raped, flayed, mutilated and murdered, in both the real and the fictional worlds, reflect and enact large-scale assaults on a besieged and traditionally feminine-identified Earth. In *The Death of Nature*, Caroline Merchant argued that the basic dynamic of the scientific revolution of early modern Europe was played out in the very structures and practices of the Witchcraze. The courtroom inquisitions, the ceaseless interrogations, the torture of women with mechanical devices: all of these precisely paralleled the emerging scientific model of men's supreme power over a female Nature, the mandate to probe and interrogate her "mysteries," to use science and mechanism as the method by which men could extract her deeply guarded secrets. Similarly, today, the torture, ravaging, mutilations and annihilations of individual women and feminized men by sex murderers, both factual and fictional, function as parallel rituals to the larger industrial, scientific, technological, and militaristic "crimes against nature," those actions which contaminate, eviscerate and consume the planet, including deforestation, species extinctions, chemical and nuclear contamination, strip mining, etc.

At the core of ecofeminist philosophy is the proposition that violence against women and violence against the earth, legitimated by both religion and science, are interconnected assaults, rooted in that characteristic eroticization of domination as well as the designation of women and nature as "other" and as objects for use, targets for exploitation and seizure/rape. The masculinization of nuclear weapons, frequently imaged as phalli aimed at virgin targets, is one of the more obvious enactments of this paradigm. Intriguingly, the connection of sex crime to nuclear devastation, is observed and even critiqued in a variety of serial killer narratives. These include: *Monsieur Verdoux* (a 1947 film where Charlie Chaplin explicitly compares serial sex murder to the mass murder so recently accomplished by the atom bomb); *Dr. Strangelove: Or How I Learned to Stop Worrying and Love the Bomb* (where the crazed Air Force commander who initiates world nuclear apocalypse is General Jack D. Ripper); *The Dead Zone* (the Stephen King novel where a psychic understands a nuclear-crazed U.S. Presidential aspirant as the "political equivalent" of a serial killer of teenage girls)

and, to a lesser degree P. D. James' *Devices and Desires* (where the feelings of disquiet aroused by a local nuclear power plant are analogized to those occasioned by a local serial killer).

Recently, in the Gulf War, the United States accomplished the mass murder of nearly 100,000 Iraqis and the ecological ruination of vast regions in Iraq and Kuwait. Before the war began, one California columnist warned against Sadaam Hussein as "Ted Bundy with chemical weapons." Of course, in terms of devastation inflicted, Ted Bundy seems to have operating on the U.S. side. This connection between serial killers and the Gulf War again informed the 1991 April Fools' Day cover of *Newsweek*. The cover portrayed the staring eyes of the nation's favorite mass killer (and Fool archetype), "Hannibal the Cannibal," to highlight a featured story, "Violence Goes Mainstream" about the unprecedented surge of mayhem, particularly against women, in all forms of popular culture. At the top of the cover, above the *Newsweek* logo, is a blurb referring to another inside story, "Apocalypse in Iraq: The Shattering of a Nation." Elsewhere ["Charting the Flow: The Construction of Meaning Through Juxtaposition in Media Texts," *Journal of Communication Inquiry* (1991)], I have identified a media practice of creating meaning through "flow," whereby a magazine cover or a television or magazine sequence must be understood as comprising a cohesive package, constructing a message through the juxtaposition of seemingly distinct items. This particular juxtaposition subtextually reminds us that the violence, multiple murder and cannibalism that run so rampant in our popular culture are linked, however subterraneanly, to the ideals and accomplishments of our political leaders and military forces and our ravenous national appetite for luxury and hence the lion's share of the world's resources, in this case, oil. The Fool (Lecter) is, after all, the disreputable alter-ego of the King (Bush). Moreover, depictions and descriptions of the legal murders of the war—soldiers buried alive by tanks, civilians bombed and so on—were censored by government decree in news coverage. Yet perhaps that violence was displaced onto a ubiquitous and accelerated output of gorenography (nonsexually explicit, but erotic and often extremely explicit violent portrayals) in mainstream representation.

Hannibal Lecter's most singular characteristic is his cannibalism and, while cannibalism has many potential symbolic meanings, I would like to focus here on its relationship to unbridled materialism as well as its status as an act prohibited by taboo. To understand why cannibalism has become a major motif in horror film and fiction since the 1960s, we might consider it as a metaphor for, in a word, consumerism. A corporate consumerist society is inherently ravenous, devouring natural resources and ever insatiable for new mass-produced goods. Perhaps Lecter (and the actual sex murderer and cannibal, Jeffrey Dahmer) so grip the collective imagination in part because they mirror gluttonous American incorporation of the land and resources (bodies) of others, most frequently, racial others. Jeffrey Dahmer, a white man, battened on the bodies of men of color; Lecter, also a white man and one particularly associated with luxury culture, by novel's end takes up residence in South America. Common consensus holds that it is modern people's respect for a taboo on cannibalism that makes us "civilized." Yet, a curious doublethink informs this, for metaphorical cannibalism is necessary to the much vaunted "American way of life."

The transgression of supposedly sacred taboos is a central dynamic in the Western tradition of knowledge (memorialized in the Apple computer logo—the artificial apple with the bite proudly taken). In Christian myth, taboo breaking is synonymous with sexual awareness and knowledge. In Sadean philosophy, taboo breaking is erotic, heroic and liberating. In techno-scientific practice, taboo breaking is all of these and also routine. "Can implies ought" is a basic technological maxim. As J. Robert Oppenheimer avowed, "It is my judgment in these things that when you see something that is technically sweet, you go ahead and do it, and you argue about what to do about it only after you have had your technical success. That's the way it was with the atomic bomb" (qtd. in [Robert J. Lifton, *The Broken Connection: On Death and the Continuity of Life*, 1979]).

In ancient thought, the breaking of a taboo (as with incest in Sophocles' *Oedipus The King*) results in *pollution*, understood as a moral impurity, manifesting in contamination, disease and disorder in the natural world (Sophocles). In modern thought, the moral factor has been deleted and pollution is itself the contamination or material impurity. Yet, contemporary pollution remains rooted in the flouting of taboo. Capitalism continuously endorses and encourages the unbounded and ever expanding pursuit of the (material) good. As those authoritative voices on the credit card commercials firmly suggest: "Don't Leave Home Without it"; "Visa takes you everywhere you want to go." Concomitantly, technology allows no limits in its quest, as a 1985 Lockheed advertisement boasts, "to penetrate the secrets of the Universe." The denial of any need for taboo, for protective restraints on economic expansion or technology's sweet tooth, has resulted, quite obviously, in an epidemic of pollution and the invention of ever greater means of mass destruction. The taboo violation embodied in the character of Hannibal the Cannibal mirrors that core cultural dynamic and ensures our spectacular obsession with his person, for "our heroes and their narratives are an index to our character and conception of our role in the universe" [Richard Slotkin, *Regeneration through Violence: The Mythology of the American Frontier 1600-1860*, 1973].

The popular embrace of mutilating, cannibalistic, serial killers in both fact and fiction suggests not only femicidal and ecocidal impulses, but also a suicidal one, a desire to be engulfed, to reach an end to commitment. Turning back once more to the *Newsweek* cover featuring Lecter, we might note the word *apocalypse* in the blurb describing the damage done to Iraq. That resonant word invites us to consider yet another related theme in serial killer narratives—the correspondence of that mythic figure to one of the most ubiquitously reiterated stories of contemporary culture—the apocalyptic narrative, the millennial hope for/dread of the end of the world.

Apocalypse Now

> "Apocalyptic thinking is in the air," University of Connecticut psychologist Kenneth Ring says. "As we approach that subjective date, 2000, images stored in the collective unconscious begin to populate our dreams and visions." And nightmares, of course.
>
> —Teresi and Hooper

> I'm twenty-seven for Christ sakes and this is, uh, how life presents itself in a bar or in a club in New York, maybe *anywhere,* at the end of the century . . .
>
> —Bret Easton Ellis, *American Psycho*

In a poem composed after the murders of 12 Black women in a small area of Boston in six months in 1979, Audre Lorde writes: "As women we were meant to bleed / but not this useless blood / my blood each month a memorial / to my unspoken sisters falling / like red drops to the asphalt / I am not satisfied to bleed / as a quiet symbol for no one's redemption / why is it our blood / that keeps these cities fertile?" While Lorde rages, other voices urge acceptance of this blood sacrifice. For example, after the Montreal Massacre, Cardinal Paul-Émile Léger stated that the death of these women must be seen as "an offering made to God" (qtd. in [Andrée Côtè, "The Art of Making it Work for You" in Louise Mallette and Marie Chalouh, *The Montreal Massacre*, translated by Marlene Wildeman, 1991]). Although this is rarely openly admitted, patriarchal culture does indeed require the ritual sacrifice of women, sometimes called witches, sometimes, prostitutes, sometimes even feminists.

These intimations of ritual sacrifice also recall an underlying theme of *The Silence of the Lambs*. The title derives from the story Lecter extracts from Starling to satisfy his sadistic taste for her most private memory. It goes like this. Two years after her father's violent death, her mother was no longer able to support the family and she, at ten the eldest child, was sent to Montana to live with her mother's cousin and her husband on their ranch. There, both lambs and horses were slaughtered and Clarice would wake at night to the screaming of the lambs. Unable to bear this, after seven months she takes one of the horses marked for death and runs away. She is caught, but does not have to return to the ranch; in a very happy ending, she and the horse get to live together at an orphanage. Through her "therapeutic" interaction with Lecter, Starling understands that her adult life has been determined by this early experience, and that she now is embarked on a continuing quest to "silence the lambs," which we understand to be equivalent to saving women endangered by sex criminals.

Long before Starling reveals her own traumatic resonance with "sacrificial" lambs to Lecter, the subject pops up in conversation. Lecter has done a sketch of Golgotha and, when Starling asks about it, he refers to Christ as the paschal lamb, the rubric under which he appears in the book of *Revelations*. In Harris' earlier novel, *Red Dragon*, references to that classic apocalyptic narrative are even more insistent. The serial killer at large is one who has adopted the name "Red Dragon" in homage to god's antithesis in *Revelations*. In nearly all serial killer fiction, the line between the killer and his pursuer continually is blurred, suggesting a false opposition between the two as well as the inherent normalcy of sexual murder. In *Red Dragon*, that same convention adheres; the imprisoned Hannibal Lecter writes to Will Graham, the FBI expert on serial killing, telling him that he knows Graham too finds pleasure in killing: "Think about it, but don't worry about it. Why shouldn't it feel good? It must feel good to God—He does it all the time, and are we not made in His image?" Currently, as the millennium approaches, many people, some with great joy and anticipation, expect God to commit the ultimate act of mass murder and ecocide—destroying the Earth with fire as prophesied in the gospel of St. Peter. Perhaps this provides a partial explanation for why more and more men are finding ways to emulate that divine role model. Mass murder, the killing of three or more people at one time, throughout 1991 was committed on average of twice monthly in this country, an unprecedented rate.

American Psycho too is rife with apocalyptic references. Just prior to her torture and murder, Bethany, a former girlfriend, tells Bateman he has hung a painting upside down and asks how long it has been that way. "A millennium," Bateman answers and then knocks her unconscious:

> I drag her back into the living room, laying her across the floor over a white Voilacutro cotton sheet and then I stretch her arms out, placing her hands flat on thick wooden boards, palms up, and nail three fingers on each hand, at random to the wood by their tips. . . . I keep shooting nails into her hands until they're both covered . . .

It is impossible to miss the references to Bethlehem and to crucifixion here. Is Ellis setting up Bateman as apocalyptic "AntiChrist?" Or can we read this moment as a cynical twist on the anticipated second coming of "Christ?" In traditional Christian iconography the divine sacrificial tortured and crucified victim is male, just as was the original lamb. The paschal lamb was the substitute for the murder of the first born son demanded by Yahweh, a tradition reenacted in the continuing sacrifice of sons in war by governmental and military fathers. Yet, as *The Silence of the Lambs* attests, in modern imagery, the passive, victimized lamb recalls the feminine body and, as *American Psycho* makes plain, though women are by no means divinized in the Christian era, we certainly are sacrificed.

Later, Bateman dines with his current girlfriend and muses:

> To Evelyn our relationship is yellow and blue, but to me it's a gray place, most of it blacked out, bombed, footage from the film in my head is endless shots of stone and any language heard is utterly foreign, the sound flickering away over new images: blood pouring from automatic tellers, women giving birth through their assholes, embryos frozen or scrambled (which is it?), nuclear warheads, billions of dollars, the total destruction of the world . . .

Such description evokes the chaos, monstrosity and reversal of apocalypse. Surely, as Ellis implies, the ascendancy of the serial killer is a harbinger of apocalypse for the culture that has immortalized him, a culture that enacts on a grand scale an attack on the feminine, women and often literally the womb (as in the crimes of Jack the Ripper), understood within our tradition to be an assault on the core source of life and, hence, the future itself.

However, another reading of these apocalyptic themes also merits some attention. Mention of the "Dragon" of the apocalypse appears as well in George Stade's *Confessions of a Lady-Killer;* only in his schema the dragon is not the serial killer, but that killer's avowed enemy, feminists, who represent a political movement capable of bringing about the collapse of civilization:

> The monster who held Samantha in thrall [the feminist Jude Karnofsky, his first victim] was the Dragon of the Apocalypse herself. Karnofsky had at her disposal all the demonic forces released by the collapse of a civilization, our civilization. (Stade, *Confessions of a Lady-Killer*)

Here then is a key toward understanding one drift of the apocalyptic references in serial killer narratives. The acceleration of violence of all types against women is a backlash phenomenon, meant to reassert threatened male power and stave off the socially transformative powers of feminism. The political apocalypse that Stade fears and so identifies with feminism is not the end of the world, but the end of the world as we know it, that is, the very world that has produced the serial killer, the world of patriarchy.

The Revenge of the Lambs

> Out of Florida's recent wave of horrific crimes comes a dark version of *Thelma & Louise* in a rare case of a female serial killer.
> —*Vanity Fair,* Sept. 1991

> Thelma and Louise Live Forever.
> —feminist T-shirt, 1991

Reality and representation intertwine once again in *Vanity Fair's* comparison between Aileen Wuornos, the prostitute accused of killing seven men in Florida, and the film sensation of 1991, *Thelma and Louise* (dir. Ridley Scott). That film is the story of two ordinary women, one of whom kills a man who has raped her friend. The killing is not required to stop the rape; it is an act of rage, revenge and perhaps even prevention. Neither woman kills anyone else in the movie. They do become road running outlaws, who, eventually, in order to avoid capture, drive their car over the cliffs of the Grand Canyon. Once women have lived outside men's law, the film suggests, once women have renounced the role of sacrificial lamb, there can be no return.

Aileen Wuornos is a lesbian who worked for years as a prostitute. She has told police that two years ago she bought a small .22 pistol to protect herself for she had been raped at least 12 times on the job, and that many men would have sex with her and then refuse to pay the $30.00 she asked. Wuornos stated that if a man tried to beat or rape her, or refused to pay her, she would kill him. At this writing, she has been convicted of one murder and given the death penalty.

Wuornos' story of continuous sexual abuse is credible. One study of street prostitutes found that 70 percent of the women interviewed had been raped on the job, and that those who had been raped had been victimized an average of eight to ten times a year. Only seven percent had sought any kind of help and only four percent had reported any of the rapes to the police. Another found 74 percent reported assaults by customers. Of these, 79 percent were beaten by a customer and 50 percent had been raped. Prostitutes were the scapegoated victims in the Jack the Ripper murders and remain a favored prey of serial killers. Police and public apathy to violence against prostitutes, from assault through murder, is well documented (Caputi, ["The Sexual Politics of Murder," *Gender & Society* (1989)]).

Although, as far as I know there never has been another case such as Wuornos', the theme of revenge, of women fighting back and serially killing those who would rape, abuse or kill them, is an increasingly prevalent theme in fiction authored by women. *Dear John,* by Susan Lee and Sondra Till Robinson (1980), is an explicit revenge tale. Kate Delling is a 28-year-old woman with a lifetime reserve of justifiable anger against men—family members, lovers, bosses. She recently has befriended a neighbor who is a high class prostitute. Within days of their meeting, that woman is beaten nearly to death by a rich and famous man. Kate begins to carry a gun. Some time later, as she walks in a park, a man tries to rape her and she kills him. Relishing this experience, she decides to advertise in a sex magazine, hoping to attract the man who assaulted her friend. After killing several other men who answer her ad, she finally locates and kills the original abuser, though not without injury to herself. The novel ends ambiguously, suggesting that she has to pay too great a price for a perhaps misguided vengeance.

No ambiguity whatsoever intrudes into two novels written ten years later, *The Weekend* by Helen Zahavi and *Mercy* by Andrea Dworkin. *The Weekend* features an ordinary Englishwoman. Bella, who is harassed by obscene phone calls and rape threats. After suffering these for some weeks, she decides that she finally has had enough and kills her harasser with no great difficulty. Having done this, she too becomes a serial killer, slaying, variously, those men who assault her. In the last scene, Bella is walking along Brighton Beach at night when a man approaches and attacks. He is himself a serial killer named "Jack" who strangles, rapes and mutilates women. But Bella is prepared with her switchblade and knifes him repeatedly until he dies. Zahavi leaves the reader with a final message:

> If you see a woman walking, if she's stepping quietly home, if you see her flowing past you on the pavement. If you'd like to break her brittle bones, and you want to hear the hopeless pleading, and you want to feel the pink flesh bruising, and you want to taste the taut skin bleeding.
>
> If, in fact, you see her and you want her.
>
> Think on. Don't touch her. Just let her pass you by.
>
> Don't place your palm across her mouth and drag her to the ground.
>
> For unknowingly, unthinkingly, unwittingly you might have laid your heavy hand on Bella. And she's woken up this morning with the knowledge that she's finally had enough.

Mercy, by Andrea Dworkin, is the most ambitious and complex of these novels. Written as unbroken monologue, save a brief prologue and epilogue in a measured, academic voice "Not Andrea," the narrator is Andrea, a woman born into an age already in thrall to mass murder: "I was born in 1946, after Auschwitz, after the bomb, I never wanted to kill, I had an abhorrence for killing but it was raped from me, raped from my brain; obliterated, like freedom" ([Andrea] Dworkin, *Mercy* [1991]). First assaulted as a child by a man in a movie theater, Andrea recounts years of sexual abuse and social complicity in its proliferation. By the age of 27, Andrea is living on the streets, inhabiting a "body packed with rage" and enunciating a political principle: "It is very important for women to kill men." She acts on this principle, going out at night to find drunken bums and kicking them to death. She envisions an army of girls who will burn down Times Square, gather *en masse* to kill abusive husbands and/or pimps, and who "are ready for Mr. Wall Street who will follow any piece of ass down any dark street; now he's got a problem it is very important for women to kill men."

Dworkin is best known for her ceaseless work against pornography, as both enactment and incitement to violence against women, and is the author, with Catherine MacKinnon of an anti-pornography civil ordinance (*Pornography and Civil Rights*). By explicitly advocating serial gender murder in *Mercy,* Dworkin dares challenges from those who defend pornography as mere representation, not equivalent to or causally connected to acts or statements in the real world. *Mercy* challenges the reader—who might find Dworkin's advocacy of male death far more shocking and reprehensible than Bret Easton Ellis' imagined depredations against women in *American Psycho* or *Guns 'N Roses* tuneful admission that "I used to love her but I had to kill her"—to examine the normalization of misogynist, lethal violence in popular culture and its defense through classic liberal principles.

Revenge is an unmistakable motif in these novels. Strangely enough, I believe that theme also more subtly pervades *The Silence of the Lambs* and that it was revenge, connected to an incest subtext, that ensured many women's fascination with the novel. As Starling, in response to Lecter's insistence, begins to tell him the story of her removal to the ranch in Montana, he immediately interrupts her narrative: "Did your foster father in Montana fuck you, Clarice" (Harris, *Silence*). She denies that he ever even tried and tells him that the real trauma she experienced there was her encounter with the slaughter of lambs and horses. Yet, the girl's waking up to horror in the night, her identification with helpless, screaming animals and her flight from the ranch beg an interpretation of these events as an allegorical rendering of incestuous assault. It was that personal atrocity that actually constituted her "worst memory of childhood." It was her own trauma around sexual assault that impelled Starling as an adult to commit to saving women endangered by male sexual abuse, that catalyzed her into tracking down and slaying offenders such as Jame Gumb. Unfortunately, as the novel sets it up, to complete that mission, she must consent to being "mind fucked" by her surrogate father, Hannibal Lecter. Incest trauma, in this schema, is indelible and the victim, how-

ever strong, must reenact it in subsequent interactions with abusive father figures.

Mercy ends with a threat: "I went out; at night; to smash a man's face in; I declared war. My *nom de guerre* is Andrea One; I am reliably told there are many more; girls named courage who are ready to kill." Whatever one thinks of the ethics of recommending or committing revenge murder, it is imperative to recognize a central motif in all of these novels: feminist reclamation and redefinition of the powers of death. For millennia, women, particularly in the Christian tradition, have been hypocritically revered as givers of life (e.g., the Virgin Mary), while at the same time banished from any commerce, on our own terms, with the powers of death. That divine power is reserved to the male God and his earthly delegates, men who "play god": political leaders; soldiers; doctors, nuclear scientists, husbands; mass murderers; serial killers.

Playing God

> I was making life-and-death decisions . . . playing God in their lives.
> —Edmund Kemper, the "Coed Killer" (qtd. in ["The Random Killers," *Newsweek* (26 November 1984)])

> I had a sense of power. A sense of destruction. . . . in the Nam you realized you had the power to take a life. You had the power to rape a woman and nobody could say nothing to you. That godlike feeling you had was in the field. It was like I was god. I could take a life. I could screw a woman.
> —anonymous Vietnam veteran, (Qtd. in [Mark Baker, *Nam: The Vietnam War in the Worlds of the Men and Women Who Fought There*, 1982])

In mainstream representation it is only very occasionally that women are given license to kill. Clarice Starling (in both novel and film versions) has the power briefly but at great cost to her soul. Several other extremely popular Hollywood films also feature lethal women. For example, *Aliens* (dir. James Cameron, 1986) and *Fatal Attraction* (dir. Adrian Lyne, 1987) present "good" women who kill, but, of course, these characters are not so subtly legitimated by the fact that they are defending home and children against vicious *female* predators. On the other hand, *Thelma and Louise* features a woman who wrathfully kills a male predator. That film aroused an enormous amount of controversy and was denigrated as "fascist" and "degrading to men" by several male reviewers—reactions that betray a deep uneasiness with women violently responding to male oppression. Predictably, a backlash film soon issued from Hollywood; women again spectacularly, but far more conventionally, kill in the highly publicized 1992 film, *Basic Instinct* (dir. Paul Verhoeven). That film, a wonder of misogynist, homophobic, paranoid fantasy, has only four female characters. All four of these female characters are bisexual or lesbian and all are remorseless, self-absorbed killers. Moreover, the "heroine" is not only fabulously wealthy and diabolically clever, but she kills men explicitly for erotic pleasure. Such plotting by no means develops a feminist conceptualization of the powers of death, but enacts a profound reversal whereby a woman is cast as a serial sex killer, that paradigm of masculinist death power. In keeping with the men's movement's emphasis on male victimization, this film invites male viewers to imagine themselves as sexual prey, not abusers, of women. Simultaneously, it functions as an act of faith in the traditional sexist belief that evil originates in and is the "instinctual" property of women.

Masculinist prohibition against female powers of death ensures the dearth of divine female Being in most contemporary religions. It underlies the fear and loathing accorded to matter, the cycles of nature and the Earth itself in the christotechnological tradition. It informs the disgust and trivialization accorded to post-menopausal women in reality as well as representation. It is at the root of masculine hysteria over the use of women in combat, and indeed in having any decision making power over war. It as well provides the fundamental motive behind anti-abortion machinations, for the "pro-life" movement is not so much in favor of life as it is dedicated to keeping the powers of death out of the hands of women. Patriarchal men have staked their lives on a belief in their exclusive mastery of death, resulting in a bizarre cultural necrophilia marked by: the worship of commodities; the generation of automata and simulacra; the artificial and often torturous prolongation of "life" through medical technology; the constancy of war; an epidemic of ecocide; the invention of the means of megadeath; and the emergence of the serial killer and mass murderer in epidemic numbers in reality, and as core fantasy icons.

In those fantasies, serial killers often become deathless. Immortality is the dominating motif in Jack the Ripper fantasies and that theme pervades the lore associated with such fictional fellows as Dr. Lecter. We see this as well in James Ellory's *Killer on the Road* (1986) where the imprisoned serial murderer concludes his narrative, "I implode into a space beyond all laws, all roadways, all speed limits. In some dark form, I will continue." The myth that the sex killer lives in perpetuity legitimates and naturalizes the endless perpetuation of sexual abuse. Significantly, the serial killer whom Bella slays in the climactic scene of *The Weekend* is named "Jack." Zahavi thus declares war against the myth of the eternal Ripper. In reclaiming the power of death, it is imperative that women declare their resolve to fight back against those who attack us with lethal intent. At the same time, we must break the grip of the immortal ripper on our

symbol system in a number of ways: by reassociating men with nurturance and the life force; by restoring dignity to death; by making matter and women once again sacred; by deconstructing the myth of the eternal sex killer; and by conjuring immortal female power.

We Walk the Back of the Tiger by Patricia A. Murphy (1988) is a lesbian-feminist novel about a male serial killer. In this, the killer of young college women is himself finally slain by Fitzie O'Donnell, a Black prostitute who paints a "red teardrop in the center of her forehead" Fitzie is "playing Goddess," the supreme subversive act in the femicidal world. She is the avatar of Kali Ma, "the Hindu Triple Goddess of creation, preservation, and destruction . . . the basic archetypal image of the birth-and-death Mother, simultaneously womb and tomb, giver of life and devourer of her children: the same image portrayed in a thousand ancient religions" [Barbara G. Walker, *The Woman's Encyclopedia of Myths and Secrets*, 1983]. The elemental Kali Ma refuses the rigid dichotomization of death and life as well as their packaging into separate and unequal gender bundles. In a world without serial murder, it is not Jack the Ripper, but Kali Ma, not Hannibal Lecter, but Thelma and Louise who live forever.

Tom Weyr (essay date 12 April 1993)

SOURCE: "Marketing America's Psychos," in *Publishers Weekly,* Vol. 240, April 12, 1993, pp. 38-41.

[*In the following essay, Weyr provides an overview of the publishing industry's views on why people read true crime, the characteristics of the market, and what components publishers look for in true-crime books.*]

What's the fatal attraction in true crime that draws so many millions to the genre? Surprisingly few sociological studies have probed the nature of American society for clues. For some of publishing's most distinguished editors, however, the roots of true crime go back a long way—and dig deep into the human psyche.

The consensus seems to be that readers relish the shudder of horror and relief. They buy books that mirror situations that could happen to them, on their block, in their town or their school. "The horror is that it could be anyone," says St. Martin's associate publisher Sally Richardson. "When I'm standing in the supermarket checkout line the guy in front of me buying olive oil may be planning to fry somebody at home with it."

"Successful true crime books take place in families very much like those of the people who are reading them," says Simon & Schuster's editor-in-chief, Michael Korda. "They carry emotions we all have and take them one step further. True crime is the legitimization of our worst voyeuristic impulses and that's a potent form of entertainment."

Passion, insanity and blood are the core of reader interest, says John Douglas of the Foul Play bookstore in New York City's Greenwich Village. The backbone of the category, he notes, "are addictive readers interested in luridness the same way that people in the Middle Ages were in drawing and quartering."

"Crime is so huge in American life," adds Knopf's Ann Close, editor of Alec Wilkinson's *A Violent Act,* "and there is something so very American about it." (Wilkinson's book was the first account of a murder published in the *New Yorker* since Truman Capote's *In Cold Blood.*)

Capote's book is always cited first when editors, publishers and booksellers talk about true crime. As Korda puts it: "Until *In Cold Blood,* very few literary heavyweights had plunged off into Midwestern Middle America. Capote and Norman Mailer, whose *Executioner's Song* is probably his best book, opened up the floodgates by making the genre respectable."

"One reason true crime does well in hardcover is that the writers are more interested in character than simply in true crime," says S & S senior editor Fred Hills. But he and other editors see market limitations for hardcover.

Hills notes that "only the authors at the very top of the genre seem to have much success in hardcover—the triumvirate of Ann Rule, Jack Olsen and Joe McGinness. Their books are marked by true-life plots and character and as such are writer-driven. But that's not true in paperbacks. And increasingly, this is becoming a paperback market."

Indeed, true crime does look back on a long and lucrative history, but it did not explode into a publishing phenomenon until the mid-'80s. Hardcover books profited from the take-off, yet it was the mass markets that supplied the fuel and turned the genre into a category. True crime paperbacks walked out of stores at such a pace that chains and specialty stores began to feature true crime sections. When Sheldon MacArthur opened the Mysterious Book Shop West in Los Angeles in 1988, he devoted 60 feet of shelf space to true crime. Jean Macmillan, who opened her Mystery Book Shop in Bethesda, Md., four years ago, gave true crime three large shelves. The stairs of every multilevel major chain store became cluttered with cardboard display dumps as everybody added true crime shelf space. (One notable exception: the 246 stores of the Crown chain that still display true crime under general nonfiction.)

And publishers have responded. St. Martin's has started a True Crime library. Zebra's Pinnacle line is aiming for two to three titles a month in 1994, making it a category akin to

romances. Time-Life has kicked off a 20-volume mail-order series after one of the best test responses ever for a new product line. Doubleday launched a true crime book club last June and reports robust response.

But success in publishing often carries the seeds of its own demise in the temptation to dump too much inferior product on the market. Nobody denies that true crime books are clogging publishing arteries, and that it is harder to sell individual titles. But there is little agreement about whether the trend has peaked.

In hardcover true crime does seem to be retrenching. "I think it has peaked in terms of the number of hardcover books publishers will do on the subject," Norton editor Star Lawrence says. "I don't see as much coming through in editorial meetings as I did four years ago. A lot of hardcover true crime has moved into paperback original publishing. The genre seems to be more paperback than it was."

"Yes, it's a difficult category because there is so much out there," says Morrow's v-p/editorial director Adrian Zackheim. "But with the right book, you can still have a bestseller."

"A lot of inferior true crime books have made the genre seem glutted," Dick Marek, senior editor at Crown, notes. "They're harder to sell, our reps tell us. Mention true crime and booksellers' eyes glaze. It's no longer true that anything sells, if it ever was. But whenever a field is crowded the cream rises. You need better stories and writers."

Booksellers concur. Many are shrinking display space for hardcover true crime books. Today Sheldon MacArthur has reduced his true crime shelf space to only 20 feet. Jean Macmillan says true crime in hardcover is a tougher sell today and accounts for only 10% of her true crime volume. "I'm not selling true crime hardbacks as well as I used to," says Kate Mattes, who runs Kate's Mystery Book Shop in Cambridge, Mass. "Hardcover sales for me peaked more than a year ago. I'm thinking seriously of discontinuing hardcover true crime books."

She probably won't. The tantalus of the big book keeps everybody coming back to see if they can replicate Ann Rule's success. Even with flagging hardcover interest, her last book, *If You Really Loved Me,* sold around 100,000 copies.

The interest and the doubt hold for the chains as well. "I buy most everything in the category" says Walden's Robert Fields, "but I don't expect to sell as many copies as I did four or five years ago. The category has plateaued, but at a relatively high level and it is still very profitable."

"Hardcover true crime books sell less well for us today than they did five years ago," B. Dalton merchandizing director

Bob Wietrack agrees, "but they're still strong sellers when authors have a track record." He blames the downtrend on publishers "publishing so much."

The readership is so numbed by TV tabloid journalism that it looks for something more gruesome. Look at Jeffrey Dahmer. All five books on him did well because the public has an insatiable need to look at the dark, dark side of this criminal activity.

—Paul Dinas

But true crime is not even as easy a sell in the paperback market as it was in the late '80s. "The trend is slowing," St. Martin's Richardson says. "We used to get 300,000-400,000 copies and that number has tapered down." But she says true crime is leveling into a strong category with steady appeal when readers are offered exceptional stories. "Today you can't slap an okay story between covers, the way you could five years ago when anything went. Now too much money is being tossed at lousy stuff."

So how do publishers shape their true crime lists in a glutted market? Richardson believes being "the first ones out of the gate" is important. "We try and get writers who are terrific reporters, who can do narrative and who have speed." For *Lethal Lolita,* the publisher, "put a *People* writer in her 20s named Maria Eftimiades on the Amy Fisher case. She delivered in three weeks. Don Davis, an old UPI hand, turned out *Deadly Lessons,* an account of the Milwaukee murders [committed by Jeffrey Dahmer], in four weeks."

At Zebra, executive editor Paul Dinas takes a far different approach. For one thing, he doesn't buy the idea of a peaking category. "Salespeople and buyers say that sales are flat and going down. But they are out of sync with the market. Buyers for stores and chains shy away from popular depiction of graphic blood, gore and forensic shots [police pictures of often horribly mutilated crime victims]. But the sales performance of titles that include them do not support the theory."

He cites a book entitled *Rites and Burials* about a California serial killer (everybody agrees that serial killers are today's hottest true crime topic). "I got a proposal from a cop and a journalist and everybody at the editorial meeting retched. It has torture, kidnapping and sex. We have pictures of torture sessions from the police. So far we've had two printings adding up to sales into the high six figures."

True crime books, Dinas says, can go a lot further than any

other media. "The readership is so numbed by TV tabloid journalism that it looks for something more gruesome. Look at Jeffrey Dahmer. All five books on him did well because the public has an insatiable need to look at the dark, dark side of this criminal activity," says Dinas.

How does Dinas find these horror stories? "I get a lot of my material from people who see our books on the racks. Journalists mostly, and some stuff from agents. I don't chase much after headlines." Writing, Dinas thinks, is not critical. "This is a story- and picture-driven market," he says, "not a writer-driven one. A lot of our authors are journalists who can tell a clear story and have all the facts. We edit more for clarity than for style, and make sure that all the bases are covered." That includes sending manuscripts to legal counsel for libel vetting and legal sanitizing.

Adds Dinas: "Crime committed for money or revenge without sex is much less commercial, so I look for the sex angle, for murder, adjudicated killers, and increasingly for multiple bodies. The manner of death has to be very violent, very visceral." But his books do not only focus on gore, Dinas insists. "Each story routinely contains a psychological evaluation or profile that explains how a human being is turned into a monster."

Dinas's views may be extreme, but he is not alone. Berkley senior editor Susan Allison, for example, says that a book about how "Johnny killed Susie because he was mad at her is not as interesting as an insane psycho killer. Family crime does well for us, the notion that kids are killed, and there was a rash of books about children killing their parents."

At Dell/Delacorte "blood and gore is only one kind of book we do," says v-p and editor-in-chief Leslie Schnur, adding that "body count books don't do as well as books that have some psychological depth." Still, the house rushed out Peter Conradi's *The Red Ripper,* an instant book on the Russian serial killer Andrei Chikatilo, which did well. The same thing held for Dell's version of the Jeffrey Dahmer case, *Milwaukee Massacre,* by Bob Dzorchak. It sold 350,000 copies and is still selling 1500 copies a month, a reflection of the category's backlist power.

"You have to look for a good story," says Avon editor-in-chief Bob Mecoy, "although not necessarily a front page national story. Family, religion and obsession drive sales. A book torn from today's headlines isn't going to interest me." True crime editors who were inundated with proposals for books on the World Trade Center bombing and the Waco, Texas, shootout and standoff between federal agents and religious cultists agree. To Michael Korda, the bombing in New York was a terrorist bombing, not a crime, "and it is hard to get interested in a book-length account of that." True crime has to be personal to work, it must "touch your heart, fears and passions." Dinas doesn't consider the bombing a true crime story, either, and thinks the Waco incident would make a book only if the cult leader is captured, tried and convicted.

Bill Grose, executive v-p and editorial director at Pocket Books, points to another trend that makes true crime profitable—regionalism. "You can make money publishing for regions, if the advance is modest and you have a sales organization that can ship enough books."

"You can target a book to a Texas audience and be successful doing so," says St. Martin's Richardson. "There are enough people in Texas willing to pay $22.95 for a true crime book set in their state." St. Martin's is betting on a book called *To Hatred Turned* that's set among rich Texas society.

Let a true crime story receive very strong regional media coverage, says Morrow's Adrian Zackheim, "and we can go out with a book and sell significant numbers in that region. We did a book called *Preacher's Girl* by Jim Shultze, set entirely in the Carolinas; we had very good sales in the South."

Regions are important to booksellers, too. Walden's Field notes that a book may not sell 300 miles from the place where the crime took place but do well in its "home town." Regional sales can keep a book profitable. "We make money on Texas books."

John Sutton, paperback buyer for the Crown chain, says that strong involvement of store managers in the book ordering process allows them "to stock books that are specific to their regions." He cites Texas and the Pacific Northwest as strong locales for true crime and says books about the regions sell well in them.

The appearance of tabloid TV shows like *A Current Affair, Hard Copy* and *Inside Edition* and the plethora of true crime movies of the week on network television is given credit by many for triggering the '80s boom in true crime. Indeed Zebra's Dinas worries about the future of the category should these shows ever go off the air. But TV can also, in some instances, hurt true crime book sales.

For St. Martin's true crime editor Charley Spicer, "TV movies play a real role in the success of true crime titles. Once a case is on TV we get another bang." Even more important, Spicer says, "Exposure on a national TV network says to the bookseller that this is prime time fare."

One of the more dramatic examples of the interaction between TV and books occurred with Vincent Bugliosi's *And The Sea Will Tell*. The Norton book was published in hardcover three weeks before the TV movie aired and the hoopla

surrounding the film scooted the book to the top of the bestseller lists.

For Dinas, TV is a "crap shoot" that depends on publishing schedules. If you're out before the TV show then it helps, if not it hurts.

Dell's Schnur thinks TV can boost sales but can also hurt sales by competing for audience time. "What it says to me is not to publish true crime as a regular category. Choose your titles with care and you'll do very well."

Avon's Mecoy concurs, arguing that TV can preempt sales of books that simply recite the facts again. But a very good TV miniseries or film can spur interest in the book simply because the electronic media can't tell the whole story as well as a book can.

Who are the readers? Generally they are middle class. For many books the female component is stronger than the male, though few scientific samples exist. Thus Spicer thinks "the majority of readers are women, perhaps because they want to know the unknown enemy."

Mecoy is less sure. He thinks readership depends on the book. Thus Olson's *Doc* had more female readers, while *Give a Boy a Gun* did better among men. He also identifies a strong teen market for true crime, citing a book he did at Dell, *Say You Love Satan* by David St. Clair, as an example. It featured a teenager involved in teen homicide.

Store owners do report on some strange customers, however. Mysterious Book Shop West is across the street from Cedars of Lebanon hospital in Los Angeles and the single biggest group of buyers for sensational true crime books are doctors, radiologists and nurses from the hospital.

"These are people who deal with illness and death every day. I can't for the life of me figure out why they want to read about it when they go home," Sheldon MacArthur says.

MacArthur also has noticed that both fledgling and experienced mystery writers utilize true crime titles for rough background material. Apparently the gory details of the lives of real murderers provide excellent grist for the mental mill. "I've even taken to putting the 'How To Write a Mystery' titles in with true crime since, at least at my store, the sale of one is usually accompanied by the sale of the other."

John Douglas keeps a subsection devoted to the Mafia, as do most other booksellers, and reports that he's had limos roll up and "and some thug in a new suit and tons of cologne walks in and says have you got that new book on Gambino, and it's clear he's never been to a bookstore before."

What does the future hold for true crime? It may be wishful thinking, but publishers and booksellers agree that psychological insight into the minds of the killers, some rational explanation for monstrous behavior, and the fallout of such crimes on the community in which they occur are the strongest components of the genre.

Ann Fabian (essay date October 1993)

SOURCE: "Crime that Pays," in *Yale Review,* Vol. 81, October, 1993, pp. 45-61.

[*In the following essay, Fabian remarks on the history of true crime writing and published confessions.*]

In the summer of 1977, the New York police finally caught "Son of Sam," a serial killer who had been preying on young women. The tabloid press had reveled in the hunt, following both the police and the killer for one long year. David Berkowitz, the man who called himself the Son of Sam, was ruled insane and locked away. Although the man was incarcerated, his story remained at large. To stop those who had seen financial opportunity in the story of the captured killer and had offered him large sums of money to tell it, the New York legislature passed a law that denied criminals the profits obtained from the sale of their stories. The law stipulated that the state would collect the revenues generated by any work which involved the sale of the criminal's rights to his own story; such funds were to be put in trust, and used to aid the criminal's victims or to defray the costs of his imprisonment.

In December 1991, the United States Supreme Court declared New York's "Son of Sam" law unconstitutional on the grounds that it violated the First Amendment. During the oral argument, an assistant attorney general reasoned that New York's law, as written, would apply even in the following hypothetical case: Suppose that Saint Augustine's *Confessions* had been published in New York. The State of New York would then be entitled to the author's profits—profits that had been piling up for sixteen hundred years or so—because he confessed to the crimes of pear stealing and keeping a concubine. Here it became apparent that the law's absurdities were literary as well as legal, and Justice Antonin Scalia dismissed the lawyer's claim as ridiculous. Nevertheless, it is hard to imagine the *Confessions* without its recollections of the future bishop's boyhood exploits in the pear orchard and his sinful life in Carthage.

Others have entered the media marketplace with only their crimes to sell. Take the recent case of Amy Fisher, the Long Island teenager who shot, but did not kill, her lover's wife. Fisher's lawyer has called her story "her only asset"; rights to that story have been aggressively marketed for staggering

fees. To those who object to Fisher's being so lavishly rewarded for her crimes, the lawyer counters that she needs the money to pay legal costs and to finance her college education.

David Berkowitz and Amy Fisher are by no means the first criminals to have stirred up controversy over the marketing of true stories of murder and crime, especially those told by the criminals themselves. Commercial publishers in the United States have long turned to the misdeeds of criminals, availed themselves of the narratives constructed for them in court during their trials, taken advantage of the protections of the First Amendment, and benefited from the popular curiosity aroused by the publicity that any crime generates. Even if crime does not pay, publishers know that stories of crime do, and they have exploited the fortuitous conjunction between the court's interest in producing true accounts of crime and punishment and their own interest in turning a profit. But at some point, as the Son of Sam law illustrates, the judicial interests of the state (punishing the criminal for the sake of his victims and of society, demonstrating the efficacy and rightness of the justice system) come into conflict with the commercial interests of publishers (making money from selling crime stories, which in effect rewards the criminal for his crime and therefore subverts justice). This clash of interests can be seen even in the fledgling commercial culture of the United States during the early nineteenth century. A number of American murderers who sold their life stories and confessions in those years helped to create the marketplace in which stories like Fisher's could be worth startling sums.

Criminal confessions have long been part of popular print culture in the United States, a fact well documented by historians. Several scholars have studied the criminal confessions and the sermons delivered at the gallows in seventeenth-century New England for signs of the decline of Puritan theocracy; others continue their research into the eighteenth century, but tend to abandon criminal narratives at century's end, when they begin to lose their strongest spiritual accents and their close ties to a religious community of readers. A different group of historians picks up criminal narratives again in the 1840s, when lurid tales of sex and murder become a staple of sensational publishing. The confessions that appeared in the first few decades of the nineteenth century, however, were neither carefully constructed histories of spiritual failings and contrition nor sensational tales of famous crimes; they were instead local stories that help us understand how authentic versions of experience came to play so central a role in our cultural marketplace. During this transitional period, when criminal confessions were neither purely religious nor purely sensational in nature, we can see criminals and publishers experimenting with ways to turn experience into money; at the same time, the authors and publishers of these pamphlets were producing meditations not only upon closeness to death, but upon authenticity, state authority, and literacy.

These murder stories were part of a world of print that was widely diffuse. Hundreds of small publisher-printers scattered around the northeastern United States put out weekly papers, almanacs, religious tracts, and schoolbooks. Because these businesses operated on tight budgets, enterprising publishers turned eagerly to local murders, to stories already publicized by gossip and the courts, and thus sure to sell briskly. Villains and victims alike were local figures, and publishers tailored their stories to suit local markets. Most of these confession pamphlets were ephemeral publications designed for a relatively small audience; the little booklets disappeared in the avalanche of sensational stories that came later. By the 1840s, market consolidation and developments in both technology and transportation were making the small worlds of local publishing obsolete, and the precisely detailed early confessions were replaced by stories designed for wide sensational appeal.

> **When hangings were moved from public squares into prison yards, . . . punishment and prisoners alike disappeared from public view. The end of public execution did not mean the end of public interest, however; printers and publishers successfully pursued the crowds who had once gathered to watch hangings but were now dispersed as so many isolated readers.**
>
> *—Ann Fabian*

When incarcerated criminals entered the local market with their printed confessions, they were also knocking at the door of the literary world—a sphere they recognized as larger and more permanent than anything they had experienced in their narrow lives. Publication offered these prisoners one kind of escape: men about to be hanged could create something that would live on after them; they could cultivate the sympathy of their readers by casting themselves as victims of state power. Although most local pamphlets chronicled ugly scenes of domestic violence—wives and children slain by furious men—publication put the criminal, not the victim, at the center of things. The dead could not speak; only the living murderer controlled the story, and could depict himself as the victim of his jailers and executioners. Of course these poor murderers were also trying to realize the cash value, however tiny, that lay in their stories. And it is here that we see in little the problem that the Son of Sam law was designed to correct.

Let me begin with the story of John Lechler, an unhappy Pennsylvanian who sometime in 1822 caught his wife Mary with his friend and neighbor Bernhart Haag. While the trouserless lover cowered in the cellar, Lechler strangled his wife. Haag then fled for home and Lechler followed, gun in hand; but when he fired at Haag through the door of his house, the aggrieved husband missed and killed Mrs. Haag instead. Before being hanged for the double murder, Lechler arranged to publish his dying confession, hoping "to raise a small pittance for the assistance of those innocent orphans who are rendered destitute by the crime of their father and the justice of their country."

Lechler's phrasing nicely gestures toward the peculiar cultural place of the criminal narrative. To confess in public, to admit guilt and acknowledge the justice of one's punishment was, on the one hand, to uphold the authority of the state and to invite the reader's approval of its workings. But Lechler's confession also invited readers to sympathize with his poor orphans and, through his unfortunate children, with him. He had killed their mother, but the state was about to kill their father. Lechler's acknowledgment of state authority was no sooner made than subverted through the reader's sympathetic identification with a criminal.

To win that sympathetic identification, Lechler tried to prevent anyone else from telling his story. He concluded his confession with words designed to damage a pirated version his jailer threatened to put out—and designed also to wring the hearts of his readers: "My good old friend, Samuel Carpenter, agrees to receive my confession, and have it published to raise a little money, after paying the printers, to educate my poor children. And I declare with my dying breath that it contains the whole truth. The jailor has frequently, as I have told several people, told me that I must give him my confession, because he gave me such good victuals—and at last I was *compelled,* for I am his poor prisoner, in chains to write a *history* for him, which he intends to have published also." He also made sure to remind his readers that he was a victim not only of the state but of a cruel and greedy jailer.

Few criminals wrote because someone forced them to do so, but many published as a defense against piracy. Lechler was one of several murderers who employed this old device of insecure authors. He was also one of many who used the power of print to control the gossip circulating outside jail cells and who recognized that their stories, if properly handled, might become economic assets. Lechler therefore turned to a friendly collaborator, and together they wrote a tale designed to make a little money. Lechler sensed that print was more powerful than speech, and he knew that his performance as a confessing murderer would be valuable to his heirs only if it appeared as a published text that could be sold.

As long as executions were public events, the condemned

were assigned roles in those staged dramas of justice and death; but there was no worldly profit to be made simply by assisting at one's own hanging. When hangings were moved from public squares into prison yards—first in Pennsylvania in 1834 and by 1845 in all the New England and Middle Atlantic states—punishment and prisoners alike disappeared from public view. The end of public execution did not mean the end of public interest, however; printers and publishers successfully pursued the crowds who had once gathered to watch hangings but were now dispersed as so many isolated readers. This served other interests as well: the authorities had worried that early nineteenth-century crowds harbored a volatile mix of classes, races, sexes, and nationalities; print could teach the necessary moral lessons without risking mob violence.

But publication was not an entirely reliable means of teaching moral lessons: superfluous information, the arousal of dangerous sensations, and sympathetic criminal narrators undermined the didactic intent of criminal literature. Many of the pamphlets printed in the early nineteenth century contained what we might call digressions on the prisoner's ability to read and write (or lack thereof) and on the professional skills of the ministers and lawyers who helped convey criminals' stories to the public. In addition, both the confessing criminals and the men who took their confessions were conscious of the advantages of turning ephemeral speech into published documents, and they also acknowledged that the value (whether economic or spiritual) of a confession was enhanced by the presence of the criminal's authentic voice. The ministers, lawyers, jailers, and reporters who compiled murder pamphlets presented themselves to the reading public without apology, but they worked hard to get the murderer onto the page, to present intimate views of criminal excess. To obtain the effect of unmediated, unedited authenticity, they turned to old devices: they claimed to take words "from the prisoner's own mouth" (or lips or tongue) or to have received documents from the prisoner's hands, using the criminal's body to authenticate his confession. In addition, such devices made it possible to represent in writing those who could neither read nor write in such a way that they appeared to be representing themselves. On the one hand, such authenticity suggested that the true-crime pamphlets might be read as simple chronicles of experience. But this carefully made structure of representation allowed murderers like Lechler to begin to interpret their lives, to admit their guilt but also to accuse their executioners.

Murderers and ministers were conscious of the many ways illiteracy entered into crimes and published confessions. Several found that the divine grace that came before execution forced them to acknowledge intellectual as well as spiritual shortcomings. "Being an illiterate man," one murderer confessed in 1797, "I kept no journal; and consequently many acts of wickedness have escaped my memory." Now that he

was appearing in print his journal of wickedness would be valuable indeed, but the trajectory of the pamphlets was not toward more careful recollection but interpretation and control. Murderers began to miss the interpretive skills that came with literacy.

John Cowan, an illiterate Cincinnati man, entered the world of print in 1835, when he published his confession to a brutal crime: in a fit of rage, he had taken an axe and chopped up his wife and two children. With the help of a man named James Allen, he produced a particularly self-conscious life and confession, although what he was conscious of was not the psychology of murder but the economic standing of murder pamphlets and the devices necessary to represent an illiterate man in print in what were supposed to be his own words. Cowan's pamphlet opened with the publisher's usual disclaimers about his intent to educate rather than to pander to a taste for the morbid, but he then reminded would-be readers that proceeds from the pamphlet would be dedicated to "the pious task of raising a monument over the grave in which repose the victims of his barbarity." So Cowan's pamphlet, a sort of monument to himself, would also raise a gravestone over his victims.

An editor introduced Cowan as "what is commonly called an illiterate man," but by the 1830s people called illiterate possessed considerable skill in reading and writing. Cowan's amanuensis acknowledged that the prisoner read the Bible, but that his only prior attempt at composition had been a "slight epistolary correspondence with his friends." The editor found Cowan's orthography "rather good," his syntax better than expected, but his skills at punctuation entirely wanting. In his prefatory remarks, he told readers that Cowan wrote best about intemperance and about the necessity and vitality of religion. While the editor attributed such rare passages of clear composition to divine inspiration, it is more likely that they reflect earthly borrowings or simple transcriptions from sermons and temperance lectures.

The preface ends with Cowan's affidavit, which awards all his property to William Doty and James Allen along with the "right in a certain manuscript, written by myself, and containing my confession and narrative of my life." But here Cowan qualifies Allen's "pious task" and asks that only one hundred dollars of the profits be set aside for his victims' gravestones. The residue, he wrote, "I freely bestow upon the said Doty and Allen." Like most such pamphlets, Cowan's based its claim to commercial value on the authenticity of his confession and on its intimate revelations of criminal behavior and violent death, but it added to this list the chance to perform a pious act of charity for the victims. Cowan also tried to control his work and its earnings from beyond the grave by designating his collaborators as his heirs.

When editors and publishers constructed their careful frames around these criminals' publications, they granted to their words, especially to the words of the illiterate, an importance rarely if ever experienced by living men. Cowan himself suddenly became more important to more people: "the children of God," namely, "clergymen and pious people, of different denominations" visited him in jail. They were persons of real power; they controlled access to culture in this world even as they presumed to influence his standing in the next. Cowan would never have used those words, but he was certainly aware of his new position, and tried to turn his brief fame to his advantage, worldly and eternal, by using his dubious entry into the public world of print to gain a sympathetic hearing.

If Cowan's soul was the prize in an evangelical contest, his authentic story was the trophy in a more secular one. But how can we be sure what is meant by *authentic?* Cowan's carefully structured and clearly written pamphlet concludes with this sample of his own writing: "I want my name signed Amedeately under this—I have it in my power to Ru two familyes in this place and sattisfy the world of its correctness. . . . I remain until Death your most humble murderer." In the manufacture of an asset designed to bring in more than the one hundred dollars needed for a tombstone, Allen clearly did more than correct Cowan's grammar. He provided the logical conventions that made sense of Cowan's life and dressed the "illiterate" man in linguistic trappings to match the black suit he described Cowan as wearing at his execution. But he did so by adopting a guise of authenticity meant to package experience for a commercial market.

Two years later, in 1837, another malefactor met his fate in Cincinnati, but the publishers of *Life and confession of John Washburn: (partner of Lovett, Jones, &c.,) the great robber and murderer!* aimed their story at a market freed from the constraints of local geography. Washburn's drama covered a good deal of territory: his *Life and confession* was sold wholesale at 38 Strawberry Street in Philadelphia, and not where the murderer lived, killed, or was executed. Washburn was the son of a poor but honest shoemaker who saw to it that his son at least learned to read. Young John then worked for his brother in a brickyard in Memphis, but he fell in with a gang of murderous thieves who took the whole of the Mississippi Valley as their criminal domain. His tale, "dictated by himself and written by a fellow prisoner," was a cold-blooded chronicle of some thirty murders: "This last murder was committed in the winter of 1828," he reported. "This murder happened in March 1833. . . . This murder I committed in July 1833." The number of his crimes and the fact that his victims were strangers set him apart from most antebellum murderers, who killed as a result of intimate or family quarrels.

Washburn insisted that his criminal calendar contained no exaggerations, and, evincing a curious moral fastidiousness,

he swore on the "Holy Evangelists of Almighty God" that his story was true. Why should a man who had forsworn the simplest social conventions about the value of human life adopt a verbal convention of veracity? Like so many confessing criminals, Washburn told his story as a narrative of conversion and vowed that, despite his criminal past, he was ready to assent to the obligations of a writer. Whether this story was true or false mattered far less than that it was he himself, the criminal, who produced it.

If he used his pamphlet to acknowledge the evil of his ways and to make some kind of restitution to his victims by warning others of the existence of heartless, impersonal killers, he also used it to effect a more secular conversion: he left off being a man of action and became a man of letters. He had lived his former life as a series of close and violent encounters; now he became a storyteller, addressing readers remote in time and place, and exercising a certain power of abstraction hitherto unknown to him. As a writer he tried to establish new grounds upon which posterity would judge his guilt or innocence: the only evidence that would endure would be the material he permitted to be published. He concluded by thanking Thomas Walker, the fellow prisoner who had written up his "particulars." Calling upon his skill as a reader, he pronounced himself "perfectly satisfied with the manner in which he has performed his services; but I have no way to recompense him for his services and kindness, except by sincerely desiring the welfare of himself and family, both in this world and the world to come, which thing I do." Washburn thus used his new role as a writer to reach beyond his life into eternity, and in this he resembles authors far greater than he.

Others with less grand aspirations tried to use print to reach outside their cells to control the rumors and gossip still circulating about their deeds. One man used his confession to admit to bestiality and incest but to deny a long list of very specific local crimes. Another complained that nasty gossip forced him into print. He had "intended to die without making any observation on his fate, or giving any particulars of his life; but there were so many idle and cruel reports in circulation, and each one ornamented with so many horrors, all told with such assurance of the truth, that he was constrained, if not on his own account, yet in consideration of his friends, for friends he has, and those dear to him, to give the public some sketch of his humble walk through life."

Amasa Walmsley published a confession not only to counter "false reports" that he had killed for revenge, but also to stop a story "stating that he had sold his body to the surgeons for rum. The story is false in all its parts. His body, the last legacy he can give to his friends, he has submitted to the disposal of his brother Uriah." While Walmsley did not specify the value of his legacy to Uriah, he did try to control the fate of his body, using his one chance to appear in print to announce that he did not want to be disinterred "for the promotion of science." Walmsley perhaps believed that the printed version of his confession would give him the last word on his remains, physical and literary. For a criminal like Walmsley such efforts were largely futile. What was his temporary assertion of power on the page compared to the state's life-and-death power over him? But for the scattered community of readers who purchased and read Walmsley's story but did not see his execution, the state's power was perhaps less certain.

Pamphlets by illiterates like Walmsley were not long on literary art. They contained narratives built around what one historian labeled "dry itineraries of dates, locations, and crimes." Such dry recitations, however, served several purposes. They provided a rough organization for the local knowledge presented in narratives by admitted illiterates, and they helped establish confessing criminals as reliable witnesses to the events of their own lives. Furthermore, precise and controlled description of local scenes lent authenticity to wild scenes of murder. Twentieth-century readers make their way through crime stories with the aid of an internalized mapping system called psychology; criminal pamphlets of the early nineteenth century used geographical markers to lead an audience familiar with the details of a neighborhood or a landscape into the less familiar terrain of violent crime.

With increasing frequency in the 1830s, however, publishers replaced references to local geography with references to other murders and murderers, removing tales from the scene of the crime and setting them instead among other stories. Antoine Le Blanc, a Frenchman convicted of a murderous spree in New Jersey, brought his confession before the public with the help of an interpreter, a printer, a publisher, and the sheriff of the county. The publisher knew Le Blanc's place in the genre, and he concluded the confession by stating that he had read the confessions of Gibbs, the pirate, as well as those of William Teller, Caesar Reynolds, and George Swearingen and recommended them to those who had perused and enjoyed Le Blanc's story. His mention of others' confessions—probably an indirect form of genre advertising—suggests that he advised Le Blanc to address himself to a new kind of audience: an audience of scattered readers who enjoyed shuddering at any representation of evil, no matter how distant, rather than a local community that gathered at the gallows to shudder at the person of the condemned, the embodiment of evil in their very midst. Pamphlets, which had once dealt with specific crimes, were now concerned with the genre of criminal publication; discussions of murder's social and moral costs were replaced by allusions to the financial success that attended telling tales of murder.

By the middle of the century, popular publishers had learned to cater to the public taste for that sort of sensational tale.

Murder and confession, as is well known, were grist for the mill of popular publishing houses like G. B. Zeiber in Philadelphia, A. R. Orton in New York, and Erastus Elmer Barclay in New Orleans. Although these narratives no longer depended on the voice of the murderer, publishers turned to their own ends the authenticating devices that had brought murderers' voices from the cell into the marketplace.

G. B. Zeiber, for example, presented an 1848 story, *Authentic narrative of the murder of Mrs. Rademacher,* as an "authentic and succinct account." Even though the story concerns a Philadelphia murder, the title page courted a national market, presenting the twelve-and-a-half-cent pamphlet as "For Sale by all the Newsmen and Periodical Agents in the United States." The pamphlet, written in the voice of an unidentified and unexplained editorial "we," tells the story of a German-born shoemaker, Charles Langfeldt, who carried out a mistaken act of revenge on the new tenants of his enemies' former home. The editor asks the reader to regard the murder not as a piece of local gossip but as an event that can create a wave of disgust in a wider audience. "But now comes the crowning horror—at the recital of which our heart grows sick, and our hand refuses to perform its office. On removing the corpse of the murdered woman, the body of the child prematurely born, was found, dead, beneath her! At the sight, one shudder of horror shook the hearts of the spectators of this direful scene with an electric spasm."

The editor's pen conducted that electricity to his readers, thus turning the readers' sensations, rather than the criminal's voice, into a marketable asset. (This emphasis on sensation may explain why the pamphlet's title names the victim rather than the killer, and why the climax of the narrative is the discovery of the victim's corpse, not the criminal's confession.) In fact, the editor never for a moment forgot that his ultimate goal was to sell, not merely to tell, the tale: when the editor assisted at the coroner's inquest, he could not avoid plugging another of Zeiber's publications; while listening to Langfeldt describe his experiences as a shoemaker wandering through Europe, "we were forcibly reminded of the policy and organization of the French prisons, so graphically and powerfully described by Eugene Sue, in his inimitable work, 'The Mysteries of Paris.'" The shoemaker with a grudge had become the tool of a sizeable literary enterprise; his tale was told to court a vast, anonymous market rather than to influence the local gossips.

Like the publishers and prisoners who struggled to realize the financial value of confession, Protestant ministers tried to establish their place in commercial markets by maintaining a presence in murder stories. In the early nineteenth century, ministers followed their erring charges into print and made sure that those who read of murder would learn of the labor of ministers: descriptions of their good works appeared on the pages of popular confessions. But ministers were not the only visitors to murderers' cells. They competed for access to stories with reporters, jailers, publishers, lawyers, and even with ministers of different denominations. Criminals were kept isolated from family and friends, but were readily available to jailers and to a coterie of professionals and experts. Criminals and their confessors needed each other, and they worked out their interdependence in the pamphlets they produced.

There were, however, a few who refused to play along with the process of confession and exposure that brought stories to the market. Catholic murderers, who reserved their confessions for priests, posed problems for the Protestant ministers who worked closely with popular publishers. These problems, however, were not insurmountable: if a murderer refused to bare his soul in public, his silence could be taken as yet another instance of Popish conspiracy. Several murder pamphlets used the criminal's silence to play into a widespread anti-Catholicism. "We understand," wrote the two men who published Thomas Barrett's confession in 1845, "that he has made a full confession to the priest, but of what nature no one can tell, as the Catholic confessional is held sacred. We have been at great pains, and have gathered all the particulars which can be obtained." The particulars included the contents of Barrett's victim's stomach—a gruesome substitute for the missing confession.

For Protestant divines, who were long accustomed to making or officiating at public confessions and to publishing their own sermons, the move to popular culture posed few problems. The career of one man, the Reverend John Stanford, illustrates both how easy it was for a minister to enter the realm of popular print culture and the difficulties he faced when prisoners refused to confess in public.

Stanford was born in England in 1754, and was ordained a Baptist minister before coming to the United States in 1785. He served as pastor of the Church of Christ in New York City from 1795 until 1801, when the church was destroyed by fire. Lacking a fixed congregation, he took under his "ministerial charge" those confined to the "various humane and criminal institutions" in New York. In 1812, Governor De Witt Clinton appointed him chaplain of the state prison in New York City, which assured Stanford unlimited access to inmates and their stories. Stanford went into prisons with an evangelical zeal that inspired his colleagues to conduct revivals in their own congregations. He recorded his daily round of visits in a diary, taking upon himself the task of charting his congregants' slow progress toward divine grace.

Stanford served his captive flock with dedication until his death in 1834. In the 1820s, he began to keep a log of the sermons he delivered to the city's institutionalized populations; and at the end of each month he tabulated the sermons he had delivered, as if demonstrating how much work he

had done. But he also began to compile a diary in which he engaged in more extensive speculation about members of his congregation and his mission to them. He took "short notes" on all those he visited, and in the late 1820s he gathered the notes together to publish a volume "to show the benefit of the institution and to magnify the riches of a Saviour's mercy to the chief of Sinners!"

Stanford carried piety, humility, and prayer into the prison, and he carried stories out: he was a conduit for the publication of several criminal biographies and confessions. When Stanford published his notes, as he did, for example, in the *Confession of James Reynolds for the Murder of Captain Wm. West,* he accomplished several things at once. The portions of his diary reprinted throughout the pamphlet documented his work as a minister without church. He also used his notes to convey knowledge about prisoners to their keepers, in effect extending the range of their surveillance from body to soul. "I shall now close these notes," he wrote after presenting Reynolds's "full disclosure." "As usual they are given to Messrs. Grant and See, of the City Prison, as their perquisite. It is requested that should their Printer obtain any other papers on the subject of James Reynolds, that they should be kept separate from these Notes, as the writer is not answerable for any other communications."

Another of Stanford's prisoners, a man who refused to make a public confession about the murder for which he was eventually hanged, became the subject of popular conjecture and, naturally, several competing pamphlets. John Johnson kept a sailors' boardinghouse in lower Manhattan. When one of his lodgers, a man named James Murray, was found murdered with a hatchet, Johnson was arrested and later tried and convicted of the slaying. Shortly after his arrest, Johnson confessed orally to the murder, but then retracted that confession and steadily refused to sign any written version of his remarks, which would have constituted a public confession. Stanford began to visit Johnson in December 1823, and he continued to urge him to confess throughout the spring of 1824. His efforts intensified in March; he recorded ten visits to the prisoner that month. In the course of the visits, Stanford read Johnson's correspondence with his wife, and he did not hesitate to comment sharply about her having included mundane reports about the livestock on their upstate farm. Her letter, he decided, "exhibits either a great want of feeling or education," and he reprinted it for his readers. Perhaps Stanford was also annoyed because in the course of the letter she advised her husband to maintain his silence and not to confess to Stanford or anyone else.

> The people say that come up from New York, that you are going to write your life, but dear father there are more of writing going than you could think of. I hope God will have a little more guide in your hand than for to let you write anything about your life. It is

bad enough now, don't let them have any speech nor any life to have printed in books when you are dead. And you have so much printed now it would take half a day for to read it. Dear husband, make your prayer to God and die innocently, as I believe you are; and make none to the public for they cannot relieve your poor soul.

Mrs. Johnson's letter shows that she understood several important things. Writing up his life would not save Johnson's soul or protect his life history from misinterpretation. This capable woman, who managed the family farm and reported its finances quite precisely, made no mention of the profits to be derived from publication; all a printed confession would do is prolong Johnson's notoriety and the family's shame. It is little wonder that Stanford, faced with this uncooperative pair, needed the occasion of Johnson's execution to launch his own pamphlet. Stanford turned Johnson's defiant silence—soon to become the silence of death—into material for publication, but even as he did so, he gave the condemned man an oddly heroic cast.

Johnson's execution was a great public event. He was escorted to the gallows by members of the cavalry, the infantry, and the clergy. A crowd of fifty thousand (including enough pickpockets to produce one long paragraph of complaints) showed up at Thirteenth Street and Second Avenue and filled the park there "to a degree that was never before witnessed. It presented as it were a solid mass of living flesh—men, women and children of all colours and descriptions." Even on the scaffold, Johnson continued to resist all pressure to confess, and went so far as to refuse to allow a clergyman to make a speech. (Nevertheless, Stanford felt it to be "his duty" to offer up a public prayer.)

Amasa Walmley had used a text to attempt to control his remains, but Johnson did not even bother to make the effort: his body was given to surgeons, who wired it to a voltaic battery "of greater force than is anywhere else recorded, (328 pairs of plates of 4 inches)." In the theater of the College of Physicians and Surgeons, the doctors made a play of the dead man's muscles. They not only reproduced "the results of Dr. Ure in Glasgow," they also managed to get a "nervous twitching of the mouth" and to make the muscles of his heart contract. So the "strangely unfeeling" man, who resisted all attempts to obtain his public confession and withheld his heart and voice from the commercial culture of his city, had his organs of speech and sentiment manipulated, when all will was absent, by electricity.

Popular culture has come a long way since Mrs. Johnson urged her husband to withhold his confession from the public because "they cannot relieve your poor soul." Nowadays, when we confess in public it is to fatten our purses, not to relieve our souls. We have created a thriving market for authentic stories, and we put a fat premium on any presentation of a criminal's own voice, whether that voice lies or tells the truth. Perhaps we relish the chance to judge the case for ourselves, or else we may prefer the experience of candor or exposure to anything so final as the truth.

Writers still collaborate with criminals and their executioners. A century and a half after Johnson's death, Truman Capote found himself waiting for two men to die so that he could finish *In Cold Blood*. According to his biographer, Capote spent two agonizing years in "suspended animation" as he waited for the State of Kansas to provide the execution that would conclude the best-seller he knew he had written. But Capote's biographer also describes the puzzled and disappointed murderers, who watched as their friend the professional author became the professional author who had befriended their enemies. The executioner, finally, was Capote's most valuable collaborator.

Publishers are still devising ways to profit from representations of crime and death, even though some commentators believe that there are no taboos left to violate. The William Kennedy Smith rape trial was televised nationally, and the plaintiff's name was revealed in the newspapers; one popular "true-crime" television program broadcast a police videotape that showed an officer being murdered (the video camera mounted in the victim's patrol car was programmed to continue taping after the policeman had left the vehicle). Perhaps the last remaining forbidden subject is the filming of an actual execution, but that, too, may soon change: in April 1992 the American Civil Liberties Union arranged to tape the execution of a convicted murderer, Robert Alton Harris, in California. The ACLU wants to show the tape in order to demonstrate how revolting capital punishment is, how it violates the constitutional ban on "cruel and unusual punishment." But if the tape is aired, punishment will once again take place in public—that is, on television—and we will have to consider that medium's extraordinary potential for producing revenue. We will also have to face a much more disturbing question: will television make execution a form of entertainment?

The same week that Harris died in California, New York lawmakers considered a bill to restrict the sale of "serial killer trading cards." When the tabloid press covered the story, however, both the power of murder to shock and to sell and the state's inability to control stories of murder were manifest. The *New York Post* filled its front page with reproductions of one set of cards, and the story inside concluded by listing the prices of four different sets, along with their manufacturers' names and addresses. One publisher boasted that his "Forty Famous Murderers to Fear," released in 1989 at ten dollars for the set, had sold out. "If you can find it now, it sells for $20. It's actually an investment," he told the *Post,* not very subtly encouraging people to buy his cards. One angry murderer, however, threatened to sue the company that had appropriated his image and story.

The rising value of serial killer trading cards suggests just how hard it is to regulate and especially to end the story of a murder. Even when the state executes the criminal, it cannot lay claim to the profits engendered by those able to recycle works of the criminal imagination, nor can it direct those revenues away from wily profiteers and into the hands of the victims or their families. Execution may complete the story of an individual criminal's life, yet free speech and the free market push the story into the land of the living, where tales of grisly deeds pass uncontrolled into our fertile imaginations.

Rosaria Champagne (essay date 1994)

SOURCE: "True Crimes of Motherhood: Mother-Daughter Incest, Multiple Personality Disorder, and the True Crime Novel," in *Feminist Nightmares: Women at Odds,* edited by Susan Ostrov Weisser and Jennifer Fleischner, New York University Press, 1994, pp. 142-58.

[*In the following essay, Champagne centers on mother-daughter abuse and incest, and the multiple personality disorders that often result. In her discussion, Champagne focuses on two books, Flora Rheta Schreiber's* Sybil *and Joan Frances Casey's* The Flock: The Autobiography of a Multiple Personality.]

PATIENT: Mother, I am frightened.

CHARCOT: Note the emotional outburst. If we let things go unabated we will soon return to the epileptoid behavior. . . . (The patient cries again: "Oh! Mother.")

CHARCOT: Again, note these screams. You could say it is a lot of noise over nothing.
  (Charcot the Clinician)

Feminism has historically relied on the mother-daughter bond as a noncontested category for women's connection and social activism. And yet, with the genre of women's true crime fiction, mother-daughter abuse shows up in every narrative gap. There are two formula plots for this genre: in the first, a white upper-middle-class woman murders her daughters; her neighbors and tennis pals are shocked; her husband didn't see it coming. (These narratives flourish in white middle-class women's magazines, such as *Redbook* and *Woman's Day*). The second model, typified by Flora Rheta Schreiber's *Sybil,* centers the mother-daughter relationship around incest, not murder.

Important elements of plot and politics distinguish this model:

the featured presence of abusive mothers; lesbianism in the bodies of women already sanctioned as heterosexual; the production of a multiple daughter, whose unproblematized discourse of confession, disclosure, and confrontation fails to reconstruct the individual (that is, humanism cannot restore the multiple to a single consciousness); and the replacement of the incestuous mother with the mother-therapist. It is this therapist-mother role that, I will argue, inscribes the misogyny that sustains mother-daughter abuse by setting up the crazy mother who "makes" a crazy daughter and then pits the crazy mother against the mother-therapist, who emerges at the narrative's close as the good and more deserving mother.

Discussions about incest and its aftereffects almost always configure a father (or father figure) perpetrator, and a daughter (or surrogate) victim/survivor. While it is absolutely true that men commit sexual abuse more often than women, women can also function as perpetrators of incest. By privileging the father-daughter incest paradigm, we successfully inscribe the "sentimental romance" of heterosexuality and cannot account for one of the signal aftereffects of incest— multiple personality disorder (MPD). MPD, only recognized by the American Psychiatric Association as an aftereffect of incest since 1980, frustrates the father-daughter incest paradigm because, at least as represented in women's true crime novels, mothers cause MPD. But, I will argue, "mothers" recast as mother-therapists also "cure" MPD by recapitulating a desperately felt belief in the healing power of motherhood.

In this essay, I will use Flora Rheta Schreiber's *Sybil* and Joan Frances Casey's *The Flock: The Autobiography of a Multiple Personality* to show how mother-daughter abuse, the open secret of women's true crime novels, troubles the nostalgic relationship between women that feminism often desperately assumes. I will focus this essay not only on the individual mothers and daughters brought to light by these novels, but also on the role of motherhood and daughterhood. Both novels show that abusive mothers assume power through the social role of motherhood. Importantly, this same social role facilitates the feminist therapists, who function as surrogate mothers, with the power to heal. Indeed, daughters who suffer from MPD find wholeness only when they shift loyalty from the evil mother to the good one, a shift often accomplished with bribes and solicitations from the mother-therapist. These mother-therapists are indeed better mothers than the sadistic mothers that precede them, but their cure comes with a price: entrapment, always, in some mother's narrative. That is, by naturalizing and idealizing the role of motherhood and its usefulness in feminist therapy, the MPD daughter is merely reinscribed in another mother's narrative—i.e., one that is not her own. Even with sanity, good daughterhood is a dead-end street.

In *Sybil,* the story of Sybil Isabel Dorsett, who was sexually, physically, and verbally abused by her mother, Hattie Dorsett, from infancy, and her relationship with the "real" Dr. Cornelia B. Wilbur (who still serves as a leading spokesperson about MPD), is narrated by Sybil herself, who, amnesiac and unaware of her sixteen other personalities, knows and feels shame because she "loses time." Vicky, Sybil's memory trace who emerges when she is twelve but knows the history of the body from the age of two, works with Dr. Wilbur as a co-analysand. The Peggys—Peggy Lou and Peggy Ann—interrupt Sybil's life and therapy to express rage and anger directed at Hattie Dorset. The other twelve personalities appear and confront Dr. Wilbur throughout Sybil's eight years of therapy, and some even try at various times to "murder" Sybil.

In therapy with Dr. Wilbur, Sybil consistently replays themes that point to child abuse—secrecy, isolation, entrapment. While the aftereffects are ever-present—the most evident of which is her severe MPD—the events themselves (ritualized incest, medical abuse, verbal abuse) are "lost" in the pre-mirror stage talk and not transferable into a comprehensible narrative for the conscious, adult Sybil. While the Peggys know that Hattie sexually abused Sybil, Sybil does not. And while Vicky knows the tale of Sybil's sad plight, she believes she is an entirely separate person from Sybil. Interestingly, even though Hattie's abuse was sadistic, ritualized, and consistent, Sybil does not remember it. She only recalls that Hattie was "at once overprotective and unsympathetic." When one of Sybil's alters "returns" her body to her, leaving Sybil to explain her amnesia to her boss, the police, or to a member of the medical community, she repeats in rote: "I am an only child and my parents are very good to me."

Hattie perpetrated incest by tying Sybil in a bondage ritual with dish towels, penetrating her with kitchen utensils, and inducing ejaculation with unnecessary enemas. She then enforced silence and repression by "erasing" the event, by veiling it with her role as mother. Hattie reportedly said, "Now don't you dare tell anybody anything about this. If you do, I won't have to punish you. God's wrath will do it for me!" (Importantly, the narrator, Flora Schreiber, writes from the psychiatrist's perspective; and so Sybil's story is really Cornelia Wilbur's story, just as Freud's case studies of his famous hysterics are his, not theirs.) The Peggys "talk" this trauma because they don't think Hattie Dorset is their mother; in fact, the fifteen other personalities that take over Sybil's body claim to have no mother at all. Thus, the alters capably read Hattie as perpetrator only because they refuse to read her as mother. For Sybil, the role and title of "mother" veils all abuse: "Sybil invested the perpetrator of the tortures with immunity from blame. The buttonhook was at fault, or the enema tip, or the other instruments of torture. The perpetrator, however, by virtue of being her mother, whom one had not only to obey but also to love and honor, was not to blame." This mother-daughter abuse is more psychologically dangerous than father-daughter abuse precisely because her ste-

reotyped social role overdetermines how her behavior will be read.

In addition to the social role that protected Hattie's abuse from discovery was her own self-projected image—as an advocate of children's rights, of all things: "Hattie Dorsett enunciated solemn strictures about exemplary child care. Never hit a child, Hattie Dorsett preached, when it is possible to avoid it, and under no circumstances hit a child on the face or head." This projected image successfully prohibits Sybil from taking seriously her therapy with Dr. Wilbur until after Hattie's death. Hattie sabotages Sybil's first relationship with Dr. Wilbur by intentionally not giving Sybil a phone message that Dr. Wilbur had to cancel an appointment. Sybil feels stood up and abandoned, as Hattie had hoped, and Hattie caps the moment with another injunction for mother-love: "Dr. Wilbur didn't really care for you. . . . She tells you one thing now. But when she gets you where she wants you, she'll tell you altogether different things. And remember young lady, she'll turn on you if you tell her you don't love your own mother." The only reason Sybil has the strength and desire to return to Dr. Wilbur after Hattie's death is because Sybil buffers Hattie's warning with Hattie's fundamentalist Christianity and its proscriptions against psychiatric help. (Hattie warned Sybil that Dr. Wilbur would "make [her] crazy . . . and then . . . put [her] in an institution because that's the way doctors make money.")

Sybil, like all abused children, was told never to tell. For this reason, she is "scared about words," and also, for this reason, she perfected a skill that afforded her nonverbal communication. For Sybil, the only terrain untouched by her mother's abuse and prohibition was drawing. When trapped, Sybil colors her way out of and into amnesia. For example, when the evangelical pastor of her family's Omaha church, hoping to involve her in church activities, asks Sybil to help him scare Satan away by painting his sermons, Sybil agrees. Because the words of the evangelical preacher scare her (Vicky tells Dr. Wilbur that, in church and in their appointments, Sybil was "scared about words"), Sybil illustrates the sermons from a "scaffold nine feet above [the preacher] at an easel covered with drawing paper and spanning the entire width of the church." Often during these sermons, Sybil would illustrate and "split" into one of her alters. This "strategy of discourse," drawing and splitting, allows Sybil to negotiate between unnamed events and their potential meanings. We see here that MPD actually helps Sybil to cope. But MPD, in its plethora of visual figures and many-voiced talk, is, ultimately, antinarrative. That is, it constitutes an endless return to the site of the mother's domination, but by reading the mother's social role over her behavior, it fails to recognize the mother as perpetrator. For Sybil, all that is left are feelings and words disconnected from agents or actors.

Psychoanalysis figures victims of MPD as almost always

physically, sexually, and psychologically abused before the age of two, before the Lacanian mirror stage, the moment when the child becomes enraptured with its separateness from its mother. While the mirror stage functions as "the origin of the origin," for the multiple daughter, this origin is nebulous. Thus Anna O's famous "talking cure" cannot aid the victim of MPD because the multiple daughter cannot retrace trauma done in the presymbolic with discourse. So even though the "drug of choice for multiples seems to be talk— the kind of talk that permits each of the separate traumas to be identified and relived," the talk produced by a multiple is abject and therefore the trauma cannot be easily abreacted. Thus, MPD discourse (presymbolic), not (narrative) name, is talk whose signifier does not reflect its signified.

Self-help theory, as represented by Ellen Bass and Laura Davis in *The Courage to Heal: A Guide for Women Survivors of Child Sexual Abuse* (referred to by the False Memory Foundation, a family-values organization in the business of discrediting incest survivors and their therapists, as the "Bible" of the incest industry and its favorite "cult" text), describes MPD as a condition produced by early childhood sexual and physical abuse that "splits" the core personality into "alters" or "multiples" who function as distinct, complex personalities and who may or may not be aware of each other. These personalities are both adaptive and defensive, using the only means available to the disempowered—manipulation of the psyche. That trauma literally shatters the child is made evident by Judith Herman, who writes that "traumatic events violate the autonomy of the person at the level of basic bodily integrity. The body is invaded, injured, defiled" ([Judith Lewis] Herman, *Trauma and Recovery,* [1992]). And it is for this reason that "the traumatic event thus destroys the belief that one can *be oneself* in relation to others" (Herman's italics). MPD is dissociation to the extreme; triggered by shame and self-loathing, it represents the release of the rage that victims/survivors embody. Those children who were tortured at a very young, preverbal age, and who have nowhere else to turn, turn inward. Dr. Wilbur adds psychological abuse ("demeaning, denigrating, or ridiculing infants and children") to the list of MPD-producing traumas. And Margaret Smith features MPD in her recent book, *Ritual Abuse,* stating that the entrapment of ritual abuse almost always results in MPD.

Because of his failure to offer escape, Willard Dorsett, Sybil's father, also serves as an accomplice to Hattie's crime. Importantly, though, he also participated in a bedtime ritual that is sometimes defined as incest. Until the age of nine, Sybil slept in a crib in her parent's bedroom and, three times a week, was forced to watch them have sex. In a list of abusive practices headed by the descriptor, "How Can I Know If I Was a Victim of Childhood Sexual Abuse," Bass and Davis include "made to watch sexual acts or look at sexual parts" as an example. Schreiber writes: "Three or four nights a week,

year in and year out, parental intercourse took place within her hearing and vision. And not infrequently, the erect penis was easily visible in the half-light." Importantly, neither the narrator nor the psychiatrist nor the patient blames Willard Dorsett for this display. Instead, Vicky tells Dr. Wilbur that "Hattie Dorsett actually wanted her daughter to look," and the doctor concurs.

Indeed, Willard is not ever made to take responsibility for his behavior, and this reader is left wondering if this omission is not an extension of male privilege—in this case the privilege of freedom from the responsibility for proper parenting. This is made especially clear in the confrontation that Dr. Wilbur has with Willard Dorsett. Dr. Wilbur commands Willard to meet her in her office (in spite of his poor health, advanced age, and difficulty traveling) under the pretense of needing more "hard evidence" to legitimate and authorize the experiences of child abuse revealed by Sybil's alters. In a chapter called "Confrontation and Verification," Dr. Wilbur stages a showdown that successfully emasculates Willard Dorsett, making clear to the reader who really wields the power of the phallus. After Dr. Wilbur feeds Willard memories from the past, his large stature seems to shrink. Like a mollusk, Willard Dorsett had always stayed within his shell, insulated in the private sea of his own concerns. He has been resolute in pursuing a path of conformity, refusing to look in any other direction. Now the mollusk, out of the sea, was steaming in hot water, its shell cracking. And just in case the drama of Dr. Wilbur's emasculation of Willard Dorsett is not readily apparent, the narrator tells us: "It was a pivotal moment, the kind that the classic Greek dramatists describe as a peripety—the moment in which the action of a drama assumes a quick catastrophic new turn, a reversal." Importantly, Willard is only held accountable for facilitating Hattie's abuse through his absence. Finally, when Dr. Wilbur repeatedly asks Willard why he allowed Hattie to raise Sybil, even when "this schizophrenic mother came very close to killing her child," Willard is reduced to repeating himself like a traumatized child: "It's a mother's place to raise a child," he chants.

Enforced voyeurism also shows up again in Sybil's life, when Sybil watches her mother sexually abuse the small children Hattie babysat for on Sundays and witnesses Hattie masturbating the adolescent, but "lower crust," lesbians at the beach. And medical records indicate forms of more recognizable child abuse: "The dislocated shoulder, the fractured larynx, the burned hand, the bead in the nose, [nearly suffocating in] the wheat crib, the black eyes, the swollen lips." Through this "training," Sybil developed other aftereffects associated with incest: eating disorders, time and memory lapses that eventually convert into MPD, the acting out of particular scenes (Peggy Lou, who breaks glass in an effort to escape Hattie's kitchen; "the blonde" who hurls herself against walls and glass doors trying to escape traumatic blows to the body);

the deep shame regarding her body and her inability to stay present; the inability to feel anger because, even after her death, Hattie won't allow it; the unexplained neurological disorders; the transference of fear from the perpetrator to the objects of abuse; and the fear of intimacy and people. Also evident was Sybil's repressed rage at the teachers who never ask, the grandparents who live above the kitchen and never hear, the family physician who knows but never tells, the father who pretends never to notice, and the religion that declares, to quote the title of Alice Miller's excellent book, "Thou shalt not be aware" of parental abuse.

With the whole culture behind her, the abusive mother is entirely unreadable; she becomes visible only when we read her through her daughter's aftereffects, such as MPD.

In *The Flock: The Autobiography of a Multiple Personality,* Joan Casey, the personality recuperated by therapist Lynn Wilson, experiences a childhood similar to Sybil's. Lynn, a social worker at a university clinic, expresses anxiety over her lack of medical credentials and consults Cornelia Wilbur, leaning on Dr. Wilbur to guide her through the process of Joan's therapy and integration. The narrative of *The Flock* is held together by this intertextual therapy-driven matriarchy: Cornelia Wilbur "mothers" Lynn Wilson, who "mothers" Joan Casey; Joan reads *Sybil* with an obsession, feels Sybil is an older sister, and encourages Joan to model Dr. Wilbur's therapy/parenting approach. (Dr. Wilbur denies that she ever used a "parenting" approach, and insists that the narrator, Flora Schreiber, embellished this role for the purpose of creating a good story.) Joan has twenty-four personalities, differing in age, gender, and sexual orientation. The personalities of Jo (withdrawn, academic, un-feminine), Renee (fun, sexual, personable), Missy (a needy six-year old), Iris (a lesbian), Joan Frances (suicidal over unrequited mother-worship), Rusty (an illiterate, misogynist boy), and Josie (a two-year-old who hurls herself into walls and through glass and, by so doing, constantly relives and performs her mother's physical abuse) function as primary storytellers in Joan Casey's life. Secrets abound in *The Flock.* Just as Sybil "quickly . . . reassured herself that what she didn't dare tell had not been told" because "she realized she would never be able to tell," so too Jo tells Lynn, "It's like I'm carrying around this huge secret that I'm never supposed to tell. But since I don't remember just what I'm supposed to keep secret, [I'm afraid] I'll tell it by mistake."

In *The Flock,* Joan's father was an incest perpetrator. Long before Missy tells Lynn that Joan was raped by her father and Josie replays the scene in Lynn's office (and breaks two of Lynn's ribs in the process), Joan's mother, Nancy, pooh-poohs her daughter's weakness, telling her, "Look at me. You don't see me running to a therapist with every little crisis. My stepfather abused me—you've seen the scars on my back from the beatings—and I came through it without a

therapist." Indeed, Joan Frances replays her mother's words in her therapist's office: "Joan Frances admitted no blankness, no multiplicity, but provided only vague statements about the ideal childhood her mother claimed she had." And while Jo has no early childhood memories of her mother and none of Missy's memories of rape, she does remember "happy" early childhood times with her father—playing driver of his car—until his erection intrudes: "Daddy's hardness under her buttocks and the hard steering wheel in her hands were equally part of the experience." In spite of father-daughter incest, Lynn (and eventually Joan) believes that her mother's physical brutality followed by emotional coldness before the age of two caused Joan's MPD. The alter Josie remembers this brutality and "desires" the repetition compulsion of blacking out by beating her head and body on the wall or floor: "One day when [Mother] screamed in rage at her two-year-old daughter, Josie found herself propelled against a wall. Josie, created in that instinctual certainty that she was about to die, remembered her terror and then a wonderful blackness that brought peace." So even though the father assumes the role of incest perpetrator in *The Flock,* it is the preverbal mother-daughter abuse that splits Joan into a multiple.

Joan embodies the abuse of the incestuous parent with the concomitant neglect and betrayal of the other parent. Unlike Sybil, who has no access to her alters when they talk with Dr. Wilbur, Joan hears the therapy sessions with Lynn, but does not have access to the behaviors of the alters when they take over the body. And so Joan watches Josie relive a rape scene, and then turns to Lynn and her husband Gordon (who becomes a co-therapist of "the flock," the term Joan uses to describe herself), saying: "Josie was raped by her father." Rusty, who hates women and is sure he will grow a penis in time to escape the body, emerges when Ray, Joan's father, initiates father-daughter camping trips. Rusty can't read because part of this incest ritual includes the "woods game," a chase of entrapment when Ray writes his lust for his daughter in the sand with his urine, which he then forces his daughter, who transmogrifies into the illiterate Rusty, to read. The frustration Rusty feels for his inability to perform the task of reading overshadows the body's fear of incest. Importantly, Rusty is raped by words he cannot read, as is evident in his repetition compulsion during therapy with Gordon (whom he calls "Dad"): "The words . . . they're everywhere, Dad. The words, Dad. They're gonna cut me. They're gonna kill me." Screaming castration anxiety, Rusty turns into Josie, and Gordon watches as Joan relives the feeling of being "cut" open with Ray's penis, the instrument of the words in the sand.

Joan manifests aftereffects that don't make sense to her because the MPD-producing trauma predates the mirror stage, the organizing moment of narrative. But even though Nancy does not perpetrate incest against her daughter as Hattie does, it is her abuse that "splits" Joan because Joan feels she cannot afford escape—either physical or emotional—from her mother.

The narrator and the therapist in both *Sybil* and *The Flock* collude against the crazy biological mothers; in the course of therapy, they become surrogate mothers. This is a dangerous move, since all mothers function as potentially abusive mothers when mother-love and mother-abuse define mothering on any terms as something that daughters literally, painfully, need. Furthermore, because mother-daughter abuse often extends "normal" mother-daughter intrusions (such as excessive medicalization), mother-love is simultaneously lethal and necessary. Thus this alliance of narrator and therapist against the abusive mother in the "battle for the daughter" misreads the role of the therapist in recovery. Narrative positioning aligns the narrator (and audience) with the female therapists who assume the role of good mothers, castigate the abusive mothers as bad mothers, and retain the role of motherhood as an unproblematic one. This collusion breaks with a fundamental distance necessary, according to Judith Herman, for the empowerment of women in therapy. According to Herman (in chapter 7 of *Trauma and Recovery*), a feminist therapist should promise to bear witness, work in solidarity with the survivor, empower the survivor by making her responsible for her decisions and for her truth-telling. But once the feminist-therapist asks for emotional support from the survivor in the form of devotion and mother-love, a dangerous boundary has been transgressed, a line Lynn Wilson has clearly crossed.

This transgression occurs because of the transference and counter-transference in therapy (processes whereby unconscious wishes and needs are swapped between client and therapist) and because, isolated, Lynn as therapist-mother starts to undergo a secondary victimization, taking on Joan's pain, isolation, and secrecy. The problem begins because Lynn feels isolated in her place of work. She makes it clear that her supervisor does not "believe" in MPD and that she is then unable to include him in the diagnostic process. Lynn writes: "The lack of support I feel among my colleagues makes me unwilling to talk with them about this case. . . . I have been taking my own uncertainty and excitement home." Lynn here manifests a particularly dangerous counter-transference; she imagines herself indispensable, the all-loving mother who alone knows what Joan needs and stands with her multiple patient against the world. This counter-transference makes Lynn take on the role of rescuer when Joan needs to learn how to help herself. Judith Herman refers to just such a therapist-patient relationship when she describes a therapist who

> come[s] to feel that she is the only one who really understands the patient, and she may become arrogant and adversarial with skeptical colleagues. As she feels increasingly isolated and helpless, the temp-

tations of either grandiose action or flight become irresistible. Sooner or later she will indeed make serious errors. It cannot be reiterated too often: *no one can face trauma alone.* If a therapist finds herself isolated in her professional practice, she should discontinue working with traumatized patients until she has secured an adequate support system. (*Trauma and Recovery;* Herman's italics)

Perhaps because *The Flock* is narrated through the journals that Lynn Wilson and Joan Casey kept throughout their six years of work together, no "error" of the kind Herman points to is disclosed. But the narrative ends abruptly with Lynn and Gordon's untimely death in a boating accident. With no (narrative) time to "process" this abandonment, *The Flock* concludes with Joan energized and alienated in her unresolved grief over her loss of the entire symbolic parental unit. This reader knows a crash and possible relapse will follow, but *The Flock* ends before such a crash occurs. Our last glimpse of Joan captures her with her husband, her son, and her tenure-track job, none of which inspires great confidence on my part.

The mother-therapist role becomes solidified when the abusive mothers, jealous of the therapists, participate in the therapist-patient relationship with their own transference. When Sybil's and Joan's mothers try to sabotage their daughters' relationships with their therapist, Dr. Wilbur and Lynn Wilson transmogrify into overly protective and threatened mothers themselves. This also functions as a kind of transference, where the crazy mothers' desire to own their daughters is projected onto the therapists themselves, who unwittingly become the characters they oppose. It is here that the therapists threaten to become "phallic mothers," as the fantasy of the phallic mother is to be everything for the child. While Dr. Wilbur shows more restraint, Lynn Wilson becomes energized and excited by her role as a surrogate mother for Joan, as is evident when she speculates in her journal:

> Gordon's and my success so far is beyond my wildest dreams. We are not only providing what the various personalities need at various times; we are also modeling good parenting and a healthy marriage for all of them. Jo and Missy both watch me carefully to see how I'll respond to their enjoyment of Gordon. Unlike her mother, I'm not envious of the relationship they have. In some respects, the mother role is not a new transition, just one newly recognized. I've known for two years of cuddling Missy and the other very young personalities that I was providing healthy maternal love. Although Renee would never accept hearing this, I mother her as well, using what I learned when my own daughters were teenagers. Like any wise mother of a teenager, I allow Renee to depend on my counsel without ever drawing attention to the

fact of her dependency. Mothering Jo is a joy, if for no other reason than her beginning to realize that, even within her own limited personality, she is a lovely young woman whom I am proud to call my daughter.

By becoming a mother again, Lynn can avoid her mid-life slump. Lynn steps into the role of motherhood without recognizing that this same social role aided and abetted Joan's trauma. Playing out the good daughter role she knows so well, Joan accepts these new parents, referring to Lynn and Gordon as her "therapist-parents." Lynn thinks of the post-integration Joan with the same "marvel [she] felt in seeing [her] first grandchild." And while Cornelia Wilbur is maternal in her own way, in her "exorcism" of Hattie Dorsett she also positions herself as the protective mother-replacement: "I'm helping you to grow up,' the doctor would [say]. 'You're getting better, and you're going to be able to use all your talents.' The incantation, the exorcising of Hattie Dorsett, would proceed: 'Your mother taught you not to believe in yourself. I'm going to help you do so.'" And here we see the ultimate danger, the feminist therapist who colludes with the patriarchal idealization of motherhood: pitting women against each other in a duel that allows the good mother to assume the very same role that constituted the evil mother and that fed her sadism. Indeed, it is the role of motherhood that conceals and therefore conditions this abuse.

By not confronting the category of motherhood and only identifying the individuals that occupy social spaces as the agents of transgression, both texts assume as neutral and natural that Hattie and Nancy were simply evil anomalies of motherhood. When Joan attempts a confrontation with her mother, through Joan's selected omission we see how she still feels trapped by her mother's expectations that she will not "remember" her mother's abuse. After telling Nancy that Ray molested and raped her, and then "steeling [herself] for [Nancy's] angry denial," Joan is amazed when her mother says: "it makes sense" and "I didn't know" and "your father always had sexual problems." Importantly, Joan doesn't ask Nancy to take responsibility for her abusive behavior. Both Dr. Wilbur and Joan advance misdirected confrontations that serve to protect the mother-roles that the mother-therapists have now assumed. It should be recalled that when Dr. Wilbur confronts Willard, Sybil isn't even in the room to hear and see herself vindicated. In Joan's case, she doesn't confront Nancy with the issue that she has spent most of her therapy dollars addressing—the physical and verbal abuse Nancy hurled at her daughter, beginning at her birth when Joan was not the boy her mother wanted, and continuing throughout Joan's adulthood until Lynn "saves" her.

These misdirected confrontations echo the problems raised by replacing the evil mothers with the good mother-therapists. Confronting the role of motherhood threatens to destroy the power of the mother-daughter relationship that Joan

and Sybil have with their therapists. Thus Joan and Sybil both become their therapists' "more-than-daughters," their narratives tying together incestuously. Mothers may die, but daughters may never be autonomous, self-generating women. Importantly, these feminist therapists do not question the role of motherhood because it threatens their place vis-à-vis their new daughters. Indeed, the signal aftereffect of mother-daughter incest after MPD is the very symbiotic dynamic that sets up the potential abuse: the utter impossibility of maintaining separate boundaries between mother and daughter. Bass and Davis quote one survivor of mother-daughter incest on this point: "For a while I didn't know where my mother left off and I began. I thought she had a psychic hold on me. I was convinced she knew every thought I had. It was like she was in my body, and she was evil. I felt I was possessed, that I was going to be taken over. I've had a real fear that if I look at all that stuff that I don't like about myself, it will be my mother inside of me."

Women's true crime novels that feature MPD daughters also feature a war of the mothers; the Gothic element of this war is made manifest when daughters never connect the abuser with the social role that commands that abuse.

Because heterosexism foundationalizes the theories that describe cultural practices, mother-daughter abuse still cannot be narrated. Father-daughter incest is almost always portrayed as an act of sexual seduction and therefore "normalized" as an obvious extension of heterosexual practice; but abusive mothers are doubly veiled, first by the power they wield and second by a culture blinded by the stereotype of mother-love. Yet although women's true crime novels offer a cultural repository for this unnarrativizable power, they do not expose the abusive mother per se; they reveal her as evil in comparison to the nurturant feminist psychotherapist who emerges at the novel's end as the good mother. What gets lost in this war of the mothers is the voices of the multiple daughters, who always speak from some mother's abyss. In both the genre of women's true crime and the discourse of the contemporary feminist recovery movement, evil mothers assume the position of an individual's problem, not a social one. Because MPD offers an important entrance into subject construction, feminist theory would do well to position daughters outside the mother's script and to read the potential abusive power inherent in the role of motherhood, instead of concealing this power in the romanticized social stereotype that refuses to name the open secret of mother-daughter bond(age).

Brenda Herrmann (essay date 3 February 1994)

SOURCE: "The Interest in Murder Multiplies But Serial Killer Buffs Say It's Not a Crime to Be Fascinated with the Dark Side of Human Nature," in *Chicago Tribune*, February 3, 1994, p. 1.

[*In the essay below, Herrmann considers society's interest in serial killers and true crime. Herrmann argues that the growing interest among teenagers and young adults stems from their desire to shock adults.*]

Who's your favorite serial killer? Jeffrey Dahmer? John Wayne Gacy? Ed Gein?

Or, if you're really in the know, maybe you'd say Jerome Brudos, Aileen Wuornos, Robert Hansen or the tag team of Leonard Lake and Charles Ng.

Whether such discussion over serial killers seems strange—or even sick—it's not all that uncommon.

In fact, with all the recent hoopla over the Charles Manson song on the latest Guns N' Roses album, the fascination with serial killers, which was once just a thing for true crime buffs, has become a mainstream craze—and big business.

There are Charles Manson T-shirts (and infant wear), encyclopedias of killers, a Time/Life book series on true crime, cassette books featuring the actual taped confessions of the likes of Texas serial killer Henry Lee Lucas, and a whole host of tabloid TV shows and talk shows offering daily doses of the latest deadly flavor of the month. Gacy's paintings even hang in art galleries.

So if you think Axl Rose is the only person with a penchant for psychos, think again. He's just the latest to take heat for the hobby.

"It's a fascination with people who step over the line," explains Valarie Jones, 33, serial killer buff and creator of the infamous True Crime Trading Cards, which immortalizes serial killers in full-color cards.

And, with stories of violence more prevalent every day, young people seem to be drawn to these twisted tales. Publishers of true crime books say there is a very strong teen and young adult market for serial killer publications.

Michaela Hamilton, 45, vice president at Simon & Schuster, handles the true crime division of the company. She chalks up the serial killer craze among young people as being part of pop culture.

"We have a generation of kids who grew up on stories of violence and crime and Gacy and Manson, just like they grew up on *The Brady Bunch*," she says, noting that her own fascination with the genre started when she read Truman Capote's *In Cold Blood* in junior high.

"Each generation has gotten progressively rougher, tougher and a little more in-your-face," Jones adds. "When you mix

that with the natural desire for young people to rebel against society, it's not surprising they love to shock their elders by debating over the 'coolest' serial killers."

Elders aren't just shocked—some, especially church groups, have protested products like the cards because they believe they are dangerous to young people's minds.

Dr. Bennett Leventhal, chairman of psychiatry at University of Chicago, disagrees.

"A fascination with killers certainly doesn't mean the crime buff will become the criminal," Leventhal says. "It's curiosity for sure and there's also a certain thrill readers get out of following the killer as he stalks and the police chase and the body count builds. . . . Some people are interested in jumping out of planes, some people read about serial killers. I certainly wouldn't check somebody into the psychiatric ward for that."

Besides, according to fans and publishers, criminals provide ideal plot lines.

"These books provide a very dramatic format for the battle between good and evil, which has always fascinated humankind," Hamilton says. "By reading them we get an insight. We may never understand what causes a person to commit murder, but trying to find out is what draws people to the genre."

Since 1966, when *In Cold Blood* was published, the interest in true crime has steadily increased.

Books like *The Want-Ad Killer* by Ann Rule (about Washington state killer Harvey Carignan, who slaughtered women he met through classified ads), have been best-sellers in both hardcover and paperback. Made-for-TV movies on the Son of Sam (David Berkowitz), the Hillside Stranglers (Kenneth Bianchi and Angelo Buono) and Bundy received high ratings.

True crime books sales kept increasing until 1990, when "a glut of poor product"—or overkill—turned off some fans, according to *Publishers Weekly*. Even so, only hardcover sales suffered and paperbacks kept selling.

With the story of Jeffrey Dahmer, serial killers went from just being of interest to the true crime fan to making the cover of *People* magazine in August 1991.

"All five books on Jeffrey Dahmer did well because the public has an insatiable need to look at the dark side of criminal activity," says Paul Dinas, executive editor at Zebra Books.

From Dahmer on, the public didn't feel the need to hide

their interest anymore, Jones notes. "Something that had been secretly read and talked about among buffs is now out in the open, at least to an extent," Jones says. "Teenagers and younger people especially get fascinated by the whole subject and that bothers some people. I mean, people still get outraged at some of the publicity these killers get, like the Guns N' Roses thing or the trading cards."

Jones is referring to Guns N' Roses 1992 *The Spaghetti Incident.* The last song on the disc, which is not mentioned in the song list, is "Look at Your Game, Girl," written by Charles Manson. At the end of the tune, Rose takes a deep breath and sighs, "Thanks, Chas."

When it became known that Manson, who was convicted of the murders of actress Sharon Tate and six others in 1969, would earn about $60,000 in royalties for every million copies of the album sold, Rose was taken to task by newspaper columnists, angry relatives of victims and even by the president of his record label, David Geffen, who said he had no knowledge that the extra song was even on the album.

"The fact that Manson would be earning money based on the fame he derived committing one of the most horrific crimes of the 20th Century is unthinkable to me," Geffen said in a released statement, where he noted that he had personally known two of the victims of the Manson massacre.

Within a week of the uproar, Geffen announced that Manson would receive no royalties and the money would go to the son of one of his victims instead, based on a 1971 court judgment regarding any money Manson may receive in the future. Geffen also said that the track would be pulled from future pressings of the GNR album. Rose followed up by saying he would donate any money he earned performing the song to an environmental group.

Rose also said in a letter released by his record company that he "just liked the song's melody and lyrics" but thought Manson to be "a sick individual."

Rose isn't the only rocker to have a penchant for Manson, however.

White Zombie bassist Sean Yseult, 26, is a true crime buff and says her fascination with killers is fueled by the lure of the dark side that lurks in all of us.

"Serial killers are part of American trash culture, the things that exist in every trailer park of this country but nobody wants to talk about," Yseult says. It's also such a common interest among bands and fans that it's always a great conversation piece, she says.

Members of underground bands like Blitzspeer have worn

Manson T-shirts for years in concerts. Evan Dando of The Lemonheads recorded a Manson song a few years back. As well, bands like Tad, The Jesus Lizard and Slayer (which recorded a song about Ed Gein), have all professed a prurient interest in serial killers. There's even a band named Sharon Tate's Baby.

In the late '80s, an Arlington Heights rock group named Macabre released a theme album about serial killers.

According to Graham Carlton, an entertainment attorney and packager who worked with Macabre, rockers just "want to push that new envelope."

"Death is a fascinating subject," Carlton explains. "But I don't think Guns N' Roses are trying to make a hero out of Manson. Axl Rose has no motive other than to sell records and get noticed and you have to admit, the song has helped them do that."

Jones says by focusing on Manson's songs or image, "people assume you are making a hero out of him and condoning his actions.

"But I think true crime tales show the public that criminals do get caught. We're not saying Manson is a hero. We're saying he got caught."

Jones adds that her cards never call for leniency or worship of killers. "If anything, our cards show the need for punishment that sticks. We point out repeatedly that most serial killers are former offenders."

While Dr. Leventhal says that following the lifestyles of serial killers doesn't have any real psychological effect, fans and publishers have noted one change in their own lives since they were hooked by true crime.

"I'm much more cautious now," Hamilton says.

"I wouldn't even put an ad in the paper when I wanted to sell my air-conditioner. I mean, I read *The Want-Ad Killer*!"

James Hitchcock (essay date Spring 1994)

SOURCE: "Murder as One of the Liberal Arts," in *American Scholar,* Vol. 63, Spring, 1994, pp. 277-85.

[*In the following essay, Hitchcock examines the history of true-crime writing as well as famous historical murders. Hitchcock argues that the genre, as well as crimes, changed after World War II.*]

When, more than 150 years ago, Thomas De Quincey enthroned murder as one of the fine arts, he did not mean the detective stories that would soon become an established genre of popular fiction, but actual crimes of the kind that dominate the popular press for a brief period, then are replaced by new atrocities.

Because they are "news," crime stories (used here to mean accounts of historical events) tend to be ephemeral and seldom attain the status of classics in the way that detective stories (here meaning fiction) sometimes do. Arthur Conan Doyle has a permanent place in the pantheon of famous writers, and Agatha Christie, Ellery Queen, Rex Stout, and a few others have realistic possibilities for minor immortality. But the names of Edmund Pearson, William Roughead, or Jonathan Goodman are totally unknown, except to the small coterie of those devoted to De Quincey's art.

Even the best crime stories are difficult to find, even in libraries or in bookstores that stock hundreds of detective stories. Only within the past few years have larger stores installed "true crime" sections, where, if one is lucky, the browser might find three or four classics amid dozens of sensationalistic accounts of the horrors of the past two decades. "True crime" apparently has become a more popular genre in recent years, but in the exact sense of "news"—publishers exploiting cases prominent in recent headlines or television clips, and featuring gore and sex.

The genuine crime story is simply a branch of history and should be treated as such. While literary merit is highly desirable, and drama welcome if it does not distract from the narrative, the true afficionado's desire is simply to know, and this requires careful, scrupulous, systematic narrative and analysis. While there can be responsible accounts of contemporary crimes in the same way that there can be responsible journalism on any subject, most true-crime reports are the equivalent of tabloid news.

Hence the afficionado somewhere draws a line marking a chronological boundary: the cases before a certain date merit serious attention, while later ones are required to undergo the usual fermentation and the test of changing tastes. That line is now best drawn at roughly the time of World War II. The connoisseur realizes that sensational cases have been coming much thicker and faster in recent decades, which is a major reason for reserving judgment on which should be taken as classics.

"Serial killers" have perhaps always done their work. But the explosion of recent ones—John Wayne Gacy, Theodore Bundy, Dean Coryll, Son of Sam, the Zodiac Killer, Jeffrey Dahmer, and a dozen more—far exceed the number that can be dredged up through even the most diligent historical research. Something, whatever it may be, has obviously happened to make this possible.

In many ways Victorian crimes continue to be the most fascinating, precisely because of the contrast between the stark evil of murder and the stiff respectability of the larger society. The Jack the Ripper murders still fascinate, as they did in 1888, partly because of the contrast between snug rooms with blazing fires, curtains drawn against the fog, and menacing horrors perpetrated amidst flickering gaslights in hidden nooks of the city. If the Victorians had not been so apparently upright, their misdeeds would be far less interesting. (The peculiar fascination of Victorian crimes, as distinct from those that came before and after, may also have something to do with the young science of photography, which rendered murderers and victims alike in blurry black and white, often with unnatural stares on their faces, in contrast to the graceful drawings of an earlier period and better photographs since.)

> **The genuine crime story is simply a branch of history and should be treated as such. . . . While there can be responsible accounts of contemporary crimes in the same way that there can be responsible journalism on any subject, most true-crime reports are the equivalent of tabloid news.**
>
> **—James Hitchcock**

Great crimes have of course been perpetrated since the beginning of history, but until the nineteenth century it is rare to find information sufficient to generate real interest. The case of Arden of Faversham, which inspired an anonymous Elizabethan play, contains interesting points of detection, but only the bare outline survives, as is true of the murder of Christopher Marlowe, for example.

Perhaps the first genuine classic is the murder, in 1678, of Edmund Berry Godfrey, a London magistrate, a sensational case at the time and one about which a good deal of information survives. But, if it belongs on the list of classics, it is a forerunner. One or two eighteenth-century cases might be considered, but it was in the nineteenth century that the crime classic came into its own, just as the detective story did.

The *Newgate Calendar* and other such sources provide a great deal of information about eighteenth-century crimes, but the compilers' interests tended to be a combination of sensationalism and moralizing, and the reader is often frustrated and tantalized by the absence of crucial information and a failure to explain enigmas. The same is true of the hardy genres of pamphlets, ballads, and broadsheets, whose factual reliability is furthermore highly suspect.

But if the classic crime itself is largely a nineteenth-century development, there are no classic works of crime writing before World War I, not even De Quincey's superficial early essays. Not only is this genre less commercially successful than its fictional counterpart, it has also been slower in developing.

The Godfrey case is an uncertain entry in the list of classics because it is necessary to draw a line between "mere" crime on the one hand and professional crime and political crime on the other. All three have their fascinations, but the motives in the latter two are much different from those in the first. The actions of professional criminals may hold drama and horror but usually lack mystery and, in any case, lack the ingredient already noticed—fascination with ordinary people doing horrendous things. Political crime—assassinations, terrorism, spying—has endless ramifications (for example, the Sacco-Vanzetti case) that impede an objective solution. Part of the fascination of the Godfrey case is that, while he may well have been murdered as part of the grim political fraud called the Popish Plot, he may also have been killed by a vengeful former defendant in his court, the very uncertainty of motive adding greatly to the fascination of the case. (Interestingly, the case of the only assassinated prime minister in British history—Spencer Percival in 1811—was not a political crime but was motivated by a personal grievance.)

The appeal of crime stories over detective stories is the same as the appeal of historical events over novels—the fact that something actually happened. A fertile imagination can concoct almost anything, to the point where the feat soon loses its dazzle, whereas lasting fascination attaches to events that really did occur.

In many ways Victorian crimes continue to be the most fascinating, precisely because of the contrast between the stark evil of murder and the stiff respectability of the larger society.

—James Hitchcock

Devotees of the crime story suffer a major disability beyond the difficulty of finding books—the stock of classics is finite, with only an occasional rediscovery of a lost case or a challenging new interpretation of a familiar one, even as fiction writers churn out an endless series of fresh works for the addicted reader.

Detection is a major part of the crime story's appeal, but the operative principles are quite different from those of the detective story. The detective novelist puts into the story precisely what the reader requires, thus creating a finite and manageable world. The crime writer, on the other hand, often does not know for certain which information is truly relevant, or he has not searched far enough. The actual detectives themselves may have been deficient in the same respect, so that important information is permanently or temporarily lost. Whereas the last page of each detective story marks a definitive solution to the puzzle, each new book about crime tends to prepare the ground for yet further ones, which either produce new facts or reinterpret familiar ones. The author of a crime story is only a provisional detective, subject to being overruled by later writers or even by the readers themselves.

In detective stories every piece of information is significant. If a paper clip is found on the floor, it will turn out either to help explain the crime or to be a misleading clue. In life, on the other hand, many facts surrounding an event are irrelevant and even professional detectives err in sifting the important from the misleading. Whereas the world of the detective story is closed, that of the crime story is practically infinite, and serious investigators must cast their nets wider and wider in search of knowledge. (Thus Jonathan Goodman, perhaps the best crime-story writer ever, solves old cases mainly by tracing the characters of the drama in contexts outside the crime itself—their past lives, their social circles, their histories after the crimes were committed.) In principle no case will ever be closed, because there is always the possibility of discovering new information or seeing the old in a new way.

If one uses fifty years as the minimum time a case must retain its interest, the following are the classics of the genre, in order of excellence:

1. The murder of Julia Wallace, Liverpool, 1931. The wife of an insurance agent was battered to death in her parlor. Her husband, Herbert, was convicted, but his conviction was overturned on appeal.

2. The Borden murders, Massachusetts, 1892. The elderly Andrew and Abigail Borden were hacked to death in their home. Lizzie, Andrew's daughter and Abigail's stepdaughter, was tried and acquitted.

3. The Jack the Ripper killings, London, 1888. A series of prostitutes (five, by most reckonings) were strangled and mutilated in the slums of East London. No one was ever charged.

4. The Road Hill House murder, Wiltshire, 1860. An infant, Francis Kent, was found dead with his throat cut in an outhouse. Some years later his half-sister Constance confessed and served a long prison term.

5. The Croydon poisonings, Surrey, 1928. Over a period of several months three members of the same family, in two different households—mother, daughter, and another daughter's husband—died by arsenic poison. No one was ever charged.

6. The Gorse Hall murder, Cheshire, 1909. An intruder burst into the home of the wealthy George Harry Storrs and stabbed him to death after a fierce struggle. Servants and family members at different times identified two different young men as the killer, both of whom were tried and acquitted.

7. The Gatton murders, Queensland, 1898. Three siblings named Murphy, driving home from a village dance, were lured or forced into a field and shot to death, the two women being raped. No one was ever charged.

8. The murder of Sir Edmund Berry Godfrey, London, 1678. After hearing evidence related to the alleged Popish Plot, Godfrey disappeared and was found battered and stabbed to death in the country. Several Catholics were executed for alleged complicity, but they were probably scapegoats.

9. The Hall-Mills murders, New Jersey, 1922. An Episcopal minister and a woman of his parish were shot and mutilated in a "lovers' lane," their love letters scattered about the bodies. Edward Hall's wife and two of her relatives were tried and acquitted.

10. The murder of William Desmond Taylor, Hollywood, 1922. A film producer was shot to death in his house, with numerous ancillary mysteries following. No one was ever charged.

11. The Tichbourne claimant, London, 1865. An Australian butcher claimed to be the lost heir to a British title and fortune. After two lengthy trials he was imprisoned for perjury.

12. The Elwell murder, New York, 1920. Joseph Bowne Elwell, man-about-town, was found shot to death in his living room. No one was ever charged.

13. The New Orleans axeman, 1918. During a period of several months, more than a dozen people were killed or menaced by a mysterious figure who broke through doors with an axe and attacked his victims in their beds. No one was ever charged.

14. The abandonment of the *Mary Celeste,* the Atlantic, 1872. An American cargo ship was found under full sail but totally abandoned, with no sign of violence. No official solution was ever offered.

15. The disappearance of Elizabeth Canning, London, 1753. A young woman disappeared from home for a month, then reappeared to say that she had been held prisoner by gypsies. The gypsies were eventually freed, and Canning was convicted of perjury and transported to Connecticut.

16. The Sandyford murder, Glasgow, 1863. A housemaid, Jessie M'Pherson, was battered to death in a kitchen. A fellow servant, Jessie M'Laghlan, was convicted and served a long prison term.

17. The burning of Evelyn Foster, Northumberland, 1931. A young woman who drove cars for hire was found near death in a field, she and her car severely burned. She claimed to have been raped and set on fire by a male passenger. No one was ever charged.

18. The Lindbergh kidnapping, New Jersey, 1932. The infant son of the great aviator was kidnapped from his nursery and later found murdered in a field. A German immigrant, Bruno Hauptmann, was executed for the crime.

19. The Edalji case, Staffordshire, 1903. George Edalji, son of the Indian vicar of a rural English parish, was imprisoned for animal mutilation and sending anonymous threatening letters. Arthur Conan Doyle later obtained his exoneration.

20. The Oscar Slater case, Glasgow, 1908. The elderly Marion Gilchrist was battered to death in her flat. Her maid and a neighbor saw the murderer leaving, and the maid identified him as Gilchrist's nephew, a prominent physician. The police rejected her claim and persuaded her instead to identify the German immigrant Oscar Slater, who was sent to prison. Some years later he also was released through the efforts of Conan Doyle.

All these cases have in common a central mystery that has retained its fascination over the decades. In most cases the murderer is unknown, or at least there is insufficient evidence.

But a case does not have to be unsolved to retain its fascination. Lizzie Borden, despite her acquittal, almost certainly killed her parents. The fascination lies in her motive, in the psychology whereby an upright spinster could brutally slaughter two people and retain her aplomb, and certain loose ends in the case make it barely conceivable that she was not guilty (for example, a mysterious man or men seen loitering near the Borden house on the morning of the murders). Frances Hall and her kin perhaps did commit murder, although the evidence was certainly insufficient to convict.

Conversely, legal conviction by no means settles a matter, as the Wallace case shows. Jessie M'Laghlan was probably no more than an accomplice after the fact to a murder committed by an elderly member of the family of her employers, and she may have been completely innocent.

Like other classics, each case possesses certain almost indefinable features that elevate it above the crimes that routinely crowd the mass media. If Elizabeth Canning was not held prisoner by gypsies, neither was she probably simply lying, and no one ever discovered what in fact she was doing for a month. The Gorse Hall case has many fascinating dimensions, including the fact that Storrs expected an attack and probably recognized his killer but refused to identify him with his dying breath, and that witnesses who saw the assailant at close range for some minutes managed to identify two different suspects at different times. (This was possibly the only classic murder case in which two different defendants were both acquitted.)

In the Tichbourne case half the evidence seemed to show that the claimant was genuine, half that he was a fraud. How the Gatton victims were persuaded to enter a dark field remains an enigma, but the case was given immortality by a contemporary hint (probably wrong) that the murderer was another member of the family. The police believed that Evelyn Foster set fire to herself, a belief vehemently rejected by her friends and family.

The Road Hill case involves little mystery—Constance Kent probably did murder her half-brother, out of hatred of her stepmother, although there are intriguing scraps of evidence that point to their father. But it is perhaps the only crime story which of itself rises above the genre and becomes a moving human tragedy, worthy of the artistry of a Greek dramatist.

Some cases fail of being classics simply because there is not enough information, for example, the murder of Sarah Meservy in Tenants Harbor, Maine, in 1877. The middle-aged woman lay strangled in her house for thirty-eight days in a village of only eighty people before her disappearance began to attract notice, and what followed was a carnival of weird anonymous letters and mysterious figures on the beach. A sea captain, Nathan Hart, was arrested and died in prison, but there are many unanswered questions.

The Wallace case remains preeminent in part because it resembles a detective story and would have been a worthy challenge to Hercule Poirot. As one commentator put it, if Herbert Wallace was not guilty, the man who committed the murder was a criminal genius and, thanks to the work of Jonathan Goodman and another writer, Roger Wilkes, that genius is now known to have been a man named Gordon Parry, an insurance agent whom Wallace had caught embezzling. Parry managed to lure Wallace away from home, murder Julia, and skillfully arrange the details to make Wallace look guilty. No writer of detective stories has ever produced a more enthralling tale, as conceded by no less an authority than Raymond Chandler, who said, "The Wallace Case is tops. It will always be tops."

The Croydon poisonings also resemble a detective story, set as they were in a small community and involving complex family relationships. Richard Whittington-Egan's book on the subject, *The Riddle of Birdhurst Rise,* is quite interesting but seriously flawed by the fact that he uncritically accepted the views of one of the two surviving natural suspects, who was understandably anxious to incriminate the other.

Crime naturally reflects the style of the age. Victorian London had, besides Jack the Ripper, more than its share of Gaslight Ghouls who could easily be the subject of Christopher Lee films—Dr. Thomas Neill Cream, who looked like a stage villain and stalked the dark streets giving poison pills to prostitutes; Kate Webster a maid who killed her elderly female employer, rendered her remains, and carried the woman's head around with her in a gladstone bag; and Mary Eleanore Pearcy, who murdered a romantic rival and the woman's infant daughter, placed their bodies in a perambulator, and trundled them for miles through the streets before dumping them at distant locations.

In the same era America provided plots sufficient for a series of Bette Davis-Joan Crawford films: the first woman to die in the electric chair, Martha Place, who hid in a closet and set upon her stepdaughter with vitriol and an axe; Theodore Durrant, who murdered two young women in a San Francisco church, hiding one body in the belfry and placing the other in plain view where the ladies' society would come upon it; and the Wardlaws, three weird but wealthy sisters who drowned a young relative in a bathtub.

Detective-story readers speak of the Golden Age between the two world wars, when the classic pattern of fictional detection was set. Obligingly the age produced its real cases: Elvira Barney, a Mayfair "bright young thing" who shot her lover (an accident, she claimed successfully) amidst stories of sex and drug orgies; Starr Faithfull (her real name), a glamorous but unstable woman found drowned on a Long Island beach; and the Taylor and Elwell cases.

Afficionados of the genre will immediately notice in the above list of classics which old warhorses have been put out to pasture—Dr. Palmer, Madeleine Smith, the Bravo case, Adelaide Bartlett, Florence Maybrick, Dr. Crippen, the Brides in the Bath, the Rattenbury case, the Snyder-Gray case, and the Thompson-Bywaters case, among others.

In most of these cases there is little doubt as to the murderer. Except for Palmer and the Brides in the Bath, each involved a love triangle, which usually does not produce a classic— the motives are too obvious to be intriguing, and the killer often acts under an emotional impulse which prevents dramatic tension from building up. The combination of murder and illicit love is an infallible formula for popularity, but for that very reason it produces cases that are famous mainly for being famous, automatically recycled in every new anthology of crime stories. Such cases are often interesting for what they reveal of the sexual mores of a particular age, but not as crimes in themselves.

Curiously, perhaps the most famous of all cases—Jack the Ripper—does not conform to most of the established rules. Serial killing has become so familiar that today the case would attract little beyond local notice and would be forgotten after a year. That it terrified London for decades and entered the realm of folklore was due in part to something extraneous— letters to the police signed "Jack the Ripper," which may not have been from the killer at all.

The detective story has been called a conservative genre in that it requires that society's laws be enforced. In crime stories, that often does not happen. But in both genres readers have a decided preference for respectable villains—murder in waterfront taverns holds little interest either in fact or in fiction. The purported diary of Jack the Ripper, published in 1993, rather implausibly identifies him as James Maybrick, a Liverpool cotton broker who was the victim in a famous poisoning case. (His wife was sent to prison, but he may have poisoned himself.) The authenticity of the book will be long debated, and until it is authenticated the most likely candidate as Jack is an obscure Polish immigrant who died in an asylum, a figure traced by Martin Fido and several other writers. Once it is accepted that the Ripper was not a sophisticated lunatic taunting the public, was not even a respectable attorney, much less Queen Victoria's grandson, a good deal of the inherent interest of the case evaporates.

Yet it has been raised to the level of immortality precisely because of the attention lavished on it. No other case has spawned a full-blown literary industry as the Ripper has— more than a dozen books (most in the past thirty years) written with a remarkable diligence of investigation and attention to detail, each adding at least a few new pieces to the familiar mosaic, every point endlessly scrutinized and debated, making it altogether in some ways the most intriguing of all crime stories, whatever its inherent limits.

Since crime stories are a species of historical writing, they contribute to the stock of historical knowledge in ways not necessarily related to crime, because they give intimate glimpses into people's lives. Legal cases, civil or criminal, force people to reveal the details of their lives in ways they would not normally do, and in ways professional historians seldom bother to record, so that every crime story lays out a small world of customs, relationships, and emotional ties not otherwise accessible—the eating habits of the Borden family, who kept feeding on the same roast of mutton day after day in the stifling August heat; the fact that in Victorian Maine a woman offended by a man's remarks showed her displeasure by pulling up his stiff shirt front (the Meservy

case); the ceaseless comings and goings, all night long, of the inhabitants of Victorian East London. Sometimes these cases yield knowledge contrary to logical assumption. Although Elizabeth Canning was a respectable young woman with much public support, London authorities from the beginning determined to give the accused gypsies justice, and they apparently did so. In 1915, for whatever reasons, the citizens of Atlanta preferred to believe that the Jewish factory manager Leo Frank killed a young employee named Mary Phagan rather than the black janitor who probably did it. (Frank was lynched.)

A disappointing conclusion from the study of crime stories is that historically there have been few great detectives. Until the mid-Victorian period there were no detectives at all, although when Godfrey's body was found in 1678, the village Dogberry who took charge of the case showed a certain sophistication in noting salient facts about its location and condition. The most famous English detective of the Victorian era, Jonathan Whicher, was forced into retirement during the Road Hill case when he expressed premature suspicion of Constance Kent. (He was the model for Sergeant Cuff in Wilkie Collins's *The Moonstone*.) The most famous Scotland Yard detective of the present century was perhaps Walter Dew, who wrote *I Caught Crippen*. But his dramatic capture of the mousy dentist after a transatlantic chase obscured the fact that Dew had originally botched the case, realizing that Crippen had murdered his wife only after the doctor had fled. The Glasgow police framed Oscar Slater, and in two English cases—Wallace and Edalji—the police willfully ignored evidence of innocence.

The greatest policemen have done well against professional criminals, but no actual detective had a brilliant record of solving "mere" crimes. (Eliot Ness, who performed so sensationally against Chicago gangsters, failed a few years later to solve the murders perpetrated in Cleveland by the Mad Butcher of Kingsbury Run.) Except for Conan Doyle, there has also never been an important case solved by a brilliant amateur. Perhaps the lone giant in the field of detection was the English pathologist Bernard Spilsbury, who testified in dozens of cases beginning with Crippen in 1910 and whom juries believed to be infallible.

Criminal fame is an unstable thing, the greatest professional criminals, like Al Capone, almost always becoming better known than the leading amateurs. Probably everyone has heard of Jack the Ripper, due mainly to the macabre name itself; and the ditty about Lizzie Borden's giving her mother forty whacks has helped insure her immortality. But probably few of the readers of the *New York Times* who used to rely on the detective story reviews of H. H. Holmes were aware that this was the pseudonym of Herman Webster Mudgett, perhaps America's greatest mass murderer (c. 1900) and Gaslight Ghoul of the first rank. (In Chicago he built a "murder castle" that included secret gas pipes, chutes, and dissecting rooms by which he could murder his female guests and dispose of their bodies.) So also Belle Gunness, the Indiana farmer of the same era, is largely unknown despite being perhaps America's greatest female mass murderer. (She lured men by matrimonial advertisements, then she killed them for their money and buried their bodies on her farm.)

Almost all the names here cited, including the entire list of classics, are Anglo-Saxons, predominantly English. In part this may be the stereotypical contrast between a snugly prosaic environment and the cheerful English character on the one hand and shocking evil on the other, a contrast that seems less pronounced in other national images. But the main reason is practical—accounts of crimes on the European Continent, much less outside the Western world, are very difficult to find in America, and any attempt to consider them comprehensively would inevitably fail.

Devotees of crime stories, unlike readers of detective stories, are often charged with having a taste for gore, presumably because most fictional murders are rather antiseptic. The charge, however, is unfair.

As in fiction, not all actual murders are bloody—the Croydon poisoning is among the most fascinating of cases—and the interest of a case does not rise in proportion to its brutality.

Strictly speaking there is no need for a criminal case to involve murder at all. A stolen penny might prove intriguing in terms of motives and methods, and in some ways disappearances are more intriguing than murders, since there is still another layer of mystery—whether the victim was or was not killed. (The most famous American disappearance, that of Judge Joseph Crater of New York in 1931, is omitted here because it was probably the work of professional criminals.) The Edalji case involved no crime worse than animal mutilation. Most of its fascination comes from the blood-curdlingly insane letters that the perpetrator sent to various people. The fate of the *Mary Celeste* may not have involved criminal action at all.

But the crime devotee must also admit that the quantity of blood is not wholly irrelevant, because brutal murders by seemingly ordinary people are more intriguing than other kinds. Lizzie Borden apparently tried to poison her parents, and had she succeeded she would probably now be forgotten. The extreme horror of her deed, in contrast to her own impeccable respectability, is what draws the spectator in and arouses curiosity about the hidden recesses of human nature.

As noted, until after World War I there was no proper literature of crime—both Jack the Ripper and Lizzie Borden waited decades for real books on their cases. In some ways Pearson, Roughead, and Lustgarten were giants, but, as with other art

forms, tastes were far different in their day. None of them did original research; they relied mainly on court testimony and newspaper accounts. Their purpose was frankly to entertain, which meant frequent witticisms, clever phrases, and a supercilious approach to the subject that suggested that both victim and perpetrator were rather ridiculous, an approach that allowed writers like James Thurber and Ring Lardner also to try their hands at the genre. (*The New Yorker's* St. Claire McKelway, who recorded "Annals of Crime," was interested mainly in professionals.) They seem to have been catering to readers who felt slightly uneasy at indulging what they felt was a prurient interest and who could justify it, as the crime writer Colin Wilson has suggested, by taking an attitude of superiority to the subject.

In a sense the "serious" approach to crime was pioneered by Conan Doyle, who researched and wrote detailed works on several cases in order to argue, successfully, the innocence of those convicted of the crimes.

The quality of crime writing has never been higher than in the last two decades, with Goodman, Bernard Taylor, Fido, and a number of others whose approach tends to be straightforward, detailed, factual, and meticulous, aimed at a solution to the mystery and not merely at an entertaining tale.

An honor roll of crime stories would include the following:

1. Bernard Taylor, *Cruelly Murdered*. A work worthy of its subject, the Road Hill Murder.

2. Victoria Lincoln, *A Private Disgrace: Lizzie Borden by Daylight*. A gripping and insightful book by a novelist who as a young girl knew the aged Lizzie by sight and understood the subtleties of Fall River society.

3. Jonathan Goodman, *The Killing of Julia Wallace*. A skillfully told account of the classic case, along with what is certainly the definitive solution.

4. John Dickson Carr, *The Murder of Sir Edmund Berry Godfrey*. An excursion by a detective novelist into the world of true crime, and a work of literary distinction. It should be supplemented by Stephen Knight's *The Killing of Justice Berry Godfrey*, which includes important new evidence.

5. Jonathan Goodman, *The Stabbing of George Harry Storrs*. An enthralling account of the neglected Gorse Hall case.

6. P. D. James and T. A. Critchley, *The Maul and the Pear Tree*. Another venture by a successful detective novelist into the field of true crime, in this case the Ratcliffe Highway murders in London in 1811, when burglars murdered two families in their homes a week apart.

7. James and Desmond Gibney, *The Gatton Mystery*. Publication of this book in an English series rescued this classic Australian crime from total oblivion in the northern hemisphere.

8. Sidney D. Kirkpatrick, *A Cast of Killers*. Fascinating account of the murder of William Desmond Taylor, based in part on the investigations of the film producer King Vidor.

9. William Kunstler, *The Minister and the Choir Singer*. The only comprehensive account of the Hall-Mills Case, although his solution lacks evidence and seems unlikely.

10. Christina Brand, *Heaven Knows Who*. A detective novelist's graceful account of the Sandyford Murder.

Not every great crime has produced its classic book. At least a half dozen of the books on Jack the Ripper are of high quality, but the field changes so quickly that none can be singled out, and the New Orleans axeman, on the whole a far more sinister figure than the Ripper but far less notorious, has never been the subject of a book. On the other hand, James and Critchley's investigations into the Ratcliffe Highway murders is a model of the genre far beyond the somewhat prosaic (by today's standards) nature of the crimes.

The omission of Colin Wilson from this list of honor requires justification, because no one has written more extensively about historic crime. Wilson sometimes shows brilliance, but his theories are usually too eccentric and speculative to be entirely helpful.

The great crime books of sixty years ago—Pearson, Roughead, Lustgarten—were the expatiations of gifted amateurs aiming to be amusing or provocative. The best crime writers today are historians, and they approach their tasks in that spirit. On the whole they succeed, and indeed their diligence, their ingenuity, and their thoroughness would shame many professional historians. Where they tend to fail, as might be expected, is in the larger historical generalizations—vague allusions to "Victorian hypocrisy" are a staple of crime writers trying to make their work "significant."

In general crime stories do not yield such significance and, while they do not lack historical meaning, it is seldom the kind that can be readily generalized. Writers with an ideological purpose tend to obscure as much as they enlighten, and William Kunstler's Hall-Mills book does not depend on his radical political philosophy. For post-1945 crimes the genre has been taken in new directions by Truman Capote's *In Cold Blood* and Norman Mailer's *The Executioner's Song*.

Those who develop a taste for crime stories may after a time want to swim on their own by plunging into the Notable British Trials Series, for which there is no American equiva-

lent. Here it is possible actually to become the detective through close attention to what witnesses had to say, straining to see aspects of the case that others have missed. This distinguished series, now defunct, was spotty, however, including some relatively uninteresting cases and omitting a number of others, such as Herbert Wallace and Constance Kent.

All the classic works above are books devoted to a single subject, which the genre absolutely requires. Given the fact that no one can be certain which facts are relevant to the crime, and given the author's obligation to be fair to the reader, crime writers should always err on the side of too much information rather than too little, so that even long essays are usually insufficient. (This in itself excludes most of the work of the trio of Pearson-Roughead-Lustgarten.)

Like most historical writing, crime stories tend to go through three phases—the first in which the author states what seems obvious (Pearson's *The Trial of Lizzie Borden*), the revisionist phase in which the errors of the first author are exposed and a new solution proposed (Edward Radin's *Lizzie Borden: The Untold Story*), and the post-revisionist phase which accepts the revisionist criticisms, points out their limitations, and offers a modified version of the original thesis (Lincoln's *A Private Disgrace*). The fascination of the Jack the Ripper Case lies partly in the fact that it has not followed this dialectic but has continued to lead in new and unexpected directions.

Omitted from the list of classics is one of America's most famous cases, the Black Dahlia Murder in Los Angeles in 1947, when the torso of a young woman was found on a vacant lot; she had been dismembered somewhere else after lengthy torture. The victim was Elizabeth Short, called the Black Dahlia after her style of dress.

The case marks the beginning of the modern era—the fact that the mutilations involved sadism and were not merely an attempt to hide the victim's identity; the fact that the murderer taunted the police by sending them the victim's personal papers; and the social context in which the deed took place—Short was an unsuccessful aspirant to film stardom, was estranged from her family in Massachusetts, and moved in the rootless circles of southern California in wartime and its direct aftermath. Modern killers have often been more brutal than most of their predecessors. and they have found it increasingly easy to carry on their work.

Classic crimes are indeed emotions recollected in tranquillity, like yellowed photographs or insects forever trapped in amber—fascinating and still capable of inducing a shiver, but safely quarantined from the viewer's emotional world, no longer able to provoke real terror.

Publishers Weekly (essay date 26 September 1994)

SOURCE: "Does True Crime Pay?," in *Publishers Weekly,* Vol. 241, September 26, 1994, p. 39.

[*In the essay below, the critic remarks on the publishing industry's views on true crime.*]

As recently as a year ago true crime was considered the hot genre in nonfiction mass market books. Now publishers question where the category is headed; many say it has run its course.

"True crime will move out of its cycle and become a less published area," declares Bantam's Irwyn Applebaum. "A lot of bad books were put out by a lot of greedy publishers in a short amount of time. After a while the titles get indistinguishable from one another."

"The category is not as big for anybody as it used to be," agrees Lou Aronica at Berkley. "The amount of titles being published has diminished the overall impact on the market. There was a time when these books sold several hundred thousand copies, now true crime is much more a category level kind of publishing and doesn't generate very big numbers."

Despite Aronica's concern about such titles, he continues to publish them with success. Citing the 100,000-copy advance of this spring's *The Murder of Bob Crane* by Robert Graysmith—which may be given a boost by Court TV as the new trial begins—Aronica comments, "I think the fact that the victim was a celebrity helped this book get out." In October Berkley will publish *Crossing the Line* by Lisa Beth Pulitzer and Joan Swirsky, about NYC serial killer Joel Rifkin.

Michaela Hamilton, v-p and editor-in-chief of Penguin USA's Signet and Onyx Books, remains optimistic. "I still have faith that the great books are going to rise to the top," says the publisher of such true crime bestsellers as Ann Rule's *Small Sacrifices* and Joe McGinniss's *Fatal Vision* and *Blind Faith,* which have all sold in the millions. "I agree that a lot of inferior products flooded the market, but I still think there's room for the right books."

At Warner Paperbacks, v-p and publisher Mel Parker notes, "We have never published very heavily in this area; being selective has paid off. I think the category can be shaky because of the proliferation of titles."

"With the exception of tried and proven authors like Ann Rule," says Pocket's Helene Atwan, "true crime does seem to be going down a little bit." Pocket's new hot true crime title is an Ann Rule original, *You Belong to Me,* which some weeks back reached the #2 spot on the *New York Times* bestseller list.

One reason for the category's decline is television, claims Dell's Leslie Schnur. "Once you can get true crime every night on TV you don't need to spend money for a book. So we choose our titles carefully. The category can still be profitable, but we don't expect the enormous numbers that we used to get."

But TV or not TV, industry players agree that the category is not going to disappear. "I think people are more fascinated than ever with the criminal justice system, partly because of its many imperfections," says Hamilton. "What publishers face is increasing competition from other media. With O.J. Simpson on the front of every magazine and newspaper, we have to seek out the enduring stories, those cases that are interesting enough that people will want to read 400 pages about them, rather than just one page in the newspaper."

Joseph Grixti (essay date Spring 1995)

SOURCE: "Consuming Cannibals: Psychopathic Killers as Archetypes and Cultural Icons," in *Journal of American Culture,* Vol. 18, Spring, 1995, pp. 87-96.

[*In the essay below, Grixti suggests why American society is consumed with serial killers and argues that popular culture's depictions of such criminals reveals underlying needs and concerns of American society.*]

> There is no longer any such thing as fiction or nonfiction, there is only narrative.
> —E.L. Doctorow (qtd. in [Shelley Fisher] Fishkin [*From Fact to Fiction: Journalism and Imaginative Writing in America,* 1985])

Early in 1992, a series of newspaper articles announced that Jeffrey Dahmer had been made the "main hero" of a comic book biography. A Milwaukee court of law had recently found Dahmer guilty of a string of violent murders involving rape, dismemberment, and cannibalism. One article (headlined "Dahmer Now a Comic Book Hero" [by Yaroslau Trofimou in *The Weekend Australian* (May 1992)]) reported that the book contained "pictures of Dahmer slicing the throats of his victims and having sex with the corpses," that it had sold out immediately in Milwaukee, Wisconsin, and neighbouring states of the American Midwest, and that a sequel was being planned. Another article reported that, in his response to protests from the relatives of Dahmer's victims, the book's publisher had insisted that he had only made $200 from the first comic book, and that the relatives would be better off "directing their wrath at those who are writing books and making movies about the killer because they will be making thousands of dollars" ("Dahmer Sequel Draws Families' Ire" [in *The Weekend Australian* (June 1992)]). In implying that levels of moral responsibility should be judged according to the amount of financial profit generated by representations of disturbing atrocities, the publisher provides a forceful reminder of the extent to which our perceptions of and reactions to mass murder and serial killing have become inseparable from the orientations of consumerism.

Criminals and Psychopaths as Cultural Icons

Jeffrey Dahmer's elevation to the rank of ambiguous monster-hero in the iconography of contemporary consumer culture forms part of a noteworthy tradition. Interest in mass murderers and serial killers is not restricted to readers of popular "true crime" paperbacks and comics, of course. Accounts involving such figures are very frequent and prominent in the mass media—in news and current affairs programmes, as well as in a range of popular entertainments. As Jane Caputi puts it [in "The New Founding Fathers: The Lore and Lure of the Serial Killer in Contemporary Culture." *Journal of American Culture* (Fall 1990)], serial killers of the late-20th century tend to "generate legends and attract cult-like behavior" in that they are "celebrated (sometimes covertly, sometimes overtly) along a cultural gamut including made-for TV movies, rock 'n' roll songs, horror fanzines, jokes, pornographic magazines such as *Hustler,* and extreme sadist publications." In a sense, such celebrations usher figures like Dahmer into a hall of fame where historical murderers acquire mythical proportions (frequently reinforced by the ascription of evocative names like Jack the Ripper, the Hillside Strangler, the Vampire of Düsseldorf, or the Night Stalker). There they rub shoulders with a long line of fictional figures created over the centuries in variously loaded attempts to come to cognitive terms with evil by visualizing and personifying its threats and horrors in reassuringly recognizable forms. Within the popular cultural domains that underlie the construction of this chamber of horrors, boundaries between fact and fiction often tend to become blurred.

Criminals, psychopaths, and murderers have consistently attracted the attention of writers and readers of all levels of fiction, but it is in popular literature that bloodthirsty murders have been most frequently contemplated. Murderers have here tended to be depicted in terms that frighten and disturb, and they have frequently (consciously or unconsciously) been made to serve ideologically weighted functions. Such functions include providing challenging reminders about the need for constant vigilance, or offering reassurance about the ultimate rightness of law-enforcement structures as guardians and embodiments of the social and moral order. As a number of commentators have pointed out, Jack the Ripper is perhaps the most influentially mythologized murderer of recent history, and fictional recreations of his crimes have dressed him up in guises ranging from that of street-cleaning avenger of decadence to bloodcurdling challenger of any smug belief in the prevalence of sanity or security in ad-

vanced urban societies. Other historical mass murderers and serial killers whose exploits have been reimagined and variously reinterpreted in fiction include Vlad the Impaler (mythologized as Dracula), Gilles de Rais (accused of sadistically torturing and murdering between 140 and 800 children as well as murdering six of his seven wives, and around whose life grew the legend of "Bluebeard"), and Elizabeth Bathory, the Hungarian Countess (fictionalized as "Countess Dracula" in a 1960s Hammer horror film) who in 1611 was convicted of killing up to 650 girls and bathing in their blood in order to halt the aging process.

Recent years have also seen a growth in the number of criminologists attempting to identify patterns in order to place such crimes within some sort of coherence—partly in response to an alarming growth in the incidence of "recreational killings" and murders involving a single killer claiming large numbers of victims. Significantly in this context, the semantic distinction between *mass murder* and *serial killing* was only developed in the 1980s. In the preface to his *Annotated Bibliography of Mass Murder,* Michael Newton notes that, with official recognition of a growing problem in the 1980s, "jargon raced ahead of understanding, and a host of experts quarreled among themselves about the proper terminology for this or that atrocity." Serial sex murders have also been the focus of attention among feminist social theorists, a number of whom have unequivocally designated the phenomenon as a symptomatic sin of patriarchy. The evidence presented in this regard is challenging and damning, in that the fascination exerted by mass and serial sex killings in late capitalist consumer societies is clearly entangled with some of the more sinister aspects of phallocentrism and fear or hatred of women. This is perhaps most obvious in the thrust and orientations of sado-masochistic publications that celebrate violence as sexual titillation— or *gorenography,* to borrow a phrase coined by U.S. traders to describe such specialty magazines as *Gore Gazette, The Splatter Times, Bill Landis' Sleazoid Express, Confessions of a Trash Fiend, Scarephanalia,* and *Fangoria.*

But the moral and cognitive problems raised by popular interest in horrific murders are wider and more complex than is suggested by the sensational and exploitative nature of many of the narratives that focus on them. According to Brian Masters [in *Killing for Company: The Case of Dennis Nilsen,* 1986]:

> The murderer takes his place in the jumbled kaleidoscope of the human condition. So, too, does his audience. For them to enjoy the display of crime, detection, retribution, while refusing to be drawn into a steady contemplation of themselves as audience, and the subterranean echoes which the case disturbs, would be fruitless and arid.

Masters draws attention to the moral tightrope that writers and readers have to negotiate while trying to make sense of the serial killer and of the disturbing issues that he or she raises. Sympathy with murder is unthinkable, Masters points out, but to avoid the pain of trying to understand is an abnegation of responsibility.

Murder and Cultural Disorientation

Perhaps the most widespread popular reactions to the recounting of horrific crimes are the more socially respectable ones of bafflement and incomprehension. "There is murder in cold blood, and murder in hot blood," declared *Newsweek* magazine in its 1957 report on the bizarre crimes of Edward Gein. "Both, at least, can be explained in human terms. But there is also a kind of murder that springs from the deep recesses of a mind so twisted that it passes human understanding. This can be murder in its most terrible, sickening form" ("The Secrets of the Farm" [*Newsweek* (2 December 1957)]). The impact that violent acts have on society at large is powerful not only because they produce fear but also, and perhaps more importantly, because they produce disorientation. In this relation, Clive Bloom has suggested in ["The House that Jack Built: Jack the Ripper, Legend and the Power of the Unknown," in *Nineteenth Century Suspense: From Poe to Conan Doyle,* edited by C. Bloom, B. Docherty, J. Gibb and K. Shand. London: Macmillan, 1988] that the "legendary power" of the violence of a figure like Jack the Ripper "acts as a gaping maw into which perception of order and rightness are sucked." One way of dealing with this uncertainty is to affirm that mass murderers and serial killers are neither civilized nor really human—i.e., to stress their monstrosity so as to perceive them as belonging to the realm of the *other*. The tendency is well illustrated in the tone and imagery that dominate the following excerpt from a "true crime" account of the atrocities committed in the mid-1980s by Richard Ramirez, the Los Angeles "Night Stalker":

> The public, even the police, can understand a crime of passion, perhaps sympathize with the killer, even if they don't approve. . . . But this bloody rampage was different. It was the sadistic, systematic slaughter of innocent people. Someone with a vampire's taste for human blood was creeping into houses in middle-class neighborhoods after dark to work nightmarish evil. And the ghoulish intruder was not satisfied simply to kill his victims; he added torture, rape and mutilation. He dehumanized his victims. It was villainy beyond ordinary comprehension; evil that truly chilled the soul. ([Clifford L.] Linedecker [*Night Stalker*, 1991])

The reaction is peculiarly modern in its implications, and it will be useful to briefly locate it in its historical context before we go any further. According to Randall McGowen, the

modern tendency to construct violence as the domain of the other owes a lot to 19th-century reforms in the English penal system. By reducing the harshness and violence of the state's patterns of punishment, McGowen suggests, the legal reformers helped to bring an end to the use of violence as a means of legitimating the state's power. Violent acts could no longer be officially attributed to God's righteousness when reformers were campaigning to circumscribe and eliminate violence from their society. The demands for reform, in other words, encouraged the development of a world view in which the existence of violence in civilized societies could be attributed exclusively to criminals—outsiders whose violent acts came to be designated as being beyond rational comprehension. We now like to believe, McGowen points out, that we cannot understand what makes one person harm another:

> Yet one consequence of the puzzle over the violence criminals do becomes an uncertainty about ourselves and our neighbors. The violent act comes to define a character as different from us, as criminal. This person appears to be outside of human community, perhaps less than human. But this boundary, seemingly so secure, begins to erode when we become aware of a neighbor's violence, or that of the police. We draw away from these offenders but remain uneasily aware that the violence we thought we had excluded from the community has found its way back into our midst. At such time we turn away or deny the characterization of the act because otherwise our very identity seems in doubt.

The events surrounding the execution of Ted Bundy, one of the most notorious *and* celebrated serial killers of recent history, in many ways illustrate some of the socio-psychological implications of this tendency. Bundy's case was particularly disorienting to many because he looked so decent and (as a handsome, intelligent former law student who had worked for the Republican party) he seemed to epitomize many of the most cherished American notions of wholesomeness. In the course of the television interview that he gave shortly before his execution, Bundy insisted on his fellowship in a universal brotherhood and attributed his transgressions to one of the less salutary components of consumer culture: "Those of us who are . . . so much influenced by violence in the media, in particular pornographic violence, are not some kind of inherent monsters. We are your sons, and we are your husbands, and we grew up in regular families" (qtd. in Caputi). This rejection of the label of "inherent monster" contrasts starkly with the ways in which Bundy was insistently being portrayed by others. As he went to the electric chair in January 1989, a carnivalesque crowd gathered outside the prison gates and waved banners announcing (among other things) "Bundy BBQ," "I like my Ted well done" and "Fry, Bundy, Fry." The crowd, echoing as it did some of the symbolic functions performed by the torch-waving crowds that so frequently rose to destroy the monster at the climax of horror movies in the 1930s, partly reflected a firm determination not to lose sight of the murderer as outsider—an unnatural growth that society had finally recognized for what it was and was now dealing with accordingly. This is also the way in which Bundy was constructed by his journalistic biographers Stephen Michaud and Hugh Aynesworth, who claimed inside knowledge of his mind on the basis of a lengthy series of taped (and usually circumspect) interviews which he granted them in prison. Elaborating on an assertion made by the prosecution during Bundy's trial that criminals are human beings and not, as popular stereotypes have it, "a hunchbacked, cross-eyed little monster slithering through the dark, leaving a trail of slime," [Stephen G.] Michaud and [Hugh] Aynesworth assert [in *The Only Living Witness,* 1989]:

> But within Ted Bundy, human being, that slithering hunchback lives, residing behind what one eminent psychiatrist has termed a psychopath's "mask of sanity." The mask is a fabrication and nothing more, but it is impenetrable by even the most skilled doctor of the mind. In Ted, the cross-eyed creature lurks on a different plane of existence and can only be seen by means of a tautology; its presence must be inferred before it can be found. . . . Only by means of his astounding capacity to compartmentalize had Bundy been able to keep the hunchback from raging through the mask and destroying him. When at last it did, *Ted* became the hunchback. No longer its protector, he and the entity fused. (Michaud and Aynesworth, italics in the original)

The imagery employed here to describe the unaccountable derives unmistakably from the literary genres of fantasy and horror fiction. The passages do not add much to our understanding of a figure like Bundy. They simply appeal to a stock of prejudices and associations based on our familiarity with fictional accounts involving things like slithering cross-eyed creatures, imprisoned Gorgons or Frankenstein monsters that turn on their jailers, or horrible hunchbacked witches disguised as "normal" people. Dr. Jekyll and Mr. Hyde also form an important part of this cluster of connotations—particularly in terms of how Mr. Hyde has popularly come to personify an alleged beast beneath the skin, what Robert Louis Stevenson called in his influential 1885 novel, "the animal within . . . licking the chops of memory [when] the spiritual side [is] a little drowsed" ([Robert Louis] Stevenson [*The Strange Case of Dr. Jekyll and Mr. Hyde*]). Designating murderers as inhuman beasts, or as having been taken over completely by the "Beast Within," is a way of distancing them from what we popularly perceive as the norm.

All this suggests that popular (and formulaic) fictionalizations of serial killers allow us to make them perform scapegoating functions analogous to those identified by René Girard [in *Violence and the Sacred,* translated by Patrick Gregory, 1977] in his description of sacrifice as serving "to protect the entire community from *its own violence*" (Girard's italics). But, as is indicated by Ted Bundy's rejection of the label of "inherent monster," the role is not assumed willingly. Nor is the process of ascribing it either innocent or unambiguous. According to Brian Masters, "people accused of vile murders who regard themselves as a cathartic release from the accumulated wickedness of mankind [. . .] deeply resent the additional burden" (*Killing for Company*).

Villains as Monstrous Attractions

"No one wants to believe ever," declared British serial killer Dennis Nilsen, "that I am just an ordinary man come to an extraordinary and overwhelming conclusion" (*Killing for Company*). Nilsen was arrested on February 9, 1983, after human remains had been identified as the cause of blocked drains outside his north London home. Body parts of several of his male victims, in various stages of dismemberment, were also found inside his house. Nilsen's private life, which jarred so starkly with his public role as civil servant, attracted a lot of public attention in the days following his arrest, and Nilsen, angry at the simplistic tone of the press accounts, even penned his own pastiche of a tabloid news report headlined: "RED MONSTER LURES YOUNG MEN TO THEIR DEATHS IN HOMOSEXUAL HOUSE OF HORROR" (*Killing for Company*). "I am always surprised and truly amazed," Nilsen declared at another stage, "that anyone can be attracted by the macabre":

> The population at large is neither "ordinary" or "normal." They seem to be bound together by a collective ignorance of themselves and what they are. They have, every one of them, got their deep dark thoughts with many a skeleton rattling in their secret cupboards. Their fascination with "types" (rare types) like myself plagues them with the mystery of why and how a living person can actually do things which may be only those dark images and acts secretly within them. I believe they can identify with these 'dark images and acts' and loathe anything which reminds them of this dark side of themselves. The usual reaction is a flood of popular self-righteous condemnation but a willingness to, with friends and acquaintances, talk over and over again the appropriate bits of the case. (*Killing for Company*)

Fictionalizing figures like Nilsen and Bundy as inhuman monsters is one way of coming to terms with the dislocations that they generate in order to preserve the preferred contours of our own identity. Popular fiction, because of its very generic and formulaic nature, frequently acts as a frame of reassurance which allows us to safely engage in this exploratory process. The process involves locating the criminal-outsiders within a tradition, and identifying their affinities with antecedents—which have in their turn been made part of a mythology. What we and our cultures are engaged in when we endeavour to contextualize serial murderers within this broader mythology is an exercise designed to allow them to be habitually perceived in the same unthreatening terms as is the case with domesticated mythic monsters like the werewolf or the vampire. It is a way of disarming threatening figures by dressing them up as circus or cinematic attractions. In other words, we are attempting to make them familiar and consumable. As Amy Taubin puts it [in "Killing Men," *Sight and Sound* (May 1991)], cinematic and other popular images of the serial killer are "a substitute and a shield for a situation so incomprehensible it must be disavowed." The argument, it bears noting, echoes Franco Moretti's account [in *Signs Taken for Wonders: Essays in the Sociology of Literary Forms,* 1983] of the socio-cultural functions performed by 19th-century horror fiction—i.e., that such literature takes up within itself determinate fears in order to transform them into other (unreal) fears, with the purpose of saving readers from having to face up to what might really frighten them (Moretti).

The moral and cognitive problems raised by popular interest in horrific murders are wider and more complex than is suggested by the sensational and exploitative nature of many of the narratives that focus on them.

—Joseph Grixti

The process can be briefly illustrated by drawing attention to some of the ways in which consumer culture has appropriated a mythical figure traditionally associated with obsessive, bloodthirsty and frequently sexually motivated serial killing—that of the vampire. In the course of the 20th century, vampires have been made the subject of a seemingly never-ending stream of both serious and comic representations in movies, books, and TV programmes. Dracula in particular has also been transmogrified into manifestations like that of the Count in *Sesame Street* (where the craving for blood has been replaced by a craving for counting numbers); Count Duckula and Quackula the Vampire Duck in children's TV cartoon programmes; (in the U.S.) a "vitamin enriched vampire cereal" called Count Chocula as well as "vampire-shaped" ice-lollies; and (on Australia's Gold Coast) a tourist attraction in the shape of "Dracula's Cabaret Restaurant" located (if one is to believe the publicity) "just a blood squirt from the Casino." Within a cultural context that engages in this type of transmutation, the exercise of designating serial killers as monsters can be read as little more

than the first step towards making them less threatening by locating them within a multilayered entertainment industry. We don't so much worry any more about being taken over and eaten by vampires and other monsters; our consumer-oriented societies have taught us how to neutralize, eat, suck, consume *them* instead. We have, in other words, learned to transform ideas and images that might challenge our everyday securities and expectations into a means of actually reaffirming them.

The implications of this assertion call for systematic unpacking, and to this end, it will be worth focusing more directly on the fascination exerted by a selection of fictional serial killers that have captured the public imagination in recent years. The figures I have chosen to discuss here are of primary interest because of the manner in which they are cognitively and culturally located at a narrative intersection between fact and fiction. They can be shown to be based on real-life murderers but they are also fictional and appear in texts that project themselves as crimethrillers—a genre that combines the literary conventions of realism (in its emphasis on verisimilitude, meticulous logic and hard-nosed accuracy of detail) and romance (in its focus on adventure and a hero's quest to overcome daunting odds and save or win a maiden in distress). The serial killers in question are Francis Dolarhyde, Jame Gumb, and Dr. Hannibal Lecter. These three villains appear in the popular novels *Red Dragon* and *The Silence of the Lambs* by Thomas Harris, a former crime reporter for the Press Association turned best-selling novelist.

Loners, Losers, and Devils

Harris approaches the task of fictionalizing serial killers by compartmentalizing the phenomenon into two distinct types. The first is the psychopathic loner who turns into a vicious beast, largely as a consequence of serious gender identity problems which are usually attributed to (at worst) cruel or (at best) neglectful mothering. The second is the serial killer as enigmatic devil and modern embodiment of evil. The prototypes are not Harris's invention, but appear to derive from a popular tendency to stereotype murderers as either "making sense" because they are "obviously" psychotic and sexually mixed up, or else, when the label doesn't appear to fit, as somehow being associated with a realm of supernatural evil. The tendency is well captured in Michaud and Aynesworth's account of popular reactions to Ted Bundy's crimes:

> Against a backdrop of mass insane homicide, Ted instead emerged as a variety of criminal genius, a nearly fictive character who wasn't stereotypically a loner or a loser—because he didn't *look* like one—and so must be something else: the incarnation of Evil. . . . Even the closer profiles of him, some well researched, others based upon presumed personal

knowledge of Ted, are suffused with a variety of awe at his works.

Harris's presentation of both the loner/loser and the demonic stereotypes of the serial killer proceeds in metaphoric terms that derive much of their force from identifiable mythical and literary associations. The killers who fit the first category are broadly associated with the mythic archetype of the werewolf. Thus, as if to highlight his conception as Americanized Mr. Hyde, the psychopathic serial killer on the loose in *Red Dragon* is called Dolarhyde and he commits his grisly multiple murders at full moon. The notion of beasts beneath the skin is given a bizarre twist in *The Silence of the Lambs,* where the psychopath (referred to as both "Buffalo Bill" and "Mr. Hide") covers himself with an outer skin sewn from the "hide" of his female victims.

Images involving murder and mayhem striking at full moon are of course deeply embedded in folklore, legends, and horror tales about werewolves and similar mutants. But, as is the case with most legends, there are also psychological and historical foundations to the imagery. It has often been noted, for instance, that serial killers frequently attack in monthly cycles. When, in the early months of 1974, the bodies of Ted Bundy's victims were being discovered at monthly intervals, the police (bizarrely) started to nickname the next expected victim according to the month—as "Miss May" or "Miss June" (Michaud and Aynesworth). Similarly, Bobby Joe Long, a serial rapist and murderer arrested in 1983, associated his compulsion to attack with lunar protomenstrual cycles, which he was claimed to experience because of a congenital dysfunction of the endocrine system. When he was 11 years old, Long had more than six pounds of tissue surgically removed from his chest in an attempt to remedy what looked like the development of female breasts. "Even now," he revealed to Joel Norris in prison

> I can always tell when it's full moon; I can't sit still; I have to pace; even the smallest thing sets me off. And I'm not the only one. All over the row, you can tell when it's the full moon, even if you can't see it from this hole. People start screaming and carrying on, you just know it's a full moon. (qtd. in Norris [*Serial Killers: The Growing Menace,* 1988])

Harris's inspiration for Jame Gumb (or "Buffalo Bill") can be traced more specifically to Edward Gein, a serial murderer from Wisconsin who made news headlines in the 1950s, and who also inspired at least two other influential updatings of the Hyde-werewolf legend, those of Norman Bates in Robert Bloch's and Alfred Hitchcock's *Psycho,* and "Leatherface" in Tobe Hooper's *Texas Chainsaw Massacre.* One of the acts in which Gein had habitually engaged before his arrest in 1957 was that of prancing around his deserted farm on moonlit evenings, wearing the faces, the hair, the breasts, and the

vaginas of his female victims. Two reasons were given for this: a secret desire for transsexual surgery for which he lacked both the courage and the funds, and a wish to recreate the form and presence of his dead mother. Other things that Gein had fashioned out of human skin and bone included a belt of nipples, a wastepaper basket, lamp shades, bowls made of skullcaps, and upholstery for his furniture. One aspect of the Gein case that had been found most shocking at the time of its discovery was what a photo-spread article in *Life* magazine at the time termed "the chilling discrepancy between Ed Gein's public and private life" ["House of Horror Stuns the Nation," *Life* (2 December 1957)]. It was this discrepancy that became the focus of attention in Gein's fictionalization as Norman Bates in Bloch's best-selling 1959 novel and in Hitchcock's influential 1960 film. Three decades later (after a period of escalating emphasis on the details of gory violation in popular literature and cinema), while there are still allusions to this duality in Gein's reappearance as "Buffalo Bill," the metaphoric emphasis, as the nickname suggests, has shifted more forcefully to the image of the predatory beast lurking beneath a grotesquely transparent mask or extraneous skin of civilization.

At the climax of *The Silence of the Lambs,* as "Buffalo Bill" prepares to close in on his quarry, he considers how it "would have been fun to hunt her for a long time—he'd never hunted one armed before" (Harris). Hunting imagery pervades Harris's novels, and details of the killers' methods of stalking their victims are given full metaphoric force—a point highlighted in the change of title in the 1986 movie version of *Red Dragon* to *Manhunter.* It is worth stressing that the metaphor is not a simple literary conceit, in that serial killers have often been noted to think of themselves as hunters. The preparations undertaken by "Buffalo Bill" to "harvest the hide" of his victims (*Silence*) echo Edward Gein's bizarrely systematic methods of hanging his dead victims' bodies by the ankles as he prepared to put their skin to personal and household use—in much the same way as the deer hunters in his district harvested and used the hide of their prey. But within the generic conventions chosen by Harris as frame for his narrative, fact has been domesticated and made to perform clearly delineated formulaic functions—creating suspense, shocking through surprise or grotesque association, evoking a tense but ultimately reassuring atmosphere in which we know that though the villains may look daunting, it is the heroes who always win the end. What Harris has achieved, in other words, is a cognitive and imaginative contextualization of a disturbing social phenomenon within a recognizable and familiar mythic tradition. The medium, to modify an old cliché, has domesticated the message, in that, as Jean Baudrillard puts it [in *Revenge of the Crystal: Selected Writings on the Modern Object and Its Destiny, 1968-1983,* edited and translated by Paul Foss and Julian Pefanis, 1990],

[T]he truth of the mass media is that they function to

neutralize the unique character of actual world events by replacing them with a multiple universe of mutually reinforcing and self-referential media. At the very limit, they become each other's reciprocal content—and this constitutes *the totalitarian 'message' of the consumer society*. (Baudrillard's italics)

The prevalence and uses of hunting imagery in the context of mass mediated entertainments like Harris's, as well as in a substantial number of popular movies that project "recreational killing" as ritualistic hunting, derives from a complex series of assumptions about human nature that deserve further elaboration. We can perhaps get closer to the implications of these assumptions and to how such entertainments serve to reinforce them with specific hegemonic purposes by considering the second type of fictionalized serial killer highlighted in Harris's novels—that of the murderer as evil genius.

Consuming the Cannibal: "Evil Be Thou My Good"

Dr. Hannibal Lecter (or Hannibal the Cannibal), has become a celebrity in his own right, especially after the phenomenal financial and Oscar-winning success of the film version of *The Silence of the Lambs,* which among other things turned Anthony Hopkins into what Dame Edna Everage would call a megastar. A great deal of the fascination exerted by this particular character can be argued to derive from the fact that he has been presented in terms that deliberately and evocatively associate him with some of the most resilient archetypes of western mythology. As was illustrated in the 1992 Oscar Awards ceremony (in which the audience burst into laughter and applause when comedian Billy Crystal, muzzled and strait-jacketed to look like the movie version of Lecter, was wheeled onto the stage), the process has served to transform the horrors and threats evoked by this figure into something reassuringly familiar and consumable.

In the two Harris best-sellers in which he appears, Lecter is described in terms that associate him with preternatural evil: ever present, ever powerful, and incomprehensible. In this sense, he can be argued to owe his appeal to what John Lanchester [in "Strangers," *London Review of Books* (11 July 1991)] has called "a kernel of wish-fulfillment." According to Lanchester, the serial murderer, precisely because he baffles comprehension, stands to remind us that there is literally nothing of which human beings are not capable, and in this sense he "fulfills a general desire to believe that the human psyche is not fully explicable." Even the unknown, in other words, is amenable to appropriation as fodder for reassurance. It is worth stressing again that what Harris is doing here is simply applying and extending metaphors that have become the stock clichés of popular "true crime" accounts. Such clichés are highlighted, for instance, in the title of Ronald Markman and Dominick Bosco's *Alone with the*

Devil, which describes a forensic psychiatrist's encounters with figures like Richard Chase (the "Vampire of Sacramento") and other killers. The publishers of this particular volume have further stressed the cliché by printing two triangular dots over the letter *v* in the word "devil" as it appears on both the title page and in the running heads throughout the volume—forming what is presumably intended as a demonic pair of umlaut-like horns. The images surrounding Harris's Lecter also echo passages like the following about Ted Bundy:

> The *idea* of Ted Bundy preys on the mind. He is his own abstraction, a lethal absurdity masquerading as a man. Nevertheless, there were times at the prison when I was enveloped in the charisma of his madness. He fascinated me like a viper motionless in a crevice; a black, palpable malignancy. . . . There is a cold, poisonous luster in Bundy's unguarded gaze . . . (Michaud and Aynesworth, italics in the original)

The first time Dr. Lecter's name is mentioned in *The Silence of the Lambs,* we are told that a "brief silence follows his name, always, in any civilized gathering." The aura he exerts disconcerts those who approach him:

> Graham wanted to see Dr. Lecter asleep. He wanted time to brace himself. If he felt Lecter's madness in his head, he had to contain it quickly, like a spill.
>
> To cover the sound of his footsteps, he followed an orderly pushing a linen cart. Dr. Lecter is very difficult to slip up on. (Harris, *Red Dragon*)

As that last sentence indicates, Lecter (unlike the other characters) is frequently described in the present tense—a technique which is presumably intended to bring him closer to the reader's present reality, as well as suggesting a timeless quality:

> Dr. Lecter's eyes are maroon and they reflect the light redly in tiny points.
>
> Lecter rose and walked over to his table. He is a small, lithe man. Very neat.
>
> Dr. Lecter seldom holds his head upright. He tilts it as he asks a question, as though he were screwing an augur of curiosity into your face. (*Red Dragon*)

The tiny red spots in Lecter's maroon eyes, and the "augur of curiosity" are just some of the ways in which Harris borrows the imagery and associations of demonology in his construction of Lecter as modernday witch-doctor and fiend. At another point we are told of Lecter's gaze that it felt as if he "was looking through to the back of [the] skull" and that his "attention felt like a fly walking around in there" (*Red Dragon*). The monstrous dimensions of this latterday lord of the flies are also underlined by the fact that he exhibits "the rarest form of polydactyly": he has six fingers on his left hand (*Silence*).

Echoes of Milton's Satan are also frequent. At one point in *Red Dragon* we are told of Lecter as he watches his jailers "from the shadowed corner of his cell" that there was "a curious grace about him, even in restraints." Lecter's thoughts, we are told in *The Silence of the Lambs,* "were no more bound by fear or kindness than Milton's were by physics. He was free in his own head." He has a "cultured voice [which] has a slight metallic rasp beneath it, possibly from disuse" (*Silence*). Before her first encounter with him, Clarice Starling, the young heroine of *The Silence of the Lambs,* is warned that if Lecter talks to her at all, he'll just be trying to find out about her: "It's the kind of curiosity that makes a snake look in a bird's nest." As the image suggests, Harris's story of the encounter between the young trainee FBI agent and the incarcerated demon doctor has its imaginative origins in the legend of Eve's temptation by the serpent. That the association is deliberate is suggested by the novel's frequent references to the symbols of Christianity, and by the fact that Starling is also watched over by an all-wise (God the) father figure in the shape of the FBI chief who makes her his protégée.

In an angry response to Starling's comment about the desirability of discovering why he's in jail and what happened to him, Lecter asserts:

> Nothing happened to me, Officer Starling. *I* happened. You can't reduce me to a set of influences. You've given up good and evil for behaviorism, Officer Starling. You've got everything in moral dignity pants—nothing is ever anybody's fault. Look at me, Officer Starling. Can you stand to say I'm evil? Am I evil, Officer Starling? (*Silence*)

"Dr. Lecter is not crazy, in any common way we think of being crazy," comments the hero of *Red Dragon,* "he did some hideous things because he enjoyed them." Harris is clearly not parsimonious in his use of references to well-known villains in order to allow the connotations they bring to rub on to his character. Besides being something of a witch-doctor, a monster, and a Jungian shadow, Lecter thus also has something of the charm and enigma of Iago as well as the epic grandeur of Milton's Satan. He is also a bit of a vampire. When Starling leaves him after their first encounter, "she suddenly felt empty, as though she had given blood"—and this while he lies on his cot "as remote from her as a stone crusader lying on a tomb" (*Silence*). In the course of his meeting with the Senator whose daughter is in mortal danger, Lecter, we are told, "took a single sip of her

pain and found it exquisite." On another occasion, his appearance in his cell conjures up images of Klaus Kinski's haunting portrayal of the vampiric count in Herzog's 1979 *Nosferatu*:

> Dr. Lecter wore the white asylum pajamas in his white cell. The only colors in the cell were his hair and eyes and his red mouth, in a face so long out of the sun it *leached* into the surrounding whiteness; his features seemed suspended above the collar of his shirt. (*Silence,* emphasis added)

Observing his "sleek dark head," Starling at another point has a vision of him as "a cemetery mink [which] lives down in a ribcage in the dry leaves of a heart." Because of her association with Lecter, Starling herself also comes to be described by the popular press in the novel as the "Bride of Dracula."

It is precisely because of the basis of his mystery and incomprehensibility in language and intertextuality that Lecter and the evil he represents have been so enthusiastically appropriated by contemporary consumer societies. "We have lived so long in foggy landscapes reflected in misty mirrors," as Wayne Booth put it [in *The Rhetoric of Fiction,* 1961], "that we have come to *like* fog." If this intertextuality constructs the demon-doctor as incomprehensible, it also encourages us to think of him as somehow supernatural and infallible. As a psychiatrist who has embraced the abyss, he is projected as knowing more about the inner depths of those around him than they care to admit to themselves. *"He sees very clearly—he damn sure sees through me,"* reflects Starling at one point in the novel. "It's hard to accept," the passage continues, "that someone can understand you without wishing you well" (*Silence,* Harris's italics).

Lecter-Lucifer, then, tempts his young female antagonist with the knowledge that will gain her recognition in a vicious world where law-enforcement officers perceive themselves in the same metaphoric terms as the criminals. "Because it's the plight that drives you," Lecter tells Starling in his letter at the end of the book, "seeing the plight, and the plight will not end, ever." Like the predatory serial killers, the police and FBI agents in the novels frequently think of themselves as being engaged in a hunt and as fighting against time to catch the predator before *he* gets to *his* prey. "The reason you caught me," shouts Lecter to taunt the police officer who had mysteriously identified him as a killer and arrested him, "is that WE'RE JUST ALIKE" (*Red Dragon*). Harris's novels and the films that followed them as a whole, in fact, project a world view that is basically an extended cliché—that of the vicious concrete jungle where life and death are visualized in predatory and counterpredatory terms, and where our last memory of peace is from the time before our birth (*Red Dragon*). Within this world, everything appears to be interpreted in terms of the unquestioned dictates of the "survival of the fittest," so that even problem solving (as Harris's heroine comes to realize) is hunting (*Silence*). The good and the bad are here projected as two aspects of an evolved "basic reptile brain"—with the difference that the bad are viewed as a virus in the social organism, while the good prefer to think of themselves as a vaccine (*Red Dragon*).

Consciously or unconsciously, the thrust of fictionalizations like these is to appropriate and package the serial killer with the ideological purpose of making him confirm the widespread belief that we all carry a destructive beast beneath our skins, and that it is only the controls of civilized order that stop us from regressing to the nasty, brutish, and short state that allegedly typified life in the state of nature. "You, too, Steve," Ted Bundy once told one of his interviewers, "could make a successful mass killer. I really think you have it in you!" (Michaud and Aynesworth). Paradoxically, this parable has become reassuring. Seeing oneself as belonging on the right side of the law is usually also associated with having had the strength to control the beast within—a feat that we are encouraged to attribute to the internalization of the rules, demands, and prohibitions of the social order. We are also reassured about the rightness of the current state of civilized society, since the monsters repeatedly emerge as the exceptions that make the rule, the chinks and cracks in the social fabric that (though they might cause momentary concern and discomfort) are actually made to remind us of the structural soundness of the fabric itself. As a exercise in social cohesion and control, this could possibly be construed as an excusable, perhaps even a necessary process.

The problem, however, is that its value-laden purposes continue to reinforce some very deeply ingrained but erroneous assumptions about the roots of human nature and about how our emotions and instincts relate to the (often poorly understood) historical patterns of evolution. The thrust of such assumptions is to perpetuate the puzzles about the sources of criminality and serial killing—since it is the puzzles themselves (and not their solutions) that fit in most comfortably within the orientations and demands of consumerism. In this sense, these are perspectives that perpetuate self-deluding bafflement and incomprehension, and as such they can also be argued to propagate communal helplessness.

George Garrett (essay date Summer 1996)

SOURCE: "Then and Now: *In Cold Blood* Revisited," in *The Virginia Quarterly Review,* Vol. 72, Summer, 1996, pp. 467-74.

[*In the essay below, Garrett discusses Truman Capote's* In Cold Blood *and its impact on the true-crime genre.*]

Now it is a matter of memory, but then it was an experience. Not simply a memorable event, but an experience lived in and through and worth remembering, one of those rare occurrences which, even after all is said and done, modified and revised by time, can be said to have changed things.

In my house, which is, among other things, a hopeless clutter and chaos of books, placed in no known or discernible order, I can go directly to it, no groping and searching, and lift Truman Capote's *In Cold Blood,* hardcover, first printing, off the shelf. Partly this is because of the unusual book jacket (slightly torn and frayed since 1965) consisting of nothing but words: title and author on front and spine; on the back, "Books by Truman Capote," a list of his nine published titles at that time, including this one. No blurbs, no photograph, fore or aft. On the end flap, "About the Author," we learn Capote's date of birth—September 30, 1924; that his first novel, *Other Voices, Other Rooms,* "was an international literary success and established the author in the first rank of contemporary writers—a position he has since sustained with additional novels and short stories, as well as his widely praised experiments in the field of reportage." The copy goes on to claim that this new book "represents the culmination of his long-standing desire to make a contribution toward the establishment of a serious new literary form: the Nonfiction Novel."

In an essay review written at the time, I quibbled with that claim, reminding other readers and myself of e. e. cummings' *The Enormous Room,* of Hemingway's *Green Hills of Africa, Death in the Afternoon,* and *A Moveable Feast,* of the whole line of books descending from Walter Lord's *A Night to Remember.* And at that moment I had ignored, and will not again, the major contribution to the form, Shelby Foote's magnificent achievement, *The Civil War: A Narrative,* which, by 1963, was two-thirds done, with the first two volumes in print. All of which only suggests that other writers had thought and were thinking at the same time in the same way—that, somehow, the traditional novel, as it came to them and was practiced, did not have the ways and means to deal honestly and artistically with large events of the past or with the mad reality of our own times, with what Capote described in an interview as "desperate, savage, violent America in collision with sane, safe, insular even smug America—people who have every chance against people who have none." The real world was, they thought, too wild for fiction, but the hard facts of it could be tamed and arranged in a narrative form, what Tom Wolfe would later call "the New Journalism."

The front flap of the jacket is equally spare and unusual, then or now. Title and subtitle, "A True Account of a Multiple Murder and Its Consequences." The text, a little over 100 words, deserves to be quoted in full:

On November 15, 1959, in the small town of Holcomb, Kansas, four members of the Clutter family were savagely murdered by blasts from a shotgun held a few inches from their faces. There was no apparent motive for the crime and there were almost no clues.

Five years, four months and twenty-nine days later, on April 14, 1965, Richard Eugene Hitchcock, aged thirty-three, and Perry Edward Smith, aged thirty-six, were hanged on a gallows in a warehouse in the Kansas State Penitentiary in Lansing, Kansas.

In Cold Blood is the story of the lives and deaths of these six people. It has already been hailed as a masterpiece.

All but the final sentence is made up of bare facts and numbers, might as well be a newspaper account, surprising in its flat tone (only the word "savagely" is an adverbial judgment call) and perhaps surprising in that it might seem to eliminate some of the suspense of the story. We are told what happened to the six principals before opening the book or reading a page.

But we knew that anyway. The last statement on the jacket is factual also. This book had been serialized in *The New Yorker* with great success. In his "Acknowledgements" Capote thanks "Mr. William Shawn of *The New Yorker*, who encouraged me to undertake this project, and whose judgment stood me in good stead from first to last."

I remember that, remember, after the first chunk of it appeared, waiting eagerly for the next issue of *The New Yorker*. People talked about it with excitement in the way that people only talk about good new movies nowadays. I couldn't wait to get my hands on the book. Didn't wait too long, either, to have acquired an expensive ($5.95) hardcover of the first printing. Waiting around for it we read all about Capote and the new book in all the magazines. I'll never forget the big spread in *Life* magazine where Capote, calm and matter-of-fact, allowed: "The book will be a classic." And in any case it was a huge and instantaneous success, a bestseller, a Book-of-the-Month Club selection (more important then than now); paperback rights were sold for an enormous sum; movie rights were promptly purchased.

It's true, Capote had enjoyed a good measure of literary fame and success ever since the appearance of *Other Voices, Other Rooms;* but this was a great leap, a *grande jete* into popular success. Fame became celebrity. Then that celebrity was at once confirmed and flaunted in 1967 by a party at the Plaza Hotel—"The Party," Gloria Steinem named it in *Vogue* magazine, "a great masked ball that would bring guests from Europe and Asia, not to mention Kansas, California, and

Harlem"—to which Capote invited 540 people, enough of them celebrities to be called (again by Gloria Steinem) "a new Four Hundred of the World."

What else about the book itself? It is a very handsomely made and designed book, beautifully printed on the best paper and with a rare and elegant full-cloth binding. Made to last. Made to be kept and appreciated. Made to tell the world: *This is real class.* Open it up and you are soon greeted on the title page by a chilling illustration, the only one in the book or jacket—two pairs of eyes, an extreme close shot in black and white, the eyes of the killers, here brooding over the story to follow. To say the eyes of these two dead young men are haunting would be an understatement. That it is, finally, their book, their story, is underscored by the epigraph, four lines asking for pity and God's mercy, from Francois Villon's "*Ballade des pendus.*"

One thing more. We soon discover that one of the people to whom the book is dedicated is Capote's old childhood friend Harper Lee, author of *To Kill a Mockingbird,* one of the best-loved stories of our time. From all the advance publicity about the making of the book, we already knew that Harper Lee had helped him in various ways in the research and socially in winning over reticent people in Kansas.

Maybe Capote lent to the "true crime" story a patina of literary respectability; but now it seems that this was coming anyway, part of the spirit of the 1960's, as was our gradual change over from concern for victims to fascination with perpetrators.

—George Garrett

The advance publicity, unusual for the time, and the carefully designed jacket copy for the book served a powerful technical purpose as well. Since we knew, more or less, what was coming to pass before reading the first words on the first page, knew that what was coming was horrific—"blasts from a shotgun held a few inches from their faces," to be followed in due course by a double hanging, Capote was free to do what he did, building his story quietly and inexorably. Building it around a classical four-part structure, he could, paradoxically, keep suspense at a high level throughout. The first three sections move along quickly and easily, intercutting back and forth between the murderers and their unsuspecting victims, then the hunters and the hunted. In the final section, "The Corner," dealing with the trial and punishment, Capote demonstrated a virtuoso magician's sleight of hand. By now all the original suspense has been dissipated, and the announced conclusion, the hanging of the killers, was obligatory. Yet he managed to get there without any diminishment of intensity or interest. The hanging scene is one of the finest of its kind, right up there with Melville's *Billy Budd* and the hanging of Popeye in William Faulkner's *Sanctuary*. With one great difference. Melville and Faulkner scrupulously avoided the dramatic cliches, working against the grain of the material. Capote pulled out all the stops: "The hangman coughed—impatiently lifted his cowboy hat and settled it again, a gesture somehow reminiscent of a turkey buzzard huffing, then smoothing its neck feathers—and Hickcock, nudged by an attendant, mounted the scaffold steps." That others present at the scene recalled the details, including the condemned men's last words, differently is not strictly relevant. It's a hell of a hanging.

Before *In Cold Blood* Capote had written—in *Other Voices, Other Rooms, The Grass Harp*, even in the lighthearted *Breakfast at Tiffany's*—romantic fables, well-removed from the world of "realistic" fiction. Even though each of these works is different from the others, all have a clear and consistent moral frame, an inversion of conventional, middle-class values. Even the lovable Holly Golightly of *Breakfast at Tiffany's* has a hard and independent core: "Good? Honest is more what I mean. Not low-type honest—I'd rob a grave, I'd steal two-bits off a dead man's eyes if I thought it would contribute to the day's enjoyment—but unto-thyself-type honest. Be anything but a coward, a pretender, an emotional crook, a whore: I'd rather have cancer than a dishonest heart." In each of these books, and most of the short stories, it is the outsiders and the outcasts who reject conventional morality and are examples of another kind of virtue. Those who manage to prosper or get along in the duplicitous world of practical matters are usually exposed as being at heart deceitful and/or self-deceived, hypocrites at best. It is these, too, who make real mischief and cause real trouble. In the end, thanks to a kind of whimsical Providence or poetic justice they get what is coming to them.

In *In Cold Blood* it is the all-American Clutter family— Herbert William Clutter, 48, the father; Bonnie, his wife; Kenyon, 15, the only son; and Nancy, 16, "the town darling"—whom destiny has selected to represent, in Capote's telling, "sane, safe, insular, even smug America—people who have every chance against people who have none." Anyone at all familiar with the world of Capote's earlier fiction knew two things, why he had chosen this subject and not another and what doom was coming to the Clutters, from the moment he first introduced Herbert Clutter. "Always certain of what he wanted in the world, Mr. Clutter had in large measure obtained it." Poor Clutter is even physically emblematic of the doom-deserving, vulnerable losers (outward and visible winners) of Capote's universe: "Though he wore rimless glasses and was of but average height, standing just under five feet ten, Mr. Clutter cut a man's-man figure. His shoulders were broad, his hair had held its dark color, his

square-jawed confident face retained a healthy-hued youthfulness, and his teeth, unstained and strong enough to shatter walnuts, were still intact." People who happened to have read Capote would read that passage and others with an awareness of his irony. People who had never read a word until the arrival of *In Cold Blood,* the huge majority of the audience that made the book a bestseller, were at once invited and allowed to take things straight, at face value. The subtext, however, is slightly camouflaged and complicated because there are some good "straights" in the story, the most important of whom, "a lean and handsome fourth-generation Kansan of forty-seven," is Alvin Adams Dewey, an agent of the Kansas Bureau of Investigation and the closest facsimile of a conventional "hero" in the book. Alvin Dewey and his family became friends of Capote in real life and was noted by Gloria Steinem in her account of "The Party" in 1967. "Alvin Dewey answered questions about problems of the Clutter case, just as dignified and direct in the Paley dining room as he had been in Kansas during the murder investigation in *In Cold Blood*." Subtext: *There are some real people out there beyond the Hudson, Dorothy. Even in a place like Kansas.* But Dewey, as a figure in the book, is treated with a respect and consideration that, otherwise, only the killers receive.

Capote is adroitly clever here, too. He inverts the old good-cop-bad-cop convention and uses it on the murderers. One, Dick Hickcock, is from the outset the most blameworthy and the least attractive, basically a bad influence on the other, Perry Smith, who is presented with deeply dimensional sympathy. Hickcock is the heavy. There is an archetypal malevolence about him with his head "halved like an apple, then put together a fraction off center," with his "left eye being truly serpentine, with a venomous, sickly-blue squint that, although it was involuntarily acquired, seemed nevertheless to warn of bitter sediment at the bottom of his nature." That's our first impression. Not too pretty, huh? You bring a serpent and an apple together in the same paragraph and you're talking Original Sin and suchlike.

Perry Smith, though he suffers from a physical deformity as the result of an accident, has an interesting look about him: "It was a changeling's face, and mirror-guided experiments had taught him how to ring the changes, how to look now ominous, now impish, now soulful; a tilt of the head, a twist of the lips, and the corrupt gypsy became the gentle romantic." Perry Smith becomes in almost every detail we are given a spooky embodiment of Capote's early fiction. What could be more perfect for a Capote protagonist than to be the child of "a lean Cherokee girl (who) rode a wild horse, a 'bucking bronco,' and her loosened hair whipped back and forth, flew about like a flamenco dancer's"? Capote gives us an empathetic and fascinating look at a murderer's psyche through his portrait of Perry Smith.

There are a number of problems, more evident in hindsight than at the time. For one thing there is the complex matter of fact and judgment. When pictures of the people involved appeared in the magazines, it was clear how much of Capote's descriptions and judgments was subjective, *literary*. The people did not look much like the people he described. Later it turned out that they did not do or say all the things he attributed to them; and some things neither he nor anyone else could have known. Still, it was wonderful reporting and charged writing. And we have become used to the other flaws in our post-Capote non-fiction narratives.

There is also the slightly more disturbing fact that neither the Clutters nor the killers were fictional constructs. They were real people. The brains and blood and hair that splatter walls of the house at River Valley Farm were real. There remains the often asked and always unanswered question, then: were the lives and deaths of these people exploited for the sake of our titillation and the author's profit? Maybe so, but by now both titillation and profit from the real sufferings of others have become so commonplace as to leave us unfit to ask that question about a book from 31 years ago. Maybe Capote lent to the "true crime" story a patina of literary respectability; but now it seems that this was coming anyway, part of the spirit of the 1960's, as was our gradual change over from concern for victims to fascination with perpetrators. Capote's book had something to do with that change of heart and values and certainly spawned a multitude of literary imitations in both fiction and non-fiction. For that reason alone *In Cold Blood* is an important book, an historical landmark. And, finally, there is another, maybe stronger claim the book makes. The "real" world of America as revealed in this story, of which Capote said at the time "It's what I really think about America," has come to pass, is far more a matter of public fact than private vision. Who today would deny that we live in a "desperate, savage, violent America (that is) in collision with sane, safe, insular, even smug America"? In that sense *In Cold Blood* can qualify as prophecy.

What was beyond prophecy, even predictability, was that this book would be the last "big" book by Truman Capote. There would be five more books in his lifetime, none without style and merit, but none of them more than minor exercises. When he died in 1984, he had been working for many years on the novel *Answered Prayers,* dealing with his rich and powerful acquaintances, the folks who came to The Party. When something was cobbled together by Random House from published excerpts and leftover bits and pieces, it was described on the jacket as "perhaps the most famous unpublished novel in contemporary American letters." The publication of *Answered Prayers* in 1987 did little or nothing to change that judgment call. Meantime, no question about it, Truman Capote's continuing claim on our attention derives from and rests in a single extraordinary volume—*In Cold Blood.*

REVIEWS OF TRUE-CRIME PUBLICATIONS

David Lodge (review date 11 January 1980)

SOURCE: "From a View to a Death," in *The Times Literary Supplement,* January 11, 1980, pp. 27-8.

[*In the following review, Lodge discusses* The Executioner's Song.]

What the American short-story writer Leonard Michaels calls "the condemned prisoner story" (in a book, *I Would Have Saved Them If I Could,* which contains and alludes to several examples of the genre) has exercised a powerful fascination over the modern literary imagination. This is not surprising. Capital punishment, and the ritual associated with it, dramatize the inevitability and finality of personal death with a stark intensity that no other action, not even terminal illness, can match. We all know that we must die, but most of the time we suppress the knowledge, or others suppress it for us; only the condemned prisoner must live with the certain knowledge of the exact day and hour at which he will pass from life to death. And, since capital punishment is a legal institution, an act through which the State asserts the sanctity of human life by taking one, it brings into consciousness the paradoxes and contradictions on which civilization is founded, and poses in an extreme and daunting way the perennial problems of evil, responsibility and justice.

Among literary polemics against capital punishment, Orwell's "A Hanging" is a classic of the documentary prose method, Oscar Wilde's "The Ballad of Reading Gaol" of the poetic. More existential in emphasis are the celebrated fabulations of Ambrose Bierce ("Occurrence at Owl Creek Bridge") and Borges ("The Secret Miracle") which stretch the instant before death to encompass an epic of desire. In the nineteenth-century novel (putting aside such cases as *The Heart of Midlothian* and *Adam Bede,* in which the machinery of the plot allows the prisoner—and thus, vicariously, the reader—a reprieve) one thinks particularly of Dickens's fascination with the subject: his gloating account of Fagin in the condemned cell, Wemmick's disconcertingly casual interview with the "Colonel" in *Great Expectations,* and the grimly ironic reversal by which the monstrous hangman Dennis in *Barnaby Rudge* meets his end. Dickens was opposed to capital punishment in principle, but was drawn irresistibly to witness, and to describe, several executions. Byron described the guillotining of three men in a letter which gave Leonard Michaels his title:

> The first turned me quite hot and thirsty, and made
> me shake so that I could hardly hold the opera glass.
> (I was close, but was determined to see, as one should

see everything, once, with attention); the second and third (which shows how dreadfully soon things grow indifferent) had no effect on me as a horror, though I would have saved them if I could.

One could go back at least as far as *Measure for Measure* (before the Renaissance, the condemned prisoner is usually a martyr, and the meaning of his story quite different). But while reading Norman Mailer's monumental and enthralling non-fiction novel about the execution of Gary Gilmore, the literary parallel which came most readily to my mind was James Boswell's account of his dealings with his client John Reid, in that volume of the Journals entitled *Boswell for the Defence* in the Yale edition. Reid, whom Boswell had succeeded in getting acquitted of a charge of sheep-stealing in his first court case, was in 1774 again charged with the same offence (then a capital one) and in spite of Boswell's eloquent defence, was found guilty and sentenced to death. Boswell, who believed the man was really guilty, urged him to confess before he died, but Reid staunchly asserted his innocence. While seeking, without much hope, to obtain a commutation of the sentence to transportation, Boswell visited his client frequently in the condemned cell, and became obsessed with the case to an extent which alarmed his wife and friends. He was deeply impressed by the calm resignation with which Reid contemplated his imminent death and the steadfastness with which he averred his innocence, but he was unable to reconcile these two facts with each other, or with his professional intuition that Reid was guilty. Although Boswell's interest was sincerely compassionate, it always hovered on the edge of the purely aesthetic. "I was desirous to have his picture done *while under sentence of death* and was therefore rather desirous that, in case a respite were to come, it should not come till he had sat his full time . . . When it was finished, and hung upon a nail to dry, it swung, which looked ominous to my fancy."

The respite, or stay of execution, does come, but upsets rather than encourages Reid, who however persists in maintaining his innocence. Boswell concocts a crazy plot to rush Reid's body from the scaffold and attempt to resuscitate him. He resolves "to know the truth by being with him to the very last minute of his life". At their final interview, with the executioner waiting to escort Reid to the scaffold, the latter again avers his innocence. "Then", says Boswell, "I shall trouble you no more upon this head. I believe you. God forbid that I should not believe a fellow man in your situation." Just before he is turned off, Reid speaks from the scaffold: "Take warning: mine is an unjust sentence." But some of the people around think he said: "Mine is a just sentence." The hangman confirms the former version, but a tantalizing, irresolvable doubt lingers to haunt Boswell.

Gary Gilmore believed he had been hanged in eighteenth-century England in a previous incarnation, but that is not

what invites a comparison between Mailer's and Boswell's versions of the condemned prisoner story; rather, it is that both Reid and Gilmore, in their different ways, by taking up an unexpected stance towards their own imminent executions, fascinated and puzzled and provoked those who observed them to the point of obsession. Both stories are as much about the observers as about the observed.

As everyone must know by now, Gary Gilmore committed two callous murders in Utah in 1976, was charged and convicted and sentenced to death, but refused to exercise the right of appeal which would have ensured either the commutation of his sentence to life imprisonment or the indefinite postponement of his execution. By refusing to play the part expected of him, by insisting upon being executed, Gilmore called the State's bluff. American society was no longer able to hide its uncertainty about what to do with proven killers behind the interminable delays and technical quibbling of the legal process. "I believe I was given a fair trial and I think the sentence is just and I am willing to accept it like a man", said Gilmore. "Don't the people of Utah have the courage of their convictions?" This was Gilmore's mock, and it was quite unanswerable except on Gilmore's own terms. The officials and lawyers of the Utah Attorney General's office accordingly put in motion the machinery for carrying out the sentence, but it made them feel uneasy, and a little foolish, that they were collaborating with Gilmore rather than punishing him, while at the same time they were taking a great deal of flak from the American Civil Liberties Union and the National Association for the Advancement of Colored People. These liberal pressure groups tried every legal device to stop Gilmore's execution because they feared it would jeopardize the lives of all the other men on Death Rows across America. Gilmore had a mock for them too.

> V. Jinks Dabney of ACLU, what a phoney-sounding name. You said in *Salt Lake Tribune* there is still a chance that Gilmore may flip-flop and change his mind about wanting to be executed. No chance, V. Jinks Dabney, no way, never. You and ACLU are the flip-flops. You take one stand on abortion, which is actually execution. You are all for that. And then you take another stand on capital punishment. You're against that. Where are your convictions, V. Jinks Dabney? Do you and ACLU know where you really stand on anything?

Remarks like that, taken from one of many tape-recorded conversations between Gilmore and his lawyers in the maximum security wing of Utah State Prison, inevitably make one wonder how and why a man capable of such wit and acumen came to be in the condemned cell at all. Gary Gilmore was a gifted artist, had an IQ of 140 and could quote Shelley (when *Newsweek* attributed the poem to him, he enjoyed the joke). But at thirty-six he had spent eighteen of his last twenty-two years in gaol, and since being sent to reform school he had never been free for longer than eight months at a stretch. He described himself mockingly as "the eternal recidivist". His crimes of robbery with violence were invariably rash, impulsive and unprofitable. He came to Utah on parole, generously sponsored by his cousin Brenda. This woman, her relatives and friends, did as much as anyone could expect and more, to assist Gary's rehabilitation.

They lent him money and clothing, found him a job, helped him buy an old car, tolerated his rough manners. But Gary was impatient: he wanted more money, a better car. He commenced a passionate affair with a young girl of nineteen, Nicole Barrett, already twice married and with two children, a beautiful but unhappy young woman whose psychological and sexual history was almost as self-destructive as Gary's own. When Gary got frustrated, over money or sex, he drank, and when he drank he got dangerous. Estranged from Nicole, and pressed for money to make the payments on his new pick-up truck, he went on a rampage and in one twenty-four-hour period robbed the tills of a filling station and a motel office, shooting their respective attendants through the head at point-blank range. He never counted his loot and when he was told, shortly after his arrest, that it scarcely amounted to $250 in all, he wept and said, "I hope they execute me for it. I ought to die for what I did."

Who could gainsay him? For a few paltry dollars, and the relief of frustration, he had laid waste the lives of two fine, decent young men, and the lives of their wives and families. The disproportion between motive and deed baffled everyone. Lawyers, police, psychiatrists, and journalists again and again probed for some secret clue to the enigma—some concealed fact, some childhood trauma, some sexual hangup; and again and again Gary gave them the same answer, but most explicitly in his last interview, a telephone conversation on the very eve of his execution: "I was always capable of murder . . . I can become totally devoid of feelings for others, unemotional". The uncomfortable idea that Gilmore compels us to contemplate is that there may be such a thing as innate evil, which can be neither explained nor expelled by conditioning. "Are you the devil?" Nicole once asked him, on an impulse, early in their relationship. He wasn't, but, as he said to her later in a remarkable letter written from prison, "I might be further from God than I am from the devil. Which is not a good thing . . . It seems that I know evil more intimately than I know goodness and that's not a good thing either. I want to get even, to be made even, whole, my debts paid (whatever it may take!) to have no blemish, no reason to feel guilt or fear. . . ." If Gilmore thought he could best achieve this by accepting his sentence, who could gainsay him? His comment on the alternative was shrewd and all too plausible; "What do I do, rot in prison? growing old and bitter and eventually work this round in my mind to where it

reads that I'm the one who's getting fucked around, that I'm just an innocent victim of society's bullshit?"

In an afterword, Norman Mailer describes *The Executioner's Song* as a true-life story told as a novel. This means more than selecting and ordering the narration of events with an eye to effects of suspense and ironic juxtaposition; and it means more than evoking atmosphere, setting and character by an artful selection of synecdochic details; it means above all presenting events as they were perceived and reflected upon by the people involved, rather than from the detached perspective of a historian. Norman Mailer has written non-fiction novels before—*The Armies of the Night, Miami and the Siege of Chicago*—but in those books he himself appeared, in the third person, as the dominant character. *The Executioner's Song* is remarkable, among Mailer's works, for the almost complete absence of the author's personality from the text. Not only does Mailer himself not appear in the story, he seldom makes his presence felt stylistically. Following the model of Truman Capote's *In Cold Blood* (1965), a book on a very similar subject for which the author coined the term "non-fiction novel", but going even further in stylistic self-effacement, Mailer tells his story very largely within the constraints of the linguistic registers of the people involved. He makes extensive use of the rhetorical device known to stylisticians as "free indirect speech", in which the narrator omits those tags, "he said", "she perceived" etc, that overtly signal his presence in the text, and describes the characters' perceptions and reflections in their own kind of language—e.g., this passage from Nicole's point of view:

> Gary came home in a sloppy old windcheater with the sleeves cut off. His pants were a mess, and he was half drunk. He told her to go over with him to Val Conlin's to examine the truck. She asked him to get cleaned up first. She didn't really want to be seen with him. He looked like he slept out in the yard.

Gilmore himself, it should be noted, is never represented in this way, as a reflector of events; he is always an object of other people's perception, and when his actions are described by the narrator, it is without any psychological interiority. The challenging enigma of his character is thus preserved, and respected, to the end. Readers, like the people associated with him, have to judge Gilmore for themselves, on the evidence of his words and deeds. An additional reason for this strategy, and for Mailer's self-effacement, was no doubt the fact that Mailer himself never met Gilmore. By the time Mailer started researching the book, Gilmore was no longer available for interview.

Although Gary Gilmore is never presented from within, he dominates the first half of the book, which is called "Western Voices": the focus is upon his character, his impact on the dull, decent society of small-town Utah, the cruel folly of his crimes, and the formation of this existential decision to die. In Part 2, "Eastern Voices" (the titles of the parts indicate the book's narrative method), the emphasis shifts somewhat from Gary to the people who surround him: guarding him, observing him, trying to get him reprieved, trying to get him executed, trying to understand him and, especially, trying to report him. The media men move into Utah in a big way, among them one Larry Schiller, a successful photographer turned agent-producer, who is sensitive about his reputation as a practitioner of morbid and unscrupulous cheque-book journalism, but determined to secure the rights to what he identifies as a story of extraordinary human interest.

Shortly after Schiller's arrival on the scene, Gary Gilmore's death-wish became a *Liebestod:* Nicole Barrett (who had taken to wandering round the walls of the prison yelling "I love you, Gary Gilmore", and had already tried cutting her wrists) succeeded in smuggling an overdose of Seconal tablets into the gaol in her vagina and the two lovers made a suicide pact that failed only because the dose was not quite big enough. Gilmore was getting upset by the delays to his execution, and was racked with jealousy on Nicole's account, as Schiller discovered when he got hold of Gary's letters to her from prison, an unbelievable haul of 1,000 pages of confession, self-analysis, reincarnation, romantic love and crude sexual fantasy.

> Schiller began to feel a little security. Even if the Supreme Court took back their stay and Gary was executed in a week or so, these letters still offered the story. He not only had the man's reason for dying but Romeo and Juliet and life after death. It might even be enough for a screen writer.

When Schiller's financial backers, ABC, drop out, he takes on the financial risk himself, aiming to collect a mass of documentation about the Gary Gilmore case, which can be handed over to a professional writer who will make a book out of it. At some point it dawns on the reader of *The Executioner's Song* that this *is* the book. Whatever odium attaches to Schiller, therefore, as an exploiter of Gary Gilmore's death, must be shared at one remove by Mailer. Mailer deals with this problem, and with the problem of his own belatedness upon the scene, boldly and effectively, by putting Larry Schiller, warts and all, in the foreground of "Eastern Voices". Thus Schiller performs the role that Mailer himself, ironically distanced by third-person narration, performs in his earlier books of reportage: not merely a reflector of events, but a consciousness in which the ethics and pragmatics of the writing project itself are laid bare. Schiller is in fact one of Mailer's finest character-creations—egotistical, unscrupulous, but human, comic and alive. Here he is, having snatched a quick vacation in Hawaii to appease his girlfriend Stephanie, dealing with bad news on the telephone

from Gilmore's lawyer; the insurers of one of Gilmore's victims have filed an order for him to make a deposition, which threatens Schiller's monopoly over his story:

> "I want you to go right into Court. If you can't block the deposition, at least file a motion that it's got to be put in bond." He smacked his fist against the night table, feeling a whole kinship with the notion of bond. "The tapes from that meeting", he said, "have got to be sealed right in the jail, and the Court has to give an order that they're not to be transcribed for so many months, blah blah, you understand what I mean, et cetera". Stephie was ready to kill him. Here it was supposed to be a vacation, and he was living on the phone. "Is this what it's going to be like when we get married?" she cried out. Was she just another woman? Was she a business deal? Schiller waved her off. Over the wire, he was practically writing out the motion. What a relief when he learned a couple of days later that the Judge agreed to seal the stuff in wax, literally, until March.

It is impossible not to admire in some degree Schiller's energy, determination and resourcefulness, or to remain completely aloof from the excitement of his wheeling and dealing. On the other hand the moral ambivalence of his position is clear, and clear to himself.

In order to get Gilmore to entrust him with the rights to his story, he must form a friendly relationship with him, but the story will have maximum value only if Gary dies at the end of it—and can one wish for a friend's, or a client's death? When Gary's brother puts the question bluntly to him, Schiller has an answer ready: "I'm here to record history, not to make it". But even as he first formulated that defence, he had the unspoken thought: "Actually, I have become part of it. All around me. I'm becoming part of the story". Like Boswell in the case of John Reid, Schiller found he had invested more of himself than he knew in the life and death of Gary Gilmore.

Whatever the impurity of Schiller's motives, his judgment of the literary potential of the Gary Gilmore story was not misplaced, and one can understand why Norman Mailer put aside his own novel-in-progress to take it on. For the abiding impression this book leaves, with me at least, is of the remarkably "literary" quality of so many of its source materials, both major and minor.

The sexual relationship between Gary and Nicole, which physical separation raised to the pitch of the romantic sublime, was of course the most important of these "gifts" to the writer, because it was structural: establishing a fundamental antithesis between inside and outside prison—then, when Nicole is confined to a psychiatric ward after her suicide attempt, between two kinds of prison, so that from being a Romeo and Juliet they become a kind of Eloise and Abelard.

On the night when he committed his first murder, Gary was driving Nicole's schizophrenic sister April around in his pick-up truck, and her distracted Gertrude Stein-like remarks provide a weirdly appropriate surrealistic chorus to his actions (e.g., "It's hard to get along if you have to wait too long. The rooms get narrow and very often there is a dog").

As the story draws towards its close, the gratuitous ironies and equivalences and symbols multiply amazingly. During the night before Gary's execution, while an extraordinary vigil-cum-party is in progress in his cell, the ACLU persuade an eccentric judge to make a last-minute stay of execution. The Attorney-General's staff retaliate with a writ of Mandamus, which will have to be heard by three judges at a higher court in Denver.

In the early hours of the morning, representatives of both sides, and one of the judges, fly over the Rockies through a storm in a small uninsured prop plane. There seems a high probability that they will all get killed in this frantic legal battle over Gary Gilmore's life, and though they make it safely to Denver, the judge has shortened his life expectancy by taking up smoking again under the strain of the flight. The stay is quashed, a last, desperate appeal to the Supreme Court fails, and Gary Gilmore goes before the firing squad (his choice of death) only a little behind schedule. Larry Schiller, one of five people Gilmore was allowed to invite to witness his execution, discovers when he gets inside the prison that he has forgotten his notebook, and has to use his cheque-book as a substitute. The prince of cheque-book journalism, compelled to write his notes on the backs of cheques! In a work of fiction the irony would seem too heavy, but if you believe it actually happened it takes your breath away.

Mailer describes *The Executioner's Song* as a "dare I say it, true life story", and "as accurate as one could make it". We know, of course, and Mailer acknowledges, that absolute truth is never attainable in human affairs; but the basic contract the non-fiction novelist makes with his readers, the guarantee that his story is based entirely on verifiable sources, does enable him to exert over them the spell of the classic realistic novel, which has been so assiduously deconstructed and to an extent discredited by contemporary criticism. *The Executioner's Song* demonstrates the undiminished power of empirical narrative to move, instruct, and delight, to provoke pity and fear, and to extend our human understanding. It is remarkable, not for the originality of its conception—*In Cold Blood* retains that prize—but for the professional skill and self-discipline with which it is composed. This is easy to underestimate. There is a nice moment in *The Armies of the Night* when Robert Lowell says, a shade patronizingly, to Mailer, "I really think you are the best journalist in America",

and Mailer replies, "Well, Cal . . . there are days when I think of myself as the best writer in America". *The Executioner's Song* certainly does not weaken that claim.

Maria Simson (review date 20 April 1992)

SOURCE: "'Who Killed My Daughter?': Lois Duncan (and Delacorte) Search for an Answer," in *Publishers Weekly,* Vol. 239, April 20, 1992, p. 19.

[*Below, Simson reviews* Who Killed My Daughter?]

"*Don't Look Behind You* (1989) was a book about a teenage girl who was chased by a hitman in a Camarro," says Lois Duncan of her 1989 YA novel. "Later that year, my eldest daughter, who was the model for the girl, was chased by a hitman driving a Camarro." The difference is that in real life, 18-year-old Kaitlyn Arquette was shot and killed. Since then, Duncan, who has 39 novels to her credit, has written only one book—*Who Killed My Daughter?: The True Story of a Mother's Search for Her Daughter's Murderer,* due from Delacorte in June.

Had Kaitlyn's death been the random killing that the police labeled it, there would have been no need for a search. But while settling her daughter's affairs, Duncan discovered from a telephone bill that calls had been made from Kaitlyn's apartment to an unlisted California number minutes *after* her death. Other discrepancies, too, led Duncan to suspect that her daughter's death was no accident.

"Soon after the murder I began having memory blackouts," says Duncan. "As I didn't want to misremember anything, I began taking daily notes"—notes that quickly began developing into a book. "It helped keep me sane. I would sit down and write a chapter in real time, but I never knew what was going to happen next."

Duncan, who used to teach journalism at the University of New Mexico, spent the next two years following up leads. When these cooled, she turned, with some skepticism, to psychic investigators who helped her pick up the trail. But these leads, too, petered out. Duncan decided that "the only way to find out the missing information was to make the story public."

This January, on what would have been Kaitlyn's 21st birthday, she mailed the manuscript to her agent, Claire Smith, who in turn sent it on to both Dell/Delacorte publisher Carole Baron and Books for Young Readers division publisher George Nicholson. "We had done a lot of business with Lois through the Books for Young Readers department, so it was natural we would see it," says Baron. Even though she did not know Duncan personally, she was well aware of her daughter's death, having been in Albuquerque at the time of the killing.

Baron hopes that the book will travel beyond the normal true-crime audience to interest any parent who is concerned about the increasing violence against children: "It doesn't matter who you are—all kids can get hurt," she says. According to associate publicity director Judy Westerman, the mainstream media, including major talk shows, have already expressed considerable interest in the book, which will no doubt bolster Duncan on her first-ever author tour.

But Delacorte sees yet another audience as well, among Duncan's original readers—young adults. "Booksellers who know her from her novels are very interested in this project, and our sales force is tapping into that," says Baron. "Young adults will have no difficulty reading the book." Everyone connected with the book remarks upon its similarities to Duncan's YA stories of murder and mystery. And when Duncan visits the ALA and the Canadian Library Association this year, she will be participating both as an adult author and as a YA author.

There is, however, one other audience and that is the one Duncan is most desperate to reach. "We've found out so much [about Kaitlyn's death] but there are still holes. We're hoping that someone out there will be able to help fill a few of those holes." With that in mind, *Who Killed My Daughter?* opens with a list of possible scenarios and unanswered questions, along with addresses for Duncan and for the New Mexico attorney general, in the hope that some reader will come forward with information that answers the question in Duncan's title.

Joe Sharkey (review date 19 March 1995)

SOURCE: "Jeffrey MacDonald's New Jury," in *The New York Times Book Review,* March 19, 1995, pp. 31-2.

[*Below, Sharkey reviews* Fatal Justice: Reinvestigating the MacDonald Murders, *in which the authors argue that Jeffrey MacDonald was wrongly convicted of murdering his wife and daughters.*]

Writers who reconstruct major murder cases quickly discover that prosecutors and the police routinely botch certain things, especially during the initial chaos at a crime scene. Particularly when the suspect looks obviously guilty, investigators can get sloppy; they cut corners, conveniently overlooking the shreds of confoundingly contradictory evidence (or amazing coincidence) that almost always turn up.

When the accused can hire the best defense lawyers, these blunders can come back to torment prosecutors who don't have their cases nailed down tight. Red-faced investigators squirm on the stand under blistering cross-examination, and the ingredients of conspiracy theories pile up neatly beside the mixing bowl.

In *Fatal Justice: Reinvestigating the MacDonald Murders,* Jerry Allen Potter and Fred Bost maintain that ineptitude, arrogance, opportunism and, perhaps, even conspiracy persuaded a jury and convinced the public that Jeffrey R. MacDonald, a Green Beret captain and Army physician, brutally murdered his wife, Colette, and their two young daughters in 1970. Dr. MacDonald, they believe, was railroaded by prosecutors and then demonized by the writer Joe McGinniss in his 1983 best seller, *Fatal Vision.*

Mr. Potter and Mr. Bost detail striking examples of spectacularly botched forensic evidence from the voluminous case records. With the ardor of defense attorneys, they marshal documentation to argue that the prosecution mishandled evidence, withheld potentially exculpatory material and even discounted confessions from other suspects.

Unfortunately, in this retrial, no cross-examination is allowed. Actions are freely interpreted and motivations freely ascribed—but the players are not given the benefit of reply. Some important sources are now dead. There were a lot of times, when I was reading this book, that I wanted to jump up and say, "I object."

But the authors did persuade me that the MacDonald trial was a sorry spectacle of gross legal ineptitude. Furthermore, the McGinniss portrait of Dr. MacDonald, so brilliantly drawn, glossed over some of the most troublesome questions about the prosecution's case. What we need is a work of painstakingly honest journalism, à la *Case Closed,* Gerald Posner's landmark re-examination of the assassination of John F. Kennedy. What Mr. Potter and Mr. Bost give us instead is courtroom advocacy.

During his trial in 1979, Dr. MacDonald, a surgeon, was depicted as a narcissistic sociopath, an amphetamine abuser and secret philanderer who in early 1970 flew into a rage and murdered his family in their home at Fort Bragg, N.C. The word "Pig" was scrawled in blood near the bodies—an interesting detail at a time when headlines were blazing over arrests in the Charles Manson murders. Dr. MacDonald, a tall, handsome, muscular man, claimed that he had been overpowered by four hippies—three men and a woman in a floppy hat—who stabbed him and then killed his wife and children while chanting "Acid is groovy."

Investigators had problems with this story even beyond the obvious one of how four doped-up hippies could so easily subdue a Green Beret to butcher his family. For one, Dr. MacDonald's wounds were not life threatening. He also behaved oddly, reacting less with grief than outrage about the unfairness of the crime to himself. He was arrested.

Amid the drug hysteria induced by the Manson murders, Dr. MacDonald became a national celebrity—and won a constituency by positioning himself in the news media as a tragic victim, a falsely accused military hero whose life was destroyed by a satanic drug cult. After a four-month Army investigation, during which technicians mishandled much of the forensic evidence, no charges were brought. Jeffrey MacDonald left the Army, took a hospital job in California, bought a fancy sports car and a $300,000 beachfront condo, and lived an apparently carefree bachelor life for several years. It all came tumbling down in 1975, when he was arrested again, partly as the result of a tireless crusade by Colette's stepfather, who firmly believed that Dr. MacDonald had got away with murder. In 1979 he was tried, convicted of the three murders and sentenced to life in prison.

Then things got really complicated.

Just before the trial, Dr. MacDonald had signed a contract with Joe McGinniss, giving him complete cooperation in exchange for a percentage of the royalties from a book about his ordeal. From prison, Dr. MacDonald, who believed that Mr. McGinniss accepted his claims of innocence, poured out his tortured thoughts in taped soliloquies for Mr. McGinniss—who had become convinced that his subject was indeed guilty. After the publication of *Fatal Vision,* with its shocking portrayal of a manipulative killer, Dr. MacDonald sued, and later received $325,000 in an out-of-court settlement. The ethics of a mutually manipulative relationship between a writer and a living character in a nonfiction work were then explored by Janet Malcolm in a celebrated series in *The New Yorker,* which excoriated Mr. McGinniss and damned journalists in general.

The lawsuit, involving the civil contract between Mr. McGinniss and Dr. MacDonald, is a side issue: Mr. Potter and Mr. Bost expend entirely too much effort trying to discredit Mr. McGinniss and not enough buttressing their arguments about ineptitudes during the criminal trial, which was over long before the McGinniss book appeared.

The most prominent of these involves a young woman named Helena Stoeckley, a defense witness who claimed to be a member of a devil-worshiping cult near Fort Bragg at the time of the murders. On various occasions (including while in therapy for drug addiction), Stoeckley had spoken publicly of recovered memories of being present at the MacDonald murders and sometimes described memories of participating in other ritual killings. She eventually came to believe that she might have been the very hippie in the floppy hat named by Dr. MacDonald as one of the killers. During the trial, Stoeckley was successfully depicted by the prosecu-

tion as a burned-out drug case. She died of cirrhosis of the liver and pneumonia in 1983.

The ritual-murder connection is what got the authors started in the first place. Mr. Potter, who had written about ritual cult murders before, says that he began exploring the case in 1985 at the behest of a MacDonald supporter, a former F.B.I. agent named Ted L. Gunderson, who had become interested in witchcraft and ritual murders of children. Early in *Fatal Justice,* the account of Mr. Potter's first meeting with Mr. Gunderson sets an overwrought conspiratorial tone (a "cold fog rising out of Chavez Ravine" pours "over the freeway like a wet ghost slithering through the Asian business district"). After digesting Mr. Gunderson's files on the case, Mr. Potter hooked up with Mr. Bost, a former Army Special Forces sergeant who was a reporter in North Carolina.

Of course, prosecutorial misconduct turns up even in cases where the defendant is found over the body holding a smoking gun. And sometimes, of course, innocent people are wrongly convicted. On rare occasions, journalistic re-examinations of such cases—CBS's *60 Minutes* has several notable credits here—have freed wrongly convicted people. But this kind of thing isn't done by making suppositions or by offering plausible alternative scenarios that can't be proved. It's done by uncovering new evidence, presenting living witnesses, uncovering solid information that stands up to tough challenge.

That is where *Fatal Justice* most falls short. At the end of the book the authors concede their inability to "penetrate this mystery." But then they shift position. Suddenly they are in the jury box evaluating their own arguments. "If we were jurors in a new trial," they conclude, "we would find Jeffrey MacDonald wrongly accused of murder." But they aren't. They're journalists, and their story—intriguing as it seems—is full of holes. Court adjourned.

David Andrew Price (review date 3 April 1995)

SOURCE: "Criminal Policy Diverted, Justice Denied," in *Wall Street Journal,* April 3, 1995, p. A12.

[*Below, Price gives Wendy Kaminer's* It's All the Rage: Crime and Culture *an unfavorable review.*]

"Debates about crime control are rarely sensible," says lawyer-turned-writer Wendy Kaminer in *It's All the Rage: Crime and Culture.* Ms. Kaminer made her mark as a social critic with her 1992 book, *I'm Dysfunctional, You're Dysfunctional,* taking on pop-psychology fads. In her new book she aims to bring sensibleness to a range of criminal-justice issues, especially the "abuse excuse" and capital punishment.

Ms. Kaminer's wit, dogged research and epigrammatically graceful writing in *I'm Dysfunctional, You're Dysfunctional* give one high hopes for *It's All the Rage.* The epigrams are still there in her latest work, but much of the rest is missing. In her denunciation of abuse excuses—such as the "black-rage" defense dreamed up by lawyers for convicted Long Island Rail Road shooter Colin Ferguson—she eschews the fresh and detailed reporting that marked her earlier work and instead relies mainly on material from press clips about the cases of Lorena Bobbitt and Lyle and Erik Menendez.

Yes, the Menendez brothers' mistrial was unjust, but Dominick Dunne already told us how and why in *Vanity Fair.* After 20 pages of Bobbitt, Menendez, Bobbitt, Menendez, one wonders why Ms. Kaminer sees the abuse excuse as having much practical significance in the first place; from this book, it appears to have done more for essayists than for criminal defendants. Even the famous black-rage defense—presumably the impetus for the title of her book—never found its way into court. (At his trial, Ferguson argued that he was innocent, not that American racism made him do it.)

Only later, in her assaults on the death penalty and the trend toward tougher sentencing policies, do we get to the book that Ms. Kaminer obviously wanted to write. (In 1993, as the book was under way, she jokingly told the *Boston Globe* that she wanted to call it "Fear of Frying.") While railing against the irrationality of today's policies, she mostly proves unable to break free of her own prejudices as a self-described "radical individualist member of the ACLU."

Her explanation for the popularity of the death penalty and other get-tough policies is that the public is ignorant and that the politicians backing those policies are opportunistic frauds. Thus, Congress and the states enacted mandatory minimum sentencing laws not out of a belief that they might do some good but "because they were effective rhetorically." Likewise, support for the death penalty is "a case study in demagoguery." And the Supreme Court has been "delusional" in allowing capital punishment.

Moreover, the effect of violent crime on victims and their families—something that the public does know about—is, for Ms. Kaminer, beside the point in these debates. "What is the difference between the grief of a mother who loses her son to murder and the grief of a mother who loses her son to a murder conviction and an execution or twenty-five years in prison, or life without parole?" she asks myopically. The grief of the survivors is "wrenching," she allows, "but is it relevant?"

Yet for all of her effort to claim the side of rationality, her arguments often don't measure up. The death penalty is "unnecessary," she says early on, because "we can incapacitate people by incarcerating them." But we don't quite "incapacitate" people by putting them behind bars—prisoners commit violence against guards and other prisoners. Also, incapacitation is not the only possible reason to consider a death sentence "necessary"; another, as expressed by Judge Alex Kozinski of the Ninth Circuit, is the belief that "those who show utter contempt for human life by committing remorseless, premeditated murder justly forfeit the right to their own life."

Ms. Kaminer also repeats the abolitionist claim that capital punishment is "applied disproportionately in cases involving white victims, clearly implying that the lives of whites are valued more highly than the lives of racial minorities." The old Wendy Kaminer would have done the legwork to find out that this claim is debated, and that analyses by Stephen Klein of the RAND Corp. and other researchers contradict it. The old Wendy Kaminer might also have noticed the oddity of the theory that juries discriminate based on the race of the victim but not based on the race of the defendant in front of them (black defendants are slightly less likely than whites to be sentenced to death, or to be executed).

While awaiting Ms. Kaminer's next work, those interested in criminal-justice controversies should check out a recent essay collection that takes an informed look at America's rising tide of cop-outs: Alan Dershowitz's *The Abuse Excuse* (1994). Mr. Dershowitz, unlike Ms. Kaminer, gets beyond Bobbitt and Menendez. He also shows why the issue matters, connecting the handful of cases that involve such excuses with broader social concerns.

Michiko Kakutani (review date 4 April 1995)

SOURCE: "I'm O.K., You're Nowhere Near O.K.," in *The New York Times,* April 4, 1995, p. C18.

[*In the review below, Kakutani argues that Wendy Kaminer's* It's All the Rage: Crime and Culture *reads more like an "impassioned polemic than a reasoned piece of analysis."*]

Wendy Kaminer's last book, *I'm Dysfunctional, You're Dysfunctional,* was a terrifically witty, intelligent and cogent assessment of the recovery movement and its implications for American society at large. In that volume, Ms. Kaminer not only sketched the history and sources of the current vogue for self-help and public confession, but also performed a devastating deconstruction of the movement's simplistic (not to mention highly narcissistic) ethos of personal growth. Her latest book, *It's All the Rage: Crime and Culture,* purports to take up where *I'm Dysfunctional, You're Dysfunctional* left off.

As Ms. Kaminer sees it, the recovery movement's emphasis on touchy-feely empathy stands in polar opposition to another popular trend in American society: the tendency to judge too harshly and to pronounce morally self-righteous judgments on others, a tendency embodied, she suggests, in increasingly vociferous calls for the death penalty, mandatory sentencing and "three strikes you're out" laws.

Yet for all their apparent contradictions, says Ms. Kaminer, the recovery movement and the current debate over criminal-justice policies have something very much in common: a high degree of irrationality. In her view, debates about crime control "are rarely sensible," but are "ruled by politics and fear and the mindless exchange of attitudes that dominates the worst talk shows, where people never exchange ideas."

"Rationality, in general, has been out of fashion in recent years," she writes. "New Agers condemn it as left-brain thinking, some feminists consider it male-identified, while some self-styled radical academics are apt to dismiss it as a pretense of objectivity; on the right, religiosity is a much more potent political force than reason. I expect that we'll proudly become even less rational as the millennium approaches; more people will report being visited by aliens or abused by Satanic cults in childhood or graced by their guardian angels. In my worst moments, I imagine that this book would be taken more seriously by a broader audience if I claimed to be channeling the spirit of a 2,000-year-old shaman or an extraterrestrial with our interests at whatever passes for its heart. But God doesn't talk to me. This is not a book of revelation."

Had Ms. Kaminer actually gone on to expand upon this theme (the decline of rationality and the reasons for this decline) or fully explored contemporary culture's obsession with criminals and crime (as evidenced in a fascination with high-profile court cases, growing fears of random violence and increasingly insistent calls for stricter crime control), she might have produced a book as original and provocative as *I'm Dysfunctional, You're Dysfunctional.* As it stands, *It's All the Rage* is peppered with some acute asides about these subjects, but Ms. Kaminer never really pulls them together into a coherent thesis. Instead, her book turns into a rambling series of predictable attacks on the death penalty, mandatory sentencing and efforts to restrict the writ of habeas corpus (which allows for Federal appeals of state court convictions).

Ms. Kaminer, who once served as a public defender in the Brooklyn criminal courts, brings considerable ardor to this discussion, though the arguments she serves up tend to be ones we've all heard many times before. She argues that "the death penalty has been applied disproportionately in cases involving white victims, clearly implying that the lives of whites are valued more highly than the lives of racial minorities." She argues that the death penalty "is considerably more expensive than life imprisonment" and that the notion

of deterrence has little effect on "violent offenders who lack the will or capacity to control their actions or on arrogant offenders who deem themselves above the law."

"Public support for capital punishment," she writes, "seems based on ignorance about how the death penalty is applied and what it does or does not achieve." She adds that most people "don't know that many death row inmates have not had fair trials, in many cases because they have not been represented by competent counsel," that they "don't know the extent of class and racial biases in capital cases" and that "they don't know that what are commonly derided as legal technicalities—rules prohibiting the use of coerced confessions or suggestive identification procedures—bear directly on questions of innocence and guilt."

Ms. Kaminer acknowledges that her speculation about public attitudes toward the death penalty is "thoroughly unscientific" and she relies heavily in this volume on carefully selected statistics as well as on anecdotal material taken from arbitrarily chosen cases, the same sort of personal testimony prized, she notes, by "the talk show culture, in which the authority of experience almost always trumps the authority of disinterested reflection."

As a result of this approach, *It's All the Rage* reads more like a piece of impassioned polemic than a reasoned piece of analysis. Some assertions in this book are pithy at the expense of thoughtfulness; "If a conservative is a liberal who's been mugged, a liberal is a conservative once arrested." Others have a vague what-if quality that fall to take into account alternative situations: "Boot camps may also pose particular problems for the juveniles they're intended to help, if they allow mingling of juvenile and adult offenders."

All in all, it's a half-baked performance that fails to live up to Ms. Kaminer's usual standards of intellectual rigor and ferocious common sense.

Joan Ullman (essay date 18 June 1995)

SOURCE: "Crimes Don't Always Pay, Especially for Writers," in *The New York Times,* June 18, 1995, p. 4.

[*In the essay below, Ullman discusses the popularity and quality of true-crime fiction.*]

When Juliet Papa's *Ladykiller* reached bookstores in the spring its publisher and writer were poised to see sales take off.

The book by Ms. Papa, a crime reporter for WINS-AM, may have seemed quite likely to become another hot-selling book about headline crimes on Long Island, in the tradition of

Lethal Lolita about Amy Fisher and *Crossing the Line: The True Story of Long Island Serial Killer Joel Rifkin.*

Ms. Papa's subject was certainly lurid enough. The *Ladykiller* of the title, Ricardo S. Caputo, had skyrocketed to fame a year earlier, after admitting on television that he had murdered his 19-year-old fiancée and three other young women 20 years ago.

Mr. Caputo said he was turning himself in because, after 20 years on the run, he began hearing voices and was again feeling the old urge to kill.

Ms. Papa spent most of last spring working on the book, putting in one day a week at the station. In eight weeks she delivered the manuscript to the publisher, St. Martin's Press, which had timed the publication of *Ladykiller* to coincide with the start of Mr. Caputo's murder trial in Nassau County. But on the eve of the trial, on Jan. 31, he pleaded guilty.

The announcement, which seemed to spell disaster for Ms. Papa's book, underscored the volatile nature of true-crime writing. "Quickie books," those that are written and published within a few weeks or months, are as perishable as the headlines that inspire them, and for writers like Ms. Papa and others on Long Island finding success in the highly competitive field can be difficult.

Ms. Papa's publisher and agent are optimistic, saying it is far too early to predict how the book will ultimately fare. The writer remains upbeat, too, talking about possibly updating her book for the three trials that Mr. Caputo may face.

Yet among others who write about true crimes, the uncertain fate of Ms. Papa's book may seem like a sign of market glut.

It takes a big-name author like Joe McGinnis or Dominick Dunne to sell a crime book, said Darnay Hoffman, a legal historian who vacations in Southampton. The proliferation of true-crime books has led many stores to set aside a section for them.

"I used to place them in the psychology section, because crimes are about psychology," said Canio Pavone, owner of two bookstores in Sag Harbor that bear his name.

St. Martin's made the so-called quickie crime books like Ms. Papa's a specialty six years ago. But the rapid popularity did not lead to unalloyed success. "The market was getting a little crowded," said Charles E. Spicer Jr., senior editor for the True Crime Library at St. Martin's.

Although demand has declined, Mr. Spicer said, crime books continue to be profitable for the house.

Most experts say sales of hardcover true-crime titles have declined, just as they have for hardcover books in every category. "Readers are more discriminating in what they buy," Ms. Papa's agent, Jane Dystal, said. "Even Ann Rule and Joe McGinnis are not selling as well as they used to."

Mr. Spicer said top-selling quickies about well-known people like Jeffrey Dahmer, Amy Fisher and O. J. Simpson had initial printings of 100,000 or more.

He pointed to the success that Maria Efftimiades, a writer from Queens, has had with two of her four truecrime books. Ms. Efftimiades's first book, *Lethal Lolita,* now in its fourth printing, was sold to NBC-TV and became the basis for one of three network movies about Miss Fisher.

Ms. Efftimiades's latest book, *The Sins of the Mother,* about Susan V. Smith, the mother from South Carolina who has been accused of killing her two sons, which was published at the same time as *Ladykiller,* had an initial printing of 300,000 and has been another hit, Mr. Spicer said.

Elizabeth Beier, who works at Berkley Publishers, is similarly bullish for *Crossing the Line: The True Story of Long Island Serial Killer Joel Rifkin,* by two writers for *The New York Times Long Island Weekly,* Lisa Beth Pulitzer and Joan Swirsky. It was published 16 months after Mr. Rifkin's arrest. He ultimately confessed to killing 17 women.

Crossing the Line, with an initial printing of 60,000, is soon to have its second printing, Ms. Beier said.

True-crime paperbacks may be profitable for the publishers, but they seem far less so for the writers. The writers say they have to work fast for little money. Ms. Dystal, who also represents Ms. Efftimiades, said payments to most nonfiction writers had been declining.

Ms. Papa, who is back full time at WINS, said she received a "low five-figure" advance for *Ladykiller.* "Put it this way," she said, "I wouldn't quit my day job."

Though she recently signed a contract for a new true-crime book, Ms. Pulitzer said, she was disappointed by her experience with her first book. "Our agent said, 'When this book comes out, you'll be in a whole different world,'" Ms. Pulitzer recounted. "Instead, our book was in and out of the news and forgotten."

Despite nibbles from Hollywood, few of these authors are as fortunate as Ms. Efftimiades. "These writers cannot count on a continuing steady stream of royalties," Ms. Dystal said.

The idea of working the Rifkin case into a book, Ms. Pulitzer said, was from a conversation with Ms. Swirsky at a press club party.

"You have a book!" said Ms. Swirsky, a nurse, psychotherapist, health and science writer and editor of a national nursing journal.

"But I don't know how to write a book," Ms. Pulitzer recounted. "I was terrified. I thought it was too overwhelming."

"I'll help you!" Ms. Swirsky said. "Call my agent."

"I've always looked for stories wherever I am," Ms. Efftimiades said. She had been vacationing in Rhode Island, when "I read about this guy accused of murdering an entire family."

"And when I came home," said Ms. Efftimiades, who has worked at several newspapers, "I pitched this story to someone at St. Martin's."

The publisher turned her down. But when the Amy Fisher case broke a few months later and Ms. Efftimiades was covering it for *People,* St. Martin's asked her about writing a book. She wrote *Lethal Lolita* in seven weeks.

St. Martin's signed her to two additional books on other high-profile Long Island crimes, *My Name Is Katherine* about the search for Katie Beers, and her own Rifkin book, *Garden of Graves,* with a main focus on the 17 missing women.

Ms. Efftimiades wrote each in four weeks. "I crashed at the end of the year," she said.

When Ms. Papa needed advice, she turned to Ms. Efftimiades, a longtime friend and fellow player on the East Hampton Artists-Writers baseball team, for pointers. In the course of her reporting, Ms. Papa also flew to Chicago and San Francisco to interview people who recalled Mr. Caputo as a fugitive.

For her book on Ms. Smith, Ms. Efftimiades struck up friendships in the Carolinas to help lead her to sources. In writing the book in 17 days, "I divided it all up into 22 chapters and would plug my notes into each chapter as I went along."

Despite their efforts none of the writers met their subjects or their families. Publishing executives said that what counts more than the writer, the reporting, accuracy or literary qualities are factors like the nature of the crime and its geography, timing and press coverage.

Ms. Efftimiades's book about Susan Smith has continued to outsell a rival account by Andrea Peyser, a columnist for *The New York Post,* that appeared a month after hers.

Although the sales of *Ladykiller* may be hurt by a lack of attention, other crime books have had an excess of publicity. Linda Wolfe, who is also a frequent vacationer on the East End, said she thought that the television movie about Robert Chambers, which was broadcast almost at the same time as the publication of her first hard-cover book, *Wasted Life,* had skimmed interest from her book.

"TV is now competing with your book," Ms. Wolfe said, "and very often it gets there faster."

"It's the difference between apples and oranges," said Steven Wick of *Newsday* and writer of *Bad Company* in 1991 about the murder of Roy Radin, a film producer from Southampton. Mr. Wick said he took a year to write the book, which was based on more than four years of reporting. "If you want to be taken seriously," Mr. Wick said, "I think you really need to delve into a story and really dig."

Ms. Papa also said it was possible to provide a quick but accurate overview. "If you're a good journalist and you're persistent," she said, "there's a lot of information you can get."

But some critics say the books lack style and sophistication. "They do a disservice to history," Mr. Caputo's lawyer, Michael Kennedy, said. "These books taint the record. Potential jurors read them and may be subliminally influenced by the errors."

Suzanne Gordon (review date 25 June 1995)

SOURCE: "Why Americans Can't Think Straight about Crime," in *Book World—The Washington Post,* Vol. XXV, No. 26, June 25, 1995, pp. 3, 13.

[*In the review below, Gordon examines Wendy Kaminer's "reflection on the problem of crime and punishment in America."*]

The title of Wendy Kaminer's sometimes unstructured but always interesting reflection on the problem of crime and punishment in America [*It's All the Rage: Crime and Culture*] is far more than a shrewd commercial calculation. It captures perfectly the author's argument: In late 20th-century America discussions of crime and punishment have been entrapped by a culture of rage and ignorance, guided not by reason—or even compassion—but by prejudice, fantasies of revenge and the most uneducated emotions. That title suggests logically the author's mission—to confront the reader with the numerous contradictions that make it difficult for our society to understand the issues of guilt and innocence, personal responsibility and societal obligation.

The author, a lawyer and freelance social critic who did a

brief stint as a public defender, frankly states that she is a card-carrying member of the ACLU and a staunch opponent of capital punishment. This viewpoint in no way detracts from the clarity of her major argument—that Americans see-saw between two extremes, "conferring too much absolution on some people and too much guilt on others."

Thus, many sympathize with the handsome, well-dressed Menendez brothers and O.J. Simpson. But the "less telegenic people on death row—poor, ill-groomed and often ill-coached by their lawyers, and, in many cases, mentally or emotionally disabled, with awful histories of abuse—are presumed to be unfettered moral agents with a capacity for self control, masters of their fates." Indeed, we are so besotted by the hard-luck stories of celebrity criminals that, Kaminer writes, we have confused questions of "guilt with questions of punishment" and allow defendants to "mitigate their guilt with evidence that should instead mitigate their sentences."

It is difficult to discuss crime in America without an excursion into the problem of television violence. Kaminer reviews the usual arguments against murder and mayhem on the tube and adds her own spin. Watching violent shows on TV makes it difficult for Americans to distinguish fact from fiction. The O.J. Simpson trial is obviously a perfect example. Is it an afternoon soap opera or a serious criminal trial?

In this discussion, Kaminer suggests that we can learn something about the effects of public consumption of violence from the history of public executions. Public executions produced not deference or greater reverence and sobriety in the public viewing them, but rowdiness and barbarity. In the 19th century they fell out of favor because "people enjoyed them too much." They thus defeated one of the main goals of the criminal justice system: "to replace untamed, private vendettas with more measured, less emotional acts of public retribution."

This theme of the confusion between public and private goals is further elaborated upon in an exploration of the conflict between the rights of victims and those of the accused. Kaminer fears that we are turning the courtroom into a therapist's office. She reminds us that the goal of a state-run system of criminal justice is not to help victims recover from the trauma of crime but to signal that crime is a "public not private concern."

This confusion between personal prejudice and public knowledge is further explored in two chapters on the death penalty—"how it is perceived and how it is applied." Kaminer argues that untested assumptions and outright bias color our views. Using a variety of surveys and polls, she contends that "the more people know [about capital punishment], the more equivocal and uncomfortable they are about support-

ing the death penalty; the less people know, the more adamant they are in support."

As an antidote to what she believes to be widespread public ignorance, Kaminer introduces some sober facts about how the death penalty is applied and to whom. Those who are sentenced to death are almost always men. Most are poor, from racial minorities, and many have been violently abused themselves. Their legal representation is often inadequate. Some are insane or retarded. Some may have been innocent.

Lest one believe that mentally incompetent people are never executed, Kaminer takes us to Louisiana. In 1984, that state medicated an insane man so that he could be considered "competent to be executed." Incompetent criminals aren't the only ones confused about the meaning of the death sentence. Kaminer tells us that some jurors have voted for the death penalty because they believe it will never actually be exercised. And before determining the sentence, many are not informed about sentencing options for defendants or eligibility for parole.

Kaminer also reviews the history of attitudes toward rehabilitation, crime control and gun control. To her, we are the perfect example of a society in which citizens fear one another so much that they perpetuate the conditions in which violence continues unchecked. The issue of gun control leads logically to a concluding chapter entitled "Virtue Talk" that highlights profound shifts in our attitudes toward government, as well as social and individual responsibility.

Today, she argues, we have given up on crime prevention, rehabilitation of criminals and the idea that society bears some responsibility for criminal behavior. Instead, pundits like William Bennett and James Q. Wilson tell the public that crime is solely a result of individual failings. The reason bad things happen to good people is that bad people with bad characters, raised by bad families, are on the loose and must be either permanently incarcerated or permanently incapacitated—i.e., killed by the state. This formulation, Kaminer believes, conveniently lets society off the hook.

Some might find Kaminer's lack of concrete recommendations disappointing. Here there is no liberal dogma to cling to, no alternative "virtue talk" to solace the insecure. Instead, the author pleads for a "nuanced view of moral agency, an ethic of relative accountability to guide us." Whether or not one agrees with all of Kaminer's arguments, this provocative book certainly accomplishes what it intended—to make readers scrutinize a web of cultural contradictions and reflect on their own and society's vicious cycle of rage and far too shallow repentance.

Darcy Frey (review date 22 October 1995)

SOURCE: "Death at an Early Age," in *The New York Times Book Review,* October 22, 1995, p. 28.

[*Below, Frey reviews* Drive-By *and* Uprising: Crips and Bloods Tell the Story of America's Youth in the Crossfire.]

On a sultry July night in 1990, in the projects of East Oakland, Calif., five teen-age boys and girls stood beneath a streetlight—talking, flirting, passing the time. Around the corner came an old green sedan. As it sped past the group, someone leaned out the window with a 45-caliber semiautomatic pistol and opened fire into the group. Two of the young people were wounded. A third, 13-year-old Kevin Reed, was shot in the groin and bled to death on the sidewalk that night. Two days later, *The Oakland Tribune* ran a story on the shooting. Even so, the particulars of Kevin's life—who he was, what he dreamed of becoming—quickly faded amid the general handwringing over Oakland's urban woes. Kevin was the city's 84th homicide victim of the year—many of those victims young black men shot down in that same East Oakland neighborhood, known to locals as "the killing zone." And so, Kevin himself was publicly reduced to a statistic and the generic subject of newspaper tributes ("An all-around great kid," Kevin's father told *The Tribune*).

The desire to render the complex, often endangered lives of inner-city teen-agers with more depth than police blotters and local newspapers usually muster has drawn dozens of nonfiction writers in recent years. The latest, *Drive-By,* comes from an Oakland journalist, Gary Rivlin, who has focused on the Kevin Reed killing in order to "explore the human side of this country's youth violence epidemic." One can see why Mr. Rivlin saw such dramatic possibilities in this apparently random act of brutality. Kevin's killers, it turned out, were fragile teen-agers themselves, one of whom—16-year-old John (Junebug) Jones—had been assaulted by six youths who had heard he was making threats against one of them. Junebug hadn't, however, and the next night—pride and body wounded—he went looking for his attackers with his friends, 15-year-old Aaron Estill and 18-year-old Anthony (Fat Tone) Davis. Junebug thought he saw them, standing under the streetlight. But as they drove by the group, Fat Tone, who was drunk and stoned at the time, opened fire on the wrong person—Kevin Reed was actually the brother of the boy who had jumped Junebug. So two cases of mistaken identity led to the death of one young man and the long imprisonment of three others—a multiple tragedy, Mr. Rivlin suggests, emblematic of the helpless fury and self-destructive codes of street justice prevailing in the inner city.

Mr. Rivlin's research is prodigious—he has interviewed every major player in the shooting—and his attitude large-hearted. He examines the murder in light of disintegrating families (Junebug and Fat Tone had absent fathers), the pressures of the crack trade (they were small-time dealers, obliged to protect their turf), bad schooling, degraded housing. Eminently well-intentioned, *Drive-By* gives us nearly 100 pages of socioeconomic background on Oakland's ghetto communities before the fateful shooting occurs—everything from a primer on the physiological effects of crack on the brain to an inquiry into whether lead from neighborhood canneries may have caused learning disabilities among area schoolchildren.

But for all the impressive marshaling of facts, Kevin, Junebug, Aaron and Fat Tone remain elusive figures, their portraits so unimaginatively drawn that the reader, too, might be guilty of mistaking one for another. At best, Mr. Rivlin's observations simply lack vividness. For example: "Junebug felt disoriented" the day after the shooting, "as if everything in his world had suddenly been turned upside down." At worst, Mr. Rivilin turns his subjects into the same sorts of journalistic abstractions he was apparently hoping to get beyond by writing his book. Junebug rationalized his drug dealing, Mr. Rivlin writes, by telling himself that "he was helping out his mother the same way a towheaded boy of yesteryear worked as a box boy after school and on Saturdays to help take the financial strain off his ma and pa." The essence of that passage may be true, but Mr. Rivlin's language is so much a part of his world and not his subject's that Junebug himself—with all the rage and hurt and teen-age fallibility that led him on his disastrous course—vanishes, and we're left with a vague approximation of inner-city adolescence, not one highly individual kid.

Uprising: Crips and Bloods Tell the Story of America's Youth in the Crossfire takes a different approach to similar material by going straight to the source. The book is a collection of interviews with 13 former gang members, who discuss life and death on the streets of Los Angeles. There are moments of brutal clarity: one interviewee, T. Rodgers, describes how his gang would prepare for drive-by shootings with a so-called drop drill. "We would yell 'Duck,' and those that were not listening would be standing, and we would tell them, 'You're dead.'" But one must hunt for such moments. From the foreword by the rap artist Ice-T, in which he declares this book "the most dramatic and major turning point in American history as far as my life is concerned," to its relentlessly hortatory tone ("It's time to stop the fighting, connect, get with one another, and get back to black. . . . Peace!"), *Uprising* can be a slog to read. One finishes the book convinced of its authentic depiction of gang life, perhaps, but hungering—as one does in all but the most artfully assembled oral histories—for a narrator who might draw some lasting wisdom from all the noise.

As Joan Didion famously wrote, we tell ourselves stories in order to live. But also one might add, to know how others live—particularly that vast group of citizens, living in poor black communities, whose experiences seem so utterly foreign to middle-class white America. And readers trying to understand this world don't want just statistics on teen-age pregnancy or the rules of drug dealing: we want to peer into people's souls and begin to understand, to know how three confused but certainly not irredeemable young men found themselves committing a drive-by shooting for which they were later ripped apart by guilt and grief. That is the stuff of high drama, which requires not merely assiduous research or verbatim testimonials, but an imaginative writer able to transform raw data into felt life on the page. After describing a jailhouse interview with Fat Tone, Mr. Rivlin writes: "I felt sympathy for this oversize kid born with the odds stacked against him, trying to survive in circumstances that were the closest thing to hell on earth that my mind could possibly imagine." But that's the problem: Mr. Rivlin could not really imagine it, or do so in a way that would bring Fat Tone's singular humanity to life.

Richard Bernstein (review date 19 December 1995)

SOURCE: "Could a Stalker Have Been Stopped?," in *The New York Times,* December 19, 1995, p. C21.

[*In the following review, Bernstein examines* The Stalking of Kristin.]

Kristin Lardner, a student at the School of the Museum of Fine Arts in Boston, was gunned down on the street on May 30, 1992. She was a vibrant, gently rebellious 21-year-old whose fatal mistake was to have gotten into a brief romance with one Michael Cartier, a young man with a rap sheet three pages long. When she tried to leave him, Mr. Cartier killed her, and then, minutes later, killed himself. George Lardner Jr., in this investigation of his daughter's murder, knows where ultimate blame should be placed: on the violent and sadistic Mr. Cartier himself. But his anger is all the greater because along the way there were many others who could have prevented the murder merely by doing their job.

Mr. Lardner, a longtime reporter for *The Washington Post,* won a Pulitzer Prize in 1993 for a series of articles on Ms. Lardner's death. Here he extends his earlier investigation, attributing complacency, ineptitude and bungling to various judges, prosecutors and parole officers who, he argues, should have gotten Ms. Lardner's murderer off the streets before he could take her life.

The Stalking of Kristin is also a more general complaint: that the prevailing attitude toward crime is subject to a host of illusions that have the effect of deflecting attention from what really needs to be done. We spend a lot of our collective time wondering where society has gone wrong, Mr. Lardner argues, at a time when most people convicted of a crime—

more than 70 percent in 1992—are either on probation or parole when they commit it.

There is "a footloose legion of convicted criminals on our streets, from petty offenders on their way up the ladder to seasoned felons who know the ropes," Mr. Lardner writes. "They know how to play the game. They know they can count on being released at any and every stage after arrest—on bond, on their own recognizance, for rehabilitation, for counseling, for supervision by probation and parole officers too busy to do any real supervising."

A father who has lost his daughter is, it could be argued, not the sort of dispassionate observer to write about that very crime. On the other hand, those who have suffered the kind of terrible loss that Mr. Lardner did are more likely to have the passion and commitment to investigate the issue thoroughly, to track down the operations of the system in every detail.

And so Mr. Lardner makes no secret of how intensely he feels the loss of his daughter, who was the youngest of his and his wife Rosemary's five children. But it is his reporter's skills that come through in *The Stalking of Kristin,* which manages to be both heartfelt and carefully documented, angry and judicious at the same time. Mr. Lardner assiduously interviewed Ms. Lardner's friends and the friends and family members of Mr. Cartier. He searches the documentary record. He talks to every official with a connection to the case.

The crucial person to understand in this story is, sadly, not Ms. Lardner but her stalker, and here Mr. Lardner, while he does his reporter's work, leaves the reader unsatisfied. He finds out about Mr. Cartier's troubled childhood, his broken family, his utterly unloving mother, his descent as a teenager into violence, especially violence against women. And yet the portrait lacks psychological depth. The impression is left that Mr. Cartier was just bad, an embodiment of malevolence and that nothing could have been done with him except to lock him up and throw away the key. Very possibly that is true. But Mr. Cartier not only killed Ms. Lardner. He killed himself as well, an act that is unexplored by Mr. Lardner but that suggests a greater mystery than he describes.

Would nothing have tamed the cruel rage of Ms. Lardner's killer? Mr. Lardner discredits the idea of rehabilitation, which certainly failed in Mr. Cartier's case, as indeed it fails in most cases. But the only real effort to rehabilitate Mr. Cartier consisted of six one-hour weekly sessions of something called "Alternatives to Violence," which Mr. Lardner, citing the recidivism rates, aptly calls "a placebo that pacifies the courts more than the convicts."

This raises a question: Could criminals be reformed by truly sustained, intelligent efforts to help them? Or, as Mr. Lardner suggests, once a child has become delinquent, is it essentially too late to do anything other than keep the rest of us out of his way? Mr. Lardner clearly believes that it is too late, but to be persuasive he needs a more sustained argument on that crucial question.

Still, his depiction of the system's failing his daughter, which is the heart of this book, is sad and alarming. Mr. Lardner recounts the many times when officials ignored the large amount of evidence showing just how dangerous Mr. Cartier was. They also neglected even to put into effect the system's own rules.

During one six-week period in the months before he met Ms. Lardner, Mr. Cartier was brought before judges three times and charged with several felonies, including grand larceny and breaking and entering, but he never served more than a few months in prison. Mr. Cartier attacked another girlfriend, Rose Ryan, with scissors. Ms. Ryan got a restraining order against Mr. Carter that he routinely violated. He then started going out with Ms. Lardner, and, when she moved to sever their relations after a few weeks, he followed her and beat her unconscious, kicking her in the head with steel-tipped shoes. Ms. Lardner complained to the police and got a restraining order of her own against Mr. Cartier.

That alone should have gotten him jailed, since he had assaulted her while on probation for prior offenses and had repeatedly violated the restraining order taken out against him by Ms. Ryan. The police did prepare a summons that should have led to Mr. Cartier's arrest. The summons sat on a desk, waiting, it seems, to be typed. It sat there for three weeks, and it was still sitting there the day Mr. Cartier shot Ms. Lardner three times in the head.

Charles Platt (review date 21 January 1996)

SOURCE: "On the Track of the Hacker," in *Book World— The Washington Post,* Vol. XXVI, No. 3, January 21, 1996, pp. 3, 7.

[*Below, Platt reviews* Takedown: The Pursuit and Capture of Kevin Mitnick, America's Most Wanted Computer Outlaw— By the Man Who Did It, *the story of Tsutomu Shimomura's efforts to catch the computer criminal Kevin Mitnick.*]

Every age has its bogeymen. A century ago, fictitious outlaw antiheroes such as Dr. Jekyll, Dr. Moreau and Captain Nemo chilled readers who were concerned about the emerging powers of science. Today, computer criminals have acquired the same dangerous aura, and Captain Nemo has been replaced by Kevin Mitnick.

Mitnick, of course, is a real person—or is he? Katie Hafner and John Markoff catalyzed his notoriety in their book *Cyberpunk,* where they portrayed him as "the darkside hacker," a nerdy recluse with a grudge against society. Mitnick later complained that this was "twenty percent fabricated and libelous," but the memorable image of a fat, moody sociopath gobbling junk food while attacking his enemies via a computer keyboard quickly gained a life of its own.

In 1994, writing for the *New York Times,* John Markoff parlayed it into front-page news. Mitnick was hiding from police following a probation violation; Markoff claimed he was "Now one of the nation's most wanted computer criminals."

This didn't fit the facts. Mitnick had never sold national secrets or raided bank accounts; his only crimes were electronic trespassing, copying software and taking away some technical manuals. Even Markoff admitted that Mitnick hadn't caused damage or profited from his actions.

Still, he did have an unusual talent for being where he wasn't supposed to be, and in 1994 he invaded the computers of security expert Tsutomu Shimomura. Shimomura was so outraged that he launched a personal quest to catch Mitnick, and John Markoff tagged along—or, as he put it, "I too became enmeshed in the digital manhunt for the nation's most wanted computer outlaw." The "manhunt" ended when Mitnick was arrested in February 1995.

Here was an interesting situation: A journalist had elevated a petty criminal to "most wanted" status, and then helped to catch him. Shortly after that, Markoff and Shimomura sold book rights to the Mitnick story for a rumored $750,000. *Takedown* is the result. The book contains hardly any new information about Mitnick, presumably because he has always refused to talk to journalists and his case has not yet been tried. Instead, the narrative is autobiographical from Shimomura's viewpoint and focuses mainly on Shimomura himself.

Unfortunately the life of a computer security expert turns out to be humorless and pedestrian compared with the life of a hacker, and *Takedown* is rather a dull book. It is also embarrassingly pompous, full of boasts about Shimomura's skills while demeaning Mitnick as an "anklebiter" who is "really more of a con man or a grifter than a hacker in the true sense of the word."

If Shimomura is a genius in his field while Mitnick is "a bit sloppy" and "prone to make mistakes," it seems odd that Mitnick penetrated Shimomura's system so easily. But even if we accept Shimomura's opinion of himself, a genius computer nerd is still a computer nerd. His primary obsession is hardware; his idea of an amusing anecdote is the time he crashed an old disk drive.

In an attempt to add human interest, the book chronicles Shimomura's efforts to steal a friend's girlfriend in spare moments when he's not pursuing Mitnick. But "human" is not synonymous with "likable," and even here Shimomura seems unappealingly smug.

The final section of the book contains some drama. Tracking Kevin Mitnick's cellular phone using a homemade bugging device of doubtful legality, Shimomura behaves like a vigilante waging an obsessional vendetta. And surely "vendetta" is the correct term: He put his entire life on hold and worked numerous 20-hour days to capture the man who had violated his privacy, wounded his vanity and teased him a little.

Yet according to Shimomura, pride was never a factor. He merely felt a selfless, general concern for computer security. He questions Mitnick's motives many times, but never his own.

At the end, when Mitnick is taken off to jail, Markoff quotes himself calling out to him, "Kevin, I hope things go OK for you." An odd statement, coming from the man who transformed a reclusive hacker into a media figure whom the police couldn't possibly ignore.

As it happens, though, things *have* gone OK for Mitnick since his arrest. All charges were dropped, except a minor one relating to possession of phone numbers, and he may even be out of jail before the Markoff-Shimomura book tour. This rather undercuts advance publicity characterizing him as a threat to global civilization. Still, Markoff should look on the bright side: As soon as Kevin Mitnick is free again he'll probably resume his habit of breaking into computers—generating fresh material for Markoff's next book.

Selwyn Raab (review date 10 March 1996)

SOURCE: "Mob Hit?," in *The New York Times Book Review,* March 10, 1996, p. 13.

[*In the review below, Raab discusses* Perfect Villains, Imperfect Heroes, *an account of Robert Kennedy's efforts against the Mafia.*]

For half a century one of the nation's premier growth industries was the Mafia. Virtually ignored by Federal and local law-enforcement agencies, America's adaptive mobsters always found new commercial enterprises to enrich themselves. When Prohibition ended in 1933, the dons and godfathers blithely switched from bootlegging into even more lavish rackets: prostitution, gambling, loan-sharking, labor racketeering and narcotics trafficking, to name just a few.

But the Mafia's golden era was disturbed when John F. Kennedy entered the White House in 1961. Kennedy surprisingly appointed his brother, Robert, as United States Attorney General, and fighting the mob became Robert Kennedy's top priority, perhaps bordering on an obsession.

One of the first prosecutors to enlist in Robert Kennedy's campaign was Ronald Goldfarb, who believes that the crusade may have led to a tragic casualty: in *Perfect Villains, Imperfect Heroes,* Mr. Goldfarb, now a Washington lawyer, concludes there is strong probability that leading mobsters plotted the assassination of President Kennedy. (I should clarify a possible conflict of interest here: in presenting his theory, Mr. Goldfarb cites disclosures and views expressed in *Mob Lawyer,* a book I wrote in 1994 with Frank Ragano, the lawyer who represented two major mob bosses and the corrupt Teamsters' Union chief, James R. Hoffa.)

Mr. Goldfarb was a 27-year-old rookie lawyer when he landed a prize job in 1961 on Robert Kennedy's nascent Organized Crime and Racketeering Section. Using new tactics, Kennedy began his assault on the mob by establishing elite investigative units that coordinated the efforts of Federal law-enforcement agencies. Because of his background as a counsel to Senate investigation committees, Mr. Goldfarb asserts, Kennedy understood, as few other officials did at the time, the true nature of the mob. It was not a loosely knit band of nonviolent criminals who served the public's harmless appetite for gambling and casino flings. It was, on the contrary, an enormously powerful organization that threatened the nation's well-being.

After three years of trial and error, Mr. Goldfarb says, Kennedy's strategy was beginning to reap results and convictions. But the death of President Kennedy on Nov. 22, 1963, and the ascension of Lyndon B. Johnson to the White House, signaled the end of Robert Kennedy's tenure at the Justice Department.

Mr. Goldfarb's account of how Robert Kennedy laid the groundwork for future successful campaigns against the Mafia is occasionally repetitious, and it is laced with minor historical errors. (He misspells Santo Trafficante's first name and mistakenly places Frank Ragano at an infamous mob meeting in Queens.) But his analysis implicating prominent mobsters in John F. Kennedy's assassination is engrossing.

There is abundant evidence from wiretaps, bugs and witnesses, Mr. Goldfarb maintains, to demonstrate that several dons were bent on revenge, convinced they had been double-crossed by the Kennedy Administration after surreptitiously supporting John Kennedy in the 1960 Presidential election and aiding the C.I.A. in conspiracies to kill Fidel Castro. Instead of rewarding the godfathers, Mr. Goldfarb tells us, the Kennedys enraged them by cracking down on their rackets and by prosecuting Hoffa, who was an important source of illegal wealth for many mobsters.

Mr. Goldfarb concedes that the passage of time may have made it impossible to construct an ironclad case that the Mafia used Lee Harvey Oswald or someone else to fire the fatal shots. But, he sums up: "There is a haunting credibility to the theory that our organized crime drive prompted a plan to strike back at the Kennedy brothers, and that Robert Kennedy went to his grave at least wondering whether—and perhaps believing—there was a real connection between the plan and his brother's assassination."

Jonathan Yardley (review date 17 July 1996)

SOURCE: "True Crime Stories: Bad Guys, on Why They Did What They Did," in *Washington Post,* No. 225, July 17, 1996, p. C2.

[*In the following review, Yardley remarks on* Bad Guys, *which gathers information on crime and criminals from interviews that Baker conducted with numerous convicted felons.*]

Mark Baker correctly notes that ordinary Americans are at once horrified by and attracted to crime and those who commit it. On the one hand, "crime is one of the most talked about social issues in America today," with public fears exacerbated by "lurid images of crime" routinely presented on television, while on the other hand "Americans have always had an attraction to criminal behavior," and "our heroes are often loners, rebels, mavericks, romanticized outlaws."

As this suggests, our fears of crime and our infatuation with criminals have little connection with reality. We actually know almost nothing about crime as it is routinely practiced and criminals as they actually are. It was with the hope of providing a few facts to clear up our fantasies that Baker interviewed several dozen prison inmates, "to put a human face on our fears, to shed some light on a very dark corner of ordinary, everyday life in this country." The criminals he spoke to had committed ordinary rather than glamorous crimes:

> I wanted to interview the people any of us might run into one day. I talked to the people who really should be feared, the ones who will jack your car at a red light, sneak into your hotel room while you're in there sleeping, prowl the hallway of your home in the middle of the night when you get up to go to the bathroom; the people who will stick up the McDonald's down the street, a drug store, bank or 7-Eleven where you shop or work; the people who will steal your credit cards, cash your paycheck, bilk you out of your savings, and gorge on your vices."

This he has done, or so at least we are to believe. A central difficulty with a book such as *Bad Guys* is that while a promise of anonymity is essential to get interviewees' cooperation, this denies the reader documentation or proof. If one is willing to take at face value the interviewer's claims for the authenticity of what he presents, there should be no problem; if one is not, it's hard not to wonder what is fact and what is fiction.

There seems no particular reason to disbelieve Mark Baker. Though a few of his interviews read like serio-comic chase scenes out of George V. Higgins or *GoodFellas,* most of what one finds here has the air of mundane reality. Those interviewed are white and black, male and female, prosperous and poor, smart and slow. Most are willing to accept responsibility for the courses they followed, and few fall back on blaming family or society or even race. As one says:

> I had a rebellious nature, but I was never influenced by older kids. No one led me astray, no one seduced me into a life of crime. These were my own internal feelings. I didn't identify with the square people, the working people. Maybe I sensed the hypocrisy. Maybe I saw the kind of respect or admiration they had for the successful outlaw. I associated with this.

Though those last three sentences have the ring of convenient introspection abetted by pop psychology, the rest of it rings true. So many of these people talk about rebellious natures and discomfort in the straight world that it's hard not to find some truth in these explanations. By the same token, a man who talks about "how people get sucked into crime," about how "you're wallowing in the crab muck with everybody else, and there you are—stuck," points to another valid explanation: the difficulty of getting out once you've gotten in.

If there is a single dominant theme, it is drugs. Either out of appetites aroused by taking them or dreams of riches inspired by selling them, almost everyone who speaks here has been touched by the drug epidemic. The living a life centered on them is not necessarily inescapable, but so many have followed it that the urgency of the problem becomes even clearer than before—in particular where the terrible effects of crack cocaine are concerned.

Of the book's three sections—one about the road to crime, one about the criminal life, one about prison—the last is the most effective and convincing. Some of the testimony about prison as a school for criminals and prison as a homosexual stalking ground is familiar, but it still has the power to persuade. *Bad Guys* isn't exactly a work of scholarship, but it tells us more about crime and criminals than we're likely to learn from an evening in front of the television set.

WRITING INSTRUCTION

William K. Beaver (essay date September 1990)

SOURCE: "Writing True-Life Crime," in *The Writer,* Vol. 103, September, 1990, pp. 17-19.

[*In the essay below, Beaver discusses how to write a successful true crime article.*]

The true-life crime genre originated in the late 19th century and has grown in popularity ever since. After nearly forty true-life detective magazines were born and died, modern magazine and book publishers discovered that a solid audience exists for the true-life crime story. Books like *The Preppie Murder* or *The Stranger Beside Me* consistently find their way to the bestseller lists.

Writing about true-life crime is not for hack writers. Finding a fresh detective story inside a crime that has already been widely covered by the media requires the skills of a sleuth and the style of a novelist. Here are seven secrets for writing successful true-life crime articles.

1. Find the perfect crime. Recognizing the perfect crime for a true-life article eventually becomes an intuitive flash. Many of the detective magazines will accept a story about almost any crime, but to increase the chance of success, search for a crime with some notoriety and color to it.

Serial killings, mass murders, and terrorist-related murders are obvious choices, but smaller crimes can also provide excellent material. Consider the following:

I queried an editor concerning the murder of a bank teller during an armed robbery. The young woman's murder was of itself interesting enough for an article, but what gave it a special twist was the brutal way the crime was committed. The assailant had started for the door to make his escape when he suddenly turned, walked back to the desk under which the teller was hiding, pulled her out, and shot her.

In writing the true-life crime story, the writer must face the worst that human beings are capable of doing. Forgetting the article and its subject sometimes takes effort, especially when you must visualize the event as you write.

The perfect true-life crime article for any of the detective magazines and for most book publishers requires another element—superlative detective work on the part of investigators. The readers of true-life crime want to know how the police solved aspects of the case that had originally stumped them. Articles editorializing what the police did wrong are best left to investigative pieces.

The third aspect of the perfect crime involves knowing the conclusion of the story. Articles about unsolved crimes, or those in which the accused is found innocent usually do not satisfy or appeal to editors or readers. Most true-life crime buffs believe in law and order, so stories in which the accused were found guilty usually stand the best chance of being accepted.

2. Develop the available information. To begin research for an article, first unravel the basic facts of the story by finding all the information that is readily available. The best method is to photocopy newspaper or magazine articles about the particular crime and use them as your starting point.

If you failed to follow the story and keep newspaper clippings as it developed, you will need to visit libraries and possibly newspaper morgues. Depending on the library, indexes may be available in which the story is listed under the subject of homicides and murders, or under the name of the victim and/or assailant.

After you gather the available information, organize it into four categories: information about the victim; the suspects; information from the police and coroner; and details of the crime scene. Correlate all the information you have collected under one of the four columns, noting what information and details are missing.

3. Interview other sources. You must find information that the press or the investigators did not reveal at the time of the crime. Start with the investigation team at the police department. Your task becomes difficult because you are trying to write about a crime on which the police have already been endlessly questioned.

You can gain the police's cooperation by emphasizing that you wish to write the article from their point of view: how did the investigators crack the case? Ask to speak with the police officer in charge of the original investigation, since he's the person with the most knowledge about the crime.

The key to a successful interview with the police, like any other interview, is to prepare carefully for it. Ask the officer to tell you about the case in his own words, recording the interview if he will permit it. As he speaks, listen for the facts you already have, and especially for new material not mentioned previously.

Don't be afraid to ask for any additional details the police have.

I have managed to obtain copies of police reports and been given access to a complete case file, which provided a wealth of information not usually given to the press.

Be sure to double-check the facts you obtained from newspaper and magazine articles. Ask the police officer about such important details as names, dates, and methods. One newspaper article about the murder of a young girl described the murder weapon as a nail file found lying on the bedroom floor, but the detective told me the actual weapon was a box-cutting knife found in the suspect's apartment.

4. Search for "color." Little details discovered during your research add immeasurably to the story. I will often go to the neighborhood of the crime scene to absorb the sights, the sounds, and the people.

If the police give you access to photographs of the crime scene, look for details like the time on the clock, the furnishings in the room, unusual photographs on the wall or table.

Ask the police if there was anything unusual about the investigation. In writing about one crime I discovered that the police tried using a psychic to find the murderer. The psychic described a scene that did not relate to the crime in question, but sounded like another crime that took place in another city.

Investigators called the police there and gave them the psychic's information. When I later wrote about the second murder, the investigators mentioned the psychic's tip (which I already knew about), and I was able to use the anecdote in my story.

The suspect is another source of color. Try to find small bits of information that show how the criminal was perceived by those around him who were unaware of his activities. These could be observations of strange behavior or awards for good behavior. In fact, once when I worked as a resumé and business writer, I found the resumé belonging to the first mass murderer I wrote about. The resumé listed four awards for exemplary performance at the hospital where he murdered seventeen patients.

5. Use fiction techniques to develop both suspense and the characters. Once you discover the color of the story and gather all the information, start to weave the elements into a tight, cohesive story. A good true-life crime article demands the same attention to setting, character, and pacing as a fictional story does.

As with all articles, the choice of the lead is vital. You must decide on the starting point from which to develop the story, and also how to work in all the details. The first true-life piece I tackled concerned a serial killer—a hospital orderly—who murdered more than fifty-four people. I had several options for the lead, but a thorough review of the material provided it for me. A coroner's office pathologist detected the smell of almonds while performing an autopsy on an accident victim who had died in the hospital. The smell of almonds sometimes indicates the presence of cyanide, but since the odor can be detected by only twenty per cent of the population, the pathologist ran a test for cyanide. The test came back positive, the pathologist had discovered a murder that later led to the arrest of the serial killer/orderly, and I had my lead.

Try to pace the piece by developing the setting so the reader can visualize as much as possible. Describe the scene of the crime, the actions of the investigators, and what is known about the victim. The most important detail, however, is to delay identification of the murderer until the last possible moment. Use suspense techniques, such as dead-end investigative leads, to build the story.

Use the same format as you would in writing fiction: the introduction, story buildup, the climax, and finally the resolution.

6. Know the required format. Most true-life crime articles use the same basic formats, but it's a good idea to write to the various magazines and request their writers' guidelines.

Ask about photographs. Does the magazine pay extra for the pictures or are they included—even expected—in the manuscript price?

Always submit the query and manuscript in professional form. Nothing will bring a rejection faster than sloppy presentation or obvious mistakes. Keep track of all source materials, including interviews and newspaper clippings. Most magazines will check your facts and will require copies of your material for their files. These will provide references in the event of a lawsuit.

7. Be on the lookout for more sources and the perfect crime. If you continue as a true-life crime writer, you must gain the confidence of your sources in the police department and the coroner's office, among others, in the same manner a newspaper journalist might. Respect their wishes.

I approached a police department for information about a crime I was writing about. Since I was unknown to them, their reception was guarded and aloof. But when they later saw how I treated the story, the next time I went back, they shared information with me that the newspaper did not have, including the film taken by a hidden camera during the bank robbery/murder.

If you are serious about writing true-life crime articles, join any legal groups in your area. I was invited to speak about the pursuit of Nazi war criminals for a discussion group that included two county coroners, several legal aides, and several investigators and attorneys, all of whom expressed a willingness to help me in the future.

Successful true-life crime writing centers on *information* and *presentation*. If you have enough information and polish your presentation, chances are you will be successful writing about the perfect crime.

Krist Boardman (essay date April 1995)

SOURCE: "Probing the Mind of the True Crime Detective," in *The Writer,* Vol. 108, No. 4, April, 1995, pp. 7-9.

[*In the essay below, Boardman offers advice on how to write an article for a true-crime magazine.*]

Nonfiction writers can never truly get inside the mind of a real person, not to the point where we know everything about him. Fiction writers are the only gods on the planet who can wholly create persons and imbue their personalities with all the complexities of real people.

Writers of nonfiction can do only what other keen observers might do: listen and record what the person says about himself and what he did, what other people said he said and did, and what they observe directly.

A true crime writer uses indirect and direct observation to describe his protagonist, but his main subject is the crime itself. The writer should never make the mistake of speculating what is in the detective's mind, unless he has reliable information to support his observations.

For the true crime article, information is assembled from courthouse and newspaper research and interviews. While characterizations of the important players in each crime are important, they should be supported by the researched material. Invented, undocumented dialogue and situations should be avoided.

The true crime article is most effective when written from the perspective of the detective. There are a number of very good reasons for this. One is that policemen and detectives love to read about themselves or others in their profession; also, other people like to read about the everyday heroes on local police forces.

Editors of true crime magazines know that cops aren't perfect either in the personal or professional aspects of their lives, but their magazines are an appropriate place to show detective work at its best. The ideal protagonist for a true crime article is a seemingly ordinary detective with extraordinary skills or just plain dogged persistence, who faces numerous obstacles in his efforts to bring a criminal to justice.

Remember also that police officers usually can't take shortcuts: They have to obey the law and follow proper procedures, or they may blow their cases. When they get frustrated, they can't just pull out high-caliber weapons and blow people's heads off, as Clint Eastwood does in the Dirty Harry movies. And they can't break into people's homes and offices with lock picks or credit cards to search for incriminating evidence and documents when new evidences is needed.

These impediments to frontier-style and private-eye justice help make a better true crime story, because the challenge of the investigation is increased. In today's real world, the investigator's techniques must remain within the confines of the law. Legal issues are very much part of the overall article, as they play an increasingly important role in the resolution of a case.

There are limits to what a beginning true crime writer can write about when describing an investigation. A fiction writer might describe a disorder in the unusual life of a homicide detective—a gambling habit, womanizing, alcoholism, problems with a relationship or with another person. This makes a more interesting story, particularly if the detective's personal problems can be woven into the main mystery. But it is not appropriate for the true crime magazine piece, unless it becomes part of the official record of the court case, which is unlikely.

If the true crime writer exposes the personal weaknesses of detectives, he may never regain the confidence and trust of officers working in that department. Furthermore, the focus of the true crime article would be straying too far from the resolution of the crime itself. Yet it is often helpful—and it makes for a more effective article—if as part of the narrative the writer does note and include a short profile of the detective. After all, readers want to know something about the main person or persons who solve the crime. That's what makes the article human and interesting.

You must try to humanize the components of your article, often despite the tendency of investigators to depersonalize everything about the investigation in their accounts of it. Anyone who has read detailed applications for search warrants and reports by detectives to their supervisors understands this. Many documents are written in stilted police bureaucratese in which the detective describes himself and his actions as the activities of "the writer," "the applicant," or "your affiant."

These detective-written narratives are usually the best sources of information about a case, barring a long interview. They should be used as guidelines to describe the progress of the investigation and as supporting documentation for your article. But you must rework the material, weaving in information from other sources to bring your article to life.

To the extent possible, official documents should also be

evaluated for information the detective may purposely not have included. There is plenty that never gets into these official records for a variety of reasons—for instance, the interplay among various persons working on the case or in the investigative unit. This kind of information can be obtained only from interviews or court transcripts of trials where it was brought out under the rules of discovery or in cross-examination in the courtroom.

For example, one of my favorite true crime articles described a detective's obsession with a human leg bone retrieved by a junkyard dog from a swamp. The detective was an unheralded policeman from a small agency who tenaciously followed up the discovery with an investigation that lasted several years. His coworkers derisively nicknamed him "Bones" and made fun of his efforts to solve what appeared to be an unsolvable crime. Yet "Bones" did go on to solve the case, much to his credit, and he removed from the streets a dangerous man who had been involved in other criminal activity.

That particular case was unusual because the detective succeeded almost in spite of the efforts of others in his department. Most detectives are not usually in such an untenable position, but are accepted members of tightly knit investigative units and are careful not to attract undue attention to themselves. Nevertheless, a resourceful crime writer may find ways to characterize the detective while working within these limits.

In addition to the constraints within police departments, there are often problem cases that prosecutors and detectives feel uncomfortable discussing even after a conviction, because of possible appeals that may be cause for retrial. If an interview can be obtained, the source will usually be reluctant to discuss anything that was not said or did not actually occur in the courtroom. Newspaper accounts of the trial and investigation will then have to serve as primary sources, unless the writer has the time and opportunity to attend the court trial himself.

Nevertheless, even with all these restrictions, detectives are talkative and anxious to explain a point that is not clear. You as the true crime writer should first study all the sources that are available so that you can ask only informed questions. You may then be able to elicit over the phone off-the-cuff remarks that will be very useful even if someone up the chain of command has refused a formal interview. This usually works best if you say at the outset that the comments will not be attributed to that particular source.

One true crime article I wrote involved a crime committed in a northern Virginia county. The suspect had family ties to a very small, remote county in the mountains of southwest Virginia that the investigator and his partner had never heard of. The detectives' trip to the county was eventful because there was no available lodging, nor could the locals understand how black and white detectives could work together. None of this material about the detectives' trip was included in official documents, but in an interview the investigator gave me material that added color, perspective, and insight into the life of the suspect.

The myriad problems real detectives face, such as pleading with supervisors for funds to travel, mistaken identities, foul-ups within the jail system, courtroom maneuverings, not to mention the craftiness and elusiveness of suspects, make up the interesting though often frustrating lives of real detectives. The more of this kind of detail a crime writer can provide, the better job he has done in profiling the work of America's frontline investigators.

Peter A. DePree (essay date December 1995)

SOURCE: "True Crime Writing: A Dynamic Field," in *The Writer*, December, 1995, pp. 16-17, 41.

[*In the following essay, DePree comments on how to write a true-crime article, stressing that an article should only be written if the crime is recent, a conviction was made, and research and photographs are available.*]

Few genres in journalism today are as exciting and profitable as true crime, whether article or book. Although this piece focuses on the true crime article, many of the techniques and methods discussed in the following six steps are readily applicable to the true crime book.

STEP ONE: *Researching the field.* Buy several true crime magazines and spend a rainy afternoon getting a feel for the slant and depth of the articles. Jot down what you liked and didn't like about them. Then, dash off a request to the editorial office of one or two of the magazines for the writers guidelines (include the requisite SASE).

STEP TWO: *Finding a crime.* Visit your local library and look in the index of the biggest newspaper in your area under the heading Murder/Manslaughter, going back about four years, and photocopy those index pages. (Most crimes more than four or five years old are too stale to fit the slant of true detective magazines.) Highlight the crimes that seem most likely to make interesting true crime pieces. The few sentences describing each article will give you a good feel for the highlights of the case. Select about half a dozen cases that look promising. As you peruse them, you will whittle down the group for one reason or another until you're left with one or two that have all the elements you need for an effective true crime piece. Most detective magazine guidelines will help you narrow them down: The crime is always murder; the "perp" (police parlance for perpetrator) has been convicted; there was a substantial investigation leading to the arrest; the crime took place reasonably near your area (important, since you'll have to go to the court to gather research); and photos are available for illustration.

STEP THREE: *Doing the research*. First, with the index as a guide, collect all available newspaper articles on the crime you've selected so you can make an outline before reading the trial transcript. Your library should have either back issues or microfilm (provided you followed Step One and picked a case no more than four years old). If there are two or more newspapers in your area that covered the crime, get copies of all of them. Often, pertinent details were printed by one paper but not the other.

STEP FOUR: *Reading the trial transcript*. Call the clerk's office of the court where the trial took place and ask for the case number on the crime and whether the transcript is available to the public (it usually is). By now you should have a three- or four-page outline based on all the articles you've read. Take your outline and a lot of paper and pens to the courthouse, and be prepared to spend a whole day reading the trial record; even a trial that lasted only three or four days can fill several bound volumes. (When I was doing research for a book on the Nightstalker serial killer case in Los Angeles, the court record was 100,000 pages long and filled three shopping carts!) Skim and make notes of the quotes and material you'll need; this will be a lot easier if you've prepared your outline carefully, since you'll already know the key names to watch for—the lead detective, prosecutor, defense attorney, victim, witnesses, responding officer, and so forth. You'll need to look for material on several different levels simultaneously: details for accuracy, dramatic quotes, colorful background, etc. There will usually be far more of these elements than you could possibly pack into an article, so you have the luxury of choosing only the very best. You may discover a brand-new form of writing frustration when you have to slash all those dramatic prosecutorial summations and subplots down to the required word count.

Use whatever form of research you're comfortable with. I find a combination of scribbling notes in my own pseudo-shorthand and dictating into a hand-held recorder suits me. (Pack enough spare batteries and tapes!) I can mumble into my recorder faster than I can write. Having photocopies made at the court is usually prohibitively expensive, so copy very selectively. As a rule of thumb, the parts of a transcript that yield the most important factual information are the opening remarks of both attorneys; the questioning of the lead detective; the testimony of expert witnesses such as forensic technicians; and the summing up of both attorneys. A couple of tips: Dates are especially important, and so are names.

Almost as important as the transcript is the court file. Specify

to the court clerk that you would like that as well as the transcript.

STEP FIVE: *Writing the article*. Reread the writers guidelines for the magazine to which you're submitting your piece, then write the kind of article *you* would find exciting and surprising (or shocking) to read. Chances are that if a particular detail, scene, or quote piques your interest, it belongs in your piece. Don't get lost in boring minutiae, but do remember that sprinkling in telling details seasons the piece and sharpens the focus.

If your detective used a K9 dog to search for evidence, you might mention that it was a Rottweiler named Butch, with a mangled ear. If the ballistics expert test-fired the gun, you could throw in that detail, noting that he fired it into a slab of gel, then retrieved the bullet and viewed it under a comparison microscope for tell-tale striations, and so on. The trial transcript is packed with details like these that make your article stand out from a "made-up" detective story.

As you're writing, watch your length. Editors are not impressed with articles that run a few thousand words over their suggested length.

STEP SIX: *Secondary wrap-up research*. True crime editors are picky about certain details, especially names (check those writers guidelines again!). If you mention "Mr. Gordon," you should specify that he is Commissioner John Gordon of the Gotham City Police Department. Change the names of witnesses or family members, for obvious reasons. Go back to the library to check the details that will give your writing authority. For instance, if the crime was committed with a shotgun and you don't know a pump-action from an over-&-under, you need to do some minor research to find out. If your crime involves DNA fingerprinting, you'll need to spend no more than an hour in the library to find enough useful facts to give your article a little snap. I recently wrote an article on a killer who was suffering from paranoid schizophrenia. In just four pages in two college psych textbooks—twenty minutes' investment of my time—I came up with more than enough facts for my piece.

What to watch out for

There are at least four articles in my computer that are almost completely written, but went nowhere. Why? Because I made stupid, unnecessary mistakes—mistakes that *you* would never make if you follow a few simple rules. The following three are non-negotiable:

1) *Never start on an article without querying the magazine first*. Nothing is quite as frustrating as writing twenty detailed pages on the Longbow rapist, only to discover that Joe

Bland already sold that piece to your target magazine a year ago. You now have a pile of perfectly good kindling.

2) *Always make doubly sure the trial transcript is available.* You should never have to invest more than one or two full days in researching the transcript and court file, but that doesn't help when on the day you need it you learn that the whole file was shipped five hundred miles away so the appeals judges could study it at their leisure. (We're talking *months* here.)

3) *Never start an article without making sure photos are available.* Etch this in stone: No true crime magazine will run an article without *at least* three photos. The minimum basics are a photo of the perp; one of the victim; one of the crime scene. These can be what I call "documentary-grade"; sometimes, even a particularly sharp photo clipped from a newspaper will suffice. But query your target magazine first, and always make sure the picture is in the public domain (i.e., a high school yearbook photo of the killer, a photo of the victim distributed to all the papers, a snapshot of the bank building where an armed robbery took place).

True crime writing might be called entry-level journalism. If you can write a tightly researched and entertaining piece following these suggestions, you'll have a better chance of success.

AUTHOR PROFILES

Robert Dahlin (essay date 18 October 1991)

SOURCE: "Joe McGinniss," in *Publishers Weekly,* Vol. 238, October 18, 1991, pp. 40-1.

[*In the following essay, Dahlin profiles true-crime writer Joe McGinniss.*]

Until the telephone rang in mid-February last year, *Cruel Doubt* hadn't been even a scribble in Joe McGinniss's notebook.

He'd signed a two-book contract with Simon & Schuster in the summer of 1988, but the subjects were not specified, and he had no desire to follow up *Fatal Vision* and *Blind Faith* with another disturbing scrutiny of a family slashed apart by murder. His commitment was only for one manuscript by the end of 1991 and the second by the end of 1994.

"I wanted to sell books like a novelist," says McGinniss of the agreement, negotiated by agent Mort Janklow. "You don't ask Philip Roth for an outline of his next book."

He's on the terrace behind his commodious home just outside Williamstown, Mass. Tall and invincibly low-key, McGinniss looks his age—48. Known as an intrepid reporter and something of a cynic, in person he seems genuine and not at all glib. His broad lawn flourishes under a late-summer sun, as do flower beds in a swirl of colors. In the distance, a steamy haze dims the lofty profile of Greylock State Reservation, which rises just a few miles south of Vermont's Green Mountain National Forest. McGinniss's wife Nancy and their young sons have just gone into town.

"I thought, why not take advantage of the brainpower in a place like Simon & Schuster?" he continues, with evident appreciation for his new publisher. Putnam had issued his previous two titles. "Why should the author alone have to come up with ideas for books? There's only a finite supply."

Amused by the notion, McGinniss cups his hands around an invisible shape about as big as a basketball, the estimated size of the book idea inventory presently available.

In fact, the first proposal did come from S & S. "Michael Korda had been struck during the 1988 Democratic Convention by the fact that Ted Kennedy was only a bit player," McGinniss says. "Kennedy had become almost obsolescent in the blink of an eye."

Korda suggested that the implosion of Kennedy's political stature had potential. McGinniss agreed, and set upon what would stretch into a year of research.

But then the telephone call came from North Carolina. The caller was Wade Smith, a former lawyer for Jeffrey MacDonald, the disgruntled protagonist, if that's the word, of *Fatal Vision.* After that book was published in 1983, MacDonald sued McGinniss for misleading and betraying him (a suit that resulted in a hung jury), and writer Janet Malcolm subsequently mounted her own broadside against him for essentially similar but more complicated reasons in a two-part *New Yorker* series in March 1989, later published by Knopf as *The Journalist and the Murderer* (1990). While difficult to live through at the time, those two unpleasant experiences seem to have left McGinniss pretty much unscarred.

The same summer McGinniss had signed with S & S, Wade Smith had taken on a new client, Bonnie Von Stein, who had been stabbed and beaten as her husband was knifed to death beside her while they slept. Smith was calling McGinniss at Von Stein's suggestion: she had read *Fatal Vision,* admired it, and wondered if the author would care to write about her own family tragedy.

A friendship had developed between McGinniss and Smith despite the MacDonald furor. At Smith's suggestion,

McGinniss flew down to Raleigh to talk with Von Stein. Within hours, he felt himself drawn—albeit reluctantly—into the case. And how could he not? Only three weeks before, Von Stein's own son Chris had been sentenced to life plus 20 years for engineering—though not executing—the deadly assault.

"I called Michael in New York, and told him I wasn't going to do the Kennedy book first," McGinniss says. "I wanted to do a story about a family in North Carolina that he'd never heard of. Michael said, 'Fine.'"

Cruel Doubt fast became a feverish priority. McGinniss plunged in, delivering half the manuscript last December, the rest in July. "Michael told me to buy a fax machine," he remarks. "I would write a page and throw it on the fax while I was writing the next page. It reminded me of working for a newspaper."

McGinniss had had plenty of experience as a journalist since earning his B.S. from Holy Cross in 1964. He'd covered sports and been a columnist for such papers as the Philadelphia *Bulletin* and the Philadelphia *Inquirer,* and had written for magazines, too—*Harper's, Sports Illustrated* and the *New York Times* magazine among them. "It was stressful doing *Cruel Doubt* so fast, but maybe I work best that way," he says, "and with Dick Snyder's push toward electronic publishing, Simon & Schuster is awesome."

The book was written so closely under the gun, and is so thoroughly up to date, that the last interviews were completed by McGinniss's research assistant, Robyn Smith, in mid-June, and the final editorial changes were made August 3—no small accomplishment for an October hardcover with a first printing of 350,000 copies.

McGinniss believes, "This book goes beyond my last two, because here was a woman who was a victim in a very real way. She was almost killed, and then the legal system treated her as though she might have been in some way responsible." Some might say she escaped death twice—and narrowly.

After the murder, the police subjected her to a polygraph test and ongoing suspicion, in part because Von Stein was heir to the $2-million estate left by her second husband, Lieth Von Stein, who was not the father of Chris or his sister Angela.

"Bonnie was also a psychological victim," McGinnis suggests, "a victim of her own son, in whom she had such faith. Nobody I've written about has had to deal with something like that.

"I saw her for the first time just about three weeks after Chris was sentenced, so all this was still raw, fresh and open,"

McGinniss recalls, "and then she took the extra step, talking to her lawyers, her psychiatrist, to her family. She urged them all to tell me the truth."

McGinniss speculates on the reasons for Von Stein's pursuit of candor in such dire circumstances. He remembers putting the question to her psychiatrist, Jean Spaulding. "I asked her what Bonnie could get out of the book. She'd get no money; she had no control over what I'd write, and it was certain to be painful. Jean said that Bonnie still didn't understand what had happened. How could her son have wanted her dead? Bonnie hoped I would be a psychological detective."

The players in the broken family that McGinniss pieced together included Chris, a drug user and an addict of the game "Dungeons & Dragons" (he had devised the assassination plot while in a narcotic haze), and Angela, whose possible role in the murder raised more cruel doubts than have ever been answered.

"Chris was eager to talk," McGinniss comments. "He's still trying to figure out how he could have done this. *All* the family wanted to talk, because they were trying to explore something they didn't understand, either."

As he proceeded, McGinniss found himself paying an expected emotional toll. "When you're learning about this horrible situation, it's hard to stay detached," he says. "After each of my last three books, I've said, 'Never again.' I don't want to write about someone hurting somebody else."

Perhaps all writers have a limited amount of empathy, he worries. "There's a cost when you take on someone's pain and live with it. A writer can build a shell around himself, but the book he'd write would be very different. How could the reader feel Bonnie's pain if I didn't?"

In the end, he acknowledges, some revelations did indeed wound Bonnie Von Stein, especially those relating to Angela.

"Bonnie read the book for the first time last weekend," McGinniss says, "and we had an emotional talk. It was a terribly painful experience for her, but she felt relieved that the full story had been told. Our conversation was intense, but cordial."

So, in the end, what justifies stirring up such anguish? "What I hope to get to is the heart of what goes on in American families," he says. "In a story like this, the dilemmas, the psychological traumas, are brought into relief. When one family member kills another, you've got the ultimate dysfunctional family. There's an exposure of a kind of emotion most of us feel on a regular basis—only here, it's brought to extremes."

No clear demarcation stands between everyday friction and a burst of violence, McGinniss observes. "There are normal stresses in family life, but some people cross that line and do damaging things. I'm personally intrigued by that moment."

Nevertheless, he plans to lay this curiosity to rest. "I hope the next story that comes to me doesn't involve people hurting people. I've written books about Alaska [*Going to Extremes*] and politics [*The Selling of the President*]. I have many other interests."

Asked if his experiences with MacDonald's lawsuit and with Malcolm's salvo in the *New Yorker* have also contributed to his desire to leave these matters behind, McGinniss says, "They haven't changed me at all, and that's because MacDonald was a special case. By many definitions, he'd be classified as a psychopath, which puts him outside the norm."

McGinniss declares that his responsibility is to the reader, not to the person whose life he is examining, and this leads him to one of Malcolm's bitterest criticisms: that he misled MacDonald into believing that he was an ally.

"How can you learn the truth about someone without keeping lines of communication open? If somebody is the primary subject of a book, it's absolutely essential to learn as much as you can. I have no apologies for the [sympathetic] letters I wrote him. I did feel bad. He'd conned me so well."

As *New Yorker* readers will remember, when Malcolm sought to interview McGinniss, he initially agreed. After a single session, however, he declined to continue.

"It quickly became apparent to me that she had an internal agenda," he says. "In the first hour, it felt like being in a bottle with a scorpion. When I told her I didn't want to talk to her any more, she wrote me a letter saying, in effect, 'You'll be sorry.'"

What he didn't know then was that Malcolm herself was being sued for libel by psychoanalyst Jeffrey Masson over quotations he claimed she'd concocted in her book, *In the Freud Archives* (1984).

As her research proceeded without his cooperation, McGinniss wagers, Malcolm became infatuated with MacDonald's view of his own mistreatment.

"For 50 years, the *New Yorker* had the reputation for printing only nice things about people," he says with a smile. "[But] even if other people didn't recognize it, she was working out difficulties of her own at my expense." In turn, he put *his* account of the contretemps before the public in a new afterword to the paperback edition of *Fatal Vision*.

However, the story hasn't quite come to a close yet.

In June, the U.S. Supreme Court ruled in the Masson-Malcolm case that an author's alterations of quotations can be viewed as libelous if they materially change the intended meaning, and thus, the justices cleared the way for Jeffrey Masson's lawsuit against Malcolm to proceed in the California courts.

In what could pass for the ultimate irony, McGinniss will cover the trial for *Vanity Fair*.

Dennis Romero (essay date 10 July 1995)

SOURCE: "New Respect for the New Centurions," in *Los Angeles Times*, July 10, 1995, pp. E1, E2.

[*In the following essay, Romero profiles true-crime writer Paul Mones.*]

Dead, mangled and strangled women stared at Paul Mones for three years while he tried to capture their horror in mere words.

He plastered their crime-scene Polaroids around his Santa Monica office and listened to Verdi operas as dark inspiration for his new true-crime book, *Stalking Justice*. Most of the victims were ornately tied up with rope, string or mini-blind chords. One was badly decomposed. Another stared at Mones, her eyes bulging with the terror that marked her last moments as a living being. They were the strangulation victims of a serial killer who stalked the streets of Virginia during the 1980s.

What makes this story special to readers is that it is a juicy, true-crime page-turner (lock your windows), and in this day of O.J. mania, it recounts the first murder case in America in which DNA testing was used successfully to get a conviction. What makes it special, even unique, to Mones is that, even as death enveloped his office, he became a changed man.

The attorney-cum-author is best known as a tireless children's-rights advocate who has had little love for the criminal justice system. It's hard to believe in a system that prosecutes abused children who kill their parents (he defended more than 200 such children) more often than it prosecutes parents who kill innocent children, he used to say.

In his first nonfiction book, *When a Child Kills* (1991), Mones decried "the mindless, insensitive, and morally bankrupt reaction of the legal system to the children's plight."

But after spending so much time under the gaze of these

hapless strangulation victims, recounting how their killer was captured, tried and executed, this self-professed '60s liberal can only say one thing: "I was wrong."

"Writing this book really opened my eyes about my own legal work," said Mones, a 43-year-old who looks a little like Frank Zappa in a businessman's haircut. "I never saw the other side."

"What I saw and heard," he wrote in *Stalking Justice,* "expanded my understanding and cracked my long-held prejudices about cops."

To see the other side, it took a year of living in Arlington, Va. He boarded with police Detective Joe Horgas, spent time at the FBI behavioral sciences unit (a few weeks after Jodie Foster was there to study for her part in *Silence of the Lambs*), visited prosecutors and shadowed DNA wizards at Lifecodes Inc. in White Plains, N.Y. (Rival Cellmark Diagnostics worked for the defense in this case.) Mones even traced the killer's every step, video camera in hand. "He was obsessive," said wife Niki, a business writer.

At one point, a police investigator asked Mones, "You really want to know what it's like to be a cop?" he recalled. The officer then played him a cassette tape of a teen-age girl being tortured by two men. "I lasted a minute and a half," Mones said, "then I shut it off."

"Those cops," he said, "have to shut off their emotion."

Mones came upon the murder story in 1989, in a phone introduction to Horgas in which, Mones said, "we hit it off." The author purchased Horgas' version of the tale for an undisclosed amount.

A masked rapist had been haunting Arlington during 1983, tying up his victims. In 1984, a woman was tied up in similar fashion and strangled. Horgas—an old-school detective from Pennsylvania who looks like he's paid his dues at local doughnut establishments—believed that whoever killed in 1984 was the same masked rapist. But a separate team of detectives in Arlington found a local man, David Vasquez, who was fingered by witnesses and who confessed to the killing.

Vasquez was tried and jailed, but it happened again in 1987: A woman was tied up and strangled.

"She was nude and lying face down across the lower half of the bed," Mones wrote. "Her face was almost completely blackened, her eyes swollen shut, and her head hung slightly over the bed's edge. A thick, dark red mucus oozed from her mouth and nose, soaking the coverlet and pooling on the gray carpet.

"A brilliantly shiny, white nylon rope . . . was tautly wrapped around her neck."

Then three more strangulation victims appeared in and around Richmond, 100 miles to the south. All Horgas could think about was the masked rapist, still on the loose. The only thing linking the masked rapist to the strangulation killings was Horgas' unparalleled memory (he pulled the suspect's name seemingly out of thin air from an old list of local trouble-makers) and a new technique called DNA fingerprinting.

After checking records, Horgas found that his suspect, Timothy Spencer, was either on parole or holed up in a low-security half-way house at the times of all the murders. He lived close to the scene of all the murders. Then there was the clincher: DNA from sperm found at several crime scenes matched that of Spencer's blood.

Spencer—eventually convicted of four murders and strongly suspected in the other—and one rape—was pronounced dead at 11:13 p.m., April 27, 1994, the victim of Virginia's electric chair and Horgas' relentless investigation. Vasquez—whose confession was attributed to his low mental abilities—was pardoned.

In his tireless efforts to get everyone from his own superiors to the Richmond police to believe that Spencer was their man, Horgas emerged as the story's hero. "I know I did a good job," he said recently, "but all the publicity is a little embarrassing."

While the case changed Mones' view of the justice system, it also fortified his view that DNA fingerprinting is to the next millennium what fingerprinting has been to the 20th Century. Here is a case where a serial murderer was captured and an innocent man was released. "This story to me was the embodiment of justice," Mones said.

He is disappointed that California is one of the few states that does not legally put DNA in the same league as fingerprints when it comes to placing suspects at the scene of a crime. He also believes that the O.J. Simpson defense team has taken advantage of the state's lack of faith when it comes to DNA.

"Some people say this is a nefarious tool of the state to deprive people of their freedom," said Mones as he sat barefoot and laid-back in his West Los Angeles home. "I think DNA fingerprinting is a terrific tool to eliminate the innocent and provide a critical piece of evidence for convicting criminals."

And the conviction of criminals is something Mones feels strongly about these days.

"He can't have a cut-and-dried position on the death penalty anymore," said Niki Mones, also 43, about her husband. (Paul Mones said he's still against capital punishment, but now better sees the other side of the argument.)

He plans to stay liberal, defend kids and speak out against child abuse. And the new book has also whetted Mones' appetite for writing fiction.

"I want to take what I learned and write a fictional novel," he said. "I don't want to be categorized."

FURTHER READING

Criticism

Boyer, Allen D. "The Trials of Dr. Sheppard." *New York Times Book Review* (8 October 1995): 26.
    Reviews *Mockery of Justice.*

Huddleston, Eugene L. "Literary Nonfiction: Extending Its Definition." *Midwest Quarterly* 33 (Spring 1992): 340-56.
    Discusses the nonfiction novel as a genre and comments on the legal problems faced by nonfiction writers.

Mortimer, Penelope. "Lusting after Ghosts." *New Statesman* (23 November 1979): 812.
    Offers an unfavorable review of Norman Mailer's *The Executioner's Song.*

Stern, Richard. "Missingeria and Literary Health." *The Georgia Review* 34 (Summer 1980): 422-27.
    Reviews Norman Mailer's *The Executioner's Song* along with several other books. Sterns argues that Mailer was concerned in the book with "the power of narrative" with creating a "grand, even a tragic pattern."

☐ Contemporary Literary Criticism

Indexes

Literary Criticism Series
Cumulative Author Index
Cumulative Topic Index
Cumulative Nationality Index
Title Index, Volume 99

How to Use This Index

The main references

Camus, Albert
  1913-1960 .. **CLC 1, 2, 4, 9, 11, 14,**
32, 69; DA; DAB; DAC; DAM DRAM,
MST, NOV; DC2; SSC 9; WLC

list all author entries in the following Gale Literary Criticism series:

BLC = *Black Literature Criticism*
CLC = *Contemporary Literary Criticism*
CLR = *Children's Literature Review*
CMLC = *Classical and Medieval Literature Criticism*
DA = *DISCovering Authors*
DAB = *DISCovering Authors: British*
DAC = *DISCovering Authors: Canadian*
DAM = *DISCovering Authors Modules*
  DRAM = *dramatists;* **MST** = *most-studied*
  authors; **MULT** = *multicultural authors;* **NOV** =
  novelists; **POET** = *poets;* **POP** = *popular/genre*
  writers; **DC** = *Drama Criticism*
HLC = *Hispanic Literature Criticism*
LC = *Literature Criticism from 1400 to 1800*
NCLC = *Nineteenth-Century Literature Criticism*
PC = *Poetry Criticism*
SSC = *Short Story Criticism*
TCLC = *Twentieth-Century Literary Criticism*
WLC = *World Literature Criticism, 1500 to the Present*

The cross-references

See also CA 89-92; DLB 72; MTCW

list all author entries in the following Gale biographical and literary sources:

AAYA = *Authors & Artists for Young Adults*
AITN = *Authors in the News*
BEST = *Bestsellers*
BW = *Black Writers*
CA = *Contemporary Authors*
CAAS = *Contemporary Authors Autobiography Series*
CABS = *Contemporary Authors Bibliographical Series*
CANR = *Contemporary Authors New Revision Series*
CAP = *Contemporary Authors Permanent Series*
CDALB = *Concise Dictionary of American Literary Biography*
CDBLB = *Concise Dictionary of British Literary Biography*

DLB = *Dictionary of Literary Biography*
DLBD = *Dictionary of Literary Biography Documentary Series*
DLBY = *Dictionary of Literary Biography Yearbook*
HW = *Hispanic Writers*
JRDA = *Junior DISCovering Authors*
MAICYA = *Major Authors and Illustrators for Children and Young Adults*
MTCW = *Major 20th-Century Writers*
NNAL = *Native North American Literature*
SAAS = *Something about the Author Autobiography Series*
SATA = *Something about the Author*
YABC = *Yesterday's Authors of Books for Children*

Literary Criticism Series
Cumulative Author Index

Abasiyanik, Sait Faik   1906-1954
See Sait Faik
See also CA 123

Abbey, Edward   1927-1989 . . . . . . CLC 36, 59
See also CA 45-48; 128; CANR 2, 41

Abbott, Lee K(ittredge)   1947- . . . . . . CLC 48
See also CA 124; CANR 51; DLB 130

Abe, Kobo
1924-1993 . . . . CLC 8, 22, 53, 81;
DAM NOV
See also CA 65-68; 140; CANR 24; MTCW

Abelard, Peter   c. 1079-c. 1142 . . . CMLC 11
See also DLB 115

Abell, Kjeld   1901-1961. . . . . CLC 15
See also CA 111

Abish, Walter   1931- . . . . CLC 22
See also CA 101; CANR 37; DLB 130

Abrahams, Peter (Henry)   1919- . . . . . CLC 4
See also BW 1; CA 57-60; CANR 26;
DLB 117; MTCW

Abrams, M(eyer) H(oward)   1912- . . . CLC 24
See also CA 57-60; CANR 13, 33; DLB 67

Abse, Dannie
1923- . . . CLC 7, 29; DAB; DAM POET
See also CA 53-56; CAAS 1; CANR 4, 46;
DLB 27

Achebe, (Albert) Chinua(lumogu)
1930- . . . . . CLC 1, 3, 5, 7, 11, 26, 51, 75;
BLC; DA; DAB; DAC; DAM MST,
MULT, NOV; WLC
See also AAYA 15; BW 2; CA 1-4R;
CANR 6, 26, 47; CLR 20; DLB 117;
MAICYA; MTCW; SATA 40;
SATA-Brief 38

Acker, Kathy   1948- . . . . CLC 45
See also CA 117; 122; CANR 55

Ackroyd, Peter   1949- . . . . CLC 34, 52
See also CA 123; 127; CANR 51; DLB 155;
INT 127

Acorn, Milton   1923- . . . . CLC 15; DAC
See also CA 103; DLB 53; INT 103

Adamov, Arthur
1908-1970 . . . . CLC 4, 25; DAM DRAM
See also CA 17-18; 25-28R; CAP 2; MTCW

Adams, Alice (Boyd)
1926- . . . . CLC 6, 13, 46; SSC 24
See also CA 81-84; CANR 26, 53;
DLBY 86; INT CANR-26; MTCW

Adams, Andy   1859-1935. . . . . TCLC 56
See also YABC 1

Adams, Douglas (Noel)
1952- . . . . CLC 27, 60; DAM POP
See also AAYA 4; BEST 89:3; CA 106;
CANR 34; DLBY 83; JRDA

Adams, Francis   1862-1893 . . . . NCLC 33

Adams, Henry (Brooks)
1838-1918 . . . . . . TCLC 4, 52; DA; DAB;
DAC; DAM MST
See also CA 104; 133; DLB 12, 47

Adams, Richard (George)
1920- . . . . . . CLC 4, 5, 18; DAM NOV
See also AAYA 16; AITN 1, 2; CA 49-52;
CANR 3, 35; CLR 20; JRDA; MAICYA;
MTCW; SATA 7, 69

Adamson, Joy(-Friederike Victoria)
1910-1980 . . . . CLC 17
See also CA 69-72; 93-96; CANR 22;
MTCW; SATA 11; SATA-Obit 22

Adcock, Fleur   1934- . . . . CLC 41
See also CA 25-28R; CAAS 23; CANR 11,
34; DLB 40

Addams, Charles (Samuel)
1912-1988 . . . . CLC 30
See also CA 61-64; 126; CANR 12

Addison, Joseph   1672-1719 . . . . LC 18
See also CDBLB 1660-1789; DLB 101

Adler, Alfred (F.)   1870-1937 . . . . . . TCLC 61
See also CA 119

Adler, C(arole) S(chwerdtfeger)
1932- . . . . CLC 35
See also AAYA 4; CA 89-92; CANR 19,
40; JRDA; MAICYA; SAAS 15;
SATA 26, 63

Adler, Renata   1938- . . . . CLC 8, 31
See also CA 49-52; CANR 5, 22, 52;
MTCW

Ady, Endre   1877-1919 . . . . TCLC 11
See also CA 107

Aeschylus
525B.C.-456B.C. . . . . CMLC 11; DA;
DAB; DAC; DAM DRAM, MST

Afton, Effie
See Harper, Frances Ellen Watkins

Agapida, Fray Antonio
See Irving, Washington

Agee, James (Rufus)
1909-1955 . . . . TCLC 1, 19; DAM NOV
See also AITN 1; CA 108; 148;
CDALB 1941-1968; DLB 2, 26, 152

Aghill, Gordon
See Silverberg, Robert

Agnon, S(hmuel) Y(osef Halevi)
1888-1970 . . . . CLC 4, 8, 14
See also CA 17-18; 25-28R; CAP 2; MTCW

Agrippa von Nettesheim, Henry Cornelius
1486-1535 . . . . LC 27

Aherne, Owen
See Cassill, R(onald) V(erlin)

Ai   1947- . . . . CLC 4, 14, 69
See also CA 85-88; CAAS 13; DLB 120

Aickman, Robert (Fordyce)
1914-1981 . . . . CLC 57
See also CA 5-8R; CANR 3

Aiken, Conrad (Potter)
1889-1973 . . . . CLC 1, 3, 5, 10, 52;
DAM NOV, POET; SSC 9
See also CA 5-8R; 45-48; CANR 4;
CDALB 1929-1941; DLB 9, 45, 102;
MTCW; SATA 3, 30

Aiken, Joan (Delano)   1924- . . . . CLC 35
See also AAYA 1; CA 9-12R; CANR 4, 23,
34; CLR 1, 19; DLB 161; JRDA;
MAICYA; MTCW; SAAS 1; SATA 2,
30, 73

Ainsworth, William Harrison
1805-1882 . . . . NCLC 13
See also DLB 21; SATA 24

Aitmatov, Chingiz (Torekulovich)
1928- . . . . CLC 71
See also CA 103; CANR 38; MTCW;
SATA 56

Akers, Floyd
See Baum, L(yman) Frank

Akhmadulina, Bella Akhatovna
1937- . . . . CLC 53; DAM POET
See also CA 65-68

Akhmatova, Anna
1888-1966 . . . . CLC 11, 25, 64;
DAM POET; PC 2
See also CA 19-20; 25-28R; CANR 35;
CAP 1; MTCW

Aksakov, Sergei Timofeyvich
1791-1859 . . . . NCLC 2

Aksenov, Vassily
See Aksyonov, Vassily (Pavlovich)

Aksyonov, Vassily (Pavlovich)
1932- . . . . CLC 22, 37
See also CA 53-56; CANR 12, 48

Akutagawa, Ryunosuke
1892-1927 . . . . TCLC 16
See also CA 117; 154

Alain   1868-1951 . . . . TCLC 41

Alain-Fournier. . . . . TCLC 6
See also Fournier, Henri Alban
See also DLB 65

Alarcon, Pedro Antonio de
1833-1891 . . . . NCLC 1

Alas (y Urena), Leopoldo (Enrique Garcia)
1852-1901 . . . . TCLC 29
See also CA 113; 131; HW

Albee, Edward (Franklin III)
1928- . . . . . . CLC 1, 2, 3, 5, 9, 11, 13, 25,
53, 86; DA; DAB; DAC; DAM DRAM,
MST; WLC
See also AITN 1; CA 5-8R; CABS 3;
CANR 8, 54; CDALB 1941-1968; DLB 7;
INT CANR-8; MTCW

Alberti, Rafael   1902- . . . . CLC 7
See also CA 85-88; DLB 108

Albert the Great   1200(?)-1280. . . . CMLC 16
See also DLB 115

Alcala-Galiano, Juan Valera y
See Valera y Alcala-Galiano, Juan

Alcott, Amos Bronson   1799-1888 . . **NCLC 1**
See also DLB 1

Alcott, Louisa May
1832-1888 . . . . . **NCLC 6, 58; DA; DAB;
DAC; DAM MST, NOV; WLC**
See also AAYA 20; CDALB 1865-1917;
CLR 1, 38; DLB 1, 42, 79; DLBD 14;
JRDA; MAICYA; YABC 1

Aldanov, M. A.
See Aldanov, Mark (Alexandrovich)

Aldanov, Mark (Alexandrovich)
1886(?)-1957 . . . . **TCLC 23**
See also CA 118

Aldington, Richard   1892-1962 . . . . . . **CLC 49**
See also CA 85-88; CANR 45; DLB 20, 36,
100, 149

Aldiss, Brian W(ilson)
1925- . . . . **CLC 5, 14, 40; DAM NOV**
See also CA 5-8R; CAAS 2; CANR 5, 28;
DLB 14; MTCW; SATA 34

Alegria, Claribel
1924- . . . . **CLC 75; DAM MULT**
See also CA 131; CAAS 15; DLB 145; HW

Alegria, Fernando   1918- . . . . **CLC 57**
See also CA 9-12R; CANR 5, 32; HW

Aleichem, Sholom . . . . **TCLC 1, 35**
See also Rabinovitch, Sholem

Aleixandre, Vicente
1898-1984 . . . . **CLC 9, 36; DAM POET;
PC 15**
See also CA 85-88; 114; CANR 26;
DLB 108; HW; MTCW

Alepoudelis, Odysseus
See Elytis, Odysseus

Aleshkovsky, Joseph   1929-
See Aleshkovsky, Yuz
See also CA 121; 128

Aleshkovsky, Yuz . . . . **CLC 44**
See also Aleshkovsky, Joseph

Alexander, Lloyd (Chudley)   1924- . . **CLC 35**
See also AAYA 1; CA 1-4R; CANR 1, 24,
38, 55; CLR 1, 5; DLB 52; JRDA;
MAICYA; MTCW; SAAS 19; SATA 3,
49, 81

Alexie, Sherman (Joseph, Jr.)
1966- . . . . **CLC 96; DAM MULT**
See also CA 138; DLB 175; NNAL

Alfau, Felipe   1902- . . . . **CLC 66**
See also CA 137

Alger, Horatio, Jr.   1832-1899 . . . . . **NCLC 8**
See also DLB 42; SATA 16

Algren, Nelson   1909-1981 . . . . **CLC 4, 10, 33**
See also CA 13-16R; 103; CANR 20;
CDALB 1941-1968; DLB 9; DLBY 81,
82; MTCW

Ali, Ahmed   1910- . . . . **CLC 69**
See also CA 25-28R; CANR 15, 34

Alighieri, Dante   1265-1321 . . . . **CMLC 3, 18**

Allan, John B.
See Westlake, Donald E(dwin)

Allen, Edward   1948- . . . . **CLC 59**

Allen, Paula Gunn
1939- . . . . **CLC 84; DAM MULT**
See also CA 112; 143; DLB 175; NNAL

Allen, Roland
See Ayckbourn, Alan

Allen, Sarah A.
See Hopkins, Pauline Elizabeth

Allen, Woody
1935- . . . . **CLC 16, 52; DAM POP**
See also AAYA 10; CA 33-36R; CANR 27,
38; DLB 44; MTCW

Allende, Isabel
1942- . . . . **CLC 39, 57, 97; DAM MULT,
NOV; HLC**
See also AAYA 18; CA 125; 130;
CANR 51; DLB 145; HW; INT 130;
MTCW

Alleyn, Ellen
See Rossetti, Christina (Georgina)

Allingham, Margery (Louise)
1904-1966 . . . . **CLC 19**
See also CA 5-8R; 25-28R; CANR 4;
DLB 77; MTCW

Allingham, William   1824-1889 . . . **NCLC 25**
See also DLB 35

Allison, Dorothy E.   1949- . . . . **CLC 78**
See also CA 140

Allston, Washington   1779-1843 . . . . **NCLC 2**
See also DLB 1

Almedingen, E. M. . . . . **CLC 12**
See also Almedingen, Martha Edith von
See also SATA 3

Almedingen, Martha Edith von   1898-1971
See Almedingen, E. M.
See also CA 1-4R; CANR 1

Almqvist, Carl Jonas Love
1793-1866 . . . . **NCLC 42**

Alonso, Damaso   1898-1990 . . . . **CLC 14**
See also CA 110; 131; 130; DLB 108; HW

Alov
See Gogol, Nikolai (Vasilyevich)

Alta   1942- . . . . **CLC 19**
See also CA 57-60

Alter, Robert B(ernard)   1935- . . . . . . **CLC 34**
See also CA 49-52; CANR 1, 47

Alther, Lisa   1944- . . . . **CLC 7, 41**
See also CA 65-68; CANR 12, 30, 51;
MTCW

Altman, Robert   1925- . . . . **CLC 16**
See also CA 73-76; CANR 43

Alvarez, A(lfred)   1929- . . . . **CLC 5, 13**
See also CA 1-4R; CANR 3, 33; DLB 14,
40

Alvarez, Alejandro Rodriguez   1903-1965
See Casona, Alejandro
See also CA 131; 93-96; HW

Alvarez, Julia   1950- . . . . **CLC 93**
See also CA 147

Alvaro, Corrado   1896-1956 . . . . **TCLC 60**

Amado, Jorge
1912- . . . . **CLC 13, 40; DAM MULT,
NOV; HLC**
See also CA 77-80; CANR 35; DLB 113;
MTCW

Ambler, Eric   1909- . . . . **CLC 4, 6, 9**
See also CA 9-12R; CANR 7, 38; DLB 77;
MTCW

Amichai, Yehuda   1924- . . . . . . **CLC 9, 22, 57**
See also CA 85-88; CANR 46; MTCW

Amiel, Henri Frederic   1821-1881 . . **NCLC 4**

Amis, Kingsley (William)
1922-1995 . . . . . **CLC 1, 2, 3, 5, 8, 13, 40,
44; DA; DAB; DAC; DAM MST, NOV**
See also AITN 2; CA 9-12R; 150; CANR 8,
28, 54; CDBLB 1945-1960; DLB 15, 27,
100, 139; INT CANR-8; MTCW

Amis, Martin (Louis)
1949- . . . . **CLC 4, 9, 38, 62**
See also BEST 90:3; CA 65-68; CANR 8,
27, 54; DLB 14; INT CANR-27

Ammons, A(rchie) R(andolph)
1926- . . . . **CLC 2, 3, 5, 8, 9, 25, 57;
DAM POET; PC 16**
See also AITN 1; CA 9-12R; CANR 6, 36,
51; DLB 5, 165; MTCW

Amo, Tauraatua i
See Adams, Henry (Brooks)

Anand, Mulk Raj
1905- . . . . **CLC 23, 93; DAM NOV**
See also CA 65-68; CANR 32; MTCW

Anatol
See Schnitzler, Arthur

Anaya, Rudolfo A(lfonso)
1937- . . . . **CLC 23; DAM MULT, NOV;
HLC**
See also AAYA 20; CA 45-48; CAAS 4;
CANR 1, 32, 51; DLB 82; HW 1; MTCW

Andersen, Hans Christian
1805-1875 . . . . **NCLC 7; DA; DAB;
DAC; DAM MST, POP; SSC 6; WLC**
See also CLR 6; MAICYA; YABC 1

Anderson, C. Farley
See Mencken, H(enry) L(ouis); Nathan,
George Jean

Anderson, Jessica (Margaret) Queale
. . . . **CLC 37**
See also CA 9-12R; CANR 4

Anderson, Jon (Victor)
1940- . . . . **CLC 9; DAM POET**
See also CA 25-28R; CANR 20

Anderson, Lindsay (Gordon)
1923-1994 . . . . **CLC 20**
See also CA 125; 128; 146

Anderson, Maxwell
1888-1959 . . . . . . **TCLC 2; DAM DRAM**
See also CA 105; 152; DLB 7

Anderson, Poul (William)   1926- . . . . **CLC 15**
See also AAYA 5; CA 1-4R; CAAS 2;
CANR 2, 15, 34; DLB 8; INT CANR-15;
MTCW; SATA 90; SATA-Brief 39

Anderson, Robert (Woodruff)
1917- . . . . **CLC 23; DAM DRAM**
See also AITN 1; CA 21-24R; CANR 32;
DLB 7

Anderson, Sherwood
1876-1941 . . . . **TCLC 1, 10, 24; DA;
DAB; DAC; DAM MST, NOV; SSC 1;
WLC**
See also CA 104; 121; CDALB 1917-1929;
DLB 4, 9, 86; DLBD 1; MTCW

Andier, Pierre
See Desnos, Robert

Andouard
See Giraudoux, (Hippolyte) Jean

Andrade, Carlos Drummond de ...... CLC 18
See also Drummond de Andrade, Carlos

Andrade, Mario de 1893-1945..... TCLC 43

Andreae, Johann V(alentin)
1586-1654 .... LC 32
See also DLB 164

Andreas-Salome, Lou 1861-1937... TCLC 56
See also DLB 66

Andrewes, Lancelot 1555-1626 .... LC 5
See also DLB 151, 172

Andrews, Cicily Fairfield
See West, Rebecca

Andrews, Elton V.
See Pohl, Frederik

Andreyev, Leonid (Nikolaevich)
1871-1919 .... TCLC 3
See also CA 104

Andric, Ivo 1892-1975 .... CLC 8
See also CA 81-84; 57-60; CANR 43;
DLB 147; MTCW

Angelique, Pierre
See Bataille, Georges

Angell, Roger 1920- .... CLC 26
See also CA 57-60; CANR 13, 44; DLB 171

Angelou, Maya
1928- .... CLC 12, 35, 64, 77; BLC; DA;
DAB; DAC; DAM MST, MULT, POET,
POP
See also AAYA 7, 20; BW 2; CA 65-68;
CANR 19, 42; DLB 38; MTCW;
SATA 49

Annensky, Innokenty (Fyodorovich)
1856-1909 .... TCLC 14
See also CA 110; 155

Annunzio, Gabriele d'
See D'Annunzio, Gabriele

Anon, Charles Robert
See Pessoa, Fernando (Antonio Nogueira)

Anouilh, Jean (Marie Lucien Pierre)
1910-1987 ...... CLC 1, 3, 8, 13, 40, 50;
DAM DRAM
See also CA 17-20R; 123; CANR 32;
MTCW

Anthony, Florence
See Ai

Anthony, John
See Ciardi, John (Anthony)

Anthony, Peter
See Shaffer, Anthony (Joshua); Shaffer,
Peter (Levin)

Anthony, Piers 1934-.. CLC 35; DAM POP
See also AAYA 11; CA 21-24R; CANR 28,
56; DLB 8; MTCW; SAAS 22; SATA 84

Antoine, Marc
See Proust, (Valentin-Louis-George-Eugene-)
Marcel

Antoninus, Brother
See Everson, William (Oliver)

Antonioni, Michelangelo 1912- ..... CLC 20
See also CA 73-76; CANR 45

Antschel, Paul 1920-1970
See Celan, Paul
See also CA 85-88; CANR 33; MTCW

Anwar, Chairil 1922-1949 .... TCLC 22
See also CA 121

Apollinaire, Guillaume
1880-1918 .... TCLC 3, 8, 51;
DAM POET; PC 7
See also Kostrowitzki, Wilhelm Apollinaris
de
See also CA 152

Appelfeld, Aharon 1932- .... CLC 23, 47
See also CA 112; 133

Apple, Max (Isaac) 1941-........ CLC 9, 33
See also CA 81-84; CANR 19, 54; DLB 130

Appleman, Philip (Dean) 1926-..... CLC 51
See also CA 13-16R; CAAS 18; CANR 6,
29, 56

Appleton, Lawrence
See Lovecraft, H(oward) P(hillips)

Apteryx
See Eliot, T(homas) S(tearns)

Apuleius, (Lucius Madaurensis)
125(?)-175(?) .... CMLC 1

Aquin, Hubert 1929-1977.......... CLC 15
See also CA 105; DLB 53

Aragon, Louis
1897-1982 ..... CLC 3, 22; DAM NOV,
POET
See also CA 69-72; 108; CANR 28;
DLB 72; MTCW

Arany, Janos 1817-1882......... NCLC 34

Arbuthnot, John 1667-1735......... LC 1
See also DLB 101

Archer, Herbert Winslow
See Mencken, H(enry) L(ouis)

Archer, Jeffrey (Howard)
1940- .... CLC 28; DAM POP
See also AAYA 16; BEST 89:3; CA 77-80;
CANR 22, 52; INT CANR-22

Archer, Jules 1915- .... CLC 12
See also CA 9-12R; CANR 6; SAAS 5;
SATA 4, 85

Archer, Lee
See Ellison, Harlan (Jay)

Arden, John
1930- ...... CLC 6, 13, 15; DAM DRAM
See also CA 13-16R; CAAS 4; CANR 31;
DLB 13; MTCW

Arenas, Reinaldo
1943-1990 ...... CLC 41; DAM MULT;
HLC
See also CA 124; 128; 133; DLB 145; HW

Arendt, Hannah 1906-1975 ..... CLC 66, 98
See also CA 17-20R; 61-64; CANR 26;
MTCW

Aretino, Pietro 1492-1556 .... LC 12

Arghezi, Tudor.................... CLC 80
See also Theodorescu, Ion N.

Arguedas, Jose Maria
1911-1969 .... CLC 10, 18
See also CA 89-92; DLB 113; HW

Argueta, Manlio 1936-............ CLC 31
See also CA 131; DLB 145; HW

Ariosto, Ludovico 1474-1533........ LC 6

Aristides
See Epstein, Joseph

Aristophanes
450B.C.-385B.C......... CMLC 4; DA;
DAB; DAC; DAM DRAM, MST; DC 2

Arlt, Roberto (Godofredo Christophersen)
1900-1942 ..... TCLC 29; DAM MULT;
HLC
See also CA 123; 131; HW

Armah, Ayi Kwei
1939- .... CLC 5, 33; BLC;
DAM MULT, POET
See also BW 1; CA 61-64; CANR 21;
DLB 117; MTCW

Armatrading, Joan 1950-.......... CLC 17
See also CA 114

Arnette, Robert
See Silverberg, Robert

Arnim, Achim von (Ludwig Joachim von
Arnim) 1781-1831 .... NCLC 5
See also DLB 90

Arnim, Bettina von 1785-1859.... NCLC 38
See also DLB 90

Arnold, Matthew
1822-1888 ..... NCLC 6, 29; DA; DAB;
DAC; DAM MST, POET; PC 5; WLC
See also CDBLB 1832-1890; DLB 32, 57

Arnold, Thomas 1795-1842 ...... NCLC 18
See also DLB 55

Arnow, Harriette (Louisa) Simpson
1908-1986 .... CLC 2, 7, 18
See also CA 9-12R; 118; CANR 14; DLB 6;
MTCW; SATA 42; SATA-Obit 47

Arp, Hans
See Arp, Jean

Arp, Jean 1887-1966.............. CLC 5
See also CA 81-84; 25-28R; CANR 42

Arrabal
See Arrabal, Fernando

Arrabal, Fernando 1932- ... CLC 2, 9, 18, 58
See also CA 9-12R; CANR 15

Arrick, Fran.................... CLC 30
See also Gaberman, Judie Angell

Artaud, Antonin (Marie Joseph)
1896-1948 ... TCLC 3, 36; DAM DRAM
See also CA 104; 149

Arthur, Ruth M(abel) 1905-1979.... CLC 12
See also CA 9-12R; 85-88; CANR 4;
SATA 7, 26

Artsybashev, Mikhail (Petrovich)
1878-1927 .... TCLC 31

Arundel, Honor (Morfydd)
1919-1973 .... CLC 17
See also CA 21-22; 41-44R; CAP 2;
CLR 35; SATA 4; SATA-Obit 24

Arzner, Dorothy 1897-1979........ CLC 98

Asch, Sholem 1880-1957 .... TCLC 3
See also CA 105

Ash, Shalom
See Asch, Sholem

Bashkirtseff, Marie   1859-1884 . . .   **NCLC 27**

Basho
See Matsuo Basho

Bass, Kingsley B., Jr.
See Bullins, Ed

Bass, Rick   1958-. . . . .   **CLC 79**
See also CA 126; CANR 53

Bassani, Giorgio   1916-. . . . .   **CLC 9**
See also CA 65-68; CANR 33; DLB 128;
MTCW

Bastos, Augusto (Antonio) Roa
See Roa Bastos, Augusto (Antonio)

Bataille, Georges   1897-1962 . . . .   **CLC 29**
See also CA 101; 89-92

Bates, H(erbert) E(rnest)
1905-1974 . . . .   **CLC 46; DAB;**
DAM POP; SSC 10
See also CA 93-96; 45-48; CANR 34;
DLB 162; MTCW

Bauchart
See Camus, Albert

Baudelaire, Charles
1821-1867 . . . .   **NCLC 6, 29, 55; DA;**
DAB; DAC; DAM MST, POET; PC 1;
SSC 18; WLC

Baudrillard, Jean   1929-. . . . .   **CLC 60**

Baum, L(yman) Frank   1856-1919 . . .   **TCLC 7**
See also CA 108; 133; CLR 15; DLB 22;
JRDA; MAICYA; MTCW; SATA 18

Baum, Louis F.
See Baum, L(yman) Frank

Baumbach, Jonathan   1933- . . . . . .   **CLC 6, 23**
See also CA 13-16R; CAAS 5; CANR 12;
DLBY 80; INT CANR-12; MTCW

Bausch, Richard (Carl)   1945- . . . . . .   **CLC 51**
See also CA 101; CAAS 14; CANR 43;
DLB 130

Baxter, Charles
1947- . . . .   **CLC 45, 78; DAM POP**
See also CA 57-60; CANR 40; DLB 130

Baxter, George Owen
See Faust, Frederick (Schiller)

Baxter, James K(eir)   1926-1972 . . . .   **CLC 14**
See also CA 77-80

Baxter, John
See Hunt, E(verette) Howard, (Jr.)

Bayer, Sylvia
See Glassco, John

Baynton, Barbara   1857-1929 . . . . . .   **TCLC 57**

Beagle, Peter S(oyer)   1939-. . . . .   **CLC 7**
See also CA 9-12R; CANR 4, 51;
DLBY 80; INT CANR-4; SATA 60

Bean, Normal
See Burroughs, Edgar Rice

Beard, Charles A(ustin)
1874-1948 . . . .   **TCLC 15**
See also CA 115; DLB 17; SATA 18

Beardsley, Aubrey   1872-1898 . . . . .   **NCLC 6**

Beattie, Ann
1947- . . . .   **CLC 8, 13, 18, 40, 63;**
DAM NOV, POP; SSC 11
See also BEST 90:2; CA 81-84; CANR 53;
DLBY 82; MTCW

Beattie, James   1735-1803 . . . .   **NCLC 25**
See also DLB 109

Beauchamp, Kathleen Mansfield   1888-1923
See Mansfield, Katherine
See also CA 104; 134; DA; DAC;
DAM MST

Beaumarchais, Pierre-Augustin Caron de
1732-1799 . . . .   **DC 4**
See also DAM DRAM

Beaumont, Francis
1584(?)-1616 . . . .   **LC 33; DC 6**
See also CDBLB Before 1660; DLB 58, 121

Beauvoir, Simone (Lucie Ernestine Marie
Bertrand) de
1908-1986 . . . .   **CLC 1, 2, 4, 8, 14, 31, 44,**
50, 71; DA; DAB; DAC; DAM MST,
NOV; WLC
See also CA 9-12R; 118; CANR 28;
DLB 72; DLBY 86; MTCW

Becker, Carl   1873-1945 . . . .   **TCLC 63:**
See also DLB 17

Becker, Jurek   1937-. . . . .   **CLC 7, 19**
See also CA 85-88; DLB 75

Becker, Walter   1950-. . . . .   **CLC 26**

Beckett, Samuel (Barclay)
1906-1989 . . . . . .   **CLC 1, 2, 3, 4, 6, 9, 10,**
11, 14, 18, 29, 57, 59, 83; DA; DAB;
DAC; DAM DRAM, MST, NOV;
SSC 16; WLC
See also CA 5-8R; 130; CANR 33;
CDBLB 1945-1960; DLB 13, 15;
DLBY 90; MTCW

Beckford, William   1760-1844 . . . .   **NCLC 16**
See also DLB 39

Beckman, Gunnel   1910-. . . . .   **CLC 26**
See also CA 33-36R; CANR 15; CLR 25;
MAICYA; SAAS 9; SATA 6

Becque, Henri   1837-1899. . . . .   **NCLC 3**

Beddoes, Thomas Lovell
1803-1849 . . . .   **NCLC 3**
See also DLB 96

Bede   c. 673-735. . . . .   **CMLC 20**
See also DLB 146

Bedford, Donald F.
See Fearing, Kenneth (Flexner)

Beecher, Catharine Esther
1800-1878 . . . .   **NCLC 30**
See also DLB 1

Beecher, John   1904-1980. . . . .   **CLC 6**
See also AITN 1; CA 5-8R; 105; CANR 8

Beer, Johann   1655-1700. . . . .   **LC 5**
See also DLB 168

Beer, Patricia   1924-. . . . .   **CLC 58**
See also CA 61-64; CANR 13, 46; DLB 40

Beerbohm, Max
See Beerbohm, (Henry) Max(imilian)

Beerbohm, (Henry) Max(imilian)
1872-1956 . . . .   **TCLC 1, 24**
See also CA 104; 154; DLB 34, 100

Beer-Hofmann, Richard
1866-1945 . . . .   **TCLC 60**
See also DLB 81

Begiebing, Robert J(ohn)   1946-. . . . .   **CLC 70**
See also CA 122; CANR 40

Behan, Brendan
1923-1964 . . . .   **CLC 1, 8, 11, 15, 79;**
DAM DRAM
See also CA 73-76; CANR 33;
CDBLB 1945-1960; DLB 13; MTCW

Behn, Aphra
1640(?)-1689 . . . . . .   **LC 1, 30; DA; DAB;**
DAC; DAM DRAM, MST, NOV,
POET; DC 4; PC 13; WLC
See also DLB 39, 80, 131

Behrman, S(amuel) N(athaniel)
1893-1973 . . . .   **CLC 40**
See also CA 13-16; 45-48; CAP 1; DLB 7,
44

Belasco, David   1853-1931 . . . .   **TCLC 3**
See also CA 104; DLB 7

Belcheva, Elisaveta   1893- . . . .   **CLC 10**
See also Bagryana, Elisaveta

Beldone, Phil "Cheech"
See Ellison, Harlan (Jay)

Beleno
See Azuela, Mariano

Belinski, Vissarion Grigoryevich
1811-1848 . . . .   **NCLC 5**

Belitt, Ben   1911-. . . . .   **CLC 22**
See also CA 13-16R; CAAS 4; CANR 7;
DLB 5

Bell, Gertrude   1868-1926. . . . .   **TCLC 67**
See also DLB 174

Bell, James Madison
1826-1902 . . . .   **TCLC 43; BLC;**
DAM MULT
See also BW 1; CA 122; 124; DLB 50

Bell, Madison Smartt   1957-. . . . . . .   **CLC 41**
See also CA 111; CANR 28, 54

Bell, Marvin (Hartley)
1937- . . . .   **CLC 8, 31; DAM POET**
See also CA 21-24R; CAAS 14; DLB 5;
MTCW

Bell, W. L. D.
See Mencken, H(enry) L(ouis)

Bellamy, Atwood C.
See Mencken, H(enry) L(ouis)

Bellamy, Edward   1850-1898 . . . . . .   **NCLC 4**
See also DLB 12

Bellin, Edward J.
See Kuttner, Henry

Belloc, (Joseph) Hilaire (Pierre Sebastien
Rene Swanton)
1870-1953 . . .   **TCLC 7, 18; DAM POET**
See also CA 106; 152; DLB 19, 100, 141,
174; YABC 1

Belloc, Joseph Peter Rene Hilaire
See Belloc, (Joseph) Hilaire (Pierre Sebastien
Rene Swanton)

Belloc, Joseph Pierre Hilaire
See Belloc, (Joseph) Hilaire (Pierre Sebastien
Rene Swanton)

Belloc, M. A.
See Lowndes, Marie Adelaide (Belloc)

Bellow, Saul
    1915- ...... CLC 1, 2, 3, 6, 8, 10, 13, 15,
        25, 33, 34, 63, 79; DA; DAB; DAC;
        DAM MST, NOV, POP; SSC 14; WLC
    See also AITN 2; BEST 89:3; CA 5-8R;
        CABS 1; CANR 29, 53;
        CDALB 1941-1968; DLB 2, 28; DLBD 3;
        DLBY 82; MTCW

Belser, Reimond Karel Maria de   1929-
    See Ruyslinck, Ward
    See also CA 152

Bely, Andrey .... TCLC 7; PC 11
    See also Bugayev, Boris Nikolayevich

Benary, Margot
    See Benary-Isbert, Margot

Benary-Isbert, Margot 1889-1979... CLC 12
    See also CA 5-8R; 89-92; CANR 4;
        CLR 12; MAICYA; SATA 2;
        SATA-Obit 21

Benavente (y Martinez), Jacinto
    1866-1954 ..... TCLC 3; DAM DRAM,
                                                    MULT
    See also CA 106; 131; HW; MTCW

Benchley, Peter (Bradford)
    1940- ..... CLC 4, 8; DAM NOV, POP
    See also AAYA 14; AITN 2; CA 17-20R;
        CANR 12, 35; MTCW; SATA 3, 89

Benchley, Robert (Charles)
    1889-1945 .... TCLC 1, 55
    See also CA 105; 153; DLB 11

Benda, Julien 1867-1956 .... TCLC 60
    See also CA 120; 154

Benedict, Ruth 1887-1948 .... TCLC 60

Benedikt, Michael 1935- .... CLC 4, 14
    See also CA 13-16R; CANR 7; DLB 5

Benet, Juan 1927-................ CLC 28
    See also CA 143

Benet, Stephen Vincent
    1898-1943 ...... TCLC 7; DAM POET;
                                                    SSC 10
    See also CA 104; 152; DLB 4, 48, 102;
        YABC 1

Benet, William Rose
    1886-1950 ..... TCLC 28; DAM POET
    See also CA 118; 152; DLB 45

Benford, Gregory (Albert) 1941-.... CLC 52
    See also CA 69-72; CANR 12, 24, 49;
        DLBY 82

Bengtsson, Frans (Gunnar)
    1894-1954 .... TCLC 48

Benjamin, David
    See Slavitt, David R(ytman)

Benjamin, Lois
    See Gould, Lois

Benjamin, Walter 1892-1940 ...... TCLC 39

Benn, Gottfried 1886-1956........ TCLC 3
    See also CA 106; 153; DLB 56

Bennett, Alan
    1934- ... CLC 45, 77; DAB; DAM MST
    See also CA 103; CANR 35, 55; MTCW

Bennett, (Enoch) Arnold
    1867-1931 .... TCLC 5, 20
    See also CA 106; 155; CDBLB 1890-1914;
        DLB 10, 34, 98, 135

Bennett, Elizabeth
    See Mitchell, Margaret (Munnerlyn)

Bennett, George Harold   1930-
    See Bennett, Hal
    See also BW 1; CA 97-100

Bennett, Hal .... CLC 5
    See also Bennett, George Harold
    See also DLB 33

Bennett, Jay 1912-................ CLC 35
    See also AAYA 10; CA 69-72; CANR 11,
        42; JRDA; SAAS 4; SATA 41, 87;
        SATA-Brief 27

Bennett, Louise (Simone)
    1919- ..... CLC 28; BLC; DAM MULT
    See also BW 2; CA 151; DLB 117

Benson, E(dward) F(rederic)
    1867-1940 .... TCLC 27
    See also CA 114; DLB 135, 153

Benson, Jackson J. 1930-........ CLC 34
    See also CA 25-28R; DLB 111

Benson, Sally 1900-1972 .... CLC 17
    See also CA 19-20; 37-40R; CAP 1;
        SATA 1, 35; SATA-Obit 27

Benson, Stella 1892-1933........ TCLC 17
    See also CA 117; 155; DLB 36, 162

Bentham, Jeremy 1748-1832 ..... NCLC 38
    See also DLB 107, 158

Bentley, E(dmund) C(lerihew)
    1875-1956 .... TCLC 12
    See also CA 108; DLB 70

Bentley, Eric (Russell) 1916-...... CLC 24
    See also CA 5-8R; CANR 6; INT CANR-6

Beranger, Pierre Jean de
    1780-1857 .... NCLC 34

Berdyaev, Nicolas
    See Berdyaev, Nikolai (Aleksandrovich)

Berdyaev, Nikolai (Aleksandrovich)
    1874-1948 .... TCLC 67
    See also CA 120

Berendt, John (Lawrence) 1939-.... CLC 86
    See also CA 146

Berger, Colonel
    See Malraux, (Georges-)Andre

Berger, John (Peter) 1926- ...... CLC 2, 19
    See also CA 81-84; CANR 51; DLB 14

Berger, Melvin H. 1927-.......... CLC 12
    See also CA 5-8R; CANR 4; CLR 32;
        SAAS 2; SATA 5, 88

Berger, Thomas (Louis)
    1924- .... CLC 3, 5, 8, 11, 18, 38;
                                                    DAM NOV
    See also CA 1-4R; CANR 5, 28, 51; DLB 2;
        DLBY 80; INT CANR-28; MTCW

Bergman, (Ernst) Ingmar
    1918- .... CLC 16, 72
    See also CA 81-84; CANR 33

Bergson, Henri 1859-1941 .... TCLC 32

Bergstein, Eleanor 1938-.......... CLC 4
    See also CA 53-56; CANR 5

Berkoff, Steven 1937-............ CLC 56
    See also CA 104

Bermant, Chaim (Icyk) 1929- ...... CLC 40
    See also CA 57-60; CANR 6, 31

Bern, Victoria
    See Fisher, M(ary) F(rances) K(ennedy)

Bernanos, (Paul Louis) Georges
    1888-1948 .... TCLC 3
    See also CA 104; 130; DLB 72

Bernard, April 1956- .... CLC 59
    See also CA 131

Berne, Victoria
    See Fisher, M(ary) F(rances) K(ennedy)

Bernhard, Thomas
    1931-1989 .... CLC 3, 32, 61
    See also CA 85-88; 127; CANR 32;
        DLB 85, 124; MTCW

Berriault, Gina 1926- .... CLC 54
    See also CA 116; 129; DLB 130

Berrigan, Daniel 1921-............ CLC 4
    See also CA 33-36R; CAAS 1; CANR 11,
        43; DLB 5

Berrigan, Edmund Joseph Michael, Jr.
    1934-1983
    See Berrigan, Ted
    See also CA 61-64; 110; CANR 14

Berrigan, Ted.................... CLC 37
    See also Berrigan, Edmund Joseph Michael,
        Jr.
    See also DLB 5, 169

Berry, Charles Edward Anderson 1931-
    See Berry, Chuck
    See also CA 115

Berry, Chuck.................... CLC 17
    See also Berry, Charles Edward Anderson

Berry, Jonas
    See Ashbery, John (Lawrence)

Berry, Wendell (Erdman)
    1934-............. CLC 4, 6, 8, 27, 46;
                                                    DAM POET
    See also AITN 1; CA 73-76; CANR 50;
        DLB 5, 6

Berryman, John
    1914-1972 ...... CLC 1, 2, 3, 4, 6, 8, 10,
                            13, 25, 62; DAM POET
    See also CA 13-16; 33-36R; CABS 2;
        CANR 35; CAP 1; CDALB 1941-1968;
        DLB 48; MTCW

Bertolucci, Bernardo 1940- .... CLC 16
    See also CA 106

Bertrand, Aloysius 1807-1841 .... NCLC 31

Bertran de Born c. 1140-1215 ..... CMLC 5

Besant, Annie (Wood) 1847-1933 ... TCLC 9
    See also CA 105

Bessie, Alvah 1904-1985........... CLC 23
    See also CA 5-8R; 116; CANR 2; DLB 26

Bethlen, T. D.
    See Silverberg, Robert

Beti, Mongo.... CLC 27; BLC; DAM MULT
    See also Biyidi, Alexandre

Betjeman, John
    1906-1984 .... CLC 2, 6, 10, 34, 43;
                            DAB; DAM MST, POET
    See also CA 9-12R; 112; CANR 33, 56;
        CDBLB 1945-1960; DLB 20; DLBY 84;
        MTCW

Bettelheim, Bruno 1903-1990 ...... CLC 79
    See also CA 81-84; 131; CANR 23; MTCW

Betti, Ugo 1892-1953 . . . . **TCLC 5**
See also CA 104; 155

Betts, Doris (Waugh) 1932- . . . . **CLC 3, 6, 28**
See also CA 13-16R; CANR 9; DLBY 82;
INT CANR-9

Bevan, Alistair
See Roberts, Keith (John Kingston)

Bialik, Chaim Nachman
1873-1934 . . . . **TCLC 25**

Bickerstaff, Isaac
See Swift, Jonathan

Bidart, Frank 1939- . . . . **CLC 33**
See also CA 140

Bienek, Horst 1930- . . . . **CLC 7, 11**
See also CA 73-76; DLB 75

Bierce, Ambrose (Gwinett)
1842-1914(?) . . . . . . **TCLC 1, 7, 44; DA;**
DAC; DAM MST; SSC 9; WLC
See also CA 104; 139; CDALB 1865-1917;
DLB 11, 12, 23, 71, 74

Biggers, Earl Derr 1884-1933 . . . . . **TCLC 65**
See also CA 108; 153

Billings, Josh
See Shaw, Henry Wheeler

Billington, (Lady) Rachel (Mary)
1942- . . . . **CLC 43**
See also AITN 2; CA 33-36R; CANR 44

Binyon, T(imothy) J(ohn) 1936- . . . . **CLC 34**
See also CA 111; CANR 28

Bioy Casares, Adolfo
1914- . . . . **CLC 4, 8, 13, 88;**
DAM MULT; HLC; SSC 17
See also CA 29-32R; CANR 19, 43;
DLB 113; HW; MTCW

Bird, Cordwainer
See Ellison, Harlan (Jay)

Bird, Robert Montgomery
1806-1854 . . . . **NCLC 1**

Birney, (Alfred) Earle
1904- . . . . **CLC 1, 4, 6, 11; DAC;**
DAM MST, POET
See also CA 1-4R; CANR 5, 20; DLB 88;
MTCW

Bishop, Elizabeth
1911-1979 . . . . . . **CLC 1, 4, 9, 13, 15, 32;**
DA; DAC; DAM MST, POET; PC 3
See also CA 5-8R; 89-92; CABS 2;
CANR 26; CDALB 1968-1988; DLB 5,
169; MTCW; SATA-Obit 24

Bishop, John 1935- . . . . **CLC 10**
See also CA 105

Bissett, Bill 1939- . . . . **CLC 18; PC 14**
See also CA 69-72; CAAS 19; CANR 15;
DLB 53; MTCW

Bitov, Andrei (Georgievich) 1937- . . . **CLC 57**
See also CA 142

Biyidi, Alexandre 1932-
See Beti, Mongo
See also BW 1; CA 114; 124; MTCW

Bjarme, Brynjolf
See Ibsen, Henrik (Johan)

Bjornson, Bjornstjerne (Martinius)
1832-1910 . . . . **TCLC 7, 37**
See also CA 104

Black, Robert
See Holdstock, Robert P.

Blackburn, Paul 1926-1971 . . . . . . **CLC 9, 43**
See also CA 81-84; 33-36R; CANR 34;
DLB 16; DLBY 81

Black Elk
1863-1950 . . . . . **TCLC 33; DAM MULT**
See also CA 144; NNAL

Black Hobart
See Sanders, (James) Ed(ward)

Blacklin, Malcolm
See Chambers, Aidan

Blackmore, R(ichard) D(oddridge)
1825-1900 . . . . **TCLC 27**
See also CA 120; DLB 18

Blackmur, R(ichard) P(almer)
1904-1965 . . . . **CLC 2, 24**
See also CA 11-12; 25-28R; CAP 1; DLB 63

Black Tarantula
See Acker, Kathy

Blackwood, Algernon (Henry)
1869-1951 . . . . **TCLC 5**
See also CA 105; 150; DLB 153, 156

Blackwood, Caroline 1931-1996 . . . **CLC 6, 9**
See also CA 85-88; 151; CANR 32;
DLB 14; MTCW

Blade, Alexander
See Hamilton, Edmond; Silverberg, Robert

Blaga, Lucian 1895-1961 . . . . **CLC 75**

Blair, Eric (Arthur) 1903-1950
See Orwell, George
See also CA 104; 132; DA; DAB; DAC;
DAM MST, NOV; MTCW; SATA 29

Blais, Marie-Claire
1939- . . . . **CLC 2, 4, 6, 13, 22; DAC;**
DAM MST
See also CA 21-24R; CAAS 4; CANR 38;
DLB 53; MTCW

Blaise, Clark 1940- . . . . **CLC 29**
See also AITN 2; CA 53-56; CAAS 3;
CANR 5; DLB 53

Blake, Nicholas
See Day Lewis, C(ecil)
See also DLB 77

Blake, William
1757-1827 . . . . **NCLC 13, 37, 57; DA;**
DAB; DAC; DAM MST, POET; PC 12;
WLC
See also CDBLB 1789-1832; DLB 93, 163;
MAICYA; SATA 30

Blake, William J(ames) 1894-1969 . . . **PC 12**
See also CA 5-8R; 25-28R

Blasco Ibanez, Vicente
1867-1928 . . . . . . **TCLC 12; DAM NOV**
See also CA 110; 131; HW; MTCW

Blatty, William Peter
1928- . . . . **CLC 2; DAM POP**
See also CA 5-8R; CANR 9

Bleeck, Oliver
See Thomas, Ross (Elmore)

Blessing, Lee 1949- . . . . **CLC 54**

Blish, James (Benjamin)
1921-1975 . . . . **CLC 14**
See also CA 1-4R; 57-60; CANR 3; DLB 8;
MTCW; SATA 66

Bliss, Reginald
See Wells, H(erbert) G(eorge)

Blixen, Karen (Christentze Dinesen)
1885-1962
See Dinesen, Isak
See also CA 25-28; CANR 22, 50; CAP 2;
MTCW; SATA 44

Bloch, Robert (Albert) 1917-1994 . . . **CLC 33**
See also CA 5-8R; 146; CAAS 20; CANR 5;
DLB 44; INT CANR-5; SATA 12;
SATA-Obit 82

Blok, Alexander (Alexandrovich)
1880-1921 . . . . **TCLC 5**
See also CA 104

Blom, Jan
See Breytenbach, Breyten

Bloom, Harold 1930- . . . . **CLC 24**
See also CA 13-16R; CANR 39; DLB 67

Bloomfield, Aurelius
See Bourne, Randolph S(illiman)

Blount, Roy (Alton), Jr. 1941- . . . . . **CLC 38**
See also CA 53-56; CANR 10, 28;
INT CANR-28; MTCW

Bloy, Leon 1846-1917 . . . . **TCLC 22**
See also CA 121; DLB 123

Blume, Judy (Sussman)
1938- . . . **CLC 12, 30; DAM NOV, POP**
See also AAYA 3; CA 29-32R; CANR 13,
37; CLR 2, 15; DLB 52; JRDA;
MAICYA; MTCW; SATA 2, 31, 79

Blunden, Edmund (Charles)
1896-1974 . . . . **CLC 2, 56**
See also CA 17-18; 45-48; CANR 54;
CAP 2; DLB 20, 100, 155; MTCW

Bly, Robert (Elwood)
1926- . . . . **CLC 1, 2, 5, 10, 15, 38;**
DAM POET
See also CA 5-8R; CANR 41; DLB 5;
MTCW

Boas, Franz 1858-1942 . . . . **TCLC 56**
See also CA 115

Bobette
See Simenon, Georges (Jacques Christian)

Boccaccio, Giovanni
1313-1375 . . . . **CMLC 13; SSC 10**

Bochco, Steven 1943- . . . . **CLC 35**
See also AAYA 11; CA 124; 138

Bodenheim, Maxwell 1892-1954 . . . **TCLC 44**
See also CA 110; DLB 9, 45

Bodker, Cecil 1927- . . . . **CLC 21**
See also CA 73-76; CANR 13, 44; CLR 23;
MAICYA; SATA 14

Boell, Heinrich (Theodor)
1917-1985 . . . . **CLC 2, 3, 6, 9, 11, 15, 27,**
32, 72; DA; DAB; DAC; DAM MST,
NOV; SSC 23; WLC
See also CA 21-24R; 116; CANR 24;
DLB 69; DLBY 85; MTCW

Boerne, Alfred
See Doeblin, Alfred

Boethius 480(?)-524(?) . . . . **CMLC 15**
See also DLB 115

Bogan, Louise
1897-1970 . . . . **CLC 4, 39, 46, 93;**
DAM POET; PC 12
See also CA 73-76; 25-28R; CANR 33;
DLB 45, 169; MTCW

Bogarde, Dirk . . . . **CLC 19**
See also Van Den Bogarde, Derek Jules
Gaspard Ulric Niven
See also DLB 14

Bogosian, Eric 1953- . . . . **CLC 45**
See also CA 138

Bograd, Larry 1953- . . . . **CLC 35**
See also CA 93-96; SAAS 21; SATA 33, 89

Boiardo, Matteo Maria 1441-1494 . . . . **LC 6**

Boileau-Despreaux, Nicolas
1636-1711 . . . . **LC 3**

Bojer, Johan 1872-1959 . . . . **TCLC 64**

Boland, Eavan (Aisling)
1944- . . . . **CLC 40, 67; DAM POET**
See also CA 143; DLB 40

Bolt, Lee
See Faust, Frederick (Schiller)

Bolt, Robert (Oxton)
1924-1995 . . . . . . **CLC 14; DAM DRAM**
See also CA 17-20R; 147; CANR 35;
DLB 13; MTCW

Bombet, Louis-Alexandre-Cesar
See Stendhal

Bomkauf
See Kaufman, Bob (Garnell)

Bonaventura . . . . **NCLC 35**
See also DLB 90

Bond, Edward
1934- . . . **CLC 4, 6, 13, 23; DAM DRAM**
See also CA 25-28R; CANR 38; DLB 13;
MTCW

Bonham, Frank 1914-1989 . . . . **CLC 12**
See also AAYA 1; CA 9-12R; CANR 4, 36;
JRDA; MAICYA; SAAS 3; SATA 1, 49;
SATA-Obit 62

Bonnefoy, Yves
1923- . . . . . . **CLC 9, 15, 58; DAM MST,**
POET
See also CA 85-88; CANR 33; MTCW

Bontemps, Arna(ud Wendell)
1902-1973 . . . . **CLC 1, 18; BLC;**
DAM MULT, NOV, POET
See also BW 1; CA 1-4R; 41-44R; CANR 4,
35; CLR 6; DLB 48, 51; JRDA;
MAICYA; MTCW; SATA 2, 44;
SATA-Obit 24

Booth, Martin 1944- . . . . **CLC 13**
See also CA 93-96; CAAS 2

Booth, Philip 1925- . . . . **CLC 23**
See also CA 5-8R; CANR 5; DLBY 82

Booth, Wayne C(layson) 1921- . . . . . **CLC 24**
See also CA 1-4R; CAAS 5; CANR 3, 43;
DLB 67

Borchert, Wolfgang 1921-1947 . . . . . **TCLC 5**
See also CA 104; DLB 69, 124

Borel, Petrus 1809-1859 . . . . **NCLC 41**

Borges, Jorge Luis
1899-1986 . . . **CLC 1, 2, 3, 4, 6, 8, 9, 10,**
13, 19, 44, 48, 83; DA; DAB; DAC;
DAM MST, MULT; HLC; SSC 4; WLC
See also AAYA 19; CA 21-24R; CANR 19,
33; DLB 113; DLBY 86; HW; MTCW

Borowski, Tadeusz 1922-1951 . . . . . . **TCLC 9**
See also CA 106; 154

Borrow, George (Henry)
1803-1881 . . . . **NCLC 9**
See also DLB 21, 55, 166

Bosman, Herman Charles
1905-1951 . . . . **TCLC 49**

Bosschere, Jean de 1878(?)-1953 . . . **TCLC 19**
See also CA 115

Boswell, James
1740-1795 . . . . . . **LC 4; DA; DAB; DAC;**
DAM MST; WLC
See also CDBLB 1660-1789; DLB 104, 142

Bottoms, David 1949- . . . . **CLC 53**
See also CA 105; CANR 22; DLB 120;
DLBY 83

Boucicault, Dion 1820-1890 . . . . . . **NCLC 41**

Boucolon, Maryse 1937(?)-
See Conde, Maryse
See also CA 110; CANR 30, 53

Bourget, Paul (Charles Joseph)
1852-1935 . . . . **TCLC 12**
See also CA 107; DLB 123

Bourjaily, Vance (Nye) 1922- . . . . **CLC 8, 62**
See also CA 1-4R; CAAS 1; CANR 2;
DLB 2, 143

Bourne, Randolph S(illiman)
1886-1918 . . . . **TCLC 16**
See also CA 117; 155; DLB 63

Bova, Ben(jamin William) 1932- . . . . **CLC 45**
See also AAYA 16; CA 5-8R; CAAS 18;
CANR 11, 56; CLR 3; DLBY 81;
INT CANR-11; MAICYA; MTCW;
SATA 6, 68

Bowen, Elizabeth (Dorothea Cole)
1899-1973 . . . . . . **CLC 1, 3, 6, 11, 15, 22;**
DAM NOV; SSC 3
See also CA 17-18; 41-44R; CANR 35;
CAP 2; CDBLB 1945-1960; DLB 15, 162;
MTCW

Bowering, George 1935- . . . . **CLC 15, 47**
See also CA 21-24R; CAAS 16; CANR 10;
DLB 53

Bowering, Marilyn R(uthe) 1949- . . . **CLC 32**
See also CA 101; CANR 49

Bowers, Edgar 1924- . . . . **CLC 9**
See also CA 5-8R; CANR 24; DLB 5

Bowie, David . . . . **CLC 17**
See also Jones, David Robert

Bowles, Jane (Sydney)
1917-1973 . . . . **CLC 3, 68**
See also CA 19-20; 41-44R; CAP 2

Bowles, Paul (Frederick)
1910- . . . . **CLC 1, 2, 19, 53; SSC 3**
See also CA 1-4R; CAAS 1; CANR 1, 19,
50; DLB 5, 6; MTCW

Box, Edgar
See Vidal, Gore

Boyd, Nancy
See Millay, Edna St. Vincent

Boyd, William 1952- . . . . **CLC 28, 53, 70**
See also CA 114; 120; CANR 51

Boyle, Kay
1902-1992 . . . . . **CLC 1, 5, 19, 58; SSC 5**
See also CA 13-16R; 140; CAAS 1;
CANR 29; DLB 4, 9, 48, 86; DLBY 93;
MTCW

Boyle, Mark
See Kienzle, William X(avier)

Boyle, Patrick 1905-1982 . . . . **CLC 19**
See also CA 127

Boyle, T. C. 1948-
See Boyle, T(homas) Coraghessan

Boyle, T(homas) Coraghessan
1948- . . . . . **CLC 36, 55, 90; DAM POP;**
SSC 16
See also BEST 90:4; CA 120; CANR 44;
DLBY 86

Boz
See Dickens, Charles (John Huffam)

Brackenridge, Hugh Henry
1748-1816 . . . . **NCLC 7**
See also DLB 11, 37

Bradbury, Edward P.
See Moorcock, Michael (John)

Bradbury, Malcolm (Stanley)
1932- . . . . **CLC 32, 61; DAM NOV**
See also CA 1-4R; CANR 1, 33; DLB 14;
MTCW

Bradbury, Ray (Douglas)
1920- . . . . . **CLC 1, 3, 10, 15, 42, 98; DA;**
DAB; DAC; DAM MST, NOV, POP;
WLC
See also AAYA 15; AITN 1, 2; CA 1-4R;
CANR 2, 30; CDALB 1968-1988; DLB 2,
8; INT CANR-30; MTCW; SATA 11, 64

Bradford, Gamaliel 1863-1932 . . . . . **TCLC 36**
See also DLB 17

Bradley, David (Henry, Jr.)
1950- . . . . . **CLC 23; BLC; DAM MULT**
See also BW 1; CA 104; CANR 26; DLB 33

Bradley, John Ed(mund, Jr.)
1958- . . . . **CLC 55**
See also CA 139

Bradley, Marion Zimmer
1930- . . . . **CLC 30; DAM POP**
See also AAYA 9; CA 57-60; CAAS 10;
CANR 7, 31, 51; DLB 8; MTCW;
SATA 90

Bradstreet, Anne
1612(?)-1672 . . . . . . **LC 4, 30; DA; DAC;**
DAM MST, POET; PC 10
See also CDALB 1640-1865; DLB 24

Brady, Joan 1939- . . . . **CLC 86**
See also CA 141

Bragg, Melvyn 1939- . . . . **CLC 10**
See also BEST 89:3; CA 57-60; CANR 10,
48; DLB 14

Braine, John (Gerard)
1922-1986 . . . . **CLC 1, 3, 41**
See also CA 1-4R; 120; CANR 1, 33;
CDBLB 1945-1960; DLB 15; DLBY 86;
MTCW

Camus, Albert
     1913-1960 .... **CLC 1, 2, 4, 9, 11, 14, 32,**
     63, 69; DA; DAB; DAC; DAM DRAM,
     MST, NOV; DC 2; SSC 9; WLC
     See also CA 89-92; DLB 72; MTCW

Canby, Vincent 1924-............. **CLC 13**
     See also CA 81-84

Cancale
     See Desnos, Robert

Canetti, Elias
     1905-1994 ...... **CLC 3, 14, 25, 75, 86**
     See also CA 21-24R; 146; CANR 23;
     DLB 85, 124; MTCW

Canin, Ethan 1960-............. **CLC 55**
     See also CA 131; 135

Cannon, Curt
     See Hunter, Evan

Cape, Judith
     See Page, P(atricia) K(athleen)

Capek, Karel
     1890-1938 ...... **TCLC 6, 37; DA; DAB;**
     DAC; DAM DRAM, MST, NOV; DC 1;
     WLC
     See also CA 104; 140

Capote, Truman
     1924-1984 ...... **CLC 1, 3, 8, 13, 19, 34,**
     38, 58; DA; DAB; DAC; DAM MST,
     NOV, POP; SSC 2; WLC
     See also CA 5-8R; 113; CANR 18;
     CDALB 1941-1968; DLB 2; DLBY 80,
     84; MTCW; SATA 91

Capra, Frank 1897-1991.......... **CLC 16**
     See also CA 61-64; 135

Caputo, Philip 1941-............. **CLC 32**
     See also CA 73-76; CANR 40

Card, Orson Scott
     1951- ...... **CLC 44, 47, 50; DAM POP**
     See also AAYA 11; CA 102; CANR 27, 47;
     INT CANR-27; MTCW; SATA 83

Cardenal, Ernesto
     1925- .... **CLC 31; DAM MULT,**
     POET; HLC
     See also CA 49-52; CANR 2, 32; HW;
     MTCW

Cardozo, Benjamin N(athan)
     1870-1938 .... **TCLC 65**
     See also CA 117

Carducci, Giosue 1835-1907...... **TCLC 32**

Carew, Thomas 1595(?)-1640........ **LC 13**
     See also DLB 126

Carey, Ernestine Gilbreth 1908-.... **CLC 17**
     See also CA 5-8R; SATA 2

Carey, Peter 1943-......... **CLC 40, 55, 96**
     See also CA 123; 127; CANR 53; INT 127;
     MTCW

Carleton, William 1794-1869...... **NCLC 3**
     See also DLB 159

Carlisle, Henry (Coffin) 1926-...... **CLC 33**
     See also CA 13-16R; CANR 15

Carlsen, Chris
     See Holdstock, Robert P.

Carlson, Ron(ald F.) 1947-........ **CLC 54**
     See also CA 105; CANR 27

Carlyle, Thomas
     1795-1881 .... **NCLC 22; DA; DAB;**
     DAC; DAM MST
     See also CDBLB 1789-1832; DLB 55; 144

Carman, (William) Bliss
     1861-1929 .... **TCLC 7; DAC**
     See also CA 104; 152; DLB 92

Carnegie, Dale 1888-1955 .... **TCLC 53**

Carossa, Hans 1878-1956......... **TCLC 48**
     See also DLB 66

Carpenter, Don(ald Richard)
     1931-1995 .... **CLC 41**
     See also CA 45-48; 149; CANR 1

Carpentier (y Valmont), Alejo
     1904-1980 .... **CLC 8, 11, 38;**
     DAM MULT; HLC
     See also CA 65-68; 97-100; CANR 11;
     DLB 113; HW

Carr, Caleb 1955(?)-............. **CLC 86**
     See also CA 147

Carr, Emily 1871-1945........... **TCLC 32**
     See also DLB 68

Carr, John Dickson 1906-1977 ...... **CLC 3**
     See also CA 49-52; 69-72; CANR 3, 33;
     MTCW

Carr, Philippa
     See Hibbert, Eleanor Alice Burford

Carr, Virginia Spencer 1929-....... **CLC 34**
     See also CA 61-64; DLB 111

Carrere, Emmanuel 1957- .... **CLC 89**

Carrier, Roch
     1937- ... **CLC 13, 78; DAC; DAM MST**
     See also CA 130; DLB 53

Carroll, James P. 1943(?)-......... **CLC 38**
     See also CA 81-84

Carroll, Jim 1951- .... **CLC 35**
     See also AAYA 17; CA 45-48; CANR 42

Carroll, Lewis .... **NCLC 2, 53; WLC**
     See also Dodgson, Charles Lutwidge
     See also CDBLB 1832-1890; CLR 2, 18;
     DLB 18, 163; JRDA

Carroll, Paul Vincent 1900-1968.... **CLC 10**
     See also CA 9-12R; 25-28R; DLB 10

Carruth, Hayden
     1921- ...... **CLC 4, 7, 10, 18, 84; PC 10**
     See also CA 9-12R; CANR 4, 38; DLB 5,
     165; INT CANR-4; MTCW; SATA 47

Carson, Rachel Louise
     1907-1964 .... **CLC 71; DAM POP**
     See also CA 77-80; CANR 35; MTCW;
     SATA 23

Carter, Angela (Olive)
     1940-1992 ...... **CLC 5, 41, 76; SSC 13**
     See also CA 53-56; 136; CANR 12, 36;
     DLB 14; MTCW; SATA 66;
     SATA-Obit 70

Carter, Nick
     See Smith, Martin Cruz

Carver, Raymond
     1938-1988 .... **CLC 22, 36, 53, 55;**
     DAM NOV; SSC 8
     See also CA 33-36R; 126; CANR 17, 34;
     DLB 130; DLBY 84, 88; MTCW

Cary, Elizabeth, Lady Falkland
     1585-1639 .... **LC 30**

Cary, (Arthur) Joyce (Lunel)
     1888-1957 ....TCLC 1, 29
     See also CA 104; CDBLB 1914-1945;
     DLB 15, 100

Casanova de Seingalt, Giovanni Jacopo
     1725-1798 .... **LC 13**

Casares, Adolfo Bioy
     See Bioy Casares, Adolfo

Casely-Hayford, J(oseph) E(phraim)
     1866-1930 .... **TCLC 24; BLC;**
     DAM MULT
     See also BW 2; CA 123; 152

Casey, John (Dudley) 1939-........ **CLC 59**
     See also BEST 90:2; CA 69-72; CANR 23

Casey, Michael 1947-.............. **CLC 2**
     See also CA 65-68; DLB 5

Casey, Patrick
     See Thurman, Wallace (Henry)

Casey, Warren (Peter) 1935-1988... **CLC 12**
     See also CA 101; 127; INT 101

Casona, Alejandro................. **CLC 49**
     See also Alvarez, Alejandro Rodriguez

Cassavetes, John 1929-1989........ **CLC 20**
     See also CA 85-88; 127

Cassian, Nina 1924-............... **PC 17**

Cassill, R(onald) V(erlin) 1919-... **CLC 4, 23**
     See also CA 9-12R; CAAS 1; CANR 7, 45;
     DLB 6

Cassirer, Ernst 1874-1945 .... **TCLC 61**

Cassity, (Allen) Turner 1929- .... **CLC 6, 42**
     See also CA 17-20R; CAAS 8; CANR 11;
     DLB 105

Castaneda, Carlos 1931(?)-......... **CLC 12**
     See also CA 25-28R; CANR 32; HW;
     MTCW

Castedo, Elena 1937- .... **CLC 65**
     See also CA 132

Castedo-Ellerman, Elena
     See Castedo, Elena

Castellanos, Rosario
     1925-1974 ...... **CLC 66; DAM MULT;**
     HLC
     See also CA 131; 53-56; DLB 113; HW

Castelvetro, Lodovico 1505-1571..... **LC 12**

Castiglione, Baldassare 1478-1529 ... **LC 12**

Castle, Robert
     See Hamilton, Edmond

Castro, Guillen de 1569-1631........ **LC 19**

Castro, Rosalia de
     1837-1885 ...... **NCLC 3; DAM MULT**

Cather, Willa
     See Cather, Willa Sibert

Cather, Willa Sibert
     1873-1947 .... **TCLC 1, 11, 31; DA;**
     DAB; DAC; DAM MST, NOV; SSC 2;
     WLC
     See also CA 104; 128; CDALB 1865-1917;
     DLB 9, 54, 78; DLBD 1; MTCW;
     SATA 30

Cato, Marcus Porcius
     234B.C.-149B.C............. **CMLC 21**

Chesnutt, Charles W(addell)
1858-1932 .... **TCLC 5, 39; BLC;**
                    DAM MULT; SSC 7
See also BW 1; CA 106; 125; DLB 12, 50,
78; MTCW

Chester, Alfred 1929(?)-1971 ...... **CLC 49**
See also CA 33-36R; DLB 130

Chesterton, G(ilbert) K(eith)
1874-1936 .... **TCLC 1, 6, 64;**
                    DAM NOV, POET; SSC 1
See also CA 104; 132; CDBLB 1914-1945;
DLB 10, 19, 34, 70, 98, 149; MTCW;
SATA 27

Chiang Pin-chin 1904-1986
See Ding Ling
See also CA 118

Ch'ien Chung-shu 1910- .... **CLC 22**
See also CA 130; MTCW

Child, L. Maria
See Child, Lydia Maria

Child, Lydia Maria 1802-1880 .... **NCLC 6**
See also DLB 1, 74; SATA 67

Child, Mrs.
See Child, Lydia Maria

Child, Philip 1898-1978 .... **CLC 19, 68**
See also CA 13-14; CAP 1; SATA 47

Childers, (Robert) Erskine
1870-1922 .... **TCLC 65**
See also CA 113; 153; DLB 70

Childress, Alice
1920-1994 .... **CLC 12, 15, 86, 96; BLC;**
        DAM DRAM, MULT, NOV; DC 4
See also AAYA 8; BW 2; CA 45-48; 146;
CANR 3, 27, 50; CLR 14; DLB 7, 38;
JRDA; MAICYA; MTCW; SATA 7, 48,
81

Chislett, (Margaret) Anne 1943- .... **CLC 34**
See also CA 151

Chitty, Thomas Willes 1926- .... **CLC 11**
See also Hinde, Thomas
See also CA 5-8R

Chivers, Thomas Holley
1809-1858 .... **NCLC 49**
See also DLB 3

Chomette, Rene Lucien 1898-1981
See Clair, Rene
See also CA 103

Chopin, Kate
.... **TCLC 5, 14; DA; DAB; SSC 8**
See also Chopin, Katherine
See also CDALB 1865-1917; DLB 12, 78

Chopin, Katherine 1851-1904
See Chopin, Kate
See also CA 104; 122; DAC; DAM MST,
NOV

Chretien de Troyes
c. 12th cent. - .... **CMLC 10**

Christie
See Ichikawa, Kon

Christie, Agatha (Mary Clarissa)
1890-1976 ...... **CLC 1, 6, 8, 12, 39, 48;**
                    DAB; DAC; DAM NOV
See also AAYA 9; AITN 1, 2; CA 17-20R;
61-64; CANR 10, 37; CDBLB 1914-1945;
DLB 13, 77; MTCW; SATA 36

Christie, (Ann) Philippa
See Pearce, Philippa
See also CA 5-8R; CANR 4

Christine de Pizan 1365(?)-1431(?) .... **LC 9**

Chubb, Elmer
See Masters, Edgar Lee

Chulkov, Mikhail Dmitrievich
1743-1792 .... **LC 2**
See also DLB 150

Churchill, Caryl 1938- .... **CLC 31, 55; DC 5**
See also CA 102; CANR 22, 46; DLB 13;
MTCW

Churchill, Charles 1731-1764 .... **LC 3**
See also DLB 109

Chute, Carolyn 1947- .... **CLC 39**
See also CA 123

Ciardi, John (Anthony)
1916-1986 .... **CLC 10, 40, 44;**
                            DAM POET
See also CA 5-8R; 118; CAAS 2; CANR 5,
33; CLR 19; DLB 5; DLBY 86;
INT CANR-5; MAICYA; MTCW;
SATA 1, 65; SATA-Obit 46

Cicero, Marcus Tullius
106B.C.-43B.C. .... **CMLC 3**

Cimino, Michael 1943- .... **CLC 16**
See also CA 105

Cioran, E(mil) M. 1911-1995 ...... **CLC 64**
See also CA 25-28R; 149

Cisneros, Sandra
1954- ..... **CLC 69; DAM MULT; HLC**
See also AAYA 9; CA 131; DLB 122, 152;
HW

Cixous, Helene 1937- .... **CLC 92**
See also CA 126; CANR 55; DLB 83;
MTCW

Clair, Rene .... **CLC 20**
See also Chomette, Rene Lucien

Clampitt, Amy 1920-1994 .... **CLC 32**
See also CA 110; 146; CANR 29; DLB 105

Clancy, Thomas L., Jr. 1947-
See Clancy, Tom
See also CA 125; 131; INT 131; MTCW

Clancy, Tom ..... **CLC 45; DAM NOV, POP**
See also Clancy, Thomas L., Jr.
See also AAYA 9; BEST 89:1, 90:1

Clare, John
1793-1864 .... **NCLC 9; DAB;**
                            DAM POET
See also DLB 55, 96

Clarin
See Alas (y Urena), Leopoldo (Enrique
Garcia)

Clark, Al C.
See Goines, Donald

Clark, (Robert) Brian 1932- .... **CLC 29**
See also CA 41-44R

Clark, Curt
See Westlake, Donald E(dwin)

Clark, Eleanor 1913-1996 .... **CLC 5, 19**
See also CA 9-12R; 151; CANR 41; DLB 6

Clark, J. P.
See Clark, John Pepper
See also DLB 117

Clark, John Pepper
1935- .... **CLC 38; BLC; DAM DRAM,**
                            MULT; DC 5
See also Clark, J. P.
See also BW 1; CA 65-68; CANR 16

Clark, M. R.
See Clark, Mavis Thorpe

Clark, Mavis Thorpe 1909- .... **CLC 12**
See also CA 57-60; CANR 8, 37; CLR 30;
MAICYA; SAAS 5; SATA 8, 74

Clark, Walter Van Tilburg
1909-1971 .... **CLC 28**
See also CA 9-12R; 33-36R; DLB 9;
SATA 8

Clarke, Arthur C(harles)
1917- .... **CLC 1, 4, 13, 18, 35;**
                    DAM POP; SSC 3
See also AAYA 4; CA 1-4R; CANR 2, 28,
55; JRDA; MAICYA; MTCW; SATA 13,
70

Clarke, Austin
1896-1974 ...... **CLC 6, 9; DAM POET**
See also CA 29-32; 49-52; CAP 2; DLB 10,
20

Clarke, Austin C(hesterfield)
1934- .... **CLC 8, 53; BLC; DAC;**
                            DAM MULT
See also BW 1; CA 25-28R; CAAS 16;
CANR 14, 32; DLB 53, 125

Clarke, Gillian 1937- .... **CLC 61**
See also CA 106; DLB 40

Clarke, Marcus (Andrew Hislop)
1846-1881 .... **NCLC 19**

Clarke, Shirley 1925- .... **CLC 16**

Clash, The
See Headon, (Nicky) Topper; Jones, Mick;
Simonon, Paul; Strummer, Joe

Claudel, Paul (Louis Charles Marie)
1868-1955 .... **TCLC 2, 10**
See also CA 104

Clavell, James (duMaresq)
1925-1994 .... **CLC 6, 25, 87;**
                            DAM NOV, POP
See also CA 25-28R; 146; CANR 26, 48;
MTCW

Cleaver, (Leroy) Eldridge
1935- ..... **CLC 30; BLC; DAM MULT**
See also BW 1; CA 21-24R; CANR 16

Cleese, John (Marwood) 1939- ..... **CLC 21**
See also Monty Python
See also CA 112; 116; CANR 35; MTCW

Cleishbotham, Jebediah
See Scott, Walter

Cleland, John 1710-1789 .... **LC 2**
See also DLB 39

Clemens, Samuel Langhorne 1835-1910
See Twain, Mark
See also CA 104; 135; CDALB 1865-1917;
DA; DAB; DAC; DAM MST, NOV;
DLB 11, 12, 23, 64, 74; JRDA;
MAICYA; YABC 2

Cleophil
See Congreve, William

Clerihew, E.
See Bentley, E(dmund) C(lerihew)

Clerk, N. W.
See Lewis, C(live) S(taples)

Cliff, Jimmy . . . . **CLC 21**
See also Chambers, James

Clifton, (Thelma) Lucille
1936- . . . . **CLC 19, 66; BLC;**
DAM MULT, POET; PC 17
See also BW 2; CA 49-52; CANR 2, 24, 42;
CLR 5; DLB 5, 41; MAICYA; MTCW;
SATA 20, 69

Clinton, Dirk
See Silverberg, Robert

Clough, Arthur Hugh 1819-1861 . . **NCLC 27**
See also DLB 32

Clutha, Janet Paterson Frame 1924-
See Frame, Janet
See also CA 1-4R; CANR 2, 36; MTCW

Clyne, Terence
See Blatty, William Peter

Cobalt, Martin
See Mayne, William (James Carter)

Cobbett, William 1763-1835 . . . . . **NCLC 49**
See also DLB 43, 107, 158

Coburn, D(onald) L(ee) 1938- . . . . . . **CLC 10**
See also CA 89-92

Cocteau, Jean (Maurice Eugene Clement)
1889-1963 . . . . **CLC 1, 8, 15, 16, 43; DA;**
DAB; DAC; DAM DRAM, MST, NOV;
WLC
See also CA 25-28; CANR 40; CAP 2;
DLB 65; MTCW

Codrescu, Andrei
1946- . . . . **CLC 46; DAM POET**
See also CA 33-36R; CAAS 19; CANR 13,
34, 53

Coe, Max
See Bourne, Randolph S(illiman)

Coe, Tucker
See Westlake, Donald E(dwin)

Coetzee, J(ohn) M(ichael)
1940- . . . . . . **CLC 23, 33, 66; DAM NOV**
See also CA 77-80; CANR 41, 54; MTCW

Coffey, Brian
See Koontz, Dean R(ay)

Cohan, George M. 1878-1942 . . . . . **TCLC 60**

Cohen, Arthur A(llen)
1928-1986 . . . . **CLC 7, 31**
See also CA 1-4R; 120; CANR 1, 17, 42;
DLB 28

Cohen, Leonard (Norman)
1934- . . . . **CLC 3, 38; DAC; DAM MST**
See also CA 21-24R; CANR 14; DLB 53;
MTCW

Cohen, Matt 1942- . . . . **CLC 19; DAC**
See also CA 61-64; CAAS 18; CANR 40;
DLB 53

Cohen-Solal, Annie 19(?)- . . . . **CLC 50**

Colegate, Isabel 1931- . . . . **CLC 36**
See also CA 17-20R; CANR 8, 22; DLB 14;
INT CANR-22; MTCW

Coleman, Emmett
See Reed, Ishmael

Coleridge, Samuel Taylor
1772-1834 . . . . . **NCLC 9, 54; DA; DAB;**
DAC; DAM MST, POET; PC 11; WLC
See also CDBLB 1789-1832; DLB 93, 107

Coleridge, Sara 1802-1852 . . . . . . **NCLC 31**

Coles, Don 1928- . . . . **CLC 46**
See also CA 115; CANR 38

Colette, (Sidonie-Gabrielle)
1873-1954 . . . . **TCLC 1, 5, 16;**
DAM NOV; SSC 10
See also CA 104; 131; DLB 65; MTCW

Collett, (Jacobine) Camilla (Wergeland)
1813-1895 . . . . **NCLC 22**

Collier, Christopher 1930- . . . . **CLC 30**
See also AAYA 13; CA 33-36R; CANR 13,
33; JRDA; MAICYA; SATA 16, 70

Collier, James L(incoln)
1928- . . . . **CLC 30; DAM POP**
See also AAYA 13; CA 9-12R; CANR 4,
33; CLR 3; JRDA; MAICYA; SAAS 21;
SATA 8, 70

Collier, Jeremy 1650-1726 . . . . **LC 6**

Collier, John 1901-1980 . . . . **SSC 19**
See also CA 65-68; 97-100; CANR 10;
DLB 77

Collingwood, R(obin) G(eorge)
1889(?)-1943 . . . . **TCLC 67**
See also CA 117; 155

Collins, Hunt
See Hunter, Evan

Collins, Linda 1931- . . . . **CLC 44**
See also CA 125

Collins, (William) Wilkie
1824-1889 . . . . **NCLC 1, 18**
See also CDBLB 1832-1890; DLB 18, 70,
159

Collins, William
1721-1759 . . . . **LC 4; DAM POET**
See also DLB 109

Collodi, Carlo 1826-1890 . . . . **NCLC 54**
See also Lorenzini, Carlo
See also CLR 5

Colman, George
See Glassco, John

Colt, Winchester Remington
See Hubbard, L(afayette) Ron(ald)

Colter, Cyrus 1910- . . . . **CLC 58**
See also BW 1; CA 65-68; CANR 10;
DLB 33

Colton, James
See Hansen, Joseph

Colum, Padraic 1881-1972 . . . . **CLC 28**
See also CA 73-76; 33-36R; CANR 35;
CLR 36; MAICYA; MTCW; SATA 15

Colvin, James
See Moorcock, Michael (John)

Colwin, Laurie (E.)
1944-1992 . . . . **CLC 5, 13, 23, 84**
See also CA 89-92; 139; CANR 20, 46;
DLBY 80; MTCW

Comfort, Alex(ander)
1920- . . . . **CLC 7; DAM POP**
See also CA 1-4R; CANR 1, 45

Comfort, Montgomery
See Campbell, (John) Ramsey

Compton-Burnett, I(vy)
1884(?)-1969 . . . . . . **CLC 1, 3, 10, 15, 34;**
DAM NOV
See also CA 1-4R; 25-28R; CANR 4;
DLB 36; MTCW

Comstock, Anthony 1844-1915 . . . . **TCLC 13**
See also CA 110

Comte, Auguste 1798-1857 . . . . **NCLC 54**

Conan Doyle, Arthur
See Doyle, Arthur Conan

Conde, Maryse
1937- . . . . **CLC 52, 92; DAM MULT**
See also Boucolon, Maryse
See also BW 2

Condillac, Etienne Bonnot de
1714-1780 . . . . **LC 26**

Condon, Richard (Thomas)
1915-1996 . . . . **CLC 4, 6, 8, 10, 45;**
DAM NOV
See also BEST 90:3; CA 1-4R; 151;
CAAS 1; CANR 2, 23; INT CANR-23;
MTCW

Confucius
551B.C.-479B.C. . . . . **CMLC 19; DA;**
DAB; DAC; DAM MST

Congreve, William
1670-1729 . . . . **LC 5, 21; DA; DAB;**
DAC; DAM DRAM, MST, POET;
DC 2; WLC
See also CDBLB 1660-1789; DLB 39, 84

Connell, Evan S(helby), Jr.
1924- . . . . **CLC 4, 6, 45; DAM NOV**
See also AAYA 7; CA 1-4R; CAAS 2;
CANR 2, 39; DLB 2; DLBY 81; MTCW

Connelly, Marc(us Cook)
1890-1980 . . . . **CLC 7**
See also CA 85-88; 102; CANR 30; DLB 7;
DLBY 80; SATA-Obit 25

Connor, Ralph . . . . **TCLC 31**
See also Gordon, Charles William
See also DLB 92

Conrad, Joseph
1857-1924 . . . . **TCLC 1, 6, 13, 25, 43, 57;**
DA; DAB; DAC; DAM MST, NOV;
SSC 9; WLC
See also CA 104; 131; CDBLB 1890-1914;
DLB 10, 34, 98, 156; MTCW; SATA 27

Conrad, Robert Arnold
See Hart, Moss

Conroy, Donald Pat(rick)
1945- . . . **CLC 30, 74; DAM NOV, POP**
See also AAYA 8; AITN 1; CA 85-88;
CANR 24, 53; DLB 6; MTCW

Constant (de Rebecque), (Henri) Benjamin
1767-1830 . . . . **NCLC 6**
See also DLB 119

Conybeare, Charles Augustus
See Eliot, T(homas) S(tearns)

Cook, Michael 1933- . . . . **CLC 58**
See also CA 93-96; DLB 53

Cook, Robin 1940- . . . . **CLC 14; DAM POP**
See also BEST 90:2; CA 108; 111;
CANR 41; INT 111

Cook, Roy
See Silverberg, Robert

Cooke, Elizabeth 1948- .... CLC 55
See also CA 129

Cooke, John Esten 1830-1886..... NCLC 5
See also DLB 3

Cooke, John Estes
See Baum, L(yman) Frank

Cooke, M. E.
See Creasey, John

Cooke, Margaret
See Creasey, John

Cook-Lynn, Elizabeth
1930- .... CLC 93; DAM MULT
See also CA 133; DLB 175; NNAL

Cooney, Ray .... CLC 62

Cooper, Douglas 1960-.......... CLC 86

Cooper, Henry St. John
See Creasey, John

Cooper, J(oan) California
.... CLC 56; DAM MULT
See also AAYA 12; BW 1; CA 125;
CANR 55

Cooper, James Fenimore
1789-1851 .... NCLC 1, 27, 54
See also CDALB 1640-1865; DLB 3;
SATA 19

Coover, Robert (Lowell)
1932- .... CLC 3, 7, 15, 32, 46, 87;
DAM NOV; SSC 15
See also CA 45-48; CANR 3, 37; DLB 2;
DLBY 81; MTCW

Copeland, Stewart (Armstrong)
1952- .... CLC 26

Coppard, A(lfred) E(dgar)
1878-1957 .... TCLC 5; SSC 21
See also CA 114; DLB 162; YABC 1

Coppee, Francois 1842-1908 ..... TCLC 25

Coppola, Francis Ford 1939-....... CLC 16
See also CA 77-80; CANR 40; DLB 44

Corbiere, Tristan 1845-1875 ..... NCLC 43

Corcoran, Barbara 1911-.......... CLC 17
See also AAYA 14; CA 21-24R; CAAS 2;
CANR 11, 28, 48; DLB 52; JRDA;
SAAS 20; SATA 3, 77

Cordelier, Maurice
See Giraudoux, (Hippolyte) Jean

Corelli, Marie 1855-1924........ TCLC 51
See also Mackay, Mary
See also DLB 34, 156

Corman, Cid...................... CLC 9
See also Corman, Sidney
See also CAAS 2; DLB 5

Corman, Sidney 1924-
See Corman, Cid
See also CA 85-88; CANR 44; DAM POET

Cormier, Robert (Edmund)
1925- .... CLC 12, 30; DA; DAB; DAC;
DAM MST, NOV
See also AAYA 3, 19; CA 1-4R; CANR 5,
23; CDALB 1968-1988; CLR 12; DLB 52;
INT CANR-23; JRDA; MAICYA;
MTCW; SATA 10, 45, 83

Corn, Alfred (DeWitt III) 1943-.... CLC 33
See also CA 104; CAAS 25; CANR 44;
DLB 120; DLBY 80

Corneille, Pierre
1606-1684 .... LC 28; DAB; DAM MST

Cornwell, David (John Moore)
1931- .... CLC 9, 15; DAM POP
See also le Carre, John
See also CA 5-8R; CANR 13, 33; MTCW

Corso, (Nunzio) Gregory 1930-... CLC 1, 11
See also CA 5-8R; CANR 41; DLB 5, 16;
MTCW

Cortazar, Julio
1914-1984 ...... CLC 2, 3, 5, 10, 13, 15,
33, 34, 92; DAM MULT, NOV; HLC;
SSC 7
See also CA 21-24R; CANR 12, 32;
DLB 113; HW; MTCW

CORTES, HERNAN 1484-1547..... LC 31

Corwin, Cecil
See Kornbluth, C(yril) M.

Cosic, Dobrica 1921- .... CLC 14
See also CA 122; 138

Costain, Thomas B(ertram)
1885-1965 .... CLC 30
See also CA 5-8R; 25-28R; DLB 9

Costantini, Humberto
1924(?)-1987 .... CLC 49
See also CA 131; 122; HW

Costello, Elvis 1955-.............. CLC 21

Cotter, Joseph Seamon Sr.
1861-1949 .... TCLC 28; BLC;
DAM MULT
See also BW 1; CA 124; DLB 50

Couch, Arthur Thomas Quiller
See Quiller-Couch, Arthur Thomas

Coulton, James
See Hansen, Joseph

Couperus, Louis (Marie Anne)
1863-1923 .... TCLC 15
See also CA 115

Coupland, Douglas
1961- .... CLC 85; DAC; DAM POP
See also CA 142; CANR 57

Court, Wesli
See Turco, Lewis (Putnam)

Courtenay, Bryce 1933-.......... CLC 59
See also CA 138

Courtney, Robert
See Ellison, Harlan (Jay)

Cousteau, Jacques-Yves 1910-..... CLC 30
See also CA 65-68; CANR 15; MTCW;
SATA 38

Coward, Noel (Peirce)
1899-1973 .... CLC 1, 9, 29, 51;
DAM DRAM
See also AITN 1; CA 17-18; 41-44R;
CANR 35; CAP 2; CDBLB 1914-1945;
DLB 10; MTCW

Cowley, Malcolm 1898-1989 .... CLC 39
See also CA 5-8R; 128; CANR 3, 55;
DLB 4, 48; DLBY 81, 89; MTCW

Cowper, William
1731-1800 ...... NCLC 8; DAM POET
See also DLB 104, 109

Cox, William Trevor
1928- .... CLC 9, 14, 71; DAM NOV
See also Trevor, William
See also CA 9-12R; CANR 4, 37, 55;
DLB 14; INT CANR-37; MTCW

Coyne, P. J.
See Masters, Hilary

Cozzens, James Gould
1903-1978 .... CLC 1, 4, 11, 92
See also CA 9-12R; 81-84; CANR 19;
CDALB 1941-1968; DLB 9; DLBD 2;
DLBY 84; MTCW

Crabbe, George 1754-1832....... NCLC 26
See also DLB 93

Craddock, Charles Egbert
See Murfree, Mary Noailles

Craig, A. A.
See Anderson, Poul (William)

Craik, Dinah Maria (Mulock)
1826-1887 .... NCLC 38
See also DLB 35, 163; MAICYA; SATA 34

Cram, Ralph Adams 1863-1942.... TCLC 45

Crane, (Harold) Hart
1899-1932 .... TCLC 2, 5; DA; DAB;
DAC; DAM MST, POET; PC 3; WLC
See also CA 104; 127; CDALB 1917-1929;
DLB 4, 48; MTCW

Crane, R(onald) S(almon)
1886-1967 .... CLC 27
See also CA 85-88; DLB 63

Crane, Stephen (Townley)
1871-1900 .... TCLC 11, 17, 32; DA;
DAB; DAC; DAM MST, NOV, POET;
SSC 7; WLC
See also CA 109; 140; CDALB 1865-1917;
DLB 12, 54, 78; YABC 2

Crase, Douglas 1944-............. CLC 58
See also CA 106

Crashaw, Richard 1612(?)-1649...... LC 24
See also DLB 126

Craven, Margaret
1901-1980 .... CLC 17; DAC
See also CA 103

Crawford, F(rancis) Marion
1854-1909 .... TCLC 10
See also CA 107; DLB 71

Crawford, Isabella Valancy
1850-1887 .... NCLC 12
See also DLB 92

Crayon, Geoffrey
See Irving, Washington

Creasey, John 1908-1973.......... CLC 11
See also CA 5-8R; 41-44R; CANR 8;
DLB 77; MTCW

Crebillon, Claude Prosper Jolyot de (fils)
1707-1777 .... LC 28

Credo
See Creasey, John

Creeley, Robert (White)
1926- ..... CLC 1, 2, 4, 8, 11, 15, 36, 78;
DAM POET
See also CA 1-4R; CAAS 10; CANR 23, 43;
DLB 5, 16, 169; MTCW

Daudet, (Louis Marie) Alphonse
1840-1897 .... **NCLC 1**
See also DLB 123

Daumal, Rene 1908-1944 .... **TCLC 14**
See also CA 114

Davenport, Guy (Mattison, Jr.)
1927- .... **CLC 6, 14, 38; SSC 16**
See also CA 33-36R; CANR 23; DLB 130

Davidson, Avram 1923-
See Queen, Ellery
See also CA 101; CANR 26; DLB 8

Davidson, Donald (Grady)
1893-1968 .... **CLC 2, 13, 19**
See also CA 5-8R; 25-28R; CANR 4;
DLB 45

Davidson, Hugh
See Hamilton, Edmond

Davidson, John 1857-1909 .... **TCLC 24**
See also CA 118; DLB 19

Davidson, Sara 1943- .... **CLC 9**
See also CA 81-84; CANR 44

Davie, Donald (Alfred)
1922-1995 .... **CLC 5, 8, 10, 31**
See also CA 1-4R; 149; CAAS 3; CANR 1,
44; DLB 27; MTCW

Davies, Ray(mond Douglas) 1944- .. **CLC 21**
See also CA 116; 146

Davies, Rhys 1903-1978 .... **CLC 23**
See also CA 9-12R; 81-84; CANR 4;
DLB 139

Davies, (William) Robertson
1913-1995 ..... **CLC 2, 7, 13, 25, 42, 75,
91; DA; DAB; DAC; DAM MST, NOV,
POP; WLC**
See also BEST 89:2; CA 33-36R; 150;
CANR 17, 42; DLB 68; INT CANR-17;
MTCW

Davies, W(illiam) H(enry)
1871-1940 .... **TCLC 5**
See also CA 104; DLB 19, 174

Davies, Walter C.
See Kornbluth, C(yril) M.

Davis, Angela (Yvonne)
1944- .... **CLC 77; DAM MULT**
See also BW 2; CA 57-60; CANR 10

Davis, B. Lynch
See Bioy Casares, Adolfo; Borges, Jorge
Luis

Davis, Gordon
See Hunt, E(verette) Howard, (Jr.)

Davis, Harold Lenoir 1896-1960 .... **CLC 49**
See also CA 89-92; DLB 9

Davis, Rebecca (Blaine) Harding
1831-1910 .... **TCLC 6**
See also CA 104; DLB 74

Davis, Richard Harding
1864-1916 .... **TCLC 24**
See also CA 114; DLB 12, 23, 78, 79;
DLBD 13

Davison, Frank Dalby 1893-1970 ... **CLC 15**
See also CA 116

Davison, Lawrence H.
See Lawrence, D(avid) H(erbert Richards)

Davison, Peter (Hubert) 1928- ..... **CLC 28**
See also CA 9-12R; CAAS 4; CANR 3, 43;
DLB 5

Davys, Mary 1674-1732 .... **LC 1**
See also DLB 39

Dawson, Fielding 1930- .... **CLC 6**
See also CA 85-88; DLB 130

Dawson, Peter
See Faust, Frederick (Schiller)

Day, Clarence (Shepard, Jr.)
1874-1935 .... **TCLC 25**
See also CA 108; DLB 11

Day, Thomas 1748-1789 .... **LC 1**
See also DLB 39; YABC 1

Day Lewis, C(ecil)
1904-1972 .... **CLC 1, 6, 10;
DAM POET; PC 11**
See also Blake, Nicholas
See also CA 13-16; 33-36R; CANR 34;
CAP 1; DLB 15, 20; MTCW

Dazai, Osamu .... **TCLC 11**
See also Tsushima, Shuji

de Andrade, Carlos Drummond
See Drummond de Andrade, Carlos

Deane, Norman
See Creasey, John

**de Beauvoir, Simone (Lucie Ernestine Marie
Bertrand)**
See Beauvoir, Simone (Lucie Ernestine
Marie Bertrand) de

de Brissac, Malcolm
See Dickinson, Peter (Malcolm)

de Chardin, Pierre Teilhard
See Teilhard de Chardin, (Marie Joseph)
Pierre

Dee, John 1527-1608 .... **LC 20**

Deer, Sandra 1940- .... **CLC 45**

De Ferrari, Gabriella 1941- .... **CLC 65**
See also CA 146

Defoe, Daniel
1660(?)-1731 .... **LC 1; DA; DAB; DAC;
DAM MST, NOV; WLC**
See also CDBLB 1660-1789; DLB 39, 95,
101; JRDA; MAICYA; SATA 22

de Gourmont, Remy(-Marie-Charles)
See Gourmont, Remy (-Marie-Charles) de

de Hartog, Jan 1914- .... **CLC 19**
See also CA 1-4R; CANR 1

de Hostos, E. M.
See Hostos (y Bonilla), Eugenio Maria de

de Hostos, Eugenio M.
See Hostos (y Bonilla), Eugenio Maria de

Deighton, Len .... **CLC 4, 7, 22, 46**
See also Deighton, Leonard Cyril
See also AAYA 6; BEST 89:2;
CDBLB 1960 to Present; DLB 87

Deighton, Leonard Cyril 1929-
See Deighton, Len
See also CA 9-12R; CANR 19, 33;
DAM NOV, POP; MTCW

Dekker, Thomas
1572(?)-1632 ..... **LC 22; DAM DRAM**
See also CDBLB Before 1660; DLB 62, 172

Delafield, E. M. 1890-1943 .... **TCLC 61**
See also Dashwood, Edmee Elizabeth
Monica de la Pasture
See also DLB 34

de la Mare, Walter (John)
1873-1956 .... **TCLC 4, 53; DAB; DAC;
DAM MST, POET; SSC 14; WLC**
See also CDBLB 1914-1945; CLR 23;
DLB 162; SATA 16

Delaney, Franey
See O'Hara, John (Henry)

Delaney, Shelagh
1939- .... **CLC 29; DAM DRAM**
See also CA 17-20R; CANR 30;
CDBLB 1960 to Present; DLB 13;
MTCW

Delany, Mary (Granville Pendarves)
1700-1788 .... **LC 12**

Delany, Samuel R(ay, Jr.)
1942- .... **CLC 8, 14, 38; BLC;
DAM MULT**
See also BW 2; CA 81-84; CANR 27, 43;
DLB 8, 33; MTCW

De La Ramee, (Marie) Louise 1839-1908
See Ouida
See also SATA 20

de la Roche, Mazo 1879-1961 ...... **CLC 14**
See also CA 85-88; CANR 30; DLB 68;
SATA 64

Delbanco, Nicholas (Franklin)
1942- .... **CLC 6, 13**
See also CA 17-20R; CAAS 2; CANR 29,
55; DLB 6

del Castillo, Michel 1933- .... **CLC 38**
See also CA 109

Deledda, Grazia (Cosima)
1875(?)-1936 .... **TCLC 23**
See also CA 123

Delibes, Miguel .... **CLC 8, 18**
See also Delibes Setien, Miguel

Delibes Setien, Miguel 1920-
See Delibes, Miguel
See also CA 45-48; CANR 1, 32; HW;
MTCW

DeLillo, Don
1936- ..... **CLC 8, 10, 13, 27, 39, 54, 76;
DAM NOV, POP**
See also BEST 89:1; CA 81-84; CANR 21;
DLB 6, 173; MTCW

de Lisser, H. G.
See De Lisser, H(erbert) G(eorge)
See also DLB 117

De Lisser, H(erbert) G(eorge)
1878-1944 .... **TCLC 12**
See also de Lisser, H. G.
See also BW 2; CA 109; 152

Deloria, Vine (Victor), Jr.
1933- .... **CLC 21; DAM MULT**
See also CA 53-56; CANR 5, 20, 48;
DLB 175; MTCW; NNAL; SATA 21

Del Vecchio, John M(ichael)
1947- .... **CLC 29**
See also CA 110; DLBD 9

de Man, Paul (Adolph Michel)
1919-1983 .... **CLC 55**
See also CA 128; 111; DLB 67; MTCW

Doctorow, E(dgar) L(aurence)
　　1931- . . . . . **CLC 6, 11, 15, 18, 37, 44, 65;**
　　　　　　　　　　　　　　　　DAM NOV, POP
　　See also AITN 2; BEST 89:3; CA 45-48;
　　　CANR 2, 33, 51; CDALB 1968-1988;
　　　DLB 2, 28, 173; DLBY 80; MTCW

Dodgson, Charles Lutwidge　1832-1898
　　See Carroll, Lewis
　　See also CLR 2; DA; DAB; DAC;
　　　DAM MST, NOV, POET; MAICYA;
　　　YABC 2

Dodson, Owen (Vincent)
　　1914-1983 . . . . **CLC 79; BLC;**
　　　　　　　　　　　　　　　　　　DAM MULT
　　See also BW 1; CA 65-68; 110; CANR 24;
　　　DLB 76

Doeblin, Alfred　1878-1957. . . . . . . **TCLC 13**
　　See also Doblin, Alfred
　　See also CA 110; 141; DLB 66

Doerr, Harriet　1910- . . . . **CLC 34**
　　See also CA 117; 122; CANR 47; INT 122

Domecq, H(onorio) Bustos
　　See Bioy Casares, Adolfo; Borges, Jorge
　　　Luis

Domini, Rey
　　See Lorde, Audre (Geraldine)

Dominique
　　See Proust, (Valentin-Louis-George-Eugene-)
　　　Marcel

Don, A
　　See Stephen, Leslie

Donaldson, Stephen R.
　　1947- . . . . **CLC 46; DAM POP**
　　See also CA 89-92; CANR 13, 55;
　　　INT CANR-13

Donleavy, J(ames) P(atrick)
　　1926- . . . . **CLC 1, 4, 6, 10, 45**
　　See also AITN 2; CA 9-12R; CANR 24, 49;
　　　DLB 6, 173; INT CANR-24; MTCW

Donne, John
　　1572-1631 . . . . **LC 10, 24; DA; DAB;**
　　　　　　　　　　　DAC; DAM MST, POET; PC 1
　　See also CDBLB Before 1660; DLB 121,
　　　151

Donnell, David　1939(?)- . . . . **CLC 34**

Donoghue, P. S.
　　See Hunt, E(verette) Howard, (Jr.)

Donoso (Yanez), Jose
　　1924-1996 . . . . **CLC 4, 8, 11, 32, 99;**
　　　　　　　　　　　　　　　　DAM MULT; HLC
　　See also CA 81-84; 155; CANR 32;
　　　DLB 113; HW; MTCW

Donovan, John　1928-1992 . . . . **CLC 35**
　　See also AAYA 20; CA 97-100; 137;
　　　CLR 3; MAICYA; SATA 72;
　　　SATA-Brief 29

Don Roberto
　　See Cunninghame Graham, R(obert)
　　　B(ontine)

Doolittle, Hilda
　　1886-1961 . . . . . **CLC 3, 8, 14, 31, 34, 73;**
　　　　　　　　　DA; DAC; DAM MST, POET; PC 5;
　　　　　　　　　　　　　　　　　　　　　　WLC
　　See also H. D.
　　See also CA 97-100; CANR 35; DLB 4, 45;
　　　MTCW

Dorfman, Ariel
　　1942- . . . . **CLC 48, 77; DAM MULT;**
　　　　　　　　　　　　　　　　　　　　HLC
　　See also CA 124; 130; HW; INT 130

Dorn, Edward (Merton)　1929-. . . **CLC 10, 18**
　　See also CA 93-96; CANR 42; DLB 5;
　　　INT 93-96

Dorsan, Luc
　　See Simenon, Georges (Jacques Christian)

Dorsange, Jean
　　See Simenon, Georges (Jacques Christian)

Dos Passos, John (Roderigo)
　　1896-1970 . . . . . . **CLC 1, 4, 8, 11, 15, 25,**
　　　　　　34, 82; DA; DAB; DAC; DAM MST,
　　　　　　　　　　　　　　　　　NOV; WLC
　　See also CA 1-4R; 29-32R; CANR 3;
　　　CDALB 1929-1941; DLB 4, 9; DLBD 1;
　　　MTCW

Dossage, Jean
　　See Simenon, Georges (Jacques Christian)

Dostoevsky, Fedor Mikhailovich
　　1821-1881 . . . . . . **NCLC 2, 7, 21, 33, 43;**
　　　　　　DA; DAB; DAC; DAM MST, NOV;
　　　　　　　　　　　　　　　　SSC 2; WLC

Doughty, Charles M(ontagu)
　　1843-1926 . . . . **TCLC 27**
　　See also CA 115; DLB 19, 57, 174

Douglas, Ellen . . . . **CLC 73**
　　See also Haxton, Josephine Ayres;
　　　Williamson, Ellen Douglas

Douglas, Gavin　1475(?)-1522. . . . . . . **LC 20**

Douglas, Keith　1920-1944 . . . . **TCLC 40**
　　See also DLB 27

Douglas, Leonard
　　See Bradbury, Ray (Douglas)

Douglas, Michael
　　See Crichton, (John) Michael

Douglas, Norman　1868-1952 . . . . . . **TCLC 68**

Douglass, Frederick
　　1817(?)-1895 . . . . **NCLC 7, 55; BLC; DA;**
　　　　　　　DAC; DAM MST, MULT; WLC
　　See also CDALB 1640-1865; DLB 1, 43, 50,
　　　79; SATA 29

Dourado, (Waldomiro Freitas) Autran
　　1926- . . . . **CLC 23, 60**
　　See also CA 25-28R; CANR 34

Dourado, Waldomiro Autran
　　See Dourado, (Waldomiro Freitas) Autran

Dove, Rita (Frances)
　　1952- . . . . **CLC 50, 81; DAM MULT,**
　　　　　　　　　　　　　　　　　　POET; PC 6
　　See also BW 2; CA 109; CAAS 19;
　　　CANR 27, 42; DLB 120

Dowell, Coleman　1925-1985. . . . . . . **CLC 60**
　　See also CA 25-28R; 117; CANR 10;
　　　DLB 130

Dowson, Ernest (Christopher)
　　1867-1900 . . . . **TCLC 4**
　　See also CA 105; 150; DLB 19, 135

Doyle, A. Conan
　　See Doyle, Arthur Conan

Doyle, Arthur Conan
　　1859-1930 . . . . **TCLC 7; DA; DAB;**
　　　　　　DAC; DAM MST, NOV; SSC 12; WLC
　　See also AAYA 14; CA 104; 122;
　　　CDBLB 1890-1914; DLB 18, 70, 156;
　　　MTCW; SATA 24

Doyle, Conan
　　See Doyle, Arthur Conan

Doyle, John
　　See Graves, Robert (von Ranke)

Doyle, Roddy　1958(?)- . . . . **CLC 81**
　　See also AAYA 14; CA 143

Doyle, Sir A. Conan
　　See Doyle, Arthur Conan

Doyle, Sir Arthur Conan
　　See Doyle, Arthur Conan

Dr. A
　　See Asimov, Isaac; Silverstein, Alvin

Drabble, Margaret
　　1939- . . . . **CLC 2, 3, 5, 8, 10, 22, 53;**
　　　　　　　　DAB; DAC; DAM MST, NOV, POP
　　See also CA 13-16R; CANR 18, 35;
　　　CDBLB 1960 to Present; DLB 14, 155;
　　　MTCW; SATA 48

Drapier, M. B.
　　See Swift, Jonathan

Drayham, James
　　See Mencken, H(enry) L(ouis)

Drayton, Michael　1563-1631. . . . . **LC 8**

Dreadstone, Carl
　　See Campbell, (John) Ramsey

Dreiser, Theodore (Herman Albert)
　　1871-1945 . . . . **TCLC 10, 18, 35; DA;**
　　　　　　　　　DAC; DAM MST, NOV; WLC
　　See also CA 106; 132; CDALB 1865-1917;
　　　DLB 9, 12, 102, 137; DLBD 1; MTCW

Drexler, Rosalyn　1926- . . . . **CLC 2, 6**
　　See also CA 81-84

Dreyer, Carl Theodor　1889-1968. . . . **CLC 16**
　　See also CA 116

Drieu la Rochelle, Pierre(-Eugene)
　　1893-1945 . . . . **TCLC 21**
　　See also CA 117; DLB 72

Drinkwater, John　1882-1937 . . . . . . **TCLC 57**
　　See also CA 109; 149; DLB 10, 19, 149

Drop Shot
　　See Cable, George Washington

Droste-Hulshoff, Annette Freiin von
　　1797-1848 . . . . **NCLC 3**
　　See also DLB 133

Drummond, Walter
　　See Silverberg, Robert

Drummond, William Henry
　　1854-1907 . . . . **TCLC 25**
　　See also DLB 92

Drummond de Andrade, Carlos
　　1902-1987 . . . . **CLC 18**
　　See also Andrade, Carlos Drummond de
　　See also CA 132; 123

Drury, Allen (Stuart)　1918- . . . . **CLC 37**
　　See also CA 57-60; CANR 18, 52;
　　　INT CANR-18

Eddison, E(ric) R(ucker)
1882-1945 . . . . TCLC 15
See also CA 109; 154

Edel, (Joseph) Leon   1907- . . . . . . CLC 29, 34
See also CA 1-4R; CANR 1, 22; DLB 103;
INT CANR-22

Eden, Emily   1797-1869 . . . . NCLC 10

Edgar, David
1948- . . . . CLC 42; DAM DRAM
See also CA 57-60; CANR 12; DLB 13;
MTCW

Edgerton, Clyde (Carlyle)   1944- . . . . CLC 39
See also AAYA 17; CA 118; 134; INT 134

Edgeworth, Maria   1768-1849. . . NCLC 1, 51
See also DLB 116, 159, 163; SATA 21

Edmonds, Paul
See Kuttner, Henry

Edmonds, Walter D(umaux)   1903- . . CLC 35
See also CA 5-8R; CANR 2; DLB 9;
MAICYA; SAAS 4; SATA 1, 27

Edmondson, Wallace
See Ellison, Harlan (Jay)

Edson, Russell. . . . . CLC 13
See also CA 33-36R

Edwards, Bronwen Elizabeth
See Rose, Wendy

Edwards, G(erald) B(asil)
1899-1976 . . . . CLC 25
See also CA 110

Edwards, Gus   1939- . . . . CLC 43
See also CA 108; INT 108

Edwards, Jonathan
1703-1758 . . . . LC 7; DA; DAC;
DAM MST
See also DLB 24

Efron, Marina Ivanovna Tsvetaeva
See Tsvetaeva (Efron), Marina (Ivanovna)

Ehle, John (Marsden, Jr.)   1925- . . . . CLC 27
See also CA 9-12R

Ehrenbourg, Ilya (Grigoryevich)
See Ehrenburg, Ilya (Grigoryevich)

Ehrenburg, Ilya (Grigoryevich)
1891-1967 . . . . CLC 18, 34, 62
See also CA 102; 25-28R

Ehrenburg, Ilyo (Grigoryevich)
See Ehrenburg, Ilya (Grigoryevich)

Eich, Guenter   1907-1972 . . . . CLC 15
See also CA 111; 93-96; DLB 69, 124

Eichendorff, Joseph Freiherr von
1788-1857 . . . . NCLC 8
See also DLB 90

Eigner, Larry. . . . . CLC 9
See also Eigner, Laurence (Joel)
See also CAAS 23; DLB 5

Eigner, Laurence (Joel)   1927-1996
See Eigner, Larry
See also CA 9-12R; 151; CANR 6

Einstein, Albert   1879-1955 . . . . TCLC 65
See also CA 121; 133; MTCW

Eiseley, Loren Corey   1907-1977 . . . . . CLC 7
See also AAYA 5; CA 1-4R; 73-76;
CANR 6

Eisenstadt, Jill   1963- . . . . CLC 50
See also CA 140

Eisenstein, Sergei (Mikhailovich)
1898-1948 . . . . TCLC 57
See also CA 114; 149

Eisner, Simon
See Kornbluth, C(yril) M.

Ekeloef, (Bengt) Gunnar
1907-1968 . . . . CLC 27; DAM POET
See also CA 123; 25-28R

Ekelof, (Bengt) Gunnar
See Ekeloef, (Bengt) Gunnar

Ekwensi, C. O. D.
See Ekwensi, Cyprian (Odiatu Duaka)

Ekwensi, Cyprian (Odiatu Duaka)
1921- . . . . . . CLC 4; BLC; DAM MULT
See also BW 2; CA 29-32R; CANR 18, 42;
DLB 117; MTCW; SATA 66

Elaine. . . . . TCLC 18
See also Leverson, Ada

El Crummo
See Crumb, R(obert)

Elia
See Lamb, Charles

Eliade, Mircea   1907-1986 . . . . CLC 19
See also CA 65-68; 119; CANR 30; MTCW

Eliot, A. D.
See Jewett, (Theodora) Sarah Orne

Eliot, Alice
See Jewett, (Theodora) Sarah Orne

Eliot, Dan
See Silverberg, Robert

Eliot, George
1819-1880 . . . . . NCLC 4, 13, 23, 41, 49;
DA; DAB; DAC; DAM MST, NOV;
WLC
See also CDBLB 1832-1890; DLB 21, 35, 55

Eliot, John   1604-1690 . . . . LC 5
See also DLB 24

Eliot, T(homas) S(tearns)
1888-1965 . . . . . CLC 1, 2, 3, 6, 9, 10, 13,
15, 24, 34, 41, 55, 57; DA; DAB; DAC;
DAM DRAM, MST, POET; PC 5;
WLC 2
See also CA 5-8R; 25-28R; CANR 41;
CDALB 1929-1941; DLB 7, 10, 45, 63;
DLBY 88; MTCW

Elizabeth   1866-1941. . . . . TCLC 41

Elkin, Stanley L(awrence)
1930-1995 . . . . . . CLC 4, 6, 9, 14, 27, 51,
91; DAM NOV, POP; SSC 12
See also CA 9-12R; 148; CANR 8, 46;
DLB 2, 28; DLBY 80; INT CANR-8;
MTCW

Elledge, Scott. . . . . CLC 34

Elliot, Don
See Silverberg, Robert

Elliott, Don
See Silverberg, Robert

Elliott, George P(aul)   1918-1980. . . . . CLC 2
See also CA 1-4R; 97-100; CANR 2

Elliott, Janice   1931- . . . . CLC 47
See also CA 13-16R; CANR 8, 29; DLB 14

Elliott, Sumner Locke   1917-1991 . . . CLC 38
See also CA 5-8R; 134; CANR 2, 21

Elliott, William
See Bradbury, Ray (Douglas)

Ellis, A. E.. . . . . CLC 7

Ellis, Alice Thomas. . . . . CLC 40
See also Haycraft, Anna

Ellis, Bret Easton
1964- . . . . CLC 39, 71; DAM POP
See also AAYA 2; CA 118; 123; CANR 51;
INT 123

Ellis, (Henry) Havelock
1859-1939 . . . . TCLC 14
See also CA 109

Ellis, Landon
See Ellison, Harlan (Jay)

Ellis, Trey   1962- . . . . CLC 55
See also CA 146

Ellison, Harlan (Jay)
1934- . . . . . . CLC 1, 13, 42; DAM POP;
SSC 14
See also CA 5-8R; CANR 5, 46; DLB 8;
INT CANR-5; MTCW

Ellison, Ralph (Waldo)
1914-1994 . . . . CLC 1, 3, 11, 54, 86;
BLC; DA; DAB; DAC; DAM MST,
MULT, NOV; WLC
See also AAYA 19; BW 1; CA 9-12R; 145;
CANR 24, 53; CDALB 1941-1968;
DLB 2, 76; DLBY 94; MTCW

Ellmann, Lucy (Elizabeth)   1956- . . . . CLC 61
See also CA 128

Ellmann, Richard (David)
1918-1987 . . . . CLC 50
See also BEST 89:2; CA 1-4R; 122;
CANR 2, 28; DLB 103; DLBY 87;
MTCW

Elman, Richard   1934- . . . . CLC 19
See also CA 17-20R; CAAS 3; CANR 47

Elron
See Hubbard, L(afayette) Ron(ald)

Eluard, Paul. . . . . TCLC 7, 41
See also Grindel, Eugene

Elyot, Sir Thomas   1490(?)-1546 . . . . . LC 11

Elytis, Odysseus
1911-1996 . . . . CLC 15, 49; DAM POET
See also CA 102; 151; MTCW

Emecheta, (Florence Onye) Buchi
1944- . . CLC 14, 48; BLC; DAM MULT
See also BW 2; CA 81-84; CANR 27;
DLB 117; MTCW; SATA 66

Emerson, Ralph Waldo
1803-1882 . . . . . NCLC 1, 38; DA; DAB;
DAC; DAM MST, POET; WLC
See also CDALB 1640-1865; DLB 1, 59, 73

Eminescu, Mihail   1850-1889 . . . . . NCLC 33

Empson, William
1906-1984 . . . . CLC 3, 8, 19, 33, 34
See also CA 17-20R; 112; CANR 31;
DLB 20; MTCW

Enchi Fumiko (Ueda)   1905-1986. . . . CLC 31
See also CA 129; 121

Ende, Michael (Andreas Helmuth)
1929-1995 . . . . CLC 31
See also CA 118; 124; 149; CANR 36;
CLR 14; DLB 75; MAICYA; SATA 61;
SATA-Brief 42; SATA-Obit 86

Endo, Shusaku
1923-1996 ...... **CLC 7, 14, 19, 54, 99;**
DAM NOV
See also CA 29-32R; 153; CANR 21, 54;
MTCW

Engel, Marian 1933-1985.......... **CLC 36**
See also CA 25-28R; CANR 12; DLB 53;
INT CANR-12

Engelhardt, Frederick
See Hubbard, L(afayette) Ron(ald)

Enright, D(ennis) J(oseph)
1920- .... **CLC 4, 8, 31**
See also CA 1-4R; CANR 1, 42; DLB 27;
SATA 25

Enzensberger, Hans Magnus
1929- .... **CLC 43**
See also CA 116; 119

Ephron, Nora 1941- .... **CLC 17, 31**
See also AITN 2; CA 65-68; CANR 12, 39

Epicurus 341B.C.-270B.C. .... **CMLC 21**

Epsilon
See Betjeman, John

Epstein, Daniel Mark 1948- .... **CLC 7**
See also CA 49-52; CANR 2, 53

Epstein, Jacob 1956- .... **CLC 19**
See also CA 114

Epstein, Joseph 1937-............. **CLC 39**
See also CA 112; 119; CANR 50

Epstein, Leslie 1938- .... **CLC 27**
See also CA 73-76; CAAS 12; CANR 23

Equiano, Olaudah
1745(?)-1797 .... **LC 16; BLC;**
DAM MULT
See also DLB 37, 50

Erasmus, Desiderius 1469(?)-1536.... **LC 16**

Erdman, Paul E(mil) 1932- .... **CLC 25**
See also AITN 1; CA 61-64; CANR 13, 43

Erdrich, Louise
1954- .... **CLC 39, 54; DAM MULT,**
NOV, POP
See also AAYA 10; BEST 89:1; CA 114;
CANR 41; DLB 152, 175; MTCW;
NNAL

Erenburg, Ilya (Grigoryevich)
See Ehrenburg, Ilya (Grigoryevich)

Erickson, Stephen Michael 1950-
See Erickson, Steve
See also CA 129

Erickson, Steve .... **CLC 64**
See also Erickson, Stephen Michael

Ericson, Walter
See Fast, Howard (Melvin)

Eriksson, Buntel
See Bergman, (Ernst) Ingmar

Ernaux, Annie 1940- .... **CLC 88**
See also CA 147

Eschenbach, Wolfram von
See Wolfram von Eschenbach

Eseki, Bruno
See Mphahlele, Ezekiel

Esenin, Sergei (Alexandrovich)
1895-1925 .... **TCLC 4**
See also CA 104

Eshleman, Clayton 1935-........... **CLC 7**
See also CA 33-36R; CAAS 6; DLB 5

Espriella, Don Manuel Alvarez
See Southey, Robert

Espriu, Salvador 1913-1985........ **CLC 9**
See also CA 154; 115; DLB 134

Espronceda, Jose de 1808-1842... **NCLC 39**

Esse, James
See Stephens, James

Esterbrook, Tom
See Hubbard, L(afayette) Ron(ald)

Estleman, Loren D.
1952- ...... **CLC 48; DAM NOV, POP**
See also CA 85-88; CANR 27;
INT CANR-27; MTCW

Eugenides, Jeffrey 1960(?)-........ **CLC 81**
See also CA 144

Euripides c. 485B.C.-406B.C. .... **DC 4**
See also DA; DAB; DAC; DAM DRAM,
MST

Evan, Evin
See Faust, Frederick (Schiller)

Evans, Evan
See Faust, Frederick (Schiller)

Evans, Marian
See Eliot, George

Evans, Mary Ann
See Eliot, George

Evarts, Esther
See Benson, Sally

Everett, Percival L. 1956-........ **CLC 57**
See also BW 2; CA 129

Everson, R(onald) G(ilmour)
1903- .... **CLC 27**
See also CA 17-20R; DLB 88

Everson, William (Oliver)
1912-1994 .... **CLC 1, 5, 14**
See also CA 9-12R; 145; CANR 20; DLB 5,
16; MTCW

Evtushenko, Evgenii Aleksandrovich
See Yevtushenko, Yevgeny (Alexandrovich)

Ewart, Gavin (Buchanan)
1916-1995 .... **CLC 13, 46**
See also CA 89-92; 150; CANR 17, 46;
DLB 40; MTCW

Ewers, Hanns Heinz 1871-1943 ... **TCLC 12**
See also CA 109; 149

Ewing, Frederick R.
See Sturgeon, Theodore (Hamilton)

Exley, Frederick (Earl)
1929-1992 .... **CLC 6, 11**
See also AITN 2; CA 81-84; 138; DLB 143;
DLBY 81

Eynhardt, Guillermo
See Quiroga, Horacio (Sylvestre)

Ezekiel, Nissim 1924-............. **CLC 61**
See also CA 61-64

Ezekiel, Tish O'Dowd 1943- .... **CLC 34**
See also CA 129

Fadeyev, A.
See Bulgya, Alexander Alexandrovich

Fadeyev, Alexander............... **TCLC 53**
See also Bulgya, Alexander Alexandrovich

Fagen, Donald 1948-............. **CLC 26**

Fainzilberg, Ilya Arnoldovich 1897-1937
See Ilf, Ilya
See also CA 120

Fair, Ronald L. 1932-............. **CLC 18**
See also BW 1; CA 69-72; CANR 25;
DLB 33

Fairbairns, Zoe (Ann) 1948- .... **CLC 32**
See also CA 103; CANR 21

Falco, Gian
See Papini, Giovanni

Falconer, James
See Kirkup, James

Falconer, Kenneth
See Kornbluth, C(yril) M.

Falkland, Samuel
See Heijermans, Herman

Fallaci, Oriana 1930-............. **CLC 11**
See also CA 77-80; CANR 15; MTCW

Faludy, George 1913-............. **CLC 42**
See also CA 21-24R

Faludy, Gyoergy
See Faludy, George

Fanon, Frantz
1925-1961 .... **CLC 74; BLC;**
DAM MULT
See also BW 1; CA 116; 89-92

Fanshawe, Ann 1625-1680 .... **LC 11**

Fante, John (Thomas) 1911-1983 ... **CLC 60**
See also CA 69-72; 109; CANR 23;
DLB 130; DLBY 83

Farah, Nuruddin
1945- ..... **CLC 53; BLC; DAM MULT**
See also BW 2; CA 106; DLB 125

Fargue, Leon-Paul 1876(?)-1947 ... **TCLC 11**
See also CA 109

Farigoule, Louis
See Romains, Jules

Farina, Richard 1936(?)-1966 .... **CLC 9**
See also CA 81-84; 25-28R

Farley, Walter (Lorimer)
1915-1989 .... **CLC 17**
See also CA 17-20R; CANR 8, 29; DLB 22;
JRDA; MAICYA; SATA 2, 43

Farmer, Philip Jose 1918-....... **CLC 1, 19**
See also CA 1-4R; CANR 4, 35; DLB 8;
MTCW

Farquhar, George
1677-1707 .... **LC 21; DAM DRAM**
See also DLB 84

Farrell, J(ames) G(ordon)
1935-1979 .... **CLC 6**
See also CA 73-76; 89-92; CANR 36;
DLB 14; MTCW

Farrell, James T(homas)
1904-1979 .... **CLC 1, 4, 8, 11, 66**
See also CA 5-8R; 89-92; CANR 9; DLB 4,
9, 86; DLBD 2; MTCW

Farren, Richard J.
See Betjeman, John

Farren, Richard M.
See Betjeman, John

Fassbinder, Rainer Werner
    1946-1982 . . . . **CLC 20**
    See also CA 93-96; 106; CANR 31

Fast, Howard (Melvin)
    1914- . . . . **CLC 23; DAM NOV**
    See also AAYA 16; CA 1-4R; CAAS 18;
    CANR 1, 33, 54; DLB 9; INT CANR-33;
    SATA 7

Faulcon, Robert
    See Holdstock, Robert P.

Faulkner, William (Cuthbert)
    1897-1962 . . . . . **CLC 1, 3, 6, 8, 9, 11, 14,
        18, 28, 52, 68; DA; DAB; DAC;
        DAM MST, NOV; SSC 1; WLC**
    See also AAYA 7; CA 81-84; CANR 33;
    CDALB 1929-1941; DLB 9, 11, 44, 102;
    DLBD 2; DLBY 86; MTCW

Fauset, Jessie Redmon
    1884(?)-1961 . . . . **CLC 19, 54; BLC;
        DAM MULT**
    See also BW 1; CA 109; DLB 51

Faust, Frederick (Schiller)
    1892-1944(?) . . . . . **TCLC 49; DAM POP**
    See also CA 108; 152

Faust, Irvin 1924- . . . . **CLC 8**
    See also CA 33-36R; CANR 28; DLB 2, 28;
    DLBY 80

Fawkes, Guy
    See Benchley, Robert (Charles)

Fearing, Kenneth (Flexner)
    1902-1961 . . . . **CLC 51**
    See also CA 93-96; DLB 9

Fecamps, Elise
    See Creasey, John

Federman, Raymond 1928- . . . . . . **CLC 6, 47**
    See also CA 17-20R; CAAS 8; CANR 10,
    43; DLBY 80

Federspiel, J(uerg) F. 1931- . . . . **CLC 42**
    See also CA 146

Feiffer, Jules (Ralph)
    1929- . . . . . . **CLC 2, 8, 64; DAM DRAM**
    See also AAYA 3; CA 17-20R; CANR 30;
    DLB 7, 44; INT CANR-30; MTCW;
    SATA 8, 61

Feige, Hermann Albert Otto Maximilian
    See Traven, B.

Feinberg, David B. 1956-1994 . . . . . . **CLC 59**
    See also CA 135; 147

Feinstein, Elaine 1930- . . . . **CLC 36**
    See also CA 69-72; CAAS 1; CANR 31;
    DLB 14, 40; MTCW

Feldman, Irving (Mordecai) 1928- . . . . **CLC 7**
    See also CA 1-4R; CANR 1; DLB 169

Fellini, Federico 1920-1993 . . . . **CLC 16, 85**
    See also CA 65-68; 143; CANR 33

Felsen, Henry Gregor 1916- . . . . **CLC 17**
    See also CA 1-4R; CANR 1; SAAS 2;
    SATA 1

Fenton, James Martin 1949- . . . . **CLC 32**
    See also CA 102; DLB 40

Ferber, Edna 1887-1968 . . . . **CLC 18, 93**
    See also AITN 1; CA 5-8R; 25-28R; DLB 9,
    28, 86; MTCW; SATA 7

Ferguson, Helen
    See Kavan, Anna

Ferguson, Samuel 1810-1886 . . . . . **NCLC 33**
    See also DLB 32

Fergusson, Robert 1750-1774 . . . . **LC 29**
    See also DLB 109

Ferling, Lawrence
    See Ferlinghetti, Lawrence (Monsanto)

Ferlinghetti, Lawrence (Monsanto)
    1919(?)- . . . . **CLC 2, 6, 10, 27;
        DAM POET; PC 1**
    See also CA 5-8R; CANR 3, 41;
    CDALB 1941-1968; DLB 5, 16; MTCW

Fernandez, Vicente Garcia Huidobro
    See Huidobro Fernandez, Vicente Garcia

Ferrer, Gabriel (Francisco Victor) Miro
    See Miro (Ferrer), Gabriel (Francisco
    Victor)

Ferrier, Susan (Edmonstone)
    1782-1854 . . . . **NCLC 8**
    See also DLB 116

Ferrigno, Robert 1948(?)- . . . . **CLC 65**
    See also CA 140

Ferron, Jacques 1921-1985 . . . **CLC 94; DAC**
    See also CA 117; 129; DLB 60

Feuchtwanger, Lion 1884-1958 . . . . . **TCLC 3**
    See also CA 104; DLB 66

Feuillet, Octave 1821-1890 . . . . . . **NCLC 45**

Feydeau, Georges (Leon Jules Marie)
    1862-1921 . . . . . **TCLC 22; DAM DRAM**
    See also CA 113; 152

Ficino, Marsilio 1433-1499 . . . . **LC 12**

Fiedeler, Hans
    See Doeblin, Alfred

Fiedler, Leslie A(aron)
    1917- . . . . **CLC 4, 13, 24**
    See also CA 9-12R; CANR 7; DLB 28, 67;
    MTCW

Field, Andrew 1938- . . . . **CLC 44**
    See also CA 97-100; CANR 25

Field, Eugene 1850-1895 . . . . **NCLC 3**
    See also DLB 23, 42, 140; DLBD 13;
    MAICYA; SATA 16

Field, Gans T.
    See Wellman, Manly Wade

Field, Michael . . . . **TCLC 43**

Field, Peter
    See Hobson, Laura Z(ametkin)

Fielding, Henry
    1707-1754 . . . . . . **LC 1; DA; DAB; DAC;
        DAM DRAM, MST, NOV; WLC**
    See also CDBLB 1660-1789; DLB 39, 84,
    101

Fielding, Sarah 1710-1768 . . . . **LC 1**
    See also DLB 39

Fierstein, Harvey (Forbes)
    1954- . . . . . **CLC 33; DAM DRAM, POP**
    See also CA 123; 129

Figes, Eva 1932- . . . . **CLC 31**
    See also CA 53-56; CANR 4, 44; DLB 14

Finch, Robert (Duer Claydon)
    1900- . . . . **CLC 18**
    See also CA 57-60; CANR 9, 24, 49;
    DLB 88

Findley, Timothy
    1930- . . . . . . **CLC 27; DAC; DAM MST**
    See also CA 25-28R; CANR 12, 42;
    DLB 53

Fink, William
    See Mencken, H(enry) L(ouis)

Firbank, Louis 1942-
    See Reed, Lou
    See also CA 117

Firbank, (Arthur Annesley) Ronald
    1886-1926 . . . . **TCLC 1**
    See also CA 104; DLB 36

Fisher, M(ary) F(rances) K(ennedy)
    1908-1992 . . . . **CLC 76, 87**
    See also CA 77-80; 138; CANR 44

Fisher, Roy 1930- . . . . **CLC 25**
    See also CA 81-84; CAAS 10; CANR 16;
    DLB 40

Fisher, Rudolph
    1897-1934 . . . . **TCLC 11; BLC;
        DAM MULT**
    See also BW 1; CA 107; 124; DLB 51, 102

Fisher, Vardis (Alvero) 1895-1968 . . . . **CLC 7**
    See also CA 5-8R; 25-28R; DLB 9

Fiske, Tarleton
    See Bloch, Robert (Albert)

Fitch, Clarke
    See Sinclair, Upton (Beall)

Fitch, John IV
    See Cormier, Robert (Edmund)

Fitzgerald, Captain Hugh
    See Baum, L(yman) Frank

FitzGerald, Edward 1809-1883 . . . . **NCLC 9**
    See also DLB 32

Fitzgerald, F(rancis) Scott (Key)
    1896-1940 . . . . **TCLC 1, 6, 14, 28, 55;
        DA; DAB; DAC; DAM MST, NOV;
        SSC 6; WLC**
    See also AITN 1; CA 110; 123;
    CDALB 1917-1929; DLB 4, 9, 86;
    DLBD 1; DLBY 81; MTCW

Fitzgerald, Penelope 1916- . . . **CLC 19, 51, 61**
    See also CA 85-88; CAAS 10; CANR 56;
    DLB 14

Fitzgerald, Robert (Stuart)
    1910-1985 . . . . **CLC 39**
    See also CA 1-4R; 114; CANR 1; DLBY 80

FitzGerald, Robert D(avid)
    1902-1987 . . . . **CLC 19**
    See also CA 17-20R

Fitzgerald, Zelda (Sayre)
    1900-1948 . . . . **TCLC 52**
    See also CA 117; 126; DLBY 84

Flanagan, Thomas (James Bonner)
    1923- . . . . **CLC 25, 52**
    See also CA 108; CANR 55; DLBY 80;
    INT 108; MTCW

Flaubert, Gustave
    1821-1880 . . . . **NCLC 2, 10, 19; DA;
        DAB; DAC; DAM MST, NOV; SSC 11;
        WLC**
    See also DLB 119

Flecker, Herman Elroy
    See Flecker, (Herman) James Elroy

Fredro, Aleksander 1793-1876..... **NCLC 8**

Freeling, Nicolas 1927- .... **CLC 38**
See also CA 49-52; CAAS 12; CANR 1, 17, 50; DLB 87

Freeman, Douglas Southall
1886-1953 .... **TCLC 11**
See also CA 109; DLB 17

Freeman, Judith 1946-............ **CLC 55**
See also CA 148

Freeman, Mary Eleanor Wilkins
1852-1930 .... **TCLC 9; SSC 1**
See also CA 106; DLB 12, 78

Freeman, R(ichard) Austin
1862-1943 .... **TCLC 21**
See also CA 113; DLB 70

French, Albert 1943- .... **CLC 86**

French, Marilyn
1929-................ **CLC 10, 18, 60;**
DAM DRAM, NOV, POP
See also CA 69-72; CANR 3, 31;
INT CANR-31; MTCW

French, Paul
See Asimov, Isaac

Freneau, Philip Morin 1752-1832.. **NCLC 1**
See also DLB 37, 43

Freud, Sigmund 1856-1939 .... **TCLC 52**
See also CA 115; 133; MTCW

Friedan, Betty (Naomi) 1921-...... **CLC 74**
See also CA 65-68; CANR 18, 45; MTCW

Friedlander, Saul 1932-........... **CLC 90**
See also CA 117; 130

Friedman, B(ernard) H(arper)
1926-........................ **CLC 7**
See also CA 1-4R; CANR 3, 48

Friedman, Bruce Jay 1930-.... **CLC 3, 5, 56**
See also CA 9-12R; CANR 25, 52; DLB 2, 28; INT CANR-25

Friel, Brian 1929-.......... **CLC 5, 42, 59**
See also CA 21-24R; CANR 33; DLB 13;
MTCW

Friis-Baastad, Babbis Ellinor
1921-1970 .... **CLC 12**
See also CA 17-20R; 134; SATA 7

Frisch, Max (Rudolf)
1911-1991 ..... **CLC 3, 9, 14, 18, 32, 44;**
DAM DRAM, NOV
See also CA 85-88; 134; CANR 32;
DLB 69, 124; MTCW

Fromentin, Eugene (Samuel Auguste)
1820-1876 .... **NCLC 10**
See also DLB 123

Frost, Frederick
See Faust, Frederick (Schiller)

Frost, Robert (Lee)
1874-1963 .... **CLC 1, 3, 4, 9, 10, 13, 15,**
26, 34, 44; DA; DAB; DAC; DAM MST,
POET; PC 1; WLC
See also CA 89-92; CANR 33;
CDALB 1917-1929; DLB 54; DLBD 7;
MTCW; SATA 14

Froude, James Anthony
1818-1894 .... **NCLC 43**
See also DLB 18, 57, 144

Froy, Herald
See Waterhouse, Keith (Spencer)

Fry, Christopher
1907- ..... **CLC 2, 10, 14; DAM DRAM**
See also CA 17-20R; CAAS 23; CANR 9, 30; DLB 13; MTCW; SATA 66

Frye, (Herman) Northrop
1912-1991 .... **CLC 24, 70**
See also CA 5-8R; 133; CANR 8, 37;
DLB 67, 68; MTCW

Fuchs, Daniel 1909-1993 .... **CLC 8, 22**
See also CA 81-84; 142; CAAS 5;
CANR 40; DLB 9, 26, 28; DLBY 93

Fuchs, Daniel 1934-.............. **CLC 34**
See also CA 37-40R; CANR 14, 48

Fuentes, Carlos
1928- ...... **CLC 3, 8, 10, 13, 22, 41, 60;**
DA; DAB; DAC; DAM MST, MULT,
NOV; HLC; SSC 24; WLC
See also AAYA 4; AITN 2; CA 69-72;
CANR 10, 32; DLB 113; HW; MTCW

Fuentes, Gregorio Lopez y
See Lopez y Fuentes, Gregorio

Fugard, (Harold) Athol
1932-......... **CLC 5, 9, 14, 25, 40, 80;**
DAM DRAM; DC 3
See also AAYA 17; CA 85-88; CANR 32, 54; MTCW

Fugard, Sheila 1932- .... **CLC 48**
See also CA 125

Fuller, Charles (H., Jr.)
1939- .... **CLC 25; BLC; DAM DRAM,**
MULT; DC 1
See also BW 2; CA 108; 112; DLB 38;
INT 112; MTCW

Fuller, John (Leopold) 1937-...... **CLC 62**
See also CA 21-24R; CANR 9, 44; DLB 40

Fuller, Margaret .... **NCLC 5, 50**
See also Ossoli, Sarah Margaret (Fuller
marchesa d')

Fuller, Roy (Broadbent)
1912-1991 .... **CLC 4, 28**
See also CA 5-8R; 135; CAAS 10;
CANR 53; DLB 15, 20; SATA 87

Fulton, Alice 1952-............... **CLC 52**
See also CA 116; CANR 57

Furphy, Joseph 1843-1912....... **TCLC 25**

Fussell, Paul 1924-............... **CLC 74**
See also BEST 90:1; CA 17-20R; CANR 8, 21, 35; INT CANR-21; MTCW

Futabatei, Shimei 1864-1909 ..... **TCLC 44**

Futrelle, Jacques 1875-1912 ...... **TCLC 19**
See also CA 113; 155

Gaboriau, Emile 1835-1873 ...... **NCLC 14**

Gadda, Carlo Emilio 1893-1973 .... **CLC 11**
See also CA 89-92

Gaddis, William
1922- ..... **CLC 1, 3, 6, 8, 10, 19, 43, 86**
See also CA 17-20R; CANR 21, 48; DLB 2;
MTCW

Gage, Walter
See Inge, William (Motter)

Gaines, Ernest J(ames)
1933- .... **CLC 3, 11, 18, 86; BLC;**
DAM MULT
See also AAYA 18; AITN 1; BW 2;
CA 9-12R; CANR 6, 24, 42;
CDALB 1968-1988; DLB 2, 33, 152;
DLBY 80; MTCW; SATA 86

Gaitskill, Mary 1954-............. **CLC 69**
See also CA 128

Galdos, Benito Perez
See Perez Galdos, Benito

Gale, Zona
1874-1938 ...... **TCLC 7; DAM DRAM**
See also CA 105; 153; DLB 9, 78

Galeano, Eduardo (Hughes) 1940-... **CLC 72**
See also CA 29-32R; CANR 13, 32; HW

Galiano, Juan Valera y Alcala
See Valera y Alcala-Galiano, Juan

Gallagher, Tess
1943- .. **CLC 18, 63; DAM POET; PC 9**
See also CA 106; DLB 120

Gallant, Mavis
1922- .... **CLC 7, 18, 38; DAC;**
DAM MST; SSC 5
See also CA 69-72; CANR 29; DLB 53;
MTCW

Gallant, Roy A(rthur) 1924- .... **CLC 17**
See also CA 5-8R; CANR 4, 29, 54;
CLR 30; MAICYA; SATA 4, 68

Gallico, Paul (William) 1897-1976 ... **CLC 2**
See also AITN 1; CA 5-8R; 69-72;
CANR 23; DLB 9, 171; MAICYA;
SATA 13

Gallo, Max Louis 1932-........... **CLC 95**
See also CA 85-88

Gallois, Lucien
See Desnos, Robert

Gallup, Ralph
See Whitemore, Hugh (John)

Galsworthy, John
1867-1933 ...... **TCLC 1, 45; DA; DAB;**
DAC; DAM DRAM, MST, NOV;
SSC 22; WLC 2
See also CA 104; 141; CDBLB 1890-1914;
DLB 10, 34, 98, 162

Galt, John 1779-1839........... **NCLC 1**
See also DLB 99, 116, 159

Galvin, James 1951-.............. **CLC 38**
See also CA 108; CANR 26

Gamboa, Federico 1864-1939...... **TCLC 36**

Gandhi, M. K.
See Gandhi, Mohandas Karamchand

Gandhi, Mahatma
See Gandhi, Mohandas Karamchand

Gandhi, Mohandas Karamchand
1869-1948 ..... **TCLC 59; DAM MULT**
See also CA 121; 132; MTCW

Gann, Ernest Kellogg 1910-1991.... **CLC 23**
See also AITN 1; CA 1-4R; 136; CANR 1

Garcia, Cristina 1958- .... **CLC 76**
See also CA 141

Gide, Andre (Paul Guillaume)
    1869-1951 . . . . **TCLC 5, 12, 36; DA;**
       DAB; DAC; DAM MST, NOV; SSC 13;
          WLC
    See also CA 104; 124; DLB 65; MTCW

Gifford, Barry (Colby) 1946- . . . . . **CLC 34**
    See also CA 65-68; CANR 9, 30, 40

Gilbert, W(illiam) S(chwenck)
    1836-1911 . . . . . **TCLC 3; DAM DRAM,**
               POET
    See also CA 104; SATA 36

Gilbreth, Frank B., Jr. 1911- . . . . **CLC 17**
    See also CA 9-12R; SATA 2

Gilchrist, Ellen
    1935- . . . . **CLC 34, 48; DAM POP;**
               SSC 14
    See also CA 113; 116; CANR 41; DLB 130;
    MTCW

Giles, Molly 1942- . . . . **CLC 39**
    See also CA 126

Gill, Patrick
    See Creasey, John

Gilliam, Terry (Vance) 1940- . . . . **CLC 21**
    See also Monty Python
    See also AAYA 19; CA 108; 113;
      CANR 35; INT 113

Gillian, Jerry
    See Gilliam, Terry (Vance)

Gilliatt, Penelope (Ann Douglass)
    1932-1993 . . . . **CLC 2, 10, 13, 53**
    See also AITN 2; CA 13-16R; 141;
      CANR 49; DLB 14

Gilman, Charlotte (Anna) Perkins (Stetson)
    1860-1935 . . . . **TCLC 9, 37; SSC 13**
    See also CA 106; 150

Gilmour, David 1949- . . . . **CLC 35**
    See also CA 138, 147

Gilpin, William 1724-1804 . . . . **NCLC 30**

Gilray, J. D.
    See Mencken, H(enry) L(ouis)

Gilroy, Frank D(aniel) 1925- . . . . **CLC 2**
    See also CA 81-84; CANR 32; DLB 7

Gilstrap, John 1957(?)- . . . . **CLC 99**

Ginsberg, Allen
    1926- . . . . . . **CLC 1, 2, 3, 4, 6, 13, 36, 69;**
      DA; DAB; DAC; DAM MST, POET;
             PC 4; WLC 3
    See also AITN 1; CA 1-4R; CANR 2, 41;
      CDALB 1941-1968; DLB 5, 16, 169;
    MTCW

Ginzburg, Natalia
    1916-1991 . . . . **CLC 5, 11, 54, 70**
    See also CA 85-88; 135; CANR 33; MTCW

Giono, Jean 1895-1970 . . . . **CLC 4, 11**
    See also CA 45-48; 29-32R; CANR 2, 35;
    DLB 72; MTCW

Giovanni, Nikki
    1943- . . . . . . **CLC 2, 4, 19, 64; BLC; DA;**
      DAB; DAC; DAM MST, MULT, POET
    See also AITN 1; BW 2; CA 29-32R;
      CAAS 6; CANR 18, 41; CLR 6; DLB 5,
      41; INT CANR-18; MAICYA; MTCW;
    SATA 24

Giovene, Andrea 1904- . . . . **CLC 7**
    See also CA 85-88

Gippius, Zinaida (Nikolayevna) 1869-1945
    See Hippius, Zinaida
    See also CA 106

Giraudoux, (Hippolyte) Jean
    1882-1944 . . . . **TCLC 2, 7; DAM DRAM**
    See also CA 104; DLB 65

Gironella, Jose Maria 1917- . . . . **CLC 11**
    See also CA 101

Gissing, George (Robert)
    1857-1903 . . . . **TCLC 3, 24, 47**
    See also CA 105; DLB 18, 135

Giurlani, Aldo
    See Palazzeschi, Aldo

Gladkov, Fyodor (Vasilyevich)
    1883-1958 . . . . **TCLC 27**

Glanville, Brian (Lester) 1931- . . . . . . **CLC 6**
    See also CA 5-8R; CAAS 9; CANR 3;
    DLB 15, 139; SATA 42

Glasgow, Ellen (Anderson Gholson)
    1873(?)-1945 . . . . **TCLC 2, 7**
    See also CA 104; DLB 9, 12

Glaspell, Susan 1882(?)-1948 . . . . . . **TCLC 55**
    See also CA 110; 154; DLB 7, 9, 78;
    YABC 2

Glassco, John 1909-1981 . . . . **CLC 9**
    See also CA 13-16R; 102; CANR 15;
    DLB 68

Glasscock, Amnesia
    See Steinbeck, John (Ernst)

Glasser, Ronald J. 1940(?)- . . . . **CLC 37**

Glassman, Joyce
    See Johnson, Joyce

Glendinning, Victoria 1937- . . . . **CLC 50**
    See also CA 120; 127; DLB 155

Glissant, Edouard
    1928- . . . . **CLC 10, 68; DAM MULT**
    See also CA 153

Gloag, Julian 1930- . . . . **CLC 40**
    See also AITN 1; CA 65-68; CANR 10

Glowacki, Aleksander
    See Prus, Boleslaw

Gluck, Louise (Elisabeth)
    1943- . . . . **CLC 7, 22, 44, 81;**
           DAM POET; PC 16
    See also CA 33-36R; CANR 40; DLB 5

Gobineau, Joseph Arthur (Comte) de
    1816-1882 . . . . **NCLC 17**
    See also DLB 123

Godard, Jean-Luc 1930- . . . . **CLC 20**
    See also CA 93-96

Godden, (Margaret) Rumer 1907- . . . **CLC 53**
    See also AAYA 6; CA 5-8R; CANR 4, 27,
      36, 55; CLR 20; DLB 161; MAICYA;
      SAAS 12; SATA 3, 36

Godoy Alcayaga, Lucila 1889-1957
    See Mistral, Gabriela
    See also BW 2; CA 104; 131; DAM MULT;
      HW; MTCW

Godwin, Gail (Kathleen)
    1937- . . . . **CLC 5, 8, 22, 31, 69;**
              DAM POP
    See also CA 29-32R; CANR 15, 43; DLB 6;
      INT CANR-15; MTCW

Godwin, William 1756-1836. . . . . . **NCLC 14**
    See also CDBLB 1789-1832; DLB 39, 104,
      142, 158, 163

Goebbels, Josef
    See Goebbels, (Paul) Joseph

Goebbels, (Paul) Joseph
    1897-1945 . . . . **TCLC 68**
    See also CA 115; 148

Goebbels, Joseph Paul
    See Goebbels, (Paul) Joseph

Goethe, Johann Wolfgang von
    1749-1832 . . . . **NCLC 4, 22, 34; DA;**
      DAB; DAC; DAM DRAM, MST,
         POET; PC 5; WLC 3
    See also DLB 94

Gogarty, Oliver St. John
    1878-1957 . . . . **TCLC 15**
    See also CA 109; 150; DLB 15, 19

Gogol, Nikolai (Vasilyevich)
    1809-1852 . . . . . **NCLC 5, 15, 31; DA;**
      DAB; DAC; DAM DRAM, MST; DC 1;
         SSC 4; WLC

Goines, Donald
    1937(?)-1974 . . . . **CLC 80; BLC;**
            DAM MULT, POP
    See also AITN 1; BW 1; CA 124; 114;
      DLB 33

Gold, Herbert 1924- . . . . **CLC 4, 7, 14, 42**
    See also CA 9-12R; CANR 17, 45; DLB 2;
      DLBY 81

Goldbarth, Albert 1948- . . . . **CLC 5, 38**
    See also CA 53-56; CANR 6, 40; DLB 120

Goldberg, Anatol 1910-1982 . . . . **CLC 34**
    See also CA 131; 117

Goldemberg, Isaac 1945- . . . . **CLC 52**
    See also CA 69-72; CAAS 12; CANR 11,
      32; HW

Golding, William (Gerald)
    1911-1993 . . . . **CLC 1, 2, 3, 8, 10, 17, 27,**
      58, 81; DA; DAB; DAC; DAM MST,
           NOV; WLC
    See also AAYA 5; CA 5-8R; 141;
      CANR 13, 33, 54; CDBLB 1945-1960;
      DLB 15, 100; MTCW

Goldman, Emma 1869-1940 . . . . . . **TCLC 13**
    See also CA 110; 150

Goldman, Francisco 1955- . . . . **CLC 76**

Goldman, William (W.) 1931- . . . . **CLC 1, 48**
    See also CA 9-12R; CANR 29; DLB 44

Goldmann, Lucien 1913-1970 . . . . . . **CLC 24**
    See also CA 25-28; CAP 2

Goldoni, Carlo
    1707-1793 . . . . **LC 4; DAM DRAM**

Goldsberry, Steven 1949- . . . . **CLC 34**
    See also CA 131

Goldsmith, Oliver
    1728-1774 . . . . . . **LC 2; DA; DAB; DAC;**
      DAM DRAM, MST, NOV, POET;
           WLC
    See also CDBLB 1660-1789; DLB 39, 89,
      104, 109, 142; SATA 26

Goldsmith, Peter
    See Priestley, J(ohn) B(oynton)

Gombrowicz, Witold
1904-1969 . . . . CLC 4, 7, 11, 49;
DAM DRAM
See also CA 19-20; 25-28R; CAP 2

Gomez de la Serna, Ramon
1888-1963 . . . . CLC 9
See also CA 153; 116; HW

Goncharov, Ivan Alexandrovich
1812-1891 . . . . NCLC 1

Goncourt, Edmond (Louis Antoine Huot) de
1822-1896 . . . . NCLC 7
See also DLB 123

Goncourt, Jules (Alfred Huot) de
1830-1870 . . . . NCLC 7
See also DLB 123

Gontier, Fernande   19(?)- . . . . CLC 50

Goodman, Paul   1911-1972 . . . . CLC 1, 2, 4, 7
See also CA 19-20; 37-40R; CANR 34;
CAP 2; DLB 130; MTCW

Gordimer, Nadine
1923- . . . . CLC 3, 5, 7, 10, 18, 33, 51, 70;
DA; DAB; DAC; DAM MST, NOV;
SSC 17
See also CA 5-8R; CANR 3, 28, 56;
INT CANR-28; MTCW

Gordon, Adam Lindsay
1833-1870 . . . . NCLC 21

Gordon, Caroline
1895-1981 . . . CLC 6, 13, 29, 83; SSC 15
See also CA 11-12; 103; CANR 36; CAP 1;
DLB 4, 9, 102; DLBY 81; MTCW

Gordon, Charles William   1860-1937
See Connor, Ralph
See also CA 109

Gordon, Mary (Catherine)
1949- . . . . CLC 13, 22
See also CA 102; CANR 44; DLB 6;
DLBY 81; INT 102; MTCW

Gordon, Sol   1923- . . . . CLC 26
See also CA 53-56; CANR 4; SATA 11

Gordone, Charles
1925-1995 . . . . . CLC 1, 4; DAM DRAM
See also BW 1; CA 93-96; 150; CANR 55;
DLB 7; INT 93-96; MTCW

Gorenko, Anna Andreevna
See Akhmatova, Anna

Gorky, Maxim . . . . TCLC 8; DAB; WLC
See also Peshkov, Alexei Maximovich

Goryan, Sirak
See Saroyan, William

Gosse, Edmund (William)
1849-1928 . . . . TCLC 28
See also CA 117; DLB 57, 144

Gotlieb, Phyllis Fay (Bloom)
1926- . . . . CLC 18
See also CA 13-16R; CANR 7; DLB 88

Gottesman, S. D.
See Kornbluth, C(yril) M.; Pohl, Frederik

Gottfried von Strassburg
fl. c. 1210- . . . . CMLC 10
See also DLB 138

Gould, Lois . . . . CLC 4, 10
See also CA 77-80; CANR 29; MTCW

Gourmont, Remy (-Marie-Charles) de
1858-1915 . . . . TCLC 17
See also CA 109; 150

Govier, Katherine   1948- . . . . CLC 51
See also CA 101; CANR 18, 40

Goyen, (Charles) William
1915-1983 . . . . CLC 5, 8, 14, 40
See also AITN 2; CA 5-8R; 110; CANR 6;
DLB 2; DLBY 83; INT CANR-6

Goytisolo, Juan
1931- . . . . . CLC 5, 10, 23; DAM MULT;
HLC
See also CA 85-88; CANR 32; HW; MTCW

Gozzano, Guido   1883-1916 . . . . PC 10
See also CA 154; DLB 114

Gozzi, (Conte) Carlo   1720-1806 . . NCLC 23

Grabbe, Christian Dietrich
1801-1836 . . . . NCLC 2
See also DLB 133

Grace, Patricia   1937- . . . . CLC 56

Gracian y Morales, Baltasar
1601-1658 . . . . LC 15

Gracq, Julien . . . . CLC 11, 48
See also Poirier, Louis
See also DLB 83

Grade, Chaim   1910-1982 . . . . CLC 10
See also CA 93-96; 107

Graduate of Oxford, A
See Ruskin, John

Graham, John
See Phillips, David Graham

Graham, Jorie   1951- . . . . CLC 48
See also CA 111; DLB 120

Graham, R(obert) B(ontine) Cunninghame
See Cunninghame Graham, R(obert)
B(ontine)
See also DLB 98, 135, 174

Graham, Robert
See Haldeman, Joe (William)

Graham, Tom
See Lewis, (Harry) Sinclair

Graham, W(illiam) S(ydney)
1918-1986 . . . . CLC 29
See also CA 73-76; 118; DLB 20

Graham, Winston (Mawdsley)
1910- . . . . CLC 23
See also CA 49-52; CANR 2, 22, 45;
DLB 77

Grahame, Kenneth
1859-1932 . . . . TCLC 64; DAB
See also CA 108; 136; CLR 5; DLB 34, 141;
MAICYA; YABC 1

Grant, Skeeter
See Spiegelman, Art

Granville-Barker, Harley
1877-1946 . . . . . . TCLC 2; DAM DRAM
See also Barker, Harley Granville
See also CA 104

Grass, Guenter (Wilhelm)
1927- . . . . . CLC 1, 2, 4, 6, 11, 15, 22, 32,
49, 88; DA; DAB; DAC; DAM MST,
NOV; WLC
See also CA 13-16R; CANR 20; DLB 75,
124; MTCW

Gratton, Thomas
See Hulme, T(homas) E(rnest)

Grau, Shirley Ann
1929- . . . . CLC 4, 9; SSC 15
See also CA 89-92; CANR 22; DLB 2;
INT CANR-22; MTCW

Gravel, Fern
See Hall, James Norman

Graver, Elizabeth   1964- . . . . CLC 70
See also CA 135

Graves, Richard Perceval   1945- . . . . CLC 44
See also CA 65-68; CANR 9, 26, 51

Graves, Robert (von Ranke)
1895-1985 . . . . . . CLC 1, 2, 6, 11, 39, 44,
45; DAB; DAC; DAM MST, POET;
PC 6
See also CA 5-8R; 117; CANR 5, 36;
CDBLB 1914-1945; DLB 20, 100;
DLBY 85; MTCW; SATA 45

Graves, Valerie
See Bradley, Marion Zimmer

Gray, Alasdair (James)   1934- . . . . . . CLC 41
See also CA 126; CANR 47; INT 126;
MTCW

Gray, Amlin   1946- . . . . CLC 29
See also CA 138

Gray, Francine du Plessix
1930- . . . . CLC 22; DAM NOV
See also BEST 90:3; CA 61-64; CAAS 2;
CANR 11, 33; INT CANR-11; MTCW

Gray, John (Henry)   1866-1934 . . . . TCLC 19
See also CA 119

Gray, Simon (James Holliday)
1936- . . . . CLC 9, 14, 36
See also AITN 1; CA 21-24R; CAAS 3;
CANR 32; DLB 13; MTCW

Gray, Spalding   1941- . . CLC 49; DAM POP
See also CA 128

Gray, Thomas
1716-1771 . . . . . . LC 4; DA; DAB; DAC;
DAM MST; PC 2; WLC
See also CDBLB 1660-1789; DLB 109

Grayson, David
See Baker, Ray Stannard

Grayson, Richard (A.)   1951- . . . . CLC 38
See also CA 85-88; CANR 14, 31, 57

Greeley, Andrew M(oran)
1928- . . . . CLC 28; DAM POP
See also CA 5-8R; CAAS 7; CANR 7, 43;
MTCW

Green, Anna Katharine
1846-1935 . . . . TCLC 63
See also CA 112

Green, Brian
See Card, Orson Scott

Green, Hannah
See Greenberg, Joanne (Goldenberg)

Green, Hannah . . . . CLC 3
See also CA 73-76

Green, Henry   1905-1973 . . . . . CLC 2, 13, 97
See also Yorke, Henry Vincent
See also DLB 15

Green, Julian (Hartridge) 1900-
See Green, Julien
See also CA 21-24R; CANR 33; DLB 4, 72;
MTCW

Green, Julien . . . . **CLC 3, 11, 77**
See also Green, Julian (Hartridge)

Green, Paul (Eliot)
1894-1981 . . . . . . **CLC 25; DAM DRAM**
See also AITN 1; CA 5-8R; 103; CANR 3;
DLB 7, 9; DLBY 81

Greenberg, Ivan 1908-1973
See Rahv, Philip
See also CA 85-88

Greenberg, Joanne (Goldenberg)
1932- . . . . **CLC 7, 30**
See also AAYA 12; CA 5-8R; CANR 14,
32; SATA 25

Greenberg, Richard 1959(?)- . . . . . . **CLC 57**
See also CA 138

Greene, Bette 1934- . . . . **CLC 30**
See also AAYA 7; CA 53-56; CANR 4;
CLR 2; JRDA; MAICYA; SAAS 16;
SATA 8

Greene, Gael . . . . **CLC 8**
See also CA 13-16R; CANR 10

Greene, Graham
1904-1991 . . . . **CLC 1, 3, 6, 9, 14, 18, 27,
37, 70, 72; DA; DAB; DAC; DAM MST,
NOV; WLC**
See also AITN 2; CA 13-16R; 133;
CANR 35; CDBLB 1945-1960; DLB 13,
15, 77, 100, 162; DLBY 91; MTCW;
SATA 20

Greer, Richard
See Silverberg, Robert

Gregor, Arthur 1923- . . . . **CLC 9**
See also CA 25-28R; CAAS 10; CANR 11;
SATA 36

Gregor, Lee
See Pohl, Frederik

Gregory, Isabella Augusta (Persse)
1852-1932 . . . . **TCLC 1**
See also CA 104; DLB 10

Gregory, J. Dennis
See Williams, John A(lfred)

Grendon, Stephen
See Derleth, August (William)

Grenville, Kate 1950- . . . . **CLC 61**
See also CA 118; CANR 53

Grenville, Pelham
See Wodehouse, P(elham) G(renville)

Greve, Felix Paul (Berthold Friedrich)
1879-1948
See Grove, Frederick Philip
See also CA 104; 141; DAC; DAM MST

Grey, Zane
1872-1939 . . . . **TCLC 6; DAM POP**
See also CA 104; 132; DLB 9; MTCW

Grieg, (Johan) Nordahl (Brun)
1902-1943 . . . . **TCLC 10**
See also CA 107

Grieve, C(hristopher) M(urray)
1892-1978 . . . . **CLC 11, 19; DAM POET**
See also MacDiarmid, Hugh; Pteleon
See also CA 5-8R; 85-88; CANR 33;
MTCW

Griffin, Gerald 1803-1840 . . . . **NCLC 7**
See also DLB 159

Griffin, John Howard 1920-1980 . . . . **CLC 68**
See also AITN 1; CA 1-4R; 101; CANR 2

Griffin, Peter 1942- . . . . **CLC 39**
See also CA 136

Griffith, D(avid Lewelyn) W(ark)
1875(?)-1948 . . . . **TCLC 68**
See also CA 119; 150

Griffith, Lawrence
See Griffith, D(avid Lewelyn) W(ark)

Griffiths, Trevor 1935- . . . . **CLC 13, 52**
See also CA 97-100; CANR 45; DLB 13

Grigson, Geoffrey (Edward Harvey)
1905-1985 . . . . **CLC 7, 39**
See also CA 25-28R; 118; CANR 20, 33;
DLB 27; MTCW

Grillparzer, Franz 1791-1872 . . . . . . **NCLC 1**
See also DLB 133

Grimble, Reverend Charles James
See Eliot, T(homas) S(tearns)

Grimke, Charlotte L(ottie) Forten
1837(?)-1914
See Forten, Charlotte L.
See also BW 1; CA 117; 124; DAM MULT,
POET

Grimm, Jacob Ludwig Karl
1785-1863 . . . . **NCLC 3**
See also DLB 90; MAICYA; SATA 22

Grimm, Wilhelm Karl 1786-1859 . . **NCLC 3**
See also DLB 90; MAICYA; SATA 22

Grimmelshausen, Johann Jakob Christoffel
von 1621-1676 . . . . **LC 6**
See also DLB 168

Grindel, Eugene 1895-1952
See Eluard, Paul
See also CA 104

Grisham, John 1955- . . **CLC 84; DAM POP**
See also AAYA 14; CA 138; CANR 47

Grossman, David 1954- . . . . **CLC 67**
See also CA 138

Grossman, Vasily (Semenovich)
1905-1964 . . . . **CLC 41**
See also CA 124; 130; MTCW

Grove, Frederick Philip . . . . **TCLC 4**
See also Greve, Felix Paul (Berthold
Friedrich)
See also DLB 92

Grubb
See Crumb, R(obert)

Grumbach, Doris (Isaac)
1918- . . . . **CLC 13, 22, 64**
See also CA 5-8R; CAAS 2; CANR 9, 42;
INT CANR-9

Grundtvig, Nicolai Frederik Severin
1783-1872 . . . . **NCLC 1**

Grunge
See Crumb, R(obert)

Grunwald, Lisa 1959- . . . . **CLC 44**
See also CA 120

Guare, John
1938- . . . . **CLC 8, 14, 29, 67;
DAM DRAM**
See also CA 73-76; CANR 21; DLB 7;
MTCW

Gudjonsson, Halldor Kiljan 1902-
See Laxness, Halldor
See also CA 103

Guenter, Erich
See Eich, Guenter

Guest, Barbara 1920- . . . . **CLC 34**
See also CA 25-28R; CANR 11, 44; DLB 5

Guest, Judith (Ann)
1936- . . . . **CLC 8, 30; DAM NOV, POP**
See also AAYA 7; CA 77-80; CANR 15;
INT CANR-15; MTCW

Guevara, Che . . . . **CLC 87; HLC**
See also Guevara (Serna), Ernesto

Guevara (Serna), Ernesto 1928-1967
See Guevara, Che
See also CA 127; 111; CANR 56;
DAM MULT; HW

Guild, Nicholas M. 1944- . . . . **CLC 33**
See also CA 93-96

Guillemin, Jacques
See Sartre, Jean-Paul

Guillen, Jorge
1893-1984 . . . . . . **CLC 11; DAM MULT,
POET**
See also CA 89-92; 112; DLB 108; HW

Guillen, Nicolas (Cristobal)
1902-1989 . . . . **CLC 48, 79; BLC;
DAM MST, MULT, POET; HLC**
See also BW 2; CA 116; 125; 129; HW

Guillevic, (Eugene) 1907- . . . . **CLC 33**
See also CA 93-96

Guillois
See Desnos, Robert

Guillois, Valentin
See Desnos, Robert

Guiney, Louise Imogen
1861-1920 . . . . **TCLC 41**
See also DLB 54

Guiraldes, Ricardo (Guillermo)
1886-1927 . . . . **TCLC 39**
See also CA 131; HW; MTCW

Gumilev, Nikolai Stephanovich
1886-1921 . . . . **TCLC 60**

Gunesekera, Romesh . . . . **CLC 91**

Gunn, Bill . . . . **CLC 5**
See also Gunn, William Harrison
See also DLB 38

Gunn, Thom(son William)
1929- . . . . **CLC 3, 6, 18, 32, 81;
DAM POET**
See also CA 17-20R; CANR 9, 33;
CDBLB 1960 to Present; DLB 27;
INT CANR-33; MTCW

Gunn, William Harrison 1934(?)-1989
See Gunn, Bill
See also AITN 1; BW 1; CA 13-16R; 128;
CANR 12, 25

Gunnars, Kristjana 1948- . . . . **CLC 69**
See also CA 113; DLB 60

Gurganus, Allan
1947- . . . . **CLC 70; DAM POP**
See also BEST 90:1; CA 135

Gurney, A(lbert) R(amsdell), Jr.
1930- . . . . **CLC 32, 50, 54; DAM DRAM**
See also CA 77-80; CANR 32

Harling, Robert 1951(?)- . . . . **CLC 53**
See also CA 147

Harmon, William (Ruth) 1938- . . . . . **CLC 38**
See also CA 33-36R; CANR 14, 32, 35;
SATA 65

Harper, F. E. W.
See Harper, Frances Ellen Watkins

Harper, Frances E. W.
See Harper, Frances Ellen Watkins

Harper, Frances E. Watkins
See Harper, Frances Ellen Watkins

Harper, Frances Ellen
See Harper, Frances Ellen Watkins

Harper, Frances Ellen Watkins
1825-1911 . . . . **TCLC 14; BLC;**
DAM MULT, POET
See also BW 1; CA 111; 125; DLB 50

Harper, Michael S(teven) 1938- . . **CLC 7, 22**
See also BW 1; CA 33-36R; CANR 24;
DLB 41

Harper, Mrs. F. E. W.
See Harper, Frances Ellen Watkins

Harris, Christie (Lucy) Irwin
1907- . . . . **CLC 12**
See also CA 5-8R; CANR 6; DLB 88;
JRDA; MAICYA; SAAS 10; SATA 6, 74

Harris, Frank 1856-1931 . . . . **TCLC 24**
See also CA 109; 150; DLB 156

Harris, George Washington
1814-1869 . . . . **NCLC 23**
See also DLB 3, 11

Harris, Joel Chandler
1848-1908 . . . . **TCLC 2; SSC 19**
See also CA 104; 137; DLB 11, 23, 42, 78,
91; MAICYA; YABC 1

Harris, John (Wyndham Parkes Lucas)
Beynon 1903-1969
See Wyndham, John
See also CA 102; 89-92

Harris, MacDonald . . . . **CLC 9**
See also Heiney, Donald (William)

Harris, Mark 1922- . . . . **CLC 19**
See also CA 5-8R; CAAS 3; CANR 2, 55;
DLB 2; DLBY 80

Harris, (Theodore) Wilson 1921- . . . . **CLC 25**
See also BW 2; CA 65-68; CAAS 16;
CANR 11, 27; DLB 117; MTCW

Harrison, Elizabeth Cavanna 1909-
See Cavanna, Betty
See also CA 9-12R; CANR 6, 27

Harrison, Harry (Max) 1925- . . . . . . **CLC 42**
See also CA 1-4R; CANR 5, 21; DLB 8;
SATA 4

Harrison, James (Thomas)
1937- . . . . . . **CLC 6, 14, 33, 66; SSC 19**
See also CA 13-16R; CANR 8, 51;
DLBY 82; INT CANR-8

Harrison, Jim
See Harrison, James (Thomas)

Harrison, Kathryn 1961- . . . . **CLC 70**
See also CA 144

Harrison, Tony 1937- . . . . **CLC 43**
See also CA 65-68; CANR 44; DLB 40;
MTCW

Harriss, Will(ard Irvin) 1922- . . . . . . **CLC 34**
See also CA 111

Harson, Sley
See Ellison, Harlan (Jay)

Hart, Ellis
See Ellison, Harlan (Jay)

Hart, Josephine
1942(?)- . . . . **CLC 70; DAM POP**
See also CA 138

Hart, Moss
1904-1961 . . . . . . **CLC 66; DAM DRAM**
See also CA 109; 89-92; DLB 7

Harte, (Francis) Bret(t)
1836(?)-1902 . . . . **TCLC 1, 25; DA; DAC;**
DAM MST; SSC 8; WLC
See also CA 104; 140; CDALB 1865-1917;
DLB 12, 64, 74, 79; SATA 26

Hartley, L(eslie) P(oles)
1895-1972 . . . . **CLC 2, 22**
See also CA 45-48; 37-40R; CANR 33;
DLB 15, 139; MTCW

Hartman, Geoffrey H. 1929- . . . . **CLC 27**
See also CA 117; 125; DLB 67

Hartmann von Aue
c. 1160-c. 1205 . . . . **CMLC 15**
See also DLB 138

Hartmann von Aue 1170-1210 . . . . **CMLC 15**

Haruf, Kent 1943- . . . . **CLC 34**
See also CA 149

Harwood, Ronald
1934- . . . . **CLC 32; DAM DRAM, MST**
See also CA 1-4R; CANR 4, 55; DLB 13

Hasek, Jaroslav (Matej Frantisek)
1883-1923 . . . . **TCLC 4**
See also CA 104; 129; MTCW

Hass, Robert
1941- . . . . **CLC 18, 39, 99; PC 16**
See also CA 111; CANR 30, 50; DLB 105

Hastings, Hudson
See Kuttner, Henry

Hastings, Selina . . . . **CLC 44**

Hatteras, Amelia
See Mencken, H(enry) L(ouis)

Hatteras, Owen . . . . **TCLC 18**
See also Mencken, H(enry) L(ouis); Nathan,
George Jean

Hauptmann, Gerhart (Johann Robert)
1862-1946 . . . . . . **TCLC 4; DAM DRAM**
See also CA 104; 153; DLB 66, 118

Havel, Vaclav
1936- . . . . **CLC 25, 58, 65;**
DAM DRAM; DC 6
See also CA 104; CANR 36; MTCW

Haviaras, Stratis . . . . **CLC 33**
See also Chaviaras, Strates

Hawes, Stephen 1475(?)-1523(?) . . . . . **LC 17**

Hawkes, John (Clendennin Burne, Jr.)
1925- . . . . . . **CLC 1, 2, 3, 4, 7, 9, 14, 15,**
27, 49
See also CA 1-4R; CANR 2, 47; DLB 2, 7;
DLBY 80; MTCW

Hawking, S. W.
See Hawking, Stephen W(illiam)

Hawking, Stephen W(illiam)
1942- . . . . **CLC 63**
See also AAYA 13; BEST 89:1; CA 126;
129; CANR 48

Hawthorne, Julian 1846-1934 . . . . . **TCLC 25**

Hawthorne, Nathaniel
1804-1864 . . . . **NCLC 39; DA; DAB;**
DAC; DAM MST, NOV; SSC 3; WLC
See also AAYA 18; CDALB 1640-1865;
DLB 1, 74; YABC 2

Haxton, Josephine Ayres 1921-
See Douglas, Ellen
See also CA 115; CANR 41

Hayaseca y Eizaguirre, Jorge
See Echegaray (y Eizaguirre), Jose (Maria
Waldo)

Hayashi Fumiko 1904-1951 . . . . **TCLC 27**

Haycraft, Anna
See Ellis, Alice Thomas
See also CA 122

Hayden, Robert E(arl)
1913-1980 . . . . . . **CLC 5, 9, 14, 37; BLC;**
DA; DAC; DAM MST, MULT, POET;
PC 6
See also BW 1; CA 69-72; 97-100; CABS 2;
CANR 24; CDALB 1941-1968; DLB 5,
76; MTCW; SATA 19; SATA-Obit 26

Hayford, J(oseph) E(phraim) Casely
See Casely-Hayford, J(oseph) E(phraim)

Hayman, Ronald 1932- . . . . **CLC 44**
See also CA 25-28R; CANR 18, 50;
DLB 155

Haywood, Eliza (Fowler)
1693(?)-1756 . . . . **LC 1**

Hazlitt, William 1778-1830 . . . . . . **NCLC 29**
See also DLB 110, 158

Hazzard, Shirley 1931- . . . . **CLC 18**
See also CA 9-12R; CANR 4; DLBY 82;
MTCW

Head, Bessie
1937-1986 . . . . **CLC 25, 67; BLC;**
DAM MULT
See also BW 2; CA 29-32R; 119; CANR 25;
DLB 117; MTCW

Headon, (Nicky) Topper 1956(?)- . . . **CLC 30**

Heaney, Seamus (Justin)
1939- . . . . . . **CLC 5, 7, 14, 25, 37, 74, 91;**
DAB; DAM POET
See also CA 85-88; CANR 25, 48;
CDBLB 1960 to Present; DLB 40;
DLBY 95; MTCW

Hearn, (Patricio) Lafcadio (Tessima Carlos)
1850-1904 . . . . **TCLC 9**
See also CA 105; DLB 12, 78

Hearne, Vicki 1946- . . . . **CLC 56**
See also CA 139

Hearon, Shelby 1931- . . . . **CLC 63**
See also AITN 2; CA 25-28R; CANR 18,
48

Heat-Moon, William Least . . . . **CLC 29**
See also Trogdon, William (Lewis)
See also AAYA 9

Hebbel, Friedrich
1813-1863 . . . . **NCLC 43; DAM DRAM**
See also DLB 129

Hichens, Robert S.   1864-1950..... **TCLC 64**
See also DLB 153

Higgins, George V(incent)
1939-................**CLC 4, 7, 10, 18**
See also CA 77-80; CAAS 5; CANR 17, 51;
DLB 2; DLBY 81; INT CANR-17;
MTCW

Higginson, Thomas Wentworth
1823-1911.................**TCLC 36**
See also DLB 1, 64

Highet, Helen
See MacInnes, Helen (Clark)

Highsmith, (Mary) Patricia
1921-1995..........**CLC 2, 4, 14, 42;**
DAM NOV, POP
See also CA 1-4R; 147; CANR 1, 20, 48;
MTCW

Highwater, Jamake (Mamake)
1942(?)-.....................**CLC 12**
See also AAYA 7; CA 65-68; CAAS 7;
CANR 10, 34; CLR 17; DLB 52;
DLBY 85; JRDA; MAICYA; SATA 32,
69; SATA-Brief 30

Highway, Tomson
1951-..... **CLC 92; DAC; DAM MULT**
See also CA 151; NNAL

Higuchi, Ichiyo   1872-1896....... **NCLC 49**

Hijuelos, Oscar
1951-.... **CLC 65; DAM MULT, POP;**
HLC
See also BEST 90:1; CA 123; CANR 50;
DLB 145; HW

Hikmet, Nazim   1902(?)-1963....... **CLC 40**
See also CA 141; 93-96

Hildegard von Bingen
1098-1179.................**CMLC 20**
See also DLB 148

Hildesheimer, Wolfgang
1916-1991..................**CLC 49**
See also CA 101; 135; DLB 69, 124

Hill, Geoffrey (William)
1932-... **CLC 5, 8, 18, 45; DAM POET**
See also CA 81-84; CANR 21;
CDBLB 1960 to Present; DLB 40;
MTCW

Hill, George Roy   1921-........... **CLC 26**
See also CA 110; 122

Hill, John
See Koontz, Dean R(ay)

Hill, Susan (Elizabeth)
1942-.. **CLC 4; DAB; DAM MST, NOV**
See also CA 33-36R; CANR 29; DLB 14,
139; MTCW

Hillerman, Tony
1925-............**CLC 62; DAM POP**
See also AAYA 6; BEST 89:1; CA 29-32R;
CANR 21, 42; SATA 6

Hillesum, Etty   1914-1943........ **TCLC 49**
See also CA 137

Hilliard, Noel (Harvey)   1929-...... **CLC 15**
See also CA 9-12R; CANR 7

Hillis, Rick   1956-.................**CLC 66**
See also CA 134

Hilton, James   1900-1954......... **TCLC 21**
See also CA 108; DLB 34, 77; SATA 34

Himes, Chester (Bomar)
1909-1984.... **CLC 2, 4, 7, 18, 58; BLC;**
DAM MULT
See also BW 2; CA 25-28R; 114; CANR 22;
DLB 2, 76, 143; MTCW

Hinde, Thomas.................**CLC 6, 11**
See also Chitty, Thomas Willes

Hindin, Nathan
See Bloch, Robert (Albert)

Hine, (William) Daryl   1936-....... **CLC 15**
See also CA 1-4R; CAAS 15; CANR 1, 20;
DLB 60

Hinkson, Katharine Tynan
See Tynan, Katharine

Hinton, S(usan) E(loise)
1950-........**CLC 30; DA; DAB; DAC;**
DAM MST, NOV
See also AAYA 2; CA 81-84; CANR 32;
CLR 3, 23; JRDA; MAICYA; MTCW;
SATA 19, 58

Hippius, Zinaida.................**TCLC 9**
See also Gippius, Zinaida (Nikolayevna)

Hiraoka, Kimitake   1925-1970
See Mishima, Yukio
See also CA 97-100; 29-32R; DAM DRAM;
MTCW

Hirsch, E(ric) D(onald), Jr.   1928-... **CLC 79**
See also CA 25-28R; CANR 27, 51;
DLB 67; INT CANR-27; MTCW

Hirsch, Edward   1950-......... **CLC 31, 50**
See also CA 104; CANR 20, 42; DLB 120

Hitchcock, Alfred (Joseph)
1899-1980.................**CLC 16**
See also CA 97-100; SATA 27;
SATA-Obit 24

Hitler, Adolf   1889-1945.......... **TCLC 53**
See also CA 117; 147

Hoagland, Edward   1932-.......... **CLC 28**
See also CA 1-4R; CANR 2, 31, 57; DLB 6;
SATA 51

Hoban, Russell (Conwell)
1925-..........**CLC 7, 25; DAM NOV**
See also CA 5-8R; CANR 23, 37; CLR 3;
DLB 52; MAICYA; MTCW; SATA 1,
40, 78

Hobbes, Thomas   1588-1679......... **LC 36**
See also DLB 151

Hobbs, Perry
See Blackmur, R(ichard) P(almer)

Hobson, Laura Z(ametkin)
1900-1986.................**CLC 7, 25**
See also CA 17-20R; 118; CANR 55;
DLB 28; SATA 52

Hochhuth, Rolf
1931-..... **CLC 4, 11, 18; DAM DRAM**
See also CA 5-8R; CANR 33; DLB 124;
MTCW

Hochman, Sandra   1936-.......... **CLC 3, 8**
See also CA 5-8R; DLB 5

Hochwaelder, Fritz
1911-1986...... **CLC 36; DAM DRAM**
See also CA 29-32R; 120; CANR 42;
MTCW

Hochwalder, Fritz
See Hochwaelder, Fritz

Hocking, Mary (Eunice)   1921-..... **CLC 13**
See also CA 101; CANR 18, 40

Hodgins, Jack   1938-.............. **CLC 23**
See also CA 93-96; DLB 60

Hodgson, William Hope
1877(?)-1918.............**TCLC 13**
See also CA 111; DLB 70, 153, 156

Hoeg, Peter   1957-................ **CLC 95**
See also CA 151

Hoffman, Alice
1952-............ **CLC 51; DAM NOV**
See also CA 77-80; CANR 34; MTCW

Hoffman, Daniel (Gerard)
1923-..................**CLC 6, 13, 23**
See also CA 1-4R; CANR 4; DLB 5

Hoffman, Stanley   1944-............ **CLC 5**
See also CA 77-80

Hoffman, William M(oses)   1939-... **CLC 40**
See also CA 57-60; CANR 11

Hoffmann, E(rnst) T(heodor) A(madeus)
1776-1822............**NCLC 2; SSC 13**
See also DLB 90; SATA 27

Hofmann, Gert   1931-............. **CLC 54**
See also CA 128

Hofmannsthal, Hugo von
1874-1929.... **TCLC 11; DAM DRAM;**
DC 4
See also CA 106; 153; DLB 81, 118

Hogan, Linda
1947-.......... **CLC 73; DAM MULT**
See also CA 120; CANR 45; DLB 175;
NNAL

Hogarth, Charles
See Creasey, John

Hogarth, Emmett
See Polonsky, Abraham (Lincoln)

Hogg, James   1770-1835........... **NCLC 4**
See also DLB 93, 116, 159

Holbach, Paul Henri Thiry Baron
1723-1789...................**LC 14**

Holberg, Ludvig   1684-1754.......... **LC 6**

Holden, Ursula   1921-............. **CLC 18**
See also CA 101; CAAS 8; CANR 22

Holderlin, (Johann Christian) Friedrich
1770-1843............**NCLC 16; PC 4**

Holdstock, Robert
See Holdstock, Robert P.

Holdstock, Robert P.   1948-........ **CLC 39**
See also CA 131

Holland, Isabelle   1920-........... **CLC 21**
See also AAYA 11; CA 21-24R; CANR 10,
25, 47; JRDA; MAICYA; SATA 8, 70

Holland, Marcus
See Caldwell, (Janet Miriam) Taylor
(Holland)

Hollander, John   1929-...... **CLC 2, 5, 8, 14**
See also CA 1-4R; CANR 1, 52; DLB 5;
SATA 13

Hollander, Paul
See Silverberg, Robert

Holleran, Andrew   1943(?)-........ **CLC 38**
See also CA 144

Hollinghurst, Alan   1954-....... **CLC 55, 91**
See also CA 114

Hollis, Jim
See Summers, Hollis (Spurgeon, Jr.)

Holly, Buddy 1936-1959 . . . . **TCLC 65**

Holmes, John
See Souster, (Holmes) Raymond

Holmes, John Clellon 1926-1988. . . . **CLC 56**
See also CA 9-12R; 125; CANR 4; DLB 16

Holmes, Oliver Wendell
1809-1894 . . . . **NCLC 14**
See also CDALB 1640-1865; DLB 1;
SATA 34

Holmes, Raymond
See Souster, (Holmes) Raymond

Holt, Victoria
See Hibbert, Eleanor Alice Burford

Holub, Miroslav 1923-. . . . . **CLC 4**
See also CA 21-24R; CANR 10

Homer
c. 8th cent. B.C.-. . . . . **CMLC 1, 16; DA;
DAB; DAC; DAM MST, POET**

Honig, Edwin 1919- . . . . **CLC 33**
See also CA 5-8R; CAAS 8; CANR 4, 45;
DLB 5

Hood, Hugh (John Blagdon)
1928- . . . . **CLC 15, 28**
See also CA 49-52; CAAS 17; CANR 1, 33;
DLB 53

Hood, Thomas 1799-1845. . . . . . . **NCLC 16**
See also DLB 96

Hooker, (Peter) Jeremy 1941-. . . . . . **CLC 43**
See also CA 77-80; CANR 22; DLB 40

hooks, bell . . . . **CLC 94**
See also Watkins, Gloria

Hope, A(lec) D(erwent) 1907- . . . . **CLC 3, 51**
See also CA 21-24R; CANR 33; MTCW

Hope, Brian
See Creasey, John

Hope, Christopher (David Tully)
1944- . . . . **CLC 52**
See also CA 106; CANR 47; SATA 62

Hopkins, Gerard Manley
1844-1889 . . . . **NCLC 17; DA; DAB;
DAC; DAM MST, POET; PC 15; WLC**
See also CDBLB 1890-1914; DLB 35, 57

Hopkins, John (Richard) 1931-. . . . . . **CLC 4**
See also CA 85-88

Hopkins, Pauline Elizabeth
1859-1930 . . . . **TCLC 28; BLC;
DAM MULT**
See also BW 2; CA 141; DLB 50

Hopkinson, Francis 1737-1791 . . . . . . **LC 25**
See also DLB 31

Hopley-Woolrich, Cornell George 1903-1968
See Woolrich, Cornell
See also CA 13-14; CAP 1

Horatio
See Proust, (Valentin-Louis-George-Eugene-)
Marcel

Horgan, Paul (George Vincent O'Shaughnessy)
1903-1995 . . . . . . **CLC 9, 53; DAM NOV**
See also CA 13-16R; 147; CANR 9, 35;
DLB 102; DLBY 85; INT CANR-9;
MTCW; SATA 13; SATA-Obit 84

Horn, Peter
See Kuttner, Henry

Hornem, Horace Esq.
See Byron, George Gordon (Noel)

Hornung, E(rnest) W(illiam)
1866-1921 . . . . **TCLC 59**
See also CA 108; DLB 70

Horovitz, Israel (Arthur)
1939- . . . . **CLC 56; DAM DRAM**
See also CA 33-36R; CANR 46; DLB 7

Horvath, Odon von
See Horvath, Oedoen von
See also DLB 85, 124

Horvath, Oedoen von 1901-1938. . . **TCLC 45**
See also Horvath, Odon von
See also CA 118

Horwitz, Julius 1920-1986. . . . . **CLC 14**
See also CA 9-12R; 119; CANR 12

Hospital, Janette Turner 1942-. . . . . **CLC 42**
See also CA 108; CANR 48

Hostos, E. M. de
See Hostos (y Bonilla), Eugenio Maria de

Hostos, Eugenio M. de
See Hostos (y Bonilla), Eugenio Maria de

Hostos, Eugenio Maria
See Hostos (y Bonilla), Eugenio Maria de

Hostos (y Bonilla), Eugenio Maria de
1839-1903 . . . . **TCLC 24**
See also CA 123; 131; HW

Houdini
See Lovecraft, H(oward) P(hillips)

Hougan, Carolyn 1943- . . . . **CLC 34**
See also CA 139

Household, Geoffrey (Edward West)
1900-1988 . . . . **CLC 11**
See also CA 77-80; 126; DLB 87; SATA 14;
SATA-Obit 59

Housman, A(lfred) E(dward)
1859-1936 . . . . . . **TCLC 1, 10; DA; DAB;
DAC; DAM MST, POET; PC 2**
See also CA 104; 125; DLB 19; MTCW

Housman, Laurence 1865-1959 . . . . . **TCLC 7**
See also CA 106; 155; DLB 10; SATA 25

Howard, Elizabeth Jane 1923- . . . **CLC 7, 29**
See also CA 5-8R; CANR 8

Howard, Maureen 1930- . . . . . **CLC 5, 14, 46**
See also CA 53-56; CANR 31; DLBY 83;
INT CANR-31; MTCW

Howard, Richard 1929- . . . . . . **CLC 7, 10, 47**
See also AITN 1; CA 85-88; CANR 25;
DLB 5; INT CANR-25

Howard, Robert Ervin 1906-1936. . . **TCLC 8**
See also CA 105

Howard, Warren F.
See Pohl, Frederik

Howe, Fanny 1940- . . . . **CLC 47**
See also CA 117; SATA-Brief 52

Howe, Irving 1920-1993. . . . . **CLC 85**
See also CA 9-12R; 141; CANR 21, 50;
DLB 67; MTCW

Howe, Julia Ward 1819-1910 . . . . . **TCLC 21**
See also CA 117; DLB 1

Howe, Susan 1937-. . . . . **CLC 72**
See also DLB 120

Howe, Tina 1937-. . . . . **CLC 48**
See also CA 109

Howell, James 1594(?)-1666 . . . . **LC 13**
See also DLB 151

Howells, W. D.
See Howells, William Dean

Howells, William D.
See Howells, William Dean

Howells, William Dean
1837-1920 . . . . **TCLC 7, 17, 41**
See also CA 104; 134; CDALB 1865-1917;
DLB 12, 64, 74, 79

Howes, Barbara 1914-1996 . . . . **CLC 15**
See also CA 9-12R; 151; CAAS 3;
CANR 53; SATA 5

Hrabal, Bohumil 1914-. . . . . **CLC 13, 67**
See also CA 106; CAAS 12

Hsun, Lu
See Lu Hsun

Hubbard, L(afayette) Ron(ald)
1911-1986 . . . . **CLC 43; DAM POP**
See also CA 77-80; 118; CANR 52

Huch, Ricarda (Octavia)
1864-1947 . . . . **TCLC 13**
See also CA 111; DLB 66

Huddle, David 1942- . . . . **CLC 49**
See also CA 57-60; CAAS 20; DLB 130

Hudson, Jeffrey
See Crichton, (John) Michael

Hudson, W(illiam) H(enry)
1841-1922 . . . . **TCLC 29**
See also CA 115; DLB 98, 153, 174;
SATA 35

Hueffer, Ford Madox
See Ford, Ford Madox

Hughart, Barry 1934-. . . . . **CLC 39**
See also CA 137

Hughes, Colin
See Creasey, John

Hughes, David (John) 1930- . . . . **CLC 48**
See also CA 116; 129; DLB 14

Hughes, Edward James
See Hughes, Ted
See also DAM MST, POET

Hughes, (James) Langston
1902-1967 . . . . . **CLC 1, 5, 10, 15, 35, 44;
BLC; DA; DAB; DAC; DAM DRAM,
MST, MULT, POET; DC 3; PC 1;
SSC 6; WLC**
See also AAYA 12; BW 1; CA 1-4R;
25-28R; CANR 1, 34; CDALB 1929-1941;
CLR 17; DLB 4, 7, 48, 51, 86; JRDA;
MAICYA; MTCW; SATA 4, 33

Hughes, Richard (Arthur Warren)
1900-1976 . . . . . . **CLC 1, 11; DAM NOV**
See also CA 5-8R; 65-68; CANR 4;
DLB 15, 161; MTCW; SATA 8;
SATA-Obit 25

Hughes, Ted
1930- . . . . **CLC 2, 4, 9, 14, 37; DAB;
DAC; PC 7**
See also Hughes, Edward James
See also CA 1-4R; CANR 1, 33; CLR 3;
DLB 40, 161; MAICYA; MTCW;
SATA 49; SATA-Brief 27

Hugo, Richard F(ranklin)
　　1923-1982 . . . . CLC 6, 18, 32;
　　　　　　　　　　　　　　　　　DAM POET
　　See also CA 49-52; 108; CANR 3; DLB 5

Hugo, Victor (Marie)
　　1802-1885 . . . . NCLC 3, 10, 21; DA;
　　　　　DAB; DAC; DAM DRAM, MST, NOV,
　　　　　　　　　　　　POET; PC 17; WLC
　　See also DLB 119; SATA 47

Huidobro, Vicente
　　See Huidobro Fernandez, Vicente Garcia

Huidobro Fernandez, Vicente Garcia
　　1893-1948 . . . . TCLC 31
　　See also CA 131; HW

Hulme, Keri　1947- . . . . CLC 39
　　See also CA 125; INT 125

Hulme, T(homas) E(rnest)
　　1883-1917 . . . . TCLC 21
　　See also CA 117; DLB 19

Hume, David　1711-1776 . . . . LC 7
　　See also DLB 104

Humphrey, William　1924- . . . . CLC 45
　　See also CA 77-80; DLB 6

Humphreys, Emyr Owen　1919- . . . . . CLC 47
　　See also CA 5-8R; CANR 3, 24; DLB 15

Humphreys, Josephine　1945- . . . . CLC 34, 57
　　See also CA 121; 127; INT 127

Huneker, James Gibbons
　　1857-1921 . . . . TCLC 65
　　See also DLB 71

Hungerford, Pixie
　　See Brinsmead, H(esba) F(ay)

Hunt, E(verette) Howard, (Jr.)
　　1918- . . . . CLC 3
　　See also AITN 1; CA 45-48; CANR 2, 47

Hunt, Kyle
　　See Creasey, John

Hunt, (James Henry) Leigh
　　1784-1859 . . . . . . NCLC 1; DAM POET

Hunt, Marsha　1946- . . . . CLC 70
　　See also BW 2; CA 143

Hunt, Violet　1866-1942 . . . . TCLC 53
　　See also DLB 162

Hunter, E. Waldo
　　See Sturgeon, Theodore (Hamilton)

Hunter, Evan
　　1926- . . . . CLC 11, 31; DAM POP
　　See also CA 5-8R; CANR 5, 38; DLBY 82;
　　　　INT CANR-5; MTCW; SATA 25

Hunter, Kristin (Eggleston)　1931- . . . CLC 35
　　See also AITN 1; BW 1; CA 13-16R;
　　　　CANR 13; CLR 3; DLB 33;
　　　　INT CANR-13; MAICYA; SAAS 10;
　　　　SATA 12

Hunter, Mollie　1922- . . . . CLC 21
　　See also McIlwraith, Maureen Mollie
　　　　Hunter
　　See also AAYA 13; CANR 37; CLR 25;
　　　　DLB 161; JRDA; MAICYA; SAAS 7;
　　　　SATA 54

Hunter, Robert　(?)-1734 . . . . LC 7

Hurston, Zora Neale
　　1903-1960 . . . . CLC 7, 30, 61; BLC; DA;
　　　　DAC; DAM MST, MULT, NOV; SSC 4
　　See also AAYA 15; BW 1; CA 85-88;
　　　　DLB 51, 86; MTCW

Huston, John (Marcellus)
　　1906-1987 . . . . CLC 20
　　See also CA 73-76; 123; CANR 34; DLB 26

Hustvedt, Siri　1955- . . . . CLC 76
　　See also CA 137

Hutten, Ulrich von　1488-1523 . . . . LC 16

Huxley, Aldous (Leonard)
　　1894-1963 . . . . . CLC 1, 3, 4, 5, 8, 11, 18,
　　　　35, 79; DA; DAB; DAC; DAM MST,
　　　　　　　　　　　　　　　NOV; WLC
　　See also AAYA 11; CA 85-88; CANR 44;
　　　　CDBLB 1914-1945; DLB 36, 100, 162;
　　　　MTCW; SATA 63

Huysmans, Charles Marie Georges
　　1848-1907
　　See Huysmans, Joris-Karl
　　See also CA 104

Huysmans, Joris-Karl . . . . TCLC 7, 69
　　See also Huysmans, Charles Marie Georges
　　See also DLB 123

Hwang, David Henry
　　1957- . . . . CLC 55; DAM DRAM; DC 4
　　See also CA 127; 132; INT 132

Hyde, Anthony　1946- . . . . CLC 42
　　See also CA 136

Hyde, Margaret O(ldroyd)　1917- . . . CLC 21
　　See also CA 1-4R; CANR 1, 36; CLR 23;
　　　　JRDA; MAICYA; SAAS 8; SATA 1, 42,
　　　　76

Hynes, James　1956(?)- . . . . CLC 65

Ian, Janis　1951- . . . . CLC 21
　　See also CA 105

Ibanez, Vicente Blasco
　　See Blasco Ibanez, Vicente

Ibarguengoitia, Jorge　1928-1983 . . . . CLC 37
　　See also CA 124; 113; HW

Ibsen, Henrik (Johan)
　　1828-1906 . . . . . . TCLC 2, 8, 16, 37, 52;
　　　　DA; DAB; DAC; DAM DRAM, MST;
　　　　　　　　　　　　　　DC 2; WLC
　　See also CA 104; 141

Ibuse Masuji　1898-1993 . . . . CLC 22
　　See also CA 127; 141

Ichikawa, Kon　1915- . . . . CLC 20
　　See also CA 121

Idle, Eric　1943- . . . . CLC 21
　　See also Monty Python
　　See also CA 116; CANR 35

Ignatow, David　1914- . . . . . . CLC 4, 7, 14, 40
　　See also CA 9-12R; CAAS 3; CANR 31;
　　　　DLB 5

Ihimaera, Witi　1944- . . . . CLC 46
　　See also CA 77-80

Ilf, Ilya . . . . TCLC 21
　　See also Fainzilberg, Ilya Arnoldovich

Illyes, Gyula　1902-1983 . . . . PC 16
　　See also CA 114; 109

Immermann, Karl (Lebrecht)
　　1796-1840 . . . . NCLC 4, 49
　　See also DLB 133

Inclan, Ramon (Maria) del Valle
　　See Valle-Inclan, Ramon (Maria) del

Infante, G(uillermo) Cabrera
　　See Cabrera Infante, G(uillermo)

Ingalls, Rachel (Holmes)　1940- . . . . . CLC 42
　　See also CA 123; 127

Ingamells, Rex　1913-1955 . . . . TCLC 35

Inge, William (Motter)
　　1913-1973 . . CLC 1, 8, 19; DAM DRAM
　　See also CA 9-12R; CDALB 1941-1968;
　　　　DLB 7; MTCW

Ingelow, Jean　1820-1897 . . . . NCLC 39
　　See also DLB 35, 163; SATA 33

Ingram, Willis J.
　　See Harris, Mark

Innaurato, Albert (F.)　1948(?)- . . CLC 21, 60
　　See also CA 115; 122; INT 122

Innes, Michael
　　See Stewart, J(ohn) I(nnes) M(ackintosh)

Ionesco, Eugene
　　1909-1994 . . . . CLC 1, 4, 6, 9, 11, 15, 41,
　　　　86; DA; DAB; DAC; DAM DRAM,
　　　　　　　　　　　　　　MST; WLC
　　See also CA 9-12R; 144; CANR 55;
　　　　MTCW; SATA 7; SATA-Obit 79

Iqbal, Muhammad　1873-1938 . . . . . TCLC 28

Ireland, Patrick
　　See O'Doherty, Brian

Iron, Ralph
　　See Schreiner, Olive (Emilie Albertina)

Irving, John (Winslow)
　　1942- . . . . . CLC 13, 23, 38; DAM NOV,
　　　　　　　　　　　　　　　　　POP
　　See also AAYA 8; BEST 89:3; CA 25-28R;
　　　　CANR 28; DLB 6; DLBY 82; MTCW

Irving, Washington
　　1783-1859 . . . . . NCLC 2, 19; DA; DAB;
　　　　　　　　　　DAM MST; SSC 2; WLC
　　See also CDALB 1640-1865; DLB 3, 11, 30,
　　　　59, 73, 74; YABC 2

Irwin, P. K.
　　See Page, P(atricia) K(athleen)

Isaacs, Susan　1943- . . . CLC 32; DAM POP
　　See also BEST 89:1; CA 89-92; CANR 20,
　　　　41; INT CANR-20; MTCW

Isherwood, Christopher (William Bradshaw)
　　1904-1986 . . . . CLC 1, 9, 11, 14, 44;
　　　　　　　　　　　　　DAM DRAM, NOV
　　See also CA 13-16R; 117; CANR 35;
　　　　DLB 15; DLBY 86; MTCW

Ishiguro, Kazuo
　　1954- . . . . . . CLC 27, 56, 59; DAM NOV
　　See also BEST 90:2; CA 120; CANR 49;
　　　　MTCW

Ishikawa, Hakuhin
　　See Ishikawa, Takuboku

Ishikawa, Takuboku
　　1886(?)-1912 . . . . TCLC 15;
　　　　　　　　　　　DAM POET; PC 10
　　See also CA 113; 153

Iskander, Fazil　1929- . . . . CLC 47
　　See also CA 102

Isler, Alan . . . . CLC 91

Ivan IV　1530-1584 . . . . LC 17

Johnson, Benjamin F. of Boo
See Riley, James Whitcomb

Johnson, Charles (Richard)
1948- .... **CLC 7, 51, 65; BLC;
DAM MULT**
See also BW 2; CA 116; CAAS 18;
CANR 42; DLB 33

Johnson, Denis 1949- .... **CLC 52**
See also CA 117; 121; DLB 120

Johnson, Diane 1934- .... **CLC 5, 13, 48**
See also CA 41-44R; CANR 17, 40;
DLBY 80; INT CANR-17; MTCW

Johnson, Eyvind (Olof Verner)
1900-1976 .... **CLC 14**
See also CA 73-76; 69-72; CANR 34

Johnson, J. R.
See James, C(yril) L(ionel) R(obert)

Johnson, James Weldon
1871-1938 .... **TCLC 3, 19; BLC;
DAM MULT, POET**
See also BW 1; CA 104; 125;
CDALB 1917-1929; CLR 32; DLB 51;
MTCW; SATA 31

Johnson, Joyce 1935- .... **CLC 58**
See also CA 125; 129

Johnson, Lionel (Pigot)
1867-1902 .... **TCLC 19**
See also CA 117; DLB 19

Johnson, Mel
See Malzberg, Barry N(athaniel)

Johnson, Pamela Hansford
1912-1981 .... **CLC 1, 7, 27**
See also CA 1-4R; 104; CANR 2, 28;
DLB 15; MTCW

Johnson, Robert 1911(?)-1938 ..... **TCLC 69**

Johnson, Samuel
1709-1784 ..... **LC 15; DA; DAB; DAC;
DAM MST; WLC**
See also CDBLB 1660-1789; DLB 39, 95,
104, 142

Johnson, Uwe
1934-1984 .... **CLC 5, 10, 15, 40**
See also CA 1-4R; 112; CANR 1, 39;
DLB 75; MTCW

Johnston, George (Benson) 1913- ... **CLC 51**
See also CA 1-4R; CANR 5, 20; DLB 88

Johnston, Jennifer 1930- .... **CLC 7**
See also CA 85-88; DLB 14

Jolley, (Monica) Elizabeth
1923- .... **CLC 46; SSC 19**
See also CA 127; CAAS 13

Jones, Arthur Llewellyn 1863-1947
See Machen, Arthur
See also CA 104

Jones, D(ouglas) G(ordon) 1929- .... **CLC 10**
See also CA 29-32R; CANR 13; DLB 53

Jones, David (Michael)
1895-1974 .... **CLC 2, 4, 7, 13, 42**
See also CA 9-12R; 53-56; CANR 28;
CDBLB 1945-1960; DLB 20, 100; MTCW

Jones, David Robert 1947-
See Bowie, David
See also CA 103

Jones, Diana Wynne 1934- .... **CLC 26**
See also AAYA 12; CA 49-52; CANR 4,
26, 56; CLR 23; DLB 161; JRDA;
MAICYA; SAAS 7; SATA 9, 70

Jones, Edward P. 1950- .... **CLC 76**
See also BW 2; CA 142

Jones, Gayl
1949- .... **CLC 6, 9; BLC; DAM MULT**
See also BW 2; CA 77-80; CANR 27;
DLB 33; MTCW

Jones, James 1921-1977 .... **CLC 1, 3, 10, 39**
See also AITN 1, 2; CA 1-4R; 69-72;
CANR 6; DLB 2, 143; MTCW

Jones, John J.
See Lovecraft, H(oward) P(hillips)

Jones, LeRoi .... **CLC 1, 2, 3, 5, 10, 14**
See also Baraka, Amiri

Jones, Louis B. .... **CLC 65**
See also CA 141

Jones, Madison (Percy, Jr.) 1925- ... **CLC 4**
See also CA 13-16R; CAAS 11; CANR 7,
54; DLB 152

Jones, Mervyn 1922- .... **CLC 10, 52**
See also CA 45-48; CAAS 5; CANR 1;
MTCW

Jones, Mick 1956(?)- .... **CLC 30**

Jones, Nettie (Pearl) 1941- .... **CLC 34**
See also BW 2; CA 137; CAAS 20

Jones, Preston 1936-1979 .... **CLC 10**
See also CA 73-76; 89-92; DLB 7

Jones, Robert F(rancis) 1934- .... **CLC 7**
See also CA 49-52; CANR 2

Jones, Rod 1953- .... **CLC 50**
See also CA 128

Jones, Terence Graham Parry
1942- .... **CLC 21**
See also Jones, Terry; Monty Python
See also CA 112; 116; CANR 35; INT 116

Jones, Terry
See Jones, Terence Graham Parry
See also SATA 67; SATA-Brief 51

Jones, Thom 1945(?)- .... **CLC 81**

Jong, Erica
1942- .... **CLC 4, 6, 8, 18, 83;
DAM NOV, POP**
See also AITN 1; BEST 90:2; CA 73-76;
CANR 26, 52; DLB 2, 5, 28, 152;
INT CANR-26; MTCW

Jonson, Ben(jamin)
1572(?)-1637 ...... **LC 6, 33; DA; DAB;
DAC; DAM DRAM, MST, POET;
DC 4; PC 17; WLC**
See also CDBLB Before 1660; DLB 62, 121

Jordan, June
1936- ..... **CLC 5, 11, 23; DAM MULT,
POET**
See also AAYA 2; BW 2; CA 33-36R;
CANR 25; CLR 10; DLB 38; MAICYA;
MTCW; SATA 4

Jordan, Pat(rick M.) 1941- .... **CLC 37**
See also CA 33-36R

Jorgensen, Ivar
See Ellison, Harlan (Jay)

Jorgenson, Ivar
See Silverberg, Robert

Josephus, Flavius c. 37-100 ...... **CMLC 13**

Josipovici, Gabriel 1940- .... **CLC 6, 43**
See also CA 37-40R; CAAS 8; CANR 47;
DLB 14

Joubert, Joseph 1754-1824 .... **NCLC 9**

Jouve, Pierre Jean 1887-1976 ...... **CLC 47**
See also CA 65-68

Joyce, James (Augustine Aloysius)
1882-1941 .... **TCLC 3, 8, 16, 35, 52;
DA; DAB; DAC; DAM MST, NOV,
POET; SSC 3; WLC**
See also CA 104; 126; CDBLB 1914-1945;
DLB 10, 19, 36, 162; MTCW

Jozsef, Attila 1905-1937 .... **TCLC 22**
See also CA 116

Juana Ines de la Cruz 1651(?)-1695 ... **LC 5**

Judd, Cyril
See Kornbluth, C(yril) M.; Pohl, Frederik

Julian of Norwich 1342(?)-1416(?) .... **LC 6**
See also DLB 146

Juniper, Alex
See Hospital, Janette Turner

Junius
See Luxemburg, Rosa

Just, Ward (Swift) 1935- .... **CLC 4, 27**
See also CA 25-28R; CANR 32;
INT CANR-32

Justice, Donald (Rodney)
1925- .... **CLC 6, 19; DAM POET**
See also CA 5-8R; CANR 26, 54;
DLBY 83; INT CANR-26

Juvenal c. 55-c. 127 .... **CMLC 8**

Juvenis
See Bourne, Randolph S(illiman)

Kacew, Romain 1914-1980
See Gary, Romain
See also CA 108; 102

Kadare, Ismail 1936- .... **CLC 52**

Kadohata, Cynthia .... **CLC 59**
See also CA 140

Kafka, Franz
1883-1924 .... **TCLC 2, 6, 13, 29, 47, 53;
DA; DAB; DAC; DAM MST, NOV;
SSC 5; WLC**
See also CA 105; 126; DLB 81; MTCW

Kahanovitsch, Pinkhes
See Der Nister

Kahn, Roger 1927- .... **CLC 30**
See also CA 25-28R; CANR 44; DLB 171;
SATA 37

Kain, Saul
See Sassoon, Siegfried (Lorraine)

Kaiser, Georg 1878-1945 .... **TCLC 9**
See also CA 106; DLB 124

Kaletski, Alexander 1946- .... **CLC 39**
See also CA 118; 143

Kalidasa fl. c. 400- .... **CMLC 9**

Kallman, Chester (Simon)
1921-1975 .... **CLC 2**
See also CA 45-48; 53-56; CANR 3

Kaminsky, Melvin 1926-
See Brooks, Mel
See also CA 65-68; CANR 16

Kerry, Lois
See Duncan, Lois

Kesey, Ken (Elton)
1935- . . . . . . **CLC 1, 3, 6, 11, 46, 64; DA;
DAB; DAC; DAM MST, NOV, POP;
WLC**
See also CA 1-4R; CANR 22, 38;
CDALB 1968-1988; DLB 2, 16; MTCW;
SATA 66

Kesselring, Joseph (Otto)
1902-1967 . . . . . **CLC 45; DAM DRAM,
MST**
See also CA 150

Kessler, Jascha (Frederick) 1929- . . . . **CLC 4**
See also CA 17-20R; CANR 8, 48

Kettelkamp, Larry (Dale) 1933- . . . . **CLC 12**
See also CA 29-32R; CANR 16; SAAS 3;
SATA 2

Key, Ellen 1849-1926 . . . . **TCLC 65**

Keyber, Conny
See Fielding, Henry

Keyes, Daniel
1927- . . . . **CLC 80; DA; DAC;
DAM MST, NOV**
See also CA 17-20R; CANR 10, 26, 54;
SATA 37

Keynes, John Maynard
1883-1946 . . . . **TCLC 64**
See also CA 114; DLBD 10

Khanshendel, Chiron
See Rose, Wendy

Khayyam, Omar
1048-1131 . . . . **CMLC 11; DAM POET;
PC 8**

Kherdian, David 1931- . . . . **CLC 6, 9**
See also CA 21-24R; CAAS 2; CANR 39;
CLR 24; JRDA; MAICYA; SATA 16, 74

Khlebnikov, Velimir . . . . **TCLC 20**
See also Khlebnikov, Viktor Vladimirovich

Khlebnikov, Viktor Vladimirovich 1885-1922
See Khlebnikov, Velimir
See also CA 117

Khodasevich, Vladislav (Felitsianovich)
1886-1939 . . . . **TCLC 15**
See also CA 115

Kielland, Alexander Lange
1849-1906 . . . . **TCLC 5**
See also CA 104

Kiely, Benedict 1919- . . . . **CLC 23, 43**
See also CA 1-4R; CANR 2; DLB 15

Kienzle, William X(avier)
1928- . . . . **CLC 25; DAM POP**
See also CA 93-96; CAAS 1; CANR 9, 31;
INT CANR-31; MTCW

Kierkegaard, Soren 1813-1855 . . . . **NCLC 34**

Killens, John Oliver 1916-1987 . . . . . **CLC 10**
See also BW 2; CA 77-80; 123; CAAS 2;
CANR 26; DLB 33

Killigrew, Anne 1660-1685 . . . . **LC 4**
See also DLB 131

Kim
See Simenon, Georges (Jacques Christian)

Kincaid, Jamaica
1949- . . . . **CLC 43, 68; BLC;
DAM MULT, NOV**
See also AAYA 13; BW 2; CA 125;
CANR 47; DLB 157

King, Francis (Henry)
1923- . . . . **CLC 8, 53; DAM NOV**
See also CA 1-4R; CANR 1, 33; DLB 15,
139; MTCW

King, Martin Luther, Jr.
1929-1968 . . . . **CLC 83; BLC; DA; DAB;
DAC; DAM MST, MULT**
See also BW 2; CA 25-28; CANR 27, 44;
CAP 2; MTCW; SATA 14

King, Stephen (Edwin)
1947- . . . . **CLC 12, 26, 37, 61;
DAM NOV, POP; SSC 17**
See also AAYA 1, 17; BEST 90:1;
CA 61-64; CANR 1, 30, 52; DLB 143;
DLBY 80; JRDA; MTCW; SATA 9, 55

King, Steve
See King, Stephen (Edwin)

King, Thomas
1943- . . . . . **CLC 89; DAC; DAM MULT**
See also CA 144; DLB 175; NNAL

Kingman, Lee . . . . **CLC 17**
See also Natti, (Mary) Lee
See also SAAS 3; SATA 1, 67

Kingsley, Charles 1819-1875 . . . . . **NCLC 35**
See also DLB 21, 32, 163; YABC 2

Kingsley, Sidney 1906-1995 . . . . **CLC 44**
See also CA 85-88; 147; DLB 7

Kingsolver, Barbara
1955- . . . . **CLC 55, 81; DAM POP**
See also AAYA 15; CA 129; 134; INT 134

Kingston, Maxine (Ting Ting) Hong
1940- . . . . **CLC 12, 19, 58; DAM MULT,
NOV**
See also AAYA 8; CA 69-72; CANR 13,
38; DLB 173; DLBY 80; INT CANR-13;
MTCW; SATA 53

Kinnell, Galway
1927- . . . . **CLC 1, 2, 3, 5, 13, 29**
See also CA 9-12R; CANR 10, 34; DLB 5;
DLBY 87; INT CANR-34; MTCW

Kinsella, Thomas 1928- . . . . **CLC 4, 19**
See also CA 17-20R; CANR 15; DLB 27;
MTCW

Kinsella, W(illiam) P(atrick)
1935- . . . . **CLC 27, 43; DAC;
DAM NOV, POP**
See also AAYA 7; CA 97-100; CAAS 7;
CANR 21, 35; INT CANR-21; MTCW

Kipling, (Joseph) Rudyard
1865-1936 . . . . . . **TCLC 8, 17; DA; DAB;
DAC; DAM MST, POET; PC 3; SSC 5;
WLC**
See also CA 105; 120; CANR 33;
CDBLB 1890-1914; CLR 39; DLB 19, 34,
141, 156; MAICYA; MTCW; YABC 2

Kirkup, James 1918- . . . . **CLC 1**
See also CA 1-4R; CAAS 4; CANR 2;
DLB 27; SATA 12

Kirkwood, James 1930(?)-1989 . . . . . . **CLC 9**
See also AITN 2; CA 1-4R; 128; CANR 6,
40

Kirshner, Sidney
See Kingsley, Sidney

Kis, Danilo 1935-1989 . . . . **CLC 57**
See also CA 109; 118; 129; MTCW

Kivi, Aleksis 1834-1872 . . . . **NCLC 30**

Kizer, Carolyn (Ashley)
1925- . . . . . **CLC 15, 39, 80; DAM POET**
See also CA 65-68; CAAS 5; CANR 24;
DLB 5, 169

Klabund 1890-1928 . . . . **TCLC 44**
See also DLB 66

Klappert, Peter 1942- . . . . **CLC 57**
See also CA 33-36R; DLB 5

Klein, A(braham) M(oses)
1909-1972 . . . . **CLC 19; DAB; DAC;
DAM MST**
See also CA 101; 37-40R; DLB 68

Klein, Norma 1938-1989 . . . . **CLC 30**
See also AAYA 2; CA 41-44R; 128;
CANR 15, 37; CLR 2, 19;
INT CANR-15; JRDA; MAICYA;
SAAS 1; SATA 7, 57

Klein, T(heodore) E(ibon) D(onald)
1947- . . . . **CLC 34**
See also CA 119; CANR 44

Kleist, Heinrich von
1777-1811 . . . . **NCLC 2, 37;
DAM DRAM; SSC 22**
See also DLB 90

Klima, Ivan 1931- . . . . . **CLC 56; DAM NOV**
See also CA 25-28R; CANR 17, 50

Klimentov, Andrei Platonovich 1899-1951
See Platonov, Andrei
See also CA 108

Klinger, Friedrich Maximilian von
1752-1831 . . . . **NCLC 1**
See also DLB 94

Klopstock, Friedrich Gottlieb
1724-1803 . . . . **NCLC 11**
See also DLB 97

Knapp, Caroline 1959- . . . . **CLC 99**
See also CA 154

Knebel, Fletcher 1911-1993 . . . . **CLC 14**
See also AITN 1; CA 1-4R; 140; CAAS 3;
CANR 1, 36; SATA 36; SATA-Obit 75

Knickerbocker, Diedrich
See Irving, Washington

Knight, Etheridge
1931-1991 . . . . **CLC 40; BLC;
DAM POET; PC 14**
See also BW 1; CA 21-24R; 133; CANR 23;
DLB 41

Knight, Sarah Kemble 1666-1727 . . . . . **LC 7**
See also DLB 24

Knister, Raymond 1899-1932 . . . . . . **TCLC 56**
See also DLB 68

Knowles, John
1926- . . . . . . **CLC 1, 4, 10, 26; DA; DAC;
DAM MST, NOV**
See also AAYA 10; CA 17-20R; CANR 40;
CDALB 1968-1988; DLB 6; MTCW;
SATA 8, 89

Knox, Calvin M.
See Silverberg, Robert

La Colere, Francois
See Aragon, Louis

Lacolere, Francois
See Aragon, Louis

La Deshabilleuse
See Simenon, Georges (Jacques Christian)

Lady Gregory
See Gregory, Isabella Augusta (Persse)

Lady of Quality, A
See Bagnold, Enid

La Fayette, Marie (Madelaine Pioche de la Vergne Comtes 1634-1693 . . . . **LC 2**

Lafayette, Rene
See Hubbard, L(afayette) Ron(ald)

Laforgue, Jules
1860-1887 . . . . **NCLC 5, 53; PC 14; SSC 20**

Lagerkvist, Paer (Fabian)
1891-1974 . . . . **CLC 7, 10, 13, 54; DAM DRAM, NOV**
See also Lagerkvist, Par
See also CA 85-88; 49-52; MTCW

Lagerkvist, Par . . . . **SSC 12**
See also Lagerkvist, Paer (Fabian)

Lagerloef, Selma (Ottiliana Lovisa)
1858-1940 . . . . **TCLC 4, 36**
See also Lagerlof, Selma (Ottiliana Lovisa)
See also CA 108; SATA 15

Lagerlof, Selma (Ottiliana Lovisa)
See Lagerloef, Selma (Ottiliana Lovisa)
See also CLR 7; SATA 15

La Guma, (Justin) Alex(ander)
1925-1985 . . . . **CLC 19; DAM NOV**
See also BW 1; CA 49-52; 118; CANR 25; DLB 117; MTCW

Laidlaw, A. K.
See Grieve, C(hristopher) M(urray)

Lainez, Manuel Mujica
See Mujica Lainez, Manuel
See also HW

Laing, R(onald) D(avid)
1927-1989 . . . . **CLC 95**
See also CA 107; 129; CANR 34; MTCW

Lamartine, Alphonse (Marie Louis Prat) de
1790-1869 . . . . . **NCLC 11; DAM POET; PC 16**

Lamb, Charles
1775-1834 . . . . **NCLC 10; DA; DAB; DAC; DAM MST; WLC**
See also CDBLB 1789-1832; DLB 93, 107, 163; SATA 17

Lamb, Lady Caroline 1785-1828 . . **NCLC 38**
See also DLB 116

Lamming, George (William)
1927- . . . . **CLC 2, 4, 66; BLC; DAM MULT**
See also BW 2; CA 85-88; CANR 26; DLB 125; MTCW

L'Amour, Louis (Dearborn)
1908-1988 . . . . **CLC 25, 55; DAM NOV, POP**
See also AAYA 16; AITN 2; BEST 89:2; CA 1-4R; 125; CANR 3, 25, 40; DLBY 80; MTCW

Lampedusa, Giuseppe (Tomasi) di . . . **TCLC 13**
See also Tomasi di Lampedusa, Giuseppe

Lampman, Archibald 1861-1899 . . **NCLC 25**
See also DLB 92

Lancaster, Bruce 1896-1963 . . . . **CLC 36**
See also CA 9-10; CAP 1; SATA 9

Lanchester, John . . . . **CLC 99**

Landau, Mark Alexandrovich
See Aldanov, Mark (Alexandrovich)

Landau-Aldanov, Mark Alexandrovich
See Aldanov, Mark (Alexandrovich)

Landis, Jerry
See Simon, Paul (Frederick)

Landis, John 1950- . . . . **CLC 26**
See also CA 112; 122

Landolfi, Tommaso 1908-1979 . . . **CLC 11, 49**
See also CA 127; 117

Landon, Letitia Elizabeth
1802-1838 . . . . **NCLC 15**
See also DLB 96

Landor, Walter Savage
1775-1864 . . . . **NCLC 14**
See also DLB 93, 107

Landwirth, Heinz 1927-
See Lind, Jakov
See also CA 9-12R; CANR 7

Lane, Patrick
1939- . . . . **CLC 25; DAM POET**
See also CA 97-100; CANR 54; DLB 53; INT 97-100

Lang, Andrew 1844-1912 . . . . **TCLC 16**
See also CA 114; 137; DLB 98, 141; MAICYA; SATA 16

Lang, Fritz 1890-1976 . . . . **CLC 20**
See also CA 77-80; 69-72; CANR 30

Lange, John
See Crichton, (John) Michael

Langer, Elinor 1939- . . . . **CLC 34**
See also CA 121

Langland, William
1330(?)-1400(?) . . . . . . **LC 19; DA; DAB; DAC; DAM MST, POET**
See also DLB 146

Langstaff, Launcelot
See Irving, Washington

Lanier, Sidney
1842-1881 . . . . . . **NCLC 6; DAM POET**
See also DLB 64; DLBD 13; MAICYA; SATA 18

Lanyer, Aemilia 1569-1645 . . . . . . **LC 10, 30**
See also DLB 121

Lao Tzu . . . . **CMLC 7**

Lapine, James (Elliot) 1949- . . . . **CLC 39**
See also CA 123; 130; CANR 54; INT 130

Larbaud, Valery (Nicolas)
1881-1957 . . . . **TCLC 9**
See also CA 106; 152

Lardner, Ring
See Lardner, Ring(gold) W(ilmer)

Lardner, Ring W., Jr.
See Lardner, Ring(gold) W(ilmer)

Lardner, Ring(gold) W(ilmer)
1885-1933 . . . . **TCLC 2, 14**
See also CA 104; 131; CDALB 1917-1929; DLB 11, 25, 86; MTCW

Laredo, Betty
See Codrescu, Andrei

Larkin, Maia
See Wojciechowska, Maia (Teresa)

Larkin, Philip (Arthur)
1922-1985 . . . . **CLC 3, 5, 8, 9, 13, 18, 33, 39, 64; DAB; DAM MST, POET**
See also CA 5-8R; 117; CANR 24; CDBLB 1960 to Present; DLB 27; MTCW

Larra (y Sanchez de Castro), Mariano Jose de
1809-1837 . . . . **NCLC 17**

Larsen, Eric 1941- . . . . **CLC 55**
See also CA 132

Larsen, Nella
1891-1964 . . . . **CLC 37; BLC; DAM MULT**
See also BW 1; CA 125; DLB 51

Larson, Charles R(aymond) 1938- . . . **CLC 31**
See also CA 53-56; CANR 4

Larson, Jonathan 1961(?)-1996 . . . . . **CLC 99**

Las Casas, Bartolome de 1474-1566 . . **LC 31**

Lasker-Schueler, Else 1869-1945 . . **TCLC 57**
See also DLB 66, 124

Latham, Jean Lee 1902- . . . . **CLC 12**
See also AITN 1; CA 5-8R; CANR 7; MAICYA; SATA 2, 68

Latham, Mavis
See Clark, Mavis Thorpe

Lathen, Emma . . . . **CLC 2**
See also Hennissart, Martha; Latsis, Mary J(ane)

Lathrop, Francis
See Leiber, Fritz (Reuter, Jr.)

Latsis, Mary J(ane)
See Lathen, Emma
See also CA 85-88

Lattimore, Richmond (Alexander)
1906-1984 . . . . **CLC 3**
See also CA 1-4R; 112; CANR 1

Laughlin, James 1914- . . . . **CLC 49**
See also CA 21-24R; CAAS 22; CANR 9, 47; DLB 48

Laurence, (Jean) Margaret (Wemyss)
1926-1987 . . . . **CLC 3, 6, 13, 50, 62; DAC; DAM MST; SSC 7**
See also CA 5-8R; 121; CANR 33; DLB 53; MTCW; SATA-Obit 50

Laurent, Antoine 1952- . . . . **CLC 50**

Lauscher, Hermann
See Hesse, Hermann

Lautreamont, Comte de
1846-1870 . . . . **NCLC 12; SSC 14**

Laverty, Donald
See Blish, James (Benjamin)

Lavin, Mary
1912-1996 . . . . **CLC 4, 18, 99; SSC 4**
See also CA 9-12R; 151; CANR 33; DLB 15; MTCW

L'Engle, Madeleine (Camp Franklin)
1918- .... **CLC 12; DAM POP**
See also AAYA 1; AITN 2; CA 1-4R;
CANR 3, 21, 39; CLR 1, 14; DLB 52;
JRDA; MAICYA; MTCW; SAAS 15;
SATA 1, 27, 75

Lengyel, Jozsef 1896-1975......... **CLC 7**
See also CA 85-88; 57-60

Lenin 1870-1924
See Lenin, V. I.
See also CA 121

Lenin, V. I. .... **TCLC 67**
See also Lenin

Lennon, John (Ono)
1940-1980 .... **CLC 12, 35**
See also CA 102

Lennox, Charlotte Ramsay
1729(?)-1804 .... **NCLC 23**
See also DLB 39

Lentricchia, Frank (Jr.) 1940-...... **CLC 34**
See also CA 25-28R; CANR 19

Lenz, Siegfried 1926- .... **CLC 27**
See also CA 89-92; DLB 75

Leonard, Elmore (John, Jr.)
1925- ...... **CLC 28, 34, 71; DAM POP**
See also AITN 1; BEST 89:1, 90:4;
CA 81-84; CANR 12, 28, 53; DLB 173;
INT CANR-28; MTCW

Leonard, Hugh.................... **CLC 19**
See also Byrne, John Keyes
See also DLB 13

Leonov, Leonid (Maximovich)
1899-1994 .... **CLC 92; DAM NOV**
See also CA 129; MTCW

Leopardi, (Conte) Giacomo
1798-1837 .... **NCLC 22**

Le Reveler
See Artaud, Antonin (Marie Joseph)

Lerman, Eleanor 1952-............ **CLC 9**
See also CA 85-88

Lerman, Rhoda 1936-............ **CLC 56**
See also CA 49-52

Lermontov, Mikhail Yuryevich
1814-1841 .... **NCLC 47**

Leroux, Gaston 1868-1927....... **TCLC 25**
See also CA 108; 136; SATA 65

Lesage, Alain-Rene 1668-1747...... **LC 28**

Leskov, Nikolai (Semyonovich)
1831-1895 .... **NCLC 25**

Lessing, Doris (May)
1919- ..... **CLC 1, 2, 3, 6, 10, 15, 22, 40,
94; DA; DAB; DAC; DAM MST, NOV;
SSC 6**
See also CA 9-12R; CAAS 14; CANR 33,
54; CDBLB 1960 to Present; DLB 15,
139; DLBY 85; MTCW

Lessing, Gotthold Ephraim
1729-1781 .... **LC 8**
See also DLB 97

Lester, Richard 1932-............ **CLC 20**

Lever, Charles (James)
1806-1872 .... **NCLC 23**
See also DLB 21

Leverson, Ada 1865(?)-1936(?) .... **TCLC 18**
See also Elaine
See also CA 117; DLB 153

Levertov, Denise
1923- ...... **CLC 1, 2, 3, 5, 8, 15, 28, 66;
DAM POET; PC 11**
See also CA 1-4R; CAAS 19; CANR 3, 29,
50; DLB 5, 165; INT CANR-29; MTCW

Levi, Jonathan.................... **CLC 76**

Levi, Peter (Chad Tigar) 1931-..... **CLC 41**
See also CA 5-8R; CANR 34; DLB 40

Levi, Primo
1919-1987 .... **CLC 37, 50; SSC 12**
See also CA 13-16R; 122; CANR 12, 33;
MTCW

Levin, Ira 1929- ..... **CLC 3, 6; DAM POP**
See also CA 21-24R; CANR 17, 44;
MTCW; SATA 66

Levin, Meyer
1905-1981 .... **CLC 7; DAM POP**
See also AITN 1; CA 9-12R; 104;
CANR 15; DLB 9, 28; DLBY 81;
SATA 21; SATA-Obit 27

Levine, Norman 1924- .... **CLC 54**
See also CA 73-76; CAAS 23; CANR 14;
DLB 88

Levine, Philip
1928- .... **CLC 2, 4, 5, 9, 14, 33;
DAM POET**
See also CA 9-12R; CANR 9, 37, 52;
DLB 5

Levinson, Deirdre 1931-........... **CLC 49**
See also CA 73-76

Levi-Strauss, Claude 1908- .... **CLC 38**
See also CA 1-4R; CANR 6, 32; MTCW

Levitin, Sonia (Wolff) 1934- .... **CLC 17**
See also AAYA 13; CA 29-32R; CANR 14,
32; JRDA; MAICYA; SAAS 2; SATA 4,
68

Levon, O. U.
See Kesey, Ken (Elton)

Levy, Amy 1861-1889........... **NCLC 59**
See also DLB 156

Lewes, George Henry
1817-1878 .... **NCLC 25**
See also DLB 55, 144

Lewis, Alun 1915-1944........... **TCLC 3**
See also CA 104; DLB 20, 162

Lewis, C. Day
See Day Lewis, C(ecil)

Lewis, C(live) S(taples)
1898-1963 ..... **CLC 1, 3, 6, 14, 27; DA;
DAB; DAC; DAM MST, NOV, POP;
WLC**
See also AAYA 3; CA 81-84; CANR 33;
CDBLB 1945-1960; CLR 3, 27; DLB 15,
100, 160; JRDA; MAICYA; MTCW;
SATA 13

Lewis, Janet 1899-.............. **CLC 41**
See also Winters, Janet Lewis
See also CA 9-12R; CANR 29; CAP 1;
DLBY 87

Lewis, Matthew Gregory
1775-1818 .... **NCLC 11**
See also DLB 39, 158

Lewis, (Harry) Sinclair
1885-1951 ..... **TCLC 4, 13, 23, 39; DA;
DAB; DAC; DAM MST, NOV; WLC**
See also CA 104; 133; CDALB 1917-1929;
DLB 9, 102; DLBD 1; MTCW

Lewis, (Percy) Wyndham
1884(?)-1957 .... **TCLC 2, 9**
See also CA 104; DLB 15

Lewisohn, Ludwig 1883-1955...... **TCLC 19**
See also CA 107; DLB 4, 9, 28, 102

Leyner, Mark 1956-.............. **CLC 92**
See also CA 110; CANR 28, 53

Lezama Lima, Jose
1910-1976 .... **CLC 4, 10; DAM MULT**
See also CA 77-80; DLB 113; HW

L'Heureux, John (Clarke) 1934-.... **CLC 52**
See also CA 13-16R; CANR 23, 45

Liddell, C. H.
See Kuttner, Henry

Lie, Jonas (Lauritz Idemil)
1833-1908(?) .... **TCLC 5**
See also CA 115

Lieber, Joel 1937-1971............ **CLC 6**
See also CA 73-76; 29-32R

Lieber, Stanley Martin
See Lee, Stan

Lieberman, Laurence (James)
1935- .... **CLC 4, 36**
See also CA 17-20R; CANR 8, 36

Lieksman, Anders
See Haavikko, Paavo Juhani

Li Fei-kan 1904-
See Pa Chin
See also CA 105

Lifton, Robert Jay 1926-.......... **CLC 67**
See also CA 17-20R; CANR 27;
INT CANR-27; SATA 66

Lightfoot, Gordon 1938-.......... **CLC 26**
See also CA 109

Lightman, Alan P. 1948- .... **CLC 81**
See also CA 141

Ligotti, Thomas (Robert)
1953- .... **CLC 44; SSC 16**
See also CA 123; CANR 49

Li Ho 791-817.................... **PC 13**

Liliencron, (Friedrich Adolf Axel) Detlev von
1844-1909 .... **TCLC 18**
See also CA 117

Lilly, William 1602-1681.......... **LC 27**

Lima, Jose Lezama
See Lezama Lima, Jose

Lima Barreto, Afonso Henrique de
1881-1922 .... **TCLC 23**
See also CA 117

Limonov, Edward 1944-........... **CLC 67**
See also CA 137

Lin, Frank
See Atherton, Gertrude (Franklin Horn)

Lincoln, Abraham 1809-1865..... **NCLC 18**

Lind, Jakov .... **CLC 1, 2, 4, 27, 82**
See also Landwirth, Heinz
See also CAAS 4

Loxsmith, John
See Brunner, John (Kilian Houston)

Loy, Mina . . . . **CLC 28; DAM POET; PC 16**
See also Lowry, Mina Gertrude
See also DLB 4, 54

Loyson-Bridet
See Schwob, (Mayer Andre) Marcel

Lucas, Craig 1951- . . . . **CLC 64**
See also CA 137

Lucas, George 1944- . . . . **CLC 16**
See also AAYA 1; CA 77-80; CANR 30;
SATA 56

Lucas, Hans
See Godard, Jean-Luc

Lucas, Victoria
See Plath, Sylvia

Ludlam, Charles 1943-1987 . . . . . **CLC 46, 50**
See also CA 85-88; 122

Ludlum, Robert
1927- . . . **CLC 22, 43; DAM NOV, POP**
See also AAYA 10; BEST 89:1, 90:3;
CA 33-36R; CANR 25, 41; DLBY 82;
MTCW

Ludwig, Ken . . . . **CLC 60**

Ludwig, Otto 1813-1865 . . . . **NCLC 4**
See also DLB 129

Lugones, Leopoldo 1874-1938 . . . . . **TCLC 15**
See also CA 116; 131; HW

Lu Hsun 1881-1936 . . . . . . **TCLC 3; SSC 20**
See also Shu-Jen, Chou

Lukacs, George . . . . **CLC 24**
See also Lukacs, Gyorgy (Szegeny von)

Lukacs, Gyorgy (Szegeny von) 1885-1971
See Lukacs, George
See also CA 101; 29-32R

Luke, Peter (Ambrose Cyprian)
1919-1995 . . . . **CLC 38**
See also CA 81-84; 147; DLB 13

Lunar, Dennis
See Mungo, Raymond

Lurie, Alison 1926- . . . . **CLC 4, 5, 18, 39**
See also CA 1-4R; CANR 2, 17, 50; DLB 2;
MTCW; SATA 46

Lustig, Arnost 1926- . . . . **CLC 56**
See also AAYA 3; CA 69-72; CANR 47;
SATA 56

Luther, Martin 1483-1546 . . . . **LC 9, 37**

Luxemburg, Rosa 1870(?)-1919 . . . . **TCLC 63**
See also CA 118

Luzi, Mario 1914- . . . . **CLC 13**
See also CA 61-64; CANR 9; DLB 128

L'Ymagier
See Gourmont, Remy (-Marie-Charles) de

Lynch, B. Suarez
See Bioy Casares, Adolfo; Borges, Jorge
Luis

Lynch, David (K.) 1946- . . . . **CLC 66**
See also CA 124; 129

Lynch, James
See Andreyev, Leonid (Nikolaevich)

Lynch Davis, B.
See Bioy Casares, Adolfo; Borges, Jorge
Luis

Lyndsay, Sir David 1490-1555 . . . . . . **LC 20**

Lynn, Kenneth S(chuyler) 1923- . . . . **CLC 50**
See also CA 1-4R; CANR 3, 27

Lynx
See West, Rebecca

Lyons, Marcus
See Blish, James (Benjamin)

Lyre, Pinchbeck
See Sassoon, Siegfried (Lorraine)

Lytle, Andrew (Nelson) 1902-1995 . . **CLC 22**
See also CA 9-12R; 150; DLB 6; DLBY 95

Lyttelton, George 1709-1773 . . . . **LC 10**

Maas, Peter 1929- . . . . **CLC 29**
See also CA 93-96; INT 93-96

Macaulay, Rose 1881-1958 . . . . . **TCLC 7, 44**
See also CA 104; DLB 36

Macaulay, Thomas Babington
1800-1859 . . . . **NCLC 42**
See also CDBLB 1832-1890; DLB 32, 55

MacBeth, George (Mann)
1932-1992 . . . . **CLC 2, 5, 9**
See also CA 25-28R; 136; DLB 40; MTCW;
SATA 4; SATA-Obit 70

MacCaig, Norman (Alexander)
1910- . . . . . **CLC 36; DAB; DAM POET**
See also CA 9-12R; CANR 3, 34; DLB 27

MacCarthy, (Sir Charles Otto) Desmond
1877-1952 . . . . **TCLC 36**

MacDiarmid, Hugh
. . . . **CLC 2, 4, 11, 19, 63; PC 9**
See also Grieve, C(hristopher) M(urray)
See also CDBLB 1945-1960; DLB 20

MacDonald, Anson
See Heinlein, Robert A(nson)

Macdonald, Cynthia 1928- . . . . . . **CLC 13, 19**
See also CA 49-52; CANR 4, 44; DLB 105

MacDonald, George 1824-1905 . . . . . **TCLC 9**
See also CA 106; 137; DLB 18, 163;
MAICYA; SATA 33

Macdonald, John
See Millar, Kenneth

MacDonald, John D(ann)
1916-1986 . . . . **CLC 3, 27, 44;
DAM NOV, POP**
See also CA 1-4R; 121; CANR 1, 19;
DLB 8; DLBY 86; MTCW

Macdonald, John Ross
See Millar, Kenneth

Macdonald, Ross . . . . . **CLC 1, 2, 3, 14, 34, 41**
See also Millar, Kenneth
See also DLBD 6

MacDougal, John
See Blish, James (Benjamin)

MacEwen, Gwendolyn (Margaret)
1941-1987 . . . . **CLC 13, 55**
See also CA 9-12R; 124; CANR 7, 22;
DLB 53; SATA 50; SATA-Obit 55

Macha, Karel Hynek 1810-1846 . . **NCLC 46**

Machado (y Ruiz), Antonio
1875-1939 . . . . **TCLC 3**
See also CA 104; DLB 108

Machado de Assis, Joaquim Maria
1839-1908 . . . . . **TCLC 10; BLC; SSC 24**
See also CA 107; 153

Machen, Arthur . . . . **TCLC 4; SSC 20**
See also Jones, Arthur Llewellyn
See also DLB 36, 156

Machiavelli, Niccolo
1469-1527 . . . . **LC 8, 36; DA; DAB;
DAC; DAM MST**

MacInnes, Colin 1914-1976 . . . . . . **CLC 4, 23**
See also CA 69-72; 65-68; CANR 21;
DLB 14; MTCW

MacInnes, Helen (Clark)
1907-1985 . . . . . **CLC 27, 39; DAM POP**
See also CA 1-4R; 117; CANR 1, 28;
DLB 87; MTCW; SATA 22;
SATA-Obit 44

Mackay, Mary 1855-1924
See Corelli, Marie
See also CA 118

Mackenzie, Compton (Edward Montague)
1883-1972 . . . . **CLC 18**
See also CA 21-22; 37-40R; CAP 2;
DLB 34, 100

Mackenzie, Henry 1745-1831 . . . . **NCLC 41**
See also DLB 39

Mackintosh, Elizabeth 1896(?)-1952
See Tey, Josephine
See also CA 110

MacLaren, James
See Grieve, C(hristopher) M(urray)

Mac Laverty, Bernard 1942- . . . . . . **CLC 31**
See also CA 116; 118; CANR 43; INT 118

MacLean, Alistair (Stuart)
1922-1987 . . . . **CLC 3, 13, 50, 63;
DAM POP**
See also CA 57-60; 121; CANR 28; MTCW;
SATA 23; SATA-Obit 50

Maclean, Norman (Fitzroy)
1902-1990 . . . . **CLC 78; DAM POP;
SSC 13**
See also CA 102; 132; CANR 49

MacLeish, Archibald
1892-1982 . . . . **CLC 3, 8, 14, 68;
DAM POET**
See also CA 9-12R; 106; CANR 33; DLB 4,
7, 45; DLBY 82; MTCW

MacLennan, (John) Hugh
1907-1990 . . . . **CLC 2, 14, 92; DAC;
DAM MST**
See also CA 5-8R; 142; CANR 33; DLB 68;
MTCW

MacLeod, Alistair
1936- . . . . . . **CLC 56; DAC; DAM MST**
See also CA 123; DLB 60

MacNeice, (Frederick) Louis
1907-1963 . . . . . . **CLC 1, 4, 10, 53; DAB;
DAM POET**
See also CA 85-88; DLB 10, 20; MTCW

MacNeill, Dand
See Fraser, George MacDonald

Macpherson, James 1736-1796 . . . . . . **LC 29**
See also DLB 109

Macpherson, (Jean) Jay 1931- . . . . . . **CLC 14**
See also CA 5-8R; DLB 53

MacShane, Frank 1927- . . . . **CLC 39**
See also CA 9-12R; CANR 3, 33; DLB 111

Macumber, Mari
See Sandoz, Mari(e Susette)

Marivaux, Pierre Carlet de Chamblain de
1688-1763 . . . . **LC 4**

Markandaya, Kamala . . . . **CLC 8, 38**
See also Taylor, Kamala (Purnaiya)

Markfield, Wallace 1926- . . . . **CLC 8**
See also CA 69-72; CAAS 3; DLB 2, 28

Markham, Edwin 1852-1940 . . . . . . **TCLC 47**
See also DLB 54

Markham, Robert
See Amis, Kingsley (William)

Marks, J
See Highwater, Jamake (Mamake)

Marks-Highwater, J
See Highwater, Jamake (Mamake)

Markson, David M(errill) 1927- . . . . **CLC 67**
See also CA 49-52; CANR 1

Marley, Bob . . . . **CLC 17**
See also Marley, Robert Nesta

Marley, Robert Nesta 1945-1981
See Marley, Bob
See also CA 107; 103

Marlowe, Christopher
1564-1593 . . . . . **LC 22; DA; DAB; DAC;**
DAM DRAM, MST; DC 1; WLC
See also CDBLB Before 1660; DLB 62

Marlowe, Stephen 1928-
See Queen, Ellery
See also CA 13-16R; CANR 6, 55

Marmontel, Jean-Francois
1723-1799 . . . . **LC 2**

Marquand, John P(hillips)
1893-1960 . . . . **CLC 2, 10**
See also CA 85-88; DLB 9, 102

Marques, Rene
1919-1979 . . . . . . **CLC 96; DAM MULT;**
HLC
See also CA 97-100; 85-88; DLB 113; HW

Marquez, Gabriel (Jose) Garcia
See Garcia Marquez, Gabriel (Jose)

Marquis, Don(ald Robert Perry)
1878-1937 . . . . **TCLC 7**
See also CA 104; DLB 11, 25

Marric, J. J.
See Creasey, John

Marrow, Bernard
See Moore, Brian

Marryat, Frederick 1792-1848 . . . . **NCLC 3**
See also DLB 21, 163

Marsden, James
See Creasey, John

Marsh, (Edith) Ngaio
1899-1982 . . . . . . **CLC 7, 53; DAM POP**
See also CA 9-12R; CANR 6; DLB 77;
MTCW

Marshall, Garry 1934- . . . . **CLC 17**
See also AAYA 3; CA 111; SATA 60

Marshall, Paule
1929- . . . . **CLC 27, 72; BLC;**
DAM MULT; SSC 3
See also BW 2; CA 77-80; CANR 25;
DLB 157; MTCW

Marsten, Richard
See Hunter, Evan

Marston, John
1576-1634 . . . . . . **LC 33; DAM DRAM**
See also DLB 58, 172

Martha, Henry
See Harris, Mark

Martial c. 40-c. 104 . . . . **PC 10**

Martin, Ken
See Hubbard, L(afayette) Ron(ald)

Martin, Richard
See Creasey, John

Martin, Steve 1945- . . . . **CLC 30**
See also CA 97-100; CANR 30; MTCW

Martin, Valerie 1948- . . . . **CLC 89**
See also BEST 90:2; CA 85-88; CANR 49

Martin, Violet Florence
1862-1915 . . . . **TCLC 51**

Martin, Webber
See Silverberg, Robert

Martindale, Patrick Victor
See White, Patrick (Victor Martindale)

Martin du Gard, Roger
1881-1958 . . . . **TCLC 24**
See also CA 118; DLB 65

Martineau, Harriet 1802-1876 . . . . **NCLC 26**
See also DLB 21, 55, 159, 163, 166;
YABC 2

Martines, Julia
See O'Faolain, Julia

Martinez, Jacinto Benavente y
See Benavente (y Martinez), Jacinto

Martinez Ruiz, Jose 1873-1967
See Azorin; Ruiz, Jose Martinez
See also CA 93-96; HW

Martinez Sierra, Gregorio
1881-1947 . . . . **TCLC 6**
See also CA 115

Martinez Sierra, Maria (de la O'LeJarraga)
1874-1974 . . . . **TCLC 6**
See also CA 115

Martinsen, Martin
See Follett, Ken(neth Martin)

Martinson, Harry (Edmund)
1904-1978 . . . . **CLC 14**
See also CA 77-80; CANR 34

Marut, Ret
See Traven, B.

Marut, Robert
See Traven, B.

Marvell, Andrew
1621-1678 . . . . . . **LC 4; DA; DAB; DAC;**
DAM MST, POET; PC 10; WLC
See also CDBLB 1660-1789; DLB 131

Marx, Karl (Heinrich)
1818-1883 . . . . **NCLC 17**
See also DLB 129

Masaoka Shiki . . . . **TCLC 18**
See also Masaoka Tsunenori

Masaoka Tsunenori 1867-1902
See Masaoka Shiki
See also CA 117

Masefield, John (Edward)
1878-1967 . . . . **CLC 11, 47; DAM POET**
See also CA 19-20; 25-28R; CANR 33;
CAP 2; CDBLB 1890-1914; DLB 10, 19,
153, 160; MTCW; SATA 19

Maso, Carole 19(?)- . . . . **CLC 44**

Mason, Bobbie Ann
1940- . . . . **CLC 28, 43, 82; SSC 4**
See also AAYA 5; CA 53-56; CANR 11,
31; DLB 173; DLBY 87; INT CANR-31;
MTCW

Mason, Ernst
See Pohl, Frederik

Mason, Lee W.
See Malzberg, Barry N(athaniel)

Mason, Nick 1945- . . . . **CLC 35**

Mason, Tally
See Derleth, August (William)

Mass, William
See Gibson, William

Masters, Edgar Lee
1868-1950 . . . . . . **TCLC 2, 25; DA; DAC;**
DAM MST, POET; PC 1
See also CA 104; 133; CDALB 1865-1917;
DLB 54; MTCW

Masters, Hilary 1928- . . . . **CLC 48**
See also CA 25-28R; CANR 13, 47

Mastrosimone, William 19(?)- . . . . . . **CLC 36**

Mathe, Albert
See Camus, Albert

Matheson, Richard Burton 1926- . . . **CLC 37**
See also CA 97-100; DLB 8, 44; INT 97-100

Mathews, Harry 1930- . . . . **CLC 6, 52**
See also CA 21-24R; CAAS 6; CANR 18,
40

Mathews, John Joseph
1894-1979 . . . . . . **CLC 84; DAM MULT**
See also CA 19-20; 142; CANR 45; CAP 2;
DLB 175; NNAL

Mathias, Roland (Glyn) 1915- . . . . . . **CLC 45**
See also CA 97-100; CANR 19, 41; DLB 27

Matsuo Basho 1644-1694 . . . . **PC 3**
See also DAM POET

Mattheson, Rodney
See Creasey, John

Matthews, Greg 1949- . . . . **CLC 45**
See also CA 135

Matthews, William 1942- . . . . **CLC 40**
See also CA 29-32R; CAAS 18; CANR 12;
DLB 5

Matthias, John (Edward) 1941- . . . . . . **CLC 9**
See also CA 33-36R; CANR 56

Matthiessen, Peter
1927- . . . . **CLC 5, 7, 11, 32, 64;**
DAM NOV
See also AAYA 6; BEST 90:4; CA 9-12R;
CANR 21, 50; DLB 6, 173; MTCW;
SATA 27

Maturin, Charles Robert
1780(?)-1824 . . . . **NCLC 6**

Matute (Ausejo), Ana Maria
1925- . . . . **CLC 11**
See also CA 89-92; MTCW

McLuhan, (Herbert) Marshall
1911-1980 . . . . **CLC 37, 83**
See also CA 9-12R; 102; CANR 12, 34;
DLB 88; INT CANR-12; MTCW

McMillan, Terry (L.)
1951- . . . . **CLC 50, 61; DAM MULT,**
NOV, POP
See also BW 2; CA 140

McMurtry, Larry (Jeff)
1936- . . . . **CLC 2, 3, 7, 11, 27, 44;**
DAM NOV, POP
See also AAYA 15; AITN 2; BEST 89:2;
CA 5-8R; CANR 19, 43;
CDALB 1968-1988; DLB 2, 143;
DLBY 80, 87; MTCW

McNally, T. M. 1961- . . . . **CLC 82**

McNally, Terrence
1939- . . . **CLC 4, 7, 41, 91; DAM DRAM**
See also CA 45-48; CANR 2, 56; DLB 7

McNamer, Deirdre 1950- . . . . **CLC 70**

McNeile, Herman Cyril 1888-1937
See Sapper
See also DLB 77

McNickle, (William) D'Arcy
1904-1977 . . . . . . **CLC 89; DAM MULT**
See also CA 9-12R; 85-88; CANR 5, 45;
DLB 175; NNAL; SATA-Obit 22

McPhee, John (Angus) 1931- . . . . . . **CLC 36**
See also BEST 90:1; CA 65-68; CANR 20,
46; MTCW

McPherson, James Alan
1943- . . . . **CLC 19, 77**
See also BW 1; CA 25-28R; CAAS 17;
CANR 24; DLB 38; MTCW

McPherson, William (Alexander)
1933- . . . . **CLC 34**
See also CA 69-72; CANR 28;
INT CANR-28

Mead, Margaret 1901-1978 . . . . **CLC 37**
See also AITN 1; CA 1-4R; 81-84;
CANR 4; MTCW; SATA-Obit 20

Meaker, Marijane (Agnes) 1927-
See Kerr, M. E.
See also CA 107; CANR 37; INT 107;
JRDA; MAICYA; MTCW; SATA 20, 61

Medoff, Mark (Howard)
1940- . . . . **CLC 6, 23; DAM DRAM**
See also AITN 1; CA 53-56; CANR 5;
DLB 7; INT CANR-5

Medvedev, P. N.
See Bakhtin, Mikhail Mikhailovich

Meged, Aharon
See Megged, Aharon

Meged, Aron
See Megged, Aharon

Megged, Aharon 1920- . . . . **CLC 9**
See also CA 49-52; CAAS 13; CANR 1

Mehta, Ved (Parkash) 1934- . . . . **CLC 37**
See also CA 1-4R; CANR 2, 23; MTCW

Melanter
See Blackmore, R(ichard) D(oddridge)

Melikow, Loris
See Hofmannsthal, Hugo von

Melmoth, Sebastian
See Wilde, Oscar (Fingal O'Flahertie Wills)

Meltzer, Milton 1915- . . . . **CLC 26**
See also AAYA 8; CA 13-16R; CANR 38;
CLR 13; DLB 61; JRDA; MAICYA;
SAAS 1; SATA 1, 50, 80

Melville, Herman
1819-1891 . . . . . **NCLC 3, 12, 29, 45, 49;**
DA; DAB; DAC; DAM MST, NOV;
SSC 1, 17; WLC
See also CDALB 1640-1865; DLB 3, 74;
SATA 59

Menander
c. 342B.C.-c. 292B.C. . . . . **CMLC 9;**
DAM DRAM; DC 3

Mencken, H(enry) L(ouis)
1880-1956 . . . . **TCLC 13**
See also CA 105; 125; CDALB 1917-1929;
DLB 11, 29, 63, 137; MTCW

Mendelsohn, Jane 1965(?)- . . . . **CLC 99**
See also CA 154

Mercer, David
1928-1980 . . . . **CLC 5; DAM DRAM**
See also CA 9-12R; 102; CANR 23;
DLB 13; MTCW

Merchant, Paul
See Ellison, Harlan (Jay)

Meredith, George
1828-1909 . . **TCLC 17, 43; DAM POET**
See also CA 117; 153; CDBLB 1832-1890;
DLB 18, 35, 57, 159

Meredith, William (Morris)
1919- . . **CLC 4, 13, 22, 55; DAM POET**
See also CA 9-12R; CAAS 14; CANR 6, 40;
DLB 5

Merezhkovsky, Dmitry Sergeyevich
1865-1941 . . . . **TCLC 29**

Merimee, Prosper
1803-1870 . . . . **NCLC 6; SSC 7**
See also DLB 119

Merkin, Daphne 1954- . . . . **CLC 44**
See also CA 123

Merlin, Arthur
See Blish, James (Benjamin)

Merrill, James (Ingram)
1926-1995 . . . . **CLC 2, 3, 6, 8, 13, 18, 34,**
91; DAM POET
See also CA 13-16R; 147; CANR 10, 49;
DLB 5, 165; DLBY 85; INT CANR-10;
MTCW

Merriman, Alex
See Silverberg, Robert

Merritt, E. B.
See Waddington, Miriam

Merton, Thomas
1915-1968 . . **CLC 1, 3, 11, 34, 83; PC 10**
See also CA 5-8R; 25-28R; CANR 22, 53;
DLB 48; DLBY 81; MTCW

Merwin, W(illiam) S(tanley)
1927- . . . . . . **CLC 1, 2, 3, 5, 8, 13, 18, 45,**
88; DAM POET
See also CA 13-16R; CANR 15, 51; DLB 5,
169; INT CANR-15; MTCW

Metcalf, John 1938- . . . . **CLC 37**
See also CA 113; DLB 60

Metcalf, Suzanne
See Baum, L(yman) Frank

Mew, Charlotte (Mary)
1870-1928 . . . . **TCLC 8**
See also CA 105; DLB 19, 135

Mewshaw, Michael 1943- . . . . **CLC 9**
See also CA 53-56; CANR 7, 47; DLBY 80

Meyer, June
See Jordan, June

Meyer, Lynn
See Slavitt, David R(ytman)

Meyer-Meyrink, Gustav 1868-1932
See Meyrink, Gustav
See also CA 117

Meyers, Jeffrey 1939- . . . . **CLC 39**
See also CA 73-76; CANR 54; DLB 111

Meynell, Alice (Christina Gertrude Thompson)
1847-1922 . . . . **TCLC 6**
See also CA 104; DLB 19, 98

Meyrink, Gustav . . . . **TCLC 21**
See also Meyer-Meyrink, Gustav
See also DLB 81

Michaels, Leonard
1933- . . . . **CLC 6, 25; SSC 16**
See also CA 61-64; CANR 21; DLB 130;
MTCW

Michaux, Henri 1899-1984 . . . . . . **CLC 8, 19**
See also CA 85-88; 114

Michelangelo 1475-1564 . . . . **LC 12**

Michelet, Jules 1798-1874 . . . . **NCLC 31**

Michener, James A(lbert)
1907(?)- . . . . **CLC 1, 5, 11, 29, 60;**
DAM NOV, POP
See also AITN 1; BEST 90:1; CA 5-8R;
CANR 21, 45; DLB 6; MTCW

Mickiewicz, Adam 1798-1855 . . . . . **NCLC 3**

Middleton, Christopher 1926- . . . . . . **CLC 13**
See also CA 13-16R; CANR 29, 54;
DLB 40

Middleton, Richard (Barham)
1882-1911 . . . . **TCLC 56**
See also DLB 156

Middleton, Stanley 1919- . . . . **CLC 7, 38**
See also CA 25-28R; CAAS 23; CANR 21,
46; DLB 14

Middleton, Thomas
1580-1627 . . . . **LC 33; DAM DRAM,**
MST; DC 5
See also DLB 58

Migueis, Jose Rodrigues 1901- . . . . . **CLC 10**

Mikszath, Kalman 1847-1910 . . . . . **TCLC 31**

Miles, Josephine (Louise)
1911-1985 . . . . **CLC 1, 2, 14, 34, 39;**
DAM POET
See also CA 1-4R; 116; CANR 2, 55;
DLB 48

Militant
See Sandburg, Carl (August)

Mill, John Stuart 1806-1873 . . **NCLC 11, 58**
See also CDBLB 1832-1890; DLB 55

Millar, Kenneth
1915-1983 . . . . **CLC 14; DAM POP**
See also Macdonald, Ross
See also CA 9-12R; 110; CANR 16; DLB 2;
DLBD 6; DLBY 83; MTCW

Newman, John Henry
1801-1890 .... NCLC 38
See also DLB 18, 32, 55

Newton, Suzanne 1936- .... CLC 35
See also CA 41-44R; CANR 14; JRDA;
SATA 5, 77

Nexo, Martin Andersen
1869-1954 .... TCLC 43

Nezval, Vitezslav 1900-1958 ..... TCLC 44
See also CA 123

Ng, Fae Myenne 1957(?)-.......... CLC 81
See also CA 146

Ngema, Mbongeni 1955- .... CLC 57
See also BW 2; CA 143

Ngugi, James T(hiong'o)........ CLC 3, 7, 13
See also Ngugi wa Thiong'o

Ngugi wa Thiong'o
1938- ..... CLC 36; BLC; DAM MULT,
NOV
See also Ngugi, James T(hiong'o)
See also BW 2; CA 81-84; CANR 27;
DLB 125; MTCW

Nichol, B(arrie) P(hillip)
1944-1988 .... CLC 18
See also CA 53-56; DLB 53; SATA 66

Nichols, John (Treadwell) 1940- .... CLC 38
See also CA 9-12R; CAAS 2; CANR 6;
DLBY 82

Nichols, Leigh
See Koontz, Dean R(ay)

Nichols, Peter (Richard)
1927- .... CLC 5, 36, 65
See also CA 104; CANR 33; DLB 13;
MTCW

Nicolas, F. R. E.
See Freeling, Nicolas

Niedecker, Lorine
1903-1970 .... CLC 10, 42; DAM POET
See also CA 25-28; CAP 2; DLB 48

Nietzsche, Friedrich (Wilhelm)
1844-1900 .... TCLC 10, 18, 55
See also CA 107; 121; DLB 129

Nievo, Ippolito 1831-1861 .... NCLC 22

Nightingale, Anne Redmon 1943-
See Redmon, Anne
See also CA 103

Nik. T. O.
See Annensky, Innokenty (Fyodorovich)

Nin, Anais
1903-1977 ..... CLC 1, 4, 8, 11, 14, 60;
DAM NOV, POP; SSC 10
See also AITN 2; CA 13-16R; 69-72;
CANR 22, 53; DLB 2, 4, 152; MTCW

Nishiwaki, Junzaburo 1894-1982 .... PC 15
See also CA 107

Nissenson, Hugh 1933-.......... CLC 4, 9
See also CA 17-20R; CANR 27; DLB 28

Niven, Larry .... CLC 8
See also Niven, Laurence Van Cott
See also DLB 8

Niven, Laurence Van Cott 1938-
See Niven, Larry
See also CA 21-24R; CAAS 12; CANR 14,
44; DAM POP; MTCW

Nixon, Agnes Eckhardt 1927- ...... CLC 21
See also CA 110

Nizan, Paul 1905-1940 .... TCLC 40
See also DLB 72

Nkosi, Lewis
1936- ..... CLC 45; BLC; DAM MULT
See also BW 1; CA 65-68; CANR 27;
DLB 157

Nodier, (Jean) Charles (Emmanuel)
1780-1844 .... NCLC 19
See also DLB 119

Nolan, Christopher 1965-.......... CLC 58
See also CA 111

Noon, Jeff 1957-................. CLC 91
See also CA 148

Norden, Charles
See Durrell, Lawrence (George)

Nordhoff, Charles (Bernard)
1887-1947 .... TCLC 23
See also CA 108; DLB 9; SATA 23

Norfolk, Lawrence 1963-.......... CLC 76
See also CA 144

Norman, Marsha
1947- .... CLC 28; DAM DRAM
See also CA 105; CABS 3; CANR 41;
DLBY 84

Norris, Benjamin Franklin, Jr.
1870-1902 .... TCLC 24
See also Norris, Frank
See also CA 110

Norris, Frank
See Norris, Benjamin Franklin, Jr.
See also CDALB 1865-1917; DLB 12, 71

Norris, Leslie 1921- .... CLC 14
See also CA 11-12; CANR 14; CAP 1;
DLB 27

North, Andrew
See Norton, Andre

North, Anthony
See Koontz, Dean R(ay)

North, Captain George
See Stevenson, Robert Louis (Balfour)

North, Milou
See Erdrich, Louise

Northrup, B. A.
See Hubbard, L(afayette) Ron(ald)

North Staffs
See Hulme, T(homas) E(rnest)

Norton, Alice Mary
See Norton, Andre
See also MAICYA; SATA 1, 43

Norton, Andre 1912- .... CLC 12
See also Norton, Alice Mary
See also AAYA 14; CA 1-4R; CANR 2, 31;
DLB 8, 52; JRDA; MTCW; SATA 91

Norton, Caroline 1808-1877...... NCLC 47
See also DLB 21, 159

Norway, Nevil Shute 1899-1960
See Shute, Nevil
See also CA 102; 93-96

Norwid, Cyprian Kamil
1821-1883 .... NCLC 17

Nosille, Nabrah
See Ellison, Harlan (Jay)

Nossack, Hans Erich 1901-1978 ..... CLC 6
See also CA 93-96; 85-88; DLB 69

Nostradamus 1503-1566 .... LC 27

Nosu, Chuji
See Ozu, Yasujiro

Notenburg, Eleanora (Genrikhovna) von
See Guro, Elena

Nova, Craig 1945-............... CLC 7, 31
See also CA 45-48; CANR 2, 53

Novak, Joseph
See Kosinski, Jerzy (Nikodem)

Novalis 1772-1801 .... NCLC 13
See also DLB 90

Nowlan, Alden (Albert)
1933-1983 .. CLC 15; DAC; DAM MST
See also CA 9-12R; CANR 5; DLB 53

Noyes, Alfred 1880-1958 .... TCLC 7
See also CA 104; DLB 20

Nunn, Kem 19(?)-................ CLC 34

Nye, Robert
1939- .... CLC 13, 42; DAM NOV
See also CA 33-36R; CANR 29; DLB 14;
MTCW; SATA 6

Nyro, Laura 1947- .... CLC 17

Oates, Joyce Carol
1938- ...... CLC 1, 2, 3, 6, 9, 11, 15, 19,
33, 52; DA; DAB; DAC; DAM MST,
NOV, POP; SSC 6; WLC
See also AAYA 15; AITN 1; BEST 89:2;
CA 5-8R; CANR 25, 45;
CDALB 1968-1988; DLB 2, 5, 130;
DLBY 81; INT CANR-25; MTCW

O'Brien, Darcy 1939-............. CLC 11
See also CA 21-24R; CANR 8

O'Brien, E. G.
See Clarke, Arthur C(harles)

O'Brien, Edna
1936- .... CLC 3, 5, 8, 13, 36, 65;
DAM NOV; SSC 10
See also CA 1-4R; CANR 6, 41;
CDBLB 1960 to Present; DLB 14;
MTCW

O'Brien, Fitz-James 1828-1862... NCLC 21
See also DLB 74

O'Brien, Flann........ CLC 1, 4, 5, 7, 10, 47
See also O Nuallain, Brian

O'Brien, Richard 1942-........... CLC 17
See also CA 124

O'Brien, Tim
1946- .... CLC 7, 19, 40; DAM POP
See also AAYA 16; CA 85-88; CANR 40;
DLB 152; DLBD 9; DLBY 80

Obstfelder, Sigbjoern 1866-1900... TCLC 23
See also CA 123

O'Casey, Sean
1880-1964 ...... CLC 1, 5, 9, 11, 15, 88;
DAB; DAC; DAM DRAM, MST
See also CA 89-92; CDBLB 1914-1945;
DLB 10; MTCW

O'Cathasaigh, Sean
See O'Casey, Sean

Ochs, Phil 1940-1976............. CLC 17
See also CA 65-68

Ovid
43B.C.-18(?) ... **CMLC 7; DAM POET;
PC 2**

Owen, Hugh
See Faust, Frederick (Schiller)

Owen, Wilfred (Edward Salter)
1893-1918 ...... **TCLC 5, 27; DA; DAB;
DAC; DAM MST, POET; WLC**
See also CA 104; 141; CDBLB 1914-1945;
DLB 20

Owens, Rochelle 1936-............. **CLC 8**
See also CA 17-20R; CAAS 2; CANR 39

Oz, Amos
1939-......... **CLC 5, 8, 11, 27, 33, 54;
DAM NOV**
See also CA 53-56; CANR 27, 47; MTCW

Ozick, Cynthia
1928-.... **CLC 3, 7, 28, 62; DAM NOV,
POP; SSC 15**
See also BEST 90:1; CA 17-20R; CANR 23;
DLB 28, 152; DLBY 82; INT CANR-23;
MTCW

Ozu, Yasujiro 1903-1963......... **CLC 16**
See also CA 112

Pacheco, C.
See Pessoa, Fernando (Antonio Nogueira)

Pa Chin .... **CLC 18**
See also Li Fei-kan

Pack, Robert 1929-.............. **CLC 13**
See also CA 1-4R; CANR 3, 44; DLB 5

Padgett, Lewis
See Kuttner, Henry

Padilla (Lorenzo), Heberto 1932-... **CLC 38**
See also AITN 1; CA 123; 131; HW

Page, Jimmy 1944-.............. **CLC 12**

Page, Louise 1955-.............. **CLC 40**
See also CA 140

Page, P(atricia) K(athleen)
1916-.... **CLC 7, 18; DAC; DAM MST;
PC 12**
See also CA 53-56; CANR 4, 22; DLB 68;
MTCW

Page, Thomas Nelson 1853-1922.... **SSC 23**
See also CA 118; DLB 12, 78; DLBD 13

Paget, Violet 1856-1935
See Lee, Vernon
See also CA 104

Paget-Lowe, Henry
See Lovecraft, H(oward) P(hillips)

Paglia, Camille (Anna) 1947-....... **CLC 68**
See also CA 140

Paige, Richard
See Koontz, Dean R(ay)

Pakenham, Antonia
See Fraser, (Lady) Antonia (Pakenham)

Palamas, Kostes 1859-1943 .... **TCLC 5**
See also CA 105

Palazzeschi, Aldo 1885-1974....... **CLC 11**
See also CA 89-92; 53-56; DLB 114

Paley, Grace
1922-....... **CLC 4, 6, 37; DAM POP;
SSC 8**
See also CA 25-28R; CANR 13, 46;
DLB 28; INT CANR-13; MTCW

Palin, Michael (Edward) 1943-..... **CLC 21**
See also Monty Python
See also CA 107; CANR 35; SATA 67

Palliser, Charles 1947-............ **CLC 65**
See also CA 136

Palma, Ricardo 1833-1919....... **TCLC 29**

Pancake, Breece Dexter 1952-1979
See Pancake, Breece D'J
See also CA 123; 109

Pancake, Breece D'J............... **CLC 29**
See also Pancake, Breece Dexter
See also DLB 130

Panko, Rudy
See Gogol, Nikolai (Vasilyevich)

Papadiamantis, Alexandros
1851-1911 .... **TCLC 29**

Papadiamantopoulos, Johannes 1856-1910
See Moreas, Jean
See also CA 117

Papini, Giovanni 1881-1956....... **TCLC 22**
See also CA 121

Paracelsus 1493-1541.............. **LC 14**

Parasol, Peter
See Stevens, Wallace

Pareto, Vilfredo 1848-1923 .... **TCLC 69**

Parfenie, Maria
See Codrescu, Andrei

Parini, Jay (Lee) 1948-........... **CLC 54**
See also CA 97-100; CAAS 16; CANR 32

Park, Jordan
See Kornbluth, C(yril) M.; Pohl, Frederik

Parker, Bert
See Ellison, Harlan (Jay)

Parker, Dorothy (Rothschild)
1893-1967 .... **CLC 15, 68;
DAM POET; SSC 2**
See also CA 19-20; 25-28R; CAP 2;
DLB 11, 45, 86; MTCW

Parker, Robert B(rown)
1932-...... **CLC 27; DAM NOV, POP**
See also BEST 89:4; CA 49-52; CANR 1,
26, 52; INT CANR-26; MTCW

Parkin, Frank 1940-.............. **CLC 43**
See also CA 147

Parkman, Francis, Jr.
1823-1893 .... **NCLC 12**
See also DLB 1, 30

Parks, Gordon (Alexander Buchanan)
1912-... **CLC 1, 16; BLC; DAM MULT**
See also AITN 2; BW 2; CA 41-44R;
CANR 26; DLB 33; SATA 8

Parnell, Thomas 1679-1718.......... **LC 3**
See also DLB 94

Parra, Nicanor
1914-...... **CLC 2; DAM MULT; HLC**
See also CA 85-88; CANR 32; HW; MTCW

Parrish, Mary Frances
See Fisher, M(ary) F(rances) K(ennedy)

Parson
See Coleridge, Samuel Taylor

Parson Lot
See Kingsley, Charles

Partridge, Anthony
See Oppenheim, E(dward) Phillips

Pascal, Blaise 1623-1662 .... **LC 35**

Pascoli, Giovanni 1855-1912...... **TCLC 45**

Pasolini, Pier Paolo
1922-1975 .... **CLC 20, 37; PC 17**
See also CA 93-96; 61-64; DLB 128;
MTCW

Pasquini
See Silone, Ignazio

Pastan, Linda (Olenik)
1932- .... **CLC 27; DAM POET**
See also CA 61-64; CANR 18, 40; DLB 5

Pasternak, Boris (Leonidovich)
1890-1960 ...... **CLC 7, 10, 18, 63; DA;
DAB; DAC; DAM MST, NOV, POET;
PC 6; WLC**
See also CA 127; 116; MTCW

Patchen, Kenneth
1911-1972 ... **CLC 1, 2, 18; DAM POET**
See also CA 1-4R; 33-36R; CANR 3, 35;
DLB 16, 48; MTCW

Pater, Walter (Horatio)
1839-1894 .... **NCLC 7**
See also CDBLB 1832-1890; DLB 57, 156

Paterson, A(ndrew) B(arton)
1864-1941 .... **TCLC 32**
See also CA 155

Paterson, Katherine (Womeldorf)
1932- .... **CLC 12, 30**
See also AAYA 1; CA 21-24R; CANR 28;
CLR 7; DLB 52; JRDA; MAICYA;
MTCW; SATA 13, 53, 92

Patmore, Coventry Kersey Dighton
1823-1896 .... **NCLC 9**
See also DLB 35, 98

Paton, Alan (Stewart)
1903-1988 ...... **CLC 4, 10, 25, 55; DA;
DAB; DAC; DAM MST, NOV; WLC**
See also CA 13-16; 125; CANR 22; CAP 1;
MTCW; SATA 11; SATA-Obit 56

Paton Walsh, Gillian 1937-
See Walsh, Jill Paton
See also CANR 38; JRDA; MAICYA;
SAAS 3; SATA 4, 72

Paulding, James Kirke 1778-1860.. **NCLC 2**
See also DLB 3, 59, 74

Paulin, Thomas Neilson 1949-
See Paulin, Tom
See also CA 123; 128

Paulin, Tom...................... **CLC 37**
See also Paulin, Thomas Neilson
See also DLB 40

Paustovsky, Konstantin (Georgievich)
1892-1968 .... **CLC 40**
See also CA 93-96; 25-28R

Pavese, Cesare
1908-1950 ..... **TCLC 3; PC 13; SSC 19**
See also CA 104; DLB 128

Pavic, Milorad 1929-............. **CLC 60**
See also CA 136

Payne, Alan
See Jakes, John (William)

Paz, Gil
See Lugones, Leopoldo

Pinkwater, Daniel Manus 1941- . . . . **CLC 35**
See also Pinkwater, Manus
See also AAYA 1; CA 29-32R; CANR 12,
38; CLR 4; JRDA; MAICYA; SAAS 3;
SATA 46, 76

Pinkwater, Manus
See Pinkwater, Daniel Manus
See also SATA 8

Pinsky, Robert
1940- . . **CLC 9, 19, 38, 94; DAM POET**
See also CA 29-32R; CAAS 4; DLBY 82

Pinta, Harold
See Pinter, Harold

Pinter, Harold
1930- . . . . . **CLC 1, 3, 6, 9, 11, 15, 27, 58,
73; DA; DAB; DAC; DAM DRAM,
MST; WLC**
See also CA 5-8R; CANR 33; CDBLB 1960
to Present; DLB 13; MTCW

Piozzi, Hester Lynch (Thrale)
1741-1821 . . . . **NCLC 57**
See also DLB 104, 142

Pirandello, Luigi
1867-1936 . . . . . . **TCLC 4, 29; DA; DAB;
DAC; DAM DRAM, MST; DC 5;
SSC 22; WLC**
See also CA 104; 153

Pirsig, Robert M(aynard)
1928- . . . . **CLC 4, 6, 73; DAM POP**
See also CA 53-56; CANR 42; MTCW;
SATA 39

Pisarev, Dmitry Ivanovich
1840-1868 . . . . **NCLC 25**

Pix, Mary (Griffith) 1666-1709 . . . . **LC 8**
See also DLB 80

Pixerecourt, Guilbert de
1773-1844 . . . . **NCLC 39**

Plaidy, Jean
See Hibbert, Eleanor Alice Burford

Planche, James Robinson
1796-1880 . . . . **NCLC 42**

Plant, Robert 1948- . . . . **CLC 12**

Plante, David (Robert)
1940- . . . . **CLC 7, 23, 38; DAM NOV**
See also CA 37-40R; CANR 12, 36;
DLBY 83; INT CANR-12; MTCW

Plath, Sylvia
1932-1963 . . . . . **CLC 1, 2, 3, 5, 9, 11, 14,
17, 50, 51, 62; DA; DAB; DAC;
DAM MST, POET; PC 1; WLC**
See also AAYA 13; CA 19-20; CANR 34;
CAP 2; CDALB 1941-1968; DLB 5, 6,
152; MTCW

Plato
428(?)B.C.-348(?)B.C. . . . . . **CMLC 8; DA;
DAB; DAC; DAM MST**

Platonov, Andrei . . . . **TCLC 14**
See also Klimentov, Andrei Platonovich

Platt, Kin 1911- . . . . **CLC 26**
See also AAYA 11; CA 17-20R; CANR 11;
JRDA; SAAS 17; SATA 21, 86

Plautus c. 251B.C.-184B.C. . . . . **DC 6**

Plick et Plock
See Simenon, Georges (Jacques Christian)

Plimpton, George (Ames) 1927- . . . . . **CLC 36**
See also AITN 1; CA 21-24R; CANR 32;
MTCW; SATA 10

Plomer, William Charles Franklin
1903-1973 . . . . **CLC 4, 8**
See also CA 21-22; CANR 34; CAP 2;
DLB 20, 162; MTCW; SATA 24

Plowman, Piers
See Kavanagh, Patrick (Joseph)

Plum, J.
See Wodehouse, P(elham) G(renville)

Plumly, Stanley (Ross) 1939- . . . . . . **CLC 33**
See also CA 108; 110; DLB 5; INT 110

Plumpe, Friedrich Wilhelm
1888-1931 . . . . **TCLC 53**
See also CA 112

Poe, Edgar Allan
1809-1849 . . . . **NCLC 1, 16, 55; DA;
DAB; DAC; DAM MST, POET; PC 1;
SSC 1, 22; WLC**
See also AAYA 14; CDALB 1640-1865;
DLB 3, 59, 73, 74; SATA 23

Poet of Titchfield Street, The
See Pound, Ezra (Weston Loomis)

Pohl, Frederik 1919- . . . . **CLC 18**
See also CA 61-64; CAAS 1; CANR 11, 37;
DLB 8; INT CANR-11; MTCW;
SATA 24

Poirier, Louis 1910-
See Gracq, Julien
See also CA 122; 126

Poitier, Sidney 1927- . . . . **CLC 26**
See also BW 1; CA 117

Polanski, Roman 1933- . . . . **CLC 16**
See also CA 77-80

Poliakoff, Stephen 1952- . . . . **CLC 38**
See also CA 106; DLB 13

Police, The
See Copeland, Stewart (Armstrong);
Summers, Andrew James; Sumner,
Gordon Matthew

Polidori, John William
1795-1821 . . . . **NCLC 51**
See also DLB 116

Pollitt, Katha 1949- . . . . **CLC 28**
See also CA 120; 122; MTCW

Pollock, (Mary) Sharon
1936- . . . . **CLC 50; DAC; DAM DRAM,
MST**
See also CA 141; DLB 60

Polo, Marco 1254-1324 . . . . **CMLC 15**

Polonsky, Abraham (Lincoln)
1910- . . . . **CLC 92**
See also CA 104; DLB 26; INT 104

Polybius c. 200B.C.-c. 118B.C. . . . . **CMLC 17**

Pomerance, Bernard
1940- . . . . **CLC 13; DAM DRAM**
See also CA 101; CANR 49

Ponge, Francis (Jean Gaston Alfred)
1899-1988 . . . . . **CLC 6, 18; DAM POET**
See also CA 85-88; 126; CANR 40

Pontoppidan, Henrik 1857-1943 . . . **TCLC 29**

Poole, Josephine . . . . **CLC 17**
See also Helyar, Jane Penelope Josephine
See also SAAS 2; SATA 5

Popa, Vasko 1922-1991 . . . . **CLC 19**
See also CA 112; 148

Pope, Alexander
1688-1744 . . . . . . **LC 3; DA; DAB; DAC;
DAM MST, POET; WLC**
See also CDBLB 1660-1789; DLB 95, 101

Porter, Connie (Rose) 1959(?)- . . . . . **CLC 70**
See also BW 2; CA 142; SATA 81

Porter, Gene(va Grace) Stratton
1863(?)-1924 . . . . **TCLC 21**
See also CA 112

Porter, Katherine Anne
1890-1980 . . . . . . **CLC 1, 3, 7, 10, 13, 15,
27; DA; DAB; DAC; DAM MST, NOV;
SSC 4**
See also AITN 2; CA 1-4R; 101; CANR 1;
DLB 4, 9, 102; DLBD 12; DLBY 80;
MTCW; SATA 39; SATA-Obit 23

Porter, Peter (Neville Frederick)
1929- . . . . **CLC 5, 13, 33**
See also CA 85-88; DLB 40

Porter, William Sydney 1862-1910
See Henry, O.
See also CA 104; 131; CDALB 1865-1917;
DA; DAB; DAC; DAM MST; DLB 12,
78, 79; MTCW; YABC 2

Portillo (y Pacheco), Jose Lopez
See Lopez Portillo (y Pacheco), Jose

Post, Melville Davisson
1869-1930 . . . . **TCLC 39**
See also CA 110

Potok, Chaim
1929- . . . . **CLC 2, 7, 14, 26; DAM NOV**
See also AAYA 15; AITN 1, 2; CA 17-20R;
CANR 19, 35; DLB 28, 152;
INT CANR-19; MTCW; SATA 33

Potter, Beatrice
See Webb, (Martha) Beatrice (Potter)
See also MAICYA

Potter, Dennis (Christopher George)
1935-1994 . . . . **CLC 58, 86**
See also CA 107; 145; CANR 33; MTCW

Pound, Ezra (Weston Loomis)
1885-1972 . . . . . . **CLC 1, 2, 3, 4, 5, 7, 10,
13, 18, 34, 48, 50; DA; DAB; DAC;
DAM MST, POET; PC 4; WLC**
See also CA 5-8R; 37-40R; CANR 40;
CDALB 1917-1929; DLB 4, 45, 63;
MTCW

Povod, Reinaldo 1959-1994 . . . . **CLC 44**
See also CA 136; 146

Powell, Adam Clayton, Jr.
1908-1972 . . . . **CLC 89; BLC;
DAM MULT**
See also BW 1; CA 102; 33-36R

Powell, Anthony (Dymoke)
1905- . . . . **CLC 1, 3, 7, 9, 10, 31**
See also CA 1-4R; CANR 1, 32;
CDBLB 1945-1960; DLB 15; MTCW

Powell, Dawn 1897-1965 . . . . **CLC 66**
See also CA 5-8R

Powell, Padgett 1952- . . . . **CLC 34**
See also CA 126

Power, Susan . . . . **CLC 91**

Powers, J(ames) F(arl)
1917- . . . . CLC 1, 4, 8, 57; SSC 4
See also CA 1-4R; CANR 2; DLB 130;
MTCW

Powers, John J(ames) 1945-
See Powers, John R.
See also CA 69-72

Powers, John R. . . . . CLC 66
See also Powers, John J(ames)

Powers, Richard (S.) 1957- . . . . CLC 93
See also CA 148

Pownall, David 1938- . . . . CLC 10
See also CA 89-92; CAAS 18; CANR 49;
DLB 14

Powys, John Cowper
1872-1963 . . . . CLC 7, 9, 15, 46
See also CA 85-88; DLB 15; MTCW

Powys, T(heodore) F(rancis)
1875-1953 . . . . TCLC 9
See also CA 106; DLB 36, 162

Prager, Emily 1952- . . . . CLC 56

Pratt, E(dwin) J(ohn)
1883(?)-1964 . . . . CLC 19; DAC;
DAM POET
See also CA 141; 93-96; DLB 92

Premchand . . . . TCLC 21
See also Srivastava, Dhanpat Rai

Preussler, Otfried 1923- . . . . CLC 17
See also CA 77-80; SATA 24

Prevert, Jacques (Henri Marie)
1900-1977 . . . . CLC 15
See also CA 77-80; 69-72; CANR 29;
MTCW; SATA-Obit 30

Prevost, Abbe (Antoine Francois)
1697-1763 . . . . LC 1

Price, (Edward) Reynolds
1933- . . . . CLC 3, 6, 13, 43, 50, 63;
DAM NOV; SSC 22
See also CA 1-4R; CANR 1, 37; DLB 2;
INT CANR-37

Price, Richard 1949- . . . . CLC 6, 12
See also CA 49-52; CANR 3; DLBY 81

Prichard, Katharine Susannah
1883-1969 . . . . CLC 46
See also CA 11-12; CANR 33; CAP 1;
MTCW; SATA 66

Priestley, J(ohn) B(oynton)
1894-1984 . . . . CLC 2, 5, 9, 34;
DAM DRAM, NOV
See also CA 9-12R; 113; CANR 33;
CDBLB 1914-1945; DLB 10, 34, 77, 100,
139; DLBY 84; MTCW

Prince 1958(?)- . . . . CLC 35

Prince, F(rank) T(empleton) 1912- . . CLC 22
See also CA 101; CANR 43; DLB 20

Prince Kropotkin
See Kropotkin, Peter (Alekseievich)

Prior, Matthew 1664-1721. . . . . LC 4
See also DLB 95

Pritchard, William H(arrison)
1932- . . . . CLC 34
See also CA 65-68; CANR 23; DLB 111

Pritchett, V(ictor) S(awdon)
1900- . . . . CLC 5, 13, 15, 41;
DAM NOV; SSC 14
See also CA 61-64; CANR 31; DLB 15,
139; MTCW

Private 19022
See Manning, Frederic

Probst, Mark 1925- . . . . CLC 59
See also CA 130

Prokosch, Frederic 1908-1989. . . . CLC 4, 48
See also CA 73-76; 128; DLB 48

Prophet, The
See Dreiser, Theodore (Herman Albert)

Prose, Francine 1947- . . . . CLC 45
See also CA 109; 112; CANR 46

Proudhon
See Cunha, Euclides (Rodrigues Pimenta) da

Proulx, E. Annie 1935- . . . . CLC 81

Proust, (Valentin-Louis-George-Eugene-)
Marcel
1871-1922 . . . . TCLC 7, 13, 33; DA;
DAB; DAC; DAM MST, NOV; WLC
See also CA 104; 120; DLB 65; MTCW

Prowler, Harley
See Masters, Edgar Lee

Prus, Boleslaw 1845-1912 . . . . TCLC 48

Pryor, Richard (Franklin Lenox Thomas)
1940- . . . . CLC 26
See also CA 122

Przybyszewski, Stanislaw
1868-1927 . . . . TCLC 36
See also DLB 66

Pteleon
See Grieve, C(hristopher) M(urray)
See also DAM POET

Puckett, Lute
See Masters, Edgar Lee

Puig, Manuel
1932-1990 . . . . CLC 3, 5, 10, 28, 65;
DAM MULT; HLC
See also CA 45-48; CANR 2, 32; DLB 113;
HW; MTCW

Purdy, Al(fred Wellington)
1918- . . . . CLC 3, 6, 14, 50; DAC;
DAM MST, POET
See also CA 81-84; CAAS 17; CANR 42;
DLB 88

Purdy, James (Amos)
1923- . . . . CLC 2, 4, 10, 28, 52
See also CA 33-36R; CAAS 1; CANR 19,
51; DLB 2; INT CANR-19; MTCW

Pure, Simon
See Swinnerton, Frank Arthur

Pushkin, Alexander (Sergeyevich)
1799-1837 . . . . . NCLC 3, 27; DA; DAB;
DAC; DAM DRAM, MST, POET;
PC 10; WLC
See also SATA 61

P'u Sung-ling 1640-1715 . . . . LC 3

Putnam, Arthur Lee
See Alger, Horatio, Jr.

Puzo, Mario
1920- . . . . . CLC 1, 2, 6, 36; DAM NOV,
POP
See also CA 65-68; CANR 4, 42; DLB 6;
MTCW

Pygge, Edward
See Barnes, Julian (Patrick)

Pym, Barbara (Mary Crampton)
1913-1980 . . . . CLC 13, 19, 37
See also CA 13-14; 97-100; CANR 13, 34;
CAP 1; DLB 14; DLBY 87; MTCW

Pynchon, Thomas (Ruggles, Jr.)
1937- . . . . . CLC 2, 3, 6, 9, 11, 18, 33, 62,
72; DA; DAB; DAC; DAM MST, NOV,
POP; SSC 14; WLC
See also BEST 90:2; CA 17-20R; CANR 22,
46; DLB 2, 173; MTCW

Qian Zhongshu
See Ch'ien Chung-shu

Qroll
See Dagerman, Stig (Halvard)

Quarrington, Paul (Lewis) 1953- . . . . CLC 65
See also CA 129

Quasimodo, Salvatore 1901-1968 . . . CLC 10
See also CA 13-16; 25-28R; CAP 1;
DLB 114; MTCW

Quay, Stephen 1947- . . . . CLC 95

Quay, The Brothers
See Quay, Stephen; Quay, Timothy

Quay, Timothy 1947- . . . . CLC 95

Queen, Ellery. . . . . CLC 3, 11
See also Dannay, Frederic; Davidson,
Avram; Lee, Manfred B(ennington);
Marlowe, Stephen; Sturgeon, Theodore
(Hamilton); Vance, John Holbrook

Queen, Ellery, Jr.
See Dannay, Frederic; Lee, Manfred
B(ennington)

Queneau, Raymond
1903-1976 . . . . CLC 2, 5, 10, 42
See also CA 77-80; 69-72; CANR 32;
DLB 72; MTCW

Quevedo, Francisco de 1580-1645. . . . LC 23

Quiller-Couch, Arthur Thomas
1863-1944 . . . . TCLC 53
See also CA 118; DLB 135, 153

Quin, Ann (Marie) 1936-1973 . . . . CLC 6
See also CA 9-12R; 45-48; DLB 14

Quinn, Martin
See Smith, Martin Cruz

Quinn, Peter 1947- . . . . CLC 91

Quinn, Simon
See Smith, Martin Cruz

Quiroga, Horacio (Sylvestre)
1878-1937 . . . . . TCLC 20; DAM MULT;
HLC
See also CA 117; 131; HW; MTCW

Quoirez, Francoise 1935- . . . . CLC 9
See also Sagan, Francoise
See also CA 49-52; CANR 6, 39; MTCW

Raabe, Wilhelm 1831-1910 . . . . TCLC 45
See also DLB 129

Rabe, David (William)
1940- . . . . . . CLC 4, 8, 33; DAM DRAM
See also CA 85-88; CABS 3; DLB 7

Rabelais, Francois
1483-1553 . . . . . LC 5; DA; DAB; DAC;
DAM MST; WLC

Rabinovitch, Sholem 1859-1916
See Aleichem, Sholom
See also CA 104

Rachilde 1860-1953 . . . . TCLC 67
See also DLB 123

Racine, Jean
1639-1699 . . . . LC 28; DAB; DAM MST

Radcliffe, Ann (Ward)
1764-1823 . . . . NCLC 6, 55
See also DLB 39

Radiguet, Raymond 1903-1923 . . . . TCLC 29
See also DLB 65

Radnoti, Miklos 1909-1944 . . . . TCLC 16
See also CA 118

Rado, James 1939- . . . . CLC 17
See also CA 105

Radvanyi, Netty 1900-1983
See Seghers, Anna
See also CA 85-88; 110

Rae, Ben
See Griffiths, Trevor

Raeburn, John (Hay) 1941- . . . . CLC 34
See also CA 57-60

Ragni, Gerome 1942-1991 . . . . CLC 17
See also CA 105; 134

Rahv, Philip 1908-1973 . . . . CLC 24
See also Greenberg, Ivan
See also DLB 137

Raine, Craig 1944- . . . . CLC 32
See also CA 108; CANR 29, 51; DLB 40

Raine, Kathleen (Jessie) 1908- . . . CLC 7, 45
See also CA 85-88; CANR 46; DLB 20;
MTCW

Rainis, Janis 1865-1929 . . . . TCLC 29

Rakosi, Carl . . . . CLC 47
See also Rawley, Callman
See also CAAS 5

Raleigh, Richard
See Lovecraft, H(oward) P(hillips)

Raleigh, Sir Walter 1554(?)-1618 . . . . LC 31
See also CDBLB Before 1660; DLB 172

Rallentando, H. P.
See Sayers, Dorothy L(eigh)

Ramal, Walter
See de la Mare, Walter (John)

Ramon, Juan
See Jimenez (Mantecon), Juan Ramon

Ramos, Graciliano 1892-1953 . . . . . TCLC 32

Rampersad, Arnold 1941- . . . . CLC 44
See also BW 2; CA 127; 133; DLB 111;
INT 133

Rampling, Anne
See Rice, Anne

Ramsay, Allan 1684(?)-1758 . . . . LC 29
See also DLB 95

Ramuz, Charles-Ferdinand
1878-1947 . . . . TCLC 33

Rand, Ayn
1905-1982 . . . . . CLC 3, 30, 44, 79; DA;
DAC; DAM MST, NOV, POP; WLC
See also AAYA 10; CA 13-16R; 105;
CANR 27; MTCW

Randall, Dudley (Felker)
1914- . . . . . . CLC 1; BLC; DAM MULT
See also BW 1; CA 25-28R; CANR 23;
DLB 41

Randall, Robert
See Silverberg, Robert

Ranger, Ken
See Creasey, John

Ransom, John Crowe
1888-1974 . . . . CLC 2, 4, 5, 11, 24;
DAM POET
See also CA 5-8R; 49-52; CANR 6, 34;
DLB 45, 63; MTCW

Rao, Raja 1909- . . . CLC 25, 56; DAM NOV
See also CA 73-76; CANR 51; MTCW

Raphael, Frederic (Michael)
1931- . . . . CLC 2, 14
See also CA 1-4R; CANR 1; DLB 14

Ratcliffe, James P.
See Mencken, H(enry) L(ouis)

Rathbone, Julian 1935- . . . . CLC 41
See also CA 101; CANR 34

Rattigan, Terence (Mervyn)
1911-1977 . . . . CLC 7; DAM DRAM
See also CA 85-88; 73-76;
CDBLB 1945-1960; DLB 13; MTCW

Ratushinskaya, Irina 1954- . . . . CLC 54
See also CA 129

Raven, Simon (Arthur Noel)
1927- . . . . CLC 14
See also CA 81-84

Rawley, Callman 1903-
See Rakosi, Carl
See also CA 21-24R; CANR 12, 32

Rawlings, Marjorie Kinnan
1896-1953 . . . . TCLC 4
See also AAYA 20; CA 104; 137; DLB 9,
22, 102; JRDA; MAICYA; YABC 1

Ray, Satyajit
1921-1992 . . . CLC 16, 76; DAM MULT
See also CA 114; 137

Read, Herbert Edward 1893-1968 . . . . CLC 4
See also CA 85-88; 25-28R; DLB 20, 149

Read, Piers Paul 1941- . . . . . . CLC 4, 10, 25
See also CA 21-24R; CANR 38; DLB 14;
SATA 21

Reade, Charles 1814-1884 . . . . NCLC 2
See also DLB 21

Reade, Hamish
See Gray, Simon (James Holliday)

Reading, Peter 1946- . . . . CLC 47
See also CA 103; CANR 46; DLB 40

Reaney, James
1926- . . . . . . CLC 13; DAC; DAM MST
See also CA 41-44R; CAAS 15; CANR 42;
DLB 68; SATA 43

Rebreanu, Liviu 1885-1944 . . . . TCLC 28

Rechy, John (Francisco)
1934- . . . . CLC 1, 7, 14, 18;
DAM MULT; HLC
See also CA 5-8R; CAAS 4; CANR 6, 32;
DLB 122; DLBY 82; HW; INT CANR-6

Redcam, Tom 1870-1933 . . . . TCLC 25

Reddin, Keith . . . . CLC 67

Redgrove, Peter (William)
1932- . . . . CLC 6, 41
See also CA 1-4R; CANR 3, 39; DLB 40

Redmon, Anne . . . . CLC 22
See also Nightingale, Anne Redmon
See also DLBY 86

Reed, Eliot
See Ambler, Eric

Reed, Ishmael
1938- . . . . CLC 2, 3, 5, 6, 13, 32, 60;
BLC; DAM MULT
See also BW 2; CA 21-24R; CANR 25, 48;
DLB 2, 5, 33, 169; DLBD 8; MTCW

Reed, John (Silas) 1887-1920 . . . . . . TCLC 9
See also CA 106

Reed, Lou . . . . CLC 21
See also Firbank, Louis

Reeve, Clara 1729-1807 . . . . NCLC 19
See also DLB 39

Reich, Wilhelm 1897-1957 . . . . TCLC 57

Reid, Christopher (John) 1949- . . . . . CLC 33
See also CA 140; DLB 40

Reid, Desmond
See Moorcock, Michael (John)

Reid Banks, Lynne 1929-
See Banks, Lynne Reid
See also CA 1-4R; CANR 6, 22, 38;
CLR 24; JRDA; MAICYA; SATA 22, 75

Reilly, William K.
See Creasey, John

Reiner, Max
See Caldwell, (Janet Miriam) Taylor
(Holland)

Reis, Ricardo
See Pessoa, Fernando (Antonio Nogueira)

Remarque, Erich Maria
1898-1970 . . . . CLC 21; DA; DAB; DAC;
DAM MST, NOV
See also CA 77-80; 29-32R; DLB 56;
MTCW

Remizov, A.
See Remizov, Aleksei (Mikhailovich)

Remizov, A. M.
See Remizov, Aleksei (Mikhailovich)

Remizov, Aleksei (Mikhailovich)
1877-1957 . . . . TCLC 27
See also CA 125; 133

Renan, Joseph Ernest
1823-1892 . . . . NCLC 26

Renard, Jules 1864-1910 . . . . TCLC 17
See also CA 117

Renault, Mary . . . . CLC 3, 11, 17
See also Challans, Mary
See also DLBY 83

Rendell, Ruth (Barbara)
1930- .... **CLC 28, 48; DAM POP**
See also Vine, Barbara
See also CA 109; CANR 32, 52; DLB 87;
INT CANR-32; MTCW

Renoir, Jean 1894-1979 .... **CLC 20**
See also CA 129; 85-88

Resnais, Alain 1922-.............. **CLC 16**

Reverdy, Pierre 1889-1960 .... **CLC 53**
See also CA 97-100; 89-92

Rexroth, Kenneth
1905-1982 ...... **CLC 1, 2, 6, 11, 22, 49;
DAM POET**
See also CA 5-8R; 107; CANR 14, 34;
CDALB 1941-1968; DLB 16, 48, 165;
DLBY 82; INT CANR-14; MTCW

Reyes, Alfonso 1889-1959 .... **TCLC 33**
See also CA 131; HW

Reyes y Basoalto, Ricardo Eliecer Neftali
See Neruda, Pablo

Reymont, Wladyslaw (Stanislaw)
1868(?)-1925 .... **TCLC 5**
See also CA 104

Reynolds, Jonathan 1942-....... **CLC 6, 38**
See also CA 65-68; CANR 28

Reynolds, Joshua 1723-1792 .... **LC 15**
See also DLB 104

Reynolds, Michael Shane 1937- .... **CLC 44**
See also CA 65-68; CANR 9

Reznikoff, Charles 1894-1976 .... **CLC 9**
See also CA 33-36; 61-64; CAP 2; DLB 28,
45

Rezzori (d'Arezzo), Gregor von
1914- .... **CLC 25**
See also CA 122; 136

Rhine, Richard
See Silverstein, Alvin

Rhodes, Eugene Manlove
1869-1934 .... **TCLC 53**

R'hoone
See Balzac, Honore de

Rhys, Jean
1890(?)-1979 .... **CLC 2, 4, 6, 14, 19, 51;
DAM NOV; SSC 21**
See also CA 25-28R; 85-88; CANR 35;
CDBLB 1945-1960; DLB 36, 117, 162;
MTCW

Ribeiro, Darcy 1922-............. **CLC 34**
See also CA 33-36R

Ribeiro, Joao Ubaldo (Osorio Pimentel)
1941- .... **CLC 10, 67**
See also CA 81-84

Ribman, Ronald (Burt) 1932- .... **CLC 7**
See also CA 21-24R; CANR 46

Ricci, Nino 1959-................. **CLC 70**
See also CA 137

Rice, Anne 1941- ..... **CLC 41; DAM POP**
See also AAYA 9; BEST 89:2; CA 65-68;
CANR 12, 36, 53

Rice, Elmer (Leopold)
1892-1967 .... **CLC 7, 49; DAM DRAM**
See also CA 21-22; 25-28R; CAP 2; DLB 4,
7; MTCW

Rice, Tim(othy Miles Bindon)
1944- .... **CLC 21**
See also CA 103; CANR 46

Rich, Adrienne (Cecile)
1929- .... **CLC 3, 6, 7, 11, 18, 36, 73, 76;
DAM POET; PC 5**
See also CA 9-12R; CANR 20, 53; DLB 5,
67; MTCW

Rich, Barbara
See Graves, Robert (von Ranke)

Rich, Robert
See Trumbo, Dalton

Richard, Keith................... **CLC 17**
See also Richards, Keith

Richards, David Adams
1950-................... **CLC 59; DAC**
See also CA 93-96; DLB 53

Richards, I(vor) A(rmstrong)
1893-1979 .... **CLC 14, 24**
See also CA 41-44R; 89-92; CANR 34;
DLB 27

Richards, Keith 1943-
See Richard, Keith
See also CA 107

Richardson, Anne
See Roiphe, Anne (Richardson)

Richardson, Dorothy Miller
1873-1957 .... **TCLC 3**
See also CA 104; DLB 36

Richardson, Ethel Florence (Lindesay)
1870-1946
See Richardson, Henry Handel
See also CA 105

Richardson, Henry Handel........ **TCLC 4**
See also Richardson, Ethel Florence
(Lindesay)

Richardson, John
1796-1852 .... **NCLC 55; DAC**
See also DLB 99

Richardson, Samuel
1689-1761 ...... **LC 1; DA; DAB; DAC;
DAM MST, NOV; WLC**
See also CDBLB 1660-1789; DLB 39

Richler, Mordecai
1931- .... **CLC 3, 5, 9, 13, 18, 46, 70;
DAC; DAM MST, NOV**
See also AITN 1; CA 65-68; CANR 31;
CLR 17; DLB 53; MAICYA; MTCW;
SATA 44; SATA-Brief 27

Richter, Conrad (Michael)
1890-1968 .... **CLC 30**
See also CA 5-8R; 25-28R; CANR 23;
DLB 9; MTCW; SATA 3

Ricostranza, Tom
See Ellis, Trey

Riddell, J. H. 1832-1906 .... **TCLC 40**

Riding, Laura................... **CLC 3, 7**
See also Jackson, Laura (Riding)

Riefenstahl, Berta Helene Amalia 1902-
See Riefenstahl, Leni
See also CA 108

Riefenstahl, Leni................ **CLC 16**
See also Riefenstahl, Berta Helene Amalia

Riffe, Ernest
See Bergman, (Ernst) Ingmar

Riggs, (Rolla) Lynn
1899-1954 ..... **TCLC 56; DAM MULT**
See also CA 144; DLB 175; NNAL

Riley, James Whitcomb
1849-1916 ...... **TCLC 51; DAM POET**
See also CA 118; 137; MAICYA; SATA 17

Riley, Tex
See Creasey, John

Rilke, Rainer Maria
1875-1926 .... **TCLC 1, 6, 19;
DAM POET; PC 2**
See also CA 104; 132; DLB 81; MTCW

Rimbaud, (Jean Nicolas) Arthur
1854-1891 ..... **NCLC 4, 35; DA; DAB;
DAC; DAM MST, POET; PC 3; WLC**

Rinehart, Mary Roberts
1876-1958 .... **TCLC 52**
See also CA 108

Ringmaster, The
See Mencken, H(enry) L(ouis)

Ringwood, Gwen(dolyn Margaret) Pharis
1910-1984 .... **CLC 48**
See also CA 148; 112; DLB 88

Rio, Michel 19(?)-............... **CLC 43**

Ritsos, Giannes
See Ritsos, Yannis

Ritsos, Yannis 1909-1990..... **CLC 6, 13, 31**
See also CA 77-80; 133; CANR 39; MTCW

Ritter, Erika 1948(?)-............. **CLC 52**

Rivera, Jose Eustasio 1889-1928... **TCLC 35**
See also HW

Rivers, Conrad Kent 1933-1968...... **CLC 1**
See also BW 1; CA 85-88; DLB 41

Rivers, Elfrida
See Bradley, Marion Zimmer

Riverside, John
See Heinlein, Robert A(nson)

Rizal, Jose 1861-1896.......... **NCLC 27**

Roa Bastos, Augusto (Antonio)
1917- ..... **CLC 45; DAM MULT; HLC**
See also CA 131; DLB 113; HW

Robbe-Grillet, Alain
1922- ...... **CLC 1, 2, 4, 6, 8, 10, 14, 43**
See also CA 9-12R; CANR 33; DLB 83;
MTCW

Robbins, Harold
1916- .... **CLC 5; DAM NOV**
See also CA 73-76; CANR 26, 54; MTCW

Robbins, Thomas Eugene 1936-
See Robbins, Tom
See also CA 81-84; CANR 29; DAM NOV,
POP; MTCW

Robbins, Tom.............. **CLC 9, 32, 64**
See also Robbins, Thomas Eugene
See also BEST 90:3; DLBY 80

Robbins, Trina 1938-............. **CLC 21**
See also CA 128

Roberts, Charles G(eorge) D(ouglas)
1860-1943.................. **TCLC 8**
See also CA 105; CLR 33; DLB 92;
SATA 88; SATA-Brief 29

Roberts, Elizabeth Madox
1886-1941 .... **TCLC 68**
See also CA 111; DLB 9, 54, 102;
SATA 33; SATA-Brief 27

Roberts, Kate 1891-1985 .... **CLC 15**
See also CA 107; 116

Roberts, Keith (John Kingston)
1935- .... **CLC 14**
See also CA 25-28R; CANR 46

Roberts, Kenneth (Lewis)
1885-1957 .... **TCLC 23**
See also CA 109; DLB 9

Roberts, Michele (B.) 1949-........ **CLC 48**
See also CA 115

Robertson, Ellis
See Ellison, Harlan (Jay); Silverberg, Robert

Robertson, Thomas William
1829-1871 .... **NCLC 35; DAM DRAM**

Robinson, Edwin Arlington
1869-1935 .... **TCLC 5; DA; DAC;**
DAM MST, POET; PC 1
See also CA 104; 133; CDALB 1865-1917;
DLB 54; MTCW

Robinson, Henry Crabb
1775-1867 .... **NCLC 15**
See also DLB 107

Robinson, Jill 1936- .... **CLC 10**
See also CA 102; INT 102

Robinson, Kim Stanley 1952- ...... **CLC 34**
See also CA 126

Robinson, Lloyd
See Silverberg, Robert

Robinson, Marilynne 1944-........ **CLC 25**
See also CA 116

Robinson, Smokey................. **CLC 21**
See also Robinson, William, Jr.

Robinson, William, Jr. 1940-
See Robinson, Smokey
See also CA 116

Robison, Mary 1949- .... **CLC 42, 98**
See also CA 113; 116; DLB 130; INT 116

Rod, Edouard 1857-1910 .... **TCLC 52**

Roddenberry, Eugene Wesley 1921-1991
See Roddenberry, Gene
See also CA 110; 135; CANR 37; SATA 45;
SATA-Obit 69

Roddenberry, Gene .... **CLC 17**
See also Roddenberry, Eugene Wesley
See also AAYA 5; SATA-Obit 69

Rodgers, Mary 1931- .... **CLC 12**
See also CA 49-52; CANR 8, 55; CLR 20;
INT CANR-8; JRDA; MAICYA;
SATA 8

Rodgers, W(illiam) R(obert)
1909-1969 .... **CLC 7**
See also CA 85-88; DLB 20

Rodman, Eric
See Silverberg, Robert

Rodman, Howard 1920(?)-1985 ..... **CLC 65**
See also CA 118

Rodman, Maia
See Wojciechowska, Maia (Teresa)

Rodriguez, Claudio 1934-......... **CLC 10**
See also DLB 134

Roelvaag, O(le) E(dvart)
1876-1931 .... **TCLC 17**
See also CA 117; DLB 9

Roethke, Theodore (Huebner)
1908-1963 ...... **CLC 1, 3, 8, 11, 19, 46;**
DAM POET; PC 15
See also CA 81-84; CABS 2;
CDALB 1941-1968; DLB 5; MTCW

Rogers, Thomas Hunton 1927- ..... **CLC 57**
See also CA 89-92; INT 89-92

Rogers, Will(iam Penn Adair)
1879-1935 ...... **TCLC 8; DAM MULT**
See also CA 105; 144; DLB 11; NNAL

Rogin, Gilbert 1929-............. **CLC 18**
See also CA 65-68; CANR 15

Rohan, Koda .... **TCLC 22**
See also Koda Shigeyuki

Rohmer, Eric................... **CLC 16**
See also Scherer, Jean-Marie Maurice

Rohmer, Sax .... **TCLC 28**
See also Ward, Arthur Henry Sarsfield
See also DLB 70

Roiphe, Anne (Richardson)
1935- .... **CLC 3, 9**
See also CA 89-92; CANR 45; DLBY 80;
INT 89-92

Rojas, Fernando de 1465-1541 ...... **LC 23**

Rolfe, Frederick (William Serafino Austin
Lewis Mary) 1860-1913...... **TCLC 12**
See also CA 107; DLB 34, 156

Rolland, Romain 1866-1944....... **TCLC 23**
See also CA 118; DLB 65

Rolle, Richard c. 1300-c. 1349 ... **CMLC 21**
See also DLB 146

Rolvaag, O(le) E(dvart)
See Roelvaag, O(le) E(dvart)

Romain Arnaud, Saint
See Aragon, Louis

Romains, Jules 1885-1972.......... **CLC 7**
See also CA 85-88; CANR 34; DLB 65;
MTCW

Romero, Jose Ruben 1890-1952 ... **TCLC 14**
See also CA 114; 131; HW

Ronsard, Pierre de
1524-1585 .... **LC 6; PC 11**

Rooke, Leon
1934- .... **CLC 25, 34; DAM POP**
See also CA 25-28R; CANR 23, 53

Roosevelt, Theodore 1858-1919.... **TCLC 69**
See also CA 115; DLB 47

Roper, William 1498-1578 .... **LC 10**

Roquelaure, A. N.
See Rice, Anne

Rosa, Joao Guimaraes 1908-1967 ... **CLC 23**
See also CA 89-92; DLB 113

Rose, Wendy
1948- .... **CLC 85; DAM MULT; PC 13**
See also CA 53-56; CANR 5, 51; DLB 175;
NNAL; SATA 12

Rosen, Richard (Dean) 1949-....... **CLC 39**
See also CA 77-80; INT CANR-30

Rosenberg, Isaac 1890-1918....... **TCLC 12**
See also CA 107; DLB 20

Rosenblatt, Joe .... **CLC 15**
See also Rosenblatt, Joseph

Rosenblatt, Joseph 1933-
See Rosenblatt, Joe
See also CA 89-92; INT 89-92

Rosenfeld, Samuel 1896-1963
See Tzara, Tristan
See also CA 89-92

Rosenstock, Sami
See Tzara, Tristan

Rosenstock, Samuel
See Tzara, Tristan

Rosenthal, M(acha) L(ouis)
1917-1996 .... **CLC 28**
See also CA 1-4R; 152; CAAS 6; CANR 4,
51; DLB 5; SATA 59

Ross, Barnaby
See Dannay, Frederic

Ross, Bernard L.
See Follett, Ken(neth Martin)

Ross, J. H.
See Lawrence, T(homas) E(dward)

Ross, Martin
See Martin, Violet Florence
See also DLB 135

Ross, (James) Sinclair
1908- ...... **CLC 13; DAC; DAM MST;**
SSC 24
See also CA 73-76; DLB 88

Rossetti, Christina (Georgina)
1830-1894 ..... **NCLC 2, 50; DAB;**
DAC; DAM MST, POET; PC 7; WLC
See also DLB 35, 163; MAICYA; SATA 20

Rossetti, Dante Gabriel
1828-1882 ..... **NCLC 4; DA; DAB;**
DAC; DAM MST, POET; WLC
See also CDBLB 1832-1890; DLB 35

Rossner, Judith (Perelman)
1935- .... **CLC 6, 9, 29**
See also AITN 2; BEST 90:3; CA 17-20R;
CANR 18, 51; DLB 6; INT CANR-18;
MTCW

Rostand, Edmond (Eugene Alexis)
1868-1918 ...... **TCLC 6, 37; DA; DAB;**
DAC; DAM DRAM, MST
See also CA 104; 126; MTCW

Roth, Henry 1906-1995 .... **CLC 2, 6, 11**
See also CA 11-12; 149; CANR 38; CAP 1;
DLB 28; MTCW

Roth, Joseph 1894-1939.......... **TCLC 33**
See also DLB 85

Roth, Philip (Milton)
1933- ...... **CLC 1, 2, 3, 4, 6, 9, 15, 22,**
31, 47, 66, 86; DA; DAB; DAC;
DAM MST, NOV, POP; WLC
See also BEST 90:3; CA 1-4R; CANR 1, 22,
36, 55; CDALB 1968-1988; DLB 2, 28,
173; DLBY 82; MTCW

Rothenberg, Jerome 1931-........ **CLC 6, 57**
See also CA 45-48; CANR 1; DLB 5

Roumain, Jacques (Jean Baptiste)
1907-1944 .... **TCLC 19; BLC;**
DAM MULT
See also BW 1; CA 117; 125

Salisbury, John
See Caute, David

Salter, James 1925- .... **CLC 7, 52, 59**
See also CA 73-76; DLB 130

Saltus, Edgar (Everton)
1855-1921 .... **TCLC 8**
See also CA 105

Saltykov, Mikhail Evgrafovich
1826-1889 .... **NCLC 16**

Samarakis, Antonis 1919- .... **CLC 5**
See also CA 25-28R; CAAS 16; CANR 36

Sanchez, Florencio 1875-1910..... **TCLC 37**
See also CA 153; HW

Sanchez, Luis Rafael 1936-........ **CLC 23**
See also CA 128; DLB 145; HW

Sanchez, Sonia
1934- ...... **CLC 5; BLC; DAM MULT;**
PC 9
See also BW 2; CA 33-36R; CANR 24, 49;
CLR 18; DLB 41; DLBD 8; MAICYA;
MTCW; SATA 22

Sand, George
1804-1876 .... **NCLC 2, 42, 57; DA;**
DAB; DAC; DAM MST, NOV; WLC
See also DLB 119

Sandburg, Carl (August)
1878-1967 .... **CLC 1, 4, 10, 15, 35; DA;**
DAB; DAC; DAM MST, POET; PC 2;
WLC
See also CA 5-8R; 25-28R; CANR 35;
CDALB 1865-1917; DLB 17, 54;
MAICYA; MTCW; SATA 8

Sandburg, Charles
See Sandburg, Carl (August)

Sandburg, Charles A.
See Sandburg, Carl (August)

Sanders, (James) Ed(ward) 1939- ... **CLC 53**
See also CA 13-16R; CAAS 21; CANR 13,
44; DLB 16

Sanders, Lawrence
1920- .... **CLC 41; DAM POP**
See also BEST 89:4; CA 81-84; CANR 33;
MTCW

Sanders, Noah
See Blount, Roy (Alton), Jr.

Sanders, Winston P.
See Anderson, Poul (William)

Sandoz, Mari(e Susette)
1896-1966 .... **CLC 28**
See also CA 1-4R; 25-28R; CANR 17;
DLB 9; MTCW; SATA 5

Saner, Reg(inald Anthony) 1931- .... **CLC 9**
See also CA 65-68

Sannazaro, Jacopo 1456(?)-1530...... **LC 8**

Sansom, William
1912-1976 ...... **CLC 2, 6; DAM NOV;**
SSC 21
See also CA 5-8R; 65-68; CANR 42;
DLB 139; MTCW

Santayana, George 1863-1952 ..... **TCLC 40**
See also CA 115; DLB 54, 71; DLBD 13

Santiago, Danny .... **CLC 33**
See also James, Daniel (Lewis)
See also DLB 122

Santmyer, Helen Hoover
1895-1986 .... **CLC 33**
See also CA 1-4R; 118; CANR 15, 33;
DLBY 84; MTCW

Santos, Bienvenido N(uqui)
1911-1996 ...... **CLC 22; DAM MULT**
See also CA 101; 151; CANR 19, 46

Sapper .... **TCLC 44**
See also McNeile, Herman Cyril

Sapphire 1950- .... **CLC 99**

Sappho
fl. 6th cent. B.C.- .... **CMLC 3;**
DAM POET; PC 5

Sarduy, Severo 1937-1993 .... **CLC 6, 97**
See also CA 89-92; 142; DLB 113; HW

Sargeson, Frank 1903-1982 .... **CLC 31**
See also CA 25-28R; 106; CANR 38

Sarmiento, Felix Ruben Garcia
See Dario, Ruben

Saroyan, William
1908-1981 ..... **CLC 1, 8, 10, 29, 34, 56;**
DA; DAB; DAC; DAM DRAM, MST,
NOV; SSC 21; WLC
See also CA 5-8R; 103; CANR 30; DLB 7,
9, 86; DLBY 81; MTCW; SATA 23;
SATA-Obit 24

Sarraute, Nathalie
1900- .... **CLC 1, 2, 4, 8, 10, 31, 80**
See also CA 9-12R; CANR 23; DLB 83;
MTCW

Sarton, (Eleanor) May
1912-1995 .... **CLC 4, 14, 49, 91;**
DAM POET
See also CA 1-4R; 149; CANR 1, 34, 55;
DLB 48; DLBY 81; INT CANR-34;
MTCW; SATA 36; SATA-Obit 86

Sartre, Jean-Paul
1905-1980 .... **CLC 1, 4, 7, 9, 13, 18, 24,**
44, 50, 52; DA; DAB; DAC;
DAM DRAM, MST, NOV; DC 3; WLC
See also CA 9-12R; 97-100; CANR 21;
DLB 72; MTCW

Sassoon, Siegfried (Lorraine)
1886-1967 .... **CLC 36; DAB;**
DAM MST, NOV, POET; PC 12
See also CA 104; 25-28R; CANR 36;
DLB 20; MTCW

Satterfield, Charles
See Pohl, Frederik

Saul, John (W. III)
1942- ...... **CLC 46; DAM NOV, POP**
See also AAYA 10; BEST 90:4; CA 81-84;
CANR 16, 40

Saunders, Caleb
See Heinlein, Robert A(nson)

Saura (Atares), Carlos 1932-....... **CLC 20**
See also CA 114; 131; HW

Sauser-Hall, Frederic 1887-1961.... **CLC 18**
See also Cendrars, Blaise
See also CA 102; 93-96; CANR 36; MTCW

Saussure, Ferdinand de
1857-1913 .... **TCLC 49**

Savage, Catharine
See Brosman, Catharine Savage

Savage, Thomas 1915- .... **CLC 40**
See also CA 126; 132; CAAS 15; INT 132

Savan, Glenn 19(?)- .... **CLC 50**

Sayers, Dorothy L(eigh)
1893-1957 ..... **TCLC 2, 15; DAM POP**
See also CA 104; 119; CDBLB 1914-1945;
DLB 10, 36, 77, 100; MTCW

Sayers, Valerie 1952- .... **CLC 50**
See also CA 134

Sayles, John (Thomas)
1950- .... **CLC 7, 10, 14**
See also CA 57-60; CANR 41; DLB 44

Scammell, Michael .... **CLC 34**

Scannell, Vernon 1922- .... **CLC 49**
See also CA 5-8R; CANR 8, 24; DLB 27;
SATA 59

Scarlett, Susan
See Streatfeild, (Mary) Noel

Schaeffer, Susan Fromberg
1941- .... **CLC 6, 11, 22**
See also CA 49-52; CANR 18; DLB 28;
MTCW; SATA 22

Schary, Jill
See Robinson, Jill

Schell, Jonathan 1943-............ **CLC 35**
See also CA 73-76; CANR 12

Schelling, Friedrich Wilhelm Joseph von
1775-1854 .... **NCLC 30**
See also DLB 90

Schendel, Arthur van 1874-1946 ... **TCLC 56**

Scherer, Jean-Marie Maurice 1920-
See Rohmer, Eric
See also CA 110

Schevill, James (Erwin) 1920-....... **CLC 7**
See also CA 5-8R; CAAS 12

Schiller, Friedrich
1759-1805 .... **NCLC 39; DAM DRAM**
See also DLB 94

Schisgal, Murray (Joseph) 1926-..... **CLC 6**
See also CA 21-24R; CANR 48

Schlee, Ann 1934-................. **CLC 35**
See also CA 101; CANR 29; SATA 44;
SATA-Brief 36

Schlegel, August Wilhelm von
1767-1845 .... **NCLC 15**
See also DLB 94

Schlegel, Friedrich 1772-1829 .... **NCLC 45**
See also DLB 90

Schlegel, Johann Elias (von)
1719(?)-1749 .... **LC 5**

Schlesinger, Arthur M(eier), Jr.
1917- .... **CLC 84**
See also AITN 1; CA 1-4R; CANR 1, 28;
DLB 17; INT CANR-28; MTCW;
SATA 61

Schmidt, Arno (Otto) 1914-1979 .... **CLC 56**
See also CA 128; 109; DLB 69

Schmitz, Aron Hector 1861-1928
See Svevo, Italo
See also CA 104; 122; MTCW

Schnackenberg, Gjertrud 1953-..... **CLC 40**
See also CA 116; DLB 120

Schneider, Leonard Alfred 1925-1966
See Bruce, Lenny
See also CA 89-92

Sierra, Gregorio Martinez
See Martinez Sierra, Gregorio

Sierra, Maria (de la O'LeJarraga) Martinez
See Martinez Sierra, Maria (de la
O'LeJarraga)

Sigal, Clancy 1926-............... **CLC 7**
See also CA 1-4R

Sigourney, Lydia Howard (Huntley)
1791-1865 .... **NCLC 21**
See also DLB 1, 42, 73

Siguenza y Gongora, Carlos de
1645-1700 .... **LC 8**

Sigurjonsson, Johann 1880-1919... **TCLC 27**

Sikelianos, Angelos 1884-1951 .... **TCLC 39**

Silkin, Jon 1930- .... **CLC 2, 6, 43**
See also CA 5-8R; CAAS 5; DLB 27

Silko, Leslie (Marmon)
1948- .... **CLC 23, 74; DA; DAC;
DAM MST, MULT, POP**
See also AAYA 14; CA 115; 122;
CANR 45; DLB 143, 175; NNAL

Sillanpaa, Frans Eemil 1888-1964... **CLC 19**
See also CA 129; 93-96; MTCW

Sillitoe, Alan
1928- .... **CLC 1, 3, 6, 10, 19, 57**
See also AITN 1; CA 9-12R; CAAS 2;
CANR 8, 26, 55; CDBLB 1960 to
Present; DLB 14, 139; MTCW; SATA 61

Silone, Ignazio 1900-1978 .... **CLC 4**
See also CA 25-28; 81-84; CANR 34;
CAP 2; MTCW

Silver, Joan Micklin 1935- .... **CLC 20**
See also CA 114; 121; INT 121

Silver, Nicholas
See Faust, Frederick (Schiller)

Silverberg, Robert
1935- .... **CLC 7; DAM POP**
See also CA 1-4R; CAAS 3; CANR 1, 20,
36; DLB 8; INT CANR-20; MAICYA;
MTCW; SATA 13, 91

Silverstein, Alvin 1933- .... **CLC 17**
See also CA 49-52; CANR 2; CLR 25;
JRDA; MAICYA; SATA 8, 69

Silverstein, Virginia B(arbara Opshelor)
1937- .... **CLC 17**
See also CA 49-52; CANR 2; CLR 25;
JRDA; MAICYA; SATA 8, 69

Sim, Georges
See Simenon, Georges (Jacques Christian)

Simak, Clifford D(onald)
1904-1988 .... **CLC 1, 55**
See also CA 1-4R; 125; CANR 1, 35;
DLB 8; MTCW; SATA-Obit 56

Simenon, Georges (Jacques Christian)
1903-1989 ...... **CLC 1, 2, 3, 8, 18, 47;
DAM POP**
See also CA 85-88; 129; CANR 35;
DLB 72; DLBY 89; MTCW

Simic, Charles
1938- .... **CLC 6, 9, 22, 49, 68;
DAM POET**
See also CA 29-32R; CAAS 4; CANR 12,
33, 52; DLB 105

Simmel, Georg 1858-1918 .... **TCLC 64**

Simmons, Charles (Paul) 1924-..... **CLC 57**
See also CA 89-92; INT 89-92

Simmons, Dan 1948-... **CLC 44; DAM POP**
See also AAYA 16; CA 138; CANR 53

Simmons, James (Stewart Alexander)
1933- .... **CLC 43**
See also CA 105; CAAS 21; DLB 40

Simms, William Gilmore
1806-1870 .... **NCLC 3**
See also DLB 3, 30, 59, 73

Simon, Carly 1945-............... **CLC 26**
See also CA 105

Simon, Claude
1913-.... **CLC 4, 9, 15, 39; DAM NOV**
See also CA 89-92; CANR 33; DLB 83;
MTCW

Simon, (Marvin) Neil
1927- .... **CLC 6, 11, 31, 39, 70;
DAM DRAM**
See also AITN 1; CA 21-24R; CANR 26,
54; DLB 7; MTCW

Simon, Paul (Frederick) 1941(?)- ... **CLC 17**
See also CA 116; 153

Simonon, Paul 1956(?)- .... **CLC 30**

Simpson, Harriette
See Arnow, Harriette (Louisa) Simpson

Simpson, Louis (Aston Marantz)
1923-.... **CLC 4, 7, 9, 32; DAM POET**
See also CA 1-4R; CAAS 4; CANR 1;
DLB 5; MTCW

Simpson, Mona (Elizabeth) 1957-... **CLC 44**
See also CA 122; 135

Simpson, N(orman) F(rederick)
1919- .... **CLC 29**
See also CA 13-16R; DLB 13

Sinclair, Andrew (Annandale)
1935- .... **CLC 2, 14**
See also CA 9-12R; CAAS 5; CANR 14, 38;
DLB 14; MTCW

Sinclair, Emil
See Hesse, Hermann

Sinclair, Iain 1943-............... **CLC 76**
See also CA 132

Sinclair, Iain MacGregor
See Sinclair, Iain

Sinclair, Irene
See Griffith, D(avid Lewelyn) W(ark)

Sinclair, Mary Amelia St. Clair 1865(?)-1946
See Sinclair, May
See also CA 104

Sinclair, May................. **TCLC 3, 11**
See also Sinclair, Mary Amelia St. Clair
See also DLB 36, 135

Sinclair, Roy
See Griffith, D(avid Lewelyn) W(ark)

Sinclair, Upton (Beall)
1878-1968 ...... **CLC 1, 11, 15, 63; DA;
DAB; DAC; DAM MST, NOV; WLC**
See also CA 5-8R; 25-28R; CANR 7;
CDALB 1929-1941; DLB 9;
INT CANR-7; MTCW; SATA 9

Singer, Isaac
See Singer, Isaac Bashevis

Singer, Isaac Bashevis
1904-1991 .... **CLC 1, 3, 6, 9, 11, 15, 23,
38, 69; DA; DAB; DAC; DAM MST,
NOV; SSC 3; WLC**
See also AITN 1, 2; CA 1-4R; 134;
CANR 1, 39; CDALB 1941-1968; CLR 1;
DLB 6, 28, 52; DLBY 91; JRDA;
MAICYA; MTCW; SATA 3, 27;
SATA-Obit 68

Singer, Israel Joshua 1893-1944 ... **TCLC 33**

Singh, Khushwant 1915-........... **CLC 11**
See also CA 9-12R; CAAS 9; CANR 6

Sinjohn, John
See Galsworthy, John

Sinyavsky, Andrei (Donatevich)
1925- .... **CLC 8**
See also CA 85-88

Sirin, V.
See Nabokov, Vladimir (Vladimirovich)

Sissman, L(ouis) E(dward)
1928-1976 .... **CLC 9, 18**
See also CA 21-24R; 65-68; CANR 13;
DLB 5

Sisson, C(harles) H(ubert) 1914-..... **CLC 8**
See also CA 1-4R; CAAS 3; CANR 3, 48;
DLB 27

Sitwell, Dame Edith
1887-1964 .... **CLC 2, 9, 67;
DAM POET; PC 3**
See also CA 9-12R; CANR 35;
CDBLB 1945-1960; DLB 20; MTCW

Sjoewall, Maj 1935-............... **CLC 7**
See also CA 65-68

Sjowall, Maj
See Sjoewall, Maj

Skelton, Robin 1925-............. **CLC 13**
See also AITN 2; CA 5-8R; CAAS 5;
CANR 28; DLB 27, 53

Skolimowski, Jerzy 1938- .... **CLC 20**
See also CA 128

Skram, Amalie (Bertha)
1847-1905 .... **TCLC 25**

Skvorecky, Josef (Vaclav)
1924- .... **CLC 15, 39, 69; DAC;
DAM NOV**
See also CA 61-64; CAAS 1; CANR 10, 34;
MTCW

Slade, Bernard................. **CLC 11, 46**
See also Newbound, Bernard Slade
See also CAAS 9; DLB 53

Slaughter, Carolyn 1946-.......... **CLC 56**
See also CA 85-88

Slaughter, Frank G(ill) 1908- ...... **CLC 29**
See also AITN 2; CA 5-8R; CANR 5;
INT CANR-5

Slavitt, David R(ytman) 1935-.... **CLC 5, 14**
See also CA 21-24R; CAAS 3; CANR 41;
DLB 5, 6

Slesinger, Tess 1905-1945 .... **TCLC 10**
See also CA 107; DLB 102

Slessor, Kenneth 1901-1971........ **CLC 14**
See also CA 102; 89-92

Slowacki, Juliusz 1809-1849 ..... **NCLC 15**

Smart, Christopher
    1722-1771 . . . **LC 3; DAM POET; PC 13**
    See also DLB 109

Smart, Elizabeth 1913-1986. . . . . . . **CLC 54**
    See also CA 81-84; 118; DLB 88

Smiley, Jane (Graves)
    1949- . . . . **CLC 53, 76; DAM POP**
    See also CA 104; CANR 30, 50;
    INT CANR-30

Smith, A(rthur) J(ames) M(arshall)
    1902-1980 . . . . **CLC 15; DAC**
    See also CA 1-4R; 102; CANR 4; DLB 88

Smith, Adam 1723-1790. . . . . **LC 36**
    See also DLB 104

Smith, Alexander 1829-1867 . . . . . **NCLC 59**
    See also DLB 32, 55

Smith, Anna Deavere 1950- . . . . **CLC 86**
    See also CA 133

Smith, Betty (Wehner) 1896-1972. . . **CLC 19**
    See also CA 5-8R; 33-36R; DLBY 82;
    SATA 6

Smith, Charlotte (Turner)
    1749-1806 . . . . **NCLC 23**
    See also DLB 39, 109

Smith, Clark Ashton 1893-1961 . . . . **CLC 43**
    See also CA 143

Smith, Dave . . . . **CLC 22, 42**
    See also Smith, David (Jeddie)
    See also CAAS 7; DLB 5

Smith, David (Jeddie) 1942-
    See Smith, Dave
    See also CA 49-52; CANR 1; DAM POET

Smith, Florence Margaret 1902-1971
    See Smith, Stevie
    See also CA 17-18; 29-32R; CANR 35;
    CAP 2; DAM POET; MTCW

Smith, Iain Crichton 1928- . . . . **CLC 64**
    See also CA 21-24R; DLB 40, 139

Smith, John 1580(?)-1631 . . . . **LC 9**

Smith, Johnston
    See Crane, Stephen (Townley)

Smith, Joseph, Jr. 1805-1844 . . . . **NCLC 53**

Smith, Lee 1944- . . . . **CLC 25, 73**
    See also CA 114; 119; CANR 46; DLB 143;
    DLBY 83; INT 119

Smith, Martin
    See Smith, Martin Cruz

Smith, Martin Cruz
    1942- . . . . . **CLC 25; DAM MULT, POP**
    See also BEST 89:4; CA 85-88; CANR 6,
    23, 43; INT CANR-23; NNAL

Smith, Mary-Ann Tirone 1944- . . . . . **CLC 39**
    See also CA 118; 136

Smith, Patti 1946- . . . . **CLC 12**
    See also CA 93-96

Smith, Pauline (Urmson)
    1882-1959 . . . . **TCLC 25**

Smith, Rosamond
    See Oates, Joyce Carol

Smith, Sheila Kaye
    See Kaye-Smith, Sheila

Smith, Stevie . . . . . . **CLC 3, 8, 25, 44; PC 12**
    See also Smith, Florence Margaret
    See also DLB 20

Smith, Wilbur (Addison) 1933- . . . . . **CLC 33**
    See also CA 13-16R; CANR 7, 46; MTCW

Smith, William Jay 1918- . . . . **CLC 6**
    See also CA 5-8R; CANR 44; DLB 5;
    MAICYA; SAAS 22; SATA 2, 68

Smith, Woodrow Wilson
    See Kuttner, Henry

Smolenskin, Peretz 1842-1885. . . . **NCLC 30**

Smollett, Tobias (George) 1721-1771 . . **LC 2**
    See also CDBLB 1660-1789; DLB 39, 104

Snodgrass, W(illiam) D(e Witt)
    1926- . . . . **CLC 2, 6, 10, 18, 68;**
                                              DAM POET
    See also CA 1-4R; CANR 6, 36; DLB 5;
    MTCW

Snow, C(harles) P(ercy)
    1905-1980 . . . . . . **CLC 1, 4, 6, 9, 13, 19;**
                                              DAM NOV
    See also CA 5-8R; 101; CANR 28;
    CDBLB 1945-1960; DLB 15, 77; MTCW

Snow, Frances Compton
    See Adams, Henry (Brooks)

Snyder, Gary (Sherman)
    1930- . . **CLC 1, 2, 5, 9, 32; DAM POET**
    See also CA 17-20R; CANR 30; DLB 5, 16,
    165

Snyder, Zilpha Keatley 1927- . . . . . . **CLC 17**
    See also AAYA 15; CA 9-12R; CANR 38;
    CLR 31; JRDA; MAICYA; SAAS 2;
    SATA 1, 28, 75

Soares, Bernardo
    See Pessoa, Fernando (Antonio Nogueira)

Sobh, A.
    See Shamlu, Ahmad

Sobol, Joshua . . . . **CLC 60**

Soderberg, Hjalmar 1869-1941 . . . . **TCLC 39**

Sodergran, Edith (Irene)
    See Soedergran, Edith (Irene)

Soedergran, Edith (Irene)
    1892-1923 . . . . **TCLC 31**

Softly, Edgar
    See Lovecraft, H(oward) P(hillips)

Softly, Edward
    See Lovecraft, H(oward) P(hillips)

Sokolov, Raymond 1941- . . . . **CLC 7**
    See also CA 85-88

Solo, Jay
    See Ellison, Harlan (Jay)

Sologub, Fyodor . . . . **TCLC 9**
    See also Teternikov, Fyodor Kuzmich

Solomons, Ikey Esquir
    See Thackeray, William Makepeace

Solomos, Dionysios 1798-1857 . . . **NCLC 15**

Solwoska, Mara
    See French, Marilyn

Solzhenitsyn, Aleksandr I(sayevich)
    1918- . . . . . . **CLC 1, 2, 4, 7, 9, 10, 18, 26,**
            34, 78; DA; DAB; DAC; DAM MST,
                                              NOV; WLC
    See also AITN 1; CA 69-72; CANR 40;
    MTCW

Somers, Jane
    See Lessing, Doris (May)

Somerville, Edith 1858-1949 . . . . . . **TCLC 51**
    See also DLB 135

Somerville & Ross
    See Martin, Violet Florence; Somerville,
    Edith

Sommer, Scott 1951- . . . . **CLC 25**
    See also CA 106

Sondheim, Stephen (Joshua)
    1930- . . . . **CLC 30, 39; DAM DRAM**
    See also AAYA 11; CA 103; CANR 47

Sontag, Susan
    1933- . . . . **CLC 1, 2, 10, 13, 31;**
                                              DAM POP
    See also CA 17-20R; CANR 25, 51; DLB 2,
    67; MTCW

Sophocles
    496(?)B.C.-406(?)B.C. . . . . . **CMLC 2; DA;**
        DAB; DAC; DAM DRAM, MST; DC 1

Sordello 1189-1269. . . . . **CMLC 15**

Sorel, Julia
    See Drexler, Rosalyn

Sorrentino, Gilbert
    1929- . . . . **CLC 3, 7, 14, 22, 40**
    See also CA 77-80; CANR 14, 33; DLB 5,
    173; DLBY 80; INT CANR-14

Soto, Gary
    1952- . . . . **CLC 32, 80; DAM MULT;**
                                              HLC
    See also AAYA 10; CA 119; 125;
    CANR 50; CLR 38; DLB 82; HW;
    INT 125; JRDA; SATA 80

Soupault, Philippe 1897-1990 . . . . . . **CLC 68**
    See also CA 116; 147; 131

Souster, (Holmes) Raymond
    1921- . . . **CLC 5, 14; DAC; DAM POET**
    See also CA 13-16R; CAAS 14; CANR 13,
    29, 53; DLB 88; SATA 63

Southern, Terry 1924(?)-1995 . . . . **CLC 7**
    See also CA 1-4R; 150; CANR 1, 55;
    DLB 2

Southey, Robert 1774-1843 . . . . **NCLC 8**
    See also DLB 93, 107, 142; SATA 54

Southworth, Emma Dorothy Eliza Nevitte
    1819-1899 . . . . **NCLC 26**

Souza, Ernest
    See Scott, Evelyn

Soyinka, Wole
    1934- . . . . **CLC 3, 5, 14, 36, 44; BLC;**
        DA; DAB; DAC; DAM DRAM, MST,
                                  MULT; DC 2; WLC
    See also BW 2; CA 13-16R; CANR 27, 39;
    DLB 125; MTCW

Spackman, W(illiam) M(ode)
    1905-1990 . . . . **CLC 46**
    See also CA 81-84; 132

Spacks, Barry (Bernard) 1931- . . . . . **CLC 14**
    See also CA 154; CANR 33; DLB 105

Spanidou, Irini 1946- . . . . **CLC 44**

Spark, Muriel (Sarah)
    1918- . . . . . **CLC 2, 3, 5, 8, 13, 18, 40, 94;**
        DAB; DAC; DAM MST, NOV; SSC 10
    See also CA 5-8R; CANR 12, 36;
    CDBLB 1945-1960; DLB 15, 139;
    INT CANR-12; MTCW

Spaulding, Douglas
See Bradbury, Ray (Douglas)

Spaulding, Leonard
See Bradbury, Ray (Douglas)

Spence, J. A. D.
See Eliot, T(homas) S(tearns)

Spencer, Elizabeth 1921- . . . . **CLC 22**
See also CA 13-16R; CANR 32; DLB 6;
MTCW; SATA 14

Spencer, Leonard G.
See Silverberg, Robert

Spencer, Scott 1945- . . . . **CLC 30**
See also CA 113; CANR 51; DLBY 86

Spender, Stephen (Harold)
1909-1995 . . . . . . **CLC 1, 2, 5, 10, 41, 91;
DAM POET**
See also CA 9-12R; 149; CANR 31, 54;
CDBLB 1945-1960; DLB 20; MTCW

Spengler, Oswald (Arnold Gottfried)
1880-1936 . . . . **TCLC 25**
See also CA 118

Spenser, Edmund
1552(?)-1599 . . . . **LC 5; DA; DAB; DAC;
DAM MST, POET; PC 8; WLC**
See also CDBLB Before 1660; DLB 167

Spicer, Jack
1925-1965 . . . . **CLC 8, 18, 72;
DAM POET**
See also CA 85-88; DLB 5, 16

Spiegelman, Art 1948- . . . . **CLC 76**
See also AAYA 10; CA 125; CANR 41, 55

Spielberg, Peter 1929- . . . . **CLC 6**
See also CA 5-8R; CANR 4, 48; DLBY 81

Spielberg, Steven 1947- . . . . **CLC 20**
See also AAYA 8; CA 77-80; CANR 32;
SATA 32

Spillane, Frank Morrison 1918-
See Spillane, Mickey
See also CA 25-28R; CANR 28; MTCW;
SATA 66

Spillane, Mickey . . . . **CLC 3, 13**
See also Spillane, Frank Morrison

Spinoza, Benedictus de 1632-1677 . . . . **LC 9**

Spinrad, Norman (Richard) 1940- . . . **CLC 46**
See also CA 37-40R; CAAS 19; CANR 20;
DLB 8; INT CANR-20

Spitteler, Carl (Friedrich Georg)
1845-1924 . . . . **TCLC 12**
See also CA 109; DLB 129

Spivack, Kathleen (Romola Drucker)
1938- . . . . **CLC 6**
See also CA 49-52

Spoto, Donald 1941- . . . . **CLC 39**
See also CA 65-68; CANR 11

Springsteen, Bruce (F.) 1949- . . . . . . **CLC 17**
See also CA 111

Spurling, Hilary 1940- . . . . **CLC 34**
See also CA 104; CANR 25, 52

Spyker, John Howland
See Elman, Richard

Squires, (James) Radcliffe
1917-1993 . . . . **CLC 51**
See also CA 1-4R; 140; CANR 6, 21

Srivastava, Dhanpat Rai 1880(?)-1936
See Premchand
See also CA 118

Stacy, Donald
See Pohl, Frederik

Stael, Germaine de
See Stael-Holstein, Anne Louise Germaine
Necker Baronn
See also DLB 119

**Stael-Holstein, Anne Louise Germaine Necker
Baronn** 1766-1817 . . . . **NCLC 3**
See also Stael, Germaine de

Stafford, Jean 1915-1979 . . . **CLC 4, 7, 19, 68**
See also CA 1-4R; 85-88; CANR 3; DLB 2,
173; MTCW; SATA-Obit 22

Stafford, William (Edgar)
1914-1993 . . . **CLC 4, 7, 29; DAM POET**
See also CA 5-8R; 142; CAAS 3; CANR 5,
22; DLB 5; INT CANR-22

Staines, Trevor
See Brunner, John (Kilian Houston)

Stairs, Gordon
See Austin, Mary (Hunter)

Stannard, Martin 1947- . . . . **CLC 44**
See also CA 142; DLB 155

Stanton, Maura 1946- . . . . **CLC 9**
See also CA 89-92; CANR 15; DLB 120

Stanton, Schuyler
See Baum, L(yman) Frank

Stapledon, (William) Olaf
1886-1950 . . . . **TCLC 22**
See also CA 111; DLB 15

Starbuck, George (Edwin)
1931-1996 . . . . **CLC 53; DAM POET**
See also CA 21-24R; 153; CANR 23

Stark, Richard
See Westlake, Donald E(dwin)

Staunton, Schuyler
See Baum, L(yman) Frank

Stead, Christina (Ellen)
1902-1983 . . . . **CLC 2, 5, 8, 32, 80**
See also CA 13-16R; 109; CANR 33, 40;
MTCW

Stead, William Thomas
1849-1912 . . . . **TCLC 48**

Steele, Richard 1672-1729 . . . . **LC 18**
See also CDBLB 1660-1789; DLB 84, 101

Steele, Timothy (Reid) 1948- . . . . **CLC 45**
See also CA 93-96; CANR 16, 50; DLB 120

Steffens, (Joseph) Lincoln
1866-1936 . . . . **TCLC 20**
See also CA 117

Stegner, Wallace (Earle)
1909-1993 . . . **CLC 9, 49, 81; DAM NOV**
See also AITN 1; BEST 90:3; CA 1-4R;
141; CAAS 9; CANR 1, 21, 46; DLB 9;
DLBY 93; MTCW

Stein, Gertrude
1874-1946 . . . . . . **TCLC 1, 6, 28, 48; DA;
DAB; DAC; DAM MST, NOV, POET;
WLC**
See also CA 104; 132; CDALB 1917-1929;
DLB 4, 54, 86; MTCW

Steinbeck, John (Ernst)
1902-1968 . . . . . . **CLC 1, 5, 9, 13, 21, 34,
45, 75; DA; DAB; DAC; DAM DRAM,
MST, NOV; SSC 11; WLC**
See also AAYA 12; CA 1-4R; 25-28R;
CANR 1, 35; CDALB 1929-1941; DLB 7,
9; DLBD 2; MTCW; SATA 9

Steinem, Gloria 1934- . . . . **CLC 63**
See also CA 53-56; CANR 28, 51; MTCW

Steiner, George
1929- . . . . **CLC 24; DAM NOV**
See also CA 73-76; CANR 31; DLB 67;
MTCW; SATA 62

Steiner, K. Leslie
See Delany, Samuel R(ay, Jr.)

Steiner, Rudolf 1861-1925 . . . . **TCLC 13**
See also CA 107

Stendhal
1783-1842 . . . . **NCLC 23, 46; DA; DAB;
DAC; DAM MST, NOV; WLC**
See also DLB 119

Stephen, Leslie 1832-1904 . . . . **TCLC 23**
See also CA 123; DLB 57, 144

Stephen, Sir Leslie
See Stephen, Leslie

Stephen, Virginia
See Woolf, (Adeline) Virginia

Stephens, James 1882(?)-1950 . . . . . . **TCLC 4**
See also CA 104; DLB 19, 153, 162

Stephens, Reed
See Donaldson, Stephen R.

Steptoe, Lydia
See Barnes, Djuna

Sterchi, Beat 1949- . . . . **CLC 65**

Sterling, Brett
See Bradbury, Ray (Douglas); Hamilton,
Edmond

Sterling, Bruce 1954- . . . . **CLC 72**
See also CA 119; CANR 44

Sterling, George 1869-1926 . . . . **TCLC 20**
See also CA 117; DLB 54

Stern, Gerald 1925- . . . . **CLC 40**
See also CA 81-84; CANR 28; DLB 105

Stern, Richard (Gustave) 1928- . . . **CLC 4, 39**
See also CA 1-4R; CANR 1, 25, 52;
DLBY 87; INT CANR-25

Sternberg, Josef von 1894-1969 . . . . . **CLC 20**
See also CA 81-84

Sterne, Laurence
1713-1768 . . . . . . **LC 2; DA; DAB; DAC;
DAM MST, NOV; WLC**
See also CDBLB 1660-1789; DLB 39

Sternheim, (William Adolf) Carl
1878-1942 . . . . **TCLC 8**
See also CA 105; DLB 56, 118

Stevens, Mark 1951- . . . . **CLC 34**
See also CA 122

Stevens, Wallace
1879-1955 . . . . **TCLC 3, 12, 45; DA;
DAB; DAC; DAM MST, POET; PC 6;
WLC**
See also CA 104; 124; CDALB 1929-1941;
DLB 54; MTCW

Stevenson, Anne (Katharine)
1933- . . . . CLC 7, 33
See also CA 17-20R; CAAS 9; CANR 9, 33;
DLB 40; MTCW

Stevenson, Robert Louis (Balfour)
1850-1894 . . . . . NCLC 5, 14; DA; DAB;
DAC; DAM MST, NOV; SSC 11; WLC
See also CDBLB 1890-1914; CLR 10, 11;
DLB 18, 57, 141, 156, 174; DLBD 13;
JRDA; MAICYA; YABC 2

Stewart, J(ohn) I(nnes) M(ackintosh)
1906-1994 . . . . CLC 7, 14, 32
See also CA 85-88; 147; CAAS 3;
CANR 47; MTCW

Stewart, Mary (Florence Elinor)
1916- . . . . CLC 7, 35; DAB
See also CA 1-4R; CANR 1; SATA 12

Stewart, Mary Rainbow
See Stewart, Mary (Florence Elinor)

Stifle, June
See Campbell, Maria

Stifter, Adalbert 1805-1868 . . . . . . NCLC 41
See also DLB 133

Still, James 1906- . . . . CLC 49
See also CA 65-68; CAAS 17; CANR 10,
26; DLB 9; SATA 29

Sting
See Sumner, Gordon Matthew

Stirling, Arthur
See Sinclair, Upton (Beall)

Stitt, Milan 1941- . . . . CLC 29
See also CA 69-72

Stockton, Francis Richard 1834-1902
See Stockton, Frank R.
See also CA 108; 137; MAICYA; SATA 44

Stockton, Frank R. . . . . TCLC 47
See also Stockton, Francis Richard
See also DLB 42, 74; DLBD 13;
SATA-Brief 32

Stoddard, Charles
See Kuttner, Henry

Stoker, Abraham 1847-1912
See Stoker, Bram
See also CA 105; DA; DAC; DAM MST,
NOV; SATA 29

Stoker, Bram
1847-1912 . . . . TCLC 8; DAB; WLC
See also Stoker, Abraham
See also CA 150; CDBLB 1890-1914;
DLB 36, 70

Stolz, Mary (Slattery) 1920- . . . . CLC 12
See also AAYA 8; AITN 1; CA 5-8R;
CANR 13, 41; JRDA; MAICYA;
SAAS 3; SATA 10, 71

Stone, Irving
1903-1989 . . . . CLC 7; DAM POP
See also AITN 1; CA 1-4R; 129; CAAS 3;
CANR 1, 23; INT CANR-23; MTCW;
SATA 3; SATA-Obit 64

Stone, Oliver (William) 1946- . . . . . . CLC 73
See also AAYA 15; CA 110; CANR 55

Stone, Robert (Anthony)
1937- . . . . CLC 5, 23, 42
See also CA 85-88; CANR 23; DLB 152;
INT CANR-23; MTCW

Stone, Zachary
See Follett, Ken(neth Martin)

Stoppard, Tom
1937- . . . . . . CLC 1, 3, 4, 5, 8, 15, 29, 34,
63, 91; DA; DAB; DAC; DAM DRAM,
MST; DC 6; WLC
See also CA 81-84; CANR 39;
CDBLB 1960 to Present; DLB 13;
DLBY 85; MTCW

Storey, David (Malcolm)
1933- . . . . . CLC 2, 4, 5, 8; DAM DRAM
See also CA 81-84; CANR 36; DLB 13, 14;
MTCW

Storm, Hyemeyohsts
1935- . . . . CLC 3; DAM MULT
See also CA 81-84; CANR 45; NNAL

Storm, (Hans) Theodor (Woldsen)
1817-1888 . . . . NCLC 1

Storni, Alfonsina
1892-1938 . . . . . TCLC 5; DAM MULT;
HLC
See also CA 104; 131; HW

Stout, Rex (Todhunter) 1886-1975 . . . CLC 3
See also AITN 2; CA 61-64

Stow, (Julian) Randolph 1935- . . CLC 23, 48
See also CA 13-16R; CANR 33; MTCW

Stowe, Harriet (Elizabeth) Beecher
1811-1896 . . . . . NCLC 3, 50; DA; DAB;
DAC; DAM MST, NOV; WLC
See also CDALB 1865-1917; DLB 1, 12, 42,
74; JRDA; MAICYA; YABC 1

Strachey, (Giles) Lytton
1880-1932 . . . . TCLC 12
See also CA 110; DLB 149; DLBD 10

Strand, Mark
1934- . . CLC 6, 18, 41, 71; DAM POET
See also CA 21-24R; CANR 40; DLB 5;
SATA 41

Straub, Peter (Francis)
1943- . . . . CLC 28; DAM POP
See also BEST 89:1; CA 85-88; CANR 28;
DLBY 84; MTCW

Strauss, Botho 1944- . . . . CLC 22
See also DLB 124

Streatfeild, (Mary) Noel
1895(?)-1986 . . . . CLC 21
See also CA 81-84; 120; CANR 31;
CLR 17; DLB 160; MAICYA; SATA 20;
SATA-Obit 48

Stribling, T(homas) S(igismund)
1881-1965 . . . . CLC 23
See also CA 107; DLB 9

Strindberg, (Johan) August
1849-1912 . . . . . . TCLC 1, 8, 21, 47; DA;
DAB; DAC; DAM DRAM, MST; WLC
See also CA 104; 135

Stringer, Arthur 1874-1950 . . . . TCLC 37
See also DLB 92

Stringer, David
See Roberts, Keith (John Kingston)

Strugatskii, Arkadii (Natanovich)
1925-1991 . . . . CLC 27
See also CA 106; 135

Strugatskii, Boris (Natanovich)
1933- . . . . CLC 27
See also CA 106

Strummer, Joe 1953(?)- . . . . CLC 30

Stuart, Don A.
See Campbell, John W(ood, Jr.)

Stuart, Ian
See MacLean, Alistair (Stuart)

Stuart, Jesse (Hilton)
1906-1984 . . . . CLC 1, 8, 11, 14, 34
See also CA 5-8R; 112; CANR 31; DLB 9,
48, 102; DLBY 84; SATA 2;
SATA-Obit 36

Sturgeon, Theodore (Hamilton)
1918-1985 . . . . CLC 22, 39
See also Queen, Ellery
See also CA 81-84; 116; CANR 32; DLB 8;
DLBY 85; MTCW

Sturges, Preston 1898-1959 . . . . TCLC 48
See also CA 114; 149; DLB 26

Styron, William
1925- . . . . CLC 1, 3, 5, 11, 15, 60;
DAM NOV, POP
See also BEST 90:4; CA 5-8R; CANR 6, 33;
CDALB 1968-1988; DLB 2, 143;
DLBY 80; INT CANR-6; MTCW

Suarez Lynch, B.
See Bioy Casares, Adolfo; Borges, Jorge
Luis

Su Chien 1884-1918
See Su Man-shu
See also CA 123

Suckow, Ruth 1892-1960 . . . . SSC 18
See also CA 113; DLB 9, 102

Sudermann, Hermann 1857-1928 . . TCLC 15
See also CA 107; DLB 118

Sue, Eugene 1804-1857 . . . . NCLC 1
See also DLB 119

Sueskind, Patrick 1949- . . . . CLC 44
See also Suskind, Patrick

Sukenick, Ronald 1932- . . . . . CLC 3, 4, 6, 48
See also CA 25-28R; CAAS 8; CANR 32;
DLB 173; DLBY 81

Suknaski, Andrew 1942- . . . . CLC 19
See also CA 101; DLB 53

Sullivan, Vernon
See Vian, Boris

Sully Prudhomme 1839-1907 . . . . . . TCLC 31

Su Man-shu . . . . TCLC 24
See also Su Chien

Summerforest, Ivy B.
See Kirkup, James

Summers, Andrew James 1942- . . . . . CLC 26

Summers, Andy
See Summers, Andrew James

Summers, Hollis (Spurgeon, Jr.)
1916- . . . . CLC 10
See also CA 5-8R; CANR 3; DLB 6

Summers, (Alphonsus Joseph-Mary Augustus)
Montague 1880-1948 . . . . TCLC 16
See also CA 118

Sumner, Gordon Matthew 1951- . . . . CLC 26

Surtees, Robert Smith
1803-1864 . . . . NCLC 14
See also DLB 21

Susann, Jacqueline 1921-1974 . . . . . . CLC 3
See also AITN 1; CA 65-68; 53-56; MTCW

Terkel, Louis   1912-
See Terkel, Studs
See also CA 57-60; CANR 18, 45; MTCW

Terkel, Studs...................... **CLC 38**
See also Terkel, Louis
See also AITN 1

Terry, C. V.
See Slaughter, Frank G(ill)

Terry, Megan   1932-................ **CLC 19**
See also CA 77-80; CABS 3; CANR 43;
DLB 7

Tertz, Abram
See Sinyavsky, Andrei (Donatevich)

Tesich, Steve   1943(?)-1996...... **CLC 40, 69**
See also CA 105; 152; DLBY 83

Teternikov, Fyodor Kuzmich   1863-1927
See Sologub, Fyodor
See also CA 104

Tevis, Walter   1928-1984 .... **CLC 42**
See also CA 113

Tey, Josephine.................. **TCLC 14**
See also Mackintosh, Elizabeth
See also DLB 77

Thackeray, William Makepeace
1811-1863 .... **NCLC 5, 14, 22, 43; DA;
DAB; DAC; DAM MST, NOV; WLC**
See also CDBLB 1832-1890; DLB 21, 55,
159, 163; SATA 23

Thakura, Ravindranatha
See Tagore, Rabindranath

Tharoor, Shashi   1956-........... **CLC 70**
See also CA 141

Thelwell, Michael Miles   1939- ..... **CLC 22**
See also BW 2; CA 101

Theobald, Lewis, Jr.
See Lovecraft, H(oward) P(hillips)

Theodorescu, Ion N.   1880-1967
See Arghezi, Tudor
See also CA 116

Theriault, Yves
1915-1983 .. **CLC 79; DAC; DAM MST**
See also CA 102; DLB 88

Theroux, Alexander (Louis)
1939-..................... **CLC 2, 25**
See also CA 85-88; CANR 20

Theroux, Paul (Edward)
1941-........ **CLC 5, 8, 11, 15, 28, 46;
DAM POP**
See also BEST 89:4; CA 33-36R; CANR 20,
45; DLB 2; MTCW; SATA 44

Thesen, Sharon   1946-............ **CLC 56**

Thevenin, Denis
See Duhamel, Georges

Thibault, Jacques Anatole Francois
1844-1924
See France, Anatole
See also CA 106; 127; DAM NOV; MTCW

Thiele, Colin (Milton)   1920- .... **CLC 17**
See also CA 29-32R; CANR 12, 28, 53;
CLR 27; MAICYA; SAAS 2; SATA 14,
72

Thomas, Audrey (Callahan)
1935-........ **CLC 7, 13, 37; SSC 20**
See also AITN 2; CA 21-24R; CAAS 19;
CANR 36; DLB 60; MTCW

Thomas, D(onald) M(ichael)
1935- .... **CLC 13, 22, 31**
See also CA 61-64; CAAS 11; CANR 17,
45; CDBLB 1960 to Present; DLB 40;
INT CANR-17; MTCW

Thomas, Dylan (Marlais)
1914-1953 ... **TCLC 1, 8, 45; DA; DAB;
DAC; DAM DRAM, MST, POET;
PC 2; SSC 3; WLC**
See also CA 104; 120; CDBLB 1945-1960;
DLB 13, 20, 139; MTCW; SATA 60

Thomas, (Philip) Edward
1878-1917 ...... **TCLC 10; DAM POET**
See also CA 106; 153; DLB 19

Thomas, Joyce Carol   1938-........ **CLC 35**
See also AAYA 12; BW 2; CA 113; 116;
CANR 48; CLR 19; DLB 33; INT 116;
JRDA; MAICYA; MTCW; SAAS 7;
SATA 40, 78

Thomas, Lewis   1913-1993 .... **CLC 35**
See also CA 85-88; 143; CANR 38; MTCW

Thomas, Paul
See Mann, (Paul) Thomas

Thomas, Piri   1928-.............. **CLC 17**
See also CA 73-76; HW

Thomas, R(onald) S(tuart)
1913- .... **CLC 6, 13, 48; DAB;
DAM POET**
See also CA 89-92; CAAS 4; CANR 30;
CDBLB 1960 to Present; DLB 27;
MTCW

Thomas, Ross (Elmore)   1926-1995 .. **CLC 39**
See also CA 33-36R; 150; CANR 22

Thompson, Francis Clegg
See Mencken, H(enry) L(ouis)

Thompson, Francis Joseph
1859-1907 .... **TCLC 4**
See also CA 104; CDBLB 1890-1914;
DLB 19

Thompson, Hunter S(tockton)
1939- .... **CLC 9, 17, 40; DAM POP**
See also BEST 89:1; CA 17-20R; CANR 23,
46; MTCW

Thompson, James Myers
See Thompson, Jim (Myers)

Thompson, Jim (Myers)
1906-1977(?) .... **CLC 69**
See also CA 140

Thompson, Judith .... **CLC 39**

Thomson, James
1700-1748 ..... **LC 16, 29; DAM POET**
See also DLB 95

Thomson, James
1834-1882 ..... **NCLC 18; DAM POET**
See also DLB 35

Thoreau, Henry David
1817-1862 ..... **NCLC 7, 21; DA; DAB;
DAC; DAM MST; WLC**
See also CDALB 1640-1865; DLB 1

Thornton, Hall
See Silverberg, Robert

Thucydides   c. 455B.C.-399B.C.... **CMLC 17**

Thurber, James (Grover)
1894-1961 .... **CLC 5, 11, 25; DA; DAB;
DAC; DAM DRAM, MST, NOV; SSC 1**
See also CA 73-76; CANR 17, 39;
CDALB 1929-1941; DLB 4, 11, 22, 102;
MAICYA; MTCW; SATA 13

Thurman, Wallace (Henry)
1902-1934 .... **TCLC 6; BLC;
DAM MULT**
See also BW 1; CA 104; 124; DLB 51

Ticheburn, Cheviot
See Ainsworth, William Harrison

Tieck, (Johann) Ludwig
1773-1853 .... **NCLC 5, 46**
See also DLB 90

Tiger, Derry
See Ellison, Harlan (Jay)

Tilghman, Christopher   1948(?)-..... **CLC 65**

Tillinghast, Richard (Williford)
1940-..................... **CLC 29**
See also CA 29-32R; CAAS 23; CANR 26,
51

Timrod, Henry   1828-1867 .... **NCLC 25**
See also DLB 3

Tindall, Gillian   1938-.............. **CLC 7**
See also CA 21-24R; CANR 11

Tiptree, James, Jr. .... **CLC 48, 50**
See also Sheldon, Alice Hastings Bradley
See also DLB 8

Titmarsh, Michael Angelo
See Thackeray, William Makepeace

Tocqueville, Alexis (Charles Henri Maurice
Clerel Comte)   1805-1859..... **NCLC 7**

Tolkien, J(ohn) R(onald) R(euel)
1892-1973 .... **CLC 1, 2, 3, 8, 12, 38;
DA; DAB; DAC; DAM MST, NOV,
POP; WLC**
See also AAYA 10; AITN 1; CA 17-18;
45-48; CANR 36; CAP 2;
CDBLB 1914-1945; DLB 15, 160; JRDA;
MAICYA; MTCW; SATA 2, 32;
SATA-Obit 24

Toller, Ernst   1893-1939.......... **TCLC 10**
See also CA 107; DLB 124

Tolson, M. B.
See Tolson, Melvin B(eaunorus)

Tolson, Melvin B(eaunorus)
1898(?)-1966 .... **CLC 36; BLC;
DAM MULT, POET**
See also BW 1; CA 124; 89-92; DLB 48, 76

Tolstoi, Aleksei Nikolaevich
See Tolstoy, Alexey Nikolaevich

Tolstoy, Alexey Nikolaevich
1882-1945 .... **TCLC 18**
See also CA 107

Tolstoy, Count Leo
See Tolstoy, Leo (Nikolaevich)

Tolstoy, Leo (Nikolaevich)
1828-1910 ...... **TCLC 4, 11, 17, 28, 44;
DA; DAB; DAC; DAM MST, NOV;
SSC 9; WLC**
See also CA 104; 123; SATA 26

Tomasi di Lampedusa, Giuseppe   1896-1957
See Lampedusa, Giuseppe (Tomasi) di
See also CA 111

Tzara, Tristan
1896-1963 . . . . CLC 47; DAM POET
See also Rosenfeld, Samuel; Rosenstock,
Sami; Rosenstock, Samuel
See also CA 153

Uhry, Alfred
1936- . . . . . CLC 55; DAM DRAM, POP
See also CA 127; 133; INT 133

Ulf, Haerved
See Strindberg, (Johan) August

Ulf, Harved
See Strindberg, (Johan) August

Ulibarri, Sabine R(eyes)
1919- . . . . CLC 83; DAM MULT
See also CA 131; DLB 82; HW

Unamuno (y Jugo), Miguel de
1864-1936 . . . TCLC 2, 9; DAM MULT,
NOV; HLC; SSC 11
See also CA 104; 131; DLB 108; HW;
MTCW

Undercliffe, Errol
See Campbell, (John) Ramsey

Underwood, Miles
See Glassco, John

Undset, Sigrid
1882-1949 . . . . TCLC 3; DA; DAB;
DAC; DAM MST, NOV; WLC
See also CA 104; 129; MTCW

Ungaretti, Giuseppe
1888-1970 . . . . CLC 7, 11, 15
See also CA 19-20; 25-28R; CAP 2;
DLB 114

Unger, Douglas 1952- . . . . CLC 34
See also CA 130

Unsworth, Barry (Forster) 1930- . . . . CLC 76
See also CA 25-28R; CANR 30, 54

Updike, John (Hoyer)
1932- . . . . . . CLC 1, 2, 3, 5, 7, 9, 13, 15,
23, 34, 43, 70; DA; DAB; DAC;
DAM MST, NOV, POET, POP;
SSC 13; WLC
See also CA 1-4R; CABS 1; CANR 4, 33,
51; CDALB 1968-1988; DLB 2, 5, 143;
DLBD 3; DLBY 80, 82; MTCW

Upshaw, Margaret Mitchell
See Mitchell, Margaret (Munnerlyn)

Upton, Mark
See Sanders, Lawrence

Urdang, Constance (Henriette)
1922- . . . . CLC 47
See also CA 21-24R; CANR 9, 24

Uriel, Henry
See Faust, Frederick (Schiller)

Uris, Leon (Marcus)
1924- . . . . CLC 7, 32; DAM NOV, POP
See also AITN 1, 2; BEST 89:2; CA 1-4R;
CANR 1, 40; MTCW; SATA 49

Urmuz
See Codrescu, Andrei

Urquhart, Jane 1949- . . . . CLC 90; DAC
See also CA 113; CANR 32

Ustinov, Peter (Alexander) 1921- . . . . CLC 1
See also AITN 1; CA 13-16R; CANR 25,
51; DLB 13

Vaculik, Ludvik 1926- . . . . CLC 7
See also CA 53-56

Valdez, Luis (Miguel)
1940- . . . . . CLC 84; DAM MULT; HLC
See also CA 101; CANR 32; DLB 122; HW

Valenzuela, Luisa
1938- . . . CLC 31; DAM MULT; SSC 14
See also CA 101; CANR 32; DLB 113; HW

Valera y Alcala-Galiano, Juan
1824-1905 . . . . TCLC 10
See also CA 106

Valery, (Ambroise) Paul (Toussaint Jules)
1871-1945 . . . . TCLC 4, 15;
DAM POET; PC 9
See also CA 104; 122; MTCW

Valle-Inclan, Ramon (Maria) del
1866-1936 . . . . . TCLC 5; DAM MULT;
HLC
See also CA 106; 153; DLB 134

Vallejo, Antonio Buero
See Buero Vallejo, Antonio

Vallejo, Cesar (Abraham)
1892-1938 . . . . TCLC 3, 56;
DAM MULT; HLC
See also CA 105; 153; HW

Vallette, Marguerite Eymery
See Rachilde

Valle Y Pena, Ramon del
See Valle-Inclan, Ramon (Maria) del

Van Ash, Cay 1918- . . . . CLC 34

Vanbrugh, Sir John
1664-1726 . . . . LC 21; DAM DRAM
See also DLB 80

Van Campen, Karl
See Campbell, John W(ood, Jr.)

Vance, Gerald
See Silverberg, Robert

Vance, Jack . . . . CLC 35
See also Vance, John Holbrook
See also DLB 8

Vance, John Holbrook 1916-
See Queen, Ellery; Vance, Jack
See also CA 29-32R; CANR 17; MTCW

**Van Den Bogarde, Derek Jules Gaspard Ulric
Niven** 1921-
See Bogarde, Dirk
See also CA 77-80

Vandenburgh, Jane . . . . CLC 59

Vanderhaeghe, Guy 1951- . . . . CLC 41
See also CA 113

van der Post, Laurens (Jan)
1906-1996 . . . . CLC 5
See also CA 5-8R; 155; CANR 35

van de Wetering, Janwillem 1931- . . CLC 47
See also CA 49-52; CANR 4

Van Dine, S. S. . . . . TCLC 23
See also Wright, Willard Huntington

Van Doren, Carl (Clinton)
1885-1950 . . . . TCLC 18
See also CA 111

Van Doren, Mark 1894-1972 . . . . . CLC 6, 10
See also CA 1-4R; 37-40R; CANR 3;
DLB 45; MTCW

Van Druten, John (William)
1901-1957 . . . . TCLC 2
See also CA 104; DLB 10

Van Duyn, Mona (Jane)
1921- . . . . CLC 3, 7, 63; DAM POET
See also CA 9-12R; CANR 7, 38; DLB 5

Van Dyne, Edith
See Baum, L(yman) Frank

van Itallie, Jean-Claude 1936- . . . . CLC 3
See also CA 45-48; CAAS 2; CANR 1, 48;
DLB 7

van Ostaijen, Paul 1896-1928 . . . . . TCLC 33

Van Peebles, Melvin
1932- . . . . CLC 2, 20; DAM MULT
See also BW 2; CA 85-88; CANR 27

Vansittart, Peter 1920- . . . . CLC 42
See also CA 1-4R; CANR 3, 49

Van Vechten, Carl 1880-1964 . . . . . . CLC 33
See also CA 89-92; DLB 4, 9, 51

Van Vogt, A(lfred) E(lton) 1912- . . . . CLC 1
See also CA 21-24R; CANR 28; DLB 8;
SATA 14

Varda, Agnes 1928- . . . . CLC 16
See also CA 116; 122

Vargas Llosa, (Jorge) Mario (Pedro)
1936- . . . . CLC 3, 6, 9, 10, 15, 31, 42, 85;
DA; DAB; DAC; DAM MST, MULT,
NOV; HLC
See also CA 73-76; CANR 18, 32, 42;
DLB 145; HW; MTCW

Vasiliu, Gheorghe 1881-1957
See Bacovia, George
See also CA 123

Vassa, Gustavus
See Equiano, Olaudah

Vassilikos, Vassilis 1933- . . . . CLC 4, 8
See also CA 81-84

Vaughan, Henry 1621-1695 . . . . LC 27
See also DLB 131

Vaughn, Stephanie . . . . CLC 62

Vazov, Ivan (Minchov)
1850-1921 . . . . TCLC 25
See also CA 121; DLB 147

Veblen, Thorstein (Bunde)
1857-1929 . . . . TCLC 31
See also CA 115

Vega, Lope de 1562-1635 . . . . LC 23

Venison, Alfred
See Pound, Ezra (Weston Loomis)

Verdi, Marie de
See Mencken, H(enry) L(ouis)

Verdu, Matilde
See Cela, Camilo Jose

Verga, Giovanni (Carmelo)
1840-1922 . . . . TCLC 3; SSC 21
See also CA 104; 123

Vergil
70B.C.-19B.C. . . . . . . CMLC 9; DA; DAB;
DAC; DAM MST, POET; PC 12

Verhaeren, Emile (Adolphe Gustave)
1855-1916 . . . . TCLC 12
See also CA 109

Walker, Ted. . . . . CLC 13
See also Walker, Edward Joseph
See also DLB 40

Wallace, David Foster　1962- . . . . CLC 50
See also CA 132

Wallace, Dexter
See Masters, Edgar Lee

Wallace, (Richard Horatio) Edgar
1875-1932 . . . . TCLC 57
See also CA 115; DLB 70

Wallace, Irving
1916-1990 . . . . . CLC 7, 13; DAM NOV,
POP
See also AITN 1; CA 1-4R; 132; CAAS 1;
CANR 1, 27; INT CANR-27; MTCW

Wallant, Edward Lewis
1926-1962 . . . . CLC 5, 10
See also CA 1-4R; CANR 22; DLB 2, 28,
143; MTCW

Walley, Byron
See Card, Orson Scott

Walpole, Horace　1717-1797. . . . . LC 2
See also DLB 39, 104

Walpole, Hugh (Seymour)
1884-1941 . . . . TCLC 5
See also CA 104; DLB 34

Walser, Martin　1927- . . . . CLC 27
See also CA 57-60; CANR 8, 46; DLB 75,
124

Walser, Robert
1878-1956 . . . . TCLC 18; SSC 20
See also CA 118; DLB 66

Walsh, Jill Paton. . . . . CLC 35
See also Paton Walsh, Gillian
See also AAYA 11; CLR 2; DLB 161;
SAAS 3

Walter, Villiam Christian
See Andersen, Hans Christian

Wambaugh, Joseph (Aloysius, Jr.)
1937- . . . . CLC 3, 18; DAM NOV, POP
See also AITN 1; BEST 89:3; CA 33-36R;
CANR 42; DLB 6; DLBY 83; MTCW

Ward, Arthur Henry Sarsfield　1883-1959
See Rohmer, Sax
See also CA 108

Ward, Douglas Turner　1930- . . . . CLC 19
See also BW 1; CA 81-84; CANR 27;
DLB 7, 38

Ward, Mary Augusta
See Ward, Mrs. Humphry

Ward, Mrs. Humphry
1851-1920 . . . . TCLC 55
See also DLB 18

Ward, Peter
See Faust, Frederick (Schiller)

Warhol, Andy　1928(?)-1987. . . . . . . CLC 20
See also AAYA 12; BEST 89:4; CA 89-92;
121; CANR 34

Warner, Francis (Robert le Plastrier)
1937- . . . . CLC 14
See also CA 53-56; CANR 11

Warner, Marina　1946- . . . . CLC 59
See also CA 65-68; CANR 21, 55

Warner, Rex (Ernest)　1905-1986. . . . CLC 45
See also CA 89-92; 119; DLB 15

Warner, Susan (Bogert)
1819-1885 . . . . NCLC 31
See also DLB 3, 42

Warner, Sylvia (Constance) Ashton
See Ashton-Warner, Sylvia (Constance)

Warner, Sylvia Townsend
1893-1978 . . . . CLC 7, 19; SSC 23
See also CA 61-64; 77-80; CANR 16;
DLB 34, 139; MTCW

Warren, Mercy Otis　1728-1814. . . NCLC 13
See also DLB 31

Warren, Robert Penn
1905-1989 . . . . CLC 1, 4, 6, 8, 10, 13, 18,
39, 53, 59; DA; DAB; DAC; DAM MST,
NOV, POET; SSC 4; WLC
See also AITN 1; CA 13-16R; 129;
CANR 10, 47; CDALB 1968-1988;
DLB 2, 48, 152; DLBY 80, 89;
INT CANR-10; MTCW; SATA 46;
SATA-Obit 63

Warshofsky, Isaac
See Singer, Isaac Bashevis

Warton, Thomas
1728-1790 . . . . LC 15; DAM POET
See also DLB 104, 109

Waruk, Kona
See Harris, (Theodore) Wilson

Warung, Price　1855-1911. . . . . TCLC 45

Warwick, Jarvis
See Garner, Hugh

Washington, Alex
See Harris, Mark

Washington, Booker T(aliaferro)
1856-1915 . . . . TCLC 10; BLC;
DAM MULT
See also BW 1; CA 114; 125; SATA 28

Washington, George　1732-1799 . . . . . . LC 25
See also DLB 31

Wassermann, (Karl) Jakob
1873-1934 . . . . TCLC 6
See also CA 104; DLB 66

Wasserstein, Wendy
1950- . . . . CLC 32, 59, 90;
DAM DRAM; DC 4
See also CA 121; 129; CABS 3; CANR 53;
INT 129

Waterhouse, Keith (Spencer)
1929- . . . . CLC 47
See also CA 5-8R; CANR 38; DLB 13, 15;
MTCW

Waters, Frank (Joseph)
1902-1995 . . . . CLC 88
See also CA 5-8R; 149; CAAS 13; CANR 3,
18; DLBY 86

Waters, Roger　1944-. . . . . CLC 35

Watkins, Frances Ellen
See Harper, Frances Ellen Watkins

Watkins, Gerrold
See Malzberg, Barry N(athaniel)

Watkins, Gloria　1955(?)-
See hooks, bell
See also BW 2; CA 143

Watkins, Paul　1964-. . . . . CLC 55
See also CA 132

Watkins, Vernon Phillips
1906-1967 . . . . CLC 43
See also CA 9-10; 25-28R; CAP 1; DLB 20

Watson, Irving S.
See Mencken, H(enry) L(ouis)

Watson, John H.
See Farmer, Philip Jose

Watson, Richard F.
See Silverberg, Robert

Waugh, Auberon (Alexander)　1939- . . CLC 7
See also CA 45-48; CANR 6, 22; DLB 14

Waugh, Evelyn (Arthur St. John)
1903-1966 . . . . . . CLC 1, 3, 8, 13, 19, 27,
44; DA; DAB; DAC; DAM MST, NOV,
POP; WLC
See also CA 85-88; 25-28R; CANR 22;
CDBLB 1914-1945; DLB 15, 162; MTCW

Waugh, Harriet　1944- . . . . CLC 6
See also CA 85-88; CANR 22

Ways, C. R.
See Blount, Roy (Alton), Jr.

Waystaff, Simon
See Swift, Jonathan

Webb, (Martha) Beatrice (Potter)
1858-1943 . . . . TCLC 22
See also Potter, Beatrice
See also CA 117

Webb, Charles (Richard)　1939- . . . . . . CLC 7
See also CA 25-28R

Webb, James H(enry), Jr.　1946- . . . . CLC 22
See also CA 81-84

Webb, Mary (Gladys Meredith)
1881-1927 . . . . TCLC 24
See also CA 123; DLB 34

Webb, Mrs. Sidney
See Webb, (Martha) Beatrice (Potter)

Webb, Phyllis　1927-. . . . . CLC 18
See also CA 104; CANR 23; DLB 53

Webb, Sidney (James)
1859-1947 . . . . TCLC 22
See also CA 117

Webber, Andrew Lloyd. . . . . CLC 21
See also Lloyd Webber, Andrew

Weber, Lenora Mattingly
1895-1971 . . . . CLC 12
See also CA 19-20; 29-32R; CAP 1;
SATA 2; SATA-Obit 26

Weber, Max　1864-1920 . . . . TCLC 69
See also CA 109

Webster, John
1579(?)-1634(?) . . . . . . LC 33; DA; DAB;
DAC; DAM DRAM, MST; DC 2; WLC
See also CDBLB Before 1660; DLB 58

Webster, Noah　1758-1843 . . . . NCLC 30

Wedekind, (Benjamin) Frank(lin)
1864-1918 . . . . . . TCLC 7; DAM DRAM
See also CA 104; 153; DLB 118

Weidman, Jerome　1913-. . . . . CLC 7
See also AITN 2; CA 1-4R; CANR 1;
DLB 28

Weil, Simone (Adolphine)
1909-1943 . . . . TCLC 23
See also CA 117

Weinstein, Nathan
See West, Nathanael

Weinstein, Nathan von Wallenstein
See West, Nathanael

Weir, Peter (Lindsay) 1944- .... CLC 20
See also CA 113; 123

Weiss, Peter (Ulrich)
1916-1982 .... CLC 3, 15, 51;
DAM DRAM
See also CA 45-48; 106; CANR 3; DLB 69,
124

Weiss, Theodore (Russell)
1916- .... CLC 3, 8, 14
See also CA 9-12R; CAAS 2; CANR 46;
DLB 5

Welch, (Maurice) Denton
1915-1948 .... TCLC 22
See also CA 121; 148

Welch, James
1940- ..... CLC 6, 14, 52; DAM MULT,
POP
See also CA 85-88; CANR 42; DLB 175;
NNAL

Weldon, Fay
1933- .... CLC 6, 9, 11, 19, 36, 59;
DAM POP
See also CA 21-24R; CANR 16, 46;
CDBLB 1960 to Present; DLB 14;
INT CANR-16; MTCW

Wellek, Rene 1903-1995 .... CLC 28
See also CA 5-8R; 150; CAAS 7; CANR 8;
DLB 63; INT CANR-8

Weller, Michael 1942- .... CLC 10, 53
See also CA 85-88

Weller, Paul 1958- .... CLC 26

Wellershoff, Dieter 1925- .... CLC 46
See also CA 89-92; CANR 16, 37

Welles, (George) Orson
1915-1985 .... CLC 20, 80
See also CA 93-96; 117

Wellman, Mac 1945- .... CLC 65

Wellman, Manly Wade 1903-1986 .. CLC 49
See also CA 1-4R; 118; CANR 6, 16, 44;
SATA 6; SATA-Obit 47

Wells, Carolyn 1869(?)-1942 ...... TCLC 35
See also CA 113; DLB 11

Wells, H(erbert) G(eorge)
1866-1946 .... TCLC 6, 12, 19; DA;
DAB; DAC; DAM MST, NOV; SSC 6;
WLC
See also AAYA 18; CA 110; 121;
CDBLB 1914-1945; DLB 34, 70, 156;
MTCW; SATA 20

Wells, Rosemary 1943- .... CLC 12
See also AAYA 13; CA 85-88; CANR 48;
CLR 16; MAICYA; SAAS 1; SATA 18,
69

Welty, Eudora
1909- ...... CLC 1, 2, 5, 14, 22, 33; DA;
DAB; DAC; DAM MST, NOV; SSC 1;
WLC
See also CA 9-12R; CABS 1; CANR 32;
CDALB 1941-1968; DLB 2, 102, 143;
DLBD 12; DLBY 87; MTCW

Wen I-to 1899-1946 .... TCLC 28

Wentworth, Robert
See Hamilton, Edmond

Werfel, Franz (V.) 1890-1945 ...... TCLC 8
See also CA 104; DLB 81, 124

Wergeland, Henrik Arnold
1808-1845 .... NCLC 5

Wersba, Barbara 1932- .... CLC 30
See also AAYA 2; CA 29-32R; CANR 16,
38; CLR 3; DLB 52; JRDA; MAICYA;
SAAS 2; SATA 1, 58

Wertmueller, Lina 1928- .... CLC 16
See also CA 97-100; CANR 39

Wescott, Glenway 1901-1987 ...... CLC 13
See also CA 13-16R; 121; CANR 23;
DLB 4, 9, 102

Wesker, Arnold
1932- .... CLC 3, 5, 42; DAB;
DAM DRAM
See also CA 1-4R; CAAS 7; CANR 1, 33;
CDBLB 1960 to Present; DLB 13;
MTCW

Wesley, Richard (Errol) 1945- .... CLC 7
See also BW 1; CA 57-60; CANR 27;
DLB 38

Wessel, Johan Herman 1742-1785 .... LC 7

West, Anthony (Panther)
1914-1987 .... CLC 50
See also CA 45-48; 124; CANR 3, 19;
DLB 15

West, C. P.
See Wodehouse, P(elham) G(renville)

West, (Mary) Jessamyn
1902-1984 .... CLC 7, 17
See also CA 9-12R; 112; CANR 27; DLB 6;
DLBY 84; MTCW; SATA-Obit 37

West, Morris L(anglo) 1916- ..... CLC 6, 33
See also CA 5-8R; CANR 24, 49; MTCW

West, Nathanael
1903-1940 ..... TCLC 1, 14, 44; SSC 16
See also CA 104; 125; CDALB 1929-1941;
DLB 4, 9, 28; MTCW

West, Owen
See Koontz, Dean R(ay)

West, Paul 1930- .... CLC 7, 14, 96
See also CA 13-16R; CAAS 7; CANR 22,
53; DLB 14; INT CANR-22

West, Rebecca 1892-1983 .. CLC 7, 9, 31, 50
See also CA 5-8R; 109; CANR 19; DLB 36;
DLBY 83; MTCW

Westall, Robert (Atkinson)
1929-1993 .... CLC 17
See also AAYA 12; CA 69-72; 141;
CANR 18; CLR 13; JRDA; MAICYA;
SAAS 2; SATA 23, 69; SATA-Obit 75

Westlake, Donald E(dwin)
1933- .... CLC 7, 33; DAM POP
See also CA 17-20R; CAAS 13; CANR 16,
44; INT CANR-16

Westmacott, Mary
See Christie, Agatha (Mary Clarissa)

Weston, Allen
See Norton, Andre

Wetcheek, J. L.
See Feuchtwanger, Lion

Wetering, Janwillem van de
See van de Wetering, Janwillem

Wetherell, Elizabeth
See Warner, Susan (Bogert)

Whale, James 1889-1957 .... TCLC 63

Whalen, Philip 1923- .... CLC 6, 29
See also CA 9-12R; CANR 5, 39; DLB 16

Wharton, Edith (Newbold Jones)
1862-1937 ...... TCLC 3, 9, 27, 53; DA;
DAB; DAC; DAM MST, NOV; SSC 6;
WLC
See also CA 104; 132; CDALB 1865-1917;
DLB 4, 9, 12, 78; DLBD 13; MTCW

Wharton, James
See Mencken, H(enry) L(ouis)

Wharton, William (a pseudonym)
.... CLC 18, 37
See also CA 93-96; DLBY 80; INT 93-96

Wheatley (Peters), Phillis
1754(?)-1784 .... LC 3; BLC; DA; DAC;
DAM MST, MULT, POET; PC 3; WLC
See also CDALB 1640-1865; DLB 31, 50

Wheelock, John Hall 1886-1978 .... CLC 14
See also CA 13-16R; 77-80; CANR 14;
DLB 45

White, E(lwyn) B(rooks)
1899-1985 .. CLC 10, 34, 39; DAM POP
See also AITN 2; CA 13-16R; 116;
CANR 16, 37; CLR 1, 21; DLB 11, 22;
MAICYA; MTCW; SATA 2, 29;
SATA-Obit 44

White, Edmund (Valentine III)
1940- .... CLC 27; DAM POP
See also AAYA 7; CA 45-48; CANR 3, 19,
36; MTCW

White, Patrick (Victor Martindale)
1912-1990 .. CLC 3, 4, 5, 7, 9, 18, 65, 69
See also CA 81-84; 132; CANR 43; MTCW

White, Phyllis Dorothy James 1920-
See James, P. D.
See also CA 21-24R; CANR 17, 43;
DAM POP; MTCW

White, T(erence) H(anbury)
1906-1964 .... CLC 30
See also CA 73-76; CANR 37; DLB 160;
JRDA; MAICYA; SATA 12

White, Terence de Vere
1912-1994 .... CLC 49
See also CA 49-52; 145; CANR 3

White, Walter F(rancis)
1893-1955 .... TCLC 15
See also White, Walter
See also BW 1; CA 115; 124; DLB 51

White, William Hale 1831-1913
See Rutherford, Mark
See also CA 121

Whitehead, E(dward) A(nthony)
1933- .... CLC 5
See also CA 65-68

Whitemore, Hugh (John) 1936- ..... CLC 37
See also CA 132; INT 132

Whitman, Sarah Helen (Power)
1803-1878 .... NCLC 19
See also DLB 1

Whitman, Walt(er)
1819-1892 ..... NCLC **4, 31**; DA; DAB;
DAC; DAM MST, POET; PC **3**; WLC
See also CDALB 1640-1865; DLB 3, 64;
SATA 20

Whitney, Phyllis A(yame)
1903- .... CLC **42**; DAM POP
See also AITN 2; BEST 90:3; CA 1-4R;
CANR 3, 25, 38; JRDA; MAICYA;
SATA 1, 30

Whittemore, (Edward) Reed (Jr.)
1919- .... CLC **4**
See also CA 9-12R; CAAS 8; CANR 4;
DLB 5

Whittier, John Greenleaf
1807-1892 .... NCLC **8, 59**
See also DLB 1

Whittlebot, Hernia
See Coward, Noel (Peirce)

Wicker, Thomas Grey   1926-
See Wicker, Tom
See also CA 65-68; CANR 21, 46

Wicker, Tom .... CLC **7**
See also Wicker, Thomas Grey

Wideman, John Edgar
1941- .... CLC **5, 34, 36, 67**; BLC;
DAM MULT
See also BW 2; CA 85-88; CANR 14, 42;
DLB 33, 143

Wiebe, Rudy (Henry)
1934- .... CLC **6, 11, 14**; DAC;
DAM MST
See also CA 37-40R; CANR 42; DLB 60

Wieland, Christoph Martin
1733-1813 .... NCLC **17**
See also DLB 97

Wiene, Robert   1881-1938 .... TCLC **56**

Wieners, John   1934- .... CLC **7**
See also CA 13-16R; DLB 16

Wiesel, Elie(zer)
1928- ...... CLC **3, 5, 11, 37**; DA; DAB;
DAC; DAM MST, NOV
See also AAYA 7; AITN 1; CA 5-8R;
CAAS 4; CANR 8, 40; DLB 83;
DLBY 87; INT CANR-8; MTCW;
SATA 56

Wiggins, Marianne   1947- .... CLC **57**
See also BEST 89:3; CA 130

Wight, James Alfred   1916-
See Herriot, James
See also CA 77-80; SATA 55;
SATA-Brief 44

Wilbur, Richard (Purdy)
1921- ... CLC **3, 6, 9, 14, 53**; DA; DAB;
DAC; DAM MST, POET
See also CA 1-4R; CABS 2; CANR 2, 29;
DLB 5, 169; INT CANR-29; MTCW;
SATA 9

Wild, Peter   1940- .... CLC **14**
See also CA 37-40R; DLB 5

Wilde, Oscar (Fingal O'Flahertie Wills)
1854(?)-1900 .... TCLC **1, 8, 23, 41**; DA;
DAB; DAC; DAM DRAM, MST, NOV;
SSC **11**; WLC
See also CA 104; 119; CDBLB 1890-1914;
DLB 10, 19, 34, 57, 141, 156; SATA 24

Wilder, Billy .... CLC **20**
See also Wilder, Samuel
See also DLB 26

Wilder, Samuel   1906-
See Wilder, Billy
See also CA 89-92

Wilder, Thornton (Niven)
1897-1975 ...... CLC **1, 5, 6, 10, 15, 35,
82**; DA; DAB; DAC; DAM DRAM,
MST, NOV; DC **1**; WLC
See also AITN 2; CA 13-16R; 61-64;
CANR 40; DLB 4, 7, 9; MTCW

Wilding, Michael   1942- .... CLC **73**
See also CA 104; CANR 24, 49

Wiley, Richard   1944- .... CLC **44**
See also CA 121; 129

Wilhelm, Kate .... CLC **7**
See also Wilhelm, Katie Gertrude
See also AAYA 20; CAAS 5; DLB 8;
INT CANR-17

Wilhelm, Katie Gertrude   1928-
See Wilhelm, Kate
See also CA 37-40R; CANR 17, 36; MTCW

Wilkins, Mary
See Freeman, Mary Eleanor Wilkins

Willard, Nancy   1936- .... CLC **7, 37**
See also CA 89-92; CANR 10, 39; CLR 5;
DLB 5, 52; MAICYA; MTCW;
SATA 37, 71; SATA-Brief 30

Williams, C(harles) K(enneth)
1936- .... CLC **33, 56**; DAM POET
See also CA 37-40R; CAAS 26; DLB 5

Williams, Charles
See Collier, James L(incoln)

Williams, Charles (Walter Stansby)
1886-1945 .... TCLC **1, 11**
See also CA 104; DLB 100, 153

Williams, (George) Emlyn
1905-1987 ...... CLC **15**; DAM DRAM
See also CA 104; 123; CANR 36; DLB 10,
77; MTCW

Williams, Hugo   1942- .... CLC **42**
See also CA 17-20R; CANR 45; DLB 40

Williams, J. Walker
See Wodehouse, P(elham) G(renville)

Williams, John A(lfred)
1925- ... CLC **5, 13**; BLC; DAM MULT
See also BW 2; CA 53-56; CAAS 3;
CANR 6, 26, 51; DLB 2, 33;
INT CANR-6

Williams, Jonathan (Chamberlain)
1929- .... CLC **13**
See also CA 9-12R; CAAS 12; CANR 8;
DLB 5

Williams, Joy   1944- .... CLC **31**
See also CA 41-44R; CANR 22, 48

Williams, Norman   1952- .... CLC **39**
See also CA 118

Williams, Sherley Anne
1944- ..... CLC **89**; BLC; DAM MULT,
POET
See also BW 2; CA 73-76; CANR 25;
DLB 41; INT CANR-25; SATA 78

Williams, Shirley
See Williams, Sherley Anne

Williams, Tennessee
1911-1983 ..... CLC **1, 2, 5, 7, 8, 11, 15,
19, 30, 39, 45, 71**; DA; DAB; DAC;
DAM DRAM, MST; DC **4**; WLC
See also AITN 1, 2; CA 5-8R; 108;
CABS 3; CANR 31; CDALB 1941-1968;
DLB 7; DLBD 4; DLBY 83; MTCW

Williams, Thomas (Alonzo)
1926-1990 .... CLC **14**
See also CA 1-4R; 132; CANR 2

Williams, William C.
See Williams, William Carlos

Williams, William Carlos
1883-1963 .... CLC **1, 2, 5, 9, 13, 22, 42,
67**; DA; DAB; DAC; DAM MST, POET;
PC **7**
See also CA 89-92; CANR 34;
CDALB 1917-1929; DLB 4, 16, 54, 86;
MTCW

Williamson, David (Keith)   1942- .... CLC **56**
See also CA 103; CANR 41

Williamson, Ellen Douglas   1905-1984
See Douglas, Ellen
See also CA 17-20R; 114; CANR 39

Williamson, Jack .... CLC **29**
See also Williamson, John Stewart
See also CAAS 8; DLB 8

Williamson, John Stewart   1908-
See Williamson, Jack
See also CA 17-20R; CANR 23

Willie, Frederick
See Lovecraft, H(oward) P(hillips)

Willingham, Calder (Baynard, Jr.)
1922-1995 .... CLC **5, 51**
See also CA 5-8R; 147; CANR 3; DLB 2,
44; MTCW

Willis, Charles
See Clarke, Arthur C(harles)

Willy
See Colette, (Sidonie-Gabrielle)

Willy, Colette
See Colette, (Sidonie-Gabrielle)

Wilson, A(ndrew) N(orman)   1950- .. CLC **33**
See also CA 112; 122; DLB 14, 155

Wilson, Angus (Frank Johnstone)
1913-1991 .. CLC **2, 3, 5, 25, 34**; SSC **21**
See also CA 5-8R; 134; CANR 21; DLB 15,
139, 155; MTCW

Wilson, August
1945- .... CLC **39, 50, 63**; BLC; DA;
DAB; DAC; DAM DRAM, MST,
MULT; DC **2**
See also AAYA 16; BW 2; CA 115; 122;
CANR 42, 54; MTCW

Wilson, Brian   1942- .... CLC **12**

Wilson, Colin   1931- .... CLC **3, 14**
See also CA 1-4R; CAAS 5; CANR 1, 22,
33; DLB 14; MTCW

Wilson, Dirk
See Pohl, Frederik

Wilson, Edmund
1895-1972 .... CLC **1, 2, 3, 8, 24**
See also CA 1-4R; 37-40R; CANR 1, 46;
DLB 63; MTCW

Wilson, Ethel Davis (Bryant)
    1888(?)-1980 . . . . **CLC 13; DAC;**
        DAM POET
    See also CA 102; DLB 68; MTCW

Wilson, John   1785-1854. . . . . **NCLC 5**

Wilson, John (Anthony) Burgess   1917-1993
    See Burgess, Anthony
    See also CA 1-4R; 143; CANR 2, 46; DAC;
        DAM NOV; MTCW

Wilson, Lanford
    1937- . . . . . **CLC 7, 14, 36; DAM DRAM**
    See also CA 17-20R; CABS 3; CANR 45;
        DLB 7

Wilson, Robert M.   1944- . . . . **CLC 7, 9**
    See also CA 49-52; CANR 2, 41; MTCW

Wilson, Robert McLiam   1964- . . . . . **CLC 59**
    See also CA 132

Wilson, Sloan   1920- . . . . **CLC 32**
    See also CA 1-4R; CANR 1, 44

Wilson, Snoo   1948- . . . . **CLC 33**
    See also CA 69-72

Wilson, William S(mith)   1932- . . . . . **CLC 49**
    See also CA 81-84

Winchilsea, Anne (Kingsmill) Finch Counte
    1661-1720 . . . . **LC 3**

Windham, Basil
    See Wodehouse, P(elham) G(renville)

Wingrove, David (John)   1954- . . . . . . **CLC 68**
    See also CA 133

Winters, Janet Lewis . . . . **CLC 41**
    See also Lewis, Janet
    See also DLBY 87

Winters, (Arthur) Yvor
    1900-1968 . . . . **CLC 4, 8, 32**
    See also CA 11-12; 25-28R; CAP 1;
        DLB 48; MTCW

Winterson, Jeanette
    1959- . . . . **CLC 64; DAM POP**
    See also CA 136

Winthrop, John   1588-1649. . . . . **LC 31**
    See also DLB 24, 30

Wiseman, Frederick   1930- . . . . **CLC 20**

Wister, Owen   1860-1938 . . . . **TCLC 21**
    See also CA 108; DLB 9, 78; SATA 62

Witkacy
    See Witkiewicz, Stanislaw Ignacy

Witkiewicz, Stanislaw Ignacy
    1885-1939 . . . . **TCLC 8**
    See also CA 105

Wittgenstein, Ludwig (Josef Johann)
    1889-1951 . . . . **TCLC 59**
    See also CA 113

Wittig, Monique   1935(?)- . . . . **CLC 22**
    See also CA 116; 135; DLB 83

Wittlin, Jozef   1896-1976 . . . . **CLC 25**
    See also CA 49-52; 65-68; CANR 3

Wodehouse, P(elham) G(renville)
    1881-1975 . . . **CLC 1, 2, 5, 10, 22; DAB;**
        DAC; DAM NOV; SSC 2
    See also AITN 2; CA 45-48; 57-60;
        CANR 3, 33; CDBLB 1914-1945;
        DLB 34, 162; MTCW; SATA 22

Woiwode, L.
    See Woiwode, Larry (Alfred)

Woiwode, Larry (Alfred)   1941- . . . **CLC 6, 10**
    See also CA 73-76; CANR 16; DLB 6;
        INT CANR-16

Wojciechowska, Maia (Teresa)
    1927- . . . . **CLC 26**
    See also AAYA 8; CA 9-12R; CANR 4, 41;
        CLR 1; JRDA; MAICYA; SAAS 1;
        SATA 1, 28, 83

Wolf, Christa   1929- . . . . **CLC 14, 29, 58**
    See also CA 85-88; CANR 45; DLB 75;
        MTCW

Wolfe, Gene (Rodman)
    1931- . . . . **CLC 25; DAM POP**
    See also CA 57-60; CAAS 9; CANR 6, 32;
        DLB 8

Wolfe, George C.   1954- . . . . **CLC 49**
    See also CA 149

Wolfe, Thomas (Clayton)
    1900-1938 . . . . . **TCLC 4, 13, 29, 61; DA;**
        DAB; DAC; DAM MST, NOV; WLC
    See also CA 104; 132; CDALB 1929-1941;
        DLB 9, 102; DLBD 2; DLBY 85; MTCW

Wolfe, Thomas Kennerly, Jr.   1931-
    See Wolfe, Tom
    See also CA 13-16R; CANR 9, 33;
        DAM POP; INT CANR-9; MTCW

Wolfe, Tom . . . . **CLC 1, 2, 9, 15, 35, 51**
    See also Wolfe, Thomas Kennerly, Jr.
    See also AAYA 8; AITN 2; BEST 89:1;
        DLB 152

Wolff, Geoffrey (Ansell)   1937- . . . . . **CLC 41**
    See also CA 29-32R; CANR 29, 43

Wolff, Sonia
    See Levitin, Sonia (Wolff)

Wolff, Tobias (Jonathan Ansell)
    1945- . . . . **CLC 39, 64**
    See also AAYA 16; BEST 90:2; CA 114;
        117; CAAS 22; CANR 54; DLB 130;
        INT 117

Wolfram von Eschenbach
    c. 1170-c. 1220 . . . . **CMLC 5**
    See also DLB 138

Wolitzer, Hilma   1930- . . . . **CLC 17**
    See also CA 65-68; CANR 18, 40;
        INT CANR-18; SATA 31

Wollstonecraft, Mary   1759-1797 . . . . . . **LC 5**
    See also CDBLB 1789-1832; DLB 39, 104,
        158

Wonder, Stevie . . . . **CLC 12**
    See also Morris, Steveland Judkins

Wong, Jade Snow   1922- . . . . **CLC 17**
    See also CA 109

Woodcott, Keith
    See Brunner, John (Kilian Houston)

Woodruff, Robert W.
    See Mencken, H(enry) L(ouis)

Woolf, (Adeline) Virginia
    1882-1941 . . . . **TCLC 1, 5, 20, 43, 56;**
        DA; DAB; DAC; DAM MST, NOV;
        SSC 7; WLC
    See also CA 104; 130; CDBLB 1914-1945;
        DLB 36, 100, 162; DLBD 10; MTCW

Woollcott, Alexander (Humphreys)
    1887-1943 . . . . **TCLC 5**
    See also CA 105; DLB 29

Woolrich, Cornell   1903-1968. . . . . . . **CLC 77**
    See also Hopley-Woolrich, Cornell George

Wordsworth, Dorothy
    1771-1855 . . . . **NCLC 25**
    See also DLB 107

Wordsworth, William
    1770-1850 . . . . **NCLC 12, 38; DA; DAB;**
        DAC; DAM MST, POET; PC 4; WLC
    See also CDBLB 1789-1832; DLB 93, 107

Wouk, Herman
    1915- . . **CLC 1, 9, 38; DAM NOV, POP**
    See also CA 5-8R; CANR 6, 33; DLBY 82;
        INT CANR-6; MTCW

Wright, Charles (Penzel, Jr.)
    1935- . . . . **CLC 6, 13, 28**
    See also CA 29-32R; CAAS 7; CANR 23,
        36; DLB 165; DLBY 82; MTCW

Wright, Charles Stevenson
    1932- . . . . **CLC 49; BLC 3;**
        DAM MULT, POET
    See also BW 1; CA 9-12R; CANR 26;
        DLB 33

Wright, Jack R.
    See Harris, Mark

Wright, James (Arlington)
    1927-1980 . . . . **CLC 3, 5, 10, 28;**
        DAM POET
    See also AITN 2; CA 49-52; 97-100;
        CANR 4, 34; DLB 5, 169; MTCW

Wright, Judith (Arandell)
    1915- . . . . **CLC 11, 53; PC 14**
    See also CA 13-16R; CANR 31; MTCW;
        SATA 14

Wright, L(aurali) R.   1939- . . . . **CLC 44**
    See also CA 138

Wright, Richard (Nathaniel)
    1908-1960 . . . . **CLC 1, 3, 4, 9, 14, 21, 48,**
        74; BLC; DA; DAB; DAC; DAM MST,
        MULT, NOV; SSC 2; WLC
    See also AAYA 5; BW 1; CA 108;
        CDALB 1929-1941; DLB 76, 102;
        DLBD 2; MTCW

Wright, Richard B(ruce)   1937- . . . . . . **CLC 6**
    See also CA 85-88; DLB 53

Wright, Rick   1945- . . . . **CLC 35**

Wright, Rowland
    See Wells, Carolyn

Wright, Stephen Caldwell   1946- . . . . **CLC 33**
    See also BW 2

Wright, Willard Huntington   1888-1939
    See Van Dine, S. S.
    See also CA 115

Wright, William   1930- . . . . **CLC 44**
    See also CA 53-56; CANR 7, 23

Wroth, LadyMary   1587-1653(?) . . . . . **LC 30**
    See also DLB 121

Wu Ch'eng-en   1500(?)-1582(?). . . . . . . **LC 7**

Wu Ching-tzu   1701-1754 . . . . **LC 2**

Wurlitzer, Rudolph   1938(?)- . . . **CLC 2, 4, 15**
    See also CA 85-88; DLB 173

Wycherley, William
    1641-1715 . . . . . **LC 8, 21; DAM DRAM**
    See also CDBLB 1660-1789; DLB 80

Literary Criticism Series
Cumulative Topic Index

This index lists all topic entries in Gale's *Classical and Medieval Literature Criticism, Contemporary Literary Criticism, Literature Criticism from 1400 to 1800, Nineteenth-Century Literature Criticism,* and *Twentieth-Century Literary Criticism.*

Age of Johnson LC 15: 1-87
Johnson's London, 3-15
aesthetics of neoclassicism, 15-36
"age of prose and reason," 36-45
clubmen and bluestockings, 45-56
printing technology, 56-62
periodicals: "a map of busy life," 62-74
transition, 74-86

AIDS in Literature CLC 81: 365-416

American Abolitionism NCLC 44: 1-73
overviews, 2-26
abolitionist ideals, 26-46
the literature of abolitionism, 46-72

American Black Humor Fiction TCLC 54: 1-85
characteristics of black humor, 2-13
origins and development, 13-38
black humor distinguished from related literary trends, 38-60
black humor and society, 60-75
black humor reconsidered, 75-83

American Civil War in Literature NCLC 32: 1-109
overviews, 2-20
regional perspectives, 20-54
fiction popular during the war, 54-79
the historical novel, 79-108

American Frontier in Literature NCLC 28: 1-103
definitions, 2-12
development, 12-17
nonfiction writing about the frontier, 17-30
frontier fiction, 30-45

frontier protagonists, 45-66
portrayals of Native Americans, 66-86
feminist readings, 86-98
twentieth-century reaction against frontier literature, 98-100

American Humor Writing NCLC 52: 1-59
overviews, 2-12
the Old Southwest, 12-42
broader impacts, 42-5
women humorists, 45-58

American Popular Song, Golden Age of TCLC 42: 1-49
background and major figures, 2-34
the lyrics of popular songs, 34-47

American Proletarian Literature TCLC 54: 86-175
overviews, 87-95
American proletarian literature and the American Communist Party, 95-111
ideology and literary merit, 111-7
novels, 117-36
Gastonia, 136-48
drama, 148-54
journalism, 154-9
proletarian literature in the United States, 159-74

American Romanticism NCLC 44: 74-138
overviews, 74-84
sociopolitical influences, 84-104
Romanticism and the American frontier, 104-15
thematic concerns, 115-37

American Western Literature TCLC 46:

1-100
definition and development of American Western literature, 2-7
characteristics of the Western novel, 8-23
Westerns as history and fiction, 23-34
critical reception of American Western literature, 34-41
the Western hero, 41-73
women in Western fiction, 73-91
later Western fiction, 91-9

Art and Literature TCLC 54: 176-248
overviews, 176-93
definitions, 193-219
influence of visual arts on literature, 219-31
spatial form in literature, 231-47

Arthurian Literature CMLC 10: 1-127
historical context and literary beginnings, 2-27
development of the legend through Malory, 27-64
development of the legend from Malory to the Victorian Age, 65-81
themes and motifs, 81-95
principal characters, 95-125

Arthurian Revival NCLC 36: 1-77
overviews, 2-12
Tennyson and his influence, 12-43
other leading figures, 43-73
the Arthurian legend in the visual arts, 73-6

Australian Literature TCLC 50: 1-94
origins and development, 2-21
characteristics of Australian literature, 21-33

Topic Index

Topic Index

Cumulative Nationality Index

Nationality Index

Nationality Index

Nationality Index

CLC-99 Title Index